NEW
AMERICAN
CROSSWORD
PUZZLE
DICTIONARY

NEW AMERICAN CROSSWORD PUZZLE DICTIONARY

EDITED BY
Albert and Loy Morehead

3rd Edition
Revised and Expanded

Prepared by
Philip D. Morehead

A SIGNET BOOK

SIGNET
Published by New American Library, a division of
Penguin Group (USA) Inc., 375 Hudson Street,
New York, New York 10014, U.S.A.
Penguin Books Ltd, 80 Strand,
London WC2R 0RL, England
Penguin Books Australia Ltd, 250 Camberwell Road,
Camberwell, Victoria 3124, Australia
Penguin Books Canada Ltd, 10 Alcorn Avenue,
Toronto, Ontario, Canada M4V 3B2
Penguin Books (NZ), cnr Airborne and Rosedale Roads,
Albany, Auckland 1310, New Zealand

Penguin Books Ltd, Registered Offices:
80 Strand, London WC2R 0RL, England

First published by Signet, an imprint of New American Library,
a division of Penguin Group (USA) Inc.

First Printing, November 1967
First Printing (New Revised and Expanded Edition), December 1986
First Printing (Third Edition, Revised and Expanded), July 2004
10   9   8   7   6   5   4   3   2   1

PREFACE

The NEW AMERICAN CROSSWORD PUZZLE DIC-
TIONARY was conceived by Albert H. Morehead, the
well-known lexicographer and games expert, and compiled
by a staff trained in the field, headed by Gerard Mosler.
Mr. Morehead was a pioneer in the crossword puzzle field,
having introduced the Cryptic (or Puns and Anagrams)
type of puzzle to the United States, and his long experince
editing dictionaries and encyclopedias made him uniquely
qualified for the task.

As veteran crossword puzzle writer Jack Luzzatto wrote
in the Introduction to the first edition: "This book is the
finest aid available for solving crossword puzzles and other
word games. It is the largest and most compendious book
of its type, as a glance at the richness and range of the
contents pages will reveal. So complete are the various
categories that even a person who is not primarily inter-
ested in crosswords could put it to use as a handy reference
guide in various fields. Special stress has been laid on the
unusual words, exactly the ones that baffle most solvers.
For the puzzle fan, this dictionary is the matchless source
par excellence, a fount of information he cannot do
without."

For the third edition, Albert and Loy Morehead's classic
has been throughly updated and designed to make finding
the right answer easier than ever.

HOW TO USE THIS DICTIONARY

The user will get the most out of this dictionary if a few
moments are spent becoming familiar with the wealth of
information contained herein.

The dictionary is divided into two sections:

SECTION I lists definitions and key words with possible answers, the answers being arranged by length. Phrases (but not hyphenated words) are alphabetized according to the main word, so that "acid neutralizer" comes after "acid" but before "acidity."

SECTION II contains listings of words under a variety of categories (user should consult the index of the section on page vii and note the categories included).

SECTION III provides help in solving Cryptic or Puns and Anagrams puzzles.

Steps to Finding the Right Word

1) Look up the definition in Section I. Usually the best approach is to look up the principal word of the definition. For example, to find "quercine seed," look up "seed"; to find "Afr. antelope," look up "antelope." If the definition asks for a plural or past tense, look up the root word.

2) See if the definition suggests one of the many general categories contained in Section II (see table of contents for listing). A few moments taken to browse through this section will greatly increase the utility of it for the solver.

Readers are encouraged to visit the author's Web site, www.philsbooks.com, for links to online crossword puzzle solving tools and other information.

Happy solving!

—*Philip D. Morehead*
Chicago, 2004

CONTENTS

SECTION I
Definitions and Answers

A

A	ABEL, ALPHA
à la—	MODE, CARTE
à la mode	IN, HIP, CHIC,
	COOL, SMART, STYLISH,
	TRENDY
A to Z	GAMUT
aa	LAVA
aardvark	ANTBEAR,
	ANTEATER, EARTHPIG
Aare, city on the	BERN(E)
Aaron death mount	HOR
Aaron relative	ABIHU, AMRAM,
	MOSES, NADAB, MIRIAM,
	ELEAZAR, ITHAMAR,
	ELISHEBA, JOCHEBED
Aaron's rod	MULLEIN
abaca	HEMP, LUPIS
abacus	SOROBAN, SUANPAN
abaddon	see HELL
abalone	ULLO, AWABI, ORMER,
	UHLLO, SEAEAR, EARSHEL
abandon	MAROON, DISCARD
abandoned	LORN, CORRUPT,
	DERELICT
abase(ment)	LOWER, SHAME,
	MEIOSIS
abash	COW, DAUNT, SHAME,
	HUMBLE
abatement	LETUP
abbé	MONK, PRIEST
abbess	AMMA
abbey	FLY, BADIA, ABADIA,
	PRIORY, NUNNERY
abbot	ABBAS, COARB
abbreviations and acronyms	see
	p. 478
ABC country	CHILE, BRAZIL,
	ARGENTINA
abdicate	RESIGN, RETIRE
abdomen	BELLY, RUMEN,
	VENTER, VISCERA
abdominal	HEMAL, CELIAC,
	COELIAC, VENTRAL
abdominal pain	GAS, COLIC,
	PYROSIS, HEARTBURN
abduct	PRESS, KIDNAP,
	SHANGHAI
Abdul the Bul Bul	AMIR
abecedary	TYRO, PRIMER
Abel's brother	CAIN, SETH
Abelard's beloved	(H)ELOISE

Abelard work	SIC ET NON
abet	EGG, FOMENT, INCITE
abhor	HATE, SCORN, DETEST,
	DESPISE, LOATHE
abhorrent	VILE, NASTY,
	HATEFUL
Abi relative	AHAZ, HEZEKIAH,
	ZECHARIAH
Abiah relative	ASHUR,
	HEZRON
Abie's girl	ROSE
Abiel	KISH, NER
abigail	ABBY, MAID
Abigail relative	AMASA, AMNON,
	DAVID, ITHRA, MERAB, NABAL,
	MICHAL, JONATHAN
Abihail relative	HURI, ELIAB,
	ESTHER, ZURIEL, ABISHUR,
	REHOBOAM
Abijah's son	ASA
ability	TALENT, CALIBER
Abimelech relative	GIDEON,
	JOTHAM, ABIATHAR
Abital relative	DAVID,
	SHEPHATIAH
abject	BASE, VILE, MENIAL,
	SCURVY
abjure	DENY, RECANT, REJECT
ablation	EROSION, REMOVAL,
	SURGERY
ablution	SIDU, WASH, WIDU,
	WUDU, WUZU
— Abner	LIL
Abner relative	NER, KISH,
	SAUL, RIZPAH, JAASIEL
Abner slayer	JOAB
abode	DAR, HUT, NEST,
	HABITAT
abode of bliss	EDEN, GOSHEN,
	ARCADIA
abode of dead	AALU, AARU,
	ARALU, HADES, ORCUS,
	SHEOL
abolitionist	LUNDY, STEVENS,
	GARRISON
abominable snowman	YETI
aboriginal	FIRST, BINGHI,
	NATIVE, INDIGENOUS
aboriginal weapon	NULLA,
	BLOWPIPE, WO(O)MERA,
	BOOMERANG
abortion	FAILURE,
	MISCARRIAGE
abound(ing)	SNY, RIFE, SNEE,
	TEEM, SWARM

about	YAY, ASTO, (IN)RE, NEAR, OR SO, SOME, ANENT, CIRCA
about-face	FLIP, UTURN, REVERSAL, TURNABOUT
above	OER, ATOP, OVER, UPON, SUPER, SUPRA
above all	MOSTLY, PRIMARILY
above water	SAFE, CLEAR, AFLOAT
abrade	RUB, FRET, CHAFE
abrading material	SAND, EMERY, CORUNDUM, SANDPAPER
abrading tool	FILE, RASP, SANDER, GRINDER
Abraham's birthplace	UR
Abraham relative	LOT, ESAU, HARAN, ISAAC, JACOB, MEDAN, NAHOR, SARAH, SHUAH, MIDIAN, TERAH, ISHBAK, ZIMRAN, ISHMAEL, JOKSHAN, KETURAH
Abraham shrine	CAABA, KAABA
abrasive	BO(A)RT, EMERY, PUMICE, CORUNDUM
abridge	RAZEE, CURTAIL, CONDENSE
abridgment	DIGEST, PRECIS, EPITOME
abrogate	ANNUL, CANCEL, RESCIND
abrupt	CURT, RUDE, BLUNT, ICTIC
abrupt flexure	GENU
Absalom's relative	AMASA, DAVID, TAMAR, MAACAH
Absalom's slayer	JOAB
abscess	BOIL, SORE, ULCER, PIMPLE, BLISTER, PUSTULE
abscond	FLEE, ELOIN, ELOPE, DECAMP, ELOIGN, LEVANT
absence permit	EXEAT, LEAVE
absent	OFF, AWAY, AWOL, ABROAD
absinthe	GENIPI, WORMWOOD
absolute	FREE, VERY, ZERO, TOTAL, UTTER, CAPTAIN
absolve	FREE, CLEAR, SHRIVE
absorb	SOAK, SUCK, DRINK, IMBIBE, TAKEIN, OCCLUDE
absorbed	LOST, RAPT, SUNK
absorbent material	GAUZE, TOWEL, SPONGE, BANDAGE, BLOTTER
abstinence	CELIBACY, CHASTITY, CONTINENCE, TEMPERANCE

abstract	ENS, BRIEF, ENTIA, COMPEND, EPITOME
abstruse	ESOTERIC, ACROMATIC
abundance	SCADS, BOUNTY, GALORE, PLETHORA
abundant	RIFE, AMPLE, COPIOUS
abuse	GALI, GALL, RAIL, GALEE, SNASH, REVILE, VIOLATE, MISTREAT
abuse of confidence	PERFIDY, BETRAYAL, INFIDELITY
abut	ADJOIN, BORDER
abutment	ALETTE
abyss	PIT, GULF, CHASM, VORAGO
Abyssinia	AXUM; see ETHIOPIA
Abyssinia, ancient capital	MEROE
Abyssinian	KAF(F)A
acacia	SANT, SUNT, BABUL, GIDYA, KIKAR, MULGA, VEREK, VYALL, BABLAH, BABOOL, GIDGEA, GIDGEE, GIDYEA
academic	MOOT, PEDANTIC
Academy Awards	see p. 505
Acadia	NOVASCOTIA
acadian	CAJUN
accelerate	REV, HASTEN, SPRINT
accent	BLAS, TONE, ACUTE, ARSIS, GRAVE, ICTUS, BROGUE, STRESS, THESES
access	ADIT, ENTRY, ENTREE
accipiter	OWL, HAWK, EAGLE
acclaim	LAUD, ECLAT, PRAISE
acclamation	CRY, SHOUT, OVATION; see CRY
acclivity	SLANT, SLOPE, TALUS
accolade	EMMY, TONY, AWARD, HONOR, OSCAR
accommodate	FIT, LEND, FAVOR, LODGE, BILLET, OBLIGE
accommodation	ROOM, BERTH, FAVOR, PLACE, LODGING(S), QUARTERS, DWELLING, CONCESSION
— accompli	FAIT
accomplish	DO, EFFECT
accomplished	ABLE, GIFTED, SKILLED
accord	UNITY, UNISON, HARMONY, AGREEMENT
accord with	BEFIT
according to	ALA, AUX, PER, ALLA
according to law	LEGAL, LICIT, LEGITIMATE

accordingly	ERGO, THUS, HENCE
accordion	MELODEON, BANDONION, CONCERTINA, SQUEEZEBOX
accost	HAIL, GREET, WAYLAY
account	TAB, TOT, BILL, TALE, STORY, BATTEL, REPORT
account access	ATM
accountant	CA, CPA, SIRCAR, AUDITOR
accounting term	ITEM, ASSET, DEBIT, ENTRY, CREDIT, LEDGER
accouter	GIRD, ARRAY, EQUIP
accumulate	FUND, MASS, AMASS, HOARD, ACCRUE
accurate	JUST, LEAL, NICE
accuse	FRAME, DELATE, INDICT, REPORT
accustom	ENURE, INURE
accustomed	USED, WONT, USUAL, REGULAR, HABITUAL
ace	JOT, ONE, TIP, AONE, TOPS, BASTO, PILOT, SPADILLE
ace hiding place	SLEEVE
ace in the —	HOLE
acerb	SOUR, TART, BITTER
aces	GREAT, TIPTOP
acetone	ACETOL, KETONE
acetylene	FOLAN, ETHINE, ETHYNE, TOLANE
ache	YEN, PAIN, PANG, THROB
Acheron tributary	COCYTUS
Achilles	PELIDES
Achilles friend	PATROCLUS
Achilles horse	XANTHUS
Achilles relative	PELEUS, THETIS
Achilles slayer	PARIS
Achilles teacher	CHIRON, NESTOR
Achilles victim	HECTOR, TROILUS
Achilles vulnerable spot	HEEL
acid	LSD, KEEN, TART, AMINO, BORIC, OLEIC, NITRIC, PECTIC, OLEATE, MURIATIC
acid neutralizer	ALKALI
acid radical	LSD, ACYL, ANION, ACETYL
acidity	ACOR
acknowledge	NOD, OWN, AVOW, ADMIT, GRUNT, CONFESS
acme	CAP, TIP, APEX, CREST, CLIMAX, HEYDAY
acolyte	PATENER, THURIFER

acorn(s)	MAST, OVEST, BELOTE, CAMATA
acquainted	VERSANT
acquiesce	CHIME, ASSENT
acquire	WIN, GAIN, REAP
acre	see p. 638
acreage	LAND, ESTATE
acrobat	NAT, GYMNAST, TUMBLER, AERIALIST
acrobat equipment	MAT, BARS, POLE, WIRE, RINGS, TRAMPOLINE
acronyms	see p. 478
acropolis	CADMEA, CITADEL, LARISSA
across	OER, OVER, TRAN(S)
across the board	TOTALLY, UTTERLY, COMPLETELY
acrostic	AGLA, PUZZLE, TELESTIC(H), WORDPLAY, ABECEDARIUS
act	LAW, ACTU, BILL, DEED, FEAT, PLAY, WORK, ACTUS, EMOTE
act out	MIME, ENACT, MIMIC, PORTRAY
acting award	EMMY, TONY, GLOBE, OSCAR
actinide series	CURIUM, FERMIUM, THORIUM, URANIUM, ACTINIUM, NOBELIUM, AMERICIUM, BERKELIUM, NEPTUNIUM, PLUTONIUM, LAWRENCIUM, MENDELEVIUM, CALIFORNIUM, EINSTEINIUM, PROTACTINIUM
action	DEED, FIGHT, WORKS, AGENCY, PRAXIS, CONDUCT
action, put into	ACTUATE
action word	VERB
active	BUSY, SPRY, AGILE, ALERT, BRISK, NIMBLE
activist org., former	SDS
actor	HAM, DOER, MIME, AGENT, SERIO, EMOTER, MUMMER, PLAYER, STAGER, HISTRIO, THESPIAN, HISTRION
actors' group	CAST, ACTRA, AFTRA, TROOP, EQUITY, TROUPE
actor's hint	CUE, LINE, PROMPT
actress	DIVA, STAR, HEROINE, INGENUE, STARLET
actual	REAL, TRUE, DEFACTO
actual, take as	POSIT

actuate	ROUSE, INCITE
acuate	POINTED, SHARPEN
acuity	WIT, EDGE
acute	KEEN, SHARP, SHREWD
A.D.	ANNO DOMINI
A.D. coiner	STBEDE
ad	*see* ADVERTISEMENT
ad hoc	INFORMAL, MAKESHIFT, TEMPORARY
ad infinitum	FOREVER, ENDLESSLY
ad lib	CASUAL, OFFHAND
adage	SAW, DICT, MAXIM
Adah relative	ESAU, JABAL, JUBAL, LAMECH
Adaiah relative	JEDIDAH
Adam (Norse)	ASKR
Adam Bede author	ELIOT
Adam relative	EVE, ABEL, CAIN, ENOS, SETH, LILITH
Adam's ale	WATER
Adam's apple	LARYNX
Adam's needle	YUCCA
Adam's teacher	RAISEL
adamant	SET, FIRM, HARD
Adamite	NUDIST, NATURIST
adapt	SUIT, ADJUST, ATTUNE
add	SUM, TOT, FOOT, TOTE, AFFIX, ANNEX, TOTAL, APPEND, THROWIN
add insult to injury	WORSEN, AGGRAVATE
add up to	MEAN, TOTAL, PRODUCE
Addams Family name	ITT, GOMEZ, LURCH, THING, COOGAN, FESTER, PUGSLEY, MORTICIA
addendum	PS, RIDER, CODICIL
adder	*see* VIPER
addict(ion)	FAN, BUFF, HOOK, USER, FIEND, HABIT, JUNKIE, MONKEY, DEVOTEE
adding machine	COMPUTER, TOTALIZER, CALCULATOR
Addison partner	STEELE
addition(s)	ELL, AFFIX, RIDER, ADDEND, ENCORE, ADDENDA, CODICIL
addle	MIRE, MUDDLE
addlepated	STUPID, IDIOTIC, MUDDLED, PINHEAD, PEABRAIN
add-on	EXTRA, ATTACHMENT
address	HAIL, TACT, GREET, ACCOST, SPEECH
Adeline	ADDY
Adenauer nickname	(DER)ALTE
adenoids	TONSILS

adept	APT, EXPERT, VERSED
adequate	DUE, FIT, MEET, AMPLE
adhere	GLUE, HOLD, CLING, CLEAVE
adherent	IST, ITE, AIDE, ALLY, VOTARY
adhesive	TAR, GUM, GLUE, EPOXY, GLUEY, GUMMY, PASTE, CEMENT
adipose	FAT, OBESE, SQUAB, SQUAT
adjective	ADNOUN
adjective ending	IC, ENT, IAL, ILE, INE, ISH, IST, ITE, IVE, OUS, ICAL
adjourn	DEFER, DELAY, SUSPEND, PROROGUE
adjudicate	TRY, HEAR, JUDGE, DECIDE
adjunct	ADDON, ANNEX, EXTRA, PARTTIME
adjust	FIT, FIX, SET, TRIM, TRUE, ALIGN, ATTUNE, SETTLE
adjutant	AIDE, STORK, ARGALA, HURGILA
adjutant bird	CRANE, STORK, ARGALA, HURGILA, MARABOU
adman	FLACK, PRMAN, BARKER, HUCKSTER, PUBLICIST
Admetus' wife	ALCESTIS
administration	REGIME, RUNNING, EXECUTIVE
administrative	CLERICAL, MANAGERIAL
admiral	KING
admiral, famous	BYRD, SPEE, DEWEY, LEAHY, HALSEY, NELSON, NIMITZ, PORTER, FARRAGUT
admiral, type of	REAR, VICE, FLEET
Admiralty island	MANUS, RAMBUTYO
admire	ESTEEM, REVERE
admirer	BEAU, SUITOR
admission	PASS, CARD, ACCESS, AVOWAL, ENTREE, TICKET
admit	OWN, ALLOW, FESS (UP), GRANT, CONCEDE
admittedly	TO BE SURE, CERTAINLY
admonish	URGE, WARN, CHIDE, EXHORT
admonisher	MONITOR

ado   FUSS, STIR, POTHER
adobe   CLAY, BRICK
adolescence   TEENS, YOUTH,
   NONAGE, PUBERTY
adolescent   TEEN, MINOR,
   CALLOW, NUBILE, SUBDEB,
   PREBETIC, TEENAGER
Adonis' beloved   APHRODITE
Adonis relative   MYRRA(H),
   CINYRAS
Adonis' slayer   BOAR
adorn   DECK, PINK, TRAP,
   BEGEM, DIGHT, BEDIZEN
Adriana servant   LUCE
Adriatic city   BARI, FIUME,
   RIMINI, VALONA, TRIESTE
adrift   ASEA, LOST
adroit   DEFT, HABILE, NIMBLE
adulation   GLORY, KUDOS,
   PRAISE
adult   MAN, GROWN, OFAGE,
   WOMAN, MATURE, NUBILE,
   GROWNUP
adulterate   MIX, ALLOY,
   DEACON, DEBASE, DEFILE,
   DILUTE, CORRUPT
advance   AID, ABET, LOAN,
   RAISE, FOSTER, PROMOTE
advance guard   VAN
advance man   AGENT
advance slowly   INCH, NOSE,
   CREEP
advanced   OLD, AGED, LATER,
   MODERN, SENIOR,
   COMPLEX, ELDERLY
advantage   BOT(E), PRO, EDGE,
   AVAIL, PROFIT, BENEFIT,
   TOEHOLD
advantage, in tennis   ADIN,
   ADOUT
advantage, one having an   IN,
   HOME TEAM
advantage, take   ABUSE, CHEAT,
   EXPLOIT
advent   COMING, ARRIVAL
adventure   GEST, RISK, GESTE,
   DARING
adventurer   GAMBLER,
   DAREDEVIL, PICAROON
adventuress   DEMIREP
adversity   BUMMER, MISHAP,
   HARDSHIP
advertisement   AD, PLUG,
   BLURB, FLYER, ADVERT,
   NOTICE, TRAILER,
   COMMERCIAL
advertisement, type of   DISPLAY,
   CLASSIFIED
advertiser   SPONSOR

advice   LORE, REDE, AVISO,
   CAVEAT, COUNSEL
adviser   SAGE, EGERIA,
   MENTOR, NESTOR, KIBITZER
advisory   WARNING
advocate   PRO, ATTY, BACK,
   ANGEL, FAVOR, BACKER,
   ATTORNEY, PROMOTER
Aeetes daughter   MEDEA
Aegean island   IOS, NIO, MELOS,
   SAMOS, TENOS, LESBOS,
   PATMOS, MYTILENE
Aegean river   STRUMA
Aegean sea   SAROS
Aegeon wife   AEMILIA
Aegeus wife   MEDEA
Aegir's wife   RAN
Aeneas friend   ACHATES
Aeneas relative   VENUS,
   CREUSA, ANCHISES,
   ASCANIUS
Aeneid poet   VERGIL, VIRGIL
Aengus mother   BOANN
Aeolian lyric poet   SAPPHO
Aeolus relative   DORUS,
   CANACA, ORSEIS, XUTHUS,
   ATHAMAS, CRETHEUS,
   HALCYONE, HIPPOTES,
   SALMONEUS
Aeschylus play   ORESTEIA,
   PERSIANS, SUPPLIANTS
Acsir   *see* NORSE GODS, *p. 649*
Aeson relative   JASON, PELIAS
affair   EVENT, LIAISON
affect   FAKE, MOVE, FEIGN,
   PUTON, UPSET, INFLUENCE
affected   FALLAL, BELOVED
affectionate   FOND, DOTING
affirm   AVER, AVOW, STATE,
   VOUCH, ASSERT, ATTEST
affirmative   AY(E), YEA, YES,
   AMEN
affix   PIN, JOIN, SEAL, STAMP
afflict(ion)   AIL, PLY, TRY, VEX,
   WOE, HURT, ONUS, CURSE,
   DISTRESS
affluence   EASE, FLOW,
   PLENTY, RICHES
affray   RIOT, BRAWL, MELEE
Afghan   DURANI
Afghan city/town   ARIA, FARAH,
   HERAT, KABUL, KALAT,
   GHAZNI, KUNDUZ, NIMRUZ,
   PANJAO, TERMIZ,
   KANDAHAR
Afghan language   DARI,
   TURKIC, PASHTO, PUSHTO,
   TURKMEN; *see* IRANIAN
Afghan measure   JERIB, KAROH

Afghan money   PUL, ABBASI,
     AMANIA, AFGHANI
Afghan mountain   KOH, SAFED,
     PAMIRS, HINDUKUSH
Afghan neighbor   IRAN, CHINA,
     INDIA, PAKISTAN,
     TAJIKISTAN, UZBEKISTAN,
     TURKMENISTAN
Afghan parliament   JIRGA,
     SHURA, WOLESI
Afghan people   TAJIK, UZBEK,
     HAZARA, PASHTUN, SISTANI
Afghan river   HARI, BALKH,
     HARUT, KABUL, LURAH,
     GHAZNI, TARNAK
Afghan ruler   KARZAI,
     TALIBAN, RABBANI,
     NAJIBULLAH
Afghanistan, capital of   KABUL
aficionado   FAN, BUFF,
     DEVOTEE
afore   ERE
aforesaid   DITTO, PRIOR, SUPRA
aforethought   PREPENSE
afraid   RAD, ADRAD, REDDE
afreet   GIANT; *see* DEMON
African carrier   TSETSE
African city/town   BO, ABA,
     ADO, EDE, FES, IWO, KANO,
     ORAN, SALE, ACCRA, AZROU,
     BEIRA, DAKAR, ENUGU,
     JINJA, NDOLA, KABWE, KITWE,
     RABAT; *see* p. 598
African desert   ERG, LIBYAN,
     NUBIAN, SAHARA,
     KALAHARI
African gulf   ADEN, GABES,
     SIDRA, GUINEA
African instrument   MBIRA,
     NANGA, REHAB, SANSI,
     ZANZE, BALAFO
African island   BIOKO, PEMBA,
     AZORES, HELENA,
     ANNOBON, BOURBON,
     MADAGASCAR
African lake   CHAD, LIFU,
     TANA, NYASA, ALBERT,
     ASSALE, DEMBEL, EDWARD,
     KARIBA, MALAWI, NASSER,
     RUDOLF, VICTORIA,
     TANGANYIKA
African language   TIV, EFIK,
     EKOI, FULA, GEEZ, GOLA,
     SAHO, TAAL, KISSI, LIMBA,
     MENDE, SERER, TEMNE,
     WOLOF, BERBER, FULANI,
     IBIBIO, BALANTE, SWAHILI;
     see BANTU, NIGER-CONGO,
     CUSHITIC, SEMITIC

African mountain   KIBO,
     ELGON, KENYA, NATAL,
     TOUBKAL, RUWENZORI,
     KILIMANJARO
African port   ORAN, ACCRA,
     DAKAR, LAGOS, TUNIS,
     LUANDA
African river   NILE, VAAL,
     CONGO, NIGER, VOLTA,
     ZAIRE, ORANGE, LIMPOPO,
     SENEGAL, ZAMBEZI
African sectarian   COPT,
     ABELITE
African tree   IFE, BAKU, BOBO,
     COLA, ODUM, ROKA, SHEA,
     ABURA, ADJAB, AFARA, BUMBO,
     DJAVE, IROKO, KHAYA, LIMBA,
     NARAS, NJAVE, OCHNA,
     OWALA, POOLI, SASSY, UNONA,
     KORINA, MAFUR(R)A, TURTOSA,
     SASSWOOD; *see* TREE
African tribe   *see* p. 735
Afrikaans   TAAL
aft   ABAFT, ASTERN
after a while   ANON, SOON,
     SHORTLY
after expenses   NET
aftereffect   WAKE
aftermath   ROWEN, ARRISH,
     EDDISH, EDGREY
afterpiece, comic   EXODE
aftersong   EPODE
Agag slayer   SAMUEL
again   BIS, EFT, ANEW, ANON,
     TWICE, ENCORE
against   CON, ANTI, VERSUS
against the law   ILLEGAL,
     ILLICIT, UNLAWFUL
agalloch   AGAR, AGGUR,
     ALOES, GAROC, TAMBAC
Agamemnon kingdom   MYCENAE
Agamemnon relative   AEROPE,
     ATREUS, ELECTRA, ORESTES,
     MENELAUS
Agamemnon, rescued by   BRISEIS
agate   ONYX, ACHATE,
     MARBLE
agave   ALOE, TULA, ISTLE,
     IXTLE, SISAL, SIZAL,
     MAGUEY, ZAPUPE
age   ERA, ELD, EON, AERA,
     RIPEN, YEARS, SENESCE
Age of Anxiety poet   AUDEN
age, of same   COEVAL
aged   OLD, ANILE, OLDEN,
     SENILE
Agena   ATLAS
agency   ARM, CIA, FBI, FDA,
     FHA, FTC, HUD, ICC, IRS,

NRA, NSA, OPA, DESK, DINT,
NASA, WING, MEANS,
MEDIUM; see U.N., NEWS
Agenor relative **EUROPA**
agent **FED, IST, SPY, AMIN,**
DOER, GMAN, NARC, TMAN,
PROXY, WALLA, MEDIUM,
WALLAH
ages **ICE, IRON, STONE,**
ATOMIC, BRONZE
agglomerate **HEAP, LUMP,**
MASS, SLAG
aggravate **NAG, TWIT, ENRAGE**
aggression **RAID, ANGER,**
ATTACK, ASSAULT,
HOSTILITY
agile **LISH, SPRY, NIMBLE,**
LISSOME, SPRINGE
agitate **FRET, STIR, CHURN,**
ROUSE
agitation **GOG, FRET, STIR,**
DITHER, POTHER
agitator **RIOTER, INCITER,**
MUTINEER, ANARCHIST
aglow **ALIT, RADIANT, SHINING**
agnomen **EPITHET, NICKNAME**
agnostic **ATHEOUS, INFIDEL,**
SKEPTIC, NESCIENT
agnus **DEI**
ago **SYNE, YORE, SINCE**
agony **WOE, PAIN, THROE**
agora coin **OBOL**
Agra tomb **TAJ(MAHAL)**
Agram **ZAGREB**
agree **GEE, YES, GIBE, JIBE,**
GRANT, TALLY, CONCUR
agreeable **LIEF, AMENE, SUENT**
agreement **MISE, COVIN, IKRAR,**
ACCORD, CARTEL, ENTENTE
agriculture goddess **CERES,**
DEMETER
Agrippina's son **NERO**
Ahab cabin boy **PIP**
Ahab relative **OMRI, AHAZIAH,**
JEHORAM, JEZEBEL,
ATHALIAH
Ahab ship **PEQUOD**
Ahasuerus' minister **(II)AMAN**
Ahaz relative **JOTHAM,**
HEZEKIAH, MANASSEH
Ahinoam spouse **SAUL, DAVID**
Aholibamah's husband **ESAU**
ai **SLOTH**
aid **ABET, HELP, ASSIST,**
SUCCOR
Aida composer **VERDI**
Aida role **AIDA, AMNERIS,**
RADAMES, RAMPHIS,
AMONASRO

aide memoire **CRIB,**
MEMO(RANDUM)
aim **END, BUTT, ACIES,**
ETELE, VISIE
— aimée **BIEN**
air **AER, ARIA, AURA, MIEN,**
TELE, TUNE, DITTY, ETHER,
OZONE, AERATE
air base, U.S. **GUAM, OFFUT,**
SCOTT, ANDREWS, LANGLEY,
LINDSEY, MAXWELL,
KIRKLAND, RANDOLPH
air component **NEON, ARGON,**
XENON, HELIUM, OXYGEN,
KRYPTON, NITROGEN
air conditioning term **BTU,**
FREON, CONDENSER
air, pert. to **AERO, AURAL**
air raid **BALBO**
air taxi **SHUTTLE**
aircraft **JET, MIG, GYRO, KITE,**
SHIP, SPAD, ZERO, STUKA,
AVION, BLIMP, DRONE, PLANE,
BOMBER, COPTER, AIRSHIP,
BALLOON, GLIDER, BIPLANE,
FIGHTER, MUSTANG,
PROPJET, AEROSTAT, AIRPLANE,
SPITFIRE, ZEPPELIN,
AEROPLANE, DIRIGIBLE,
MONOPLANE
aircraft carrier **HORNET,**
MIDWAY, RANGER,
TRUMAN, VINSON, AMERICA,
FLATTOP, LANGLEY,
STENNIS, INTREPID,
SARATOGA, YORKTOWN,
FORRESTAL, KITTYHAWK,
ENTERPRISE
aircraft designer **FOKKER,**
CURTISS, SIKORSKY
aircraft group **WING,**
SQUADRON
aircraft part **BAY, GUN, FLAP,**
HOOD, KEEL, NOSE, SKEW,
TAIL, WING, STICK, STRUT,
CABANE, ELEVON, RUDDER,
AILERON, AIRFOIL, BLISTER,
COWLING, NACELLE
air-driven **PNEUMATIC**
airfoil **FIN, WING**
Air Force mascot **FALCON**
airline **LOT, TACA, DELTA,**
PANAM, USAIR, VARIG,
CANJET, COMAIR, IBERIA,
QANTAS, SABENA, UNITED,
EASTERN, FINNAIR,
AEROFLOT, ALITALIA,
AMERICAN, MEXICANA
airplane **see AIRCRAFT**

airplane accident victim, famous
    CLINE, CROCE, HOLLY,
    MILLER, NELSON, REDDING,
    VANZANT
airplane shelter   HANGAR
airport   JFK, ORLY, LOGAN,
    OHARE, DULLES, GANDER,
    MIDWAY, NARITA, REAGAN,
    CROYDON, GATWICK,
    KENNEDY, PEARSON, SCHIPOL,
    SHANNON, CIAMPINO,
    DEGAULLE, HEATHROW,
    IDLEWILD, FIUMICINO,
    LAGUARDIA, STAPLETON,
    TEMPELHOF
airport abbr.   ETA, ETD
airport codes   see p. 493
airport name part   INTL
airport part   APRON, PYLON,
    STRIP, TOWER, HANGAR,
    RUNWAY, TARMAC
airport sight   LIMO
airship   *see* AIRCRAFT
airtight   HERMETIC
airy   AERIAL, JAUNTY,
    ETHEREAL
ait   ILE, EYOT, HOLM, ISLE(T)
Ajax relative   TELAMON
Akan language   TWI, TCHI, TSHI
akin   SIB, AGNATE, COGNATE,
    GERMANE
Alabama   see also p. 615
Alabama city/town   PELL, TROY,
    SELMA, MOBILE, GADSDEN,
    ANNISTON
Alabama Indian   CREEK,
    POARCH, CHOCTAW,
    SHAWNEE, CHEROKEE
Alabama lake   LAY, WEISS,
    JORDAN, HARDING
Alabama river   ELK, PEA,
    COOSA, CAHABA, LITTLE,
    MOBILE, SIPSEY, TENSAW
Aladdin monkey   ABU
Aladdin servant   GENIE
—alai   JAI
alameda   MALL, WALK
Alamo hero   BOWIE, CROCKETT
alarm   SOS, LARUM, PANIC,
    SIREN, TOCSIN
alas   ACH, HEU, OCR, OME,
    VAE, OIME, OHONE,
    OCHONE, OTOTOI
Alaska   see also p. 615
Alaskan city/town   NOME,
    KENAI, SITKA, BETHEL,
    KODIAK, SEWARD, VALDEZ
Alaskan glacier   MUIR, GUYOT,
    BERING

Alaskan highway   ALCAN
Alaskan island   HALL, KING,
    KUIU, UNGA, KAYAK, KISKA,
    OTTER, SANAK, UMNAK,
    KODIAK, ETOLIN, YAKOBI,
    AFOGNAK, NUNIVAK,
    PRIBILOF
Alaskan lake   CLARK, SELAWIK,
    BECHAROF
Alaskan mountain   ADA, BEAR,
    BONA, COOK, HAYES, KENAI,
    MCKINLEY
Alaskan mountain range   BAIRD,
    BROOKS, TAYLOR, WARING,
    ALEUTIAN
Alaskan native   ALEUT
Alaskan river   TAKU, FIRTH,
    KOBUK, MEADE, STONY,
    WHITE, YUKON, COPPER,
    TANANA, KOYUKUK,
    SUSITNA, PORCUPINE
Alaskan volcano   KISKA,
    KATMAI, PAVLOF, TANAGA
Albania, capital of   TIRANA
Albanian   GHEG
Albanian city/town   BERAT,
    KORCA, KUKES, VLORA,
    DURRES
Albanian dialect   G(H)EG, TOSK
Albanian king   ZOG(U)
Albanian lake   OHRID, PRESPA,
    SCUTARI, BURRINTIT
Albanian money   LEK, FRANC,
    QINTAR
Albanian neighbor   GREECE,
    SERBIA, MACEDONIA
Albanian river   DRIN, ISHM,
    OSUM, BUENE, SEMAN,
    DEVOLL, VIJOSE
albatross   NELLY, GOONEY
Alberta   see also p. 614
Alberta city/town   ACME, ADEN,
    ALIX, IRMA, MILO, OLDS,
    OYEN, BANFF, BOYLE, EDSON,
    FAUST, HABAY, HANNA,
    HILDA, HYTHE, LEDUC, RYLEY,
    BARONS, CEREAL, CHATEH,
    IRVINE, JASPER, MOMONT,
    SUNDRA, TILLEY, VULCAN,
    WOKING, CALGARY, CONKLIN,
    RALSTON, WABASCA, COLD
    LAKE, EDMONTON
Alberta lake   COLD, GULL,
    SLAVE, CLAIRE, LEGEND,
    LOUISE, PIGEON, UTIKUMA,
    PAKOWSKI, PEERLESS,
    PRIMROSE, ATHABASCA
Alberta mountain   HOUSE,
    TROUT, CASTLE, ROBSON,

	WALLACE, COLUMBIA, ASSINIBOINE
Alberta river	BOW, HAY, PEACE, SLAVE, SMOKY, BATTLE, WAPITI, RED DEER, WABASCA, ATHABASCA, SASKATCHEWAN
Albion	ENGLAND
Alceste composer	GLUCK
Alcestis relative	ADMETUS
Alcides	HERCULES
Alcinous garden	SCHERIA
Alcmene relative	PERSEUS, HERACLES, AMPHITRYON
alcohol	ALKY, AMYL, ETHAL, ETHYL, IDITE, IDITOL, STEROL, TALITE; see DRINK, LIQUOR
alcohol solid	STERIN, STEROL
alcoholic	SOT, WINY, BEERY, VINIC
Alcott heroine	JO, AMY, MEG, BETH
alcove	BAY, NOOK, BOWER, NICHE, ORIEL, RECESS
alder	ARN, ALISO, ALNUS
alderman	BAILIE
ale	see BEER
alee, opposite of	STOSS
alembic	STILL, RETORT
alert	TELL, WAKY, WARN, ALARM, AWARE, SIREN, WARNING, WATCHFUL, ON ONES TOES
Aleutian island	FOX, RAT, ADAK, ATTU, NEAR, UNIMAK, UNALASKA
alewife	SHAD; see HERRING
Alexander battle site	ISSUS
Alexander father	PHILIP
Alexander kingdom	MACEDON(IA)
Alexander tutor	ARISTOTLE
Alexander victory	TYRE, IRBIL, ISSUS, MILETUS, GRANICUS
Alexander wife	ROXANA
alfalfa	LUCERN(E)
Alfonso queen	ENA
alfresco	OPENAIR, OUTDOOR
alfresco meal	ROAST, PICNIC, BARBECUE
alga(e)	FUCI, NORI, DASYA, FUCUS, ALARIA, DESMID, DIATOM
Algeria	NUMIDI, POMARIA
Algeria, capital of	ALGIERS, ELDJAZAIR
Algerian city/town	BONE, ORAN, BLIDA, BORDJ, MEDEA, SETIF, ANNABA, SKIKDA, ALGIERS, TINDOUF

Algerian desert	ERG, IGUIDI, SAHARA
Algerian language	ARABIC, BERBER
Algerian measure	TARRI, TERMIN
Algerian money	DINAR
Algerian mountain	AISSA, TAHAT
Algerian neighbor	MALI, LIBYA, NIGER, MOROCCO, TUNISIA, MAURITANIA
Algerian weight	ROTL, UCKIA
Algernon	ALGY
Algiers district	KASBA, CASBAH, KASBAH
Algonquian language or tribe	FOX, SAC, CREE, SAUK, ABNAKI, MICMAC, OJIBWA, ARAPAHO, MAHICAN, PAMLICO, SHAWNEE, CHEYENNE, DELAWARE, ILLINOIS, MENOMINI, POWHATAN
Ali Baba brother	CASSIM
Ali Baba helper	MORGIANA
Ali Baba password	SESAME
Ali's descendants	ALID(E)S
Ali's wife	FATIMA
alias	AKA, ELSE, NAME, EPITHET, PENNAME
alibi	PLEA, EXCUSE, PRETEXT
Alice	ALYS
Alice name	FLO, MEL, RAYE, VERA, LAVIN, CARRIE
Alice's cat	DINAH
alien	GER, METIC, MARTIAN, STRANGE, OUTSIDER
alienate	WEAN, ESTRANGE
alienist	SHRINK, PSYCHIATRIST
align	TRAM, TRUE, DRESS, RANGE
alike	AKIN, SAME, EQUAL
aliment	see FOOD
alimentary canal	ENTERON
alive	SPRY, ALERT, QUICK, LIVING
alkali	LYE, REH, SODA, USAR, POTASH
alkali metals	CESIUM, SODIUM, LITHIUM, FRANCIUM, HYDROGEN, RUBIDIUM, POTASSIUM
alkaline earth metals	BARIUM, RADIUM, CALCIUM, BERYLLIUM, MAGNESIUM, STRONTIUM
alkaloid	CERINE, CODEIN, ESERIN, THEINE, CAFFEIN, CODEINE, ESERINE, CAFFEINE

all	TOTAL, WHOLE, ENTIRE	allspice	PIMENTO
all alternative	NONE	allude	HINT, IMPLY, ADVERT
all —	OUT, SET, EARS	allure	TICE, TOLE, TOLL,
All in the Family character			DECOY, TEMPT, ENTICE
EDITH, ARCHIE, GLORIA,		allusion	INKLING, INNUENDO
LIONEL, LOUISE, REINER,		almighty	CREATOR, SUPREME,
OCONNOR, MEATHEAD,			INVINCIBLE
STAPLETON		almond emulsion	AMARIN,
All in the Family producer LEAR,			ORGEAT, AMARINE
KANTER, LACHMAN		almost	NIGH, ANEAR, NEARLY
All Quiet on the Western Front		alms	DOLE, CORBAN,
author	REMARQUE		MAUNDY, HANDOUT
All Saints' Day eve HALLOWEEN		alms chest	ARCA, RELIQUARY
All's Well That Ends Well		aloe	LILY, AGAVE, MAGUEY
character	DIANA, LAFEU,	aloe substance	ALOIN, PICRA
HELENA, BERTRAM,		alone	LORN, SOLA, SOLE,
LAVACHE, PAROLLES			SOLO, SOLUS
alla —	BREVE	aloof	COOL, ABACK, REMOTE
Allah	see GOD	alpaca-like animal	LLAMA,
allay EASE, SLAKE, ASSUAGE,			VICUNA, GUANACO
PALLIATE		alpha and —	OMEGA
allegation CLAIM, CHARGE,		alphabet	ABC(S), OGAM,
ACCUSATION			OGUM, OGHAM, SARADA,
Allegheny city/town OLEAN,			FUTHORC, CROSSROW
WARREN, PITTSBURGH		alphabet character	RUNE
allegiance	FEALTY	alphabet, phonetic ECHO, GOLF,
allegory EMBLEM, APOLOG,			KILO, LIMA, MIKE, PAPA,
ANAGOGE, PARABLE,			XRAY, ZULU, ALPHA, BRAVO,
APOLOGUE			DELTA, HOTEL, INDIA,
allergic AVERSE, SENSITIVE			OSCAR, ROMEO, TANGO,
allergy ATOPY, REACTION			QUEBEC, SIERRA, VICTOR,
allergy cause DUST, MITE,			WHISKY, YANKEE, CHARLIE,
MOLD, POLLEN, DANDER			FOXTROT, UNIFORM,
allergy symptom ITCH, RASH,			JULIETTE, NOVEMBER
HIVES		alphabets	TEMA, LATIN,
alley MIB, LOKE, WYND, TEWER			OGHAM, ONMUN, OSCAN,
Alley Oop character OOLA			RUNIC, THERA, ATTICA,
alliance UN, EEC, OAS, AXIS,			BRAHMI, CARIAN, HANKUL,
BLOC, NATO, OASS, OPEC,			LYDIAN, NASHKI, ARAMAIC,
ASEAN, SEATO, SHAPE,			CHALCIS, MILETUS,
LEAGUE, ENTENTE			MOABITE, PAHLAVI,
allice SHAD, ALEWIFE			PALMYRA, SABAEAN,
allied AKIN, AGNATE,			UMBRIAN, CYRILLIC,
COGNATE			ETRUSCAN, FALISCAN,
alligator ALBERT; see			LIBYANIC, SUMERIAN,
CROCODILE			CUNEIFORM, GLAGOLITIC,
alligator pear AVOCADO			PHOENICIAN; see p. 623
allot DOLE, METE, CAVEL,		Alphaeus relative	JAMES
GRANT		Alpine	NORDIC
allotment see PORTION		Alpine dress	DIRNDL,
allow LET, LOW, GRANT,			LEDERHOSEN
ENDURE		Alps	see MOUNTAINS
allowance BOT(E), DOLE, ODDS,		Alps pass	see PASS
TARE, TRET, ARRAS, STINT,		also	EIK, EKE, PLUS, DITTO
MARGIN		altar	ED, ARA, BOMOS,
alloy PIG, BRASS, INVAR, STEEL,			HAIKAL, VEDIKA, CHANTRY
ALNICO, BRONZE, PEWTER,		altar boy	ACOLYTE, THURIFER
SOLDER, AMALGAM, MIXTURE,		altar cloth	PALL(A), DOSSAL,
CARBOLOY; see p. 690			HAPLOMA

altar part	BEMA, MENSA, GRADIN, RIDDEL, SEPTUM, DIPTYCH, PISCINA, RETABLE, PREDELLA, TRIPTYCH
alter	GELD, VARY, MUTATE
alter ego	SELF, FRIEND
altercation	SPAT, TIFF, FRACAS, DISPUTE, QUARREL, SQUABBLE
alternate	OTHER, WAVER, ROTATE, OSCILLATE
alternative	OR, ANDOR, CHOICE, OPTION, SUBSTITUTE
alternator	DYNAMO, GENERATOR
although	EEN, ALBEIT
altogether	INTOTO, WHOLLY
altruism	CHARITY, HUMANITY, GENEROSITY
altruist	SAMARITAN
alula	SQUAMA
aluminum ore	MICA, KAOLIN, SPINEL, ALUNITE, BAUXITE, CORUNDUM, CRYOLITE, FELDSPAR, TURQUOISE
alumni	GRADS, PUPILS
always	AYE, E(V)ER
amadou	PUNK, TINDER
Amalekite king	AGAG
amaryllis	AGAVE, AMOLE, DAFFY, GUACO, JONQUIL, DAFFODIL, NARCISSUS
Amata relative	LATINIA, LAVINIA
amateur	TYRO, NOVICE, DABBLER, NEOPHYTE
amazed	AGAPE, STUNNED, STARTLED
amazing	UNCANNY, REMARKABLE
Amazon discoverer	PINZON
Amazon estuary	PARA
Amazon port	MANAUS
Amazon queen	ANTIOPE, HIPPOLYTA
Amazon tributary	APA, ICA, JARI, NAPO, PARA, PARU, JURUA, JUTAI, NEGRO, PURUS, XINGU, JAVARI, MADERIA, TAPOJOS, HUALLAGA, TROMBETAS
ambassador	ELCHI, VAKIL, ELCHEE, LEGATE, NUNCIO
amber	RESIN, LAMMER, SUCCIN, ELECTRUM, MEDREGAL
ambit	SCOPE, SPHERE
amble	PADNAG
ambrosia	MANNA, NECTAR

ambush	TRAP, BLIND, WAYLAY
amend	BEETE, REPAIR, REVISE
amendment	RIDER, CODICIL
amends, make	ATONE
ament	CHAT, IDIOT, MORON, CATKIN, CATTAIL, GOSLING
amerce	FINE, MULCT, AFFEER
American	GRINGO, YANK(EE)
American artist	(MAN) RAY, WOOD, CURRY, HOMER, MOSES, PEALE, SHAHN, SLOAN, BENTON, CALDER, CATLIN, EAKINS, HOPPER, ROTHKO, STUART, AUDUBON, CASSATT, OKEEFFE, POLLOCK, SARGENT, MACLEISH, ROCKWELL, REMINGTON
American Graffiti diner	MELS
American Graffiti name	CURT, JOHN, TOAD, CAROL, STEVE, DEBBIE, LAURIE, DREYFUS
American Indian	*see* NATIVE AMERICAN
American playwright	MAMET, ODETS, MILLER, ONEILL, WILDER, KAUFMAN, SAROYAN, SHERWOOD, WILLIAMS
American poet	POE, AUDEN, BENET, FROST, MOORE, PLATH, POUND, LOWELL, MILLAY, PARKER, LINDSAY, STEVENS, WHITMAN, SANDBURG, TEASDALE, WHITTIER, LONGFELLOW
American writer	AGEE, JONG, KING, RAND, ALGER, CRANE, LEWIS, OATES, OHARA, STEIN, STOWE, TWAIN, TYLER, WELTY, WOLFE, CAPOTE, CLANCY, COOPER, FERBER, IRVING, LONDON, PROULX, RUNYON, SONTAG, UPDIKE, DREISER, FARRELL, HAMMETT, HURSTON, THOREAU, THURBER, CRICHTON, DOCTOROW, FAULKNER, MELVILLE, MICHENER, MITCHELL, MORRISON, SINCLAIR, SPILLANE, VONNEGUT, HEMINGWAY, MCCULLERS, STEINBECK, FITZGERALD
amide, *pert. to*	AMIC
Amiens river	SOMME
amino acid	LYSIN, SERIN, VALIN, ALANIN, LYSINE, SERINE, VALINE, ALANINE, GLYCINE

Amish	MENNONITE	Anatolia	see TURKEY
amiss	AWRY, AGLEY, ASTRAY	Anatolian language	LUIAN,
ammonia compound	AMIN,	LUVIAN, LUWIAN, LYCIAN,	
	AMIDE, AMINE		LYDIAN, HITTITE
ammunition	AMMO, AMMU,	anatomy	FRAME(WORK),
	SHOT	BIOLOGY, ZOOTOMY,	
amnesia	FUGUE		STRUCTURE
amnesty	STAR, PARDON,	ancestor	SIRE, MANU, ELDER,
	REPRIEVE		ATAVUS, BELSIRE
Amon relative	JOSIAH	ancestral	AVAL, AVITAL
Amon-Re relative	MUT	ancestral spirit	ANITO, LARES
Amos 'n' Andy name	AMOS,	Anchises relative	AENEAS
ANDY, MAMA, CALHOUN,		anchor	FIX, MOOR, AFFIX,
	KINGFISH	BOWER, KEDGE, DROGUE,	
amount	FECK, MISE, RISE,		GRAPNEL, KILLICK
	RATAL	anchor chain	CABLE
amour-propre	VANITY	anchor lifter	DANDY, CAPSTAN
ampersand	AND, ALSO, PLUS	anchor part	ARM, CAT, PEE,
amphibian	HYLA, ANURA,	PALM, RING, TORE, CROWN,	
ANURAN, APODA,		FLUKE, SHANK, TOROID	
CAUDATA, CAUDATE,		anchorite	HERMIT, STYLITE
COSTATA, URODELA,		ancient	OLD, AGED, EARLY,
CAECILIA, SALIENTIA; see p. 672		OLDEN, ARCHAIC, ARCHEAN	
Amphion relative	ZEUS, NIOBE,	and	PLUS, AMPERSAND
	ANTIOPE	and others	ETALII
amphitheater	OVAL, ARENA,	and so on	ETC, USW
CAVEA, CIRQUE		Andes	see MOUNTAINS
ample	WALLY, COPIOUS	Andes grass	ICHU
amplify	PAD, SWELL	Andes region	PUNA, PUNO
amputate	LOP, SEVER	andiron	(FIRE)DOG, HESSIAN
Amram relative	AARON,	Andorran language	CATALAN
MOSES, MIRIAM		Andorran money	FRANC,
amulet	CHARM, SAFFI(E),		PESETA
FETISH, MERIAT, SCARAB,		Andrews,—	DANA, JULIE
PERIAPT, TALISMAN		Andromache husband	HECTOR
Amun-Re wife	MUT	Andromeda's rescuer	PERSEUS
Amur tributary	ZEYA, ARGUN,	Andy Capp character	FLO
SHIKA, BUREYA, KUMARA,		Andy's friend	AMOS
USSURI, SONGHUA		Andy Griffith Show name	ANDY,
amuse	DIVERT, REGALE,	OTIS, PYLE, GOMER, BARNEY,	
	DELIGHT	HOWARD, KNOTTS, NABORS,	
amusement park	BUSCH,	TAYLOR, THELMA, AUNTBEE	
EPCOT, SIX FLAGS,		anecdote(s)	ANA, TALE, STORY
UNIVERSAL, DISNEYLAND		anemic	PALE, PALLID
Amy's sister	JO, MEG, BETH	anemone	POLYP
anadem	WREATH, CHAPLET,	anent	(IN)RE, WITH, ABOUT,
	GARLAND		BESIDE
Anah husband	ESAU	anesthetic	GAS, DULL, ETHER,
anal	RECTAL	COCAIN, OPIATE, CHLORAL,	
analgesic	ANODYNE; see	DEMEROL, PROCAIN,	
	ANESTHETIC	STOVAIN, NOVOCAIN,	
analogous	AKIN, LIKE, SIMILAR	XYLOCAIN, NOVOCAINE	
analyze	ASSAY, PARSE, DISSECT	angel	MAH, EBLIS, SIJIL, URIEL,
Ananias wife	SAPPHIRA	AZRAEL, BELIAL, CHERUB,	
anarchist	RADICAL,	SERAPH, SIJILL, ABADDON,	
AGITATOR, NIHILIST,		GABRIEL, ISRAFIL, LUCIFER,	
	TERRORIST	MICHAEL, SAMMAEL	
anathema	CURSE, HATED,	anger	IRE, GALL, HUFF, RILE,
	ACCURSED	ROIL, PIQUE, CHOLER	

angle **ELL, ZIG, AXIL, CANT,**
HADE, ARRIS, ELBOW,
SLANT, CORNER
angle measure **GRAD, DEGREE,**
RADIAN
angle, type of **ACUTE, RIGHT,**
OBTUSE, REFLEX, VERTEX,
STRAIGHT
Angles' hero **OFFA**
Anglo-Saxon letter **EDH, ETH,**
WEN, WYN, YOK, WYNN,
YOGH
Anglo-Saxon money **ORA**
Anglo-Saxon official **REEVE,**
GEREFA
Anglo-Saxon poem **BEOWULF**
Angola, capital of **LUANDA**
Angola exclave **CABINDA**
Angolan city/town **UIGE,**
KUITO, LUCAPA, LUENA,
SUMBE, CAXITO, HUAMBO,
LOBITO, LUANDA, CABINDA,
LUBANGO, MALANJE,
BENGUELA
Angolan language *see* **BANTU**
Angolan money **LWEI, ESCUDO,**
KWANZA, MACUTA,
ANGOLAR, CENTAVO
Angolan mountain **MOCO,**
TCHEVIRA
Angolan neighbor **CONGO,**
ZAIRE, ZAMBIA, NAMIBIA
Angolan port **LOBITO,**
LUANDA, BENGUELA
Angolan river **CONGO, CUITO,**
KASAI, CUANZA, CUNENE,
KWANDO, KWANGO,
CUBANGO, ZAMBEZI
angry **HOT, MAD, HUFF,**
IRATE, RABID, WROTH,
IREFUL, SNUFFY
anguish **WOE, PAIN, AGONY**
angular **EDGY, ZIGZAG,**
POINTED
animal **ZOON, BIPED, BEAST,**
BRUTE; *see p. 660*
animal cry or sound **ARF, BAY,**
HUM, LOW, MEW, MOO, TAP,
YAP, BARK, BARR, BELL, BLAT,
BRAY, GOWL, HISS, HOWL,
JUCK, JUKE, MEWL, PULE, ROAR,
YAUP, YAWL, YAWP, YELP,
BLEAT, CHIRR, CHURR, GROWL,
GRUNT, MIAOU, MIAOW,
NEIGH, SNARL, SNORT, WHINE,
BALLOW, BOWWOW, SQUEAK,
SQUEAL, WHINNY, TIRALEE; *see*
BIRD; *see p. 701*
Animal Farm author **ORWELL**

animal in literature **BABE, BAMBI,**
JUMBO, WINNIE; *see p. 630*
animal life **BIOTA, FAUNA**
animal, many-footed **DECAPOD,**
HEXAPOD, OCTOPOD
animator **AVERY, HANNA,**
JONES, STONE, TERRY,
PARKER, BARBERA, CULHANE,
FRELENG
animosity **VENOM, ENMITY,**
HATRED, RANCOR
animus **MIND, SOUL, SPIRIT**
ankle, *pert. to* **TARSAL,**
TALARIC
ankle(s) **CUIT, HOCK, TALI,**
QUEET, TALUS, TARSI,
TARSUS
Anna relative **MARY**
Annabel Lee author **POE**
Annapolis student **PLEBE**
annatto seeds **ACHIOTE**
anneal **HEAT, TEMPER,**
TOUGHEN
annex **ADD, ELL, APPEND**
Annie Oakley **PASS, FREEBIE**
annihilate **KILL, EFFACE,**
DESTROY
anniversary *see p. 718*
anno— **DOMINI**
annotate **GLOSE, GLOSS,**
GLOZE, COMMENT
annotation **NOTE, RUBRIC,**
APOSTIL, EXEGESIS,
FOOTNOTE
announce **CERN, BRUIT,**
HERALD, STEVEN
announcement **AD, BAN(S),**
BAN(NS), BLURB, NOTICE,
GAZETTE, TIDINGS, BULLETIN
announcer **DJ, MC, EMCEE,**
DEEJAY
annoy **IRK, NAG, NOY, TRY,**
VEX, BORE, FASH, FIKE, GALL,
HARRY, STURT, TEASE,
MOLEST, PESTER
annual **BOOK, MASS, PLANT,**
YEARLY, ETESIAN
annuity **RENTE, PENSION,**
STIPEND, TONTINE
annul **CASS, UNDO, VOID,**
ELIDE, ERASE, CANCEL,
REVOKE
annular **CYCLIC, RINGED**
Annus Mirabilis poet **DRYDEN**
anodyne **OPIATE, PACIFIER,**
SEDATIVE
anoint **OIL, ANELE, SALVE,**
BALSAM, CHRISM
anomalous **ODD, ABERRANT**

anon   SOON, AGAIN, BEDEEN,
SHORTLY
ansa   HANDLE
answer   REPLY, RETORT,
YES SIR, COMEBACK
answerable   LIABLE
ant   EMMET, KELEP, MAXIM,
MINIM, NURSE, QUEEN,
SAUBA, SLAVE, AMAZON,
DRIVER, NEUTER, REDANT,
WORKER, BULLDOG, ERGATES,
FORAGER, PISMIRE,
REPLETE, ACULEATA
ant genus   ATTA, ECITON,
LASIUS, PONERA, FORMICA
antacid   TUMS, ALKALI,
ROLAID
antagonist   FOE, ENEMY, RIVAL
Antarctic bay   PRYDZ, ELTANIN,
AMUNDSEN, PORPOISE
Antarctic cape   AGASSIZ,
MACKINTOSH
Antarctic explorer   BYRD, METZ,
FUCHS, RONNE, SCOTT,
THIEL, MURDEN, RYMILL,
OUSLAND, AMUNDSEN,
KRISTENSEN, SHACKLETON
Antarctic glacier or ice shelf   GETZ,
ROSS, WEST, ABBOT, MERTZ,
ALMERY, DALTON, DIBBLE,
DOTSON, FIMBUL, LARSEN,
WORDIE, HEIBERG, LAMBERT,
RENNICK, SKELTON,
FILCHNER, SKYTRAIN,
BEARDMORE, SHACKLETON
Antarctic island   BURKE, SIPLE,
BISCOE, CARNEY, LATADY,
SMYLEY, SPAATZ, WRIGHT,
BERKNER, CHARCOT,
SEYMOUR, THURSTON
Antarctic mountain   COMAN,
FAURE, MINTO, TONEY,
EREBUS, SEELIG, SIDLEY,
VINSON, JACKSON,
MARKHAM, MENZIES
Antares   MARS, MSTAR
ante   PAY, POT, BLIND, KITTY,
STAKE
anteater   ANTBEAR, TAMANDU
antecedent(s)   PRIOR, ANCESTRY
antelope   see p. 661
antelope, fabulous   BAGWYN
antelope genus   ORYX, KOBUS,
OZANNA
antelope, young   CALF
antenna   HORN, PALP, YAGI,
TOUCH, AERIAL, CERCUS,
FEELER
antenna, end of   CLAVA

anteroom   HALL, FOYER, LOBBY
anthelion   HALO, ANTISUN
anthem   HYMN, MOTET,
CANTATA
anther   POLLEN, STAMEN
anthocyanin   (O)ENIN
anthology   ANA, CORPUS,
GARLAND
antiaircraft   FLA(C)K, ACKACK,
BOFORS
antibiotic   MYCIN, STREPTO,
NEOMYCIN, PENICILLIN
antic   DIDO, CAPER, PRANK
antidote   SERUM, TOXIN,
CACOON, EMETIC, REMEDY
antigen disabler   TCELL
Antigone relative   CREON,
ISMENE, JOCASTA, OEDIPUS
Antigua and Barbuda, capital of
ST JOHNS
Antiguan money   DOLLAR
antimacassar   TIDY, DOILY
antimony   KOH(O)L, SURMA,
SOORMA
Antiope son   AMPHION
antipasto   RELISH, APPETIZER
antiphon   HYMN, ANSWER,
RESPONSE
antiquated   PASSE, ARCHAIC
antiquity   ELD, YORE
antiseptic   EGOL, BORAX, IODIN,
IODOL, SALOL, CRECOL,
IODINE, THYMOL, BROMINE,
CHLORINE
antisubmarine vessel   CORVET
antitoxin   SERA, SERUM,
ANTIGEN, ANTIVENIN
antler   BEZ, DAG, BROW, HORN,
SNAG, DAGUE, TRESTINE
antler parts   TINE, PRONG,
ROYAL, CROCHE, VELVET
antlered animal   DEER, MOOSE
Antoninus reign year (AD 138–161)
CXL, CXLI, CXLV, CLX,
CLXI
Antony and Cleopatra character
EROS, IRAS, SEXTUS, OCTAVIA,
CHARMIAN
Anu husband   ANAT
Anubis   HERMES
anvil   AMBOS, INCUS, STITH,
TEEST, STITHY
anxiety   HOE, CARE, FEAR,
ANGOR, PANIC
any   ALL, ARY, ONI, SOME
Apache chief   MANGAS,
COCHISE, GERONIMO,
VICTORIO
Apache drink   TISWIN

Apache tribe   KIOWA, LIPAN, TONTO, CIBECUE, JICARILLA, MESCALERO

apart   AROOM, ASIDE, ENISLED

apartment   PAD, COOP, FLAT, ROOMS, SUITE, DINGLE, DUPLEX, STANZA

apartment house   INSULA, TENEMENT

apathy   ACEDIA, PHLEGM, TORPOR, DOLDRUMS

ape   COPY, MIME, MOCK, DRILL, ORANG, BABOON, GIBBON, OURANG, SIMIAN, MANDRILL; see p. 665

ape genus   PAN, SIMIA

ape man   AKUT

aperçu   DIGEST, OUTLINE

aperture   *see* OPENING

apex   ACME, CUSP, APOGEE, CACUMEN

apex, belonging to   APICAL

apex covering   EPI

apex, rounded   RETUSE

aphasia   ALALIA, MUTISM

aphorism   SAW, ADAGE, MAXIM, SUTRA, DICTUM, EPIGRAM

aphrodisiac   CELERY, GARLIC, GINGER, PRUNES, SNAILS, OYSTERS, TRUFFLES

Aphrodite   VENUS, URANIA

Aphrodite lover   ARES, ANCHISES

Aphrodite relative   EROS, DIONE, AENEAS

Aphrodite temple site   PAPHOS

apiece   PER, EACH

aplomb   TACT, POISE, SURETY

Apocrypha   *see p. 515*

apogee   ACME, APEX, CLIMAX

Apollo   HELIOS, SUNGOD, PHOEBUS

Apollo astronaut   *see p. 742*

Apollo birthplace, oracle site   DELOS

Apollo, giant killed by   OTUS

Apollo instrument   BOW, LYRE

Apollo, *pert.* to   DELIAN

Apollo priest   ABARIS, CALCHAS

Apollo relative   ION, LETO, DIANA, IAMUS, LATONA, ARTEMIS

Apollo's spring   CASTALIA

apologue   MYTH, FABLE, ALLEGORY

apoplexy   ESCA, STROKE

apostate   RAT, RECREANT, RENEGADE, TURNCOAT

apostle   NERI, REMI, ELIOT, ANSCAR, XAVIER, PATRICK, SCHOLAR, ULFILAS

apostles of Christ   JOHN, JUDE, LEVI, PAUL, JAMES, JUDAS, PETER, SIMON, ANDREW, CEPHAS, PHILIP, THOMAS, DIDYMUS, MATTHEW, ISCARIOT, MATTHIAS, THADDAEUS, BARTHOLOMEW

apostolic manual   DIDACHE

apothecary   CHEMIST, DRUGGIST, PHARMACIST

apothecary measure   DRAM, GRAIN, MINIM, SCRUPLE

apothegm   SAW, AXIOM, ADAGE, DICTUM, SAYING

Appalachian range   GREEN, WHITE, RAMAPO, CATSKILLS, BLUE RIDGE, CUMBERLAND, ALLEGHENIES

appalling   AWFUL, TERRIBLE

apparatus   GEAR, TOOL, DEVICE, GADGET

apparel   GARB, RAIMENT

apparent   OVERT, PLAIN, PATENT, EVIDENT, OBVIOUS

apparition   GHOST, SHADE, SPECTER, REVENANT

appealing   CATCHY, ATTRACTIVE

appear   LOOM, KITHE

appearance   AIR, MIEN, GUISE, PHASM, OSTENT

append   ADD, AFFIX, ATTACH

appendage, appendix   ALA, TAB, TAIL, CAUDA, RIDER, ADJUNCT, CODICIL, ADDENDUM

Appenine range   ROMAN, TUSCAN, ABRUZZI, UMBRIAN, LUCANIAN, LIGURIAN

Appenine pass   CISA, FUTA, GIOVI, PESCARA, SCHEGGIA, BOCCHETTA

appetite   ZEST, GUSTO, OREXIS

appetite, abnormal   PICA, ASITIA, B(O)ULIMIA

appetizer   CANAPE, APERITIF, ANTIPASTO

appetizing   SAVORY

applaud   CLAP, LAUD, CHEER, EXTOL, PRAISE

applauders   CLAQUE

applause   HAND, OVATION, CLAPPING

applause word   OLE, HEAR, BRAVO

apple   CRAB, LOVE, POME, GOLDEN, PIPPIN, RUSSET, CODLING, COSTARD, WINESAP,

	JONATHAN, PEARMAIN, DELICIOUS, MCINTOSH
apple acid	MALIC
apple part	BASIN
apple product	ANONA, CIDER, POMACE
appliance	IRON, OVEN, DRYER, MIXER, RANGE, DEVICE, FRIDGE, BLENDER, FREEZER, MACHINE, TOASTER, CANOPENER
apply	USE, LAYON, RUBIN, APPOSE, IMPOSE, RELATE, SLAPON, PERTAIN
appoint	SET, NAME, EQUIP, ORDAIN
appointment	DATE, SLOT, TRYST, HIRING, NAMING, MEETING, ELECTION
apportion	DEAL, DOLE, METE
apposite	APT, FIT, RIGHT, PROPER, GERMANE, RELEVANT
appraise	RATE, ASSAY, VALUE, ASSESS, EVALUE
appraiser	ASSAYER, ASSESSOR, SURVEYOR
apprehend	NAB, FEAR, GRASP, GRIPE, INTUE, INTUIT
apprentice	SNOB, TYRO, ROOKIE, TRAINEE, NEOPHYTE
approach	WAY, ADIT, (A)NEAR, ACCESS, IMPEND
approbation	FAVOR, ASSENT, PRAISE, PLAUDIT
appropriate	APT, MEET, ALLOT, STEAL, USURP
approve	PASS, AGREE, GRANT, ENDORSE, SUPPORT, SANCTION, AUTHORIZE
apricot(s)	UME, ANSU, ANZU, MEBOS
apron	BRAT, DICK, TIER, BARVEL, BISHOP, HOOVER, RUNWAY
apropos	FIT, TIMELY, FITTING
apt	FIT, PAT, DEFT, MEET, LIKELY, FITTING
apteryx	MOA, KIWI, RATITE
aptitude	BENT, GIFT, FLAIR, TALENT
Apulia capital	BARI
aquamarine	BLUE, BERYL
aquarium	BOWL, TANK, GLOBE
aquarium fish	CICHLID
aquavitae	BRANDY, LIQUOR
aqueduct	CANAL, CONDUIT
aqueduct of Sylvius	ITER
aquiline	BEAKED, HOOKED

Arab	BROWN, GAMIN, HORSE, SEMITE, URCHIN
Arabia	ARABY
Arabian	see also SAUDI ARABIAN
Arabian chieftain	AMIR, EMIR, RAIS, REIS, AMEER, EMEER, SAY(Y)ID, SEY(Y)ID
Arabian clothing	ABA
Arabian colony	ADEN
Arabian drink	BOSA, BOZA, BOOZA, BOUZA
Arabian lyric	G(H)AZEL
Arabian measure	BARID, CUDDY, TEMAN, ZUDDA, FARSAIKH, FARSANG, MARHALA, NUSFIAH
Arabian measure (ancient)	DEN, SAA, FERK, KIST, CABDA, CAFIZ, MILLE, QASAB, ASSBAA, FEDDAN, GHALVA, QASABA, CAPHITE
Arabian Nights characters	AGIB, AMINE, CANEM, FATIMA, HAROUN, SINBAD, ALADDIN, ALIBABA, BADOURA, HOUSSAIN, MORGIANA, SCHARIAN
Arabian poet & romance	ANTAR(A)
Arabian script	CUFIC, KUFIC, NESK(H)I
Arabian tent village	DOUAR
Arabian weight	BAHAR, CHEKI, KELLA, MAUND, TOMAN, MISKAL, BOKARD
Arabian weight (ancient)	ROTL, NASCH, NEVAT, OCQUE, OUKIA
Arabic alphabet	BA, FA, HA, RA, TA, YA, ZA, DAD, DAL, AYN, JIM, KAF, KHA, LAM, MIM, NUN, SAD, SIN, THA, WAW, ZAY, ALIF, DHAL, SHIN, GHAYN
arable	LAINE, FERTILE, TILLABLE
arachnid	ACERATA; see SPIDER, SCORPION, MITE, TICK, FLEA
Arafat org.	PLO
Aram relative	MASH
Arawakan language	MOJO, BAURE, CAMPA, TAINO, GOAJIRO
arbiter	UMPIRE, OVERMAN, REFEREE
arbitrary	THETIC, DESPOTIC
arbitrator	MEDIATOR, GOBETWEEN, CONCILIATOR
arbor	BOWER, RAMADA, PERGOLA

arboreal	SYLVAN, DENDRAL
arc	BOW, CURVE
arcade	LOGGIA, PORTICO, ARCATURE
arcadian	RUSTIC, BUCOLIC
arcanum	ELIXIR, SECRET, MYSTERY
arch	COY, SLY, OGEE, CHIEF, HANCE, OGIVE, VAULT, IMPISH
archangel	SATAN, URIEL, GABRIEL, MICHAEL, RAPHAEL
archbishop	HATTO, ANSELM, BECKET, RAMSEY, CRANMER, PONTIFF, PRIMATE
archeological find	TOMB
archer	CLIM, CLYM, TELL, BOWER, CUPID, TEUCER
archery term	BUTT, WAND, CLOUT
archetype	IDEA, TYPE, IDEAL, MODEL, PATTERN
archfiend	SATAN
architect	BUILDER, CREATOR, FOUNDER, PLANNER, DESIGNER, ENGINEER
architect, famous	*see p. 537*
architectural feature	ANTA, CYMA, SOCLE, FRIEZE, PLINTH
architecture, type of	DORIC, GREEK, IONIC, LATIN, ROMAN, TUDOR, COPTIC, EMPIRE, FLORID, GOTHIC, LANCET, MOSLEM, NORMAN, ROCOCO, TUSCAN, BAUHAUS, BAROQUE, BOURBON, CLASSIC, MOORISH, REVIVAL, RHENISH, GEORGIAN, BYZANTINE, RENAISSANCE, ROMANESQUE, POSTMODERNIST
Arctic	ICY, POLAR, GALOSH
Arctic town	NUUK, THULE
arctic cover	ICESHEET
Arctic explorer	BYRD, COOK, BYLOT, DAVIS, WEBER, ANDREE, BAFFIN, BURTON, DELONG, NANSEN, NOBILE, HEARNE, HUDSON, UEMURA, BARENTS, BENNETT, FIENNES, WRANGEL, AMUNDSEN, ANDERSON, MALAKHOV, SCORESBY, MACMILLAN
Arctic island	BANKS, BYLOT, DEVON, BAFFIN, WRANGEL, MELVILLE, VICTORIA, ELLESMERE, NOTTINGHAM, RESOLUTION

Arctic mountain	NEWTON, BARBEAU
ardor	ELAN, FIRE, ZEAL, FERVOR
area	TREF, TRACT, AREOLA, PURLIEU
arena	BOWL, CAGE, OVAL, RING, RINK, SAND, TURF, DROME, LISTS, STADIUM
Ares relative	ERIS, HERA
Argentina, capital of	BUENOSAIRES
Argentine city/town	AZUL, JUJUY, JUNIN, MORON, SALTA, TIGRE, PARANA, RAWSON, TRELEW, ZARATE, CORDOBA, LAPLATA, MENDOZA, ROSARIO, MERCEDES, MAR DEL PLATA
Argentine measure	VARA, BRAZA, GALON, LEGUA, FENEGA, FRASCO, LASTRE, QUADRA, MANZANA
Argentine money	PESO, CENTAVO, AUSTRALE
Argentine mountain	CHANI, MAIPO, DUMUYO, PALERMO, ACONCAGUA, TUPUNGATO
Argentine neighbor	CHILE, BRAZIL, BOLIVIA, URUGUAY, PARAGUAY
Argentine province	CHACO, JUJUY, SALTA, CHUBUT, MENDOZA, TUCUMAN
Argentine river	CHICO, LIMAY, NEGRO, CHUBUT, PARANA, SALADO, BERMEJO, LAPLATA, MENDOZA, NEUQUEN, TUNUYAN, COLORADO
Argentine tree	TALA, AJARI, AMBAY, TIMBO
Argentine weight	LIBRA, QUINTAL
Argo crew member	MOPSUS, TIPHYS, ANCAEUS, POLYDEUCES
argonaut	JASON, ACASTUS, MELEAGER
Argos, princess of	OANAE
argot	*see* SLANG
argue	ARGY, MOOT, WORD, REBUT
argument	AGON, FUSS, TIFF, WORDS, DEBATE, HASSLE, POLEMIC
argus-eyed	VIGILANT, WATCHFUL
aria	AIR, SOLO; *see* SONG
aria part	CAVATINA, CABALETTA
Ariadne father	MINOS

Ariadne loved **THESEUS**
arid **DRY, VAPID, JEJUNE,**
    STERILE
Ariel master **PROSPERO**
Aries **RAM**
Arikara **REE**
arise **MOUNT, REBEL, APPEAR**
arista **AWN, BEARD**
aristocrat **LORD, PEER, BOYAR,**
   NOBLE, GRANDEE, HIDALGO
Aristophanes work **BIRDS,**
   FROGS, PEACE, WASPS,
   CLOUDS, WEALTH
Aristotle's father **AMYNTAS**
Aristotle's home town **STAGIRA**
Aristotle's teacher **PLATO**
Aristotle's work **ETHICS,**
   ORGANON, POETICS
Arizona *see p. 615*
Arizona city/town **MESA, YUMA,**
   TEMPE, TUCSON, NOGALES
Arizona dam **DAVIS, HOOPER,**
   COOLIDGE
Arizona desert **YUMA, PAINTED**
Arizona Indian **HOPI, TEWA,**
   YUMA, MOQUI, YAQUI,
   APACHE, MOHAVE, NAVAHO,
   NAVAJO, PAIUTE, QUECHAN,
   COCOPAH
Arizona lake **MEAD, ALAMO,**
   APACHE, CANYON, HAVASU,
   SANCARLOS
Arizona mountain **ORD, BAKER,**
   ELDEN, WOODY, GRAHAM,
   LEMMON, PASTORA,
   HUALAPAI, MAZATZAL
Arizona river **GILA, SALT,**
   SANPEDRO, VERDE, VIRGIN,
   COLORADO
ark **ASYLUM, COFFER**
ark driver **AHIO**
ark landing place **ARARAT**
Arkansas *see also p. 615*
Arkansas lake **BEAVER,**
   CONWAY, DEGRAY, NIMROD,
   WINONA, GREESON, NORFOLK,
   MITTWOOD, OUACHITA
Arkansas mountain **BLUE,**
   BOSTON, POTEAU,
   MAGAZINE, OUACHITA
Arkansas river **RED, BLACK,**
   WHITE, ARKANSAS,
   OUACHITA
arm **GIB, JIB, LIMB, EQUIP,**
   GARDY, OXTER, BRANCH,
   PINION, FORTIFY, TENTACLE
arm of sea **BAY, LOCH, FIRTH,**
   FJORD, FRITH
arm, part of **ULNA, ELBOW,**

OXTER, RADIUS, AXILLA,
   FOREARM, BRACHIUM
arm, *pert. to* **BRACHIAL**
armadillo **APAR, PEBA, TATU,**
   APARA, POYOU, TATOU,
   MATACO, PELUDO, DASYPUS,
   TATOUAY
Armageddon author **URIS**
armed band **HOST, POSSE**
Armenia **HAYASDAN**
Armenia, capital of **ERIVAN,**
   YEREVAN
Armenian city/town **KAMO,**
   ARTIK, ARARAT, GYUMRI,
   HRAZDAN, ALAVERDI,
   VANADZOR
Armenian lake **VAN, SEVAN**
Armenian money **DRAM,**
   LOUMA
Armenian mountain **ARARAT,**
   ARAGATS
Armenian neighbor **IRAN,**
   RUSSIA, TURKEY, GEORGIA,
   AZERBAIJAN
Armenian river **ARPA, ARAKS,**
   DEBED, HRAZDAN,
   EUPHRATES
Armenian money **DRAM**
armful **LOCK, TAFFLE**
armistice **TRUCE**
armor *see also p. 504*
armor, arm & leg **JAMB, CUISH,**
   JAMBE, ARMLET, CUISSE,
   GREAVE, TUILLE, AILETTE,
   CHAUSSE, JAMBEAU,
   ROUNDEL, BRASSARD,
   BRASSART, GAUNTLET,
   PALLETTE, PAULDRON,
   SABBATON, SOLLERET,
   VAMBRACE
armor bearer **ARMIGER,**
   CUSTREL
armor, body **TACE, ACTON,**
   CULET, TASSE, BYRNIE,
   CORIUM, LORICA, TASSET,
   TONLET, BROIGNE, HAUBERK,
   LAMBOYS, SURCOAT,
   DEMISUIT, DOSSIERE,
   GAMBESON, PANSIERE,
   PLASTRON
armor, full suit **BARD, MAIL,**
   WEED, BARDE, CUIRASS,
   PANOPLY, JAZERANT,
   PLACCATE
armor, head & neck **COIF, HELM,**
   ARMET, GALEA, VISOR,
   BEAVER, CAMAIL, CASQUE,
   GALERA, GORGET, HEAUME,
   HELMET, MORION, SALLET,

	SECRET, BASINET, GALERUM,	arrive	HENT, LAND, LIGHT
	GALERUS, (A)VENTAIL,	arrogance	HUBRIS, HYBRIS
	BURGONET, CABASSET,	arrogant	HIGH, LORDLY,
	GORGERIN		UPPISH, CAVALIER
armor, horse	POITREL,	arrogate	GRAB, CLAIM, USURP
	CHAMFRON, CRINIERE,	arrow	FLO, BARB, BOLT, DART,
	CROUPIERE		SELF, VIRE, FLANE, ROVER,
armpit	AXILLA		SHAFT, SUMPIT(AN)
arms	see also pp. 502, 619	arrow case	QUIVER
army	FYRD, HERD, HERE, HOST,	arrow maker	BOWYER, FLETCHER
	IMPI, LEGION, TROOPS,	arrow part	NOCK, PILE, STELE
	MILITARY	arrow poison	INEE, UPAS,
army division	MORA, SQUAD,		URALI, ANTIAR, CURARE,
	COHORT, LEGION, COMPANY,		WOORALI, WOORARA; see
	MANIPLE, PLATOON,		POISON
	INFANTRY, REGIMENT	arrowroot	PIA, MUSA, ARARU,
army engineer	SAPPER, SEABEE,		CANNA, TACCA, ARARAO,
	PIONEER		MARANTA, TAPIOCA
aroid	ARAD, ARUM, TARO,	arrow-shaped	BELOID
	TANIA, KONJAK, TANIER	arroyo	RUN, BAYOU, BROOK,
aroma	AURA, NIDOR, SAVOR,		CREEK, GULLY, HONDO
	BOUQUET	ars —	NOVA, ANTICA,
aromatic	BALMY, SPICY,		MAGICA
	PIQUANT, PUNGENT	arsenic mixture	SPEISS,
aromatic plant	DILL, MACE,		ERINITE, ORPIMENT
	MINT, NARD, SAGE, ANISE,	arsonist	PYRO, TORCH,
	BASIL, CARUM, TANSY,		FIREBUG
	GINSENG	art	ARS, WIT, WILE, KNACK,
aromatic substance	TOLU,		TRADE
	BUCCO, BUCHU, MYRRH,	art style	see PAINTING
	ARALIA, BALSAM	Artaxerxes composer	ARNE
around	NEAR, ABOUT, CIRCA	Artemis	DELIA, DIANA,
Around the World in 80 Days			PHOEBE
name	FOGG, NIVEN,	Artemis birthplace	DELOS
	CANTINFLAS,	Artemis relative	LETO, ZEUS,
	PASSEPARTOUT		LATONA, APOLLO
Around the World in 80 Days		Artemis victim	ORION
producer	TODD	artery	WAY, AORTA, ATERIA,
arouse	FIRE, STIR, PIQUE,		AVENUE, CAROTID; see VEIN
	ACCITE	artful	SLY, WILY, DOWNY,
arpeggio	RUN, ROULADE		POLITIC
arquebus prop	CROC	Artful Dodger	JACK DAWKINS
arraign	PEACH, ACCUSE,	arthritis help	ACTH,
	INDICT, INDITE, IMPEACH		ASPIRIN(E), CORTISONE
arrange	FIX, PLAN, PLAT,	arthritis type	GOUT, SEPTIC,
	ETTLE, SCORE, STAGE,		RHEUMATOID
	DAIKER, DISPOSE	Arthur's enemy	MORDRED
arrangement	FILE, INDEX,	Arthur's fool	DAGONET
	TAXIS	Arthur's queen	GUINEVERE
arrangement, pert. to	TACTIC	Arthur's relative	IGRAINE
arrant	BAD, UTTER, BRAZEN,	Arthur's weapon	RON,
	VAGRANT		PRIDWIN, EXCALIBUR
array	DECK, ACIES, ADORN,	Arthurian lady	ENID, ELAINE
	PAREL, DEPLOY, APPAREL	Arthurian town	AVALON,
arrears	DEB(I)T		ASTOLAT, CAMELOT
arrest	NAB, VAG, HALT, SIST,	artichoke	CANADA, CYNARA,
	STAY, PINCH, STUNT,		CHOROGI, GIRASOL
	COLLAR, DETAIN	article	ITEM, TERM, PIECE,
arris	PIEN(D)		CLAUSE, OBJECT, EDITORIAL

articles	*see p. 582*
articulate	JOIN, UTTER, VOCAL, JOINTED
artifice	RUSE, CRAFT, DODGE, GUILE, TRICK, FINESSE
artificial	FAKE, SHAM, FAKED, FALSE, PASTE, ERSATZ
artillery man	GUN(NER), TOPECHEE
artist(e)	DAB, ACTOR, ADEPT, BRUSH, ETCHER, FICTOR, SKETCHER; *see* PAINTER, SCULPTOR
artistic	ARTY, CREATIVE, INVENTIVE, IMAGINATIVE
artless	NAIF, RUDE, NAIVE, SEELY, GAUCHE
arts and —	CRAFTS, LETTERS, SCIENCES
arum	ARAD, TARO, AROID, CALLA, STARCH
as	QUA, LIKE, THUS, SINCE, WHILE
as a rule	MOSTLY, GENERALLY
as if	QUA, QUASI
As Time Goes By choreographer	THARP
As You Like It character	DUKE, CELIA, PHEBE, AMIENS, AUDREY, JAQUES, LEBEAU, OLIVER, ROSALIND
As You Like It forest	ARDEN
asafetida	HING, LASER, FERULA, NARTHEX
asbestos	ABISTON, AMIANTH
ascent	RIST, UPGO, SLOPE, STEEP, STIPE
ascetic	MUNI, YATI, YOGI, SADHU, YOGIN, ESSENE, HERMIT, AUSTERE, DERVISH
ascot	TIE, SCARF, NECKTIE
Asenath husband	JOSEPH
ash(es)	CHAR, SORB, ARTER, EMBER, ROWAN, VAREC, SINTER, WICKEN
ashen	WAN, PALE, LIVID
Asher relative	ARA, GAD, JACOB, SERAH, ZILPAH
ash fruit	KEY, ROWAN, SAMARA
Asherite chief	IMNA
Asia, highest point	EVEREST
Asia, largest city	TOKYO
Asia, largest country	RUSSIA
Asia, largest island	NEWGUINEA
Asia, largest lake	CASPIAN
Asia, longest river	CHANG, YANGTZE
Asia, lowest point	DEADSEA

Asia, smallest country	MALDIVES
Asia Minor ancient country	AEOLIA
Asian	HUN, SERE, THAI, TATAR, BURMAN, INDIAN, KOREAN, CHINESE, ORIENTAL
Asian plague	CHOLERA
Asian title	AGA; *see* TITLE
Asian tree	ACLE, ASAX, ASOK, AUTE, DITA, KOZO, AEGLE, ASOKA, DURIO, MESUA, SIRIS, WAMPI, ZYLIA, NYSSA, MEDLAR, WAMPEE
aside	OFF, APART, WHISPER
asinine	INANE, SILLY, STUPID, IDIOTIC
ask	SUE, THIG, FRAYN, SPEER, SPERE, ENTREAT
ask for	BEG, SUE, DEMAND, ENTREAT, REQUEST
askew	WRY, AGEE, ALOP, AWRY
asp	URAEUS; *see* VIPER
aspect	MIEN, SIDE, VULT, ANGLE, FACET, PHASE
aspen	POPLAR, TREMBLE
asperse	SKIT, SLUR, LIBEL, MALIGN, VILIFY, SLANDER
aspersion	SLUR, INNUENDO
asphalt	TAR, PITCH, BITUMEN
asphyxia	APN(O)EA
aspire	AIM, HOPE, COVET, CRAVE
ass	DOLT, MOKE, BURRO, CUDDY, DICKY, JENNY, KIANG, KULAN, KYANG, NEDDY, CUDDIE, DICKEY, DONKEY, JENNET, KIYANG, KOULAN, ONAGER, QUAGGA, FUSSOCK, JACKASS, LONGEAR, ZEBRASS
assail	PELT, BESET, MOLEST
Assamese dialect	AO, KHAMI, LHOTA
Assamese native	AO, AKA, AHOM
assassin	CAIN, THUG, SICARIAN
assassin, famous	RAY, AMIR, CAIN, RUBY, BOOTH, GODSE, OSWALD, SIRHAN, CHAPMAN, GUITEAU, CZOLGOSZ
assassination victim	HEE, TAL, DIEM, KING, LONG, ARKAN, EVERS, RABIN, SADAT, VILLA, ALNAIF, CAESAR, DOUMER, FAISAL, GANDHI, KABILA, LENNON, SOMOZA, COLLINS, HUSSEIN, MADERO, KENNEDY,

LINCOLN, LUMUMBA, MASSOUD, NGOUABI, TROTSKY, MCKINLEY, MALCOLMX, RASPUTIN, TRUJILLO, FERDINAND

assault BLITZ, ONSET, SIEGE, STORM, BUFFET, THRUST

assay TRY, TEST, ANALYSIS

assaying cup TEST, CUPEL

assemblage BODY, HERD, LEVY, LEVEE, CAUCUS, THRONG; *see* BEVY

assemble MEET, HUDDLE, MUSTER, COLLECT

assembly HUI, BEVY, DIET, AGORA, COVEN, FORUM, GEMOT, PLENA, COVINE, GEMOTE, PLENUM, SABBAT, SESSION

assembly hall KIVA, ESTUFA

assembly, legislative DAIL, DUMA, RAAD, SEIM, SEJM, SEYM, YUAN, BOULE, JUNTA, CORTES, SENATE, COMMONS, KNESSET, LAGTING, RIGSDAG, RIKSDAG, CHAMBERS, CONGRESS, STORTING

assembly place PNYX, AGORA

assent NOD, AMEN, GRANT, ACCEDE

assert AFFY, AVER, POSIT, STATE, THREAP, THREEP

assess BOTE, IMPOSE; *see* TAX

assessor JUDGE, MUFTI, RATER

asset ESTATE, PROPERTY

assign ALLOT, CAVEL, REFER

assignment JOB, BEAT, DUTY, POST, TASK, ROUND

assimilate ABSORB, DIGEST

assist *see* AID

assistance ALMS, DOLE

assistant(s) AID, CAD, AIDE, CREW, HAND, STAFF, SECOND

assize WRIT, COURT, DECREE

associate MIX, MONK, MOOP, CRONY, HOBNOB, SOCIUS

association BOND, BUND, GILD, HONG, ARTEL, GUILD, HANSE, LODGE, UNION, CARTEL, CONGER, GRANGE

association football SOCCER

assortment FONT, BATCH, SUNDRIES

assuage CALM, EASE, ABATE, ALLAY, SLAKE

assume ENDUE, FEIGN, INFER, USURP, ARROGATE

assumed name ALIAS, INCOGNITO, PSEUDONYM

assurance WORD, BRASS, APLOMB

assure PLEDGE, SICKER, WITTER

Assyria(n) ASHUR, ASSUR, ASSHUR

Assyrian capital CALAH, KALAKH, NINEVEH

Assyrian city HARA, OPIS, AKKAD, ARBELA

Assyrian ruler P(H)UL, SARGON, SEMIRAMIS

aster DAISY; *see* FLOWER

asterism URSA MAJOR, USRA MINOR

astern AFT, BAFT, REAR, ABAFT

asteroid *see p. 740*

Astolat, Lily Maid ELAIN(E)

astound STUN, FERLY, SHOCK

astral SIDEREAL

astray LOST, AMISS

astringent ALUM, COTO, KATH, PIPI, BORAL, STERN, CATECHU, STYPTIC(AL)

astrologer JOTI, JOSHI, JOTISI, CHALDEAN

astrology term APHETA, ALMUTEN, ANARETA

astronaut SPACEMAN, COSMONAUT; *see p. 742*

astronaut, female RIDE, ACTON, LUCID, DUNBAR, FISHER, RESNIK, SEDDON

astronaut killed on Challenger JARVIS, MCNAIR, SMITH, RESNICK, SCOBEE, ONIZUKA, MCAULIFFE

astronaut term AOK, NOMINAL

astronomer, famous *see p. 538*

astronomical URANIC

astronomical instrument ABA, ARMIL, SECTOR, ORRERY, SEXTANT

astronomical measure PARSEC, AZIMUTH

astronomy, muse of URANIA

Astyanax parent HECTOR, ANDROMACHE

asunder APART, ATWAIN

Aswan SYENE

asylum ARK, HOME, HAVEN, BEDLAM

at once NOW, STAT, INSTANTLY

Atalanta relative MILANION

atelier SHOP, STUDIO, WORKSHOP

atelier item	**PALETTE**	attempt	**MIRD, OSSE, STAB,**
Athaliah relative	**AHAZIAH**		**ESSAY, ETTLE, EFFORT**
Athamas relative	**INO, HELLE,**	attend	**SEE, GOTO, FOCUS,**
	NEPHELE, PHRIXUS		**LISTEN**
Athapascan language	**HUPA,**	attendant(s)	**GILLY, SUITE,**
	APACHE, NAVAJO,		**THANE, THEGN, TRAIN,**
	CHIPPEWA		**VALET, DONZEL, GILLIE,**
atheist	**INFIDEL, AGNOSTIC**		**VERGER**
Athena epithet	**ALEA, ARELA,**	attended	**SAW, WASAT**
	ERGANE, HIPPIA, PALLAS,	attendee	**GOER**
	MINERVA	attention	**EAR, GAUM, HEED**
Athena's shield	**(A)EGIS**	attention sound	**PST, AHEM,**
Athenian	**ATTIC, METIC**		**PSST, COUGH**
Athenian general	**CIMON,**	attentive	**WARY, TENTY, TENTIE**
	CLEON, NICIAS	attenuate	**THIN, DILUTE,**
Athenian ruler	**CLEON, DRACO,**		**RAREFY**
	ARCHON, CODRUS,	attest	**VOUCH, WITTEN,**
	CECROPS, THESEUS, PERICLES		**CERTIFY**
Athens part	**AGORA,**	attic	**LOFT, SOLAR, SOLER,**
	ACROPOLIS, KERAMIKOS		**DORMER, GARRET, TALLET,**
athlete	**TURNER, GYMNAST**		**GRENIER**
athletic event	**AGON, GAME,**	Attila	**HUN, ATLI, ETZEL**
	MEET, RACE, OLYMPICS	Attila's wife	**GUDRUN**
athwart	**OVER, AGAINST**	attire	*see* **CLOTHING**
Atlas	**BONE, MAPS, AGENA,**	attitudinize	**POSE, MINCE**
	TITAN	attorney	**VAKIL, VAKEEL,**
atlas letters	**SSR**		**ADVOCATE**
Atlas relative	**MAIA, HYAD(E),**	Attorney General, U.S.	*see p. 699*
	PLEIAD, CALYPSO	attract	**DRAW, LURE**
ATM transaction	**DEP, WDL,**	attraction	**DAHLIA, MAGNET**
	DEPOSIT, WITHDRAWAL	attribute	**OWE, TYPE, IMPUTE,**
atmosphere	**AURA, MAUVE,**		**ASCRIBE, FEATURE**
	OZONE	attrition	**WEAR, GRIEF, REGRET**
atmospheric pressure, of	**BARIC**	attune	**KEY, ADAPT, PITCH,**
atom	**ISOBAR, ISOSTERE;** *see*		**ACCORD**
	JOT	au naturel	**RAW, NUDE,**
atom part	**ION, KAON, MUON,**		**NAKED, UNCLAD,**
	PION, GLUON, MESON,		**UNADORNED**
	QUARK, BARYON, LEPTON,	auction	**CANT, ROUP, SALE,**
	NEURON, PHOTON, PROTON,		**VEND, BRIDGE, HAMMER,**
	NEUTRON, NUCLEUS,		**VENDUE**
	ELECTRON, NEUTRINO	audience	**EAR, PIT, EARING,**
atomic attack date	**ADAY**		**PUBLIC, HEARING**
atone	**ABY(E), EXPIATE,**	audit	**SCAN, VERIFY,**
	REDEEM		**ACCOUNT, SITIN(ON)**
Atreus' slayer	**AEGISTHUS**	audition	**TRYOUT, HEARING**
atrium	**FOYER, VESTIBULE**	auditory	**OTIC, AURAL**
atrium-like	**SKYLIT**	Auel heroine	**AYLA**
attach	**FIX, PEND, AFFIX,**	auger	**BORE(R), GIMLET,**
	APPEND		**WIMBLE**
attaché case	**TASHIE**	augment	**EKE, SWELL, VOWEL**
attached	**FOND, ADNATE,**	augur	**BODE, SEER, AUSPEX**
	SESSILE	augury	**OMEN, PORTENT**
attack	**FIT, FRAY, RAID, BESET,**	August 1st	**GULE, LAMMAS**
	BLITZ, BRASH, ONSET, SIEGE,	Augustus reign year (27BC–14AD)	
	SPASM, STRIKE, COMEAT	**II, IV, IX, VI, XI, XV, XX, III, VII,**	
attack, kind of	**RAID, BLITZ,**	**XII, XIV, XIX, XVI, XXI, XXV,**	
	SIEGE, SNEAK, SURPRISE	**VIII, XIII, XVII, XXII, XXIV,**	
attar	**ITR, OIL, OTTO**	**XXVI**	

auk   ALCA, POPE, URIA, ARRIE, MURRE, ROTCH, AUKLET, LUNGIE, MARROT, PUFFIN, ROTCHE, STRANY, DOVEKIE, GUILLEMOT
— au lait   CAFE
aunt   TIA, TANTA, TANTE
Auntie —   MAME
aureate   GOLDEN, ORNATE
aureole   HALO, GLORY, NIMBUS
auric acid salt   AURATE
auricle   EAR, PINNA, ATRIUM
aurochs   TUR, URUS, BISON
aurora   EOS, DAWN
aurorian   EOAN, ROSEATE
auspice   EGIS, CARE, OMEN, AEGIS
auspicious   BENIGN, DEXTER
Austral island   RAPA, RURUTU, TUBUAI, RIMATARA
Australasia   OCEANIA
Australia   OZ
Australia, capital of   CANBERRA
Australian   OSSIE
Australian aborigine   GOA, HAPU, BUSHMAN
Australian bird   EMU, KOEL, COOEE, COOEY, GALAH, BROLGA, DRONGO
Australian city/town   AYR, MOE, MANLY, PERTH, BURNIE, CAIRNS, SYDNEY, GEELONG, ADELAIDE, BRISBANE, CANBERRA, GOLD COAST, MELBOURNE
Australian cry   COOEE, COOEY
Australian dame   EDNA
Australian food   KAI
Australian hut   MIAM, MIMI, WURLY, GUNWA, MIAMIA, WURLEY
Australian lake   AULD, DORA, EYRE, NASH, CAREY, COWAN, FROME, NEALE
Australian money   CENT, DOLLAR
Australian mountain   ISA, BLUE, ZEIL, BRUCE, COOKE, MAGNET, NEWMAN, CONSUELO, PAINTER, REMARKABLE
Australian river   SWAN, BARWON, MURRAY, DARLING, FITZROY, GLENELG, HERBERT, BELYANDO, FLINDERS
Australian state   TASMANIA, VICTORIA, QUEENSLAND

Australian tree   KARI, HAKEA, KARRI, NONDA, WILGA
Australian weapon   NULLA, WO(O)MERA, BOOMERANG
Austria, capital of   VIENNA
Austrian city/town   GRAZ, LINZ, WELS, WIEN, BADEN, VIENNA, MODLING, SALZBURG, INNSBRUCK, KLAGENFURT
Austrian language   GERMAN, SLOVENE
Austrian measure   FASS, FUSS, JOCH, MASS, MUTH, HALBE, LINIE, MEILE, METZE, PFIFF, PUNKT, ACHTEL, BECHER, KLAFTER, VIERTEL
Austrian money   CENT, DUCAT, KRONE, FLORIN, HELLER, KREUZER, GROSCHEN, SCHILLING
Austrian mountain pass   LOIBL, BRENNER, PLOCKEN
Austrian neighbor   ITALY, GERMANY, HUNGARY, SLOVAKIA, SLOVENIA, SWITZERLAND, CZECH REPUBLIC
Austrian river   INN, MUR, ENNS, DONAU, DRAVA, TRAUN, DANUBE
Austrian ruler   ZITA , ALBERT, CHARLES, JOSEPH
Austrian weight   MARK, SAUM, UNZE, DENAT, KARCH, PFUND, STEIN, PFENNIG, CENTNER
authentic   REAL, TRUE, GENUINE, ORIGINAL
author   see p. 624
authority   RULE, SWAY, POWER, RIGHT, SAYSO
auto accident victims, famous   DEAN, KIDD, WHITE, ALLMAN, COCHRAN
auto body style   COUPE, SEDAN, TUDOR, WAGON, HARDTOP, HATCHBACK
auto court   MOTEL
autobiography   VITA, MEMOIR(S)
autocrat   TSAR, MOGUL, TORSE, DESPOT
automaton   GOLEM, ROBOT, ANDROID
automobile   BUS, CAR, AUTO, HACK, JEEP, TAXI, TRAM, COACH, COUPE, LORRY, SEDAN, TRUCK, CAMION, HEARSE,

automobile designer JALOPY, JITNEY, JALLOPY, MOTORCAR, ROADSTER, AMBULANCE, CABRIOLET, CHARABANC; *see p. 726*

automobile designer BENZ, DAIMLER, STUDEBAKER

automobile, early REO, NASH, EDSEL, HUDSON, MODELT, MAXWELL, PACKARD

automobile, inferior BOMB, CRATE, EDSEL, LEMON, WRECK, FLIVVER

automobile model BUG, LTD, CAMRY, CIVIC, IROC, ALERO, EDSEL, FOCUS, JETTA, ACCORD, ALTIMA, AURORA, BEETLE, ESCORT, IMPALA, MALIBU, RABBIT, SATURN, SENTRA, TAURUS, TORINO, CENTURY, COROLLA, CORVAIR, ELANTRA, LESABRE, MODELT, BRAVADA, EXTERRA, MUSTANG, CAVALIER, CORVETTE, INTREPID, VOYAGER, EXPLORER, EXCURSION, SILHOUETTE

automobile noise PING, RATTLE

automobile part BOOT, PLUG, TRIM, BRAKE, CHOKE, BONNET, BUMPER, CLUTCH, FENDER, STATOR, TIEROD, CHASSIS, STARTER, IGNITION; *see* VEHICLE

automobile racing driver FOYT, HILL, WARD, HANKS, JONES, KEECH, SNEVA, UNSER, MEARS, PETTY, PROST, RAHAL, SENNA, SNEVA, ASCARI, BURTON, FANGIO, MARLIN, BRABHAM, MONTOYA, WALTRIP, ANDRETTI; *see also p. 703*

automobile racing term LAP, WIN, CARD, FORM, LANE, SHOW, TAPE, PLACE, PURSE, PYLON, SILKS, FINISH, STAKES, STRETCH, HANDICAP

autumn FALL

autumn color RUST

auxiliary verb MAY, SHALL

available FREE, OPEN, ONCALL, ACCESSIBLE

avalanche SLIDE, LA(U)WINE

avast STAY, STOP, CEASE

ave HAIL, FAREWELL

avenge VISIT, REQUITE, RETALIATE

avengement WRATH

avenger GOEL, NEMESIS

avenging spirit FURY, ALECTO, ERINYS, MAGAERA

avenue *see* STREET

average PAR, NORM, SOSO, MEDIAL

avert FEND, PARRY, SHEER, THWART

Avesta part YASNA, GATHAS, YASHTS, VENDIDAD, VISPERED

Avestan demigod YIMA

aviator, famous EARHART, RICKENBACKER

avifauna BIRDS, ORNIS

— avis RARA

avocado COYO, PEAR, CHENIN, PERSEA

avocado sauce GUACAMOLE

avocation HOBBY, CALLING

avoid SHUN, EVADE, EVITE, ESCHEW

await PEND, STAY, TARRY

awake(n) (A)IDAW, STIR, ALERT

award DSC, DSM, DSO, EMMY, MEED, OBIE, TONY, BONUS, GENIE, MEDAL, OSCAR, CONFER, LAUREL; *see p. 505*

aware HEP, RECK, UP ON, WISE

away OFF, GONE, HYNE, HENCE, ABSENT

— and away UP, FAR

aweather, opposed to ALEE

awful BAD, POOR, DREADFUL

awkward GAWKY, INEPT, CLUMSY, GAUCHE

awkward one LOUT, GALOOT, BUNGLER

awl FID, BROD, DART, AUGER, ELSIN, BODKIN, STABBER

awn(ed) ILE, AVEL, BARB, ARISTA(TE)

awning TILT, CANOPY, SEMIAN, VELARIUM

awry CAM, AGEE, AJEE, AGLEY, GLEED

ax BILL, CELT, HACHE, ONCIN, FASCES, MACANA, POLEAX, BOUCHER, HALBERD, HATCHET, TWIBILL, FRANCISC, LOCHABER, PARTISAN, TOMAHAWK

axilla, *pert. to* ALA(R)

axiom MAXIM, TRUISM, APHORISM

axis, axle HUB, PIN, ARBOR, PIVOT

axis, *pert. to* AXILE

aye-aye LEMUR(OID)

Azerbaijan, capital of BAKU

Azerbaijani city/town **BAKU,**
AGDAM, GANCA, YAVLAX,
LANKARAN, SUMQAYIT,
XANKANDI
Azerbaijani money **MANAT**
Azerbaijani neighbor **IRAN,**
RUSSIA, ARMENIA, GEORGIA
Azerbaijani river **KURA, ARAKS**
Azores island **PICO, CORVO,**
FAIAL, FLORES
Azores town **ANGRA, HORTA**
Aztec hero(ine) **NANA, NATA**
Aztec language **NAHUATL**
Aztec temple **TEOPAN,**
TEOCALLI
Azubah husband **ASA, CALEB**
azure **SKY, BLUE, CERULEAN**

B

B **BEE, BRAVO**
baal **IDOL, MOLOCH**
Babbitt **ISAAC, IRVING, GEORGE**
babble(r) **BLAB, BLAT(E),**
BROOK, HAVER, GLAVER,
JABBER, HAVEREL
Babel **DIN, SCHEME**
Babel site **SHINAR**
Babism founder **BAB, SHIRAZ**
baboon *see* **APE**
baboon-headed god **HAPI, THOTH**
babul **GUM, GARAD, ACACIA**
baby **TOT, BABE, TOTO, WEAN,**
CHILD, HUMOR, SPOIL,
INFANT, PAMPER, SUCKLING
baby carriage **PRAM, BUGGY,**
STROLLER, PERAMBULATOR
baby food **PAP**
baby seat **LAP**
baby's equip. **BIB, DOLL, TALC,**
BOTTLE, DIAPER, RATTLE,
TEETHER, LAYETTE
Babylonian predecessor **SUMER,**
AKKAD, SHINAR
Babylonian Adam **ADAPA**
Babylonian city **CALNO, ERECH,**
LARSA, CALNEH, CUNAXA,
CUTHAH, LAGASH, NIPPUR,
SIPPAR, SHIRPURLA; *see p. 589*
Babylonian myth *see p. 648*
Babylonian numeral **SAROS**
Babylonian ruler **HAMMURABI**
babysitter **AMAH, AYAU,**
NANNY, NURSE, AUPAIR
bacalao **CODFISH, GROUPER**
baccarat term **COUP, BANCO,**
PUNTER, NATURAL

Bacchae, Bacchante **M(A)ENAD**
bacchanal **ORGY, FEAST,**
REVELRY
bacchanal cry **EVOE**
Bacchus **DIONYSUS**
Bacchus relative **SEUS, SEMELE,**
PRIAPUS
bachelor **AGAMIST, COELEBS**
back **AFT, AID, FRO, ABET,**
HIND, NOTA, REAR, NOTUM,
STERN, DORSUM, TERGUM,
ENDORSE, SPONSOR
back again **REBORN**
back and — **FORTH**
back country **BUSH, STICKS**
back, lying on **SUPINE**
back off **EBB, YIELD, GIVE IN,**
RETREAT, REVERSE
back out **WELSH, CANCEL,**
RENEGE, WITHDRAW
back, *pert. to* **NOTAL, DORSAL,**
TERGAL
back, toward **RETRAD, RETRAL**
backache **LUMBAGO, SCIATICA**
backbite **SASS, MALIGN, VILIFY**
backbone **GRID, CHINE,**
NERVE, RIDGE; *see* SPINE
backer **ANGEL, SPONSOR**
backfire **FAIL, RECOIL,**
GOWRONG, MISCARRY
backgammon **TABLES,**
TRICTRAC
backslide **SLIP, LAPSE,**
REVERT, RELAPSE
backtalk **LIP, SASS, RETORT**
backwater **BAYOU, STICKS,**
BOONDOCKS
bacon **LARD, JAMON, PRIZE,**
SPECK, RASHER
bacon, cover with **BARD**
Bacon work **NOVUM,**
ORGANUM
bacteria **GERM, AEROBE,**
COCCUS, VIBRIO, SARCINA
bacteriologist's wire **OESE**
bad **ILL, EVIL, POOR, VILE,**
WICKED, SINFUL
bad blood **ANIMUS**
bad dream **INCUBUS,**
NIGHTMARE
bad luck **EVIL, MISHAP,**
AMBSACE
bad trip **BUMMER**
badge **MON, PLAQUE, INSIGNE**
badge, shoulder **EPAULET**
badger **BAIT, FRET, BROCK,**
CHEVY, HECKLE, PESTER; *see*
WEASEL
Badger State **WI, WISCONSIN**

badinage	CHAFF, BANTER
baffle	BALK, FOIL, POSE, ELUDE
bag	NAB, SAC, CYST, GRIP,
	POKE, ASCUS, BOGUE, DILLI,
	POCKY, PURSE, CHAGUL,
	SACHET, MUSETTE,
	KNAPSACK, RETICULE
bag man	PIPER
bag net	FIKE, FYKE
bagatelle	TRIFLE
bagel topping	LOX,
	CREAMCHEESE
baggage	HUSSY, SAMAN,
	WENCH, DUNNAGE
baggage carrier	PORTER,
	REDCAP
bagpipe	DRONE, MUSETTE
bagpipe music	SKIRL, PIBROCH
bagpipe part	LILL, DRONE,
	CHANTER
bagpipe player	PIPER, SKIRLER
Baha'i founder	BAHAULLAH
Baha'i principle	UNITY
Bahaman aborigine	LUCAYO,
	LUCAYAN
Bahamas, capital of	NASSAU
Bahamas island	CAT, LONG,
	ABACO, EXUMA, ANDROS,
	INAGUA, ACKLINS, CROOKED,
	ELEUTHERA
Bahamas money	DOLLAR
Bahrain, capital of	MANAMA
Bahrain money	FILS, DINAR
bail	BOND, HOOP, LADE,
	SURETY
bailiff	REEVE, GEREFA
bailiwick	FIELD, DOMAIN,
	SPHERE, DISTRICT,
	JURISDICTION
bait	HANK, DECOY, SHRAP,
	BERLEY, CAPELIN
bait, drop	DAB, DIB
bake	FIRE, PARCH, ANNEAL,
	HARDEN
baked —	ALASKA
baker	FLY, OST, OAST, OVEN,
	HORNERO
baker's tool	PAN, BRAKE,
	WHISK, TURNER, SPATULA,
	ROLLINGPIN
baking pit	IMU, UMU, HUTCH
Balaam's steed	ASS
balance	ATRY, REST, POISE,
	SCALE, SANITY
balance	REST, POISE, SCALE,
	TOTAL, WEIGH, SETTLE,
	RESIDUE, REMAINDER,
	EQUILIBRIUM
Balance, The	LIBRA

balance of sentence	PARISON
balance weight	RIDER,
	BALLAST
balcony	LOGE, LANAI,
	LOGGIA, GALLERY,
	TERRACE, MEZZANINE
bald	BARE, NAKED,
	GLABROUS, HAIRLESS
Balder's killer	HOD, HOTH,
	LOKI, HODER, HOTHR
Balder relative	ODIN, FRIGG,
	NANNA
baldness	ACOMIA, ALOPECIA
bale	EVIL, HARM, PACK, PYRE
Balearic island	IBIZA,
	CABRERA, MAJORCA,
	MINORCA, FORMENTERA
Balearic Islands language	
	CATALAN
balk	COND, FOIL, REAR,
	REEST, IMPEDE
Balkan	SERB, SLAV, BULGAR,
	SLOVENE
Balkan province (ancient Roman)	
	DACIA, EPIRUS, ACHAEA,
	MOESIA, THRACE, ILLYRIA,
	PANNONIA
Balkan river	DRIN
Balkan state	BOSNIA, GREECE,
	SERBIA, TURKEY, ALBANIA,
	CROATIA, ROMANIA,
	BULGARIA, SLOVENIA,
	MACEDONIA
ball	ORB, CLEW, GOLI, KNUR,
	PROM, TICE, DANCE, PINDA,
	PELLET
ball, hit	LOB, BOWL, BUNT,
	SWAT
ballad	LAI, LAY, DERRY
Ballard novel	CRASH
ballet dancer	see p. 540
ballet term	BAR, PAS, JETE,
	PLIE, TOUR, BRISE, COUPE,
	FERME, FONDU, PIQUE, POINT,
	CAMBRE, CHASSE, CRAINE,
	DEGAGE, ECARTE, EFFACE,
	OUVERT, PENCHE, RELEVE,
	ALLONGE, BALANCE,
	BOURREE, CISEAUX,
	CROISEE, FOUETTE, ASSEMBLE,
	CABRIOLE, GLISSADE,
	PARTERRE, POSITION,
	ARABESQUE, ENTRECHAT,
	PIROUETTE
balloon part	CAR, BASKET,
	GONDOLA, NACELLE
ballpark	see BASEBALL
ballyhoo	PLUG, TOUT, NOISE,
	PUFFERY

balm	SALVE, BALSAM, ANODYNE
balmy	MAD, SOFT, BLAND, SILLY, SWEET
baloney	JIVE, HOGWASH, NONSENSE
Baltic language	LATVIAN, LITHUANIAN; *see* FINNO-UGRIC
Baltic port	KIEL, RIGA, MALMO, MEMEL, REVAL, GDANSK, STETTIN, TALLINN
Baltic Sea country	LATVIA, POLAND, SWEDEN, DENMARK, ESTONIA, FINLAND, GERMANY, LITHUANIA
Baltimore heater	LATROBE
Baluchistan capital	QUETTA
Baluchistan city/town	BELA, DADU, MACH, NUSHKI, PISHIN, MASTUNG, BARKHAN, LORALAI
Baluchistan language	BRAHUI, PASHTO, SINDHI, BALOCHI
Baluchistan people	MARI, REKI, BALOCHI, PASHTUN
Baluchistan river	HAB, DASHT, HINGOL, MASHKEL
Baluchistan state	KALAT, KHARAN, LASBELA
Baluchistan tribe	REKI
balustrade	PARAPET, RAILING
Balzac novel	PERE GORIOT, EUGENIE GRANDET
Bambi	DEER
Bambi author	SALTEN
Bambi name	ENA, GOBO, THUMPER
bamboo, pickled shoots	ACHAR
bamboozle	FOOL, HOAX, CHEAT, HUMBUG, DECEIVE
ban	BAR, TABOO, FORBID, INTERDICT
Bana daughter	USHA
banal	FLAT, CORNY, TRITE, TRIVIAL
banana	FEI, MUSA, ENSETE, PLANTAIN
banana plant	MUSA, ABACA, PESANG
band	MOB, BELT, FESS, ZONA, COMBO, FACIA, PATTE, STRIA, CLAVUS, FASCIA, FILLET, LIGULA, RADULA, REGULA, TAENIA
bandage	SPICA, STUPE, LIGATE
bandit	PAD, CACO, HOOD, TORY, CATERAN, LADRONE, TULISAN
bandleader	DOC, RICH, SHAW, WEBB, WELK, BASIE, BLOCH, KRUPA, NORVO, SOUSA, DORSEY, HERMAN, KENTON, MILLER, OLIVER, VALLEE, WARING, CHORAGI, SPANIER, STRAUSS, GOODMAN; *see* CONDUCTOR
bane	NEMESIS
Banff lake	LOUISE
banger	LIE, SAUSAGE
Bangladesh, capital of	DACCA, DHAKA
Bangladesh city/town	FENI, DHAKA, PABNA, KHULNA, BARISAL, COMILLA, JESSORE, KUSIYARA, CHITTAGONG
Bangladesh language	BENGALI
Bangladesh money	TAKA
Bangladesh neighbor	INDIA, MYANMAR
Bangladesh river	KALNI, NAGAR, PUSUR, SURMA, TISTA, GANGES, JAMUNA, MEGHNA
bangle	ANKLET, CIRCLET
banish	OUST, EXILE, EXPEL
bank	BERM, BRAE, CAJA, DUNE, RELY, RIPA, BERME, DIGUE, SHORE
bank employee	RUNNER, TELLER
bank, fishing	HAAF
bank job	HEIST, HOLDUP, STICKUP
bank, *pert. to*	LITTORAL, RIPARIAN
bankbook	PASSBOOK
banker	BANYA, SARAF, MELLON, MORGAN, SHROFF
banknote	BILL
bankroll	WAD, ANGEL, BACKER, SPONSOR
bankrupt	FAIL, BROKE, QUISBY
banner	LABRUM; *see* FLAG
banquet	SUP, DIFFA, JUNKET, REGALE, SPREAD
banter	JOSH, TWIT, BORAK, CHAFF, ASTEISM
Bantu language	ILA, BUBI, FANG, GUHA, LUBA, PEDI, SUTO, VILI, XOSA, ZULU, BEMBA, GANDA, KAMBA, KONGO, MAKUA, NGALA, RONGA, RUNDI, SOTHO, SWAZI, XHOSA, MBUNDU, NYANJA, RUANDA, SEPEDI, THONGA, TSWANA, KIKONGO, LINGALA, SWAHILI, FANGBULU, KIMBUNDU

Bantu people   GOGO, YAKU, ZULU, DUALA, (M)PONDO, SWAZI, BASUTO; see p. 735
banyan   BUR(R)
baptize   CHRISTEN; see NAME
bar   FID, TIE, LOOP, MUNT, PAWL, RAIL, REIN, ROSE, SESS, SNIB, BETTY, BLOCK, BRIDE, DETER, ESTOP, INGOT, JIMMY, SHOAL, STEEK, BISTRO, HINDER, STRIPE, SALOON, TAVERN
bar, door   RISP, STANG
bar feature   PIANO
bar money   BONK
barb   JAG, NAG, FLUE, HARL, HERL, RAMUS, SPINE
Barbados, capital of   BRIDGETOWN
Barbados money   DOLLAR
Barbados native   BIM
barbarian   HUN, GOTH, ALIEN, VANDAL
Barbarossa   FREDERICK
barbarous   FELL, RUDE, CRUDE, CRUEL, ROUGH, BRUTAL, SAVAGE, HEATHEN
Barbary state   ALGERIA, MOROCCO, TRIPOLI, TUNISIA
barber   FISH, SHAVE, FIGARO, SHAVER, TONSOR, COMPOSER
Barber of Seville character   BERTA, FIGARO, ROSINA, BARTOLO, ALMAVIVA
Barbie boyfriend   KEN
Barbuda, capital of   STJOHNS
Barcarolle composer   CHOPIN, OFFENBACH
bard   SCOP, DRUID, RUNER, SCALD, SKALD, VATES, SAGAMAN, MINSTREL
bard of Avon   SHAKESPEARE
bare   BALD, NUDE, NAKED, STARK, STRIP
bargain   DEAL, HUCK, KOOP, PRIG, TROG, DICKER, HAGGLE, HIGGLE, NIFFER, PALTER
barge   HOY, PRAM, SCOW, CASCO, LUNGE, LURCH, PRAAM, SCOLD, SHREW, WHERRY, LIGHTER
bark   BAST, DITA, HIDE, RIND, ROSS, SKIN, TAPA, YABA, FOAM, YEAST; see p. 682
barn   MEW, BYRE, AMBAR, LATHE, SKIPPER
Barnaby Rudge's raven   GRIP

barnacle   ACORN, BALANID
Barney Miller name   SOO, FISH, NICK, STAN, CHANO, ARTHUR, LINDEN, SCANLON
barnstorm   TOUR, STUMP, AVIATE
Barnum act   JUMBO, (TOM)THUMB
barometric line   ISOBAR
barony   HAN, FIEF
barrack(s)   BILLET, CAN(N)ABA, BIVOUAC
barracuda   SPET, BARRY, SENET, BECUNA, PICUDA, SENNET
barrel   TUN, CADE, KNAG, TIERCE
barrel part   LAG, RUNG, CHIMB, CHIME, STAVE, GA(U)NTRY
barrel-maker   COOPER, TUBBER, TUBMAN
barren   DULL, EILD, GELD, SECK, YELD, DRAPE, EFFETE, HISTLE, STERILE
barren land   REH, USAR, DESERT
barricade   BAR, ABATIS, PALISADE
Barrie character   NANA, PETER, WENDY, TIGER LILY, TINKERBELL, CAPTAIN HOOK
Barrie play   MARYROSE, PETERPAN
barrier   DAM, PALE, TREBLE
barrister   LAWYER, COUNSEL, ATTORNEY
barrow   CART, KURGAN, TUMULUS
Barrymore,—   DREW, JOHN, ETHEL, LIONEL, MAURICE
bartender   MIXER, SKINKER, TAPSTER
barter   MONG, SWAP, TROG, TROKE, NIFFER, TRAFFIC
Bartered Bride character   HANS, MUFF, AGNES, KEZAL, MARIE, MISHA
Bartered Bride composer   SMETANA
base   BAD, BAG, CAMP, VILE, CAITIFF, SERVILE
base, architectural   DADO, SOCLE, PATTEN, PLINTH
base, attached by   SESSILE
base on balls   PASS, WALK
baseball   see also p. 704
baseball league   AMERICAN, NATIONAL
baseball, home run leaders   FOXX, MAYS, MIZE, RUTH, SOSA, BELLE, BONDS, KINER, MARIS,

FOSTER, MANTLE, THOME, WILSON, FIELDER, GRIFFEY, MCQUIRE, ANDERSON, GONZALEZ, GREENBERG, RODRIGUEZ

baseball managers and executives DARK, HOUK, MACK, MELE, FRICK, GRIMM, HANEY, KEANE, LOPEZ, TERRY, TORRE, VEECK, ALSTON, BARROW, CRONIN, ECKERT, HARRIS, LANDIS, MARTIN, MCGRAW, RICKEY, RIGNEY, YAWKEY, ZIMMER, DRESSEN, HUGGINS, JOHNSON, STENGEL, BOUDREAU, COCHRANE, COMISKEY, DUROCHER, GRIFFITH

baseball stadiums, American League EDISON, FENWAY, JACOBS, ORIOLE, SAFECO, YANKEE, NETWORK, SKYDOME, COMERICA, COMISKEY, HUMPHREY, KAUFFMAN, ARLINGTON, TROPICANA

baseball stadiums, National League PNC, SHEA, BUSCH, COORS, DODGER, MILLER, TURNER, BANKONE, CINERGY, OLYMPIC, WRIGLEY, QUALCOMM, VETERANS, PROPLAYER, MINUTE MAID, PACIFIC BELL

baseball stadiums, former EBBETS, MUNICIPAL, POLOGROUNDS

baseball team   NINE; see p. 706

baseball term   BAG, BAT, BOX, ERA, FAN, FLY, HIT, OUT, RBI, RUN, BALK, BUNT, DECK, FOUL, MUFF, NINE, SACK, SAFE, SAVE, SLAB, WALK, BENCH, CATCH, CLOUT, FORCE, FRAME, HOMER, LINER, MOUND, PITCH, PLATE, POPUP, STEAL, STICK, SWING, BATTER, DOUBLE, DUGOUT, RUBBER, RUNNER, SINGLE, STRIKE, TRIPLE, BLOOPER, BULLPEN, CLEANUP, DIAMOND, FIELDER, INFIELD, SLUGGER, SQUEEZE, GROUNDER, OUTFIELD, PINCHHIT, SACRIFICE; see PITCH

baseball trio   EVERS, CHANCE, TINKERS

basement   CELLAR
Bashemath husband   ESAU
bashful   COY, SHY, BLATE, HELOE, VERECUND

basic   ROOT, PRIMARY, ESSENTIAL
basic reading   CANON
basilica   CANOPY, LATERAN
basin   PAN, FONT, TALA, LAVER, STOUP, HOLLOW, LAVABO, LEKANE, MARINA, CUVETTE
basis   FOND, AXIOM, PREMISE
bask   SUN, APRICATE
basket   PED, KISH, SKEP, DILLI, GRATE, MAUND, SERON, BIGGIN, DOSSER, GABION, HAMPER, HOPPET, JICARA, KIPSEY, PEGALL, CRESSET, PANNIER
basket, fish   CAUL, CAWL, KIPE, WEEL, CRAIL, CREEL
basket, fruit   CABA(S), FRAIL, MOLLY, POTTLE, PUNNET, TAPNET
basket material   RUSH, WOOD, OSIER, RAFFIA, RATTAN, SPLINT, WICKER, WILLOW
basket of coals   CORB, CORF
basket, sports   GOAL, CESTA
basketball   see also p 707
basketball coach   MOE, DALY, KARL, SHUE, BROWN, FITCH, MOTTA, RILEY, SLOAN, ATTLES, HARRIS, NELSON, RAMSAY, HOLZMAN, JACKSON, MACLEOD, WILKENS, AUERBACH, FRATELLO
basketball inventor   NAISMITH
basketball player   CAGER, GUARD, CENTER, FORWARD, HOOPMAN, CAGESTER; see p. 707
basketball team   FIVE; see p. 707
basketball term   NET, CAGE, DUNK, FOUL, HOOK, HOOP, PASS, LAYUP, TIPIN, WEAVE, BUCKET, DUNKER, FREEZE, JUMPER, TRAVEL, DRIBBLE, KEYHOLE, PALMING, REBOUNDING, WALKING, TURNOVER, BACKBOARD
basketful   WASH
basketry term   RAND, OSIER, SLATH, SCALLOM
basketwork   TEE, SLEW, WALE, SLA(R)TH
Basque   WAIST, SCOTER, IBERIAN, BISCAYAN, EUSCARIAN
Basque city/town   IRUN, EIBAR, BERMED, BILBAO, SESTAO, TOLOSA, GASTEIZ, VITORIA
Basque game   PELOTA

Basque province	ALVA, SOULE, BISCAY, LABOURD, NAVARRA, VISCAYA
bass	LOW, DEEP, VIOL, GRAVE, BASSO, DRONE, BURDEN, VIOLONE
bass (fish)	BOGA, ROCK, REDEYE, BARFISH
bast	BARK, RAMIE, PHLOEM
baste	SEW, DRAB, LARD, SLEW, TACK, CUDGEL
basto	CARD, QUEEN
Basutoland	see LESOTHO
bat	CLUB, HARPY, ALIPED, CUDGEL, RACKET, VAMPIRE
batfish	DIABOLO
bath(s)	BAIN, STEW, SAUNA, THERM(AE)
bath, type of	BUBBLE, SPONGE, JACUZZI, SWEDISH, TURKISH, WHIRLPOOL
Bath's river	AVON
bathe	LAVE, TOSH, CLEAN
bathhouse	BAGNIO, CABANA
bathing suit	TONGA, BIKINI, TRUNKS, MAILLOT
bathroom	WC, LOO, HEAD, TOILET
bathroom fixture	TUB, BASIN, BIDET, POTTY, STOOL, URINAL, COMMODE
Bathsheba relative	URIA, DAVID, URIAH, ANMIEL, NATHAN, SHIMEA, SHOBATH, SOLOMON
bathtub item	DUCKY, LOOFAH, BATHTOY
baton	ROD, STICK, SCEPTER
batten	RIB, REEPER
batter	RAM, MAUL, PASTE, SLOPE
battering ram	CORVUS, TEREBRA
battery	CELL, PILE, PARAPET
battery term	GRID, POST, CHARGER
battery size	AA, AAA
battle	COPE, FRAY, AFFRAY, HOSTING
battle cry	ABU, ABOO, BANZAI
battle formation	ACIES, HERSE, DEPLOY, PHALANX
Battle Hymn of the Republic author	HOWE, WARD, JULIA
battle of wits	REPARTEE
battle site	IVRY, JENA, STLO, VAUX, ZAMA, ADOWA, ALAMO, BULGE, CRECY, IPSUS, ISSUS, MARNE, SEDAN,

	SOMME, VALMY, YPRES, ARBELA, BATAAN, CANNAE, CRESSY, SADOWA, SENLAR, SHILOH, VERDUN, DUNKIRK, MARENGO, PLATAEA, SALAMIS, BOSTOGNE, HASTINGS, SKAGERAK, WATERLOO, SKAGERRAK, TRAFALGAR; see individual wars
battle-ax	SHREW, TWIBIL(L), GISARME, HATCHET, VIRAGO
battlefield	ARENA, CHAMP, SECTOR, TERRAIN, THEATER
battlement	CRENEL, MERLON, PINION
battleship	see SHIP
bauble	TOY, GEWGAW, MAROTTE
Baucis' husband	PHILEMON
Bauhaus founder	GROPIUS
Bavarian city	MUNICH, NURNBERG, AUGSBURG, BAYREUTH
Bavarian king	LUDWIG
Bavarian river	EGER, ISAR, MAIN, ILLER
bawdy	LEWD, OBSCENE, INDECENT
bawl	see CRY
bay	ISE, RED, VOE, COIL, COVE, KARA, BIGHT, CORAL, INLET, BISCAY, GALWAY, LAUREL, SAGAMI, TASMAN, UNGAVA, DONEGAL, SALERNO, THUNDER
Baylor U. city	WACO
Bay State	MA, MASSACHUSETTS
bay window	ORIEL
bayou	INLET
bazaar	FAIR, SOOK, SOUK, AGORA, GINZA
be temporarily	ACTAS
beach	PLAYA, SHORE, SHILLA, STRAND
beach craft	LST
beach, famous	BONDI, MALIBU, TAHITI, VIRGINIA, BLACKPOOL
beachcomber	DRIFTER
beachfront locale	RESORT
beachwear	THONG, TONGA, BIKINI, MONOKINI, SWIMSUIT, SWIMWEAR
beacon	PIKE, FANAL, PHAROS, CRESSET
Beaconsfield	DISRAELI
beads	ROSARY, CHAPLET

beak	NEB, NIB, BILL, TUTEL	beauty parlor	SALON
beak part	GENA	beauty treatment	RUB, SET,
beam	RAY, SILE, CABER,		WAVE, FACIAL, MUDPACK,
	STRUT, GIRDER, LINTEL,		MASSAGE, MANICURE,
	RAFTER, TEMPLET, TEMPLATE		PEDICURE, PERMANENT
beam type	XRAY, LASER,	beaver	CASTOR
	PROTON, NEUTRON,	beaver skin	PLEW
	ELECTRON	Beaver State	OR, OREGON
bean	SOY, URD, FABA, LIMA,	beaver, young	KIT
	SOYA, MUNGO, PINTO,	because	AS, SINCE, INASMUCH
	TONKA, ADZUKI, LEGUME,	bêche-de-mer	TREPANG
	HARICOT; see p. 685	beck and —	CALL
bean curd	TOFU	becket	GROMMET
beans, pile of	HILL	Beckett work	GODOT,
Beantown	BOSTON		MOLLOY, UNNAMABLE
bear	DUBB, URSA, BRUIN,	becoming	FIT, PROPER,
	YIELD, ENDURE, GRIZZLY,		SEEMLY
	ICEBEAR, SUNBEAR	bed	COT, KIP, BUNK, CRIB,
bear down	LEAN, PRESS(URE)		DOSS, DONGA, PALLET
bear, famous	(GENTLE)BEN	bed and —	BOARD,
bear, young	CUB		BREAKFAST
heard	AWN, FUZZ, ARISTA,	bedclothes	CASES, LINEN,
	BARBET, BYSSUS, GOATEE,		SHEETS, PILLOWS, BLANKETS
	SHADOW	bedlam	RIOT, MELEE, UPROAR
bearded	AWNY, HAIRY,	bedmaker	RIVER, STREAM
	BARBATE	Bedouin	ARAB, HARB, RIFF,
bearer	TOTER, SIRDAR		NOMAD, BERBER, RIFFIAN
bearing	AIR, MIEN, ORLE, PORT	bedridden	ABED, LAIDUP
bearings	STANCE,	bee	DOR, BIKE, GYNE, HIVE,
	ORIENTATION		KING, DRONE, KARBI,
beast	LOUT, BRUTE		MASON, QUEEN, BUMBEE,
beast of burden	OX, YAK,		BUMBLE, KILLER, NEUTER,
	CAMEL, LLAMA; see ASS,		WORKER, ANDRENA,
	HORSE		BUMBLER, BUMMLER,
beastly	VILE, FERAL, BRUTAL		KOOTCHA, ACULEATA,
beat	LAM, TAN, CANE, DRUB,		HONEYBEE
	LACE, LASH, WELT, WHIP,	bee genus	APIS, APIDAE,
	PULSE, ROUND, CUDGEL,		BOMBUS, APOIDAE,
	LARRUP, POMMEL, RHYTHM,		TRIGONA
	SWINGE, SWITCH, THRASH,	bee, pert. to	APIAN
	BELABOR; see TACK,	beech	FAGUS, RAULI, ROBLE
	ACCENT, DEFEAT	beechnuts	MAST
beat it	SCRAM, GETLOST	beef	COW, BULL, CARP, MEAT,
beater	RAB, BATTEN		STEER, BRAWN, BULLY,
Beatle	JOHN, PAUL, RINGO,		GRIPE, MUSCLE; see CATTLE
	STARR, GEORGE, LENNON,	beef cut	RIB, LOIN, RUMP,
	HARRISON, MCCARTNEY		CHUCK, ROUND, SADDLE,
Beatles manager	EPSTEIN		BRISKET, SIRLOIN; see ROAST,
Beatrice lover	DANTE,		STEAK
	BENEDICT	beefy	MEATY, STOUT, BRAWNY
beau	BLADE, FLAME, SWAIN	beehive	SKEP, APIARY
beau monde	JETSET	beekeeper	APIARIAN, SKEPPER
beautician	(HAIR)STYLIST,	Beelzebub	SATAN
	MANICURIST	beer	ALE, BEER, BOCK, BREW,
beautiful	FAIR, COMELY,		GYLE, KVAS, MEAD, QUAS,
	LOVELY, PRETTY		SUDS, CHANG, KVASS, LAGER,
beautiful woman	DOLL, LULU,		POMBE, STOUT, PORTER,
	PERI, HELEN, NYMPH, VENUS,		PANGASI, NEARBEER,
	LOOKER, KNOCKOUT		METHEGLIN

beer ingredient	HOPS, MALT, YEAST, BARLEY		HOMYEL, MAHILYOW, VITSYEBSK
beer maker	BUSCH, PABST	Belarus money	KOPEK,
Beeri relative	JUDITH		R(O)UBLE
Beethoven birthplace	BONN	Belarus neighbor	LATVIA,
Beethoven opera	FIDELIO		POLAND, RUSSIA, UKRAINE,
Beethoven sonata	TEMPEST,		LITHUANIA
	ARCHDUKE, KREUTZER,	Belarus river	DVINA, NEMAN,
	PATHETIC, MOONLIGHT		DNIEPER, PRIPYAT
Beethoven symphony	CHORAL,	belch	BURP, ERUCT(ATE)
	EROICA, PASTORAL	beldam(e)	see HAG
beetle	DOR(R), BORER, LYCID,	Belgian	FLEMING, WALLOON
	CHAFER, PRUNER, SCARAB,	Belgian artist	RUBENS,
	WEEVIL, FIREFLY, JUNEBUG,		BRUEGEL, VANDYCK,
	LADYBUG; see p. 678		VANEYCK, MAGRITTE
beetle genus	AMARA, LARIA,	Belgian city/town	HUY, SPA,
	SAGRA, CLERUS, IPIDAE,		BOOM, BALEN, GHENT,
	LYCTUS, PTINUS, SILPHA,		LIEGE, VORST, YPRES,
	ADELOPS, AGRILUS,		ANTWERP, OSTENDE
	GYRINUS, LUCANUS, VEDALIA	Belgian language	DUTCH,
before	ERE, AFORE, PRIOR,		FRENCH, FLEMISH
	EARLIER, EARLYON	Belgian measure	AUNE, PIED,
befuddled	ATSEA, BAFFLED,		PERCHE
	PERPLEXED	Belgian neighbor	FRANCE,
beg	SORN, CADGE, ENTREAT;		GERMANY, LUXEMBOURG,
	see ASK		NETHERLANDS
beget	EAN, SIRE	Belgian river	LYS, LEIE, MAAS,
beggar	FAKIR, LAZAR,		YSER, MEUSE, RUPEL, SENNE,
	MENDICANT, PANHANDLER		DENDER, OURTHE, SAMBRE,
Beggar's Opera author	GAY		SCHELDE
Beggar's Opera character	LUCY,	Belgian ruler	ALBERT,
	SUKY, DIANA, JENNY, POLLY,		CHARLES, LEOPOLD,
	LOCKIT, PEACHUM,		BAUDOUIN
	MACHEATH	Belgian money	EURO, BELGA,
beggary	WANT, PENURY		FRANC
begin	FANG, OPEN, ARISE	Belgian weight	LIVRE,
beginner	TYRO, NOVICE,		CHARGE, CHARIOT
	ROOKIE	Belgium, capital of	BRUSSELS
beginning	ALPHA, FRONT,	belief(s)	FAY, ISM, DOXY,
	ONSET, ORIGIN, INITIAL,		CREDO, CREED, DEISM,
	NASCENT		DOGMA(TA), FAITH, TENET,
begone	OUT, VIA, SCAT,		TROTH
	AROINT	believe	DEEM, HOLD, TROW
beguile	LURE, VAMP, WILE,	believer	IST, DEIST, OMNIST
	WISE, COZEN	belittle	DIS, DERIDE, PUT
behave	ACT, KEEP, DEPORT,		DOWN
	COMPORT, CONDUCT	Belize	HONDURAS
behest	BID, ORDER, MANDATE	Belize, capital of	BELMOPAN
behind	AFT, SLOW, ABAFT,	Belize district	CAYO, TOLEDO,
	AREAR, TARDY, ASTERN		COROZAL
behold	LA, LO, SEE, ECCE,	Belize money	DOLLAR
	ESPY, VISE, VOILA	Belize neighbor	MEXICO,
being(s)	ENS, ESSE, LIFE, ENTIA,		HONDURAS, GUATEMALA
	FRONT, HUMAN, ANTEAL,	Belize river	HONDO, BELIZE,
	ENTITY		SARSTOON
Bela Lugosi pet	BAT	bell	GONG, CODON, KNELL,
Belafonte word	DAYO		TOCSIN, CAMPANA,
Belarus, capital of	MINSK		CAMPANE, SQUILLA
Belarus city/town	MINSK,	bell set	CHIME, CARILLON

bell town	**ADANO**	Benjamin relative	**ARD, EHI,**
belladonna	**ATROPIN,**		**BELA, ROSH, JACOB**
	MANICON, ATROPINE	Benjamite	**ADER, AHER, JEUZ**
bell-bottom feature	**FLARE**	bent	**BIAS, HOOK, FLAIR,**
belle	**DEB, MAJA, PERI**		**KNACK, TASTE**
Bellini opera	**NORMA, PIRATA,**	Beowulf's victim	**GRENDEL**
(I) PURITANI, SONNAMBULA		bequest	**DOT, GIFT, DOWRY,**
belly	**RIFF, WOMB, PLEON,**		**LEGACY**
	THARM, TUMMY, PAUNCH,	berate	**JAW, WIG, CHEW,**
	VENTER, MIDRIFF		**CHIDE, SCOLD, REVILE,**
bellyache	**CARP, MOAN,**		**CENSURE, CHEWOUT**
	GRIPE, GROUSE	Berber	**MOOR, RIFF, HAMITE**
belong	**INHERE, PERTAIN**	Berber language	**RIF, DRAA,**
below	**ALOW, NEATH, UNDER,**		**SIWI, KABYLE, LIBYAN,**
	SOTTO		**SHAWIA, TUAREG, ZENAGA,**
belt	**OBI, LACE, SASH, ZONE,**		**ZENETE, BERABER,**
	SMITE, CESTUS, CINGLE,		**GUANCHE, SAHARAN,**
	CORDON, GIRDLE,		**TAMASHEK**
	BALDRIC(K), CEINTURE	bereave	**STRIP, WIDOW,**
— Ben Adhem	**ABOU**		**DIVEST, DESPOIL**
bench	**BAR, PEW, BANC, DAIS,**	bereft	**LORN, DEPRIVED**
	ZYGA, ZYGON, EXEDRA,	berg	**ICE, FLOE, BARROW**
	SETTEE, THWART	Berg opera	**LULU, WOZZECK**
bend	**BOW, NID, SAG, FLEX,**	Bergen's dummy	**SNERD**
	KINK, LOUT, WARP, BULGE,	Bergman, —	**INGMAR, INGRID**
	CROOK, CURVE	Bering Sea river	**YUKON**
— bene	**NOTA**	Berlin river	**HAVEL, SPREE**
beneath	**BELOW, UNDER,**	Berlin Stories musical	**CABARET**
	SOTTO	Bermuda, capital of	**HAMILTON**
benedict	**GROOM**	— Berra	**YOGI**
benediction	**SHEMA, BENISON**	berry	**PASA, BACCA, CUBEB,**
benefaction	**ALMS, BOON, GIFT**		**GRAPE, TOMATO, CURRANT,**
benefactor	**ANGEL, DONOR,**		**MADRONA;** see **FRUIT**
	PATRON, SPONSOR	berserk	**MAD, AMOK,**
benefice	**ANNAT, GLEBE**		**ENRAGED**
beneficial	**GOOD, SALUTARY**	berth	**BED, JOB, BUNK, DOCK,**
beneficiary	**HEIR, USER,**		**SLIP, LOWER, UPPER, BILLET**
	DONEE, LEGATEE	beseech	**BEG, SUE, PRAY,**
benefit	**BOON, BOOT, AVAIL,**		**ADJURE, APPEAL, OBTEST,**
	PROFIT		**ENTREAT**
Bengal city	**PATNA,**	beset	**SIT, HARRY, OBSESS**
	CALCUTTA	besides	**AND, TOO, YET, ALSO,**
Ben-Hur author	**WALLACE**		**ELSE, INBY, OVER, THEN,**
Ben-Hur rival	**MESSALA**		**EXCEPT**
benign	**SUAVE, GENIAL,**	besiege	**BESET, OBSIDE,**
	GENTLE		**PESTER, PLAGUE**
Benin, capital of	**COTONOU,**	besmear	**DAUB, SOIL, TAINT**
	PORTONOVO	besmirch	**TAR, SOIL, DIRTY,**
Benin city/town	**SAVE, KANDI,**		**SULLY, DEFAME, TARNISH**
	ABOMEY, COTONOU,	besom	**MOP, BROOM,**
	PARAKOU		**HEATHER**
Benin, formerly	**DAHOMEY**	bespangle	**STAR, STUD,**
Benin language	see **GUR**		**ENSTAR**
Benin money	**FRANC**	best	**ACME, AONE, BEAT,**
Benin native	**FON**		**MOST, TOPS, CREAM, ELITE,**
Benin neighbor	**TOGO, NIGER,**		**CHOICE, OUTWIT, UTMOST**
	NIGERIA, BURKINA FASO	bet	**GO, POT, ANTE, PUNT,**
Benin river	**MONO, SOTA, NIGER,**		**WAGE, HEDGE, STAKE,**
	OUEME, MEKROU, ALIBORI		**WAGER, MILIEU, PARLAY**

bet, fail to pay   **WELCH, WELSH**
bête noire   **BANE, BUGABOO,**
       BUGBEAR
betel   **BUYO, SIRI, ARECA,**
     BONGA, BUNGA, SIRIH
Beth's sister   **JO, AMY, MEG**
betray   **BLAB, SELL, SILE, TRAP,**
     PEACH, RATON, SNARE,
     TRICK, REVEAL, SQUEAL
betrayal comment   **ET TU**
betrayer   **RAT, JUDAS,**
     SEDUCER, TRAITOR
betroth   **AFFY, EARL, TOKEN,**
     PLEDGE, PLIGHT
better   **TOP, (A)MEND, EMEND,**
     REFORM, OUTCLASS
betting system   **PARLAY,**
     PARIMUTUEL
betting term   **ODDS, PUNT,**
     TOUT, WAGER, BOOKIE,
     PARLAY
between   **AMELL, AMONG,**
     INTER, MESNE
betwixt and —   **BETWEEN**
bevel   **CANT, EDGE, REAM,**
     MITER, MITRE, SNAPE,
     ASLANT
beverage   **ADE, ALE, POP, TEA,**
   BEER, COKE, NEHI, SODA,
WINE, CIDER, COCOA, MORAT,
   NEGUS, PEPSI, NECTAR,
POSSET, LIQUOR, POTABLE;
     see **DRINK**
Beverly Hillbillies name   **JED,**
   EBSEN, HOMER, PEARL,
GRANNY, JETHRO, ELLYMAY
bevy   **NYE, HERD, PACK, WISP,**
   BATCH, BROOD, CHARM,
   COVEY, DROVE, FLOCK,
PLUMP, SIEGE, SKEIN, SUITE,
   SWARM, BAZAAR, COVERT,
   DESERT, FLIGHT, GAGGLE,
   MUSTER, SPRING; *see p. 523*
bewail   **CRY, WEY, WEEP,**
     GRIEVE, LAMENT
beware   **SHUN, AVOID, ESCHEW**
bewildered   **ASEA, DAZED,**
     ADDLED, AMAZED
bewitch   **HEX, CHARM,**
     ENAMOR, THRILL,
     ENCHANT, ENSORCEL
Bewitched name   **ADAM, YORK,**
   LARRY, DARRIN, ENDORA,
     SARGENT, TABITHA,
SAMANTHA, MOOREHEAD,
     MONTGOMERY
Beyoglu   **PERA**
beyond   **BY, PAST, ULTRA,**
     YONDER

bezel   **RIM, EDGE, SEAL,**
     FACET, TEMPLET
Bhagavad —   **GITA**
Bhutan, capital of   **THIMPHU,**
     TASHICHHO
Bhutan language   **NEPALI,**
     DZONGKHA
Bhutan money   **NGULTRUM**
Biafran leader   **OJUKWU**
bias   **PLY, BENT, CANT, SWAY,**
     SLANT, SLOPE
biased person   **BIGOT**
Bible   **BOOK, TEXT, WORD,**
   WRIT, GOSPEL; *see also p. 515*
Bible version   **DOUAY, ITALA,**
     TARGUM, HEXAPLA,
REVISED, TYNDALE, VULGATE,
   PESHITTA, TETRAPLA,
   WYCLIFFE, KING JAMES
Biblical pronoun   **THEE, THOU**
bicker   **SPAT, CAVIL, QUIBBLE**
bicycle   **BIKE, TANDEM**
bid   **ENJOIN, INVITE, TENDER;**
     see **BRIDGE**
bier   **PYRE, TABUT, COFFIN,**
     LITTER
bifurcation   **WYE, FORK,**
     BRANCH
Big Five   **CHINA, ITALY, JAPAN,**
     FRANCE, RUSSIA
bight   **BAY, COVE, GULF, LOOP**
bigot   **ZEALOT, FANATIC**
bikini   **ATOLL, TONGA**
bile   **GALL, VENOM, CHOLER,**
     SPLEEN
Bilhah husband   **JACOB**
Bilhah relative   **DAN, NAPHTALI**
bilk   **GYP, HOAX, CHEAT, TRICK**
bill   **ACT, DUN, LAW, NEB, NIB,**
     PEE, TAB, BEAK, CARD,
   MENU, NOTE, POSTER, TICKET,
     PLACARD; *see p. 640*
bill and —   **COO**
bill, rare   **TWO**
billet   **JOB, POST, BERTH,**
     LODGE
billhook   **DHAW**
billiards term   **CUE, BAFF, BALK,**
     BANK, KISS, POOL, REST,
   SPOT, BAIZE, CAROM, CHALK,
     MASSE, SIGHT
billingsgate   **ABUSE, OBLOQUY**
billow   **SEA, WAVE, SURGE,**
     SWELL, ROLLER
bin   **ARK, CANCH, KENCH**
binaural   **STEREO**
bind   **WAP, LINK, TAPE, TILE,**
     TRUSS, UNITE, COHERE,
   SECURE, SWATHE, CONFINE

binder	**TYER**
binding	**YAPP**
bingo	**KENO, BEANO, LOTTO**
biography	**LIFE, VITA, MEMOIR**
biological	**BIOTIC(AL)**
biological term	**GENE, RIMA**
biological weapons	**VHF, EBOLA,**
	PLAGUE, ANTHRAX,
	MARBURG, BOTULISM,
	SMALLPOX, TULAREMIA
biologist	*see p. 538*
birch	**BIRK, CANE, FLOG, TREE,**
	ALDER, STICK, BETULA
bird	**AVES, AVIS, IBIS, DIVER,**
	ORNIS, TURCO, BARBET,
	DOPPER, GORLIN, HOOTER,
	NESTER, PEEPER, PULLUS,
	RAPTOR, SOARER, ANT BIRD,
	CHEEPER, CHIRPER, FLAPPER,
	FLOPPER, JACAMAR,
	MANAKIN, AVIFAUNA,
	FLAMINGO, LYREBIRD,
	TAPACOLO; see p. 673
bird cry	**CAW, COO, CRAW,**
	HONK, PEEP, SING, CHEEP,
	CHIRM, CHIRP, CHUCK,
	CLUCK, QUACK, TWEET,
	CACKLE, GAGGLE, GOBBLE,
	SQUAWK, TRUMPET
bird, extinct	**MOA, DODO, JIBI,**
	MAMO; see p. 673
bird, flightless	**EMU, MOA,**
	DODO, EMEU, KAGU, KIWI,
	RHEA, WEKA, DIDUS, NANDU,
	MOORUP, RAPHUS,
	APTERYX, OSTRICH, RATITE,
	WOODHEN, KIWIKIWI,
	NOTORNIS, CASSOWARY
bird, mythological	**ROC, RUKH,**
	PH(O)ENIX, SIMORG(H),
	SIMURG(H)
bird nest materials	**MUD, HAIR,**
	MOSS, TWIG, FIBRE, GRASS,
	LICHEN, SALIVA
bird of Juno	**PEACOCK**
bird of Jupiter	**EAGLE**
bird, *pert. to*	**AVIN, AVIAN,**
	AVINE, OSCINE
bird, small	**TIT, TODY, WREN,**
	BLUET, FINCH, PEWEE, PIPIT,
	SERIN, SYLPH, VIREO, TOMTIT
bird talk	**CHITTER**
bird, talking	**CROW, MINA,**
	MYNA, PARROT; see
	SONGBIRD
bird, young	**NESTLING,**
	FLEDGLING
birdhouse	**COTE, NEST,**
	AVIARY

birth	**ORIGIN, GENESIS,**
	LYINGIN, DELIVERY,
	NATIVITY
birth, before	**PRENATAL,**
	PREPARTUM
birth, by	**NE(E)**
birth, of one's	**NATAL**
birthday suit	**BUFF, NUDE, SKIN**
birthmark	**MOLE, N(A)EVUS**
birthright	**HERITAGE,**
	PATRIMONY
birthstones	*see p. 718*
bis	**AGAIN, TWICE, ENCORE,**
	REPEAT
biscuit	**BUN, RUSK, PANAL,**
	WAFER, BISQUE, SIMNEL,
	PANTILE, RATAFIA,
	MACAROON
bishop	**ABBA, POPE, ALFIN,**
	AILIUS, PONTIFF, PRELATE,
	PRIMATE
bishop's assistant	**COAD,**
	VICAR, VERGER
bishop's attire	*see* **VESTMENTS**
bishop's headgear	**MITRE**
bishop's seat	**SEE, APSE, BEMA,**
	LAWN, DIOCESE
bistro	**BAR, PUB, TAVERN**
bit	**ACE, FID, JOT, ORT, WEE,**
	ATOM, GLIM, IOTA, MITE,
	MOTE, PART, SNAP, WHIT,
	SPECK, MORSEL, SIPPET,
	PALLION
bite	**NIP, CHAM, CHEW,**
	GNAW, KNIP, NOSH, SNAP,
	ZING, CHAMP, WHEAL,
	MORSEL
biting	**ACID, ACRID, CRISP,**
	CAUSTIC, MORDANT
bitstock	**BRACE**
bitter	**AMER, AMAR, BILE,**
	HATE, ACERB, ACRID, AIGRE
bittern	**KAKKAK; see HERON**
bitterness	**RUE, ACOR, ATTER,**
	MARAH, ACRIMONY
bitumen	**TAR, PITCH,**
	ASPHALT
bivalve	**CLAM, MUSSEL,**
	OYSTER
bivouac	**CAMP, BARRACKS**
bizarre	**ODD, OUTRE, QUEER,**
	DAEDAL, ODDISH
Bizet opera	**CARMEN,**
	PEARLFISHERS
blab	**GOSSIP, TATTLE,**
	PRATTLE
black	**DHU, JET, EBON, INKY,**
	SABLE
black and —	**TAN, BLUE, WHITE**

black art	MAGIC, SORCERY	blast	BUB, BANG, FLAW,
black congresswoman, first			GALE, ATTACK
	CHISHOLM	blatant	GLIB, GROSS, VOCAL,
Black Death	PLAGUE		COARSE
black diamond	COAL	blaze	LOW, MARK, GLOW,
black eye	SHINER		FLARE
black gold	OIL	blazer	JACKET
black hole	MACHO	bleach	BLANCH, CHLORE,
Black Maria	(PADDY)WAGON		WHITEN, ETIOLATE
Black Power leader	BROWN,	bleak	RAW, BLAE, BLAY, BLEA,
	NEWTON		ABLET, DREAR(Y)
Black Prince	EDWARD	bleared	INKY, DUSKY,
Black Sea	EUXINE, PONTUS		RHEUMY
Black Sea city	ANAPA, VARNA,	bleary-eyed	TEARY, RHEUMY
	YALTA, ODESSA	bleb	BULLA, BUBBLE, BLISTER,
Black Sea peninsula	CRIMEA		PUSTULE
Black Shirt	NAZI, FASCIST	blemish	FLAW, SLUR, TASH,
blackball	BOYCOTT		AMPER, TACHE, BRUISE,
blackbird	MERL(E), LAZYBIRD;		MACULE, STIGMA
	see CROW	blench	PALE, SHUN, AVOID,
blacken	INK, SOOT, JAPAN,		ELUDE, QUAIL, SHIRK,
	SHINE, DEFAME		FLINCH, RECOIL
blackguard	GAMIN, KNAVE,	blenny	POUT, GUNNEL,
	VILLAIN		SHANNY, ROCKEEL
blackhead	DUCK, PLUG,	bless	SAIN, BENSH, EXTOL,
	COMEDO, PIMPLE		HALLOW, PRAISE, BEATIFY
blackheart	CHERRY	blessed	HOLY, SACRE, DIVINE,
blackjack	MUG, COSH		SACRED
blackjack term	ACE, HIT, TEN,	blessing	BOON, SAIN, GRACE,
	CHECK, STAND		BENISON, BENEFICE
blacklist	BOYCOTT, EXCLUDE,	blight	NIP, ROT, RUIN, RUST,
	OSTRACIZE		SMUT, SOKA, MILDEW
blacklist org.	HUAC	blind	SEEL, DECOY, SHADE,
blackmail	EXTORT(ION),		SHUTTER
	SQUEEZE	blind alley	IMPASSE, DEAD
blackout	SKIT, FAINT		END, CULDESAC
blacksmith	LOHAR, SHOER,	blind as a —	BAT
	SMITHY, STITHY, FARRIER	blind, printing for	BRAILLE
blacksmith tool	ANVIL, FORGE,	blinder	SEEL, WINKER,
	HARDY, SWAGE, FULLER		BLINKER
blade	BIT, OAR, EDGE, LEAF,	blindness	CECITY, ANOPSIA
	TANG, DANDY, SABRE,	blink	PINK, WINK, NICTATE,
	SPIRE, SWORD		TWINKLE
blain	SORE, BULLA, BUSTER	bliss	KEF, KIF, KEIF, KIEF, KIFF,
blame	CHOP, ONUS, FAULT,		HEAVEN, RAPTURE, ECSTASY
	GUILT, ODIUM, SNAPE,	blissful	HOLY, SEELY,
	ASCRIBE, CENSURE		ECSTATIC
bland	FLAT, MILD, SUAVE,	blister	BLEB, BLAIN, BLURE,
	URBANE		BULLA(E)
blandish	COAX, CAJOLE,	blithe	GAY, AIRY, JOVIAL
	FLATTER, WHEEDLE	blizzard	BURA(N), PURGA
blanket	BROT, COTTA,	bloat	SWELL, TUMEFY,
	MANTA, QUILT, SHEET,		DISTEND, INFLATE
	CORONA, PONCHO, SERAPE,	bloated	TUMID, TURGID
	STROUD, TILPAH	blob	WEN, MASS, BLEMISH
— Blas	GIL	bloc	RING, CABAL, FACTION
blasé	BORED, JADED	block	BAN, BAR, DAM, NOG,
blaspheme	CURSE, SWEAR,		VOL, BITT, DOOK, FOIL,
	PROFANE		QUAD, CHECK, PERCH,

DENTEL, DENTIL, HINDER, MUTULE, STYMIE

blockade   BESIEGE, ISOLATE

blockhead   ASS, LUG, OAF, MOKE, DUNCE, NINNY

blond(e)   FAIR, FLAXEN, TOWHEAD

blond bombshell   HARLOW, MONROE, MANSFIELD

blonde, type of   ASH, HONEY, PEROXIDE, PLATINUM

blood   GORE, SERA, CRUOR, ICHOR, SERUM, PLASMA

blood —   BANK

— blood   COLD

blood carrier   VEIN, AORTA, ARTERY

blood cell   *see* CELL

blood disease   LEUKEMIA

blood emulsion   CHYLE

blood, lack of   AN(A)EMIA

blood money   CRO, GALANAS

blood, *pert. to*   H(A)EMAL, H(A)EMIC

blood poisoning   SEPSIS, PYEMIA, TOXEMIA

blood system   ABO

blood vessel   *see* VEIN

bloodless   PALE, ANEMIC

bloodsucker   FLEA, TICK, LEECH, LOUSE, BEDBUG, VAMPIRE, HORSEFLY, PARASITE

bloodthirsty   MURDEROUS, SANGUINARY

bloody   GORY, CURSED

bloom   DOWN, PRIME, FLOWER, HEYDAY

Bloomsbury resident   WOOLF, KEYNES

blooper   SLIP, BONER, ERROR, LAPSE

blossom   BUD, BLOOM, FLOWER

blot   BLUR; *see* STAIN

blot out   DELE(TE), EFFACE

blotch   BLEB, BLAIN, BULLA, SPLAT, MACULA, MOTTLE

blouse   TOP, MIDDY, CAMISA, GUIMPE, MIDDIE, SLIPON, CAMISOLE, PULLOVER, GARIBALDI

blow   HIT, CONK, COUP, CRIG, DINT, GALE, HUFF, ONER, PANT, SWAT, WAFT, VAUNT, DISASTER

blow away   KILL, SHOOT, ASTOUND

blow up   ENLARGE, EXPLODE, INFLATE

blow-by-blow   FULL, DETAILED, THOROUGH

blowfish   PUFFER

blubber   CRY, FAT, WAIL, FENKS, SPECK, LIPER

blubber, strip   FLENSE

bludgeon   BAT, CLUB, MACE, BILLY

blue   LOW, SAD, DOWN, GLUM, DISMAL, EROTIC; *see p. 531*

Blue Eagle   NRA

Bluebeard's wife   FATIMA

bluebell   COWSLIP, HAREBELL

bluebird genus   IRENA, SIALIA

bluebottle   BLOWFLY

Bluefin   *see* TUNA

Bluegrass State   KY, KENTUCKY

bluejacket   MARINE, SAILOR, SOLDIER

blue-pencil   EDIT, CORRECT

blueprint   MAP, PLAN, PLOT, DRAFT, TRACE

blues   DUMPS, MEGRIMS, SADNESS, DOLDRUMS

blues singer   SIMS, WOLF, ESTES, (SON) HOUSE, (BESSIE) SMITH, HOOKER, PATTON, WATERS, BROONZY, JOHNSON, JEFFERSON

bluff   BRAG, CURT, HOAX, RUDE, CLIFF, STEEP, CRUSTY

blunder   ERR, BULL, GAFF, SKEW, SLIP, BONER, BOTCH, ERROR, MISDO, BUNGLE

blunt   DULL, RUDE, BLATE, GRUFF, OBTUND, OBTUSE, ASSUAGE

blush   BLOOM, FLUSH, ROUGE, TINGE, MANTLE, REDDEN

bluster   RANT, ROAR, BULLY, BRAVADO, SWAGGER

Bnai —   BRITH

boa   ABOMA, ANACONDA

boar head   HURE

board(s)   EATS, LODGE, MEALS, PANEL, PLANK, STAGE, COUNCIL

— and board   BED

board a vehicle   EMBUS, EMPLANE, ENTRAIN

board game   *see* GAMES

board game ending   ENDGAME

boast   BOG, GAB, BRAG, CROW, RAVE, GLOAT, PREEN, VAUNT, FLAUNT, BOMBAST, SWAGGER

boaster   JINGO, BRAVADO, BRAGGART, RODOMONT

boastful air   PARADO

boat	*see* SHIP	Boer language	TAAL,
boatman	PHAON, CHARON		AFRIKAANS
Boaz wife	RUTH	bog	FEN, GOG, MIRE, MOOR,
Boaz relative	OBED, RUTH		OOZE, QUAG, SYRT, MARSH,
bob	DIP, JOG, NOD, RAP,		SWAMP, MORASS, SLOUGH
	CURTSY, HAIRDO, DUCK,	boggle	JIB, SHY, BALK,
	JERK, FLOAT, PENDANT,		ALARM, SCARE
	SHILLING	bogus	FAKE, SHAM, PHON(E)Y
bobbin	PIN, PIRN, REEL,	Bohème character	MIMI,
	CLUNY, SPOOL		COLLINE, MUSETTA,
bobcat	LYNX		RODOLFO, MARCELLO,
bobolink	SORA, REEDBIRD,		SCHAUNARD
	RICEBIRD	Bohème composer	PUCCINI
bobwhite	COLIN, QUAIL	Bohemia	CECHY
Boccaccio book	DECAMERON	bohemian	ARTY, SLAV, CZECH,
bode	AUGUR, PORTEND,		GYPSY, ARTIST
	PRESAGE	Bohemian city	PLZEN, PRAHA,
bodice	VEST, WAIST, BASQUE		PILSEN, PRAGUE
bodkin	DAGGER, NEEDLE,	Bohemian girl	ARLINE
	STILETTO	Bohemian hero	HUS(S)
body	BOLE, BULK, FORM,	Bohemian river	EGER, ELBE,
	DEHA, KHET, LICH, MASS,		LABE, OHRE, MOLDAU,
	RUPA, SOMA, STEM, TORSO,		VLTAVA
	CORPSE, CORPUS, LICHAM,	boil	STY, COCT, KYLE, RAGE,
	CADAVER, CARCASS		SORE, STEW, TEEM, PLOOK,
body hugger	BRA(SSIERE)		BUBBLE, DECOCT, SEETHE,
body motion, *pert. to*	GESTIC		ESTUATE
body of men	ARMY, MASS,	boiler	TANK, COPPER,
	NAVY, CORPS, FORCE, POSSE		RETORT, ALEMBIC,
body opening	FORAMEN,		CA(U)LDRON
	ORIFICE, FENESTRA	boiler plate	SPUT
body part	ARM, HIP, LEG,	bok—	CHOY
	BACK, BONE, BUST, CELL,	bold	DERF, PERT, RASH,
	CHAP, DUCT, FOOT, HAND,		NERVY, BRAZEN, HEROIC,
	HEAD, LIMB, LOIN, NECK,		MALAPERT
	RUMP, SKIN, VEIN, ANKLE,	bole	DOSE, STEM, CRYPT,
	BELLY, BLOOD, BOSOM,		TRUNK
	CHEST, KNEE, ELBOW, GLAND,	Boléro composer	RAVEL
	GROIN, JOINT, LYMPH,	bolide	METEOR, MISSILE
	NERVE, ORGAN, PENIS, SERUM,	Bolivia, capital of	LAPAZ,
	THIGH, TORSO, TRUNK,		SUCRE
	WAIST, WRIST, ANTRUM,	Bolivian city/town	ORURO,
	ARMPIT, ARTERY, BREAST,		TARUA, PUNATA, VIACHA,
	DORSUM, FINGER, GULLET,		TRINIDAD
	HAUNCH, THORAX,	Bolivian language	AYMARA,
	ABDOMEN, PLECTRUM,		QUECHUA
	SHOULDER, EPIDERMIS	Bolivian money	PESO, TOMINE,
body, *pert. to*	SOMAL,		CENTAVO, BOLIVIANO
	SOMATIC	Bolivian mountain	JARA,
body politic	WEAL, STATE,		PUPUYA, SAJAMA, SORATA,
	NATION		ILLAMPU, ILLIMANI
body segment	SOMITE,	Bolivian river	BENI, ABUNA,
	MEROSOME, METAMERE,		BAURES, MAMORE, GUAPORE
	SOMATOME	boll	POD, BULB, KNOB,
bodyguard	THANE, ESCORT,		ONION, SWELL
	MUSCLE, TORPEDO	boll weevil	PICUDO
Boeing	ENOLA	Bolshevik	RED, LENIN,
Boeotian city	THEBES		TROTSKY, ANARCHIST
Boer general	BOTHA, HERTZOG	bolster	AID, PROP, PILLOW

bolt BAR, PIN, LOCK, PAWL, SIFT, SLOT, ELOPE, FLASH, FASTEN, SCREEN, WINNOW
— and bolts NUTS
bolus CUD, CLOD, LUMP, MASS
bomb EGG, VONE, VTWO, ABOMB, HBOMB, SHELL, ASHCAN, PETARD, AEROSOL, GRENADE
bomb, kind of ATOM(IC), STINK, WATER, ASHCAN, FISSION, FUSION, NEUTRON, HYDROGEN
bombard SHELL, STRAFE
bombardment RAFALE, BARRAGE
bombast ELA, GAS, RANT, BOAST, TUMOR, BLUSTER, FUSTIAN
bombastic TUMID, TURGID, FLOWERY, OROTUND, POMPOUS
bomber see AIRPLANE
bombyx ERI(A), MOTH
bon — AMI, MOT, VIVANT, VOYAGE
bon mot QUIP, WITTICISM
bon vivant EPICURE
bona — FIDE
Bonaparte LOUIS, LUCIEN, JEROME, NAPOLEON
bond TIE, VOW, BAIL, DUTY, GLUE, YOKE, NEXUS, ESCROW, PLEDGE, VALENCE
Bond creator FLEMING
Bond movie DRNO, GOLDENEYE, MOONRAKER, OCTOPUSSY, GOLDFINGER, THUNDERBALL
bond(s)man ESNE, PEON, SERF, CHURL, HELOT, SLAVE, THRALL, VASSAL, VILLEIN
bond-stone PERPEND
bone OS(SO); see p. 501
bone, pert. to ULNAR, OSTEAL
bone scraper XYSTER
boner FLUB, GOOF, SLIP
bonnet CAP, HOOD, LEGHORN
— bono CUI, PRO
bonus TIP, MEED, AWARD, CUMSHAW, PREMIUM, PRESENT
bony HARD, LANK, LEAN, STIFF, OSSEOUS, SKELETAL
boo HISS, HOOT, JEER, RAZZ
boob ASS, DUNCE, NITWIT
booby LOSER, PRIZE, STUPID
boodle LOOT, SWAG, LOLLY

book MO, MS, LOG, MSS, VOL, HORA, OPUS, TOME, ALDUS, BIBLE, CODEX, DIARY, FOLIO, HORAE, LIBER, MANUAL, MISSAL, PRIMER, PSALTER
book, famous LOLITA, ULYSSES, PALEFIRE
book part LEAF, PAGE, COVER, INDEX, SPINE, TITLE, JACKET, BINDING, CHAPTER, FLYLEAF, CONTENTS, FOREWORD
book, science fiction EON, COSM, DAWN, DUNE, MARS, SLAN, FLESH, RADIX, VALIS, MUTANT, TRITON, SOLARIS, FLATLAND, FOUNDATION
bookbinding material SKIVER, VELLUM, BUCKRAM, MOROCCO
bookbinding method YAPP, GROLIER
bookish ERUDITE, PEDANTIC, STUDIOUS
bookkeeper ACTUARY, ACCOUNTANT
bookkeeping see ACCOUNTING
booklet BROCHURE, PAMPHLET
boom JIB, DRUM, ROAR, SPAR, SPRIT
boomerang KILEY, KYLIE, RECOIL, RESILE, BACKFIRE, RICOCHET
boon GAY, BENE, FAVOR, GRANT, JOVIAL
Boone, — PAT, DANIEL
boor OAF, NUP, CARL, CLOD, KERN, LOUT, MOME, CHURL, KNUFF, LOOBY, CARLOT, GROBIAN
boorish RUDE, GAWKY, VULGAR
boost ABET, KITE, LIFT, EXALT, HOIST, ELEVATE
boot KICK, SHOE, SOCK, KAMIK, BOOTEE, BOOTIE, CRAKOW, MUCLUC, MUKLUK, PEDULE, BOTTINE, COTHURN, CRAKOWE, GAMBADO, HESSIAN, RECRUIT, TOPBOOT, BALMORAL, HALFBOOT, MUCKLUCK, NAPOLEON; see SHOE
boot — CAMP
booth SUQ, LOGE, SOOK, SOUK, CRAME, STALL
bootleg ALKY, POTEEN, WHISKY, MOONSHINE

bootlick	FAWN, TOADY, FLATTER	Botswana, capital of	GABORONE
booty	FANG, GAIN, LOOT, PELF, PREY, SWAG	Botswana money	PULA, RAND
		bottle	JUG, KIT, PIG, VIAL, CRUET, CRUSE, FLASK, PHIAL, CARAFE, CARBOY, FLAGON, MAGNUM, CANTEEN, COSTREL, JEROBOAM, REHOBOAM
borax	TINCAL		
Bordeaux wine	MEDOC, CLARET, GRAVES, LUSSAC, MOULIS, MARGAUX, PAUILLAC		
border	HEM, MAT, TIP, ABUT, BRIM, LINE, RAND, BRINK, FLANK, FOREL, MARGE, SKIRT, VERGE, MARGIN, PURFLE, FLOROON	bottom	BED, BASE, LEES, SOLE, DREGS, FLOOR, NADIR, PLAYA, GROUND
		bough(s)	ARM, LIMB, TWIG, SHOOT, SPRIG, SHROUD, RAMAGE
bore	IRK, DRAG, TIDE, EAGRE, ENNUI, PRICK, PIERCE	boulevard	DRIVE, AVENUE, CONCOURSE
boredom	ENNUI, TEDIUM	boulevard cowboy	CABBIE, CAB DRIVER
boredom, express	SIGH, YAWN		
borer	AWL, BIT, AUGER, BEETLE, GIMLET, WIMBLE	— de Boulogne	BOIS
		bounce	FIRE, LEAP, SACK, EJECT, VERVE, RECOIL, SPRING
born	NE(E), NATE, NASCENT		
Borneo native	DYAK		
borough	BORG, BURG	bound	HOP, DART, LOPE, SCUD, SKIM, LIMIT, STEND, DELIMIT
borrow	COPY, KICK, ADOPT, STEAL		
borrowed stock	BAER	boundary	LINE, MERE, METE, AMBIT, LIMIT
Boru defeats Danes	MXIV		
bosh	END, ROT, JOKE, POOH, TRIVIA, NONSENSE, RUBBISH	bounder	CAD, CUB, RAKE, ROUE, SNOB
		bounds	AMBIT, COMPASS
Bosnia and Herzegovina, capital of	SARAJEVO	bounty	BOON, GIFT, MEED, BONUS, GRANT, PRIZE, LARGESS(E)
Bosnia and Herzegovina money	MARK		
boss	BAAS, CAPO, KNOB, KNOP, STUD, UMBO, MASTER	Bounty captain	BLIGH
		Bounty mate	CHRISTIAN
boss, political	LONG, RUEF, WEED, CRUMP, DALEY, HAGUE, HANNA, TWEED, CURLEY	bouquet	ODOR, POSY, AROMA, POSEY, NOSEGAY
		bouquet part	ROSE, DAISY
Boston	HUB, BACK BAY, BEANTOWN	bourne	GOAL, LIMIT, BROOK, STREAM
		bout	TURN, ESSAY, MATCH, ROUND, SETTO
Boston author	ALCOTT, EMERSON, HAWTHORNE, LONGFELLOW	boutique	SHOP(PE), BAZAAR
		boutonniere	POSY, BOUQUET, CORSAGE
Boston district	BACK BAY, BEACON HILL	Bovary	*see* MADAME BOVARY
Boston family	CABOT, ELIOT, FILENE, LOWELL	bovine	DULL, STOLID; *see* OX
		bow	ARC, NOD, ARCH, BEND, PROW, RODD, STEM, CURVE, DEFER, SALAM, STOOP, CURTSY, ONAGER, SALAAM, LONGBOW, QUARREL, ARBALEST, BALLISTA, CATAPULT, CROSSBOW, MANGONEL, TREBUCHET
Boston orchestra	BSO, POPS		
Boston team	BRUINS, RED SOX, CELTICS		
botanical terms	*see p. 688*		
botanist	RAY, BROWN, HALES, THOME, MENDEL, HELMONT, LINNAEUS, PRIESTLEY		
		bowdlerize	CENSOR, EXPURGATE
botch	MUX, FLUB, MESS, BUNGLE		
bother	AIL, FUSS, PEST, TODO, HARRY, TEASE, MEDDLE, MOLEST, PESTER	bowed	ARCATE, ARCUATE(D)
		bowel purge	CATHARSIS

bowels PITY, RUTH, COLON, ENTRAIL, INTESTINE

bower NOOK, ARBOR, KNAVE, ANCHOR, GROTTO

Bowery Boys member DELL, HALL, HALOP, GORCEY, JORDAN, PUNSLEY

bowfin AMIA, LAWYER, DOGFISH, MUDFISH

bowing term see VIOLIN

bowl PAN, ARENA, BASIN, DEPAS, JORUM, KITTY, MAZER, TANOA, ACERRA, BEAKER, CENSER, CHAWAN, THURIBLE

Bowl, college football SUN, ROSE, SUGAR, COTTON, FIESTA, ORANGE, TANGERINE

bowler HAT, DERBY, KEGLER

bowlers BOHN, DUKE, OZIO, ROTH, VOSS, WEBB, ZAHN, AULBY, DAVIS, WEBER, CARTER, ANTHONY, MCGRATH, STRAMPE, HARDWICK

bowling BOCCIE, TENPINS, DUCKPINS, NINEPINS, SKITTLES

bowling term JACK, LANE, ALLEY, BREAK, FRAME, GREEN, SPARE, SPLIT, GUTTER, STRIKE, KINGPIN

box BIN, ARCA, BINN, CASE, CIST, CUFF, ETUI, INRO, LOGE, SEAT, SLAP, SLUG, SPAR, SWAT, TILL, CADDY, CAPSA, CHEST, CRATE, FIGHT, PUNCH, CASKET, COFFER, CAISSON, TRUMMEL, CANISTER

box office GATE, TAKE, RECEIPTS

boxer DOG, PUG, MAULER, FIGHTER, SLUGGER, PUGILIST

boxers, famous see p. 708

boxing RING, SAVATE

boxing, pert. to FISTIC

boxing promoter (BOB)ARUM, (DAN)DUVA, (DON)KING, (TEX)RICHARD

boxing term KO, JAB, REF, TKO, BELL, BOLO, BOUT, CARD, HOOK, KAYO, MATCH, ROUND, SETTO, CESTUS

boy BUB, LAD, TAD, TOT, GROOM, YOUTH, SHAVER, see MAN, MALE

boy king TUT

Boy Scout founder BADENPOWELL

Boy Scout gathering CAMPOREE, JAMBOREE

Boy Scout group DEN, PACK, TROOP, PATROL

boycott SHUN, BLACKBALL, BLACKLIST, OSTRACIZE

boyfriend BEAU, LOVER, ESCORT, STEADY

boyhood YOUTH, PUBERTY

boyish PUERILE

Boys Town neighbor OMAHA

BPOE member ELK

Brabant princess ELSA

brace LEG, DUO, TWO, GIRD, PAIR, PROP, STAY, SHORE, TRUSS, CRUTCH, STIFFEN

brace and a half see THREE

bracelet BAND, BANGLE, ARMLET, WRISTLET

bracer TONIC, STIMULANT

bracket CLASS, SHELF, STRUT, CORBEL, CONSOLE

bract GLUME, PALEA, PALET, SPADIX, SPATHE

Brady Bunch name JAN, GREG, MIKE, BOBBY, CAROL, CINDY, PETER, MARCIA, FLORENCE

brag CROW, RAVE, YELP, BOAST, PREEN, STRUT, VAPOR, VAUNT, SWAGGER

braggart GASBAG, GASCON, BOASTER, BRAGGER, WINDBAG, BLOWHARD

Bragi wife IDUN

Brahma ATMAN

Brahman AYA, PUNDIT

Brahms symphony key DMAJOR, FMAJOR, CMINOR, EMINOR

braid CUE, PLAT, TRIM, BREDE, INKLE, LACET, ORRIS, PLAIT, QUEUE, TRESS

brain MIND, INTELLECT

brain, parts of FALX, GYRI, LOBE, PONS, ROOT, STEM, GYRUS, CORTEX, MEDULLA, CALLOSUM, CEREBRUM, CEREBELLUM

brain term PAN, PIA, ALBA, DURA, HARN, ITER, LURA, OBEX, PYLA, TELA, UTAC

brainchild IDEA, PLAN, FANCY

brake BUR(R), CURB, DRAG, BLOCK, BRUSH, DELAY

brake part DISK, DRUM, SHOE

Bram Stoker work DRACULA

branch ARM, BROG, FORK, LIMB, RAME, RAMUS, SPRIG, VIMEN, RAMIFY, RUNNER, STOLON

branched RAMAL, RAMATE, RAMOSE, RAMOUS, CLADOSE

branchia **GILL**
brand **CHOP, FLAW, KIND,**
MARK, SEAR, LABEL, STAIN,
STAMP, TAINT; STIGMA
brandish **WIELD, FLAUNT,**
FLOURISH
brandy **MARC, COGNAC;** *see*
LIQUOR
brash **BOLD, HASTY, SAUCY**
Brasilia designer **NEUMEYER**
brass **ALOY, NERVE,**
OFFICER(S)
brass hat **GENERAL, OFFICER**
brass tacks **FACTS, ESSENTIALS**
brassiere **UPLIFT, BANDEAU,**
FALSIES
brassiere inventor **JACOB**
brat **IMP, BANTLING**
brave **BOLD, DARE, DEFY,**
FACE, GAME, MANLY, STIFF,
DARING, HEROIC, INDIAN
Brave Bulls author **LEA**
Brave New World author **HUXLEY**
Brave New World drug **SOMA**
bravo **BIS, OLE, RAH, THUG**
brawl **ROW, SHINDY;** *see*
FIGHT
brawny **HARD, TOUGH,**
SINEWY
bray **MIX, CRUSH, GRIND,**
HEEHAW
brazen **PERT, NERVY, SASSY,**
CHEEKY
Brazil, capital of **BRASILIA**
Brazil discoverer **CABRAL**
Brazilian aborigine **ANDOA,**
CARIB
Brazilian city/town **RIO, BAHIA,**
BELEM, NATAL, MACEIO,
MANAUS, OLINDA, RECIFE,
SANTOS, GOIANIA,
ARACAJU, ITABUNA, VITORIA,
BRASILIA, CURITIBA,
SALVADOR, SAOPAULO
Brazilian Indian **MURA, PURU,**
TUPI, ACROA, ARARA,
CARIB, GUANA, ZAPARO,
TAPUYAN
Brazilian islands **MARACA,**
MARAJO, CAVIANA
Brazilian measure **MOIO,**
PASSO, TONEL, CUARTA,
TAREFA; *see* **PORTUGUESE**
MEASURE
Brazilian money **REIS, CONTO,**
CENTAVO, MILREIS,
MOIDORE, CRUZEIRO
Brazilian river **ICA, ACRE,**
DOCE, FEIO, ITAPI, AMAZON,

IGUACU, URUGUAY,
PARAGUAY, PARNAIBA
Brazilian state **ACRE, PARA,**
AMAPA, BAHIA, CEARA,
GOIAS, PIAUI, PARANA,
ALGOAS, PARAIBA,
RORAIMA, SERGIPE
Brazilian tree **APA, ANDA,**
ARACA, MURURE, WALLABA,
ANDAASSU
Brazilian weight **ONCA, LIBRA,**
ARROBA, OITAVA, ARRATEL,
QUILATE, QUINTAL
Brazos, city on the **WACO,**
FREEPORT
Brazos tributary **LITTLE,**
PALUXY, NAVASOTA
breach **GAP, RENT, RIFT, SLAP,**
CLEFT, CRACK, RUPTURE
bread **BUN, AZYM, CUSH,**
DIKA, LOAF, PAIN, PIKI,
PONE, ROLL, RUSK, BATCH,
KISRA, MANNA, SCONE,
BREWIS, MATZOS, PANADA,
SIPPET, MANCRET,
MATZOTH, POBBLES
bread part **RIND, CRUMB, CRUST**
bread spread **JAM, OLEO, JELLY,**
BUTTER, MARGARINE
bread type **RYE, AZYM, CORN,**
BLACK, CAROB, WHEAT,
WHITE, BANANA, RAISIN
bread plate **PATEN**
breadbasket **MIDWEST**
breadfruit **KAJ, TERAP,**
JA(C)KFRUIT
breadth **SPAN, GIRTH, WIDTH,**
EXTENT
break **BOON, HINT, RUIN,**
SNAP, CRACK, HIATUS,
RECESS, SIESTA, CAESURA,
RUPTURE
break in **STAVE, INITIATE**
break off **END, CEASE,**
DETACH, TERMINATE
break up **PART, DIVIDE,**
DIVORCE, SEPARATE, FALL
APART
breaker **BILLOW, COMBER,**
ROLLER
breakfast item **EGG(S), HAM,**
BACON, JUICE, TOAST,
DANISH, MUFFIN, RASHER
breakup **SPLIT, DISPERSION,**
SEPARATION
breakwater **COB, DAM, DIKE,**
MOLE, PIER, QUAY, JETTY
bream **TAI, CHAD, SCUP,**
PORGY, SHINER, SUNFISH

breast CHEST; *see* BODY
breastbone STERNUM
breastplate URIM, ARMOR,
EPHOD, THORAX
breastwork FORT, REDAN,
DICKEY, SCHERM, PARAPET,
RAMPART
breath ANDE, HUFF, LIFE,
PECH, PRANA, PNEUMA,
HALITUS, SNOACH
breathe LIVE, PANT, PUFF,
WHEEZE, RESPIRE
breather REST, BREAK, PAUSE
breathing GASP, RALE,
PNEUMA, STRIDOR
breathless AGOG, WINDED,
EXCITED, GASPING,
PANTING
breech BORE, BUTT, REAR,
BLOCK
breechcloth MALO, CLOUT,
GSTRING
breeches TREWS, BRITCHES,
JODHPURS, TROUSERS
breed ILK, KIND, RACE, REAR,
SIRE, BEGET, HATCH, RAISE,
PROGENY
breeding CULTURE, LINEAGE,
REARING
breeze AIR, AURA, FLAW,
GUST, PIRR, STIR, WIND,
ZEPHYR
Bremen river WESER
Breslau WROCLAW
Breslau river ODER, OSAR
breve MARK, NOTE, WRIT,
BRIEF, MINIM, ORDER
— breve ALLA
brevet PATENT, LICENSE
breviary ORDO, DIGEST,
PORTAS, COMPEND,
EPITOME, PORTASS
brew MIX, PLOT, STEW,
FOMENT, CONCOCT
brewer TEAPOT
brewer's equipment TUN, KILN,
MILL, OAST, COPPER, KETTLE
brewer's material CORN, HOPS,
MALT, YEAST, BARLEY
brewing CYLE, GAAL, GAIL,
GYLE, MALTING
brewing term CHIT, TRUB,
WORT, COUCH, GRIST
bribe SOP, BAIT, SWAG,
GRAFT, GRAVY, TEMPT,
BOODLE, PAYOLA, SUBORN,
DANEGELD
bric-a-brac CURIO, VERTU,
VIRTU, BIBELOT

brick NOG, DOBE, DOBY,
DOOK, MARL, ADOBE
brick carrier HOD
bricklayer MASON
bridal wreath SPIREA
bride KALLAH
Bridewell GAOL, JAIL, PRISON
bridge ARCH, JULA, LINK,
PONS, PONT, SPAN, MAGAS,
PONTOON
bridge part ARCH, DECK, PIER,
SHOE, CABLE, CROWN,
PYLON, TRUSS, HANGAR,
CAISSON, TRESSEL, TRESTLE,
SPANDREL
bridge (game) term BYE, LEG,
SET, BOOK, DUCK, ECHO,
JUMP, OPEN, PASS, SLAM,
VOID, SHIFT, TRICK,
DOUBLE, RUBBER, NOTRUMP;
see CARD TERM
bridge type ARCH, BEAM,
GIRDER, BASCULE,
PONTOON, TRESTLE
bridge, famous *see p. 613*
Bridges BEAU, JEFF, LLOYD
bridle BIT, CURB, BRANK,
CAPER, STRUT, BRANKS,
PILLORY, SNAFFLE
brief CURT, PITHY, TERSE,
CONCISE, LACONIC,
SUMMARY
brigand BANDIT, LATRON
Brigham Young U. site PROVO
bright APT, GAY, GLEG, KEEN,
NAIF, ANIME, LUCID, NITID,
SHARP, SHINING
brightness NITOR, SHEEN,
ACUMEN
Bright's disease NEPHRITIS
brilliance ECLAT, LUSTER,
GLITTER, ORIENCY
brilliant GEM, SIGNAL,
DIAMOND, RADIANT
brim POKE, SKIRT; *see* EDGE
— and brimstone FIRE
brine SEA, MAIN, SALT,
BRACK, OCEAN, TEARS,
PICKLE
bring FETCH, INCUR,
COMMAND, CONDUCT
bring forth EAN, BEAR, YEAN,
BEGET, HATCH
bring out EDUCE, ELICIT,
LAUNCH, REVEAL, RELEASE
brink END, EVE, DITCH,
MARGE, MARGIN
briny SALTY, SALINE
brisk LIVE, PERK, SPRY, YARE,

ALERT, FLEET, KEDGE,
PERKY, RAPID, SHARP, NIMBLE,
CHEERY, ALLEGRO
bristle   RIB, SETA, BRUSH,
PREEN, PRIDE, SPINE, STRUT,
CHAETA, PALPUS, RUFFLE
bristly   HISPID, SETOSE
Britain   UK, ALBION,
BRITANNIA
Britain, capital of   LONDON
— B'rith   BNAI
British   *see* ENGLISH
British Columbia   *see also p. 614*
British Columbia city/town   USK,
HOPE, ATLIN, DUNCAN,
KASLO, QUICK, WELLS, LIKELY,
NAKUSP, NELSON, SURREY,
TELKWA, YOUBOU, BURNABY,
ENDERBY, NANAIMO,
QUESNEL, LILLOOET,
RICHMOND, VICTORIA,
VANCOUVER
British Columbia lake   ATLIN,
ARROW, BABINE, CHILKO,
STUART, QUESNEL, FRANCOIS,
HARRISON, KOOTENAY,
OKANAGAN, TETACHUCK,
WILLISTON
British Columbia mountain(s)
COAST, ROCKY, COPPER,
ROBSON, SKEENA, CARIBOO,
CASSIAR, OMINECA, PURCELL,
SELKIRK, HAZELTON,
MONASHEE, WADDINGTON
British Columbia river   DEAN,
NASS, ISKUT, LIARD, PEACE,
FINLAY, FRASER, SKEENA,
PARSNIP, STIKINE,
COLUMBIA, CHILCOTIN,
MACKENZIE, LILLOOET,
THOMPSON
Briton(s)   BRIT, CELT, JUTE,
PICT, ANGLE, ICENI
Brittany   ARMORICA
Britten opera   GLORIANA,
BILLYBUDD, PETERGRIMES,
ALBERTHERRING
brittle   FROW, WEAK, CRISP,
FRAIL, FROWY, FICKLE
broach   AIR, AWL, VENT,
BEGIN, RIMER, VOICE,
LAUNCH, REAMER, PUBLISH
broad   WIDE, GENERAL,
LIBERAL, SWEEPING
broadcast   AIR, SHOW, SCREEN,
TELEVISE, TRANSIT,
PUBLICIZE
Broadway sign   SRO
brogan   BOOT, SHOE, STOGY

brogue   *see* ACCENT
broil   ROW, GRILL, MELEE,
SCRAP, FRACAS, SCORCH
broker   AGENT, FACTOR,
JOBBER, SCHATCHEN
bromide   SAW
bronco   MUSTANG; *see* HORSE
Brontë   ANNE, EMILY,
CHARLOTTE
Brontë character   EYRE, JANE,
CATHY, EDGAR
Brontë pseudonym   BELL, ELLIS,
CURRER
Bronx cheer   RAZZ, RASPBERRY
bronze   AES
brooch   PIN, OUCH, CAMEO,
CLASP, FIBULA, PECTORAL
brood   FRY, NID, NYE, SIT,
BEVY, MOPE, NEST, NIDE,
COVEY, HATCH, LITTER
brook   RUN, BEAR, BECK, RILL,
ABIDE, CREEK, STAND,
RILLET, RUNNEL
broom   COW, MOP, SWAB,
BESOM, HIRSE, WHISK
broth   BROO, SOUP,
BOUILLON, CONSOMME
brothel   BAGNIO, BORDEL
brother   FRA, PAL, SIB, MONK,
BILLY, CADET, FRIAR,
FELLOW, FRATER, SIBLING
brotherhood   CLAN, SODALITY
brow   TOP, BREE, EDGE, SNAP,
CREST, RIDGE
browbeat   BULLY, HECTOR
brown   TAN, COOK, SEAR,
TOAST, SUNTAN, OATMEAL
browned   TANNED, RISSOLE
brownie —   POINTS
Browning home   ASOLO
browse   BRUT, CROP, FEED,
GRAZE, NIBBLE, PASTURE
bruise   BRAY, DENT, HURT,
MAUL, TUND, CRUSH, ICTUS,
SHINER, CONTUSE, SQUEEZE
bruised   HURT, LIVID, HUMBLE
bruit   TELL, NOISE, RUMOR,
HEARSAY
Brunei, capital of   BANDAR(SERI
BEGAWAN)
Brunei city/town   LABU, SERIA,
MUARA, BANGAR, BELAIT
Brunei money   DOLLAR
Brunhild relation   ATU, ERDA,
ASLAUG, SIGURD
brush   TIP, FRAY, CLEAN,
COPSE, FIGHT, FITCH,
SCOPA(E)
brusque   CURT, RUDE, BLUFF,

BLUNT, GRUFF, TERSE, ABRUPT

brutal CRUEL, FERAL, CARNAL, COARSE, SAVAGE, BESTIAL

et tu —? BRUTE

Brythonic CORNISH

bubble AIR, BEAD, BLEB, BOIL, BOLL, GLOB, BLAIN, CHEAT, SEETHE

bubbly, make AERATE

buccaneer PIRATE, VIKING, CORSAIR, PICAROON

buck TOP, NOB, DUDE, STAG, TOFF, DANDY, SWELL, DOLLAR, RESIST

bucket SOE, TUB, BOWK, PAIL, STOP, SCOOP, SKEEL

Buckeye State OH, OHIO

buckle BLEND, TACH, WARP, CLASP, TACHE

buckler TARGE, SHIELD

bucolic IDYL, RURAL, RUSTIC, PASTORAL

bud GEM, IMP, PAL, CION, GERM, KNOP, BEGIN, GEMMA, GRAFT, SPROUT, BEGINNING

Buddha FO, JATAKA, GAUTAMA

Buddha's wife AHALYA

Buddhist language PALI

Buddhist monk BO, LAMA, BONZE, MAHATMA

Buddhist mountain EMEI(SHAN), OMEI(SHAN)

Buddhist sacred tree PIPAL, SACREDFIG

Buddhist site DEERPARK

Buddhist term DOSA, KARMA, TORAN, DUKKHA, NARAKA, NIRVANA, SAMUDAYA

buddy PAL, CHUM, PARTNER

budget BAG, PACK, PLAN, BUNCH, PACKET

buff FAN, SKIN, FIEND, POLISH

buff, in the NUDE, NAKED

buffalo ARNA, ARNI, ARNEE, BISON; see OX

Buffalo Bill CODY

buffet BOX, SLAP, TOSS, SMITE

buffoon FOOL, JAPE, ZANY, ANTIC, CLOWN, DROLL, MIMER, ANDREW, JESTER

bug MITE, ANNOY, NEEDLE; see INSECT

bugaboo GOGA, GOGO, JUMBO, MUMBO

bugbear BOGY, OGRE, GOBLIN

bugle call MESS, POST, TAPS, TATO(O), COLORS, RECALL, TATTOO, RETREAT, TANTARA, ASSEMBLY REVEILLE

build COOT, FORM, REAR, ERECT, RAISE

building ADOBE, TAPIA, INSULA, EDIFICE

building material PISÉ, WOOD, ADOBE, BRICK, STEEL, STONE, MORTAR, STUCCO, CONCRETE

building part BAY, ELL, ROOF, WING, ANNEX, ATTIC, QUOIN, CELLAR

bulb BUD, CORM, KNOB, LAMP, GLOBE, TUBER

Bulba, — TARAS

Bulgaria, ancient capital OHRID, PRESLAV

Bulgaria, capital of SOFIA

Bulgarian city/town RUSE, VARNA, PLEVEN, PLOVDIV

Bulgarian measure KRINA, LEKHA

Bulgarian money LEV, LEW, DINAR, STOTINKA

Bulgarian mountain MUSALA

Bulgarian river VIT, MESTA, TIMOK, DANUBE, STRUMA, MARITSA

Bulgarian ruler DUS(H)AN, SIMEON, MARGARITA

Bulgarian weight OKA, ORE, TOVAR

bulge BAG, BUG, JUT, HUMP, KNOB, BLOAT, SWELL

bulging FULL, TUMID, CONVEX, GIBBOUS

bulk BODY, BOUK, MASS, GROSS, SHAPE, VOLUME

bull OX, COP, APIS, HAPI, SLIP, BOBBY, ERROR, PEELER, BLUNDER, SOLECISM

bull writer POPE

bulldoze COW, DIG, RAM, BULLY, FORCE, SCOOP, BROWBEAT

bullet BALL, SHOT, SLUG, DUMDUM, PELLET, TRACER

bullet sound PHIT, PHUD, PHUT, PING

bullfight CORRIDA

bullfight cry OLE

bullfight term CAPA, COLETA, MULETA, VERONICA

bullfighter TORERO, MATADOR, PICADOR, TOREADOR

bullion BAR, MASS, INGOT, BILLOT
bull-like TAURINE
bullring ARENA
bull's-eye DAISY, CENTER, TARGET
bully COW, BRAVO, SCARE, VAPOR, HECTOR, SHANNY
bulwark BAIL, FORT, SCONCE, BASTION, CITADEL, PARAPET, RAMPART
bum HOBO, IDLER, TRAMP
bump JOLT, OUST, COLLIDE
bump into HIT, MEET, RUN INTO
bump off DO IN, KILL, WASTE, MURDER
bumper BEADLE, BUNGLE, BLUNDER
bumpkin CLOD, HICK, LOUT, RUBE, YOKEL
bumpy ROUGH, UNEVEN
bun JAG, WIG, CAKE, ROLL, STEM, TAIL, STALK
bunch LOT, BALE, TUFT, WISP, CROWD, FAGOT, SHEAF
bund DAM, DIKE, QUAY, LEAGUE
bundle BALE, BOLT, HANK, PACK, FADGE, FAGOT, SHEAF, PACKET
bung CORK, PLUG, SHIVE, STOPPER
bungle ERR, GOOF, BOTCH
bunk COT, BERTH, HOKUM, LODGE, SLEEP
bunker BIN, ABRI, CRIB, HAZARD, SANDHOLE
bunting FLAGS, TOWHEE, COWBIRD, ORTOLAN
Bunyan ox BABE
buoy CAN, DAN, NUN, NUT, BELL, SPAR, FLOAT, LIGAN, RAISE
buoyancy FLO(A)TAGE
buoyant GAY, LIGHT, LILTING
burbot see COD
burden TAX, BIRN, CARE, CARK, LADE, LOAD, ONUS, CARGO, CUMBER, FARDEL
burdened LADEN, LOADED, FRAUGHT
bureau DESK, CHEST, AGENCY, OFFICE, DRESSER
bureaucracy RED TAPE, CITY HALL
bureaucrat OFFICIAL, FUNCTIONARY
bureaucratese CANT, JARGON, GOBBLEDYGOOK

burgeon BUD, SHOOT, SPROUT
burglar requirement STEALTH
burglar's tool BAR, PICK, JIMMY
Burgundy wine MACON, CHABLIS, POUILLY, MACONNAIS, MEURSAULT, CHAMBERTIN, MONTRACHET
burial place AHU, LOW, GRAVE, BARROW, KURGAN, TUMULUS, CEMETERY, NECROPOLIS
buried HIDDEN, SUNKEN, IMBEDDED
burke MURDER, SUFFOCATE
Burkina Faso, capital of OUAGADOUGOU
Burkina Faso money FRANC
burl KNOT, LUMP, PIMPLE
burlesque FARCE, REVUE, COMEDY, OVERDO, PARODY
burly BULKY, HUSKY, OBESE, STOUT
Burma see MYANMAR
burn ASH, CHAR, RILL, SERE, BROOK, CENSE, SCALD, SINGE, SCORCH, CONSUME, CREMATE
burn preventer SPF, SUNBLOCK
burner BUDE, ETNA, ARGAND, BUNSEN
burning (A)FIRE, ARSON, CALID, EAGER, IRATE, ARDENT
burning bush WAHOO
burnisher see POLISHER
Burns and Allen Show names HAL, HARRY, GEORGE, GRACIE, MORTON, BLANCHE, VONZELL
burnt CHARRED, SCORCHED
burp BELCH, ERUCTATE
burp — GUN
burr NUT, POD, HALO, RING, BRIAR, WHIRR, CIRCLE, CORONA
burrow DIG, HOLE, MINE, MOIL, ROOT, TUBE, NUZZLE, TUNNEL
burrowing animal MOLE, GOPHER, MARMOT, SURICAT(E)
bursa SAC
burst POP, REND, ERUPT, REAVE, SPLIT, VOLLEY, EXPLODE
Burundi, capital of BUJUMBURA
Burundi city/town NGOZI, BURURI, GITEGA

Burundi money	FRANC, CENTIME
Burundi native	HUTU, BANTU, PYGMY, TUTSI, WATUSI
bury	CACHE, EARTH, INTER, INURN, INHUME
bus	COACH, JITNEY, AUTOCAR, OMNIBUS, CHARABANC
bus customer	FARE, RIDER
bus part	REAR
Bus Stop author	INGE
Bus Stop character	ELMA, VERA, CHERIE, GRACE, VIRGIL, BEAUREGARD
Bus Stop star	LANGE, MONROE
bush	TOD, BOSH, CLUMP, SHRUB, BOSCAGE
bush leagues	MINORS
bushing	PINTLE
bush-league	AMATEUR(ISH)
bushy	DUMOSE, DUMOUS
business	FEAT, FIRM, GEAR, LINE, CHORE, CRAFT, STINT, TRADE, AFFAIR, ERRAND
buss	DECK, KISS, DRESS, SMACK
bust	BOSOM, DEMOTE
bustard	KORI
bustard genus	OTIS
bustle	ADO, FISK, FUSS, TODO, HYPER, DITHER, FLURRY, POTHER
bustling	BUSY, ASTIR, ACTIVE
busy	TAKEN, ACTIVE, HECTIC, ON THE GO, EVENTFUL, OCCUPIED
busy, be	HUM
busybody	SNOOP, MEDDLER, QUIDNUNC
but	BAR, YET, MERE, ONLY, SAVE, STILL
butcher	KILL, CUTUP, SLAUGHTER
butcher's cut	LOIN, FILET, FLANK
butcher's tool	GAFF, SKEWER, CLEAVER, GAMBREL
butchery	CARNAGE, SHAMBLES, SLAUGHTER
butler	SERVANT, SPENCER, STEWARD
butt	RAM, TUP, BUNT, CASK, GOAD, PUSH, STUB, STUMP
butter	GHI, GHEE, FULWA, MAHUA, BEURRE, PHULWA
— and butter	BREAD
Butterfield 8 author	OHARA
butterfingers	OAF

butterfish	POMFRET
butterfly	IO, KIHO, ARGUS, COMMA, ELFIN, SATYR, WHITE, ZEBRA, APOLLO, COPPER, DANAID, URSULA, VIOLET, ADMIRAL, DANAINE, EMPEROR, JUNONIA, MONARCH, VANESSA, VICEROY, HESPERID, WANDERER; see p. 677
butterfly genus	COLIAS, MORPHO, PIERIS, THECLA
buttery	LARDER, PANTRY, SPENCE
buttocks	BUM, ARSE, BUTT, PRAT, RUMP, SEAT, BEHIND, DERRIERE
button	BUD, BOSS, HOOK, KNOB, KNOP, STUD, BADGE, OLIVE, FASTEN
button part	SHANK
buttonhole	GRAB, LOOP, ACCOST, CORNER, EYELET, WAYLAY
buttress	PIER, PROP, STAY, OUTCAST
buxom	BUILT, BUSTY, SONSY, ROBUST, SHAPELY, STACKED
buyer	CHAP, AGENT, EMPTOR, VENDEE
buying urge	EMACITY
Buzi relative	EZEKIEL
buzz	HUM, WHIR(R), PHONE NUMBER; see SOUND
buzz off	LEAVE, SCRAM, DEPART
buzzard	PERN, TESA, GLEDE; see HAWK
buzzer	BEE, BELL, ALARM, HOWLER, SIGNAL
buzzword	CATCHPHRASE
by	AGO, PER, VIA, NEAR, PAST, WITH, ASIDE, CLOSE, BESIDE
by way of	PER, VIA, THRU
bygone	PAST, YORE, OLDEN, FORMER
Byron poem	LARA, BEPPO, CORSAIR, DONJUAN, MANFRED
bystander	see SPECTATOR
byword	MOTO, PROVERB
Byzantine	COMPLEX, DEVIOUS, INTRICATE
Byzantine capital	NICAEA, ISTANBUL, BYZANTIUM, CONSTANTINOPLE
Byzantine coin	BESANT, BEZANT, BYZANT

C

C	**GAMMA, CHARLIE, HUNDRED**
C mark	**CEDILLA**
Caaba city	**MECCA**
caama	**ASSE**
cab	**HACK, TAXI, ARABA, HANSOM**
cabal	**BLOC, PLOT, JUNTO, CLIQUE, INTRIGUE**
cabbage	**COS, CHOU, COLE, KAIL, KALE, KEAL, COLZA, KRAUT, SAVOY**
cabin	**HUT, SHED, BERTH, CABAN, COACH, HOVEL, CABANA, SALOON, SHANTY**
cabin boy	**GRUMMET**
cabinet	**BUHL, BAHUT, BUREAU, CLOSET, ALMIRAH, ETAGERE, WHATNOT, MINISTRY**
cabinet, African-Americans	**ESPY, RICE, BROWN, HARRIS, HERMAN, PIERCE, POWELL, WEAVER**
cabinet, first woman	**PERKINS**
cabinet post	**DOE, DOT, HEW, HHS, HUD, ARMY, NAVY, LABOR, STATE, ENERGY, DEFENSE, JUSTICE, COMMERCE, INTERIOR, TREASURY**
cabinet, woman member	**DOLE, RENO, HILLS, HOBBY, KREPS, FOLSOM, HARRIS, HERMAN, MARTIN, OLEARY, HECKLER, PERKINS, SHALALA, ALBRIGHT**
cable	**GUY, CORD, WIRE, COAXIAL, PAINTER**
cable channel	**AMC, APL, BET, CNN, DSC, HBO, MTV, TBS, TLC, TWC, USA, CNBC, ESPN, CSPAN;** see **NETWORK**
— and caboodle	**KIT**
caboose	**CAB, CAR, HACK, GALLEY**
Caca brother	**CACUS**
cacao	**BROMA, COCKER**
cache	**BURY, HIDE, STOW, STORE, TROVE, CONCEAL**
cachet	**SEAL, STAMP, WAFER**
cacique	**CHIEF, PRINCE, SACHEM**
cactus	**TUNA, AGAVE, NOPAL, CARDON, CEREUS, CHOLLA,**

	MESCAL, MEZCAL, PEYOTE, CARDONA, OPUNTIA, SAGUARO, OCOTILLO
cactus fruit	**TUNA, SABRA, COCHAL**
Cacus sister	**CACA**
cad	**HEEL, KNAVE, BOUNDER**
cadaver	**BODY, STIFF, COR(P)SE, CARCASS**
Caddoan Indian	**REE, PAWNEE**
caddy	**BOX, CAN, CHEST, CARRIER**
cadence	**LILT, PACE, TONE, CLOSE, METER, RHYTHM**
cadet	**SON, PLEB(E), JUNIOR**
cadge	**BEG, MOOCH, SPONGE**
Cadiz	**GADES**
Cadmus city	**THEBES**
Cadmus relative	**INO, AGENOR, EUROPA, SEMELE, HARMONIA**
caduceus	**WAND, STAFF, SCEPTER**
Caen river	**ORNE**
Caesar	**NERO, OTHO, GAIUS, GALBA, TITUS, JULIUS, TYRANT, EMPEROR, AUGUSTUS, AUTOCRAT, CLAUDIUS, DOMITIAN, TIBERIUS, VESPASIAN, VITELLIUS**
Caesar foe	**CASCA, BRUTUS, POMPEI, CASSIUS**
Caesar last words	**ET TU, BRUTE**
Caesar mistress	**EUNOE, CLEO(PATRA)**
Caesar relative	**ATIA, AURELIA**
Caesar, river crossed by	**RUBICON**
Caesar saying	**VENI, VIDI, VICI**
caesura	**REST, BREAK, PAUSE**
cafe	**DINER, BISTRO, BARROOM, CABARET, CANTEEN**
café au —	**LAIT**
cafeteria	**DINER, CANTEEN, AUTOMAT**
caffeine	**THEIN, THEINA, THEINE**
caffeine source	**TEA, COLA, COCOA, COFFEE**
cage	**GIG, MEW, HUTCH**
cagey	**SLY, SHIFTY, CUNNING**
cahoots	**LEAGUE, PARTNERS**
caiman	**JACARE;** see **CROCODILE**
Cain's relative	**EVE, ABEL, ADAM, SETH, ENOCH, JUBAL**
Cain's land	**NOD**

Cain's victim **ABEL**
Caine captain **QUEEG**
Caine Mutiny author **WOUK**
Cairo shopping district **MOUSSKY**
caisson disease **BENDS**
caitiff **BASE, MEAN, VILE**
cajole **COAX, PALP, CHEAT,**
DECOY, TEASE, BUTTER,
ENTICE, BEGUILE, FLATTER,
WHEEDLE
cake **WIG, FARL, FLOE, PONE,**
TART, WIGG, ANGEL, BATTY,
POORI, SCONE, TORTE, WAFER,
HARDEN, JUMBAL, JUMBLE,
SIMNEL, SPONGE, STOLLEN
cake type **BUNDT, FRUIT,**
POUND, LAYER, WHITE,
SPONGE
Calais English counterpart **DOVER**
calamitous **SAD, DIRE, EVIL,**
HAPLESS
calamity **WOE, BLOW, WRACK,**
MISERY, DISASTER
calcium compound **LIME, TUFA,**
HEPAR, GYPSUM, APATITE,
CALCITE, CALICHE, PLASTER
calculate **AIM, RATE, FRAME,**
TALLY, RECKON, COMPUTE
calculator **LOG, TABLE, ABAC,**
ABACUS
calculus **TARTAR,**
(GALL)STONE
Calcutta measure **KUNK, RAIK**
Calcutta weight **DHAN, PANK**
caldron **POT, BOILER, KETTLE**
Caleb companion **JOSHUA**
Caleb relative **ACHSAH**
Caledonia **SCOTLAND**
calendar **LOG, ORDO, DIARY,**
DOCKET, ALMANAC,
JOURNAL; *see p. 717*
calendar abbreviation **APR,**
AUG, DEC, FEB, FRI, MAR,
MON, JAN, JUN, JUL, NOV,
OCT, SAT, SEP, SUN, THU,
TUE, WED
calendar type **JULIAN,**
GREGORIAN
calf **BOB, DOGY, DOGIE,**
FATLING
calf, *pert. to* **SURAL**
calf meat **VEAL**
Caliban master **PROSPERO**
Caliban mother **SYCORAX**
caliber **BORE, GAUGE,**
METTLE, DIAMETER
calico **SALLO(O)**
California *see also p. 615*
California bay **MORRO,**

CARMEL, BODEGA, MISSION,
HALFMOON
California city/town **ANA,**
DALY, NAPA, FRESNO,
ANAHEIM, BELMONT,
OAKLAND, ONTARIO,
PASADENA
California college **USC, UCLA,**
DAVIS, MILLS, IRVINE,
HAYWARD, POMONA
California county **INYO, KERN,**
LAKE, MONO, NAPA, YOLO,
YUBA, BUTTE, GLENN, KINGS,
MARIN, MODOC, ALPINE,
COLUSA, FRESNO, MADERA,
NEVADA, ORANGE, PLUMAS,
SHASTA, SIERRA, SOLANO,
TULARE, VENTURA
California Indian **HUPA, MONO,**
POMO, YANA, CAHTO,
KARUK, MAIDU, MIWOK,
WIYOK, YUROK, MOHAVE,
OHLONE, PAIUTE, SHASTA,
TOLOWA, TONGVA,
WASHOE, WINTUN, YOKUTS,
CHUMASH, MISSION,
SALINAN, CAHUILLA,
SHOSHONE
California military base **EDWARDS,**
MATHER, TRAVIS, MOFFETT,
PRESIDIO, PENDLETON
California park **REDWOOD**
California river **EEL, MAD, PIT,**
LOST, NOYO, YUBA,
SALMON, CUYAMA, SALINAS,
COLORADO
California valley **NAPA, SIMI,**
SQUAW, HIDDEN
Caligula reign year (AD37–41) **XL,**
XLI
caliph **ALI, IMAM, OMAR,**
OTHMAN
calk **NAP, COPY, STOP,**
CLOSE, CHINESE
call **BAN, BID, DUB, CITE,**
NAME, SOOK, TERM, YELL,
CLEPE, PHONE, ROUSE, TITLE,
VISIT, ELICIT, INVITE,
MUSTER, SUMMON; *see* **CRY**
— and call **BECK**
call a bluff **DARE, FACE**
call forth **EVOKE, ELICIT,**
KINDLE
call into question **IMPUGN**
Call of the Wild dog **BUCK,**
DAVE, CURLY, DOLLY,
SPITZ, SOLLEKS
call to cows **SOOK**
call to horse **HUPP**

call to mind EVOKE, RECALL
call to prayer ADAN, AZAN
call to witness OBTEST
call up BUZZ, RING, ENLIST
calla ARUM, LILY
called NAMED, STYLED, DUBBED, YCLEPT
caller GUEST, SUITOR, VISITOR
calligrapher PENMAN, SCRIBE
calling JOB, LINE, TRADE, METIER, (A)VOCATION
calling, alternative to RAISING, CHECKING
Calliope relative ERATO
Callisto relative ARCAS
callous HARD, HORNY, TOUGH
callus CORN, CLAVUS
calm LOWN, LULL, ABATE, ALLAY, STILL, STOIC, PLACID, SERENE, PLACATE
calorie THERM(E)
Calpurnia husband CAESAR
calumet (PEACE)PIPE
calumniate BELIE, DEFAME, MALIGN, REVILE, VILIFY
calumny SLUR, ABUSE, LIBEL, SLANDER
Calvary ARAM, GOLGOTHA
Calvinist BEREAN
calyx CUP, HUSK, SEPAL
cam COG, LOBE, CATCH, WIPER, TAPPET, TRIPPET
cambio coin(s) LIRA, LIRE
Cambodia, capital of PHNOMPENH
Cambodian city/town KULEN, SUONG, TAKEV, KAMPOT, PURSAT
Cambodian language KHMER
Cambodian money RIEL
Cambodian neighbor LAOS, VIETNAM, THAILAND
Cambria WALES
Cambridge college MIT, HARVARD
Cambridge exam TRIPOS
Cambridge student SIZAR, SIZER, CANTAB, OPTIME, WRANGLER
camel OONT, DELOUL, MEHARI, BACTRIAN
camel driver SARWAN
camel genus CAMELUS
camel hair ABA
Camelot see ARTHURIAN
camera BOX, SLR, PRESS, REFLEX, BROWNIE
camera equipment DOLLY, FLASH, FILTER, TRIPOD

camera part LENS, STOP, FINDER, SHUTTER, DIAPHRAGM
Cameroon, capital of YAOUNDE
Cameroon city/town WUM, EDEA, TIKO, KUMBA, DOUALA, GAROUA
Cameroon language FANG, BANTU, FULANI, SUDANIC
Cameroon money FRANC
Cameroon neighbor CAR, CHAD, CONGO, GABON, NIGERIA
Cameroon river NYONG, YAOUNDE
Camille actress GARBO
Camille author DUMAS
Camille character ARMAND
Camorra MAFIA
camp BOMA, POST, ETAPE, LAGER, TABOR, LAAGER, ZAREBA, BIVOUAC
camp, pert. to CASTRAL
campaign DRIVE, JIHAD, STUMP, CRUSADE, BARNSTORM, ELECTIONEER
camphor ALANT, APIOL, BORNEOL, MENTHOL
campus QUAD, YARD, FIELD
Camus work PLAGUE, STRANGER
can JUG, MAY, TIN, JAIL, PRESERVE
can, imperfect FLIPPER, SWELLER, SPRINGER
can opener (PULL) TAB
Canaan relative HAM, CUSH, HETH, NOAH, SIDON
Canada see also p. 614
Canada, capital of OTTAWA
Canada goose OUTARDE
Canada, lower QUEBEC
Canadian CANUCK
Canadian actors, famous FOX, FORD, DURBIN, MASSEY, PIDGEON, SHATNER, PICKFORD, SUTHERLAND
Canadian airport DORVAL, GANDER, MIRABEL, PEARSON, GATINEAU
Canadian city/town HULL, BANFF, GUELPH, REGINA, BRANDON, CALGARY, HALIFAX, NANAIMO, SUDBURY, TORONTO, MONTREAL
Canadian Indian CREE, DENE, TAKU, HAIDA, SIOUX, TINNE, MICMAC, SARCEE

Canadian island FOGO, BANKS, DEVON, BAFFIN, MANSEL, VICTORIA

Canadian lake ERIE, HURON, LOUISE, NIPIGON, WINNIPEG

Canadian money CENT, DIME, DOLLAR, LOONIE, TWONIE, QUARTER

Canadian mountain LOGAN, ROBSON, CARIBOO, SELKIRK

Canadian national park YOHO, BANFF, FUNDY, JASPER, KLUANE, GLACIER, NAHANNI, KOOTENAY

Canadian rebel RIEL

Canadian river LIARD, PEACE, SLAVE, YUKON, ALBANY, FRASER, NELSON, OTTAWA, SEVERN, DUBAWNT, SAGUENAY, MACKENZIE, ATHABASKA

canal RIO, SOO, DUCT, ERIE, KIEL, SUEZ, ZANJA, MEATUS, PANAMA, STRAIT, CHANNEL, CONDUIT, WELLAND

canape SOFA, COUCH, DIVAN, APPETIZER

canary ERIFF

Canary island LOBOS, GOMERA, HIERRO, GRACIOSA, LAPALMA, TENERIFE

canasta play MELD, FREEZE

cancel BLOT, DELE, VOID, ANNUL, ERASE, DELETE, EFFACE, REPEAL, REVOKE, POSTMARK

cancer CRAB, TUMOR, GROWTH, SARCOMA

candid BLUNT, FRANK, NAIVE, HONEST, ARTLESS

candidate NOMINEE, ASPIRANT

candidate list SLATE, BALLOT, TICKET

candle DIP, WAX, TEST, TAPER, BOUGIE, CIERGE

candle part WAX, WICK, SNAST, TALLOW

candle type VOTARY, VOTIVE, PASCHAL

candlenut tree AMA, KUKUI, BANKUL

candlestick JESSE, CRUSIE, GRADIN, LAMPAD, LUSTRE, SCONCE, PRICKET, GIRANDOLE

candy KISS, DULCE, LOLLY, SWEET, TAFFY, BONBON, CIMBAL, COCKLE, COMFIT, DRAGEE, CONFECT, NOUGAT, CARAMEL, FONDANT, PRALINE, YINGLING, SWEETMEAT

cane FLAY, FLOG, WHIP, STEM, STICK, PUNISH, RATTAN, MALACCA

— canem CAVE

canine CUR, PUG, PUP, FANG, FICE, CUSPID; see DOG

Canio's wife NEDDA

canister CASE, CADDY, CALIN

canker ROT, RUST, SORE, DECAY, TAINT, FUNGUS, MILDEW

cannabis HEMP; see DRUG

Cannery Row author STEINBECK

cannon KRAG, ASPIC, DRAKE, MOYEN, SAKER, BERTHA, CULVER, FALCON, FOWLER, LICORN, MINNIE, MORTAR, POMPOM, TREPAN, BASTARD, BAZOOKA, BOMBARD, HACKBUT, LANTACA, LOMBARD, MOYENNE, ROBINET, TEREBRA, UNICORN, CULVERIN, HOWITZER

cannon part ANSE, BORE, CHASE, RIMBASE, TAMPION, CASCABEL, LINSTOCK, TRUNNION

cannonade BLITZ, SALVO, BARRAGE

cannonball RACE

canny WARY, SHREWD

canoe KIAK, KAYAK, DUGOUT, PITPAN; see VESSEL

canon LAW, HYMN, LAUD, RULE, SONG, AXIOM, NODUS

canonical hours NONE, SEXT, LAUDS, PRIME, TIERCE, COMPLIN, ORTHRON, ORTHROS, VESPERS

canonicals see VESTMENTS

canopied SHADED

canopy SKY, COPE, DAIS, VAULT, TESTER, AWNING

cant see SLANG, TILT

cantankerous CROSS, CRANKY, GRUMPY, ORNERY

cantankerous person GROUCH, CURMUDGEON

cantata ORATORIO; see SONG

canteen PX, FLASK, FLACON

canter RUN, PACE, RACK, WHINER

Canterbury archbishop see ARCHBISHOP

canticle ODE, HYMN, LAUD, SONG
canto AIR, FIT, PACE, FYTTE, PASSUS
canton STATE, QUARTER, DISTRICT
canvas DUCK, SAIL, TARP, TENT, TUKE, SCRIM, TEWKE, WIGAN
canvass POLL, SIFT, STUDY, SURVEY
canyon GAP, VALE, GULCH, ARROYO, CANADA
canyon mouth ABRA
CaO LIME
cap FEZ, LID, TAJ, TAM, TOP, COIF, CORK, KEPI, BERET, MUTCH, EXCEL, TUQUE, BARRET, BIGGIN, BONNET, CALPAC, COCKUP, MOBCAP, PILEUS, PINNER, CALOTTE, CALPACK, CHECHIA, COMMODE, FLANDAN, MONTERO, BALMORAL, BARRETTE, BIGGONET, SKULLCAP, YARMULKA; see HAT
capable APT, ABLE, SKILLED, COMPETENT
capacity BENT, SIZE, KNACK, SKILL
cape ANN, COD, MAY, NES, RAS, COPE, FEAR, HORN, HUKE, NAZE, NESS, ROBE, SCAW, SKAW, SABLE, BERTHA, DOLMAN, DOMINO, SONTAG, TIPPET, VISITE, HATTERAS, MANTILLA, PELERINE
Cape Verde, capital of PRAIA
Cape Verde island SAL, FOGO, MAIO, BRAVA
Cape Verde money ESCUDO, CENTAVO
Capek character ROBOT
Capek play RUR
caper HOP, DIDO, ROMP, ANTIC, FRISK, PRANK, GAMBOL, PRANCE, TITTUP
capillary see VEIN
capital CITY, MAIN, BASIC, FATAL, STOCK, LETTER, PRIMAL; see p. 586
capital punishment see EXECUTION
Capitoline trio JUNO, JUPITER, MINERVA
caprice FAD, KINK, WHIM, QUIRK, VAGARY, WHIMSEY

capricious FICKLE, ERRATIC, FLIGHTY
Capricorn star DABIH, DENEB, GIEDI, ALGEDI, ALSHAT, NASHIRA
— Caps SNO
capsize UPEND, UPSET, OVERTURN
capstan DRUM, HOIST, LEVER, WINCH, WINDLASS
capsule POD, PILL, PEARL, THECA, CACHET, SHEATH
captain AHAB, RAIS, REIS, BLIGH, QUEEG, SOTNIK
captain's command TROOP, BATTERY, COMPANY
captain's insignia EAGLE
caption TITLE, LEADER, LEGEND, HEADING
captious CROSS, TESTY, CARPING
captivate CHARM, ALLURE, ENAMOR, ENCHANT, ENSLAVE
capture BAG, COP, NAB, NET, PRIZE, SNARE, ARREST
caput TOP, HEAD, DOOMED
car see CABIN, AUTOMOBILE
car rack item SKI, BICYCLE
Caradoc BALA
caravan TREK, CAFILA, SAFARI
caravansary see INN
carbine see GUN
carbohydrate SUGAR, STARCH
carbon COAL, COKE, COPY, LEAD, SOOT
carbuncle RUBY, GARNET, PIMPLE, ANTHRAX
card ACE, PAM, SIX, TEN, TUM, TWO, WAG, COMB, DAME, FOUR, JACK, JASZ, KING, NINE, NOBS, SODA, TREY, BASTO, BOWER, DEUCE, HONOR, JOKER, KNAVE, MENEL, PEDRO, TAROC, TAROT, TEASE, ZENER, POSTAL, TAROCCO
card games see p. 586
card, tarot SUN, FOOL, MOON, STAR, DEATH, DEVIL, TOWER, WORLD, ARCANA, HERMIT, LOVERS, CHARIOT, JUSTICE
card term BID, CAT, CUT, GIN, PIG, POT, DEAL, DECK, DROP, HAND, MELD, PACK, PASS, SUIT, VOLE, BLIND, BLITZ, CHECK, ENTRY, HONOR, KITTY, KNOCK, RAISE, SMEAR, TRUMP, WIDOW, BRELAN,

RENEGE, TENACE; see
BRIDGE, CANASTA, POKER
cardinal ROY, CHIEF, LEGER,
DATARY, RITTER, SHEHAN,
CUSHING, MCGUIGAN,
MCINTYRE, SPELLMAN
cardinal point EAST, WEST,
NORTH, SOUTH
care CARK, HEED, RECK, TEND
careen TIP, YAW, CALK, CANT,
HEEL, KEEL, LIST, TILT
career RUN, RUSH, CALLING,
LIFEWORK, VOCATION
carefree GAY, BLITHE
careful WARY, CHARY, LEERY
careless LAX, LASH, RASH,
CASUAL, REMISS
care-less attitude APATHY
caress HUG, PET, CODDLE,
COSSET, DANDLE, NUZZLE
caretaker KEEPER, CURATOR,
TRUSTEE, CUSTODIAN
cargo LAST, LOAD, GOODS,
LADING, PORTAGE
Caribbean island AVES, CUBA,
ARUBA, NASSAU, TOBAGO,
BARBUDA, BONAIRE,
CURACAO, GRENADA,
JAMAICA, ANGUILLA,
BARBADOS, DOMINICA
caricature SKIT, FARCE,
PARODY, TAKEOFF
caries DECAY
Carmen composer BIZET
Carmen role CARMEN,
ZUNIGA, DONJOSE, MICAELA
Carmichael song STARDUST
carmine RED, CRIMSON
carnage HAVOC, BLOODSHED
carnival FETE, FEAST, REVEL
carnivorous insect MANTIS
carol LAY, NOEL; see SONG
caroler WAIT
Caroline Islands YAP, TRUK,
CHUUK, PALAU, KOSRAE,
POHNPEI
carom SHOT, REBOUND,
RICOCHET
Caron role GIGI
carousal ORGY, BINGE, REVEL,
SPREE, JAMBOREE
carouse BIRLE, BOOZE, BOUSE
carp NAG, CAVIL, NIBBLE,
CENSURE
carp(-like fish) ID, ASP, CHI, IDE,
KOI, BLAY, CHUB, DACE, KIYI,
ORFE, RUDD, SPOT, BLEAK,
BREAM, GIBEL, GOBIO, HITCH,
LOACH, MINIM, MINNY, PIRAI,

ROACH, TENCH, CHEVIN,
GOBID, MAHSIR, MAHSUR,
MINNOW, TAUTOG,
FATHEAD, GOBIOID, GUAVINA,
GUDGEON, MAHSEER,
MORWONG, OLDWIFE, PINFISH,
PINHEAD, FALLFISH
carpe — DIEM
carpel LEAF, PISTIL, SOREMA
carpenter ANT, FRAMER,
JOINER, WRIGHT
carpenter's tool AWL, SAW,
ADZE, BEVEL, LEVEL, PLANE,
CHISEL, HAMMER
carpet MAT, HERAT, TAPET,
TAPIS, TAPETE, WILTON,
DRUGGET; see RUG
carriage FLY, GIG, MIEN, PORT,
SHAY, POISE, CALASH,
MANNER; see VEHICLE
carrier HAMAL, BEARER,
PORTER, REDCAP; see
AIRLINE
Carroll, Lewis, character ALICE,
SNARK, HATTER, WALRUS,
DORMOUSE, JABBERWOCK,
TWEEDLEDEE, TWEEDLEDUM
carrot DRIAS
carry LUG, BEAR, HOLD, RIDE,
TOTE, FERRY, FETCH
— and carry CASH
carry away ELATE, REMOVE,
TRANSPORT
carry off RAPE, ABDUCT
carry on WAGE, CAPER,
CUTUP, CONDUCT
carry-on TOTE(BAG)
cart see VEHICLE
cartel PACT, POOL, TRUST
Carter library location ATLANTA,
GEORGIA
Carthage capital CARALIS
Carthage, of PUNIC
Carthage ruler DIDO, BARCA,
HANNIBAL
cartilage GRISTLE
cartographer MAPPER,
MERCATOR
cartoon EPURE, DESIGN,
SKETCH
cartoon character BC, HANS,
JEFF, LUCY, MUTT, POGO,
SHOE, TOON, ABNER, ANNIE,
DONDI, FRITZ, HAGAR,
JIGGS, LINUS, PLUTO, SLATS,
ARCHIE, BATMAN, DENNIS,
HERMAN, MICKEY, SLUGGS,
BLONDIE, DAGWOOD,
PEANUTS, GARFIELD

cartoon term	CEL, PANEL
cartoonist	see ANIMATOR; see p. 538
cartridge	SHELL, CASING
carve	SHAPE, CHISEL, INCISE, SCULPT
carving	CAMEO, SCRIVE
casaba	MELON, CANTALOUPE
Casablanca character	SAM, ILSE, RICK, LOUIS, LASZLO, UGARTE, VICTOR, FERRARI, RENAULT
case	ETUI, INRO, ETWEE, FOREL, TRIAL, CARTON, FORELL, PETARD, SHEATH
case, grammatical	DATIVE, ABLATIVE, GENITIVE, LOCATIVE, VOCATIVE, ACCUSATIVE
cash	DUST, CLEAR, DARBY, HONOR, MONEY, SPECIE
cash and —	CARRY
cashier	DROP, FIRE, OUST, EXPEL, BURSAR, PURSER, TELLER
casing	SHOE, COVER, LINER, SHEATH(ING)
casino	TEN, TWO, PINK
casino table cover	FELT, LAYOUT
cask	KEG, TUB, TUN, VAT, BOSS, BUTT, CADE, RIER, BARECA, FIRKIN, TIERCE
cask part	LAG, BILGE, CHIMB, CHIME
casket	BOX, PYX, TYE, COFFIN, SHRINE
Caspian Sea river	EMBA, KURA, URAL, ARAKS, TEREK, VOLGA
cassava	AIPI, JUCA, MANIOC, TAPIOCA
casserole	STEW, RAGOUT, RAMEKIN
Cassiopeia relative	CEPHEUS, ANDROMEDA
cassock	SOUTANE; see VESTMENT
cast	TOT, JILT, JUNK, MOLD, MOLT, SHED, SPEW, TINT, TOSS, FUSIL, SLING
cast aside	ABANDON, DISCARD
cast off	DUMP, SHED, SLOUGH, DISCARD
cast out	OUST, EJECT, EXPEL, EVICT
castaway	WAIF, MAROON, PARIAH, DERELICT
caste	DOM, MAL, MEO, AHIR,

	BAIS, GOLA, JATI, KOLI, KORI, KULI, MAGI, MALI, PASI, RANK, TELI, CLASS, GRADE, SUDRA, VARNA, BANIAN, CHETTY, LOHANA, PARIAH, RAJPUT, VAISYA, BRAHMAN
caste mark	BOTTU
caster	VIAL, CRUET, PHIAL, WHEEL, HURLER, ROLLER
castigate	BEAT, PUNISH, CENSURE, REPROVE, LAMBASTE
Castilian queen	ISABELLA
castle	ROOK, MORRO, CHATEAU, WINDSOR, ELSINORE, FORTRESS; see FORT
castle part	KEEP, MOAT, TOWER, DONJON
castor	HAT, BEAN, STAR, CRUET, BEAVER
Castor and Pollux	TWINS, GEMINI, DIOSCURI
Castor and Pollux, mother of	LEDA
Castor's slayer	IDAS
castrate	FIX, LIB, GELD, SPAY, ALTER, DESEX, UNMAN, NEUTER, STERILIZE
castrated animal	OX, GIB, HOG, STAG, CAPON, BARROW, EUNUCH, WETHER, GELDING, CASTRATO
casual(s)	IDLE, CHANCE, LOAFERS, OFFHAND
casualty	MISHAP, VICTIM, ACCIDENT
casuarina	TOA, AGOHO, AGOJO, BELAH, BELAR, HEOAK, BEEFWOOD
cat	GIB, KIT, PUS, TAB, TOM, KITT, PUSS, FELID, KITTY, MEWER, MOGGY, PUSSY, QUEEN, TABBY, TOMMY, FELINE, GIBCAT, KITTEN, KITTIE, MEWLER, MOUSER, NEUTER, PURRER, PUSSIE, THOMAS, TOMCAT, LIONCEL; see p. 663
— the cat	BELL
cat breed	MAU, REX, MANX, KORAT, MANUL, TABBY, ANGOLA, ANGORA, BIRMAN, BOMBAY, OCICAT, SPHYNX, BOBTAIL, BURMESE, PERSIAN, SIAMESE, BALINESE, PARAGUAY, HIMALAYAN, SHORTHAIR, ABYSSINIAN
cat call	MEW, MIAOW; see CRY
cat genus	FELIS
cat in cartoon	TOM, MILO, FELIX

cat, wild   LEO, EYRA, LION,
LYNX, PARD, PUMA, CHAUS,
CHITA, OUNCE, TIGER,
BOBCAT, CAFFER, CHETAH,
COUGAR, JAGUAR, KAFFIR,
LIONET, LUCERN, MARGAY,
OCELOT, PARDAL, SERVAL,
CARACAL, CHEETAH,
GUEPARD, LEOPARD, LIBBARD,
LIONESS, PANTHER, TIGRESS;
see CIVET
cat, young   KIT, PUSS, KITTY,
PUSSY, KITTEN, CATLING
cataclysm   HAVOC, DELUGE,
DEBACLE, DISASTER
catacomb   TOMB, CRYPT,
VAULT, LOCULUS
catafalque   BIER, SCAFFOLD
catalog(ue)   FILE, LIST, ROTA,
CANON, INDEX, CENSUS,
ROSTER
catapult   HURL, ONAGER,
BALISTA, PROJECT,
BALLISTA, SCORPION
cataract   CAST, LINN, FALLS,
CALIGO, CASCADE
catarrh   COLD, RHEUM
catastrophe   RUIN, CALAMITY,
DISASTER, CATACLYSM
catcall   BOO, RAZZ
catch   KEP, NAB, NET, TRAP,
GRAB, HAUL, HOOK, PAWL,
SNAG, CLICK, INCUR, DETENT,
ENTRAP, PELVIS, SNATCH,
RATCHET
catch on   TAKE, CLICK
Catch 22 author   HELLER
Catch 22 name   ARKIN, DANBY,
BALSAM, GARFUNKEL,
YOSSARIAN
catchall   BAG, BASKET, CLOSET
catching   VIRULENT,
CONTAGIOUS, INFECTIOUS
catchword   CUE, SLOGAN,
STARTER
category   CASTE, CLASS,
GENRE, GENUS, FAMILY,
RUBRIC, SPECIES
cater   FEED, PANDER, PURVEY,
PROVIDE
caterpillar   WERI, ERUCA,
CANKER, LOOPER, WOUBIT,
CUTWORM, WEBWORM,
INCHWORM, SPANWORM; see
MOTH, BUTTERFLY
catfish   POUT, RAAD, WELS,
BAGRE, DORAD, DORAS,
HASSAR, TANDAN, ASPREDO,
CANDIRU, FIDDLER, SILURID

Catfish Row resident   BESS,
CLARA, CROWN, PORGY,
SPORTINGLIFE
catgut   CORD, THARM, VIOLIN
cathartic   ALOE, ALOIN,
CASSIA, EMETIC, PHYSIC,
CALOMEL, GAMBOGE,
LAXATIVE, PURGATIVE
Cathay   CHINA
cathedral   DOM, DUOMO,
SOBOR, CHURCH, LATERAN,
MINSTER
cathedral, famous   ELY, REIMS,
AMIENS, STJOHN,
CHARTRES, NOTREDAME
cathedral official   DEAN, CANON
Catholic Church schism   MLIV
Catholic, Greek   UNIAT(A)
Catholic title   FRA
catkin   RAG, AMENT, SPIKE
catnip   NEP, NIP, CATMINT
cat's-paw   DUPE, GULL, TOOL,
CULLY, STOOGE
cattle   FAT, NOT, AVER, BOSS,
BUCK, CALF, COWS, DOGY,
GOUR, KINE, NOWT, OXEN,
QUEY, AIVER, ANGUS,
CUSHA, DEVON, DOGIE,
KERRY, PODDY, SANGA, SANGU,
SLINK, STEER, STIRK, STOCK,
VACHE, ANKOLE, ANKOLI,
AUROCS, BEEVES, CABREE,
CALVER, CANNER, CATALO,
DEXTER, DODDIE, HAWKEY,
HAWKIE, HEIFER, JERSEY,
MOILEY, MOOLEY, MULLEY,
SUSSEX, VEALER, BERENDO,
BIGHORN, BRAHMAN,
BRAHMIN, CATTALO,
GRASSER, SLINKER,
GUERNSEY, HEREFORD,
HOLSTEIN, LONGHORN
cattle dealer   DROVER, RANCHER
cattle disease   GID, BOTS,
LOCO, GARGET, NAGANA,
ANTHRAX, MURRAIN
cattle, young   CALF, HEIFER,
YEARLING
catwalk   BRIDGE
Caucasian   UDIC, ARYAN,
TATAR
Caucasian language   LAZ, UDI,
ANDI, AVAR, ADIGHE,
GEORGIAN
caucus   POWWOW, MEETING
Caudillo   FRANCO
ca(u)ldron   POT, RED, VAT,
BOILER, COPPER, KETTLE
caulking material   TAR, OAKUM

cause	AIM, END, HOTI, ORIGIN	CD, make a	BURN
cause, person with a	ACTIVIST	cease	HALT, QUIT, STAY,
causerie	CHAT, TALK, PLEAD,		AVAST, PETER
	APERCU, DÉBATE, PARLEY	cease and —	DESIST
causeuse	SOFA, TETEATETE	cease to exist	UNBE
causeway	DIKE, PATH, CAUSEY	ceaselessly	ONEND,
caustic	LYE, ALUM, LIME,		ETERNALLY, ENDLESSLY
	ACRID, BITING, PHENOL,	Cecrops city	ATHENS
SEVERE, ERODENT, MORDANT,		Cecrops daughter	HERSE
	PUNGENT, PYROTIC	Cecrops successor	THESEUS
cauterize	BURN, SEAR, BRAND	cede	DEED, FORGO, GRANT,
caution	CARE, WARN,		WAIVE, YIELD, ASSIGN
	ADVICE, TIPOFF	Cedric ward	ROWENA
cautious	SHY, WARY, CANNY,	ceiling	DOME, ROOF, COVER,
	CHARY, FABIAN		VAULT, CANOPY, CUPOLA
— cava	VENA	celebrate	KEEP, HONOR,
cavalier	PROUD, KNIGHT,		HALLOW, OBSERVE
	HAUGHTY	celebrated	NOTED, FAMOUS,
Cavalleria Rusticana character			EMINENT, RENOWNED
	LOLA, ALFIO	celebrity	VIP, LION, NAME,
Cavalleria Rusticana composer			STAR, ECLAT
	MASCAGNI	celerity	HASTE, HURRY, SPEED
cavalry	TURM(A), HUSSARS,	celestial	HOLY, DIVINE,
	LANCERS		URANIC, ANGELIC
cavalry weapon	LANCE, SABER	celibacy	CHASTITY
cavalryman	ULAN, SOWAR,	celibate	CHASTE, SINGLE,
SPAHI, UHLAN, HUSSAR,		VIRGIN, BACHELOR, SPINSTER
	SPAHEE, DRAGOON	cell	EGG, KIL, GERM, KILL,
cave(rn)	DEN, GROT, LAIR,		GROUP, VAULT, SPORE,
WEEM, ANTRE, CROFT,		CYTODE, GAMETE, NEURON(E)
CRYPT, CAVITY, GROTTO,		cell division	SPIREM(E)
	RECESS	cell part	LININ, ENERGID,
cave —	CANEM		NUCLEUS, PLASTID,
cave dweller	BAT, BEAR,		VACUOLE
HERMIT, EREMITE,		cella	NAOS, SERDAB
	TROGLODYTE	cellar	VAULT, BUTTERY,
cave explorer	SPELUNKER		BASEMENT
cave, famous	LURAY,	celt	AX, CHISEL
LASCAUX, MAMMOTH,		Celt	IR, ITH, MIL, NAR, EBER,
	CARLSBAD	ERSE, GAEL, KELT, MANX,
cave, inhabiting a	SPEL(A)EAN		BRETON, MIDEDH
caveat	CAUTION, WARNING	Celtic	ERSE, MANX, WELSH,
caveman	TROGLODYTE	BRETON, GAELIC, KELTIC,
caviar	ROE, IKRA		CORNISH, GAULISH
caviar fish	STERLET,	Celtic church center	IONA
	STURGEON	Celtic lord	TANIST
cavil	CARP, HAFT, BICKER,	cement	GLUE, LUTE, PASTE,
	CENSURE, QUIBBLE	PUTTY, MORTAR, SOLDER
cavity	PIT, VUG, DENT, VOOG,	cemetery	LITTEN, BONEYARD,
VUGG, VUGH, ANTRA,		CATACOMB, GRAVEYARD
DRUSE, FOSSA, GEODE,		cenobite	NUN, MONK, FRIAR,
LUMEN, SINUS, ANTRUM,			ESSENE
	ATRIUM, POCKET	cenoby	ABBEY, PRIORY,
cavort	DIDO, CAPER, PRANK		CONVENT
Cawdor castle site	NAIRN	Censor, The (Roman)	CATO
Cawdor, thane of	MACBETH	censure	FLAY, BLAME, CHIDE,
cay	REEF, ISLET	KNOCK, SLATE, TARGE
cayenne	WHIST, CANARY,	census	POLL, COUNT, SURVEY
PEPPER, COPEPOD, CAPSICUM		census figure	STAT

cent   SOU, PENNY, COPPER
centaur   CHIRON, NESSUS
centaur father   IXION
center   HUB, CORE, NAVE,
        FOCUS, HEART, PIVOT,
                        NUCLEUS
center, away from   DISTAL
center, toward   ENTAD, MESIAL
centerpiece   EPERGNE
central   MID, AXIAL, FOCAL,
              NUCLEAR, PIVOTAL
C. Afr. Republic, capital of
                          BANGUI
C. Afr. Republic money   FRANC
C. Afr. Republic president
              DACKO, BOKASSA
C. Amer. bird   GUAN, JACU,
      SYLPH, TURCO, CONDOR
C. Amer. country   BELIZE,
        PANAMA, HONDURAS,
      COSTA RICA, GUATEMALA,
      NICARAGUA, EL SALVADOR
C. Amer. tree   ULE, EBOE,
                          AMATE
Central Park fountain   BETHESDA
century plant   PITA, AGAVE,
                        MAGUEY
Cepheus relative   ANDROMEDA,
                      CASSIOPEIA
ceramic   see CHINA
cerate   WAX, LARD, SALVE
cereal   BRAN, CORN, RICE,
        GRITS, GRUEL, MAIZE,
      WHEAT, FARINA, HOMINY,
              SECALE, OATMEAL
cerebral   MENTAL,
                  INTELLECTUAL
cerebral palsy   DIPLEGIA,
        EPILEPSY, NEURALGIA
cerebral person   EGGHEAD,
                  INTELLECTUAL
cerebral thrombosis   STROKE
cerebrate   THINK, PONDER,
                      COGITATE
ceremony   FORM, POMP, RITE,
                          RITUAL
Ceres parent   OPS, SATURN
certain   ONE, YEA, SURE,
                    TRUE, FIXED
certainly   IWIS, NATCH,
      SURELY, INDEED, OFCOURSE
certificate   SCRIP, STOCK,
        DIPLOMA, VOUCHER
certify   OK, OKAY, VOUCH,
        ATTEST, DEPOSE, EVINCE,
                        LICENSE
cerumen   EARWAX
cervine   DOE, DEER, ELK, STAG,
                    see p. 664

cessation   END, STAY, STOP,
        DEATH, PAUSE, DESITION
cesspool   SINK, SUMP, SINKER
c'est la —   VIE, GUERRE
cetacean   see WHALE, DOLPHIN
Ceylon   see SRILANKA
Chad, capital of   NDJAMENA
Chad money   FRANC
Chad mountains   TIBESTI
Chad neighbor   CAR, LIBYA,
      NIGER, SUDAN, NIGERIA,
                      CAMEROON
Chad river   KEBI, CHARI,
                        LOGONE
Chad town   ATI, BOL, MAO,
      DOBA, ARADA, MOUNDOU
chafe   RUB, VEX, FRET, FROT,
              GALL, ABRADE
chaff   PUG, BRAN, HUSK,
      HULLS, TRASH, BANTER
chaffer   SIEVE, DICKER,
              HAGGLE, HIGGLE
chaffinch   CHINK, SPINK
chatty   SCALY, ACEROSE,
              PALEATE, TRIVIAL
chain   FOB, TYE, GYVE, TORC,
      TETHER, TORQUE, MANACLE,
                        SHACKLE
chair   KAGO, SEAT, SEDAN,
      STOOL, ROCKER, SPEAKER
chair part   RUNG, SPLAT
chairwoman   MADAM
chalcedony   ONYX, SARD,
      AGATE, CHERT, PRASE
Chaldean city   UR
chalice   AMA, CUP, BOWL,
      AMULA, CALIX, GRAIL
challenge   DARE, DEFY, GAGE,
      CARTEL, QUESTION
challenge response   CAN SO
chamber   ODA, KIVA, ODAH,
      ROOM, CAMERA, LOCULUS
chamfer   BEVEL, GROOVE,
                        FLUTING
chamois   AOUDAD, SHAMMY
champ   CHEW, MUNCH
champion   ACE, BACK, HERO,
      VICTOR, ESPOUSE, PALADIN;
                    see p. 708
chance   HAP, LOT, FATE, LUCK,
      ODDS, RISK, OCCUR, HAZARD,
      KISMET, RANDOM, FORTUNE
chancel   BEMA, JUBE
chancel garb   ALB
chancel part   BEMA, JUBE,
                        RAILING
change   CTS, COIN, FLUX,
      MUTA, VARY, ALTER,

MORPH, SHIFT, MODIFY,
MUTATE, OBVERT
changeable   FICKLE, PROTEAN,
VARIANT
changeling   ELF, OAF, DOLT,
DUNCE, DOUBLE, RINGER
channel   GAT, BAND, DIKE,
DUCT, LEAF, PIPE, RACE,
TUBE, CHUTE, FLUME, STRIA,
ALVEUS, FURROW, GROOVE,
GUTTER, MEDIUM, SLUICE,
STRAIT, CONDUIT, STATION;
see TELEVISION
Channel Islands   SARK, JERSEY,
ALDERNEY, GUERNSEY
Channel Islands measure   CABOT
chant   MELE, CRONE, INTONE,
INTROIT, CANTICLE,
RESPONSE
chanticleer   COCK, ROOSTER
chantry   ALTAR, CHAPEL,
SHRINE
chaos   NU, PO, NUN, PIE, APSU,
KORE, MESS, VOID, ABYSS,
BABEL, HAVOC
Chaos relative   EREBUS
chaotic   SNAFU, MUDDLED
chap   GUY, MAN, COVE, KIBE,
CHINK, CRACK, KEREL,
SPRAY
chapel   CHOIR, BETHEL,
CHANTRY, ORATORY,
SISTINE
chaperon   DUE(N)NA, ESCORT
chaplet   ANADEM, FILLET,
ROSARY, WREATH
Chaplin wife   OONA
chapped   KIBY, KIBED, SPLIT,
CRACKED
chapter   PART, LOCAL, LODGE,
BRANCH, SECTION
char   SEAR, SCORCH
character   ROLE, RUNE, ETHOS,
NEUME, REPUTE
charade   PUZZLE, RIDDLE,
PANTOMIME
charge   FEE, COST, ONUS,
DEBIT, ADJURE, INDICT
charge, opp. of   RETREAT, RUN
AWAY
charger   MOUNT, PLATE,
STEED, PLATTER
chariot   BIGA, RATH, WAIN,
CURRE, ESSED, RATHA,
ESSEDA, ESSEDE
charioteer   (BEN)HUR, JEHU,
PILOT, AURIGA, DRIVER
charisma   IT, GIFT, CHARM,
POWER, APPEAL

charitable   BENIGN, HUMANE
charity   ALMS, DOLE, DONEE,
MERCY, ALTRUISM
charlatan   FAKE(R), QUACK,
EMPIRIC
Charlemagne kin   PEPIN,
MARTEL, ROLAND,
ORLANDO
Charlemagne knight   PALADIN,
DOUZEPER
Charlemagne sword   JOYEUSE
Charles River school   MIT,
HARVARD
charleyhorse   CRAMP
charm   MAGIC, AMULET,
ENAMOR, ENCHANT,
PERIAPT, CHARISMA,
SWASTIKA; see FETISH
Charon river   STYX
Charpentier opera   LOUISE
chart   MAP, PLAT, PLOT,
GRAPH, TABLE, CHEMA,
DIAGRAM, MERCATOR
charter   LET, DEED, HIRE,
RENT, GRANT, LEASE,
PATENT
Charteris detective   (THE)SAINT
chary   SHY, WARY, PRUDENT,
CAUTIOUS
Charybdis, rock opposite   SCYLLA
chase   HUNT, REPEL, FOLLOW,
PURSUE, PURSUIT
chasm   GAP, GLUT, GULF,
REFT, ABYSS, CLEFT, FLUME,
GORGE, CREVAS, HIATUS,
RAVINE
chassis   BODY, FRAME,
NACELLE, ARMATURE,
BODYWORK, SKELETON
chaste   PURE, MODEST, VESTAL
chasten   ABASH, SMITE,
HUMBLE
chastise   TRIM, BLAME, SLATE,
TAUNT, SWINGE, CENSURE
chastity   VIRTUE, CELIBACY
chasuble   see VESTMENT
chat   GAB, CHIN, COZE, TOVE,
PRATE, CONFAB
chat room term   IM, CALL,
LURK, SEND, MESSAGE
chatelaine   PIN, CLASP,
BROOCH
chattel   GOODS, SLAVE,
EFFECTS
chatter   GAB, GAS, YAP, BLAT,
CLAP, CLAT, PRATE, BABBLE,
JABBER; see TALK
chatterer   JAY, MAG, PIET
chatty   PYOT, TALKATIVE

Chaucer inn **TABARD**	WOODY, DANSON, KELSEY,
Chaucer pilgrim **NUN, COOK,**	FRASIER, KIRSTIE, REBECCA,
MONK, CLERK, FRIAR, REEVE,	HARRELSON
KNIGHT, MILLER, PARSON,	cheese **BLEU, BLUE, BRIE,**
SQUIRE, THOPAS, YEOMAN,	**DICK, EDAM, FETA, JACK,**
SHIPMAN, FRANKLIN,	**BRICK, COLBY, CREAM,**
MERCHANT, MANCIPLE,	**GOUDA, GRANA, SWISS,**
PARDONER, PRIORESS,	**ASIAGO, BARRIE, DUNLOP,**
SUMMONER	**GRATIN, MYSOST, ROMANO,**
cheap **VILE, PALTRY, SHODDY,**	**BOURSIN, CHEDDAR,**
SCHLOCK, NOMINAL	**COTTAGE, FONTINA,**
— cheap **DIRT**	**GRUYERE, RICOTTA,**
cheapskate **MISER, PIKER,**	**SAPSAGO, STILTON,**
NIGGARD	**AMERICAN, BELPAESE,**
cheat **BAM, CON, FOB, FUB,**	**MUENSTER, PARMESAN,**
GIP, GYP, BILK, CLIP, DUFF,	**TILSITER, CAMEMBERT,**
GULL, MUMP, SCAM, SWIZ,	**EMMENTHAL, JARLSBERG,**
COZEN, GOUGE, RENIG,	**LIMBURGER, PROVOLONE,**
SHARK, SHARP, STING, WELCH,	**ROQUEFORT, GORGONZOLA,**
CHISEL, CONMAN, DIDDLE,	**MOZZARELLA, LIEDERKRANZ**
RENEGE, SHARPER, SWINDLE	cheesy **CASEOUS**
check **NIP, TAB, CURB, REIN,**	chemical compound **ALUM,**
STAY, BLOCK, STUNT,	**AMID, AMIN, AZIN, IMID,**
BRIDLE, STUMER	**SALT, SODA, AMIDE, AMINE,**
check part **DATE, PAYEE,**	**AZINE, AZOLE, BORID,**
AMOUNT, SIGNATURE	**CERIA, ESTER, IMIDE, IMINE,**
checkerboard-like **TESSELATE**	**NITER, NITRE, BORIDE,**
checkered **PIED, VAIR, PLAID,**	**IODIDE, ISOMER, POTASH,**
MOSAIC	**ANATASE, DRYBONE,**
checkers **DAM(E)S, DRAUGHTS**	**INOSITE, LEUCINE, METAMER,**
checkers opening **ALMA, DYKE,**	**POTASSA, STEARATE**
FIFE, CROSS, DENNY, KELSO,	chemical element *see p. 521*
BOSTON, DUNDEE, NAILOR,	chemical radical **BUTYL, ETHYL,**
SOUTER, BRISTOL	**TOLYL, METHYL, OXALYL,**
checkers term **DAM, HUFF,**	**BENZOYL, CARBONYL**
KING, CROWN	chemical term **BOND, ANION,**
checking block **SPRAG**	**ALKALI, ALCOHOL, ISOTOPE,**
checkmate **STOP, UNDO,**	**POLYMER, VALENCE,**
BAFFLE, SCOTCH, STYMIE,	**CATALYST, COMPOUND**
THWART	chemical weapon **GE, VX,**
checkup **MEDICAL, PHYSICAL**	**SARIN, LABUN, SOMAN,**
cheek(s) **CHAP, GALL, GENA,**	**CYANIDE, MUSTARD,**
JAMP, JOLE, JOWL, BRASS,	**CHLORINE, LEWISITE,**
BUCCA, NERVE, SAUCE	**PHOSGENE**
cheek, *pert. to* **GENAL, MALAR,**	chemise **SARK, SLIP, CYMAR,**
BUCCAL	**SHIFT**
cheer **OLE, RAH, CLAP, LAUD,**	chemist *see p. 538*
ROOT, VIVA, BOOLA, BRAVO,	cherish **PET, DOTE, PRIZE,**
ELATE, ENCORE, HOORAY,	**ESTEEM, FOSTER, REVERE**
HURRAH, PRAISE, APPLAUD	cherry **DUKE, FUJI, GEAN,**
cheerful **GLEG, PERT, ROSY,**	**MOREL, RUDDY, MORELL,**
JOLLY, PEART, BLITHE,	**CAPULIN, MARASCA,**
HILARY	**OXHEART, SIANGKI**
cheerless **DRAB, GLUM,**	Cherry City **SALEM**
DREAR, DISMAL, DREARY,	chess champion **TAL, EUWE,**
GLOOMY	**ANAND, KARPOV, LASKER,**
Cheers name **SAM, LONG,**	**FISCHER, SMYSLOV, SPASSKY,**
NORM, RHEA, CARLA, CLIFF,	**ALEKHINE, KASPAROV,**
COACH, DIANE, WENDT,	**STEINITZ, PETROSIAN**

chess move   BB, KB, RB, BK, KK, QK, RK, BQ, KQ, QQ, RQ, BR, KR, QR, RR, BKB, BQB, KTB, KTK, RKB, RQB, BKKT, BQKT, KTKB, KTKR, KTKT, KTQB, KTQR, QQKT, RKKT, RQKT

chess term   MATE, PIRC, CHECK, DEBUT, PRISE, CASTLE, FIDATE, GAMBIT, ENPRISE, JADOUBE

chessman   KING, PAWN, ROOK, HORSE, PIECE, QUEEN, BISHOP, CASTLE, KNIGHT

chest   ARK, ARCA, CASE, CIST, KIST, BAHUT, BOSOM, COFFER, LOCKER, THORAX

chestnut   LING, RATA, LINGKO, MARRON

chevron   RANK, ANGLE, STRIPE

chew   BITE, CHAM, GNAW, QUID, CHAMP, MUNCH, CHAVEL

chewink   FINCH, TOWHEE

— chi   TAI

chic   NATTY, NIFTY, DAPPER, MODISH, ELEGANT, STYLISH

Chicago   WINDY CITY, SECOND CITY

Chicago airport   MDW, ORD, MIEGS, OHARE, MIDWAY

Chicago district   LOOP

Chicago Seven   DAVIS, RUBIN, HAYDEN, WEINER, FROINES, HOFFMAN, DELLINGER

Chicago sports team   CUBS, BEARS, BULLS, STING, WHITE SOX

Chicago stadium   UNITED, WRIGLEY, COMISKEY, SOLDIER FIELD

chicanery   RUSE, WILE, CAVIL, INTRIGUE

Chicano, prominent   BAKER, BARELA, CHACON, CHAVEZ, MAGNON, SEGUIN, WARREN, ALMARAZ, CANALES, CORTINA, GALARZA, PARSONS, PERALES, RAMIREZ, OLIVAREZ

chick pea   BUB, GRAM, CHICH, CICER

chicken   HEN, COCK, BIDDY, FRYER, LAYER, POULT, BROILER, ROASTER

chicken breed   RED, JAVA, ASEEL, MALAY, ANCONA, BANTAM, BRAHMA, COCHIN, FLECHE, GALLUS, HOUDAN, JERSEY, LAMONA, POLISH,

SULTAN, SUSSEX, TURKEN, BANDARA, BUCKEYE, CAMPINE, CORNISH, DORKING, FRIZZLE, HOLLAND, LEGHORN, MATROUH, MINORCA, STYRIAN, SUMATRA, ARAUCANA, CATALANA, CUBALAYA, DELAWARE, WYANDOTTE

chicken feed   CORN, MEAL, GRAIN, BARLEY, CHANGE, PEANUTS

chicken out   QUIT, GIVE UP, RENEGE

chicle   GUM, LATEX, SAPOTA

chicory   ENDIVE, SUCCORY

chide   RATE, SCOLD, BERATE, REPROVE

chief(tain)   AGA, JAM, MIR, AMIR, ARCH, DATO, DATU, HEAD, JARL, MAIN, MORO, RAIS, RAJA, RANA, REIS, SYED, SYUD, TYEE, YARL, ZAIM, ZIPA, ALDER, AMEER, DATTO, ELDER, FRIST, POMBO, PRIME, RAJAH, THANE, VITAL, ATAMAN, HETMAN, CAPITAL, SUPREME

Chief Justice   see SUPREME COURT

chiefly   MAINLY, MOSTLY, LARGELY

chilblain   KIBE, PERNIO

child(ren)   CUB, IMP, KID, TAD, TOT, ARAB, BABE, BABY, BATA, BRAT, CHIT, TIKE, TYKE, BAIRN, CHICK, GAMIN, CHILDE, INFANT, MOPPET, URCHIN, PROGENY

child, foster   DALT, NORRY, NURRY

childbirth   LABOR, LYINGIN, DELIVERY, CONFINEMENT

childish   NAIVE, ASININE, PUERILE, IMMATURE, INFANTILE

childless   BARREN, INFERTILE

childlike   MEEK, NAIVE, DOCILE

Chile, capital of   SANTIAGO

Chilean city/town   LOTA, ANGOL, ARICA, MAIPU, PENCO, RENCA, TALCA, TEMUCO, SANTIAGO

Chilean lake   TORO, RANCO, BLANCO, PALENA, YELCHO

Chilean measure   VARA, LEGUA, LINEA, CUADRA, FANEGA

Chilean money　　PESO, COLON,
　　LIBRA, CONDOR, ESCUDO,
　　　　　　　　　CENTAVO
Chilean mountain　　　MACA,
　CONICO, RINCON, COPIAPO,
　　　　　　　　　PALPANA
Chilean peninsula　　HARDY,
　LACUY, TUMBES, STAINES,
　　　　　　　　　WHARTON
Chilean president　　UGARTE,
　　ALLENDE, ESCOBAR,
　　　　　　　　　PINOCHET
Chilean river　　LOA, ITATA,
　MAIPO, MAULE, BIOBIO,
　　　　　　　　　COPIAPO
Chilean tree　　ULMO, QUINA,
　　　　　　　　　MUERMO
chill　　ICE, NIP, AGUE, ALGOR,
　GELID, RIGOR, FREEZE,
　　　　　　　　　SHIVER
chilling　　　　　　ONICE
chilly　　ICY, RAW, COLD, COOL,
　ALGID, BLEAK, GELID
chime　　RIM, BELL, EDGE,
　　AGREE, HARMONY
chimera　　FANCY, MIRAGE,
　　　　　　　　　FANTASY
chimney　　LUM, FLUE, VENT,
　　　　　　　　　TEWEL
chimney piece　　PAREL, MANTEL
chin　　　　　　　BUCCULA
China　　　　　　CATHAY
China, capital of　　PEKING,
　　　　　　　　　BEIJING
china　　DELF(T), CERAMIC,
　DRESDEN, FAIENCE,
　CROCKERY, EGGSHELL, see
　　　　　　　　　PORCELAIN
chine　　SILK, CREST, RIDGE,
　　　　　　　　　SPINE
Chinese　　MAIO, SINO, SERIC,
　SINIC, CATAJA, JOHNNY,
　MONGOL, CATAJAN
Chinese aborigine　　MAN, YAO,
　　MIAO, MANTZU
Chinese city/town　　AMOY,
　LUDA, SIAN, ZIBO, KIRIN,
　TZEPO, ANSHAN, CANTON,
　FUSHUN, KALGAN, TSINAN
Chinese dialect　　WU, YI, MIN,
　AMOY, BUYI, TONG, HAKKA,
　FOOTOW, SWATOW,
　MANDARIN, CANTONESE,
　　　　　　　　　PEKINGESE
Chinese dynasty　　WU, HAN,
　SHU, SUI, WEI, CHIN, CHOU,
　GHOS, HSIA, LIAO, MING,
　SUNG, TANG, TSIN, YUAN,
　　CHING, SHANG

Chinese factory　　　　HONG
Chinese government seat　　HIEN
Chinese instrument　　KIN, ERHU,
　PIPA, XIAO, SHENG
Chinese island　　AMOY, MACAU,
　MATSU, HAINAN, TAIWAN,
　DONGSHA, HUNGTOW,
　　　　　　　　　PINGTAN
Chinese lake　　TAI, HONGZE,
　POYANG, ZANGBO,
　DONGTING, QINGHAI
Chinese language　　WA, YI,
　MIAO, SHAN, UIGUR,
　CHUANG, KAZAKH, MONGOL,
　TIBETAN, MANDARIN
Chinese leader　　HU, LI, LIU,
　HUA, MAO, ZHU, DENG,
　PENG, YANG, ZHAO, ZHOU,
　ENLAI, JIANG, ZEMIN,
　RONGJI, SHAOQI, ZEDONG,
　ZIYANG, GUOFENG,
　TSETUNG, YAOBANG,
　XIANNIAN, XIAOPING,
　　　　　　　　　SHANGKUN
Chinese martial art　　KENDO,
　KYUDO, KUNG FU, TAI CHI
Chinese measure　　HO, HU, LI,
　MU, PU, TU, FEN, TOU, CHEK,
　CHIH, KISH, TSUN, CHANG,
　　CHING, SHENG
Chinese money　　LI, PU, FEN,
　CASH, CENT, JIAO, TAEL,
　TIAO, YUAN, RENMINBI
Chinese mountain　　KONGUR,
　LUSHAN, GONGGA,
　MUZTAG, YUSHAN, EVEREST
Chinese poet　　LI PO, LAO ZI,
　　　　　　　　　LI TAI PO
Chinese province　　ANHUI,
　GANSU, HEBEI, HENAN,
　HUBEI, HUNAN, JILIN, FUJIAN,
　HAINAN, SHANXI, YUNNAN,
　　SICHUAN, SHANDONG
Chinese region　　MACAO, TIBET,
　GUANGXI, HONGKONG,
　　　　　　　　　XINJIANG
Chinese river　　XI, AMUR,
　CHANG, HUANG, MEKONG,
　ZANGBO, SALWEEN, SONGHUA
Chinese season　　CHIU, CHUN,
　　HSIA, TUNG
Chinese society　　HUI, HOEY,
　　TONG, BOXER
Chinese state　　　　TSAO
Chinese tree　　ECHO, ICHO, KIRI,
　TUNG, LICHI, GINGKO,
　　GINKGO, LITCHI
Chinese way　　　　　TAO
Chinese weight　　LI, FEN, HAD,

KIN, TAN, YIN, CHIN, MACE,
SHIH, TAEL, CATTY, PICUL
Chinese year   OX, DOG, PIG,
RAT, GOAT, HARE, HORSE,
SHEEP, SNAKE, TIGER,
DRAGON, MONKEY, RABBIT,
ROOSTER
chink   BORE, RIFT, RIMA, RIME,
CRACK, CRANNY
chinky   RIMAL, RIMOSE,
RIMOUS
chip   BIT, NIG, NICK, CHECK,
CRISP, FLAKE, SPALL,
GALLET, COUNTER
chip away at   ERODE
chip for snacks   FRITO
chipmunk   CHIPPY, HACKEE
chipper   ADZ, SPRY, COCKY,
PERKY
chirp   PEW, PUE, PEEP, PIPE,
CHEEP
chisel   GAD, CELT, PARE,
CHEAT, DROVE, SCULP,
SLICK, POMMEL
chit   IOU, INFANT, VOUCHER
chivy   CRY, NAG, GAME,
HUNT, CHASE, PURSUE
chlorophyll   ETIOLIN
chock   BLOCK, CLEAT, WEDGE
chocolate mixing stick   MOLINET
chocolate powder   PINOLE
choice   OPT, AONE, PICK,
RARE, CREAM, ELITE, PRIME,
OPTION, PICKED, SELECT,
NOMINEE
choice location   FORK, POLL,
BALLOT, REFERENDUM
choir singer   CHORIST(ER); see
SINGER
choir type   MIXED,
ACAP(P)ELLA
choir vestment   COTTA,
SURPLICE
choke   DAM, GAG, CLOG,
QUAR, BURKE, WORRY,
STIFLE
choking victim, famous   ELLIOT
choler   IRE, BILE, FURY, RAGE,
ANGER, WRATH, SPLEEN
choleric   FIERY, HUFFY, IRATE,
TESTY
cholesterol   HDL, LDL, LIPID
choose   OPT, CULL, VOTE,
ADOPT, ELECT, OPTATE,
SELECT, DESTINE
— and choose   PICK
chop   AXE, HEW, LOP, CHIP,
DICE, HACK, JOWL, SNIG,
CARVE, MINCE

Chopin's country   POLAND
Chopin's lover   SAND
chord   TRIAD, TRINE,
HARMONY
chore   JOB, CHAR, DUTY,
CHARE, STINT
choreographer   see p. 539
chorus   CHOIR, ACCORD,
BURDEN, UNISON, REFRAIN
chorus girl   CHORINE,
STEPPER, ROCKETTE
Chosen   COREA, KOREA
Christ's word on cross   ELOI
christen   NAME, CLEPE,
BAPTIZE
— Christi   ANNO
Christian   GENTILE, BELIEVER
Christian feast   AGAPE
Christian Science founder   EDDY
— Christie   ANNA
Christina   XINA
Christmas   NOEL, XMAS,
YULE(TIDE)
Christmas Carol author   DICKENS
Charistmas Carol character
TINY TIM, MARLEY, SCROOGE,
CRATCHIT, FEZZIWIG
chromosome   IDANT
chronicle   ANNAL, DIARY,
ANNALS, RECORD,
ACCOUNT
chrysalis   KELL, PUPA, NYMPH,
COCOON, AURELIA
chrysanthemum   MUM, KIKU,
POMPOM, POMPON,
ANEMONE, COSTMARY,
FEVERFEW
chubby   FAT, OBESE, PLUMP,
ROTUND
chuck   FOOD, GRUB, HURL
chuckle   CLUCK, CACKLE,
GIGGLE, TITTER, CHORTLE
chum   PAL, BUDDY, CRONY,
FRIEND
chunk   GOB, WHANG, WHANK,
GOBBET
chunky   LUMPY, SQUAT,
STOUT, STOCKY
church   KIL, FANE, KIRK, TERA,
CRYPT, SAMAJ, BETHEL,
CHAPEL, MOSQUE, PAGODA,
TEMPLE, MINSTER, MISSION,
BASILICA, ECCLESIA,
CATHEDRAL
church jurisdiction
SEE, PARISH, DEANERY, DIOCESE
church leader   ARIUS, PAPAS,
ORIGEN, HIERARCH
Church of England   ANGLICAN

church official **ELDER, BEADLE, LECTOR, SEXTON, VERGER, SACRIST(AN); see CLERGY**
church part **NEF, PEW, APSE, BEMA, KURK, NAVE, ALTAR, BENCH, STALL, PARVIS, CHANCEL, ORATORY, STEEPLE, SACRISTY, TRANSEPT**
church property **GLEBE**
Churchill relative **SARAH, SOAMES**
churchman **DEAN, POPE, ABBOT, BISHOP, DEACON, PRIEST, RECTOR, PRELATE, PRIMATE, CARDINAL; see CLERGY**
churchyard **PARVIS**
churl **OAF, BOOR, CARL, LOUT, CEORL, KNAVE, VILLEIN**
churlish **DOUR, SOUR, SULKY, SURLY, SORDID, SULLEN**
chute **DUCT, FLUME, RAPIDS**
Chuuk **TRUK, HOGOLU**
Chuuk island **TOL, UDOT, UMAN, WENO, FEFAN, DUBLON**
CIA directors **BUSH, CASEY, COLBY, GATES, SMITH, TENET, DEUTCH, DULLES, MCCONE, RABORN, SOUERS, TURNER, WEBSTER, WOOLSEY**
ciborium **PYX, CANOPY, COFFER**
Cid author **CORNEILLE**
Cid horse **BABIECA**
Cid name **RUY, DIAZ**
Cid sword **COLADA**
Cid wife **ISMENA**
cider **QUAS, PERRY**
cigar **ROPE, TOBY, CLARO, SEGAR, STOGY, CORONA, STOGIE, CHEROOT, CULEBRA, PANATELA**
cigarette **CIG, FAG, BIRI, BUTT, CUBES, GASPER**
cigarette brand **KENT, TRUE, CAMEL, SALEM, DUNHILL, WINSTON, MARLBORO, PALLMALL, PIEDMONT, CHESTERFIELD**
cinch **GRIP, BREEZE, FASTEN**
cinder(s) **ASH, SCAR, SLAG, ASHES, DROSS, EMBER, GLEED, SCORIA, CLINKER**
cion **BUD, GRAFT, SCION, SHOOT**
Cipango **JAPAN**
cipher **NIL, CODE, NULL,**

ZERO, AUGHT, OUGHT, NAUGHT, MONOGRAM
Circe's island **AEAEA, AIAIA**
Circe's kin **MEDEA, AEETES**
circle **ORB, CIRC, DISK, EDDY, GIRD, HALO, HOOP, LOOP, NIMB, RING, GLOBE, RHOMB, CIRQUE, CLIQUE, CORDON, GIRDLE, ROTATE**
circle dance **HORA**
circle part **ARC, CHORD, CENTER, RADIUS, SECANT, SECTOR, SEGMENT, TANGENT**
circuit **LAP, TOUR, EYRE, ZONE, AMBIT, CYCLE, ORBIT, ROUTE, DETOUR**
circuitous **MAZY, DEVIOUS, SINUOUS**
circular **AD, BILL, FLIER, ORBED, ROUND, MAILER, ANNULAR, DISCOID, PAMPHLET**
circulate **BRUIT, DEFUSE, ROTATE, SPREAD**
circumference **GIRT, AMBIT, GIRTH, VERGE**
circumlocution **AMBAGE, VERBIAGE**
circumspect **WARY, CHARY, DISCREET**
circumstance **FACT, STATE, STRAIT, DETAIL, FACTOR, EPISODE**
circus **BIGTOP, CIRCLE, CIRQUE, CARNIVAL, COLISEUM**
circus employee **SPIELER**
circus equipment **NET, RING, TENT, TRAPEZE**
circus post **META**
cirque **CWM, CIRC, CORRIE, RECESS, EROSION**
Cisco Kid character **CISCO, DIABLO, PANCHO**
cistern **BAC, SAC, VAT, SUMP, WELL**
— cit. **OP, LOC**
citadel **ARX, FORT, ALAMO, TOWER, CASTLE, FORTRESS**
cite **CALL, QUOTE, ADDUCE, MUSTER, SUBPOENA**
cities, foreign see p. 593
cities, U.S. see p. 598
citizen **CIT, VOTER, NATIVE, BURGHER, DENIZEN, OPPIDAN, RESIDENT**
Citizen Kane name **SUSAN, FOSTER, GETTYS, LELAND, CHARLES, ROSEBUD,**

JEDEDIAH, THATCHER, BERNSTEIN

citron   LIME, ETROG, LEMON, CEDRAT, ETHROG

city URBS, BURGH, POLIS, STADT

city division   WARD, BOROUGH, DISTRICT

city, evil   SODOM, BABYLON, GOMORRAH

city named for a general   RENO

City of Angels   BANGKOK

City of Bridges   BRUGES

City of David   JERUSALEM

City of Kings   LIMA

City of Light   PARIS

City of Seven Hills   ROME

city of the dead   NECROPOLIS

city, *pert. to*   CIVIC, URBAN, MUNICIPAL

civet   FOSSA, GALET, GENET, RASSE, ZIBET, BONDAR, MUSANG, PAGUMA, ZIBETH, NANDINE, PERFUME, VIVERRA; *see* CAT

civic   LAY, CIVIL, SUAVE, URBAN, OPPIDAN, SECULAR

civic group   ELKS, LIONS, ROTARY

civil   LAY, HEND, CIVIC, HENDE, SUAVE, POLITE, URBANE

Civil Rights Memorial designer   LIN

Civil War battle   SHILOH, ATLANTA, BULLRUN, CORINTH, MALVERN, ANTIETAM, FAIROAKS, FRANKLIN, MANASSAS, APPOMATOX, BOONVILLE, NASHVILLE, VICKSBURG, CEDAR CREEK, CHARLESTON, COLD HARBOR, GETTYSBURG, PETERSBURG, WILDERNESS, CHATTANOOGA, CHICKAMAUGA, MURFREESBORO, SPOTSYLVANIA, FREDERICKSBURG, LOOKOUT MOUNTAIN, CHANCELLORSVILLE

Civil War commander   COX, LEE, HILL, HOOD, POLK, POPE, BANKS, BRAGG, BUELL, CANBY, CROOK, EARLY, EWELL, FLOYD, FOOTE, GRANT, LOGAN, MAURY, MEADE, MOSBY, PRICE, SCOTT, SYKES, BARRON, BUFORD, BUTLER, CUSTER, HOOKER, PORTER, SLOCUM, STUART, SUMNER, FORREST, JACKSON, PICKETT, MCCLELLAN

Civil War veteran   GAR

civilian   NONCOMBATANT

civilian clothes   CITS, MUFTI, CIVVIES

civilization   CULTURE

civilize   POLISH, REFINE, EDUCATE

claim   LIEN, EXACT, TITLE, USURP, ALLEGE, ARROGATE

clam   MYA, RAZOR, MACTRA, QUAHOG, COQUINA, GEODUCK, GOEDUCK, MOLLUSK, QUAHAUG, QUOHAUG, SHIPWORM, LITTLENECK, CHERRYSTONE

clam-digging locale   SHORE

clambake   PICNIC, COOKOUT

clamor   DIN, BERE, BUNK, NOISE, VOCAL

clamp   BOLT, VICE, VISE, BRACE, CLASP, GLAND

clan   GEN, OBE, SET, SIB, GENS, SEPT, SIOL, AYLLU, CASTE, GENOS, PHYLE, TRIBE, CLIQUE, FAMILY

clan, head of   ALDER, THANE, TANIST

clandestine   SLY, PRIVY, SECRET, FURTIVE

clang   TONK, JANGLE, STROKE

clangor   DIN, HUBBUB, UPROAR

clannish   SECRET, TRIBAL

clap   BLOW, APPLAUD

claret   BLOOD, MEDOC, GRAVES, BORDEAUX, SAUTERNE

clarify   FREE, CLEAR, RENDER, DEPURATE

clarinet   PIBGORN, HORNPIPE, STOCKHORN, CHALUMEAU

clarinet register   BREAK, THROAT, CLARINO, CLARION, CHALUMEAU

clarinet socket   BIRN

Clark   ROY, DICK

clash   JAR, COLLIDE, CONFLICT

clasp   HUG, HASP, OUCH, TACH, CINCH, MORSE, TACHE, BUCKLE, ENFOLD, INFOLD

class   ILK, CLAN, KIND, RACE, RANK, SORT, TYPE, CASTE, GENUS, ORDER, FAMILY, GENERA, HEIMIN, PHYLUM, KINGDOM, SEMINAR, SPECIES

classic **MODEL, SIMPLE, ANTIQUE, STYLISH, MASTERPIECE**
classical **PURE, ATTIC, CHASTE**
classical language **GREEK, LATIN, SANSKRIT**
classification **FILE, TAXIS, SYSTEM, CATEGORY**
classify **LIST, RANK, RATE, SORT, TYPE, GRADE, LABEL, ASSORT, TICKET, CATALOG**
clatter **DIN, RATTLE**
Claudia husband **PILATE**
clause **PLANK, PROVISO**
clavichord **SPINET**
clavier **PIANO, KEYBOARD**
claw(s) **HOOK, UNCI, CHELA, GRIFF, TALON, UNCUS, CHELAE, NIPPER, SCRAPE, UNGUIS, UNGULA**
clay **PUG, WAD, BOLE, LOAM, LUTE, TILE, ADOBE, ARGIL, BRICK, CRETA, LOESS, OCHER, OCHRE, TASCO, KAOLIN, SAGGAR, SAGGER, KAOLINE**
clay bed **GA(U)LT**
clay layer **SLOAM, SLOOM**
clayey **BOLAR, MALMY, LUTOSE**
clean **FAY, MOP, DUST, TRIM, BREAM, EMPTY, CHASTE, KOSHER, WET MOP**
cleaner **MOP, SOAP, BROOM, BRUSH, PURER, DUSTER, LOOFA(H), RAMROD, SCALER, SPONGE, VACUUM, SWEEPER**
cleanse **PURGE, PURIFY, DETERGE**
cleanser **SOAP, ARIEL, BORAX, DETERGENT, DISINFECTANT**
clear **FAY, NET, RID, FAIR, FREE, LUCID, SUNNY, ACQUIT, AWEIGH, LIMPID, LUCENT, GRAPHIC**
— and clear **LOUD**
clearing **SART, GLADE, MILPA, ASSART**
cleat **KEVEL, PITON, SPIKE, STRIP, BATTEN, BOLLARD**
cleavage **GULF, CLEFT, FISSION**
cleave **REND, RIVE, CLING, SPLIT, ADHERE, BISECT, SUNDER**
cleaver **FROE, FROW**
cleft **FENT, REFT, RIFT, RIMA, RIVA, CLOVEN, FORKED**
Clemenceau nickname **TIGER, TIGRE**
clement **MILD, LENIENT**

Clemens, Samuel **MARK, TWAIN**
clench **GRIP, HOLD**
Cleopatra's attendant **IRAS**
Cleopatra's country **EGYPT**
Cleopatra's lover **ANTONY, CAESAR**
Cleopatra's needle **OBELISK**
clergy **ABBE, DEAN, CANON, CLERK, PADRE, PRIOR, RABBI, VICAR, CLERIC, CURATE, DIVINE, PARSON, PASTOR, PRIEST, RECTOR;** see **CHURCHMAN**
clergy residence **MANSE, RECTORY, VICARAGE, PARSONAGE**
clerical collar **RABATO**
clerk **AGENT, SCRIBE, TELLER**
clever **DEFT, HEND, CANNY, HENDE, SMART, ARTFUL, HABILE, VULPINE**
clew **CUE, BALL, HINT, SKEIN**
cliche **SAW, TRUISM, FORMULA, PLATITUDE**
click **AGREE;** see **DETENT**
client **USER, BUYER, PATRON, CONSUMER, CUSTOMER**
clientele **TRADE, CUSTOMERS, PATRONAGE**
cliff **CRAG, KLIP, SCAR, BLUFF, CLEVE, SCARF**
climax **ACME, APEX, APOGEE, SUMMIT, ZENITH**
climb **SHIN, SOAR, GRIMP, SCALE, SPEEL, ASCEND, ASCENT, CLAMBER**
climbing gear **CLEAT, PITON, CRAMPON, CARABINER**
clime **REALM, TRACT, REGION**
clinch **HUG, GRIP, NAIL, CLAMP, RIVET, CLENCH**
cling **HANG, RELY, STICK, TRUST, ADHERE, COHERE**
Clinton's ditch **ERIE(CANAL)**
Clio field **HISTORY**
Clio relative **ERATO**
clip **CUT, MOW, BARB, PARE, SNIP, TRIM, PRUNE, SHEAR, WHACK**
clique **SET, CLUB, GANG, RING, CABAL, JUNTO, COTERIE**
cloaca **PRIVY, SEWER**
cloak **ABA, HAP, CAPA, HIDE, MASK, PALL, WRAP, BLIND, CAPOT, CHOGA, MANTA, CAPOTE, JOSEPH, MANTLE, PONCHO, SARAPE, SERAPE, SHIELD, VISITE, PELISSE, CARDINAL, MANTILLA;** see **CAPE**

cloak and —   DAGGER
clock   NEF, BELL, DIAL, TIME,
              METER, TIMER, VERGE,
                                WATCH
clock part   DIAL, HAND, PAWL,
        BUNDY, CHIME, PEISE,
    DETENT, PALLET, PENDULUM
Clockwork Orange word   GLOM,
        DROOG, SOLVO, VIDDY,
            BOLSHY, NADSAT
clod   SOD, BOOR, DOLT, LOAM,
        LUMP, CLUMP, EARTH
clog(s)   JAM, BALK, CURB,
        GETA, CHOKE, SABOT,
    CHOPIN, GALOSH, DAGGLE,
        PATTEN, CHOPINE
cloister   CELL, STOA, ABBEY,
        CLOSE, FRIARY, PRIORY,
        CONVENT, NUNNERY
clone ancestor   ORTET
clone member   RAMET
close   CAM, HUG, CALK, CODA,
        DITT, NEAR, NIGH, SEAL,
        SEAM, SEEL, SHUT, TAUT,
        DENSE, ESTOP, FINAL,
        MUGGY, STIVY, CHINSE,
        FINALE, STINGY, STUFFY,
        NIGGARD, OCCLUDE
close ranks   SERRY
closefisted   CHEAP, TIGHT,
    FRUGAL, STINGY, MISERLY
closet   WC, EWRY, AMBRY,
        CUDDY, EWERY, LOCKER
closet item   RACK, HANGER,
                SKELETON
closure   LIEN, CLOSING,
                STOPPAGE
clot   GEL, GOB, JELL, LUMP,
        MASS, CRUOR, THICKEN,
                COAGULATE
cloth   BRIN, PATA, CRAPE,
    TAPET, CHEYNEY; see p. 535
cloth, blemish in   RIP, SNAG,
        TEAR, AMPER
clothe   TOG, DECK, GARB,
        GIRD, VEST, ARRAY, DRAPE,
        ENDUE, INVEST
clothed   CLAD, ATTIRED
clothes   GARB, WEAR, DRESS,
        ATTIRE, OUTFIT, RAIMENT,
        APPAREL, ENSEMBLE,
                WARDROBE
clothes stand   RACK, TREE
clothes, work   APRON, DENIM,
        SMOCK, UNIFORM,
                COVERALL
clotheshorse   FOP, DANDY,
                BRUMMEL
clothing   RIG, BRAT, DUDS,

        GARB, GEAR, RAGS, TOGS,
    ARRAY, BUREL, DICKY, DRESS,
    HABIT, KHAKI, LUNGI, SLOPS,
        SMOCK, ATTIRE, DICKEY,
    FINERY, KHAKEE, LUNGYI,
        OUTFIT, TIGHTS, APPAREL,
            CORSLET, COSTUME,
    HARNESS, NEGLIGE, PAISLEY,
        RAIMENT, REGALIA,
        ROMPERS, TOGGERY,
        VESTURE, CLEADING,
        CORSELET, FRIPPERY,
        NEGLIGEE, OVERALLS,
        PINAFORE; see p. 743
clothing store   TOGGERY,
            HABERDASHERY
cloud(s)   COMA, RACK, SCUD,
    SMUR, CIRRI, NUBIA, RACKS,
    VAPOR, CIRRUS, CUMULI,
    NEBULA, NIMBUS, STRATI,
    CUMULUS, NEBULAE,
    STRATUS, NUBECULA
cloudburst   DELUGE,
                DOWNPOUR
cloudless   CLEAR, SUNNY
cloudy   DIM, HAZY, FOGGY,
    FILMY, LOWERY, OVERCAST
clout   BUMP, CUFF, NAIL, SLAP,
        SWAT, PATCH, POWER,
                INFLUENCE
cloven   CLEFT, SPLIT
cloven-footed   FISSIPED
clover   HAGI, HUBAM, MEDIC,
        SULLA, ALSIKE, LADINO,
    NARDOO, ALFALFA, MELILOT,
        TREFOIL, SHAMROCK
clown   HOB, BOZO, GOFF,
    ZANY, PUNCH, JESTER,
        RUSTIC, BUFFOON
clownish   GAWKY, LOUTISH
cloy   CLOG, FILL, GLUT, PALL,
    SATE, GORGE, SATIATE,
                SURFEIT
cloying   SWEET, SUGARY
club   BAT, KIRI, MACE, MERE,
    PATU, POLT, BILLY, STAFF,
    STICK, WADDY, CUDGEL,
    LIBBET, MACANA, MARREE,
    NULLAH, TAIAHA, BLUDGEON,
        BLACKJACK, SHILLALAH,
    KNOBKERRIE; see GOLF; see p. 503
club, social   USO, DOES, ELKS,
    TEAM, BRITH, LAMBS, LIONS,
        LODGE, MOOSE, ORDER,
    ZONTA, FRIARS, MASONS,
    ROTARY, KIWANIS, SOCIETY,
        SOROSIS, SORORITY
clubfoot   TALIPED, TALIPES
club-shaped   CLAVATE

clue	CUE, KEY, TIP, HINT	Coast Guard member	ENS(IGN), SPAR
clump	CLOD, MOTT, TUFT, TURB, BUNCH, MOTTE, PATCH	coast, *pert. to*	ORARIAN, LITTORAL, RIPARIAN
clumsily, move	FLOB, PLOD, CLUMP	coaster	BOB, LUGE, SLED, ROLLER(COASTER)
clumsy	AWK, GAUCHE, OAFISH, AWKWARD	coat	ABA, FUR, TOG, HAIR, HIDE, PELT, RIND, SKIN,
clumsy person	OX, OAF, BULL, SWAB, KLUTZ, LUMMOX		WOOL, CLOAK, CRUST, GLAZE, LAYER, PARKA, PLATE,
cluster	NEP, CYME, TUFT, BUNCH, CLUMP, SORUS, SPRIG, ANADEM, RACEME		TERNE, ANORAK, CAFTAN, COATEE, KAFTAN, PATINA, PELAGE, SURCOAT, SURTOUT,
clutch	CLUM, GRIP, HOLD, GRASP		WRAPPER, MACKINAW, PINAFORE, GABARDINE,
clutter	MESS, JUMBLE, LITTER, DISORDER		GABERDINE, INVERNESS, REDINGOTE; *see* OVERCOAT
Clytemnestra lover	AEGISTHUS	coat part	LAPEL, SKIRT, SLEEVE
Clytemnestra relative	LEDA, ELECTRA, ORESTES, AGAMEMNON	coat with flour	DREDGE
		coax	JOLE, EGG, CANT, LURE, CAJOLE, ENTICE, WHEEDLE
coach	BUS, FLY, STAGE, TUTOR, JARVEY, CARRIER, DILIGENCE; *see* HACK	cobble	MEND, PAVE, BOTCH, PATCH
coach dog	DALMATIAN	cobbler	SOLER, SUTOR, SOUTER, CRISPIN
Coach names	JUDY, KELLY, DAUBER, HAYDEN, LUTHER, VANDAM, VANDYKE	cobbler's tool	AWL, LAST, ROZET
coachman	FLY, JEHU, WHIP, PILOT, DRIVER	cobra	NAG, HAJE, NAGA, NAIA, NAJA, MAMBA, RINGHALS; *see* VIPER
coagulate	GEL, SET, CAKE, CLOT, CURD, JELL, CURDLE, POSSET, CONGEAL	cobweb	NET, TRAP, SNARE
coagulant	RENNET, STYPTIC	Coca-Cola founder	(ASA)CANDLER
coal	COB, JET, BASS, COKE, DUFF, SMUT, SWAD, EMBER, CARBON, CINDER, LIGNITE	cocaine	COKE, DUST, SNOW
		cocaine source	COCA, CUCA
		Cochin China	VIETNAM
coal box	DAN, HOD, SCUTTLE	cock	TAP, HEAP, RICK, PRIME, FAUCET
coal dust	ASH, CULM, DUFF, SMUT, SLACK	cockade	KNOT, ROSETTE
coal refuse	ASH, COOM, CULM, SLAG, SMUT, SOOT, COOMB, CINDER, CLINKER	cockatoo	ARARA, GALAH, CORELLA
		cockcrow	DAWN, DAYBREAK
coal size	EGG, NUT, PEA, STOVE, WALLSEND	cocker	PET, CODDLE, FONDLE, PAMPER, SPANIEL
coal tar derivative	PITCH, CREOSOL, BITUMEN, CREOSOTE, TOLUENE, TOLUOL(E)	cockeyed	AWRY, DRUNK, CROOKED
		cockle	GITH, KILN, OAST, SHELL
		cockney worker	ARRY
coalesce	BLEND, MERGE	cockpit	CAB, NOSE, ARENA, CABIN, NACELLE
coalition	AXIS, BLOC, UNION, LEAGUE, MERGER	Cockpit of Europe	BELGIUM
		cocktail	*see p. 564*
coals, rake over the	CENSURE, CRITICIZE	cocky	PERT, PERKY, PROUD, JAUNTY
coarse	RUDE, CRASS, CRUDE, GROSS, RIBALD, VULGAR	coconut	COCO, PATE, COPRA, NARGIL, NOGGIN
coast	RIPA, BEACH, GLIDE, SLIDE, SEASIDE	coconut fiber	COIR, KOIR, KYAR, COIRE
Coast Guard boat	CUTTER	cocoon	POD, CLEW, KELL

cod(-like fish) **BIB, CUSK, GADE, HAKE, HAIK, LING, LOTA, ODAX, POOR, POUT, TUSK, GADID, GADUS, SCROD, SPRAG, TORSK, BURBOT, GADOID, HADDIE, LAWYER, MURRAY, TOMCOD, WACHNA, BACALAO, BEARDIE, CODFISH, CODLING, DOGFISH, EELPOUT, HADDOCK, KEELING, POLLACK, POLLOCK, WHITING, STOCKFISH**

cod, *pert.* to **GADOID**
COD part **ON, CASH, DELIVERY**
coddle **BABY, PAMPER**
code **KEY, LAW, RULE, CODEX, CIPHER**
code word **DAH, DOT, KEY, SESAME**
codfish, young **SPRAG, CODLING**
codger **CUSS, CHURL, MISER, NIGGARD**
codicil **RIDER, SEQUEL, DIPLOMA**
coerce **COW, CURB, BULLY, FORCE, COMPEL**
— Coeur **SACRE**
Coeus relative **LETO**
coffee **MUD, RIO, CAFE, JAVA, MOCHA, BRAZIL, SANTOS, CHICORY, SUMATRA, SUCCORY, ESPRESSO, CAPPUCCINO**
coffee bean **NIBS**
coffee companion **DONUT, DANISH**
coffee cup **FINJAN**
coffee cup holder **ZARF**
coffee grind **DRIP, FINE, PERC, SILEX, COARSE, VACUUM**
coffee grinder **MILL**
coffee shop **CAFE, DINER, TEAROOM**
coffeemaker **URN, SILEX, PERCOLATOR**
coffeepot part **BIGGIN**
coffer **ARK, DAM, PYX, CHEST, CAISSON**
coffin **BIER, CASKET, LITTER, PINEBOX**
cog **GEAR, PAWL, CHEAT, CHUCK, TENON, TOOTH, WHEEDLE**
cogent **VALID, POTENT, STRONG**
cogitate **CHEW, MULL, THINK**
cognate **AKIN, ALLIED, RELATED**

cognizance **KEN, HEED, NOTICE**
cognizant **HEP, ONTO, AWAKE, AWARE**
cognomen **NAME, EPITHET, SURNAME**
coheir **(CO)PARCENER**
cohere **BIND, CLING, STICK**
coiffure **HAIRDO**
coign **ANGLE, CORNER**
coil **CAP, ANSA, CLUE, CURL, LOOP, ROLL, WIND, HELIX, QUERL, TWINE, TWIST, WHORL**
coin **JOE, CASH, MINT, BRASS, INVENT, SPECIE, TALENT;** *see p. 638*
coin box **PYX, TILL, METER**
coin edge **NIG, (K)NURL**
coin roll **ROULEAU**
coincide **FIT, JIBE, AGREE, TALLY**
colander **SIEVE, BOLTER, STRAINER**
cold **ICY, RAW, ROUP, ALGID, GELID, RHEUM, CORYZA, FRIGID, CATARRH**
cold blood **SANGFROID**
cold sore **HERPES**
cold weather clothing **BOOTS, PARKA, ANORAK, GLOVES, EARMUFFS, THERMALS**
cole *see* **CABBAGE**
Cole **NATALIE, NAT(KING)**
cole — **SLAW**
Cole Porter character **KATE**
Cole Porter musical **CANCAN, JUBILEE, KISS ME KATE**
Coleridge river **ALPH**
Colette heroine **GIGI**
Colette novel **DUO, GIGI, SIDO**
collaborator **LAVAL, QUISLING**
collapse **FALL, RUIN, CAVEIN, DOWNFALL**
collar **LEI, NAB, CANG, ETON, RING, RUFF, CATCH, FANON, ORALE, CANGUE, DICKY, BERTHA, CARCAN, CHOKER, DICKEY, GORGET, RABATO, REBATO, TORQUE, CARCANET**
collate **ALIGN, GATHER, COMPARE, COMPILE**
collation **TEA, MEAL, REPAST, LUNCHEON**
colleague **COMRADE, PARTNER, ASSOCIATE**
collect **BAG, MASS, LEVY, REAP, AMASS, GLEAN, GARNER, PRAYER, SHEAVE, COMPILE**

collected CALM, COOL, SERENE, COMPOSED
collection ANA, SET, CLAN, HEAP, MASS, RAFT, STACK, SYLVA, CORPUS, ROSARY, SORITE, THRONG, DOSSIER, SORITES; see BEVY; see p. 523
collective COOP, KOLKHOZ
collector's item CURIO, RARITY
colleen GIRL, LASS, MAID
college TOL, GUILD, LYCEE, BREVET, LYCEUM, NORMAL, ACADEMY, SEMINARY
college building GYM, LAB, DORM, FRAT
college class LECTURE, SEMINAR, TUTORIAL
college grounds LAWN, QUAD, CAMPUS
college officer DON, DEAN, BEADLE, BURSAR, DOCENT, REGENT, PROCTOR, REGISTRAR
college student COED, SOPH, FROSH, PLEBE, JUNIOR, SENIOR, FRESHMAN, SOPHOMORE
college term QUARTER, SEMESTER, TRIMESTER
colleges and nicknames see p. 524
collide BUMP, CRASH, CANNON, HURTLE
collier see MINER
collision CRASH, PILEUP, CONFLICT, FENDERBENDER
colloid GEL, SOL
colloquialism IDIOM
colloquy TALK, PARLEY, CONFERENCE
collude PLOT, SCHEME, CONNIVE
Colombia, capital of BOGOTA
Colombian city/town CALI, PASTO, NEIVA, BOGOTA, CUCUTA, IBAGUE, ZARZAL, PEREIRA, MANIZALES
Colombian district META, CAUCA, CESAR, CHOCO, HUILA, ARAUCA, BOYACA, CALDAS, NARINO, VAUPES, BOLIVAR, CORDOBA
Colombian gulf URABA, CUPICA, TIBUGA
Colombian lake UVA, CHAIRA, LAGUNA
Colombian money PESO, REAL, CONDOR, CENTAVO
Colombian mountain CHITA, HUILA, PURACE, TOLIMA

Colombian neighbor PERU, BRAZIL, PANAMA, ECUADOR, VENEZUELA
Colombian river META, CAUCA, ATRATO, VAUPES, CAQUETA, ORINOCO, VICHADA, APAPORIS, GUAVIARE, PUTUMAYO, MAGDALENA
Colombian volcano PASTO, PURACE
Colombian weight SACO, CARGA, LIBRA, QUILATE, QUINTAL
colonel's command BRIGADE
colonel's insignia EAGLE
colonizer ANT, OECIST, SETTLER, PLANTER
colonnade STOA, PORTICO, TERRACE
color(s) DYE, HUE, FLAG, TINT, PAINT, SHADE, TINGE, BANNER, ENSIGN; see p. 531
color blindness DALTONISM
color brilliance CHROMA
color, primary RED, BLUE, GREEN, INDIGO, ORANGE, VIOLET, YELLOW
color vehicle MAGILP, MEGILP
Colorado see also p. 615
Colorado city/town ASPEN, CRAIG, CORTEZ, DENVER, PUEBLO, BOULDER, DURANGO, GREELEY
Colorado county BACA, BENT, LAKE, MESA, PARK, WELD, YUMA, DELTA, EAGLE, KIOWA, LOGAN, OTERO, OURAY, ROUTT, CUSTER, GILPIN, MOFFAT, SUMMIT
Colorado Indian UTE, PUEBLO
Colorado lake BARR, CLAY, TWIN, AVERY, HENRY, GRANBY
Colorado mountain BALD, MESA, BAKER, ETHEL, SHEEP, ELBERT, SILVER, ZIRKEL
Colorado park ESTES, MESA, VERDE
Colorado river ELK, PINOS, SLATE, YAMPA, MANCOS, LARAMIE, ARKANSAS, COLORADO
Colorado tributary GILA, GREEN
colorful VIVID
coloring agent DYE, PIGMENT
colorist PAINTER
colorless WAN, DRAB, DULL, PALE, ASHEN, CLEAR, ALBINO, PALLID

colossus	TITAN
Colossus sculptor	CHARES
Columbia	US(A), AMERICA
Columbia river fish	SALMON
Columbia tributary	SNAKE, KOOTENAY
Columbus's captain	PINZON
Columbus's place	GENOA, PALOS
Columbus's ship	NINA, PINTA, SANTA MARIA
Columbus's son	DIEGO
column	LAT, ANTA, FUST, LOSS, TENS, DORIC, IONIC, STELE, TORSE, TORSO, PILLAR, PROFIT, PILASTER
column figure	TELAMON, ATLANTES, CARYATID
column, ring of annulated	BAGUE
columnist	see JOURNALIST
coma	STUPOR, TRANCE, CATALEPSY
Comanche	SNAKE, PADUCA; see p. 730
comb	CARD, RAKE, CREST, CURRY, RIDGE, TEASE
combat	COPE, DUEL, TILT, FIGHT, JOUST, STOUR, SKIRMISH
combative	WARLIKE, MILITANT, PUGNACIOUS, AGGRESSIVE
combination	CABAL, JUNTO, TRUST, UNION, CARTEL, LEAGUE, MERGER, FACTION
combine	MIX, WED, JOIN, POOL, RING, BLEND, MARRY, CARTEL, SPLICE
combustible	FIERY; see FUEL
come	SUE, NEAR, (A)RISE, ENSUE, REACH, ACCRUE, ADVENE, ARRIVE
come and —	GO
come about	TACK, OCCUR, HAPPEN
come across	PAYUP, DELIVER, DISCOVER
come around	AGREE, ACCEPT, ASSENT
come back	RECUR, RETURN
come by	GET, GAIN, OBTAIN
come clean	(CON)FESS
come down	ALIGHT
comd down with	GET, CATCH, DEVELOP
come forth	JET, GUSH, SPEW, ISSUE, EMERGE, EMERSE, EMANATE
come in	ENTER

come into view	LOOM, RISE
come short	MISS
come to	TOTAL, AWAKE(N), REVIVE
come to grief	FAIL, FALL
come to pass	OCCUR, HAPPEN, TRANSPIRE
comeback	ANSWER, RETORT, RIPOSTE, RECOVERY
comedian	WAG, WIT, BUFF, CARD, ZANY, BUFFO, ANTIC, CLOWN, COMIC, JOKER, PANIC, JESTER, BUFFOON, FARCEUR
comedians, famous	see p. 539
comedown	DIP, FALL, CRASH, DOWNER, DESCENT
comedy	FARCE, HUMOR, SATIRE, TRAVESTY, SLAPSTICK
comedy, muse of	THALIA
Comedy of Errors character	LUCE, PINCH, AEGEON, ANGELO, DROMIO, ADRIANA, SOLINUS
comely	FAIR, BUXOM, PRETTY, SEEMLY
come-on	BAIT, LURE
comestible	FOOD, EDIBLE, VICTUAL
comet part	COMA, HEAD, TAIL, TRAIN
Comet partner	CUPID
comet path	ORBIT
comets	see p. 741
comfit	see CANDY
comfort	SOP, EASE, REPOSE, SOLACE, CONSOLE
comfortable	COSH, COZY, FEIL, SNUG, LITHE, PLEASING
comforter	PUFF, QUILT, SCARF, PACIFIER
comic(al)	ZANY, DROLL, FUNNY, ABSURD, RISIBLE; see COMEDIAN
comic strip	see CARTOON
coming	DUE, ADVENT, ARRIVAL
command	BID, HEST, FIAT, ORDER, BEHEST, ENJOIN, DICTATE, MANDATE
commander	AGA, CID, AGHA, CAID, QAID, SIRDAR, ALCAIDE
commandeer	SEIZE, HIJACK
Commandments, Ten	DECALOG(UE)
commando	RAIDER, GREENBERET

comme il — FAUT
commence OPEN, BEGIN, START
commencement START, OPENING, INCEPTION, GRADUATION
Commencement Bay city TACOMA
commend KEN, LAUD, EXTOL, COMMIT
commensurate EVEN, EQUAL, ACCORDANT
comment(ary) NOTE, ASIDE, GLOSS, GEMARA, POSTIL, REMARK, DESCANT, EXEGESIS, GLOSSARY, SCHOLION
commentator CRITIC, ANCHOR, REVIEWER, COLUMNIST
commerce TRADE, BARTER, TRAFFIC
commercial AD(VERT), SPOT, TRADING, MERCANTILE
comminate BAN, CURSE, THREATEN
comminute MILL, CRUSH, GRIND
commiseration PITY, RUTH, EMPATHY
commissary PX, CANTEEN
commission PROXY, BREVET, CHARGE, DEPUTE, ORDAIN
commit ASSIGN, CONSIGN, ENTRUST, INTRUST
committee GROUP, PANEL, JUNTA
commodious ROOMY, SPACIOUS
commodity WARE, GOODS, STAPLE, PRODUCT
common LOW, PLEB, JOINT, PLAIN, TRITE, USUAL, COARSE, MUTUAL, ORNERY, VULGAR, CURRENT, GENERAL, PLEBEIAN
Common Market EEC
Common Sense author PAINE
commoner PLEB, PROLE, CITIZEN
commonly ALOT, USUALLY, GENERALLY, FREQUENTLY
commonplace BANAL, PROSY, TRITE, CLICHE, TRUISM, BROMIDE, HUMDRUM, PROSAIC
commotion ADO, CHOP, FUSS, STIR, TODO, FUROR, BUSTLE, CLAMOR, HUBBUB, POTHER, WELTER

commune ANS, ATA, EDE, EPE, MIR SHAR, IMPART, KOLHOZ, KIBBUTZ, KOLKHOZ, TOWNSHIP
communion HOST, MASS, SECT, HOUSEL, RAPPORT, VIATICUM, EUCHARIST
communion item AMA, PIX, PYX, HOST, FANON, PATEN, WAFER, EULOGIA
communist RED, COMRADE, LEFTIST
Communist leader TITO, HUSAK, DUBCEK; see RUSSIAN
Communist newspaper PRAVDA, WORKER, IZVESTIA
community MIR, TOWN, VILLAGE
Comoros, capital of MORONI
Comoros island MOHELI, ANJOUAN, MAYOTTE
Comoros money FRANC
compact BOND, ETUI, HARD, TRIG, DENSE, SOLID, CASTEL, VANITY, COVENANT
companion PAL, PEER, MATE, CRONY, ESCORT, SPOUSE, ACHATES, COMPEER, CONSORT, PARTNER
company CIE, LTD, BAND, BODY, FERE, FIRM, TROOP, TROUPE, BATTERY, PHALANX
company name, part of CO, INC, LLC
comparative THAN, EQUAL, RELATIVE
compare EVEN, LIKEN, SEMBLE, COLLATE
comparison SIMILE, ANALOGY, PARABLE
compartment BAY, BIN, CELL, CABIN, LOCKER, SECTION
compass GYRO, AMBIT, GAMUT, SWEEP, ENCLOSE, TRAMMEL
compass part VANE, GIMBAL, BINNACLE
compass point NE, NW, SE, SW, ENE, ESE, NNE, NNW, SSE, SSW, WNW, WSW, R(H)UMB
compassion RUE, PITY, RUTH, GRACY, MERCY
compeer EQUAL, MATCH
compel MAKE, FORCE, IMPEL, COERCE
compendium BRIEF, DIGEST, PRECIS, SUMMARY, SYLLABUS

compensate	PAY, ATONE, REPAY, TALLY
compensation	UTU, BALM, REWARD, SALARY, REDRESS
compete	VIE, COPE, MATCH, EMULATE
competent	APT, SANE, ADEPT, CAPAX
competition	FEIS, MATCH, STRIFE, RIVALRY
competitor	VIER, RIVAL, OPPONENT
compilation	*see* COLLECTION
compile	EDIT, SELECT, ARRANGE, COLLATE
complacent	SMUG, BLASE, COCKY
complain	CARP, FRET, FUSS, KICK, GRIPE, WHINE, GROUSE, REPINE, GRUMBLE
complaisant	CIVIL, SUAVE, POLITE, AFFABLE, LENIENT
complement	SET, UNIT, OFFSET
complementry	MATCHING
complete	END, QUITE, THORO, TOTAL, UTTER, PLENARY
completely	FULLY, IN ALL, IN TOTO, WHOLLY
complex	MAZE, MIXED, KNOTTY, NETWORK, TANGLED, MANIFOLD, SYNDROME, INTRICATE
complexion	HUE, BLEE, TINT, TINGE
complicate	INTORT, TANGLE, WORSEN, PERPLEX
complicated	KNOTTY, COMPLEX, TANGLED
complication	NODE, NODI, NODUS, SNARL
complicity	COLLUSION
compliment	LAUD, EXTOL, EULOGY
complimentary	FREE, KIND, GRATIS, GRACIOUS
comply	OBEY, ADAPT, ACCEDE
component	PART, UNIT, FACTOR, ELEMENT, INTEGRAL
comport	ACT, BEHAVE, DEMEAN, INVOLVE
composed	COOL, QUIET, SOBER, WROTE
composers, famous	*see p. 539*
composers' group	ASC, BMI, ASCAP
composite	COLLAGE, MONTAGE

composition	NOME, OPUS, CENTO, ESSAY, PIECE, SCENA, THEME; *see* MUSIC
compositor	TYPO, PRINTER
composure	MIEN, POISE, QUIET, REPOSE, BALANCE
compound	MIX, OLIO, AMIDE, OXIDE, FARRAGO, MIXTURE
comprehend	GET, SEE, GRASP, LATCH, SENSE
comprehension	KEN, GRIP, GRASP, COMMAND, MASTERY
compress	PAD, STUPE, DIGEST, REDUCE, SHRINK, ABRIDGE, BANDAGE, CURTAIL, DEFLATE, PLEDGET, SQUEEZE, CONDENSE
comprise	EMBODY, INCLUDE
compromise	BARGAIN, MEDIATE, NEGOTIATE
compulsion	FORCE, DURESS, STRESS
compulsory service	DRAFT, ANGARY, ANGARIA, SLAVERY
compunction	QUALM, REGRET, SCRUPLE
compute	TALLY, TOTAL, ASSESS, FIGURE, RECKON
computer	PC, CPU, MAC, ENIAC, LAPTOP, TABLET, UNIVAC, DESKTOP, PALMTOP, NOTEBOOK, PORTABLE, MACINTOSH, MAINFRAME, PROCESSOR, WORKSTATION
computer key	ALT, DEL, END, ESC, HELP, HOME, SHIFT, OPTION, RETURN, CONTROL
computer language	ADA, JAVA, LISP, LOGO, UNIX, ALGOL, BASIC, COBOL, LINUX, PILOT, PASCAL, PROLOG, SNOBOL, FORTRAN
computer maker	DEC, HAL, IBM, MAC, VAX, DELL, AMIGA, APPLE, ATARI, ENIAC, ABACUS, ANALOG, UNIVAC, DIGITAL, GATEWAY
computer operating system	CPM, DDS, UNIX, LINUX, MACOS, WINDOWS
computer pattern	FRACTAL
computer program	APP(LICATION)
computer term	IO, BIT, BUG, CPU, CRT, DOS, GUI, LAN, RAM, ROM, BAUD, BETA, BIOS, BOOT, BYTE, CHIP, DATA, DISK, FIFO, FILE, GIGO, PORT,

ASCII, CDROM, CRASH,
DEBUG, MODEM, BUFFER,
CURSOR
comrade PAL, CHUM, BILLY,
BUDDY, CRONY, TOVARICH
con ANTI, TAKE, CHEAT,
STING, STUDY, VERSUS,
AGAINST
con — BRIO, MOTO, AMORE
concatenate JOIN, LINK,
CHAIN, UNITE, CONNECT
concave DISHED, HOLLOW
concave molding SCOTIA
conceal WRY, FEAL, HIDE,
MASK, PALM, VEIL, CACHE,
CLOAK, ELOI(G)N
concealed COVERT, HIDDEN,
INNER, LATENT, PERDU,
SECRET, VEILED, COVERED,
LARVATE, CAMOUFLAGED
concede ADMIT, GRANT,
YIELD
conceit FLAM, VANITY,
EGOTISM
conceited person PRIG, SNOB,
EGO(T)IST, PEACOCK
conceive PLAN, BRAIN, FRAME,
IDEATE, IMAGINE
concentrate AIM, FIX, FOCUS,
SYRUP, UNIFY, ELIXIR,
DISTILL, ESSENCE, EXTRACT,
CONDENSE
concentration camp *see* PRISON
CAMP
conception IDEA, FANCY,
IMAGE, NOTION
concern CARE, FIRM, SAKE,
WORRY, AFFAIR, REGARD,
RELATE
concerning RE, FOR, ANEN,
INRE, ABOUT, ANEN(S)T
concert hall ODEON, ALBERT,
FISHER, LYCEUM, MASSEY,
ACADEMY, CARNEGIE
conch CHANK, SHELL,
COCKLE, WINKLE
conciliate EASE, PACIFY,
APPEASE, PLACATE
conciliatory GENTLE, IRENIC,
WINNING
concise CURT, BRIEF, PITHY,
TERSE, SUCCINCT
conclave CLOSET, MEETING
conclude REST, INFER,
DEDUCE, FINISH, SETTLE,
TERMINATE
conclusion END, CODA, FINIS,
RESULT, OUTCOME,
DECISION

conclusive FINAL, COGENT,
TELLING
concoct MIX, BREW, COOK,
HATCH
concord PACT, AMITY,
TREATY, EUPHONY,
RAPPORT
concordat TREATY, COMPACT,
ENTENTE
concourse MALL, CROWD,
THRONG
concrete HARD, REAL, BETON,
ACTUAL, CEMENT, MORTAR
concubine DASI, HETAERA,
ODALISK, MISTRESS
concur JIBE, AGREE, ASSENT
concussion SHOCK, IMPACT
condemn BAN, DOOM, FILE,
BLAME, DECRY, CENSURE
condense CUT, DECOCT,
DISTIL, SHRINK, DISTILL,
COMPRESS
condescend DEIGN, FAVOR,
STOOP
condign FITTING, SUITABLE
condiment SOY, CAPER, CHILI,
CUMIN, CURRY, COMINO,
HYSSOP, PEPPER, RELISH,
CANELLA, CAYENNE,
MUSTARD, PIMENTO,
CAPSICUM, CARDAMOM,
CARDAMON, CHARLOCK; *see*
SEASONING, SPICE
condition IF, TERM, FACET,
PHASE, PLIGHT, STATUS,
PROVISO, STIPULATION
condolence PITY, SYMPATHY
condone PARDON, FORGIVE
condor *see* VULTURE
conduce AID, LEND, TEND,
EFFECT
conduct RUN, CONVEY,
CONVOY, DEMEAN, ESCORT,
MANAGE
conductor CAD, MUTI, WIRE,
DAVIS, GUIDE, MEHTA,
OZAWA, SOLTI, SZELL,
ABBADO, BOULEZ, LEADER,
WALTER, BEECHAM, CARRIER,
KARAJAN, MAESTRO,
ORMANDY, CICERONE,
BERNSTEIN, LEINSDORF,
SCHERCHEN, STOKOWSKI,
TOSCANINI; *see*
BANDLEADER
conduit ADIT, DUCT, MAIN,
DRAIN, CHANNEL
cone COP, CONOID, CORNET,
FUNNEL, VOLCANO, STROBILE

— cone **SNO**
cone-shaped **CONIC, CONOID, PINEAL, CONICAL**
coney **DUPE, GULL, HARE, DAMAN, HYRAX, RABBIT**
confection *see* **CANDY**
confederate **REB, ALLY, REBEL, UNITE, ABETTOR, PARTNER;** *see* **CIVIL WAR**
Confederate money **BLUEBACK**
Confederate president **DAVIS**
confederation **BUND, UNION, LEAGUE**
confer **DUB, AWARD, ENDOW, BESTOW, PARLEY, CONSULT**
conference **SYNOD, BIGTEN, CAUCUS, CONFAB, PALAVER**
conference site **LOCARNO**
confess **OWN, ADMIT, REVEAL, SHRIVE**
confession **CREDO, CREED, AVOWAL, SHRIFT**
confessional **BOOTH**
Confessions author **ROUSSEAU**
confidant(e) **CRONY, FRIEND, INTIMATE**
confide **AFFY, TRUST, COMMIT, ENTRUST, INTRUST**
confident **SURE, SECURE, CERTAIN**
confidential **PRIVY, SECRET, ESOTERIC**
confine **BOX, DAM, HEM, PEN, CAGE, COOP, JAIL, CHECK, CRAMP, LIMIT, BORDER, INTERN**
confined **ILL, ABED, PENT**
confinement **CUSTODY, CAPTIVITY, DETENTION, CHILDBIRTH**
confirm **RATIFY, VERIFY, ENDORSE**
confirmation **RITE, SACRAMENT**
confiscate **SEIZE, ESCHEAT, IMPOUND**
conflagration **FIRE, BLAZE**
conflict **WAR, BOUT, FRAY, OPPOSE, STRIFE**
conflicting **CONTRARY, OPPOSING**
conform **FIT, ADAPT, COMPLY**
conformist **YESMAN, STICKLER**
confound **FAZE, STUN, BAFFLE, NONPLUS**
confront **DEFY, FACE, BRAVE**
Confucius principle **TAO**
Confucius work **ANNALS, I CHING, CHUN CHIU**

confuse **ABASH, BEMUSE, FUDDLE, JUMBLE, FLUSTER, NONPLUS**
confused **ASEA, MUZZY, WESTY, ADDLED**
confusion **ADO, MESS, MOIL, BABEL, CHAOS, MELEE, SNAFU, BEDLAM, JUMBLE, TOHU(BOHU)**
confute **REBUT, REFUTE, DISPROVE**
congeal **GEL, SET, JELL, HARDEN, PECTIZE**
congenial **KINDRED, FRIENDLY, AGREEABLE**
congenital **INBORN, INNATE, NATIVE**
conger *see* **EEL**
conglomerate **AMASS, MERGER, SYNDICAT(E), CORPORATION, MULTINATIONAL**
Congo, capital of **KINSHASA, BRAZZAVILLE**
Congo city/town **KAYES, MPOUYA, OWANDO, ZANAGA**
Congo discoverer **CAM, CAO**
Congo, former name **ZAIRE**
Congo language *see* **BANTU**
Congo leader **ADOULA, MOBUTU, YOULOU, LUMUMBA, TSHOMBE, KASAVUBU**
Congo money **FRANC**
Congo national park **ODZALA**
Congo neighbor **CAR, GABON, ZAIRE, ANGOLA, CABINDA, CAMEROON**
Congo people **BANTU, SIMBA, BALALI, BATEKE, BAVILI, HAMITE**
Congo river **DJA, CONGO, ALIMA, KADEI, NGOKA, NIARI, NKENI, UBANGI**
Congo tributary **UELE, KASAI, LINDI, UBANGI, ARUWIMI, LUALABA, LUAPULA**
congratulate **LAUD, SALUTE, MACORIZE**
congregation **FOLD, FLOCK, PARISH, TEMPLE**
congress **MOD, DIET, DUMA, RADA, SETAN, MAILIS, SOVIET**
conic section **CIRCLE, ELLIPSE, PARABOLA, HYPERBOLA**
conifer **FIR, YEW, PINE, CEDAR, LARCH, SPRUCE**

conjecture ETTLE, POSIT, THEORY, SURMISE

conjugal MARITAL, CONNUBIAL, MATRIMONIAL

conjunction AND, BUT, NOR, TIE, JOIN, THEN, ANDOR, SINCE, UNION

conjuncture CRISIS

conjure up EVOKE, INVOKE, SUMMON

conjuror MAGE, DOWSER, SHAMAN, VOODOO, WIZARD, EXORCIST, MAGICIAN

connect FIX, GLUE, JOIN, LINK, AFFIX, COUPLE

Connecticut *see also p. 615*

Connecticut city/town CANAAN, HAMDEN, PUTNAM, DANBURY, NORWALK, NORWICH, MERIDEN, NEWHAVEN, STAMFORD

Connecticut college YALE, HARTT, HARTFORD

Connecticut Indian NIPMUC, PEQUOT, MOHEGAN, PAUGUSSET

Connecticut river BYRAM, MYSTIC, SALMON, THAMES, HOUSATONIC

connection TIE, BOND, LINK, NEXUS

connective tissue FASCIA, TENDON, CARTILAGE

connive ABET, CONSPIRE

connoisseur EXPERT, EPICURE, (A)ESTHETE, GOURMET, AUTHORITY

connote MEAN, IMPLY

connubial MARITAL, CONJUGAL

conquer LICK, CRUSH, DEFEAT, MASTER, SUBDUE, OVERCOME

conqueror HERO, VICTOR

Conrad novel LORDJIM, VICTORY, NOSTROMO

consanguinity KINSHIP, AFFINITY

conscience QUALM, SCRUPLE

conscious WARE, AWAKE, AWARE, SENTIENT

consciousness SENSES, CONCERN, AWARENESS

conscript LEVY, DRAFT, MUSTER, DRAFTEE, RECRUIT

consecrate SAIN, BLESS, TABOO, ANOINT, HALLOW

consecrated OBLATE, SACRED

consecutive ENSUING, SEQUENT, SUCCESSIVE

consensus ACCORD

consent NOD, AGREE, ACCEDE, COMPLY, CONCUR

consequence END, IMPORT, RESULT, SEQUEL, OUTCOME

consequently SO, ERGO, HENCE

conservative SAFE, TORY, DIEHARD, RIGHTIST

consider DEEM, MUSE, RATE, STUDY, TREAT, REFLECT

consideration FEE, CARE, HEED, PRICE, ESTEEM, REASON

considering WHEN, SINCE

consign COMMIT, REMAND

consignee BROKER, FACTOR, RECEIVER

consignment CARGO

consist of INCLUDE, COMPRISE

consistency DENSITY, HARMONY

consolation SOP, BOOBY, SOLACE

console CALM, BRACE, CHEER, CABINET, COMFORT

consolidate FUSE, KNIT, MERGE, COMBINE

consommé BROTH

consonant LENE, SURD, LENIS, ATONIC, DENTAL, FORTIS, SONANT, SPIRANT

consort MATE, SPOUSE, PARTNER

consortium CARTEL, SYNDICATE

conspectus DIGEST, SYNOPSIS

conspicuous OVERT, PATENT, SIGNAL, BLATANT, SALIENT

conspiracy COUP, PLOT, CABAL, JUNTO, INTRIGUE

conspirator BRUTUS, FAWKES, CASSIUS, SABOTEUR

conspire PLOT, CABAL, SCHEME, COLLUDE, COMPLOT

constable COP, BULL, SLOP, BEADLE, BAILIFF

constant FAST, LOYAL, STILL, STAUNCH

Constant novel ADOLPHE

Constantine birthplace NIS(H)

Constantinople *see ISTANBUL*

constellation *see p. 741*

consternation FEAR, PANIC, ALARM, DISMAY, HORROR

constipated COSTIVE, STUCKUP

constituency	**VOTERS, ELECTORATE**
constituent	**PART, VOTER, ELECTOR, COMPONENT**
constitution	**CODE, HEALTH, MAKEUP, NATURE, CHARTER, IRONSIDES**
constitution part	**BYLAW, ARTICLE, PREAMBLE, AMENDMENT**
constitutional	**WALK, BASIC, LEGAL, LAWFUL**
constraint	**BOND, FORCE, DURESS**
constrict	**CHOKE, CRAMP, LIMIT, NARROW, SHRINK, ASTRINGE**
constrictor	**BOA, SPHINCTER**
construct	**BUILD, ERECT, DEVISE**
construction worker	**MASON, NAVVY, ROOFER, SEABEE, RIVETER**
construe	**INFER, PARSE, ANALYZE**
consult	**ADVISE, CONFER**
consultant	**EXPERT, ADVISOR**
consume	**EAT(OF), USE, BURN, WEAR, SPEND, WASTE**
consumer	**USER, BUYER**
consummate	**END, SHEER, WHOLE, ARRANT, ACHIEVE**
consumption	**USE, TABES, WASTE, PHTHISIS**
contact	**ABUT, TOUCH, SYZYGY**
contagion	**VIRUS, VECTION, EPIDEMIC, INFECTION**
contagious	**CATCHING, INFECTIOUS**
contain	**HOLD, CHECK, EMBODY, SUBSUME**
container	**BAG, BOX, CAN, CUP, JAR, TIN, TUB, URN, VAT, CAGE, CASE, VASE, PHIAL, POUCH, BOTTLE, CARBOY, CARTON**
contaminate	**SPOIL, SULLY, TAINT, DEFILE, POISON, POLLUTE**
contemn	**SCORN, SPURN, DESPISE**
contemplate	**BROOD, STUDY, THINK**
contemporaneous	**COEVAL, CURRENT**
contemporary	**COEVAL, MODERN**
contempt, show	**GECK, SCORN, SNEER, SNIFF, SNORT**
contemptible	**LOW, BASE, MEAN, VILE, SORRY, ABJECT**
contemptuous sound	**BAH, HISS, HOOT, PFUI, RAZZ, PHOOEY, CATCALL**
contend	**VIE, WAR, COPE, DEAL, ARGUE, CLAIM, COMPETE**
— contendere	**NOLO**
content	**GIST, SATED, REPLETE**
contention	**FEUD, STRIFE, DISPUTE**
contest	**WAR, AGON, BOUT, DUEL, FRAY, ARGUE, JOUST, ROLEO, AFFRAY, DEBATE, DISPUTE, TOURNEY**
contestant(s)	**ENTRY, FIELD, PLAYER, ENTRANT, CONTENDER**
context	**MILIEU, SETTING, SITUATION, ENVIRONMENT**
contiguous	**NEAR, ADJACENT, TOUCHING**
continent	**NA, SA, AFR, EUR, AMER, ASIA, SOBER, AFRICA, CHASTE, AUSTRAL, EURASIA, LEMURIA, ATLANTIS, CASCADIA, ANTARCTICA**
contingency	**CASE, EVENT, CHANCE**
contingent	**IFFY, RELIANT, DEPENDANT, CONDITIONAL**
continual	**CONSTANT, INCESSANT**
continuation	**SEQUEL, RESUMPTION**
continue	**LAST, ABIDE, ENDURE, PERDURE, PERSIST**
continued	**SERIAL, CHRONIC**
continuous	**NONSTOP, CONSTANT, UNBROKEN, INCESSANT**
continuously	**EVER, ALWAYS**
contort	**WARP, GNARL, TWIST, DEFORM, DISTORT**
contour	**LINE, SHAPE, OUTLINE, PROFILE**
contraband	**HOT, BOOTLEG, ILLEGAL**
contraceptive	**IUD, PILL, JELLY, CONDOM, RUBBER, DIAPHRAGM**
contract	**DEAL, HIRE, KNIT, CATCH, INCUR, SHRINK**
contraction	**EEN, EER, OER, TIS, AINT, ARNT, CANT, ISNT, WONT, ARENT, MAYNT, SHANT, SPASM, TWERE, ELISION, SYNCOPE, SHORTHAND**

contractor	BUILDER, SUPPLIER, OUTWORKER
contradict	DENY, BELIE, REBUT, IMPUGN, NEGATE, GAINSAY
contradiction	DENIAL, NEGATION, REBUTTAL
contraption	GISMO, GADGET, GIMMICK
contrary	UNRULY, FROWARD, OPPOSED
contrast	COMPARE
contribute	GIVE, CHIP IN, DONATE
contribution	TAX, ALMS, BOON, GIFT, INPUT, TITHE, PRESENT
contrite	SORRY, RUEFUL
contrivance	PLANT, PLOT, DEVICE, GIMMICK
contrive	PLOT, HATCH, DEVISE, MANAGE
control	CURB, HANK, SWAY, CHECK, REIGN, STEER
controversial	ERISTIC, POLEMIC(AL)
controversy	DEBATE, DISPUTE, QUARREL
controvert	DENY, REFUTE, GAINSAY
contumacious	UNRULY, REBELLIOUS
contumely	ABUSE, INSULT
contusion	BRUISE
conundrum	POSER, ENIGMA, RIDDLE
convene	SIT, MEET, CONVOKE
convenient	HANDY, USEFUL
convent	MATH, MUTH, ABBEY, NUNNERY, CLOISTER
convention	RULE, USAGE, CONGRESS, ASSEMBLY
conventional	NOMIC, FORMAL, PROPER
converge	MEET, FOCUS, UNITE
conversant	HEP, VERSED, FAMILIAR
conversation	CHAT, DIALOG, PALAVER, CAUSERIE
converse	RAP, CHAT, TALK, COMMUNE, OPPOSITE
convert	GER, ALTER, ANSAR, PROSELYTE
convex	BOWED, ARCHED, GIBBOUS
convey	BEAR, CEDE, CARRY, ASSIGN, TRANSFER
conveyance	CAR, DEED, DEMISE, PIPAGE, WAFTAGE

conveyor belt	APRON
convict	CON, LAG, FELON, LIFER, TERMER, CONDEMN
convince	ASSURE, PERSUADE
convinced	SURE, CERTAIN, WONOVER
convincing	VALID, COGENT, SUASION
convivial	GAR, FESTAL, GENIAL
convocation	SYNOD, COUNCIL, ASSEMBLY
convoke	CALL, CONVENE, ASSEMBLE
convolution	COIL, TWIST, WHORL
convoy	PILOT, GUARD, ESCORT, CONDUCT
convulsion	FIT, SPASM, THROE
cony	*see* CONEY
coo	CURR, CHIRR, CHOUGH, MURMUR
— and coo	BILL
cook	CHEF, SHIR(R), PREPARE, MAGIRIST
Cook island	ATIU, MAUKE, MANUAE, NASSAU, MITIARO, PENRHYN, TAKUTEA, MANIHIKI, PUKAPUKA, SUWARROW, RAROTONGA
cooker	OVEN, GRILL, STOVE, BROILER, TOASTER, BARBECUE, MICROWAVE
cookie	OREO, SNAP, WAFER, BISCUIT, MACAROON
cooking	CUISINE, MAGIRICS
cooking apparatus	ETNA, OVEN, PLATE, RANGE, STOVE, TIMER, ELEMENT, HIBACHI, HOTPLATE, MICROWAVE
cooking odor	NIDOR
cooking term	*see p. 561*
cooking utensil	PAN, POT, WOK, OLLA, KETTLE, SPIDER, TUREEN, ZESTER, GRIDDLE, SKILLET
cookout	FRY, ROAST, BARBECUE
cool	ICY, CALM, CHILL, GELID, NERVY, PLACID, COMPOSED
cooler	JAIL, CLINK, SNOCONE
Coolidge Dam river	GILA
coolie	PORTER, CARRIER
cooling apparatus	FAN, FRIDGE, FREEZER
coop	MEW, PEN, STY, COTE, CASE, JAIL, HUTCH, ENCASE
Cooper	GARY, ALICE, JACKIE
cooperative	COOP, ARTEL,

MUTUAL, HELPFUL,
COLLECTIVE
Cooperstown, first inductee
TYCOBB
cop   BULL, FLIC, BOBBY,
PEELER, GENDARME; see
POLICE
cop —   A PLEA
copal   ANIME, RESIN
cope   GETBY, VAULT, HACKIT,
HANDLE, MANAGE, SURVIVE
Cope Book author   (AUNT)ERMA
Copenhagen park   TIVOLI
copious   LUSH, PROFUSE,
REPLETE
cop-out   EXCUSE, EVASION
copper   CU, AES, CENT,
CUPRUM; see COP
copper alloy   BRASS, AROIDE,
BRONZE, ORMOLU, OROIDE,
RHEOTAN, PINCHBECK
copper center   AROA
Copperfield   see DAVID
COPPERFIELD
copse   BOSK, HOLT, COPPICE
Coptic clergyman   AMBA, ANBA
copy   APE, DUPE, CLONE,
DITTO, DRAFT, MODEL,
TRACE, CARBON, ECTYPE,
MIRROR, PARROT, ESTREAT
copyist   SCRIBE, SCRIVENER
copyright   PATENT
copyright violation   PIRACY,
PLAGIARY, PLAGIARISM
coquette   FLIRT
coral   POLYP, ZOOID, FUNGIA,
PORITE, OCULINA,
TUBIPORA, TUBIPORE
cord   AEA, AGAL, LINE, RAIP,
ROPE, WELT, HEDDLE,
PIPING, TENDON, TORSADE
cordage fiber   see FIBER
Cordelia's kin   LEAR, REGAN,
GONERIL
cordial   WARM, ARDENT; see
LIQUEUR
cordon   BELT, CORD, CIRCLE
core   AME, GIST, NAVE, NIFE,
PITH, HEART, NOWEL
Corinth   BIMARIS
Corinthian general   PISANDER
Corinthian king   POLYBUS
Coriolanus character   CAIUS,
TITUS, TULLUS, NICANOR,
VALERIA, VIRGILIA,
VOLUMNIA
cork   FLOAT, SHIVE, BOBBER,
STOPPLE
Cork County port   COBH

cormorant   SHAG, DUIKER,
DUYKER, GORMAW, PLOTUS,
ANHINGA
corn   SALT, MAIZE, CLAVUS,
MEALIE, NUBBIN
corn part   COB, EAR, HUSK,
SPIKE, STALK, STOVER,
TASSEL, TUCKET
cornea   see EYE
corned beef   BULLY, BRISKET
corned beef partner   CABBAGE
corned beef sandwich   REUBEN
corner   NOOK, TREE, ANGLE,
HERNE, INGLE, NICHE
cornerstone   COIN, COYN,
COIGN, QUOIN, COIGNE
cornice   DRIP, ASTRAGAL
Cornish prefix   LAN, ROS, TRE
cornmeal   MASA, SOFK, GRITS,
SOFKI, HOMINY, SOFKEE
corny   BANAL, MUSHY, TRITE
corolla   PETAL(S), PERIANTH
corona   AURA, HALO, CIGAR,
FILLET, AUREOLA, AUREOLE,
SCYPHUS
coronach   DIRGE, THRENODY
coronary   STROKE
coronet   BURR, CROWN, TIARA,
ANADEM, DIADEM
corporal   NCO
Corporal, Little   NAPOLEON
corporate   JOINT, COMMON,
UNITED
corporation   MERGER, SYNDIC
corporeal   HYLIC, SOMAL,
BODILY, SOMATIC
corpse   LICH, MUMMY, STIFF,
CADAVER, CARCASS
corpulent   BURLY, OBESE, PORTLY
corral   PEN, STY, HERD,
ATAJO, POUND
correct   MEND, EDIT, OKAY,
AMEND, EMEND, RIGHT,
ADJUST, ARIGHT, REMEDY,
REVISE, CHASTEN
correspond   FIT, JIBE, AGREE,
TALLY, WRITE
correspondent   PENPAL, SCRIBE,
WRITER, SECRETARY
corridor   HALL, AISLE,
HALLWAY, PASSAGE(WAY)
corrode   EAT, PIT, BURN, ETCH,
GNAW, RUST, DECAY, ERODE
corrosive   ACID, CAUSTIC,
MORDANT
corrugated   FLUTED, RUGATE,
RUGOSE, GROOVED
corrupt   VILE, SPOIL, TAINT,
VENAL, DEBASE, VITIATE

corruption	**GRAFT, TAINT, VENALITY**
corsage	**WAIST, BODICE, BOUQUET, NOSEGAY**
corsair	**PIRATE, PICAROON**
corset	**BUSK, STAY(S)**
corset tightener	**LACE**
cortege	**TRAIN, RETINUE**
cortex	**BARK, RIND**
corundum	**RUBY, EMERY, TOPAZ, AMETHYST, SAPPHIRE**
corvine	*see* **CROW**
Cos Island, *pert. to*	**COAN**
Cosa Nostra	**MAFIA, FAMILY**
Cosby Show names	**RUDY, THEO, CLAIR, CLIFF, DENISE, SONDRA, BLEDSOE, VANESSA, HUXTABLE**
Così fan —	**TUTTE**
cosmetic(s)	**KOHL, KUHL, HENNA, PAINT, ROUGE, CERUSE, MASCARA, WARPAINT**
cosmic order	**RITA**
cosmonaut	*see* **ASTRONAUT**
cosmos	**GLOBE, WORLD, UNIVERSE**
Cossack	**RUSS, TURK, TATAR**
Cossack chief	**ATAMAN, HETMAN**
Cossack regiment	**POLK, PULK**
Cossack squadron	**SOTN(I)A**
cosset	**PET, LAMB, CODDLE, FONDLE**
cost	**LOSS, RATE, PRICE, CHARGE**
Costa Rica, *capital of*	**SANJOSE**
Costa Rica city/town	**LIMON, GRECIA, NICOYA, SAN JOSE, ALAJUELA, PUNTARENAS**
Costa Rican measure	**FANEGA, CAJUELA**
Costa Rican money	**COLON, CENTIMO**
Costa Rican leader	**ARIAS, TREJOS, CALDERON**
Costa Rican peninsula	**OSA, NICOYA**
Costa Rican volcano	**BARBA, IRAZU**
Costa Rican weight	**CAJA**
costly	**DEAR, EXPENSIVE**
costume	**RIG, GETUP;** *see* **CLOTHING**
cot	**BED, CRIB**
cote	**SHED, SHELTER**
Côte d'Azur	**RIVIERA**
coterie	**SET, JUNTO, CIRCLE, CLIQUE**

cottage	**BARI, CABIN, CHALET, BUNGALOW**
cotton	*see* **FIBER, FABRIC**
cotton machine	**GIN, MULE, BALER, LINTER, WILLOW**
cotton measure	**LEA, HANK**
cotton thread	**LISLE**
couch	**HIDE, LAIR, SOFA, DIVAN, SETTEE, DAVENPORT**
cougar	**PUMA, PANTHER;** *see p. 863*
cough	**HACK, TUSSIS**
cough drop	**PASTIL, TROCHE, LOZENGE, PASTILLE**
cough up	**ANTE, CHIPIN, CONTRIBUTE**
council	**FONO, FORUM, JUNTA, SYNOD, WITAN, CABINET**
council head	**MAYOR**
councillor	**FAIPULE**
counsel(or)	**REDE, WARN, CHIDE, EGERIA, LAWYER, MENTOR, NESTOR, PROCTOR**
count	**TOT, EARL, GRAF, RELY, COMES, SCORE, TALLY, TOTAL, CENSUS, RECKON**
Count of Monte Cristo	**DANTES**
Count of Monte Cristo author	**DUMAS**
count on	**LEAN, RELY, DEPEND**
countenance	**ABET, FACE, VISAGE, SANCTION**
counter	**BAR, CHIP, CHECK, SHELF, TOKEN, GEIGER, CONTEND, RESPOND**
counteract	**CHECK, NEGATE, OFFSET, THWART**
counterfeit	**FAKE, SHAM, BOGUS, FORGE, PHONY**
counterirritant	**MOXA**
countermand	**REVOKE, RESCIND**
counterpart	**COPY, TWIN, DOUBLE, PENDANT, REPLICA**
countersink	**REAM, BEVEL, CHAMFER**
countertenor	**ALTO, FALSETTO**
countless	**MYRIAD, UNTOLD, INNUMERABLE**
countries and capitals	*see p. 586*
countrified	**RURAL, RUSTIC**
country	**LAND, PAIS, VALE, WILD, REALM, WEALD**
country, *pert. to*	**RURAL, RUSTIC, AGRESTIC**
countryman	**BOOR, SWAIN, RUSTIC, CITIZEN, PATRIOT, COMPATRIOT**
county	**AMT, LAN, FLYKE, SHIRE, PARISH;** *see p. 591*

county official **SHERIFF**	courtly **HEND, AULIC, HENDE,**
coup **BLOW, FEAT, SCOOP,**	**ELEGANT**
PUTSCH, STROKE	courtship **SUIT, WOOING**
coup de — **ETAT, GRACE**	courtyard **PATIO, ATRIUM,**
couple **DUO, TWO, DYAD,**	**SQUARE**
PAIR, SPAN, BRACE, TWINS,	Cousteau ship **CALYPSO**
GEMINI	couturier **DIOR, PUCCI, RICCI,**
coupled **GEMEL, YOKED,**	**CARDIN, CHANEL, BALMAIN,**
WEDDED, GEMELED	**CASSINI, GIVENCHY,**
couplet **DISTICH**	**BALENCIAGA**
courage **GRIT, GUTS, SAND,**	cove **CHAP, INLET, FELLOW;**
NERVE, PLUCK, SPUNK,	*see* **BAY**
VALOR, METTLE	covenant **BOND, PACT,**
courageous **BOLD, BRAVE,**	**TREATY, PROMISE**
GUTSY, DARING, HEROIC	cover(ing) **CAP, LID, CEIL,**
courier **GUIDE, ESTAFET(TE)**	**COSY, GARB, HIDE, HUSK,**
course **LAP, LEG, WAY, ROAD,**	**MASK, PEEL, PELT, RIND, SEAL,**
ROTE, SOUP, TACK, CYCLE,	**SKIN, QUILT, SHADE,**
ROUTE, SALAD, TREND,	**KECKLE, PELAGE, SHEATH,**
ENTREE, DESSERT, SEMINAR	**TEGMEN, THATCH,**
course, school **BOT, ENG, MED,**	**SHEATHE, TEGUMEN**
ANAT, ARCH, BIOL, ECON,	cover a bet **FADE**
MATH, TRIG, ZOOL, PREMED	covered **AWASH, FLOODED**
courser **STEED**	coverlet **PALL, QUILT, THROW,**
court(s) **BAR, SUE, WOO, DARI,**	**AFGHAN, SPREAD**
FORA, LEET, ROTA, YARD,	covert **HIDDEN, SECRET**
CURIA, CURRY, DAIRO,	covet **ENVY, PINE, CRAVE,**
FORUM, FAVOR, GEMOT, PATIO,	**YISSE**
GEMOTE, PALACE, PARVIS,	covetous **GREEDY, ENVIOUS,**
PROBATE, TRIBUNAL	**JEALOUS**
court action **SUIT, TRIAL,**	covey **BEVY, BROOD, FLOCK**
APPEAL	cow **BOSSY, BULLY, DAUNT,**
court assistant **EYRE, JURY,**	**BOVINE;** *see* **CATTLE**
AMALA, AMLAH, CLERK,	cow crossbreed **DZO, ZUM**
CRIER, MACER, BEADLE,	coward **CUR, SISSY, CRAVEN,**
ELISOR, BAILIFF, TALESMAN	**CAITIFF, DASTARD,**
court crier's call **OYES, OYEZ**	**POLTROON**
court decision **VERDICT**	cowardly **TIMID, CRAVEN,**
court game **SQUASH, TENNIS,**	**YELLOW, CHICKEN**
HANDBALL, JAIALAI,	cowboy **GAUCHO, HERDER,**
BADMINTON, BASKETBALL,	**RINGER, LLANERO,**
RACQUETBALL	**PUNCHER, VAQUERO**
court official **DA, ATT, CLERK,**	cowboy movie **OATER,**
JUDGE, FISCAL, JURIST,	**WESTERN**
BAILIFF, JUSTIVE, ATTORNEY,	cower **QUAIL, CRINGE,**
BARRISTER	**SHRINK**
court order **BOND, WRIT,**	cowfish **TORO, DUGONG,**
ARRET, EDICT, CITATION,	**GRAMPUS, MANATEE**
MANDAMUS, SUBPOENA	cowgirl **DUDINE, DUDETTE**
court, *pert. to* **AULIC**	cowl **COUS, HOOD, AMICE**
court president **FOUD**	cowrie **SHELL, WAMPUM**
court session **ASSIZE, SITTING**	cowslip **BLUEBELL, PRIMROSE**
courteous **KIND, CIVIL,**	coxcomb **FOP, NOB, DUPE,**
URBANE	**TOFF, DANDY, SWELL**
courtesan **LAIS, THAIS,**	coy **ARCH, CHARY, DEMURE**
HETAERA	coyote *see* **WOLF**
courtesy **FAVOR, GRACE,**	coypu **NUTRIA**
CHIVALRY, CIVILITY	cozen **CON, BILK, CHEAT,**
courtier **NOBLE, TOADY**	**TRICK, DECEIVE**

cozy SNUG, HOMEY, QUILT
CPU word UNIT, CENTRAL, PROCESSING
crab UCA, BLUE, MAIA, MAJA, ZOEA, JUPPA, MAIAN, RACER, YABBY, ZOAEA, ZOOEA, BUSTER, CANCER, HERMIT, PARTAN, PEELER, SPRITE, YABBER, YABBIE, BUCKLER, FIDDLER, LIMULID, MUDCRAB, PANFISH, PEA CRAB, SHEDDER, BLUECRAB, FROGCRAB, GRAPSOID, KING CRAB, LADY CRAB, LAND CRAB, LIMULOID, OCHIDORE, OCYPODAN, RANINIAN
crab genus ANOMURA, GRAPSUS, LIMULUS, OCYPODE, CAMBARUS, PORTUNUS
crack CHAP, COKE, JOKE, KIBE, RIFT, SNAP, CHINK, CLEFT, COCAINE
cracker POPPER, BISCUIT, BREAKER, SALTINE
crackerjack ACE, WHIZ
crackers MAD, LOCO, NUTS, CRAZY, BANANAS
crackle SNAP, SPUTTER, CREPITATE
crackpot NUT, CRANK, LUNATIC
cradle BED, CRIB, SLEE, CADRE, CRECHE, INFANCY
— cradle CATS
cradle song LULLABY
craft ART, GUILE, TRADE, METIER, POLICE, TALENT
craftsman MASON, NAVVY, SMITH, ARTIST, WRIGHT, ARTISAN
crafty SLY, FOXY, WILY, ARTFUL, TRICKY
crag TOR, SCAR, ARETE, BRACK
crake CREX, CROW, RAIL, SORA
cram RAM, WAD, PACK, STUFF
cramp ART, KINK, SPASM, STITCH
crane JIB, COOT, GRUS, JENNY, SARUS, BROLGA, CHUNGA, CARIAMA, GOLIATH, LIMPKIN, SERIEMA, WHOOPER; see LIFTING
cranium SKULL
crank NUT, BEND, BRACE, WINCH, HANDLE, CAPRICE, CRACKPOT

cranky CROSS, TESTY, GROUCHY
cranny NOOK, CHINK, FISSURE
craps see DICE
crash FAIL, BURST, CLOTH, LINEN, FAILURE
crasher INTRUDER
crass CRUDE, GROSS, COARSE, STUPID, VULGAR
Cratchit's employer SCROOGE
Cratchit's job CLERK
Cratchit's son (TINY)TIM
crate BOX, CRADLE, ENCASE, HAMPER
crate maker CASER
crater PIT, CONE, LINNE, CAVITY, CALDERA
cravat TIE, ASCOT, SCARF
crave LONG, PINE, COVET, HANKER
craven see COWARD
craving YEN, HUNGER, THIRST
craw MAW, CROP, BELLY, GULLET, GIZZARD
crawl FAWN, INCH, TEEM, CREEP, GROVEL
crayfish YABBY; see LOBSTER
crayon CHALK, PASTEL, PENCIL
craze FAD, RAGE, FUROR, MANIA, MADDEN
crazed DAFT, CUCKOO, INSANE, DEMENTED
crazy REE, AMOK, DAFT, LOCO, LUNY, DAFFY, DOTTY, LOONY, MANIC, POTTY, WACKY
cream TOP, BEST, ECRU, ELITE
cream — ALE, SODA
crease FOLD, RUCK, RUGA, SEAM, TUCK, CRIMP, STRIA
create MAKE, BEGET, BUILD, PRODUCE
creator GOD, AUTHOR, DEMIURGE
creature BEING, MINION, WRETCH
creche figure CRIB, LAMB, MAGI, MARY, INFANT, JOSEPH, MANGER, SHEPHERD
credence FAITH, TRUST, BELIEF
credentials PAPERS, DIPLOMA, VOUCHER, CERTIFICATE
credenza BUFFET, SIDEBOARD
credit TICK, TRUST, IMPUTE, ASCRIBE
credit transfer GIRO
creditor DEBTEE, LENDER
credo TENET, BELIEF

creed NICENE, APOSTLES; *see* BELIEF
creek GEO, GIO, RIA, RUN, KILL, VLEI, BAYOU, BROOK, STREAM
creel CORF, BASKET
creep FAWN, INCH, CRAWL, TINGLE
creeper IVY, VINE, WORM, SNAKE
creeping REPENT, REPTANT
creepy EERIE, WEIRD, CRAWLY
cremate BURN, CALCINE
cremation SUTTEE
Cremona craftsman AMATI, GUARNERI
Creole patois GOMBO, GUMBO
crescent(-shaped) CEE, CUSP, LUNE, MOON, LUNAR, LUNATE, LUNULA
cresset TORCH, LANTERN
Cressida lover TROILUS
crest TOP, TOR, COMB, PEAK, TUFT, ARETE, CROWN, RIDGE
crested PILEATE, CRISTATE(D)
crestfallen GLUM, DEJECTED, DOWNCAST
Cretan CANDIOT(E)
Cretan cape BUSA, KRIO, SUDA, SIDERO
Cretan city/town CANEA, SPILI, VAMOS, IRAKLION
Cretan department CANEA, IRAKLION, LASITHION
Cretan guardian TALOS
Cretan king MINOS
Cretan mountain IDA
Cretan princess ARIADNE
Crete CANDIA
cretin IDIOT, MORON
crevice RIME, CLEFT, CRANNY
crew MEN, MOB, BAND, GANG, OARS, TEAM, HANDS, OARSMAN
crib BIN, PONY, TROT, CRATCH, CRECHE
cribbage term GO, PEG, CRIB, NOBS, HEELS, LURCH
cricket GRIG, STOOL, INSECT
cricket term BAT, BYE, LEG, ONS, OFFS, OVER, SLIP, TICE, YORK, EDGER, MIDON, PITCH, BOWLER, CREASE, GOOGLY, WICKET, YORKER
crier HERALD, MUEZZIN
crime SIN, VICE, ARSON, FELONY, SIMONY
Crimean city YALTA

criminal HOOD, YEGG, FELON, NOCENT, OUTLAW, CULPRIT, CONVICT, GANGSTER
crimp FURL, FRIZ(Z), CREASE, GOFFER
crimson LAC, RED, CARMINE, HARVARD
cringe FAWN, COWER, QUAIL, WINCE
crinkle CRUMPLE
cripple(d) HALT, HOCK, LAME, IMPAIR, DISABLE
crisis RUB, HEAD, PASS, PINCH, CRUNCH
crisp CURT, TERSE, BRITTLE
crisscross MESH, CROSSING
criterion NORM, TEST, CANON, STANDARD, TOUCHSTONE
critic BOOER, CARPER, CENSOR
critic, famous LAHR, EBERT, SIMON, SISKEL, CASSIDY, STEINBERG
critical NICE, ACUTE, EXACT, EXIGENT
criticism REVIEW, CENSURE, ZOILISM
criticize PAN, RAP, CARP, FLAY, REAM, CAVIL, ROAST, SLATE
critics SHAW, AUDEN, JAMES, PATER, DRYDEN
critique REVIEW, COMMENTARY
croak CAW, DIE, CROUP
Croatia, capital of ZAGREB
Croatian SLAV, CROAT, SLOVENE
Croatian city/town PULA, ZARA, SPLIT, ZADAR, IADERA, OSIJEK, RIJEKA, ZAGREB
Croatian money KUNA, LIPA
Croatian mountains PAPUK, AGORJE, VELEBIT
Croatian river KUPA, RASA, CETINA
Croatian soldier PANDOUR
crochet KNIT
crochet stitch LOOP, CHAIN, PIQUE, TRICOT
crocodile GOA, CROC, YAKI, GATOR, CAIMAN, CAYMAN, GAVIAL, JACARE, MUGGER, YACARE, ALLIGATOR
crocodile genus GAVIALIS
crocus IRIS
Croesus' land LYDIA
croft FARM, TORP, CRYPT, VAULT

— and croft	TOFT	crowd	JAM, MOB, CRAM,
cromlech	DOLMEN		HERD, RUCK, TURB, CRAMP,
Cromwell	NOLL, IRONSIDES		PRESS, SERRY
crone	EWE, HAG, WITCH,	crowd member	EXTRA, SUPER
	BELDAM(E)	crow-like	CORVINE
Cronus	TITAN, SATURN	crown	BAY, CAP, TAJ, ATEF,
Cronus relative	GAEA, ZEUS,		PATE, POLL, CREST, TIARA,
	TETHYS, URANUS		CORONA, DIADEM, CORONET,
crony	PAL, CHUM, MATE,		PSCHENT, CORONATE
	BUDDY	Crown colony	HONGKONG
crook	BEND, CANE, HOOK,	crown prince	HEIR, DAUPHIN,
	PEDA, CURVE, PEDUM,		ATHELING
	CROSIER, POTHOOK	crow's nest cry	LANDHO
— or crook	HOOK	crucial	URGENT, CRITICAL
crooked	KAM, WRY, AGEE,	crucial point	CRUX, PIVOT,
	AWRY, BENT, ASKEW,		CRISIS
	AKIMBO, CORRUPT	crucible	TEST, TRIAL, CRUSET,
crooner	(DON) HO, BING,		RETORT
	COMO, PERRY, CROSBY,	Crucible setting	SALEM
	MARTIN, SINATRA	crucifix	see CROSS
crop(s)	MAW, CRAW, RABI,	crucifixion place	CALVARY
	REAP, ROWEN, GEBBIE,	crucify	HANG, EXECUTE,
	HARVEST		TORTURE
crop up	ARISE, RECUR	crude	RAW, CRASS, COARSE,
crop worker	PICKER, REAPER		VULGAR
croquet	ROQUE	crude person	BOOR, BEAST,
croquet term	ARCH, HOOP,		BRUTE, YAHOO
	JAWS, BISQUE, WICKET	cruel	FELL, FERAL, SAVAGE,
Crosby	BOB, BING, GARY,		BESTIAL, UNKIND, SADISTIC,
	CATHY		HEARTLESS
crosier	CROOK, STAFF	cruet	AMA, VIAL, GEMEL,
cross	TAU, ANKH, CRUX,		CRUSE, CASTER, AMPULLA,
	EDGY, ROOD, SPAN, IRATE,		BURETTE
	LATIN, TESTY, TRIAL, CELTIC,	cruise	SAIL, COAST, VOYAGE,
	FYLFOT, POTENT, MALTESE,	cruising	ASEA
	SALTIER, SALTIRE, SWASTIKA	cruller	CAKE, DONUT
cross out	EX, CUT, DELE,	crumb	BIT, ORT, SCRAP, MORSEL
	CANCEL, DELETE	crumble	DECAY, BRACKLE
cross section	SLICE, SAMPLE	crumbly	FRIABLE
cross threads	WEFT, WOOF	crumple	ROOL, RUCK,
cross timber	SPALE		RUMPLE, SCRUNCH,
crossbeam	TRAVE, TREVE		WRINKLE
crosseye(d)	SQUINT,	crunch	CHEW, CRUSH, GRIND,
	STRABISMAL, STRABISMUS		MUNCH
crosspiece	RUNG, CLEAT,	cruor	GRUME
	EVENER	crusade	CAUSE, GRIND,
cross-stroke	SERIF		JAHAD, JIHAD, CAMPAIGN
crosswise	ABEAM,	Crusade, First, date	MCIV
	DIAGONALLY	crusader	PILGRIM, RICHARD,
crotch	FORK, HOOK		TANCRED, TEMPLAR
crotchety	ODD, QUEER, FITFUL	crusader foe	TURK, SALADIN,
crouch	COWER, SQUAT,		SARACEN
	STOOP	crush	BRAY, MASH, FLAME,
crouton	SIPPET		PRESS, QUASH, QUELL,
crow	DAW, KAE, CROW, ROOK,		SUBDUE
	BOAST, CHOUGH, HOODIE,	Crusoe author	DEFOE
	KOKAKO, CORVINE,	crust	SCAB, SCALE, CORTEX
	JACKDAW, KOKAKOO	crust ingredient	LARD, FLOUR,
crowbar	PRY, JIMMY		BUTTER

crustacean   **CRAB, ALIMA, MYSID, MYSIS, PRAWN, SHRIMP, SLATER, SOWBUG, SQUILL, ASELLUS, GRIBBLE, LOBSTER, MACRURA, MYSIDAE, ONISCUS, PILLBUG, SQUILLA, COPEPODA, CUMACEAN, EPICARID, LERNAEAN;** see p. 667

crusty   **HARSH, SURLY**

crutch   **PONY, PROP, SUPPORT**

cry   **BOO, FAD, SOB, ABOO, CALL, CROW, MEWL, MOAN, OYES, OYEZ, PULK, RAGE, RALE, ROAR, WAIL, WEEP, YELL, YOHO, COOEE, COOEY, GROAN, HALLO, HOLLA, HOLLO, LARUM, SHOUT, SNORE, TRILL, WHOOP, ALARUM, BOOHOO, CLAMOR, HALLOO, HUBBUB, PLAINT, SCREAM, SCROOP, SHRIEK, SHRILL, SNIVEL, UPROAR, YOICKS, HALLOOA, SCREECH, TALLYHO;** see BIRDS, **ANIMAL, SOUND;** see p. 701

— and cry   **HUE**

cry of approval   **BIS, BRAVO, HURRAH;** see **CHEER**

cry of pain   **OW, OUCH, YELP**

Cry the Beloved Country author   **PATON**

crying source   **THROAT**

crypt   **TOMB, VAULT**

cryptic   **OCCULT, SECRET, OBSCURE**

crystal   **ICE, CLEAR, MACLE, DIAMOND**

crystalline   **SHEER, GLASSY, PELLUCID, DIAPHANOUS, TRANSPARENT**

crystallize   **SET, FORM, JELL, HARDEN, CONGEAL**

crystal gaze   **SCRY**

cub   **FRY, PUP, COLT, LIONET**

Cub Scout group   **DEN**

Cuba, capital of   **HAVANA**

Cuban bay   **NIPE, PIGS, HONDA, MAISI**

Cuban cape   **CRUZ, PEPE**

Cuban city/town   **MORON, REGLA, HAVANA, HOLGUIN, CAMAGUEY, GUANTANAMO**

Cuban dance   **R(H)UMBA, HABANERA**

Cuban measure   **KILO, VARA, LIBRA, TAREA, CORDEL, MEDIDA**

Cuban money   **PESO**

Cuban province   **GRANMA, HOLGUIN, CAMAGUEY, GUANTANAMO**

Cuban river   **CAUTO, SANPEDRO**

Cuban rum   **BACARDI**

Cuban secret police   **PORRA**

Cuban tree   **JIQUE, JIQUI**

cube   **DIE, DICE, NASIK, TESSERA, TESSELLA**

cubicle   **CELL, NICHE, ALCOVE, CARREL**

cubitus   **ULNA, FOREARM**

Cuchulain kin   **LUG, EMER, CONNLA, SUALTAM, DECHTIRE**

cuckoo   **ANI, MAD, COEL, KOEL, COOEE, CRAZY, KOKIL, COUCAL, KOKILA, LOURIE, MALKOHA, TOURACO, RAINBIRD**

cucumber   **CUKE, PEPO, PEPINO, PICKLE, GHERKIN**

cud   **CHEW, QUID, BOLUS, RUMEN**

cud-chewing animal   see **RUMINANT**

cuddle   **HUG, NESTLE, SNUGGLE**

cuddy   **ASS, CLOSET, DONKEY, STUPID**

cudgel   **BAT, CLUB, DRUB, BASTE, STAVE, TOWEL**

cue   **NOD, ROD, TIP, HINT, TAIL, PRESA, PROMPT, SIGNAL**

cuff   **SLAP, SMACK, BUFFET, POMMEL, MANACLE**

cuff fastener   **TAB, LINK, STUD, BUTTON**

cuff, off the   **OFFHAND, IMPROMPTU**

cui —   **BONO**

cuirass   **ARMOR, LORICA, BREASTPLATE**

cuisine   **COOKERY, KITCHEN**

cuisine type   **THAI, CAJUN, HAUTE, NOUVELLE**

cull   **DUPE, SIFT, GLEAN, PLUCK, SELECT, WINNOW**

culm   **STEM, SLACK, REFUSE**

culmination   **ACME, APEX, AUGE, NOON, APOGEE, CLIMAX, VERTEX, ZENITH**

— culotte   **SANS**

culpable   **GUILTY, BLAMABLE**

culprit   **FELON, OFFENDER**

cult   **FAD, ISM, SECT, MANIA**

cultivate   **EAR, HOE, FARM,**

PLOW, TILL, NURSE, HARROW, RATOON
cultivated REFINED, HIGHBROW
cultivating tool HOE, PICK, RAKE, SPADE, HARROW
cultivation JUM, GOOM, JOOM, TILTH
cultivation method JHUM
culture AGAR, ARTS, POLISH, TILLAGE
cultured person EGGHEAD, SCHOLAR, INTELLECTUAL
culvert DRAIN, SEWER
cumbersome CLUMSY, UNWIELDY
cummerbund SASH
cuneiform CUNEAL
cuneiform writing SUSIAN, ELAMITE, HITTITE
cunning ART, SLY, CUTE, FOXY, WILY, DEDAL, GUILE, ARTFUL, CALLID, CRAFTY, DAEDAL, VULPINE
cup AMA, DOP, TIG, TYG, DOPP, LOTA, TASS, CALYX, CHARX, CRUSE, CUPEL, DEPAS, GODET, GRAIL, LOTAH, MAZER, COTULA, HOLMOS, NOGGIN, TROPHY
cupbearer HEBE, SAKI
Cupid DAN, AMOR, EROS, LOVE, PUTTO
Cupid partner COMET
Cupid sweetheart PSYCHE
Cupid's mother VENUS
cupidity GREED, AVARICE
cupola DOME, TURRET, LANTERN
cup-shaped PEZIZOID
cupholder ZARF
cur DOG, MUT(T), FEIST, HOUND, MONGREL
curare URALI, OORALI, OURALI
curassow MITU
curate see CLERGY
curator WARDEN
curb REIN, CHECK, BRIDLE, REPRESS
curd CRUD, CASEIN(E), CONGEAL
curdle SAM, POSSET, RENNET, CLABBER
cure TAN, CORN, HEAL, SALT, SMOKE, PICKLE; see REMEDY
cure-all ELIXIR, NOSTRUM, PANACEA
Curia court ROTA, SIGNATURA
Curia official DATARY

curio VIRTU, GEWGAW, BIBELOT, KNICKKNACK
curiosity ODDITY, RARITY, WONDER
curious ODD, NOSY, PRYING, SNOOPY
curl COIL, FEAK, FRIZ, KINK, TRESS, BERGER, MARCEL, RINGLET
curlew SNIPE, WHAUP, GODWIT
curling term HOG, TEE, HACK, PORT, SOOP, WICK, BESOM, HOUSE, BUTTON, PATLID, POTLID
curly UNDY, WAVY, KINKY, OUNDY
curmudgeon CRAB, GNOF, GROUCH
currant RISSEL
currant syrup CASSIS
currency CHANGE; see MONEY
currency, word on GOD, UNUM, PLURIBUS
current AC, DC, EDDY, RIFE, TIDE, RAPID, COURSE, STREAM, PRESENT
current, ocean NINO, PERU, BLACK, NATAL, ALASKA, ARCTIC, KURILE, AGULHAS, MONSOON, OKHOTSK, OYASHIO, ALEUTIAN, BANGUELA, CANARIES, CAPEHORN, FALKLAND, HUMBOLDT, LABRADOR, TSUSHIMA
Currier's partner IVES
curry DRESS, GROOM, SPICE
curse HEX, DAMN, JINX, OATH, SWEAR, REVILE, ANATHEM, MALISON, ANATHEMA
cursory HASTY, CASUAL
curt BLUNT, BRUSK, GRUFF, SQUAB, SNIPPY, BRUSQUE
curtail LOP, PARE, REDUCE
curtain SCRIM, BAMBOO, SCREEN, VALANCE, CYCLORAMA
curtain material LENO, GAUZE, NINON, SCRIM, TAPIS
curtsy DIP, SALAAM, SCRAPE
curve ARC, BOW, ESS, SNY, ARCH, BEND, HOOK, OGEE, CROOK, SINUS, ELLIPSE, PARABOLA
curve section ARC
curved NOWY, ADUNC, ARCHED, CONVEX, CONCAVE

Cush relative HAM, SEBA, NIMROD

cushion PAD, COAD, PILLOW, SOFTEN, BOLSTER, HASSOCK

Cushitic language AGAU, BEJA, GALA, GOFA, KAFA, ZALA, ALABA, AWIYA, BILIN, BURJI, GALLA, OMETO, QUARA, DARASA, HARURO, KHAMIR, QABENA, SIDAMO, SOMALI, WOLAMO, BASKETO, JANJERO, KAMBATTA, SAHOAFAR

cusp EDGE, HORN, PEAK, POINT

cuss CURSE, SWEAR

custard FLAN, PAPAW, TIMBALE

custard apple ATES, ANNONA, SWEETSOP

Custer's horse VIC

custodian CUSTOS, JAILER, WARDEN, CURATOR, JANITOR

custody CARE, TRUST, CHARGE, DURANCE

custom(s) TAX, URE, CESS, DUTY, LEVY, TOLL, WONT, MORES, RITUS, SUNNA, USAGE, DASTUR, SUNNAH, TARIFF

customary USUAL, COMMON, WONTED, REGULAR, HABITUAL

customer(s) TRADE, BEBACK, CLIENT, PATRON, BUSINESS

cut DOD, HEW, LOP, MOW, NIP, DICE, DOCK, DODD, ETCH, FELL, GASH, HACK, KERF, REAP, SLIT, SNEE, SNIP, SNUB, TRIM, CARVE, SCARP, SEVER, SHEAR, SLASH, SLICE, SLISH, CLEAVE, ESCARP, LESION, TREPAN, ESCARPE

— cut CREW

cut and dried ROUTINE

cut down RASEE, RAZEE

cut in half HALVE, BISECT, REDUCE, SECANT

cut of meat CHOP, LOIN, RIBS, RUMP, CHINE, CHUCK, FLANK, SHANK, STEAK, CUTLET, BRISKET, SIRLOIN, SHOULDER

cut off LOP, SNIP, ALONE, ELIDE, ROACH

cutback SKIMP, REDUCTION, ECONOMIZE

cute TWEE, BONNY, CANNY, PRETTY

cutlery FORK, KNIFE, SPOON, FLATWARE, TABLEWARE

cut-rate CHEAP, BARGAIN, REDUCED

cutter SLED, KNIFE, SLOOP

cutting KEEN, SCION, SHARP, BITING, SECANT, INCISAL, MORDANT

cutting tool AX, ADZ, AXE, BUR, DIE, HOB, SAW, SAX, ADZE, BOLO, BURIN, KNIFE, MOWER, RAZOR, CHASER, CHISEL, SCYTHE, SHEARS, SICKLE, MACHETE

cuttlefish SEPIA, SQUID, OCTOPUS, BELEMNITE

Cy Young awards see p. 704

Cyaxares subject MEDE

Cybele OPS, RHEA

Cybele's consort ATYS, ATTIS

Cybele relative GAEA, HERA, JUNO, ZEUS, CRONUS, SATURN, URANUS

Cyclades IOS, KEA, KEOS, MILO, DELOS, MELOS, NAXOS, PAROS, SYROS, THIRA, TINOS, ANDROS, AMORGOS, KITHNOS, SERIFOS

cycle BIKE, ROUND, SAROS, PERIOD, BICYCLE

cycle per second HERTZ

cyclist RIIS, ROCHE, FIGNON, LEMOND, DELGADO, HINAULT, PANTANI, ULLRICH, INDURAIN , ARMSTRONG

cyclist stunt DROP, WHEELIE

cyclone LOW, BAGUIO, VORTEX, TORNADO, TWISTER, TYPHOON

Cyclopes ARGES, BRONTES, POLYPHEMUS

Cyclops defeater NOMAN, ODYSSEUS

cylinder INKER, BARREL, GAVION, PISTON, PLATEN

cylindrical TOROSE, TUBULAR

cyma GOLA, GULA, OGEE

cymbal(s) TAL, ZEL, PIATTI

Cymbeline's kin CLOTEN, IMOGEN

Cymric WELSH, BRETON

cynic TIMON, DOUBTER, SKEPTIC

cynical SURLY, MOROSE, ASCETIC, DOUBTING

cynicism IRONY, SARCASM

Cynthia LUNA, CINDY, DIANA, ARTEMIS

cypress LAWN, CEDAR, GILIA

cyprinoid fish *see* CARP
Cyprus cape GATA, GRECO, ANDREAS
Cyprus, capital of NICOSIA
Cyprus city/town DHALI, CITIUM, PAPHOS, LARNACA, NICOSIA, LEFKOSIA, LIMASSOL
Cyprus measure OKA, PIK, CASS, KOUZA, KARTOS, MEDIMNO
Cyprus money LIRA, POUND
Cyprus mountain OLYMPUS
Cyprus weight OKA, MOOSA, KANTAR
Cyrano de Bergerac author ROSTAND
Cyrano de Bergerac sore point NOSE
cyst BAG, SAC, WEN, POUCH
czar IVAN, PAUL, BASIL, PETER, DYNAST, FEODOR, TYRANT, DICTATOR, NICHOLAS
Czech author CAPEK, HAVEL, KAFKA
Czech composer SUK, HABA, FRIML, DVORAK, FIBICH, JANACEK, SMETANA, TOMASEK, VITASEK
Czech language CZECH, SLOVAK
Czech measure LAN, SAH, JITRO, KOREC, LATRO, LOKET, STRYCH
Czech money KC, DUCAT, HALER, HELLER, KORUNA
Czech president BENES, HAVEL, MASARYK, NOVOTNY, SVOBODA
Czech Republic, capital of PRAHA, PRAGUE
Czech Republic city/town BRNO, MOST, NOVY, PISEK, PLZEN, TABOR, PRAGUE, OSTRAVA
Czech Republic mountain(s) CERNA, ORLICE, LUSATIAN
Czech Republic neighbor POLAND, AUSTRIA, GERMANY, SLOVAKIA
Czech Republic river ELBE, LABE, ODER, OHRE, MARCH, MOLDAU, MORAVA, OSLAVA, UHLAVA, VLTAVA, BEROUNKA

D

D DELTA, DALETH, DENSITY
dab PAT, PECK, POKE, STAB, DIBBLE

dabble TOY, POTTER, TRIFLE, TINKER
dabbler TYRO, DUFFER, AMATEUR, TRIFLER, SCIOLIST
dabchick GREBE, DIPPER
dad PA(PA), DAUD, POPS, PATER, FATHER
Dadaist ARP, BALL, ERNST, GROSZ, TZARA, ARAGON, BRETON, PICABIA, DUCHAMP
daddle FIST, HAND
dado DIE, BASE, SOLIDUM
Daedalus' son ICARUS
daffodil JONQUIL, NARCISSUS
daffy SILLY, GOOFY, WACKY, SCREWY
daft CRAZY, SILLY, FOOLISH
Dagda relative BODB, ANGUS, BRIGIT, OENGUS
dagger CRIS, DIRK, KRIS, BALAS, BOWIE, KATAR, SKEAN, ANLACE, BODKIN, CREESE, STYLET, BAYONET, KHANJAR, PONIARD, STILETTO
— and dagger CLOAK
Dahl character (WILLY) WONKA
Dahomey *see* BENIN
daily ADAY, DIURNAL
dainty CATE, NESH, CHOICE, MIGNON, PETITE, TIDBIT, DELICACY
daiquiri ingredient RUM, LIME, SUGAR, LEMON
dairy LACTARIUM
dairy maid DEY(E), GOWAN
dairy product MILK, CREAM, BUTTER, CHEESE
dais PODIUM, ESTRADE, ROSTRUM
daisy GOWAN, OXEYE, SHASTA, GERBERA, MARGUERITE
— daisy UPSY
Dakota *see* SIOUX
Dakota Terr. capital YANKTON
dale GLEN, VALE, DINGLE
Dallas school SMU
dally LAG, TOY, DELAY, FLIRT, LOITER, TRIFLE
dam PEN, DIKE, SADD, SUDD, WAER, WEIR, GARTH, PARENT
dam, famous *see p. 613*
damage MAR, HARM, HURT, IMPAIR, INJURE
damages claim TROVER
daman *see* CONEY

Damascus king	ARETAS	Danish county	FYN, RIBE,
Damascus river	ABANA		ARHUS, VEJLE, VIBORG,
dame	LADY, MADAM,		BORNHOLM
	MATRON	Danish island	ALS, ERO, FAN,
damn	DOOM, CURSE,		FEJ, FEM, FYN, MAN, OMO,
	CONDEMN		MORS, SAMS, ROMO, LAESO,
Damocles weapon	SWORD		AMAGER, ANHOLT, HESSEL,
Damon's friend	PYTHIAS		SEJERO
damp	WET, DANK, HUMID,	Danish measure	FOD, MIL, POT,
	MOIST, MUGGY		ALEN, FAVN, RODE, ALBUM,
dampen	DEG, WET, MOISTEN		LINJE, TOMME, TONDE,
damsel	GIRL, MAIDEN		ACHTEL, LANDMIL, OLTONDE,
Danae lover	ZEUS		VIERTEL
Danae relative	PERSEUS,	Danish money	DKR, ORE,
	ACRISIUS		ORAS, KRONE, SKILLING
dance	BAL, HOP, BALL, PROM,	Danish parliament	RIGSDAG,
PARTY, COTILL(I)ON; *see p. 643*			FOLKETING
dance gear	TUTU, TIGHTS,	Danish river	RYE, ARNA, SUSA,
	LEOTARD		GELSA, STORA, GUDENE,
dance, muse of	POLYMNIA,		SKJERN
POLYHYMNIA, TERPSICHORE		Danish ruler	CNUT, ERIK,
dance step	PAS; *see* BALLET		GORM, KNUT, OLAF, SWEYN,
dance teacher	MURRAY,		CANUTE, MARGARET,
	ASTAIRE		VALDEMAR, WALDEMAR,
dance type	TAP, TOE, GOGO,		CHRISTIAN, FREDERICK,
	BELLY, APACHE, BALLET,		MARGRETHE
	FLAMENCO	Danish speech	STOD
dancer	ALMA, ALMEH, GEISHA,	Danish weight	ES, LOD, ORT,
	HOOFER, CHORINE,		VOG, MARK, PUND, UNZE,
	DANSEUR, STEPPER,		KVINT, CENTNER, LISPUND,
	DANSEUSE, FIGURANT,		QUINTIN
STRIPPER, ECDYSIAST; *see p. 540*		dank	WET, DAMP, HUMID,
Dancer group	REINDEER		MOIST
Dancer partner	PRANCER	Danse —	MACABRE
dandelion seed	CYPSELA	Dante deathplace	RAVENNA
dander	IRE, IDLE, ANGER,	Dante's Inferno first word	NEL
	WRATH, STROLL, TEMPER,	Dante muse	BEATRICE
	DANDRUFF	Dante patron	SCALA
dandruff	SCURF, DANDER,	Dante work	INFERNO,
	FLAKES, FURFUR		PARADISE, PURGATORY,
dandy	FOP, BEAU, BUCK, DUDE,		DIVINE COMEDY
	FINE, JAKE, TOFF, SWELL	Danube	DUNA, DONAU, ISTER
Dane	JUTLANDER	Danube city	ULM, LINZ, WIEN,
danger	RISK, PERIL, HAZARD		VIENNA
danger signal	SOS, ALARM	Danube tributary	INN, OLT,
dangerous	RISKY, UNSAFE,		VAH, ENNS, HRON, ISAR,
	PARLOUS, PERILOUS		LECH, NAAB, PRUT, RABA,
Daniel's companion	MESHACH,		SAVA, DRAVA, ILLER, ISKER,
	ABEDNEGO, SHADRACH		MARCH, NITRA, SIRET, TISZA,
Danish	*see also* DENMARK		MORAVA, SIRETUL
Danish cheese	ELBO, TYBO,	Danzig	GDANSK
	DANBO, FYNBO, MOLBO,	Daphne's father	LADON
	MARIBO, MYCELLA	Daphne's lover	CHLOE
Danish city/town	ARHUS,	dapper	CHIC, NATTY, NIFTY
	VEJLE, ALBORD, ODENSE,	dapper one	DAN
	TARNBY, COPENHAGEN	dapple(d)	PIED, SPOT, FLECK
Danish composer	GADE,	Dard	SHINA, KAFIRI,
	KUHLAU, NIELSEN,		KHOWAR, PISACA, KASHMIRI
	NORGARD, RIISAGER	Dardanus' brother	IASION

dare	DEFY, FACE, OSSE, RISK, BRAVE, VENTURE	David servant	ILAI
daring	BOLD, BRAVE, HARDY, INTREPID	David victim	URIAH, GOLIATH
		Davis	BETTE, COLIN, SAMMY, ANDREW
Darius defeat place	ISSUS	davit	SPAR, CRANE
dark	EBON, DUSKY, MIRKY, MURKY, SWART, UNLIT, DISMAL, SOMBRE	daw	see CROW
		dawdle	LAG, IDLE, POKE, DALLY
Dark Continent	AFRICA	dawn	DEW, EOS, MORN, SUNUP, AURORA
darken	DIM, BLACKEN, EBONIZE, OBSCURE	dawn, pert. to	EOAN
darkness	DUSK, MIRK, MURK, GLOOM, NIGHT	dawn, signal of	COCK, LARK, ROOSTER, COCKCROW
darling	PET, ROON, CHERI(E), ACUSHLA, ASTHORE	Dawson's river	YUKON
		day	AGE, ERA, YOM, DIES
darn	MEND, PATCH	day before	EVE
dart	BARB, BOLT, FLIT, SKYT, ARROW, SCOOT, ELANCE, MISSILE	Dayak people	IBAN
		daybreak	DAWN, MORN, AURORA, SUNRISE
D'Artagnan friend	ATHOS, ARAMIS, PORTHOS	daydream	FANCY, REVERY, REVERIE
Darwin ship	BEAGLE	daze	STUN, TRANCE, STUPEFY, BEWILDER
Darwin theory	EVOLUTION		
dash	ELAN, LACE, SOSH, TINGE, TOUCH, TRACE, VERVE, HURTLE, HYPHEN, SOUPCON	dazzle	STUN, BLIND, GLARE
		D day	see NORMANDY INVASION
		DDE	see EISENHOWER
		— de combat	HORS
dashing	GAY, BRAVE, SHOWY, FLASHY, JAUNTY	de facto	ACTUAL
dastard	CAD, COWARD, CRAVEN	de novo	ANEW, AGAIN, AFRESH
data	FACTS, INPUT, FIGURES	deacon	see CLERGY
date	IDES, NONE, COURT, NONES, TRYST, CALENDS, OUTMODE	dead	FEY, FLAT, GONE, LATE, (A)MORT, INERT, NAPOO, ASLEEP, CARNAGE, EXPIRED
date line on coin	EXERGUE	dead, abode of	HELL, HADES, SHEOL
date, out of	PASSE, EXPIRED, OBSOLETE		
		dead end	IMPASSE, CULDESAC
dated	OLD, PASSE	Dead Sea fortress	MASADA
datum	FACT	Dead Sea river	JORDAN
daub	APPLY, PAINT, SMEAR, PLASTER	Dead Souls author	GOGOL
		dead tree(s)	DRIKI, RAMPIKE
daughter	HUA, BINT, FILLE	deadbeat	BUM, IDLER, LEECH, SPONGE(R)
daunt	AWE, COW, DAW, AMATE	deaden	DAMP, MUTE, NUMB
dauntless	BRAVE, DARING, GALLANT	deadener	MUTE, BAFFLE; see ANESTHETIC
davenport	SOFA, COUCH, SETTEE	deadlock	TIE, DRAW, IMPASSE
David Copperfield name	DORA, HEEP, ROSA, AGNES, BETSY, BARKIS, DARTLE, MICAWBER, PEGGOTTY, URIAH HEEP	deadly	MORT, FATAL, LETHAL, MORTAL
		deadly sins	ENVY, LUST, ANGER, PRIDE, SLOTH, GLUTTONY, COVETOUSNESS
David's captain	JOAB	deadpan	BLANK, POKERFACE
David relative	OZEM, AMNON, JESSE, TAMAR, MAACAH, MICHAL, ABSALOM, ITHREAM, SOLOMON, ADONIJAH, BATHSHEBA	deaf	SURD, BARREN, MUFFLED
		deaf and —	DUMB
		deal	COPE, DOLE, GIVE, ALLOT, TRADE, HANDLE
		— deal	NEW, FAIR

dealer **AGENT, COPER, HOUSE, BROKER, COOPER, CUTLER, DRAPER, MERCER, MONGER, TRADER, VINTNER**

dealing **TRAFFIC, COMMERCE, EXCHANGE**

dean **DECAN, DOYEN, ELDER, DOYENNE**

Dean **DAFFY, DIZZY, JAMES, JIMMY**

dean, *pert. to* **DECANAL**

dear **LOVED, COSTLY, VALUED, PRECIOUS**

dearth **WANT, FAMINE, DROUGHT, PAUCITY**

death **END, MORT, FINIS, DEMISE, DECEASE, PASSING**

— and death **LIFE**

Death Becomes Her star **STREEP**

death god **MORS**

death note **MORT**

death notice **OBIT(UARY)**

death, put to *see* **EXECUTE**

deathless **IMMORTAL**

deathwatch **VIGIL**

debacle **ROUT, DISASTER**

debar **DENY, SHUT, STOP, DETER**

debase **ALLOY, LOWER, DEFILE, DEMEAN, DEGRADE**

debate **AGON, MOOT, CANVASS**

debauchee **RAKE, ROUE, SATYR, LECHER**

debauchery **ORGY, RIOT, CAROUSAL, INDULGENCE, INTEMPERANCE**

debenture **BOND**

debility **ATONY, FRAILTY**

debonair **SUAVE, JAUNTY, ELEGANT**

Deborah husband **LAPIDOTH**

debris **RUINS, SCREE, LITTER, JETSAM, FLOTSAM, RUBBISH**

debt **DUE, IOU, DUTY, ARREARS**

Debussy work **LAMER, REVERIE, GOLLIWOG, CLAIRDELUNE**

decadence **DECAY, DECLINE**

Decameron Tales author **BOCCACCIO**

decamp **LAM, BOLT, ELOPE, SCRAM, LEVANT, VAMOSE, ABSCOND, VAMOOSE**

— de camp **AIDE**

decant **DRAW, POUR, ELUTRIATE**

decanter **EWER, CROFT, CARAFE**

decay **ROT, BLET, CONK, SPOIL, CARIES, PUTREFY**

decayed **GONE, PUTRID, ROTTEN**

deceased **DEAD, GONE, LATE, DEFUNCT, (DE)PARTED**

deceit **LIE, SHAM, WILE, COVIN, FEINT, FRAUD, GUILE**

deceitful **SLY, WILY, FALSE, ARTFUL**

deceive **BILK, DUPE, FLAM, GULL, SILE, COZEN, TRICK, GAMMON, HUMBUG, ILLUDE**

deceiver **LIAR, FAKER, TRAPAN, SHARPER, IMPOSTOR**

decency **DECORUM, PROPRIETY**

decent **FAIR, MODEST, PROPER, SEEMLY**

deception **FAKE, HOAX, JAPE, RUSE, SHAM, WILE**

deceptive **VAGUE, HOLLOW, TRICKY, SERENIC**

decide **CERN, ELECT, RESOLVE**

decided **SET, SETTLED**

decimal **TEN(TH), REPETEND**

decimate **KILL, SLAY, BURKE**

decipher **READ, SOLVE, DECODE**

decision **TKO, ARRET, DECREE, VERDICT, JUDGMENT, SENTENCE**

deck **PACK, POOP, ADORN, CARDS, DIZEN, ORLOP**

declaim **RANT, RAVE, ORATE, BLEEZE, BLOVIATE**

declaration **OATH, AVOWAL, MISERE**

Decl. of Independence signer **LEE, HALL, HART, PACA, PENN, READ, ROSS, RUSH, ADAMS, CHASE, CLARK, FLOYD, GERRY, HEWES, LEWIS, LYNCH, PAINE, SMITH, STONE, WYTHE, CLYMER, ELLERY, HOOPER, MCKEAN, MORRIS, MORTON, NELSON, RODNEY, TAYLOR, WALTON, WILSON, BRAXTON, HANCOCK, HEYWARD, HOPKINS, SHERMAN, WHIPPLE, WOLCOTT, BARTLETT, FRANKLIN, GWINNETT, HARRISON, RUTLEDGE, STOCKTON, THORNTON, WILLIAMS, JEFFERSON, HOPKINSON, HUNTINGTON, WITHERSPOON**

declare	BID, AVER, AVOW, MELD, STATE, AVOUCH	deer genus	RUSA, CERVUS, MAZAMA, MOSCHUS
decline	DIP, EBB, FADE, SINK, DEMUR, DROOP, SLUMP, SPURN, TABES, REFUSE, SUBSIDE	deer meat	VENISON
		deer, *pert. to*	DAMINE, CERVINE
		deer pouch	BELL
declivity	SCARP, SLANT, SLOPE, CALADE	deer secretion	MUSK
		deer, small	DEERLET, CHEVROTAIN
decompose	ROT, DECAY, SPOIL		
decor	SCENERY	deer sound	BELL
decorate	DECK, ADORN, BEDECK, MINIATE	deer tail	FLAG, SCUT
		deer, young	FAWN
decoration	BADGE, PURFLE, RIBBON, TINSEL, APPLIQUE; *see* AWARD	defame	DECRY, LIBEL, MALIGN, VILIFY, SLANDER
		default	FAIL, MORA, WELCH, BREACH, ARREARS, FORFEIT
decorous	STAID, DEMURE, SEEMLY		
decorum	DIGNITY, ETIQUETTE	defeat	BEST, FOIL, LIKE, MATE, ROUT, WHOMP, WORST, SUBDUE, FAILURE, SHELLAC, TROUNCE
decoy	BAIT, LURE, TOLE, PLANT, CAPPER		
decrease	EBB, WANE, ABATE, LESSEN, RECEDE, DWINDLE	defect	BUG, FLAW, SCOB, SNAG, DESERT
decree	ACT, LAW, BULL, FIAT, WILL, WRIT, ARRET, CANON, EDICT, IRADE, UKASE, DICTUM, FIRMAN, MANDATE	defective	FAULTY, FLAWED, MANQUE, IMPERFECT
		defective item	DUD, LEMON
		defector	RAT, RENEGADE, TURNCOAT
decrepit	WEAK, SENILE, WORN(OUT)	defend	GUARD, SHIELD, UPHOLD, JUSTIFY, PROTECT, SUPPORT, CHAMPION
decry	BLAME, CENSURE, CONDEMN, DENOUNCE		
dedicate	DEVOTE, HALLOW, INSCRIBE	defendant	REUS, ACCUSED, CHAMPION
dedication	ENVOY, DEVOTION, INSCRIPTION, ALLEGIANCE	defense	PLEA, ALIBI, PALISADE, SEPIMENT
deduce	DEEM, INFER, DERIVE, CONCLUDE	defenseless	OPEN, NAKED, HELPLESS
deduct	BATE, FAIK, REBATE	defensible	TENABLE
deductive	APRIORI, DERIVATIVE	defer	DELAY, YIELD, PUTOFF, RETARD, POSTPONE
deed(s)	ACTA, CEDE, COUP, FACT, FAIT, FEAT, GEST(E), STROKE	deference	FEALTY, HOMAGE, RESPECT
deem	HOLD, JUDGE, OPINE	defiance	DARING, BOLDNESS, CONTEMPT, INSOLENCE, RESISTANCE
deep	LOW, SEA, BASS, DARK, WISE, ABYSMAL, ABYSSAL, PROFOUND		
		defiant	BOLD, DARING, INSOLENT, BELLIGERENT
deep-seated	INBRED, INNATE, INTRINSIC, ENTRENCHED	deficiency	DEARTH, ULLAGE, DEFICIT
deer	DOE, ELK, ROE, AXIS, FAWN, HART, HIND, MAHA, MUSK, NAPU, PUDU, REIN, SIKA, SPAY, STAG, ADDRA, GEMUL, KAKAR, KAKUR, MARAL, RATWA, ROYAL, SPADO, CERVID, CHITAL, GUEMUL, RASCAL, SAMBAR, SAMBUR, THAMIN, WAPITI, BROCKET, CARIBOU, CERVOID, MUNTJAC, SAMBHUR, VENISON	deficiency disease	DROPSY, SCURVY, RICKETS, BERIBERI, PELLAGRA
		deficient	SHORT, LACKING, WANTING, INCOMPLETE
		defile	PASS, SOIL, SPOIL, RAVINE, PROFANE
		define	FIX, LIMIT, OUTLINE
		definite	EXACT, CERTAIN
		definition part	ANT(ONYM), SYN(ONYM), ETYM(OLOGY)

deflate **LOWER, COLLAPSE**
deflect **VEER, AVERT, DIVERT, SWERVE**
deflower **RAPE, RAVISH**
Defoe character **MOLL, CRUSOE, FRIDAY**
deform **MAR, MAIM, WARP, CONTORT**
deformity **FLAW, DEFECT, IMPERFECTION**
defraud **GYP, BILK, GULL, CHEAT, COZEN, CHOUSE**
defray **PAY, COVER**
defrost **MELT, THAW, DEICE**
deft **APT, ADROIT, CLEVER**
defunct **DEAD, GONE, EXTINCT**
defy **DARE, BEARD, FLOUT, DISOBEY**
dégagé **CASUAL, RELAXED, DETACHED**
degenerate **PERVERT, DEPRAVED**
degrade **ABASE, LOWER, DEMEAN**
degree(s) **AB, BA, BS, CE, DD, EE, MD, ME, BAC, BFA, BSC, DDS, DSC, DVM, EDD, EST, LLB, LLD, MBA, NTH, PHD, RATE, STEP, BLITT, CLASS, LITTD, PITCH, RADIAN**
dehydrate **DRY, JERK, PARCH**
Deianira's husband **HERCULES**
deify **ADORE, EXALT, EXTOL, GLORIFY, WORSHIP, SANCTIFY**
deign **STOOP, CONDESCEND**
Deiphobus' slayer **MENELAUS**
Deirdre's abductor **NAISI**
Deirdre's father **PHELIM**
Deirdre's guardian **CONCHOBAR**
deity **GOD, NUMEN, GODDESS,**
see p. 645
déjà vu **PARAMNESIA**
dejected **SAD, GLUM, DOWNCAST**
dejection **GLOOM, DESPAIR, SADNESS**
Delaware see also p. 615
Delaware city/town **DOVER, NEWARK, SMYRNA, MILFORD, SEAFORD, WILMINGTON**
Delaware Indian **NANTICOKE**
Delaware river **DUCK, LOVE, MILL, CEDAR, SMYRNA, DELAWARE, POCOMOKE**
delay **MORA, SLOW, WAIT, DEFER, MORAE, STALL, ARREST, DETAIN, LINGER**

dele **CANCEL, EXCISE, REMOVE**
delectable **CUTE, TASTY, CHARMING, DELICIOUS**
delegate **AGENT, ENVOY, DEPUTY, LEGATE**
delete **DELE, ERASE, EXCISE, CANCEL, EXPUNGE**
deletion **DELE, APOCOPE, EXCISION, OMISSION**
deli spread **MAYO, OLEO, BUTTER, MUSTARD**
deliberate **THINK, WEIGH, PONDER**
Delibes work **LAKME, NAILA, COPPELIA**
delicacy **CATE, TIDBIT, FINESSE**
delicate **FINE, FRAIL, DAINTY, FRAGILE**
delicious **TASTY, YUMMY, SAVORY, LUSCIOUS**
delight **GLEE, AMUSE, CHARM, ELATE, MIRTH, REVEL**
Delilah's lover **SAMSON**
delineate **DRAW, LIMN, SKETCH**
delinquency **FAULT, FAILURE**
delinquent **JD, PUNK, FAILING, CARELESS, CRIMINAL, NEGLIGENT, ANTISOCIAL**
delirious **MAD, REE, RAVING**
delirium tremens **DTS, JIMJAMS**
deliver **RID, CEDE, FREE, SEND, UTTER, YIELD, RESCUE, LIBERATE**
delivery **MODE, MANNER, RELIEF, RESCUE, SUPPLY, TRANSFER, CHILDBIRTH**
dell **DALE, GLEN, VALE, DINGLE**
Delphi **KASTRI**
Delphic deity **APOLLO, DIONYSUS**
Deiphic priestess **PYTHIA**
Deiphic stone **OMPHALOS**
delude **DUPE, FLAM, GULL, CHEAT, TRICK, DECEIVE**
deluge **FLOOD, SPATE, PLETHORA**
delusion **MOHA, MIRAGE, VISION**
deluxe **ELEGANT, ELABORATE, LUXURIOUS, SUMPTUOUS**
delve **DIG, DIP, GRUB, MINE, PROBE, SPADE**
demand **DUN, NEED, WANT, CLAIM, INSIST, SOLICIT**
demanding **STRICT, ARDUOUS, EXACTING, DIFFICULT**

demean	ABASE, HUMBLE, DEGRADE
demeanor	AIR, MIEN, CARRIAGE
demented	MAD, LOCO, CRAZY, LOONY, INSANE, DERANGED
demerit	GIG, FAULT
Demeter	CERES, IOULO
Demeter relative	CORA
demigod	HERO, IDOL, SATYR
demise	DEATH, BEQUEST, DECEASE
democracy, world's largest	INDIA
democracy, world's smallest	SANMARINO
demodulate	DETECT
demolish	RASE, RAZE, RUIN, UNDO, LEVEL, WRECK
demon(s)	ALP, DEV, IMP, JIN, NAT, AITU, ATUA, BALI, DEVA, DUIN, HAGG, JANN, JINN, MARA, OGRE, RAHU, SOBK, WADE, WATE, AFRIT, ANITU, ASURA, DEUCE, FIEND, GENIE, GHOUL, JINNI, LAMIA, TROLL, ABIGOR, AFREET, AFRITE, DAEDAL, DAITYA, GOBLIN; see DEVIL
demoness	LILITH, INCUBUS, SUCCUBA
demonstrable	SURE, CERTAIN, PROVABLE, APODICTIC, DEDUCIBLE
demonstrate	SHOW, MARCH, PROVE, PICKET
demonstration	DEMO, SHOW, TEST, MARCH, PROOF, RALLY, SITIN, DISPLAY, PROTEST
demonstrative	OPEN, WARM, DEICTIC, EFFUSIVE
demoralize	CONFUSE, DISCOURAGE
demote	BUST, BREAK, LOWER, DEGRADE, DOWNGRADE
Dempsey	MAULER, MANASSA
demur	WAVER, OBJECT, PROTEST
demure	COY, MIM, SHY, PRIM, STAID
den	CAVE, DIVE, LAIR, CAVEA, STUDY, CAVERN
denature	ALTER, WEAKEN
denial	REFUSAL, REJECTION
denizen	CITIZEN, HABITUE
Denmark	THULE; see also DANISH
Denmark, capital of	COPENHAGEN
Denmark neighbor	SWEDEN, GERMANY
Dennis the Menace names	JAY, RUFF, ALICE, HENRY, NORTH, GEORGE, KEARNS, MARTHA, WILSON
denomination	SECT, CLASS, CHURCH, SCHOOL
denote	MEAN, IMPLY, PORTEND
denouement	END, OUTCOME
denounce	DECRY, ACCUSE, EXPOSE, CENSURE
dense	DULL, CLOSE, CRASS, HEAVY, THICK, OBTUSE
dent	NICK, NOTCH, EFFECT
dental	ORAL, ODONTIC
dentine	IVORY
dentist's tool	BURR, DRILL, SCALER, FORCEPS
denture	PLATE, TEETH, BRIDGE
denude	BARE, STRIP
Denver	AURARIA
deny	ABJURE, DISOWN, NEGATE, REFUSE, GAINSAY
depart	DIE, EXIT, VADE, SCRAM, BEGONE, DECAMP, MAKE OFF, VAMO(O)SE
department store	MART, EMPORIUM
department store, famous	SAKS, MACYS, GIMBELS, NORDSTROM, BLOOMINGDALES
departure	EXIT, EXODUS, HEGIRA, OUTGANG
depend	LEAN, RELY, HINGE
dependent	WARD, MINION, PROTEGE, SPONGER, SUBJECT, CONTINGENT
depict	DRAW, ETCH, LIMN, PORTRAY
depilate	HUSK, PLUCK, SHAVE
depilatory	NAIR, RUSMA
deplete	DRAIN, EMPTY, EAT INTO, EXHAUST
deplore	RUE, (BE)WAIL, GRIEVE, LAMENT
deport	BAN, CARRY, EXILE, EXPEL, BANISH
depose	AVER, OUST, DISBAR, REMOVE, UNSEAT, DETHRONE
deposit	BED, ORE, FLOT, GUHR, LEES, LODE, MARL, SILT, ARGOL, CACHE, DELTA, DREGS, GEEST, LOESS, PLACER, PLAQUE, SINTER,

	TARTAR, ALLUVIA, CALCULUS, SEDIMENT
deposition	AFFIDAVIT, TESTIMONY
depository	SAFE, CACHE, DEPOT, VAULT
depot	BASE, ARMORY, STATION, ENTREPOT
deprave	CORRUPT, DEBAUCH, PERVERT, VITIATE
deprecate	REGRET, DEPLORE, PROTEST
depreciate	LESSEN, CHEAPEN, DECLINE, DEVALUE, RUN DOWN, BELITTLE, DISPARAGE
depredate	ROB, LOOT, SPOIL
depress	DENT, SINK, DAMPEN, SADDEN
depressed	SAD, BLUE, GLUM, DEJECTED, DOWNCAST
depression	COL, DIP, PIT, BLUES, DUMPS, ENNUI, FOVEA, GLOOM, SWALE
depression symptom	GRIEF, ANXIETY, DISTRESS, SHUTDOWN
deprive	STRIP, DIVEST
deprived	REFT, SHORN, BEREFT
depth	DEEP, HOLE, ABYSS
depth charge	ASHCAN
depth finder	SONAR, SOUNDER
deputy	AGENT, ENVOY, PROXY, VICAR, FACTOR
derange	CRAZE, UPSET, DEMENT
derby	EPSOM, BOWLER, KENTUCKY; see p. 711
derelict	WAIF, SLACK, TRAMP, WRECK, ASTRAY, CASTAWAY
deride	see MOCK
derision	BOO, HISS, HOOT, RAZZ, IRONY, SCORN, MOCKERY, CATCALL
derisive term	CHUFF, FADGE, CUTTLE, DRAZEL, DURGEN, FRIBBLE
derivation	ROOT, SEED, CRADLE, ORIGIN, SOURCE, ETYMOLOGY
derive	DRAW, TRACE, DEDUCE
dernier cri	RAGE, CRAZE, VOGUE, FASHION, LAST WORD
derogatory	ADVERSE, INSULTING, DEFAMATORY
derrick	RIG, CRANE, DAVIT, STEEVE
derrick part	GIN, JIB, LEG, BEAM, BOOM, SPAR, PULLEY

dervish	AGIB, FAKIR, FAQ(U)IR
descendants	GENS, SONS, ISSUE, (S)CIONS, PROGENY
descendants, same mother	ENATE
descent	BIRTH, SCARP, SLOPE
describe	DRAW, DEPICT, RELATE, NARRATE
descriptive	VIVID, GRAPHIC, COLORFUL
descry	KEN, ESPY, BETRAY
Desdemona's attendant	EMILIA
Desdemona's husband	OTHELLO
desecrate	ABUSE, DEFILE, POLLUTE
desert	DUE, ERG, QUIT, WILD, LEAVE, WASTE, BARREN, ABANDON
desert, famous	see p. 613
Desert Fox	ROMMEL
desert, pert. to	EREMIC
desert vision	MIRAGE
desert watering place	OASIS
deserted	ALONE, LONELY, DESOLATE
deserter	RAT, AWOL, BOLTER, RUNAWAY, RECREANT, RENEGADE, TURNCOAT
deserve	EARN, RATE, MERIT
desiccated	DRY, ARID, SERE
design	AIM, END, PLAN, MOTIF, THEME, INTENT(ION), CREATE, SCHEME
designate	ASSIGN, SELECT, APPOINT; see NAME
designer	STYLIST, CREATOR, PLANNER, ARCHITECT
designer, famous	PRADA; see COUTURIER
designing	ARTFUL, CRAFTY, SCHEMING
desire	YEN, HOPE (FOR), LUST, URGE, WANT, COVET, CRAVE, ASPIRE, LIBIDO
desirous	FAIN, KEEN, EAGER, WISHFUL
desist	STOP, CEASE, FORBEAR
— and desist	CEASE
desk	AMBO, PULPIT, LECTERN, ROLLTOP, SECRETARY
desolate	LORN, RAZE, SACK, BLEAK, DREARY
despair	MISERY, ANGUISH
desperado	THUG, BRAVO, OUTLAW
despicable	LOW, BASE, MEAN, VILE, ODIOUS, HATEFUL
despise	ABHOR, SPURN, CONTEMN
despoil	ROB, STRIP, RAVAGE

despondent LOW, SAD, BLUE
despot CZAR, TSAR, TYRANT,
  AUTOCRAT, DICTATOR
dessert ICE, PIE, CAKE, TART,
  SWEET, TORTE, AFTERS,
  MOUSSE, TRIFLE, SHERBET;
  see p. 562
destination AIM, END, GOAL
destiny LOT, DOOM, EURE,
  FATE, KARMA, KISMET
destitute LORN, POOR, NEEDY
destroy EAT (INTO), RUIN,
  RASE, SACK, UNDO, TOTAL,
  TRASH, WRECK
destroyed SMIT, KAPUT
destroyer HUN, SIVA, VANDAL,
  WARSHIP, SABOTEUR
destructible FRAIL, FRAGILE
destruction STRY, TALA,
  HAVOC, STROY, WRACK
desuetude DISUSE
desultory FITFUL, RANDOM,
  ERRATIC
detach WEAN, SEVER, SUNDER
detached ALOOF, APART,
  SEPARATE, INDIFFERENT
detail(s) ITEM, NICETY,
  PATROL, ITEMIZE, SPECIFY,
  MINUTIAE
detain NAB, CHECK, DELAY,
  ARREST, INTERN
detect ESPY, NOSE, SPOT, SENSE
detection ability NOSE
detective TEC, DICK, BEAGLE,
  SLEUTH, TAILER, GUMSHOE,
  HAWKSHAW
detectives in literature and TV *see
  p. 629*
detector BUG, NOSE, RADAR,
  SONAR, DOWSER, FEELER,
  ANTENNA, TENTACLE
detent DOG, PAWL, STOP,
  STUD, CATCH, CLICK,
  RATCHET
detente TRUCE, CEASEFIRE
deter DETAIN, HINDER,
  PREVENT
detergent SOAP, SAPONIN,
  CLEANSER
deteriorate DECAY, IMPAIR,
  WORSEN
determine FIX, JUDGE,
  DECIDE, RESOLVE
determined SET, FIRM,
  DOGGED, RESOLUTE
detest HATE, ABHOR,
  LOATHE, DESPISE
detestable ODIOUS, HATEFUL,
  EXECRABLE

dethrone OUST, DEPOSE,
  UNSEAT, OVERTHROW
detonator CAP, FUSE, SQUIB,
  TRIGGER, EXPLODER
detour BYPASS, DIVERT,
  DEVIATION
detract DEROGATE,
  DISPARAGE
detritus SCREE, TALUS, DEBRIS
Detroit team LIONS, TIGERS,
  PISTONS
Deucalion relative HELLEN,
  PYRRHA, CLYMENE
devastate RAZE, SACK, WASTE
develop EVOLVE, MATURE,
  UNFOLD
development EVENT, CHANGE,
  GROWTH, PROJECT
Devi UMA, KALI, DURGA,
  GAURI, CHANDI, PARVATI,
  BHAIRAVI
Devi consort SIVA
Devi father HIMAVAT
deviate ERR, YAW, HADE,
  WARP, SHIFT, STRAY,
  MUTATE, SWERVE, DIGRESS
device PLAN, PLOY, MOTTO,
  EMBLEM, GADGET,
  IMPLEMENT
devil BENG, DEIL, DULE,
  CHORT, DEUCE, EBLIS,
  HUGON, SATAN, AZAZEL,
  BELIAL, DICKENS, LUCIFER,
  SHAITAN, SHEITAN; *see* DEMON
devilfish RAY, MANTA, SKATE
devil-may-care RASH, MADCAP,
  HEEDLESS, RECKLESS
devious SHIFTY, TRICKY,
  WINDING, TORTUOUS
devise AIM, WILL, FRAME,
  SCHEME, CONCOCT
devoid EMPTY, VACANT,
  LACKING
Devon river EXE
devotee FAN, IST, BUFF, YATI,
  BIGOT, VOTARY, ZEALOT,
  IDOLATOR
devotion ARDOR, PIETY,
  FEALTY, FERVOR, NOVENA
devour BOLT, WOLF, GORGE,
  CONSUME
devouring AVID
devout HOLY, GODLY, PIOUS
dewlap FOLD, PALEA, WATTLE
dewy MOIST, RORAL, RORIC
dexterity ART, KNACK,
  FINESSE
dexterous APT, DEFT, HANDY,
  ADROIT

diabetic's medicine INSULIN
diabolic WICKED, IMPIOUS
diacritic BREVE, TILDE, ACCENT, MACRON, UMLAUT, DIERESIS
diadem *see* CROWN
diagnostic TEST, ANALYTIC(AL)
diagonal BIAS, ASLANT, OBLIQUE
diagram PLAT, CHART, DRAFT, EPURE, SKETCH
dialect CANT, ARGOT, IDIOM, LINGO, JARGON, PATOIS
dialogue CHAT, LINES, SCRIPT, CONVERSATION
diameter BORE, MODULE, CALIBER
diamond GEM, ICE, BO(A)RT, RHOMB, CARBON, LOZENGE; *see* BASEBALL
diamond dust BORT
diamond, famous HOPE, PITT, MATAN, DUDLEY, DUTOIT, HORNBY, KOLLUR, NASSAK, ORLOFF, PIGOTT, REGENT, CHAPADA, DEBEERS, EUGENIE, JUBILEE, STEWART, TENNANT, TIFFANY, CULLINAN, KOHINOOR
diamond part CULET
diamondback RATTLER, TERRAPIN
Diana DELIA, ARTEMIS
Diana's parents LATONA, JUPITER
diaper DIDY, NAPPY, NAPKIN, NAPPIE
diaphanous THIN, GAUZY, SHEER
diaphragm, *pert. to* PHRENIC
diarist NIN, FRANK, PEPYS, BURNEY
diary LOG, RECORD, DAYBOOK, DIURNAL, JOURNAL
Diaspora GOLAH, GALUTH
diatribe SCREED, TIRADE, HARANGUE, JEREMIAD
Diblaim relative GOMER
dice CHOP, CUBE, MINCE
dice term COG, JOE, CISE, COME, DICK, FADE, MISS, NICK, ROLL, SICE, SISE, BONES, CRAPS, FIELD, POINT, SHOOT, BOXCAR, PHOEBE, AMBSACE, NATURAL
Dick Tracy character TESS

Dick van Dyke Show names ROB, ALAN, BUDDY, JERRY, LAURA, MOREY, REINER, PETRIE, SALLY, MILLIE, THOMAS, ROSEMARIE
Dickens characters *see p. 629*
Dickens illustrator PHIZ
Dickens pen name BOZ
dicker BARTER, HAGGLE, BARGAIN
dickey BIB, COLLAR, DONKEY, RUMBLE, VESTEE
dictator DESPOT, TYRANT
dictator, famous AMIN, PERON, SULLA, CAESAR, FRANCO, HITLER, MIKADO, SHOGUN, STALIN, SALAZAR, TRUJILLO, MUSSOLINI
dictionary LEXICON, WORDBOOK, VOCABULARY
dictum MAXIM, SAYING
dido ANTIC, CAPER, GAMBOL
Dido ELISSA
Dido lover AENEAS
Dido relative ANNA, BELUS
die DOD, TAT, CUBE, DADO, SICCA, STAMP, EXPIRE, PERISH, TESSERA
— die SINE
diehard FOGY, TORY, HARDNOSE, MOSSBACK, STUBBORN
— diem CARPE
Dies — IRAE
diet BANT, FARE, LOCAL, LOFAT, ATKINS, REGIME(N), CONGRESS
differ VARY, DEVIATE, DISSENT, DISAGREE
difference ODDS, EPACT, NUANCE
different OTHER, DIVERS, SUNDRY, UNLIKE, DIVERSE, DISTINCT
difficult HARD, TOUGH, ARDUOUS, STUBBORN, DEMANDING, LABORIOUS
difficulty FIX, JAM, RUB, KNOT, NODE, PICKLE, SCRAPE, DILEMMA
diffident COY, SHY, MODEST
diffuse STREW, STROW, WORDY, PROLIX
dig GET, JAB, GRUB, MINE, PION, POKE, ROOT, DELVE, SPADE, TAUNT, SHOVEL, POTSHOT, UNEARTH
digest ABSORB, APERCU, PRECIS, EPITOME, PANDECT

digestive juice	PAPAIN, PEPSIN, RENNIN
digging tool	HOE, LOY, PICK, SPUD, SCOOP, SPADE, DREDGE, SHOVEL, MATTOCK
digit	TOE, CIPHER, FINGER, INTEGER, NUMERAL
dignified	LOFTY, NOBLE, SEDATE, STATELY
dignity	HONOR, POISE, WORTH, REPUTE, DECORUM, GRAVITY, MAJESTY, EMINENCE
digress	STRAY, RAMBLE, DEVIATE
dike	DITCH, JETTY, LEVEE
dilapidated	RATTY, RUNDOWN
dilate	SWELL, WIDEN, DISTEND
dilatory	LAX, SLOW, TARDY, REMISS
dilemma	FIX, JAM, PICKLE, QUANDARY
— of a dilemma	HORN(S)
dilettante	POSEUR, AMATEUR, DABBLER
dill	ANET, ANISE, FENNEL
dilly	DARB, LULU, PEACH
dillydally	DELAY, TARRY, HESITATE
dilute	THIN, WATER, RAREFY, WEAKEN
dim	FADE, BLEAR, DUSKY, FAINT
dime —	NOVEL, ADOZEN
dimension	SIZE, EXTENT, VOLUME, MEASURE, CAPACITY
diminish	EBB, BATE, PLOY, SINK, WANE, ABATE, PETER, TAPER
diminished	WANY, LESSENED
diminutive suffix	*see p. 694*
dimple	GELASIN
dimwit	DUNCE, IDIOT
— and dine	WINE
din	NOISE, CLAMOR, RACKET, UPROAR
dine	EAT, SUP, FEAST, EAT OUT, HAVE A MEAL
dinghy	SABOT; *see* BOAT
dingle	DALE, DELL, GLEN
dingy	DRAB, GRIMY, OURIE
dining room	MESS, OECUS, SPENCE, CENACLE, REFECTORY
dinosaur	SAURIAN; *see* LIZARD
dint	DENT, MARK, FORCE
diocese	*see* BISHOP'S SEAT

Dione children	PELOPS, APHRODITE
Dionne quintuplets	MARIE, CECILE, EMELIE, YVONNE, ANNETTE
Dionne quintuplet parents	OLIVA, ELZIRE
Dionysus follower	MAENAD
Dionysus relative	ZEUS, SEMELE, PRIAPUS
Dioscuri	ANAX, TWINS, ANACES, CASTOR, POLLUX
dip	DAP, DIB, BAIL, DOPP, DUNK, LADE, DOUSE, MERSE
diploma	DEGREE, SHEEPSKIN, CERTIFICATE
diplomacy	TACT, FINESSE, PROTOCOL
diplomat	ENVOY, CONSUL, LEGATE, NUNCIO, ATTACHE, EMISSARY, MINISTER, PROXENUS
diplomatic	ARTFUL, POLITIC, TACTFUL
dipper	URSA, LADLE, SCOOP, SPOON, PIGGIN
Dirce's husband	LYCUS
Dirce's victim	ANTIOPE
dire	FATAL, FUNEST, URGENT, FATEFUL, FEARFUL
direct	AIM, CONN, OPEN, LEVEL, PILOT, POINT, STEER
direction	*see* COMPASS POINT
directly	SOON, PROMPTLY
director	HEAD, LEADER, MANAGER; *see p. 540*
directory	LIST, ORDO, BLUEBOOK, REGISTER
dirge	KEEN, LINOS, LINUS, LAMENT, TRENTAL, THRENODY
dirigible	*see* AIRCRAFT
dirk	*see* DAGGER
dirt	SOD, LOAM, SILT, SOIL, EARTH, FILTH, GRIME
dirt —	CHEAP
dirty	FOUL, DINGY, FILTHY, GRIMY, MUDDY
Dis	HADES, ORCUS, PLUTO
disable	SAP, LAME, MAIM, GRUEL
disadvantage	DRAWBACK, HANDICAP, DETRIMENT, PREJUDICE
disagree	CLASH, DIFFER, CONTEND
disagreeable	MEAN, CROSS, TESTY, ORNERY
disagreeing	ATODDS, DIFFERING

disagreement **ROW, TIFF, SPAT,** **FIGHT, SCRAP, DISPUTE**	disconnect **UNDO, SEVER,** **DETACH**
disappear **VANISH, EVANESCE**	disconnected **CUT OFF,**
disappoint **FAIL, JILT,** **LETDOWN, DISTRESS,** **DISPLEASE**	**OFFLINE, SEVERED,** **DETACHED**
	disconsolate **SAD, FORLORN**
disappointment **BLOW,** **LETDOWN**	discontinue **STOP, CEASE,** **DESIST, SUSPEND**
disapprove **VETO, REJECT,** **CONDEMN, CRITICIZE,** **TURN DOWN**	discord **JAR, ERIS, ODDS,** **STRIFE, FRICTION**
	discordant **AJAR, OFFKEY,** **JARRING**
disapproval expression **TSK(TSK),** **TUTTUT**	discount **AGIO, BATTA,** **IGNORE, REBATE**
disarray **DISORDER,** **CONFUSION**	discourage **DAUNT, DETER,** **DAMPEN, DEJECT,** **DEPRIVE**
disavow **DENY, DISOWN,** **RECANT**	
disband **DISPERSE, BREAKUP,** **SCATTER**	discourse **HOMILY, SERMON,** **DESCANT, PR(A)ELECT,** **RHETORIC**
disbeliever **THOMAS, ATHEIST,** **SKEPTIC**	discourtesy **INSULT, SLIGHT,** **DISRESPECT**
disburse **PAY, SPEND, EXPEND**	discover **(E)SPY, DISCERN,** **UNEARTH**
disc *see* **DISK**	
disc — **JOCKEY**	discoverer, famous *see p. 540*
discard **JUNK, MOLT, SCRAP,** **SLUFF, REJECT, ABANDON**	discovery **FIND, ESPIAL,** **DETECTION**
discarded **OFFCAST,** **REDUNDANT**	discredit **SLUR, SHAME,** **DISGRACE, DISHONOR,** **DISPARAGE**
discern **KEN, ESPY, DESCRY,** **DETECT**	
discerning **ASTUTE, SHREWD,** **SAPIENT**	discreet **WARY, DEMURE,** **CAREFUL**
discernment **TACT, ACUMEN**	discrepancy **GAP, EPACT,** **VARIANCE**
discharge **ARC, DROP, EMIT,** **FIRE, OUST, SACK, EJECT,** **EXPEL**	discrete **DISTINCT, SEPARATE**
	discretion **TACT, SKILL,** **JUDGMENT**
disciple **CHELA, PUPIL,** **FOLLOWER;** *see* **APOSTLE**	discriminate **SECERN,** **PREJUDGE, DISTINGUISH**
disciplinarian **TYRANT,** **MARTINET**	discriminating **PICKY, CHOOSY,** **REFINED, CRITICAL**
discipline **DRILL, ORDER,** **FERULE**	discrimination **BIAS, TASTE,** **RACISM, INEQUITY,** **INSIGHT, PREJUDICE,** **PERCEPTION**
discipliner **DEAN**	
disclaim **DENY, ABJURE,** **DISOWN**	
disclose **BARE, EXPOSE,** **REVEAL**	discus **DISK, QUOIT**
	discuss **MOOT, TREAT,** **DEBATE, DILATE, DISSERT**
discolored **DOTY, LIVID,** **USTULATE**	discussion **DEBATE, PALAVER,** **SEMINAR, SESSION,** **SQUABBLE**
discombobulate **ADDLE,** **POTHER, RATTLE, RUFFLE,** **CONFUSE, FLUSTER, PERTURB**	
	discussion group **FORUM,** **PANEL, SEMINAR**
discomfit **JAR, UPSET,** **EMBARRASS**	disdain **SCORN, SPURN,** **DESPISE, SNEER AT,** **CONTEMPT**
discomfort **PAIN, MALAISE,** **DISTRESS**	
disconcert **FAZE, ABASH,** **RATTLE, DISTURB,** **PERTURB**	disease **MAL, MALADY,** **AILMENT, ILLNESS,** **DISORDER**

disease carrier   RAT, INSECT, TSETSE, VECTOR, MOSQUITO

disease, cause of   GERM, VIRUS, MICROBE, BACILLUS, BACTERIA, PATHOGEN

disease, *pert. to*   CLINIC, LOIMIC

diseases   see p. 533

disembark   LAND, DEBUS, GETOFF, DEPLANE, DETRAIN

disembowel   GUT, DRAW, HULK, EVISCERATE

disencumber   RID, FREE, DETACH

disengage   FREE, PART, WEAN

disentangle   CARD, FREE, UNDO, RAVEL

disfigure   MAR, SCAR, DEFACE, DEFORM, MANGLE, UGLIFY

disgrace   BLOT, ABASE, ODIUM, SHEND, STIGMA, SCANDAL

disguise   MASK, MUMM, SHAM, VEIL, CLOAK, SCREEN

disgust   REPEL, OFFEND, SICKEN, REPULSE

disgusting   ODIOUS, FULSOME, HATEFUL

dish   BOWL, LANX, COMAL, CRUSE, GRAIL, PATEN, PLATE, SERVE, VIAND, PATINA, SAUCER, TUREEN, VESSEL, CHARGER, COMPOTE, PLATTER, RAMEKIN, COMPOTIER; *see* MENU

dishabille   NEGLIGEE

dishearten   AMATE, DAUNT, DETER

dishevel   MUSS, RUMPLE, TOUSLE

dishonest   FALSE, LYING, CORRUPT, CHEATING, DECEITFUL, INSINCERE

dishonor   SHAME, BLACK EYE, DISGRACE, DISCREDIT

disinclined   AVERSE, RELUCTANT

disinfectant   IODIN, LYSOL, CRESOL, IODINE, PHENOL, CHLORINE, PEROXIDE

disintegrate   DECAY, BREAKUP, CRACKUP, CRUMBLE

disinter   DIGUP, EXHUME, UNBURY, UNEARTH

disk   CD, EP, LP, DVD, ATEN, DIAL, PUCK, SPUT, CDROM, PATEN, PLATE, WAFER, HARROW, RECORD, SEQUIN, PLATTER

dislike   HATE, AVERSION, DISTASTE

dislocate   SPLAY, LUXATE, DISJOINT, DISPLACE

disloyal   FALSE, UNTRUE, FAITHLESS

disloyal person   INGRATE, TRAITOR, CHEATER, INFORMER, TURNCOAT

dismal   DRAB, DREAR(Y), SOMBRE

dismantle   RAZE, STRIP, UNRIG

dismay   FAZE, APPAL, DAUNT, APPALL

dismiss   CAN, FIRE, OUST, DEMIT, REMUE, IGNORE, CASHIER

dismissal   CONGE, OUSTER, REMOVAL

dismounted   ALIT, DISLODGED

Disney character   CLEO, HUEY, DAISY, DEWEY, DUMBO, GOOFY, LOUIE, PLUTO, DONALD, MICKEY, MINNIE, THUMPER

Disney film   BAMBI, ALADDIN, FANTASIA, PINOCCHIO, SNOW WHITE, CINDERELLA, LITTLE MERMAID

disorder   MESS, DERAY, SNARL, JUMBLE, LITTER, CLUTTER

disorderly   MESSY, UNTIDY, CHAOTIC

disown   REJECT, DISAVOW, DISCLAIM

disparage   *see* SLANDER

disparity   CONTRAST, CONFLICT

dispassionate   COOL, EVEN, LEVEL

dispatch   KILL, NOTE, POST, SEND, CABLE, HASTE, WASTE

dispel   OUST, EJECT, BANISH, RUB OUT

dispensary   CLINIC, PHARMACY

dispensation   RELEASE, EXEMPTION, PROVISION, ABSOLUTION

dispense   DOLE, EXEMPT, FOREGO

disperse   SPREAD, SCATTER

displaced person   DP, EXILE, EVACUEE, REFUGEE

display   AD, POST, SHEW, ARRAY, VAUNT, EVINCE, FLAUNT, OSTENT, PARADE, EXHIBIT

displease   MIFF, ANGER, ANNOY, PIQUE, OFFEND, PROVOKE

displeasure	ANGER, PIQUE	distaff side	FEMALE, WOMAN,
dispose (of)	BIAS, SELL, DITCH,		WEAKER SEX
	GROUP, PLACE, POSIT	distance meter	ODOMETER
disposed	BENT, PRONE,	distant	FAR, YON, AFAR,
	READY, TENDING		AWAY, ALOOF, BEYOND,
disposition	BENT, MOOD,		REMOTE
	NATURE, TENDENCY	distaste	DISLIKE, AVERSION
dispossess	OUST, EJECT,	distend	SWELL, DILATE,
	EVICT, DIVEST		EXPAND, INFLATE, STRETCH
disprove	REBUT, NEGATE,	distended	TURGID, BLOATED,
	REFUTE		SWOLLEN
disputatious	ERISTIC,	distill	BREW, DRIP, DECOCT
	CONTENTIOUS	distilling device	STILL,
dispute	CARP, FLITE, BICKER,		RETORT, ALEMBIC, MATRASS
	DEBATE, HAGGLE, HIGGLE	distinct	CLEAR, PLAIN,
disputed area	RUHR, SAAR,		EVIDENT
	CHACO, SABAH, KASHMIR,	distinction	HONOR,
	DAMANSKY		PROMINENCE
disquiet	FRET, UNEASE,	distinguish	SEE, MARK,
	ANXIETY		SECERN, DISCERN, MAKE
disquisition	ESSAY, INQUIRY,		OUT, CLASSIFY, TELL APART
	TREATISE	distinguished	FAMOUS,
Disraeli novel	SYBIL, TANCRED		EMINENT
disregard	OMIT, SKIP, WAIVE,	distort	WARP, SLANT, TWIST,
	IGNORE		DEFORM
disrepair	DECAY, ATROPHY	distraint	NA(A)M, POIND
disreputable	SEAMY, SHADY,	distraught	UPSET, CRAZED,
	UNSAVORY		FRANTIC, CONFUSED
disrepute	SHAME, TAINT,	distress	PAIN, AGONY, GRIEF,
	INFAMY, OBLOQUY,		UPSET, ANGUISH, TROUBLE
	DISGRACE	distress signal	SOS, ALARM,
disrespectful	RUDE, IMPOLITE		MAYDAY
disrobe	STRIP, UNDRESS	distribute	JOB, DEAL, DOLE,
disrupt	UPSET, DISTURB		METE, ALLOT, RATION
dissect	STUDY, CUT UP,	district	GAU, SOC, AREA, BELT,
	PARSE, DIVIDE, ANALYZE		MIAO, PALE, SOKE, WARD,
dissemble	LIE, PRETEND		WICK, ZONE, FIELD, CANTON,
disseminate	SOW, STREW,		SECTOR, CIRCUIT, DEMESNE,
	SPREAD		PRECINCT; see p. 591
dissenter	ANTI, HERETIC,	District of Columbia	see
	SECTARY, RECUSANT		WASHINGTON
dissertation	ESSAY, TRACT,	distrust	DOUBT, SUSPICION
	SERMON, THESIS,	disturb	VEX, FAZE, ROIL,
	TREATISE		STATIC, HECKLE, MOLEST
dissimilar	UNLIKE, DIFFERENT,	disturbance	ROW, RIOT,
	DISPARATE		FRACAS, HUBBUB, TUMULT
dissimulate	FEIGN, PRETEND	ditch	SAP, DIKE, FOSS, HOLL,
dissipate	FADE, SPEND, WASTE,		JILT, MOAT, RINE, TAJO,
	DISPEL, DIFFUSE, SCATTER		DRAIN, FLUME, FOSSE, ZANJE,
dissipated person	RAKE, ROUE,		RELAIS, SLUICE, DISCARD
	DEBAUCHEE	ditto	TOO, ALSO, COPY,
dissolute	LAX, LEWD, LOOSE,		SAME, LIKEWISE
	RAKISH	diuretic target	EDEMA
dissolute person	RAKE, ROUE	diurnal	DAILY, DAYTIME
dissolve	MELT, VANISH,	divagate	STRAY, WANDER,
	DISBAND		DIGRESS
dissonant	ATONAL	divan	SOFA, COURT, CANAPE,
dissuade	DETER, REPEL,		LEEWAN, SALOON, SETTEE
	DEHORT	dive	DEN, DROP, FLIP, SPIN,

SWAN, GAINER, HEADER,
SALOON, SHEBEEN, BACKFLIP
dive in   TRY, BEGIN, START
diver   AUK, LOON, GREBE,
FROGMAN, PENGUIN,
AQUANAUT
diver's disease   BENDS
diver's equipment   TANK,
CHUTE, SCUBA, AIRHOSE,
SNORKEL, AQUALUNG,
FLIPPERS, LIFELINE
diverge   FORK, VARY, DEVIATE
diversion   GAME, SPORT,
PASTIME
diversity   RANGE, VARIETY
divert   AMUSE, PARRY,
DECEIVE
divest   BARE, DOFF, TIRL
STRIP, DENUDE, DEPRIVE
divide   FORK, REND, RIVE,
ALLOT, HALVE, BISECT,
SUNDER, TRISECT
divided   REFT, APART, CLEFT,
SPLIT, PARTITE
dividend   PLUM, BONUS,
MELON, SHARE
divider   BUNTON, MERIST,
COMPASS
divination   OMEN, SORS,
AUGURY, SORTES,
DOWSING, PALMISTRY
divination, *pert. to*   FATIDIC
divine   HOLY, FANCY, GUESS,
SACRED, GODLIKE,
SUPERNAL
divine being   *see* GOD,
GODDESS
Divine Comedy author   DANTE
Divine Comedy setting   HELL,
RING, PARADISE,
PURGATORY
divine word   GRACE, LOGOS
diving bird   AUK, LOON, SMEW,
GREBE, DUCKER
diving equipment   *see* DIVER
divining rod   WAND, DOWSER
divinity   GOD, JAH, IDOL,
DEITY, NUMEN, YAHWE,
ADONAI, ELOHIM, GODHEAD,
JEHOVAH, THEOLOGY
division   HIEN, MEER, MERE,
SECT, HSIEN, BUREAU,
COHORT, EOGAEA, SCHISM,
MITOSIS, SEGMENT,
FRACTION
divorce   GET(T), PART, SPLIT,
TALAK
divorce allowance   ALIMONY,
SUPPORT, PALIMONY

divorce bill   GETT
divorce grounds   ALIMONY,
CRUELTY, INCOMPATIBILITY
divulge   BARE, TELL, REVEAL,
DISCLOSE
Dixie composer   EMMETT
Dixie(land)   SOUTH
— dixit   IPSE
Dixon partner   MASON
dizziness   SCOTOMY, VERTIGO
dizziness, *pert. to*   DINIC(AL)
dizzy   GIDDY, SILLY, FOOLISH
dizzy, fool   REEL, SEESTARS
Djibouti, capital of   DJIBOUTI
Djibouti language   ARABIC,
FRENCH; *see* CUSHITIC
Djibouti money   FRANC,
DOLLAR
Djibouti neighbor   YEMEN,
ERITREA, SOMALIA,
ETHIOPIA
DNA element   BASE, GENE,
CODON, PURINE, PYRMIDINE
Dnieper city   KIEV, ORSHA,
SMOLENSK
Dnieper tributary   PSEL, SOZH,
SULA, DESNA, PSIOL
do   FARE, MAKE, CHEAT,
PERFORM
do away with   KILL, ERASE,
ABOLISH
do (oneself) in   KILL, END IT,
SNUFF, MURDER
do up   WRAP
do without   SPARE, FOREGO,
ABSTAIN
Dobie Gillis Show names
DENVER, DWAYNE, HICKMAN,
MAYNARD
docile   TAME, GENTLE, PLIANT
dock   BOB, CUT, PEN, BANG,
CLIP, FINE, LAND, PIER,
QUAY, SLIP, BASIN, BERTH,
JETTY, WHARF, DEDUCT
docket   LABEL, AGENDA,
CALENDAR
dockworker   LUMPER,
STEVEDORE
dockworker's union   ILA
doctor   MD, HAKIM, LEECH,
MEDIC, QUACK, TREAT,
HUKAMA, INTERN, MEDICO,
TAMPER, CORONER, FALSIFY,
INTERNE, SURGEON
doctor, type of   OCULIST,
SURGEON, INTERNIST,
OSTEOPATH, UROLOGIST,
ONCOLOGIST, PODIATRIST,
NEUROLOGIST,

OPTOMOTRIST,	
RADIOLOGIST,	
CHIROPRACTOR,	
GYNECOLOGIST,	
OBSTETRICIAN,	
PERDIATRICIAN	
doctor's org.	AMA
Dr. J	ERVING, JULIUS
Dr. Seuss character	CAT,
LORAX, GRINCH, HORTON,	
YERTLE	
Doctor Zhivago part	LARA,
YURY, PASHA	
doctrinaire	ISMY, DOGMATIC
doctrine	ISM, CULT, RITE,
SECT, CREED, DOGMA,	
MAXIM, TENET, CULTUS,	
THEORY	
document	WRIT, PAPER,
SCRIP, INSTRUMENT	
document holder	FILE,
DOSSIER, HANAPER	
doddering	SENILE
Dodecanese Island	COO, CASO,
LERO, SIMI, LIPSO, LISSO,	
PATMO, TILOS, CALCHI,	
CALINO, NISIRO	
dodge	DUCK, EVADE, PARRY
Dodgers' old field	EBBETTS
dodo	FOGY, FOSSIL
doe	see DEER
— d'oeuvre	CHEF, HORS
dog	CUR, MUT, PUP, BITCH,
CANIS, POOCH, PUPPY,	
WHELP, BOWWOW, CANINE,	
WIENER, MONGREL	
dog breed	see p. 662
dog chops	FLEWS
dog command	BAD, BEG, SIC,
SIT, STAY, TOHO	
dog cry	ARF, BARK, WOOF; see
p. 701	
dog, famous	ASTA, CLEO, NEIL,
TIGE, ODIE, TOBY, YUKI,	
ARGOS, ARGUS, BELKA, BENJI,	
KELLY, LAIKA, LASSIE,	
NIPPER, RASCAL, CHECKERS,	
RIN TIN TIN; see p. 630	
dog genus	CUON, CYON,
THOS, CANIS	
dog in White House	HER, HIM,
FALA, FIDO, MIKE, BUDDY,	
HEIDI, MILLIE, CHARLIE, KING	
TUT, SHANNON, TIMAHOE,	
CHECKERS, PUSHINKA	
dog in comics	REN, PLUTO,
ROVER, DUNCAN, SNOOPY,	
MARMADUKE, HEATHCLIFF	
dog, pert. to	CANINE

dog's place	LAP, KENNEL
dog star	SIRIUS, PROCYON
dog, wild	CUON, CYON, DIEB,
DHOLE, DINGO, GUARA,	
PIDOG, AGUARA, COYDOG,	
JACKAL, KOLSON, KOLSUN,	
PYEDOG, AGOUARA; see WOLF	
dog, young	PUP, WHELP
dogfight	BRAWL, CLASH,
MELEE, SCRAP	
dogfish	TOPE, BOWFIN,
BURBOT, ROSSET	
doghouse	KENNEL
dogma	ISM, CREED, DICTA,
TENET, DOCTRINE	
dogs, group of	MUTE, PACK,
LEASH, KENNEL, LITTER	
dogwood	KOUSA, OSIER,
CORNEL, CORNUS,	
BUNCHBERRY	
doldrums	CALM, LULL, BLUES
dole	ALMS, METE, GRIEF,
RELIEF	
Dole running mate	KEMP
doleful	SAD, DISMAL,
MOURNFUL	
doll	TOY, CUTIE, MAMMET,
MAUMET, PUPPET, MANIKIN	
dollar	BEAN, BILL, BUCK,
TALER, WHEEL, SIMOLEON;	
see MONEY; see p. 638	
dolly	CART, TRUCK
dolorous	SAD, DOLEFUL,
FORLORN	
dolphin	SUSU, UNIE, BOUTO,
DORADO, PALACH, PORPUS,	
SOOSOO, TURSIO, DELPHIN,	
NARWHAL, PELLOCK,	
PULLOCK, SNUFFER,	
GAIRFISH, NARWHALE,	
PORPOISE	
dolphin, famous	FLIPPER
dolphin genus	INIA,
PHOCAENA, TURSIOPS	
dolt	ASS, OAF, CLOD, COOT,
LOUT, NOWT, NUMP,	
DUNCE, NINNY, NUMPS	
domain	BOURN, REALM,
BARONY, BOURNE, DEMENE,	
ESTATE, DEMESNE, BAILIWICK	
Dombey's suitor, Miss	TOOTS
dome	PATE, ROOF, CONCHA,
CUPOLA, THOLOS	
domelike	DOMY, ARCHED
domestic	HOMY, MAID, TAME,
HOMEY, LOCAL, NATIVE,	
SERVANT	
domesticate	TAME, BREAK,
CIVILIZE	

domicile	HOME, ABODE, HOUSE, DWELLING	doodle	DRAW, CHEAT, SKETCH, CARTOON, SCRIBBLE
dominate	BOSS, RULE, CONTROL	doodlesack	BAGPIPE
domineer	BOSS, BULLY, HECTOR	doohickey	DINGUS, DOODAD, GADGET, DINGBAT
— Domini	ANNO	doom	FATE, RUIN, CONDEMN
Dominica, capital of	ROSEAU	doomed	FATED, KAPUT
Dominica money	DOLLAR	door	GATE, TRAP, ENTRY,
Dominica river	ROSEAU		HATCH, INLET, JANUA,
Dominican	FRIAR, JACOBIN		DINGLE, FUSUMA, PORTAL,
Dominican Republic, capital of			POSTERN
	SANTODOMINGO	door, god of	JANUS
Dominican Republic island		door opener	SLIMJIM
	BEATA, SAONA	door part	JAMB, KNOB, RAIL,
Dominican Republic measure ONA,			SASH, SILL, LATCH, PANEL,
	TAREA		STILE, ALETTE, CASING,
Dominican Republic money PESO			LINTEL, MULLION
Dominican Republic province		doorkeeper, doorman	HASP,
AZUA, DUARTE, SAMANA,			TILER, TYLER, PORTER,
DAJABON, PERAVIA, SALCEDO			JANITOR, OSTIARY,
Dominican Republic town AZUA,			CONCIERGE
BANI, MOCA, NAGUA, NEIBA,		dope	INFO, JUNK, DUMMY,
SEIBO, LAROMANA, SANTIAGO			OPIATE; see DRUGS
dominion	SWAY, DUCHY,	doppelganger	DOUBLE,
REALM, COLONY, EMPERY,			WRAITH, DUPLICATE
PROVINCE		Doris consort	NEREUS
domino	BONE, HOOD, MASK,	Doris offspring	NEREID, THETIS
AMICE, CLOAK		dormant	INERT, ASLEEP,
Don Carlos author/composer			LATENT, TORPID
VERDI, SCHILLER		dormer	ATTIC, LUTHERN,
Don Carlos role	EBOLI, PHILIP		SKYLIGHT
Don Giovanni character ANNA,		dormitory	DORM, HALL,
ELVIRA, OTTAVIO,			HOSTEL, QUARTERS
LEPORELLO		dormouse	LOIR, LEROT
Don Giovanni composer MOZART		dorsal	BACK, NOTAL, TERGAL
Don Juan	RAKE, ROUE	Dos Passos trilogy	USA
Don Juan mother	INEZ	dose	PILL, PO(R)TION
Don Quixote author CERVANTES		dosser	DORSAL, PANNIER
Don Quixote's horse ROSINANTE		dossier	DATA, FILE, RECORD
Don Quixote's lady DULCINEA		Dostoyevsky novel	IDIOT,
Don Quixote's squire SANCHO			POSSESSED
Don River	DUNA, TANAIS	dot	IOTA, DOWER, DOWRY,
Don tributary	CHIR, SOSNA,		SPECK, PERIOD, SPECKLE,
DONETS, KHOPER, MANYCH			STIPPLE
donate	GIVE, BESTOW, CHIPIN,	dote	LIKE, ADORE, DRIVEL
KICKIN, CONTRIBUTE		dote on	LOVE, ADORE, SPOIL,
Donau	see DANUBE		PAMPER
Donetsk	STALINO, YUZOVKA	doting	FOND, LOVING
Donizetti opera LUCIA, ELIXIR,		dotted	PIED, SEME, PINTO,
(DON)PASQUALE			PIEBALD
donkey	see ASS	dotty	CRAZY, DIPPY, WACKY
donnybrook	MELEE, FRACAS,	double	KA, DUAL, TWIN,
RUCKUS, RUMPUS,		COVER, GEMEL, BINATE,
FREEFORALL		DUPLEX, STANDIN,
donor	ANGEL, GIVER,		UNDERSTUDY
GRANTOR, CONTRIBUTOR		double meaning	EQUIVOKE,
doodad	DINGUS, GADGET,		AMBIGUITY
GEWGAW	double vision	DIPLOPIA

double-cross **RATON, CHEAT, BETRAY**

double-dealing **DUPLICITY, TREACHERY**

double-play trio **EVERS, CHANCE, TINKER**

double-reed instrument **OBOE, SHALM, SHAWM, BASSOON, BOMBARD**

double's work **STUNT**

doublet **COUPLET, POURPOINT**

doubloon **ONZA**

doubt **SCRUPLE, DISTRUST**

doubter **THOMAS, SKEPTIC**

doubtful **IFFY, SHAKY, UNSURE, DUBIOUS, UNLIKELY, SUSPICIOUS**

dough **DUFF, SPUD, MONEY, PASTE, BATTER**

doughboy **GI, YANK, SCALLOP, INFANTRY**

doughnut **TIRE, BAGEL, DUNKER, SINKER, BEIGNET, CRULLER, SIMBALL**

doughty **BOLD, BRAVE, VALIANT**

dour **SOUR, MOROSE, SULLEN**

douse **SOAK, DRENCH, PUTOUT, QUENCH, SATURATE**

dove **NUN, KUKU, LUPE, CULVER, CUSHAT, KUKUPA, POUTER, NAMAQUA, RINGDOVE**

Dove — **SONO**

dovekie **ALLE, ROTCH, ROTGE, ROTCHE; see AUK**

Dover cliffs **CHALKY**

Dover counterpart **CALAIS**

dovetail **FIT, JOIN(T), TENON**

dowager **WIDOW, MATRON**

dowdy **SEEDY, TACKY, SHABBY, SLOVENLY**

dowel **PIN, COAK**

dower **DOS, FUR, DOWRY, ENDOW, ENDUE**

down **NAP, SAD, ALOW, DOWL, DUNE, FUZZ, PILE, DUVET, EIDER, PRONATE**

Down East **MAINE**

Down Under **ANZAC, AUSTRALIA, NEW ZEALAND**

downcast **SAD, GLOOMY, DEJECTED**

downfall **RUIN, DEFEAT, DEMISE, FAILURE**

downgrade **BUST, LOWER, DEBASE, DEMOTE, REDUCE**

downhearted **SAD, DEJECTED, DEPRESSED**

downpour **SPATE, DELUGE, TORRENT, CLOUDBURST**

downright **UTTER(LY), TOTAL(LY), COMPLETE(LY)**

downtime **REST, RANDR**

downwind **ALEE, LEEWARD**

downy **PILAR, LANATE, VILLOUS**

dowry **DOS, DOT, GIFT, DOWER**

doxology **DOXA, KAINYN, KADDISH**

doxy **ISM, CREED, HUSSY, WENCH, TROLLOP, DOCTRINE, MISTRESS**

doyen **DEAN, SENIOR**

doze **NAP, DORM, CATNAP, DROWSE, SNOOZE**

drab **DUN, DULL, DINGY, DOWDY, BORING, LACKLUSTER**

Dracula **VAMPIRE**

Dracula author **BRAM STOKER**

draft **ALE, LEVY, SWIG, TASS, INDUCT, POTION, SKETCH, CONSCRIPT**

draft animal **OX(EN), MULE, HORSE, ELEPHANT**

draft org. **SSS**

draft, vehicle requiring **GLIDER**

draftee **ROOKIE, RECRUIT, INDUCTEE, CONSCRIPT**

drag **LUG, TOW, TUG, HALE, HAUL, SNIG, TUMP, BOTHER**

dragnet **APB, WEB, TRAWL, TRAINEL**

Dragnet credits background **BADGE**

Dragnet name **JOE, BILL, JACK, WEBB, HARRY, FRIDAY, GANNON, MORGAN**

dragon **ORC, KETU, RAHU, DRAKE, LADON, DUENNA, FAFNIR, WIVERN, BASILISK**

dragon slayer **CADMUS, GEORGE**

drain **SAP, SUMP, SEWER, CLOACA, CULVERT, DEPLETE, VITIATE**

drained **TIRED, SAPPED, EXHAUSTED**

drake *see* **DUCK**

dram **NIP, SLUG, DRAFT**

drama **NOH, AUTO, MIME, PLAY, STAGE, BUSKIN, KABUKI, NOGAKU**

dramatic **STAGY, VIVID, SCENIC, THEATRICAL**

dramatic, be **EMOTE**
dramatic situation **CRUX,**
CRISIS
dramatis personae **CAST,**
ROLES, CHARACTERS
dramatist **LIBRETTIST,**
PLAYWRIGHT
dramatist, famous *see p. 625*
dramatize **ADAPT, EMOTE,**
ENACT
drapery **ARRAS, CANOPY,**
CURTAIN, VALANCE
drastic **DIRE, SEVERE,**
EXTREME
Dravidian language **KUI, KOTA,**
MALE, NAIR, TODA, TULU,
GONDI, KHOND, MALTO,
NAYAR, ORAON, TAMIL,
BRAHUI, KODAGU, KURUKH,
TELUGU, KANNADA,
CANARESE, KANARESE,
MALAYALAM
draw **TIE, TOW, WIN, HALE,**
LIMN, TOLE, DEPICT, SIPHON
draw and — **QUARTER**
draw back **WINCE, RESILE**
draw forth **EDUCE, DERIVE,**
ELICIT
draw out **ELICIT, STRETCH,**
EXTRACT, PROLONG,
PROTRACT
draw tight **BIND, COUL, FRAP**
drawback **HANDICAP,**
OBSTACLE
drawbridge **BASCULE,**
PONTLEVIS
drawer(s) **BIN, TILL, SHORTS,**
PANTIES, DRAFTSMAN
drawing **PLAN, CHART,**
DESIGN, DOODLE, SKETCH,
CARTOON, DIAGRAM,
LOTTERY, DEPICTION
drawing room **SALA, SALON,**
PARLOR
drawing tool **CURVE, RULER,**
CRAYON, FUSAIN, PASTEL,
PENCIL, TSQUARE
drawn **TAUT, TENSE, TIRED,**
LENGTHY
dray **VAN, CART, WAGON**
dread **AWE, FEAR, TERROR**
dreadful **BAD, AWFUL,**
HORRID, HIDEOUS,
FEARFUL, TERRIBLE
dream **HOPE, MUSE, REVE,**
FANCY, VISION, FANTASY,
REVERIE
Dream Girl playwright **RICE**
dreamer **ROMANTIC, VISIONARY**

dreams, interpretation of
ONEIROLOGY
dreamy **VAGUE, PENSIVE,**
SURREAL, WISTFUL
dreary **DREE, BLEAK, DISMAL,**
DREICH, DREIGH
dredge **DRAG, SIFT, SPRINKLE**
dregs **FAEX, LEES, MARC,**
SCUM, SILT, DRAFF, DROSS,
MAGMA, SALIN, DUNDER,
SORDES, VINASSE
Dreiser character **CLYDE,**
CARRIE, JENNIE
drench **SOAK, DOUSE, SOUSE**
drenched **WET, ASOP, DEWED**
dress **DAB, DUB, NIG, TAN,**
TAW, TOG, GOWN, SACK,
BANIA, FROCK, HABIT, SHIFT,
TUNIC, PREEN, BANIAN,
BANYAN, CAMISE, CLOTHE,
CHEMISE, TEAGOWN; *see*
CLOTHING, DESIGNER
dress style **MAXI, MINI, SACK,**
TENT, ALINE, CIITON,
KIRTLE, MUUMUU, PANT SUIT
dressed **CLAD, GARBED,**
SUITED, CLOTHED
dresser **CHEST, VALET,**
BUREAU, VANITY
dressing **GAUZE, STUPE,**
DOSSIL, BANDAGE,
GARNISH, PLASTER,
COMPRESS, STUFFING,
VINAIGRETTE
dressing gown **ROBE, CAMISE,**
DUSTER, KIMONO, NEGLIGE,
WRAPPER, NEGLIGEE,
PEIGNOIR
dressmaker **MODISTE,**
COUTURIER(E), SEAMSTRESS
dressmaking term **HEM, FACE,**
GORE, PURL, BASTE,
GATHER, STITCH, APPLIQUE
dressy **CHIC, FANCY, SHOWY,**
CLASSY, FORMAL, MODISH,
ELEGANT, STYLISH
Dreyfus supporter **ZOLA**
dribble **LEAK, DROOL,**
BOUNCE, SLAVER, SLABBER,
TRICKLE
dried **SERE**
dried food **HAY, COPRA, JERKY,**
PRUNE, RAISIN, BILTONG,
CHARQUI, PEM(M)ICAN
drift **FLOAT, TENOR, TREND,**
COURSE, CURRENT
drifter **BUM, HOBO, TRAMP,**
VAGRANT, VAGABOND
drill **AWL, BORE, BURR,**

AUGER, TRAIN, GIMLET, PIERCE
drill command   HALT, MARCH, ATEASE, ABOUTFACE, QUICKTIME, ONTHEDOUBLE
drink   ADE, BIB, AVA, LAP, NIP, NOG, PEG, POP, SIP, SOT, BOZA, COLA, GULP, GROG, HOMA, KAVA, NEHI, NIPA, SLUG, SODA, SWIG, TOPE, ASSAI, BOUSE, BUMBO, MORAT, NEGUS, NURSE, QUAFF, SWILL, TONIC, BRACER, CAUDLE, GUZZLE, IMBIBE, KUMISS, NECTAR, POSSET, PTISAN, TIPPLE; see p. 563
drinkable   SAFE, POTABLE
drinker   SOT, LUSH, SOUSE, TOPER, BIBBER, BOOZER, TIPPLER, TOSSPOT
drinking horn   RHYTON
drinking place   see TAVERN
drinking vessel   see CUP, GLASS
drip   LEAK, OOZE, SEEP, SILE, CREEP
drive   LANE, RIDE, URGE, FORCE, IMPEL, MOTOR, STEER
drive away   SHOO, BANISH
drive back   ROUT, REPEL, REPULSE
drive crazy   CRAZE, MADDEN, DERANGE
drive in   TAMP, HAMMER
drive, kind of   (MINI)DISK, CDROM
drive out   ROUT, EXPEL
drivel   DOTE, DROOL, SLAVER
driver   JEHU, WHIP, CABBY, HAMMER, SARWAN, MOTORIST, CHAUFFEUR; see GOLF
driving   DYNAMIC, ZEALOUS, AMBITIOUS
drizzle   RAIN, SMUR(R), MIZZLE
droll   ODD, ZANY, WAGGISH
dromedary   CAMEL, DELOUL, MEHARI
drone   BEE, HUM, IDLER, MONOTONE
drool   DRIVEL, SLAVER, SLOBBER
droop   LAG, SAG, WILT, SLOUCH
drop   BIT, DAP, SIE, SYE, BEAD, DRIB, FALL, PLOP, SINK, GUTTA, MINIM, GLOBULE
drop in   CALL, STOP, VISIT
dropsy   EDEMA, HYDROPS

dross   SCUM, SLAG, DREGS, SPRUE, SCORIA, SINTER, SULLAGE
drought   SOKA, DEARTH, ARIDITY
drove   HERD, PACK, RODE, ATAJO
drown   FLOOD, INUNDATE, SUBMERGE
drowse   NAP, NOD, DOZE, DOVER
drowsy   SLEEPY, LETHARGIC
drub   BEAT, CUDGEL, THRASH
drudge   FAG, GRUB, HACK, MOIL, PLOT, TOIL, LABOR, SLAVE
drudgery   CHORE, RATRACE
drug   ICE, KAT, KEF, KIF, LSD, PCP, POT, ACID, BANG, COCA, COKE, DOPE, DOSE, HASH, HEMP, JUNK, KHAT, KIEF, MDMA, METH, SINA, SNOW, ALOES, BENNY, BHANG, CRACK, CRANK, GANJA, GLASS, GRASS, HORSE, JALAP, MECON, OPIUM, SMACK, SPEED, SULFA, UPPER, COCAIN, CHARAS, DOWNER, FAGINE, HEROIN, OPIATE, REEFER, VALIUM, ALCOHOL, ANODYNE, COCAINE, ECSTASY, HASHISH, SECONAL, CANNABIS, DILANTIN, METHADON, MORPHINE, NARCOTIC, NICOTINE, QUAALUDE, MARIJUANA, MESCALINE
drug company   ENDO, BAYER, LILLY, MERCK, ORTHO, ROCHE, WYETH, PFIZER, COLGATE
drug reaction   HIGH, TRIP
drug seller   DEALER, PUSHER
drugget   MAT, RUG, CARPET
drugstore   PHARMACY, APOTHECARY
drum   DUB, BEAT, DRUB, THROB, REPEAT; see PERCUSSION
drumbeat   DIAN, FLAM, RUFF, TATOO, RAPPEL, RUFFLE, TATTOO, BERLOQUE
Drums Along the Mohawk hero   GIL
drumstick   LEG, TAMPON
drunk   APE, CUT, GAY, LIT, OUT, ACED, BLUE, GONE, HAZY, HIGH, ICED, KISK,

NOLO, PIED, SOSH, TOXY,
ABUZZ, AGLOW, BALMY,
BARMY, BEERY, BIFFY, BLIND,
BOOZY, DEWED, DIPSY,
DOPED, FLAKO, FRIED, HAPPY,
HOSED, LACED, LOOPY,
LUBED, OILED, PINKO, POTTO,

	POTTY, RUMMY, SOGGY,
	TIPSY, ADDLED, ALKIED,
	BAGGED, BELTED, BLOTTO,
	BLOWED, BOMBED,
	BUMMED, CANNED, CORKED,
	DUMPED, GLASSY, GLAZED,
	HOPPED, JAGGED, LOADED,
	LOOPED, MELLOW, NIPPED,
	PASTED, PISSED, PRIMED,
	PUTRID, SAUCED, SOAKED,
	SOTTED, SOUSED, STEWED,
	STINKO, STONED, TIDDLY,
	WASTED, ZONKED, BLASTED,
	BLITZED, DECAYED,
	PLOTZED, ROARING,
	SKUNKED, SLOSHED,
	SQUIFFY, WRECKED,
	PLOUGHED, TOTALLED,
	PLASTERED, PIXILATED
drunkard	SOT, LUSH, SOAK,
	WINO, TOPER, BARFLY,
PICKLED, TIPPLER, ROUNDER,
	TOSSPOT, EMBALMED,
	FISHEYED
drunk driving	DUI, DWI
drupe	TRYMA
dry	SEC, ARID, BAKE, BLOT,
	BRUT, SERE, WIPE, AREFY,
	SOBER, SCORCH, SICCATE
DST start, stop	MAR, OCT
— du jour	PLAT
dual	TWIN, BINARY, DOUBLE
dub	NAME, TITLE, KNIGHT
dubious	LEERY, SHADY,
	VAGUE, DOUBTFUL
Dublin theater	ABBEY
ducal family	WELF
Duchess of Windsor	WALLIS,
	WARFIELD
duck	DIP, DODGE, EVADE,
	MERSE
duck —	SOUP
duck eggs, Chinese	PIDAN
duck, young	DUCKLING
ducklike	ANATINE
ducks	ANAS, COLK, COOT,
DOGS, DOGY, SKEW, TEAL,
BUNTY, DILLY, DRAKE, EIDER,
SCAUP, CANARD, DIPPER,
GARROT, MARECA, QUANDY,
SCOTER, ZUISIN, CANETON,
	DUNBIRD, GADWALE,

	GADWALL, GADWELL,
MALLARD, OLD WIFE, PINTAIL,
	POCHARD, SAWBILL,
	SCOOTER, TWISTER,
WIDGEON, BALDPATE,
GARGANEY, OLD SQUAW,
	SHOVELER
duct	VAS, FLUE, VASA, AORTA,
	CANAL, LEMNA, MAETUS,
	CONDUIT
dude	FOP, DANDY, HOMBRE,
	MACARONI
Dudevant	SAND
dudgeon	PET, ANGER, PIQUE
duds	TOGS, CLOTHES,
	TRAPPINGS
due	FIT, HAK, DEBT, HAKH,
	OWED, REWARD, DESERTS,
	PAYABLE
duel	TILT, JOUST, COMBAT,
	HOLMGANG
dueler, famous	BURR, HAMILTON
dues	FEE, CHARGE,
	ASSESSMENT
duet	DUO, PAIR, TWOSOME
dugout	ABRI, BANCA,
	FOXHOLE, PIRAGUA,
	PIROGUE
dukedom	DUCHY
dull	DRY, DUN, MAT, DRAB,
	DUNS, LOGY, BLUNT,
	MATTE, PROSY, STOGY,
	TERNE, BORING, OBTUND,
	OBTUSE, PROSAIC, TEDIOUS
dullard	OAF, BOOR, LOUT,
	DUNCE
Dumas hero(ine)	ATHOS,
	ARAMIS, PORTHOS,
	DARTAGNAN
Dumas novel	CAMILLE
dumb	MUTE, SILENT
— and dumb	DEAF
dumbfound	STUN, AMAZE,
	BOGGLE, ASTONISH
dummy	DUPE, MUTE, TOOL,
	FRONT, PROXY
dump	DROP, JUNK, PILE,
	CHUCK, DITCH, DISCARD
dumpling)s)	KNISH, DIM SUM,
	GNOCCHI
dumpy	PUDGY, SQUAT
dun	ASK, TAN, GRAY,
	MOUND, SWARTHY
dunce	ASS, OAF, COOT, DOLT,
DOPE, LOUT, BOBBY, FRONT,
MORON, NINNY, PROXY,
	PONTIC
dunderhead	BOZO, FOOL, JERK,
	DUNCE, NUMSKULL

dune	DENE, HILL, RIDGE, TWINE, (SAND)BANK		STUNT, TROLL, BANTAM, DROICH, DURGAN, MIDGET, SPRITE, MANIKIN
dung	DOR, TATH, UPLA, MANURE, ORDURE, DROPPING, EXCREMENT	dwarfs, seven	DOC, DOPEY, HAPPY, GRUMPY, SLEEPY, SNEEZY, BASHFUL
dungeon	PIT, CELL, JAIL, PRISON, OUBLIETTE	dwell	BIDE, HARP, LIVE, STAY, STOP, LODGE
dupe	BILK, CULL, FOOL, GULL, HOAX, PAWN, COZEN, CULLY, SUCKER	dweller	TENANT, RESIDENT
		dwelling	HOME, ABODE, DOMICILE
Dupin creator	POE	dwindle	EBB, ABATE, PETER
duplicate	COPY, STAT, TWIN, XEROX, DOUBLE, REPEAT	dyad	PAIR
duplicating machine	DITTO, RONEO, XEROX, COPIER, MIMEO(GRAPH)	dye	AAL, ANGO, ANIL, HINO, TINT, WELD, WOAD, WOLD, YPIL, AURIN, EOSIN, STAIN, TINGE, WOALD, ANATTA,
duplication	COPY, PRINT, REPLICA, FACSIMILE		ANATTO, ARCHIL, AURINE, CERISE, EOSINE, MADDER,
duplicity	FRAUD, DECEIT		ORCHAL, ORCHIL, TANNIN,
durable	TOUGH, STABLE, LASTING		ANNATTA, ANNATTO, ANNOTTO, ARNATTO,
duration	SPAN, TERM, LENGTH		ORSELLE
duress	COERCION	dye plant	AMIL, ANIL, CHAY,
during	WHILE, WITHIN, PENDING		SUMAC, INDIGO, MADDER, ANCHUSA
dusk	SUNSET, EVENFALL, GLOAMING, TWILIGHT, CREPUSCLE	dyed-in-the-wool	TOTAL
		dyeing method	BATIK
dusky	DIM, FUSC, DARK, SWART(HY)	Dylan Thomas home	WALES
		dynamite inventor	NOBEL
dust	ASH, COOM, SOOT, BRISS, COOMB, STIVE, STOUR, POWDER	dynamo	WHIRLWIND; see MOTOR
		dynasty	REALM, KINGDOM; see CHINESE
dust remover	(DRY) MOP	dyspepsia	INDIGESTION
Dustin Hoffman role	LENNY, LOMAN, RATSO, RIZZO, KRAMER, DOROTHY		
Dutch	see also NETHERLANDS		**E**
Dutch painter	GOGH, HALS, HEDA, KALF, LELY, MEER, BOSCH, STEEN, LEYDEN, BRUEGEL, VAN EYCK, VAN GOGH, VERMEER, MONDRIAN, RUISDAEL, REMBRANDT	E	EAST, ECHO, ENERGY, EPSILON
		each	PER, EVERY, APIECE
		eager	AGOG, AVID, FAIN, KEEN, YARE, ARDENT
Dutch philosopher	SPINOZA	eagle	ERN(E), GIER, ETANA, HARPY, SCOUT, AQUILA, FALCON
Dutch statesman	GROTIUS		
Dutch treat	TULIP		
dutch uncle	OOM, MENTOR	eagle, young	EAGLET
Dutch woman	FROU(W)	eagre	BORE, WAVE
dutiful	LOYAL, DOCILE, OBEDIENT, COMPLIANT	ear	LUG, SPICA, SPIKE, HANDLE, SPICAE
duty	CESS, LEVY, CHORE, DEVOIR, DHARMA, EXCISE, IMPOST, TARIFF, LASTAGE	ear, part of	WAX, LOBE, AMBOS, ANVIL, CANAL, HELIX, INCUS, PINNA, SCALA,
Dvorak symphony	NEW WORLD		CONCHA, HAMMER, LOBULE,
dwarf	ELF, FAY, NIX, URF, PIXY, PUCK, RUNT, SHEE, CRILE, GNOME, PIGMY,		STAPES, TEGMEN, TRAGUS, AURICLE, CERUMEN, COCHLEA, EARDRUM,

	LOBULUS, MALLEUS, SACCULE, STIRRUP
ear, *pert. to*	OTIC, AURAL, AURIC, LOBAR, BINOTIC, BINAURAL
earache	OTALGY, OTALGIA
eardrum	TYMPANUM
earful	TIP, GOSSIP, TALKINGTO
earl	JARL, NOBLE(MAN)
earlier	ELDER, PRIOR, PREVIOUS
early	AHEAD, FIRST, FORWARD, INITIAL, PREMATURE, PRIMITIVE
earmark	SIGN, ALLOT, BRAND, SIGNAL, SET ASIDE
earn	EKE, WIN, GAIN, MERIT
earnest	EAGER, ARDENT
earnest money	ARLES, ARRHA, PLEDGE, HANDSEL
earnings	WAGES, PROFITS, SALARIES
Earp brothers	JAMES, WYATT, MORGAN, VIRGIL, WARREN
earring	HOOP, PENDANT, GIRANDOLE
earth	ERD, GEO, BYON, CLAY, DIRT, GAEA, GAIA, LOAM, MARL, SOIL, GLEBE, TERRA
earth, *pert. to*	GEAL, TERRENE
earth surface	SIAL, SIMA, HORST, EPIGENE
earthenware	POT, OLLA, DELF(T), RAKU, CHINA, JASPER, CROCKERY, PORCELAIN
earthly	MUNDANE, SECULAR, TEMPORAL
earthquake	SEISM, TREMOR, TEMBLOR
earthquake, *pert. to*	SEISMIC
earthquake site	ASSAM, CUTCH, KANSU, QUITO, TOKYO, ALEPPO, ISCHIA, LISBON, MESSINA
earthwork	DIKE, FORT, AGGER, MOUND, REDAN, RIDGE
earthy	GROSS, CARNAL, COARSE, NATURAL
earwax	CERUMEN
ease	CALM, ALLAY, QUIET, RELIEF
easel	TRIPOD
East	LEVANT, ORIENT, SUNRISE
East Indian herb	PIA, CHAY, CHOY, SOLA, GINGER, SESAME, ROSELLE
East Indian language	*see* DRAVIDIAN
East Indian plant	AMIL, CHAY, JUTE, SUNN, AMBARY, COLEUS, DERRIS, SESAME, TURMERIC, PATCHOULI
East Indian shrub	SOLA, CUBEB, MADAR, MALOO, MUDAR, SOLAG, MUDDAR
East Indian tree	BO, DAK, ENG, JAK, NIM, SAL, AMLA, ASAK, AULA, BIJA, BITI, DHAK, DILO, DUKU, JACK, KINO, NEEM, NIPA, POON, TEAK, TOON, ACANA, DHAVA, DHAWA, KHAIR, KOKAN, LANSA, MAHUA, MELIA, MOHWA, NIEPA, PALAS, PIPAL, PULAS, ROHAN, ROHUN, SIRIS, SISSU, BANYAN, CACHOU, DEODAR, EMBLIC, LANSAT, LANSEH, LEBBEK, SISSOO, CATECHU, MARGOSA, MASTTREE; *see* INDIAN TREE
east, *pert. to*	EOAN, ASIAN
Easter	EED, PAAS, PACE, PASCH(A)
Easter, *pert. to*	PASCHAL
East Timor, capital of	DILI
East Timor hero	GUSMAO
East Timor money	DOLLAR, RUPIAH
eastern	ASIATIC, ORIENTAL
Eastern Catholic	UNIAT(E)
Eastern Orthodox synod	SOBOR
East European	*see* EUROPEAN
easy	SOFT, FACILE, SIMPLE, EFFORTLESS
— and easy	FREE
easy job	SNAP, CINCH, SINECURE
easy to understand	EVIDENT, OBVIOUS
eat	DIET, GNAW, RUST, ERODE, DEVOUR, INGEST
eat greedily	LAB, BOLT, GULP, GORGE, RAVEN, RAVIN, GOBBLE, RAVINE
eat one's words	RECANT, RETRACT
eatable	EDIBLE, ESCULENT
eatery	*see* RESTAURANT
eating away	CAUSTIC, ERODENT
eating, *pert. to*	DIETARY
eating place	*see* RESTAURANT
ebb	NEAP, SINK, WANE, RECEDE, REFLUX
ebb and flow	(A)ESTUS

Eber relative	PELEG, JOKTAN, SHELAH
ebony	INKY, BLACK, PITCHY
eccentric	ODD, GINK, CRANK, KOOKY, OUTRE, QUEER, MISFIT, UNICUM, ERRATIC, ODDBALL
ecclesiastic	CLERIC, PRIEST, PRELATE
ecclesiastical	SACRED, CLERICAL, PRIESTLY
ecclesiastical hours	*see* CANONICAL HOURS
ecclesiastical vestment	*see* VESTMENT
echo	APE, DITTO, ITERATE, RESOUND
éclat	FAME, GLORY, RENOWN, SPLENDOR
eclipse	DIM, DARKEN, OBSCURE, SURPASS
eclipse part	PENUMBRA
eclipse type	LUNAR, SOLAR, TOTAL, PARTIAL
eclogue	IDYL(L), PASTORAL
ecology	BIONOMICS, ECOSYSTEM
economical	FRUGAL, THRIFTY
ecru	TAN, BEIGE, YELLOW
ecstasy	BLISS, RAPTURE, DELIGHT
Ecuador, capital of	QUITO
Ecuadorian city/town	LOJA, MANTA, QUITO, CEUNCA, AMBATO, MACHALA, GUYAQUIL, ESMERALDAS, PORTOVIEJO
Ecuadorian Indian	CARA, ANDOA, ARDAN, KECHUA, QUECHUA
Ecuadorian island	PUNA, PINTA, BALTRA, PINZON, WENMAN
Ecuadorian language	SPANISH, JIVAROAN, QUECHUA(N)
Ecuadorian measure	CUADRA
Ecuadorian money	SUCRE, CONDOR, DOLLAR, CENTAVO
Ecuadorian province	LOJA, NAPO, AZUAY, CANAR, ELORO, CARCHI, GUAYAS, MANABI, BOLIVAR, PASTAZA
Ecuadorian river	NAPO, TIGRE, GUAYAS, MACUMA, MORONA, CURARAY, PASTAZA, SANTIAGO
Ecuadorian volcano	SANGAY, CAYAMBE, COTOPAXI
ecumenical	GLOBAL, GENERAL, CATHOLIC, UNIVERSAL
ecumenical council	BASLE, LYONS, TRENT, NICAEA, VIENNE, EPHESUS, LATERAN, VATICAN
eczema	HERPES, TETTER, DERMATITIS
edacity	GREED, VORACITY
Eddie Cantor girl	IDA
eddo	ROOT, TARO
eddy	SWIRL, VORTEX, WHIRLPOOL
edema	TUMOR, DROPSY, SWELLING
Eden, country east of	NOD
Eden's river	GIHON, PISON
edentate	SLOTH, AARDVARK, ANTEATER; *see p. 667*
edge	HEM, LIP, RIM, BRIM, ODDS, SILL, ARRIS, BRINK, MARGE, PICOT, RUCHE, SIDLE, VERGE, LABRUM, LIMBUS, SELVAGE
edgewise	ASKANCE, SIDEWAYS
edging	FRILL, PICOT, RUCHE, FRINGE, LIMBUS, FLOUNCE, FURBELOW, TRIMMING
edgy	TENSE, NERVOUS
edible	EATABLE, ESCULENT, COMESTIBLE
edict	*see* DECREE
edifice	*see* BUILDING
Edison invention	LAMP, BATTERY, WAXPAPER, MIMEOGRAPH, PHONOGRAPH
Edison middle name	ALVA
edit	AMEND, EMEND, REDACT, REVISE, CORRECT
edition	EXTRA, FIRST, ISSUE, STRIPE, BULLDOG, PRINTING
editorialize	INDITE, COMPOSE, EXPOUND, EXPATIATE
Edom	ESAU, SEIR
Edomite city	PAU, SELA
Edomite noble	UZ, BELA, IRAM, TEMAN
educate	EDIFY, TEACH, TRAIN, INSTRUCT, ENLIGHTEN
educated	ERUDITE, LEARNED, LITERATE
educational institution	*see* SCHOOL
educator	TUTOR, MENTOR, TEACHER, PEDAGOGUE, PROFESSOR, INSTRUCTOR
educator, famous	HALL, KERR, MANN, DEWEY, ELIOT,

JAMES, POUND, ROYCE, SETON, ANGELL, BASCOM, BUTLER, CONANT, GILMAN, HARPER, MATHER, PALMER, FLEXNER, FROEBEL, HOPKINS, NEILSON, PEABODY

educe EVOKE, INFER, ELICIT

eel GRIG, SNIG, ELVER, MORAY, CONGER, CUCHIA, FAUSEN, MUR(A)ENA; see LAMPREY

eel genus ANGUILLA

eel, young ELVER

eelpout LING, BLENNY, BURBOT

cerie WEIRD, CREEPY, SPOOKY, MACABRE, UNCANNY

efface ERASE, DELETE, EXPUNGE

cffect ISSUE, RESULT, MEANING

effective ACTIVE, COGENT, TELLING, EFFICIENT

effects GOODS, THINGS, PROPERTY

effeminate EPICENE, UNMANLY, WOMANISH

effervesce FIZZ, FOAM, FROTH, AERATE, BUBBLE

effete ARID, JADED, SPENT, STERILE, DECADENT

efficient ABLE, CAPABLE, COMPETENT, EFFECTIVE

cffigy GUY, DOLL, ICON, IDOL, STATUE

effluvium AURA, FLATUS, MIASMA

effort DINT, ASSAY, NISUS, TRIAL, CONATUS

effrontery GALL, BRASS, CHEEK, AUDACITY, TEMERITY, IMPUDENCE

effulgence LUSTER, RADIANCE, SPLENDOR

effusive GUSHY, EXUBERANT

eft EVAT, EVET, NEWT, LIZARD, TRITON

egg(s) NIT, OVA, ROE, CELL, CHEX, OVUM, OVULE, PIDAN, CAVIAR, EMBRYO

egg collector OOLOGIST

egg foo — YUNG

egg grade JUMBO, LARGE, GRADEA, MEDIUM

egg-laying mammal ECHIDNA, ANTEATER, PLATYPUS

egg on GOAD, SPUR, URGE, INCITE

egg part YOLK, GLAIR, SHELL, WHITE, ALBUMEN, LATEBRA

egg-shaped OOID, OVAL, OVATE, OVOID, OVIFORM

egis SHIELD, AUSPICES

Eglah relative DAVID, ITHREAM

ego SELF, ATMAN, JIVATMA

egoism IISM, PRIDE, VANITY, CONCEIT

egotistic SMUG, VAIN, COCKY, STUCK UP, CONCEITED

egregious GROSS, FLAGRANT

egress EXIT, ISSUE, OUTLET

egret *see* **HERON**

Egypt MIZRAIM

Egypt, ancient city SAIS, TANIS, AMARNA, MEMPHIS

Egypt, capital of CAIRO

Egypt conqueror LYBIANS, NUBIANS, PTOLEMY, NAPOLEON

Egypt, *pert. to* COPTIC

Egyptian city/town GIZA, SAIS, SUEZ, ASWAN, BENHA, CAIRO, LUXOR, SOHAG, TAHTA, RASHID, PORT SAID

Egyptian desert LIBYAN, SAHARA, SKETIS, ARABIAN

Egyptian disease SIWA, SUEZ, ASWAN, MINYA, BILHARZIA

Egyptian dynasty PEPI, SETI, UNAS, MENES, NECHO, AHMOSE, CHEOPS, DARIUS, MAMLUK, NARMER, RAMSES, FATIMID, PTOLEMY, TULUNID

Egyptian gods *see p. 647*

Egyptian language COPTIC; *see* ARABIC, HAMITIC

Egyptian measure PIK, RO(U)B, ABDAT, ARDEB, FARDE, KILAH, SAHME, AURURE, FEDDAN, KEDDAH, ROBHAN, DARIBAH, MALOUAH

Egyptian measure (ancient) KHET, THEB, CUBIT, ARTABA, SCHENE, CHORYOS

Egyptian money MINA, GIRSH, POUND, RIYAL, MEDINO, TALENT, DRACHMA, PIASTER, MILLIEME

Egyptian oasis SIWA, DAKHLA, KHARGA, FURAFRA

Egyptian province GIZA, QENA, SUEZ, ASWAN, ASYUT, CAIRO, MINYA, SOHAG, MATRUH, REDSEA, BEHEIRA

Egyptian ruins LUXOR, ABYDOS, AMARNA, KARNAK,

THEBES, MEMPHIS, SAKKARA, BERENICE, PYRAMIDS	Elbe tributary EGER, ELDE, ISER, OHRE, HAVEL, MULDE,
Egyptian ruler TUT, FUAD,	SAALE, VLTAVA
NIKI, PEPI, SETI, ABBAS,	elbow BEND, NOOP, ANCON,
KHUFU, MENES, NECHO,	ANGLE, CROWD, JOINT,
ZOSER, AMASIS, AHMOSI,	NUDGE, JOSTLE
APRIES, CHEOPS, HATASU,	elbow bone ULNA, RADIUS,
HOPHRA, KAPHRE, NAGUIB,	HUMERUS
NASSER, RAMSES, SHISAK,	eld YORE
SNEFRU, HARMHAB,	elder IVA, DEAN, WAMP,
OSORKON, PSAMTIK,	PRIOR, SENIOR
PTOLEMY, SESHONK,	eldest AINE(E), EIGNE, SENIOR
THUTMOSE	eldritch EERIE, WEIRD
Egyptian weights OKA, OKE,	Eleanor ELLA, NELL, NORA
HEML, OKIA, ROTL, KERAT,	elect OPT, CHOOSE, CHOSEN,
UCKIA, KANTAR, QUINTAL	SELECT
Egyptian weights (ancient) KAT,	election POLL, RUNOFF,
KET, KHAR, DEBEN, OKIEH	PRIMARY, SELECTION
eider DOWN, DUCK	electioneer STUMP, CAMPAIGN
eidolon ICON, IDEAL, IMAGE	elector VOTER, ELISOR
eighth note UNCA, QUAVER	Electra relative ORESTES,
eight-sided figure OCTAGON	AGAMEMNON,
eighty FOUR SCORE	CLYTEMNESTRA
Einstein birthplace ULM	electric VOLTAIC, THRILLING
Eire ERIN, IRELAND	electric particle (AN)ION,
— Eireann DAIL	CATION, KATION
Eisenhower library location	electric unit AMP, BEL, MHO,
KANSAS, ABILENE	OHM, REL, DYNE, ELOD,
ejaculate CRY(OUT), BLURT,	PERM, VOLT, WATT, FARAD,
EJECT, EXCLAIM	HENRY, WEBER, AMPERE
eject EMIT, OUST, SPEW, VOID,	electricity JUICE, POWER
EVICT, SPURT, BOUNCE	electrify SHOCK, CHARGE,
eke ADD, IMP	THRILL
El — Brujo AMOR	electrode ANODE, CATHODE,
El Cid see CID	THERMION
El Salvador, capital of	electrolysis part (AN)ION
SANSALVADOR	electronic device IC, CHIP,
El Salvador city/town IZALCO,	DIODE, LASER, MASER,
CORINTO, METAPAN,	RESISTOR, CAPACITOR,
NOBASCO, ACAJUTLA	TRANSISTOR
El Salvador money COLON,	electronic instrument MOOG,
DOLLAR, CENTAVO	DXVII, ONDES (MARTENOT),
El Salvador mountain SANTAANA	SAMPLER, THEREMIN,
El Salvador river LEMPA	SYNTH(ESIZER)
Elam capital SUSA, SHUSHAN	electronic tube TRIODE,
Elam's father SHEM	PENTODE, TETRODE,
elan ZIP, DASH, ZEST, ZING,	KENATRON, KLYSTRON,
ARDOR, GUSTO, VIGOR	MAGNETRON, THYRATRON
eland see ANTELOPE	electroplating element RHODIUM
elapse PASS, EXPIRE	eleemosynary FREE, GRATIS,
elastic SUPPLE, BUOYANT,	CHARITABLE
SPRINGY, TENSILE,	elegance LUXE, GRACE, POLISH
RESILIENT	elegant FINE, POSH, RICH,
elate EXALT, GLADDEN	GENTEEL, REFINED,
elated RADE, JOYFUL,	DIGNIFIED
GLEEFUL	elegy DIRGE, NENIA, LAMENT
Elatha son BRES	element AIR, FIRE, RECT,
Elbe city MELNIK, DRESDEN,	PART, EARTH, WATER,
HAMBRUG	FACTOR, ISOTOPE; see p. 521

elemental, elementary **BASIC,
PRIMAL, PRIMER, SIMPLE,
PRIMARY**
elementary abbrev. **ATWT**
elephant **COW, BULL, HINE,
HATHI, DUMBO, JUMBO,
ROGUE, TUSKER, KOOMKIE,
LOXODON, PACHYDERM**
elephant driver **MAHOUT**
elephant genus **ELEPHAS**
elephant prod **ANKUS**
elephant trap **KHEDA**
elephant, young **CALF**
elephantine **HUGE, CLUMSY,
IMMENSE, MASSIVE,
PONDEROUS**
elevate **BUOY, LIFT, EXALT,
RAISE, HEIGHTEN**
elevation **MESA, MOUND,
MOUNT, RIDEAU, PLATEAU**
elevator **CAGE, LIFT, HOIST,
SPOUT, AIRFOIL**
elevator pioneer **OTIS, ELISHA**
elf **FAY, HOB, IMP, NIX, PERI,
PIXY, PUCK, FAIRY, GNOME,
NIXIE, OUPHE, PIXIE, GOBLIN,
KOBOLD, SPRITE, BROWNIE,
ERLKING**
elfin **FEY**
Elgin marble **FRIEZE**
elicit **EDUCE, EVOKE,
EXTRACT**
Eli relative **HOPHNI,
ICHABOD, PHINEHAS**
Elia **LAMB**
Eliam relative **BATHSHEBA**
elicit **EDUCE, EVOKE,
EXTRACT**
elide **DELE, OMIT, SLUR**
eligible **FIT, NUBILE,
SUITABLE, COMPETENT,
DESIRABLE**
Elijah **ELIA, LIGE, ELIAS**
Elimelech relative **RUTH,
NAOMI, MAHLON**
eliminate **RID, OMIT, ERASE,
EXPEL, REMOVE, EXCRETE,
SECRETE**
Eliot character **BEDE, CASS,
ROMOLA**
Eliot novel **RAMOLA, ADAM
BEDE, MIDDLEMARCH, SILAS
MARNER**
Elisheba husband **AARON**
elision **SYNCOPE, OMISSION**
elite **PICK, CREAM**
elite military group **SEAL**
elixir **RASA, SOMA, HAOMA,
AMRITA, POTION,**

**ARCANUM, NOSTRUM,
PANACEA**
Elixir of Love role **ADINA,
BELCORE, NEMORINO**
Elizabeth **LIZ, BETH, BETTY,
LIZZIE**
Elizabeth I **(GL)ORIANA**
Elizabeth I advisor **CECIL**
Elizabeth I parent **ANNE,
HENRY, BOLEYN**
Elizabeth II child **ANNE,
ANDREW, EDWARD,
CHARLES**
Elizabeth II relative **MARK,
DIANA, SARAH, ANDREW,
GEORGE, PHILIP, MARGARET**
elk *see p. 664*
Elkanah relative **SAMUEL**
ell **WING, CUBIT**
ellipse **OVAL, CURVE**
ellipsis **SYNCOPE**
elliptic **OVAL, OVATE,
OBLONG**
elliptical **OVAL, BRIEF, OVATE,
OBLONG, CONCISE**
elm **ULMUS, W(H)AHOO**
elm fruit **KEY, SAMARA**
Elon relative **ADAH, ESAU,
BASHEMATH**
elongated **LINEAR, PROLATE**
elope **FLEE, ESCAPE, ABSCOND**
eloquence **ORATORY,
RHETORIC**
elucidate **CLARIFY, EXPLAIN**
elude **JINK, SHUN, DODGE,
EVADE**
elusive **EELY, SLICK, SLIPPERY**
Elysian **HAPPY, BLISSFUL**
emaciation **TABES, WASTE,
ATROPHY**
e-mail type **SPAM**
emanation(s) **AURA, BLAS,
AURAE, NITON**
emancipate **FREE, MANUMIT,
RELEASE**
emancipator **ABE, FREER,
MOSES, LINCOLN**
emasculate **GELD, WEAKEN,
CASTRATE**
embalm **MUMMIFY, PRESERVE**
embalming fluid **FORMALIN**
embankment **DAM, BUND,
DIKE, DYKE, DIGUE, LEVEE,
STAITHE**
embark **SHIP, BOARD**
embarrass **VEX, FAZE, ABASH**
embassy **MISSION, LEGATION**
embassy official **AIDE,
ATTACHE**

embellish	DECK, GILD, PINK, ADORN, BEDECK, GARNISH
embellished	ORNATE
ember	ASH, COAL, ISEL, IZLE, SPARK, CINDER, CLINKER
embezzle	PECULATE, DEFALCATE
— and Embia	ASKR
embitter	FESTER, RANKLE
emblem	BAR, FLAG, MACE, SIGN, BADGE, EAGLE, TOTEM, DESIGN, FASCES, SYMBOL, INSIGNE, INSIGNIA
embodiment	IMAGE, AVATAR, EPITOME, INCARNATION
emboss	STUD, CHASE, RAISE, ENGRAVE
embrace	HUG, HASS, ADOPT, CLASP, ENARM, INARM, ACCEPT, CARESS, EMBODY, WELCOME
embrocation	ARNICA, LINIMENT
embroider	TAT, PURL, BREDE, COUCH, DECORATE
embroidery equipment	CREWEL, TABORET, TAMBOUR
embroil	MIXUP, MUDDLE
embryo	CELL, GERM, FETUS
emend	EDIT, ALTER, REVISE
emerald	SMARAGD; see GEM
Emerald Isle	EIRE, ERIN, IRELAND
emerge	RISE, ISSUE, EMANATE
emergency	PASS, PINCH, CRISIS, CLUTCH, STRAIT, URGENCY
emergency equipment	JACK, FLARE, SPARE
emery	ABRASIVE, CORUNDUM
emetic	ALUM, ALOIN, IPECAC, MUSTARD, CATHARTIC
emigrant	ALIEN, EMIGRE, COLONIST
emigre(e)	ALIEN, EXILE, REFUGEE
eminence	FAME, HILL, NOTE, REPUTE
eminent	NOTED, FAMOUS, EXALTED
emirate	AJMAN, DUBAI, QATAR, KUWAIT, BAHRAIN, FUJAIRA, SHARJAH, ABUDHABI
emissary	SPY, AGENT, ENVOY, (DE)LEGATE
emit	REEK, SHED, ERUCT, EXUDE
Emmentaler	SWISS, GRUYERE
emmer	SPELT, WHEAT
emollient	ALOE, BALM, SALVE
emolument	PAY, FEE, WAGE, SALARY, STIPEND
emotion	ONDE, PATHOS, PASSION
emotional	MOVING, TOUCHING
empathy	AFFINITY
emperor	CZAR, TSAR, TZAR, AKBAR, MOGUL, TENNO, KAISER, MIKADO, PADISHAH
emphasis	ICTUS, ACCENT, STRESS
empire	RULE, SWAY, KINGDOM
Empire State	NY, NEW YORK
employ	USE, HIRE, PLACE, ENGAGE
employee(s)	MAN, HAND, HELP, STAFF, WORKER, PERSONNEL
employer	BOSS, JOSS, USER, HIRER
employment	JOB, WORK, PLACE, TRADE
emporium	MART, SHOP, STORE, MARKET
empower	VEST, ENDOW, ENABLE, ENTITLE, DEPUTIZE, AUTHORIZE
empress	CZARINA
empty	BARE, IDLE, TOOM, VAIN, VOID, BLANK, DRAIN, INANE, DEVOID, UNPACK, VACANT, DEPLETE, VACUOUS, DEPLETED
emu	RHEA, RATITE, CASSOWARY; see p. 676
emulate	APE, VIE, RIVAL, STRIVE
en masse	AS ONE, AS A WHOLE
en route	ON THE WAY
— en scène	MISE
enact	PASS, ACTOUT, PERFORM, PORTRAY
enamelware	LIMOGES, CLOISONNE
enamored	FOND, SMITTEN
encamp	TENT, PITCH, BIVOUAC
enchant	CHARM, BEWITCH, DELIGHT, ENTHRAL(L)
enchantress	HAG, CIRCE, MEDEA, SIREN, WITCH
encircle	HEM, ORB, GIRD, GIRT, EMBAY, ENVIRON
enclose	MEW, PEN, CAGE, CASE, WRAP, FENCE, HEDGE, INCASE, CORRAL, ENCLAVE
enclosure	STY, BAWN, COOP,

YARD, ATAJO, KRAAL, SEKOS, CANCHA, CORRAL, STOCKADE

encomium ELOGE, PRAISE, EULOGY, TRIBUTE, PANEGYRIC

encompass GIRD, ENVELOP, INCLUDE, COMPRISE, ENCIRCLE, SURROUND

encore BIS, AGAIN, REAIR, REPEAT

encounter MEET, BATTLE, ENGAGE, COMEUPON

encourage EGG, ABET, URGE, BOOST, BRACE, ELATE, FOSTER

encroach IMPINGE, INFRINGE, TRESPASS

encumber LOAD, BURDEN, IMPEDE, SADDLE

encumbrance LIEN, LOAN, CLAIM, BURDEN, MORTGAGE

end AIM, DIE, TIP, CODA, FINE, REAR, STUB, BOURN, FINIS, OMEGA, FINALE, INTENT, RESULT, THIRTY, REMNANT

end, tending to TELIC

endanger RISK, (IM)PERIL

endangered species TIGER, DUGONG, OCELOT, CHEETAH, GORILLA, LEOPARD, BARBIRUSA, ORANGUTAN

endearment term HON, BABE, BABY, DEAR, DOLL, HONEY, SUGAR, DARLING, SWEETIE

endeavor AIM, TRY, VIE, ESSAY, NISUS

ending FINIS, FINALE, FINISH, PERIOD, CLOSURE

endive CHICORY, WITLOOF, ESCAROLE

endless ETERN(AL), UNDYING, INFINITE, PERPETUAL

endocrine gland PINEAL, TESTIS, ADRENAL, OVARIES, THYROID, PANCREAS, PITUITARY

endorse BACK, SIGN, RATIFY, SECOND, APPROVE, SANCTION

endorsement OK, NOD, VISA, VISE, BACKING, APPROVAL

endow VEST, GRACE, BESTOW, INVEST

endowed ABLE, BUXOM, GIFTED

endowment BOON, DOWER, GRANT, TALENT, FELLOWSHIP

endue VEST, DOWER, DIGEST, INVEST

endurance STAMINA, FORTITUDE

endure BEAR, BIDE, DREE, LAST, WEAR, ABIDE, BROOK, PERSIST

Endymion lover SELENE

Endymion relative CALYCE, AETOLUS

enema CLYSTER

enemy FOE, RIVAL, FOEMAN, ADVERSARY

enemy type SWORN, MORTAL, PUBLIC

energetic KEEN, VIVID, ACTIVE, LIVELY

energy PEP, VIM, ZIP, BENT, ERGAL, POWER, VIGOR, METTLE, POTENCY, STHENIA

energy, lack of ATONY, INERTIA

energy unit BTU, ERG, RAD, ERGON, JOULE, MEGERG

enervate SAP, DRAIN, WEAKEN

enfeeble UNMAN, WEAKEN

enforce COMPEL, IMPOSE

Enforcer FRANK, NITTI

enfranchise SETFREE, LIBERATE

engage BOOK, HIRE, MESH, ENLIST, OCCUPY, RETAIN, BETROTH, CHARTER, AFFIANCE

engaged AT IT, BUSY, KNEEDEEP, OCCUPIED, PROMISED

engagement DATE, TROTH, PROMISE, BETROTHAL

engaging WINNING, WINSOME, CHARMING

engender SIRE, BEGET, BREED, PROMOTE, GENERATE

engine GIN, HEMI, MOGUL, MOTOR, DIESEL, YARDER, MACHINE, TURBINE; see WEAPON

engine cleaner STP

engine part see MOTOR

engineer SAPPER, SEABEE, CONTRIVE

engineer, type of ELEC, MECH, CIVIL, CHEMICAL, ELECTRICAL, MECHANICAL

England ALBION, ANGLIA

England, capital of LONDON

English LIMEY, SAXON, BRITISH, SILURES, SASSENACH

English alphabet AR, EF, EL, EM,
EN, EX, WY, BEE, CEE, CUE,
DEE, ESS, GEE, JAY, KAY, PEE,
TEE, WYE, ZED, ZEE, AITCH,
DOUBLEU

English artist OPIE, MOORE,
MILLAIS, TURNER, EPSTEIN,
HOGARTH, REYNOLDS

English Channel swimmers
TOTH, WEBB, BURGESS,
SULLIVAN, TIRABOSCHI

English city/town ELY, YORK,
DOVER, LEEDS, EALING,
LONDON, OXFORD, BRISTOL,
BROMLEY, LAMBETH,
COVENTRY, CAMBRIDGE,
LIVERPOOL, MANCHESTER

English county AVON, KENT,
YORK, DERBY, DEVON,
ESSEX, WILTS, DORSET,
DURHAM, SURREY, SUSSEX,
CORNWALL, MIDLANDS

English dramatist SHAW,
WILDE, MARLOWE,
SHAKESPEARE

English explorer ROSS, CABOT,
BAFFIN, RALEIGH,
FROBISHER

English measure PIN, CRAN,
COOM, PIPE, CHAIN, COOMB,
COVER, JUGUM, FIRKIN,
RUNLET, VIRGATE; see
MEASURE

English money ANGEL, BODLE,
CROWN, DRAKE, GROAT,
PENNY, PLACK, POUND,
BAWBEE, FLORIN, GUINEA,
CAROLUS, JACOBUS,
UNICORN, ATCHISON,
FARTHING, SHILLING,
HALFCROWN, SOVEREIGN;
see MONEY

English playwright BARRIE,
DRYDEN, JONSON, PINTER,
MARLOWE

English poet GRAY, POPE,
AUDEN, BLAKE, BYRON,
DONNE, ELIOT, KEATS, SWIFT,
DRYDEN, JONSON, MILTON,
CHAUCER, SITWELL,
ROSSETTI, TENNYSON

English port DOVER,
MARGATE

English prince HARRY,
ANDREW, EDWARD, PHILIP,
CHARLES, WILLIAM

English river CAM, DEE, DON,
EXE, URE, AVON, TRENT,
HUMBER, THAMES

English school ETON, RUGBY,
HARROW, STPAULS

English sport RUGBY, CRICKET

English royal house YORK,
TUDOR

English ruler ANNE, BELI,
BRUT, EDWY, JOHN, EDRED,
HENRY, JAMES, ALFRED,
CANUTE, EDMUND,
EDWARD, EGBERT, GEORGE,
HAROLD, CHARLES,
RICHARD, STEPHEN, WILLIAM,
VICTORIA, ETHERLRED,
ELIZABETH

English statesman LAW, EDEN,
GREY, PEEL, PITT, DERBY,
HEATH, MAJOR, NORTH,
ATTLEE, GEORGE, PELHAM,
WILSON, ASQUITH, BALDWIN,
BALFOUR, CANNING,
GRAFTON, RUSSELL, WALPOLE,
ABERDEEN, DISRAELI,
GODERICH, PERCEVAL,
PORTLAND, ROSEBERY,
THATCHER, CALLAGHAN,
CHURCHILL, GLADSTONE,
MACDONALD, MACMILLAN,
MELBOURNE, SHELBURNE,
CHAMBERLAIN,
PALMERSTONE

English university LEEDS,
EXETER, OXFORD,
CAMBRIDGE

English weight KIP, KEEL,
BARGE, CLOVE, FAGOT,
STONE, CENTAL, FIRKIN,
POCKET

English writer MORE, DEFOE,
DOYLE, HARDY, MILNE,
SHUTE, WAUGH, WELLS,
WOOLF, AUSTEN, CONRAD,
BRONTE, FOWLES, HUXLEY,
SAYERS, STERNE, ORWELL,
DICKENS, FORSTER, FORSYTH,
GOLDING, KIPLING,
LECARRE, TOLKIEN,
MURDOCH, CHRISTIE,
FIELDING, THACKERY,
TROLLOPE

Englishman LIMEY, SAXON,
COCKNEY, SASSENACH

engrave ETCH, RIST, CARVE,
CHASE, INFIX, CHISEL,
INCISE, STIPPLE

engraver, famous BLAKE,
DURER, DAUMIER,
HOGARTH, MANTEGNA

engraving CUT, PRINT,
ETCHING, INTAGLIO

engraving, *pert. to*	**GLYPTIC**	entail	**CALLFOR, INVOLVE**
engraving tool	**BURIN, STYLE,**	entangle	**MESH, SNARL,**
	MATTOIR		**ENMESH, ENTRAP,**
engrossed	**RAPT, ABSORBED**		**RAFFLE**
engulf	**WHELM, ABSORB,**	entente	**TREATY, CONCORD**
	SWALLOW	enter	**LIST, ADMIT, ENROL,**
enhance	**AUGMENT,**		**START, ENROLL, INSERT,**
	HEIGHTEN, INTENSIFY		**RECORD, TYPEIN**
Enid husband	**GERAINT**	enterprise	**PUSH, PROJECT,**
enigma	**EGMA, REBUS,**		**VENTURE, ENDEAVOR**
	PUZZLE, RIDDLE, SECRET,	entertain	**FETE, HOST, AMUSE,**
	CONUNDRUM		**DIVERT, REGALE**
enigmatic	**CRYPTIC,**	entertainer(s)	**HOST, HETAERA,**
	BAFFLING, PUZZLING		**HETAIRA, HOSTESS,**
enisle	**ISOLATE**		**COURTESAN**
enjoin	**BID, ORDER, FORBID**	entertainment	**FUN, MASQUE,**
enjoy	**LIKE, SHARE, RELISH**		**PASTIME, AMUSEMENT,**
enjoyment.	**ZEST, GUSTO,**		**DIVERSION**
	RELISH	enthrall	**ENSLAVE, CAPTIVATE**
enlarge	**REAM, BLOWUP,**	enthusiasm	**ESTRO;** *see* **ZEAL**
	DILATE, EXPAND, DISTEND	enthusiast	**BUG, FAN, IST,**
enlighten	**EDIFY, INFORM,**		**BUFF, ADDICT, ZEALOT,**
	EDUCATE		**DEVOTEE, FANATIC**
enlist	**JOIN, ENROLL, RECRUIT**	enthusiastic, become less	**COOL**
enliven	**ELATE, ROUSE,**	entice	**BAIT, COAX, LURE,**
	ANIMATE		**TOLE, COZEN, PIQUE, TEMPT,**
enmity	**ANIMUS, MALICE,**		**ALLURE, BECKON, CAJOLE,**
	RANCOR		**INVEIGH**
ennead	**NINE**	entire	**ALL, GAMUT, TOTAL,**
Enoch relative	**EVE, ADAM,**		**WHOLE, COMPLETE**
	CAIN, EDNA, ENOS, IRAD,	entirely	**INTOTO, WHOLLY**
	JARED, METHUSELAH	entity	**ENS, BEING, ENTIA,**
enormity	**OUTRAGE,**		**ESSENCE**
	IMMENSITY	entomb	**BURY, INTER, INURN**
enormous	**HUGE, IMMENSE,**	entourage	**ROUT, TRAIN,**
	COLOSSAL		**RETINUE, FOLLOWERS**
Enos' relative	**EVE, ABEL,**	entr'acte	**INTERVAL,**
	ADAM, CAIN, SETH, ENOCH,		**INTERLUDE, INTERMISSION**
	KENAN, MAHALEL	entrails	**GUTS, OFFAL, BOWELS,**
enough	**BAS, BUS, ENOW,**		**UMBLES, VISCERA**
	AMPLE, BASTA, DROP IT	entrance	**ADIT, DOOR, GATE,**
enrage	**IRK, ROIL, ANGER,**		**DEBUT, STILE, ACCESS,**
	MADDEN, INCENSE		**PORTAL, INGRESS**
enrapture	**PLEASE, BEWITCH,**	entrant	**ENTRY, CONTENDER,**
	DELIGHT, ENCHANT		**CONTESTANT**
enrich	**ADORN, ENDOW,**	entreat	**BEG, PRAY, HALSE,**
	ENHANCE		**PLEAD, ADJURE, HALSEN,**
enroll	**ENTER, ENLIST,**		**SOLICIT**
	IMPANEL, REGISTER	entrepreneur	**TYCOON,**
ensemble	**CAST, SUIT(E),**		**MAGNATE, PROMOTER,**
	TROUPE, COSTUME		**CAPITALIST, IMPRESARIO,**
ensign	**FLAG, BANNER,**		**INDUSTRIALIST**
	STANDARD	entrepreneur, famous	*see p. 541*
enslave	**ADDICT, ENTHRALL,**	entry	**ITEM, NOTE, DEBIT,**
	SUBJUGATE		**CREDIT, MINUTE**
ensnare	**NET, WEB, LURE,**	entwine	**WEAVE, ENLACE,**
	BENET, DECOY, SNIGGLE		**WREATHE**
ensue	**FOLLOW, RESULT,**	enumerate	**LIST, TELL, TICK,**
	SUCCEED		**COUNT, NUMBER**

enunciate STATE, UTTER,
DECLARE
enure HARDEN, ACCUSTOM
envelop WRAP, ENFOLD,
INFOLD, INWRAP, SHROUD,
SWADDLE
envelope POD, SACK, SHELL,
SHEATH, CAPSULE, WRAPPER
envious GREEN(EYED),
JEALOUS
environment MILIEU, PURLIEU
environmental GREEN,
ECOLOGICAL
environs EXURBS, LOCALE,
SETTING, SUBURBS,
VICINITY, OUTSKIRTS
envisage EXPECT, FORESEE
envision PICTURE, VISUALIZE
envoy NUNCIO, (DE)LEGATE,
DIPLOMAT, EMISSARY,
MESSENGER, AMBASSADOR
envy ONDE, COVET, SPITE,
GRUDGE
enzyme ASE, FICIN, KINASE,
LOTASE, MUTASE, OLEASE,
PAPAIN, PEPSIN, RENNIN,
ZYMASE, AMYLASE,
MALTASE, PTYALIN, TRYPSIN,
DIASTASE, INSULASE
eon ERA, OLAM, EPOCH
Eos DAWN, AURORA
epaulet PATCH, INSIGNIA
epee *see* FENCING
Ephah husband CALEB
ephemeral MORTAL,
TRANSIENT, EVANESCENT,
TRANSITORY
Ephraim relative EZER, ELEAD,
JACOB, BERIZH, JOSEPH,
REPHAH, ASENATH, SHEERAH,
MANASSEH, SHUTHELAH
epic EDDA, EPOS, POEM,
SAGA, ENEID, ILIAD, AENEID,
EPOPEE, HEROIC, BEOWULF,
HOMERIC, ODYSSEY,
KALEVALA, RAMAYANA,
SAKUNTALA
Epictetus STOIC
epicure FRIAND, GOURMET,
GOURMAND, SYBARITE
epicurean APICIAN, SYBARITE
epidemic FLU, PEST, PLAGUE
epidermis BARK, SKIN,
INTEGUMENT
epigram ADAGE, MAXIM,
(BON)MOT
epigraph MOTTO
epilepsy FIT, SEIZURE,
CATALEPSY, GRANDMAL

episode EVENT, INCIDENT
epistle NOTE, LETTER, MISSIVE
epitaph word HIC, RIP, HERE,
LIES, JACET
epithet NAME, OATH, CURSE,
BYNAME, AGNOMEN
epitome BRIEF, DIGEST,
SUMMARY, SYNOPSIS
epoch AGE, EON, ERA, BALA,
ECCA, LIAS, MALM, MUAV,
CHAZY, ERIAN, UINTA,
ARENIG, KAIBAB, OOLITE,
SERIES, FORMATION
equable CALM, EVEN, SERENE,
STEADY
equal ISO, TIE, EVEN, FERE,
LIKE, MEET, PARI, PEER, TIED,
ALIKE, MATCH, COMPEER
equality PAR(ITY), ISONOMY
equanimity COOL, POISE,
SERENITY
equation part ROOT, TERM,
SCALAR, CONSTANT,
VARIABLE
equation type LINEAR,
INTEGRAL, ALGEBRAIC,
QUADRATIC
equator-crossed country CONGO,
GABON, KENYA, BORNEO,
BRAZIL, UGANDA, ECUADOR,
COLOMBIA
Equatorial Guinea, capital of
MALABO
Equatorial Guinea island BIOKO,
ELOBEY, PAGULU,
CORISCO
Equatorial Guinea language FANG,
CRIOLO; *see* MANDE
Equatorial Guinea money FRANC
Equatorial Guinea neighbor
GABON, CAMEROON
Equatorial Guinea river BENITO
Equatorial Guinea town BATA,
KOGO, MBINI
Equatorial Guinea tribe FULA,
SUSU, MALINKE
Equatorial Guinea weight AKEY,
PISO, UZAN, BENDA, SERON
equilibrium PARITY,
BALANCE, COMPOSURE
equine *see* HORSE, ASS
equip FIT, RIG, GIRD, OUTFIT,
ACCOUTRE
equipage TRAIN, OUTFIT,
RETINUE
equipment RIG, GEAR, TACKLE
equitable FAIR, JUST, HONEST
equity JUSTICE, FAIRNESS,
INTEREST

equivocal	VAGUE, EVASIVE, AMBIGUOUS, MISLEADING
equivocate	EVADE, FENCE, HEDGE, PALTER
Er relative	JUDAH, TAMAR
era	AGE, SAKA, CYCLE, EPOCH, GROUP, PERIOD, CENOZOIC, MESOZOIC, PALEOZOIC
eradicate	RID, ROOT, ERASE, LEVEL, UPROOT, EPILATE
erase	BLOT, DELE, CANCEL, DELETE, EFFACE
eraser	RUBBER
ere	BEFORE, RATHER, SOONER
Erebus	HADES
erect	REAR, TALL, BUILD, RAISE
ergo	HENCE, THEREFORE
Erin	EIRE, IRELAND, HIBERNIA
Erinyes	ALECTO, FURIES, MAGAERA, TISIPHONE
Eris	DISCORD
Eris relative	ARES, NEMESIS
Eritrea, capital of	ASMARA
Eritrean city/town	KEREN, NAKFA, ASMARA, AKORDAT
Eritrean language	AFAR, NARA, SAHO, BILEN, TIGRE, ARABIC, KUNAMA, AMHARIC, ENGLISH, TOBEDAWI, TIGRINYA
Eritrean money	CENT, NAKFA
Eritrean neighbor	SUDAN, YEMEN, DJIBOUTI, ETHIOPIA
Eritrean peninsula	DAHLAK
Eritrean river	GASH, ANSEBA, BARAKA
ermine	FUR, STOAT, WEASEL
erode	EAT, WEAR, CORRODE
Eroica composer	BEETHOVEN
Eroica key	EFLAT
Eros	AMOR, LOVE, CUPID
erosion	ABRASION, FRICTION
erotic	SEXY, BAWDY, CARNAL, AMATIVE, AMATORY, AMOROUS, PAPHIAN
err	SIN, SLIP, STRAY, WANDER, MISTAKE
errand	TASK, MISSION
errand boy/girl	PAGE, CADDIE, RUNNER, BELLBOY, BELLHOP, BUTTONS
erratic	ODD, WAYWARD, PECULIAR, ECCENTRIC
erroneous	WRONG, MISTAKEN
error(s)	BULL, TYPO, BONER, GAFFE, ERRATA, MISCUE, ERRATUM, SOLECISM
— and error	TRIAL

ersatz	SYNTHETIC, ARTIFICIAL, SUBSTITUTE
Erse	IRISH, SCOTS, GAELIC
erudite	WISE, LEARNED, SCHOLARLY
erupt	EMIT, BURST
eruption	RASH, BLAST, BLOWUP, OUTBURST
Esau	EDOM
Esau relative	ADAH, ELON, ISAAC, JACOB, JALAM, JEUSH, KORAH, REUEL, JUDITH, ELIPHAZ, REBECCA
escalator inventor	RENO
escapade	DIDO, CAPER, PRANK
escape	LAM, FLEE, LEAK, OOZE, ELUDE, EVADE, DECAMP, ABSCOND
eschatology subject	DEATH
eschew	SHUN, FORGO, ABSTAIN
escort	BEAU, USHER, CONVOY, DUENNA, SQUIRE, CONDUCT, RETINUE
escrow	BOND, DEED, CONTRACT
esculent	EDIBLE, EATABLE
escutcheon	ARMS, CREST, SHIELD
Eskimo	see p. 730
Eskimo dog	HUSKY, MALAMUTE
Eskimo hut	IGLU, IGLOO
esophagus	GULA, GULLET, WEASAND
esoteric	INNER, ARCANE, MYSTIC, OCCULT
espalier	LATTICE, TRELLIS, PALISADE
especially	MAINLY, REALLY, CHIEFLY, PRIMARILY
Esperanto	see LANGUAGE
espionage	SPYING, INTELLIGENCE
esplanade	GLACIS, WALKWAY, PROMENADE
espouse	ABET, ADOPT, MARRY
esprit	MORALE, SPIRIT
esquire	ESCORT, LAWYER, ATTENDANT
essay	TRY, TEST, CHRIA, PAPER, THEME, TRACT, THESIS, ATTEMPT, TREATISE
essayist	LAMB, CAPEK, PATER, WOOLF, CATHER, IRVING, ORWELL, CARLYLE, EMERSON, THOREAU
essence	ENS, GIST, PITH, RASA, ATTAR, BEING, SCENT, AMRITA, EXTRACT, PERFUME

essential   MUST, BASAL, BASIC,
VITAL
establish   SET, BASE, FOUND,
PROVE, SETTLE, VERIFY
establishment   FIRM, AGENCY,
COMPANY
estate   ALOD, RANK, ALLOD,
DAIRA, MANOR, TALUK,
ASSETS, DOMAIN, LEGACY,
HOLDING, ALLODIUM
esteem   HONOR, PRIDE, PRIZE,
ADMIRE, REPUTE, CHERISH
ester   ETHER, ACETIN, IODIDE,
OLEATE, STEARIN, SILICATE
Ester festival   PURIM
Esther husband   XERXES,
AHASUERUS
estimate   GAGE, METE, RATE,
ASSAY, AUDIT, ASSESS,
RECKON, APPRAISE
estimation   ESTEEM, REGARD,
APPRAISAL, CRITICISM
Estonia, capital of   TALLINN
Estonian city/town   NARVA,
PARNU, TARTU, TALLINN
Estonian island   MUHU, KIHNU,
RUHNU, VORMSI, HIIUMAA,
SAAREMAA
Estonian measure   TUN, ELLE,
LIIN, SULD, TOLL, FADEN,
SAGENE
Estonian money   EEK, SENT,
KROON, ESTMARK
Estonian neighbor   LATVIA,
RUSSIA, FINLAND
Estonian river   NARVA, PARNU,
KASARI
Estonian weight   NAEL, PUUD
estrade   DAIS
estrange   WEAN, SPLIT,
DIVERT, ALIENATE
estrus   HEAT, FRENZY
estuary   RIA, LOCH, PARA,
FIORD, FIRTH, FJORD, FRITH,
INLET, PLATA
étagère   WHATNOT
etch   CUT, SCORE, CHISEL,
ENGRAVE
Eteocles kingdom   THEBES
Eteocles relative   JOCASTA,
OEDIPUS, LAODAMAS,
POLYNICES
eternal   AGELESS, FOREVER,
INFINITE, TIMELESS
Eternal City   ROME
eternity   (A)EON, OLAM,
INFINITY
Ethan Frome wife   ZEENA
Ethbaal relative   JEZEBEL

ether   SKY, ESTER, SPACE
ethereal   AERY, AIRY, AERIAL,
DELICATE, HEAVENLY
ethical   MORAL, RIGHT, HONEST
Ethical Culture founder   ADLER
Ethiopia   CUSH, ABYSSINIA
Ethiopia, capital of   ADDIS
ABABA
Ethiopia, capital (former)   MEROE
Ethiopian city/town   ASWA,
ZULA, ASOSA, ASSAB,
AWASA, HARAR, JIMMA,
SODDU, ASMARA, GONDER,
NAZRET
Ethiopian island   DAHLAK
Ethiopian lake   TANA, ZWAI,
ABAYA, CHAMO, ASSALE,
RUDOLF, TURKANA, STEFANIE
Ethiopian language   GEEZ,
GALLA, GHESE, TIGRE,
ARABIC, SOMALI, AMHARIC,
TIGRINYA, OROMINGA,
GUARAGINGA; see SEMITIC
Ethiopian measure   TAT, CUBA,
KUBA
Ethiopian money   BESA, BIRR,
CENT, GIRSH, TALARI,
ASHRAFI
Ethiopian neighbor   KENYA,
SUDAN, ERITREA, SOMALIA,
DJIBOUTI
Ethiopian people   AFAR, KALA,
BEJAS, DANAKIL, SOMALIS
Ethiopian princess   AIDA,
ANDROMEDA
Ethiopian province   BALE, SHOA,
ARUSI, HARAR, KAFFA,
TIGRE, WALLO, GOJJAM,
GONDER, SIDAMO, ERITREA,
WALLAGA
Ethiopian river   OMO, ABAY,
BARO, DAWA, WABI, AKOBO,
FAFAN, MAREB, ATBARA,
BARAKA, TAKKAZE
Ethiopian ruler   RAS, ABUNA,
NEGUS, MEMNON,
CANDACE, MENELIK, SELASSIE
Ethiopian weight   KASM, NATR,
OKET, ALADA, NETER,
WAKEA, WOGIET
ethnic   FOLK, RACIAL
etiolate   BLANCH, BLEACH,
WHITEN
etiquette   DECORUM,
PROPRIETY
Eton rival   HARROW
Etruscan god   see p. 650
eucalyptus   YATE, KARRI,
JARRAH, MALLEE

Eucharist	*see* **COMMUNION**	Eve relative	**ABEL, ADAM,**
eugenics pioneer	**GALTON**		**CAIN, ENOS, SETH**
eulogy	**ELOGE, PRAISE,**	Eve tempter	**SERPENT**
	ENCOMIUM	even	**SAME, FLUSH, LEVEL,**
Eumenides	**FURIES, ERINNYES**		**PLANE, PLUMB, SQUARE,**
Eunice relative	**TIMOTHY**		**UNIFORM**
Euphemia	**EPPY**	evening	**DEN, DUSK, VESPER,**
Eurasian mountain range	**URALS**		**GLOAMING**
Euripides play	**ION, HELEN,**	evensong	**VESPERS**
MEDEA, BACCHAE,		event	**GALA, AFFAIR, EPISODE,**
CYCLOPS, ELECTRA,			**INCIDENT**
ORESTES, ALCESTIS		eventual	**FINAL, ULTIMATE**
Europa's lover	**ZEUS**	ever	**AYE, EER, ALWAYS**
Europe, highest point	**GORA**	Everest climber	**NORGAY,**
	ELBRUS		**HILLARY, TENZING**
Europe, largest city	**MOSCOW**	Everglade State	**FL(A), FLORIDA**
Europe, largest country	**RUSSIA**	Evergreen State	**WA(SH),**
Europe, largest island	**GREAT**		**WASHINGTON**
	BRITAIN	evergreen	**BOX, ATLE, BAGO,**
Europe, largest lake	**CASPIAN**		**MORA, PIXY, TAWA, THEA,**
Europe, longest river	**VOLGA**		**UPAS, WHIN, ATLEE, BIRMA,**
Europe, lowest point	**CASPIAN**		**BOLDO, BOLDU, BUXUS,**
Europe, smallest country			**CATHA, CLOVE, ERICA, FURZE,**
VATICAN (CITY)			**GORSE, PIXIE, PYXIE, THUJA,**
European	**BALT, DANE, FINN,**		**TOYON, NUTMEG, CALABA,**
LAPP, LETT, POLE, SERB,			**PEUMUS, SPRUCE, TOLLON,**
SLAV, CROAT, CZECH, GREEK,			**ARBUTUS, CONIFER**
SWEDE, SWISS, FRANK,		everlasting	**ETERN(E), OLAMIC,**
SLOVAK			**AGELONG, ETERNAL**
European Economic Community		every	**ALL, EACH**
see **COMMON MARKET**		everyday	**DAILY, USUAL,**
Eurydice relative	**IOLE,**		**COMMON**
	ORPHEUS	everywhere	**UBIQUE, ALLOVER**
eustachian tube	**SALPINX**	evict	**OUST, SACK, EXPEL**
evacuate	**MOVE, VOID, EMPTY**	evidence	**SIGN, PROOF,**
evade	**BILK, FOIL, SHUN,**		**TESTIMONY**
AVOID, DODGE, ELUDE,		evident	**CLEAR, PLAIN,**
PARRY, SHIRK, SHUNT, PALTER			**PATENT, APPARENT,**
evaluate	**GAGE, ASSAY,**		**PALPABLE**
GAUGE, PRICE, ASSESS,		evil	**MAL, BASE, HARM, MALA,**
APPRAISE			**VICE, VILE, WRONG,**
evanescent	**AIRY, FLEETING,**		**MALIGN**
EPHEMERAL, TRANSIENT		evil eye	**HEX, JINX, CURSE,**
Evangeline author	**LONGFELLOW**		**WHAMMY**
Evangeline home	**ACADIA**	evil intent	**DOLUS, MALICE**
evangelist	**JOHN, LUKE, MARK,**	evil person	**DEMON, DEVIL,**
SMITH, GANTRY, GRAHAM,			**VILLAIN, EVILDOER**
SUNDAY, APOSTLE, FALWELL,		evil spirit	*see* **DEMON**
MATTHEW, ROBERTS,		Evita role	**CHE, EVA, JUAN,**
PREACHER, MCPHERSON,			**PERON**
MISSIONARY		evoke	**EDUCE, ELICIT,**
Evans, Mary Ann	**ELIOT**		**SUMMON**
evaporate	**DRY, VANISH**	evolve	**(D)EDUCE, DERIVE,**
evasion	**TRICK, ESCAPE,**		**UNFOLD**
ELUSION, AVOIDANCE		ewe	**YOW, CRONE, THEAVE;**
evasive	**SHIFTY, TRICKY,**		*see* **SHEEP**
ELUSIVE		ex	**(OLD)FLAME, FORMER**
eve	**DUSK, SUNDOWN,**	ex cathedra	**OFFICIAL(LY),**
TWILIGHT		— ex machina	**DEUS**

ex post facto	LATER, AFTER THE FACT	exchange medium	SHOE, SYCEE, SCHUIT
exacerbate	IRE, IRK, ENRAGE, WORSEN, PROVOKE, IRRITATE	exchange premium	AGIO
		exchange words	ARGUE, FIGHT, QUARREL
exact	LEVY, BLEED, WREST, DEMAND, EXTORT, ESTREAT, LITERAL	exchequer	FISC, FISK, TREASURY
		excise	CUT(OUT), TAX, DUTY, TOLL, REMOVE
exactly	JUSTSO, NOLESS, RIGHTON, PRECISELY	excite	ROIL, WHET, ELATE, ROUSE, AGITATE, ENTHUSE
exaggerate	PUFF, MAGNIFY, STRETCH, EMBROIDER		
exaggeration	HYPERBOLE, EMBROIDERY	excited	AGOG, ASTIR, MANIC, ATINGLE
exalt	ELATE, EXTOL, RAISE, DIGNIFY, ELEVATE	excitement	FURY, FUROR, FRENZY, FURORE, PASSION
exalted	HIGH, LOFTY, NOBLE, EMINENT	exclaim	CRY, SHOUT, EJACULATE
examination	GRE, SAT, TAT, ORAL, QUIZ, TEST, AUDIT, PROBE, STUDY, TRIAL, BIOPSY, GREATS, TRIPOS, TRYOUT, AUTOPSY, CATECHISM	exclamation	see p. 702
		exclude	BAR, OMIT, DEBAR, DEPORT, BLACKBALL
		exclusive	ONLY, POSH, SOLE, SELECT, UNIQUE
examine	PRY, SPY, TRY, SCAN, CHECK, GRADE, APPOSE, PALPATE	excoriate	FLAY, PARE, CHAFE, ABRADE
		excrement	DUNG, FECES, MANURE
example	CASE, PINK, MODEL, SAMPLE, PARADIGM, SPECIMEN	excrescence	CORN, WART, STUD, GROWTH
exasperate	IRK, TRY, VEX, RILE, ANGER, ANNOY, INFURIATE	excrete	EGEST, EXUDE, EVACUATE
		exculpate	CLEAR, ACQUIT, ABSOLVE, EXONERATE
excavate	DIG, GRUB, MUCK, PION, SCOOP, DREDGE, UNEARTH	excursion	TOUR, TREK, JAUNT, SALLY, JUNKET, OUTING
excavation	PIT, HOLE, MINE, SHAFT, STOPE, HOLLOW	excuse	PLEA, ALIBI, REMIT, ESSOIN(E), CONDONE
exceed	CAP, BEST, PASS, EXCEL, OUTDO, BETTER	execrate	HATE, ABHOR, DETEST
excel	STAR, SHINE, SURPASS, STANDOUT	execute	DO, HANG, SIGN, LYNCH, SCRAG, ACHIEVE, PERFORM; see KILL
excellence	CLASS, MERIT, VIRTU		
excellent	DEF, AONE, RARE, TOPS, PRIME, SUPER, DELUXE, SELECT, TIPTOP, WORTHY	execution	CHAIR, STAKE, HALTER, NOYADE, LYNCHING
		executioner	HANGMAN, HEADSMAN
except	BAR, BUT, OMIT, SAVE, EXCLUDE	executive	CEO, COO, MANAGER, OFFICER, DIRECTOR, OFFICIAL, OVERSEER, PRESIDENT
exceptional	SPECIAL, UNUSUAL		
excerpt	QUOTE, EXTRACT, PASSAGE, CITATION		
excess	GLUT, EPACT, LUXUS, SPATE, NIMIETY, SURPLUS, PLETHORA	exemplar	COPY, MODEL, PATTERN
		exemplary	IDEAL, MODEL, PERFECT, TYPICAL, ADMIRABLE
excessive	UNDUE, INORDINATE		
exchange	PIT, SWAP, BANDY, TRADE, BARTER, BOURSE, MARKET, RIALTO, SWITCH	exemplify	EMBODY, TYPIFY, REPRESENT
		exempt	EXON, FREE, IMMUNE

exemption GRACE, ESSOIN(E), IMPUNITY

exercise PLY, URE, TASK, YOGA, DRILL, EXERT, NISUS, PRAXIS, CALISTHENICS

exert STRAIN, EXERCISE

Exeter man EXON

exfoliate CAST(OFF), PEEL, SHED

exhale EMIT, EXUDE

exhaust FAG, SAP, JADE, TIRE, DRAIN, SPEND, WASTE, DEPLETE

exhausted BEAT, DONE, WEAK, ALLIN, SPENT, WEARY, EFFETE

exhibit SHOW, SALON, DISPLAY, GALLERY

exhibition PARADE, PAGEANT, SPECTACLE

exhilarated GLAD, ELATED

exhort EGG, PROD, URGE, INCITE

exhume UNEARTH, DISINTER

exigency NEED, DEMAND

exigent URGENT, EXACTING, PRESSING

exiguous THIN, MEAGER, SLENDER

exile OUST, EXPEL, BANISH, DEPORT, EXPULSION

exist AM, BE, IS, ARE, LIVE, ENDURE, BREATHE

existence ENS, ESSE, BEING, CONDITION

existence, pert. to ONTAL, NOUMENAL

existentialist BUBER, CAMUS, MARCEL, SARTRE, JASPERS, HEIDEGGER

existentialist statement I AM

existing ALIVE, BEING, EXTANT

exit END, DEATH, LEAVE, DEMISE, DEPART, EGRESS

exit line TATA, SEE YA, BYE BYE

exodus FLIGHT, HEGIRA

Exodus author URIS

Exodus character ARI

Exodus locale SINAI

exonerate CLEAR, ACQUIT, ABSOLVE, EXCULPATE

exorbitant UNDUE, EXCESS, USURIOUS, EXCESSIVE

exorcist target DEMON

exorcize EXPEL, BANISH

exordium PROEM, PREFACE, OPENING

exotic ODD, ALIEN, FOREIGN, STRANGE

expand FLAN, SWELL, DILATE, DISTEND, INFLATE

expanse SEA, AREA, REACH, SCOPE, SWEEP, TRACT

expansion GROWTH, INCREASE

expatriate EXILE, BANISH

expect HOPE, WAIT, WEEN, WISH, AWAIT

expectant ATIP, EAGER, HOPEFUL

expedient FIT, PROPER, STOPGAP

expedite HIE, HURRY, SPEED, HASTEN, ADVANCE

expedition TREK, CHASE, JAUNT, QUEST, SAFARI, SHIKAR, CARAVAN, CRUSADE, SUFFARI

expeditious QUICK, SWIFT, PROMPT, SPEEDY

expel OUST, EJECT, EVICT, DEPORT

expend PAY, USE, WASTE, CONSUME

expendable NEEDLESS, REPLACEABLE

expense COST, PRICE, OUTLAY

experience FEEL, HAVE, LIVE, UNDERGO

experience, seem to DREAM

experiment TRY, TEST, TRIAL

experimental TEST, PILOT, TRIAL

expert ACE, PRO, DEFT, ONER, WHIZ, ADEPT, CRACK

expertise ART, SKILL, KNOWHOW

expiate ATONE, PURGE, SHRIVE

expire DIE, END, CEASE, PERISH

explain REDE, WISE, CLEAR, GLOSS, DEFINE

explicit CLEAR, LUCID, PRECISE, POSITIVE

explode POP, FIRE, BURST, DETONATE, FULMINATE

exploit CLIP, DEED, FEAT, GEST, MILK, TOUR, GESTE, TRADE ON

explore PROBE, SURVEY, EXAMINE, DISCOVER

explorer see ARCTIC, ANTARCTIC; see also p. 541

explosion BANG, BLAST, BLOWUP, FLAREUP, OUTBURST, DETONATION explosive   CAP, TNT, AMMO, BOMB, MINE, PETN, SOUP, GAINE, FIERY, NITRO, TENSE, AMATOL, PETARD, TONITE, CORDITE, LIGNOSE, LYDDITE, DYNAMITE, MELINITE, PENT(H)RITE

exponent   INDEX, BACKER, ADVOCATE

export   SEND, SHIP

expose   AIR, BARE, REVEAL, UNMASK

exposition   FAIR, SHOW, DISPLAY

expository   EXEGETIC

expound   REVEAL, EXPLAIN

express   ASAP, STATE, UTTER, EXPLICIT

expression   MIEN, TERM, IDIOM, ASPECT, PHRASE, SAYING, ATTICISM, LOCUTION

expression, facial   GRIN, LEER, PHIZ, POUT, SCOWL, SMILE, SMIRK, GRIMACE

expressive   ELOQUENT

expulsion   OUSTER, REMOVAL, EJECTION

expurgate   CENSOR, CLEANSE

exquisite   FINE, ACUTE, CHOICE, PERFECT

extend   EKE, JUT, LIE, REACH, RENEW, WIDEN, BEETLE, DEPLOY

extenuate   EXCUSE, LESSEN, DIMINISH, PALLIATE

exterior   ECTAL, OUTER, EXTRINSIC

exterminate   DESTROY, ANNIHILATE

external   OUTER, FOREIGN

extinct   DEAD, DEFUNCT

extinct animal   MOA, DODO, KIWI, MAMO, URUS, QUAGGA, MAMMOTH, DINOSAUR, MASTODON, STEGODON; *see p. 660*

extinguish   DOUSE, DOWSE, QUELL, SNUFF, QUENCH, STIFLE, SMOTHER

extirpate   DELE, RAZE, ROOT, STUB, UPROOT

extol   LAUD, EXALT, PRAISE

extort   MILK, BLEED, EXACT, WREST, WRING

extra   ODD, OVER, PLUS, SUPE, ADDED, SPARE, SUPER, INSERT, SURPLUS, BUCKSHEE

extract   ATAR, DRAW, OTTO, ATTAR, OTTAR, DISTIL, ELICIT, EVULSE, REMOVE, ESSENCE, ESTREAT, PERICOPE

extracts   ANALECTA, ANALECTS

extraneous   ALIEN, OUTER, EXOTIC

extraordinary   UNCO, GREAT, NOTABLE, UNCOMMON, REMARKABLE

extrapolate   INFER, CONJECTURE

extravagance   ERA, WASTE

extravagant   LUSH, OUTRE, PLUSH, FAROUT, LAVISH, ROCOCO, BAROQUE, PRODIGAL

extravaganza   REVUE, BLOWOUT, SPECTACLE

extreme   FINAL, ULTRA, SEVERE, DRASTIC, RADICAL

extremity   END, TRIP, TOE, EDGE, FOOT, HAND, LIMB, POLE, TAIL

extricate   FREE, RELEASE, LIBERATE

extrinsic   ALIEN, FOREIGN, EXTERNAL

extrovert   OUTGOING

extrude   FORM, EJECT, EXPEL

exuberant   LAVISH, PROFUSE

exudation   GUM, LAC, SAP, AURA, PITCH, RESIN, SUDOR

exude   EMIT, LEAK, OOZE, REEK, DISCHARGE

exult   CROW, GLORY, REJOICE

eye(s)   EE, BUD, EEN, ORB, SEE, UTA, GLIM, HILA, OGLE, HILUM, LAMPS, OPTIC, SIGHT, STARE, OCULUS, PEEPER, STEMMA, VISION, OCELLUS

eye, black   MOUSE, SHINER

eye, easy on the   CUTE, BONNY, COMELY, PRETTY, BEAUTIFUL, ATTRACTIVE

eye makeup   KOH(O)L, LINER, SHADOW, MASCARA

eye, part of   BREE, IRIS, LENS, UVEA, CILIA, ORBIT, PUPIL, CORNEA, EYELID, RETINA, SCLERA, VISION, EYEBALL, EYEBROW, EYELASH, GLABELLA

eye problem   STY, CAST, ANOPIA, MYOPIA, CATARACT, GLAUCOMA, ASTIGMATISM; *see DISEASE*

eye protector PATCH, VISOR, BLINDER, BLINKER, GOGGLES
eye, *rel. to* CORNEAL, RETINAL
eyeglass(es) LENS, SPEX, SPECS, OCULAR, GOGGLES, MONOCLE, LORGNETTE, SPECTACLES
eyeglasses part ROCKER, TEMPLE
eyelash(es) CILIA, CILIUM
eyelet GROMMET, LOOPHOLE
eyes, type of DOE, EVIL, GREEN, ALMOND, SHIFTY, SQUINT, DEEPSET, SOULFUL
eyesore DEFECT, BLIGHT, FRIGHT, BLEMISH
eyetooth FANG, CANINE, CUSPID
eyewitness OBSERVER, BYSTANDER, SPECTATOR
eyot ALT, ILE, ISLE(T)
eyrie NEST
Ezekiel's four beasts ANIEL, AZRIEL, HANIEL, KAFZIEL
Ezekel relative BUZI

F

F EF(F), LOUD, FORTE, FAILING, FOXTROT
Fabius victim HANNIBAL
fable MYTH, YARN, APOLOG, LEGEND, PARABLE, ALLEGORY, APOLOGUE
fable author AESOP, GRIMM, BIDPAI, PILPAY, ANDERSEN
fabric CLOTH, STUFF, TEXTILE, MATERIAL, STRUCTURE; *see* p. 535
fabric merchant DRAPER, MERCER
fabricate COIN, MAKE, ERECT, FEIGN, FORGE, DEVISE, SCHEME, CONCOCT
fabrication LIE, FAKE, FABLE, FICTION, FORGERY
fabulist ADE, LIAR, (A)ESOP, HARRIS, POTTER, THURBER, TOLKIEN, LAFONTAINE
fabulous MYTHICAL, LEGENDARY
façade FACE, FRONT
face MAP, MUG, PAN, DARE, DIAL, PHIZ, PUSS, FACET, REVET, SNOOT, FACADE, VISAGE, SURFACE

face card JACK, KING, HONOR, KNAVE, QUEEN, PICTURE
face downward PRONE, PRONATE
face, part of JAW, CHIN, EYES, NOSE, BEARD, CHEEK, DIMPLE
facelift MAKEOVER, RENOVATION
face-off SHOWDOWN, CHALLENGE
facet BEZEL, BEZIL, CULET, COLLET
facetious DROLL, WITTY, WAGGISH
face-to-face VISAVIS, TETEATETE
facial WAXING, SKINPEEL
facile APT, DEFT, EASY, ADROIT
facility EASE, KNACK, MEANS, BUILDING, DEXTERITY
facing LINER, FORNENT, COVERING, OPPOSITE, TRIMMING
facsimile COPY, REPLICA, LIKENESS
fact(s) DATA, FAIT, FIAT, DATUM, FACTO, TRUTH
faction BLOC, SECT, SIDE, CABAL, JUNTO, CLIQUE
factious DIVISIVE, PARTISAN, SEDITIOUS
facto IPSO
factor GENE, PART, AGENT, BASIS, BROKER
factory MILL, SHOP, PLANT, WORKS, WORKSHOP
Facts of Life names JO, BLAIR, CLORIS, TOOTIE, NATALIE
factual REAL, TRUE, ACTUAL
faculty BENT, KNACK, SENSE, TALENT
fad CRY, MODE, RAGE, CRAZE, FANCY, STYLE
fade DIE, DIM, PALE, WILT, WITHER
Faerie Queen author SPENSER
Faerie Queen character ATE, UNA, ALMA, TALUS, AMORET, DUESSA, ACRASIA
Faerie Queen composer PURCELL
Fafnir brother REGIN
Fafnir slayer SIGURD, SIEGFRIED
fag RUMP, STUB, TIRE, SLAVE, EXHAUST
fagot TWIGS, BUNDLE, FASCINE

fail	EBB, FLOP, LOSE, MISS, FLUNK
failing	FAULT, DEFECT, FOIBLE, WEAKNESS
fail-safe	RELIABLE, RISKFREE, FOOLPROOF
failure	DUD, BUST, FLOP, FIASCO
fain	GLAD, EAGER, CONTENT
faineant	LAZY, IDLE(R), LOAFER, DONOTHING
faint(ing)	DIM, FADE, WEAK, SWELT, SWOON, FEEBLE
fair	JUST, MELA, SOSO, BAZAR, CLEAR, FERIA, BAZAAR, BLONDE, KERMIS, KERMESS
fair and —	SQUARE
Fair —	DEAL
fair (of weather)	CLEAR, SUNNY, CLOUDLESS
fair-lead	WAPP
fairly	QUITE, JUSTLY, RATHER
fairway	see GOLF
fairy	ELF, FAY, MAB, NIZ, UNA, PERI, PIXY, PUCK, SHEE, VILA, VILY, DRYAD, NIXIE, PIXIE, SYLPH, TROLL, OBERON, SPRITE, TITANIA
fairy fort	LIS(S), SHEE, SIDHE
fairy queen	MAB, UNA, TITANIA
fairy tale writer	GRIMM, ANDERSEN, PERRAULT
faith	CULT, DOXY, CREED, DOGMA, TENET, TROTH
faith, pert. to	PISTIC
faithful	LEAL, TRUE, LIEGE, LOYAL, STA(U)NCH
faithless	FALSE, UNTRUE, DISLOYAL
fake(r)	HOAX, SHAM, FEINT, BOGUS, FRAUD, PHON(E)Y, POSEUR, SPURIOUS, COUNTERFEIT
fakir	YOGI, SWAMI, ASCETIC
falcon	FALCO, HOBBY, SAKER, FANNER, JERKIN, KEELIE, LAGGAR, LANNER, LUGGAR, MERLIN, SHAHIN, KESTREL, SAKERET, SHAHEEN
falcon-headed god	RA, MONT, HORUS, KHONS, MENTU
fall(s)	LIN, SAG, SIN, DROP, LINN, PLAP, PLOP, PLUP, SILE, SLIDE, SPILL, AUTUMN, PLUNGE, TOPPLE, CASCADE, EQUINOX, CATARACT; see WATERFALL
fall back	RECEDE, RETREAT

fall behind	LAG
fall forward	PITCH, TOPPLE
fall guy	DUPE, PATSY, STOOGE
fall to pieces	CRUMBLE
fall upon	BESET, POUNCE, ASSAULT
fallacy	IDOLA, IDOLUM, SOPHISM
fallible	WEAK, FRAIL, MORTAL
falling out	ROW, RIFT, TIFF, FIGHT, QUARREL
falling sickness	EPILEPSY, GRANDMAL
fallopian tube	OVIDUCT, SALPINX
fallout	RESULT, UPSHOT
fallow	IDLE, BARREN, UNTILLED
false	FAKE, SHAM, BOGUS, NOTSO, WRONG, PSEUDO, UNTRUE, SPURIOUS
false-hearted	FICKLE
falsehood	FIB, LIE, BUNK, FLAM, FRAUD, CANARD
Falstaff composer	VERDI
Falstaff's friend	HAL, NYM, PETO, PISTOL
falter	HAW, WAVER, DODDER, TOTTER, STAMMER
fame	ECLAT, GLORY, HONOR, KUDOS, RENOWN, REPUTE, PRESTIGE
fame partner	FORTUNE
famed	NOTED, FAMOUS, EMINENT, NOTABLE, CELEBRATED
familiar	BOLD, COSY, CLOSE, TRITE, VERSANT
family	ILK, CLAN, GENS, LINE, SEPT, CINEL, GENOS, STOCK, TRIBE, STIRPS, LINEAGE
family, famous	ESTE, ASTOR, DORIA, SOONG, DUPONT, MEDICI, KENNEDY, ROTHSCHILD, ROCKEFELLER
family member	DAD, MOM, POP, SIS, UNC, AUNT, MAMA, PAPA, UNCLE, AUNTIE, COUSIN
Family Ties names	FOX, ALEX, ELYSE, STEVEN, MALLORY, JENNIFER
family tree	LINE(AGE), PEDIGREE
famine	DEARTH, HUNGER, SCARCITY
famous	NOTED, EMINENT, RENOWNED
fan	OGI, BUFF, FREAK, PUNKA,

BLOWER, FOMENT, PUNKAH, ROOTER, VOTARY, ZEALOT, DEVOTEE
— fan tutte COSI
fanatic NUT, BIGOT, JINGO, MANIC, RABID, MANIAC, ZEALOT, DEVOTEE, PARTISAN
fanciful ANTIC, QUAINT, BIZARRE, WHIMSICAL, CAPRICIOUS
fancy IDEA, WHIM, QUIRK, SHINE, FOIBLE, IDEATE, MEGRIM, NOTION, VAGARY, VISION, CAPRICE, CHIMERA, REVERIE, WHIMSEY
fane CHURCH, SHRINE, TEMPLE, SANCTUARY
fanfare BLAST, SALUTE, TANTARA, FLOURISH
fang TUSK, BOOTY, TALON, TOOTH
fanon VANE, ORALE, INFULA, MANIPLE, CORPORAL
fantastic QUEER, UNREAL, BIZARRE, FANCIFUL
fantasy HOPE, DREAM, FANCY, WHIMSY, CAPRICE, ROMANCE, ILLUSION, PHANTASM
far REMOTE, DISTANT
far and — AWAY, WIDE
far out COOL, NEAT, OFFBEAT, RAD(ICAL)
farce MIME, SKIT, EXODE, COMEDY, PARODY, MOCKERY, TRAVESTY
farcical COMIC, ABSURD, LUDICROUS
fare PAY, DIET, MENU, BOARD, TOKEN, THRIVE
farewell AVE, CIAO, LAST, VALE, ADIEU, ADIOS, ALOHA, ANATH, CONGE, LEAVE, CONGEE, SOLONG
farfetched FORCED, REMOTE, STRAINED, UNLIKELY
farflung WIDE, BROAD, FAROFF, DISTANT, SWEEPING
farina MEAL, FLOUR, STARCH
farinaceous MEALY, STARCHY
farinaceous food SAGO, SALEP
farm TILL, TORP, WERF, CROFT, HARAS, MAINS, RANCH, BARTON, CHACRA, KOLKHOZ, HACIENDA
farm building BARN, BYRE, SHED, SILO, STABLE, ONSTEAD
farm implement PLOW, BALER,

FLAIL, HARROW, REAPER, SEEDER, TEDDER, COMBINE, PLANTER, TRACTOR, SCARIFIER
farm letters EIEIO
farm out LET, HIRE, ASSIGN, DELEGATE, OUTSOURCE, SUBCONTRACT
farm, pert. to VILLATIC
farmer MEO, HIND, KHOT, RYOT, TYTY, KULAK, SOWER, COTTER, TILLER, GRANGER
farmyard WERF, BARTON
faro term CASE, HOCK, SODA
Faroe Islands SAND, SVIN, BORDH, VAGAR, SEYSTUR, TREYM, SUDHUR
farrago OLIO, JUMBLE, MEDLEY
farrier BLACKSMITH
farrow PIG, LITTER
Farouk father FUAD
Farsi speaker IRANI
farthest UTMOST, ENDMOST, EXTREME
fascia BAND, BELT, SASH, TAENIA
fascinate CHARM, ALLURE, BEWITCH, ENCHANT
Fascist RAS, NAZI, MUSSO, HITLER, FRANCO, FALANGIST, MUSSOLINI
fashion FAD, MOLD, MODE, RAGE, MODEL, SHAPE, STYLE, VOGUE, DESIGN; see DESIGNER
fashion magazine GQ, ELLE, VOGUE, GLAMOUR, COSMO(POLITAN)
fashion model CINDY, NAOMI, TIEGS, CHERYL, TWIGGY, BRINKLEY
fashionable CHIC, NOBBY, SMART, MODISH, STYLISH
fast DIET, FIRM, LENT, APACE, EMBER, FLEET, QUICK, RAPID, SWIFT, CARENE, DHARNA, PRESTO, ABSTAIN, ALLEGRO, RAMADAN
fast and — LOOSE
fast time LENT
fasten FIX, PIN, TIE, ZIP, BOLT, GLUE, LOCK, NAIL, SEAL, SNIB, TACK, BELAY, RIVET, BATTEN
fastener NOG, NUT, PEG, PIN, BITT, BRAD, CLIP, HASP, HOOK, SNAP, STUD, CLAMP, CLEAT, DOWEL, STRAP, BUTTON, CLEVIS, COTTER, HALTER, STAPLE, ZIPPER
fastidious NICE, FUSSY,

QUEASY, FINICAL,
GOURMET, PRECISE
fat   FOZY, LARD, LIPA, OILY,
SUET, ADEPS, ELAIN, ESTER,
FUBSY, OBESE, OLEIN, PUDGY,
STOUT, ELAINE, GREASE,
OLEINE, TALLOW, ADIPOSE,
PINGUID, PORCINE,
STEARIN(E)
fat person   FUB, FATTY,
CHUBETTE
fat, *pert. to*   OLEIC, ADIPIC,
GREASY, ADIPOSE
fatal   FEY, MORT, FERAL,
DEADLY, FUNEST, LETHAL,
MORTAL
fatality   DEATH, CASUALTY
fate   LOT, DOOM, KARMA,
MOIRA, KISMET
Fate(s)   NONA, CLOTHO,
DECUMA, MOIRAI, PARCAE,
ATROPOS, LACHESIS
fateful   DIRE, BANEFUL,
OMINOUS
fathead   CLOD, FOOL, DUNCE,
IDIOT, STUPID
father   ABU, DAD, POP, ABBA,
ABOU, PAPA, PERE, POPS,
SIRE, BEGET, DADDY, PADRE,
PATER
Father Knows Best names   BUD,
JIM, KITTEN, WYATT,
YOUNG, MARGARET,
PRINCESS
father, relating to   AGNATE,
PATERNAL
fathom   DELVE, GRASP, PLUMB,
PROBE, SOUND
fatigue   FAG, SAP, BORE, JADE,
TIRE, WEARY
Fatima relative   ALI, ANNE,
SEID, SAYID, FATIMID,
MOHAMMED, BLUEBEARD
fatten   FEED, STUFF, BATTEN,
ENRICH
fatty   OILY, SUETY, GREASY,
ADIPOSE
fatty acid source   PALM, TUNA,
OLIVE, PEANUT, SUNFLOWER
fatuous   INANE, ASININE
faubourg   SUBURB, BANLIEU
faucet   TAP, BIBB, COCK, SPILE,
SPIGOT, ROBINET
fault   FLAW, CULPA, ERROR,
DEFECT, FOIBLE, BLEMISH
faultfind   NAG, CARP, CAVIL,
KNOCK, CENSURE, CRITICIZE
faultfinder   MOMUS, CENSOR,
CRITIC

faultless   IDEAL, MODEL,
PERFECT, FLAWLESS,
IMPECCABLE
faulty   BAD, FLAWED,
PECCANT
faun   SATYR, PANISK, SILENUS
fauna partner   FLORA
Faust character   HELEN,
WAGNER, GRETCHEN,
MARGARET
Faust writer   GOETHE,
GOUNOD, MARLOWE
faux pas   SLIP, GAFFE; *see*
ERROR
favor   BIAS, BOON, GRACE,
LEAVE, TOKEN, OBLIGE,
PREFER, BENEFIT
favorable   PRO, AUSPICIOUS,
PROPITIOUS
favorite   PET, HERO, IDOL,
MINION
favoritism   BIAS, NEPOTISM
fawn   DOE, DEER, TOADY,
CRINGE, GROVEL
fawning   SERVILE, SUBMISSIVE
fax   SEND, TRANSMIT
fay   *see* ELF, FAIRY
faze   DAUNT, WORRY, RATTLE,
RUFFLE, DISTURB,
DISCONCERT
FBI agent   FED, GMAN
FBI director   GRAY, BURNS,
FINCH, FLYNN, FREEH,
CLARKE, HOOVER, KELLEY,
MUELLER, PICKARD,
WEBSTER, SESSIONS,
RUCKELSHAUS
FDR agency   CCC, FWA, NRA,
OES, TVA, WPA
FDR home   HYDEPARK
FDR dog   FALA
FDR loser   DEWEY, HOOVER,
LANDON, WILLKIE
fealty   HOMAGE, LOYALTY
fear   AWE, FUNK, DREAD,
QUALM, WORRY, PHOBIA,
ANXIETY
fearful   PAVID, TIMID, AFRAID,
CRAVEN, TREPID
fearless   BOLD, BRAVE,
DARING, HEROIC, IMPAVID,
INTREPID
fearsome   SCARY, CHILLING,
ALARMING, TIMOROUS
feasible   POSSIBLE, WORKABLE
feast   FOY, MAS, FETE, LUAU,
UTAS, AGAPE, ARVAL,
PURIM, REGALE, AHAAINA,
BANQUET

Feast of Lanterns	BON		ANORTHITE, MOONSTONE,
Feast of Tabernacles	SUKKOTH		LABRADORITE
feat	ACT, DEED, GEST,	felicitous	APT, HAPPY, TIMELY
	STUNT, TRICK	felid	see CAT
feather(s)	DOWN, HULU, TUFT,	feline	CAT, SLY, WILY, CATTY
	EIDER, PENNA, PINNA,	fell	DROP, CRUEL, TOPPLE,
	PLUMA, QUILL, REMEX,		CUTDOWN, CUT, HEW, HIDE,
	PINION, PLUMAGE, REMIGES,		PELT, SKIN, DEADLY, SAVAGE
	TECTRIX	fellow	CAD, EGG, GUY, LAD,
featherbrained	DIZZY, SIMPLE,		BOZO, CHAP, DICK, MATE,
	FOOLISH		PEER, BLADE, CULLY, CHAPPY,
feathered	PLUMY, WINGED,		CHAPPIE
	FLEDGED, PENNATE	fellowship	AMITY, SOCIETY,
featherlike	PINNATE,		BONHOMIE, INTIMACY,
	PLUMATE		SODALITY, COMMUNION
feature	FILM, STAR, MOTIF,	felon	CON, OUTLAW,
	TRAIT, ASPECT		CULPRIT, CONVICT,
fecund	FERTILE, FRUITFUL,		WHITLOW, CRIMINAL
	PROLIFIC	felonious	BASF, WRONG,
fed	GMAN, TMAN		SINFUL, ILLEGAL
fed up	BORED, DISGUSTED	felony	RAPE, ABUSE, ARSON,
Federalist author	JAY,		CRIME, MURDER, MAIMING,
	MADISON, HAMILTON		OFFENSE, KIDNAPPING,
federate	UNITE		MANSLAUGHTER,
federation	UNION, LEAGUE,		EMBEZZLEMENT
	ALLIANCE	female	GAL, SHE, MOM, SIS,
fee	TIP, AGIO, DUES, FEOD,		AUNT, DAME, DOLL, GIRL,
	FIEF, TOKE, TOLL, AMOBER,		LADY, LASS, BROAD, CHICK,
	CHARGE, RETAINER		NIECE, WENCH, MOTHER,
feeble	PUNY, WEAK, ANILE,		SISTER, DISTAFF, FEMININE,
	DOTTY, DEBILE, FLABBY,		DAUGHTER; see GIRL,
	INFIRM		WOMAN
feed	OATS, AGIST, CATER,	female animal	COW, DAM,
	GRAZE, COSHER, FODDER,		DOE, DRI, EWE, GIN, HEN,
	FORAGE		NAK, PEN, REE, ROE, SHE, SOW,
feedback	INPUT, RUMBLE,		TEG, GILN, GYNE, HIND, JILL,
	STATIC, COMMENT,		MARE, NAGA, SLUT, URSA,
	REACTION		ARNEE, BIDDY, BITCH,
feedbox	MANGER, TROUGH		JENNY, TABBY, VIXEN, JENNET
feeding, forced	GAVAGE	feminine	FEMALE, WOMANLY,
feel	PALP, GROPE, SENSE,		EFFEMINATE
	TOUCH	feminine side	YING
feeler	PALP, BARBEL, PALPUS,	feminist, famous	CARY, CATT,
	TACTOR, PEDATE,		LYON, PAUL, WOLF, ABZUG,
	ANTENNA, TENTACLE		AD(D)AMS, BLACK, PARKS,
feeling	TOUCH, EMOTION,		STONE, TRUTH, CHOPIN,
	PASSION, SENSATION		GILMAN, SANGER, ANTHONY,
feet, having	PEDATE		CHICAGO, FRIEDAN,
feet, *pert. to*	PEDAL, PODAL,		STANTON, GINSBURG,
	PEDARY		WATTLETON
feign	ACT, FAKE, SHAM,	femme fatale	SIREN, LORELIE,
	PRETEND, SIMULATE,		MATAHARI
	DISSEMBLE	fen	BOG, MARSH, SWAMP,
— Fein	SINN		MORASS
feint	MOCK, SHAM, TRICK,	fence	HAHA, OXER, PARR,
	PRETENSE		RAIL, FAGIN, HEDGE, STILE,
feisty	TESTY, FRISKY		HAWHAW, PALING, RADDLE,
feldspar	KAOLIN, ODINITE,		SCRIME, PALISADE
	SILICATE, ADULARIA,	fence part	PALE, POST, RAIL,

STAKE, STILE, PALING, PICKET
fencer's cry HAI, HAY, SASA, TOUCHE, ENGARDE
fencing term PEL, BUTT, EPEE, FOIL, TUCK, VOLT, APPEL, CARTE, LUNGE, PARRY, PUNTO, SABER, SIXTE, SWORD, BUTTON, OCTAVE, QUARTE, QUINTE, RAPIER, REMISE, RIPOST, TIERCE, TOUCHE, ENGARDE, REPRISE, RIPOSTE, SECONDE, SEPTIME, PLASTROM
fend WARD, AVERT, PARRY
fender BUMPER, SHIELD, MUDGUARD
fennel HEMP, HERB, ANISE
Fenns' father LOKI
Fenns' slayer VIDAR
Fenway Park team REDSOX
feral WILD, SAVAGE, UNTAMED
Ferdinand wife ISABELLA
ferment BARM, BREW, FRET, SOUR, ZYME, YEAST, LEAVEN, SEETHE
fermented drink ALE, BEER, MEAD, NIPA, SAKE, WINE, CIDER, KVASS, PERRY, KUMISS
fermenting agent YEAST, ENZYME, LEAVEN, BACTERIA
fermenting mixture BUB, WORT
fern HEII, NITO, TARA, BRAKE, NARDO, PITAU, PONGA, TODEA, NARDOO, BRACKEN, ELKHORN, WOODSIA, POLYPODY, STAGHORN
fern part SORI, FROND, SORUS, SPORE, CROSIER
ferocious FELL, WILD, FIERCE
Ferrara family ESTE
ferret PRY, SEARCH, WEASEL, POLECAT
ferry BAC, FORD, PONT, SHUTTLE
ferryman CHARON
fertile RICH, FECUND, PINGUID, FRUITFUL
fertilization site OVULE
fertilize ENRICH, FECONDATE, POLLINATE
fertilizer MARL, GUANO, ALINIT, MANURE, COMPOST, NITRATE
ferule ROD, RULER, STICK
fervency, fervor ZEAL, ZEST, ARDOR
fervent HOT, AVID, KEEN,

ARDENT, HEATED, EARNEST, GLOWING
festal GAY, GALA, JOLLY, MERRY, JOYOUS
fester GNAW, RANKLE, ULCERATE
festival ALE, BON, BUSK, FAIR, FETE, GALA, HOLI, MELA, PUJA, VOTA, BODHI, DELIA, FAIRE, FERIA, HALOA, PURIM, SEDER, DIWALI, FIESTA, HOOLEE, KERMIS, OPALIA, PESACH, SUCCOS, DEWALEE, KERMESS, RAMADAN, SUKKOTH, SHAVUOTH
festive GAY, GALA, MERRY, JOLLY, JOVIAL, JOYOUS
festoon see GARLAND
fetch GET, MAKE, BRING, GOFOR, BEWORTH
fetching ALLURING, CHARMING, ENGAGING, APPEALING, ATTRACTIVE
fetid FOUL, OLID, RANK, FUSTY, PUTRID, RANCID, NOISOME
fetish OBI, JUJU, MOJO, OBIA, ZEME, ZEMI, ANITO, CHARM, OBEAH, TOTEM, GRIGRI, MASCOT, VOODOO
fetor STINK, MIASMA, STENCH
fetter CUFF, GYVE, IRON, HOBBLE, MANACLE, SHACKLE
fetus EMBRYO
fetus part CAUL, DOWN, LANUGO, CHORION
feud FIFE, FRAY, BROIL, AFFRAY, VENDETTA
feudal land FEOD, FEUD, FIEF, MANOR, DEMESNE, BENEFICE
feudal, opposed to AL(L)OD, AL(L)ODIUM
feudal payment HERIOT, RELIEF, TALLAGE, HEREGELD
feudal service AVERA
feudal tenant ESNE, LEUD, SERF, BORDER, COTTER, VASSAL, COTTIER, SOCAGER
feudalism HELOTRY, SERFDOM, VASSALAGE
fever AGUE, HEAT, CAUMA, PYREXIA, TERTIANA
fever type DANDY, DENGUE, JUNGLE, TYPHUS, YELLOW, MALARIA, QUARTAN, QUINTAN, SCARLET, TERTIAN, TROPICAL, UNDULATING

feverish	HECTIC, FEBRILE, PYRETIC
few	CURN, CURRAN
fez	*see* CAP
fiasco	MESS, BOTCH, DEBACLE, FAILURE, WASHOUT
fiat	EDICT, ORDER, DECREE
fiber	NOIL, STAPLE, STRANT, THREAD, NATURE; *see p. 535*
fiber plant	ALOE, FLAX, HEMP, DM, SANA, SUNN, CAROA, ISTLE, IXTLE, RAMIE, SISAL, COTTON
fickle	ERRATIC, FLIGHTY, MOONISH, UNSTABLE, VOLATILE, INCONSTANT
fiction	LIE, MYTH, TALE, YARN, FABLE, NOVEL, FIGMENT
fiction type	NOIR
fictitious	BOGUS, FALSE, UNREAL, MYTHICAL, SPURIOUS
fiddle	*see* STRING INSTRUMENT
Fiddler on the Roof name	GOLDE, MOTEL, TEVYE, TOPOL, YENTE
— fide	BONA
Fidelio character	ROCCO, JAQUINO, LEONORE, FLORISTAN, MARZELLINE
Fidelio composer	BEETHOVEN
fidelity	FEALTY, LOYALTY, DEVOTION, ALLEGIANCE
fidget	TOSS, FRET, JITTER, SQUIRM
fidgety	NERVOUS, RESTIVE, RESTLESS
fiduciary	TRUSTEE
field	LEA, ACRE, AGER, PADI, RAND, WONG, CROFT, GLEVE, RANGE, ROWEN, CAMPUS, DOMAIN, SPHERE, SAVANNA
field glass(es)	BINOCLE, TELESCOPE, BINOCULARS
fiend	*see* DEMON
fiendish	DEMONIC, HELLISH, SATANIC, DEVILISH, DIFFICULT
fierce	WILD, SAVAGE, VIOLENT
fiery	HOT, ARDENT, FERVID, BLAZING
fiesta	*see* FESTIVAL
fifth columnist	QUISLING, TURNCOAT

fifty-fifty	EVEN, EQUAL, TOSSUP
fig	BIT, FEG, FICO, FIGO, AMATE, BREBA, ELEME, ELEMI, FICUS, PIPAL, PIPUL, CARICA, PEEPAL, PEEPUL
fight	BOUT, CLEM, DUEL, FEUD, FRAY, TILT, BRAWL, JOUST, MELEE, SCRAP, SETTO, AFFRAY, BARNEY, FRACAS, RASSLE, RUMPUS, RUCTION, SCUFFLE
fighter	PUG, SPAD, ZERO, BOXER, WARRIOR, PUGILIST
fighting	ATWAR, COMBAT, WARFARE, HOSTILITY
figleaf	THRION
figurative	FLORID, ORNATE, FLOWERY, SYMBOLIC, ALLEGORIC
figure of speech	IRONY, TROPE, MERISM, SIMILE, MELOSIS, ZEUGMA, LITOTES, EPITROPE, METAPHOR, METONYMY, OXYMORON, HENDIADYS, HYPERBOLE
figurine	BUST, DOLL, STATUE, TANAGRA, STATUETTE
Fiji, capital of	SUVA
Fiji discoverer	TASMAN
Fiji island	GAU, KORO, VITI, VANUA, OVALAU, YASAWA, KANDAVU, TAVEUNI
Fiji language	BAUAN
Fiji money	DOLLAR
Fiji town	BA, LAMI, NADI, SUVA
filament	BRIN, DOWL, HAIR, HARL, FIBER, HARLE, ELATER, FIBRIL, STRAND, TUNGSTEN
filbert	HAZEL(NUT)
filch	NIM, LIFT, PINCH, SWIPE, PILFER, PURLOIN
file	RASP, EMERY, CARLET, RECORD, DOSSIER, QUANNET
file-sharing system	KAZAA, NAPSTER, LIMEWIRE
Filipino	*see* PHILIPPINE
fill	PAD, GLUT, QUAR, SATE, GORGE, STUFF
filler, newspaper	BALAAM
fillet	ORLE, SNOOD, LISTER, REGULA, TAENIA
film	BRAT, SCUM, XRAY, LAYER, MOVIE, CINEMA, PATINA, TALKIE, FEATURE
film term	PAN, CLIP, REEL, SYNC, DOLLY, CREDIT,

(UN)RATED, MOVIOLA; *see* MOVIE

filmy   HAZY, GAUZY, GOSSAMER

filter   OOZE, SEEP, SIEVE, PURIFY, STRAIN

filth   DIRT, MUCK, SMUT, GRIME

filthy   LEWD, MIRY, VILE, DIRTY, MUCKY, NASTY, SLIMY, SMUTTY, OBSCENE, SQUALID, UNCLEAN

fin   FIVER, PINNA, FLIPPER, PINNULE

finagle   CHEAT, WANGLE, MANEUVER

final   END, LAST, TELIC, ULTIMATE

finale   END, CODA, CLOSE, FINIS

finally   ENFIN, ATLAST, INTHEEND

finance   BACK, FUND, UNDERWRITE

financial   FISCAL, MONETARY

financier   BANKER, TYCOON, CAPITALIST

financier, famous   RYAN, ASTOR, COOKE, GOULD, GREEN, MELLON, MORGAN, CORNING, MERRILL, HARRIMAN, ROTHSCHILD

finch   CIRL, FINK, KATE, NOAP, OLPH, PAPE, YITE, JOREE, JUNCO, SERIN, SPINK, TARIN, TERIN, TWITE, BURION, CANARY, LINNET, ROLLER, SISKIN, TOWHEE, BUNTING, CHEWINK, ORTOLAN, REDPOLL, CARDINAL, GROSBEAK, HAWFINCH, LONGSPUR, SNOWBIRD, CROSSBILL; *see p. 675*

find   GET, DETECT, LOCATE, LIGHTON

find out   CATCH, LEARN, DETECT, EXPOSE, REVEAL, DISCOVER

finding   VERDICT, JUDGMENT, DISCOVERY

fine   CRO, LEVY, RARE, ABWAB, MULCT, AMERCE, IMPOST, MINUTE, SCONCE, GALANAS

finesse   ART, TACT, CRAFT, SKILL, CUNNING

finest   BEST, PRIME

Fingal relative   MORNA, COMHAL, FERGUS, OSSIAN

Fingal's Cave location   STAFFA

Fingal's kingdom   MORVEN

Fingal's sword   LUNO

finger   HOOF, DIGIT, INDEX, THUMB, PINKY, DACTYL, MEDIUS, POLLEX, THENAR, KNUCKLE, MINIMUS, POINTER

Finger Lakes   KEUKA, CAYUGA, OWASCO, SENECA, CANANDAIGUA

finger, part of   NAIL, LUNULA, LUNULE, UNGUAL, UNGUIS, PHALANX

fingerprint   ARCH, LOOP, MARK, WHORL, LUNULE

finial   EPI, TEE, TOP, APEX

finicky   FUSSY, DAINTY, PRISSY

finish   END, WIN, KILL, SHOW, PLACE, ENDING, FINALE

finjan holder   ZARF

fink on   *see* INFORM

Finland   SUOMI

Finland, capital of   HELSINKI

Finland, *pert. to*   SUOMIC, SUOMISH

Finlandia composer   SIBELIUS

Finnish bath   SAUNA

Finnish city/town   KEMI, OULU, PORI, SALO, ESPOO, TURKU, VANTAA, TAMPERE, HELSINKI

Finnish island   ALAND, KARLO, KIMITO, VALLGRUND

Finnish lake   INARI, SAIMAA, KEITELE, PIELINEN, OULUJARVI

Finnish language   *see* FINNOUGRIC

Finnish measure   KANNU, TUNNA, TUNLAND

Finnish money   EURO, PENNI, MARKKA

Finnish province   HAME, KYMI, OULU, ALAND, LAPPI, VAASA, KUOPIO, MIKKELI, UUSIMAA

Finnish river   TANA, IUOKI, MUONIO, TORNIO, KITINEN, KALAJOKI

Finno-Ugric language   KOMI, LAPP, VEPS, KAREL, VOGUL, MAGYAR, OSTYAK, VOTYAK, ZYRIAN, FINNISH, LAPPISH, MORDVIN, PERMIAN, CHEREMIS, ESTONIAN, KARELLAN, LIVONIAN, HUNGARIAN

fir   ABIES, SAPIN, BALSAM

fire	AGNI, CHAR, ELAN, SACK, IGNIS, ANNEAL, IGNITE, KINDLE	fish, fossil	DIPNOI, ELLOPS, DIPNOAN
fire and —	BRIMSTONE	fish, marine	CUSK, HAKE, LING, SCUP, SHAD, GRUNT, SKATE, BLENNY, BONITO, TARPON
fire god	AGNI, ATAR, LOKI, SIVA, KAMA, VESTA, VULCAN		
fire worshiper	PARSE, GHEBER, PARSEE	fish measure	MEASE
		fish, poisonous	FUGU
firearm	see GUN, RIFLE	fish, raw	SUSHI, SASHIMI
firebug	ARSONIST, INCENDIARY, PYROMANIAC	fish sauce	ALEC, GARUM
		fish, small	FRY, BRIT, DACE, SMELT, SPRAT, DARTER, MINNOW, SARDINE
firecracker	SQUIB, PETARD, SNAPPER		
fireman	VAMP, STOKER	fish, type of	FRY, HAG, BARB, CAJI, GOBY, HAKU, HUSS, LANT, MAPO, OPAH, RAUN, SAPO, SILE, TANG, CRAVO, HOUND, LANCE, MIDGE, SCROD, SKATE, TETRA, ANGLER, BICHIR, CARIBE, DORADO, MYXINE, POPEYE, REDFIN, REMORA, SLIMER, TAILER, WEEVER, AROWANA, CHALACO, FOXFISH, HAGFISH, JUGULAR, LUPHIID, MUDHAKE, PEGADOR, PIRHANA, POISSON, POMFRET, RATTAIL, SANDEEL, SURGEON, TELEOST, XIPHIAS, CHARACIN, DRAGONET, HUMANTIN, PIRARUCU, GRENADIER, see p. 668
fireplace	FOGON, GRATE, INGLE, HEARTH		
fireplace part	HOB(B), FLUE, JAMB, SPIT, GRATE, JAMBE, SHELF, TONGS, FENDER, HEARTH, MANTEL, SCREEN, ANDIRON, FIREDOG, REREDOS		
fireplug	HYDRANT		
firewater	LIQUOR, WHISKY		
firewood	LENA, BAVIN, FAGOT, BILLET, FAGGOT		
fireworks	CAP, BOMB, GERB(E), SQUIB, FIZGIG, PETARD, RIPRAP, ROCKET, SALUTE, TORPEDO		
firing line command	AIM, FIRE, LOAD(ANDLOCK), READY		
		fish, young	FRY, FINGERLING
firm	MUI, FAST, HARD, RIGID, TIGHT, STANCH, COMPANY, STAUNCH	fisherman	EELER, SQUAM, ANGLER, NETTER, SEINER, WEIRER, PISCATOR
firmament	SKY, VAULT, WELKIN	fisherman garment	PEACOAT
		fishhook	FLY, GIG, BARB, GAFF, ANGLE, DRAIL, KIRBY, FIZGIG, SEDGE, HACKLE, SPROAT
firn	ICE, NEVE, SNOW		
first	CHIEF, DEBUT, PRIME, PRIMAL, CAPITAL, INITIAL, ORIGINAL	fishing equipment	BOB, NET, ROD, BUNT, CORF, FLEW, FLUE, FYRE, GAFF, GILL, HERL, PIRN, POLE, REEL, TROT, WEEL, WEIR, CREEL, DRAKE, FLOAT, NYMPH, QUILL, SEINE, SNELL, TRAWL, TROLL, BULTER, EELPOT, TACKLE, TONKIN, BOULTER, HARPOON, SPILLER, TRAMMEL
first day of the month	CAL, KAL, CALENDS		
First Lady	MAMIE, JACKIE, ELEANOR; see p. 700		
first mortal	EVE, ADAM, YAMA		
firstborn	AYNE, EIGNE		
first-class	ACE, AONE, TOPS, DELUXE, PALMARY		
firth	ARM, KYLE, LOCH, FIORD, FJORD, ESTUARY	fishy	FUNNY, SHADY, DUBIOUS, DOUBTFUL, SUSPICIOUS
fiscal	NUMMARY, MONETARY, FINANCIAL		
fish	FIN, ANGLE, DRAIL, TRAWL, TROLL, SEARCH	fissure	RENT, RIFT, RIMA, RIME, SLIT, CHASM, CHINK, CLEFT, SULCUS
fish, cyprinoid	see CARP		
fish, fly for	HARL, HERL, SEDGE, CAHILL, CLARET, HACKLE	fist(s)	NIEF, MITT, DUKES, NIEVE, MAULEY

fit	APT, FAY, PET, HUFF, MESH, NEST, RIPE, SUIT, ADAPT, EQUIP, FADGE, SPELL, SPASM, OUTFIT, TANTRUM
fitful	SPORADIC, SPASMODIC
fits and —	STARTS
fitting	APT, DUE, PAT, MEET, RIGHT, PROPER, SUITABLE, AUSPICIOUS
five	CEE, FIN, VEE, FIVER, PEDRO, MASHIE, PENTAD, QUINTET
Five Civilized Nations	CREEK, CHOCTAW, CHEROKEE, SEMINOLE, CHICKASAW
Five Nations (Iroquois)	CAYUGA, MOHAWK, ONEIDA, SENECA, ONONDAGA
five-dollar bill	FIN, VEE, FIVER
five-year period	LUSTER, LUSTRUM
fix	SET, MEND, REDO, FREEZE, REPAIR, SETTLE
fixation	MANIA, OBSESSION
— fixe	IDEE, PRIX
fixed	SET, RIGID, FROZEN, STABILE
fixed-income person	RENTIER
fizz	HISS, BUBBLE, SPARKLE
fizzle	FAIL, HISS, FLOP, MISFIRE
fizzy, make	AERATE
flabbergast	STUN, ABASH, BOGGLE, ASTONISH, CONFOUND
flabby	SOFT, WEAK, FLACCID
flaccid	LAX, LIMP, FLABBY
flag	ALEM, FANE, IRIS, JACK, PINE, SINK, TIRE, BRUTE, ROGER, BANNER, BURGEE, COLORS, CORNET, ENSIGN, FANION, GUIDON, PENNON, BUNTING, PENNANT, BANDEROL, GONFALON, STANDARD, BANDEROLE, (JOLLY) ROGER
flag part	FLY, FIELD, UNION, CANTON
flagellants	ALBI
flagon	JUG, EWER, STOUP, CARAFE
flagrant	RANK, CRYING, GLARING, EGREGIOUS
flagstone	SHALE, SLATE, PAVING
flail	BEAT, THRESH
flair	GIFT, KNACK, STYLE, VERVE, BRAVURA
flake	CHIP, RACK, FLECK, SCALE, SPALL, SPAWL, LAMINA
flaky	DIPPY, SCALY, SQUAMOSE
flam	LIE, HOAX, TRICK, HUMBUG, CLAPTRAP
flamboyant	SHOWY, ORNATE, POMPOUS
flame	FIRE, ZEAL, BLAZE
Flanders battlesite	YPRES
Flanders capital	GHENT
flank	LEER, LISK, LOIN, SIDE
flap	LAP, TAB, TAG, LOMA, SLAT, LAPPET, FLUTTER
flare	FUSE, BLAZE, FUSEE, SPLAY, TORCH, SIGNAL
flash	BOLT, LEVIN, SPEED, SPURT, DAZZLE
Flash Gordon name	AURA, DALE, MING, ARDEN, SONYA, ZARKOV
flashlight	TORCH
flashy	GAUDY, SHOWY, RAFFISH
flask	OLPE, BETTY, CRUSE, GIRBA, FIASCO, FLACON, FLAGON, MATARA, CANTEEN, COSTREL, MATRASS, GOATSKIN
flat	MOL, EVEN, BROKE, LEVEL, MOLLE, PLANE, STALE, SUITE, OBLATE, INSIPID, PLANATE
flatfish	*see* RAY, FLOUNDER
flatten	RAZE, CRUSH, SUBDUE, CONQUER
flatten out	CLAP, PLATTEN
flatter	OIL, FAWN, PALP, TOADY, ADULATE
flatterer	TOADY, SYCOPHANT
flattery	OIL, BLARNEY, PALAVER
Flaubert heroine	EMMA
Flaubert novel	SALAMMBO
flaunt	SHOW, WAVE, PARADE, DISPLAY
flavor	GUST, LACE, TANG, TONE, AROMA, SAPOR, SAVOR, SEASON
flavorful	SAPID, SAVORY
flavoring	MINT, ANISE, ONION, TANSY, BURNET, CICELY, FENNEL, GINGER, BITTERS, EXTRACT, JUNIPER, SAFFRON, VANILLA, CINNAMON, ESTRAGON, GALANGAL, LAVENDER, LICORICE, TARRAGON, VANILLIN; *see* HERB, SPICE

flavorless	FLAT, VAPID, INSIPID, TASTELESS		BAMBAM, BARNEY, BARBERA, PEBBLES, BAMMBAMM
flaw	RIFT, BREAK, FAULT, DEFECT, BLEMISH	flip	PERT, SNAP, TOSS
flawless	PERFECT, FAULTLESS	flip result	HEADS, TAILS
flax	TOW, FLIX, LINUM, BYSSUS	flip through	SCAN, BROWSE, PERUSE
flax, prepare	RET	flippant	BOLD, GLIB, PERT,
flaxlike	TOWY		SASSY, SAUCY, BRASSY
flay	BEAT, CANE, SKIN, WHIP, ASSAIL	flirt	FLIP, OGLE, WINK, COQUET
flea	LOP, FLECH, FLECK,	flit	GAD, DART, SKIM
	CHIGOE, JIGGER, PODURA,	float	BOB, BUOY, CORK, RAFT,
	REDBUG, CHIGGER, PULICID		SWIM, WAFT, DRIFT,
flea genus	PULEX, DAPHNIA		PONTOON
fleck	SPOT, SPECK, TITTLE	floating	AWASH, ADRIFT,
Fledermaus character	ADELE,		NATANT
	FALKE, FRANK, ALFRED	flock	HERD, PACK, BROOD,
fledgling	INFANT, NESTLING		DROVE, HORDE, SHOAL,
flee	LAM, RUN, BOLT,		SWARM, TROOP, HIRSEL; see
	DECAMP, DESERT		BEVY
fleece	ABB, NAP, PILE, SKIN,	flog	CAT, TROUNCE; see BEAT
	WOOL, MULCT, SHEAR,	flogging	TOKO, WHIPPING
	SWINDLE	flood	SEA, BORE, TIDE, EAGRE,
fleet	FAST, NAVY, ARGOSY,		SPATE, DELUGE, FRESHET
	ARMADA, ARMADO,	flooded	BUSY, AWASH,
	FLOTILLA		SWAMPED
Fleet Center player	CELTIC	floodgate	CLOW, SLUICE
fleeting	BRIEF, EPHEMERAL,	floor	DECK, DALLE, LEVEL,
	TRANSIENT, TRANSITORY		STORY, PLANCH, STOREY,
flemish	COIL; see DUTCH		ENTRESOL, MEZZANINE
flesh	BODY, PULP; see MEAT	flora and fauna	BIOTA,
fleshpot(s)	LUXURY,		GODDESS(ES)
	COMFORT, BROTHEL	Florence family	MEDICI
fleshy	FAT, PULPY, CARNAL,	florid	ROSY, GAUDY, SHOWY,
	SARCOUS		ORNATE
fleur-de —	LIS	Florida	see also p. 615
flexible	AGILE, LITHE, WITHY,	Florida beach	VERO, COCOA,
	LIMBER, LISSOM, PLIANT,		DELRAY, BOYNTON,
	SUPPLE, LISSOME, TENSILE		DAYTONA, POMPANO
flick	FLIP, SNAP, FLECK,	Florida city/town	DADE,
	FLOUNCE		MIAMI, OCALA, TAMPA,
Flicka creator	OHARA		NAPLES, HIALEAH, ORLANDO
flier	ACE, PILOT, PLUNGE	Florida fish	CAXI, BONACI,
flight	HOP, ROUT, EXODUS,		BONITO, TARPON, TETARD,
	HEGIRA, SCUTTLE,		GROUPER, SNAPPER,
	STAMPEDE; see BEVY		MACKEREL
flight, put to	ROUT	Florida Indian	SEMINOLE
flightless bird	see BIRD	Florida river	INDIAN,
flighty	BARMY, GIDDY,		PERDIDO, ST JOHNS
	FRIVOLOUS	Florida team	GATORS
flimflam	LIE, HUMBUG,	Florida tree	MABI, ACOMA,
	RUBBISH		JOCUM, BUSTIC, JOCUMA
flimsy	SLIM, FRAIL, SLIGHT	Florida university	HEED, NOVA,
flinch	SHY, QUAIL, BLENCH		STETSON
fling	CAST, DART, HURL	Florida vacation area	KEYS,
flint	CHERT, SILICA; see ROCK		MIAMI (BEACH)
flintlock	FUSIL; see RIFLE	flotilla	FLEET, ARMADA
Flintstones names	FRED, DINO,	Flotow opera	MARTHA
	BETTY, HANNA, WILMA,	flotsam and —	JETSAM

flounce JUMP, RUFFLE, TOTTER, TUMBLE, FALBALA

flounder(-like fish) DAB, BUTT, SOLE, BRILL, FLUKE, WHIFF, WITCH, PLAICE, TURBOT, DABLOID, HALIBUT, PETRALE, TOPKNOT

flour AT(T)A, MEAL, FARINA, PINOLE

flour, coat with DREDGE

flourish WAX, FLAUNT, PARAPH, THRIVE, FANFARE, FUSTIAN, ROULADE, TANTARA, TANTIVY

flow RUN, FLUX, ISSUE, SPOUT, EFFUSE

— and flow EBB

flower CYME, BLOOM, CREAM, ELITE, SPIKE, UMBEL, CORYMB, FLORET, RACEME, BLOSSOM, PANICLE, THYRSUS; see p. 681

flower arrangement IKEBANA

flower part KNOT, STEM, AMENT, BRACT, CALYX, OVARY, OVULE, PETAL, SEPAL, STYLE, ANTHER, CARPEL, PISTIL, POLLEN, SPADIX, SPATHE, STAMEN, STIGMA, COROLLA, EPICARP, EXOCARP, PETIOLE, FILAMENT, PERICARP

flowerless plant FERN, MOSS, LICHEN

flowery FLORID, ORNATE, FLAMBOYANT

flowing FLUX, FLUENT, SMOOTH, CURSIVE

flu BUG, COLD, VIRUS, INFECTION

flu combatant VACCINE

flu symptom AGUE, FEVER, CHILLS

flu variety ASIAN, HONGKONG

fluctuate VEER, WAVE(R), VIBRATE

flue DUCT, FUNNEL, CHIMNEY

fluent FREE, GLIB, FACILE, COPIOUS

fluff NAP, DOWN, FLOC, LINT, PUFF, FLOSS, PRIMP, MISCUE

fluid GAS, SAP, FLUX, ICHOR, SERUM, LIQUOR, PLASTIC

fluidity unit RHE

fluke BARB, HOOK, CLEEK

flume RACE, CHUTE, GORGE, SHUTE, SLUICE

flummox THWART, CONFUSE, PERPLEX, CONFOUND

flunky SNOB, GOFER, LACKEY, MENIAL

flurry ADO, STIR, GUST, COMMOTION

flush GLOW, BLUSH, PLANE, DRENCH, LAVISH

fluster FUDDLE, DITHER, POTHER, CONFUSE, EMBARRASS

flute GROOVE, CHANNEL; see p. 642

fluting PIPING, CHAMFER, GADROON

flutter FLAP, FLIP, FLIT, WAVE, HOVER, BUSTLE, QUIVER

flux FUSE, ROSIN, SOLDER

fly MIDGE, CADDIS, GADFLY, TSETSE, BLOWFLY, BLACKFLY, FRUITFLY, HOUSEFLY; see p. 678

fly genus PHORA, ASILUS, CEPHID, MUSCAE, TIPULA, DIOPSIS

fly, to DART, FLAP, FLIT, SCUD, SOAR, WHIR, WING, GLIDE, AVIATE

flycatcher PINA, PEWEE, PITTA, BECARD, PEEWEE, PHOEBE, PIPIRI, TYRANT, YETAPA, COTINGA, TOMFOOL, KINGBIRD, KINGTODY

Flying Cloud REO

Flying Dutchman composer WAGNER

Flying Dutchman role ERIK, MARY, SENTA, DALAND, DUTCHMAN

Flying Nun names ANA, ELSIE, FIELD, SALLY, SIXTO, CARLOS, BERTRILLE

flying saucer UFO

foam BARM, FIZZ, FUME, SCUM, SUDS, FROTH, SPUME

focal point, focus HUB, AXIS, CORE, CRUX, NUCLEUS

focus HUB, MEET, HEART, CENTER, CONVERGE

fodder HAY, GRAM, OATS, BARIT, FORGE, STRAW, VETCH, SILAGE, STOVER, ENSILAGE; see FORAGE

foe see ENEMY

fog RAG, HAAR, HAZE, MIST, MURK, ROKE, SMOG, BEDIM, BRUME

foggy MISTY, MURKY, CLOUDY, BRUMOUS

foghorn SIREN(E)

foible FLAW, VICE, FAULT, FAILING, FRAILTY

foie — GRAS

foil BALK, EPEE, STUMP, BAFFLE, BANANA, DEFEAT, STOOGE

foist FOB, PALM

fold LAP, PEN, PLY, COTE, FAIL, FLAP, PLIE, RUGA, TUCK, CRIMP, DRAPE, FLOCK, PLAIT, PLEAT, PLICA, CREASE

folded RUGATE, PLICATE

folder FILE, COVER, WALLET, DIRECTORY

foliage LEAVES, LEAFAGE, UMBRAGE

folk KIN, KOLO, RACE, NATION, PEOPLE

folkway(s) MOS, MORES, CUSTOM(S)

follow DOG, TAG, HEEL, OBEY, TAIL, ACT ON, CHASE, ENSUE, HOUND, STALK, TRACE, TRAIL

follower IST, ITE, APER, BUFF, HEELER, MINION, VOTARY, DEVOTEE, ADHERENT

follow-up REVIEW, SEQUEL

folly LUNACY, FATUITY

foment ABET, BREW, SPUR

fond LOVING, TENDER, DEVOTED

Fonda JANE, HENRY, PETER

fondle PET, CARESS, COSSET, DANDLE, PAMPER, STROKE

fondness GRA, LOVE

font BOWL, TYPE, BASIN, LAVER, STOUP, ORIGIN, SOURCE, SPRING

food KAI, PAP, CHOW, DIET, EATS, FARE, GRUB, MENU, MESS, CATES, MANNA, SNACK, TABLE, AMRITA, FORAGE, PABLUM, TEREFA, TEREFE, VIANDS, ALIMENT, CUISINE, AMBROSIA, VICTUALS; see p. 561

food fish COD, EEL, BASS, CARP, CAXI, CERO, HAKE, LING, PIKE, SCUP, SHAD, SOLE, TUNA, HILSA, PERCH, SCROD, SMELT, SNOOK, TROUT, TUNNY, MULLET, PLAICE, ROBALO, SALMON, TURBOT, ALEWIFE, HALIBUT, HERRING, POMPANO, SARDINE, SNAPPER, MACKEREL

fool ASS, OAF, SAP, DOLT, GABY, JERK, NIZY, RACA, SIMP, ZANY, CLOWN, DUMMY, DUNCE, NINNY, JESTER

foolhardy RASH, BRASH, DARING, RECKLESS

foolish RASH, DAFT, ZANY, BALMY, BARMY, GOOFY, INANE, SAPPY, SILLY, HARISH, ASININE

foolproof (FAIL)SAFE, INFALLIBLE

foot PAD, PAW, PES, PUD, BASE, CHECK, IONIC, TOTAL, TREAD

foot ailment CORN, GOUT, WART, BUNION, CALLUS, PODAGRA

foot part TOE, ARCH, HEEL, INCH, SOLE, VOLA, PELMA, TALUS, INSTEP, TOENAIL

foot, poetic IAMB, ARSIS, DACTYL, IAMBIC, IAMBUS, ANAPEST, SPONDEE, TROCHEE, CHORIAMB, TRIBRACH

football RUGBY, RUGGER, SOCCER, BLADDER, PIGSKIN; see SOCCER

football coaches & players see p. 708

football division EAST, WEST, CAPITOL, CENTRAL, CENTURY, EASTERN, WESTERN, AMERICAN, NATIONAL

football team JETS, RAMS, BEARS, BILLS, COLTS, LIONS, BROWNS, CHIEFS, EAGLES, ELEVEN, GIANTS, OILERS, SAINTS, TITANS, BENGALS, BRONCOS, COWBOYS, FALCONS, JAGUARS, PACKERS, RAIDERS, VIKINGS, CHARGERS, DOLPHINS, PANTHERS, PATRIOTS, REDSKINS, SEAHAWKS, STEELERS, CARDINALS, BUCCANEERS; see also p. 525

football term END, RUN, BACK, CLIP, DOWN, KICK, PASS, PLAY, PUNT, SACK, BLOCK, GUARD, CENTER, FUMBLE, HUDDLE, KICKER, ELEVEN, ONSIDE, PUNTER, SAFETY, TACKLE, DEFENSE, HOLDING, LATERAL, OFFENSE, OFFSIDE, TURNOVER, INTERCEPTION

footing TOEHOLD

footless APOD(AL)

footlike PEDATE

footman	VALET, LACKEY, MENIAL, FLUNKEY	Ford	*see* AUTOMOBILE
footnote	GLOSS, APOSTIL, COMMENT	Ford	EDSEL, HENRY, GERALD, HARRISON
footnote marker	OBELUS, ASTERISK	Ford Library location	ANN ARBOR, MICHIGAN
footpad	HOOD, THUG, WHYO, BANDIT, BRIGAND	forebear	PARENT, ANCESTOR
footprint	PAD, STEP, TRACK, TREAD	foreboding	OMEN, PALL, AUGURY, PRESAGE
footstalk	STRIG, PEDICEL	forecaster	TOUT, TIPSTER, DOPESTER
footstool	MORA, STOOL, CRICKET, HASSOCK, OTTOMAN, TABORET	forefather	SIRE, ANCESTOR
		forego	DENY, WAIVE, RESIGN
		forehead	BROW, SINCIPUT
footwear	*see* SHOE	foreign	ALIEN, EXOTIC, STRANGE, OVERSEAS
fop	BEAU, DUDE, DANDY, SWELL, MACARONI, POPINJAY	foreign words	*see p. 565*
		foreigner	ALIEN, HAOLE, EMIGRE, GRINGO, OUTSIDER
foppish	CHIC, SILLY, CHICHI, LADEDA, FOOLISH, DANDYISH	foremost	CHIEF, LEADING
		foremost part	BOW, VAN, ACRON, FRONT, LEADING
for fear that	LEST		
for	PRO, INFAVOR	forerun	SCOUT, HERALD, PIONEER, PRELUDE
for the most part	MAINLY, LARGELY	foresee	DIVINE, PREDICT
forage	ERS, GUAR, RAID, PROG, RAPE, GRASS, SULLA, ALSIKE, LUCERN, MARAUD, RUSSUD, ALFALFA, BERSEEM; *see* FODDER	foreskin	PREPUCE
		forest	GAPO, WOLD, ARDEN, COPSE, GROVE, GUBAT, SELVA, SILVA, TAIGA, WEALD, WOODS, SHERWOOD
		forest, *pert. to*	SILVAN, SYLVAN, NEMORAL
foray	RAID, SALLY, INROAD, MARAUD	foretell	BODE, SPAE, AUGUR, INSEE, PREDICT, PRESAGE
forbear	HOLD, CEASE, PAUSE, DESIST, ABSTAIN	forever	AKE, AYE, EER, ETERN(E)
forbearance	PITY, MERCY, PATIENCE, RESTRAINT, TOLERANCE	forever and —	ADAY
		foreword	PREFACE, PROLOGUE, INTRODUCTION
forbid	BAN, TABU, TAPU, VETO, DEBAR, TABOO, ENJOIN	forfeit	KEN, FINE, LOSE, LAPSE, DEODAND
forbidden	KAPU, TABU, TREF, TABOO, T(E)REFA, ILLICIT	forge	COIN, MINT, ANVIL, SHAPE, SMITHY, STITHY, FALSIFY, BLOOMERY, COUNTERFEIT
forbidden city	LHASA, MECCA, PEKING	forger	FAKER, COPYCAT, IMPOSTOR, COUNTERFEITER
forbidding	GRIM, STERN	forget	OMIT, NEGLECT, OVERLOOK
force	OD, VIM, VIS, ARMY, BIOD, BIRR, DINT, ELOD, ODYL, CORPS, DRIVE, IMPEL, POSSE, SINEW, VIGOR, COMPEL, DURESS, ENERGY, PANTOD	forgetfulness	LETHE, AMNESIA, OBLIVION
		forgive	REMIT, EXCUSE, PARDON
force, unit of	DYNE, NEWTON, POUNDAL	forgiveness	PARDON, AMNESTY, REPRIEVE
forceful	GUTSY, VITAL, COGENT, STRONG, POWERFUL	forgiving	CLEMENT, PLACABLE
		fork	DIG, PAY, TINE, PRONG, BRANCH, CROTCH, FURCATE, JUNCTION
forceps	TONGS, PINCERS, NIPPERS		
forces	TROOPS, PERSONNEL		

forked	BIRD, CLEFT, ZIGZAG, FURCATE, LITUATE
forked tongue animal	RATTLER
forlorn	ALONE, BEREFT, DESOLATE
form	MOLD, RUPA, BLANK, EIDOS, MODEL, RITUAL, TAILLE
form, *pert. to*	MODAL
formal	BALL, PRIM, PROM, STIFF, STRICT, DISTANT
formalism	PUNCTILIO
formality	DECORUM, FORMULA, REDTAPE, CEREMONY, PROTOCOL, PROPRIETY
format	FORM, PLAN, SETUP, STYLE, DESIGN, LAYOUT, MAKEUP, CONFIGURE, ARRANGEMENT
formation	FILE, LINE, BALBO, BIOME, HERSE, ORDER, COLUMN, ECHELON
former(ly)	EX, NEE, ERST, ONCE, PRIOR, WHILOM, QUÓNDAM
former days	ELD, PAST, YORE
formidable	ARDUOUS, AWESOME, FEARFUL, DAUNTING
formless	ARUPA, VAGUE, CHAOTIC, AMORPHOUS, SHAPELESS
Formosa	TAIWAN
formula	LAW, LURRY, MANTRA, RECIPE
formulaic	FIXED, RIGID, TRITE
formulate	FRAME, DEVISE, CONCOCT
forsake	QUIT, LEAVE, DESERT, DISOWN, VACATE, ABANDON, RENOUNCE
Forseti's father	BALDER
Forseti palace	GLITNIR
Forster subject	INDIA
fort	PA, DIX, DUN, ORD, PAH, COTA, DOON, KEEP, KNOX, KOTA, POST, SILL, BLISS, BRAGG, COTTA, HENRY, CASTLE, DONJON, EUSTIS, SCONCE, SUMTER, ALCAZAR, CITADEL, BASTILLE, MARTELLO
— and forth	BACK
forthwith	NOW, ANON, (EFT)SOON
fortification	LIS(S), REDAN, TALUS, ABATIS, BASTION, RAMPART, RAVELIN, REDOUBT

fortitude	GRIT, GUTS, PLUCK, SPUNK, COURAGE, STAMINA, STRENGTH, TENACITY
fortuitous	CASUAL, CHANCE
fortunate	SRI, ROSY, SHRI, BLEST, FAUST, SHREE, DEXTER
fortune	HAP, LOT, BAHI, FATE, TYCHE, RICHES, WEALTH
fortune-teller	SEER, AUGUR, GYPSY, SIBYL, ORACLE, PALMIST, SPAEMAN, HARUSPEX
forum	*see* ASSEMBLY
forward	BOLD, SEND, SHIP, AHEAD, BRAZEN, TRANSMIT
fossil	FOG(E)Y, DOLITE, PINITE, CRINITE, CALAMITE, DINOSAUR
foster	REAR, CHERISH, PROMOTE
Foster, Jodie roll	NELL
foul	RANK, VILE, NASTY, FILTHY
foul play	VILLAINY, TREACHERY
foulmouthed	PROFANE
foul-smelling	OLID, FETID, REEKY, NOISOME
found	SET, CAST, BASE, MOLD, ENDOW, CREATE
foundation	BED, BASE, BASIS, CORSET, GIRDLE, RIPRAP, BEDROCK
founder	FAIL, FALL, SLIP, STUMBLE, CREATOR, PRODUCER, INSTIGATOR, ORIGINATOR
foundling	WAIF, EPPIE
foundry	SMITHY, IRONWORKS
fountain	JET, FONS, FONT, KELD, SYKE, WELL, BIMINI, SOURCE, SPRING
Four H, meaning	HEAD, HANDS, HEART, HEALTH
Four Horsemen	WAR, DEATH, FAMINE, LAYDEN, MILLER, CROWLEY, PESTILENCE, STUHLDREHER
fourscore	EIGHTY
fourteen days	FORTNIGHT
fourteen pounds	STONE
fourth estate	MEDIA, PRESS
fowl	HEN, COCK, DUCK, GUAN, JACU, KEET, MITU, RYPE, BIDDY, CAPON, KOKLA, LOWAN, MALEO, BANTAM, BRAHMA, BRAMAH, GROUSE, HOUDAN, LEIPOA, PIGEON,

PULLET, SULTAN, TURKEY, CHICKEN, DORKING, GALEENY, GOBBLER, LEGHORN, MEGAPOD, MOORHEN, PEACOCK, CURASSOW, PHEASANT, PARTRIDGE, PTARMIGAN
fowl genus   CRAX, PIPILE, ORTALUS, RASORES
fowl, young   POULT, CHICK(EN), FLAPPER
fox   TOD, KIT, ASSE, CAAMA, SWIFT, VIXEN, ZERDA, BAGMAN, CORSAC, FENNEC, LOWRIE, RENARD
fox genus   VULPES
fox, young   CUB, KIT, PUP
foxy   SLY, WILY, CRAFTY, VULPINE
foyer   HALL, LOBBY, VESTIBULE
Fra Diavolo composer   AUBER
fracas   see FIGHT
fraction   PART, SCRAP, MOIETY, ALIQUOT, DECIMAL, SEGMENT
fractious   UNRULY, PEEVISH
fragile   FRAIL, BRITTLE
fragment   ANA, BIT, ORT, SNIP, WISP, SCRAP, SHARD, SHERD
fragmentary   BROKEN, PATCHY, PARTIAL
Fragonard painting   SWING, BATHERS
fragrant   BALMY, OLENT, SWEET, SCENTED, AROMATIC
frail   DAME, GIRL, WEAK, WISPY, WOMAN, FEEBLE, SLIGHT, FRAGILE, DELICATE
frailty   SIN, FLAW, FAULT, FOIBLE
frame(work)   RIG, RACK, SESS, CADRE, HERSE, SETUP, SHELL, TRUSS, TENTER, CHASSIS, STENTER, TABORET, TRESSEL, TRESTLE, CONFINES, SKELETON
frame of mind   BENT, MOOD, HUMOR, TEMPER
framer's need   MAT
framework   CADRE, SHELL, CONFINES, SKELETON
France   GAUL; see FRENCH
France, capital of   PARIS
franchise   SOC, SORE, VOTE, LICENSE
Franciscan   CAPUCHIN, MINORITE

Franco-Prussian War battle   METZ, SEDAN, GRAVELOTTE
frangible   DELICATE, BREAKABLE
frank   OPEN, BLUNT, NAIVE, CANDID, EXEMPT, SINCERE
Frankenstein author   SHELLEY
frankfurter   WEENY, HOTDOG, WIENER
frankincense   THUS, OLIBANUM
Frankish king   PEPIN, CLOVIS, CHARLEMAGNE
Frankish vassal   LEUD, LITUS
frankness   CANDOR, BLUNTNESS, FREEDOM
Franks, pert. to   SALIC
frantic   WILD, FRENETIC
Frasier names   ROZ, EDDIE, NILES, KELSEY, BULLDOG, GRAMMER
fraternal group   ELKS, MOOSE, ROTARY, PYTHIAS, ODD FELLOW, (FREE) MASONS
fraternity   CLUB, LODGE, GREEKS, SORORITY
fraternity member   DELT(A), SIGMA, FRATBOY
fraternize   ASSOCIATE, COLLABORATE
fraud   CON, FAKE, HOAX, JAPE, RUSE, SHAM, BUNCO, COVIN, COZENAGE
fraudulent   FAKE, PHONY, DEVIOUS, DECEITFUL
fraught   BESET, LADEN
fray   RUB, WEAR, CHAFE, RAVEL; see FIGHT
frazzle   VEX, FRAY, WEAR, SHRED
freak   WHIM, QUIRK, CAPRICE
freckle   LENTIGO
free   RID, REDD, CLEAR, LOOSE, EXEMPT, GRATIS, LOOSEN, MANUMIT
free and —   EASY, CLEAR
freedman   LAET, LATIN, THANE
free-for-all   CLEM, FRAY, MELEE, SETTO, RUMBLE
freeloader   BUM, SPONGER, DEADBEAT, PARASITE
freeman   CEORL, CHURL, THANE, THEGN, VILLEIN
freeway   ARTERY, HIGHWAY, PARKWAY, THRUWAY, INTERSTATE
freeze   ICE, NIP, CHILL, GELATE, CONGEAL
freight   CARGO, LADING

freighter TRAMP, TANKER, LIGHTER, STEAMER
French GALLIC, ROMANCE
French artist DORE, DUFY, GROS, COROT, DEGAS, LEGER, MANET, MONET, BRAQUE, INGRES, RENOIR, SEURAT, CEZANNE, CHAGALL, CHARDIN, DAUMIER, MATISSE, ROUAULT, UTRILLO
French author SUE, GIDE, HUGO, LOTI, ZOLA, CAMUS, DUMAS, RENAN, VERNE, DESADE, FRANCE, RACINE, SARTRE, COCTEAU
French beverage THE, VIN
French city/town GEX, PAU, ALES, CAEN, FOIX, LYON, METZ, NICE, STLO, BLOIS, BREST, DIJON, LILLE, NANCY, NIMES, PARIS, REIMS, ROUEN, TOURS, VICHY, AMIENS, CALAIS, CANNES, LEMANS, NANTES, RENNES, TROYES, ANTIBES, AVIGNON, BOURGES, DUNKIRK, LEHAVRE, LIMOGES, LOURDES, ORLEANS, BORDEAUX, GRENOBLE, MARSEILLE, TOULOUSE, VERSAILLES
French composer LALO, BIZET, DINDY, FAURE, RAVEL, SATIE, BOULEZ, GOUNOD, RAMEAU, BERLIOZ, DEBUSSY, DELIBES, POULENC, MASSENET
French department AIN, LOT, VAR, AUBE, AUDE, CHER, EURE, GARD, GERS, JURA, NORD, ORNE, TARN, AISNE, DOUBS, DROME, INDRE, ISERE, LOIRE, MARNE, MEUSE, RHONE, SOMME, YONNE, ALLIER, ARIEGE, CANTAL, CREUSE, LANDES, LOZERE, MANCHE, NIEVRE, SARTHE, SAVOIE, VENDEE, VIENNE, VOSGES
French direction EST, SUD, NORD, OUEST
French district CORSE, ALSACE, CENTRE, AQUITAINE, AUVERGNE, BRETAGNE, LIMOUSIN, LORRAINE, PICARDIE, ACQUITAINE
French greeting SALUT
French island RE, YEU, USANT, HYERES, OLERON
French leader BLUM, COTY, HUGH, AURIOL, FAURE, GOUIN, GREVY, BRIAND, CARNOT, CHIRAC, DOUMER, LEBRUN, LOUBET, PETAIN, PHILIP, THIERS, BIDAULT, MAZARIN, DEGAULLE, MACMAHON, POINCARE, POMPIDOU, DOUMERGUE, MILLERAND, MITTERAND, DESCHANEL, CLEMENCEAU
French measure POT, LIEUE, LIGNE, MINOT, PINTE, ARPENT, HEMINE, PERCHE, CHOPINE, POISSON
French money ECU, SOL, SOU, EURO, AGNEL, FRANC, LIARD, LOUIS, OBOLE, BESANT, CENTIME, SOLIDUS, NAPOLEON
French mountain JURA, MONT, BLANC, FOREZ, MEZENC, VOSGES, AUVERGNE, MONTBLANC
French native BRETON, GASCON, NORMAN
French philosopher CARO, CAMUS, COMTE, TAINE, PASCAL, SARTRE, BERGSON, DIDEROT, ROUSSEAU, VOLTAIRE, DESCARTES
French Revolution leader MARAT, CLOOTS, DANTON, HEBERT
French Revolution month *see p. 717*
French river OISE, ADOUR, LOIRE, MARNE, RHONE, SAONE, SEINE, YONNE, GARONNE
French royal family CAPET, VALOIS, ORLEANS, BOURBON, CAROLINGIAN
French ruler ODO, HUGH, JOHN, EUDES, HENRY, LOUIS, BARRAS, PHILIP, ROBERT, CHARLES, LOTHAIR, RUDOLPH, NAPOLEON; *see* FRANKISH
French singer PIAF, PONS, CALVE, SABLON, TRENET, VIARDOT, AZNAVOUR
French song ALOUETTE
French territory ALOFI, BELEP, ADELIE, CROZET, GUIANA, MAYOTTE, REUNION, TUAMOTU
French weight GROS, MARC, ONCE, LIVRE, TONNE
French wine region LOIRE, RHONE, ALSACE, BORDEAUX, BURGUNDY, CHAMPAGNE
French words *see p. 566*

frenzy	**AMOK, RAGE, FUROR, MANIA**
frequent	**OFT(EN), HAUNT, RESORT, HABITUAL**
frequently	**OFT, ALOT, MUCH, OFTEN**
fresh	**RAW, FACY, FLIP, PERT, BRISK, NOVEL, SASSY, SPICK, VIVID, RECENT**
freshet	**FLOOD, SPATE**
freshman	**FROSH, PLEBE, NOVICE**
freshness indicator	**ODOR**
fret	**FUSS, STEW, CHAFE, WORRY**
fretful	**GROUCHY, PEEVISH, PETULANT**
Freudian terms	**ID, EGO, SUPEREGO, UNCONSCIOUS**
Frey's home	**ALFHEIM**
Frey's wife	**GERDA, GERTH**
Freya relative	**FREY, ODIN, NJORD**
friable	**CRISP, SHORT, BRITTLE**
friar	**FRA, MONK, TUCK, ABBOT, FRATER, LISTER, SERVITE**
friction	**RUB(BING), ABRASION**
Friday source	**FRIGGA**
friend	**AMI, AMY, DOG, PAL, AMIE, CHUM, KITH, MATE, AMIGO, BUDDY, CRONY, DAMON, QUAKER, ACHATES, PYTHIAS, INTIMATE, PLAYMATE**
Friendly Islands	**EUA, TOFUA, TONGA, VAVAU, HAAPAI**
— friends	**AMONG**
Friends names	**COX, JOEY, ROSS, MONICA, PHOEBE, RACHEL, KUDROW, ANISTON, CHANDLER**
friendship	**AMITY, COMITY**
Frigg	**FRIA**
Frigg relative	**VE, ODIN, FULLA, BALDER**
fright(en)	**AWE, FLEY, FUNK, GAST, ALARM, PANIC, SCARE**
frightened	**AFRAID, SCARED**
frightful	**GRIM, SCARY, FEARFUL, GHASTLY, HORRIBLE**
frigid	**ICY, COLD, ICED, FORMAL, GLACIAL**
frill	**RUFF, JABOT, RUCHE, RUFFLE, FALBALA, FLOUNCE, FURBELOW**
fringe	**EDGE, LOMA, THRUM, BORDER, TASSEL**

Frisbee term	**WAS, WAX, WAFT, WANE, WARP, WELL, WASTE, WEDGE, WHELM**
frisk	**CAPER, FROLIC, GAMBOL, SEARCH, TITTUP**
frisky	**SPRY, PEPPY, LIVELY, PLAYFUL**
fritter	**CAKE, DALLY, WASTE, DAWDLE**
frivolous	**PETTY, SILLY, TRIVIAL**
frock	**COAT, GOWN, ROBE, DRESS, SMOCK, TUNIC**
frog	**RANA, FROSH, FROSK, PEEPER, AGLOSSA, HYLIDAE, PADDOCK, TADPOLE, BULLFROG, FERREIRO, LINGUATA;** see **TOAD**
frog, young	**TADPOLE, POLLIWOG**
frolic	**FUN, DIDO, LARK, PLAY, ROMP, CAPER, FRISK, SPORT, SPREE, CAVORT, GAMBOL**
from	**EX, AWAY, HENCE, OUTOF, WHENCE**
From Here to Eternity character	**ALMA, KERR, PREW, CLIFT, FATSO, KAREN, ANGELO, MILTON, SINATRA, BORGNINE, LANCASTER**
Frome wife	**ITU, ZEENA**
front	**VAN, FACE, FORE, DUMMY, FACADE, STOOGE, OBVERSE**
frontal	**METOPIC**
frontier-like	**WILD, LAWLESS**
frontiersman	**CODY, EARP, BOONE, BOWIE, CLARK, LOGAN, CARSON, CROCKETT, HICKOK**
frost	**ICE, HOAR, RIME, ICEUP**
frosting	**ICING**
frosty	**ICY, COLD, RIMY, ALOOF, FRORE, HOARY, DISTANT**
froth	**FOB, BARM, FOAM, SCUM, SUDS, SPUME, YEAST, LATHER**
frown	**LOUR, LOWER, SCOWL, GLOWER, GRIMACE**
frozen	**ICY, FRORE, GELID, GLACE, FRAPPE, GLACIAL, GLACIATED**
frozen dessert	**ICE, FRAPPE, MOUSSE, SORBET, SHERBET, SPUMONI**
frugal	**CHARY, CHEAP, SPARE, PRUDENT, THRIFTY**

frugality	THRIFT, ECONOMY, PARSIMONY
fruit	NUT, CONE, CROP, PEPO, POME, AKENE, BERRY, DRUPE, GOURD, YIELD, ACHENE, AECIUM, LEGUME, LOMENT, NUTLET, PROFIT, TELIUM, DESSERT, ETAERIO, SILICLE, SILIQUE, SYNCARP, UTRICLE; *see* FRUITS
fruitcake	SIMNEL
fruitful	FECUND, FERTILE, PROLIFIC, PRODUCTIVE, PROFITABLE
fruition	END, OUTCOME, REALIZATION
fruitless	VAIN, BARREN, STERILE
fruits	FIG, HAW, HIP, DATE, LIME, PEAR, PLUM, SLOE, ACORN, APPLE, GRAPE, GUAVA, LEMON, MANGO, MELON, OLIVE, PEACH, BANANA, CHERRY, CITRON, CITRUS, LOQUAT, ORANGE, QUINCE, TOMATO, APRICOT, AVOCADO, COCONUT, KUMQUAT, PUMPKIN, TANGELO, TANGERINE; *see p. 685*
fruity	NUTTY, CARPIC
frustrate	BALK, DASH, FOIL, SCOTCH, THWART
fry	SAUTE, FRIZZ(LE)
fuddy-duddy	DODO, FOGY, DOTARD
fuel	GAS, LOG, LOX, OIL, PAB, CHIP, COAL, COKE, PEAT, PEET, UPLA, WOOD, STOKE, BUTANE, PETROL, STERNO, ALCOHOL, BRIQUET, CHARCOAL, KEROSENE
Fugard heroine	LENA
fugitive	MAROON, ESCAPEE, RUNAGATE, RUNAWAY
"Fugitive" premiere station	ABC
fugue part	DUX, COMES, PEDAL, THEME, ANSWER, STRETTO
fulcrum	AXIS, PROP, PIVOT
fulfill	EFFECT, GRATIFY, REALIZE, EXECUTE, SATISFY
full	SATED, OROTUND, PLENARY, REPLETE
full-blooded	RUDDY, ARDENT, FLORID, HEARTY, SANGUINE
full-blown	LUSH, ADULT, MATURE, COMPLETE

fullness	PLENUM, SATIETY, SURFEIT, PLETHORA
Fulton's steamboat	CLERMONT
fumble	DROP, FLUB, GROPE, BUNGLE
fume	FRET, RAGE, RAVE, REEK, SMELL, SMOKE
fumigant	PASTILLE, DEODORANT, DEODORIZER
fumigate	SANITIZE, DISINFECT
fuming	RAGING, ENRAGED, FURIOUS
fun	PLAY, JINKS, SPORT, JOLLITY, AMUSEMENT, DIVERSION, MERRIMENT
function	ACT, USE, DUTY, ROLE, SINE, WORK, EVENT, PARTY, COSINE, TANGENT
fund	CACHE, KITTY, STOCK, STORE, SUPPLY
fund type	SLUSH, TRUST
fundamental	BASAL, BASIC, VITAL, PRIMAL, RADICAL, ORGANIC, ELEMENTAL
fundraiser	RAFFLE, BENEFIT, CARWASH, BAKE SALE
funds, illegal	PELF, BOOTY
funeral	BURIAL, EXEQUIES
funeral director	MORTICIAN
funereal	SAD, DARK, FERAL, DISMAL, GLOOMY, SOMBER
fungus	BUNT, KNOT, MOLD, PUFF, PUNK, RUST, SMUT, WART, ERGOT, FOMES, IRPEX, MOREL, MOULD, MUCOR, PHOMA, PORIA, UREDO, VALSA, VERPA, YEAST, AGARIC, AMADOU, CAEOMA, FUMAGO, MILDEW, ZYTHIA, AMANITA, BLEWITS, BOLETUS, STEREUM, TRUFFLE; *see* MUSHROOM
funk	FEAR, MOOD, PANIC, COWARD, TEMPER
funnel	CONE, FLUE, CHANNEL
funnies	*see* CARTOON
funny	ODD, COMIC, DROLL, AMUSING, HUMOROUS
fur	CAT, DOG, FOX, KID, BEAR, CALF, FLIX, GOAT, HAIR, HARE, LAMB, LYNX, MINK, MOLE, PELT, FLEW, PONY, SEAL, SKIN, VAIR, WOLF, CIVET, FITCH, GENET, KOALA, LLAMA, OTTER, PAHMI, PANDA, SABLE, SHEEP, SKUNK, STOAT, ALPACA, BADGER, BEAVER, DESMAN, ERMINE, FISHER, JACKAL, JAGUAR, MARMOT, MARTEN,

MONKEY, NUTRIA, OCELOT,
PELAGE, PELTRY, RABBIT,
SUSLIK, VICUNA, WEASEL,
WOMBAT, CARACAL,
CHEETAH, CRIMMER,
FITCHEW, GUANACO,
HAMSTER, KARAKUL,
KRIMMER, LEOPARD,
MINIVER, MUSKRAT,
OPOSSUM, RACCOON,
WALLABY
fur tycoon ASTOR
Furies *see* ERINYES
furious MAD, ANGRY, WROTH,
RAGING, FRENZIED
furnace KILN, OVEN, TUEL,
FORGE, SMITHY, STITHY,
SMELTER, CREMATORY
furnace part TUE, BOSH,
FAULD, GRATE, TEWEL,
TUYERE, CRUCIBLE
furnish PLY, CATER, ENDOW,
EQUIP, PLENISH
furnishings RIG, GEAR, DECOR
furniture EQUIPAGE, FIXTURES
furniture maker CANER
furor ADO, RAGE, CRAZE,
MANIA, FRENZY, TUMULT
furrow RUT, PLOW, RILL,
SEAM, CHASE, DRILL, RILLE,
STRIA, GROOVE, SULCUS,
TRENCH
furrowed RIVOSE, RUTTED,
STRIATE
furry BUSHY, HAIRY, NAPPY,
FLEECY, LANATE, PILEOUS
further AID, AND, TOO, YET,
ABET, ELSE, MORE
furthermore TOO, ALSO, PLUS,
BESIDES
furtive SLY, WARY, SNEAKY
fury IRE, RAGE, WRATH,
FRENZY
fuse FRIT, WELD, MERGE,
SMELT, ANNEAL, SOLDER
fusilade BURST, SALVO,
BARRAGE
fusion UNION, MERGER,
COALITION
fuss ADO, FIKE, STIR, TODO,
PREEN, BUSTLE, FANTOD,
FIDGET, POTHER
fuss, make a CLAMOR
fussy PRISSY, FINICAL
fusty MOLDY, STALE, STUFFY
futile IDLE, VAIN, OTIOSE,
USELESS
future LATER, COMING,
HEREAFTER, POSTERITY

future star FIND, COMER,
STARLET, DISCOVERY
futurist SEER
fuzzy VAGUE, BLURRED,
UNCLEAR
fylfot SWASTIKA

G

G GEE, GOLF, GAMMA, GIMEL
Gaal relative EBED
gab CHAT, MOUTH, PRATE
gable DORMER, PINION,
AILERON
Gabon, capital of LIBREVILLE
Gabon city/town OYEM,
BEOUE, BITAM, MOANDA,
MOUILA, NDJOLE, OVENDO
Gabon ethnic group PUNU,
CHIRA, LUMBU, ADOUNA,
PAHOUIN
Gabon language FRENCH;
see BANTU
Gabon money FRANC
Gabon president BONGO
Gabon river SEBE, GABON,
OGOOUE, NGOUNIE
Gabon tribe FANG, BANTU,
BATEKE, ESHIRA, BAPOUNOU
Gabor EVA, MAGDA, ZSAZSA
gad ROAM, ROVE, PROWL,
RAMBLE
Gad relative ERI, AROD, OZNI,
ARELI, ASHER, HAGGI,
JACOB, ZILPAH
gadget GISMO, IPSES, OOJAH,
CLANTH, DINGUS, DOODAD,
FIDFAD, FRAMUS, GOWSER,
HOODUS, JIGGER, JIGGUS,
JIMJAM, KAJODY, STROMM,
WIDGET, WINDGE, CHINGUS,
DINGBAT, DINGLET, GIMMICK,
KADIGAN, SNIVVIE
gadoid *see* COD
Gaea relative CHAOS, TITAN,
URANUS
Gael(ic) CELT, ERSE, MANX,
SCOT, IRISH, CELTIC, KELTIC,
SCOTCH, GADHELIC,
GOIDELIC
gaff HOAX, HOOK, SP(E)AR,
FLEECE, GAMBLE
gaffe BONER, ERROR,
BLUNDER, FAUXPAS
gag QUIP, SCOB, CHOKE,
RETCH, MUFFLE, MUZZLE,
SQUELCH

gage	PAWN, PLUM, GLOVE, WAGER
gaiety	FUN, JOLLITY
gain	GET, NET, WIN, EARN, LUCRE, PROFIT
gainful	PAID, PAYING, LUCRATIVE, REWARDING
gainsay	DENY, IMPUGN, REFUTE
Gainsborough painting	BLUE BOY, MARKET CART, MORNING WALK
gait	RUN, LOPE, PACE, RACK, TROT, VOLT, WALK, AMBIT, AMBLE, CANTER, GALLOP, SHAMBLE
gaiter	SPAT, PUTTEE, LEGGING
gala	FETE, FESTAL, FIESTA, BANQUET, FESTIVE
Galahad relative	ELAINE, LANCELOT
Galatea's lover	ACIS, PYGMALION
gale	GUST, WIND, BLAST, STORM
Galilee town	CANA, NAZARETH
Galileo home	PISA
gall	VEX, BILE, FRET, ANNOY, RANCOR
gallant	HERO, BRAVE, LOVER, NOBLE, KNIGHT, SQUIRE
galleon	CARAC(K), CARRACK; see VESSEL
galleries	MET, MONA, TATE, PRADO, LOUVRE, UFFIZI, HERMITAGE
gallery	POY, LOFT, ALURE, SALON, ARCADE, LOGGIA, PIAZZA, PUBLIC, SOLLAR, VERANDA
galley	AESC, BARGE, PROOF, BIREME, DRUDGE, DROMOND, KITCHEN, TRIREME
gallic	FRENCH, GAULISH
gallinaceous	RASORIAL; see FOWL
Gallo family	GINO, MATT, JULIO, ERNEST
gallon	GAWN
gallop	RUN, LOPE, PELT, AUBIN, TANTIVY
gallows	NOOSE, GIBBET, YARDARM
galoot	SAP, GOOF, JERK, LOUT, KLUTZ
galore	PLENTY
Galsworthy character	FLEUR,

	IRENE, JOLYON, SOAMES, ANNETTE
Galsworthy novel	TOLET, FORSYTE, JOCELYN
galvanize	SHOCK, ENERGIZE
Galway Bay islands	ARAN
gam	LEG, POD, HERD, SCHOOL
gambado	LEAP, PRANK
Gambia, The, capital of	BANJUL, BATHURST
Gambian city/town	BAKAU, BANJUL, YUNDUM, BRIKAMA
Gambian language	WOLOF, MANDINKA
Gambian money	DALASI
Gambian neighbor	SENEGAL
Gambian river	GAMBIA
Gambian tribe	FULA, JOLA, WOLOF, FULANI, MALINKE, MANDINKA, SERAHULI
gamble	BET, RISK, STAKE, WAGER
gambler	DICER, SHARK, SHARP, SHILL, BETTOR, PUNTER, TINHORN, SHILLABER
gambling assistant	TOUT, RAKER, DEALER, CROUPIER
gambling game	DICE, FARO, KENO, PICO, BINGO, MONTE, POKER, STUSS, BACCARAT, ROULETTE, BLACKJACK
gambling house	RENO, CASINO, MONACO, LASVEGAS
gambol	DIDO, ROMP, CAPER, FRISK, FROLIC, CURVET
Gambrinus invention	BEER
game	FUN, BOLD, LAME, LUDI, SPORT, FROLIC, CONTEST, PASTIME, WILLING; see p. 586
game bird	DUCK, GUAN, RAIL, QUAIL, SNIPE, GROUSE, PLOVER, PHEASANT, PARTRIDGE
game fish	BASS, CERO, SCAD, TUNA, SARGO, TROUT, BONITO, MARLIN, SALMON, TARPON
game name	SEGA, SONY, XBOX, ATARI, GAMEBOY, NINTENDO, PLAYSTATION
game piece	DIE, PIN, MAN, BALL, TILE, TOKEN, DOMINO, COUNTER
game show host	FINN, CLARK, PERRY, SAJAK, STEIN, WHITE, BARKER, BARRIS, COOMBS, CULLEN, DAWSON, TREBEK, EUBANKS, RAYBURN,

WALLACE, WOOLERY,
DAVIDSON, TOMARKEN,
MARTINDALE
gamekeeper RANGER, WARDEN
games GO, TAG, DICE, FARO,
POOL, BINGO, CHESS, CRAPS,
DARTS, JACKS, LOTTO,
GHOSTS, MAJONG, HANGMAN,
MAHJONG, MARBLES, PACHISI,
ANAGRAMS, BACCARAT,
CHARADES, CHECKERS,
DOMINOES, DRAUGHTS,
MONOPOLY, ROULETTE,
SCRABBLE, HOPSCOTCH,
PARCHEESI, TICTACTOE,
BACKGAMMON,
CATEGORIES; see p. 586
gamin TAD, ARAB, BRAT,
PUNK, WAIF, URCHIN
Gandhi title MAHATMA
gang MOB, BAND, CREW,
RING, CABAL, SQUAD
gang up UNITE, COMBINE,
CONSPIRE, TAKESIDES
Ganges city BENARES,
CALCUTTA
Ganges tributary SON, GOGRA,
GUNTI, GANDAK
gangster MUG, GOON, HOOD,
THUG, WHYO, YEGG,
TOUGH, GORILLA, HOODLUM,
MAFIOSO, TORPEDO
gangway RAMP, AISLE, PLANK
gannet SULA, BOOBY, GOOSE,
SOLAN, MARGOT
ganoid fish see GAR, BOWFIN,
STURGEON
Ganymede relative ILUS, TROS
gap GULF, BREAK, M(E)USE,
MUSET, SHARD, BREACH,
HIATUS, LACUNA
gape GAWK, OGLE, YAWN,
OSCITATE
gaping AJAR, GAPPY, RICTUS,
RINGENT
gar(-like fish) IHI, BALAO,
SAURY, SNOOK, BELONE,
BONACI, GANOID, GARFISH,
GARPIKE, HALFBEAK
garage MEW, CARPORT
garb see CLOTHING
garbage JUNK, OFFAL, SWILL,
TRASH, MIDDEN, REFUSE
garble MIXUP, JUMBLE,
MUDDLE, CONFUSE,
CORRUPT, DISTORT
Garbo movie CAMILLE,
CONQUEST, NINOTCHKA,
GRANDHOTEL

garden EDEN, PLOT, ARBOR,
GARTH, PATCH, HERBARY,
OLITORY, ORCHARD,
PLEASANCE
Garden City CHICAGO
garden tool HOE, HOSE, RAKE,
SPADE, DIBBLE, (H)EDGER,
TROWEL
Gargantua author RABELAIS
Gargantua character
PANTAGRUEL
gargle WASH, RINSE, SWISH,
MOUTHWASH
garland LEI, ANADEM, FILLET,
WREATH, CHAPLET,
FESTOON
garlic CIVE, MOLY, RAMSON
garment ROBING; see
CLOTHING
garner EARN, REAP, HOARD,
STORE, GATHER, ACQUIRE,
COLLECT, HARVEST
garnet PYROPE, OLIVINE,
ESSONITE, MELANITE
garnish DECK, LARD, TRIM,
ADORN, BEDECK, RELISH,
DECORATE
garret LOFT, ATTIC, SOLER
garrison POST, BILLET,
OUTPOST, BARRACKS,
PRESIDIO
garrulous VOLUBLE,
TALKATIVE
gas BRAG, DAMP, DRUG, FUEL,
NEON, EXAN, OXAN, ARGON,
ETHER, ETHYL, FREON,
OXANE, RADON, XENON,
ARSINE, BUTANE, FLATUS,
HELIUM, KETONE, ETHANE,
PETROL, BENZENE, KRYPTON,
METHANE, PROPANE,
STIBINE, FLUORINE,
PHOSGENE
gash CUT, HACK, SLIT, SLASH
gasket ORING, SEALER
gasoline NAPALM,
PETROL(EUM)
gasoline brand BP, ARCO, ESSO,
SHELL, AMOCO, EXXON
gasoline type NOLEAD,
REG(ULAR), PREMIUM
gasp PANT, PUFF, HEAVE,
WHEEZE
gastropod see SNAIL
gate BAB, SPRUE; see DOOR
gatekeeper PORTER,
DOORMAN, CONCIERGE
gatepost DURN
Gates' wife MELINDA

gateway DAR, PYLON, TORAN,
TORII, SLUICE, TORANA
Gath hero GOLIATH
gather LEK, CULL, AMASS,
GLEAN, PLAIT, SHEVE, SHIRR,
GARNER, MUSTER, SHEAVE,
COLLATE
gathering BEE, CROWD, PARTY,
RALLY, MEETING,
ASSEMBLY, ASSEMBLAGE
gaudy SHOWY, FLASHY,
GARISH, TAWDRY, VULGAR
gauge RATE, SIZE, JUDGE,
CALIBER, MEASURE,
APPRAISE, ESTIMATE,
EVALUATE
Gaugin autobiography NOA
NOA
Gauguin island TAHITI
Gauguin wife METTE
Gaulish people REMI, CELTS,
BELGAE, SEQUANI
gaunt SICKLY, HAGGARD; see
LEAN
gauntlet CUFF, GLOVE
gauntlet, throw down the DARE,
DEFY, CHALLENGE
gauze NET, LENO, CREPE,
LISSE, MARLI, SCRIM, TULLE,
BAREGE, TISSUE, CHIFFON
gauzy FILMY, SHEER
Gawain relative LOT, GARETH,
GAHERIS, MORDRED,
AGRAVAIN
gawk GAPE, GAZE, STARE
gay AIRY, HAPPY, JOLLY,
MERRY, RIANT, JOCUND,
LIVELY
gaze GAWK, OGLE, PEER,
STARE
gazelle see ANTELOPE
Gdansk DANZIG
gear CAM, COG, KIT, GARB,
DUFFEL, PINION, TACKLE
gecko see LIZARD
gee GOSH, GOLLY
gee, opp. to HAW
Gehenna PIT, HELL, HADES,
INFERNO
geisha DANCER, HOSTESS
gelastic RISIBLE
gelatin AGAR, ASPIC, COLLIN,
COLLOID
Gelderland city EDE
gem ICE, JET, JADE, ONYX,
OPAL, RUBY, SARD, AGATE,
AMBER, BALAS, BERYL,
CAMEO, PEARL, PRASE, TOPAZ,
GARNET, IOLITE, JASPER,

LIGURE, MUFFIN, PLASMA,
PYROPE, SCARAB, SPINEL,
BURMITE, DIAMOND,
EMERALD, PERIDOT,
HEMATITE, SAPPHIRE; see
JEWEL, STONE
gem face BEZEL, CULET,
FACET, TABLE
gem setting OUCH, PAVE,
BEZEL, CHATON
Gem State ID, IDAHO
Gemini TWINS, CASTOR,
POLLUX
gender SEX, BEGET, NEUTER,
FEMININE, MASCULINE
gene DNA, RNA
genealogy TREE, LINAGE,
DESCENT, LINEAGE,
PEDIGREE
general RIFE, BROAD, USUAL,
COMMON, PANDEMIC,
INCLUSIVE, UNIVERSAL
generally ALWAYS, OVERALL,
ASARULE
generals BOR, GRANT,
ANDERS, PATTON, BRADLEY,
SHERMAN, PERSHING,
SHERIDAN, MACARTHUR; see
CIVIL WAR
generate MAKE, BEGET, BREED,
PRODUCE, ENGENDER
generation AGE, DESCENT
generator DYNAMO
generosity CHARITY,
ALTRUISM, LARGESSE
generous AMPLE, LAVISH,
LIBERAL, UNSELFISH,
CHARITABLE
genesis BIRTH, ORIGIN,
CREATION
Genesis locale ARARAT
Genesis son ENOS
Geneva lake LEMAN
Geneva river RHONE
genial WARM, AFFABLE,
AMIABLE, CORDIAL,
FRIENDLY, PLEASANT
genie see DEMON
genius GIFT, TALENT, ABILITY
Genoese family DORIA
Genoese money JANE
genre KIND, SORT, TYPE,
CLASS, STYLE, SPECIES
genteel NICE, POLITE,
REFINED, COURTEOUS
gentile GOY, PAGAN,
HEATHEN
gentle MILD, SOFT, TAME,
BALMY, DOCILE, PLACID

gentleman   SER, SIR, BABU,
    TOFF, BABOO, SENOR,
    GALLANT, YOUNKER
Gentlemen Prefer Blondes author
    LOOS
Gentlemen Prefer Blondes name
    JANE, PIGGY, COBURN,
    MONROE, CHARLES,
    LORELEI, MARILYN, RUSSELL
genuine   REAL, LEGIT, VALID,
    HONEST, SINCERE,
    AUTHENTIC
genus   *see* CLASS
geode   VUG, VOOG, VUGG,
    VUGH, DRUSE, CAVITY,
    NODULE
geographer   KANT, MELA,
    VAREN, VIDAL, BUACHE,
    CLUVEL, RITTER, STRABO,
    THALES, APIANUS, BRUNHES,
    MUNSTER, PTOLEMY,
    HUMBOLDT, MERCATOR
geological division   ERA, KOME,
    EPOCH, PERIOD, SERIES,
    SYSTEM
geological epoch   BALA, CULM,
    DYAS, ECCA, LIAS, MALM,
    MOINE, DOGGER, EOCENE,
    MIOCENE, HOLOCENE,
    PLIOCENE
geological era   AZOIC,
    ARCHEAN, CENOZOIC,
    MESOZOIC, ALGONKIAN,
    PALEOZOIC
geological formation(s)   IONE,
    STRATA, STRATUM,
    TERRANE, TERRENE
geological period   LYAS,
    PERMIAN, CAMBRIAN,
    DEVONIAN, JURASSIC,
    SILURIAN, TERTIARY,
    TRIASSIC, QUATERNARY
geologist   HUXLEY, STRABO
geology term   AGE, BED, ERA,
    CREEP, MAGMA
geometric figure   CUSP, ANGLE,
    RHOMB, CIRCLE, OBLONG,
    SQUARE, TRIGON, ELLIPSE,
    POLYGON
geometric solid   CONE, CUBE,
    LUNE, PRISM, SPHERE,
    PYRAMID, CYLINDER
geometrician   EUCLID, THALES
geometry term   PI, LOCI, SINE,
    CHORD, LOCUS, PLANE,
    SOLID, SECANT, VERSOR,
    TANGENT, THEOREM
Georgia (country), capital of
    TBILISI

Georgia (country) city/town
    GAGRA, BATUMI, KASHURI,
    KUTAISI, RUSTAVI,
    SOKHUMI, TBILISI
Georgia (country) money   GEL,
    LARI, TETRI
Georgia (country) mountain   LIKH,
    LOMIS, SHKHARA
Georgia (country) neighbor
    RUSSIA, TURKEY, ARMENIA,
    BLACKSEA, AZERBAIJAN
Georgia (country) river   BZYB,
    RIONI, ARAGUI, INGURI,
    KHRAMI, KODORI, ALAZANI
Georgia (state)   *see also p. 615*
Georgia (state) city/town   ROME,
    MACON, ALBANY, ATHENS,
    DALTON, PLAINS, ATLANTA,
    AUGUSTA
Georgia (state) Indian   CREEK,
    CHEROKE
Georgia (state) island   JEKYLL,
    SAPELO, WASSAW,
    OSSABAW, SKIDAWAY
Georgia (state) lake   BANKS,
    WEISS, BURTON, CARTERS,
    CHATUGE, SINCLAIR
Georgia (state) river   FLINT,
    OCONEE, ALTAMAHA,
    SAVANNAH
Georgia (state) swamp
    OKEFENOKEE
Georgia (state) university   EMORY,
    MERCER, OGLETHORPE
Geraint wife   ENID
geranium   RUTA
Gerda's husband   FREY
germ   BUG, SEED, SPORE,
    VIRUS, MICROBE, BACTERIA;
    see SEED
German   HUN, BOCHE, JERRY,
    KRAUT, ALMAIN, TEUTON;
    see p. 570
German artist   MARC, DURER,
    ERNST, GROSZ, MALER,
    HOLBEIN, BECKMANN,
    ALTDORFER
German city/town   ULM, BONN,
    JENA, KIEL, KOLN, ESSEN,
    HALLE, MAINZ, AACHEN,
    BERLIN, BREMEN, ERFURT,
    MUNICH, COLOGNE,
    DRESDEN, HAMBURG, LEIPZIG,
    POTSDAM, ZWICKAU,
    BAYREUTH, DORTMUND,
    HANNOVER, STUTTGART,
    WIESBADEN
German composer   BACH,
    WEBER, WEILL, BRAHMS,

HANDEL, WAGNER, STRAUSS,
SCHUMANN, BEETHOVEN,
HINDEMITH, MENDELSSOHN
German dynasty SAXON,
HAPSBURG, CAROLINGIAN,
HOHENSTAUFEN
German kingdom HESSE,
SAXONY, HANOVER, PRUSSIA
German leader EBERT, HEUSS,
LUBKE, TALER, BRANDT,
ERHARD, ADENAUER,
BISMARCK
German measure AAM, FASS,
FUSS, STAB, ZOLL, EIMER,
FUDER, KANNE, KETTE,
MAASS, MASSEL, MORGEN,
STRICH, KLAFTER, SCHEFFEL
German money EURO, GROT,
MARK, T(H)ALER, PFENNIG,
BLAFFERT
German neighbor FRANCE,
POLAND, AUSTRIA,
DENMARK, NETHERLANDS,
SWITZERLAND
German poet HEINE, HESSE,
RILKE, GOETHE, SCHILLER
German river EMS, EDER, ELBE,
ODER, HAVEL, RHINE, SAALE,
SPREE, WESER, DANUBE
German rulers OTTO, EBERT,
HENRY, ADOLPH, ALBERT,
ARNULF, CONRAD, HITLER,
JOSEPH, RUDOLF, RUPERT,
CHARLES, FRANCIS, LEOPOLD,
LOTHAIR, RUDOLPH,
THERESA, CONRADIN,
MATTHIAS, FREDERICK,
SIGISMUND, WENCESLAUS
German state HESSE, BERLIN,
BREMEN, BAVARIA,
HAMBURG, SAXONY,
SAARLAND, THURINGIA
German weight LOT, PFUND,
STEIN, CENTNER
German words *see p. 570*
German writer BOLL, MANN,
GRIMM, HESSE, KAFKA,
BRECHT, GOETHE, JUNGER,
REMARQUE
germane APT, AKIN, FITTING,
RELEVANT, PERTINENT
Germanic language TAAL,
DUTCH, DANISH, GERMAN,
GOTHIC, ENGLISH, FAROESE,
FLEMISH, FRISIAN, SWEDISH,
YIDDISH, FRANKISH,
TEUTONIC, AFRIKAANS,
ICELANDIC, NORWEGIAN,
SCANDINAVIAN

Germany, capital of BERLIN
germfree CLEAN, ASEPTIC,
STERILIZED, ANTISEPTIC
germinate GROW, SPROUT
Gershwin IRA, GEORGE
Gershwin song HIHO, SOON,
OH KAY, VODKA, SWANEE,
WHO CARES
gest(e) DEED, EXPLOIT,
ADVENTURE
Gestapo chief HIMMLER
gesture NOD, MIME, WAVE,
TOKEN, ACTION, MOTION
get NAB, EARN, GAIN,
ATTAIN, OBTAIN, SECURE
get back to ANSWER, RESPOND
get by COPE, SURVIVE
get down EAT, SWALLOW
get it? SEE
get off SEND, DESCEND,
DISMOUNT
get out SCAT, SHOO, SCRAM,
SKIDOO, VAMOSE, DEPLANE,
DETRAIN, SALVAGE,
SKIDDOO, VAMOOSE
get past ELUDE, ESCAPE
Get Smart names DON,
ADAMS, CHIEF, BROOKS,
FELDON, MAXWELL
get well HEAL, RECOVER
getaway LAM, ESCAPE, FLIGHT
get-together BEE, TEA, PARTY,
SOCIAL, REUNION
Gettysburg general LEE, MEADE
getup OUTFIT, COSTUME
get-up-and — GO
gewgaw TOY, GAUD, BAUBLE,
FEGARY, TRIFLE, TRINKET
Ghana, capital of ACCRA
Ghanian city/town WA, AXIM,
KADE, TEMA, ACCRA,
KUMASI, OBUASI, SALAGA,
TAMALE
Ghanian language *see KWA,*
GUR
Ghanian money CEDI, PESEWA
Ghanian neighbor TOGO,
IVORYCOAST, BURKINAFASO
Ghanian native GA, EWE,
AKAN, GUAN, FANTI,
GONJA, GURMA, ASHANTI,
DAGOMBA
Ghanian park BIA, MOLE,
DIGYA, KAKUM
Ghanian river BIA, TANO,
VOLTA
ghastly GRIM, LURID, PALLID,
MACABRE
ghetto SLUM, QUARTER

ghost KER, BHUT, HANT, JUBA,
WAFF, LARVA, LEMUR,
MANES, SHADE, SPOOK,
UMBRA, CASPER, SHADOW,
WRAITH, EIDOLON,
PHANTOM, SPECTER; see SPIRIT
ghoulish GRISLY, GHASTLY,
MACABRE, FIENDISH
GI YANK, DOGFACE,
JARHEAD, SOLDIER
giant(ess) ANAK, BANA, ETEN,
GROA, LOKI, NATT, NORN,
SAPH, SUKR, URTH, YMER,
YMIR, ATLAS, BALOR, GYGES,
JUMBO, ORION, SKULD, TITAN,
BESTLA, BUNYAN, FAFNIR,
ANTAEUS, CYCLOPS,
GOLIATH, MAMMOTH,
TITANIC, GARGANTUA
giant killer JACK, DAVID,
APOLLO
Giant's family OTTS
Giant ranch REATA
gibberish JABBER, JARGON,
CHATTER, TWADDLE,
CLAPTRAP, MUMBOJUMBO
gibbet GALLOWS, SCAFFOLD
gibbon see APE
gibe RIB, JEER, FLEER, SNEER,
TAUNT
Gibraltar CALPE
Gibson garnish ONION
giddy DIZZY, WOOZY,
FLIGHTY, FRIVOLOUS
gift DOW, SOP, TIP, ALMS,
BOON, DOLE, ENAM, BONUS,
LEGACY, TALENT, HANDSEL
gifted ABLE, BRAINY,
TALENTED
gig JOB, NAP, WHIM, CHAISE
gigantic HUGE, VAST,
IMMENSE, MAMMOTH,
MASSIVE, TITANIC,
COLOSSAL, ENORMOUS
giggle LAUGH, TITTER,
CHUCKLE, SNICKER
Gil Blas author LESAGE
Gilbert and Sullivan actor
SAVOYARD
Gilbert and Sullivan operetta
MIKADO, PIRATES, IOLANTHE,
PATIENCE, PINAFORE
Gilbert Island BERU, MAKIN,
TARAWA, ABAIANG,
NONOUTI, ABERBAMA,
TABITEUEA, BUTARITARI
gild DORE, ENRICH, AUREATE
Gilda's father RIGOLETTO
— in Gilead BALM

Gilead relative ULAM,
JEPHTHAH
Gilgit language SHINA
gill GUT, BROOK, WATTLE
Gilligan's Island names TINA,
LOVEY, BACKUS, DENVER,
GINGER, HOWELL, LOUISE,
MARYANN, SKIPPER,
THURSTON, PROFESSOR
gin NET, SLOE, (EN)TRAP,
RUMMY, SNARE, GENEVA,
SCHNAP(P)S
ginger SPICE, CURCUMA,
CARDAMOM
Ginger's partner FRED
Gioconda MONA LISA
Gioconda painter DA VINCI
Giotto work MURAL,
MADONNA
gipsy see GYPSY
giraffe see RUMINANT
gird BIND, GIBE, EQUIP, SCOFF
girder BEAM, TBAR, TEAR,
IBEAM, TRUSS
girdle OBI, BAND, BELT, CEST,
SASH, ZONA, CESTUS,
CINGLE, CORSET; see ENCLOSE
girl SIS, CHIT, DAME, JILL,
LASS, MAID, MINX, MISS,
SNAB, BELLE, FRAIL, SKIRT,
DAMSEL, HOYDEN, MAIDEN,
TOMBOY, COLLEEN; see
WOMAN, FEMALE
Girl Scout DAISY, BROWNIE
Girl Scouts founder LOW
girlfriend MOLL, STEADY,
SQUEEZE
girth BELT, SIZE, CINCH,
GIRDLE, RESTRAINT,
CIRCUMFERENCE
gist NUB, CORE, CRUX, PITH,
POINT, KERNEL, ESSENCE
give GIE, AWARD, GRANT,
ASSIGN, BESTOW, CONFER,
DONATE, IMPART
give and — TAKE
give away REVEAL, DISCLOSE
give out END, FAIL, TIRE,
ALLOT, OFFER, ASSIGN
give up CEDE, QUIT, LETGO,
WAIVE, YIELD, FORSAKE,
RENOUNCE, SURRENDER,
CAPITULATE
gizzard CRAW, GIBLET,
THROAT, STOMACH
glacial deposit AS, OS, ASAR,
KAME, OSAR, PAHA, ESCAR,
ESKAR, ESKER, PLACER,
MORAINE

glacial ice	FIRN, NEVE, SERAC
glaciation stage	CARY, GUNZ,
RISS, WURM, ACHEN, IOWAN,	
SAALE, ELSTER, MINDEL,	
MANKATO, VALDERS	
glacier	ICECAP, PIEDMONT
glacier, facing a	STOSS
glad	HAPPY, PLEASED,
CHEERFUL	
gladiator trainer	LANISTA
gladly	FAIN, LIEF, READILY,
WILLINGLY	
glance	LEER, LOOK, PEEK,
SCAN, SKIM, APERCU,	
GLIMPSE	
gland	ADEN, GLANS, PINEAL,
SPLEEN, THYMUS, CAROTID,	
PAROTID, THYROID,	
EXOCRINE, PANCREAS,	
PROSTATE, ENDOCRINE,	
HOLOCRINE, LYMPHATIC,	
MEROCRINE, PITUITARY	
gland, edible	RIS, NOIX
gland secretion	BILE, GALL,
SALIVA, CERUMEN,	
CHALONE, AUTACOID; see	
HORMONE	
glare	LOOK, STARE, GLOWER
glaring	RANK, PLAIN,
VIVID, BRAZEN, BRIGHT,	
BLATANT, EVIDENT,	
OBVIOUS	
glass	CALX, FRIT, LENX, PANE,
PONY, FRITT, SMALT, UVIOL,	
CULLET, GOBLET, MIRROR,	
RUMMER, STRASS, CRYSTAL,	
LALIQUE, OPALINE, PARISON,	
SNIFTER, TUMBLER,	
OBSIDIAN	
glass ingredient	FRIT, LIME,
SAND, SODA, ALKALI,	
POTASH, SILICA, ZAFFIR	
glasses	see EYEGLASSES
glassmaker	GLAZIER
glassmaker's rod	PONTY,
PUNTY, PONTIL	
glassy	CLEAR, VITRIC,
CRYSTAL, HYALINE,	
VITREOUS, TRANSPARENT	
Glaucus' father	MINOS,
SISYPHUS	
Glaucus' slayer	AJAX
glaze	COAT, FILM, GLOSS,
ENAMEL, VENEER, COATING	
gleam	RAY, BEAM, GLOW,
GLINT, GLOZE, LUSTER,	
GLISTEN	
glean	REAP, GATHER,
COLLECT	

glee	JOY, MIRTH, GAIETY,
DELIGHT, ELATION	
glen	DALE, DELL, VALE,
DINGLE, VALLEY	
glib	OILY, BLAND, FACILE,
FLUENT	
glide	SKI, SCUD, SKID, SKIM,
SKIP, SLIP, SKATE, SLIDE,	
SASHAY	
glimmer	GLEAM, SHINE,
FLICKER	
glimpse	PEEK, PEEP, GLANCE,
FORETASTE	
glint	FLASH, GLEAM
glisten	SHINE, GLEAM,
GLITTER, SPARKLE,	
CORUSCATE	
glitter	FLASH, GLINT,
GLISTEN, SPANGLE, SPARKLE	
gloat	CROW, BOAST, EXULT,
REVEL	
global position figure	
LAT(ITUDE), LONG(ITUDE)	
globe	ORB, BALL, CLEW,
EARTH, SPHERE	
globule	BEAD, BLOB, DROP
gloom	MURK, BLUES, DUMPS
gloomy	SAD, WAN, BLUE,
DARK, DOUR, MURK, ADUSK,	
FERAL, DREAR(Y), MOROSE	
glorify	LAUD, EXALT, EXTOL,
PRAISE	
glorious	SUPERB, SPLENDID
glory	FAME, EXALT, KUDOS,
RENOWN, SPLENDOR	
gloss	SHEEN, EXCUSE,
EXEGESIS	
glossary	CLAVIS, LEXICON
glossy	GLIB, GLACE, NITID,
SLICK	
glottal stop	STOD, CATCH,
STOSS	
glove	CUFF, MITT, CESTUS,
SLIPON	
glove compartment	CUBBY
glove shape	TRANK
glow	BLAZE, EXCEL, FLUSH,
RUTILATE	
glower	FROWN, SCOWL,
GRIMACE	
glowing	ARDENT, ASHINE,
CANDENT, LAMBENT	
Gluck opera	ORFEO, ARMIDA
glucoside	GEIN, RUTIN,
ESTEVIN	
glue	GUM, AGAR, PASTE,
CEMENT, MUCILAGE	
glum	LOW, SAD, SOUR, SULKY,
MOROSE, GLOOMY, SULLEN	

glut	CLOY, CRAM, FILL, PACK, SATE, GORGE, STUFF, EXCESS, SURFEIT
glutton	HOG, PIG, HELLUO, GOURMAND, CORMORANT
gluttonous	HUNGRY, PIGGISH, VORACIOUS
gluttony	GREED, EDACITY, VORACITY
gnarl	NUR, KNUR, NURR, SNAG, GROWL, KNURR
gnat	MIDGE; see FLY
gnaw	BITE, CHEW, FRET, ERODE, NIBBLE, CORRODE, TORMENT
gnome	see ELF
Gnostic	MANDEAN
gnu	KOKOON; see ANTELOPE
go	DIE, GAE, MOVE, QUIT, STIR, SUIT, LEAVE
go around	ORBIT, ROTATE, REVOLVE
go astray	ERR, SIN, ABERRATE
go away	SCAT, SHOO, SCRAM, LEAVE, DEPART
go beyond	OVERSTEP
go by	PASS
go off	MADDEN, EXPLODE
Goa capital	PANJIM, PANAJI
goad	EGG, GAD, PROD, SPUR, URGE, ANKUS, PRICK, STICK
go-ahead	OK(AY), ALL CLEAR, GREEN LIGHT
goal	AIM, META, POST, TAPE, BOURN, THULE, BOURNE
goat	KID, TUR, IBEX, JAAL, KRAS, TAHR, TEGG, THAR, BILLY, NANNY, PASAN, ANGORA, CAPRID, JHARAL, PASANG, MARKHOR
goat genus	CAPRA
goat, get one's	IRK, RILE, ANNOY, GETTO
goat, young	KID
goatish	CAPRINE, HIRCINE
goatsucker	PISK, POTOO, BULLBAT, OILBIRD, GUACHARO, NIGHTJAR, POOR WILL, NIGHTHAWK, WHIPPOORWILL
gob	TAR, LUMP, MASS, SAILOR, SEAMAN
gobble	JOLLOP
go-between	AGENT, MEDIATOR, MIDDLEMAN
Gobi Desert	SHAMO, HANHAI
goblet	TASS, BOCAL, HANAP, CHALICE; see GLASS

goblin	NIS, BHUT, POOK, PUCA, PUCK, NISSE; see ELF
god(s)	DI, DEI, DII, DEUS, IDOL, DEITY, TOTEM, PARAGON; see p. 645
God	IAM, JAH, JHVH, YHVH, ALLAH, ADONAI, ELOHIM, YAHWEH, JEHOVAH
god, false	BAAL, DAGON, BAALIM, MAMMON, MOLOCH
goddess	DEA, STAR(LET); see GRACES, NORNS, HORAE; see p. 645
godfather	PADRINO, SPONSOR
godless	PAGAN, IMPIOUS, ATHEISTIC
godlike	DIVINE
godly	PIOUS, DEVOUT
Godot	NO SHOW
godparent	CUMMER, SPONSOR
Goethe character	FAUST, MIGNON, WERTHER, MEPHISTOPHELES
Goethe's city	WEIMAR
Goethe work	FAUST, EGMONT
Gog and —	MAGOG
go-getter	DOER, HUSTLER, ACHIEVER
Gogol work	OVERCOAT, DEADSOULS, TARASBULBA
Goidelic language	ERSE, MANX
going away request	WRITE
goiter	STRUMA
gold	AU, ORO, SOL, CYME, GILT, AURUM, ORMOLU
Gold Coast	GHANA
Gold Coast negro	GA
gold coin	LATU, LION, LIRA, OBAN, TALI, ANGEL, DARIC, DUCAT, EAGLE, KRONE, LOUIS, MOHUR, OBANG, SCUDO, TOMAN, GUINEA, PISTOLE, DOUBLOON, IMPERIAL
gold digger	VAMP, FLIRT, MINER
gold, imitation	OROIDE, ORMOLU, PINCHBECK
golden	AURIC, DURRY, AUREATE
Golden Age	MILLENNIUM
golden apple character	IDUN, ATLAS, LADON, PARIS, HESPERID, APHRODITE
Golden Fleece character	JASON, MEDEA, AEETES, ARGONAUT
Golden Girls names	ROSE, BETTY, WHITE, ARTHUR, SOPHIA, BLANCHE, DOROTHY, BEATRICE

Golden State **CA, CALIFORNIA**	good news **GOSPEL, EVANGEL**
golf *see also p. 710*	goods **FEE, BONA, STOCK,**
golf club **IRON, WOOD, CLEEK,**	**WARES, WRACK, FREIGHT**
SPOON, WEDGE, DRIVER,	goods in sea **LAGAN, LIGAN,**
MASHIE, PUTTER, BRASSIE,	**JETSAM, LAGEND, FLOTSAM**
MIDIRON, NIBLICK	goof **ERR, DOLT, BONER,**
golf club part **TOE, FACE, GRIP,**	**BLUNDER**
HEAD, HEEL, NECK, NOSE,	goon **HOOD, THUG, RUFFIAN,**
HOSEL, SHAFT	**HOODLUM**
golf course part **TEE, TRAP,**	goose **DUPE, GULL, NENE,**
GREEN, ROUGH, BUNKER,	**WAVY, BRANT, CHAJA,**
HAZARD, DOGLEG, FAIRWAY	**SOLAN, GANDER, GREYLAG,**
golf organization **PGA, USGA**	**GRAYLAG, SCREAMER**
golf term **OB, LIE, PAR, PUT,**	goose egg **ZERO**
TEE, TOE, YIP, BAFF, BONE,	goose genus **CHEN, ANSER**
CHIP, FORE, HOOK, LOFT,	goose, young **GOSLING**
NOSE, PUTT, YIPS, BOGEY,	Gopher State **MN, MINNESOTA**
BOGIE, DIVOT, EAGLE, LINKS,	Gorbachev wife **RAISA**
PITCH, ROUGH, SLICE,	gore **CRUOR, INSET, GUSSET;**
BIRDIE, BISQUE, DORMIE,	*see STAB*
SCLAFF, STANCE, MULLIGAN	gorge **CLOY, GLUT, KHOR,**
golf tournament **(L)PGA, OPEN,**	**CHASM, FLUME, GULLY,**
PROAM, RYDER, SKINS,	**KLOOF, STRID, TANGI,**
MASTERS, SENIORS	**CANYON, CLOUGH, RAVINE**
Golgotha **CALVARY**	Gorgon **MEDUSA, STHENO,**
Goliath's home **GATH**	**EURYALE, JEZEBEL**
Goliath slayer **DAVID**	Gorgon parents **CETO,**
Gomer husband **HOSEA**	**PHORCYS**
gomuti **EJOO, PALM, SAGO,**	gorilla **GOON, THUG, BRUTE;**
ARENGA	*see APES*
gondola **CABIN**	gospel **JOHN, LUKE, MARK,**
gondolier **BOATMAN**	**DOGMA, TRUTH, EVANGEL,**
gondolier's song **BARCAROLE**	**MATTHEW, EVANGILE,**
gone **AGO, OUT, PAST, YORE**	**SYNOPTIC**
Gone with the Wind character	gossamer(y) **THIN, FILMY,**
OHARA, RHETT, ASHLEY,	**GAUZY, DIAPHANOUS**
BUTLER, MELANIE,	gossip **CAT, EME, GUP, DIRT,**
SCARLETT	**TALE, ONDIT, CLAVER,**
Gone with the Wind location	**NORATE, TATTLE, KLAT(S)CH**
TARA	Goth **BERIG, EURIC, ALARIC,**
Goneril relative **LEAR, REGAN,**	**FILIMER, RODERICK,**
ALBANY, CORDELIA	**LEOVIGILD, THEODORIC**
gong **TOCSIN, TAM(TAM)**	Gottfried relative **ELSA**
goober **PEANUT**	gouge **ROUT, CHEAT, FRAUD,**
good **BON, BEIN, MORAL,**	**EXTORT, SWINDLE**
PUCKA, PUKIKA, SOUND,	goulash **STEW, RAGOUT,**
VALID	**MULLIGAN**
Good Book **BIBLE**	Gounod opera **FAUST, ROMEO**
Good Queen Bess **ORIANA,**	gourd **PEPO, MELON, SQUASH,**
ELIZABETH	**PUMPKIN, CALABASH;** *see*
good-bye **AVE, CIAO, TATA,**	**FRUITS**
ADIEU, ALOHA, SOLONG,	gourmand **EPICURE, GLUTTON**
FAREWELL	gourmet **EPICURE,**
good-for-nothing **BUM, ORRA,**	**GASTRONOME**
IDLER, LOAFER, WASTREL	gout **BLOB, GOUT, CULVERT,**
good-looking **FAIR, COMELY,**	**GONAGRA, PODAGRA**
PRETTY, HANDSOME	govern **RUN, CURB, RULE,**
good-natured **AMIABLE,**	**REIGN, GUIDE, BRIDLE,**
PLEASANT	**DIRECT**

governess	NANNY, TUTOR, DUENNA
government	RULE, SWAY, STATE, POLITY, REGIME(N), DOMINION
government control	REGIE
governor	BEY, DEY, VALI, WALI, PASHA, PILOT, TUPAN, DYNAST, EPARCH, REGENT, SATRAP, SHERIF, SHOGUN, TUCHUN, TYCOON, VAIVOD, VOIVOD, KHEDIVE, SHEREEF, VICEROY, VOIVODE, HOSPODAR, REGULATOR
gown	ROBE, DRESS, FROCK, MANTUA
Goya subject	MAJA
grab	HOG, TAKE, ANNEX, SEIZE, CLUTCH, SNATCH, CAPTURE
grabber	CLAW, TONGS
Gracchus brother	GAIUS
grace	TACT, ADORN, CHARM, FAVOR, MERCY, PARDON
graceful	FEAT, GENT, GAINLY, SVELTE, SYLPHIC
graceless	GAWKY, CLUMSY, AWKWARD, INELEGANT
Graces	AGLAIA, THALIA, CHARITES, EUPHROSYNE
Graces parents	ZEUS, EURYNOME
Gracie Mansion resident	see NEW YORK CITY MAYOR
gracious	GENIAL, URBANE
grade	MARK, RANK, RATE, SORT, STEP, APLUS, CLASS, LEVEL, SLANT
gradual	SLOW, STEADY, MEASURED, MODERATE
graduate	GRAD, PASS, ALUMNA, ALUMNUS, DIPLOMATE
graduated	SCALAR
graduation sight	CAP, GOWN, TASSEL, MORTARBOARD
Graeae	ENYO, DEINO, PEMPHREDO
Graeae relatives	CETA, GORGONS, PHORCYS
Graf —	SPEE
graft	BUD, IMP, CION, SLIP, BRIBE, CLAVE, SCION, SHOOT, INARCH, KICKBACK, BAKSHEESH
grail	AMA, CUP, CHALICE, SANGREAL
grain	BIT, BRAN, DURA, MEAL, MILO, SAME, SEED, DOORA,

	DOURA, DURRA, GRIST, SPECK, WHEAT, DHURRA, HEGARI, TEMPER; see CEREAL
grammar	SYNTAX, WORDING, PHRASING
grammatical term	MODE, MOOD, PARSE, TELIC, ACTIVE, COPULA, FINITE, GENDER, ARTICLE, JUSSIVE, PASSIVE, SUBJECT, SYNESIS, PARADIGM, PARTICLE, PREDICATE, SYLLEPSIS; see CASE, TENSE
granary	BIN, CRIB, GOLA, GUNJ, SILO, GUNGE, JAGIR, GRANGE, JAGEER, JAGHIR
grand	LOFTY, PIANO, AUGUST, STATELY, IMPOSING, MAJESTIC
grand mal	EPILEPSY
grand, opposite of	MODEST
grandchild	OY(E)
grandfather	ATAVUS, GRAMPS, GRANDPA
grandmother	NANA, GRANMA, GRANNY, GRANDMA
grandparental	AVAL
grandson	NEPOTE
grandstand	STUNT, SHOWOFF, BLEACHERS
Granite State	NH, NEW HAMPSHIRE
grant	CEDE, GIFT, GIVE, ENAM, MISE, AWARD, CONFER, DEMISE, PATENT, PERMIT, REMISE, CHARTER, CONCEDE, SUBSIDY
grant source	NEA, NEH
grantor	DONOR
granular	GRAINY
grape	UVA, BACO, UGNI, GAMAY, PINOT, SIRAH, TOKAY, VITIS, MALAGA, MUSCAT, MUSKAT, RAISIN, WAMPEE, CATAWBA, CONCORD, FURMINT, MALMSEY, CABERNET, DOLCETTO, GRENACHE, MALVASIA, NEBBIOLO, PALOMINO, PROSECCO, RIESLING, RULANDER, SEMILLON, SYLVANER, SAUVIGNON, ZINFANDEL, CHARDONNAY
grape disease	ESCA, APOPLEXY
grape growing site	VINERY, VINEYARD
grape syrup	DIBS, MUST, SAPA, STUM

grapefruit	POMELO, SHADDOCK		JERRY GARCIA, ROBERT HUNTER
grapelike	UVAL, UVIC	gratify	SATE, PLEASE, ARRIDE
Grapes of Wrath author	STEINBECK	gratinate	BROWN, CRISP
		grating	GRID, RASP, GRILL, RASPY, GRILLE, HOARSE, LATTICE
Grapes of Wrath names	AL, MA, JIM, TOM, JOAD, NOAH, OKIE, ROSE, CASEY, CONNIE, SHARON		
		gratis	FREE, ONTHEHOUSE
		gratitude	THANKS
grapevine	RUMOR, PIPELINE, RUMOR MILL	gratuitous	FREE, GRATIS
		gratuity	FEE, TIP, BOON, VAIL, PILON, CUMSHA(W), BAKSHEESH
graph	CHART, DIAGRAM, FLOWCHART		
graph line(s)	AXIS, AXES	grave	DULL, ETCH, CARVE, FOSSE, MOUND, SOBER, STAID, SUANT, BARROW, SEDATE, SOMBER; see TOMB
graphic	REAL, VIVID		
graphite	KISH, LEAD, PLUMBAGO		
		graveclothes	SHROUD, CEREMENT
grapnel	DRAG, ANCHOR, GRAPLIN		
		gravel	OS, ESKER, BEACH, GEEST, BALLAST
grapple	GRASP, CLUTCH, WRESTLE		
		graven	CARVED, ETCHED, SCULPTED
— gras	FOIE		
grasp	KEN, SEE, GRAB, GRIP, HENT, HOLD, CLASP, EREPT, SEIZE, CLUTCH, UNDERSTAND	gravestone	SLAB, STELA, STELE, MARKER, STELAE, STELAI
		graveyard	BONEYARD, CEMETERY
grass	HAY, POA, AIRA, ALFA, BOHO, BOJO, CANE, COIX, DISS, DOOB, DOUB, ICHU, JAVA, LAWN, MAND, NETI, PILI, RHIA, ULLA, ADLAI, ADLAY, ALANG, AVENA, BROME, COGON, OTATE, STIPA, BAMBOO, DARNEL, FESCUE, ESPARTO, EULALIA, TIMOTHY; see CEREAL	gravity	WEIGHT, SOLEMNITY
		gravy	JUS, SAUCE, PROFIT
		gray	DULL, HOAR, ASHEN, HOARY, STEEL; see p. 531
		graze	RUB, FEED, NICK, AGIST, TOUCH, BROWSE, GLANCE
		grease	OIL, LARD, MORT, SAIM, SUET, BRIBE, AXUNGE
		greasewood	CHICO, ORACHE, CHAMISO, HOPSAGE
grasshopper	CAGN, DRUM, GRIG, WETA, BRUKE, RACER, ROACH, STICK, CHANGA, EARWIG, EMPUSA, LOCUST, MANTID, MANTIS, PHASMA, BLATTID, CATYDID, CRACKET, CRICKET, DRUMMER, GRYLLID, KATYDID, KNOCKER, MANTOID, PROPHET, STICKBUG	greasy	OILY, FATTY, PINGUID
		greasy spoon	CAFE, EATS, DINER, EATERY
		great	BARO, SUPER, AUGUST, MICKLE
		Great Barrier island	OTEA
		Great Britain, capital of	LONDON
		Great Commoner	CLAY, PITT, BRYAN, STEVENS
grasshopper genus	BLATTA, GRYLLUS	Great Expectations author	DICKENS
grassland	LEA, MEAD, VELD, PAMPA, RANGE, SWARD, VELDT, PASTURE, PRAIRIE, SAVANNA	Great Expectations name	JOE, PIP, ABEL, PIRRIP, BENTLEY, ESTELLA, HAVISHAM, MAGWITCH
grate	JAR, RASP, CHARK, CREAK, GRIDE, ABRADE, IRRITATE	Great Lake	ERIE, HURON, ONTARIO, MICHIGAN, SUPERIOR
grateful	BEHOLDEN, THANKFUL	Great Lakes fish	PIKE, CISCO, TULLIBEE, MUSKELLUNGE
Grateful Dead member	MICKEY HART, PHIL LESH, BOB WEIR,	great number	LAC, HEAP, HOST, LAKH, GALAXY, LEGION

Great White Father **PRESIDENT**	**CYCLADES, SPORADES,**
Great White Way **RIALTO,**	**DODECANESE;** *see p. 603*
BROADWAY	Greek region **CRETE, ATTICA,**
Greater Antilles island **CUBA,**	**EPIRUS, THRACE, THESSALY**
CAYMAN, JAMAICA,	Greek measure **PIK, ACAENA,**
NAVASSA, HISPANIOLA,	**BACHEL, BARILE, COTULA,**
PUERTORICO	**GRAMME, KOILON, PALAME,**
grebe **FINFOOT, PYGOPOD,**	**STADION, STREMMA**
DABCHICK, DIDAPPER	Greek measure (ancient) **BEMA,**
Greece **ELLAS, ACHAEA,**	**POUS, CHOUS, PYGON,**
ACHAIA, ATTICA, HELLAS;	**DICHAS, ACAENA, ORGYIA,**
see **GREEK**	**AMPHORA, STADIUM**
Greece, capital of **ATHENS**	Greek money **EURO, OBOL,**
greed **AVARICE, AVIDITY,**	**LEPTON, STATER, DRACHMA**
EDACITY, CUPIDITY	Greek mountain **OETA, OSSA,**
greedy **GRIPPLE, COVETOUS,**	**ATHOS, OTHRYS, PINDUS,**
ESURIENT	**CYLLENE, OLYMPUS,**
Greek **ATTIC, ARGIVE,**	**PARNASSUS, ERYMANTHUS**
AEOLIAN, GRECIAN,	Greek neighbor **TURKEY,**
HELLENE, HELLENIC	**ALBANIA, BULGARIA,**
Greek alphabet **MU, NU, PI, XI,**	**MACEDONIA**
CHI, ETA, PHI, PSI, RHO, TAU,	Greek philosopher **ZENO,**
BETA, IOTA, ZETA, ALPHA,	**PLATO, TIMON, THALES,**
DELTA, GAMMA, KAPPA,	**DIOGENES, SOCRATES,**
OMEGA, SIGMA, THETA,	**ARISTOTLE**
LAMBDA, EPSILON, OMICRON,	Greek poet **ION, ARION,**
UPSILON	**HOMER, HESIOD, PINDAR,**
Greek author **ZENO, AESOP,**	**SAPPHO, CORINNA,**
HOMER, PLATO, TIMON,	**ANACREON, MENANDER**
ALCMAN, HESIOD, PINDAR,	Greek river **PENEUS, ALPHEUS,**
SAPPHO, STRABO, THALES,	**ACHELOUS, CEPHISUS,**
ALCAEUS, PLUTARCH	**ARAKHTHOS**
Greek city/town **ARTA, CANEA,**	Greek sea **CRETE, AEGEAN,**
CORFU, DRAMA, KHIOS,	**IONIAN, MIRTOON**
LAMIA, VATHY, VOLOS,	Greek statesman **PERICLES,**
ATHENS, EDESSA, KHALKI,	**ARISTIDES**
KILKIS, KOZANI, LEVKAS,	Greek warrior **AJAX, ACAMAS,**
PATRAS, PYRGOS, RHODES,	**ACHILLES, DIOMEDES,**
SERRAI, SPARTA, VEROIA,	**ODYSSEUS**
XANTHI, MYTILENE	Greek weight **MNA, OKA,**
Greek dialect **AEOLIC, ATTIC,**	**MINA, LITRA, DRAMME,**
DORIC, IONIC, KOINE,	**OBULUS, STATER, DRACHMA**
MINOAN, AEOLIAN, CYPRIAN,	Greek weight (ancient) **DIOBOL,**
CYPRIOT, BOEOTIAN,	**CHALCON**
MYCENEAN	green **RAW, VERD, LEAFY,**
Greek dramatis **THESPIS,**	**CALLOW, VERDANT;**
MENANDER, AESCHYLUS,	*see p. 531,* **MONEY**
EURIPIDES, SOPHOCLES,	Green Acres names **EB, EVA,**
ARISTOPHANES	**SAM, FRED, LISA, DORIS,**
Greek gulf **ARTA, KHANIA,**	**EDDIE, GABOR, ALBERT,**
MESARA, ARGOLIS,	**OLIVER**
CORINTH, LAKONIA, MESSINI,	Green Gables girl **ANNE**
SARONIC, SALONIKA,	Green Hornet sidekick **KATO**
THERMAIC, TORONAIC,	green light **OK, OKAY, PERMIT,**
KIPARISSIA	**GOAHEAD**
Greek house **FRAT**	Greenland, capital of **NUUK,**
Greek island **CHIOS, CRETE,**	**GOTHAB**
SAMOS, EUBOEA, IONIAN,	Greenland town **ETAH, THULE,**
LEMNOS, LESBOS, THASOS,	**GODHAVN**

Green Mansions author	HUDSON
Green Mansions name	ABEL, RIMA
Green Mountain State	VT, VERMONT
greenhorn	TYRO, IKONA, ROOKIE
Greenland settlement	ETAH
greet(ing)	HI, AVE, HAIL, ALOHA, HELLO, NETOP, ACCOIL, CURTSY, SALUTE, WELCOME
gregarious	SOCIAL, FRIENDLY, OUTGOING, SOCIABLE
gremlin	BUG, JINX, GNOME
Grenada, capital of	STGEORGES
Grenada island	HOG
Grenada money	DOLLAR
grenade	BOMB, SHELL
Grendel slayer	BEOWULF
Grenoble river	ISERE
greyhound	SALUKI, WHIPPET
griddle	PAN, GRILL
griddle cake	CRUMPET, PANCAKE
grief	WOE, DOLE, TEEN, DOLOR, MISERY
Grieg hero(ine)	ASE, GYNT, PEER, ANITRA
grievance	BEEF, GRIPE, SCORE, GRAVAMEN
grieve	CRY, MOURN, LAMENT, SADDEN, DISTRESS
grievous	INTENSE, FLAGRANT
grill	GRID, QUIZ, RACK, BROIL, TAVERN, GRATING, HIBACHI
grim	SET, DOUR, STERN, MACABRE
Grim Reaper	DEATH
grimace	MOW, MOUE, MOWE, POUT, FLEER, SCOWL, SMIRK, MURGEON
grime	DIRT, SMUT, SOOT, COLLY, FILTH
Grimm character	GRETEL, HANSEL, (TOM) THUMB, RAPUNZEL, SNOW WHITE
grind	BRAY, CHEW, CRAM, GRIT, HONE, MILL, WHET, CRUSH, GNASH, RAT RACE
grinder	GRIT, HONE, MANO, MILL, MOLAR, TOOTH, METATE, MORTAR, MULLER, PESTLE
grip	BAG, LUG, HOLD, CLAMP, CLASP, GRASP, CLUTCH, HANDLE, VALISE, CONTROL, STAGEHAND

gripe	BEEF, BITCH, MUTTER, GRUMBLE, COMPLAIN
grippe	FLU, COLD
grisly	GRIM, MORBID, GHASTLY, GRUESOME
grist	MEAL
grist for the —	MILL
grit	SAND, NERVE, PLUCK, GRAVEL, METTLE
grits	KASHA, HOMINY
groggy	DRUNK, TIPSY, SLEEPY
grommet	RING, LOOP, BECKET, EYELET
groom	PAGE, SAIS, SICE, SYCE, CURRY, TRAIN, OSTLER, EQUERRY, HOSTLER, BENEDICT
groove	RUT, CHASE, CROZE, FLUTE, SCARF, STRIA, RABBET, RAGGLE, RUNNEL, SULCUS
grooved	LIRATE, STRIATE
grope	FEEL, PROBE, FUMBLE
Gropius school	BAUHAUS
gross	ICKY, RANK, CRASS, CRUDE, VULGAR, GLARING
grotesque	ODD, FREAK, GOTHIC, BIZARRE
grotto	see CAVE
grouch	CRAB, SULK, GRUMBLE(R), CURMUDGEON
grouchy	CROSS, TESTY, GRUMPY
ground	SET, LAND, SOIL, BASIS, FOUND, TERRAIN
ground breaker	HOE, PICK, SHOVEL
grounded	ASHORE, KEPTIN
groundhog	MARMOT, WOODCHUCK
Groundhog Day	CANDLEMAS
groundless	BASELESS, UNFOUNDED
grounds	LEES, BASIS, DREGS, PROOF, CAMPUS, ESTATE, REASON, GARDENS, RESIDUE, SEDIMENT
group	ERA, NYE, SET, BAND, BLOC, BODY, CREW, TEAM, CADRE, CLASS, CORPS, FLEET, GENUS, CLAQUE, MUSTER, PHYLUM, SUBSET, DIORAMA; see BEVY
grouper	GAG, CONY, HIND, MERO, CONEY, GUASA, SCAMP, AGUAJI, BONACI, CHERNA, GROPER, HAPUKU, WARSAW, GOURAMI, SEABASS, WHAPUKU

groupie	FAN, FOLLOWER
grouse	GRUMBLE, COMPLAIN;
	see PHEASANT
grouse, young	CHEEPER
grove	HOLT, TOPE, COPSE,
	NEMUS
grovel	FAWN, WORM, COWER
grow	WAX, BREED, RAISE,
	ACCRUE, MATURE, SPROUT,
	THRIVE
growing out	ENATE
Growing Pains names	BEN(NY),
	GOLD, LUKE, MIKE, CAROL,
	JASON, NOBLE, MAGGIE,
	SEAVER, CHELSEA, CHRISSY,
	DICAPRIO
growl	YAR, GIRN, GNAR,
	GURL, YARR, YIRR, SNARL,
	GRUMBLE
grown	ADULT, MATURE
growth	WEN, CORN, MOLE,
	WART, POLYP, TUMOR,
	CANCER, CLAVUS
grub	DIG, CHOW, EATS,
	LARVA, ASSART
grubby	DINGY, DIRTY,
	SHABBY
grudge	ENVY, PIQUE, SPITE,
	ANIMUS, MALICE, ILLWILL
gruel	ATOLE, BURGOO,
	CAUDLE, LOBLOLLY
grueling	HARD, TOUGH,
	TAXING, ARDUOUS
gruesome	GRIM, GRISLY,
	MACABRE
gruff	RUDE, HARSH, SURLY
grumble	HONE, GRIPE,
	GROWL, GROUCH, MUTTER
grunt	RONCO, SNORT; *see*
	SNAPPER
Guam	GUAHAN
Guam, capital of	AGANA
Guam port	APRA
guano	MANURE, TUATARA
guarantee	BOND, CAGE, AVAIL,
	SURETY, WARRANT,
	SCHOLIUM
guard	TILE(R), WATCH,
	BANTAY, CONVOY, FENDER,
	GHAFIR, PATROL, PICKET,
	SENTRY, SHIELD, DRABANT,
	OSTIARY, SENTINEL
guard dog	SNARLER,
	SHEPHERD
guarded	WARY, LEERY,
	CAUTIOUS
guardhouse	BRIG, HOOSEGOW
guardian	ARGUS, CUSTOS,
	WARDEN, CURATOR,

	TRUSTEE, TUTELAR,
	CERBERUS
Guatemala, capital of	
	GUATEMALA CITY
Guatemala city town	COBAN,
	FLORES, JALAPA, SALAMA,
	SOLOLA, ZACAPA, CUILAPA,
	JUTIAPA
Guatemala lake	IZABAL,
	ATITLAN, PETENITZA
Guatemala language	GARIFUNA;
	see MAYAN
Guatemala money	PESO,
	CENTAVO, QUETZAL
Guatemala mountain	TACANA,
	ATITLAN, ACATENANGO
Guatemala neighbor	BELIZE,
	MEXICO, HONDURAS,
	ELSALVADOR
Guatemala president	PONCE,
	CEREZO, MENDEZ, AREVALO,
	ESTRADA, SERRANO
Guatemala river	MOTAGUA,
	POLOCHIC, SARSTOON
Gudrun's husband	ATLI, HELGI,
	HERWIG, SIGURD, SIEGFRIED
guerrilla(s)	MAQUI, REBEL,
	MAQUIS, CHETNIK,
	FEDAYEE, PARTISAN
guess	DIVINE, THEORY,
	SURMISE, CONJECTURE
guessing game	POKER,
	CHARADE; *see p. 586*
guest	CALLER, VISITOR
guffaw	BRAY, LAUGH,
	HEEHAW
Guiana	*see* GUYANA,
	SURINAME
guide	KEY, PIR, AIRT, CLEW,
	LEAD, PILOT, SCOUT, STEER,
	CONVOY, LEADER, SHIKARI,
	CICERONE, SHIKAREE
guidebook	ORDO, BAEDEKER,
	MICHELIN, VADEMECUM
guided missile	*see p. 742*
guidon	FLAG, PENNANT
Guidonian note	UT, ARE, ELA,
	BEMI, BEFA, ELAMI, CEFAUT,
	FEFAUT, ALAMIRE, CESOLFA,
	DELASOL, DESOLRE,
	GAMMAUT
guild	HUI, TONG, HANSE,
	LIANA, EPIPHYTE, PARASITE
guile	WILE, CRAFT, DECEIT,
	CUNNING, TRICKERY,
	DUPLICITY
guileless	NAIVE, CANDID,
	ARTLESS, SINCERE
guilt	SIN, CRIME, CULPA

guiltless   CLEAR, INNOCENT, BLAMELESS
guilty   NOCENT, ATFAULT, CULPABLE
Guinea, capital of   CONAKRY
Guinea city   BOKE, LABE, BEYLA, BOFFA, MAMOU, KANKAN, KINDIA, CONAKRY, NZEREKORE
Guinea, Equatorial   *see* EQUATORIAL GUINEA
Guinea language   SUSU, FRENCH, FULANI, MANDINGO
Guinea money   KORI, SYLI
Guinea neighbor   MALI, LIBERIA, SENEGAL, IVORYCOAST, SIERRALEONE
Guinea river   MILO, NIGER, FATALA, KOLENTE
Guinea-Bissau, capital of   BISSAU
Guinea-Bissau city/town   BELI, GABU, CATIO, PICHE, SALIM, BISSAU, CACHEU
Guinea-Bissau language   CRIOULU
Guinea-Bissau money   FRANC
Guinea-Bissau neighbor   GUINEA, SENEGAL
Guinea-Bissau river   GEBA, FARIM, CACHEU, CORUBAL
Guinea-Bissau tribe   FULANI, MANJAK, BALANTE, MANDINKA
Guinevere's husband   ARTHUR
Guinevere's lover   LANCELOT
guise   FORM, MIEN, SHAPE, ASPECT
guitar   *see* STRING INSTRUMENT
guitarist   SOR, BYRD, FISK, KING, BREAM, FARLOW, HOOKER, WATSON, CLAPTON, HENDRIX, SEGOVIA, CHRISTIAN, WILLIAMS, FELICIANO, REINHARDT
gulch   GULLY, ARROYO, CANYON, COULEE, RAVINE
gulf   ARTA, MORO, VIBO, ABYSS, ALBAY, BIGHT, CHASM, DAVAO, DULCE, SAROS, TONKIN
Gulf sight   OILER, TANKER
Gulf State   TEXAS, ALABAMA, FLORIDA, LOUISIANA, MISSISSIPPI
gull   COB, MEW, COBB, DUPE, SKUA, CHEAT, CULLY, PEWIT, BONXIE, HOODIE, JAEGER, PEEWIT, TEASER, ICEGULL

gull genus   XEMA, LARID
gullet   MAW, CRAW, FAUCES, SWALLOW
gullible   NAIVE, TRUSTING, CREDULOUS
Gulliver's Travels author   SWIFT
Gulliver's Travels name   YAHOO, LAPUTA, LEMUEL, LILLIPUT, HOUYHNHNM
gulls, *pert. to*   LARINE
gully   NALA, SIKE, WADI, DONGA, ARROYO, NULLAH
gulp   BOLT, DOWN, SWIG, SWALLOW
gum   AMRA, KINO, CAROB, LATEX, LOBAN, MATTI, MYRRH, TUART, XYLAN, ACACIA, ACACIN, BALATA, CHICLE, GHATTI, KARAYA, TUPELO, WATTLE, ACACINE
gumbo   OCRA, OKRA, SOUP
gum disease   GUMBOIL, GINGIVITIS
gums, *pert. to*   ULETIC, GINGIVAL
gun   DAG, GAT, REV, ROD, BREN, COLT, DAGG, HAIK, HAKE, IRON, PIAT, ROER, STEN, YGUN, BARIL, BETSY, LUGER, MAXIM, MINIE, RIFLE, BARKER, CHASER, DRAGON, HEATER, JEZAIL, JINGAL, MAGNUM, MAUSER, MUSKET, PISTOL, ROSCOE, TUPERA, BARETTA, BULLDOG, CARBINE, DUNGEON, GATLING, SHOTGUN, FIRELOCK, PISTOLET, TROMBONE
gun part   NAB, PIN, BEAD, BOLT, BORE, BUTT, COCK, LOCK, GOMER, SIGHT, STOCK, BARREL, BREECH, HAMMER, CHAMBER, TRIGGER, CYLINDER, MAGAZINE
gunfire   SALVO, RAFALE, VOLLEY, BROADSIDE, FUSILLADE
gung ho   AVID
gunman   THUG, HITMAN, TORPEDO, GANGSTER
Gunnar relative   GUDRUN, SIGURD, GUTHRUN, BRUNHILD
gunpowder   TEA, NITER
Gunsmoke name   DOC, MATT, THAD, KITTY, NEWLY, ARNESS, FESTUS, WEAVER, CHESTER

Gunther relative	HAGEN, GUTRUNE, BRYNHILDE, GRIMHILDE
gunwale	GUNL
Gur language	GURMA, MOSSI, BARIBA, SENUFO, DAGBANE, DAGOMBA, GURUNSI
gurgle	BICKER, BURBLE
Gurkha sword	KUKRI
gurnard(-like fish)	TUB, ELLECK, BATFISH, TUBFISH, VOLADOR
guru	MASTER, TEACHER, MAHARISHI
gush	FLOW, RUSH, SPOUT, SPURT
gust	FLAW, RUSH, BLAST, SQUALL
gusto	ELAN, ZEST, PALATE, RELISH
gut	GULLY, INTESTINE
guts	PLUCK, BOWELS, COURAGE, INNARDS
gutta	SOH, DROP, SIAK, MINIM
gutter	CURB, SLUM, DITCH, CULLIS, TROUGH
guttural	GRUM, GRUFF, HUSKY, VELAR, HOARSE, THROATY
guy	CHAP, ROPE, FELLOW
Guy Fawkes Day month	NOV(EMBER)
guy rope	STAY, VANG
Guyana, capital of	GEORGETOWN
Guyana city	ENMORE, LETHEM, LINDEN, SUDDIE, BARTICA, CHARITY
Guyana Falls	KAIETEUR
Guyana language	URDU, HINDI, CREOLE, ENGLISH
Guyana money	CENT, DOLLAR
Guyana mountain	AMUKU, EBINT, KAMOA, KANUKU, MERUME, POTARO, WOKRAMA
Guyana neighbor	BRAZIL, SURINAME, VENEZUELA
Guyana river	ABARY, WAINI, BARAMA, CUYUNI, PURUNI, BERBICE, MAZARUNI
gym feat	KIP(P), CROSS, LEVER, SCALE
gymnast	ACROBAT, ATHLETE, TUMBLER
gymnast, famous	GUTSU, SAWAO, SZABO, AMANAR, CONNOR, KORBUT, RETTON, TURNER, VIDMAR, GAYLORD, CHUKARIN,

	COMANECI, LATYNINA, CASLAVSKA
gymnastics coach	BELA KAROLYI
gymnastics event	BARS, FLOOR, HORSE, RINGS, VAULT, BALANCE, TUMBLING, TRAMPOLINE, ACROBATICS
gymnastics, father of	JAHN
gymnastics term	KIP, BUCK, ROUNDOFF, HANDSTAND
gyp	CHEAT, CONGAME, SWINDLE
gypsum	YESO, GESSO
gypsy	ROM, RYE, CALE, CALO, CHAI, CHAL, RANI, ROMI, APTAL, CAIRD, NOMAD, ROMNI, GITANO, ROAMER, ROMANY, SELUNG, TSIGANE, BOHEMIAN
gyrate	SPIN, TURN, TWIRL, WHIRL, ROTATE, REVOLVE
gyre	WHIRL, VORTEX

H

H	AITCH, HOTEL
H-shaped	ZYGAL
habeas corpus	WRIT
habile	APT, ABLE, CLEVER
habiliment	DRESS, ATTIRE, CLOTHING
habit	RUT, GARB, MODE, WONT, USAGE, ATTIRE, COSTUME
habitable	LIVABLE, PLEASANT
habitual	USUAL, COMMON, WONTED, CHRONIC, ROUTINE
habituate	USE, DRILL, ENURE, INURE, ADDICT, FREQUENT
habitué	USER, REGULAR, FREQUENTER
hack	CAB, NAG, CHOP, GASH, GRUB, HAGG, TAXI, COUGH, DEVIL, DRUDGE, WRITER, MATTOCK
hackle(s)	CUT, COMB, DANDER, HAGGLE, MANGLE, TEMPER, HATCHEL, FEATHERS
hackneyed	WORN, BANAL, STALE, STOCK, TRITE
Hades	DIS, AALU, AARU, DUAT, IALU, ARALU, AYARU, ORCUS, PLUTO, EREBUS, TARTARUS; see HELL
Hades relative	RHEA, ZEUS,

CRONUS, POSEIDON,
PERSEPHONE
Hadrian reign year (AD117–138)
CXIX, CXX, CXXI, CXXV, CXXX
hag   FURY, GIGG, CRONE,
HARPY, SHREW, VECKE,
VIXEN, BELDAM, VIRAGO,
HARRIDAN, STRUMPET
Hagar relative   ISHMAEL,
ABRAHAM
haggard   WAN, DRAWN, GAUNT
Haggard novel   SHE, MARIE
Haggith husband   DAVID
haggle   PRIG, CAVIL, PALTER,
BARGAIN, CHAFFER,
QUIBBLE
Hagia —   SOPHIA
haha   WALL, FENCE, LAUGH,
TE(E)HEE
hail   AVE, AHOY, POUR,
AVAST, SLEET, SALUTE,
GRAUPEL
Hailey novel   HOTEL, AIRPORT
hair   FUR, MOP, NAP, DOWN,
FUZZ, LOCK, PILE, POLL,
SHAG, CRINE, ROACH, TRESS,
LANUGO, THATCH, VELLUS
Hair co-writer   RADO
hair fastener   PIN, CLIP,
BODKIN, HAIRPIN,
BARRETTE
hair product   COMB, BRUSH,
HENNA, RINSE, CURLER,
POMADE, SHAMPOO
hair, remove   BOB, TRIM,
(D)EPILATE
hair remover   NAIR, NEET,
RUSMA, DEPILATOR
hair shirt   CILICE
hairdo   BOB, AFRO, GLIB, PERM,
BRAID, STYLE, MARCEL,
BEEHIVE, CREWCUT,
HAIRCUT, PAGEBOY,
PIGTAIL, SHINGLE, DUCKTAIL,
PONYTAIL, POMPADOUR
hairdresser   BARBER, FRISEUR,
STYLIST, COIFFEUR,
COIFFEUSE
hairdressing term   BUN, SET,
COIF, PERM, TETE, WAVE,
BANGS, RINSE, MARCEL,
POODLE, SHINGLE, PAGEBOY,
SHAMPOO, COIFFURE,
POMPADOUR
hairless   BALD, PELON,
GLABROUS
hairpiece   RAT, WIG, FALL,
ROLL, PERUKE, TOUPEE
hairy   NAPPY, PILAR, COMATE,

COMOSE, PILOSE, CILIATE,
CRINITE, HIRSUTE, VILLOSE,
VILLOUS, CRINATED
Haiti, capital of   PORTAUPRINCE
Haitian city   ASQUIN, LIMBE,
HINCHE, JACMEL,
DESDUNES, GONAIVES
Haitian language   CREOLE
Haitian money   FRANC,
GOURDE, CENTIME
Haitian president   AVRIL,
ESTIME, ARISTIDE,
DUVALIER, MAGLOIRE,
TROUILLOT
Haitian religion   VODOU
Haitian river   ARTIBONITE
halberd   AX, GLAIVE, POLEAX,
GISARME
Halcyone relative   CEYX
hale   DRAG, HAUL, WELL,
HEARTY, ROBUST, HEALTHY
Halévy opera   (LA)JUIVE
half   DEMI, HEMI, SEMI,
MOIETY
half-breed   MULE, GRIFF, METIS,
GRIFFE, LADINO, MESTEE,
MUSTEE, MESTIZO, METISSE,
MULATTO
half-eaten   SEMESE
half-moon   ARC, LUNE(TTE),
CRESCENT
half note   MINIM
halfpenny   MAG
halibut   see FLATFISH
Halifax native   HALIGONIAN
hall(s)   AULA, DORM, SAAL,
XYST, ATRIA, FOYER,
ODEON, XYSTUS
hallowed   HOLY, SACRED
hallucination   AUTISM,
CHIMERA, FANTASY,
DELUSION
hallucinogen   LSD, ACID,
CAAPI, PEYOTE, MESCALINE
hallway   ENTRY, FOYER,
CORRIDOR, VESTIBULE
halo   AURA, NIMB, BROUGH,
CORONA, NIMBUS,
AUREOLA, AUREOLE
halogen   IODINE, BROMINE,
ASTATINE, CHLORINE,
FLUORINE
halt   HOLD, LAME, LIMP, STEM,
STOP, CEASE, HOBBLE
ham   EMOTE, GAMMON,
RASHER, AMATEUR,
OVERACT
Ham relative   CUSH, PHUT,
CANAAN

hamburger PATTY, TARTARE,
SALISBURY (STEAK)
Hamite AFAR, GALLA, TIBBU,
BERBER, TUAREG, DANAKIL,
GUANCHE
Hamitic language see BERBER,
CUSHITIC
hamlet MIR, BURG, DORP,
TREF, ALDEA, THORP,
CLACHAN
Hamlet character HAMLET,
YORICK, HORATIO, LAERTES,
OPHELIA, CLAUDIUS,
GERTRUDE, POLONIUS
Hamlet relative CLAUDIUS,
GERTRUDE
Hamlet site DENMARK,
ELSINORE
Hamlet's friend HORATIO
Hamlet's girlfriend OPHELIA
Hamlet's slayer LAERTES
hammer BEAT, MAUL, POUND,
BEETLE, FULLER, MALLET,
OLIVER, PLEXOR, SLEDGE
hammer part CLAW, HEAD,
PEEN, POLL
hamper PED, CRAMP, MAUND,
FETTER, HINDER, IMPEDE,
TRAMMEL; see BASKET
Hampshire HANTS
Hamutal relative JOSIAH,
ZEDEKIAH
Hananiah relative AZUN
hand PUD, DEAL, MANO,
NEAF, NIEF, MANUS, NIEVE,
SCRIPT, LABORER, APPLAUSE
hand, part of FIST, LOOF,
PALM, VOLA, FINGER,
THENAR
hand, pert. to VOLAR, CHIRAL,
MANUAL, THENAR
handbag CABA, GRIP, PURSE,
CLUTCH, VALISE, SATCHEL
handbill LEAF, FLIER, FLYER,
POSTER, DODGER, LEAFLET
handbook TOME, GUIDE,
MANUAL, BAEDEKER,
CATECHISM
handcart BARROW
handcuff DARBY, FETTER,
NIPPERS, MANACLE
Handel work NERO, SAUL,
ALMIRA, CAESAR, ESTHER,
XERXES, JEPHTHA, MESSIAH,
ORLANDO, RINALDO,
AGRIPPINA, PARTENOPE
handicap ODDS, RACE, HINDER
handkerchief HANKIE,
SUDARY, FOULARD,

SUDARIUM, VERNICLE,
VERONICA
handkerchief border FORRE
handle EAR, LUG, PAW, ANSA,
BALL, BOOL, DEAL, HAFT,
HANK, HILT, TANG, TOAT,
TOTE, HELVE, SNATH,
SNEAD, SWIPE, TREAT, WIELD,
BECKET, SNATHE
handled DEALT, ANSATE,
PALMED
hand-me-down USED,
SECONDHAND
handout DOLE, GIFT, LEAFLET,
DONATION
handsome BRAW, BONNY,
COMELY, LIBERAL,
GOODLOOKING
handspring TUMBLE,
CARTWHEEL
handstone MANO
handwriting SCRIPT,
PENMANSHIP
handwriting on the wall MENE,
TEKEL, UPHARSIN
handy DEFT, ADROIT, HABILE,
CONVENIENT
hang PEND, LOLL, DRAPE,
DROOP, HOVER, DANGLE,
IMPEND, STRING UP
hang ten SURF
hangar SHED, SHELTER
hanger-on LEECH, TOADY,
HEELER, PARASITE
hanging PENDENT, PENSILE,
SESSILE
Hanging Gardens site BABYLON
hangnail WHITLOW
hangout DEN, HAUNT,
RETREAT
hang-up PROBLEM, NEUROSIS,
INHIBITION
hank RAN, COIL, LOOP, SKEIN
hankering YEN, ITCH, DESIRE
Hannah relative SAMUEL,
ELKANAH
Hannibal battle site ZANA,
CANNAE
Hannibal conqueror SCIPIO
Hannibal's father BARCA,
HAMILCAR
Hans JOHN, JOHANNES
haphazard CASUAL, RANDOM,
AIMLESS
hapless ILLFATED, UNLUCKY
happen FARE, OCCUR, BEFALL,
BETIDE, CHANCE
happening CASUS, EVENT,
INCIDENT

happiness JOY, BLISS, ELATION, FELICITY

happy COSH, GLAD, FAUST, BLITHE, JOYOUS

happy as — ACLAM

Happy-Days names IRV, PAT, RON, BAIO, LORI, MORK, HENRY, ARNOLD, CHACHI, FONZIE, HOWARD, JOANIE, MORITA, POTSIE, WINKLER

happy-go-lucky EASY, CASUAL, CAREFREE, EASYGOING, NONCHALANT

harakiri SUICIDE, SEPPUKU

Haran relative LOT, ABRAM, ISCHA, NAHOR, TERAH, MILCAH

harangue RANT, ORATE, SPIEL, SCREED, TIRADE, DIATRIBE

harass NAG, BAIT, JADE, RIDE, BESET, HECKLE, PESTER

harbinger OMEN, HERALD, FORETELL

harbor BAY, COVE, PIER, PORT, HAVEN, HITHE, CONCEAL

hard STERN, FLINTY, STEELY, ADAMANT, ARDUOUS, CALLOUS, PETROUS

hard-boiled TOUGH, CALLOUS, CYNICAL, SEASONED

harden GEL, SET, KERN, ENURE, INURE, STEEL, TEMPER, INDURATE

hardheaded TOUGH, SHREWD, STUBBORN

hardly BARELY, RARELY, SCARCELY

hard-pressed BESET, HARASSED, STRICKEN

hardship NEED, WANT, RIGOR, TRIAL, STRAITS, POVERTY, ADVERSITY

hardtack BREAD, TOMMY, PANTILE

hardware GUNS, TOOLS, FIREARMS, WEAPONS, WEAPONRY, HOUSEWARES

hardwired INNATE, BUILTIN

hardwood ASH, ELM, OAK, IPIL, TEAK, BEECH, BIRCH, EBONY, MAPLE, HICKORY, MAHOGANY

hardy HALE, TOUGH, STURDY, DURABLE

Hardy character CLYM, JUDE, TESS

Hardy locale WESSEX

hare(-like rodents) BUN, WAT, BAWD, CONY, HARE, PIKA,

BUNNY, CUTTY, DAMAN, HYRAX, LAPIN, DASSIE, MALKIN, MAUKIN, RABBIT, TAPETI, FLEMISH, LEPORID, LEVERET, RATHARE

hare genus LEPUS, PEDETES

harebrained GIDDY, FLIGHTY, FOOLISH

harem ODA, SERAI, ZENANA, SERAGLIO

hark HEAR, HEED, LIST, ATTEND, LISTEN

harlot of Jericho RAHAB

harm MAR, BALE, BANE, DERE, HURT, DAMAGE, INJURE, SCATHE

harmful ILL, NOXAL, NOCENT, BANEFUL, NOISOME, NOXIOUS

harmful influence NOXA, UPAS

harmless SAFE, RISKFREE, INNOCUOUS

harmonica MOUTHORGAN

harmonious CORDIAL, MUSICAL, ORDERLY, SPHERAL, BALANCED

harmonize SET, AGREE, BLEND, ATTUNE

harmony KEY, SYNC, CHIME, COSMOS, UNISON, CONCORD

harness RIG, GEAR, TAME, ARMOR, EQUIP, GRAITH, INSPAN, CALTROP

harness part BIT, TUG, HAME, REIN, BLIND, TRACE, BILLET, BRIDLE, COLLAR, HALTER, TERRET, CRUPPER

Harold and Maude name MAUDE, (RUTH)GORDON

harp KOTO, LYRE, NANGA, TRIGON, SAMBUKE, DULCIMER, PSALTERY

Harp constellation LYRA

harp (on) NAG, DWELL, REPEAT

harpoon SPEAR, JAVELIN

harpsichord SPINET, VIRGINAL, BEDSPRINGS

Harpy NAG, AELLO, BUZZARD, CELAENO, OCYPETE, PODARGE

harquebus support CROC

harrier NUISANCE

harrow CHIP, DRAG, TILL

harrow part DISC, TOOTH

Harrow rival ETON

harry BESET, TEASE, HARASS, PESTER

Harry Potter author (JK)ROWLING

Harry Potter character **DUDLEY, RUBEUS HAGRID, DRACO MALFOY, PERCY NEVILLE, PETUNIA, RON WEASLEY, HERMIONE GRANGER, ALBUS DUMBLEDORE**
Harry Potter term **MUGGLE, SEEKER, QUAFFLE, HOGWARTS, QUIDDITCH**
harsh **DURE, GRIM, ACERB, CRUEL, STERN, COARSE, RASPING**
hart *see* **DEER**
Harte, Bret play **AHSIN**
hartebeest *see* **ANTELOPE**
harum-scarum **RASH, WILD, RECKLESS**
Harvard president **ELIOT, PUSEY, CONANT, LOWELL**
harvest **CROP, KIRN, RABI, REAP, RABBI, YIELD, GARNER**
harvest machine *see* **FARM**
Harvey author **CHASE**
Harvey character **DOWD, POOKA, ELWOOD**
hash **CHOP, MINCE, BUNGLE, JUMBLE**
hash joint **DINER, EATERY**
hashish **HEMP, BHANG, CANNABIS**
hassle **FRAY, MELEE, RUCKUS**
hassock **TUT, PESS, TUFT, STOOL**
haste(n) **HIE, DASH, HURRY, SCAMP, SPEED**
hasty **RASH, BRASH, QUICK, URGENT, HURRIED**
hasty pudding **HASH, MUSH, SEPON, SUP(P)AWN**
hat **DIP, FEZ, LID, TAM, BAKU, CADY, COIF, FELT, FLAT, KADY, KATY, KEPI, TILE, TOPI, BENJY, BENNY, BERET, BOXER, BUSBY, CADDY, DERBY, DICER, GIBUS, MILAN, SQUAM, STRAW, TERAI, TOPEE, TOQUE, BEAVER, BOATER, BONNET, BOWLER, CASTOR, CLAQUE, CLOCHE, COCKUP, FEDORA, PANAMA, RAFFIA, SAILOR, SCONCE, SLOUCH, TOPHAT, TOPPER, TRILBY, BANDEAU, BRIMMER, CAUBEEN, CHAPEAU, HOMBURG, LEGHORN, PETASOS, PETASUS, PILLBOX, PORKPIE, SALACOT, SALAKOT, SUNDOWN, TARBUSH, TRICORN, BEARSKIN,**
CAPELINE, OPERAHAT, SOMBRERO, TARBOOSH, TARBOUSH, SOUWESTER; *see* **HEADWEAR, CAP**
hatch **PLAN, PLOT, DEVISE, CONCOCT**
hatchet **AX(E), MOGO, TOMAHAWK**
hatchet man **KILLER, ASSASSIN**
hatchway **DOOR, SCUTTLE**
hate **DOSA, MISO, ABHOR, ODIUM, DETEST, LOATHE, MALICE, RANCOR, AVERSION**
hateful **ODIOUS, HEINOUS, HOSTILE, EXECRABLE, LOATHSOME, OBNOXIOUS, REPUGNANT, REPULSIVE, ABOMINABLE**
Hatfield foe **MCCOY**
haughty **PROUD, SNOOTY, STUCKUP, ARROGANT, CAVALIER, CONCEITED**
haul **LUG, TOW, TUG, DRAG, HALE, SWAG, TOTE, BOOTY, BOUSE, TRICE**
hauler **DRAY, MOVER, CARTER, SHIPPER**
haunch **HIP, HUCKLE, BUTTOCK**
haunt **DEN, DIVE, NEST, SPOOK, OBSESS, PURLIEU, RETREAT, FREQUENT**
have something **EAT**
haven **LEE, PORT, HITHE, ASYLUM, HARBOR, REFUGE, SHELTER, SANCTUARY**
havoc **HOBB, RUIN, CHAOS, MAYHEM, CONFUSION**
haw **HEM, SLOE, BERRY, FRUIT, EYELID, FALTER**
Hawaii *see also p. 615*
Hawaii author **MICHENER**
Hawaii discoverer **GAETANO**
Hawaii Five-O name **KIMO, LORD, ZULU, DANNO, DANNY, STEVE, CHEFONG, MCGARRETT**
Hawaiian bay **HILO, HALAWA, KAHANA, KIHOLO, MAMALA, WAIMEA, WAIPIO, KANAPOU**
Hawaiian beach **EWA, SUNSET, WAIKIKI, KAWAILOA**
Hawaiian bird **IO, OO, IIWI, KOAE, MAMO, OMAO, OOAA, PALILA**
Hawaiian city **AIEA, HILO, KAPAA, LANIA, OHIO, KAILUA, MAKAHA, MOKAPU, WAIMEA, KANEOHE,**

Hawaiian fish   MOLOKAI, WAILUKU, HONOLULU
Hawaiian fish   AHI, AKU, AWA, ULUA, AKULE
Hawaiian island   KURE, MAUI, OAHU, KAUAI, KAULA, LANAI, HAWAII, NECKER, NIIHAU, MOLOKAI, HONOLULU
Hawaiian language   *see* POLYNESIAN
Hawaiian mountain   KAALA, REDHILL, MAUNAKEA
Hawaiian royalty   ALII
Hawaiian tree   KOA, AULU, NAIO, OHIA, AALII, LEHUA, ILIAHI
hawk   GOS, IOA, IWA, EYAS, KAHU, KITE, ASTUR, FALCON, OSPREY, SHIKRA, TERCEL, FRIGATE, GOSHAWK, HAGGARD, HARRIER, KESTREL, MANOWAR, TIERCEL, CARACARA; *see* BUZZARD
hawk genus   IO, BUTEO, PANDION, ACCIPITER
hawk, young   EYAS
hawker   ROWEN, CADGER, COSTER, PEDLAR, CHAPMAN, PEDDLER, HUCKSTER
Hawkeye   IOWAN; *see* MASH
Hawkeye State   IA, IOWA
hawser   BITT, BOLLARD
hawthorn   HAW, MAY, A(I)GLET, AZAROLE, COCKSPUR
Hawthorne birthplace   SALEM
Hawthorne character   HESTER, PRYNNE
hay   CHAFF, CLOVER, ALFALFA, TIMOTHY
hayfield   RAKH
hayseed   HICK, RUBE, RUSTIC
haystack   COB, MOW, COIL, GOAF, PIKE, RICK
haywire   AMOK, WILD, CRAZY, SNAFU
Hayworth role   SADIE
hazard   DARE, RISK, PERIL, STAKE, DANGER, JEOPARDY
haze   FOG, FILM, GLIN, MIST, PALL, SMOG, BRUME
hazel   A(I)GLET
Hazel names   BOOTH, BURKE, SUSIE, BAXTER, GEORGE, HAROLD, MILLIE, BARBARA, DOROTHY, SHIRLEY
hazelnut   FILBERT

hazy   FOGGY, MISTY, VAGUE, OBSCURE
HBO competitor   *see* CABLE
head   NOB, NUT, TOP, VAN, BEAN, CONK, LEAD, NOLL, PASH, PATE, POLL, TETE, WITS, CAPUT, CHIEF, FRONT, SKULL, CAPITA, MAZARD, NODDLE, NOGGIN, NOODLE, CRANIUM
head —   TO TOE
head, membrane covering   CAUL, OMENTUM
head off   AVERT, LEAVE, DEPART, DIVERT
head of state   *see* CHIEF
head, part of   EAR, EYE, JAW, FACE, HAIR, JOWL, NOSE, BRAIN, CHEEK, CROWN, FRONS, INION, MOUTH, NARES, SCALP, SINUS, BASION, BREGMA, MENTUM, OCULUS, THORAX, THROAT, VERTEX, EYEBROW, EYELASH, OCCIPUT, ANTINION, CALVARIA, FOREHEAD, SINCIPUT
head type   POINTY
headache   HASSLE, MEGRIM, MIGRAINE
headband   AGAL, FILLET, DIADEM, TAENIA, CIRCLET
headdress   WIG, AMIT, POUF, TIARA, DIADEM, TURBAN, COMMODE, COIFFURE
headhunter   AGENT, DAYAK
heading   ENE, WNW, DRIFT, TITLE, CAPTION
headland   RAS, CAPE, NAZE, NESS, BLUFF
headless   ETETE
headless man   BROM, NICK, BONES
headline   STAR, BANNER, SCREAMER, STREAMER
headliner   LEAD, STAR, ATTRACTION
headlong   HASTY, RASH, RECKLESS
headman   BOSS, CHIEF, HETMAN, INDUNA, SACHEM
headmaster   RECTOR, PRINCIPAL
headpiece   CAP, HAT, ARMET, BRAINS, HALTER, HELMET, HEADSTALL
headquarters   HQ, BASE, SEAT
headstone   STELE, BARROW,

DOLMEN, CROMLECH, GRAVESTONE
headstrong RASH, WAYWARD, WILLFUL, OBSTINATE
headway PROGRESS
headwear BOW, AGAL, POUF, TIAR, CROWN, MITER, MITRE, SHAKO, SNOOD, TIARA, DIADEM, FILLET, HENNIN, TURBAN, WIMPLE, HAVELOCK, HEADGEAR, STEPHANE; see HAT, CAP, HOOD
heady RASH, GIDDY, SPICY, PUNGENT, AROMATIC, RECKLESS, IMPETUOUS, EXHILARATING
healer ASA, QUACK, DOCTOR, SHAMAN
healing IATRIC, CURATIVE, REMEDIAL, MEDICINAL, THERAPEUTIC
healing sign SCAB
healing substance BALM, CURE(ALL), DRUG, REMEDY, NOSTRUM, PANACEA, MEDICINE
health SHAPE, FITNESS, WELFARE, WELLBEING
healthy HALE, SANE, SOUND, ROBUST, SALUBRIOUS
heap COB, LOTS, PILE, RAFF, RAFT, AMASS, LOADS, MOUND, STACK, CONGERIES
hear LIST(EN), HARK(EN), HEARKEN
hearer AUDITOR, LISTENER
hearing OYER, PROBE, TRIAL, INQUEST, AUDIENCE
hearken HEAR, HEED, HIST, LIST, ATTEND, LISTEN
hearsay TALK, RUMOR, GOSSIP, REPORT
hearse BIER
Hearst captor SLA
heart AB, COR(E), GIST, HATI, PITH, BOSOM, BREAST, CARDIA, KERNEL, TICKER
heart and — SOUL
heart disease ANGINA, CARDITIS, CORONARY
heart regulator PACEMAKER
heartache WOE, PAIN, GRIEF, SORROW
heartbeat PULSE, THROB, FLUTTER
heartburn PYROSIS, CARDIALGIA
hearten CHEER, GLADDEN

heartfelt DEEPEST, GENUINE, SINCERE
hearth LING, INGLE, FIRESIDE
heartily INLY, WARMLY, WHOLLY
heartless COLD, CRUEL, HARSH, UNKIND, CALLOUS, PITILESS, MERCILESS
heartrending MOVING, TOUCHING
heart-shaped CORDATE, CARDIOID
heart-shaped leaf tree LINDEN
heartsick SAD, ANGUISHED, DEPRESSED
heartthrob HUNK, LOVER, LOOKER, DREAMBOAT
heartwarming MOVING, TOUCHING, REWARDING, GRATIFYING
hearty HALE, WELL, LUSTY, ROBUST, SAILOR, VIGOROUS
heat RUT, NUKE, WARM, ZEAL, ARDOR, CALOR, CAUMA, FEVER, TEPOR, ESTRUS
— heat DEAD
heat maker OVEN, STOVE, BOILER, BURNER, WARMER
heat unit BTU, THERM, CALORY, CALORIE
heated ANGRY, FIERY, CANDENT
heater ETNA, OVEN, STOVE, BUNSEN, PISTOL, RETORT; see GUN
heath BENT, GRIG, LING, MOOR, PIPE, BESOM, ERICA, GORSE, BRUYERE, HEATHER
heathen PAGAN, PAYNIM, INFIDEL
heather LING, ERICA, GORSE
heave CAST, RECK, FLING, RETCH, SCEND, SWELL, VOMIT
heaven(s) SKY, CIEL, AALU, AARU, EDEN, SION, ZION, URANO, (A)ETHER, WELKIN, VALHALLA
heavenly HOLY, DIVINE, EDENIC, URANIC, ANGELIC, SERAPHIC, SUPERNAL
heavenly being AFA, ANGEL, CHERUB, SERAPH(IM)
heavenly body SUN, MOON, STAR, COMET, METEOR, PLANET, ASTEROID
heavy DENSE, INERT, GRAVE, LADEN, LEADEN, WEIGHTY

heavyweight	**VIP, BOXER, BIGWIG, FIGHTER, PUGILIST**
Heber relative	**SHUAH**
Hebrew	**JEW, SEMITE, ISRAELITE**
Hebrew alphabet	**HE, PE, AIN, MEM, NUN, SIN, TAV, TAW, VAU, WAW, ALEF, AYIN, BETH, CAPH, ELEF, KAPH, KOPH, QOPH, RESH, SADE, SHIN, TETH, YODH, ALEPH, CHETH, GIMEL, ZAYIN, DALETH, LAMEDH, SAMEKH;** *see p. 623*
Hebrew marginal note	**KRI, QRI, KERE, KERI, QERE, Q(U)ERI**
Hebrew measure	**CAB, KAB, HIN, KOR, LOG, BATH, EPHA, EZBA, OMER, REED, SEAH, CUBIT, EPHAH, HOMER**
Hebrew month	*see p. 717*
Hebrew weight	**MINA, BEKA, REBA, BEKAH, REBAH, SHEKEL**
Hebrides	**(H)EBUDAE**
Hebrides island	**COLL, IONA, MULL, RHUM, SKYE, ISLAY, LEWIS, TIREE, HARRIS**
heckle	**BAIT, ANNOY, TAUNT, NEEDLE**
hectic	**FEBRILE, FEVERED, FEVERISH**
hector	**BAIT, HUFF, BULLY, PESTER, HARASS, BROWBEAT**
Hector relative	**PRIAM, HECUBA, ANDROMACHE**
Hecuba relative	**PARIS, PRIAM, HECTOR, TROILUS, CASSANDRA**
hedge	**HEM, REW, ROW, BOMA, WAVER, RADDLE**
hedgehog	**TENREC, URCHIN, ECHINOS, PORCUPINE**
heed	**MIND, NOTE, OBEY, RECK, HARKEN**
heedful	**MINDFUL, ATTENTIVE, WATCHFUL**
heedless	**DEAF, CARELESS, UNMINDFUL, OBLIVIOUS**
heel	**CAD, CALX, OBEY, TILT, LOUSE, CAREEN, BOUNDER**
— Heep	**URIAH**
heft	**PULL, WEIGHT, INFLUENCE**
hefty	**HEAVY, WEIGHTY**
hegira	**FLIGHT, JOURNEY**
hegira destination	**MEDINA**
height	**ACME, PITCH, CLIMAX, SUMMIT, STATURE**

heighten	**ADDTO, ENHANCE, INCREASE, INTENSIFY**
heinous	**ODIOUS, HATEFUL, ABOMINABLE**
heir	**HERES, SCION, HAERES, HERITOR, LEGATEE, PARCENER, INHERITOR**
heirloom	**KEEPSAKE, HERITABLE**
Heisman Trophy winners	*see p. 710*
heist	**THEFT, HOLDUP, ROBBERY, BURGLARY**
Helah husband	**ASHUR**
held	**TENUTO, GRIPPED, INCUSTODY**
Helen of Troy's abductor	**PARIS**
Helen of Troy relative	**ION, LEDA, DORUS, HERMIONE, MENELAUS**
Helen of Troy's suitor	**AJAX, PARIS**
helical	**TORSE, SPIRAL**
helicopter	**GIRO, ROTOR, CHOPPER, WHIRLYBIRD**
Helios	**APOLLO, SUNGOD, HYPERION**
Helios relative	**CIRCE, ARTEMIS, HYPERION**
helix	**COIL, SNAIL, WHORL, SPIRAL, MOLLUSK**
hell	**PIT, ABYSS, SHEOL, NARAKA, TOPHET, ABADDON, AVERNUS, GEHENNA, INFERNO;** *see* **HADES**
— hell	**CATCH, RAISE**
Hellas	**GREECE**
hellbender	**SPREE, DEBAUCH**
hellcat	**SHREW, VIXEN, WITCH, VIRAGO**
Hellespont swimmer	**LEANDER**
hellhound	**FIEND, CERBERUS**
hellish	**STYGIAN, DEVILISH, FIENDISH, INFERNAL**
helm	**WHEEL, RUDDER, TILLER**
helmet	**ARMET, CASQUE, HEAUME, MORION, SALADE, SALLET, BASINET, BURGONET**
helmet-shaped	**GALEATE**
helmsman	**COX(ON), PILOT, TILLER, STEERER, COXSWAIN**
Héloïse husband	**ABELARD**
helot	**ESNE, SERF, SLAVE**
help	**AID, ABET, TIDE, STAFF, REMEDY, SECOND, SUCCOR**
helper	**CUE, AIDE, ALLY, ASSIST(ER), SECOND**
helpful	**OFUSE, USEFUL, BENEFICIAL, COOPERATIVE**

helpless **LOST, WEAK, FEEBLE, IMPOTENT, DEPENDENT**
helpmate **MATE, WIFE, SPOUSE, HUSBAND**
helter-skelter **CHAOTIC, HAYWIRE**
Helvetic **SWISS**
hem **EDGE, BORDER, MARGIN, SELVAGE**
hem and haw **ER, UM, HEDGE, FALTER**
hem in **BESET, FENCE, INVEST**
Hemingway character **NICK, ADAMS, BRETT, PILAR**
Hemingway nickname **PAPA**
hemlock **KEX, YEW, CASH, CONIUM, VALERIAN**
hemp **DA, IFE, PUA, SUN, TOW, KEEF, PITA, POOA, SUNN, ABACA, BHANG, DAGGA, GANJA, GUNJA, MURVA, SISAL, SIZAL, AMBARI, CHARAS, GANJAH, GUNJAH, MOORVA**
hen **FOWL, LAYER, PULLET, SITTER, CHICKEN, POULARD**
hen, young **PULLET**
hence **SO, OFF, AWAY, ERGO, THEN, THEREFORE**
henchman **TOADY, LACKEY, SQUIRE**
henpeck **NAG, DOMINEER**
Henry II adversary **BECKET**
Henry II wife **ELEANOR**
Henry IV birthplace **PAU**
Henry IV character **PETO, HENRY, PERCY, POINS, SCROOP, FALSTAFF**
Henry V character **GREY, YORK, ALICE, EXETER, ISABEL, BEDFORD**
Henry VI character **JOAN, LUCY, TALBOT, MARGARET, WOODVILLE**
Henry VIII child **MARY, EDWARD, ELIZABETH**
Henry VIII's wives **ANNE, JANE, PARR, ARAGON, BOLEYN, CLEVES, HOWARD, SEYMOUR, CATHERINE**
hep **ONTO, AWARE, WISETO**
hepatica **LIVERWORT**
Hepburn **AUDREY, KATHERINE**
Hepburn/Tracy comedy **DESK SET, ADAMS RIB, PAT AND MIKE**
hepcat **BEATNIK, HIPSTER**
Hera relative **ARES, RHEA, ZEUS, JUPITER**

herald **CRIER, USHER, BLAZON**
heraldry see p. 619
herb **RUE, ALOE, DILL, LEEK, RAPE, RUTA, SAGE, ANISE, BASIL, CRESS, SEDGE, TANSY, THYME, CATNIP, CELERY, ENDIVE, GINGER, POTATO, SAVORY, SESAME, CARAWAY, CHERVIL, CHICORY, GINSENG, PARSLEY, POTHERB;** see p. 685
herb genus **AMMI, GEUM, SIUM, AJUGA, APIUM, CICER, SEDUM**
herb, mythical **MOLY**
Hercules **ALCIDES, HERACLES, HERAKLES**
Hercules death site **OETA**
Hercules feat **BOAR, IOLE, HYDRA, NESSUS, HESIONE**
Hercules horse **ARION**
Hercules relatives **HEBE, ZEUS, ALCMENE, DEIANERA**
herd **GAM, MOB, POD, CAV(V)Y, DROVE, FLOCK, SHOAL, CAVIYA, CORRAL, MANADA, REMUDA, SOUNDER**
herdsman **SENN, COWBOY, DROVER, GAUCHO, VACHER, VAQUERO, RANCHERO**
here **NOW, HITHER, PRESENT**
here lies **HICJACET**
hereafter **LATER, BEYOND, AFTERLIFE**
hereditary **FAMILY, INBORN, INBRED, INNATE, LINEAL, GENETIC, ANCESTRAL**
hereditary factor **DNA, GEN, RNA, GENE**
heredity **GENETICS**
heresy **ARIANISM, DONATISM, MONTANISM, GNOSTICISM**
heretic **PERVERT, DISSENTER**
heretic, famous **ARIUS, CYRIL, ATHANASIUS**
heretofore **ERST, ERENOW, QUONDAM**
heritage **LEGACY, BEQUEST, PATRIMONY**
hermaphrodite **SCRAT, ANDROGYNE**
Hermes **MERCURY**
Hermes equipment **PETASOS, TALARIA, CADUCEUS**
Hermes relative **PAN, MAIA, ZEUS, HERSE, CHIONE, AGLAUCUS**
hermetic **MYSTIC, SEALED, AIRTIGHT**

Hermione relative **DORUS, HELEN, ORESTES, MENELAUS**
hermit **LONER, SANTON, ASCETIC, EREMITE, RECLUSE, STYLITE, ANCHORITE**
hermitage **ASHRAM, RETREAT, CLOISTER, MONASTERY**
hernia **BREACH, RUPTURE**
hero **IDOL, LEAD, LION, STAR, TOOA, DEMIGOD, PALADIN, CHAMPION**
Hero's lover **LEANDER**
Herod relative **SALOME, ANTIPAS, HERODIAS**
Herodias relative **HEROD, SALOME, ANTIPAS**
heroic **EPIC(AL), GALLANT, VALIANT**
heroic poem *see* **EPIC**
heroin **SNOW, HORSE, SMACK**
heron **QUA, HERN, SOCO, EGRET, GUARA, HERNE, QUAWK, UMBER, KOTUKU, BITTERN, SQUACCO, BOATBILL, SHOEBILL, SHOEBIRD, UMBRETTE, HAMMERKOP;** *see* **GANNET**
heron genus **ARDEA**
herpes **SORE, TETTER, ZOSTER, SIMPLEX, LABIALIS**
herring(-like fish) **BANG, BRIT, SHAD, ALLIS, ALOSA, BRITT, CHIRO, CISCO, DORAB, HILSA, MARAY, MATIE, SMELT, SPRAT, ALLICE, BUNKER, GARVIE, TWAITE, ALEWIFE, ANCHOVY, BUGFISH, BUGHEAD, CLUPEID, LONGJAW, MOONEYE, SARDINE, MENHADEN, PILCHARD**
Herzegovina *see* **BOSNIA**
Hesiod work **THEOGONY, WORKS AND DAYS**
hesitant **CHARY, TIMID, WAVERING, RELUCTANT**
hesitate **HAW, HEM, DEMUR, WAVER, FALTER, TEETER**
hesitation sound **ER(R), UH, UM**
Hesperides **AEGLE, HESPERE, ERYTHEIA**
Hesperides parents **CETO, ATLAS, NIGHT, EREBUS, PHORCYS**
Hesperus parent **EOS, ASTRAEUS**
Hess **MYRA, RUDOLF**
Hestia parent **RHEA, CRONUS**

het up **AGOG, JUMPY, ONEDGE, EXCITED, JITTERY**
heterogeneous **MISC, VARIED, DIVERSE, ASSORTED**
hew **AX, CUT, CHOP, FELL, GASH, HACK, CLEAVE**
Hezekiah relative **ABI**
hex **JINX, CURSE, SPELL, WITCH, HOODOO**
heyday **PEAK, GLORY, PRIME**
Heyerdahl book **KONTIKI**
Hi and Lois child **DOT, DITTO**
hiatus **COL, GAP, LULL, BREAK, CHASM, LACUNA**
hibachi **GRILL, BRAZIER, BARBECUE**
hibernate **SLEEP, WINTER, HOLEUP**
hibernate opposite **GESTIVATE**
hibernating animal **BAT, BEAR, MARMOT, LEMMING, HEDGEHOG, SQUIRREL, WOODCHUCK**
hibiscus **ILAU, BOLA, PURAU, MAHAGUA, MAJAGUA, BALIBAGO**
hibiscus ring **LEI**
hick **RUBE, YOKEL, HAYSEED**
hidden **INNER, PERDU, ARCANE, COVERT, LATENT**
hide(s) **KIP, FELL, MASK, PELT, SKIN, VEIL, CACHE, JUFTI, ENCODE, SCREEN**
hideaway, hideout **DEN, FORT, HOLE, LAIR, RETREAT**
hidebound **OBSTINATE, PAROCHIAL, INFLEXIBLE**
hideous **UGLY, SCABROUS, REPULSIVE, REVOLTING**
hie **RUSH, HURRY, SPEED, HASTEN**
hierarchy **RANK, ORDER, LADDER**
high **ALT, DEAR, ALOFT, LOFTY, DRUNK, COSTLY, SOUSED, SOARING**
high and dry **MAROONED, STRANDED**
high flyer **SST**
High Noon name **AMY, WILL, KANE, KELLY, COOPER, HARVEY**
high priest **AARON**
high spot **ACME, APEX, CLIMAX**
highbrow **SNOB, EGGHEAD, SERIOUS, LONGHAIR, INTELLECTUAL**
high-class **POSH, TONY, ELITE,**

RITZY, SWANKY, SWISH, DELUXE, QUALITY

highest point APEX, PEAK, APOGEE, FINIAL, VERTEX, ZENITH

high-handed ARROGANT, CAVALIER, AUTOCRATIC

highland accessory KILT, TREWS, SPORRAN, CLAYMORE

highlander GAEL, SCOT, TARTAN

highlight ACCENT, STRESS, UNDERLINE

highly VERY, VASTLY, GREATLY, LARGELY

high-strung TENSE, NERVOUS

high-toned LOFTY, MODISH, QUALITY

highway ITER, PIKE, ALCAN, AVENUE, FREEWAY

highwayman PAD, BRIGAND, LADRONE, HIJACKER

hijacker CAPTOR, TERRORIST

hike TREK, WALK, BOOST, TRAMP, DECAMP

hilarious GAY, MERRY, RIOTOUS

hill COP, KOP, TOR, BRAE, BULT, DAGH, DENE, DOWN, DUNE, HOLT, KAME, KNAP, LOMA, MESA, PAHA, RATH, TUMP, BUTTE, KNOLL, KOPJE, MORRO, MOUND, COPPLE, CUESTA, LOMITA, TERTRE

Hillary's companion NORGAY

Hillary's feat EVEREST

hillbilly RUBE, RUSTIC

hillock TOFT, TUMP, KNOLL, MOUND, HUMMOCK

hillside BRAE, SLOPE

hilltop TOR, KNAP, PEAK, CREST, SUMMIT

hilt HAFT, HELVE, HANDLE

Himalayan country JAMMU, NEPAL, TIBET, BHUTAN, SIKKIM, KASHMIR

Himalayas see MOUNTAINS

hind BACK, REAR; see DEER

hinder BALK, DELAY, DETER, CUMBER, HAMPER, IMPEDE, THWART

Hindi dialect BRAJBASHA

hindrance BAR, HITCH, BARRIER, OBSTACLE, DIFFICULTY, IMPEDIMENT

Hindu SER, BABU, JAIN, SEIK, SIKH, JAINA, TAMIL, GENTOO

Hindu beverage AMRITA

Hindu calendar see p. 718

Hindu essence SAT, KARMA, AMRITA

Hindu holy city BENARES

Hindu mythology see p. 650

Hindu sacred writings VEDA, AGAMA, TANTRA

Hindu title MIR, RAO, SRI, BARA, NAIK, SIDI, BURRA, SAHIB; see TITLE

Hindustani language URDU, HINDI

hinge AXIS, BUTT, HARR, JOINT, PIVOT

hinge part PINTLE

hint CUE, TIP, CLEW, CLUE, IMPLY, INKLE, TRACE, ALLUDE, TIPOFF

hinterland INLAND, LOCALITY, VICINITY, BOONDOCKS

hip COXA, ILIA, HAUNCH, HUCKLE

hip, pert. to ILIAC, SCIATIC

Hippocrates birthplace KOS

hippopotamus, young CALF

hire LET, RENT, LEASE, EMPLOY, ENGAGE, SALARY, SIGNUP, TAKEON, CHARTER, (RE)STAFF

hired labor TOGT

hirsute BUSHY, HAIRY, PILOSE, SHAGGY, BRISTLY

historian ANTIQUARY, ARCHIVIST

historian, famous see p. 541

historical PAST, REAL, FACTUAL

history LORE, PAST, ANNALS, RECORD, MEMOIR

history muse CLIO

hit BOP, BOFF, CUFF, SLUG, SOCK, CLOUT, SMITE, LARRUP, POMMEL

hit or miss RANDOM, AIMLESS, HAPHAZARD

hit, something to JACKPOT

hitch TUG, LIMP, SNAG, CATCH, DELAY, GLITCH, HOBBLE

hitchhike THUMB

hitherto TO NOW, (UN)TIL NOW

Hitler rank CORPORAL

Hitler wife EVA, BRAUN

Hittite ancestor HETH, (K)HATTI

hive(s) GUM, RASH, SKEP, SWARM, UREDO, APIARY

hoard   SAVE, AMASS, CACHE, STASH, STORE

hoarder   ANT, MISER, NIGGARD, PACKRAT

hoarfrost   RAG, RIME

hoarse   ROKY, GRUFF, HUSKY, ROUPY, CROAKY, RAUCOUS, THROATY

hoarseness   ROUP

hoary   OLD, GRAY, WHITE, ANCIENT

hoax   BAM, GULL, RUSE, SHAM, FRAUD, SPOOF, CANARD, HUMBUG

hobble   LIMP, HITCH, FETTER, HAMPER, HINDER

hobby   FAD, PASTIME, SIDELINE, AVOCATION, DIVERSION

hobgoblin   IMP, BOGY, PUCK, BOGEY, SPRITE, BUGBEAR

hobnob   MIX, MINGLE, CONSORT, HANGOUT, SOCIALIZE

hobo   BUM, STIFF, TRAMP, DRIFTER, VAGRANT

hock   HAM, HOX, PAWN, GAMBREL

hockey   HURLEY, SHINNY, HURLING

hockey coaches   DAY, HART, BLAKE, ARBOUR, BOWMAN, DEMERS, GORMAN, IMLACH, SATHER

hockey penalty   HOOKING, CLIPPING, SLASHING, TRIPPING

hockey players & teams   see p. 710

hockey position   WING, CENTER, GOALIE, FORWARD

hockey term   CAGE, PUCK, BULLY, CAMAN, ICING, GOALIE, CAMMOCK, FACEOFF

hod filler   MORTAR

hodgepodge   HASH, MESS, OLIO, OLLA, CENTO, MEDLEY, FARRAGO

hoe   HACK, TILL, WEED, WARREN, PREPARE

hog   GRAB, CORNER, CONTROL; see SWINE

Hogan's Heroes name   CLARY, CRANE, KINCH, KLINK, BANNER, DAWSON, LEBEAU, MCLARY, WERNER, NEWKIRK, SCHULTZ, KLEMPERER

Hogan's Heroes setting   STALAG

hogtie   BIND, CURB, FETTER, HAMPER

hogwash   HOOEY, HOKUM, SWILL, REFUSE, BALONEY

hoist   GIN, BOOM, DROP, JACK, LIFT, REAR, CRANE, DAVIT, HEAVE, SLING, WINCH, CAPSTAN, DERRICK, UPRAISE, WINDLASS

hoity-toity   POSH, SNOOTY

hokum   BUNK, HOOEY, HUMBUG, HOGWASH, CLAPTRAP

hold   FIX, OWN, BITE, GRIP, STAY, AVAST, BELAY, CLASP, GRASP, HATCH, THINK, CLUTCH, DETAIN, STORAGE

hold on   ENDURE, PERSIST, CONTINUE

— hold on   PUT A

hold up   ROB, PROP, DELAY, DETAIN, ENDURE, SUPPORT, SURVIVE

holder   DOP(P), OWNER, TENANT

holding   SEAT, ASSET, TENURE, PROPERTY

holdup   MUG, PROP, RAID, SNAG, DELAY, HEIST, HITCH, HIJACK, STICKUP, ROBBERY

hole   EYE, PIT, BORE, DENT, GEAT, GIME, LILL, PORE, SCYE, SLOT, VOID, SPRUE, SIPAPU

— in the hole   ACE

holiday(s)   TET, XMAS, FEAST, FERIA, FERIE, STPAT, EASTER, FIESTA, RECESS, NONLEDAY

Holland   see NETHERLANDS

hollow   PIT, DENT, GORE, GULF, HOWE, BIGHT, FALSE, FOVEA, SCOOP, DIMPLE

holly   ASSI, HOLM, ILEX, MATE, ACEBO, DAHOON, YAUPON, CASSINA, CASSINE

Hollywood   TINSELTOWN; *see also* MOVIE, FILM

Hollywood street   VINE, SUNSET

Hollywood ten   COLE, MALTZ, SCOTT, BESSIE, LAWSON, ORNITZ, TRUMBO, DMYTRYK, LARDNER, BIBERMAN

Holmes actors   BRETT, MOORE, MASSEY, WONTNER, RATHBONE, TREVILLE

Holmes author   DOYLE

Holmes companion   WATSON

holy   DIVINE, SACRED, BLESSED, SAINTLY, HALLOW(ED), CONSECRATED

Holy City   KIEV, ROME, ZION,
LHASA, MECCA, MEDINA,
BENARES, HARDWAR,
VARANASI, JERUSALEM
Holy Grail   SANGRAAL
Holy Grail castle   MONSALVAT
Holy Grail seeker   GALAHAD
Holy Land   PALESTINE
holy man   SADH, FAKIR,
SADHU
Holy Roman emperor   KARL,
OTTO, WIDO, FRANZ, LOUIS,
ARNULF, JOSEPH, KONRAD,
LOTHAR, LUDWIG, RUDOLF,
WENZEL, CHARLES, LEOPOLD,
FREDERIC
Holy Writ   BIBLE
homage   DUTY, HONOR,
RESPECT, TRIBUTE,
REVERENCE
home   NEST, ROOF, ABODE,
ASTRE, HEARTH, HABITAT,
HOSPICE
Home Sweet Home poet   PAYNE
homebody   RECLUSE
homecoming   RETURN,
REUNION
homely   UGLY, PLAIN, RUSTIC,
SIMPLE
homemaker   HOUSEWIFE
Homer birthplace   CHIOS
Homer work   ILIAD, ODYSSEY
Homer character   AJAX, HELEN,
PARIS, PRIAM, HECTOR,
NESTOR, ULYSSES, ACHILLES,
MENELAUS, ODYSSEUS
homesick   BLUE, LONGING,
WISTFUL, NOSTALGIC
homesickness   LONGING,
NOSTALGIA, MELANCHOLY
homespun   PLAIN, SIMPLE
homestead   TOFT, MESSUAGE
homey   COZY, FAMILIAR,
FRIENDLY, INTIMATE
homily   TALK, SERMON,
LECTURE
hominy   SAMP, GRITS
— homo   ECCE
homogeneous   SAME, ALIKE,
UNIFORM
homosexual   GAY, INVERT,
EPICENE, LESBIAN
Honduran city   LIMA, YORO,
CEIBA, DANLI, ROATAN,
TRUJILLO, YUSCARAN,
CHOLUTECA, TEGUCIGALPA
Honduran lake   YOJOA
Honduran measure   VARA,
MILLA, TERCIA

Honduran money   CENTAVO,
LEMPIRA
Honduran neighbor   GUATEMALA,
NICARAGUA, ELSALVADOR
Honduran river   COCO, ULUA,
AGUAN, JALAN, PATUCA,
SULACO, CHOLUTECA
Honduras, capital of   TEGUCIGALPA
hone   FILE, WHET, STROP,
SHARPEN
honest   GOOD, TRUE, FRANK,
SINCERE, UPRIGHT
honesty   CANDOR, PROBITY,
INTEGRITY
honey   MEL, DEAR, MELL,
DARLING
honey drink   MEAD, MORAT,
PIMENT
honeycombed   FAVOSE,
RIDDLED
honeyeater   OO, IAO, IHI, BEAR,
MOHO, POOH, MAOMAO,
BELLBIRD
honeyed   SILKY, SWEET,
SMOOTH, SUGARY
Honeymooners name   KEAN,
ALICE, RALPH, CARNEY,
NORTON, TRIXIE, GLEASON,
KRAMDEN, MEADOWS
Hong Kong bay   DEEP,
REPULSE, DISCOVERY
Hong Kong city   TAIPO,
KOWLOON, ABERDEEN,
VICTORIA
honky-tonk   DIVE, SALOON,
CABARET
honor   ACE, TEN, JACK, KEEP,
KING, QUEEN, CREDIT,
ESTEEM, DIGNITY, RESPECT
honorable   NOBLE, WORTHY,
UPRIGHT
honorarium   FEE, TIP, REWARD
honorary   TITULAR, EMERITUS
Honshu city   GIFU, KOBE,
KURE, KYOTO, OSAKA,
TOKYO, KAWASAKI,
YOKOHAMA
hood   HOW, COWL, BIGGIN,
CALASH, CAMAIL, CAPOTE,
SURTOUT; see GANGSTER
hoodlum   see GANGSTER
hoodoo   HEX, JINX, JYNX,
JONAH
hoodwink   CON, DUPE, FOOL,
SEEL, BLIND, DELUDE,
DECEIVE
hooey   BUNK, HUMBUG,
NONSENSE
hoof   CLEE, UNGUIS, UNGULA

hoofer DANCER
hook GAFF, CLEEK, POPPER, CRAMPON, HAMULUS
hook and — CROOK, LADDER
hookah NARGILE
hooked ADUNC, HAMUS, GAFFED, HAMATE, HAMOSE, CLEEKED, FALCATE, ADUNCOUS, AQUILINE, FALCATED
hookey player TRUANT
hooligan SPIV, THUG, TOUGH, ROWDY, RUFFIAN
hoopla HYPE, BALLYHOO
hoopoe UPUPA
hoosegow see JAIL
Hoosier State IN(D), INDIANA
Hoover dam lake MEAD
hop LEAP, CAPER, BOUND, SPRING
hope LONG, SPES, FAITH, TRUST, ASPIRE, CHANCE, PROSPECT
hopeful ROSY, ASPIRANT, EXPECTANT, PROMISING
hopeless BAD, VAIN, BLEAK, INEPT, FUTILE, FORLORN, DEJECTED
Hopi MOKI, MOQUI, PUEBLO
hopscotch stone PEEVER
Hora(e) DIKE, CARPO, HOURS, EIRENE, THALLO, EUNOMIA
horde MOB, GANG, MASS, PACK, DROVE, SWARM, THRONG
horizon SCOPE, SKYLINE, AZIMUTH
horizontal FLAT, FLUSH, LEVEL, PLANE, PRONE
horizontal timber LINTEL
hormone ESTRIOL, ESTRONE, GASTRIN, INSULIN, THEELIN, ANDROGEN, ESTROGEN, LIPOCAIC, SECRETIN, ADRENALIN, CORTISONE, ESTRADIOL, PROGESTIN, PROLACTIN, THYROXINE
hormone medicine ACTH
horn DAG, CUSP, BUGLE, CORNU, FRENCH, PRONG, ANTLER, BASSET, RHYTON, SHOFAR, ENGLISH
horn tissue SCUR, KERATIN
hornbill TOCK, HOMRAI
horned animal GNU, RAM, BULL, IBEX, STAG, RHINO, SHEEP, CATTLE, BUFFALO, UNICORN, ANTELOPE; see ANTLER

hornet VESPID; see WASP
hornless NOT, MULEY, POLEY, DODDIE, MULLEY, POLLED, ACEROUS
horny CALOUS, CORNEOUS
horrible BAD, VILE, DIRE, GRIM, AWFUL, NASTY, GRISLY, GHASTLY
horrid UGLY, VILE, NASTY, HATEFUL
horrify REPEL, APPAL(L), SICKEN
horror DREAD, SHOCK, DISGUST, AVERSION, REVULSION
hors d'oeuvre TAPA, CANAPE, STARTER, ZAKUSKA, ANTIPASTO, APPETIZER
horse GRI, NAG, COLT, FOAL, HACK, MARE, PLUG, PONY, BLOCK, FILLY, FRAME, MOUNT, PACER, STEED, BRONCO, CAYUSE, DOBBIN, JENNET, CHARGER, GELDING, PALFREY, TRESTLE, STALLION; see p. 663
horse, command to GEE, HAW, HUP, PROO, WHOA, GIDDAP
horse disease GID, BOTS, LOCO, FARCY, FRUSH, SURRA, VIVES, HEAVES, LAMPAS, NAGANA, SPAVIN, SURRAH, THRUSH, DOURINE, LAMPERS, QUITTOR, MALANDERS
horse, famous LOCO, FURY, LUCKY, SCOUT, DIABLO, FLICKA, SILVER, TOPPER, MARSHAL, RAWHIDE, TRIGGER, CHAMPION, BUTTERMILK; see p. 630
horse genus EQUUS
horse part FROG, HOCK, HOOF, FRUSH, SHANK, CANNON, GASKIN, INSTEP, STIFLE, CORONET, FETLOCK, PASTERN
horse training school MANEGE
horse, young COLT, FOAL, FILLY, YEARLING
horsefly TABANID
horsehair SETON, SNELL, TOUPEE
horseman RIDER, GAUCHO, JOCKEY, CABALLERO
horsemanship MANEGE, EQUITATION
horseshoe part CALK
horseshoeing frame TRAVE

hortatory **WARNING, ADVISORY**
Horus **RA**
Horus head **HAWK**
Horus parent **ISIS, OSIRIS**
hose **SOCK(S), ANKLET,**
BOOTEE, BOOTIE, MOGGAN,
HOSIERY, STOCKING(S)
Hosea relative **GOMER**
hospice **INN, REFUGE,**
SHELTER
hospitable **OPEN, WARM,**
CORDIAL, RECEPTIVE
hospital **ASYLUM, CLINIC,**
HOSPICE, SICKBAY,
INFIRMARY, SANATORIUM
hospital attendant **RN, AIDE,**
NURSE, INTERN(E),
ORDERLY, THERAPIST
hospital section **ER, OR, WARD,**
CLINIC, PAVILION,
EMERGENCY
host(ess) **PYX, ARMY, ARRAY,**
CROWD, HORDE, PATEN,
USHER, WAFER, LEGION,
THRONG, BONIFACE
hostage **PAWN, PLEDGE,**
CAPTIVE
hostel **INN, HOTEL, TAVERN,**
HOSPICE
hostility **ANIMUS, ENMITY,**
ILLWILL
hostler **GROOM**
hot **NEW, SEXY, ANGRY,**
FIERY, MUGGY, SPICY,
SULTRY, INTENSE, PEPPERY,
THERMAL
hot-blooded **LUSTY, ARDENT,**
INTENSE, SPIRITED
hot dog **FRANK, WIENER,**
WIENIE, FRANKFURTER
hot food **CURRY, CAYENNE,**
TABASCO, JALAPENO
hot iron **CAUTER(Y)**
hot item **LOOT, SALSA**
hotel **INN, LODGE, HOSTEL(RY)**
hotel chain **OMNI, HYATT,**
HILTON, RAMADA, WESTIN,
DAYSINN, WYNDHAM,
SHERATON
hotel facility **SPA**
hotel guest **PATRON,**
TRAVELER, TRANSIENT
hotheaded **RASH, FIERY,**
TESTY, WILLFUL
hothouse **NURSERY,**
GREENERY
Hottentot **GONA, KORA,**
NAMA, DAMARA, GRIQUA,
SAN DAWE

hound **NAG, HUNT, CHASE,**
WORRY, HARASS, PLAGUE;
see **DOG**
hourly **HORAL, FREQUENT**
house **ECO, HUT, CASA, COTE,**
HOME, IGLU, ROOF, ABODE,
BAHAY, IGLOO, TEMPE,
TUPEK, VILLA, CASINO,
GAZEBO, MAISON,
COTTAGE, MANSION
— house **DOSS**
House, longest serving members
YATES, CANNON, CELLER,
PATMAN, SABATH, VINSON,
RAYBURN, WHITTEN
House speakers **ORR, BELL,**
BOYD, CLAY, COBB, REED,
BANKS, BYRNS, CLARK, CRISP,
DAVIS, FOLEY, GROW,
MACON, WHITE, ALBERT,
COLFAX, DAYTON, GARNER,
KEIFER, MARTIN, ONEILL,
RAINEY, BARBOUR,
RAYBURN, GINGRICH,
HASTERT
household **FAMILY, MENAGE**
housewife **HAUSFRAU,**
HOMEMAKER
housing **FRAME, LODGING,**
SHELTER, COVERING
hovel **HUT, HUTCH, SHACK,**
LEANTO
hover **FLIT, DRIFT, FLOAT,**
WAVER, LINGER, FLUTTER
however **BUT, YET, STILL,**
THO(UGH)
howl **BAY, KEEN, YOWL,**
BELLOW; *see* **CRY**
hoyden **ROMP, TOMBOY**
hub **AXIS, CORE, NAVE,**
FOCUS, HEART, BOSTON,
CENTER
Hub team **SOX, CELTICS**
hubbub **ADO, DIN, STIR,**
TODO, CLAMOR, TUMULT,
UPROAR
Huckleberry Finn author **(MARK)**
TWAIN, CLEMENS
Huckleberry Finn charcters **JIM,**
TOM, THE DUKE, THE KING,
DAUPHIN
huckster **PEDLAR, HAWKER,**
VENDOR, PEDDLER
huddle **MEET, CROWD,**
GROUP, CAUCUS, CROUCH,
CLUSTER
Hudson River city **TROY,**
TIVOLI, NEW YORK,
YONKERS, WEST POINT

hue CRY, DYE, TINT, TONE, COLOR, SHADE, TINGE
hue and — CRY
huff PANT, PUFF, SNIT, SULK, TEMPER, WHEEZE
huff and — PUFF
hug CLASP, CUDDLE, ENFOLD, EMBRACE
huge VAST, ENORM, GIANT, GIGANTIC
Hugo wife ADELE
Huguenot leader CONDE, ADRETS, MORNAY, COLIGNY
hull POD, HUSK, CALYX, SHUCK
hullabaloo ADO, DIN, FLAP, TODO, CLAMOR, HUBBUB, TUMULT, UPROAR, BALLYHOO
hum BURR, BUZZ, DRONE, BUMBLE
human HOMO, SOUL, WIGHT, MORTAL, PERSON, ADAMITE, EARTHLY, EARTHLING
humane KIND, CARING, TENDER, MERCIFUL
humanitarian ALTRUIST, DOGOODER
humanity MERCY, CHARITY, MANKIND, SYMPATHY
Humber estuary ABUS
humble MEEK, POOR, ABASE, LOWLY, DEBASE, DEMEAN, MODEST, DEGRADE, SUBMISS, RETIRING
humble pie CROW, NOMBLES, NUMBLES
humbled, be EATCROW, EATDIRT
humbug BOSH, FLAM, HOAX, FRAUD, GAMMON
humdinger PIP, LULU, ONER, DILLY, WINNER
humdrum DRAB, DULL, BORING, ROUTINE, PROSAIC
humid WET, DANK, MOIST, MUGGY, STICKY, SULTRY
humiliate ABASE, ABASH, SHAME, DEMEAN, HUMBLE, DEGRADE, BRING DOWN
humility MODESTY, MEEKNESS
hummingbird CARIB, SYLPH, TOPAZ, HERMIT, HUMMER, COLIBRI, JACOBIN, PUFFLEG, SNOWCAP, WARRIOR, COQUETTE
hummingbird genus SAPPHO
hummock HILL, HUMP, KNOLL, MOUND, MOUNT, HILLOCK

humor FUN, WIT, BABY, BILE, MOOD, WHIM, CATER, FANCY, LYMPH, COMEDY, PHLEGM, INDULGE
humorist ADE, NYE, WAG, WIT, COBB, NASH, ADAMS, ALLEN, BAKER, TWAIN, ROGERS, THURBER, BENCHLEY, COMEDIAN
humorous DROLL, FUNNY, JOKEY, WITTY, JOCOSE, AMUSING, COMICAL
hump HEAP, HILL, KNOB, PILE, BULGE, RIDGE
humpbacked GIBBOUS
Humperdinck opera HANSEL AND GRETEL
Hun ATLI, BOCHE, ETZEL, ATTILA, GERMAN, VANDAL
Hunchback of Notre Dame QUASIMODO
Hunchback of Notre Dame author HUGO
hundred HECTO, CENTUM
Hundred Years' War battles CRECY, CALAIS, ORLEANS, POITIERS, AGINCOURT
hundred-eyed monster ARGUS
Hungarian MAGYAR
Hungarian city EGER, GYOR, PECS, MISKOLC, SZEGED, SZOLNOK, BUDAPEST
Hungarian composer ERKEL, LEHAR, LISZT, BARTOK, KODALY, KURTAG, LIGETI, JOACHIM, DOHNANYI
Hungarian county VAS, PEST, ZALA, BEKES, FEJER, HEVES, TOLNA, NOGRAD, SOMOGY, BARANYA, BUDAPEST
Hungarian lake BALATON
Hungarian language see FINNO-UGRIC
Hungarian leader KUN, DOBI, MARY, NAGY, LOUIS, KADAR, ALBERT, KAROLYI, STEPHEN, ULASZLO
Hungarian measure HOLD, JOCH, YOKZ, METZE
Hungarian money FT, GARA, PENGO, FILLER, FORINT, GULDEN
Hungarian mountain BUKK, KEKES, MATRA, BAKONY
Hungarian neighbor SERBIA, AUSTRIA, CROATIA, ROMANIA, UKRAINE, SLOVAKIA
Hungarian plain (GREAT)ALFOLD

Hungarian river SIO, DUNA, EGER, ZALA, KAPOS, KOROS, TISZA, DANUBE

Hungary, capital of BUDAPEST

hunger YEN, CLEM, ITCH, NEED, PICA, PINE, ACORIA, BULIMY, DESIRE, FAMINE, YEARNING

hungry AVID, KEEN, EAGER, UNFED, STARVED, FAMISHED, RAVENOUS

hunk LUMP, SLAB, CHUNK, PIECE, SLICE

hunt SEEK, TRAP, POACH, STALK, TRACK, TRAIL, FERRET, FOLLOW, SHIKAR

hunter JAGER, ORION, JAEGER, NIMROD, SHIKARI, TRAPPER

hunter's cry TIVY

hunting CHASE, VENERY

hunting dog ALAN(D), HOUND, BASSET, BEAGLE, SETTER, POINTER, SPANIEL

huntress DIANA, SKADI, ARTEMIS, ATALANTA

hurdle SNAG, BARRIER, OBSTACLE

hurdy-gurdy LIRA, ROTA, ORGAN

hurl PASH, TOSS, CHUCK, FLING, HEAVE, PITCH, LAUNCH

hurling, game similar to LACROSSE

hurly-burly CHAOS, BUSTLE, TURMOIL

hurrah OLE, VIVA, CHEER

hurricane STORM, TEMPEST, CYCLONE, TORNADO, TYPHOON

hurricane name FIFI, HUGO, CAROL, DAVID, DIANE, FLORA, FLOYD, HAZEL, HILDA, JANET, MITCH, CONNIE, HATTIE

hurricane part EYE

hurry HIE, RUN, DASH, RUSH, TEAR, TROT, DRIVE, HASTE, SESSA, HASTEN, SCURRY

hurt MAR, ACHE, DERE, HARM, PAIN, IMPAIR, LESION

hurtful CRUEL, NOCENT, CUTTING, MALEFIC, NOISOME

hurtle CAST, DASH, HURL, RACE, RUSH, FLING, CAREER

husband RO, GROOM, OLDMAN, SANNUP, GOODMAN; see SPOUSE

husband's brother LEVIR

husbandry THRIFT, TILLAGE, GEOPONICS

hush (H)SH, CALM, ALLAY, SHUSH

husk BRAN, HULL, LEAM, CHAFF, SHUCK

hussy DOXY, MINX, SLUT, TART, TRAMP, WENCH, WANTON, TROLLOP

hustings COURT, STUMP, PLATFORM

hustler DYNAMO, SHARP(ER), GAMBLER, SWINDLER

hut COT, BARI, COTE, CRAL, ISBA, MIAM, MIMI, SHAD, SKEO, CABIN, HOGAN, HOVEL, JACAL, SHACK, TOLDO, LEANTO, MIAMIA

hutch BIN, PEN, COOP, CREST, WARREN

Huxley novel ANTIC HAY, CROME YELLOW, POINT COUNTER POINT

hyacinth MUSK, CAMAS

hybrid MIX, CROSS, MIXED, CREOLE, FUSION, MIXTURE, MONGREL; see CROSSBREED

Hyde's other half JEKYLL

hydrate SLAKE

hydrocarbon TOLAN, BUTANE, CYMENE, MELENE, ETHANE, OCTANE, OLEFIN, PINENE, METHANE, PROPANE, RETENE, TERPENE, TOLUENE

hydroelectric see PLANT

hydrogen compound IMINE, HYDRIDE

hydrometer scale BRIX

hymn ODE, LAUD, SONG, CHANT, PAEAN, PSALM, MANTRA, ANTHEM, CANTICLE

hyperbole ELA, AUXESIS

hyperbolic function COSH, COTH, CSCH, SECH, SINH, TANH

Hyperion relative GE, EOS, HELIOS, SELENE, URANUS

hypnosis tool WATCH, PENTOTHAL

hypnotic ACETAL, LUMINAL, MESMERIC, SOOTHING, SOPORIFIC

hypnotic state COMA, TRANCE

hypnotism inventor MESMER

hypochondria HYPS

hypocrisy CANT, DECEIT, PRETENSE, DUPLICITY

hypocrite	FRAUD, CHARLATAN	Icelandic mountain	HEKLA, SNOEFELL, BARDHAR
hypothesis	GUESS, THEORY, PREMISE	Icelandic river	HOFSA, THJORSA
hysteria	FIT, PANIC, FRENZY, MADNESS	Icelandic tale	EDDA
hysterical	WILD, FRANTIC, HILARIOUS	Ichabod rival	BROM, BONES
		icon	see IMAGE
		ictus	FIT, ACCENT, STROKE, UPBEAT

I

		icy	COLD, GELID, FRIGID, FROSTY, GLACIAL, ICECOLD, SUBZERO
		id	EGO, PSYCHE
I	EGO, ONE, IOTA, SELF, INDIA	Idaho	see also p. 615
I have spoken	DIXI	Idaho city	BOISE, NAMPA, LEWISTON, POCATELLO
I Love Lucy names	BALL, DESI, FRED, LUCY, ARNAZ, ETHEL, RICKY, VANCE, VIVIAN, FRAWLEY	Idaho Indian	DELAWARE, NEZ PERCE, SHOSHONE
		Idaho mountain	WAUGH, MORMON, SADDLE, CARIBOU, LOOKOUT, TWIN PEAKS
I Remember Mama star	DUNNE		
Iago's wife	EMILIA		
Iberia	SPAIN		
Iberia author	MICHENER	Idaho river	FORK, SNAKE, STJOE, LOCHSA, SALMON, SELWAY, BIGLOST, BRUNEAU, PAYETTE
ibex	see GOAT		
Ibsen character	ASE, GYNT, NORA, PEER, ERDAL, HEDDA, ROSMER, ELLIDA		
		idea	EIDOS, FANCY, NOTION, SCHEME, INKLING
Ibsen play	GHOSTS, PEER GYNT, DOLLS HOUSE, HEDDA GABLER	ideal	HERO, IDOL, MODEL, PARAGON, PERFECT, UTOPIAN
Icarus relative	ERIGONE, DAEDALUS		
		ideal state	EDEN, ICARIA, OCEANA, UTOPIA, EREWHON
ICBM	see p. 742		
ice	BERG, FIRN, FLOE, GRUE, NEVE, SISH, BRASH, FROST, LOLLY, SERAC, BISQUE, PAYOLA, SHERBET	idealist	ANIMIST, DREAMER, OPTIMIST, ROMANTIC
		idealize	DEIFY, ELEVATE
		idée fixe	MANIA, THING, OBSESSION
ice cream	GLACE, GELATO		
ice cream dish	FRAPPE, SUNDAE, PARFAIT, MILKSHAKE	identical	ONE, SAME, TWIN, ALIKE
		identification	ID, TAG, CARD, BADGE, BRAND, LABEL, MARKER, LICENSE
ice mass	PAN, BERG, CALF, FLOE, PACK, GLACIER, GROWLER, ICEBERG		
		identify	SEE, NAME, SPOT, DETECT, EQUATE, MAKEOUT, CLASSIFY
ice skater	see SKATER		
iceberg	FLOE, GROWLER, LETTUCE		
		identity	SELF, PERSONALITY
iced	DID IN, GELID, GLACE, FRAPPE, FROSTED	ideology	ISM, DOGMA, THEORY
Iceland, capital of	REYKJAVIK	Ides of March victim	CAESAR
Icelandic bay	FAXA, HUNA	idiocy	FOLLY, AMENTIA, ANOESIA, FATUITY
Icelandic city	NES, VIK, HOFN, AKUREYRI, REYKJAVIK		
		idiom	CANT, ARGOT, DIALECT, LOCUTION, PARLANCE
Icelandic measure	FET, ALIN, LINA, FERFET, POTTUR, FERALIN, FERMILA, OLTUNNA		
		idiosyncrasy	QUIRK, FOIBLE, PECULIARITY
Icelandic money	IKR, AURAR, EYRIR, KRONA	idiot	OAF, AMENT, MORON, CRETIN

idle   OFF, SIT, LAZE, LAZY, LOAF, FUTILE, GAMMER, LOITER, OTIANT, OTIOSE; *see* INERT

idleness   SLOTH, LAZINESS

idler   SPIV, DRONE, SLACKER

idol   CROM, LION, ZEMI, PAGOD, FETISH, IDOLON, IDOLUM, PAGODA, SYMBOL, TERAPH, EIDOLON

idolater   PAGAN

idolatry   SUTTEE, ANIMISM, DEMONISM, ADULATION

idolize   ADORE, ADMIRE, REVERE, WORSHIP

idyll   ECLOGUE, PASTORAL

Idylls of the King name   ENID

if not   ELSE, NISI, UNLESS

iffy   DICEY, RISKY, CHANCY, TENTATIVE

ignite   STIR(UP), LIGHT, KINDLE, INFLAME, PROVOKE

ignoble   LOW, BASE, VILE, MEAN

ignominious   SORDID, SHAMEFUL

ignominy   SHAME, INFAMY, DISGRACE, DISHONOR

ignorance   TAMAS, NESCIENCE

ignore   OMIT, SNUB, NEGLECT, OVERLOOK, DISREGARD

iguana   *see* LIZARD

Iliad author   HOMER

Iliad character   AJAX, ARES, HELEN, NESTOR, PRIAM, HECTOR, CALCHAS, STENTOR, ULYSSES, ACHILLES

ilk   SORT, KIND, TYPE, STRIPE

ill   ABED, EVIL, SICK, AMISS, BADLY, POORLY, UNWELL, WICKED

ill will   HATE, SPITE, VENOM, ANIMUS, MALICE, RANCOR

ill-fated   DOOMED, UNLUCKY

ill-mannered   RUDE, COARSE, IMPOLITE

ill-tempered   PUXY, CROSS, SURLY, CRANKY, SULLEN, PEEVISH

ill-treatment   ABUSE

illegal   BANNED, ILLICIT, UNLAWFUL

illegitimate   ILLICIT, BASTARD

Illinois   *see also p. 615*

Illinois city   PANA, ZION, CAIRO, AURORA, DEKALB, JOLIET, MOLINE, NORMAL, PEORIA, QUINCY, SKOKIE, URBANA, CHICAGO, WHEATON, EVANSTON, KANKAKEE, ROCKFORD, WAUKEGAN, WILMETTE

Illinois lake   FOX, REND, CALUMET, MICHIGAN

Illinois river   FOX, MUDDY, OHIO, ROCK, SNAKE, SPOON, WABASH, ILLINOIS, KANKAKEE, SANGAMON, DES PLAINES, MISSISSIPPI

Illinois school   DEPAUL, COLUMBIA, ROOSEVELT

illiterate   IGNORANT, UNTAUGHT

illness   MALADY, AILMENT, DISEASE, DISORDER, SICKNESS

illuminate   LIGHT(UP), CLARIFY, ELUCIDATE

illusion   TULLE, MIRAGE, CHIMERA, FANTASY

illusory   FALSE, UNREAL, DECEPTIVE

illustrate   CITE, DRAW, SHOW, EXPLAIN, PICTURE, POINTUP

illustrator   DORE, DUFY, SENDAK, CHAGALL, ROCKWELL, BEARDSLEY

illustrious   FAMED, FAMOUS, MEMORABLE

Illyricum   CROATIA

image   FORM, ICON, IKON, SIGIL, EFFIGY, RECEPT, STATUE, REPLICA; *see* IDOL

imaginary   UNREAL, FICTIVE

imagination   IDEA, DREAM, FANCY, NOTION, VISION

imagine   SEE, WIS, WEEN, IDEATE, SURMISE

imbalance   INEQUITY, DISPARITY

imbecile   FOOL, AMENT, ANILE, MORON, CRETIN, DOTARD, FATUOUS

imbibe   BIB, SIP, GULP, DRINK

imbroglio   PLOT, ENTANGLEMENT

imbue   TINCT, TINGE, INFUSE, INGRAIN, INSPIRE, PERVADE

imitate   APE, ECHO, MIME, MIMIC

imitation   COPY, SHAM, APISM, BOGUS, MIMESIS, MIMICRY

imitator   APE(R), MIMIC, FORGER, PARROT, COPYCAT

immaculate   PURE, PERFECT, FLAWLESS, SPOTLESS

immaterial   TRIVIAL, IRRELEVANT

immature RAW, GREEN, CALLOW, NEANIC, UNRIPE, PUERILE

immediate DIRECT, URGENT, INSTANT, PRESSING

immediately NOW, PDQ, ANON, STAT, PRESTO, PRONTO, PROMPTLY

immense HUGE, VAST(Y), IMMENSE, GALACTIC

immerse DIP, DUCK, DUNK, DOUSE, STEEP, ENGROSS

immigrant ALIEN, METIC, GRIFFIN, WETBACK

immobile FIXED, STILL, STATIC, SESSILE, IMMOBILE, MOTIONLESS

immoderate UNDUE, EFFUSIVE, EXCESSIVE

immodest BOLD, BRAZEN, FORWARD

immolate BURN, SACRIFICE

immoral WICKED, CORRUPT, DEPRAVED, DISSOLUTE

immortal ENDLESS, ETERNAL, UNDYING, PERPETUAL

immovable SET, FIXED, RIGID, PERMANENT

immune EXEMPT, PROTECTED

immunity trigger ANTIGEN

immunizing substance SERUM, HAPTEN, TOXOID, HAPTENE, VACCINE

immure CONFINE, SHUT UP, WALL IN, ISOLATE, SECLUDE

immutable FIRM, ETERNAL, CHANGELESS, ABSOLUTE

imp see ELF, DEMON

impact JAR, BLOW, BRUNT, CRASH, FORCE, SHOCK, EFFECT

impair MAR, HARM, SPOIL, DAMAGE, VITIATE

impale FIX, GORE, SPIT, STAB, SPEAR, SPIKE

impalpable SUBTLE, SHADOWY, INSUBSTANTIAL

impart TELL, SHARE, CONVEY, PASSON, DIVULGE

impartial FAIR, JUST, NEUTRAL, UNBIASED, OBJECTIVE

impasse CULDESAC, DEADLOCK

impassioned FIERY, ARDENT, FERVENT

impassive CALM, BLANK, STOIC, PLACID, STOLID

impatience HASTE, EAGERNESS

impatient KEEN, EAGER, ANXIOUS

impeach ACCUSE, IMPUGN, INDICT, CHARGE

impeccable PERFECT, FLAWLESS, FAULTLESS

impecunious POOR, BROKE, MONEYLESS

impede BLOCK, ESTOP, HAMPER, STYMIE, THWART

impediment DRAG, CHECK, HITCH, BARRIER, OBSTACLE

impel PUSH, DRIVE, PROPEL

impending COMING, FUTURE, LOOMING, IMMINENT

impenetrable DENSE, SOLID, OPAQUE, IMPERVIOUS

imperative LAW, RULE, VITAL, URGENT, CRUCIAL

imperceptible FAINT, MINUTE, UNSEEN, INVISIBLE

imperfect CRUDE, FLAWED, FAULTY

imperfection BLOT, FLAW, VICE, FAULT, DEFECT, BLEMISH, FAILING

imperial GRAND, REGAL, MAJESTIC

imperil RISK, HAZARD, ENDANGER, JEOPARDIZE

imperious BOSSY, ARROGANT, SUPERIOR

impersonal COOL, ALOOF, REMOTE, DISTANT, DETACHED

impersonate APE, COPY, POSE, MIMIC, EMBODY, TAKE OFF

impertinent FLIP, PERT, RUDE, SASSY, SAUCY, MALAPERT

impetuous HOT, RASH, BRASH, HASTY, IMPULSIVE

impetus SPUR, DRIVE, FORCE, MOTIVE, THRUST, MOTIVATION

impiety SIN, APOSTASY, BLASPHEMY, PROFANITY, IRREVERENCE

impinge INVADE, ENCROACH, TRESPASS

impious GODLESS, PROFANE

impish ELFIN, ELVISH, PUCKISH, MISCHIEVOUS

implacable COOL, RIGID, CALLOUS, PITILESS

implant FIX, ROOT, GRAFT, ENROOT, ENGRAFT, INSPIRE, INSTILL

implement KIT, TOOL, EQUIP, DEVICE, ENFORCE, UTENSIL; *see p. 719* implicate LINK, FINGER, CONNECT, INVOLVE

implication ALLUSION, INFERENCE, INNUENDO

implicit, implied TACIT, INNATE, DEDUCED, INHERENT

implore BEG, PLEAD, BESEECH, ENTREAT

imply HINT, MEAN, GETAT, ENTAIL, CONNOTE

impolite RUDE, BOORISH, ILLMANNERED

impolitic UNWISE, TACTLESS, IMPRUDENT

import DRIFT, TENOR, INTENT, WEIGHT

importance VALUE, WEIGHT, ESSENCE, SUBSTANCE

important KEY, MAIN, CHIEF, MAJOR, PRIME, VITAL, EMINENT

important person VIP, MOGUL, WHEEL, BIGWIG, PLAYER, BIG SHOT, NOTABLE, CELEBRITY

impose FOB, LAY, LEVY, PALM, FOIST, ENTAIL, IMPUTE, OBTRUDE

impossible ICANT, NOCANDO, HOPELESS

impost see TAX

impostor SHAM, FAKER, FRAUD, PHONY, QUACK, PHONEY, RINGER, CHARLATAN

impotent WEAK, INEPT, STERILE, HELPLESS, POWERLESS

impound HOLD, POIND, SEIZE, CONFISCATE

impractical USELESS, UNREALISTIC

imprecation OATH, CURSE

impregnable FIRM, SECURE, INVINCIBLE

impregnate SOAK, STEEP, DRENCH, SATURATE, FERTILIZE

impresario AGENT, PROMOTER

impress DENT, LEVY, MARK, DRAFT, PRINT, STAMP

impression IDEA, MARK, STAMP, EFFECT, FEELING, IMPRINT, INKLING, OPINION

Impressionist composer RAVEL, DELIUS, DEBUSSY, GRIFFES, RESPIGHI

Impressionist painter DEGAS, MANET, MONET, RENOIR, SISLEY, BAZILLE, CEZANNE, MORISOT, PISSARO

impressive NOTABLE, AWESOME, IMPOSING, STRIKING

imprint ETCH, MARK, PRESS, STAMP, EMBOSS

imprison CAGE, JAIL, QUAD, IMMURE, CONFINE

imprisonment LIMBO, DURESS, DURANCE

improbable DUBIOUS, DOUBTFUL, UNLIKELY

impromptu ADHOC, ADLIB, OFFHAND, EXTEMPORE

improper RUDE, UNFIT, WRONG, RISQUE, INDECENT

improve AMEND, EMEND, REVISE, ADVANCE

improvement STEPUP, UPTURN, ADVANCE, UPGRADE, PROGRESS, RECOVERY

improvise PONG, VAMP, ADLIB, INVENT, CONTRIVE

imprudent RASH, HASTY, UNWISE, CARELESS

impudence LIP, GALL, BRASS, CHEEK, NERVE

impudent BOLD, FLIP, PERT, BRASH, FRESH, SAUCY

impugn ACCUSE, CHARGE, CHALLENGE

impulse SPUR, URGE, WHIM, NISUS, MOTIVE, IMPETUS

impulsive RASH, SNAP, IMPETUOUS

impunity EXEMPTION

impure BAWDY, DIRTY, AMORAL, TAINTED, UNCLEAN, POLLUTED

impurity DIRT, DROSS, FILTH, LEWDNESS, OBSCENITY

impute (A)RET, IMPOSE, ASCRIBE

in IN, HOT, CHIC, AMONG, AT HOME, ENTREE, ALAMODE, ARRIVED, POPULAR

in arrears LATE, OWING, BEHIND, OVERDUE

in addition AND, TOO, ALSO, PLUS, BESIDES, FURTHER

in agreement ASONE, UNITED, LIKEMINDED

in case IF, LEST

in due course ANON, SOON, SHORTLY

in fact TRULY, INDEED, DEFACTO

in favor	FOR, PRO	Inca ruler	HUASCAR,	
in love	GAGA, SMITTEN		ATAHUALPA	
in other words	IDEST	incalculable	VAST, UNTOLD,	
in person	LIVE		COUNTLESS	
in place of	INLIEU, INSTEAD	incandescent	REDHOT,	
in progress	CURRENT,		GLOWING, RADIANT	
	ONGOING	incantation	CHARM, SPELL,	
in re	ABOUT, ANENT,		PRAYER, CANTRAP,	
REGARDING, CONCERNING			CANTRIP	
in reserve	ONICE, ONHOLD	incapable	INEPT, UNABLE,	
in spite of	MAUGRE, DESPITE		POWERLESS	
in that case	THEN	incapacitate	LAME, LAYUP,	
in the bag	SEWN UP, CERTAIN		INJURE, DISABLE	
in the end	ATLAST, FINALLY	incarcerate	JAIL, INTERN,	
in the manner of	ALA		LOCKUP, CONFINE,	
in the raw	BARE, NUDE,		IMPRISON	
	NAKED	incarnation	EMBODIMENT,	
in time	ATEMPO, SOMETIME,		PERSONIFICATION	
	EVENTUALLY	incendiary	FIREBUG,	
inability	FAILURE,		ARSONIST	
IMPOTENCE, INCAPACITY		incense	GUM, JOSS, MATTI,	
inaccurate	WRONG, INEXACT,	MYRRH, SPICE, ENRAGE,		
	MISTAKEN	STACTE, OLIBANUM		
Inachus daughter	IO	incentive	SPUR, MOTIVE,	
inaction	INERTIA, IDLENESS,		IMPULSE	
	LETHARGY	inception	START, ORIGIN,	
inactive	LATENT, STATIC,		OUTSET	
DORMANT, FAINEANT; see		incessant	NONSTOP,	
	IDLE, INERT		CONSTANT	
inactivity	APATHY, STASIS,	inch	EDGE, CRAWL, CREEP	
	IDLENESS	incident	EVENT, EPISODE	
inadequate	SCANT(Y),	incidental	MINOR, CASUAL,	
LACKING, UNEQUAL,			CHANCE	
	DEFICIENT	incidentally	OBITER, APROPOS	
inamorata	LOVER, MISTRESS	incinerate	BURN, (IN)CREMATE	
inane	VOID, SILLY, VAPID,	incinerator	FURNACE,	
	ABSURD, IDIOTIC		CREMATORY	
inanimate	DEAD, INERT,	incipient	EARLY, INITIAL,	
	LIFELESS		EMBRYONIC	
inappropriate	INAPT, WRONG,	incision	CUT, GASH, SLIT,	
IMPROPER, UNBECOMING			NOTCH	
inarticulate	DUMB, MUTE,	incisive	KEEN, ACUTE, SHARP,	
	APHONIC		BITING	
inasmuch	SINCE, BECAUSE	incite	EGG, ABET, GOAD,	
inattention	NEGLECT,	PROD, SPUR, URGE, IMPEL,		
OVERSIGHT, DISTRACTION		ROUSE, FOMENT, SUBORN		
inattentive	DEAF, REMISS,	inclement	BAD, FOUL, RAINY,	
CARELESS, HEEDLESS,			WINDY, STORMY	
	UNMINDFUL	inclination	BEND, BENT, BIAS,	
inaugurate	OPEN, SET UP,	GRADE, SLANT, TASTE,		
INDUCT, INSTAL(L), SWEAR			LEANING	
	IN	incline	CANT, HILL, LEAN,	
inauspicious	ILL, OMINOUS,	RAMP, TEND, TILT, SLOPE,		
UNTIMELY, UNPROMISING		TREND, VERGE, DEVIATE		
inborn	INNATE, NATIVE,	inclined	APT, SKEW, PRONE,	
CONNATE, INHERENT			DISPOSED	
Inca	QUECHUAN	include	TAKEIN, CONTAIN,	
Inca capital	CUSCO, CUZCO		COMPRISE	
Inca conqueror	PIZARRO	inclusive	BROAD, GENERIC	

incognito **SECRETLY, DISGUISE(D)**
incoherent **CONFUSED,**
   RAMBLING, DISJOINTED
income **PAY, WAGE, RENTE,**
   SALARY, USANCE, ANNUITY,
   PENSION, STIPEND
incomparable **PEERLESS,**
   UNRIVALED, MATCHLESS
incomplete **SHY, SHORT,**
   LACKING, PARTIAL,
   DEFICIENT
inconclusive **UNCERTAIN,**
   UNSETTLED
incongruous **ODD, INAPT,**
   STRANGE
inconsequential **MINOR,**
   SLIGHT, TRIVIAL
inconsiderate **UNKIND,**
   SELFISH, TACTLESS
inconstant **FICKLE, MUTABLE,**
   VOLATILE, CAPRICIOUS
inconstant, be **RENEGE**
inconvenience **BOTHER,**
   HASSLE, PUTOUT, TROUBLE,
   NUISANCE
incorporate **MERGE, EMBODY,**
   CONTAIN, INCLUDE
incorrect **OFF, FALSE, WRONG,**
   UNTRUE, ERRONEOUS
increase **UP, EKE, WAX, RISE,**
   ACCRUE, DILATE, STEP UP,
   TREBLE, GREATEN
incredible **ABSURD, AMAZING,**
   IMPLAUSIBLE
incredulity **DOUBT, WONDER,**
   UNBELIEF, SKEPTICISM
incriminate **CONNECT,**
   INVOLVE, IMPLICATE
incubate **SIT, BROOD, HATCH,**
   CONCOCT
incubus **DUSE, DEMON,**
   SPIRIT, NIGHTMARE
inculcate **IMBUE, INSTIL**
incumbency **TENURE**
incumbent **SERVING, SITTING,**
   IN OFFICE, OCCUPANT
incur **RUNUP**
incursion **RAID, FORAY,**
   INROAD
indebted **OBLIGED, BEHOLDEN**
indebtedness **OWING,**
   OBLIGATION
indecent **LEWD, RACY, RISQUE,**
   OBSCENE, IMMODEST
indecision **HESITANCY,**
   INCERTAINTY
indecorous **RUDE, UNSEEMLY**
indeed **ARU, WIS, AROO, IWIS,**
   AROON, REALLY, VERILY

indefinite **DIM, HAZY, LOOSE,**
   VAGUE
indefinite amount **ANY, FEW,**
   SOME
indelible **LASTING,**
   PERMANENT
indelicate **CRASS, CRUDE,**
   GROSS, ROUGH, COARSE,
   TACTLESS, UNSEEMLY
indemnify **PAY, ASSURE,**
   REDEEM
indent **ALIGN, NOTCH,**
   IMPRESS
indentation **NICK, CRENA,**
   DINGE, NOTCH, CRENAE,
   MARGIN, CRENELET
independent **FREE,**
   AUTONOMOUS
indescribable **INEFFABLE**
indestructible **DURABLE,**
   ROCKHARD, PERMANENT,
   RESISTANT
indeterminate **VAGUE,**
   IMPRECISE, UNCERTAIN
index **PIP, FIST, MARK, TABLE,**
   GNOMON, POINTER
India, capital of **NEWDELHI**
Indian, American *see* **NATIVE**
   AMERICAN; *see p. 730*
Indian caste *see* **CASTE**
Indian city **AGRA, DELHI,**
   JAMMU, SURAT, BHOPAL,
   BOMBAY, JAIPUR, KANPUR,
   MADRAS, MYSORE, NAGPUR,
   BENARES, CALCUTTA,
   GWALIOR, JODHPUR,
   LUCKNOW, AMRITSAR,
   BANGALORE
Indian language **KHASI;**
   see **INDIC, DRAVIDIAN,**
   MUNDA
Indian leader **NAIK, ASOKA,**
   NEHRU, GANDHI, SHASTRI
Indian measure **GUZ, JOW, KOS,**
   BEGA, HATH, JAOB, KOSS,
   BIGHA, COVID, CROSA,
   DRONA, GARCE, HASTA,
   GEERAH, MUSHTI, UNGLEE
Indian money **DAM, LAC, PIE,**
   ANNA, DAWM, FELS, HOON,
   LAKH, PICE, TARA, CRORE,
   FANAM, MOHUR, PAISA,
   RUPEE, PAGODA
Indian mountain **ABIL, GHATS,**
   KAMET, ZASKAR, DAPSANG
Indian music **RAGA**
Indian pass **BOLAN, GUMAL,**
   KHYBER
Indian river **BEAS, MAHI, RAVI,**

INDUS, TAPTI, CHENAB, | indirect   OBLIQUE,
GANGES, JHELUM, SUTLEJ, | CIRCUITOUS, ROUNDABOUT
YAMUNA, KRISHNA, | indiscreet   NOSY, UNWISE,
NARMADA, GODAVARI | RECKLESS, TACTLESS,
Indian state   GOA, ASSAM, | IMPRUDENT
BIHAR, DELHI, JAMMU, | indiscretion   SLIP, FOLLY,
KERALA, ORISSA, PUNJAB, | GAFFE, LAPSE, PECCADILLO
SIKKIM, GUJARAT, | indiscriminate   RANDOM,
HARYANA, KASHMIR, | ARBITRARY, HAPHAZARD
MANIPUR, MIZORAM, | indispensable   VITAL, CRUCIAL,
TRIPURA | ESSENTIAL, REQUISITE
Indian tree   BEL, DAR, AMRA, | indisposed   SICK, LOATH,
BAEL, ANJAN, ARUSA, | LAIDUP, POORLY, UNWELL,
DADAP, HOGPLUM; see EAST | RELUCTANT
INDIAN, WEST INDIAN | indisposition   AILMENT, ILLNESS,
Indian weight   SER, DHAN, | MALAISE, AVERSION
PALA, PICE, RATI, TOLA, | indisputable   CERTAIN,
ADPAO, BAHAR, MAUND, | APOD(E)ICTIC, UNDENIABLE
RATTI, CHITTAK | indistinct   DIM, LOW, HAZY,
Indiana   see also p. 615 | FAINT, FOGGY, VAGUE,
Indiana city   GARY, PERU, | BLURRY, UNCLEAR, OBSCURE
PAOLI, GOSHEN, KOKOMO, | indite   PEN, WRITE, (IN)SCRIBE
MARION, MUNCIE, WABASH, | individual   ONE, BION, SELF,
WARSAW, ELKHART, | SOLE, BEING
HAMMOND, RICHMOND, | indivisible   ONE, UNITED
LAFAYETE, EVANSVILLE | Indochina   LAOS, VIETNAM,
Indiana Indian   MIAMI | CAMBODIA
Indiana lake   LEMON, MONROE, | Indo-Chinese people   LAO, TAI,
SHAPER, FREEMAN, | SHAN
WAWASEE | indoctrinate   BRIEF, IMBUE,
Indiana river   OHIO, WHITE, | TRAIN, COACH, INSTILL,
WABASH, ELKHART, | INSTRUCT
TIPPECANOE | Indo-European   ARYA(N)
Indic language   PALI, BHILI, | Indo-European language   URDU,
ORIYA, VEDIC, NEPALI, | CZECH, GREEK, HINDI,
PAHARI, SANSKRIT, | LATIN, WELSH, CELTIC,
SINHALESE, RAJASTHANI | DANISH, FRENCH, GERMAN,
indicate   BODE, MARK, NOTE, | POLISH, ROMANY, ENGLISH,
POINT TO | ITALIAN, LATVIAN, PERSIAN,
indication   CLUE, OMEN, | RUSSIAN, SPANISH, SWEDISH,
SIGN(AL), WARNING | YIDDISH, ALBANIAN,
indicator   DIAL, SIGN, VANE, | ARMENIAN, SANSKRIT,
ARROW, GAUGE, POINTER, | ICELANDIC, NORWEGIAN,
REGISTER | PORTUGESE; see p. 621
indict   PEACH, ACCUSE, | indolence   SLOTH, TORPOR,
ARRAIGN, IMPEACH | LAZINESS
indifference   APATHY, | indolent   LAZY, SORN, OTIOSE,
LETHARGY | SUPINE, TORPID, LISTLESS
indifferent   COLD, COOL, SOSO, | indomitable   TOUGH,
BLASE, STOIC, NEUTRAL, | RESOLUTE, DETERMINED,
STOICAL | INVINCIBLE
indigenous   INNATE, NATIVE, | Indonesia, capital of   (D)JAKARTA
EDAPHIC, ENDEMIC | Indonesian city/town   DILI,
indigent   POOR, NEEDY, | AMBON, JAMBI, MEDAN,
DESTITUTE | KUPANG, MANADO, PADANG,
indignation   IRE, ANGER, | BANDUNG, CILACAP,
RESENTMENT | JAKARTA, KENDARI,
indignity   SHAME, INSULT, | MATARAM, SEMARANG,
SLIGHT, AFFRONT | SURABAJA

Indonesian island   BALI, JAVA, CERAM, TIMOR, BORNEO, BANGKA, FLORES, LOMBOK, MADURA, SUMATRA, SULAWEST

Indonesian language   *see* PACIFIC ISLANDS

Indonesian measure   BOUW, KILAN, TAKAR, GANTANG, TJENKAL

Indonesian money   RP, SEN, RUPIAH

Indonesian mountain   KRAKATOA

Indonesian neighbor   GUINEA, MALAYSIA, SINGAPORE

Indonesian orchestra   GAMELAN

Indonesian river   BUNI, HARI, MUSI, SIAK, DIGUL, UJING, BARITO, DJAMBI

Indonesian tribe   DANI, JAYA, BATAK, SASAK,

Indonesian weight   TJI, HOEN, TALI, WANG, PICUL, REAAL, KOJANG, KULACK

indubitable   SURE, CERTAIN, DEFINITE, DOUBTLESS

induce   LEAD, URGE, CAUSE, REASON, BRINGON

inducement   BRIBE, CARROT, MOTIVE, INCENTIVE

inductance unit   HENRY

indulge   PET, CODDLE, PAMPER, PETTLE, GRATIFY

indulgent   KIND, LENIENT, SELFISH, TOLERANT

industrial   TRADE, MODERN, DEVELOPED, MANUFACTURING

industrialist   BARON, TYCOON, MAGNATE, FINANCIER, CAPITALIST

industrious   BUSY, ACTIVE, OPEROSE, DILIGENT, HARDWORKING

industry   LABOR, TRADE, BUSINESS, COMMERCE, DILIGENCE

inebriate   SOT, TIGHT, TIPSY, TOPER, SQUIFFY, INTOXICATE

inedible   BAD, SPOILED, UNEATABLE

inefficient   INEPT, BUNGLING, WASTEFUL, INCOMPETENT

inept   CLUMSY, AWKWARD

inert   DEAD, DULL, AMORT, LATENT, SUPINE

inertia   TORPOR, APATHY, LETHARGY

inevitable   FATED, CERTAIN, UNAVOIDABLE

inexorable   HARD, STERN, INEVITABLE, UNYIELDING

inexperienced   LAY, RAW, GREEN, NAIVE, CALLOW

infamous   BAD, EVIL, WICKED, NOTORIOUS

infamy   ODIUM, SHAME, ATROCITY, VILLAINY

infancy   YOUTH, BABYHOOD, CHILDHOOD

infant   TOT, BABE, BRAT, CHIT, WEAN, BAIRN, CHRISOM, PAPOOSE

infantryman   ASKAR, ZOUAVE, DOGFACE, CHASSEUR, DOUGHBOY

infatuate   BESOT, CHARM, ENAMOR

infatuated   GAGA, TAKEN, FOOLISH, SMITTEN, LOVESICK

infatuation   LOVE, RAVE, CRUSH, PASSION

infect   DIRTY, TAINT, CORRUPT, CONTAMINATE

infection   STREP, TAINT

infer   DEDUCE, GATHER, PRESUME, SURMISE

inference   SURMISE, ILLATION

inferior   LOW, POOR, LOWER, MINOR, PETTY, SHODDY

infernal   DAMNED, HELLISH, SATANIC, DEVILISH, CHTHONIC, FIENDISH

inferno   FIRE, HELL, BLAZE, HADES, GEHENNA, FIRESTORM

Inferno author   DANTE

infertile   ARID, BARREN, STERILE, CHILDLESS

infertility   ARIDITY, STERILITY

infest   SWARM, RIDDLE, OVERRUN

infidel   PAGAN, KAFFIR, ATHEIST, HEATHEN, HERETIC, SARACEN

infidelity   ADULTERY, BETRAYAL, DISLOYALTY

infielder   BASEMAN, SHORTSTOP

infiltrate   ENTER, GETINTO, PERMEATE, PENETRATE

infinite   VAST, ENDLESS, BOUNDLESS

infinitesimal   TINY, MINUTE, MINUSCULE

infinity   OLAM, ANATA, ETERNITY

infirm	ILL, SICK, ANILE, FRAIL, SENILE, DECREPIT
infirmary	CLINIC, SICKBAY; *see* HOSPITAL
infirmity	FRAILTY, ILLNESS, SICKNESS
inflame	FAN, RILE, INCITE, IGNITE, MADDEN, RANKLE
inflammable	PICEOUS
inflammable substance	PUNK, AMADOU, TINDER
inflammation	STY, ITIS, CROUP, RUBOR, ANGINA, GARGET, IRITIS, OMITIS, QUINSY, ULITIS, CATARRH, COLITIS, ILEITIS, PINKEYE, UVEITIS, CYSTITIS, MASTITIS, PHLEGMON
inflate	PUFF, RAISE, SWELL, BLOWUP, DILATE, MAGNIFY, ESCALATE
inflated	GASSY, TUMID, BLOATED
inflect	BEND, CURVE, MODULATE
inflection	TONE, SHADE, NUANCE, CADENCE
inflexible	GRIM, IRON, RIGID, STARK, DOGGED, ADAMANT
inflict	DEAL, WREAK, IMPOSE
in-flight	MIDAIR
inflorescence	CYME, AMENT, WHORL, RACEME, SPADIX
influence	PULL, SWAY, CLOUT, IMPEL, AFFECT, INDUCE, WEIGHT
influential	POWERFUL, PROMINENT
influenza	FLU, GRIP, CORYZA, GRIPPE, CATARRH
influx	ENTRY, FLOOD, ARRIVAL, ILLAPSE
inform	RAT, SING, DELATE, RATOUT, SQUEAL, APPRIZE
informal	EASY, CASUAL, RELAXED, FAMILIAR
informant	SPY, MOLE, SNEAK
information	DATA, DOPE, ITEM, LORE, NEWS, AVISO, DOSSIER
information, kind of	INSIDE
informative	NEWSY, EXPLICIT
informed	HEP, HIP, AWARE, WISE(TO)
informer	SPY, FINK, NARK, STOOL, PIGEON, SNITCH, DELATOR
infraction	BREACH, VIOLATION, INFRINGEMENT
infrequency	RARITY
infringe	BREAK, FLOUT, BREACH, PIRATE, VIOLATE
infringement	BREACH, PIRACY, VIOLATION
infuriate	RILE, ANGER, ANNOY, PEEVE, ENRAGE, MADDEN, IRRITATE
infuse	BREW, FILL, STEEP, INSTIL(L), IMPART, SUFFUSE, PERMEATE
infusion	TEA, WORT, TISANE, TINCTURE
Inge play	PICNIC, BUS STOP
ingenious	CLEVER, D(A)EDAL, INVENTIVE, RESOURCEFUL
ingenue	STARLET, DEBUTANTE
ingenuity	WIT, SKILL, ORIGINALITY
ingenuous	FRANK, NAIVE, SIMPLE, TRUSTING
ingest	EAT, DOWN, CONSUME, SWALLOW
ingot	BAR, PIG, SHOE, SYCEE
ingrained	INNATE, DEEPSEATED
ingratiate	TOADY, INSINUATE
ingratiating	SMARMY, FAWNING, WINNING, CHARMING
ingredient	ITEM, PART, FACTOR, ELEMENT, FEATURE, COMPONENT
ingress	ENTRY, WAYIN, ACCESS, ENTRANCE
inhabit	LIVE IN, OCCUPY, POPULATE
inhabitant	CIT, ITE, INMATE, CITIZEN, DENIZEN, RESIDENT
inhale	SNIFF, BREATHE, INSPIRE
inherent	BASIC, INBORN, INNATE
inherit	RECEIVE, COMEINTO
inheritance	LEGACY, BEQUEST, HERITAGE, PATRIMONY
inheritor	*see* HEIR
inhibit	BAR, CURB, ENJOIN, HAMPER, REPRESS
inhospitable	HARSH, HOSTILE
inhuman	FELL, SAVAGE, BRUTAL, BESTIAL
inimical	ADVERSE, HOSTILE
inimitable	UNIQUE, PEERLESS, MATCHLESS
iniquitous	BAD, EVIL, UNJUST, WICKED

iniquity	SIN, EVIL, VICE, CRIME
initial(s)	FIRST, CIPHER, MONOGRAM
initiate	HAZE, OPEN, BEGIN, EPOPT, FOUND, START, EPOPTA, INDUCT
initiative	IDEA, LEAD, PLAN, SCHEME, ENTERPRISE
injection	HYPO, SHOT, ENEMA, SYRETTE
injection material	INSULIN
injudicious	UNWISE, IMPRUDENT
injunction	BAN, ORDER, COMMAND, MANDATE, SANCTION
injure	MAR, HARM, LAME, MAIM, TEEN, IMPAIR, SCATHE
injurious	TOXIC, HARMFUL, NOISOME, NOXIOUS
injury	ILL, TEEN, TORT, WOUND, LESION, MAYHEM, TRAUMA
injustice	BIAS, WRONG, INEQUITY
ink	DAUB, TONER, BLACKEN
ink-like	EBON
inkling	CLUE, HINT, SUSPICION
inlaid work	BUHL, MOSAIC, NIELLO, TARSIA
inland sea	ARAL, BLACK, CASPIAN
inlay	INSET, INSERT, FILLING
inlet	BAY, RIA, VOE, ZEE, COVE, BAYOU, BIGHT, FIORD, SLOUGH
inmate	CONVICT, OCCUPANT, PRISONER
inn	KAAN, KAUN, KHAN, FONDA, HOTEL, LODGE, MOTEL, SERAI, HOSTEL, IMARET, POSADA, TABARD, TAVERN, AUBERGE, HOSPICE, LOCANDA, CHOULTRY, HOSTELRY
innards	see ENTRAILS
innate	INBORN, NATIVE, NATURAL
inner	BEN, ENTAL, ESOTERIC
Inner Mongolia capital	HOHHOT
innkeeper	HOST, PADRONE, BONIFACE, PUBLICAN
innocence	BLUET, VIRTUE, NAIVETE
innocent	NAIF, PURE, SAFE, NAIVE, CHASTE, SIMPLE,

	GULLIBLE, HARMLESS, GUILTLESS
innocuous	SAFE, BLAND, HARMLESS
innovation	CHANGE, NOVELTY, ORIGINALITY
innuendo	HINT, ALLUSION, OVERTONE, UNDERTONE
innumerable	MYRIAD, UNTOLD, INFINITE, COUNTLESS
inoculate	IMMUNIZE, VACCINATE
inoculation	JAB, SHOT, SERUM, VACCINE
inopportune	ILLTIMED, UNTIMELY
inordinately	VERY, OVERLY
input	KEY(IN), SAY, ENTER, EFFORT, CONTRIBUTION
inquest	INQUIRY, INVESTIGATION
inquire	ASK, SEEIF, SNOOP, FINDOUT
inquiring	NOSY, PROBING, CURIOUS
inquiry	INQUEST, INVESTIGATION
inquisition	PROBE, INQUEST, INVESTIGATION
inquisitive	NOSY, PRYING, SNOOPY, CURIOUS
inroad	RAID, FORAY, INVASION
insane	MAD, LUNY, BATTY, CRAZY, DOTTY, LOON(E)Y
insanity	FOLIE, MANIA, LUNACY, AMENTIA, MADNESS, VESANIA, DEMENTIA, PSYCHOSIS
insatiable	AVID, GREEDY, RAVENOUS, VORACIOUS
inscribe	MARK, WRITE, ENROLL, ENGRAVE
inscription	RUNE, ENVOY, LEGEND, EPITAPH, EXERGUE, GRAFFITO
inscrutable	ENIGMATIC, MYSTERIOUS, UNREADABLE
insect	IMAGO, NYMPH, HUMMER, AURELIA, CREEPER, FISHMOTH, CHILOPOD, DIPLOPOD, FIREBRAT, LACEWING, MILLEPED, MYRIAPOD, PAUROPOD, DRAGONFLY, SILVERFISH; see p. 676
insect body part	COXA, HEAD, WING, PALP, ACRON, CLAVA,

NOTUM, FEELER, LABIUM, PALPUS, STEMMA, TARSUS, THORAX, OCELLUS, ABDOMEN

insect-eating animal MOLE, SHREW, DESMAN, TENREC, AARDVARK, ANTEATER, HEDGEHOG, INSECTIVORE

insect stage EGG, PUPA, IMAGO, LARVA, NYMPH, REDIA, COCOON, INSTAR, PREPUPA, SUBIMAGO

insecticide BHC, DDT, ALDRIN, ENDRIN, LINDANE, CRYOLITE, NICOTINE, ROTENONE, ARSENICAL, PARATHION, PESTICIDE

insecure RISKY, SHAKY, TIMID, UNSAFE, WOBBLY, ANXIOUS, UNSOUND

inseminate SOW, (IM)PLANT

insensible, insensitive INERT, CALLOUS, NUMB(ED), COMATOSE, UNCARING, UNFEELING, INDIFFERENT

insert(ion) GODET, IMMIT, INLAY, INSET, PANEL

inset INLAY, PANEL, INSERT

inside WITHIN, INDOOR(S), INTERIOR, INTERNAL

inside out EVERTED, REVERSED, THOROUGH(LY)

insidious SLY, ARCH, CUNNING

insight KEN, ACUMEN

insignia BADGE, MEDAL, EMBLEM

insignificant PUNY, PETTY, PALTRY, TRIVIAL

insincere UNTRUE, TWOFACED, DECEITFUL, DISHONEST, HYPOCRITICAL

insinuate HINT, IMPLY, SUGGEST, INTIMATE

insipid DRY, DULL, FLAT, PROSY, JEJUNE

insist VOW, AVER, CLAIM, PRESS, SWEAR, ASSERT, DEMAND, PERSIST

insolence CHEEK, AUDACITY, IMPUDENCE

insolent RUDE, SASSY, CHEEKY, IMPUDENT

insolvent BUST, BROKE, RUINED, BANKRUPT

insomnia VIGILANCE, WAKEFULNESS

insouciant COOL, CAREFREE, CARELESS

inspect SCAN, AUDIT, CHECK, STUDY, OVERSEE

inspection CHECK, REVIEW, SCRUTINY, EXAMINATION

inspector EXAMINER, OVERSEER

inspiration IDEA, MUSE, FLASH, INSIGHT, AFFLATUS, INHALATION

inspire STIR, MOVE, IMBUE, AROUSE, EXCITE, INHALE

instability FLUX, WAVERING, SHAKINESS

install INDUCT, INVEST, ORDAIN, INSTATE

instance CASE, EXAMPLE, OCCASION

instant POP, WINK, JIFF(Y), TRICE, DIRECT, IMMEDIATE

instead ELSE, LIEU, RATHER

instigate EGG, ABET, SPUR, CAUSE, INCITE, PROMPT, SUBORN, PROVOKE

instill FILL, INFUSE, INSPIRE

instinct BENT, GIFT, KNACK, TALENT

instinct type ANIMAL, CARNAL

institute FOUND, SETUP, SOCIETY, INTRODUCE, FOUNDATION, ORGANIZATION

instruct BRIEF, COACH, EDIFY, TEACH, IMPART, EDUCATE

instruction LESSON, COUNSEL, TUITION

instructor COACH, LECTOR, LECTURER; *see* TEACHER

instrument DEED, WILL, AGENT, MEANS, MEDIA, ORGAN, AGENCY, DEVICE, GADGET, MEDIUM, DOCUMENT; *see* p. 642

insubordinate UNRULY, DEFIANT, MUTINOUS, REBELLIOUS, DISOBEDIENT

insubstantial THIN, WEAK, FRAIL, FLIMSY, SLIGHT

insufferable UNBEARABLE, INTOLERABLE

insufficient MEAGER, SCARCE, SKIMPY, LACKING, INADEQUATE

insular NARROW, LIMITED, ISOLATED

insulate CUTOFF, (EN)ISLE, SHIELD, ISOLATE

insulation MICA, TAPE, FILLING, PADDING,

ASBESTOS, CAULKING, ROCK
WOOL, ISOLATION

insulin discoverer   BEST,
BANTING

insult   CAG, FIG, SLUR,
RUFFLE, AFFRONT

insurance term   RISK, POLICY,
ANNUITY, TONTINE,
ENDOWMENT

insurance type   AUTO, FIRE,
LIFE, TERM, THEFT, HEALTH,
ANNUITY, FLOATER,
MEDICAL, NOFAULT,
TONTINE, ACCIDENT,
BURGLARY, HOSPITAL,
PROPERTY, COLLISION,
LIABILITY

insure   COVER, ASSURE,
GUARANTEE, INDEMNIFY,
UNDERWRITE

insurgence   RIOT, REVOLT,
MUTINY, UPRISING,
INSURRECTION

insurgent   REBEL, RISER,
RIOTER, UPSTART,
MUTINEER

insurrection   MUTINY, REVOLT,
UPRISING, REVOLUTION

intact   WHOLE, COMPLETE,
INTEGRAL, INONEPIECE

intaglio   DIE, ENGRAVE,
ENGRAVING

intangible   VAGUE, ELUSIVE,
ABSTRACT, ETHEREAL

integer   NORM, DIGIT, FIGURE,
NUMERAL

integral   BASIC, VITAL, WHOLE,
PRIMARY, ESSENTIAL

integrate   ADD, MIX, FUSE,
BLEND, UNITE, COMBINE

integrity   HONOR, HONESTY,
PROBITY

integument   ARIL, DERM, HIDE,
HUSK, RIND, SKIN, SHELL,
TESTA

intellect   MIND, NOUS, INWIT,
MAHAT, SENSE, NOESIS,
REASON

intellectual   MENTAL, NOETIC,
EGGHEAD

intelligence   WIT, HEAD, MIND,
SENSE, ACUMEN, BRAINS,
SMARTS, CLEVERNESS

intelligent   KEEN, QUICK,
SMART, ASTUTE, BRAINY,
BRIGHT, CLEVER, GIFTED

intelligentsia   EGGHEADS,
LITERATI, ILLUMINATI

intelligible   CLEAR, LUCID, PLAIN

intemperance   GREED, EXCESS,
GLUTTONY, HEDONISM

intemperate   WILD, RAKISH,
SEVERE, EXTREME,
EXCESSIVE

intend   AIM, TRY, MEAN,
ETTLE, SUPPOSE, INTEREST

intended   MEANT, FIANCE(E),
FUTURE, BETROTHED

intense   DEEP, KEEN, VIVID,
SHARP, ARDENT, STRONG,
FORCEFUL

intensify   DEEPEN, ENHANCE,
SHARPEN, HEIGHTEN

intensifying word   ITSELF

intensity   FORCE, DEPTH,
POWER, VIGOR

intensive   ACUTE, ALLOUT,
THORO(UGH)

intent   BENT, EARNEST,
SINCERE; see INTENTION

intention   AIM, END, GOAL,
PLAN, POINT, OBJECT,
TARGET

intentional   PLANNED,
WILLFUL, DELIBERATE

inter   BURY, INURN, ENTOMB,
INHUME

intercede   PLEAD, MEDIATE,
ARBITRATE

intercessor   BISHOP, PLEADER,
ADVOCATE, MEDIATOR,
PARACLETE

interchange   SWAP, TRADE,
JUNCTION

interdict   BAN, BAR, VETO,
TABOO, ENJOIN, PROSCRIBE

interest   WEAL, PIQUE, SHARE,
USURY, BEHALF, MOTIVE,
USANCE

interface   GUI, LINK

interfere   BUTTIN, HINDER,
IMPEDE, MEDDLE,
OBSTRUCT, INTERVENE

interference   HUM, MUSH,
RAIN, SNOW, BLOOM, FLARE,
GHOST, NOISE, STATIC,
JAMMING

interim   DIASTEM; see
INTERVAL

interior   CORE, HEART, INNER,
INLAND, INTERNAL

interject   INSERT, INTERPOSE,
INTERPOLATE

interjection   see EXCLAMATION

interlock   JOIN, KNIT, LINK,
MESH

interloper   MEDDLER,
INTRUDER

interlude	JIG, PASO, BREAK, PAUSE, VERSET, INTERIM, ENTRACTE
intermediary	AGENCY, MEDIUM, ARBITER, REFEREE, MEDIATOR, GOBETWEEN
intermediate	MEAN, MESNE, MEDIAN, MIDDLE
interment	BURIAL, FUNERAL
intermezzo	ENTRACTE, INTERLUDE
interminable	ENDLESS, INCESSANT, PERPETUAL
intermingle	MIX, FUSE, BLEND
intermission	STOP, BREAK, PAUSE, RECESS, INTERVAL
intermittent	FITFUL, RECURRENT, SPASMODIC
internal	INNER, INSIDE, INWARD, INTERIOR
international	GLOBAL, UNIVERSAL, WORLDWIDE
internet	WEB, WWW
interpolate	INSERT
interpose	INSERT, BUTTIN, MEDDLE, MEDIATE, ARBITRATE, INTRODUCE
interpret	READ, REDE, RENDER, EXPOUND, CONSTRUE
interpretation	READING, VERSION, ANALYSIS, CONSTRUAL, RENDITION
interpreter	EXEGETE, LATINER, DRAGOMAN, LING(UI)STER
interrogate	QUIZ, GRILL, PROBE, QUESTION
interrogation	PROBE, INQUIRY, INTERVIEW
interrogation mark	EROTEME
interrogative	HOW, WHO, WHY, WHAT, WHEN, WHERE
interrupt	STOP, BREAK, CHECK, BUTT IN, HORN IN, DISRUPT, INTRUDE, SUSPEND
interruption	AHEM, BREAK, PAUSE, OUTAGE
intersect	CUT, MEET, CROSS, DECUSSATE
intersection	FORK, CROSSING, JUNCTION
interstice	PORE, CHINK, STOMA, AREOLA, AREOLE, SPIRACLE
intertwine	KNIT, LACE, WEAVE, ENLACE, PLEACH
interval	GAP, REST, BREAK, LAPSE, HIATUS, LACUNA, CAESURA, INTERIM
intervene	OCCUR, BUTTIN, HAPPEN, MEDDLE, MEDIATE, ARBITRATE, INTERFERE
intervening	MESNE, BETWEEN
interweave	MAT, PLA(I)T, PLASH, TWINE, RADDLE
interview	TALKTO, MEETING, QUESTION
interviewer	KING, ROSE, ASKER, FROST, WALLACE
intestinal	ENTERIC
intestine(s)	GUT, ILEA, BOWEL, COLON, BOWELS, VISCERA, ENTRAILS
intimate	COSY, DEAR, HINT, NEAR, WARM, CLOSE, IMPLY, PRIVATE, FRIENDLY, PERSONAL
intimidate	AWE, COW, ABASH, BULLY, DAUNT, COERCE, BUFFALO
intolerable	PAINFUL, UNBEARABLE, INSUFFERABLE
intolerance	BIAS, BIGOTRY, PREJUDICE
intolerant	BIASED, NARROW, BIGOTED
intone	SING, CHANT, CROON, RECITE
intoxicate	ELATE, SOUSE, POISON, INEBRIATE
intoxicated	see DRUNK
intractable	KNOTTY, THORNY, WILLFUL, STUBBORN, FRACTIOUS, OBSTINATE
intransigent	STUBBORN, INFLEXIBLE
intrepid	BOLD, BRAVE, DARING, PLUCKY, FEARLESS
intricate	MAZY, D(A)EDAL, KNOTTY, TRICKY, COMPLEX, GORDIAN
intrigue	WILE, AMOUR, CABAL, AFFAIR, BRIGUE, SCHEME
intrinsic	TRUE, BASIC, NATIVE, INHERENT
intrinsically	PERSE, BASICALLY
introduce	IMMIT, USHER, BROACH, INSERT, LAUNCH, PRESENT
introduction	PROEM, ISAGOGE, PREFACE, PRELUDE, PREAMBLE, FOREWORD
introductory	INITIAL, OPENING, EXORDIAL, PRELIMINARY
introit	HYMN, PSALM, ANTHEM

intrude	CRASH, BUTTIN, MEDDLE, TRESPASS
intuition	ESP, HUNCH, SENSE, INSIGHT
intuitive	INNATE, NOUMENAL, INSTINCTIVE
inundate	FLOOD, SWAMP, ENGULF, OVERWHELM
inundation	see FLOOD
inure	HARDEN, TOUGHEN
invade	RAID, VIOLATE
invader	HUN, GOTH, MARTIAN
invalid	NULL, SICK, VOID, FALSE, INFIRM, SICKLY, DISABLED
invalidate	ANNUL, CANCEL, NULLIFY
invaluable	DEAR, PRECIOUS, PRICELESS
invariable	FIXED, STEADY, UNIFORM, CONSTANT
invariably	EVER, ALWAYS
invasion	RAID, FORAY, ATTACK, INROAD, ASSAULT, TRESPASS
invective	ABUSE, CURSE, TIRADE
inveigh	RAIL, CENSURE
inveigle	COAX, LURE, ENTICE
invent	COIN, FORGE, DEVISE
invention	LIE, TALE, CREATION
inventor	CREATOR, ARCHITECT, ORIGINATOR
inventor, famous	see p. 541
inventory	LIST, STOCK, STORE, RECORD, REGISTER
inverse	CONTRARY, OPPOSITE
inversion	FLEXURE, DOUBLING, REVERSAL
invert	UPSET, OVERTURN
invest	ARM, DON, ADORN, ENDOW, ENDUE, INDUE, CLOTHE, ORDAIN, BESIEGE
investigate	PROBE, STUDY, EXAMINE, EXPLORE, INDAGATE
investigation	PROBE, STUDY, HEARING, INQUEST, INQUIRY, EXAMINATION
investigator	EXAMINER, RESEARCHER
investiture	INDUCTION, INSTALLATION
investment	ASSET, SIEGE, CAPITAL, VENTURE, SPECULATION
investor	BACKER, PATRON, SPONSOR, DEPOSITOR, FINANCIER, CAPITALIST
inveterate	CHRONIC, HABITUAL, HARDENED
invigorate	BRACE, REFRESH, ANIMATE, ENERGIZE
invigorating	BRISK, CRISP, TONIC, BRACING
invincible	UNBEATABLE
inviolate	INTACT, SACRED, UNBROKEN
invisible	APHAN, UNSEEN, IMPERCEPTIBLE
Invisible Man author	WELLS
invitation	CALL, CARD, INVITE
invite	ASK, BID, SUE, CALL, TEMPT, SUMMON, ATTRACT, SOLICIT
inviting	HOMEY, ALLURING, ENTICING, ATTRACTIVE
invocation	CHARM, SPELL, PRAYER
invoke	CITE, QUOTE, RAISE, SUMMON
involuntary	REFLEX, AUTOMATIC, RELUCTANT, COMPULSIVE, OBLIGATORY
involve	LAP, COIL, ENTAIL, EMBROIL, INCLUDE
involved	KNOTTY, COMPLEX, INTRICATE, IMPLICATED
invulnerable	SAFE, IMMUNE, SECURE
inward	ENTAD, INTERNAL
Io watcher	ARGUS
iodine source	KELP
Ionian island	CORFU, PAXOS, LEVKAS, ITHACA, KITHIRA, CEPHALONIA, ZAKINTHOS
iota	see JOT
Iowa	see also p. 615
Iowa city/town	ADEL, LEON, ALBIA, BOONE, LOGAN, ONAWA, OSAGE, CRESCO, ELDORA, GARNER, SIDNEY, TIPTON, VINTON, WAUKON, DAVENPORT, DES MOINES, WATERLOO
Iowa college town	AMES
Iowa Indian	FOX, SAC, SAUK
Iowa lake	EAGLE, STORM, SPIRIT, RATHBUN, TRUMBULL, CORALVILLE
Iowa school	COE, CLARK, DRAKE, LORAS, DUBUQUE, VENNARD, GRINNELL
Iowa river	BOYER, CEDAR, SKINK, RACCOON, BIGSIOUX,

DESMOINES, MISSOURI,
MISSISSIPPI
ipecac EVEA, MADDER
ipecac source EVEA
Iphigenia relative ELECTRA,
ORESTES
ipse — DIXIT
— Irae DIES
Iran ELAM, PERSIA
Iran, capital of TEH(E)RAN
Iranian city BAM, ILAM, SARI,
YAZD, AHVAZ, RASHT,
KASHAN, KERMAN, MASULE,
SHIRAZ, TABRIZ, TEHRAN,
ESFAHAN, MASHDAD
Iranian language FARSI,
GALCHA, PASHTO, PUSHTO,
TADJIK, TAJIKI, AVESTAN,
BALUCHI, KURDISH,
OSSETIC, PAHILAVI, PERSIAN,
SOGDIAN
Iranian measure GUZ, MOU,
ZAR, MANSION
Iranian money PUL, KRAN,
LARI, POUL, RIAL, DARIC,
DINAR, MOHUR, SHAHI,
TOMAN, ASHRAFI, PAHLEVI
Iranian mountain ELBURZ,
NEZWAR, ZAGROS
Iranian neighbor UAE, IRAQ,
OMAN, TURKEY, PAKISTAN,
AZERBAIJAN, AFGHANISTAN,
TURKMENISTAN
Iranian river MAND, ATREK,
KARUN, SAFID, KARKHEH
Iranian weight ZAR, DRAM,
DUNG, SANG, ABBAS,
DINAR, MAUND, BATMAN,
GANDUM, KARWAR,
NAKHOD, ABBASSI
Iraq, capital of BAGHDAD
Iraqi city FAO, HAI, HIT, KUT,
AMARA, BASRA, DOHUK,
ERBIL, MOSUL, NAJAF, RUTBA,
ZAKHO, ABADAN, KIRKUK,
TAKRIT
Iraqi language ARABIC; see
IRANIAN
Iraqi measure MISHARA
Iraqi money FILS, DINAR
Iraqi neighbor IRAN, SYRIA,
JORDAN, KUWAIT, TURKEY,
SAUDIARABIA
Iraqi river ZAB, TIGRIS,
DIYALA, EUPHRATES
Iraqi ruler ARIF, SHAH,
SADDAM, HUSSEIN
irascible HOT, EDGY, BRASH,
TESTY, TOUCHY

irate MAD, ANGRY, WROTH,
PIQUED
ire - FURY, RAGE, ANGER,
PIQUE
Ireland, Irish EIRE, ERIN, ERSE,
IRENA, EIRANN, HIBERNIA,
EMERALD ISLE; see also
NORTHERN IRELAND
Ireland, capital of DUBLIN
Ireland, Northern, capital of
BELFAST
iris FLAG, GLAD, IRID, IXIA,
CROCI, SEDGE, CROCUS,
FREESIA, GLADDON,
GLADIOLUS
Irish church KIL
Irish city/town CORK, NAAS,
TRIM, CAVAN, ENNIS, SLIGO,
CARLOW, DUBLIN, GALWAY,
TRALEE, LIMERICK,
WATERFORD
Irish clan FOX, DALY, DERB,
EGAN, GELL, LACY, BYRNE,
DOYLE, FLYNN, HYNES,
KELLY, NAVIN, WALSH,
WHITE
Irish county CORK, MAYO,
CLARE, KERRY, LOUTH,
MEATH, SLIGO, CARLOW,
DUBLIN, GALWAY, OFFALY,
KILDARE, LEITRIM, DONEGAL,
KILKENNY, LIMERICK,
TIPPERARY, WATERFORD
Irish dramatist SHAW, BEHAN,
SYNGE, WILDE, YEATS,
OCASEY, STEELE, BECKETT
Irish hero FINN, GOLL, RORY,
FIONN, FENIAN, FERGUS
Irish kingdom MEATH, ULSTER,
MUNSTER, CONNACHT,
LEINSTER
Irish language GAELIC
Irish law DAER, SAER
Irish measure BANDLE,
FATHMUR
Irish money RAP, EURO,
PENCE, POUND, SHILLING
Irish party IRA, SINN FEIN
Irish river LEE, BANN, NORE,
SUIR, BOYNE, BARROW,
SLANEY, OCONNOR,
SHANNON
— 's Irish Rose ABIE
Irish writer REID, SHAW,
BEHAN, JOYCE, MOORE,
SYNGE, WILDE, YEATS,
OCASEY, BECKETT
Irish writing OGAM, OGUM,
OGHAM

Irishman	**PAT, AIRE, CELT, HARP, MICK, PADDY, TEAGUE, MILESIAN, HIBERNIAN**
irk	**IRE, VEX, ANNOY, CHAFE, NETTLE, IRRITATE**
irksome	**TRYING, TEDIOUS, TIRESOME**
iron	**GOOSE, PRESS, STEEL, DRIVER, FERRUM, MANGLE, MASHIE, FERRITE, NIBLICK**
iron out	**RECTIFY, SMOOTHEN**
iron, *pert. to*	**FERRIC, FERROUS**
ironclad	**ARMORED, MONITOR, WARSHIP, MERRIMAC, FOOLPROOF, UNBREAKABLE**
ironic(al)	**SARCASTIC, SARDONIC**
irons	*see* **FETTER**
Ironsides	**CROMWELL**
ironworks	**SMELTER(Y)**
irony	**SATIRE, PARADOX, SARCASM**
Iroquois tribe	**ERIE, HURON, MINGO, CAYUGA, MOHAWK, ONEIDA, SENECA, WYANDOT, CHEROKEE, ONANDAGA, TUSCARORA**
irrational	**INANE, ABSURD**
irrational number	**SURD**
Irrawaddy tributary	**MU, MALI, NMAI, MYITNGE**
irregular	**WILD, EROSE, ATYPIC, CASUAL, FITFUL, SPOTTY, UNEVEN, ERRATIC, GUERRILLA**
irregularity	**ANOMALY, ABNORMALITY**
irreligious	**PAGAN, UNHOLY, GODLESS, IMPIOUS, PROFANE, AGNOSTIC, ATHEISTIC**
irreparable	**LASTING, HOPELESS, PERMANENT, IRREVERSIBLE**
irrepressible	**WILD, UNRULY**
irreproachable	**BLAMELESS, IMPECCABLE**
irresistible	**STRONG, ALLURING, ENTICING, APPEALING, OVERWHELMING**
irresolute	**WEAK, FICKLE, HESITANT, INDECISIVE**
irrevocable	**FINAL, BINDING, IMMUTABLE**
irrigate	**WET, HOSE, FLUSH, WATER**
irritable	**EDGY, CROSS, TESTY, BITCHY, TOUCHY, PRICKLY**
irritate	**IRE, IRK, VEX, GALL, RILE, CHAFE, HECTOR, NEEDLE, NETTLE, RANKLE, PROVOKE**
Irving hero	**GARP**
Isaac relative	**EDOM, ESAU, JACOB, SARAH, SARAI, ABRA(HA)M, REBEKAH**
Isaac's well	**ESEK**
Isaiah	**ESAY**
Isaiah relative	**AMOZ**
Ishmael	**PARIAH, OUTCAST**
Ishmael relative	**TEMA, DUMAH, HADAD, HAGAR, JETUR, KEDAR, MASSA, ABDEEL, MIBSAM, MISHMA, MAHALATH**
isinglass	**AGAR, MICA, KANTEN**
Isis relative	**HORUS, OSIRIS, NEPHTHYS**
Islam	**SUFISM, WAHABISM, MOHAMMEDANISM**
Islam feast day	**ASHURA**
Islam, Five Pillars of	**HAJJ, SAWM, SALAT, ZAKAT, SHAHADAH**
Islam principle	**IJMA**
Islamic	**MOSLEM, MUSLIM, MOHAMMEDAN**
Islamic month	*see p. 717*
Islamite	**SUFI, MOSLEM, MUSLIM, SHIITE, SUNNITE**
island	**AIT, CAY, ILE, KEY, EYOT, HOLM, ILOT, ISLE, ISLA, REEF, ATOLL, ISLET, ISOLA, INSULA;** *see p. 603*
island divided by equator	**SUMATRA**
island, *pert. to*	**INSULAR**
Isle of Man capital	**DOUGLAS**
ism	**DOXY, DOGMA, TENET, BELIEF, SYSTEM, THEORY, DOCTRINE**
isolate	**DETACH, ENISLE, IMMURE**
Isolde's lover	**TRISTAN, TRISTRAM**
Israel	**ZION, JACOB, CANAAN, PALESTINE**
Israel, capital of	**JERUSALEM**
Israeli city	**HAIFA, RAMIA, HEBRON, NABLUS, JERICHO, TELAVIV, BEERSHEBA**
Israeli lake	**HULEH, TIBERIAS**
Israeli leader	**MEIR, PERES, RABIN, ESHKOL, SHAMIR, BENGURION**
Israeli money	**MIL, NIS, AGORA, POUND, PRUTA, SHEKEL**

Israeli mountain **RAMON, TABOR, CARMEL, MEIRON**
Israeli native **SABRA**
Israeli river **ZIN, BESOR, HEMAR, PARAN, RAMON**
Israelite **JEW, SION, ZION, HEBREW**
Israelite king *see p. 516*
Israelite tribes *see p. 518*
issue **DOLE, EMIT, EXIT, FLUX, METE, ENSUE, EGRESS, EDITION, EMERGE, PROGENY, PUBLISH**
issue, take **DIFFER, DISAGREE**
Istanbul district **PERA, FANAR, BEYOGLU**
isthmus **KRA, BALK, NECK, STRAIT**
Italian **LATIN, OSCAN, ROMAN, PICENE, SABINE, TUSCAN**
Italian author **ECO, DANTE, MORAVIA, BOCCACCIO**
Italian city **ALES, BARI, COMO, PISA, ROME, GENOA, LUCCA, MILAN, PARMA, RIETI, SIENA, TURIN, UDINE, MODENA, NAPLES, PESARO, SAVONA, VENICE, VERONA, BOLOGNA, BOLZANO, BRESCIA, CATANIA, CREMONA, FERRARA, MANTOVA, PALERMO, PERUGIA, RAVENNA, SALERNO, TRIESTE, VITERBO, BRINDISI, FLORENCE, PIACENZA, SIRACUSA**
Italian composer **LULLY, TOSTI, VERDI, MENOTTI, PUCCINI, ROSSINI, MASCAGNI, PAGANINI, SCARLATTI, DONIZETTI**
Italian dramatist **GOLDONI, PIRANDELLO**
Italian family **ASTI, ESTE, CENCI, DORIA, DONATI, MEDICI**
Italian island **ELBA, CAPRI, PONZA, GIGLIO, ISCHIA, LIPARI, SALINA, SICILY, USTICA**
Italian lake **COMO, GARDA, ALBANO, LUGANO, BOLSENA, MAGGIORE, BRACCIANO, TRASIMENO**
Italian leader **MORO, LEONE, SEGNI, CIAMPI, VICTOR, CAMILLO, COSSIGA, EINAUDI, GASPERI, GRONCHI, HUMBERT, MAZZINI, PERTINI, SARAGAT, UMBERTO, SCALFARO, GARIBALDI, MUSSOLINI**
Italian measure **CANNA, PALMO, PUNTO, STAIO, MIGLIO,**

MOGGIO, RUBBIO, TAVOLA, BRACCIO
Italian money **EURO, LIRA, LIRE, TARI, SCUDO, SOLDO, ZECHIN(O)**
Italian mountain **CAVO, ROSA, VISO, BLANC, CENIS, CHIANTI**
Italian painter **RENI, LIPPI, LOTTO, ROSSI, SPADA, VINCI, ANDREA, GIOTTO, TITIAN, VASARI, BELLINI, RAPHAEL, TIEPOLO, UCCELO, CAGLIARI, CORREGGIO, DONATELLO, BOTTICELLI, CARVAGGIO, MODIGLIANI**
Italian patriot **CAVOUR, MAZZINI, GARIBALDI**
Italian poet **DANTE, TASSO, ARIOSTO, MANZONI, PETRARCA, PETRARCH**
Italian region **LAZIO, MARCHE, MOLISE, PUGLIA, SICILY, UMBRIA, VENETO, ABRUZZI, LIGURIA, TUSCANY, CALABRIA, CAMPANIA, LOMBARDY, PIEDMONT, SARDINIA**
Italian river **PO, ADDA, ARNO, DORA, LIRI, OGUO, PADUS, PIAVE, TIBER, MINCIO, TANARO, TEVERE, TICINO, VOLTURNO**
Italian singer **GIGLI, PATTI, PINZA, CALLAS, CARUSO, CORELLI, TEBALDI, PAVAROTTI**
Italian sub ingredient **HAM, CHEESE, SALAMI, BOLOGNA, LETTUCE, MORTADELLA**
Italian weight **ONCIA, DENARO, GANDUM, LIBBRA, OTTAVA**
Italian wine **ASTI, CORVO, SOAVE, BAROLO, CHIANTI, MARSALA, FRASCATI, BARDOLINO, LAMBRUSCO, VALPOLICELLA**
Italian words *see p. 569*
Italic languages **LADIN, LATIN, OSCAN, CREOLE, FRENCH, CATALAN, ITALIAN, ROMANCE, ROMANIC, ROMANSH, SPANISH, FRIULIAN, UMBRIAN, VENETIC, FALISCAN, RUMANIAN, PROVENCAL, ROUMANIAN, SARDINIAN, PORTUGUESE**
Italy, capital of **ROME**
itch **YEN, RIFF, URGE, CRAVE, MANGE, PSORA, ECZEMA, SCABIES, PRURITUS**

item	UNIT, DATUM, ENTRY, DETAIL, AGENDUM	Jack and —	JILL
		Jack Sprat diet	LEAN
itemize	LIST, DETAIL, ENUMERATE	jackal	DIEB, THOS; see DOG
		jackal-headed god	ANUBIS
iterate	ECHO, HARP, REPEAT, RETELL	jackass	DOLT, JERK, DONKEY
		jacket	TUX, BAJU, ETON,
Ithra relative	AMASA		JUMP, JUPE, PEEL, RIND,
itinerant	HOBO, TRAMP, ROVING, DRIFTER, NOMADIC, ROAMING, VAGRANT		SACK, SKIN, BADJU, BANIA, GREGO, PARKA, POLKA, TUNIC, TWEED, WAMUS,
itinerary	TOUR, ROUTE, CIRCUIT, SCHEDULE		ANORAK, BADJOO, BANIAN, BANYAN, BLAZER, BOLERO,
itself	PERSE		CASING, GANSEY, REEFER,
Ivan the Terrible wife	ANASTASIA		SACQUE, TUXEDO, WAMMUS, WARMUS, BEDGOWN,
Ivanhoe author	SCOTT		DOUBLET, NORFOLK,
Ivanhoe character	BOEUF, CRONE, GURTH, ISAAC, WAMBA, CEDRIC, ROWENA, ULRICA		PALETOT, PEACOAT, SPENCER, SURCOAT, WRAPPER, CAMISOLE,
ivory	EBUR, TUSH, TUSK, DENTINE		CARDIGAN, JAQUETTE, MACKINAW; see COAT
Ivory Coast	COTEDIVOIRE	jack-of-all-trades	TINKER,
Ivory Coast, capital of	ABIDJAN, YAMOUSSOUKRO		HANDYMAN
		Jackson novel	RAMONA
Ivory Coast city/town	MAN, DALOA, BOUAKE, GAGNOA, ABIDJAN, KORTHOGO	Jacob relative	DAN, GAD, EDOM, ESAU, LEAH, LEVI, ASHER, DINAH, JUDAH,
Ivory Coast lake	KOSSOU		JOSEPH, RACHEL, REUBEN,
Ivory Coast language	see KWA, GUR, MANDE		SIMEON, ZEBULUN, BENJAMIN, ISSACHAR, NAPHTALI
Ivory Coast money	FRANC, CENTIME	Jacobin	FRIAR, PIGEON, RADICAL, DOMINICAN
Ivory Coast mountain	NIMBA	jade	NAG, TIT, MARE, SLUT,
Ivory Coast river	KOMOE, BANDAMA, SASSANDRA		TIRE, YAUD, GREEN, HUSSY, STONE, WEARY, WOMAN,
ivory tower	ACADEMIA		HARASS, MURRHINE, NEPHRITE,
ivy	VINE, CLIMBER, CREEPER		ROSINANTE
Ivy League college	ELI, PENN, YALE, BROWN, CORNELL, HARVARD, COLUMBIA, DARTMOUTH, PRINCETON	jaded	BLASE, BORED, TIRED, CYNICAL
		jaeger	SKUA, ALLAN, SHOOL, HUNTER, TEASER, SEABIRD, MARLINESPIKE
Iwo —	JIMA	Jael relative	SHUA, HEBER
Ixion offspring	CENTAUR	jag	BUN, DAG, BARB, PINK, SNAG, TEAR, NOTCH, SPREE, TOOTH
		jagged	ZAG, ZIG, CLEFT, EROSE, RAGGED, SERRATE(D)

J

J	JAY, JULIET	jaguar	see CAT
jab	DIG, BLOW, POKE, PUNCH	jai alai	PELOTA
jabber	YAP, TALK, BABBLE, GOSSIP, NATTER, CHATTER, PRATTLE	jai alai term	BLE, CESTA, CANCHA, QUANTE, REBOTE, FRONTON
Jabberwocky word	WABE, MIMSY, SLITHY, UFFISH, VORPAL, BRILLIG	jail	CAN, JUG, PEN, BRIG, CAGE, CELL, COOP, GAOL, QUOD, STIR, TANK, CLINK,
jack	NOB, PAM, MULE, NOBS, BOWER, HOIST, KNAVE, OPENER, RABBIT, TINKER		POKEY, COOLER, INSIDE, LOCKUP, SLAMMER, CALABOOSE

jailer	**SCREW, GAOLER, WARDEN, TURNKEY**
Jakarta	**BATAVIA**
jalopy	**HEAP, CRATE, WRECK, HOTROD, RATTLETRAP**
jam	**FIX, RAM, CRAM, MESS, CRUSH, STICK, SCRAPE, CONSERVE, GRIDLOCK, QUANDARY**
Jamaica, capital of	**KINGSTON**
Jamaican city/town	**NEGRIL, FALMOUTH, KINGSTON**
Jamaican mountain	**BLUE, DOLPHINHEAD**
Jamaican river	**BLACK, GREAT, MINHO**
jamb	**ALETTE**
James relative	**JUDE**
Jane's mate	**TARZAN**
jangle	**JAR, CLANG, CLASH, BICKER**
janitor	**SUPER, PORTER, SEXTON, CONCIERGE, CARETAKER, CUSTODIAN**
Japan, capital of	**TOKYO**
Japan(ese)	**AINO, AINU, NIPPON, CIPANGO**
Japanese admiral	**ITO, OKA, TOGO, OKADA, UGAKI, NAGANO, NOMURA, OIKAWA, SUZUKI, TOYODA, SHIMADA, YAMAMOTO**
Japanese city/town	**TSU, UBE, GIFU, KOBE, KOFU, MITO, NAHA, NARA, OITA, OTSU, AKITA, CHIBA, FUKUI, KOCHI, KYOTO, OSAKA, OTARU, SAKAI, TOKYO, URAWA, AOMORI, NAGANO, NAGOYA, TOYAMA, FUKUOKA, SAPPORO, KANAZAWA, KAWASAKI, NAGASAKI, YOKOHAMA, HIROSHIMA, KITAKYUSHU**
Japanese drama	**NOH, KABUKI, NOGAKU**
Japanese emperor	**JIMMU, TENNO, MIKADO, AKIHITO, HIROHITO, MUTSUHITO, YOSHIHITO**
Japanese food	**MISO, SOBA, TOFU, UDON, SUSHI, SASHIMI, TEMPURA, SUKIYAKI, TERIYAKI**
Japanese garment	**OBI, GETA, TABI, ZORI, HAORI, HAPPI, KIMONO, YUKATA**
Japanese instrument	**BIWA, FUYE, KOTO, S(H)AMISEN**
Japanese island(s)	**OKI, GOTO, SADO, AWAJI, AMAMI, HONSHU, KERAMA, KYUSHU, RYUKYU, AMAKUSA, KOSHIKI, OKINAWA, SHIKOKU, HOKKAIDO, BONINTSUSHIMA**
Japanese lake	**BIWA, TAZAWA, TOWADA, CHUZENJI, INAWASHIRO**
Japanese martial art	**JUDO, AIKIDO, KARATE, HAPKIDO, JUJITSU**
Japanese measure	**BU, GO, JO, MO, RI, SE, TO, BOO, CHO, RIN, SHO, SUN, TAN, HIRO, KOKU, SHAKU, TSUBO**
Japanese military service	**YOBI**
Japanese money	**BU, RIN, SEN, YEN, OBAN, TEMPO, ICHIBU, ITZEBU**
Japanese mountain	**ASO, ZAO, FUJI, HAKU, KUJU, NASU, ASAHI, ASAMA, IWAKI, IWATE, UNZEN, BANDAI, CHOKAI, GASSEN, HAKKEN, HODAKA, KARIBA, KOMAGA, NANTAI, ONTAKE, TESHIO, SHIRANE, DAIMANJI, FUJIYAMA**
Japanese painting school	**KANO, TOSA, SHIJO, SESSHU, UKIYOE**
Japanese peninsula	**IZU, OKI, NOTO, MIURA, OSUMI**
Japanese period	**EDO, NARA, ASUKA, HEIAN, MEIJI, SHOWA, TAIRA, HEISEI, TAISHO, YAMATO, NAMBOKU, SENGOKU, ASHIKAGA, FUJIWARA, KAMAKURA, MOMOYAMA, MUROMACHI**
Japanese port	**KOBE, KURE, MOJI, OMUTA, OTARU, KOKURA, TOBATA, TOYAMA, YAWATA**
Japanese prime minister	**MORI, SATO, TOJO, IKEDA, KAIFU, KISHI, OBUTI, OKADA, INUKAI, KONOYE, TANAKA, KOIZUMI, NAKASONE, HASHIMOTO**
Japanese river	**ARA, EDO, INA, ONO, FUJI, KINO, MUKO, NAKA, OANI, TAMA, TONE, YODO, AGANO, OMONO, MOGAMI, OBITSU, SAGAMI, TOKACHI, YOSHINO, KITAKAMO**

Japanese ruler **JIMMU, JUNGO,**
KEIKI, MEIJI, SAIWA, TENNO,
MIKÁDO, NAGAKO, TAISHO
Japanese sport **SUMO, KENDO**
Japanese tree **G(O)UMI, KIAKI,**
KEYAKI
Japanese weight **MO, FUN, KIN,**
RIN, SHI, KATI, KWAN, NIYO,
MOMME, PICUL
Japanese writing **KANA**
Japanese-American **ISSEI, KIBEI,**
NISEI, SANSEI
Japheth relative **GOMER**
jar **JUG, URN, EWER, JOLT,**
OLLA, BANGA, CADUS,
CLASH, CROCK, CRUSE,
MASON, STEAN, STEEN,
DOLIUM, GOGLET, HYDRIA,
KALPIS, PELIKE, AMPHORA,
TERRINE; see **VASE**
Jared relative **ENOCH**
jargon **CANT, ARGOT, IDIOM,**
LINGO, PATTER; see **SLANG**
jasmine **BELA, JESSAMY,**
GARDENIA, JESSAMINE
Jason relative **AESON, MEDEA,**
CREUSA, PELIAS, ATHAMAS
Jason ship **ARGO**
Jason teacher **CHIRON**
jaundice **RANCOR, ICTERUS**
jaundiced **JADED, BIASED,**
YELLOW, CYNICAL
jaunt **TRIP, SALLY, OUTING,**
EXCURSION
jaunty **CHIC, PERK, COCKY,**
PERKY, SHOWY, DAPPER,
MODISH, RAKISH, SPRUCE
Java capital **JAKARTA**
Javanese city/town **BANDUNG,**
CILACAP, JAKARTA,
SAMARANG, SURABAYA
Javanese language **KAVI, KAWI,**
SASSAK
Javanese measure **AMAT, HOEN,**
PAAL, TALL, WANG, PICUL
javelin **JERID, JEREED;** see
SPEAR
jaw **MAW, CHAP, JOWL,**
GONION, MAXILLA,
MANDIBLE
jaw, pert. to **GNATHIC**
jawbone **JOWL, CHOPS,**
MAXILLA
Jayhawk State **KS, KANSAS**
jazz **JIVE, ENLIVEN,**
POPULARIZE
jazz musician **BIRD, FATS,**
MONK, PRES, BAKER, DAVIS,
DIZZY, FATHA, HINES, KRUPA,

LOUIS, MILES, ROACH,
TATUM, YOUNG, COOTIE,
DJANGO, MINGUS, PARKER,
WALLER, WATERS, SATCHMO,
MULLIGAN, ELLINGTON
jazz style **BOP, RAG, BEBOP,**
SWING, RAGTIME,
DIXIE(LAND)
jazz term **LICK, RIFF, SCAT,**
SOLO, COMBO, CHORUS
jazz up **HOKE, REVIVE,**
ENLIVEN
jealous **WARY, GREEN,**
ENVIOUS, PROTECTIVE
Jeannie, I Dream of, names **EDEN,**
TONY, LARRY, ROGER,
AMANDA, HAGMAN, SHELDON
jeans **LEVIS, DENIMS**
Jedidah relative **AMON, JOSIAH**
jeer see **MOCK**
Jeeves name **BERTIE,**
WOOSTER, WODEHOUSE
— and Jeff **MUTT**
Jefferson home **MONTICELLO**
Jeffersons names **TOM, HELEN,**
JENNY, ROKER, GEORGE,
LIONEL, LOUISE, HEMSLEY,
JESSICA, SANFORD
Jehoshaphat relative **ASA**
Jehovah see **GOD**
Jehovah's witness founder
RUSSELL
jejune **DRY, ARID, FLAT,**
STALE, BARREN, INSIPID
Jekyll's other half **HYDE**
jell **SET, CONGEAL, CRYSTALLIZE**
jelly **JAM, ASPIC, CANDY,**
GUAVA, PECTIN
jellyfish **JELLY, QUARL,**
EPHYRA, MEDUSA, ACALEPH,
AURELIA, MEDUSAN,
SUNFISH, ACALEPHE
jeopardize **RISK, EXPOSE,**
IMPERIL, ENDANGER
jeopardy **RISK, PERIL, DANGER,**
THREAT, HAZARD
jeremiad **LAMENT, TIRADE**
Jeremiah relative **HAMUTAL**
Jericho betrayer **RAHAB**
Jericho, land opposite **MOAB**
Jericho rebuilder **HIEL**
jerk **TUG, GITT, YANK,**
DUMMY, HITCH, TWITCH,
WRENCH
jerkin **COAT, VEST**
Jerusalem **SION, ZION, ARIEL**
Jerusalem artichoke **GIRASOL**
Jerusalem mountain **SION,**
ZION, MORIAH, OLIVET

Jesse relative   DAVID, ABIGAIL
jest   GAG, MOT, JAPE, JIBE,
    JOKE, QUIP, SALLY, BANTER
jester   GOLIARD; see BUFFOON
jester's cap   COXCOMB
Jesuit   CASUIST, SCHEMER
Jesuit founder   LOYOLA
Jesus   LAMB, AGNUS, LOGOS,
    CHRIST, SAVIO(U)R,
    REDEEMER
jet   EBON, GUSH, SPEW, BLACK,
    RAVEN, SABRE, SPOUT,
    STREAM
jet engine   JATO, ATHODYD
Jethro relative   ZIPPORAH
jetsam   LAGAN, LIGAN,
    DEBRIS, LAGEND,
    DRIFTWOOD
— and jetsam   FLOTSAM
Jetsons name   JANE, JUDY,
    ASTRO, BLANC, BUZZI,
    ROSIE, GEORGE, ORBITY,
    SPACELY
jettison   DUMP, JETSAM,
    ABANDON, DISCARD
jetty   DOCK, MOLE, PIER,
    QUAY, WHARF, STARLING
Jew   ESSENE, HEBREW, SEMITE,
    ISRAELITE
jewel   BIJOU, LOUPE, PRIZE,
    TRINKET; see GEM
jewelry   ICE, QUOIN, JEWELS,
    BIJOUTERIE
jewelry expert   LAPIDARY,
    APPRAISER, GEMOLOGIST
jewelry, mock   LOGIE, PASTE,
    STRASS
jewelry, piece of   PIN, RING,
    TIARA, BROOCH, DIADEM,
    EARRING, PENDANT,
    TRINKET, BRACELET,
    NECKLACE
Jewish   JUDAIC; see HEBREW,
    ISRAELI
Jewish holiday   PURIM, PESACH,
    YOMTOV, SUKKOT(H),
    SHAVUOT, CHANUKAH,
    HANUKKAH, YOM KIPPUR,
    ROSH HASHANA
Jewish marriage contract
    KETUBAH
Jewish month   see p. 717
Jewish prayer book   MAHZOR,
    SIDDUR, MACHZOR
Kewish women's org.   HADASSAH
jezebel   VIRAGO
Jezebel relative   AHAB,
    JEHORAM, ATHALIAH
jib   SHY, BALK, BOOM, SPAR

jibe   FIT, RIB, DIG, AGREE,
    CRACK
jibing   INTUNE
jiffy   SEC(OND), TICK, TRICE,
    MOMENT, INSTANT
jig   LEAP, CAPER, (FISH)HOOK
jigger   CUB, FLEA, SAIL, SHOT,
    TICK, CHIGOE, TACKLE
jihad   WAR, CRUSADE, HOLY
    WAR
jill   GIRL, DARLING,
    SWEETHEART
— and Jill   JACK
jilt   DROP, DUMP, LEAVE,
    CASTOFF
— Jima   IWO
jimmy   PRY, JACK, LEVER,
    CROWBAR
jingle   DITTY, VERSE, TINKLE,
    DOGGEREL
jingo   RADICAL, WARRIOR,
    CHAUVINIST
jingoism   CHAUVINISM,
    PATRIOTISM
jinks   PRANKS, HORSEPLAY
jinx   HEX, JONAH, HOODOO
jipijapa hat   PANAMA
jitney   BUS, NICKEL
jitters   CREEPS, NERVES,
    DITHERS, JIMJAMS
jittery   EDGY, JUMPY, HECTIC
Jo's sister   AMY, MEG, BETH
Joan of Arc   PUCELLE
Joan of Arc birthplace   DOMREMY
Joan of Arc victory site   ORLEANS
Joash relative   GIDEON
job   GIG, LINE, POST, TASK,
    WORK, CHORE, HEIST, STINT,
    CALLING, POSITION
Job relative   KEZIA, JEMIMA
Job's comforters   ELIHU,
    BILDAD, ZOPHAR, ELIPHAZ
Job's tears   COIX, TEARGRASS
job training   ONSITE
Jocasta relative   LAIUS,
    OEDIPUS, ETEOCLES,
    POLYNEICES
Jochebed relative   AARON,
    AMRAM, MOSES, MIRIAM
jockey   CHEAT, CRUMP,
    RACER, RIDER, RUBIN,
    KUSNER, MANEUVER
— jockey   DISC
jockey, famous   DAY, BAEZA,
    SMITH, BAILEY, PINCAY,
    SANTOS, CORDERO,
    HARTACK, STEVENS,
    MCCARRON, SHOEMAKER
jockey's uniform   SILKS, COLORS

jocose	DROLL, MERRY, PLAYFUL
jocular	FUNNY, WITTY, WAGGISH, HUMOROUS
jocund	GAY, MERRY, JOYFUL
Jodie Foster film	NELL, CARNY, FOXES, SIESTA, MAVERICK
jog	HOD, SHOG, TROT, DUNCH, NUDGE, REMIND
John	IAN, EOAN, EOIN, HANS, IVAN, SEAN
John Brown's Body author	BENET
John the Baptist relative	JESUS, ZACHARY, ELIZABETH, ZACHARIAH
John the Baptist site	ENON
Johnson library location	TEXAS, AUSTIN
Johnson (Samuel) work	RAMBLER, RASSELAS
join	AFFY, JERL, MELD, WELD, YOKE, MERGE, MITER, MITRE, UNITE, ATTACH, ENLIST, RABBET, SPLICE
joined	WED, UNITED
joint	COXA, DUAL, GENU, KNEE, LINK, NODE, SEAM, ELBOW, HINGE, NEXUS, SCARF, SPALD, SPAUL, TENON, WRIST, SPAULD, ARTHRON
jointly	ASONE, TOGETHER
joist	BEAM, TRUSS, SUPPORT
joke	GAG, KID, MOT, PUN, RIB, BAUR, JAPE, JEST, JOSH, QUIP, TWIT, SALLY, TEASE
joker	DOR, WAG, WIT, CARD, CLOWN, PUNSTER, JESTER, BUFFOON, FARCEUR
Joktan relative	EBAL, OBAL
jolly	YAWL, MERRY, JOCUND
jolt	JAR, JERK, SHOCK, JOUNCE
Jonas relative	PETER
Jonathan father	SAUL
Jonathan victory site	GEBA
Jonson (Ben) comedy	FOX, VOLPONE, ALCHEMIST
Jordon, ancient city	SELA, PETRA, GERASA, JARASH
Jordan, capital of	AMMAN
Jordanian city/town	MAAN, AQABA, AMMAN, IRBID, ZARQA
Jordanian money	DINAR
Jordanian river	ZARQA, JORDAN
Joseph relative	JUDE, MARY, TOLA, JACOB, JAMES, JESUS, RACHEL, EPHRAIM, MANASSEH
Joshua's altar mountain	EBAL
Joshua tree	YUCCA
jostle	JOG, MAUL, ELBOW, BUFFET, HUSTLE
jot	ACE, BUT, TAD, IOTA, MITE, MOTE, NOTE, WHIT, TITTLE
journal	LOG, DIARY, PAPER, RECORD, DIURNAL, TRUNNION
journalism	PRESS, FOURTHESTATE
journalist	EDITOR, NEWSMAN, REPORTER
journalist, famous	see p. 542
journey	EYRE, HIKE, ITER, RIDE, TOUR, TREK, TRIP, JAUNT, JUNKET, TRAVEL, VOYAGE, ODYSSEY
journeyman	JOBBER, WORKER, WORKMAN
joust	BOUT, TILT, TOURNEY
jousting site	LISTS
jovial	GAY, HAPPY, JOLLY, CHEERY, CHEERFUL
jowl	JAW, CHAP, CHIN, CHOP, CHEEK, DEWLAP, WATTLE
joy	GLEE, ZEST, BLISS, MIRTH, DELIGHT, RAPTURE
Joyce character	BLOOM, MOLLY, ROWAN, DEDALUS, LEOPOLD, HUMPHREY, EARWICKER
Joyce novel	ULYSSES, DUBLINERS
joyous	GAY, GLAD, MERRY, RIANT, BLITHE, ELATED, FESTAL
jubilee	FESTIVAL, ANNIVERSARY
Judah (Judaea) city	ADAR, ENAM
Judah relative	ER, MAAZ, ONAN
Judas	BETRAYER
Judas's replacement	MATTHIAS
Judea, capital of	JERUSALEM
Judean king	ASA, AHAZ, AMON, HEROD, JEHORAM, MANESSEH
Judean notable	HEROD, PILATE
judge(s)	TRY, UMP, CADI, CAZI, CAZY, DEEM, DOOM, FOUD, KADI, KAZI, KAZY, RATE, BENCH, HAKIM, JUDEX, MINOS, AEACUS, CRITIC, PUISNE, UMPIRE, ALCALDE,

see p. 542

	ARBITER, REFEREE, JUDICIARY;
	see JURIST
judgment	DOOM, VIEW,
	ARRET, AWARD, VERDICT,
	DECISION
judiciary	BENCH
judicious	WISE, ASTUTE,
	POLITIC, PRUDENT
Judith relative	ESAU, KORAH
Judy's husband	PUNCH
jug	URN, EWER, LOTA, OLPE,
	TOBY, BUIRE, LOTAH,
	FLAGON, LOCKUP, PITCHER
Juggernaut	VISHNU, KRISHNA
juggle	RIG, MANAGE,
	ORGANIZE
juice	JUS, SAP, MUST, RHOB,
	SAPA, STUM, SURA
juicy	FRIM, RACY, MOIST,
	TASTY, SUCCULENT
juju	CHARM, TABOO,
	AMULET, FETISH
jujube	BER, ELB, JELLY,
	GUMDROP, LOZENGE
jukebox	WURLITZER
julep ingredient	MINT, SUGAR,
	SYRUP, BRANDY,
	BOURBON
Juliet confessor	LAURENCE
Juliet relative	TYBALT,
	CAPULET
Juliet's fiancé	PARIS
Juliet's lover	ROMEO
Julius Caesar character	CINNA,
	ANTONY, BRUTUS, MARCUS,
	PORTIA, CASSIUS, OCTAVIUS,
	CALPURNIA
jumble	PI, MIX, PIE, HASH,
	MESS, OLIO, MEDLEY,
	FARRAGO
jumbled type	PI(E)
jumbo	HUGE, ELEPHANT,
	GIGANTIC
jump	BOB, HOP, BUCK, JERK,
	LEAP, SKIP, BOUND, START,
	VAULT
jumper	BLOUSE, ROMPER,
	HURDLER
jumpy	EDGY, TENSE, SCARED,
	JITTERY, NERVOUS, SKITTISH
junction	FORK, LINK, SEAM,
	JOINT, UNION, CROSSING,
	INTERSECTION
juncture	SEAM, JOINT, SUTURE
June 6, 1944	DDAY
jungle	MAZE, FOREST, TANGLE
Jungle Book author	KIPLING
Jungle Book character	KAA,
	AKELA, MOWGLI

junior	FILS, CADET, PUISNE
juniper	CADE, EZEL, GORSE,
	R(A)ETEM, SAVIN(E)
junk	BOAT, SCRAP, TRASH,
	DISCARD, RUBBISH
junket	OUTING, PICNIC,
	JOURNEY, EXCURSION
junkie	FIEND, ADDICT
Juno, Jupiter	*see p. 645*
junta	CABAL, JUNTO, CLIQUE,
	COUNCIL, FACTION
Jupiter moon	IO, EUROPA,
	CALLISTO, GANYMEDE;
	see p. 740
Jupiter space probe	PIONEER(X),
	VOYAGER
Jupiter wife	HERA, JUNO
— jure	IPSO
jurisdiction	SOC, SOKE,
	VENUE, CONTROL
jurisprudence	LAW
jurist, famous	KEY, ELEN,
	HAND, GAIUS, NIZER,
	SOLON, DARROW, ERSKIN,
	HOLMES, LANDIS, SIRICA,
	CARDOZO, SAVIGNY;
	see JUSTICE
juror(s)	PANEL, TALESMAN,
	VENIREMAN
jury	PANEL, PETIT, GRAND,
	VENIRE
just	DUE, FAIR, ONLY,
	MORAL, BARELY, HONEST,
	SIMPLY, UPRIGHT,
	IMPARTIAL
justice	EQUITY, FAIRNESS,
	JUSTNESS, RIGHTNESS
justice, chief	JAY, TAFT,
	CHASE, STONE, TANEY,
	WAITE, WHITE, FULLER,
	HUGHES, VINSON, WARREN,
	MARSHALL
justification	EXCUSE, REASON,
	DEFENSE
justify	ACQUIT, EXCUSE,
	ABSOLVE, WARRANT,
	VINDICATE, RATIONALIZE
Justine author	SADE
jut	ABUT, BULGE, PROJECT,
	PROTRUDE
jute	DESI, HEMP, DAISEE
jute fabric	MAT, GUNNY,
	BURLAP, SACKING
Juvenal work	SATIRES
juvenile	CHILD, YOUNG,
	UNRIPE, IMMATURE,
	YOUTHFUL, INFANTILE,
	YOUNGSTER
juxtapose	ADJOIN, COMPARE

K

K	KAY, KAPH, KILO, KING, KAPPA
kachina tribe	HOPI, PUEBLO
Kafka character	KLAMM, SAMSA, FRIEDA, GREGOR, JOSEPH(K)
Kafka novel	TRIAL, CASTLE, AMERIKA
kaiser	WILHELM
kale	see CABBAGE
kama —	SUTRA
Kampuchea	CAMBODIA
kangaroo	ROO, JOEY, BOOMER, WALLABY, PADEMELON
kangaroo bear	KOALA
kangaroo, young	JOEY
Kansas	see also p. 615
Kansas city	ALMA, ERIE, IOLA, GOVE, HAYS, TROY, COLBY, HOXIE, LAKIN, LYONS, PAOLA, PRATT, SEDAN, BELOIT, EUREKA, GIRARD, HOLTON, LARNED, LYNDON, MARION, NEWTON, NORTON, OAKLEY, OLATHE, OSWEGA, SENECA, TOPEKA, WICHITA
Kansas Indian	FOX, KAW, SAC, KIOWA, OSAGE, MUNSEE, PAWNEE, WICHITA, COMANCHE, CHIPPEWA, KICKAPOO, POTAWATOMI
Kansas lake	PERRY, CHENEY, KIRWIN, POMONA, WILSON, MELVERN, MILFORD, TORONTO, WACONDA, WEBSTER
Kansas mountain	SUNFLOWER
Kansas river	ELK, FALL, OSAGE, KANSAS, PAWNEE, SALINE, SOLOMON, ARKANSAS
Kapek play	RUR
kapok source	CEBA
kaput	FINI, OVER, RUINED, FINISHED
Karamazov Brothers	IVAN, DMITRI, ALYOSHA, SMERDYAKOV
karate instructor	SENSEI
— Karenina	ANNA
karma	FATE, LUCK, CHANCE, DESTINY
Kashmir capital	MUZAFFARABAD
Kashmiri language	see DARD
Katanga leader	TSHOMBE

Kate and Allie names	CHIP, CURTIN, JENNIE, STJAMES
Katzenjammer Kids	HANS, FRITZ
kayak	CANOE, UMIAK, OOMIA(C)K
Kazakhstan, capital of	AKMOA, ASTANA
Kazakhstan cities	ORAL, AQTAU, SEMEY, AKTOBE, ALMATY, ARALSK, ATYRAU, ALMAATA, PAVLODAR
Kazakhstan desert	BARSUKI, MUYUNKUM, BETPAKDALA
Kazakhstan lake	TENGIZ, ZAISAN, BALKHASH
Kazakhstan money	TENG(G)E
Kazakhstan neighbor	CHINA, RUSSIA, KYRGYZSTAN, UZBEKISTAN, TURKMENISTAN
Kazakhstan river	ILI, EMBA, URAL, ISHIM, TOBOL, IRTYSH, SYRDARYA
Keats	ADONAIS
Keats poem	ODE, LAMIA, HYPERION, ISABELLA
keel	FIN, LIST, TILT, CAREEN, CARINA, RUDDLE
Keeling Island	COCOS
keen	GARE, GLEG, NEAT, TART, WAIL, ACRID, ACUTE, DIRGE, EAGER, SHARP, SNELL, ASTUTE
keenness	EDGE, ZEST, ACIES, ARDOR
keep	SAVE, TEND, RETAIN, CUSTODY; see FORT
keep company	HOBNOB, CONSORT, HANGOUT
keep from	AVOID, DETER, DISSUADE
keep going	PERSIST
keep out	BAN, BAR, EXCLUDE
keeper	NAB, TILER, MAHOUT, RANGER, CURATOR; see JAILER
keepsake	RELIC, TOKEN, MEMENTO, SOUVENIR
keg	TUN, VAT, CADE, CASK, FIRKIN, BREAKER, GROWLER
Keller teacher	SULLIVAN
Kelly	GENE, EMMETT
kelp	ASH, KOBU, VARIC, WRACK, SEAWEED
Kemo —	SABE
ken	SCOPE, KNOWLEDGE
Kennedy Library location	BOSTON, MASSACHUSETTS
Kennedy Space Center site	CANAVERAL

kennel HUT, DRAIN, HOVEL, HUTCH, SEWER, STALL, GUTTER

Kentucky *see also p. 615*

Kentucky capital FRANKFORT

Kentucky city/town INEZ, CADIZ, DIXON, HYDEN, MCKEE, PARIS, ALBANY, BENTON, HARLAN, IRVINE, LONDON, LOUISA, MARION, WARSAW, MOREHEAD, FRANKFORT, LEXINGTON, LOUISVILLE

Kentucky Derby *see p. 711*

Kentucky lake DEWEY, NOLIN, BARKLEY

Kentucky mountain BLACK

Kentucky river OHIO, GREEN, ROUGH, BARREN, LICKING, ROLLING, KENTUCKY, TENNESSEE, CUMBERLAND

Kenya, capital of NAIROBI

Kenya city/town LAMU, WAJIR, ISLOLO, KISUMU, KITALE, LODWAR, MOYALE, NAKURU, MOMBASA, NAIROBI

Kenya desert CHALBI

Kenya lake NATRON, VICTORIA

Kenya language BANTU, KAMBA, SWAHILI

Kenya money KSH, CENT, SHILLING

Kenya neighbor SUDAN, UGANDA, SOMALIA, ETHIOPIA, TANZANIA

Kenya river ATHI, DAUA, MARA, TANA, EWASO, GALANA

Kenya tribes LUO, MERU, KAMBA, KISII, LUHYA, KIKUYU, KALENJIN

kerchief CURCH, SCARF, BANDANA, BABUSHKA

Kerensky overthrower LENIN

kernel NUT, PIT, CORE, GIST, PITH, SEED

ketch JACK, SHIP, YAWL

ketone IRONE, CARONE, ACETONE, BUTYRONE

kettle SUKY, BILLY, CALDRON, POTHOLE, CAULDRON

kettledrum NAKER, TABOR, ATABAL, NAGARA, TIMBAL, ATTABAL, TIMBALE, TIMPANI

Keturah husband ABRAHAM

key CAY, CLUE, CODE, CRUX, ISLE, PONY, DITAL, ISLET, PITCH, CLAVIS, COTTER, SPLINE, TAPPER, TONALITY

key part BIT, BOW, PIN, WEB, LOOP, STEM, COLLAR

keyboard MANUAL, CLAVIER, PEDALIER; *see PIANO*

keynote THEME, TONIC

keystone ROOT, BASIS, WEDGE, SAGITTA, SUPPORT, FOUNDATION

Keystone State PA, PENN(SYLVANIA)

khan AGA, ALI, INN, CHAM, PRINCE

Khoisan BUSHMAN, HOTTENTOT

Khond language KUI

Kibbutz COMMUNE, COLLECTIVE, COOPERATIVE

kibitz BUTTIN, HORNIN, MEDDLE, COMMENT

kibitzer OBSERVER, OUTSIDER

kibosh VETO, SCRAG

kick BOOT, HACK, PORR, PUNT, GRIPE, SPURN, RECOIL, THRILL

kick — BACK

kick off BEGIN, START

kick out FIRE, OUST, SACK, REMOVE, DISCARD

kickback CUT, BRIBE, PAYOFF, PAYOLA, REWARD, RAKEOFF

kickoff need TEE, SETUP

kid LAD, RIB, JOSH, SUEDE, TEASE, BANTER, (Y)EARLING

kidnap SEIZE, ABDUCT, RAVISH, SNATCH, SHANGHAI

kidnapping victim, famous HAMM, FRIED, KLAAS, PEARL, FRANKS, HEARST, SINATRA, LINDBERGH

kidneys, *pert. to* RENAL, NEPHRIC

kill DOIN, PREY, SLAY, VETO, CANCEL, MURDER, BUMPOFF, DISPATCH

killer BRAVO, HITMAN, SLAYER, ASSASSIN

killing FATAL, PURGE, BATTUE, DEADLY, MURDER, POGROM, CARNAGE, HOMICIDE, SLAUGHTER

killing, make a SUCCEED

killjoy DAMPER, SPOILSPORT, WET BLANKET

Kilmer poem TREES

kiln OST, LEER, LEHR, OAST, OVEN, TILER(Y)

kilt TUCK, PLEAT, SKIRT, PHILIBEG

kilter, out of	CHAOTIC, TOPSYTURVY	kitchen	GALLEY, COOKERY, CUISINE, SCULLERY
kin	SIB(S), FOLKS, FAMILY, PEOPLE, SIBLINGS, RELATIONS	kitchen fixture	OVEN, SINK, RANGE, STOVE, FRIDGE, ICEBOX
kind	ILK, TYPE, GENOS, GENRE, GENUS, SEELY, BENIGN, GENIAL, GENTLE, SPECIES	kitchen utensil	CORER, DICER, LADLE, MIXER, RICER, SCOOP, SIEVE, BEATER, FUNNEL, GRATER, JUICER,
kindle	TIND, WHET, ROUSE, SPUNK, INCITE, IGNITE, INSPIRE		OPENER, PEELER, SPATULA, COLANDER; see COOKING
kindling	PUNK, AMADOU, FIREWOOD	kite	GLED, SOAR, GLEAN, GLEDE, ELANET, PUTTOCK
kindness	BOON, GRACE, LENITY	kite genus	ELANUS, MILVUS
kindred	KIN, SIB, AKIN, KITH, BLOOD, FAMILY, COGNATE	kith and —	KIN
king	REX, REY, ROI, KRAL, SOPHY, REGULUS, PADISHAH	kitty	POT, ANTE, POOL, WIDOW, STAKE; see CAT
King Arthur	see ARTHURIAN	kleptomaniac	THIEF, FILCHER
King Henry	see HENRY	klutz	GALOOT
King John character	BIGOT, ARTHUR, BLANCH, ELINOR, CONSTANCE	knack	ART, FEAT, HANG, FLAIR, SKILL, TRICK, TALENT
king, pert. to	REG(N)AL	knapsack	KIT, PACK, BINDLE, MOCHILA, HAVERSACK
kingdom	REALM, DOMAIN, EMPIRE, MONARCHY	knave	NOB, PAM, JACK, NOBS, BOWER, CHURL, LOREL, LOSEL, ROGUE, SCAMP
kingfisher	TODY, HALCYON, KOOKABURRA	knead	ELT, MALAX, PETRIE, MASSAGE
kingfisher genus	ALCEDO, DACELO	knee	GENU, HOCK, JOINT
kingly	REGAL, ROYAL, MAJESTIC	knee part	DIB, HOCK, ROTULA, PATELLA, HAMSTRING
kink	BEND, HOOK, PULL, CRICK, CROOK, CURVE, QUIRK	knickknack	TOY, GAUD, CURIO, BAUBLE, DOODAD, GEWGAW, TRINKET
kinky	CURLY, QUIRKY, TWISTED, ECCENTRIC	knickknack holder	SHELF, WHATNOT
kinship	NASAB, ENATION, AFFINITY, AGNATION	knife	DAH, DAO, DOW, SNY, ULU, BOLO, CHIV, DHAO, DIRK, KRIS, SHIV, SNEE, STAB,
kiosk	BOOTH, STALL, STAND		BLADE, BOWIE, CHIVE,
Kipling birthplace	BOMBAY		FLEAM, BARLOW, BETRAY,
Kipling character	KAA, KIM, DASS, EGAN, AKELA, BALOO, DURGA, HARVEY		BODKIN, CARVER, CATLIN, LANCET, CATLING, HACHOIR, STILETTO; see DAGGER
Kipling work	KIM, JUNGLEBOOK	knife cover	SHEATH, SCABBARD
— Kippur	YOM	knife part	HAFT, TANG
Kiribati, capital of	(SOUTH) TARAWA	knight(s)	DUB, SIR, BEVIS, EQUES, RITTER, EQUITES, PALADIN, TEMPLAR,
Kiribati money	DOLLAR		BANNERET; see p. 659
Kish relative	SAUL	knit	TIE, BIND, JOIN, UNITE, PUCKER
kismet	DOOM, FATE, DESTINY	knitting term	PURL, SLEY,
kiss	BUSS, PECK, SMACK, CARESS, OSCULATE, SUCKFACE	knob	GAUGE, STITCH NUB, BOSS, KNOP, NODE, STUD, UMBO, KNURL,
kisser	LIP		FINIAL, NUBBLE
kit	LOT, SET, TUB, GEAR, PACK, BUCKET, OUTFIT	knobbed	NODAL, NODOSE, TOROSE
kit and —	CABOODLE		

knobby **BUMPY, HILLY, KNOTTY, NUBBLY, TOROSE, STUDDED, TUBEROSE**

knock **HIT, PAN, RAP, TAP, BLOW, STRIKE, CRITICIZE**

knock down **DECK, FLOOR**

knockout **KO, TKO, BASH, KAYO, LULU, STUNNER**

knoll **KNAP, TOFT, MOUND, HUMMOCK**

knot **NEP, BEND, BURL, KNAG, KNAR, KNOR, KNUR, LOOP, LUMP, MILE, NODE, NODI, NOIL, NOYL, REEF, SNAG, GNARL, GNARR, HITCH, KNAUR, KNURL, MOUSE, NODUS, AMORET, GRANNY, TREFOIL, BOWLINE, SHEEPSHANK**

knot, remove **ENODATE, UNRAVEL**

knotty **NODOSE, NODOUS, COMPLEX, PUZZLING**

knout **FLOG, WHIP**

know **DEN, WIS, WOT, WIST, INTUIT**

know-how **SAVVY, EXPERTISE, SAVOIR FAIRE**

knowing **HIP, ONTO, WISE, SCIENT, GNOSTIC**

know-it-all **SMARTY, EGGHEAD, WISEACRE**

knowledge **KEN, KITH, LORE, OLOGY, NOESIS, WISDOM, SCIENTIA**

knowledgeable **HEP, HIP, WISE, INFORMED, EDUCATED, CONVERSANT**

know-nothing **DUNCE, IDIOT, AGNOSTIC, IGNORAMUS**

knuckle **JOINT**

knuckle down **OBEY, YIELD, GIVEIN**

knucklehead **CLOD**

Kojak name **THEO, FRANK, RIZZO, TELLY, SAVALAS, STAVROS, SAPERSTEIN**

kooky **KINKY, LOOPY, SILLY, WACKY**

Koran chapter **SURA(H)**

Koran scholar **ULEMA**

Korea **CHOSEN**

Korea (North), capital of **PYONGYANG**

Korea (North) city **NAMPO, SINUJU, HAMHUNG, SERIWON, SUNCHON, CHONGJIN**

Korea (North) mountain **ORYIN, HUISAEK, KWANMA, KANGNAM**

Korea (North) river **YALU, IMJIN, TUMEN, HOCHON, YESONG, TAEDONG**

Korea (South), capital of **SEOUL**

Korea (South) cities **BUSAN, NUYEO, DAEGU, MASAN, MAKPO, PUSAN, TAEGU, INCHON, TAEJON, KWANGJU**

Korea (South) mountain **CHIRI, HALLA, SORAK, KEBANG**

Korea (South) river **HAN, KUM, NAKTONG**

Korean leader **SAM, WOO, CHUN, JONG, JUNG, KWON, PARK, RHEE, SUNG**

Korean money **WON, CHON, HWAN**

kosher **CLEAN, PROPER, GENUINE, LEGITIMATE**

kosher, opposite of **TREFI(A)**

kowtow **BOW, SCRAPE, GROVEL**

Krazy — **KAT**

Krishna **VISHNU, JUGGERNAUT**

Kronos wife **RHEA**

Kubla Khan river **ALPH**

kudos **FAME, AWARD, GLORY, PRAISE, RENOWN**

Kukla friend **FRAN, OLLIE**

Kurd **GUTI**

Kuril island **URUP, ITURUP, AHUMAHU, KUNASHIR**

Kuwait, capital of **KUWAIT CITY**

Kuwait city **QASR, HAWALLI, SABIYAH, ALJAHRAH**

Kuwait dynasty **ALSABAH**

Kuwait money **KD, FILS, DINAR**

Kuwait neighbor **IRAQ, SAUDI ARABIA**

kvetch **WHINE, COMPLAIN**

Kwa language **GA, EDO, EWE, FON, IBO, KRU, AGNI, AKAN, IGBO, NUPE, BASSA, GREBO, YORUBA**

Kyrgyzstan, capital of **BISHKEK**

Kyrgyzstan money **SOM**

L

L **EL(L), LIMA, FIFTY, LAMBDA**

La Boheme composer **PUCCINI**

La Boheme character **MIMI, BENOIT, COLLINE, RODOLFO, SCHAUNARD**

La Valse composer   RAVEL
lab subject   RAT, CHIMP,
     MOUSE, GUINEAPIG
Laban relative   LEAH, RACHEL,
     REBEKAH
label   TAG, FILLET, INFULA,
     LAPPET, PASTER, STICKER
labor   *see* WORK
labor leader   BUCK, BIKEL,
     GREEN, HOFFA, LEWIS,
     MEANY, QUILL, QUINN,
     FRIEND, REUTHER, SWEENEY,
     PETRILLO
labor union   *see* UNION
laboratory   LAB, WORKROOM
laboratory utensil   RETORT,
     ALEMBIC, CRUCIBLE, TEST
     TUBE
labored   STUDIED, AFFECTED,
     DIFFICULT, STRENUOUS
laborer   ESNE, HAND, HELP,
     ORRA, PEON, TOTY, NAVVY,
     PROLE, COOLIE, FELLAH,
     SEGGON, TOILER, BRACERO
laborious   ARDUOUS,
     STRENUOUS, PROTRACTED
labyrinth   WEB, MAZE, JUNGLE
labyrinthine   MAZY, COMPLEX,
     DAEDAL, TORTUOUS,
     INTRICATE
lace   BEAT, LASH, ADORN,
     AGLET, BRAID, CLUNY,
     FILET, GRILL, LACIS, ORRIS,
     SNARE, AIGLET, EDGING,
     GRILLE, ALENCON, GUIPURE,
     MACRAME, MALINES,
     TATTING, FILIGREE
lace, make   TAT
lace, place for a   EYELET
lacerate   CUT, RIP, REND,
     TEAR, LANIATE
lachrymose   TEARY, WEEPY,
     TEARFUL
lack   NEED, WANT, DEARTH,
     FAMINE, DEFICIT,
     SCARCITY
lackadaisical   BLASE, CASUAL,
     RELAXED, LISTLESS,
     EASYGOING
lackey   SLAVE, TOADY,
     FLUNKY, FOOTMAN,
     SERVANT
lacking   SHY, SANS, SHORT,
     DEVOID, INNEED
lackluster   DRAB, DULL,
     BORING, DREARY
laconic   CURT, BRIEF, TERSE,
     CONCISE
Laconi(c)a, capital of   SPARTA

lacquer   DUCO, GLOSS, JAPAN,
     ENAMEL, VARNISH
lacus asphaltites   DEADSEA
lad   BOY, CHILD, SONNY,
     YOUTH, SHAVER, STRIPLING
ladder   STY, STEE, TREE, SCALE,
     STEPS, POMPIER, HIERARCHY
ladder part   RUNG, STEP,
     ROUND, SPOKE, STAVE,
     RUNDLE
lade   DIP, BAIL, LOAD, BURDEN
ladies' man   BEAU, DANDY,
     GALLANT
lading   CARGO
ladle   DIP, BAIL, GEAT, SCOOP,
     SHANK, DIPPER
Ladrone Islands   WANSHAN; *see*
     MARIANAS
lady   BIBI, BURD, DAME,
     BEEBEE; *see* MADAM
Lady of the Lake author   SCOTT
Lady of the Lake name   DHU,
     ELLEN, NIMUE, VIVIAN
ladykiller   DONJUAN,
     CASANOVA
ladylike   SOFT, WEAK,
     DEMURE, GENTEEL,
     FEMININE, WELLBRED
Laertes relative   OPHELIA,
     ULYSSES, POLONIUS
lag   DRAG, BREAK, DALLY,
     PAUSE, TARRY, TRAIL
laggard   IDLER, DAWDLER,
     LOITERER, STRAGGLER
lagoon   HAFF, TARN, MERE,
     LIMAN
Lagoon Islands   *see* TUVALU
laic   LAY, CIVIL, LAYMAN,
     SECULAR, TEMPORAL
lair   DEN, CAVE, HAUNT,
     BURROW, COVERT, WARREN
laissez-faire   LAX, LENIENT,
     TOLERANT
Laius relative   JOCASTA,
     OEDIPUS
lake   LOCH, MERE, SHAT,
     SHOG, TARN, LOUGH,
     SHOTT, LAGOON, SALINA; *see*
     p. 612
Lake George   HORICON
Lake State   MI, MICHIGAN
Lakshmi consort   VISHNU
lam   BEAT, FLEE, FLOG,
     SCRAM, ESCAPE, FLIGHT,
     THRASH
lama   MONK, DALAI, TESHU
lamb   (Y)EAN, SHEEP, COSSET,
     FATLING, (Y)EANLING
Lamb pseudonym   ELIA

lambaste	BEAT, SCOLD, CHEWOUT
lambskin	BUDGE, VELLUM
lame	HALT, WEAK, CRIPPLE(D), DISABLE(D), HALTING, SPAVINED
lamebrain	SAP, NINNY
Lamech relative	ADAH, CAIN, NOAH, JABAL, JUBAL, TUBAL, NAAMAH, ZILLAH, METHUSELAH
lament	CRY, RUE, WEY, HONE, KEEN, MOAN, PINE, WAIL, WEEP, MOURN, DIRGE, BEWAIL, GRIEVE, REPINE
lamentation	LINOS, TANGI, PLAINT, PLANGOR
lamina	see LAYER
laminated	COATED, COVERED, LAYERED
Lammas Day	GULE
lamp	JET, BULB, DAVY, GLIM, TORCH, ARGAND, CRUSIE, GEORDIE, LAMPION, LUCERNE, LUCIGEN
lamp part	HARP, WICK, BURNER, CHIMNEY, CRESSET
lamp, waving of	ARATI
lampblack	SOOT
lampoon	SKIT, SPOOF, SQUIB, PARODY, SATIRE, TAKEOFF
lamprey	RAMPER; see EEL
lance	DART, OPEN, PIKE, SHAFT, SLASH, SPEAR, PIERCE, JAVELIN
Lancelot beloved	ELAINE, GUINEVERE
Lancelot relative	BORS, BORT
lancer	U(H)LAN, HUSSAR
lancet	see KNIFE
land	ALOD, DOAB, DUAB, FELL, GISH, GORE, MULK, ODAL, UDAL, UNAL, ARADA, ARADO, ARDER, GLEBE, SOLUM, TILTH, TRACT, VELDT, WEALD, ALIGHT, ASSART, DEBARK, STEPPE, TUNDRA, PRAIRIE, ALODIUM
land, barren	GALL, WASTE, DESERT
land measure	see MEASURE
Land of Plenty	GOSHEN
Land of Rising Sun	JAPAN
land, pert. to	AGRARIAN, GEOPONIC
land, reclaimed	POLDER, NOVALIA
landed	ALIT, PRAEDIAL

landholder	THANE, THEGN, ZAMINDAR
landing	KEY, DOCK, GHAT, PIER, QUAI, QUAY, GHAUT, JETTY, LEVEE, WHARF
landlord	HOST, LAIRD, OWNER, LEASER, BONIFACE, INNKEEPER
landmark	COPA, MERE, CAIRN, MEITH, SENAL
landowner	LAIRD
landowner state	LANDED
landscape	VISTA, SURVEY, PAYSAGE, SCENERY
landslide	SNOWSLIDE, AVALANCHE
Landslide —	LYNDON
lane	WAY, PATH, WYND, ALLEY
— lang syne	AULD
language	LIP, CHIB, IDIOM, TONGUE, DIALECT, DICTION, PARLANCE; see p. 621
language, artificial	RO, IDO, VOLAPUK, ESPERANTO
languid	LAZY, SLOW, INDOLENT, LISTLESS, LEISURELY
languish	FLAG, PINE, WASTE, SUFFER
languor	KEF, KAIF, KEEF, KIEF, KIFF, BLUES, ENNUI, TORPOR
lanky	LEAN, GAUNT, GANGLY, SLENDER
lantern	LAMP, LOUVER, CRESSET
lanthanide series	CERIUM, ERBIUM, TERBIUM, THULIUM, EUROPIUM, LANTHANUM, LUTETIUM, SAMARIUM, NEODYMIUM, YTTERBIUM, DYSPROSIUM, GADOLINIUM, PROMETHIUM
lanyard	CORD, ROPE, THONG
Laomedon kingdom	TROY
Laomedon relative	ILUS, PRIAM, TITHONUS
Laos, capital of	VIENTIANE
Laotian city	ATTAPU, SARAVAN, VIENTIANE
Laotian language	LAO
Laotian money	AT(T), KIP
Laotian mountain	BIA
Laotian people	KHA, YUN
Laotian plain	JARS
Laotian river	OU, DON, THA, MEKONG, BANGTAI
lap	LEG, LICK, KNEE, TOUR, ROUND, SLURP, CIRCUIT

lapel   FLAP, COLLAR, REVER(S)
lapidary   CUTTER, JEWELER, ENGRAVER, POLISHER
Lapland city/town   KOLA, KIRUNA
Lapland country   NORWAY, SWEDEN, FINLAND
Lapland lake   INARI, IMANDRA, TORNEALVEN
lappet   FLAP, FOLD, LOBE, LABEL, DEWLAP, INFULA, WATTLE
lapse   ERR, GAP, PASS, SIN(K), SLIP, FALTER, SLIPUP, BLUNDER, VENALITY; see INTERVAL
larceny   THEFT, ROBBERY, STEALING
larceny type   GRAND, PETTY
larch   PINE, LARIX, SPRUCE, CONIFER
lard   FAT, OIL, GREASE
larder   SPENCE, STORE, PANTRY, BUTTERY
large   BIG, FULL, HUGE, AMPLE, GREAT, DECUMAN, OUTSIZE, COLOSSAL
large amount   SEA, SLEW, SCADS, OODLES
large, at   FREE, LOOSE, ABROAD, GENERALLY
largely   MAINLY, MOSTLY, CHIEFLY
largesse   GIFTS, CHARITY, GRATUITY, GENEROSITY
lariat   LAZO, ROPE, LASSO, NOOSE, REATA, RIATA
lariat eye   HONDA, HONDO(O)
lark   SPREE, FROLIC; see SONGBIRD
lark genus   ALAUDA
larva   BOT(T), CRAB, GRUB, MAWK, SLUG, TURK, REDIA, VELUM, CADDIS, GENTLE, MAGGOT, TUSSAH, WABBLE, WARBLE, CADDICE, CADELLE, CODWORM, FLYBLOW, PLANULA, PLUTEUS, WIGGLER, CERCARIA, GLOWWORM, NAUPLIUS, PEARSLUG, TORNARIA, WRIGGLER; see WORM
larynx   VOICEBOX
Las Vegas venue   MGM GRAND, MIRAGE, SAHARA, CAESARS, RIVIERA
lascivious   LEWD, WANTON, LUSTFUL
laser inventor   TOWNEE

lash   TIE, BIND, DASH, FLOG, KNUT, WALE, YERK, QUIRT, WHALE; see WHIP
lass, lassie   see GIRL
lassitude   LANGUOR, LETHARGY
lasso   see LARIAT
last   END, DURE, FINAL, OMEGA, ENDURE, FINALE, NEWEST, ULTIMATE
last but one   PENULT
Last Mohican   UNCAS
Last of the Mohicans author   COOPER
Last of the Mohicans character   NATTY, BUMPPO, HAWKEYE
Last Supper   C(O)ENA; see COMMUNION
Last Supper artist   DAVINCI
lasting   DURABLE, PERMANENT
lastly   ENFIN, FINALLY
latch(ing)   HOOK, BELAY, SNECK, LASKET
late   NEO, NEW, DEAD, SERO, TARDY, RECENT
latent   COVERT, HIDDEN, DORMANT, QUIESCENT
later   ANON, AFTER, SEE YA
lateral   SIDEWAYS, SIDEWISE
latest   LAST, NEWEST, CURRENT, PRESENT
latex   PUAN
latex source   POPPY, MILKWEED
lath   RAIL, SLAT, SPALE, SPLINT
lather   FOAM, SCUM, SUDS, FROTH, SPUME, FRENZY
Latin   ROMAN, ITALIAN
Latin trio   AMO, AMAS, AMAT, VENI, VIDI, VICI
Latin words   see p. 571
latitude   ROOM, SCOPE, WIDTH, EXTENT, LEEWAY, BREADTH, AUTONOMY, LOCATION, COORDINATE
Latona relative   DIANA, APOLLO
Latter-Day Saint   MORMON
lattice   BOWER, GRILLE, SCREEN, TRELLIS, CANCELLI
Latvia, capital of   RIGA
Latvian   LETT(IC), LETTISH
Latvian city/town   RIGA, JURMALA, LIEPAJA, DUNABURG, DAUGAVPILS
Latvian measure   KANNE, STOOF, KULMET
Latvian money   LAT(S), RUBLIS, SANTIMS, KAPEIKA

Latvian neighbor	RUSSIA, BELARUS, ESTONIA, LITHUANIA	law student	ONEL
		lawful	JUST, LEGAL, LICIT, ENNOMIC, OFFICIAL, LEGITIMATE
Latvian river	ABAVA, DUBNA, VENTA, IECAVA, DAUGAVA, LIELUPE	lawgiver	DRACO, SOLON, MINOS, MOSES
laud	HYMN, EXTOL, PRAISE, GLORIFY	lawless	UNRULY, ANARCHIC, CRIMINAL
laudable	WORTHY, ADMIRABLE, EXEMPLARY	lawmaker	see LEGISLATOR
laugh(s)	HEH, HAHA, HOWL, ROAR, FLEER, CACKLE, GUFFAW, GIGGLE, HAWHAW, TITTER, CHORTLE, SNICKER	lawman	COP, MAN, FUZZ, GMAN, TMAN, COPPER, MARSHAL, OFFICER, SHERIFF, TROOPER, POLICEMAN
		lawn	PLOT, GLADE, SWARD, BATISTE, CAMBRIC
laughable	see COMIC	lawnmower	HAYTER
laughing	RIANT, RIDENT	lawsuit	CASE, CLAIM, ACTION, CHARGE, GRIEVANCE, COMPLAINT, LITIGATION
laughingstock	BUTT, CLOWN		
laughter, pert. to	GELASTIC		
launch	FIRE, SEND, LANCE, SHOOT, PROPEL, UNVEIL, LIFTOFF, TAKEOFF, DISPATCH, INTRODUCE; see SHIP	lawyer	ESQ, JURIST, LEGIST, PORTIA, COUNSEL, ADVOCATE, ATTORNEY, BARRISTER, COUNSELOR, SOLICITOR
launder	WASH, (DRY)CLEAN, CENSOR, PURIFY, TRANSFER		
laundry equipment	IRON, SOAP, DRIER, BLEACH, MANGLE, WASHER	lawyer, TV	AMY, PERRY MASON, BEN MATLOCK, ALLY MCBEAL
		lax	SLACK, CARELESS, SLIPSHOD, NEGLIGENT
Laura's husband	ROB		
laurel	ANIBA, CASSY, WICKY, DAPHNE, CAJEPUT, CASSYTHA	laxative	ALOIN, CASSIA, PHYSIC, APERIENT, CATHARTIC, PURGATIVE
laurels	FAME, GLORY, HONOR, KUDOS		
lava	AA, ASH, BOMB, MAGMA, COULEE, LATITE, SCORIA, TAXITE, LAPILLUS, PAHOEHOE	lay	BET, LAIC, DITTY, PLACE, BALLAD, LAICAL, ASCRIBE, SECULAR
		lay away	SAVE, HOARD
lavabo	BASIN, TOWEL, WASHBOWL	lay down	BET, WAGER
		lay into	BEAT, LASH, SCOLD
lavatory	BOWL, BASIN, LAVABO, RESTROOM	lay off	FIRE, IDLE, FURLOUGH
		lay up	HEAP, HOARD, STORE
Laverne and Shirley names	CINDY, LENNY, PENNY, SHOTZ, FEENEY, CARMINE, DEFAZIO, SQUIGGY, MARSHALL	layer	PLY, COAT, TIER, CORTEX, LAMINA, PATINA, STRATA, VENEER, PROVINE, STRATUM
lavish	HEAP, LUSH, RICH, BESTOW, LIBERAL, PROFUSE, ABUNDANT, PROLIFIC, PLENTIFUL, EXTRAVAGANT	laziness	SLOTH, INDOLENCE
		lazy	IDLE, SLOW, OTIOSE, INDOLENT, SLOTHFUL
law	ACT, FAS, JUS, LEX, ADAT, CODE, JURE, RULE, TORA, CANON, DROIT, EDICT, SALIC, TORAH, TALION, TALMUD, DECALOG, STATUTE, DECALOGUE	lazy one	BUM, LUSK, DRONE, IDLER, LOAFER, LAZYBONES
		lazy Susan	(TURN)TABLE
		LBJ dogs	HER, HIM
		lea	MEAD, SWARD, MEADOW, PASTURE
law code	PANDECT, DECALOG(UE)	leach	BLEED, EXTRACT, LIXIVIATE
law firm employee	PARA(LEGAL), CLERK	lead	WAD, CLUE, HEAD, PILOT, PLUMB, PRESA, GALENA, SINKER, SOLDER, PLUMBUM, PRECENT
law, pert. to	LEGAL, FORENSIC		
law qualifier	DRACONIAN		

lead astray	DECEIVE, MISGUIDE	learning	KEN, LORE, WISDOM, CULTURE, ERUDITION
lead, in cards	FALSECARD	lease	LET, HIRE, RENT, CONVEY, DEMISE, CHARTER
lead up to	PAVE, PREPARE		
leaden	GRAY, HEAVY, GLOOMY, SOMBER, SULLEN	leash	CURB, JESS, LUNE, LYAM, REIN, ROPE, BRACE, LONGE, THONG, TETHER, CONTROL
leader	DUX, VAN, DUCE, CHIEF, GUIDE, SNELL, CANTOR, FUHRER, CAUDILLO	least	FEWEST, MINIMUM
		leather	ELK, KID, BOCK, CALF, CUIR, NAPA, ROAN, YUFT, ALUTA, JUFTI, MOCHA, SUEDE, BULGAR, LEVANT, OXHIDE, SKIVER, VELLUM, CANEPIN, CHAMOIS, COWHIDE, MOROCCO, SHAGREEN
leadership	GUIDANCE		
leading	VAN, MAIN, AHEAD, CHIEF, STELLAR, FORE(MOST), PRINCIPAL, PREEMINENT		
leaf	OLA, OLE, FOIL, OLAY, OLLA, PAGE, PAUN, BRACT, FOLIO, FROND, SEPAL, SHEET, LAMINA, SPATHE, LAMELLA, TENDRIL	leather, convert into	TAN, TAW
		leave	EXIT, PAGE, QUIT, SCUD, WILL, ADIEU, CONGE, EXEAT, VACATE, MAKE OFF, TAKE OFF, CLEAR OUT, FURLOUGH, RUN ALONG
leaf part	PEN, RIB, AXIL, VEIN, BLADE, COSTA, STOMA, MIDRIB, STIPEL, PAGINA, PETIOLE, STIPULE, STOMATA, TENDRIL	Leave It to Beaver names	DOW, JUNE, TONY, WARD, EDDIE, JERRY, LUMPY, WALLY, WHITEY, CLEAVER, MATTHEWS
leaf shape	OVATE	leave off	STOP, CEASE, DESIST
leaflet	FLYER, PINNA, TRACT, (HAND)BILL	leave out	OMIT, ELIDE, EXCEPT, IGNORE, EXCLUDE
leafy	FOLIOSE	leaven	BARM, ZYME, YEAST
league	BLOC, BUND, PACT, HANSE, COMBINE, ENTENTE; *see p. 706*	leaves	BUKA, FOLIAGE
		leave-taking	ADIEU, CONGE(E), PARTING, FAREWELL
Leah relative	LEVI, DINAH, JACOB, JUDAH, LABAN, RACHEL, REUBEN, SIMEON, ZEBULUN, ISSACHAR	leavings	ORTS, CHAFF, DRAFF, DREGS, RESIDUE; *see* REFUSE
		Lebanese city	TYRE, HALBA, SIDON, ZAHLE, ALMINA, BEIRUT, ZAHLAH, TRIPOLI
leak	OOZE, SEEP, SPILL		
lean	BONY, LANK, RELY, GAUNT, LANKY, SPARE, SCANTY, SCRAWNY	Lebanese language	ARABIC
		Lebanese money	LIRA, POUND, PIASTER
Leander's lover	HERO		
leaning	BENT, SLOPE, OBLIQUE, PENCHANT, INCLINATION	Lebanese neighbor	SYRIA, ISRAEL
		Lebanese river	MUSA, DAMAR, LITANI
lean-to	HUT, SHED, SHACK, LINTER	Lebanon, capital of	BEIRUT
leap	LOUP, LOWP, SKIP, FRISK, LUNGE, SALTO, STEND, VAULT, CURVET	lecher	ROUE, SATYR, DEBAUCHEE
		lecherous	RANDY, LUSTFUL, SENSUAL
leap year	BISSEXTILE	lectern	AMBO, DESK, PULPIT
Lear character	KENT, TRAY, REGAN, ALBANY, GONERIL, CORDELIA	lecture	TALK, SERMON, SPEECH, HOMILY, ADDRESS
learn	CON, HEAR, STUDY, UNEARTH, DISCOVER, MEMORIZE	lecturer	DOCENT, LECTOR, READER
		Leda's child	HELEN, CASTOR, POLLUX
learned	WISE, ERUDITE, EDUCATED, LETTERED, LITERATE	Leda's lover	SWAN, ZEUS
learned person	*see* SAGE	ledge	CAY, BERM, LODE, REEF, SILL, APRON, BERME, SHELF

ledger item	ASSET, DEBIT, ENTRY, CREDIT
Lee's horse	TRAVELER
leech	SAIL, TOADY, PARASITE
leek	BULB, ALLIUM, SCALLION
leer	GRIN, OGLE, SMIRK, SNEER
leery	WARY, CHARY, DUBIOUS, GUARDED
lees	DRAF, DREGS, DROSS, MOTHER
Leeward islands	NEVIS, BARBUDA, ANTIGUA, GUADELOUPE, ST KITTS, MONTSERRAT
leeway	SCOPE, SPACE, MARGIN, FREEDOM, LATITUDE
left	KAY, PORT, WENT, LARBOARD
left-hand (page)	LEVO, VERSO
left-handed	INEPT, LEFTY, CLUMSY, SOUTHPAW CAR(HANDED), MORGANATIC
leftist	RED, LIBERAL, RADICAL
leftover	ORT, SCRAP, MORSEL, REMNANT
leftovers, prepare	REHEAT, REWARM, WARM UP
lefty	SOUTHPAW
leg	GAM, PEG, PIN, GAMB, LIMB, GAMMON
leg covering	PUTTY, GAITER, PEDULE, PUTTEE, LEGGING(S)
leg part	CRUS, KNEE, SHIN, ANKLE, SHANK; see BONE
leg, pert. to	SURAL, CRURAL
legacy	GIFT, WILL, BEQUEST
legal	LEAL, JURAL, LICIT, VALID, LAWFUL
legal action	RES, CASE, SUIT, LAWSUIT, LITIGATION
legal aid	PARA(LEGAL)
legal tender	CASH, COIN, MONEY, SPECIE, CURRENCY
legal term	RES, ACTA, BILL, LIEN, MORA, PLEA, TORT, WRIT, DROIT, INREM, VENUE, APPEAL, CAVEAT, DELICT, SEIZIN, SUMMONS, DEMURRER, SUBPOENA
legalize	PERMIT, SANCTION, AUTHORIZE
legate	ENVOY, NUNCIO
legation	EMBASSY, MISSION
legato opposite	STACCATO
legend	MYTH, SAGA, FABLE, MOTTO, CAPTION, FICTION
legendary	EPIC, FAMOUS, FABULOUS, RENOWNED
legerdemain	MAGIC, TRICKS, SLEIGHT (OF HAND)
legging	COCKER, COGGER, GAITER, PUTTEE, GAMBADO
legible	CLEAR, READABLE, DECIPHERABLE
legion	ARMY, CROWD, HORDE, MULTITUDE
legislate	MAKE, ENACT
legislator	DRACO, MINOS, MOSES, SOLON, DEPUTY, SENATOR
legislature	see ASSEMBLY
legitimate	REAL, LEGAL, LICIT, VALID, GENUINE
legume	PEA, POD, BEAN, GUAR, PULSE, LOMENT, SOYBEAN
legwear	CHAPS, SHAPS, SPATS, GARTER, GAMASHES, SUSPENDERS; see PANTS, LEGGING
lei	WREATH, GARLAND
leisure	EASE, REST, TOOM, OTIUM, REPOSE
leisurely	EASY, RELAXED, LAIDBACK, TART
lemony	TART
lemur	LORI, MAKI, VARI, AVAHI, INDRI, KOKAM, LORIS, POTTO, SIFAC, ADAPID, AYEAYE, COLUGO, MACACO, MOHOLI, SIFAKA, LEMURID, TARSIER
lemur genus	ADAPIS, INDRIS
Lena tributary	ALDAN, VITIM
lend	GIVE, LOAN, IMPART, LET OUT, ADVANCE
length	EXTENT; see MEASURE
lengthen	EXTEND, PROLONG, STRETCH, ELONGATE
lengthening	ECTASIS
lengthwise	ONEND, LONGWAYS
lengthy	LONG, PROLIX, EXTENDED
lenient	MILD, GENTLE, CLEMENT, MERCIFUL
Leningrad	PETROGRAD, ST PETERSBURG
lenitive	SOOTHING
lens	ADON, GLASS, TORIC, CONVEX, CORNEA, CONCAVE, MENISCUS
Leoncavallo opera	ZAZA, BOHEME, PAGLIACCI
Leonidas country	SPARTA

leopard	OUNCE, OCELOT, PANTHER; *see* CAT		MISSIVE, LANDLORD; *see* ALPHABET
leotard	TIGHTS	letter, Anglo-Saxon	EDH, ETH, WEN, THORN
leper	LAZAR, PARIAH, OUTCAST	lettered	LEARNED,
leprechaun	ELF, FAIRY, GOBLIN		EDUCATED, LITERATE
leprosy	LEPRA	lettuce	COS, BIBB, SALAD,
Les Misérables author	HUGO		ENDIVE, CELTUCE, ICEBERG,
Les Misérables character	JAVERT, FANTINE, VALJEAN	letup	ROMAINE LULL, PAUSE, RESPITE,
Lesage novel	(GIL)BLAS		ABATEMENT
lesbian	GAY, EROTIC, SAPPHO	Levantine boat	JERM
Lesbos poet	ARION, SAPPHO, ALCAEUS, LESCHES	levee	DIKE, QUAY, DURBAR; *see* EMBANKMENT, LANDING
lese majesty	OUTRAGE, TREASON, INDIGNITY	level	KO, AIM, EVEN, RASE, RAZE, FLUSH, GRADE,
Lesotho, capital of	MASERU		PLANE, STEADY
Lesotho city/town	HLOTSE, LIBONO, MASERU, MAFETENG	lever	BAR, PRY, CANT, PEVY, CRANK, PEAVY, PEDAL, PRIZE, GAFFLE, TAPPET
Lesotho money	LOTI, LISENTE, MALOTI	Levi relative	JACOB, KOHATH, MERARI, GERSHON,
Lesotho river	ORANGE, CALEDON, DINAKENG	leviathan	JOCHEBED VAST, WHALE,
less	FEWER, MINUS		MONSTROUS, SEA MONSTER
lessee	RENTER, TENANT	levity	HUMOR, FRIVOLITY
lessen	BATE, FADE, THIN, ABATE, MINIFY, REDUCE, MITIGATE, PETER (OUT)	levy lewd	DRAFT, MUSTER; *see* TAX CADGY, LUSTFUL, INDECENT
lesser	MINOR, SMALLER	Lewis and Clark goal	ORIGON
Lesser Antilles island	TOBAGO, VIRGIN, LEEWARD, BARBADOS, TRINIDAD, WINDWARD	lexicographer lexicographer interest	ROGET, EDITOR, WORDMAN, COMPILER COINAGE, NEW WORD(S)
lesson	LECTURE, EXERCISE	lexicon	GLOSSARY, WORDLIST, DICTIONARY
let	ALLOW, PERMIT; *see* LEASE	Lhasa palace	POTALA
let it stand	STET	liability	DEBT, DUTY,
let off	FREE, EMIT, ACQUIT, EXCUSE		BURDEN, CHARGE, HANDICAP, OBLIGATION
let out	EMIT, TELL, UNPEN, DISMISS, DIVULGE, RELEASE	liable	APT, BOUND, EXPOSED, SUBJECT
let up	EASE, ABATE, RELAX	liaison	LINK, AMOUR, AFFAIR,
letdown	BLOW, COMEDOWN, ANTICLIMAX, DISAPPOINTMENT	liana	CONTACT CIPO, SIPO, LIBURNUM
lethal	*see* FATAL	liar	FAKE, FRAUD, PHONY,
lethargic	DULL, LAZY, TORPID, LANGUID, SLUGGISH		FIBBER, ANANIAS, WERNARD
lethargy	COMA, SOPOR, APATHY, STUPOR, TORPOR, INERTIA, LANGUOR	libel	MUD, DEFAME, CALUMNY, SLANDER, ROORBACK
Lethe	OBLIVION	liberal	FREE, WHIG, AMPLE,
Leto relative	COEUS, DIANA, APOLLO, ARTEMIS		LAVISH, BROAD, COPIOUS, GENEROUS, TOLERANT
let's —	ROLL	liberate	FREE, RANSOM,
letter	EDH, BULL, LINE, MEMO, NOTE, RUNE, BRIEF, DEMIT, BILLET, PARAPH, TENANT, UNCIAL, CAPITAL, EPISTLE,	Liberia, capital of Liberian cities	REDEEM, MANUMIT MONROVIA KLE, HARPER, KAKATA, YAKEPA, ZORZOR,

ZWEDRU, GBARNGA, MONROVIA, SASSTOWN
Liberian language *see* KWA, MANDE
Liberian leader **TAYLOR**
Liberian money **CENT, DOLLAR**
Liberian neighbor **GUINEA, IVORY COAST, SIERRA LEONE**
Liberian people **GI, KRA, KRU, VAI, VEI, GOLA, GORA, KRAHN**
Liberian river **LOFA, CESTOS, CAVALLA**
libertine **RAKE, ROUE, DESADE, DEBAUCHEE**
liberty **FREEDOM, AUTONOMY**
library **ANA, STORE, MORGUE**
libretto **BOOK, STORY, WORDS**
Libya, capital of **TRIPOLI**
Libyan city **BRAK, GHAT, JALU, SURT, BERDI, KUFRA, CYRENE, TRIPOLI, BENGHAZI**
Libyan desert **SAHARA**
Libyan leader **QADDAFI**
Libyan measure **PIK(E), BOZZE, JABIA, MATTARO**
Libyan money **DINAR, DIRHAM**
Libyan people **BERBER, TOUBOU, TUAREG**
license **GRANT, PATENT, PERMIT, FREEDOM, LIBERTY, AUTHORITY**
license issuer **DMV**
licentious **LEWD, WICKED, DISSOLUTE**
lichen **USNEA, ARCHIL, ORCHIL, EVERNIA, LUNGWORT**
lichen derivative **ARCHIL, LITMUS, PERSIS, CUDBEAR**
licit **LEGAL, VALID, LAWFUL**
lick **LAP, BEAT, FLOG, WHIP, TASTE, THRASH**
licking **HIDING, BEATING**
lid **CAP, TOP, COVER, OPERCULUM**
lie **FIB, SIT, FLAM, LAZE, LIGE, LOLL, REST, INHERE, FICTION, RECLINE, UNTRUTH, FALSEHOOD**
lie in wait **LURK, SKULK**
Liebestraum composer **LISZT**
Liechtenstein, capital of **VADUZ**
Liechtenstein money **FRANC, RAPPEN**
Liechtenstein neighbor **AUSTRIA, SWITZERLAND**
Liechtenstein river **RHINE**

lied **(ART)SONG**
lieutenant **LUFF, LOOEY, LOOIE, JEMADAR, SHAVETAIL**
lieutenant's command **PLATOON**
lieutenant colonel's command **BATTALION**
life **VIE, BIOS, DAYS, VITA, ANIMA, BIOTA, BREATH, CAREER**
life and — **LIMB, DEATH**
life jacket **MAE WEST**
Life of Riley names **BABS, CISSY, MOOSE, PEGGY, WALDO, BENDIX, DANGLE, CHESTER, GLEASON, HONEYBEE, MILLICENT**
life, *pert. to* **VITAL, BIOTIC(AL)**
life preserver **DONUT, MAEWEST**
life principle **JIVA, ATMAN, PRANA**
life science **ANATOMY, BIOLOGY, ECOLOGY, ZOOLOGY**
lifeless **DEAD, FLAT, AMORT, AZOIC, INERT, DEFUNCT, EXTINCT**
lifelike **NATURAL, REALISTIC**
Lifestyles of the Rich and Famous emcee **LEACH, ROBIN**
lifetime **AGE, DAYS, DURATION, EXISTENCE**
lift(ed) **HEFT, HOVE, PERK, EXALT, HEAVE, HOIST, RAISE, STEAL, ELEVATOR**
lifting engine **RAM, JACK, CRANE, DAVIT, HOIST, JENNY, NORIA, SAKIEH, SHADOFF**
ligament **BOND, DESMO, TAENIA**
ligature **TIE, BOND, TAENIA, THREAD**
light **ARC, AIRY, GLIM, HALO, LAND, LUNT, NEON, FANAL, FLARE, FLASH, KLEIG, LASER, LEGER, MATCH, TAPER, TORCH, CANDLE, CORONA, IGNITE, ILLUME, NIMBUS, SCONCE, CRESSET;** *see* **LAMP, LANTERN**
light unit **LUX, PYR, PHOT, LUMEN, CARCEL, HEFNER**
lighter **HOY, SCOW, SPILL**
light-headed **DIZZY, FAINT, GIDDY, WOOZY, WOBBLY**
lighthearted **FUN(NY), GAY, HAPPY, CAREFREE, CHEERFUL, HUMOROUS**

lighthouse	FANAL, PHARE, BEACON, PHAROS
lightning	BOLT, LAIT, FLASH, LEVIN, FIREBALL, WILDFIRE
lights out	TAPS, BEDTIME
ligulate	LORATE
like	AKIN, ENJOY, RELISH, COGNATE
like new	MINT
likelihood	ODDS, CHANCE
likely	APT, PRONE, SEEMLY, PROBABLE
like-minded	ONE, INACCORD
liken	EQUATE, RELATE, COMPARE
likeness	ICON, GUISE, IMAGE, EFFIGY, ANALOGY
likewise	TOO, ALSO, ITEM, DITTO, BESIDES
liking	FANCY, TASTE, FONDNESS
lilac	PRIM, MAUVE, PRIVET, SYRINGA, PIPETREE
Lilliputian	TINY, SMALL, DWARF
lilt	SWING, RHYTHM, CADENCE
lily	LIS, ALOE, ARUM, SEGO, CALLA, DATIL, HOSTA, LOTUS, TUCKY, TULIP, WOKAS, YUCCA, DAGGER, GUNKIA, SMILAX, BAYONET, HYACINTH
Lily Maid of Astolat	ELAINE
limb	ARM, FIN, LEG, WING, BOUGH, BRANCH, MEMBER
limber	SPRY, AGILE, LITHE, PLIANT, SUPPLE, PLIABLE
lime	CAO, CALX, CITRUS, LINDEN
limelight	FAME, RENOWN, ATTENTION, PUBLICITY
limestone	CAEN, CALP, LIAS, MALM, TUFA, CHALK, OOLITE
limey	BRIT(ON), SAILOR, ENGLISHMAN
limicoline bird	SNIPE, PLOVER
limit	EDGE, PALE, SPAN, TERM, BOURN, STENT, STINT, BORDER, BOURNE, CONFINE
limitless	VAST, INFINITE, BOUNDLESS
limn	DRAW, DEPICT, SKETCH, PORTRAY, DESCRIBE
limousine	LIMO, SEDAN
limp	LAX, HALT, FLABBY, FLIMSY, FLOPPY, HOBBLE, FLACCID

limpid	CLEAR, PELLUCID
Lincoln assassin	BOOTH
Lincoln debater	DOUGLAS
Lincoln relative	MARY, TODD, ROBERT, WILLIE
Lindbergh	ANNE, CHARLES
Lindbergh book	WE
linden	LIN, LIME, LIND, LINN, TEIL, TEYL, TILIA, BASSWOOD
line	CUE, DRY, ROW, WAD, CORD, EDGE, FILE, RANK, TROT, AGONE, CERIF, QUEUE, SERIF, SNELL, STEAN, STRIA, CERIPH, CORDON, EARING, PATTER, SECANT, STEENE, STRIAE, VECTOR, MARLINE
lineage	STEM, BLOOD, STOCK, STRAIN, DESCENT, PEDIGREE; see FAMILY
lined	RULED, STRIATE(D)
linen	CREA, LAWN, CRASH, SCRIM, TOILE, BYSSUS, DAMASK, DOWLAS, NAPERY, SHEETS, BATISTE, CAMBRIC, DRABBET, HOLLAND, LINGERIE
linen measure	CUT, HEER
liner	FACING, VESSEL, STEAMER
liner, famous	FRANCE, LIBERTE, CARONIA, OLYMPIC, TITANIC, AMERICA, GERMANIC, SYLVANIA, BRITANNIC, LUSITANIA, NORMANDIE, MAURETANIA, ILE DE FRANCE, (QUEEN) MARY, (QUEEN) ELIZABETH, UNITED STATES
linger	LAG, DALLY, DWELL, TARRY, DAWDLE, LOITER
lingerie	see UNDERWEAR
lingo	see JARGON
linguist	POLYGLOT
lining	GASKET, BUSHING, DOUBLURE, WAINSCOT
link(s)	YOKE, CHAIN, NEXUS, COPULA, COUPLE, COURSE, CONJOIN, CONNECT, CATENA(T)E
lint	TENT, FUZZ, FLUFF
lion	CAT, LEO, IDOL, ARIEL, SIMBA; see CAT
lion killed by Hercules	NEMEAN
lion of God	ALI
lion, young	CUB
lion-headed god(dess)	SEKHMET, NEFERTUM

lion's share	BULK, BEST PART, MAJORITY
lip	RIM, EDGE, SASS, FLANGE, LABIUM
lip ornament	LABRET, PELELE
lip, *pert. to*	LABIAL
lip service	MALARKY, HYPOCRISY
Lip, The	LEO, DUROCHER
liquefied	FUSIL(E), POTATE
liquefy	RUN, FUSE, MELT, THAW
liqueur	ANIS, MARC, RAKI, AURUM, CACAO, CREME, NOYAU, PEACH, SNAPS, ANANAS, BANANA, CASSIS, CHERRY, FRAISE, GENEPI, KIRSCH, KÜMMEL, MENTHE, MISTRA, PERNOD, POUSSE, SNAPPS, STREGA, CORDIAL, CURACAO, NOYEAUX, PARFAIT, RATAFIA, SLOEGIN, ABSINTHE, ANISETTE, AMARETTO, PRUNELLE, SCHNAPPS, TIA MARIA; *see* LIQUOR
liquid	CLEAR, FLUID, RUNNY, WATER, SMOOTH
liquid measure	*see* MEASURE
liquidate	PAY, KILL, PURGE, SETTLE, AMORTIZE
liquor	GIN, RUM, RYE, BENO, BOOF, OWSE, RHUM, TIFF, KEFIR, PISCO, VODKA, ARRACK, BRANDY, COGNAC, GENEPI, KUMISS, MASTIC, MESCAL, PULQUE, SCOTCH, WHISKY, YVETTE, AQUAVIT, BACARDI, BOURBON, DAMIANA, QUETSCH, RASPAIL, TEQUILA, WHISKEY, ADVOCAAT, ARMAGNAC, CALVADOS, CLEANRUM, DRAMBUIE, APPLEJACK, SLIVOVITZ; *see* BEER, DRINK, LIQUEUR
liquor, bad	BOUSE, BOWSE, SLIPSLOP
Lisbon river	TAGUS
lissome	LITHE, LIMBER, NIMBLE, SVELTE
list	TIP, ALBE, CANT, CAST, HARK, HEEL, LEAN, LEET, PLOW, ROTA, TILT, ALBUM, INDEX, PANEL, SLATE, TABLE, AGENDA, CAREEN, ROSTER, TARIFF, CATALOG, REGISTER
list ender	ETC, ETAL(II)

list preceder	COLON, INTERALIA
listen	BUG, HARK, HEAR, HEED, HIST, OBEY, HARKEN, EAVESDROP
listener	EAR, BUGGER, AUDITOR
listing	ROLL, TABLE, REGISTER
listless	LIMP, LANGUID, LETHARGIC, SPIRITLESS
listlessness	ENNUI, APATHY, DOLDRUMS
litany	EKTENE, PRAYER, ROGATION
literal	EXACT, STRICT, VERBAL, PROSAIC, VIRTUAL, EXPLICIT
literary	BOOKISH, LITERATE, FICTIONAL
literate	LEARNED, CULTURED, LETTERED
literature, characters in	*see p. 626*
lithe	AGILE, PLIANT, SUPPLE, SVELTE, LISSOME, FLEXIBLE
lithograph	PRINT, CHROMO
lithographer	REDON, BONNARD, HOKUSAI, KOLLWITZ
Lithuania, capital of	VILNIUS
Lithuanian city	ALYTUS, KAUNAS, VILNIUS, KLAIPEDA, SIAULIAI
Lithuanian money	LIT(AS), LITU, CENTU, MARKA, RUBLE, CENTAS, FENNIG, OSTMARK, TALONAS, AUKSINAS
Lithuanian mountain	MEDVEGALIS
Lithuanian neighbor	LATVIA, POLAND, RUSSIA, BELARUS
Lithuanian river	JURA, MUSA, NERIS, VENTA, DUBYSA, MERKYS, MINIJA, SESUPE
litigant	SUER, ACCUSER, DEFENDANT, PLAINTIFF
litigate	SUE, GOTOCOURT
litigation	CASE, ACTION, LAWSUIT
litigious	TOUCHY, CONTENTIOUS
litter	BIER, MESS, BROOD, CABIN, MULCH, TRASH, DEBRIS, FARROW, CLUTTER
little	SMA, WEE, POCO, PUNY, PETIT, MINUTE, PALTRY
Little Boy Blue painter	MONET
Little Corporal	NAPOLEON

Little Dipper	KOCAB, YILDUN, PHERKAD, POLARIS
Little Joe	FOUR
Little Mermaid character	SEAHAG
Little Nemo cartoonist	MCCAY
Little Russia	UKRAINE
Little Women	JO, AMY, MEG, BETH, MARCH
Little Women author	ALCOTT
littoral	SHORE, COAST(AL), STRAND
liturgy	MASS, RITE, RITUAL
litus	SERF, COLONUS
livable	HABITABLE
live	ARE, DWELL, EXIST, QUICK, RESIDE, TEEMING
live alone	BACH
live together	COHABIT
live wire	HUSTLER, GOGETTER
livelihood	JOB, KEEP, BREAD, LIVING, MEANS, UPKEEP, SUPPORT
livelong	WHOLE, ENTIRE
lively	VIR, KEEN, PERK, PERT, SPRY, VIVO, YARE, AGILE, BRISK, CANTY, DESTO, PEART, PERKY, VIVID, NIMBLE, ANIMATO
lively person	GRIG, DYNAMO
liven	CHEER
liver	FOIE, HEPAR, TOMALLEY
liver, *pert. to*	HEPATIC
Liverpool river	MERSEY
livery	HABIT, COLORS, COSTUME, UNIFORM
livestock	*see* CATTLE
livid	WAN, BLAE, PALE, ASHEN, PALLID
living	WAGE, ALIVE, QUICK, TRADE, EXTANT, INCOME, EXISTING
lixivium	LYE, LEACH
lizard	GILA, GECKO, SKINK, IGUANID, MONITOR, SAURIAN, BASILISK, SCORPION, CHAMELEON; *see p. 671*
lizard genus	UTA, AGAMA, DRACO, SEKKO, AMEIVA, ANGUIS, ANOLIS, MABUYA, EUMECES, GEKKOTA, IGUANID, LACERTA, PYGOPUS, TEIIDAE, VARANUS, ZONURID, ZONURUS, LACERATE, LYGOSOMA
lizardlike	SAURIAN
llama	LAMA, PACO, ALPACA, VICUNA, GUANACO

lo	SEE, ECCE, LOOK, BEHOLD
load	CARK, LADE, ONUS, CARGO
loaded	FULL, RICH, WEALTHY, WELLOFF, AFFLUENT, BURDENED
loaf	BAP, CAKE, IDLE, LOLL, MIKE, LOITER, LOUNGE
loafer	BUM, SHOE, DRONE, IDLER, LOUNGER, VAGRANT
loam	MARL, MALM, LOESS, REGUR
loan	PREST, ADVANCE
loan shark	USURER, SHYLOCK, MONEYLENDER
loan shark vice	USURY
loan source	FHA, SBA
loath	AVERSE, RELUCTANT
loathe	HATE, ABHOR, DETEST
loathsome	FOUL, VILE, HATEFUL, REPULSIVE, DETESTABLE
lobby	HALL, FOYER, ANTEROOM, VESTIBULE
lobbyist	RAINMAKER
lobster	DAD, ERYON, HOMARD, CRAWDAD, CRAWFISH, CRAYFISH
lobster box	CAR
lobster genus	ASTACUS, MACRURA
lobster ovary	CORAL
local	CHAPTER, EDAPHIC, TOPICAL
locale	SITE, SCENE, VENUE
locality	AREA, SPOT, ZONE, LOCUS, PLACE, PURLIEU
locate	PUT, SET, FIND, PLACE, TRACE, SITUATE, POSITION
location	SITE, SPOT, PLACE, POSITION, SITUATION
lock	JAG, TAG, CURL, FRIB, HASP, WISP, TRESS, COTTER, DETENT, RINGLET
lock part	BOLT, WARD, STUMP, TUMBLER, CYLINDER
locker	KIST, AMBRY, CHEST, CLOSET, STOREROOM
lockjaw	TETANUS, TRISMUS
locks, Panama Canal	GATUN
loco	NUTS, CRAZY, NUTTY
locomotive	DOLLY, DUMMY, MOGUL, TEXAS, BIGBOY, DINKEY, MIKADO, PACIFIC, PRAIRIE, SANTAFE, SWITCHER; *see* TRAIN
locus	PLACE, POINT
locust	*see* GRASSHOPPER

lode **LEAD, REEF, VEIN, LEDGE, RIDER, SCRIN**
lodestar **POLARIS**
lodge **INN, BOARD, CABIN, ROOST, BILLET, QUARTER;** *see* **TENT**
lodger **ROOMER, TRANSIENT**
lodging **ABODE, ROOMS, ROOST, QUARTERS**
loft **LOB, ATTIC, GARRET, GALLERY, MANSARD**
lofty **TALL, HAUGHTY, SOARING, ELEVATED, SUPERCILIOUS**
log **VIGA, DIARY, RECORD, TIMBER**
log-cutting area **SAWPIT**
logarithm inventor **NAPIER**
logarithm unit **BEL, MANTISSA**
loge **BOX, BOOTH, STALL**
loggerhead **DUNCE, TURTLE**
loggerheads, at **AT ODDS, STYMIED, FIGHTING**
loggia **ARCADE, GALLERY, PORTICO**
logic term **LEMMA, PONENT, SALTUS, ORGANON, PREMISS, SORITES, SUMPTION, SUBALTERN**
logical **SOUND, RATIONAL, SENSIBLE, PLAUSIBLE**
logroller **BIRLER, DECKER**
Lohengrin composer **WAGNER**
Lohengrin role **ELSA, ORTRUD, HEINRICH, FRIEDRICH**
loincloth **MALO, MARO, DHOTI, LUNGI, PAGNE, DHOOTI**
Loire river city **BLOIS, TOURS, NANTES, ORLEANS**
Lois relative **EUNICE**
loiter **HAWM, IDLE, POKE, SAUNTER;** *see* **LINGER**
Loki relative **HEL(A), NARE, VALI, NERVE, SIGYN, FENRIS**
Loki's victim **BALDER**
London **AGUSTA**
London monument **GOG, EROS, MAGOG, NEEDLE, NELSON, CENOTAPH, VICTORIA**
London museum **TATE, BRITISH, HAYWARD, WALLACE, TUSSAUD**
London park **HYDE, REGENTS, BATTERSEA, KEW (GARDENS)**
London quarter **SOHO, ADELPHI, CHELSEA, MAYFAIR, HOLBORN, LAMBETH, BELGRAVIA**

London river **THAMES**
London street **BOND, BAKER, FLEET, SAVILE, STRAND, DOWNING, HAYMARKET, PICCADILLY**
Lone Ranger's companion **TONTO**
Lone Ranger's horse **SILVER**
Lone Star State **TX, TEXAS**
loneliness **SOLITUDE, DESOLATION**
lonely **LOST, FORLORN, DESOLATE, SOLITARY**
lonesome **LONELY, DESOLATE**
long **YEN, ACHE, PANT, PINE, COVET, CRAVE, YEARN, ASPIRE, DESIRE, HANKER, PROLIX**
long ago **ELD, YORE(TIME)**
Long Island county **KINGS, NASSAU, QUEENS, SUFFOLK**
long live **VIVA, VIVE, EVVIVA**
long time **EON, AGES**
longanimity **PATIENCE, ENDURANCE**
longevity **AGE, LIFETIME**
Longfellow town **ATRI**
long-suffering **PATIENT, TOLERANT, FORBEARING**
long-winded **WORDY, PROLIX, TEDIOUS, VERBOSE, RAMBLING**
longing **YEN, ACHE, DESIRE, CRAVING**
longshoreman **DOCKER, LUMPER, STEVEDORE**
look **CON, EYE, KEN, PRY, SEE, GAZE, HIST, LEER, MIEN, OGLE, PEEK, PEEP, PEER, PORE, SCAN, SKEW, VIEW, GLARE, ASPECT, GANDER, GLANCE**
look after **TEND, SEETO**
look back **RECALL, REMEMBER**
look into **PROBE, EXAMINE, EXPLORE**
look the other way **IGNORE, OVERLOOK**
lookout **WORRY, CONNER;** *see* **GUARD**
loom **TOOL, WEAVE, APPEAR, VESSEL**
loom part **LAM, BEAM, CAAM, MAIL, PIRN, REED, SHED, SLEY, WARP, WEFT, EASER, GRIFF, HEALD, BATTEN, HEDDLE, LINGOE, PICKER, ROLLER, TEMPLE, HARNESS, SHUTTLE, TREADLE**
loon **LOWN, DIVER, WABBY, PYGOPOD;** *see* **GREBE**

loon genus **GAVIA**
loony **MAD, DAFT, NUTS, BATTY, CRAZY**
loop **EYE, ANSA, PURL, BIGHT, BRIDE, HONDA, NOOSE, PICOT, TERRY, PARRAL, PARREL, CIRCUIT, GROMMET**
Loop team **SOX, CUBS, FIRE, BEARS, BULLS**
loophole **CHINK, M(E)USE, PRETEXT**
loose(n) **LAX, EASE, LEWD, LIMP, UNDO, BAGGY, RELAX, UNTIE, REMISS, WANTON, AT LARGE**
— and loose **FAST**
loose ends, at **UNCERTAIN, UNSETTLED**
loot **HAUL, SACK, BOOTY, RIFLE, SPOIL(S), PLUNDER, RANSACK**
lop **CHOP, POLL, SNED, SNIP, PRUNE, SNATHE**
lopsided **ALOP, ALIST, ASKEW**
loquacious **GLIB, GABBY, WINDY, CHATTY, GOSSIPY, VOLUBLE**
loquat **BIWA, MEDLAR, NISPERO**
lord **MAR, KAAN, KAUN, KAWN, KHAN, PEER, LAIRD, LIEGE, PALATINE;** see **NOBLE**
Lord High Executioner **KOKO**
Lord Jim author **CONRAD**
Lord of the Rings author **TOLKIEN**
Lord of the Rings character **BILBO, FRODO, GIMLI, PIPPIN, ARAGORN, BAGGINS, GANDALF, GALADRIEL**
Lord of the Rings composer **SHORE**
Lord of the Rings director **JACKSON**
Lord's Day **SUNDAY, SABBATH**
Lord's Prayer **PATER(NOSTER)**
Lord's Supper see **COMMUNION**
lordly **NOBLE, HAUGHTY, ARROGANT, DIGNIFIED**
lore **LARE, WISDOM, LEARNING**
Lorna Doone character **TOM, ALAN, RIDD, LORNA**
lorry **TRUCK**
Los Angeles team **RAMS, KINGS, ANGELS, LAKERS, DODGERS, RAIDERS, CLIPPERS**
lose **AMIT, FAIL, MISS, MISLAY, FORFEIT, MISPLACE**

lose it **GOAPE, GOBANANAS**
lose weight **DIET, SLIM**
loser **VICTIM**
loss **COST, HURT, DEATH, DEBIT, DAMAGE, DEFEAT, DEMISE, BEATING, DEFICIT, PASTING**
lost **ASEA, GONE, (A)STRAY, MISLAID**
lost, something that can be **CAUSE**
Lost Horizon author **HILTON**
Lost Horizon country **SHANGRILA**
lot **HAP, DOOM, FATE, SCAD, SLEW, SLUE, SHARE, HAZARD, PARCEL, DESTINY**
Lot relative **MOAB, HARAN, GARETH, GAWAIN, MILCAH, WAHELA**
lotion see **OINTMENT**
lots **MUCH, HEAPS, LOADS, PILES, PLENTY**
lottery **KENO, BINGO, LOTTO, CHANCE, RAFFLE, DRAWING, NUMBERS, TOMBOLA**
lotus see **LILY**
loud **FORTE, NOISY, SHOWY, SHRILL, VULGAR**
loud and — **CLEAR**
loudmouthed **BRASH, BLATANT, BOISTEROUS**
loudness unit **DB, PHON, SONE, DECIBEL**
loudspeaker **CONE, WOOFER, MONITOR, TWEETER**
Louis XIV nickname **SUN KING**
Louisiana see also p. 615
Louisiana city **JENA, MANY, HOUMA, BENTON, EDGARD, MINDEN, RUSTON, BASTROP**
Louisiana Indians **CHOCTAW, COUSHATTA**
Louisiana mountain **DRISKILL**
Louisiana native **CAJUN**
Louisiana native **CAIJAN, CREOLE, ACADIAN**
Louisiana river **RED, SABINE, MISSISSIPPI**
Louisiana university **TULANE**
lounge **LAZE, LOLL, SOFA, DIVAN, LOBBY, SETTEE, RECLINE**
louse **NIT, RAT, CRUMB, COOTIE, PALMER, PSOCID, COLLIER, MORPION, PSOCINE**
lousy **AWFUL, ROTTEN, TERRIBLE**
lout **HOB, OAF, BOOR, GAWK, YAHOO**

louver	SLAT, SLIT, TRANSOM, ABATVENT	luck	HAP, LOT, CESS, CHANCE, HAZARD
love	GRA, LOO, WOO, DEAR, DOAT, DOTE, AMOR, ZEAL, ZERO, ADORE, AMOUR, ENAMOR, DARLING	luck, bad	CESS, JINX, DEUCE, WANION
		luck, *pert. to*	ALEATORY
		lucky	CANNY, TIMELY, FORTUNATE
Love Boat names	ACE, JULIE, VICKI, GOPHER, MACLEOD, MERRILL, STUBING, SPELLING	lucky piece	CHARM, AMULET, HORSESHOE
love, make	WOO, COURT, SPOON	lucky stroke	FLUKE
		lucrative	GAINFUL, PROFITABLE
lover	JO, GRA, BEAU, FLAME, LEMAN, ROMEO, SPARK, SWAIN, MINION, AMORIST, GALLANT, PARAMOUR	lucre	GAIN, PELF, MONEY, RICHES, WEALTH
		Lucretia's rapist	SEXTUS
		ludicrous	COMIC, ABSURD, RISIBLE
Love's Labour's Lost character	DULL, MOTH, BOYET, MARIA, BEROWNE, COSTARD, MARCADE, ROSALINE, KATHARINE	lug	EAR, TOW, DRAG, HAUL, PULL, CARRY, BLOCKHEAD
		luggage	BAGS, TRAPS, BAGGAGE
loving	FOND, DOTING, EROTIC, AMATIVE, AMATORY, AMOROUS	lugubrious	SAD, GLOOMY, SOMBER, DEPRESSING
		lukewarm	TEPID
low	BAS, MOO, BASE, BLUE, ORRA, VILE, HUMBLE, MENIAL	lull	CALM, HUSH, RESPITE
		lullaby	SONG, REFRAIN, CRADLESONG
Low Country	BELGIUM, HOLLAND, LUXEMBOURG, NETHERLANDS	lullaby start	TOORA
		lulu	ONER, BEAUT
lowbred	BASE, RUDE, CRUDE, COARSE, VULGAR	lumber	WOOD, PLOD, CLUMP, TIMBER, TRUDGE
lower	DIP, LOOM, LOUR, VAIL, ABASE, SCOWL, DEBASE, DEMOTE, GLOWER, NETHER	Lumber State	ME, MAINE
		lumberman	LOGGER, SAWYER, TOPPER, GIRDLER
lowest point	NADIR, PERIGEE	lummox	LOON, LOUT, DUNCE, LOOBY, LUBBER
lowland	HOLM, PLAIN, BOTTOM	lump	NUB, WAD, BURL, CLOD, CLOT, NODE, SWAD, TUMOR
lowly	MEAN, MEEK, POOR, HUMBLE	lunacy	MADNESS, INSANITY
lox	OXYGEN, SALMON	lunar	*see* MOON
loyal	LEAL, TRUE, STA(U)NCH	lunar calendar event	TET
loyalty	TROTH, HOMAGE, PIETAS	lunatic	CRAZY, INSANE, MADMAN
Loyalty Island	MARE, UVEA, LIFOU	luncheon	TIFFIN, UNDERN
		lunchroom	CAFE, DINER, EATERY, COUNTER
lozenge	RHOMB, CACHOU, JUJUBE, MASCLE, PASTIL, ROTULA, TROCHE, DIAMOND, PASTI(L)LE	lung disease	TB, CANCER, ASTHMA, PHTHISIS, EMPHYSEMA, BRONCHITIS
LSD	ACID	lung part	PLEURA, VOMICA, ALVEOLA
LSD source	ERGOT	lung sound	RALE, BRUIT, RATTLE
luau fare	POI	lunge	DIVE, FOIN, GRAB, SWIPE, ATTACK, CHARGE
lubricant	OIL, DOPE, LUBE, CASTOR, GREASE, UNGUENT, GRAPHITE, VASELINE	lurch	JOLL, ROLL, SWAB, PITCH, CAREEN
lubricate	OIL, LUBE, GREASE	lure	BAIT, SPOON, ENTICE, MINNOW, SEDUCE, PLUNKER, SPINNER, WIGGLER
lucid	SANE, CLEAR, SOBER, COGENT, LIMPID, RATIONAL		
Lucifer	DEVIL, MATCH, SATAN		

lurid	RED, WAN, PALE, VIVID, GARISH	lynx	PISHU, BOBCAT, CARACAL; *see* CAT
lurk	HIDE, PROWL, SKULK, SNEAK	lyre	ASOR, HARP, TRIGON, CITHARA, SACKBUT
luscious	MOIST, TASTY, SUCCULENT	lyric(al)	ODE, ALBA, ODIC, MELIC; *see* POEM
lush	JUICY, LAVISH, VERDANT, LUXURIANT	lyricist	CAHN, HART, KAHN, DAVID, DIETZ, DUBIN,
lust	ACHE, ENVY, ITCH, YEARN, HUNGER		GREEN, COMDEN, FIELDS, MERCER, YELLEN, DESYLVA,
luster	GLAZE, GLOSS, SHEEN, SCHILLER		GILBERT, HARBURG, HEYWARD, GERSHWIN,
lusterless	DIM, MAT(TE), MATT		SONDHEIM, HAMMERSTEIN
lustful	LEWD, RANDY, CARNAL	Lysander's lover	HERMIA
lustrous	NAIF, NITID, SILKY		
lusty	BURLY, BRAWNY, HEARTY, ROBUST		**M**
lute	MUD, CLAY, SEAL; *see* p. 642	M	EM, MU, MIKE
Lutheran Church founder	LUTHER	Maacah relative	ASA, DAVID,
Luxembourg, capital of	LUXEMBOURG		ABIJAH, ABSALOM, REHOBOAM
Luxembourg city/town	KAYL,	Mac rival	MS, PC, SUN,
MAMER, WILTZ, MERSCH,			MICROSOFT
PETANGE, REDANGE,		macabre	LURID, WEIRD,
CAPELLEN, CLERVAUX		GRISLY, MORBID, GHASTLY,
Luxembourg money	EURO,		GHOULISH
FLUX, FRANC		macadam	TAR, PAVING, ASPHALT
Luxembourg river	SURE, EISCH,	Macao island	TAIPA, CALOANE
ALZETTE		Macao money	AVO, PATACA
luxuriant	LUSH, RANK, RICH,	macaque	KRA, MONKEY,
LAVISH, ORNATE, FERTILE		RHESUS, WANDEROO
luxuriate	BASK, THRIVE,	macaroni	ZITI, DANDY,
WALLOW		DITALI, FORATI, STELLE,
luxurious	LUSH, POSH, RICH,	FUSILLI, GNOCCHI; *see* PASTA
COMFY, PLUSH, DELUXE,		macaroon	COOKY, BISCUIT,
OPULENT		RATAFIA
luxury	EASE, COMFORT,	macaw	ARA(RA), PARROT,
OPULENCE		MARACAN
Luzon bay	LAMON, MANILA,	Macbeth character	ROSS,
LINGAYEN		ANGUS, BANQUO, DUNCAN,
Luzon mountain	PULOG	HECATE, LENNOX, FLEANCE,
Luzon people	ATA, TAGAL,	MACDUFF, MALCOLM
ARIPAS, IGOROT, KALINGA,		Macbeth locale	GLAMIS
TAGALOG		Macbeth rank	THANE
Luzon river	AGNO, PASIG,	MacDonald (Jeanette) costar	
CAGAYAN, PAMPANGA		EDDY, NELSON
Lydian capital	SARDES, SARDIS	mace	CLUB, STAFF, STICK,
Lydian king	GYGES, CROESUS		SCEPTRE
Lydian language	ANATOLIC	mace-bearer	BEDEL, MACER,
Lydian ruler	ARDYS, GYGES,		BEDELL
CROESUS, OMPHALE		macedoine	SALAD, MEDLEY,
lye	BUCK, CAUSTIC,		MIXTURE
LIXIVIUM		Macedon(ia), ancient capital	PELLA
lying	FALSE, DISHONEST	Macedonia, capital of	SKOPJE
lymph fluid	PLASM	Macedonia city	STIP, BITOLA,
lymphocyte	BCELL	PRILEP, SKOPJE, TETOVO,
Lynette knight	GARETH	KUMANOVO

Macedonia king **PHILIP,**
PERSEUS, ALEXANDER
Macedonia neighbor **GREECE,**
SERBIA, ALBANIA, BULGARIA
Macedonia river **OMA,**
VARDAR, STRUMICA
macerate **VEX, PINE;** see **SOAK**
Macheath's wife **POLLY**
machete **BOLO, KNIFE, PANGA**
Machiavelli book **PRINCE, ART**
OF WAR, MANDRAKE
Machiavellian **WILY, ASTUTE,**
CRAFTY
— machina **DEUSEX**
machinate **PLAN, PLOT,**
DEVISE, SCHEME, CONSPIRE
machination **PLAN, PLOT,**
SETUP, CABAL, DESIGN,
SCHEME, INTRIGUE
machine **RIG, TOOL, DRILL,**
LATHE, MOTOR, PARTY,
ROBOT, DEVICE, ENGINE,
GADGET, AUTOMATON
machine gun **STEN, MAXIM,**
GATLING, THOMPSON
machine part **CAM, COG, GIB,**
HUB, AXLE, GEAR, PAWL,
ROTOR, VALVE, PISTON,
SOLENOID
Machir relative **GILEAD**
machismo **MANHOOD,**
VIRILITY, MANLINESS
macho **VIRILE, MASCULINE**
Mackenzie tributary **RED, PEEL,**
LIARD, PEACE, ATHABASCA
mackerel(-like fish) **AKU, CERO,**
PETO, TUNA, TUNNY,
WAHOO, BONITA, BONITO,
CHEBOG, ESPADA, GASCON,
MARLIN, SAUREL, SIERRA,
TINKER, CAVALLA, ESCOLAR,
ESPADON, GEELBEC, OILFISH,
PINTADO, VOLADOR,
ALBACORE, KINGFISH,
SAILFISH, SKIPJACK
mackerel, young **SPIKE,**
TINKER, BLINKER
mackinaw **BOAT, COAT,**
BLANKET
macrocosm **WORLD, UNIVERSE**
maculate **SPOT, STAIN,**
BLOTCH, DEFILE, BLEMISH,
SPECKLE
mad **SORE, CRAZY, IRATE,**
RABID, INSANE, BANANAS,
FRANTIC, FURIOUS
Mad About You names **IRA,**
BURT, HUNT, PAUL, JAMIE,
DEBBIE, REISER, SYLVIA

Madagascar, capital of
ANTANANARIVO
Madagascar city/town **IHOSY,**
MAHABO, BETROKA,
MOROMBE, TOLIARA
Madagascar language **MALAGASY**
Madagascar money **FRANC,**
CENTIME
Madagascar river **IKOPA,**
MANGOKY, ONILAHY,
BETSIBOKA
madam **MUM, DONA, FRAU,**
MAAM, DONNA, MILADY,
SENORA
Madame Bovary author **FLAUBERT**
Madame Bovary character **EMMA**
Madama Butterfly author
BELASCO, PUCCINI
Madama Butterfly character
BONZE, CIOCIO(SAN), SUZUKI,
PINKERTON, SHARPLESS
madcap **RASH, CRAZY,**
RECKLESS, IMPULSIVE
madden **ANGER, ENRAGE,**
INFURIATE
madder **DYE, EVEA, RUBIA,**
IPECAC, GARANCE,
MUNJEET
made up **FAKE, FALSE,**
INVENTED, FABRICATED
Madeira wine **BUAL, MALMSEY,**
SERCIAL, VERDELHO,
RAINWATER
madhouse **ZOO, BABEL,**
ASYLUM, BEDLAM
madman **MANIAC, LUNATIC**
madness see **INSANITY**
Madras **CHENNAI**
Madrid museum **PRADO,**
REINA SOFIA
madrigal **GLEE, SONG**
Maecenas **PATRON**
maelstrom **EDDY,**
WHIRLPOOL
maenad **NYMPH**
maestro **ACE, WHIZ, EXPERT,**
MASTER, TEACHER,
CONDUCTOR
mafia **BLACKHAND, COSA**
NOSTRA
mafioso **DON, GOODGUY,**
RACKETEER
magazine **PULP, DEPOT, SLICK,**
STORE, GLOSSY, JOURNAL
Magellan ship **SANTIAGO,**
TRINIDAD, VICTORIA
maggot **MAWK;** see **LARVA**
Magi **CASPAR, GASPAR,**
MELCHIOR, BALTHAZAR

Magi, gifts of   GOLD, MYRRH,
FRANKINCENSE
magic   OBI, JADU, JUJU, MAYA,
RUNE, GOETY, JADOO,
OBEAH, GOETIC, HOODOO,
VOODOO, CONJURY,
GRAMARY(E)
Magic Mountain author   MANN
Magic Mountain character   HANS
CASTORP
Magic Mountain sanatorium locale
DAVOS, SWITZERLAND
magic word   PRESTO, SESAME
magical   ENCHANTING,
PARANORMAL,
SUPERNATURAL
magician   WIZ, MAGE, MAGI,
CIRCE, MAGUS, WITCH,
MAGIAN, MERLIN, SHAMAN,
WIZARD, HOUDINI,
WARLOCK, KLINGSOR
Maginot line, opp. to   LIMES,
WESTWALL, SIEGFRIED
magisterial   POMPOUS,
MASTERFUL
magistrate   AG(H)A, CADI,
DOGE, FOUD, EDILE, EPHOR,
JUDGE, MAYOR, AEDILE,
ARCHON, BAILIE, CENSOR,
CONSUL, PRETOR, SYNDIC,
PRAETOR, PREFECT,
TRIBUNE; see JUDGE
magnanimous   BIG, NOBLE,
GENEROUS
magnate   COB, VIP, BARON,
MOGUL, NABOB, SHOGUN,
TYCOON
magnet   LURE, ALNICO,
LODESTONE
magnetic   ALLURING,
ELECTRIC, MESMERIC,
ATTRACTIVE
magnetic unit   WEBER,
MAXWELL
magnetism   PULL, ALLURE,
GRAVITY, MESMERISM,
ATTRACTION
magnetize   SWAY, CHARM,
ATTRACT, INFLUENCE
magnificat   HYMN, POEM,
SONG
magnificence   POMP, GLORY,
GRANDEUR, SPLENDOR
magnificent   GRAND, SUPERB,
STATELY
magnify   LAUD, EXALT, BLOW
UP, ENLARGE
magnifying glass   LOUPE
magnifying glass inventor   BACON

magnitude   SIZE, SCALE,
EXTENT, ENORMITY
magnolia   SHRUB, YULAN
Magnolia State   MS,
MISS(ISSIPPI)
— Magnon   CRO
Magog partner   GOG
magpie   MUG, PIAT, PIE(T),
PIOT, PYET, CISSA, MADGE,
SIRGANG
magpie genus   PICA
Magwitch (Dickens)   ABEL
Magyar   UGRIAN, HUNGARIAN
— Mahal   TAJ
maharaja wife   MAHARANI,
MAHARANEE
mahatma   ARHAT, GANDHI,
ARAHAT
mah-jongg piece   TILE
mahogany   CAJU, SIPO, TOON,
CAOBA, NARRA
Maia relative   ATLAS, HERMES,
PLEIONE
maid   AMA, IYA, AMAH, AYAH,
EYAH, BONNE, WENCH,
SLAVEY, ABIGAIL, ANCILLA,
MATRANEE
Maids, The, playwright   GENET
maiden   NEW, LASS, MISS,
FIRST, MISSY, DAMSEL,
LASSIE, VIRGIN, COLLEEN
maiden name indicator   NEE
maidenhead   HYMEN,
VIRGINITY
maidenly   SHY, MODEST,
GIRLISH, VIRGINAL
mail   IM, DA(U)K, DAWK, POST,
SEND, ARMOR, EMAIL,
LETTER(S), MESSAGE, LISTSERV
mailman   CARRIER, POSTMAN
maim   MAR, LAME, MANGLE,
SCOTCH, CRIPPLE
main   DUCT, CHIEF, FORCE,
MIGHT, VITAL, CRIPPLE,
DISABLE
— and main   MIGHT
Main Street author   LEWIS
Maine   see also p. 615
Maine city/town   SACO, YORK,
ORONO, AUBURN, BANGOR,
CAMDEN, AUGUSTA, BELFAST,
PORTLAND, ROCKLAND,
LEWISTON, BIDDEFORD,
FARMINGTON
Maine Indian   MICMAC,
MALISEET, PENOBSCOT
Maine lake   GRAND, SEBAGO,
RANGELEY, MOOSEHEAD,
CHAMBERLAIN, CHESUNCOOK

Maine mountain BLUE,
ABRAHAM, KATAHDIN
Maine river BEAR, ELLIS,
MOOSE, SANDY, MACHIAS,
STCROIX, KENNEBEC,
AROOSTOOK, PENOBSCOT
Maine school BATES, COLBY,
NASSON, BOWDOIN
mainly MOSTLY, CHIEFLY,
LARGELY
maintain AVER, AVOW, HOLD,
KEEP, CLAIM, ASSERT,
UPHOLD, PRESERVE
maintenance CARE, UPKEEP,
ALIMONY, SUPPORT
maitre d'hotel BUTLER,
STEWARD, HEADWAITER
maize CORN
majestic GRAND, REGAL,
AUGUST, STATELY
majesty DIGNITY, SPLENDOR
— majesty LESE
major KEY, MAIN, CHIEF,
FOREMOST
Major Barbara author SHAW
major's insignia OAKLEAF
majordomo BUTLER,
STEWARD, SENESCHAL
majority AGE, BULK, MOST,
MATURITY, SENIORITY
make DO, EARN, FORM,
MOLD, FORCE
make a killing WIN, SCORE
make a living EARN
make believe FEIGN, PRETEND
make do EKE, MANAGE
make eyes at OGLE, FLIRT
make fast BELAY, SECURE,
TIGHTEN
make fun of MOCK, TWIT,
DERIDE, RIDICULE
make known AIR, REVEAL,
DIVULGE, DISCLOSE
make love PET, WOO, SPOON,
COHABIT, MAKEOUT
make money EARN, PROFIT
make nervous RUFFLE,
AGITATE, FLUSTER
make off BOLT, FLEE, ELOPE,
LEAVE, ESCAPE, RUN AWAY
make out DO, FARE, SPOT,
DESCRY, DISCERN
make over REDO, REVAMP,
CONVERT, REBUILD,
RENOVATE
make public AIR, BARE,
DISCLOSE
make up INVENT, LAYOUT,
COMPOSE

maker DOER, CREATOR
makeshift STOPGAP,
EXPEDIENT
makeup BLUSH, ROUGE,
FORMAT, LAYOUT, POWDER,
SHADOW, MASCARA, LIPSTICK
maladroit INEPT, GAUCHE,
AWKWARD, UNGAINLY
malady ILL, WOE, AILMENT,
DISEASE, ILLNESS
Malagasy see MADAGASCAR
malaise UNEASE, DISQUIET,
DISCOMFORT
malapropos IMPROPER,
UNTIMELY
malaria MIASM(A), QUARTAN,
PALUDISM
malaria treatment ATEBRIN,
QUININE, ATABRINE
malarky HOKUM, BALONEY,
BUNCOMBE, NONSENSE
Malawi, capital of LILONGWE
Malawi city/town DOWA,
CHOLO, MZUZU, ZOMBA,
GALAKA, BLANTYRE,
LILONGWE
Malawi language CHICHEWA
Malawi money KWACHA,
TAMBALA
Malawi mountain MLANJE
Malawi neighbor ZAMBIA,
TANZANIA, MOZAMBIQUE
Malawi river BUA, SHIRE,
BUKURU
Malawi tribes YAO, SENA,
CHEWA, LOMWE, NGONI,
TONGA, NGONDE, NYANJA,
TUMBUKO
Malayan see MALAYSIAN
Malaysia, capital of
KUALALUMPUR
Malaysian cities IPOH, MUAR,
GEMAS, KANGAR, MELAKA,
KUANTAN, SEREMBAN
Malayan language JAXUN,
MALAY, SAKAI, TAMIL,
BAHASA, TELUGU
Malayan money ORA, SEN,
TRA(H), RINGGIT, TAMPANG
Malaysian people IBAN,
BANJAU, JAKUN MALAY,
MURUT, SEMOI, SEMANG,
BIDAYUH, KADAZAN,
MELANAU, ORANGASLI
Malaysian river BARAM,
JOHOR, LUPAR, PULAI,
PAHANG, RAJANG
Malaysian state JOHOR,
KEDAH, PERAK, SABAH,

PAHANG, PENANG, PERLIS,
SARAWAK
Malaysian village   KAMPONG
Maldives, capital of   MALE
Maldives currency   RUFIYAA
Maldivian language   DIVEHI
male   HIM, MACHO, MANLY,
VIRILE; *see* MAN, BOY
male animal   *see specific animal*
malediction   CURSE, MALISON
malefactor   FELON, CRIMINAL,
EVILDOER
malevolence   EVIL, MALICE,
ILLWILL
malevolent   EVIL, FELL, MEAN,
NASTY, WICKED
malfeasance   MISCONDUCT
Mali, capital of   BAMAKO
Mali city/town   KATI, NARA,
MOPTI, SEGOU, BAMAKO,
SIKASSO
Mali lake   DEBO, NIANGAY,
FAGUIBINE
Mali language   ARABIC,
FRENCH, TUAREG,
BAMBARA, SONGHAI; *see* GUR
Mali money   FRANC
Mali neighbor   NIGER, GUINEA,
ALGERIA, SENEGAL, IVORY
COAST, MAURITANIA,
BURKINA FASO
Mali people   DOGON,
BAMBARA, FULANI, TUAREG,
SONGHAI, SENOUFOU
Mali river   BANI, BAGOE,
NIGER, BATING
malice   PIQUE, SPITE, VENOM,
GRUDGE, RANCOR, SPLEEN
malicious   MEAN, CATTY,
CRUEL, NASTY, VICIOUS,
SPITEFUL
malign   ABUSE, LIBEL, DEFAME,
VILIFY, ASPERSE, BANEFUL
malignant   EVIL, HEINOUS,
VICIOUS
malinger   SHIRK, SKULK, TRUANT
malingerer   IDLER, DODGER,
TRUANT
mall   ALLEE, AVENUE,
PROMENADE
malleable   SOFT, DOCILE,
DUCTILE, TENSILE
mallet   TUP, MADGE, GAVEL,
BEETLE; *see* HAMMER
mallet sport   POLO, HOCKEY
mallow   HOCK, OKRA, MALVA,
ALTHEA, COTTON,
ALTHAEA, GARANCE,
HOLLYHOCK

malodorous   FETID, STINKY,
STINKING
malt drink   *see* BEER
malt grains   DRAFF
Malta, capital of   VALLETTA
Maltese city/town   MOSTA,
QORMI, RABAT, NAXXAR,
QRENDI, ZEJTUN, VALLETTA,
BIRKIRKARA
Maltese island   GOZO, COMINO
Maltese measure   SALM(A)
Maltese money   LIRA
mammal   PRIMATE, SUCKLER;
see p. 660
mammals, aquatic   *see p. 666*
man   HOMO, BIPED, HUMAN,
SAHIB, STAFF, VALET,
HOMBRE, FORTIFY, SERVANT;
see MALE
man and —   WIFE
man, elderly   DODO, FOGY,
CRONE, CODGER, DOTARD,
GAFFER, GEEZER, NESTOR,
SENIOR
man, handsome   FOP, BEAU,
ADONIS, APOLLO
man of brass   TALOS
man of learning   PUNDIT,
SAVANT, WISE MAN
man of letters   POET, SAVANT,
SCHOLAR
Man of a Thousand Faces
CHANEY
man's rival   MACHINE
Man Without a Country   NOLAN
manacle   FETTER, HAMPER,
SHACKLE, HANDCUFF
manage   TEND, DIGHT, GETBY,
DIRECT, HANDLE, MAKE DO,
WANGLE, CONTRIVE
manageable   RULY, TAME,
YARE, DOCILE, WIELDY
manager   AGENT, GERENT,
GRIEVE, SYNDIC, STEWARD,
OPERATOR, IMPRESARIO
Manasseh relative   JACOB,
ASRIEL, GILEAD, JOSEPH,
MACHIR, ASENATH,
EPHRAIM
manatee   DUGONG, COWFISH,
SEACOW, HALICORE,
SIRENIAN
Manchuria, capital of   MUKDEN
Manchurian city/town   JEHOL,
DAIREN, TALIEN, CHENGTEN
Manchurian river   AMUR, LIAO,
YALU, ARGUN, USSURI,
SONGHUA
mandarin   BRAHMIN, OFFICIAL

mandarin's home	YAMEN, YAMUN
mandate	ORDER, REIGN, TENURE, GOAHEAD, PERMISSION
mandatory	BINDING, COMPULSORY, OBLIGATORY
Mande language	VAI, KONO, LOMA, MANO, SUSU, DYULA, MENDE, KPELLE, BAMBARA, MALINKE
mane	JUBA, SHAG, BRUSH, CREST, STUBBLE
maned	CRINED, JUBATE
manege	HORSEMANSHIP
maneuver	COUP, PLAN, PLOT, TACTIC, SCHEME, CONTRIVE, EXERCISE
maneuverable	YARE
mange	SCABIES
manger	BIN, CRIB, CRATCH, CRECHE, TROUGH
mangle	IRON, MAIM, MAUL, GARBLE, CALENDAR
mangrove	BACAO, BACAUAN
mangy	SCABBY, SCURVY, SQUALID
manhandle	PAW, MAUL, ILLTREAT
Manhattan	see NEW YORK
Manhattan buyer	MINUIT
Manhattan hotel	PLAZA, WALDORF, WARWICK
mania	FAD, CRAZE, FRENZY, PASSION
maniac	MADMAN, FANATIC, LUNATIC
manifest	LIST, SHOW, OVERT, ARRANT, ATTEST, EVINCE, PATENT, WAYBILL
manifesto	CREDO, EDICT, STATEMENT, DECLARATION
manifold	MANY, DIVERSE
man(n)ikin	DUMMY, DWARF, MODEL
manioc	JUCA, YUCA, STARCH, CASSAVA, MANIHOT
maniple	FANO(N), FANUM, ORALE
manipulate	RIG, USE, WORK, CONTROL, OPERATE, INFLUENCE
Manitoba	see also p. 614
Manitoba city/town	ALTONA, ARBORG, BALDUR, KENTON, LUNDAR, VASSAR, VIRDEN, BRANDON, NINETTE, SELKIRK, SOLURIS, WINNIPEG
Manitoba lake	DOG, GODS, KNEE, SLOW, SWAN, CROSS,

	PAINT, CHITEK, ELLIOT, ISLAND, MOLSON, OXFORD, CHARRON, DAUPHIN, ETAWNEE, GUNISAO, NUELTIN, PELICAN, SETTING, TADOULE, MANITOBA, REINDEER, SIPIWESK, WATERHEN, WINNIPEG, CORMORANT, WINNEPEGOSIS
Manitoba rebel	RIEL, LOUIS
Manitoba river	DOG, RED, GODS, SEAL, HUDWIN, NELSON, WEAVER, CARIBOU, DAUPHIN, BIGSTONE, WINNIPEG, CHURCHILL, SASKATCHEWAN
mankind	HUMANITY
manly	MACHO, VIRILE, MASCULINE
manna	BOON, LERP, GODSEND, WINDFALL
mannequin	see MANIKIN
manner(s)	AIR, AURA, MIEN, MODE, WONT, MORES, METHOD, CONDUCT, ETIQUETTE
mannerism	TICK, QUIRK, TRAIT, GESTURE
mannerly	CIVIL, POLITE
mannish	ANDRIC, VIRILE, MASCULINE
Manoah relative	SAMSON
manor	ESTATE, DEMESNE
manqué	FAILED, USELESS
mansard	ATTIC, GARRET
manservant	GROOM, VALET, ANDREW, BUTLER, JEEVES; see SERVANT
mansion	DOME, YALI, MANOR, VILLA
manslaughter	HOMICIDE
manta	RAY, CAPE, SHAWL, DEVILFISH
mantel	LEDGE, SHELF, LINTEL
mantle	see CLOAK
mantra	HYMN, CHANT, CHARM, SPELL, BYWORD, SLOGAN
manual	HAND, HANDBOOK, PHYSICAL, TEXTBOOK
manual training	SLOID, SLOYD
manufacture	MAKE, CREATE, INVENT, CONCOCT, PRODUCE, PRODUCTION
manumit	FREE, LIBERATE, EMANCIPATE
manure	DUNG, MUCK, GUANO, ORDURE

manuscript(s)   MS(S), CODEX,
     FOLIO, SCRIPT, SCROLL,
          CODICES
Manxman   CELT, GAEL
many   LOT, GOBS, LOTS,
     LOADS, MAINT, REAMS,
          SCADS, MYRIAD
many-colored   PIED, MOTLEY,
               RAINBOW
Mao Tse Tung relative   LINA,
     MAUMAU, CHIANGCHING
Mao's successor   HUA
Maori war   WAIKATO, TARANKI
Maori warrior   HAUHAU,
               RINGATU
map(s)   PLAN, PLAT, ATLAS,
     CHART, GRAPH, INSET
maple genus   ACER
mar   SCAR, DAMAGE, DEFACE,
               BLEMISH
Marat killer   CORDAY
marathon   EPIC, RACE,
     LENGTHY, NONSTOP
marathon runner   ROE, ROP,
     COTE, HILL, MOTA, ROBA,
     AGUTA, DEMAR, JIFAR,
KAGWE, LAGAT, MEJIA, NDETI,
OKAYO, SILVA, SMITH, TANUI,
WAITZ, BENOIT, BONGJU,
CHEBET, GORMAN, PANFIL,
PIPPIG, BURFOOT, HUSSEIN,
KUSCSIK, LOROUPE, NDEREBA,
     PETROVA, RODGERS,
     UNETANI, MARKOVA,
               OKSANEN
Marathon victor   MILTIADES,
               ETHIOPIANS
marauder   HUN, VITI, RAIDER,
               VANDAL
marble(s)   MIB, MIG, TAW,
     ALAY, DUCK, MARL, MIGG,
AGGIE, ALLEY, RANCE, RANSE,
     MARMOR, RINGER,
CARRARA, CIPOLIN, SHOOTER
Marceau character   BIP
march   DEMO, WALK, ETAPE,
     RALLY, STRUT, TRAMP,
STRIDE, ADVANCE, PROTEST
March King   SOUSA
March of Dimes cause   POLIO
Marco Polo city   VENICE
Marco Polo relative   MAFFEO,
               NICCOLO
Mardi Gras festival site   RIO,
     PARIS, NEW ORLEANS
mare   YAUD; see HORSE
Margaret   MEG, PEG, MADGE,
GRETA, MARGE, PEGGY,
               MAGGIE

margin   HEM, LIP, RIM, EDGE,
     RAND, BRINK, LIMIT, VERGE,
          BORDER, LEEWAY
margin, slim   HAIR, NOSE
marginal   MINOR, TRIVIAL,
               INSIGNIFICANT
Marianas discoverer   MAGELLAN
Marianas Islands   LADRONE
Marianas island   GUAM, ROTA,
     PAGAN, GUGUAN, SAIPAN,
TINIAN, AGRIHAN, AGUIJAN
marigold   ASTER, CAPER,
               CRAZ(E)Y
marijuana   POT, HEMP, JOINT,
     ROACH, REEFER; see DRUG
Marilyn Monroe feature   MOLE
marina   DOCK, BASIN, HARBOR
marina site   BAY, INLET
marinade   SALT, WINE, BRINE,
          PICKLE, VINEGAR
marinate   CORN, CURE, SOAK,
     PICKLE, PRESERVE
marine   JOLLY, NAVAL,
     GYRENE, JARHEAD,
OCEANIC, PELAGIC; see
               SOLDIER
marine organism   SALPA,
     BUGULA, PEDATA, PLOIMA,
SEAFAN, ACTINIA, BRYOZOA,
     CRINOID, ROTIFER,
     TREPANG, VELELLA,
PHORONIS; see CORAL
mariner   GOB, SAILOR,
     SEAMAN, JACKTAR
marionette   DOLL, DUMMY,
               PUPPET
mariposa relative   SEGOLILY
marital   MARRIED, NUPTIAL,
     SPOUSAL, WEDDED
marjoram   HERB, MINT,
               OREGANO
mark   SCAR, BRAND, STAIN,
     STAMP, TALLY, STIGMA,
     SYMBOL, STIGMATA
mark, diacritical   TIL, WING,
     BREVE, PRIME, TILDE, VOLLE,
ACCENT, MACRON, UMLAUT,
     CEDILLA, DI(A)ERESIS
mark, printers'   DELE, STET,
     CARET, SCHWA, PILCROW,
               VIRGULE
mark, reference   FIST, HAND,
     STAR, INDEX, OBELI,
DAGGER, DIESIS, OBELUS,
     FLEURON, OBELISK,
POINTER, SECTION, ASTERISK,
               ASTERISM
Mark Antony lover   CLEO(PATRA)
Mark Antony wife   OCTAVIA

Mark's wife	**ISOLDE**
markdown	**CUT, DISCOUNT,**
	REDUCTION
marked	**XD IN, OBVIOUS,**
	STRIKING, NOTICEABLE
marker(s)	**DAN, IOU, PEG, TAB,**
	TAG, CHIP, CHIT, META,
	LABEL, PYLON, STAKE, STELA,
	STELE, SCORER, STELAE,
	STELAI, COUNTER
market	**SUQ, FORA, GUNJ,**
	MART, SELL, SOOK, SOUK,
	VEND, AGORA, BAZAR,
	FORUM, GUNGE, PASAR,
	TRONE, BAZAAR, RIALTO,
	EMPORIUM
marksman	**SHOT, SNIPER,**
	HAWKEYE, SHOOTIST
Marley's partner	**SCROOGE**
maroon	**CLARET, DESERT,**
	ENISLE, STRAND, ABANDON
Marquand character	**MOTO,**
	APLEY, WAYDE, HARROW,
	PULHAM, GOODWIN
marquee	**TENT, AWNING,**
	CANOPY
marquetry	**MOSAIC**
marriage	**MOTA, MUTA,**
	UNION, WEDDING,
	WEDLOCK, NUPTIALS,
	MATRIMONY
marriage, absence of	**AGAMY**
marriage notice	**BAN(NS)**
marriage settlement	**DOS,**
	DOT(E), MAHR, DOW(E)RY
marriageable	**NUBILE**
married	**WED, MATED,**
	COVERT, CONJUGAL
Married with Children names	**AL,**
	BUD, PEG, BUCK, DARCY,
	KATEY, KELLY, MARCY,
	SAGAL, BEARSE, ONEILL,
	FAUSTINO, APPLEGATE,
	CHRISTINA, JEFFERSON
marrow	**CORE, PITH, KEEST,**
	LOVER, SPOUSE, MEDULLA
marry	**WED, WIVE, HITCH,**
	UNITE, ESPOUSE
Mars, *pert. to*	**AREAN,**
	MARTIAN
Marseillaise composer	**(DE)LISLE**
marsh	**BOG, FEN, JEEL, MIRE,**
	MOOR, MOSS, QUAG, SLUE,
	LERNA, LIMAN, PINSK, SWALE,
	MORASS, MUSKE OR
	MUSKEG, PRIPET, SAUNA,
	MAREMMA, PONTINE
marsh bird	**COOT, RAIL, SORA,**
	SNIPE, STILT, BITTERN

marsh fever	**HELODES**
marsh gas	**METHANE**
marshall	**NEY, FOCH, ARRAY,**
	PETAIN, ROMMEL,
	ARRANGE
Marshall Islands, capital of	
	MAJURO
Marshall Islands chain	**RALIK,**
	RATAK
marshy	**BOGGY, PALUDAL,**
	PALUDINE
marsupial	**JOEY, KOALA,**
	YAPOK, JERBOA, POSSUM,
	WOMBAT, OPOSSUM,
	WALLABY, ANTEATER,
	KANGAROO, BANDICOOT; *see*
	p. 666
marsupial genus	**MARMOSA,**
	DASYURUS, MACROPUS,
	TARSIPES, DIDELPHIS
mart	**SALE, SHOP, STORE,**
	BAZAAR, MARKET,
	EMPORIUM
marten	**SABLE, FISHER**
martial art	**JUDO, AIKIDO,**
	JUNGDO, KARATE, KUNG FU,
	TAI CHI, BUSHIDO, HAPKIDO,
	JUJITSU, HWA, RANG DO,
	TWE KWAN DO
Martin Luther King cause	
	NONVIOLENCE
Martin Luther King phrase	**I**
	HAVE A DREAM
martinet	**DESPOT, RAMROD,**
	TYRANT, STICKLER
martini ingredient	**GIN, LEMON,**
	OLIVE, ONION, VODKA
Martinique capital	**FORT DE**
	FRANCE
Martinique volcano	**PELEE**
marvel	**WONDER, MIRACLE,**
	PRODIGY
marvelous	**SPLENDID,**
	STUNNING, WONDROUS
Marx Brothers	**CHICO,**
	GUMMO, HARPO, ZEPPO,
	GROUCHO
Marx Brothers film	**DUCK**
	SOUP, COCOANUTS, ROOM
	SERVICE, HORSE FEATHERS
Mary relative	**JAMES, JESUS,**
	JOSES, JOSEPH, CLEOPHAS
Mary Tyler Moore Show names	**LOU,**
	TED, MARY, ASNER, GAVIN,
	GRANT, RHODA, CLORIS,
	HARPER, MURRAY, NIVENS,
	SUEANN, LEACHMAN,
	RICHARDS, GEORGETTE
Maryland	*see also p. 615*

Maryland city/town **BELAIR, DENTON, EASTON, ELKTON, TOWSON, ANNAPOLIS, BALTIMORE, ROCKVILLE**

Maryland college **BOWIE, LOYOLA, TOWSON, GOUCHER, JOHNSHOPKINS**

Maryland county **KENT, CECIL, HOWARD, TALBOT, CALVERT, CERROLL, CHARLES, GARRETT, HARFORD**

Maryland founder **CALVERT**

Maryland Indian **PISCATAWAY**

Maryland mountain **MEADOW, BACKBONE**

Maryland river **CHESTER, POTOMAC, CHOPTANK, MONOCACY, PATUXENT, POCOMOKE, NANTICOKE, SUSQUEHANNA**

Mascagni opera **IRIS, CAVELLERIA, RUSTICANA**

Mascagni character **LOLA, ALFIO, LUCIA, TURIDDU, SANTUZZA**

masculine **MALE, MANLY, MANNISH**

masculine side **YANG**

mash **PAP, PULP, CRUSH, POUND, PUREE, SMASH**

Mash actor **ALDA, FARR, SWIT, FRANK, MCLEAN, MORGAN, ROGERS, STIERS, FARRELL**

Mash characters **BJ, BLAKE, BURNS, RADAR, PIERCE, POTTER, HAWKEYE, HOTLIPS, KLINGER, MULCAHY, TRAPPER, HOULIHAN, HUNNICUT, MARGARET, WINCHESTER**

Mash producers **GELBART, METCALFE, REYNOLDS**

mask **HIDE, LOUP, COVER, VISOR, DOMINO, SCREEN, CONCEAL**

masker **MUMMER**

masochism **SADISM**

mason see **STONECUTTER**

masonry **TILE, BRICKWORK**

masque **BALL, COMUS**

masquerade **MUM(M), MASQUE, RIDOTTO, DISGUISE**

mass **GOB, WAD, BULK, BOLUS, TUMOR, GATHER, MATTER**

Mass part **PAX, CREDO, KYRIE, GLORIA, GOSPEL, LAVABO, COLLECT, EPISTLE, GRADUAL, INTROIT, PREFACE,** **SANCTUS, SECRETA, FRACTION**

Massachusetts see also p. 615

Massachusetts cape **ANN, COD**

Massachusetts city/town **LEE, ADAMS, AYER, HULL, ACTON, ADAMS, SALEM, BOSTON, DEDHAM, GROTON, LOWELL, MALDEN, NEWTON, WOBURN, QUINCY, REVERE, AMHERST, ANDOVER, BELMONT, CHELSEA, CONCORD, HOLYOKE, MEDFORD, MELROSE, METHUEN, TAUNTON, PLYMOUTH, CAMBRIDGE, WORCESTER**

Massachusetts college **MIT, SMITH, TUFTS, EMERSON, HARVARD, HOLY CROSS, RADCLIFFE**

Massachusetts county **DUKES, ESSEX, BRISTOL, HAMPDEN, NORFOLK, SUFFOLK, FRANKLIN, PLYMOUTH, BERKSHIRE, HAMPSHIRE, MIDDLESEX, WORCESTER, BARNSTABLE**

Massachusetts Indian **NIPMUC, ABENAKI, PONKAPOAG, WAMPANOAG, PENNACOOK**

Massachusetts island **ELIZABETH, NANTUCKET, NO MANS LAND, CHAPPAQUIDDICK, MARTHAS VINEYARD**

Massachusetts mountain **GREYLOCK**

Massachusetts music festival **TANGLEWOOD**

Massachusetts river **MILL, SWIFT, AGAWAM, HOOSIC, MYSTIC, NASHUA, CHARLES, CONCORD, CHICOPEE, TAUNTON, MERRIMACK, CONNECTICUT**

massacre **POGROM, BUTCHER, CARNAGE**

massage **RUB, KNEAD, RUBDOWN**

massage method **SHIATSU, SWEDISH, FRICTION, KNEADING, DEEPTISSUE, EFFLEURAGE, MYOTHERAPY, TAPOTEMENT, PETRISSAGE**

Massenet opera **MANON, THAIS, SAPPHO, WERTHER**

massive **HUGE, VAST, BULKY, COLOSSAL, IMPOSING**

mast **NUTS, ACORNS, BEECHNUTS, CHESTNUTS;** see **SHIP PART**

master **BOY, BAAS, BOSS, LORD, RULE, EMCEE, LEARN, SUBDUE, CAPTAIN;** see **TEACHER**

master, pert. to a **HERILE**

masterful **EXPERT, WILFUL, SKILLED, DESPOTIC**

mastermind **BRAIN(S), HATCH, DEVISE, PLAN(NER)**

masterpiece **OPUS, CHEF(DOEUVRE)**

mastery **GRIP, SWAY, CONTROL**

mastic **RESIN, CEMENT, LIQUOR**

masticate **GUM, CHAW, CHEW, MANDUCATE**

mastiff **ALAN, BULLDOG, WATCHDOG**

mat **PAD, RUG, YAPA, BANIG, DOILY, SNARL, MATRIX, PETATE**

matador **TORERO, TOREADOR;** see **BULLFIGHTING**

match **FIT, PEER, AGREE, FUSEE, MARRY, TALLY, VESTA, LUCIFER**

matchless **PEERLESS, UNEQUALED, UNRIVALED**

matchmaker **BROKER, SHADCHAN**

mate **PAL, CHUM, FERE, BREED, BUDDY, MATCH, FELLOW, SPOUSE, REPRODUCE**

— mater **DURA, STABAT**

material **DATA, STUFF, MATTER, CONTENT;** see **FABRIC**

materialize **APPEAR, SHOWUP**

mathematical **EXACT, PRECISE, ACCURATE**

mathematical instrument **ABACUS, COMPASS, VERNIER, COMPUTER, CALCULATOR**

mathematical term **PI, LOG, COSH, SECH, SINE, SINH, SURD, TANH, NABLA, RADIX, RATIO, COSINE, RADIAN, SCALAR, TENSOR, VECTOR, VESSOR, FACIEND, FACIENT, OPERAND, CONSTANT, QUADRANT, VARIABLE**

mathematician see p. 542

mathematics, branch of **TRIG, CONICS, ALGEBRA, GEODESY, CALCULUS,**

GEOMETRY, ARITHMETIC, TRIGONOMETRY

matin **AUBADE**

matinee **LEVEE, SOIREE**

matriarch **MATRON, DOWAGER**

matriculate **ENTER, ENROL(L), REGISTER**

matrimonial **MARITAL, NUPTIAL, CONJUGAL, CONNUBIAL**

matrimony **MARRIAGE, NUPTIALS**

matrix **DIE, CAST, MOLD, WOMB, GANGUE**

matron **DAME, WIFE, WIDOW**

matronly **SEDATE, DIGNIFIED, MENOPAUSAL**

matter **PUS, RES, BEAR, HYLE, PITH, COUNT, ISSUE, STUFF, TOPIC, AFFAIR, IMPORT**

matter, source of all **YLEM**

matter-of-fact **DULL, LITERAL, PROSAIC**

Matthew home town **CAPERNAUM**

mattress **TICK, FUTON, PALLET**

mattress maker **SEALY, SERTA, SIMMONS**

mattress stuffing **DOWN, CEIBA, FLOCK, KAPOK**

mature **AGE, DUE, RIPE, ADULT, RIPEN, EVOLVE, MELLOW, PAYABLE**

Mau Mau country **KENYA**

Maude names **BEA, BAIN, ARTHUR, VIVIAN, WALTER, BADDELEY, HERMIONE**

maudlin **MUSHY, SAPPY, TEARY, SYRUPY, SENTIMENTAL**

Maugham character **SALLY, PHILIP, WYLIE, MILDRED**

Maugham work **RAIN, CIRCLE, RAZORS EDGE, CAKES AND ALE**

maul **PAN, PAW, BEAT, CLUB, SLAM, ATTACK, MANGLE**

Mauna — **LOA**

Mauritania, capital of **NOUAKCHOTT**

Mauritania city/town **ALEG, ATAR, NEMA, BOGUE, KAEDI, KIFFA, NOUAKCHOTT**

Mauritanian money **MRO, OUGUIYA**

Mauritanian neighbor **MALI, SENEGAL**

Mauritanian people   **MOORS,
PEULS, WOLOF, PULAAR,
SONINKE**
Mauritanian river   **SENEGAL**
Mauritius   **ILE DE FRANCE**
Mauritius, capital of   **PORTLOUIS**
Mauritius city/town   **MOKA,
BELAIR, VACOAS, TEMARIN**
Mauritius island   **FLAT, ROUND,
AGALEGA, GABRIEL,
SERPENT, MASCARENE,
RODRIGUES**
Mauritius languages   **URDU,
HAKKA, HINDI, CREOLE,
FRENCH, ENGLISH, BOJPOORI**
Mauritius money   **RUPEE**
mausoleum   **TOPE, CRYPT,
STUPA, VAULT, CATACOMB;**
   see **TOMB**
maverick   **CALF, WAIF, DOGIE,
LONER, REBEL, ECCENTRIC**
mawkish   **SAPPY, SOPPY,
SLUSHY, CLOYING,
SENTIMENTAL**
maxim   **SAW, ADAGE, AXIOM,
GNOME, MORAL, MOTTO,
CLICHE, TRUISM, PROVERB**
Maximilian realm   **HRE**
maximum   **CAP, LIMIT,
(UT)MOST, CEILING,
GREATEST**
may   **CAN, PRIME, HEYDAY,
MAIDEN**
May Day   **SOS, BELTANE,
BEALTINE**
Maya   **DEVI, MAGIC, SAKTI,
ILLUSION**
Mayan city   **TIKAL, COPAN,
UXMAL, RIOBEC, MAYAPAN,
PALENQUE**
Mayan people   **MAM, CHUJ,
TECO, IXIL, ACATEC,
CHOLAN, CHORTI, KEKCHI,
QUICHE**
Mayan year   **TUN, HAAB**
mayflower   **RED, ARBUTUS,
ANEMONE, COWSLIP,
HAWTHORN, MARIGOLD**
mayfly   **DUN, DRAKE**
mayhem   **CHAOS, HAVOC,
BEDLAM, CONFUSION,
MUTILATION**
mayor   **KMET, HIZZONER**
maze   **WEB, MESS, JUNGLE,
MUDDLE, WARREN,
LABYRINTH**
mazel —   **TOV**
McDonald's creator   **(RAY) KROC**
McGuffey book   **READER**

McSorley's Bar painter   **SLOAN**
— me tangere   **NOLI**
mea —   **CULPA**
meadow   **LEA, LAWN, MEAD,
VEGA, HAUGH, PASTURE**
meager   **BARE, LEAN, PUNY,
SCANT, LENTEN, SCANTY,
SPARSE**
meal   **ATA, TEA, ATTA, BRAN,
CENA, MASA, BEVER, FLOUR,
LUNCH, DINNER, FARINA,
PINOLA, PINOLE, REPAST,
TIFFIN**
mealy   **PALE, SPOTTY, PALLID,
UNEVEN, FARINOSE**
mealymouth   **HYPOCRITE**
mealymouthed   **OILY,
UNCTUOUS, HYPOCRITICAL**
mean   **AIM, LOW, MID, BASE,
NORM, POOR, WISH, AGENT,
IMPLY, NASTY, DENOTE,
ENTAIL, INTEND, MEDIAN,
MEDIUM, SCURVY, UNKIND,
AVERAGE, INVOLVE,
SQUALID**
meander   **ROAM, WIND, SNAKE,
RAMBLE, WANDER, ZIGZAG**
meaning   **GIST, SENSE, TENOR,
DESIGN, IMPORT, INTENT,
PURPOSE, PURPORT**
meaning, *pert. to*   **LITERAL,
SEMANTIC**
meaningful   **PITHY, TELLING,
ELOQUENT, IMPORTANT**
meaningless   **EMPTY, FUTILE,
POINTLESS, INSIGNIFICANT**
means   **WAY, DINT, FUNDS,
AGENCY, ASSETS, AVENUE,
COURSE, INCOME, METHOD,
WEALTH, CAPITAL**
meantime   **WHILST;** *see*
INTERVAL
measles   **ROSEOLA, RUBELLA,
RUBEOLA**
measly   **PUNY, PETTY, SMALL,
MEAGER, PALTRY, SCANTY,
STINGY**
measure   **GAGE, METE, PAGE,
SCAN, GAUGE, EXTENT**
measure, ancient   **AS, MINA,
OMER, CUBIT, EPHAH, LIBRA,
OBOLOS, PONDUS, SHEKEL,
TALENT, DRACHMA,
STADION, STADIUM**
measure, metric   **ARE, KILO,
LITER, METER, HECTARE,
CENTIARE, DECALITER,
DECAMETER, DECILITER,
DECIMETER, KILOLITER,**

KILOMETER, CENTILITER,
CENTIMETER, HECTOLITER,
HECTOMETER, MILLIMETER;
see p. 631
measure, U.S. & British   *see p. 631*
(*for other countries see specific
entry*)
Measure for Measure character
ELBOW, FROTH, LUCIO,
ANGELO, JULIET, POMPEY,
ESCALUS
measuring device   LOG, ROD,
DIAL, GAGE, POLE, RULE,
TAPE, CHAIN, CLOCK, GAUGE,
METER, RULER, STADIA,
CALIPER, SEXTANT, TRANSIT,
CALIPER, DIPSTICK,
YARDSTICK
meat   BEEF, LAMB, MEAL,
PORK, VEAL, FLESH, TRIPE,
KERNEL, MUTTON, VENISON;
see CUT, MENU
meat dish   LOAF, STEW, STEAK,
RISSOLE, POT ROAST,
HAMBURGER, STROGANOFF,
WELLINGTON
meat, dried   JERKY, BILTONG,
CHARQUI, PEM(M)ICAN
meat on skewer   CABOB,
KABOB, KEBAB, SHAS(H)LIK
meat, spiced   SALAMI,
BOLOGNA, SAUSAGE,
PASTRAMI
meatless   LENTEN, MAIGRE,
VEGETARIAN
Mecca shrine   KAABA
mechanic   REPAIRMAN
mechanical   MOTOR, REFLEX,
POWERED, AUTOMATIC
mechanics   STATICS,
DYNAMICS, KINETICS,
WORKINGS
— mecum   VADE
medal   *see* AWARD
meddle   PRY, MELL, SNOOP,
TAMPER, INTRUDE,
INTERFERE
meddler   PEST, GREMLIN,
BUSYBODY, NUISANCE
meddlesome   NOSY, PRYING,
CURIOUS, OFFICIOUS
Medea relative   JASON, AEETES
Medea victim   CREON,
CREUSA, GLAUCE
Medean king   CAMBYSES
media   TV, FILM, MOVIE,
PRESS, PRINT, RADIO,
TELEVISION
medial   MIDDLE, AVERAGE

median   PAR, MEAN, MESAL,
MESNE, MESIAL, AVERAGE
mediate   UMPIRE, REFEREE,
ARBITRATE, INTERCEDE
mediator   UMPIRE, ARBITER,
REFEREE, GOBETWEEN,
NEGOTIATOR
medic   DOC, HEALER
medical   IATRIC, CHECKUP,
CURATIVE, PHYSICAL
medical group   AMA
medical instrument   PROBE,
FORCEPS, SCALPEL, SYRINGE,
CATHETER, (STETHO)SCOPE,
THERMOMETER
medical school class   ANAT(OMY)
medicate   TREAT
medication   DRUG, PILLS,
REGIMEN, TABLETS,
THERAPY, MEDICINE,
TREATMENT, PRESCRIPTION
Medici   PIERO, COSIMO,
LORENZO, GIULIANO
medicinal   IATRIC, CURATIVE,
HEALING, REMEDIAL
medicinal plant   AGAR, ALOE,
HERB, ANISE, JALAP, ORRIS,
SENNA, TANSY, ARNICA,
COHOSH, CROTON, IPECAC,
GINSENG
medicine   CURE, DRUG, PILLS,
PHYSIC, REMEDY,
MEDICATION
medicine branch   SURGERY,
ONCOLOGY, PODIATRY,
NEUROLOGY, RADIOLOGY,
GYNECOLOGY, OBSTETRICS,
PEDIATRICS, PSYCHIATRY,
DERMATOLOGY,
ORTHOPEDICS
medicine man   PEAI, PEAY,
PIAY, BASIR, KAHUNA,
PIACHE, SHAMAN, ANGEKOK
medicine, type of   SPACE,
SPORTS, GENERAL,
CLINICAL, FORENSIC,
HOLISTIC, INTERNAL,
PEDIATRIC, VETERINARY
medieval   CRUEL, BARBAROUS,
OLD(FASHIONED)
mediocre   SOSO, AVERAGE,
MIDDLING, ORDINARY
meditate   MULL, MUSE,
PONDER
meditation sound   OM
meditative   MUSING, PENSIVE,
THOUGHTFUL
Mediterranean country   EGYPT,
ITALY, LIBYA, SPAIN,

FRANCE, GREECE, ISRAEL,
TURKEY, ALGERIA, LEBANON,
MOROCCO, TUNISIA
Mediterranean island ELBA,
CAPRI, CRETE, MALTA,
CYPRUS, LESBOS, LIPARI,
RHODES, SICILY, CORSICA,
MAJORCA, BALERIC,
CYCLADES, SARDINIA,
SPORADES, DODECANESE
Mediterranean Sea MARE
NOSTRUM, MARE INTERNUM
Mediterranean sea AEGEAN,
IONIAN, ADRIATIC,
LIGURIAN, TYRRHENIAN
medium TOOL, MEAN(S),
AGENT, AGENCY, PSYCHIC;
see MEDIA
medley MIX, OLIO, CENTO,
FARRAGO, MELANGE,
PASTICCIO, POTPOURRI
Medusa GORGON, JELLYFISH
Medusa relative CETO,
STHENO, EURYALE, PHORCYS
Medusa's slayer PERSEUS
meed GAIN, REWARD,
BRIBERY
meek TAME, TIMID, DOCILE,
HUMBLE, MODEST
meet(ing) GAM, SIT, DATE,
FACE, RALLY, SYNOD,
TRYST, CAUCUS, INDABA,
SEANCE, SEEMLY, SESSION,
SEMINAR
meeting need AGENDA
Meg's sister JO, AMY, BETH
megrim WHIM, VERTIGO,
HEADACHE, MIGRAINE
Mehitabel companion ARCHIE
Mehitabel creator MARQUIS
Mehta ZARIN, ZUBIN
Mein Kampf author HITLER
Meistersinger EVA, HANS,
ZORN, DAVID, SACHS,
POGNER, SIXTUS, WALTHER
Mekong LANCANG
melancholy LOW, SAD, DOWN,
BLUE(S), DOLOR, DREAR,
GLOOMY, MISERY, RUEFUL
Melanesian island FIJI,
SOLOMON, VANUATU,
ADMIRALTY
melange MIX, OLIO, BREW,
BLEND, MIXTURE
meld FUSE, BLEND, MERGE,
UNITE
Meleager relative ALTHEA,
OENEUS
melee see FIGHT

mellow RIPE, SOFT, RIPEN,
SOFTEN, MATURE
melodious TUNY, ARIOSE,
ARIOSO, DULCET, TUNEFUL
melodrama BATHOS,
SHOCKER, THRILLER,
TEARJERKER
melodramatic OVERDONE,
HISTRIONIC
melody AIR, LAY, ARIA, SONG,
TUNE, MELOS, STRAIN,
MELISMA
melon PEPO, CASABA,
HONEYDEW, CANTALOUP(E)
melt RUN, FUSE, FUZE, SWALE,
SWEAL, RENDER, CLARIFY
melting pot CRUCIBLE
Melville work OMOO, MARDI,
TYPEE, PIERRE, MOBY DICK
Melville character PIP, AHAB,
BARTLEBY, QUEEQUEG,
STARBUCK
member ARM, LEG, LIMB,
PART, ORGAN, FELLOW
membership BODY, SEAT,
AFFILIATION, ASSOCIATION
membrane PIA, WEB, CAUL,
FILM, RUGA, TELA, VELA,
MATER, VELUM
memento RELIC, TOKEN,
KEEPSAKE, SOUVENIR
Memnon slayer ACHILLES
memoir LOG, RECORD,
JOURNAL, BIOGRAPHY
memorable NOTABLE,
STRIKING
memorandum CHIT, MEMO,
NOTE, BRIEF, MINUTE
memorial RIP, XAT, CA(I)RN,
TOMB, SHRINE, TROPHY,
EPITAPH
memory ROTE, RECALL,
RETENTION, REMINISCENCE
memory loss AMNESIA
memory, pert. to MNESIC,
MNEMONIC
memory trace ENGRAM
Memphis god PTAH
Memphis street BEALE
menace PEST, BULLY, PERIL,
DANGER, HAZARD,
THREAT(EN)
menacing DIRE, SCARY,
ALARMING, MINATORY
menage DOMICILE,
QUARTERS, HOUSEHOLD,
HUSBANDRY
menagerie ZOO,
ANIMALFARM, PETTINGZOO

mend	FIX, DARN, HEAL, KNIT, PATCH, COBBLE, RELINE, REPAIR	mercury	HG, QUICKSILVER
		Mercury	AZOTH, HERMES
		Mercury's wand	CADUCEUS
mendacious	FALSE, LYING, UNTRUE	mercy	PITY, RUTH, LENITY, CHARITY, CLEMENCY, COMPASSION
mendacity	LIE(S), DECEIT, DISHONESTY	mercy killing	EUTHANASIA
mender	TINKER, COBBLER	mere	FEN, LAKE, ONLY, POND, POOL, MARSH, SHEER, SIMPLE
mendicant	BAUL, DANDI, DANDY, FAKIR, FRIAR, BEGGAR, FAKEER, PAUPER	
Menelaus relative	HELEN, ATREUS, HERMIONE, AGAMEMNON	merely	JUST, ONLY, PURELY, SIMPLY
		merge	WED, FUSE, BLEND
		merger	UNION, FUSION, COMBINE
menial	see SERVANT	Mérimée story	CARMEN
meniscus	DISK, LENS, CARTILAGE	merit	EARN, MEED, VALUE, WORTH, DESERVE, WARRANT
Menlo Park inventor	TAE, EDISON	
Mennonite sect	AMISH, WISLER	Merlin mistress	VIVIAN
menopause	CLIMACTERIC	mermaid	SIREN, MERROW
Menotti character	BEN, BOB, BABA, JOHN, LUCY, TOBY, TODD, MAGDA, AMELIA, ANNINA, MONICA, CARMELA, MICHELE, PINKERTON	Merrimack enemy	MONITOR
		merriment	FUN, GLEE, FROLIC, GAIETY, JOLLITY
		merry	GAY, JOLLY, JOCOSE, FESTIVE
Menotti opera	AMAHL, CONSUL, MEDIUM, TELEPHONE, GLOBOLINKS	merry andrew	CLOWN, JESTER
		Merry Widow composer	LEHAR
mental	NOETIC, PHRENIC, CEREBRAL	Merry Wives of Windsor character NYM, ANNE, FORD, PAGE, CAIUS, FENTON, PISTOL, FALSTAFF, QUICKLY, SHALLOW, SLENDER	
mental condition	LUNACY, MADNESS, DEMENTIA, NEUROSIS, PARANOIA, PSYCHOSIS	
		merry-go-round	CAROUSEL, WHIRLIGIG, WHIRLYGIG
mentality	MIND(SET), ATTITUDE	mesa	BUTTE, PLATEAU
		mescal	AGAVE, MAGUEY, PEYOTE, PEYOTL
mentally ill	CRAZY, DISTURBED, PSYCHOTIC	
		mesh	NET(TING), WEB, LATTICE, NETWORK, INTERLOCK
mention	CITE, NAME, REFER, ALLUDE	
menu	BILL, CARTE	mesmeric	HYPNOTIC, MAGNETIC
menu items and terms	see p. 561	
Merab husband	ADRIEL	Mesopotamia	IRAK, IRAQ
mercenary	VENAL, GREEDY, HESSIAN, ARMATOLI, HIRELING	Mesopotamian city	URFA, EDESSA, NIPPUR, BABYLON
		mess	PI, CLAT, CHOW, BOTCH, SNAFU, BUNGLE, MUDDLE, REPAST, CLUTTER, DISORDER
merchandise	SELL, GOODS, WARE(S), PRODUCE	
merchant	SETH, COSTER, DEALER, MONGER, SUTLER, TRADER, VENDOR, PEDDLER	mess up	FLUB, GOOF
		message	MEMO, NOTE, WORD, POINT, LETTER, REPORT, MEANING
Merchant of Venice character GOBBO, TUBAL, PORTIA, ANTONIO, JESSICA, NERISSA, SHYLOCK, BASSANIO		
		messenger	PAGE, ENVOY, HERALD, HERMES, NUNCIO, COURIER, MERCURY, EMISSARY
merciful	KIND, HUMANE, TIMELY, LENIENT, SIMPATICO, COMPASSIONATE	
		Messiah	JESUS, CHRIST, SAVIO(U)R

Messiah composer   **HANDEL**
messy   **NASTY, UNTIDY,**
CLUTTERED, UNPLEASANT
metal   **TIN, GOLD, IRON, LEAD,**
STEEL, COPPER, BRONZE,
SILVER, ALUMINUM; see p. 689
metal sheet   **FOIL, LAMINA,**
LATTEN
metal slip   **SCISSEL**
metal suit   **MAIL, HAUBERK;**
see p. 504
Metalious novel   **PEYTON PLACE**
metallic   **TINNY**
metallic element   see p. 521
metalworker   **SMITH, VULCAN,**
WELDER, RIVETER,
TINSMITH, GOLDSMITH,
SILVERSMITH, METALLURGIST
metalworking tool   **DIE, ANVIL,**
DRILL, LATHE, SWAGE,
TONGS
Metamorphoses author   **OVID**
metaphor   **TROPE, SIMILE,**
ANALOGY
metaphysical   **ABSTRACT,**
ABSTRUSE, ESOTERIC
mete   **DOLE, GIVE, ALLOT,**
APPORTION, ADMINISTER
meteor   **FIREBALL,**
FALLINGSTAR,
SHOOTINGSTAR
meteor, famous   **LYRID, URSID,**
BOLIDE, CYGNID, LEONID,
PISCID, TAURID, AQUARID,
ARIETID, GEMINID,
ORIONID, PERSEID,
DRACONID, VIRGINID
meteoric   **RAPID, SWIFT,**
DAZZLING, DRAMATIC
meteorite   **TEKTITE, AEROLITE,**
SIDERITE
meteorite, famous   **HOBA, LUCE,**
LOKET, AIGLE, SIENA,
WESTON, ELBOGEN, HATFORD,
ORGUEIL, TEKTITE,
TUNGUSKA
meter   **GA(U)GE, RHYTHM,**
CADENCE
method   **WAY, MODE, PLAN,**
ORDER, SCHEME, SYSTEM,
FORMULA, PROCEDURE
methodical   **FORMAL, LOGICAL,**
PRECISE, ORDERLY
Methodism founder   **WESLEY**
Methuselah relative   **NOAH,**
LAMECH
meticulous   **EXACT, FUSSY,**
CAREFUL, DETAILED,
PEDANTIC, SCRUPULOUS

metier   **JOB, TRADE,**
VOCATION, PROFESSION
Metis lover   **SELENE**
Metis relative   **ZEUS, TETHYS**
metric   see **MEASURE, WEIGHT;**
see p. 631
metrical foot   see **VERSE FORM**
metro   **EL, SUBWAY**
metropolis   **CITY, CONURBATION**
metropolitan   **URBAN, EPARCH,**
OPIDAN, (ARCH)BISHOP
Metropolitan Opera head   **BING,**
ABBEY, VOLPE, LEVINE,
GATTI CASAZZA
Mets' home   **SHEA**
mettle   **GRIT, GUTS, PLUCK,**
SPUNK, SPIRIT
mew   **DEN, BARN, SHED,**
GARAGE, STABLES
Mexican   **AZTEC, CHICANO**
Mexican city/town   **LEON,**
LAPAZ, TEPIC, ALAMOS,
CANCUN, COLIMA, JALAPA,
JUAREZ, MERIDA, OAXACA,
TOLACA, CORDOBA,
COZUMEL, DURANGO,
MORELIA, NOGALES,
PACHUCA, TAMPICO,
TIJUANA, ACAPULCO,
MAZATLAN, GUADALAJARA
Mexican clothing   **MANGA,**
PONCHO, SERAPE, CHIRIPA,
SOMBRERO
Mexican lake   **CHAPALA,**
CUITZEO, TEXCOCO,
PATZCUARO
Mexican measure   **VARA, BARIL,**
CARGA, JARRA, LABOR,
LEGUA, LINEA, SITIO,
FANEGA, PULGADA
Mexican money   **PESO, REAL,**
TLAC, CLACO, TLACO,
AZTECA, CENTAVO, PIASTER
Mexican mountain   **COLIMA,**
ORIZABA, MALINCHE,
CITLALTEPETL,
POPOCATEPETL
Mexican musical group   **MARIACHI**
Mexican neighbor   **US(A),**
BELIZE, GUATEMALA
Mexican people   see p. 732
Mexican president   **GIL, DIAZ,**
ORDAZ, DELEON, ALEMAN,
CALLES, HUERTA, JUAREZ,
MADERO, MADRID, MATEOS,
GORTARI, QUESADA
Mexican river   **TULA, BABIA,**
HONDO, NAZAS, RAMOS,

YAQUI, BALSAS, FUERTE,
SALADO, SONORA,
CONCHOS, PANUCO,
RIOBRAVO, GRIJALVA,
SANTIAGO, RIOGRANDE
Mexican state **COLIMA,**
MEXICO, PUEBLA, SONORA,
CHIAPAS, DURANGO,
HIDALGO, JALISCO,
MORELOS, NAYARIT, SINALOA,
TABASCO, YUCATAN,
CAMPECHE, COAHUILA,
GUERRERO, TLAXCALA,
VERACRUZ
Mexican tree **AMAPA, DRAGO,**
EBANO, GUAYULE,
MESQUIT(E)
Mexican weight **ONZA,**
CARGA, LIBRA, MARCO,
ADARME, ARROBA, OCHAVA,
TERCIO
Mexico, capital of **MEXICO**
CITY
Meyerbeer opera **AFRICAINE**
mezzanine **ENTRESOL**
MGM founder **LOEW**
MGM lion **LEO**
Miami team **HEAT, DOLPHINS**
mica **DAZE, TALC, NACRITE,**
SILICATE, ISINGLASS,
MUSCOVITE
Michal husband **DAVID,**
PHALTI
Michala father **IMLA**
Michelangelo birthplace **CAPRESE**
Michelangelo work **DAVID,**
PIETA, SISTINE CHAPEL
Michener novel **SPACE,**
ALASKA, HAWAII, IBERIA,
MEXICO, POLAND, AIRPORT,
CENTENNIAL
Michigan *see also p. 615*
Michigan city/town **TROY,**
FLINT, WARREN, DETROIT,
LANSING, LIVONIA, PONTIAC,
PORTAGE, SAGINAW,
ANNARBOR, DEARBORN,
KALAMAZOO
Michigan college **MICHIGAN,**
WAYNESTATE
Michigan Indian **MIAMI,**
OTTAWA, WYANDOT,
CHIPPEWA, POTAWATOMI
Michigan lake **ELK, GUN,**
BURT, ERIE, GLEN, HURON,
OTSEGO, PLATTE, STCLAIR,
MICHIGAN, SUPERIOR
Michigan river **DEAD, PINE,**
BLACK, BRULE, GRAND,

HURON, PAWPAW, AUSABLE,
DETROIT, STCLAIR,
ESCANABA, MANISTEE,
MONTREAL, MUSKEGON,
KALAMAZOO, MENOMINEE
microbe(s) **GERM, VIRUS,**
BACTERIA
Micronesia, capital of **PALIKIR**
Micronesia island **YAP, CHUUK,**
PALAU, KOSRAE, GILBERT,
POHNPEI, CAROLINE,
MARIANAS, MARSHALL
Micronesia languages **YAPESE,**
CHUUKESE, KOSRAEAN,
POHNPEIAN
Micronesia money **DOLLAR**
microphone **MIKE**
microphone shield **GOBO**
microscopic **TINY, MINUTE,**
INFINITESIMAL
microspores **POLLEN**
midday **NOON**
middle **HUB, MESAL, MESNE,**
MIDST, WAIST, CENTER,
CENTRY, MEDIAL, MESIAL,
CENTRAL
Middle East **UAE, IRAN, IRAQ,**
OMAN, BURMA, EGYPT,
INDIA, QATAR, SUDAN, SYRIA,
YEMEN, CYPRUS, ISRAEL,
JORDAN, KUWAIT, PERSIA,
TURKEY, BAHRAIN,
LEBANON, SAUDI ARABIA
Middle East group **PLO**
middle ground **FENCE,**
GRAYAREA
middle names *see p. 555*
middle school student **TEEN**
middle, toward the **MES(I)AD**
middleman **AGENT, BROKER,**
RETAILER, GOBETWEEN
middling **FAIR, SOSO, MODEST,**
AVERAGE, MEDIOCRE
Mideast expert **ARABIST**
Midgard serpent slayer **THOR**
midge **FLY, GNAT**
midget **RUNT, SNIP, DWARF,**
PIGMY, PYGMY
— midi **APRES**
Midnight Cowboy name **BUCK,**
RATSO, RIZZO, VOIGT,
HOFFMAN
midship, off **ABEAM**
midshipman **MIDDY, PLEBE,**
REEFER
Midsummer Night's Dream
character
MOTH, PUCK, EGEUS, FLUTE,
SNOUT, COBWEB, HELENA,

HERMIA, OBERON, QUINCE,
THISBE, THESIUS, TITANIA,
LYSANDER
midway cry   WHEE, STEP
(RIGHT) UP
midwife   DHAI, DULA, GAMP,
GRANNY, HEBAMME,
PARTERA
mien   AIR, LOOK, GUISE, POISE,
ASPECT, MANNER, OSTENT
might   FORCE, POWER, VIGOR,
ENERGY, POTENCY,
STRENGTH
might and —   MAIN
mighty   FELL, VERY, POTENT,
STRONG, VALIANT,
PUISSANT
mignonette   DYER, WELD,
RESEDA
migraine   MEGRIM, HEADACHE
migrant   OKIE, NOMAD,
DRIFTER, VAGRANT,
WETBACK
migrate   ROAM, TREK, DRIFT,
WANDER
migration   TREK, EXODUS
migratory   ROVING, NOMADIC,
PEREGRINE
migratory worker   JOAD, OKIE,
ARKIE, BRACERO, WETBACK
Mikado writer   GILBERT,
SULLIVAN
Mikado character   KOKO,
YUMYUM, POOHBAH,
KATISHA, NANKIPOO
Mikado's court   DAIRI
Milan opera house   (LA)SCALA
Milanion relative   ATALANTA
Milcah relative   HUZ, HARAN,
NAHOR, REBEKAH
mild   MOY, SHY, MEEK, SOFT,
BLAND, PLACID, LENIENT,
MODERATE
mildew   MOLD, MUST,
MOULD, BLIGHT
mile, nautical   KNOT, NAUT
milestone   EVENT, HERMA,
STELE, PILLAR, LANDMARK,
HIGHPOINT
milieu   SCENE, CLIMATE,
ENVIRON, SETTING,
AMBIANCE
militant   RADICAL, WARLIKE,
ACTIVIST, COMBATANT,
AGGRESSIVE
military   ARMY, MARTIAL,
WARLIKE
military academy   ANNAPOLIS,
WEST POINT, KINGS POINT

military leaders   *see* GENERALS,
CIVIL WAR; *see p. 542*
military review (journal)   JANES
military school student   CADET,
PLEBE, ENSIGN
military unit   CADRE, SQUAD,
COMPANY, PLATOON,
DIVISION, REGIMENT,
BATTALION, DETACHMENT
militate   WEIGH, OPERATE,
FUNCTION
militate against   OPPOSE,
COUNTER
militia   POSSE, RESERVES,
SOLDIERY
milk   LAC, CURD, SKYR, TYRE,
BEEST, BLEED, LEBAN, LEBEN,
TAYIR, KUMISS, CLABBER,
LACTOSE, BEESTINGS,
COLOSTRUM
milk, kind of   RAW, HOMO,
SKIM, FRESH, CONDENSED,
EVAPORATED
milk part   CURD, WHEY,
SERUM, CASEIN, PLASMA
milk, *pert. to*   LACTIC,
LACTEAL
milkless   YELD
milksop   FOOL, SISSY,
COWARD, WEAKLING
milkweed   SOMA, SPURGE,
ANGLEPOD, STAPELIA
milkwort   SENEGA
Milky Way   GALAXY
Milky Way black space   COALSACK
mill   (K)NURL, QUERN,
GRINDER, ARRASTRA
millet   BUDA, CUMBU,
MILIUM; *see* GRASS
millimeter, 1000th part   MICRON
milliner   HATTER
millisecond   SIGMA
millstone   BUHR, ONUS,
BURDEN
millstone support   RYND
millwheel part   AWE, LADE
Milne character   PIM, ROO,
POOH, ROBIN
Milton work   COMUS, SAMSON,
ALLEGRO, LYCIDAS,
PENSEROSO
mime   APERY, MIMIC, IMITATE
mimeograph   STENCIL,
DUPLICATE
mimic   APE(R), MIMA, MIME,
MOCK, SHAM, QUASI,
PSEUDO
mimicry   PARODY, MIMESIS,
IMITATION

mimosa SHRUB, ACACIA, SOAPBARK
minaret caller MUEZZIN
mince CHOP, DICE, SHRED, SIMPER
mincemeat ingredient BEEF, PEEL, SUET, APPLE, CLOVE, ALMOND, JUMBLE, PUNISH, RAISIN, CURRANT
mind CARE, HEED, OBEY, NOUS, RECK, SOUL, TEND, WITS
mind, *pert. to* MENTAL, PHRENIC
Mindanao island SAMAL, BASILAN, DINAGAT, SIARGAO, CAMIGUIN
Mindanao river AGUSAN, PULANGI
mind-blowing AMAZING, AWESOME, ASTOUNDING
mindful WARY, ALERT, AWARE, HEEDFUL
mindless DULL, STUPID, TEDIOUS, HEEDLESS, POINTLESS
mine DIG, PIT, SAP, LODE, VEIN, STOPE, QUARRY
mine (Fr.) AMOI
miner PITMAN, SAPPER, COLLIER, SANDHOG
mineral ORE; see p. 689
mineral jelly VASELINE, PETROLATUM
Minerva ATHENA
minesweeper TRAWLER, PARAVANE
Ming's planet MONGO
mingle MIX, MELL, BLEND, MERGE
miniature MINI, MODEL, SMALL, LITTLE, DIMINUTIVE
minim DASH, DROP, MITE
minimize LESSEN, REDUCE, PLAYDOWN, UNDERRATE
minimum LEAST, LOWEST, MEREST
mining term GOB, LOB, NOG, TUB, ADIT, DAMP, GOAF, PILE, SUMP, WHIM, WHIN, ASTEL, HUTCH, RESUE, SPRAG, STOPE, STULL, STULM, WINZE, SOLLAR
mining tool GAD, DAVY, SPAD, STEIL, JUMPER, TREPAN, MANDREL, MANDRIL
minion CRONY, GOFER, FOLLOWER

minister AID, CATER, SERVE, VIZI(E)R, PREMIER; see CLERGY
ministry CLERGY, OFFICE, FUNCTION
mink VISON, KOLINSKY
Minnihaha love HIAWATHA
Minnesota see also p. 615
Minnesota city/town ADA, MORA, ANOKA, FOLEY, AITKIN, CHASKA, BAGLEY, DULUTH, OLIVIA, ROSEAU, STPAUL, WADENA, WASECA, WINONA, BEMIDJI, MOORHEAD, ROCHESTER
Minnesota Indian SIOUX, DAKOTA, OJIBWA, OJIBWE, CHIPPEWA
Minnesota lake MUD, RED, CASS, DEER, GULL, LONG, NETT, RENO, RICE, BIRCH, EMILY, HERON, LEECH, RAINY, TROUT, WOODS, ITASCA, PELICAN, SUPERIOR, MILLELACS
Minnesota mountain EAGLE, CUYUNA, MESABI, MISQUAH, VERMILLION
Minnesota river RUM, ROCK, ROOT, SAUK, CEDAR, RAINY, TERRE, KETTLE, REDLAKE, STCROIX, CHIPPEWA, WILDRICE, MINNESOTA, VERMILION, MISSISSIPPI
Minnesotan GOPHER
minor PETTY, YOUTH, LESSER, UNDERAGE
minor suit CLUBS, DIAMONDS
minority NONAGE, PUPILAGE, ALTERNATIVE
Minos relative ARIADNE, PHAEDRA, PASIPHAE
Minotaur slayer THESEUS
minstrel BARD, BHAT, SCOP, ARIOI, RIMER, RUNER, SKALD, GLEEMAN, GOLIARD, JONGLEUR, NANKIPOO
mint BALM, COIN, SAGE, BASIL, CLARY, FRESH, STAMP, THYME, CATNIP, HYSSOP, INVENT, SAVORY, DITTANY, FORTUNE, POTHERB
minus LESS, SANS, WITHOUT
minuscule amount BIT, JOT, ATOM, DROP, IOTA, SPECK
minute(s) WEE, ACTA, MEMO, TINY, SMALL, DETAIL, RECORD, ACTA, NOTES, RECORD

minutiae	TRIVIA, DETAILS
minx	GIRL, JADE, TART, HUSSY
miracle	ANOMY, MARVEL, WONDER
miracle site	CANA, FATIMA, LOURDES
miraculous	AMAZING, MARVELOUS, WONDERFUL
mirage	SERAB, VISION, DELUSION, HALLUCINATION
Miranda's father	PROSPERO
mire	see MUD
Miriam relative	HUR, AARON, AMRAM, MOSES
mirror	GLASS, CRYSTAL, IMITATE, REFLECT, SPECULUM
mirth	GLEE, GAIETY, JOLLITY, HILARITY, LAUGHTER
misadventure	MISHAP, ACCIDENT
misanthrope	CURMUDGEON
misbegotten	BASTARD, ILLEGITIMATE
miscalculate	ERR, MISJUDGE
miscarriage	ABORTION
miscarry	FAIL, ABORT, BACKFIRE
miscellaneous	MIXED, SUNDRY, VARIED, DIVERSE, ASSORTED
miscellany	see MEDLEY
mischief	HOB, DIDO, HAVOC, PRANK, WRACK, CANTRIP
mischievous	PESKY, IMPISH, WICKED, PLAYFUL, PUCKISH, ROGUISH
misconduct	MISBEHAVIOR, MALFEASANCE
miscreant	HERETIC, INFIDEL, CRIMINAL, OFFENDER
miscue	SLIP, ERROR, MISTAKE
misdeed	SIN, CRIME, WRONG, OFFENSE
misdemeanor	SIN, CRIME, DELICT, OFFENSE, INFRACTION
mise-en-scène	SET(TING), DIRECTION
miser	CHURL, HUNKS, NABAL, MARNER, NIGGARD, SCROOGE
miserable	SAD, DISMAL, MEAGER, MEASLY, PALTRY, FORLORN, UNHAPPY, DEJECTED
miserly	MEAN, GNEDE, TIGHT, STINGY, NIGGARD

misery	WOE, PAIN, AGONY, DOLOR, CHAGRIN, DISTRESS
misfire	FAIL, BACKFIRE, MISCARRY
misfit	LOSER, QUOOB
misfortune	BADLUCK, HARDSHIP, ADVERSITY
misgiving	FEAR, DOUBT, QUALM, SCRUPLE
misguided	UNWISE, FOOLISH, ILL ADVISED, INJUDICIOUS
mishandle	BOTCH, BUNGLE, MESS UP
mishap	ACCIDENT, CALAMITY
mishmash	MESS, OLIO, JUMBLE, MUDDLE, FARRAGO, HODGEPODGE
Mishnah section	ABOT, MOED, ABOTH, NASHIM, ZERAIM, NEZIKIN, PERAKIM, SEDARIM
misinform	LIETO, DELUDE, DECEIVE, MISLEAD
misjudge	ERR, MISDEEM, MISCALCULATE
mislay	LOSE, MISPLACE
mislead	DELUDE, DECEIVE
mismanage	BOTCH, BUNGLE, MESSUP
mismatch	MISFIT, DISPARITY
misprint(s)	TYPO, ERRATA
misrepresent	BELIE, GARBLE
miss	FAIL, ESCAPE; see GIRL
Miss America	see p. 507
misshapen	WARPED, DEFORMED, CONTORTED, DISTORTED
missile	BALL, BOLA, BOLT, BOMB, DART, SHOT, SLUG, GRAPA, GRAPE, KILEY, SHAFT, SHELL, ATLATL, BULLET, DUMDUM, PELLET, WOMERA, GRENADE, OUTCAST, TORPEDO, SHRAPNEL, BOOMERANG, PROJECTILE; see ROCKET; see p. 742
missile site	SILO
missing	AWOL, LOST, ABSENT, LACKING, TRUANT
mission	TASK, ALAMO, ERRAND, CALLING, EMBASSY, CONSULATE
mission control	OPS
mission person	LEGATE
Mississippi	see also p. 615
Mississippi city/town	IUKA, YAZOO, BILOXI, FULTON, OXFORD, PURVIS, TUNICA, TUPELO, DECATUR, JACKSON, NATCHEZ,

NOXUBEE, WIGGINS,	mistreat HARM, ABUSE
GULFPORT, MERIDIAN,	mistress DAME, LEMAN,
GREENVILLE	MADAM, MINION,
Mississippi explorer DESOTO	PARAMOUR
Mississippi Indian OSAGE,	mistrust DOUBT, SUSPECT,
YAZOO, CHOCTAW,	SUSPICION
NATCHEZ, SHAWNEE,	misty ROKY, BRUMOUS,
CHEROKEE, CHICKASAW,	NEBULOUS
MERRIMACK	misunderstanding ODDS,
Mississippi mountain WOODALL	MIXUP, CONFUSION,
Mississippi river LEAF, WOLF,	DISPARITY, IMBROGLIO
BAYOU, BOGUE, CREEK,	misuse ABUSE, WASTE,
PEARL, PIERRE, BIG BLACK,	SQUANDER
YALOBUSHA, PASCAGOULA,	mite ATOM, DITE, IOTA,
TENNESSEE, MISSISSIPPI	MOTE, ATOMY, ACARI(NA);
Mississippi River source	*see* TICK
(LAKE)ITASCA	mitigate EASE, ABATE, ALLAY,
Mississippi river tributary RED,	TEMPER, ASSUAGE
IOWA, OHIO, ROCK, BLACK,	mitt PAW, HAND, GLOVE
WHITE, ARKANSAS, CHIPPEWA,	mix MENG, STIR, TEER,
ILLINOIS, MISSOURI,	ADDLE, KNEAD, GARBLE,
WISCONSIN	MINGLE, SCRAMBLE
missive MEMO, NOTE, BILLET,	mix up, mix-up FIGHT, SNAFU,
LETTER, EPISTLE	GARBLE, MINGLE, TANGLE
Missouri *see also* p. 615	mixed MIXY, VARIED,
Missouri city/town AVA, LINN,	DIVERSE, ASSORTED
TROY, EDINA, LAMAR,	mixed blood, person of METIS,
MACON, OZARK, PARIS,	LADINO, MESTEE, MUSTEE,
ROLLA, KAHOKA, POTOSI,	MESTIZO, METISSE, MULATTO
IRONTON, LINNEUS, OSCEOLA,	mixer SODA, TONIC, WATER
PALMYRA, SEDALIA,	mixture HASH, MONG, OLIO,
STLOUIS, CARTHAGE,	MAGMA, MEDLEY,
COLUMBIA	AMALGAM, FARRAGO,
Missouri Indian FOX, SAUK,	MELANGE
OSAGE	Mnemosyne MEMORY
Missouri mountain TAUMSAUK	Mnemosyne lover ZEUS
Missouri river SALT, OSAGE,	Mnemosyne relative GAEA,
PLATTE, CURRENT,	MUSES, URANUS
MEREMEC, CHARITON,	— mo SLO
MISSOURI, DESMOINES,	Moab father LOT
MISSISSIPPI	moan CARP, GRIPE, GROAN,
misspelling CACOGRAPHY	WHINE, BEWAIL
misstep SLIP, TRIP, FAUX PAS	moat FOSS, DITCH, FOSSE,
mist FOG, RAG, HAZE, SMOG,	GRAFF
SMUR, BRUME, MISLE,	mob ROUT, RUCK, BOODLE,
VAPOR, SEREIN	RABBLE, THRONG,
mistake(s) BULL, GOOF, SLIP,	CANAILLE, RIFFRAFF
TYPO, BONER, LAPSE,	mobile FREE, FLUID,
BARNEY, ERRATA, BLOOPER,	MOVABLE, FLEXIBLE,
ERRATUM	PORTABLE
mistaken WRONG,	mobilize RALLY, DRUMUP,
ERRONEOUS	MUSTER, ASSEMBLE
mister DON, PAN, SIR, BABU,	mobster THUG, HEAVY,
HERR, MIAN, SIRE, BABOO,	HOODLUM, GANGSTER
SAHEB, SAHIB, SENOR,	Moby Dick author MELVILLE
SIGNOR, MONSIEUR; *see* TITLE	Moby Dick character PIP,
Mister Ed names ALAN, LANE,	AHAB, STUBB, ISHMAEL,
CAROL, ROCKY, YOUNG,	QUEEQUEG, STARBUCK
WILBUR, WINNIE	Moby Dick ship PEQUOD

moccasin PAC, LOAFER,
   SLIPPER, LARRIGAN
mock APE, GIBE, JAPE, JEER,
  JIBE, RAZZ, FLEER, FLOUT,
SCOFF, SPOOF, TAUNT, DERIDE
mockery SHAM, FARCE, SCORN,
   DERISION, RIDICULE,
          TRAVESTY
mockingbird MOCKER
mod IN, TRENDY
Mod Squad name ADAM, LINC,
   PETE, JULIE
mode FAD, FORM, FLAIR, STYLE,
  VOGUE, MANNER, FASHION
mode, musical MAJOR, MINOR,
  DORIAN, IONIAN, LYDIAN,
  AEOLIAN, LOCRIAN,
         PHRYGIAN
model SIT, BASE, COPY, NORM,
  POSE, TYPE, IDEAL, SITTER,
  MANIKIN, PARAGON,
  MANNIKIN, PARADIGM,
  MANNEQUIN; see FASHION
Model T TINLIZZIE
moderate COOL, MILD, ABATE,
  SOBER, LESSEN, SOFTEN,
  STEADY, TEMPER, LENIENT,
        MITIGATE
modern NEO, NEW, LATE,
  NOVEL, UPTODATE
modernize RETOOL, REVISE,
  UPDATE, RENOVATE
modest SHY, MEEK, PLAIN,
  TIMID, DEMURE, HUMBLE,
  SIMPLE, BASHFUL, RETICENT
modesty indication HEMLINE,
       NECKLINE
modify VARY, ALTER, AMEND,
  EMEND, REVISE, TEMPER
modish IN, CHIC, SMART,
  STYLISH, FASHIONABLE
modiste COUTURIER
modulate CURB, VARY,
  ATTUNE, CHANGE, TEMPER,
  MODERATE, TRANSFORM
module PART, UNIT,
  SECTION, COMPONENT
modus operandi WAY,
  METHOD, PROCEDURE
modus vivendi WAYOFLIFE,
    COMPROMISE
mogul RULER, TYCOON,
  MAGNATE, AUTOCRAT
Mogul emperor AKBAR, BABAR,
  BABER, BABUR, JEHAN
Mohammed birthplace MECCA
Mohammed burial place MEDINA
Mohammed relative ALI, SAID,
  SEID, ABBAS, AISHA, AMINA,

SAUDA, SAYID, AYESHA,
  FATIMA, JINNAH, KADIJA,
    SHERIF, ZAYNAB
Mohammed supporters ANSAR
Mohammedan see MUSLIM
Mohawk, city on the UTICA
moiety HALF, PART, SHARE
Moirae see FATES
moiré WAVY
moist WET, DAMP, DANK,
  DEWY, UVID, HUMID, RORIC
moisten WET, MOIL, SOAK,
  BEDEW, DAMPEN, SPONGE
moisture FOG, WET, HUMOR,
  VAPOR, WATER, HUMIDITY
moisturizer ingredient ALOE,
    GLYCEROL
majo CHARM, POWER, SPELL,
  AMULET, VOODOO
molasses TREACLE, TRIACLE
mold CAST, MUST, KNEAD,
  FUNGUS, MATRIX, MILDEW,
    PATTERN
Moldavia MOLDAU; see
    MOLDOVA
molding CYMA, GULA, OGEE,
  TORI, CONGE, OVOLI,
  OVOLO, SPLAY, TORUS, FILLET,
  LISTEL, REGLET, REGULA,
  SCOTIA, CAVETTO, ECHINUS,
  REEDING, ASTRAGAL
molding edge AR(R)IS
Moldova MOLDAVIA
Moldova, capital of CHISINAU,
    KISHINEV
Moldovan city/town BALTI,
  KAGUL, TIGHINA, CHISINAU
Moldovan language GAGAUZI,
    MOLDOVAN
Moldovan money MDL, LEU
Moldovan neighbor ROMANIA,
    UKRAINE
Moldovan river BAC, PRUT,
  RAUT, BOTNA, IAPUG,
  COGALNIC, DNIESTER
moldy HOAR, MOSY, FUSTY,
  MUCID, MUSTY, STALE
mole SPY, PIER, QUAY, JETTY,
  NEVUS, TALPA, TAUPE,
    LENTIGO
mole-like TALPOID
molecule part ION, ATOM,
    (AN)ION
molest VEX, FRET, ABUSE,
  ANNOY, CHAFE, HARASS,
    PESTER
Molière character ORGON,
  ALCESTE, JOURDAIN,
    TARTUFFE

Molière play	**MISER,**		**SEWAN, SUGAR, UHLLO,**
TARTUFFE, MISANTHROPE			**BOODLE, BUNDLE, COWRIE,**
Moll Flanders author	**DEFOE**		**DINERO, MAZUMA, MONKEY,**
mollusk	*see p. 680*		**MOOLAH, SEAWAN, SHEKEL,**
mollycoddle	**SPOIL, COSSET,**		**SPENSE, TANNER, TENDER,**
PAMPER, INDULGE			**TENNER, WAMPUM, CABBAGE,**
Molnar play	**LILIOM**		**CENTURY, LETTUCE,**
molt	**MEW, CAST(OFF), SHED,**		**SAWBUCK, SCRATCH,**
EXUVIATE, SLOUGH			**SHEKELS, TWOBITS,**
molten	**MELTED, LIQUIFIED**		**SIMOLEONS;** *see p. 638*
molten rock	*see* **LAVA**	money box	**ARCA, SAFE, TILL,**
Moluccas	**SPICE, MALUKU**		**COFFER, DRAWER, REGISTER**
Moluccas island	**ARU, KAI, OBI,**	money, make	**EARN, MINT**
BURU, LETI, SULA, BABAR,		money market	**BOURSE,**
BACAN, BANDA, CERAM,			**EXCHANGE**
WETAR, TIDORE, MOROTAI,		moneyed	**RICH, WEALTHY,**
TERNATE, HALMAHERA			**WELLOFF, AFFLUENT,**
moment	**SEC, TICK, JIFF(Y),**		**WELLTODO**
FLASH, TRICE,		moneylender	**USURER,**
IMPORT(ANCE)			**MAHAJAN, SHYLOCK**
momentarily	**ANON, SOON,**	monger	**DEALER, TRADER**
INASEC		Mongol	**HU, ELEUT, KALKA,**
momentous	**BIG, NOTABLE,**		**MOGUL, TATAR, BURIAT,**
HISTORIC			**BURYAT, KALMU(C)K,**
momentum	**DRIVE, FORCE,**		**KHALKHA**
THRUST		Mongol conqueror	**TAMERLANE,**
mon —	**DIEU**		**TIMURLENK,**
Mona Lisa artist	**(DA)VINCI,**		**GENGHIS(KHAN)**
LEONARDO		Mongol dynasty	**YUAN**
Monaco, capital of		Mongol emperor	**KUBLAI (KHAN)**
MONACO(VILLE)		Mongolia, capital of	
Monaco dynasty	**GRIMALDI**		**ULANBATOR, ULAANBAATAR**
Monaco money	**FRANC,**	Mongolia, Outer	**URGA**
CENTIME		Mongolian city/town	**TES,**
Monaco princess	**GRACE,**		**BERH, HOVD, ALTAY,**
CAROLINE, STEPHANIE			**MORON, OLGIY, BULGAN,**
monad	**ATOM, UNIT, ENTITY**		**DARBAN**
monarch	**RULER, CALIPH,**	Mongolian money	**MNT,**
SULTAN; *see* **KING, QUEEN,**			**MONGO, TUGRIK, TUGRUC,**
EMPEROR, EMPRESS			**TOGROOG**
monarchist	**ROYALIST**	Mongolian river	**TES, ULDZ,**
monastery	**MATH, TERA,**		**ORHON, TESIYN, DZAVHAN,**
ABBEY, RIBAT, TEKKE,			**KERULEN, SELENGA,**
TEKYA, CENOBY, FRIARY,			**HOBDOGOL**
MANDRA, PRIORY, VIHARA,		Mongolic language	**KALKA,**
NUNNERY, LAMASERY			**BURYAT, KHALKA,**
— monde	**HAUT**		**KALMUCK, KHALKHA,**
monetary	**FISCAL, NUMMARY,**		**MONGOLIAN**
FINANCIAL, PECUNIARY		mongolism	**DOWNS, IDIOCY**
money *(see also specific countries*		mongoose	**URVA, MANGUE**
for currencies)	**AES, BIT, BOB,**	mongrel	**CUR, DOG, MUT(T),**
FIN, RED, TIN, BEAD, CASH,			**TYKE, HYBRID**
COIN, CUSH, DUST, GELT,		moniker	**(NICK)NAME**
JACK, KALE, LARI, MOSS,		monition	**NOTICE, CAUTION,**
PELF, PLUM, QUID, ROLL,			**SUMMONS, WARNING**
ULLO, BEANS, BREAD, BUCKS,		monitor	**CHECK, SPY ON,**
CHIPS, COWRY, DEUCE,			**LIZARD, SCREEN,**
DOUGH, FIVER, GRAND, GRIGS,			**OBSERVE(R), IRONCLAD,**
LARIN, LUCRE, MOOLA,			**SUPERVISE, SUPERVISOR**

Monitor adversary **MERRIMACK**	Montague enemy **CAPULET**
monitor type **CGA, EGA, LED,**	Montana *see also p. 615*
RGB, (S)VGA, PLASMA	Montana city/town **BUTTE,**
monk **FRA, ABBE, LAMA, SUFI,**	**DILLON, HELENA, SCOBEY,**
ABBOT, ARHAT, BONZE,	**SHELBY, BOZEMAN, EKALAKA,**
FAKIR, FRIAR, LOHAN, PRIOR,	**ROUNDUP, BILLINGS,**
ARAHAT, BHIKKY, PONGYI,	**MISSOULA**
SANTON, CALOYER, DERVISH,	Montana Indian **CREE, CROW,**
TALAPOIN	**SIOUX, SALISH, CHEYENNE,**
monk settlement **SCETE, SKETE**	**CHIPPEWA, KOOTENAI,**
Monkees movie **HEAD**	**BLACKFEET, GROSVENTRE,**
monkey **JOCKO, RHESUS,**	**ASSINIBOINE**
SIMIAN, MACAQUE; *see p. 665*	Montana mountain **KIPP,**
monkey business **MISCHIEF**	**KOCH, CRAZY**
monkey genus **AOTUS, CEBUS,**	Montana river **SUN, MILK,**
MIDAS, ATELES, GALAGO,	**RUBY, TETON, JUDITH,**
MACACA, COLOBUS,	**MARIAS, POWDER, TONGUE,**
MACACUS, SAIMIRI	**BIGHOLE, BIGHORN,**
monkey puzzle **PINON**	**MADISON, MISSOURI,**
Mon-Khmer language **WA, MON,**	**YELLOWSTONE**
JAKUN, KHASI, KHMER,	Monte Cristo *see* **COUNT OF**
SAKAI, PALAUNG,	**MONTE CRISTO**
CAMBODIAN	Montenegro **CRNAGORA,**
monkshood **ATIS, ACONITE**	**TSERNAGORA;** *see* **SERBIA**
monogram **RLS, RWE, TSE,**	**AND MONTENEGRO**
CIPHER, INITIALS	Montenegro, former capital **CETINJE**
monograph **ESSAY, PAPER,**	Monteverdi opera **ORFEO,**
THESIS, TREATISE	**ULYSSES**
monolith **DOLMEN, MENHIR,**	Montezuma's captor **CORTEZ**
PILLAR, OBELISK	Montezuma's revenge **RUNS,**
monolithic **HUGE, MASSIVE,**	**DIARRHEA**
COLOSSAL	month **ULT, ABIB, INST,**
monologue **SPEECH, SOLILOQUY**	**ULTIMO, INSTANT;** *see p. 718*
monopolize **HOG, SEW UP,**	monthly **MENSAL, MENSES,**
CORNER, CONTROL,	**MENSTRUAL**
ENGROSS, DOMINATE	Montreal team **EXPOS,**
monopoly **POOL, TRUST,**	**CANADIENS**
CARTEL, APPALTO,	Montreal World's Fair **EXPO**
SYNDICATE	monument **CARN, LECH,**
monotone **DRONE**	**CAIRN, STELE, TABUT,**
monotonous **DRAB, FLAT,**	**DOLMEN, MENHIR, RECORD,**
DREARY, HUMDRUM,	**SHRINE, CENOTAPH,**
TEDIOUS, TIRESOME	**CROMLECH**
monotony **ENNUI, TEDIUM,**	monumental **BIG, EPIC,**
BOREDOM	**COLOSSAL, HISTORIC**
mons — **PUBIS, VENERIS**	mooch **BEG, BUM, AMBLE,**
monsoon **TORRENT,**	**CADGE, PROWL, SLOUCH,**
CLOUDBURST	**SAUNTER**
monster **ORC, GILA, GOUL,**	mood **VEIN, HUMOR, TEMPER,**
GOWL, OGRE, BRUTE,	**MORALE, DISPOSITION**
GHOUL, HYDRA, RAHAB,	moody **GLUM, SULKY, TESTY,**
TERAS, ELLOPS, KRAKEN,	**MOROSE, IRRITABLE**
GRENDEL; *see p. 659*	moon **ORB, GAZE, LUNA,**
monstrosity **EVIL, FREAK,**	**CRESCENT;** *see* **SATELLITE**
HORROR, MONSTER,	moon goddess **LUNA, HECATE,**
OUTRAGE, TERATISM	**HEKATE, PHOEBE, SELENE,**
monstrous **EVIL, HUGE, UGLY,**	**CYNTHIA, ARTEMIS, ASTARTE**
HIDEOUS, INHUMAN,	moon, *pert. to* **LUNAR,**
ENORMOUS, ATROCIOUS	**SELENIC**

moon phase	NEW, FULL, GIBBOUS, LUNETTE
moon plains	MARIA
moon sea	COLD, RAINS, CRISES, NECTAR, SHOWERS, MOISTURE, SERENITY, FECUNDITY, TRANQUILITY
moon-shaped	LUNATE
moon valley	RILL, CLEFT, RILLE
moon's age	EPACT
Moonlight Sonata composer	BEETHOVEN
moonshine	WHISKY, BOOTLEG, FUSTIAN, HOME BREW
moor	FEN, BRAE, FELL, LINK, HEATH, LANDE, TIEUP, ANCHOR, FASTEN, MUSLIM, SECURE
Moor	BERBER, MOSLEM, MUSLIM, BEDOUIN, OTHELLO, SARACEN, MOROCCAN
mooring place	DOCK, PORT, SLIP, BERTH, HARBOR, MARINA
Moorish	MORISCO, MORESQUE, MORISCAN, MAURESQUE
moose genus	ALCES
moot	MEETING, PROPOSE, ARGUABLE, DEBATABLE
mop	SWAB, SWOB, WASH, WIPE, MERKIN, SCOVEL
mope	FRET, MOON, PINE, POUT, SULK, BROOD
moppet	FOP, FRY, TAD, DOLL, GIRL, CHILD
moral	JUST, MAXIM, RIGHT, ETHICAL, UPRIGHT, VIRTUOUS
morale	CHEER, NERVE, SPIRIT, CONFIDENCE
moralistic	PREACHY, DIDACTIC
morality	ETHICS, MORALS, PRINCIPLES
morals	ETHICS, STANDARDS, PRINCIPLES
morass	see MARSH
moratorium	HALT, GRACE, PAUSE, FREEZE, CESSATION
Moravia	see CZECH REPUBLIC
morbid	GLOOMY, GRISLY, MACABRE, MOROSE
mordant	ACID, ACRID, BITING, ACERBIC, CAUSTIC, CUTTING, EROSIVE, CORROSIVE
more	BIS, PIU, TOO, ELSE, PLUS, EXTRA, ENCORE, EXCESS
more or less	ABOUT, NEARLY, SOMEWHAT, APPROXIMATE(LY)
More's island	UTOPIA
moreover	TOO, ALSO, BESIDES, LIKEWISE, FURTHERMORE
— Morgana	FATA
morgue	MORTUARY, DEADHOUSE
Moriarty foe	HOLMES
moribund	DYING, WANING, EXPIRING, DECLINING
Mork greeting	NANUNANU
Mork's planet	ORK
Mormon	SMITH, YOUNG, DANITE
morning	AM, MATIN, UMAGA, MATINAL; see DAWN
morning glory	KOALI, IPOM(O)EA, BINDWEED
morning song	ALBA, MATIN, AUBADE, MATTINS
Moroccan city	FES, FEZ, SAFI, SALE, OUJDA, RABAT, AGADIR, DAKHLA, ERFOUD, MEKNES, TANTAN, TIZNIT, TANGIER, MARRAKECH, MARRAKESH, CASABLANCA
Moroccan money	OKIA, RIAL, DIRHAM
Moroccan mountain	RIF(F), ATLAS
Moroccan neighbor	SPAIN, ALGERIA
Moroccan river	DRAA, SOUS, RHERIS, TENSIFT, MOULOUYA
Moroccan weight	ROTL, GERBE, KINTAR
Morocco, capital of	RABAT
moron	AMENT, IDIOT, IMBECILE
morose	SAD, BLUE, DOUR, GLUM, GRUM, SOUR, MOODY, SULKY, SURLY, SULLEN
Morrison novel	JAZZ, BELOVED, TARBABY
Morse Code symbol	DAH, DIT, DOT, DASH
morsel	BIT, ORT, SOP, BITE, CRUMB, SCRAP, TIDBIT
mortal	MAN, FATAL, HUMAN, DEADLY, LETHAL
mortality	DEATH, HUMANITY
mortar	COMPO, CANNON, CO(E)HORN

mortar and —	PESTLE		BAGWORM, BEEMOTH,
mortar tray	HOD		BUDWORM, CODLING,
mortgage	LIEN, LOAN,		CRAMBID, DRINKER,
	PLEDGE, WADSET		FOOTMAN, PSYCHID,
mortification	SHAME,		PUGMOTH, PYRALID,
INDIGNITY, DEGRADATION			TINEOID, TORTRIX,
mortify	SHAME, DEGRADE,		TUSSOCK, TUSSORE, URANIID,
TAKEDOWN, HUMILIATE			WAXMOTH, YAMAMAI,
mortuary	MORGUE, CHARNEL,		ARMYWORM, BOLLWORM,
	CREMATORY		FORESTER, HAWKMOTH,
mosaic	INLAY, MUSIVE,		LUNAMOTH, PLUTELLA,
	COLLAGE, TESSERA		SILKWORM
Mosaic law	TORA(H)	moth genus	TINEA, ARCTIA,
mosaic materials	TILE,		PLUSIA, AGROTIS, ATTACUS,
	SMALTO, TESSERA		CRAMBUS, JUGATAE, PYRALIS
Moscow building	GUM,	moth-eaten	WORN (OUT),
	KREMLIN		SHABBY
Moscow park	GORKI	mother	MA, DAM, AMMA,
Moscow square	RED, PUSHKIN		MAMA, MATER, MOMSY,
Moselle city	METZ, TRIER,		MATRON, ABBESS; see DREGS
	TREVES, KOBLENZ	mother-of-pearl	NACRE
Moselle tributary	ORNE, SAAR,	mother-of-pearl source	ABALONE
	SURE, MEURTHE	motherhood	MATERNITY
Moses mountain	NEBO	motherly	MATERNAL
Moses relative	AARON,	motif	IDEA, LOGO, THEME,
JETHRO, MIRIAM, ELIEZER,			DESIGN
GERSHOM, ZIPPORAH		motion	FLUX, WAVE, ACTION,
Moses' spies	IGAL, CALEB,		SIGNAL, GESTURE,
NAHBI, GADDIEL			PROPOSAL, MOVEMENT
Moslem	see ISLAMIC	motion, pert. to	MOTIVE,
mosque	JAMI, OMAR, MASJID		KINETIC
mosque head	IMAM	motion picture	see MOVIE
mosque part	MIHRAB,	motion, producing	MOTILE,
MIMBAR, MINARET			MOTIFIC
mosquito	CULICID, SKEETER,	motionless	FIXED, INERT,
	STEGOMYIA		STILL, FROZEN, STATIC
mosquito genus	AEDES, CULEX	motivate	INDUCE, PROMPT,
moss	BRYUM, MNIUM, MUSCI,		INSPIRE
LICHEN, EPIPHYTE,		motivation	SPUR, CAUSE,
BRYOPHYTE, CARRAGEEN			IMPETUS, INFLUENCE
mossy	OLD, BOGGY, DATED,	motive	SPUR, CAUSE, THEME,
GREEN, HOARY, MARSHY			REASON, SPRING, IMPULSE,
most	GREATEST, MAJORITY		PURPOSE, INCENTIVE
mostly	MAINLY, LARGELY,	motley	VARIED, DIVERSE,
ASARULE, CHIEFLY			COLORFUL
mot	QUIP, EPIGRAM,	motmot	MOMOT, ROLLER,
REPARTEE, WITTICISM			KIROMBO
mote	IOTA, SPECK, TRACE	motor	CRUISE, ENGINE,
motel	INN, LODGE, CABINS		TURBINE
moth	PUG, MOCH, SLUG,	motor part	CAM, COIL, GEAR,
EGGAR, EGGER, MICRO,			ROTOR, PISTON, STATOR,
PLUME, SWIFT, WITCH,			IGNITION, CAPACITOR
BOGUNG, BOMBYX, BUGONG,		motorbike	MOPED
CODLIN, COSSID, DAGGER,		Motown	DETROIT
ERMINE, HERALD, IOMOTH,		mottled	PIED, ROEY, PINTO,
LAPPET, MILLER, PSYCHE,			DAPPLED, PIEBALD
QUAKER, RUSTIC, SPHINX,		motto	SAW, ADAGE, MAXIM,
TINEAN, TINEID, TUSSAH,			BYWORD, SLOGAN,
TUSSER, ARCTIID,			PRECEPT, CATCHWORD

mound   AHU, TEE, DENE, DHER, DUNE, HEAP, HILL, HUMP, PILE, TELL, TERP, TUMP, KNOLL, BARROW, TUMULUS

mount   RISE, BOARD, CLIMB, GETON, SCALE, SETUP, SWELL, ASCEND, LAUNCH

Mount of Olives   OLIVET

Mount Rushmore faces   LINCOLN, JEFFERSON, ROOSEVELT, WASHINGTON

Mount Vesuvius city   POMPEII

mountain   GAE, KAF, KOP, BERG, HEAP, PILE, BUTTE, STACK, SIERRA

mountain lion   PUMA, COUGAR, PANTHER

mountain pass   see PASS

mountain sickness   PUNA, VETA

Mountain State   MONTANA

mountaineer   SHERPA, CLIMBER, ALPINIST

mountainous   LOFTY, PEAKY, ROCKY, CRAGGY, RUGGED

mountains and mountain ranges see p. 611

mountaintop   ACME, APEX, CONE, PEAK, SUMMIT

mountebank   QUACK, EMPIRIC

mourn   RUE, SIGH, WAIL, WEEP, BEWAIL, GRIEVE, LAMENT

mourner   MUTE, WEEPER, PENITENT

mournful   SAD, SOMBER, DESPONDENT

mourning clothes   BLACK, WEEDS, SABLES, BOMBASINE, SACKCLOTH

mouse   VOLE, SHREW, GERBIL; see RODENT

mouser   CAT, OWL

mousy   DRAB, QUIET, TIMID

mouth(s)   OS, GOB, MUN, ORA, ABRA, BOCA, LADE, BOCCA, CODON, DELTA, FRITH, INLET, STOMA, VOICE, DECLAIM, ESTUARY

mouth part   GUM(S), LIP, TOOTH, UVULA, VELUM, LABIUM, PALATE, RICTUS, TONGUE, GINGIVA, OMPHALOS, UNDERLIP, UPPERLIP

mouthful   BITE, GOBBET

mouthpiece   PAWN, AGENT, BOCAL, PUPPET, SPOKESMAN

mouthward   ORAD

mouthwash   GARGLE, COLLUTION

mouth-watering   TASTY, SAVORY, DELICIOUS, DELECTABLE

movable   MOBILE, PORTABLE

move   GO, ACT, AWE, LEAD, PUSH, STIR, WALK, BUDGE, IMPEL, AFFECT

move over   INDENT

move sidewise   EDGE, SLUE, SIDLE

move slowly   EDGE, INCH, WORM

move to and fro   WAG, FLAP, SWAY

movement   MOTO, CAUSE, MUDGE, TAXIS, TEMPO, THEME, ACTION, MOTION, RHYTHM, CRUSADE

movie   FILM, FLICK, CINEMA, TALKIE, CARTOON, MUSICAL, QUICKIE, WESTERN, NEWSREEL, MELODRAMA

movie, cult   BRAZIL, FREAKS, REPOMAN, SCARFACE, ERASERHEAD

movie director's command   CUT, TAKE, PRINT, ACTION, CAMERA, LIGHTS

movie directors, famous   see p. 540

movie expense   RETAKE

movie, famous   see p. 505

movie part   LEAD, HEAVY, INGENUE

movie process   TODDAO, CINERAMA, CINEMASCOPE

moving   MOTILE, ELOQUENT, PATHETIC, STIRRING, TOUCHING

moving staircase   ESCALATOR

mow   CLIP, DESS, GOAF, LOFT, MATH, CUT(DOWN), (HAY)STACK

mower   HAYTER, REAPER, SCYTHE, SICKLE

Mowgli friend   BEAR, AKELA, BALOO

moxie   GUTS, NERVE

Mozambique, capital of   MAPUTO

Mozambique city/town   MOMA, TETE, BEIRA, PEMBA, MAPUTO, NACALA, XAIXAI, CHIMOIO, NAMPULA, LICHINGA

Mozambique money   CENTAVO, METICAL

Mozambique mountain   NAMULI

Mozambique neighbor **ZAMBIA, TANZANIA, ZIMBABWE, SWAZILAND, SOUTHAFRICA**

Mozambique river **BUZI, SAVE, LURIO, REVUE, LIGONHA, LIMPOPO, LUGENDA, MESSALO, ZAMBEZI**

Mozambique people **SENA, MAKUA, CHOKWE, MANYIKA, SHANGAAN**

Mozart cataloguer **KO(E)CHEL**

Mozart opera **COSI, FIGARO, MAGIC FLUTE, DON GIOVANNI**

Mozart Requiem key **D MINOR**

Mozart's city **SALZBURG**

much **LOT(S), ALOT, PLENTY**

Much Ado About Nothing
character **HERO, JOHN, PEDRO, ANTONIO, BEATRICE, CLAUDIO, LEONATO, BENEDICK**

mucilage **GOO, GUM, GLUE, PASTE, ARABIN, ADHESIVE**

muck **DIRT, MIRE, FILTH, MANURE**

mucous **SLIMY, VISCOUS, BLENNOID**

mud **MIRE, MUCK, OOZE, SILT, SLOB, SALSE, SLIME, SLUDGE**

muddle **MESS, SOSS, ADDLE, SNAFU, BUNGLE, FIASCO, EMBROIL**

muddled **DIZZY, JUMBLED, UNCLEAR, CONFUSED**

muddy **DINGY, ROILY, SLIMY, DAGGLE, SLUDGY, TURBID**

muezzin **CRIER**

muff **FUR, FLUB, MISS, BOTCH, CREST, BOLLIX, BUNGLE, GOOF UP, WARMER**

muffin **BUN, COB, GEM, ROLL, POPOVER**

muffle **GAG, MUTE, OVEN, WRAP, DAMPEN, DEADEN, STIFLE**

muffler **MUTE, SCARF**

mug **CUP, NOG, JACK, PUSS, TOBY, STEIN, NOGGIN**

mugger **THUG, ATTACKER, ASSAILANT**

muggy **DANK, WARM, HUMID, CLAMMY, STICKY, SULTRY**

Muhammed Ali **(CASSIUS)CLAY**

mulatto **METIS, CREOLE, GRIFF(E), GRIQUA**

mulberry **FUSTIC, MURREY, SYCAMINE**

mulct **FINE, AMERCE, PUNISH**

mule **MARE, HINNY, SLIPPER, TRACTOR, SHAVETAIL**

mulish **OBDURATE, STUBBORN, OBSTINATE**

mull **MUSE, THINK, PONDER**

mulligan **STEW**

multifarious **VARIED, DIVERSE, ASSORTED**

multiple **MANY, SEVERAL, MANIFOLD, NUMEROUS**

multiplication **GROWTH, INCREASE, PROCREATION**

multitude **MOB, HOST, HORDE, GALAXY, LEGION, MYRIAD**

multitudinous **MANY, MANIFOLD, NUMEROUS**

mum **ALE, BEER, MUTE, QUIET, STILL, MOTHER, SILENT**

mumble **CHEW, MURMUR, MUTTER**

mumbojumbo **IDOL, SPELL, FETISH, JARGON, GIBBERISH**

mummer **ACTOR, MASKER, PARADER**

mummify **DRY, PRESERVE**

munch **CHEW, CHOMP, MASTICATE**

Munda language **HO, ASURI, JUANG, KORKU, KORWA, GADABA, KHARIA, SAVARA, MUNDARI, SANTALI, KHERWARI**

mundane **CARNAL, COSMIC, EARTHLY, TERRENE, WORLDLY, TEMPORAL**

Munich river **ISAR**

municipal **CIVIC, URBAN, METROPOLITAN**

municipality **CITY, TOWN, METROPOLIS**

munificent **LAVISH, LIBERAL, PROFUSE, GENEROUS**

munitions **ARMS**

Munster dragon **SPOT**

mural **FRESCO, FRIEZE**

murder **KILL(ING), SLAY(ING), BURKE, NOYADE, BUMPOFF, EXECUTE, HOMICIDE**

murder fine **CRO, MURDRUM, BLOODWIT(E)**

murder victims, famous **GAYE, TOSH, MINEO, CURTIS, GEORGE, LENNON, WALTER**

murderer **KILLER, SLAYER, ASSASSIN**

murk **DARK, GLOOM**

murky **DARK, FOGGY, CLOUDY, OBSCURE**

murmur   HUM, BUZZ, CURR, PURR, MUTTER, WHISPER
muscle   BEEF, DURA, SWAY, TELA, THEW, BRAWN, CLOUT, FORCE, POWER, SINEW, INFLUENCE
muscles   BICEPS, FLEXOR, TENDON, TENSOR, DELTOID, DILATOR, ERECTOR, GLUTEUS, TRICEPS, ABDUCTOR, ADDUCTOR, EXTENSOR, LIGAMENT, PECTORAL, DIAPHRAGM, SPHINCTER;
     see p. 500
musclelike   MYOID, RIPPLED
muscular   BEEFY, BURLY, THEWY, BRAWNY, TOROSE
muse   MULL, REVE, PIERIS, PONDER
Muses   CLIO, ERATO, THALIA, URANIA, EUTERPE, CALLIOPE, POLYMNIA, MELPOMENE, TERPSICHORE
museum   RYKS, TATE, CLUNY, FIELD, FREER, GETTY, PITTI, PRADO, LOUVRE, UFFIZI, GALLERY, CLOISTERS, HERMITAGE
mush   PAP, SAMP, SEPON, ATOLE, SUPAWN; see PORRIDGE
mushroom   CEPE, MOREL, AGARIC, BUTTON, FUNGUS, AMANITA, TRUFFLE, TOADSTOOL
mushy   SOFT, SAPPY, SOGGY, SPONGY, MAUDLIN, MAWKISH
music   AIR, LAY, TUNE, MELODY, HARMONY
music hall   GAFF, BIJOU, EMPIRE, PALACE, ALHAMBRA, COLISEUM, WINDMILL, PALLADIUM, HIPPODROME
musical   MELIC, LYRIC(AL), CANOROUS, MELODIOUS;
     see p. 644
musical directions   see p. 641
musical event   CONCERT, RECITAL, MUSICALE, PERFORMANCE
musical forms   see p. 643
musical group   DUO, BAND, SOLO, TRIO, CHOIR, NONET, OCTET, CHORUS, SEPTET, SEXTET, KAPELLE, QUARTET, QUINTET, ORCHESTRA
musical instruments   see p. 642

musical part   ALTO, BASS, BASSO, CANTO, MEZZO, TENOR, SOPRANO, BARITONE, BARYTONE, CONTRALTO
musical play   CATS, HAIR, MAME, MONA, SARI, ANNIE, EVITA, FANNY, OH KAY, SALLY, SUNNY, CANCAN, EILEEN, GREASE, KISMET, CABARET, CANDIDE, FIREFLY, JUBILEE, MAYTIME, NEW MOON, PAL JOEY, ROBERTA, CAROUSEL, OKLAHOMA, SHOW BOAT;
     see p. 644
musical term   see p. 640
musicale   SOIREE, CONCERT, PROGRAM(ME), SYMPHONY
musician   see p. 643
musket   CULVERIN; see GUN
musketeer   ATHOS, ARAMIS, PORTHOS, DARTAGNAN
muskmelon   MANGO, ATIMON, CASABA, CANTALOUPE
Muslim   HANIF; see ISLAM
muslin   MULL, ADATI, MOSAL, SHELA, BATISTE, ORGANDY, NAINSOOK, TARLETAN
muss   ROW, MESS, MUDDLE, RUMPLE, TANGLE, TOUSLE, DISHEVEL, DISORDER
mussel   UNIO, NAIAD, MUCKET, MUSCLE, MYTILID, MYTILUS, UNIONID, DEERHORN
Mussolini   MUSSO, (IL)DUCE
must   MA(U)N, MOLD, SAPA, STUM, MILDEW
mustard   WOAD, RUNCH, CRESS, RADISH, TURNIP, CHARLOCK
musteline animal   MINK, OTTER, RATEL, MARTEN, WEASEL, POLECAT, WOLVERINE
muster   CALL, LEVY, LIST, MEET(ING), POLL, ROLL, GATHER, SUMMON, COLLECT, ASSEMBLE, MOBILIZE
musty   RANK, FETID, FUSTY, MOLDY, STALE
mutable   FICKLE, VARIABLE, CHANGEABLE, INCONSTANT
mutate   VARY, ALTER, CHANGE, TRANSFORM
mute   MUM, DUMB, LENE, SURD, DEADEN, MUFFLE, SILENT, VOICELESS

mutilate   MAIM, GARBLE,
MANGLE, CRIPPLE,
DISFIGURE
mutiny   RISE, REVOLT,
SEDITION, UPRISING,
INSURGENCE
mutiny, famous   CAINE, EAGLE,
BOUNTY, AMISTAD
mutt   CUR, MONGREL; see DOG
Mutt and —   JEFF
Mutt's friend   JEFF
mutter   MUMBLE, MURMUR,
GRUMBLE, COMPLAIN
mutual   JOINT, COMMON,
RECIPROCAL
muzzle   GAG, FACE, ROOT,
SNOUT, MUFFLE, SILENCE
My Fair Lady author   LOEW, SHAW
My Fair Lady character   ELIZA,
HENRY, HIGGINS, HEPBURN,
HARRISON, HOLLOWAY
Myanmar   BURMA
Myanmar, capital of   YANGON,
RANGOON
Myanmar chief   BO(H), WUN,
WOON
Myanmar city   HAKA, PAAN,
PEGU, MAGWE, TAVOY,
LOIKAW, SITTWE, YANGON,
BASSEIN, MANDALAY
Myanmar language   see
MONKHMER, TIBETO-
BURMAN
Myanmar measure   BYEE, SEIT,
TENG
Myanmar money   PYA, KYAT
Myanmar mountain   PEGU,
DAWNA, ARAKAN
Myanmar native   WA, LAI, MON,
CHIN, SHAN, KAREN,
KACHIN, BURMESE, RAKHINE
Myanmar neighbor   LAOS,
CHINA, INDIA, THAILAND
Myanmar river   MALI, LEMRO,
NIMAI, SHWELI, MYITNGE,
SALWEEN, SITTANG,
CHINDWIN, IRRAWADDY
Myanmar state   MON, CHIN,
SHAN, KAREN, KAYAH,
KACHIN, RAKHINE
Myanmar weight   MOO, VIS,
KYAT, VISS, TICAL,
ABUCCO, PEIKTHA
myrtle   AUSU, GUAVA, PENDA,
CAJEPUT
mysterious   ODD, ARCANE,
OCCULT, CRYPTIC, FURTIVE,
SHADOWY, STRANGE,
ESOTERIC

mystery   RUNE, ARCANA,
ENIGMA, PUZZLE, RIDDLE,
ARCANUM, WHODUNIT,
SACRAMENT
mystery writer   CALEB CARR,
ARTHUR CONAN DOYLE, PD
JAMES, NGAIO MARSH, REX
STOUT, DOROTHY SAYERS,
IAN FLEMING, ERLE STANLEY
GARDNER, DASHIELL
HAMMETT, RUTH RENDELL,
RAYMOND CHANDLER, ROSS
MACDONALD, GK
CHESTERTON, ELLERY
QUEEN
mystic(al)   SUFI, YOGI,
COVERT, OCCULT, SHAMAN,
SUFIST, TAOIST, CABALIC,
ESOTERIC
mystify   STUMP, BAFFLE,
STYMIE, PERPLEX, BEWILDER
mystique   AURA, CHARISMA
myth   SAGA, FABLE, LEGEND,
FICTION
mythical   FABLED, FABULOUS,
INVENTED, IMAGINARY
mythology   LEGEND, MYTHOS,
FOLKLORE; see p. 645

N

N   EN, NU, NUN, NOVEMBER
Naamah relative   REHOBOAM
nab   BAG, LIFT, NAIL, NICK,
ARREST, COLLAR, SNATCH,
CAPTURE
Nabisco brand   RITZ
nabob   NAWAB, BIGWIG,
GOVERNOR, PLUTOCRAT
Nabokov novel   ADA, DAR,
GIFT, PNIN, LOLITA,
PALEFIRE
NaCl   SALT
Na-Dene language   HAIDA,
TLINGIT, ATHAPASCAN
nadir   PITS, DEPTHS, BOTTOM,
LOWPOINT
nadir, *opp. of*   ZENITH
nag   HARRY, SCOLD, SHREW,
BADGER, HASSLE, HECTOR,
PLAGUE, HENPECK; see HORSE
Nahor relative   (B)UZ, HAZO,
ABRAM, GAHAM, HARAN,
TERAH, CHESED, KEMUEL,
MAACAH, MILCAH,
BETHUEL, JIDLAPH, PILDASH
naiad   NYMPH, OREAD

nail(s) HOB, BRAD, CLAW,
SPAD, STUD, TACK, CLOUT,
SPRIG, TALON, TENTER,
UNGUES, UNGUIS,
UNGULA(E), ACRONYX; see
NAB

naïve RAW, GREEN, CANDID,
SIMPLE, ARTLESS,
IMMATURE

naked BARE, NUDE, PLAIN,
UNCLAD, EXPOSED, INVALID

naked, run STREAK

name DUB, NOUN, ONYM,
TERM, ALIAS, CLEPE, NOMEN,
TITLE, EPONYM, AGNOMEN,
APPOINT, CACONYM,
ENTITLE, EPITHET, MONIKER,
COGNOMEN, NOMINATE

name, female ADA, ANN, ECA,
IDA, INA, MAE, ANNE, ALMA,
ANNE, DORA, ETTA, KATE,
LISA, LOLA, MARY, NORA,
VERA, ANITA, CELIA, DAISY,
ELENA, FANNY, IRENE, SALLY

name, male ABE, ELI, IAN, IRA,
PAT, ADAM, ALAN, AMOS,
CARL, DANA, DION, EMIL,
ENOS, ERIC, EVAN, EZRA,
HANS, JACK, JAKE, JOEL, JOHN,
JUDE, LEON, LUKE, MARK,
NEIL, OTTO, OWEN, PAUL,
BASIL, HIRAM, HOMER,
ALBERT, DONALD, GEORGE,
OLIVER, STEVEN, WARREN,
CHARLES

named CITED, YCLEPT,
YCLEPED, APPOINTED

nameless BASTARD,
UNNAMED, UNKNOWN,
ANONYMOUS

namely VIZ, SCIL, ID EST, TO
WIT, SCILICET, VIDELICET

name names RAT, SING

names, famous see p. 537

namesake EPONYM,
HOMONYM

Namibia, capital of WINDHOEK

Namibia city/town OPUWO,
OTAVI, OUTJO, RUNDU,
ARANOS, OSHAKATI,
REHOBOTH, WINDHOEK

Namibian desert NAMIB

Namibian money DOLLAR

Namibian mountain GAMS

Namibian people SAN, NAMA,
BASTER, DAMARA,
HERERO, OWAMBO,
TSWANA, KAVANGO,
CAPRIVIAN

Namibian river FISH, CUNENE,
ORANGE, ZAMBEZI,
OKAVANGO

Naomi relative RUTH,
MAHION, CHILION,
ELIMELECH

Nana's hero NATA

nanny NURSE

naos CELLA

nap DOZE, WINK, ZIZZ,
DROWSE, SIESTA, SNOOZE

nap, coarse GIG, RAS, PILE,
SHAG, TEASEL, TEASLE,
TEAZEL, TEAZLE

nape PALL, NUCHA, SCRUFF,
NIDDICK

Naphtali prince ENAN

napkin BIB, DIDIE, DIAPER,
SERVIETTE

Napoleon birthplace AJACCIO

Napoleon relative ELIZA,
JEROME, LUCIEN, CAROLINE,
JOSEPHINE

Napoleon's isle ELBA,
CORSICA, HELENA

Napoleon victory JENA, LODI,
WAGRAM, MARENGO,
AUSTERLITZ

Napoleonic Wars battles JENA,
NILE, EYLAU, ASPERN,
WAGRAM, LEIPZIG, MARENGO,
BORODINO, WATERLOO,
AUERSTADT, FRIEDLAND,
TRAFALGAR, AUSTERLITZ

Narcissus lover ECHO

narcotic DOWNER, SEDATIVE,
TRANQUILIZER; see DRUG

nard SALVE, OINTMENT

narrate SPIN, TELL, RECITE,
RELATE, RECOUNT,
DESCRIBE

narrative PLOT, SAGA, TALE,
STORY, ACCOUNT

narrow LIMIT, ANGUST,
REDUCE, LINEAL, STRAIT

— and narrow STRAIGHT

narrow-minded PETTY, BIASED,
BIGOTED

narthex PORCH, VESTIBULE

nary NO, NOTANY

nasal NARIAL, NARINE,
RHINAL

nascency BIRTH, ORIGIN,
GENESIS

nasty FOUL, MEAN, FILTHY,
HORRID, VICIOUS

natal INBORN, INNATE,
NATIVE

natant FLOATING, SWIMMING

nation   **LAND, STATE, PEOPLE,
COUNTRY, GENTILITIAL**
national   **CITIZEN, FEDERAL**
National Guard   **MILITIA**
National Socialist   **NAZI**
native   **ITE, RAW, SON, TAO,
BORN, NATAL, INBORN,
INNATE, DENIZEN, ENDEMIC,
NATURAL, INDIGENE;**
see p. 730
native American   **ALEUT,
INDIAN, AMERIND**
native American (Indian), prominent
**GALL, INCA, JACK, TYEE,
BANKS, GUESS, PARKER,
SACHEM, CACIQUE, CAZIQUE,
JOSEPH, SEATTLE,
GERONIMO, SAGAMORE,
SEQUOYAH, BLACKHAWK,
DULL KNIFE, CRAZY HORSE,
SITTING BULL**
native American (Indian) languages
see p. 621
native American (Indian) money
PEAG(E), PIMAN, WAMPUM
native American (Indian) tribes
see p. 730
NATO country   **ITALY, SPAIN,
CANADA, FRANCE, GREECE,
NORWAY, POLAND, TURKEY,
BELGIUM, DENMARK,
GERMANY, HUNGARY,
ICELAND, PORTUGAL,
LUXEMBOURG,
NETHERLANDS, UNITED
STATES, CZECHREPUBLIC,
UNITED KINGDOM**
natty   **CHIC, TRIM, SHARP,
SMART, SPRUCE**
natural   **RAW, BORN, CRUDE,
USUAL, INBORN, INNATE,
NATIVE, NORMAL, GENUINE,
ORDINARY, BIOLOGICAL,
UNAFFECTED**
naturalist   **GRAY, MUIR, SAKS,
BEEBE, BREHM, LINNE, PLINY,
AKELEY, CARVER, DARWIN,
FRESIA, JORDAN, MENDEL,
ANDREWS, ANIMIST,
AUDUBON, BURBANK,
DEVRIES, LAMARCK, LINDLEY,
THOREAU, BOTANIST,
LINNAEUS, BIOLOGIST**
naturalize   **ADOPT, CONVERT**
naturally   **OFCOURSE,
ARTLESSLY**
nature   **ILK, TYPE, OUSIA,
ESSENCE**
naught   **NIL, ZERO, NOTHING**

naughty   **BAD, WICKED,
WILLFUL, CONTRARY,
MISCHIEVOUS**
Nauru   **PLEASANT**
Nauru, capital of   **YAREN**
Nauru money   **DOLLAR**
nausea   **PALL, QUALM,
WAMBLE, DISGUST**
nauseate   **UPSET, REVOLT,
SICKEN**
nauseated   **PUKY, REVOLTED**
nauseating   **WAUGH,
REVOLTING, DISGUSTING**
nautical   **NAVAL, MARINE,
OCEANIC, TARRISH,
MARITIME**
nautical equipment   **HELM,
SONAR, NIGGER, TOGGLE,
CAPSTAN, COMPASS, GRAPNEL,
PELORUS, SEXTANT,
BINNACLE;** *see* **ROPE**
nautical measure   **KNOT, DEPTH**
nautical term   **AYE, AHOY,
ALEE, ALOW, ATRY, DYCE,
OHOY, ABAFT, ABEAM, MORE,
AVAST, ASTERN**
nautilus   **MOLLUSK,
ASTRONAUT**
Nautilus captain   **NEMO**
Navajo   **DINE**
Navajo dwelling   **HOGAN**
Navajo neighbor   **HOPI**
Naval Academy   **ANAPOLIS**
naval battles   **CORAL, LEYTE,
MYLAE, LEPANTO,
TRAFALGAR**
navel   **NOMBRIL, UMBILICUS**
navigate   **SAIL, PILOT, STEER,
DIRECT**
navigation aid   **BUOY, LORAN,
RACON, RADAR, SONAR**
navigator   **COOK, DIAS, ERIC,
GAMA, KEIF, ROSS, CABOT,
DRAKE, BAFFIN, BERING,
DAGAMA, HUDSON,
TASMAN, RALEIGH**
navy   **FLEET, ARMADA,
FLOTILLA, SQUADRON**
Navy mascot   **GOAT**
Nazi leader   **LEY, HESS, HITLER,
FU(E)HRER, GOERING,
HIMMLER, GOEBBELS,
HEYDRICH**
Nazi police   **SS, SIPO, KRIPO,
GESTAPO**
NCO   **SARGE(ANT), CORPORAL**
ne plus ultra   **ACME, SUMMIT**
near   **DEAR, NIGH, ABOUT,
CLOSE**

Near East country   **EGYPT, SYRIA, ISRAEL, JORDAN, TURKEY, LEBANON**

nearby   **CLOSE, ATHAND, HARDBY**

nearly   **ALLBUT, ALMOST**

nearsighted   **MYOPIC, PURBLIND**

nearsighted person   **MYOPE**

neat   **PRIM, TIDY, TOSH, TRIG, TRIM, NATTY, SOIGNE, SPRUCE**

Nebraska   *see also p. 615*

Nebraska city/town   **ORD, ALMA, BUTTE, OMAHA, PONCA, WAHOO, GERING, LINCOLN, MADISON, OSCEOLA, OSHKOSH, TEKAMAH, HASTINGS, HOLDREGE, TECUMSEH, PAPILLION**

Nebraska college   **DOANE, BELLEVUE, HASTINGS, WESLEYAN**

Nebraska Indian   **PONCA, SIOUX, WINNEBAGO**

Nebraska river   **LOUP, SNAKE, WHITE, NEMAHA, PLATTE, ELKHORN, PUMPKIN, MISSOURI, NIOBRARA**

nebula   **GALAXY, CLUSTER, SUPERNOVA**

nebulous   **HAZY, MISTY, VAGUE, CLOUDY, UNCLEAR, IMPRECISE**

necessarily   **PERFORCE, INEVITABLY**

necessary   **MUST, BASIC, VITAL, REQUIRED, ESSENTIAL, REQUISITE**

necessitate   **COMPEL, DEMAND, ENTAIL, OBLIGE, REQUIRE**

necessity   **NEED, WANT, ESSENTIAL, REQUISITE, REQUIREMENT**

neck   **PET, KISS, NUCHA, NUQUE, SPOON, CERVIX, COLLUM, SCRUFF, STRAIT, ISTHMUS**

necklace   **BAND, CARCAN, CHOKER, STRAND, TORQUE, BALDRIC, RIVIERE, SAUTOIR, CARCANET**

neckline   **DECOLLETE**

necktie party   **HANGING, LYNCHING**

neckwear   **BIB, BOA, BOW, TIE, RUFF, ASCOT, JABOT, BOWTIE, CARCAN, CHOKER,** **COLLAR, CRAVAT, TUCKER, NECKTIE, CARCANET, PEIGNOIR**

necrology   **OBIT(UARY)**

necromancy   **MAGIC, SORCERY**

necropolis   **CEMETERY, GRAVEYARD**

nectar   **AMBROSIA**

need   **LACK, WANT, PENURY, STRAIT, REQUIRE, STRAITS**

needle   **SEW, GOAD, HYPO, PROD, BODKIN, HECKLE, STYLUS, OBELISK**

— and needles   **PINS**

needle maker   **EYER**

needlefish   **GAR, PIPEFISH**

needle-shaped   **ACUATE, ACERATE, ACEROSE, ACICULAR, SPICULAR**

needlework   **SEWING, SAMPLER, EMBROIDERY, PETITPOINT**

needy   **POOR, INDIGENT, DESTITUTE**

ne'er-do-well   **LOSEL, DRIFTER, WASTREL**

nefarious   **EVIL, WICKED, DESPICABLE**

Nefertiti husband   **PHARAOH**

negate   **DENY, UNDO, CANCEL, NULLIFY, REVERSE**

negation   **VETO, DENIAL, OPPOSITE, REPUDIATION**

negative   **NAW, NEY, NIX, NON, NOT, NEIN, NOPE, NYET, MINUS**

negative ion   **ANION**

negative pole   **CATHODE**

neglect   **MISS, OMIT, SHIRK, FORGET, SLIGHT, DEFAULT**

neglectful   **LAX, REMISS, CARELESS, DERELICT**

negligee   **ROBE, (NIGHT)GOWN, PEIGNOIR**

negligent   **LAX, SLACK, REMISS, CARELESS, DERELICT**

negligible   **MINOR, SLIGHT, TRIVIAL, UNIMPORTANT**

negotiate   **DEAL, PARLE, TREAT, PARLEY, BARGAIN**

Negrito   **AETA, AKRA**

Negro   **IBO, KRU, AKIM, ALUR, EFIK, EGBA, IGBO, KROO, BANTU, BLACK, HAUSA, ETHIOP, HAUSSA, HUBSHI, NUBIAN, YORUBA**

neigh   **(W)HINNY, NICKER**

neighbor   **ABUT, TOUCH, ADJOIN, BORDER ON**

neighborhood   **AREA, REGION,**

PURLIEU, LOCALITY,
VICINITY, ENVIRONS
neighboring NEXT, NEARBY,
ADJACENT, ADJOINING
neither companion NOR
Nelson victory site NILE
nemesis BANE, CURSE,
PLAGUE, AVENGER
neophyte TYRO, NOVICE,
AMATEUR, CONVERT,
TRAINEE
neoteric NEW, MODERN,
RECENT
Nepal, capital of KATHMANDU
Nepalese city/town ILAM,
KUSMA, LAHAN, DHARAN,
MUSTANG, POKHARA,
LALITPUR, KATHMANDU,
BIRATNAGAR
Nepalese language NEWARI; see
INDIC
Nepalese money MOHAR,
RUPEE
Nepalese mountain MAKALU,
EVEREST, MANASLU,
ANNAPURNA
Nepalese neighbor CHINA,
INDIA
Nepalese people RAI, LIMBU,
MAGAR, NEWAR, BHOTIA,
INDIAN, GURUNG, SHERPA,
TAMANG, TIBETAN
Nepalese river KOSI, KUSI,
MODI, SETI, RAPTI, GANDAK,
KARNALI, KAURIALA
nephew NEVE, VASU, NEPOTE
nepotism BIAS, PATRONAGE,
FAVORITISM
Neptune LER, POSEIDON
Neptune relative OPS, CRONUS,
MEDUSA, SATURN, TRITON,
AMPHITRITE
Neptune spear TRIDENT
Ner relative ABNER
Nereus relative DORIS,
NEREID, THETIS
Nero reign year (AD 54-68) LV,
LIV, LVI, LVX, LVII, LVIX,
LVXI, LVXV
Nero relative OCTAVIA,
POPPAEA, CLAUDIUS,
AGRIPPINA
Nero victim LUCNA, SENECA
Nero Wolfe author STOUT
nerve FACE, GALL, GUTS,
BRASS, CHEEK, CRUST,
PLUCK, DARING, COURAGE,
AUDACITY, TEMERITY,
INSOLENCE

nerve cell NEURON
nerve cell process AXON(E),
NEURITE, DENDRITE
nerve layer(s) ALVEI, ALVEUS
nerve tissue GLIA, NEUROGLIA
nerves VAGI, TENIA, VAGUS,
MYELON, TAENIA,
GANGLION
nervous EDGY, JUMPY, TENSE,
FEARFUL, JITTERY, PANICKY,
SKITTISH
nervous disorder TIC, CHOREA,
ANEURIA, EPILEPSY,
NEUROSIS, PARALYSIS
nervy BOLD, BRASH, GUTSY
nest DEN, NID, AERY, BYKE,
EYRY, DRAY, DREY, NIDE,
NIDI, AERIE, NIDUS
nest egg FUND, HOARD,
STOCK, RESERVE, SAVINGS
nestle COSYUP, CUDDLE,
NUZZLE, SNUGGLE
nestling EYAS, POULT, SQUAB
Nestor SAGE, TYRO
net GIN, FYKE, KELL, CLEAR,
LACIS, SEINE, SNARE, STENT,
TRAWL, FILLET, SAGENE,
RETICLE, SPILLER
nether LOWER, UNDER
Netherlands HOLLAND; see
also DUTCH
Netherlands, capital of
THEHAGUE, AMSTERDAM
Netherlands Antilles ARUBA
Netherlands city/town EDE,
ASSEN, DELFT, GOUDA,
HAGUE, ARNHEM, LEIDEN,
ZWOLLE, HAARLEM,
UTRECHT, FLUSHING,
AMSTERDAM,
ROTTERDAM
Netherlands island TEXEL,
AMELAND, FRISIAN
Netherlands language TAAL,
AFRIKAANS
Netherlands leaders JONG,
NASSAU, BEATRIX, JULIANA,
ZIJLSTRA
Netherlands measure EL, AAM,
AUM, KAN, KOP, ZAK, DUIM,
VOET, MUDDE, ROEDE, STOOP,
BUNDER, MAATJE, MUTSJE,
STREEP, SCHEPEL
Netherlands money DOIT,
DUIT, EURO, OORD, FLORIN,
GULDEN, STIVER, DAALDER,
GUILDER
Netherlands neighbor BELGIUM,
GERMANY

Netherlands river	LEK, EEMS,	New Brunswick	ACADIA; *see*
MAAS, MARK, ROER, WAAL,			*also p. 614*
HUNSE, USSEL, MEUSE, REGGE,		New Brunswick bay	FUNDY,
RHINE, VECHT, DOMMEL		GRAND, VERTE, CHALEUR,	
Netherlands territories	SABA,	SHEPODY, MIRAMICHI	
ARUBA, BONAIRE,		New Brunswick city/town	ASTLE,
CURACAO, ANTILLES		GEARY, LORNE, MINTO,	
Netherlands weights	ONS,	DIEPPE, SHEILA, ST JOHN,	
LOOD, POND, GREIN,		JUNIPER, MONCTON,	
KORREL, WICHTJE		FREDERICTON	
netlike	MESHY, RETLARY	New Brunswick island	FOX,
nettle	BUG, IRK, VEX, FRET,	DEER, HERON, MISCOU,	
RUFFLE, IRRITATE		PORTAGE, CAMPOBELLO,	
network	WEB, MESH, RETE,	GRANDMANAN	
RETIA, PLEXUS, LATTICE		New Brunswick lake	GRAND,
network (TV)	WB, ABC, CBS,	UTOPIA, OROMOCTO	
FOX, NBC, PBS, UPN, USA,		New Brunswick mountain	BALD,
WEB, GRID, MESH, RETE,		BLUE, TODD, CARLETON,	
RETIA, PLEXUS, RESEAU; *see*		PLEASANT	
CABLE		New Brunswick river	CANAAN,
neuron part	AXON, DENDRITE	SALMON, STCROIX,	
neurotic	PHOBIC, HUNG UP,	TOBIQUE, MIRAMICHI,	
FIXATED, NERVOUS		NEPISIGUIT, RESTIGOUCHE	
neuter	DESEX, NEUTRAL,	New England state	MAINE,
SEXLESS		VERMONT, CONNECTICUT,	
neutral	PALE, DRAB, ALOOF,	RHODE ISLAND, NEW	
UNBIASED		HAMPSHIRE,	
neutralize	ANNUL, CANCEL,	MASSACHUSETTS	
DEFUSE, NEGATE, OFFSET,		New Englander	YANKEE
NULLIFY, DEACTIVATE		New Deal agency	CCC, FCA,
Nevada	*see also p. 615*	NRA, SSA, TVA, WPA, FDIC,	
Nevada city/town	ELY, ELKO,	NLRB	
RENO, EUREKA, FALLON,		New Guinea islands	AROE,
PIOCHE, LASVEGAS,		BUKA, PAPUA; *see* PAPUA	
LOVELOCK, PARADISE		NEW GUINEA	
Nevada Indian	PAIUTE,	New Guinea river	FLY, SEPIK
WASHOE, SHOSHONE		New Guinea victory	GONA
Nevada lake	MEAD, RUBY,	New Hampshire	*see also p. 615*
TAHOE, CARSON, MOHAVE,		New Hampshire, New Jersey, New	
MASSACRE		Mexico, New York information	
Nevada mountain	JOB,		*see p. 615*
KAWICH, GRANITE,		New Hampshire city/town	
WHEELER, BOUNDARY,		DOVER, KEENE, EXETER,	
CHARLESTON		NASHUA, CONCORD,	
Nevada river	CARSON,	LACONIA, NEWPORT, OSSIPEE,	
TRUCKEE, COLORADO,		ROCHESTER, MANCHESTER	
HUMBOLDT		New Hampshire Indian	ABENAKI,
never	ATNOTIME	PENNACOOK	
never-never	TIBS(EVE)	New Hampshire island	DUCK,
nevertheless	BUT, YET, STILL,	WHITE	
EVENSO, ANYHOW,		New Hampshire lake	SQUAM,
ANYWAY, HOWEVER		OSSIPEE, SUNAPEE,	
nevus	MOLE, FRECKLE,	UMBAGOG, NEWFOUND,	
LENTIGO, BIRTHMARK		NABANUSIT, WINNIPESAUKEE	
new	RAW, LATE, FRESH,	New Hampshire mountain	BLUE,
NOVEL, MODERN, RECENT,		ADAMS, WHITE, CANNON,	
NEOTERIC, ORIGINAL,		SMARTS, PROFILE, CARDIGAN,	
ADDITIONAL		KEARSARGE, MONADNOCK,	
New —	DEAL	WASHINGTON	

New Hampshire river **COLD,**
GALE, SACO, BAKER, ELLIS,
EXETER, WARNER, OSSIPEE,
ASHUELOT, MERRIMACK,
CONNECTICUT,
PISQUATAQUA, SALMON
FALLS

Newhart Show names **JERRY,**
PEEPER, POSTON, VICTOR,
PHILLIP

New Hebrides *see* **VANUATU**

New Jersey *see also p. 615*

New Jersey city/town **SALEM,**
CAMDEN, NEWARK,
HOBOKEN, PARAMUS,
TEANECK, TRENTON,
PATERSON, ELIZABETH,
PRINCETON, HACKENSACK,
JERSEY CITY

New Jersey Indian **LENAPE,**
CHEROKEE, POWHATAN

New Jersey lake **BUDD, ECHO,**
UNION, MOHAWK, OWASSA,
TAPPAN

New Jersey river **TOMS,**
BATSTO, HUDSON, RAMAPO,
WADING, MAURICE, MULLICA,
PASSAIC, PEQUEST,
RARITAN, DELAWARE

New Jersey university **RUTGERS,**
PRINCETON, SETON HALL

New Mexico **CIBOLA;** *see also p. 615*

New Mexico artists' colony **TAOS,**
SANTAFE

New Mexico city/town **MORA,**
TAOS, AZTEC, RATON,
CLOVIS, GALLUP, SANTA FE,
CARLSBAD, LAS VEGAS,
MOSQUERO, LAS CRUCES, LOS
ALAMOS, ALBUQUERQUE

New Mexico Indian **APACHE,**
NAVAJO, PUEBLO

New Mexico mountain **OSHA,**
SHIP, BLACK, BRAZOS,
GROUSE, TAYLOR, WHEELER,
MOGOLLON, WHITEWATER

New Mexico river **GILA,**
CHACO, PECOS, PUERCO,
SAN JUAN, CANADIAN,
CIMARRON, RIO GRANDE

New Testament *see p. 519*

New York City **GOTHAM,**
BIGAPPLE

New York City area **SOHO,**
BOWERY, HARLEM, TRIBECA,
EASTSIDE, FLATBUSH,
WESTSIDE, CHINATOWN,
WALL ST(REET), CONEY
ISLAND, TIMES SQUARE

New York City borough **BRONX,**
QUEENS, BROOKLYN,
RICHMOND, MANHATTAN,
STATEN ISLAND

New York City mayor **(ED)KOCH**

New York City street **WALL,**
CANAL, BOWERY, HOUSTON,
MADISON, BROADWAY

New York City subway **BMT,**
IND, IRT

New York city team **JETS,**
METS, GIANTS, KNICKS,
RANGERS, YANKEES

New York City tunnel **BATTERY,**
HOLLAND, LINCOLN,
MIDTOWN

New York *see also p. 615*

New York city/town **OVID,**
RYE, ERIE, ROME, TROY,
DELHI, NYACK, UTICA,
ALBANY, CARMEL, ELMIRA,
GOSHEN, ITHACA, OSWEGO,
BATAVIA, BUFFALO,
JAMAICA, MINEOLA, NEW
YORK, YONKERS, BREWSTER,
CATSKILL, FLUSHING,
HERKIMER, SYRACUSE,
OCEANSIDE, ROCHESTER,
COOPERSTOWN,
SCHENECTADY, WHITE
PLAINS, POUGHKEEPSIE

New York Indian **CAYUGA,**
MOHAWK, ONEIDA, SENECA,
ONONDAGA, TUSCARORA

New York island **FIRE, LONG,**
PLUM, ELLIS, STONY,
GALLOO, RIKERS, STATEN,
SHELTER, VALCOUR,
RANDALLS, GRENADIER,
MANHATTAN

New York lake **ERIE, KEUKA,**
CAYUGA, CROTON, FINGER,
GEORGE, ONEIDA, OTSEGO,
PLACID, SENECA, TUPPER,
ONTARIO, SARANAC,
ONONDAGA, SARATOGA,
CHAMPLAIN, TICONDEROGA

New York mountain **MARCY,**
POCONOS, HAYSTACK,
CATSKILLS, ADIRONDACKS

New York river **DEER, BLACK,**
TIOGA, BEAVER, CAYUTA,
HUDSON, MOHAWK,
OSWEGO, SALMON,
CHEMUNG, GENESEE,
NIAGARA, SARANAC,
STREGIS, CANISTEO,
CHENANGO, DELAWARE,
SCHOHARIE

New York team **JETS, METS, GIANTS, KNICKS, YANKEES**
New Zealand **OCEANIA**
New Zealand bay **BREAM, HAWKE, MASON, TASMAN, MERCURY, PEGASUS, HALFMOON**
New Zealand bird **KEA, MOA, TUI, HUIA, KAKI, KIWI, WEKA**
New Zealand, capital of **WELLINGTON**
New Zealand city/town **LEVIN, TAUPO, NAPIER, NELSON, TIMARU, DUNEDIN, MANUKAU, ROTORUA, AUCKLAND, GISBORNE, HAMILTON, HASTINGS, TAKAPUNA, TAURANGA, WELLINGTON**
New Zealand island **PITT, BOUNTY, SNARES, RUAPUKE, STEWART**
New Zealand lake **OHAU, HAWEA, TAUPO, TEANAU, PUKAKI, WANAKA, TEKAPO, WAKATIPU**
New Zealand language **MAORI**
New Zealand money **DOLLAR**
New Zealand mountain **COOK, EGMONT, AORANGI, TARANAKI, TARAWERA**
New Zealand river **GREY, ORETI, WAIAU, BUTLER, CLUTHA, MOHAKA, RAKAIA, WAIRAU, WAITAKI, WANGANUI**
New Zealand tree **KI, TI, AXE, AUTE, KARO, KOPI, MAHO, MAKO, MIRO, PUKA, RATA, RIMU, TAWA, TORO, TORU, TUTU, WHAU, HINAU, KAURI, MAHOE, MAIRE, MAPAU, MAPOU, TOWAI, AKEAKE, KAMAJU, KARAKA, TARATA, TOTARA, MAKOMAKO**
newborn **BABY, INFANT, NEONATE, YEANLING**
newcomer **NOVICE, ROOKIE, STRANGER, GREENHORN**
newfangled **FRESH, NOVEL, ORIGINAL**
Newfoundland *see also p. 614*
Newfoundland bay **HARE, BONNE, TABLE, WHITE, CANADA, SAGLEK, TRINITY, GROSWATER, HERMITAGE, PLACENTIA**
Newfoundland cape **RAY, PINE, RACE, STJOHN, CHIDLEY, ANGUILLE, HARRISON**

Newfoundland city/town **GANDER, WABANA, STJOHNS, LABRADOR**
Newfoundland airport **GANDER**
Newfoundland mountain **CIRQUE, THORESBY, GROSMORNE, SYLVESTER**
Newfoundland river **EAGLE, GOOSE, BRANCH, FRASER, GANDER, HUMBER, STPAUL, GILBERT, PINWARE, STLEWIS, CHURCHILL, SALMONIER**
newly **AFRESH, LATELY, RECENTLY**
newlywed **BRIDE, GROOM, BENEDICT, HONEYMOONER**
newness **NOVELTY, FRESHNESS**
news **WORD, GOSSIP, REPORT, HEARSAY, TIDINGS**
news agency **AP, UP, INS, UPI, JIJI, TASS, ANETA, DOMEI, HAVAS, KYODO, CETEKA, REUTERS**
news medium **TV, RADIO, RUMOR, GOSSIP, BULLETIN, GRAPEVINE**
newsletter **BULLETIN, CIRCULAR**
newsman **ANCHOR, REPORTER, JOURNALIST;** *see p. 542*
newspaper **RAG, DAILY, SHEET, WEEKLY, GAZETTE, JOURNAL, TABLOID**
newspaper term **OPED, ROTO, ESSAY, EXTRA, FUDGE, OBITS, SCOOP, BALAAM, BANNER, BYLINE, COLUMN, COMICS, FILLER, SPORTS, SPREAD, ARTICLE, HEADLINE, MAGAZINE, STREAMER, EDITORIAL, CROSSWORD, SUPPLEMENT**
newsperson **CUB, REPORTER, COLUMNIST, JOURNALIST**
newsstand **KIOSK**
newt **EFT;** *see* **SALAMANDER**
next **THEN, AFTER, LATER, PROCHAIN, PROCHEIN**
next to **NEAR, ALMOST, BESIDE, NEARLY**
nexus **TIE, LINK**
Niagara Falls survivors **BOYA, LEACH, TAYLOR, LUSSIER**
nib **BEAK, BILL, POINT**
nibble **EAT, NIP, BITE, GNAW, KNAB, KNAP, PECK, SNACK, MORSEL**

Nibelung	DWARF(S)		ZARIA, IKERRE, NGURU,
Nicaragua, capital of	MANAGUA		IBADAN, ILORIN, KADUNA,
Nicaraguan author	ALEGRIA		MUSHIN, OSHOGBO,
Nicaraguan city/town	LEON,		OGBOMOSHO
BOACO, RIVAS, ESTELI,		Nigerian lake	CHAD, KAINJI
MASAYA, OCOTAL, SOMOTO,		Nigerian language	EDO, IBO,
GRANADA, MANAGUA,		EFIK, HAUSA, YORUBA; see	
JINOTEPE, CHINANDEGA			KWA
Nicaraguan island	CORN,	Nigerian money	NAIRA
OMETEPE, ZAPATERA		Nigerian mountain	GOTEL,
Nicaraguan lake	MANAGUA,	DIMLANG, MANDARA	
	NICARAGUA	Nigerian park	KAMUKU,
Nicaraguan measure	SUERTE,		YANKARI
ESTAJAL, MANZANA		Nigerian people	ARO, IBO, TIV,
Nicaraguan money	CENTAVO,	IJAW, IBIBIO, KANURI,	
	CORDOBA		YORUBA
Nicaraguan mountain	MADERA,	Nigerian river	RIMA, BENUE,
MOCOTON, SASLAVA,			NIGER, KADUNA,
MOMOTOMBO, CONCEPCION			SOKOTO, GONGOLA,
Nicaraguan river	COCO, MAIZ,		KOMADUGU
MICO, WAWA, GRANDE,		niggard(ly)	CHURL, MISER,
SIQUIA, SANJUAN,		PIKER, MEAGER, SCANTY,	
ESCONDIDO			STINGY
nice	FINE, GOOD, KING,	niggle	NAG, GNAW, DOUBT,
FUSSY, CAREFUL, FINICKY,		QUALM, WORRY, FIDDLE,	
PLEASANT			TROUBLE
nicety	DETAIL, SUBTLETY	night	EVE, NOX, NYX, NATT,
niche	see NOOK		NOTT, DEATH
nick	CUT, CHIP, DENT,	night and —	DAY
NOTCH, SCORE, TALLY		night club	BOITE, DISCO,
nickel	JITNEY	BISTRO, CABARET,	
nickname	HANDLE, EPITHET,		ROADHOUSE
MONI(C)KER, PETNAME,		nightcap	HOW, COWL, BIGGIN
DIMINUTIVE, SO(U)BRIQUET		nightfall	DUSK
Nick Charles' dog	ASTA	nighthawk	BULLBAT,
Nick Charles' wife	NORA		GOATSUCKER
nicotinic acid	NIACIN	nightingale	BULBUL, THRUSH,
nifty	SMART, CLASSY,	PHILOMEL, SONGBIRD	
	STYLISH	nightmare	ALP, MARA,
Niger, capital of	NIAMEY		INCUBUS, EPHIALTES
Niger cities	BILMA, DJADO,	nightshade	MOREL, DATURA,
DOSSO, AGADEZ, MARADI,			HENBANE, PETUNIA,
NIAMEY, TAHOUA, ZINDER			SOLANUM, MANDRAKE,
Niger language	HAUSA,		BELLADONNA
DJERMA, SONGHAI		nightstick	CLUB, BILLY,
Niger money	FRANC		TRUNCHEON
Niger mountain	GREBOUN	nightwalk(er)	THIEF,
Niger neighbor	CHAD, MALI,		NOCTAMBULIST
BENIN, LIBYA, NIGERIA,		Nike	ATHENA, VICTORIA
BURKINA FASO		Nike logo	SWOOSH
Niger-Congo language	IJO,	Nike rival	PUMA, REEBOK
HAUSA, DJERMA; see GUR,		Nile	ABBAI
KWA, MANDE		Nile city/town	GIZA, QENA,
Nigeria, capital of	ABUJA	SAIS, ASWAN, ASYUT, CAIRO,	
Nigeria, former capital	LAGOS	MEROE, TANIS, TANTA,	
Nigerian cities	ABA, EDE, IFE,	THEBES, KHARTOUM,	
IWO, OYO, BAGA, KANO,			OMDURMAN
ORON, ABUJA, BENIN, ENUGU,		Nile island	RODA
GWOZA, LAGOS, NGALA,		Nile source	LAKETANA

Nile tributary	ABAY, SOBAT, ATBARA, KAGERA, BLUE NILE, WHITE NILE
nimble	YAR, DEFT, SPRY, AGILE, LISSOM, SUPPLE, VOLANT, LISSOME
nimbus	AURA, HALO, GLORIA, AUREOLA
Nimrod parent	CUSH
nincompoop	DOLT, FOOL, IDIOT, NITWIT, SIMPLETON
ninepins	KAYLES, BOWLING, SKITTLE(S)
Niobe relative	PELOPS, AMPHION, TANTALUS
Niotic language	LUO, LWO, ALUR, BARI, NUER, TESO, DINKA, LANGO, MASAI, NANDI, ACHOLI
nip	CUT, SIP, BITE, DRAM, PECK, CATCH, DRINK, PINCH, STEAL
nip and —	TUCK
nipper	KID, LAD, CLAW, TYKE, CHILD, FORCEPS, GLASSES, PINCERS, TWEEZERS
nipple	DUG, PAP, TIT, TEAT, PAPILLA
Nippon	JAPAN
nippy	COLD, BITING, CHILLY
nirvana	HEAVEN, PARADISE
niter	SALT, NATER, NITRATE, SALTPETER, SUGARSAND
nitpick	CARP, CAVIL, QUIBBLE
nitpicker	CRITIC, CAVILLER, QUIBBLER
nitrate	SALT, ESTER, NITER, SALTPETER
nitric	AZOTIC
nitrogen	AZO(TE)
nitwit	BOOB, FOOL, IDIOT, BOOBY, MORON
nix	NO, NAY, NOPE, NEGATE
nixie	FAIRY, KELPIE, NEGATE, REFUSE, SPRITE
Njorth relative	FREY
no	NAB, NAW, NAY, NIX, NOPE, NOWISE
Noah, *pert. to*	NOETIC, NOACHIAN
Noah relative	HAM, ARAM, SHEM, LAMECH, JAPHETH
Nobel prize	see p. 508
nobility	PEERS, PEERAGE, DIGNITY, GRANDEUR, ARISTOCRACY
noble	DON, DUC, SIR, DAME, DOGE, DUKE, EARL, GRAF, JARL, KAMI, KUGE, LADY, LORD, PEER, BARIN, BARON, COUNT, MURZA, THANE, DAIMIO, MILADY, RITTER, YONKER, DUCHESS, GRANDEE, HIDALGO, MARQUIS, PEERESS, BARONESS, CONTESSA, COUNTESS, MARQUISE, VISCOUNT
noble gases	NEON, ARGON, RADON, XENON, HELIUM, KRYPTON
nobody	NOONE, UNKNOWN, NONENTITY
nocturnal	NIGHT(LY)
nocturnal animal	BAT, COON, LEMUR, RATEL, TAPIR, JACKAL, WEASEL, (O)POSSUM, RAC(C)OON, TARSIER
nod	BOB, BOW, DIP, BECK, DOXE, SIGN, WINK, CONCUR, DROWSE, NUTATE, SIGNAL, SNOOZE, WAGGLE, DRIFTOFF
Nod, west of	EDEN
nodding	NUTANT, ANNUENT
node	KNOB, KNOT, LUMP, JOINT, KNUR(L), NODULE, SWELLING
nodular	LUMPY, KNOTTY, NODOSE, GNARLED, STUDDED
nodule	KNOT, LUMP, JOINT
noggin	CUP, MUG, GILL, HEAD, PAIL, PATE
no-good	KAPUT, WRETCH, WASTREL
noh actor	TOMO, WAKI, SHITE, TSURE, KOKATA, KYOGEN
noh play	KAMI, KIRK, KYOJO, OKINA, SHURA, GENDAI, KYOGEN, KATSURA, KICHIKU
noh songs	UTAI, RONGI, SASHI
— noire	BETE
noise	DIN, FLAP, ROTE, BABEL, BRUIT, CLAMOR, HUBBUB, RACKET
noisemaker	HORN, RATTLE, CLAPPER
noisome	FETID, NOXIOUS
noisy	LOUD, CLAMANT, RAUCOUS, STRIDENT
nomad	ARAB, KURD, SLEB, GYPSY, ROVER, TRAMP, BEDOUIN, SARACEN, SCENITE, ITINERANT
nomenclature	LIST, NAME, GLOSSARY, CATALOG(UE)
nominal	PAR, TOKEN, SLIGHT, TITULAR

nominate	NAME, SUBMIT, PROPOSE, SUGGEST
nomination	PROPOSAL, SUGGESTION
nominee	APPLICANT, CANDIDATE, CONTENDER
— non	SINE, QUA
non compos mentis	INSANE
nonage	INFACY, MINORITY
nonbeliever	PAGAN, ATHEIST, INFIDEL, AGNOSTIC
nonchalant	COOL, BLASE, CASUAL, OFFHAND
nonclerical	LAICAL
noncommissioned officer	CPL, NCO, CORPORAL, SERGEANT
noncommittal	VAGUE, EVASIVE, NEUTRAL
nonconformist	REBEL, BEATNIK, HERETIC, SECTARY, RECUSANT
none	NANE, NARY, NO ONE, NOT ONE, NOTHING
nonentity	NIL, CIPHER, NULITY
nonesuch	ONER, RARITY, NONPAREIL
nongypsy	GAJO
non-Jew(s)	GOI, GOY(IM), GENTILE
nonlearner	OLD DOG
non-Islamic	RAIA, RAYAH, GIAOUR, KAFFIR, ZENDIK
nonpareil	ONER, NONSUCH, PARAGON, NONESUCH, PEERLESS
nonpartisan	NEUTRAL, UNBIASED, NONALIGNED, INDEPENDENT
non-PC	SUN, IMAC, APPLE
nonplus	STUMP, PUZZLE, PERPLEX, UNNERVE, CONFOUND
nonprofessional	LAY, LAIC
nonsense	ROT, BLAH, FISH, POOH, HOOEY, TRIPE, DRIVEL, TWADDLE, FLUMMERY, FOLDEROL, MALARKEY
nonsense creature	GOOF, SMOO, GOLUK, SHMOO, SNARK, BOOJUM
nonsensical	INANE, SILLY, ABSURD, FOOLISH, IRRATIONAL, RIDICULOUS
nonstop	CEASELESS, CONTINUOUS
noodles	MEIN, FARFEL, FERFEL, LAKSHEN; *see* PASTA

nook	DEN, WRO, CANT, COVE, HERNE, NICHE, ALCOVE, CRANNY, RECESS
noon	MIDDAY, MERIDIAN
noose	LOOP, LEASH, HALTER
norm	RULE, MODEL, AVERAGE, PATTERN, STANDARD, CRITERION
Norma —	RAE
normal	USUAL, AVERAGE, REGULAR, ROUTINE, TYPICAL, HABITUAL, CUSTOMARY
Normandy capital	ROUEN
Normandy founder	ROLF, ROLLO
Normandy landing	DDAY, GOLD, JUNO, UTAH, OMAHA, SWORD
Norse gods	AESIR; *see p. 649*
Norse colony	JOMS
north(ern)	POLAR, ARCTIC, BOREAL
North America, highest point	MCKINLEY
North America, largest city	MEXICO CITY
North America, largest country	CANADA
North America, largest island	GREENLAND
North America, largest lake	SUPERIOR
North America, longest river	MISSISSIPPI
North America, lowest point	DEATH VALLEY
North Carolina, North Dakota	*see also p. 615*
North Carolina city/town	SYLVA, BURGAW, DURHAM, LENOIR, MANTEO, MURPHY, NEWTON, OXFORD, SHELBY, SPARTA, WINTON, RALEIGH, TARBORO, ASHEBORO, CARTHAGE, ASHEVILLE, CHARLOTTE, GREENSBORO
North Carolina cape	FEAR
North Carolina Indian	HALIWA, LUMBEE, SAPONI, COHARIE, CHEROKEE, MEHERRIN, WACCAMAW
North Carolina island	ROANOKE, HATTERAS
North Carolina lake	LONG, PUNGO, THORPE, CATFISH, WACCAMAW
North Carolina mountain	GUYOT, MITCHELL

North Carolina river   DAN,
HAW, TAR, NEUSE, ROCKY,
TRENT, CHOWAN, PEEDEE,
YADKIN, CAPEFEAR
North Carolina school   UNC,
DUKE, CHAPEL HILL
North Dakota city/town   MOTT,
FARGO, MINOT, ROLLA,
RUGBY, LAKOTA, MEDORA,
GRAFTON, BISMARCK,
WAHPETON, WILLISTON,
GRAND FORKS
North Dakota lake   FAN, VAN,
ETTA, LONG, OAHE, TURTLE,
DARLING, TSCHIDA
North Dakota butte   CLARK,
WHITE, SENTINEL
North Dakota Indian   SIOUX,
MANDAN, ARIKARA,
HIDATSA, CHIPPEWA
North Dakota river   RED, PARK,
GOOSE, GREEN, HEART,
JAMES, MAPLE, SOURIS,
DESLACS, MISSOURI,
PIPESTEM, SHEYENNE,
WILDRICE
North Pole discoverer   PEARY
North Sea river   DEE, TAY,
ELBE, TEES, TYNE, FORTH,
MEUSE, RHINE, HUMBER,
THAMES
North Star   POLARIS,
LODESTAR
northern   BOREAL
Northern Cross   CYGNUS
Northern Ireland   *see* IRISH
Northern Ireland capital   BELFAST
Northern Ireland city/town   DERRY,
BANGOR, BELFAST
Northern Ireland county   DOWN,
DERRY, ANTRIM, ARMAGH,
TYRONE, PAULATUK,
FERMANAGH
Northern Rhodesia   ZAMBIA
northerner   YANKEE
Northumberland river   ALN(E),
TYNE
Northwest Territories   *see also*
p. 614
Northwest Territories cape
BATHURST, MACKENZIE
Northwest Territories city/town
WHATI, DELINE, HOLMAN,
TULITA, AKLAVIK, WEKWETI,
WRIGLEY, YELLOWKNIFE
Northwest Territories island
BANKS, RICHARDS, VICTORIA
Northwest Territories river   BACK,
LIARD, THELON, MACKENZIE

Norway, capital of   OSLO
Norway, rulers of   ERIC, INGE,
OLAF, OLAV, OSCAR,
HAAKON, HARALD, MAGNUS,
SIGURD, SVERRE,
CHRISTIAN, HAARFAGER
Norwegian author   HAMSUN
Norwegian city/town   BODO,
OSLO, HAMAR, MOLDE,
SKIEN, VADSO, VARDO,
BERGEN, TROMSO, ARENDAL,
KIRKENES, STAVANGER,
TRONDHEIM, HAMMERFEST,
LILLEHAMMER
Norwegian fjord   AND, BOKA,
OSLO, VEST, FOLDA, KONGS,
SOGNE, VARANGER,
HARDANGER
Norwegian island   SOR, SENJA,
VANNA, KARMOY, KVALOY,
SOROYA, HINNOYA,
MAGEROYA
Norwegian lake   ROS, MJOSA
Norwegian language   LAPP,
SAMI, BOKMAL, NYNORSK,
RIKSMAAL, LANDSMAAL
Norwegian measure   FOT, MAL,
ALEN, MAAL, SKIEPPE
Norwegian money   ORE, KRONE
Norwegian mountain(s)   KJOLEN,
TELEMARK, GLITTERTIND
Norwegian river   OTRA, SIRA,
TANA, GLAMA, LAGEN,
REISA, DRAMSELVA
Norwegian territory   JANMAYAN,
SVALBARD
Norwegian weight   LOD, MARK,
FUND
nose   NEB, PUG, BEAK, NASUS,
SCENT, SNIFF, SNOOP,
MUZZLE
nose part   NARE, VOMER,
SEPTUM
nose, push with   NUDDLE
nose type   PUG, SNUB, ROMAN,
NASUTE, SIMOUS, AQUILINE
nosebleed   EPISTAXIS
nosegay   POSY, BOUQUET,
CORSAGE, COLLECTION
nosey   PRYING, CURIOUS,
SNOOPING, MEDDLESOME
Nosey Parker   SNOOP,
MEDDLER
nosferatu   UNDEAD
nosh   EAT, SNACK, NIBBLE,
NOURISH
nostalgia   LONGING,
MELANCHOLY,
NOSTOMANIA, HOMESICKNESS

nostrils	NARES	notoriety	FAME, INFAMY,
nostrils, of	NARIC, NARIAL,		DISREPUTE
	NARINE	notorious	ARRANT,
— Nostrum	MARE		FLAGRANT, INFAMOUS
not	NEGATIVE	notwithstanding	THO, YET,
not buy	RENT, LEASE		MAUGRE, DESPITE,
not dull	COLORFUL,		(AL)THOUGH
	INTERESTING	nought	NIL, ZERO, CIPHER,
not for	AGIN		NOTHING
not in so many words	TACIT	noun	APTOTE, GERUND,
not level	ASLANT, ASLOPE		VERBAL, SUBSTANTIVE
not long ago	OFLATE,	nourish	FEED, FOSTER,
	RECENTLY		SUCCOR
not own	RENT, LEASE	nourishing	ALMA, RICH,
not sure	RISKY, UNCERTAIN		ALIBLE, NUTRITIOUS
notable	VIP, FAMOUS,	nourishment	FOOD, MANNA,
	EMINENT, PROMINENT		ALIMENT, PABULUM,
notarize	ATTEST, CERTIFY		NUTRI(M)ENT
notary	CLERK, SCRIVENER,	nouveau —	RICHE
	SECRETARY	Nova Scotia	ACADIA; see also
notation	ENTRY, GLOSS,		p. 614
	COMMENT	Nova Scotia bay	MIRA, FUNDY,
notch	GAP, JAG, PEG, CARF,		JORDAN, MAHONE,
	DENT, DINT, KERF, NICK,		COBEQUID, CHIGNECTO,
	NOCK, CRENA, SCORE,		CHEDABUCTO
	CRENAE	Nova Scotia cape	SABLE, SPLIT,
notched	CRENATE,		BRETON, GEORGE
	SERRATE(D)	Nova Scotia city/town	CANSO,
note	IOU, CHIT, FAME, HEED,		DIGBY, MABOU, TRURO,
	LOAN, MARK, MEMO, TONE,		DEBERT, MACCAN,
	BILLET, POSTIL, RENOWN,		PICTOU, SYDNEY, TUSKET,
	APOSTIL, MISSIVE, OBSERVE,		ARICHAT, BADDECK,
	SCHOLIUM, APOSTILLE;		HALIFAX, DARTMOUTH,
	see SCALE		SHELBURNE
notebook	LOG, PAD, CAHIER,	Nova Scotia island	LONG,
	JOURNAL		BRIER, ANDREW, LAHAVE,
noted	FAMOUS, EMINENT,		MCNUTT, MOUTON, PICTOU,
	RENOWNED, CELEBRATED		SCATARIE
noteworthy	SPECIAL,	Nova Scotia mountain	EIGG,
	STRIKING, SIGNIFICANT		NUTTBY
nothing	NIL, NIX, NUL(L),	Nova Scotia river	MIRA,
	ZERO, NIHIL, CIPHER,		LAHAVE, MEDWAY, MERSEY,
	NAUGHT, TRIFLE		ROSEMAY, CARLETON,
nothing but	MERE, ONLY		ANNAPOLIS
nothing like	DISTINCT,	novel	NEW, BOOK, RARE,
	DIFFERENT		FRESH, RECENT, FICTION,
notice	SEE, CITE, HEED, MARK,		ROMANCE, STRANGE,
	CLOCK, DETECT, REGARD,		UNUSUAL; see p. 626
	REVIEW, DISCERN	— novel	DIME
noticeable	CLEAR, PLAIN,	novel necessity	PLOT,
	EVIDENT, OBVIOUS		SETTING, PROTAGONIST
notification	AVISO, ADVICE,	novelist	WRITER; see p. 624
	WARNING	novelty	FAD, NEWNESS,
notify	TELL, ALERT, ADVISE,		CURIOSITY
	INFORM, APPRISE,	novice	CUB, TYRO, ROOKIE,
	LET KNOW		ACOLYTE, AMATEUR,
notion	BEE, IDEA, VIEW,		BEGINNER, NEOPHYTE
	WHIM, CURIO, FANCY,	novitiate	NOVICE, TRAINEE,
	INKLING		NEOPHYTE, POSTULANT

now   **NOO, HERE, TODAY,
ATONCE, EXTANT, PRONTO,
PRESENT(LY)**
noxious   **FOUL, NASTY, TOXIC,
NOCENT, HARMFUL,
NOISOME, MEPHITIC**
nozzle   **JET, ROSE, VENT,
GIANT, TUYERE**
nub   **CORE, CRUX, GIST, KNOT,
LUMP, HEART**
nubile   **RIPE, ADULT, OFAGE,
MATURE, MARRIAGEABLE**
nuclear accident site   **TSURUNGA,
CHERNOBYL, TOKAIMURA**
nuclear device   **ABOMB,
REACTOR**
nuclear event   **ATEST**
nucleus   **CORE, GERM, CADRE,
HEART, CENTER, KERNEL**
nude   **BARE, NAKED, UNCLAD,
STRIPPED**
nudge   **JOG, GOAD, KNUB,
POKE, PROD**
nudist   **ADAMITE, NATURIST**
nugatory   **VAIN, FUTILE,
INVALID, USELESS,
WORTHLESS**
nugget   **HUNK, LUMP, SLUG,
CHUNK**
nuisance   **BANE, BORE, PEST,
PLAGUE, BOTHER, PLAGUE,
TROUBLE**
null   **NIL, VOID, EMPTY,
INVALID**
null and —   **VOID**
nullify   **UNDO, VETO, VOID,
CANCEL, NEGATE, REPEAL,
ABROGATE**
numb   **DULL, DEAD(EN),
FREEZE, FROZEN**
number   **LAC, LAKH, SURD,
TEEN, UNIT, COUNT, DIGIT,
STEEN, CIPHER, FIGURE,
SCALAR, ALIQUOT,
AMOUNT, COMPUTE, INTEGER**
number 2   **ASST, ASSISTANT**
numerate   **READ, TELL, COUNT,
TALLY, NUMBER**
numerous   **LOTS, MANY,
SCADS, GALORE, MYRIAD,
MANIFOLD, MULTIPLE**
Numidian city/town   **CIRTA,
HIPPO**
numskull   **DOLT, DUNCE,
MORON, NITWIT,
MEATHEAD**
nun   **CLARE, ABBESS, SISTER,
MINORESS, VOTARESS**
Nun relative   **JOSHUA**

nun's abode   **CONVENT,
NUNNERY, MONASTERY**
nun's dress   **BARB, HABIT,
WIMPLE**
nuns, order of   **MARIST,
DOMINICAN, LORETTINE,
MARYKNOLL**
Nunavut   *see also p. 614*
Nunavut city/town   **ARVIAT,
IQALUIT, IGLOOLIK,
KIMMIRUT, RESOLUTE,
NANISIVIK**
Nunavut island   **COATS,
DEVON, BAFFIN, MARBLE,
VICTORIA, ELLESMERE**
nuncio   **LEGATE**
nunnery   *see* **CONVENT**
nuptial   **BRIDAL, GENIAL,
MARITAL, SPOUSAL,
HYMENEAL, CONNUBIAL**
nuptials   **WEDDING, MARRIAGE**
nurse   **AMA, IYA, AMAH, AYAH,
BABA, EYAH, FEED, NUSS,
REAR, TEND, BONNE, NANNY,
FOSTER, SUCKLE, LACTATE,
NUTRICE**
nursery   **CRECHE, HOTHOUSE,
GREENHOUSE**
nursery furniture   **CRIB,
PLAYPEN, BASSINET,
CHANGING TABLE**
nursery rhyme characters   *see p. 630*
nurture   **FEED, REAR, RAISE,
FOSTER, CHERISH, NOURISH,
CULTIVATE**
nut   **BEN, COLA, KOLA, PILI,
ACORN, BETEL, KAROO,
LICHI, PECAN, PINON,
ALMOND, BRAZIL, CASHEW,
LICHEE, LITCHI, WALNUT,
HICKORY, LUNATIC**
Nut son   **RA**
nut(s), *pert. to*   **NUCAL**
— and bolts   **NUTS**
Nutmeg State   **CT,
CONN(ECTICUT)**
nutria   **COYPU**
nutritional, nutritive   **ALIBLE,
TROPHIC**
nutritional figure   **RDA**
nuts   **GAGA, BATTY, CRAZY,
WACKY**
nutshell   **DIGEST, CAPSULE,
OUTLINE, SYNOPSIS**
nutty   **GAGA, NUTS, BATTY,
CRAZY, MEATY, WACKY,
CUCKOO, BONKERS, HAYWIRE**
nuzzle   **NESTLE, CUDDLE,
SNUGGLE**

nylons	HOSE, SHEERS, HOSIERY, STOCKINGS
nymph	MAIA, NAIS, DRYAD, HOURI, LARVA, NAIAD, NIXIE, OREAD, SYLPH, KELPIE, NEREID, ONDINE, UNDINE, LORELEI, OCEANID, PLEIADES
nymphet	LOLITA
Nyx daughter	ERIS

O

O	ZERO, OMEGA, OSCAR, OXYGEN, OMICRON
oaf	BOOR, DOLT, GAWK, LOUT, RUBE, BUMPKIN
oafish	CRUDE, INEPT, VULGAR, BOORISH
oak	CORK, HOLM, ILEX, EMORY, ROBLE, ROBUR, CERRIS, ENCINA, DURMAST, QUERCUS
oak fruit	MAST, ACORN, CAMATA, BELLOTE
oakum, seal with	CA(U)LK
oar	ROW, BLADE, ROWER, SCULL, SWEEP, PADDLE, PROPEL
oar holder	LOCK, THOLE, POPPET, OARLOCK, ROWLOCK
oar part	LOOM, PALM, PEEL, WASH
oarsman	ROWER, STROKE, SCULLER
oasis	OJO, ELIM, WADI, WADY, DOUMA, REFUGE, SPRING
oat	AVENA, HAVER; see CEREAL
oater	WESTERN
oath	BAN, ODS, VOW, AITH, DARN, DANG, DRAT, EGAD, GOSH, HECK, LAWK, OONS, SWOW, BEDAD, BEGAD, CURSE, LAWKS, ZOOKS, CRIKEY, CRIPES, SBLOOD, ZOUNDS, SERMENT; see CRY, EXCLAMATION
oatmeal	BURGOO, PORRIDGE
oats	AVENA, GROATS
Ob tributary	KET, TOM, CHULYM, IRTYSH
obdurate	FIRM, HARD, MULISH, ADAMANT, CALLOUS, INFLEXIBLE
obeah	CHARM, FETISH, TALISMAN

Obed relative	DAVID, JESSE
obedience	DUTY, DEFERENCE, SUBMISSION
obedient	DOCILE, DUTIFUL, COMPLIANT, TRACTABLE
obeisance	CONGEE, HOMAGE, DEFERENCE; see BOW
obelisk	PYLON, NEEDLE, PILLAR, MONOLITH
Oberon's messenger	PUCK
Oberon's wife	TITANIA
obese	FAT, PLUMP, PUDGY, PURSY, PORTLY, PYRNIC, ADIPOSE, LIPAROUS, CORPULENT
obesity	FATNESS, LIPOSIS, ADIPOSIS, CORPULENCE
obey	MIND, HEED, COMPLY, FOLLOW, SUBMIT
obfuscate	DARKEN, CONFUSE, OBSCURE
obi	see SASH
obiter dictum	ASIDE, REMARK, COMMENT, OPINION
obituary	NOTICE, MEMORIAL, NECROLOGY
object	AIM, END, CARP, GOAL, ITEM, KICK, MIND, CAVIL, DEMUR, POINT, THING, INTENT, DISSENT, PROTEST, PURPOSE
object of art	CURIO, VIRTU, BIBELOT
objection	CAVIL, SCRUPLE
objectionable	VILE, HORRID, OBNOXIOUS, OFFENSIVE
objective	AIM, GOAL, TARGET, PURPOSE, DETACHED
objects, biblical	URIM, THUMMIM
objurgate	CHIDE, DECRY, BERATE, REBUKE, REPROVE, UPBRAID, CASTIGATE
oblation	OFFERING
obligate	BIND, MAKE, COMPEL, REQUIRE
obligated	FORCED, BEHOLDEN, COMPELLED
obligation	DUE, IOU, TIE, BOND, DEBT, DUTY, MUST, ONUS, PROMISE
obligatory	BINDING, REQUIRED, MANDATORY, COMPULSORY
oblige	MAKE, COMPEL, PLEASE, GRATIFY, REQUIRE
obliging	HELPFUL, COURTEOUS, ACCOMMODATING

oblique	AWRY, CANT, ASKEW, SLANT, BEVEL, SLOPT, ASLANT	obsolescence	DISUSE, ARCHAISM
obliterate	RAZE, ANNUL, EFFACE; see ERASE	obsolete	OLD, DATED, PASSE, ARCHAIC, DISUSED, OUTMODED
oblivion	VOID, LETHE, LIMBO, STUPOR, NIRVANA, FORGETFULNESS	obstacle	BAR, RUB, SNAG, HITCH, HURDLE, BARRIER
oblivious	UNAWARE, HEEDLESS, IGNORANT	obstinate	SET, HARD, MULISH, ORNERY, WILLFUL, CONTRARY, RENITENT, STUBBORN
oblong	LOZENGE, RECTANGLE, RECTANGULAR		
obloquy	ABUSE, SHAME, INFAMY, DISGRACE	obstreperous	LOUD, NOISY, UNRULY, RIOTOUS, CLAMOROUS, BOISTEROUS
obnoxious	GROSS, HATEFUL, OFFENSIVE, REPUGNANT	obstruct	DIT, DAM, CLOG, DITT, FOIL, BLOCK, CHOKE, HINDER, IMPEDE, RETARD
oboe	REED, WIND, WOOD, SHAWM, SURNAY, HAUTBOY; see p. 642		
		obstruction	HITCH, BARRIER, OBSTACLE, HINDRANCE
obscene	RAW, FOUL, LEWD, DIRTY, GROSS, COARSE, SMUTTY, NAUGHTY, INDECENT	obtain	GET, WIN, EARN, FANG, GAIN, SECURE, ACQUIRE, PROCURE
		obtund	DULL, BLUNT, DEADEN
obscure	DIM, FOG, DARK, BEDIM, CLOUD, LOWLY, MURKY, VAGUE, DARKEN, DARKLE, OCCULT, CRYPTIC, ECLIPSE, OVERSILE	obtuse	DULL, DENSE
		obverse	FACE, FRONT
		obverse, opp. of	VERSO, REVERSE
		obviate	PREVENT, WARD OFF, FORESTALL
obscurity	GLOOM, DARKNESS, ANONYMITY	obvious	OVERT, PLAIN, PATENT, EVIDENT
obsequies	WAKE, RITES, EXEQUY, FUNERAL	occasion	SELE, TIME, CAUSE, EVENT, NONCE, MOTIVE
obsequious	BOWED, ABJECT, FAWNING, TOADYING, SUBMISSIVE		
		occasional	ODD, ORBA, RARE, ANTRIN, SPORADIC
observance	RITE, RULE, CUSTOM, PRACTICE, PERFORMANCE	occasionally	RARELY, SELDOM, SOMETIMES
		Occident	WEST
observant	ALERT, VIGILANT, WATCHFUL, ATTENTIVE, PERCEPTIVE	Occident, opp. of	EAST, ORIENT
		occidental	PONENT, WESTERN, HESPERIAN
observation	REMARK, COMMENT, SCRUTINY, WATCHING, PERFORMANCE, SURVEILLANCE	occlude	SHUT, BLOCK, CLOSE, ABSORB, OBSTRUCT
		occult	HIDDEN, MYSTIC, ORPHIC, SECRET, CRYPTIC, ESOTERIC
observatory	HALE, LICK, DUNLAP, HOOKER, YERKES, AGASSIZ, CORDOBA, PALOMAR		
		occultism	MAGIC, CABALA
		occupancy	USE, TERM, TENURE, TENANCY, RESIDENCE
observe	EYE, SEE, MARK, NOTE, OBEY, SPOT, ABIDE, BEHOLD, REMARK, DISCERN, MENTION, CELEBRATE		
		occupant	INMATE, RENTEE, TENANT, RESIDENT, INCUMBENT
observer	VIEWER, WITNESS, SPECTATOR	occupation	JOB, CALL, WORK, CRAFT, TRADE, METIER, EMPLOYMENT, PROFESSION
obsess	HAUNT, FIXATE, CONSUME, PREOCCUPY		
obsession	MANIA, PASSION, FIXATION, IDEE FIXE	occupied	BUSY, ENGAGED, EMPLOYED

occupy	USE, FILL, EMPLOY, ENGAGE, ENGROSS
occur	PASS, LIGHT, APPEAR, BEFALL, BETIDE, HAPPEN
occurrence	CASE, EVENT, INCIDENT, HAPPENING
ocean	SEA, DEEP, MAIN, BRINE, ARCTIC, INDIAN, PACIFIC, ATLANTIC, ANTARCTIC; *see* SEA
oceania	MALAYA, AUSTRALIA, MELANESIA, POLYNESIA, MICRONESIA, NEW ZEALAND
oceanic	VAST, DIPS(E)Y, MARINE, PELAGIC
ocelot	TIGER (CAT), LEOPARD (CAT)
ocher	SIL, CLAY, TIVER, RADDLE, REDDLE, RUBRIC
octave	UTAS, UTIS, EIGHT
Octavia	TAVE, TAVY
Octavia's husband	ANTHONY
octopus	POLYP, POULP(E), SCUTTLE, DEVILFISH
octopus genus	POLYPUS
octoroon	METIS, MESTEE, MUSTEE
ocular	LENS, VISUAL, OPTIC(AL)
odalisque	SLAVE, CONCUBINE
odd	AWK, RUM, ORRA, DROLL, QUEER, RUMMY, AZYGO(U)S, STRANGE, PECULIAR, SINGULAR, ANOMALOUS
Odd Couple names	EDNA, JACK, TONY, FELIX, MYRNA, OSCAR, UNGER, GLORIA, LEMMON, KLUGMAN, MATTHAU, RANDALL
oddity	FREAK, QUIRK, FOIBLE, VAGARY
odd-job man	JACK, JOEY, SWAMPER
odds	CHANCES, PROBABILITY
odds and ends	ORTS, SCRAPS, REMNANTS, SUNDRIES, MISCELLANY
oder	VIADUA
Oder tributary	BOBR, NYSA, WARTA, NEISSE, KACZAWA
Odin home	VALHALLA
Odin relative	VE, BOR, TIU, TYR, FRIA, GRID, JORD, SIGI, THOR, TYRR, VALI, VILI, FRIGG, NANNA, BALDER
Odin's wolf	GERE, GERI
odious	HATEFUL, HEINOUS, LOATHSOME, REPUGNANT
odium	HATE, HATRED, DISGUST, LOATHING
odontology	DENTISTRY
odor	FOGO, FUME, NOSE, REEK, AROMA, FETOR, FUMET, NIDOR, SCENT, BOUQUET
odorless	AOSMIC, UNSCENTED
Odysseus	*see* ULYSSES
odyssey	QUEST, VOYAGE, JOURNEY, WANDERING
Odyssey author	HOMER
Odyssey character	IRUS, SIREN, ELPENOR
Oedipus relative	LAIUS, ISMENE, JOCASTA, ANTIGONE, ETEOCLES
Of Human Bondage author	MAUGHAM
Of Human Bondage character	CAREY, SALLY, PHILIP, MILDRED
Of Mice and Men author	STEINBECK
Of Mice and Men character	SLIM, CANDY, CURLY, GEORGE, LENNIE
off	AGEE, AWAY, WRONG, SKEWED
— off the old block	CHIP
off limits	TABU, TABOO, BANNED
off-the-set quarters	TRAILER
offal	GURRY, WASTE, CRUMBS, REFUSE, CARRION, GARBAGE, RUBBISH
offbase	AWOL, ON LEAVE
offbeat	ODD, KOOKY, WACKY, UNUSUAL
offend	CAG, SIN, VEX, MIFF, CHAFE, PIQUE, INSULT, NETTLE, SLIGHT, AFFRONT, OUTRAGE
offender	PERP, CULPRIT
offense	SIN, MALA, TORT, CRIME, DELICT, MALUM, WRONG, DELICT, FELONY, INSULT, UMBRAGE
offensive	RUDE, UGLY, ATTACK, ABUSIVE, IMPOLITE, INSULTING, AGGRESSIVE
offer	BID, EXTEND, TENDER, PROFFER, PROPOSE
offering	ALMS, GIFT, TRIBUTE, OBLATION
offhand	CURT, ADLIB, CASUAL, CAVALIER, INFORMAL, EXTEMPORE, IMPROMPTU

office **DUTY, POST, RANK,
BUREAU, FUNCTION, POSITION**
office, remove from **OUST,
DEPOSE, RECALL**
office station **DESK, CUBICLE**
officer **COP, ENS, NEO, EXON,
DEWAN, DIWAN, MACER,
AVENER, BAILIE, BEADLE,
DEPUTY, LICTOR, PARNAS,
TINDAL, BAILIFF, SHERIFF,
CONSTABLE**
officer, military **NCO, SGT,
MATE, MAJOR, ATAMAN,
CORNET, ENSIGN, HETMAN,
SIRDAR, YEOMAN, ADMIRAL,
CAPTAIN, COLONEL,
GENERAL, MARSHAL,
NAVARCH, PROVOST,
CORPORAL, SERGEANT,
CENTURION, COMMANDER,
COMMODORE, SUBALTERN,
LIEUTENANT**
official **KUAN, KWAN, VOGT,
EDILE, HAJIB, AEDILE,
FORMAL, SATRAP, TRIBUNE,
DIGNITARY, AUTHORIZED**
officialdom **BUREAUCRACY**
officiate **OVERSEE, PRESIDE**
officious **BOSSY, PUSHY,
INTRUSIVE, OVERBEARING**
offing, in the **AT HAND,
FUTURE, NEARBY**
offish **ALOOF**
offset **SPUR, SHOOT, BRANCH,
BALANCE, COMPENSATE**
offshoot **CON, SLIP, SPUR,
STEM, SCION, BRANCH**
offshore **ABROAD, SEAWARD**
offspring **HEIR, CHILD, ISSUE,
PROGENY**
often **ALOT, FREQUENTLY**
ogee **MOLDING**
ogle **GAZE, LEER, LOOK,
EYE(BALL), STARE, WATCH**
ogre **BOG(E)Y, DEMON, FIEND,
GIANT, TROLL, TYRANT**
ogygian **AGED, ANCIENT,
PRIMEVAL**
Ohio *see aslo p. 615*
Ohio city/town **LIMA, AKRON,
CADIZ, EATON, XENIA,
ATHENS, CANTON, CELINA,
DAYTON, ELYRIA, KENTON,
MARION, MEDINA, TOLEDO,
URBANA, BUCYRUS,
OTTAWA, POMEROY,
WAUSEON, COLUMBUS,
DEFIANCE, SANDUSKY,
CLEVELAND, CINCINNATI**

Ohio college town **ADA**
Ohio lake **ERIE, DOVER,
BERLIN, DILLON, INDIAN,
BUCKEYE, LORAMIE,
DELAWARE, PIEDMONT**
Ohio mountain range
ALLEGHENY
Ohio river **MAD, OHIO,
HURON, MIAMI, MAUMEE,
SCIOTO, TIFFIN, CHAGRIN,
HOCKING, AUGLAIZE,
CUYAHOGA, SANDUSKY,
MUSKINGUM, TUSCARAWAS**
Ohio school **KENT, KENYON,
NOTREDAME**
oil **BAY, BEN, FAT, HOP, RUE,
TIL, BALM, CADE, CHIA,
GHEE, LARD, LUBE, MACE,
NARD, OLEO, SUPA, TUNG,
ATTAR, BENNE, BRIBE, BUCHU,
IRONE, KAPOK, MADIA,
OLEUM, ORRIS, SEBUM,
TANSY, TUNNY, ACEITE,
AJOWAN, ANOINT, ASARUM,
BALSAM, CARAPA, CASSIA,
CASTOR, CETENE, COSTUS,
CURCAS, LOTION, NEROLI,
SAFROL, ARACHIS, LINSEED,
PERILLA, RAVISON,
LAVENDER; *see* FAT, GAS**
oil of — **OLAY**
oil, *pert. to* **OLEIC**
oil source **COD, TIL, PALM,
POON, RAPE, BEN(NE), OLIVE,
SHALE, ALMOND, COTTON,
PEANUT, RAMTIL, SESAME,
SOYBEAN, BLUBBER**
oilskin **SLICKER**
oily **FATTY, SLICK, GREASY,
PINGUID, UNCTUOUS**
ointment **BALM, NARD, SALVE,
CARRON, CERATE, POMADE,
UNGUENT, VASELINE**
Ojibway secret order **MIDE**
OK, okay **GO, JAKE, RIGHT,
ROGE**
OK Corral gang member **DOC,
EARP, WYATT, CLANTON,
MCLAURY**
okapi relative **GIRAFFE**
Oklahoma *see also p. 615*
Oklahoma city/town **ADA, JAY,
ALVA, ENID, HUGO, ALTUS,
ATOKA, PERRY, TULSA,
IDABEL, LAWTON, MANGUM,
NORMAN, NOWATA,
OKEMAH, POTEAU, VINITA,
WEWOKA, EUFAULA,
SAPUPA, WATONGA**

Oklahoma Indian   FOX, KAW,
OTO(E), SAG, IOWA, APACHE,
CADDO, KIOWA, MIAMI,
MODOC, OSAGE, PONCA,
YUCHI, CAYUGA, OTTAWA,
PAWNEE, PEORIA, QUAPAW,
SENECA, WICHITA, ARAPAHO,
CHOCTAW, SHAWNEE,
TONKAWA, CHEROKEE,
CHEYENNE, COMANCHE,
DELAWARE, KIALEGEE,
KICKAPOO, MUSKOGEE,
SEMINOLE, CHICKASAW,
KEETOOWAH, WYANDOTTE,
THLOPTHLOCCO

Oklahoma lake   KAW, HUGO,
EUCHA, HULAH, CANTON,
TEXOMA, WISTER

Oklahoma mountain
BLACKMESA

Oklahoma river   RED, GRAND,
BEAVER, LITTLE, NEOSHO,
WASHITA, ARKANSAS,
CANADIAN, CIMARRON,
ILLINOIS, KIAMICHI,
VERDIGRIS

old   ELD, AGED, AULD, GRAY,
WORN, ANILE, HOARY,
STALE, SENILE, ANCIENT,
ANTIQUE, ELDERLY,
OGYGIAN

old boy   CHAP

old country   EUROPE,
MOTHERLAND

Old Curiosity Shop character   NELL;
see p. 629

Old Faithful   GEYSER

old hand   PRO, VET, EXPERT,
VETERAN

old maid   SPINSTER

old sod   ERIN, IRELAND

Old Testament   see p. 515

old times   ELD, YORE,
QUONDAM

old woman   HAG, CRONE,
BELDAM, GAMMER

olden   PAST, BYGONE,
ANCIENT

old-fashioned   DATED, FUSTY,
PASSE, DEMODE, FOGRAM,
SQUARE

Oldsmobile model   ALERO,
AURORA, SILHOUETTE,
BRAVADA

old-timer   VET(ERAN)

oleaceous tree   ASH, LILAC,
OLIVE, FORSYTHIA

oleander   ROSEBAY

oleo   SPREAD, MARGARINE

oleoresin   TOLU, ANIME,
ELEMI, BALSAM

olio   MESS, OLLA, STEW,
MEDLEY, MELANGE

Oliver Twist character   see p. 629

ollapodrida   HASH, OLIO, STEW,
MEDLEY

Ollie's friend   FRAN, KUKLA

Olympian   ATHLETE, GODLIKE

Olympic events (winter)   LUGE,
HOCKEY, SKIING, CURLING,
SKATING, BIATHLON,
SKELETON, BOBSLEDDING,
SNOWBOARDING

Olympic events (summer)   RUN,
JUMP, SHOT, WALK, FIELD,
RELAY, TRACK, VAULT,
BOXING, DISCUS, DIVING,
HAMMER, HURDLES, JAVELIN,
SHOT PUT, HIGH JUMP,
LONG JUMP, MARATHON,
SWIMMING, DECATHLON, POLE
VAULT, HEPTATHLON,
STEEPLECHASE

Olympic motto words   ALTIUS,
CITIUS, FORTIUS

Olympic site (summer)   ROME,
PARIS, SEOUL, TOKYO,
ATHENS, BERLIN, LONDON,
MOSCOW, MUNICH, SYDNEY,
ANTWERP, ATLANTA, ST
LOUIS, HELSINKI, MONTREAL

Olympic site (winter)   OSLO,
NAGANO, CALGARY,
CORTINA, CHAMONIX,
GRENOBLE, SARAJEVO, ST
MORITZ

Olympic sport, former   GOLF,
POLO, ROQUE, RUGBY,
CRICKET, CROQUET, RACKETS

Olympic sport, demonstration
BUDO, BANDY, GLIDING,
KORFBALL

Oman, capital of   MUSCAT

Oman city/town   SUR, DANK,
DUQM, BARKA, HAYMA,
NIZWA, SOHAR, MASQAT,
MUSCAT, NAKHAL, RUSTAQ

Oman language   URDU, FARSI,
ARABIC, BALUCHI;
see INDIC

Oman money   GAJ, GOZ, RIAL,
GHAZI, MAHMUDI

Oman neighbor   IRAN, YEMEN,
SAUDI ARABIA

Omar Khayyam work   RUBAIYAT

— and omega   ALPHA

omen   SIGN, AUGUR, WRAITH,
AUSPICE; see PRESAGE

ominous	GRAVE, BODEFUL, FATEFUL, MENACING, SINISTER
omission	CUT, APOCOPE, DEFAULT, ELISION, SYNCOPE, OVERSIGHT
omit	DELE, DROP, PASS, SKIP, ELIDE, DELETE, EXCEPT, EXCLUDE, SLIGHT, NEGLECT
omnia vincit —	AMOR
omnibus	BUS, COACH, READER, ANTHOLOGY, COLLECTION
omnipresent	UNIVERSAL, UBIQUITOUS
on	AT, BY, ATOP, UPON, ABOVE, ONWARD, FORWARD, HAPPENING
on pins and needles	TENSE, NERVOUS
on tap	NEXT, TOCOME
on the —	LAM, OUT(S), CUFF, SKIDS
— on the market	DRUG
on the rocks	ICED, FAILED, RUINED, AGROUND, WRECKED
on time	SHARP, PROMPT, PUNCTUAL(LY)
Onassis yacht	CHRISTINA
once	ANCE, ANES, ERST, WHILOM, QUONDAM; see FORMER
once more	AGAIN, AFRESH, ENCORE
once-over	SCAN, GLANCE, REVIEW, SURVEY, SCRUTINY
oncoming	NEARING, LOOMING, APPROACHING
one	ACE, AIN, UNI, MONO, UNIT(ED)
O'Neill character	ANNA, DION, EBEN, ABBIE, JONES
O'Neill relative	OONA, CHAPLIN, CHARLIE
one-piece suit	SARONG
oner	LULU, RARITY, RARA AVIS
onerous	HEAVY, TEDIOUS, BURDENSOME
one-sided	BIASED, PARTIAL
ongoing	CURRENT, CONTINUING
onion	CEPA, CIVE, LEEK, CHIVE, CIBO(U)L, SHALLOT, ESCHALOT, SCALLION
onion genus	ALLIUM
online forum terms	QM, POST, HANDLE, MESSAGE
onlooker	WATCHER, WITNESS, BYSTANDER, SPECTATOR
only	BUT, LONE, MERE, SAVE, SOLE, SIMPLY
onomatopoetic	ECHOIC, IMITATIVE
onrush	BIRR, RUSH, WAVE, SURGE, STAMPEDE
onset	START, ATTACK, ASSAULT, OUTBREAK
onslaught	RUSH, DRIVE, ATTACK, ASSAULT, OFFENSIVE
Ontario	see also p. 614
Ontario city/town	PERTH, BARRIE, GUELPH, LONDON, OTTAWA, PICTON, SARNIA, SIMCOE, WHITBY, COBOURG, NAPANEE, PAISLEY, SUDBURY, TORONTO, WINDSOR, HAMILTON, KINGSTON, ETOBICOKE, KITCHENER, STRATFORD
Ontario island	PARRY, BARRIE, AMHERST, TORONTO, WALPOLE, COCKBURN, CHRISTIAN, FLOWERPOT
Ontario lake	ERIE, SEUL, EAGLE, HURON, RAINY, RIDEAU, SIMCOE, ABITIBI, MUSKOKA, NIPIGON, ONTARIO, KAWARTHA, NIPISSING
Ontario river	DON, GRAND, HUMBER, MOOSE, TRENT, ALBANY, OTTAWA, RIDEAU, SEVERN, THAMES, ENGLISH, ST LAWRENCE
onto	ON, HEP, AWARE, WISETO
onward	AHEAD, FORTH, FORWARD
onyx	NICOLO; see CHALCEDONY
oodles	LOTS, PILES, HEAPS, LOADS, SCADS
oomph	VIGOR
ooze	MUD, FLOW, GOOK, LEAK, MIRE, SEEP, SEIP, SIPE, SYPE, EXUD(AT)E, GLEET, SLIME, SLUDGE, SEDIMENT
opaque	DULL, DENSE, OBSCURE, DIFFICULT
open	AJAR, FREE, AGAPE, BARED, FRANK, OVERT, UNTIE, BROACH, CANDID, EXPOSED, HONEST, PATENT, PUBLIC, UNLOCK, UNSEAL, VACANT, LIBERAL

open-and-shut **CLEAR, EVIDENT, OBVIOUS**
open — policy **DOOR**
openhearted **FRANK, CANDID, CORDIAL, GENEROUS**
open-minded **TOLERANT, UNBIASED, RECEPTIVE**
opener **PRY, SESAME, CHURCHKEY**
opening **BUR, GAP, BOLE, BORE, BURR, HOLE, PORE, RIFT, RIMA, SLIT, SLOT, VENT, CLEFT, GRIKE, SINUS, STOMA, CAVITY, EYELET, GAMBIT, HIATUS, MEATUS, FORAMEN, ORIFICE, STOMATA**
opera composer **BIZET, VERDI, GOUNOD, HANDEL, MOZART, WAGNER, MENOTTI, PUCCINI, ROSSINI, SMETANA, STRAUSS, MASSENET, HUMPERDINCK**
opera, famous **AIDA, FAUST, LAKME, MANON, NORMA, THAIS, TOSCA, CARMEN, ERNANI, OTELLO, RIENZI, SALOME, ELEKTRA, FIDELIO, WOZZECK, ARABELLA, FALSTAFF, TRAVIATA, TURANDOT, BUTTERFLY, CAPRICCIO, DONCARLOS, RIGOLETTO, TROVATORE, ROSENKAVALIER**
opera hat **GIBUS, TOPPER**
opera house **MET, LYRIC, (LA) SCALA, (LA) FENICE, GARNIER, COVENT GARDEN, METROPOLITAN**
opera singers *see p. 543*
opera star **DIVA, DIVO**
operate **RUN, WORK, MANAGE, CONDUCT**
operation **ACT(ION), PROCESS, SURGERY, VENTURE, BUSINESS, MANEUVER**
operative **SPY, AGENT, RUNNING, WORKING, FUNCTIONAL**
operetta composer **FRIML, LEHAR, HERBERT, ROMBERG, STRAUSS, SULLIVAN, OFFENBACH**
Ophelia relative **LAERTES, POLONIUS**
Ophelia's love **HAMLET**
ophidian **ASP, COBRA;** *see p. 671*
opiate **DRUG, NARCOTIC, SEDATIVE, ANALGESIC**
opine **HOLD, THINK, BELIEVE**

opinion **DOOM, DOXY, IDEA, VIEW, CREDO, TENET, BELIEF, NOTION, OUTLOOK, JUDGMENT**
opinionated **BIASED, BIGOTED, DOGMATIC, PREJUDICED**
opium derivative **HEROIN, CODEINE, MORPHINE**
opium source **POPPY**
opossum **QUICA, YAPO(C)K;** *see* **MARSUPIAL**
opponent **FOE, ANTI, ENEMY, RIVAL, ADVERSARY**
opportune **APT, TIMELY, APROPOS, AUSPICIOUS**
opportunist **INVESTOR, ENTREPRENEUR**
opportunity **HENT, BREAK;** *see* **CHANCE**
oppose **BUCK, DEFY, FACE, CROSS, IMPUGN, OPPUGN, CONTEST, COUNTER, DISSENT**
opposed **ANTI, AVERSE, AGAINST**
opposite **ANTI, POLAR, CONTRA, COUNTER, FORNENT, ANTIPODE, CONTRARY, CONVERSE, ANTIPODAL**
opposition **FOE, RIVAL, ENEMY, HOSTILITY, RESISTANCE**
oppress **CRUSH, WEIGH, BURDEN, MOLEST, AFFLICT, HARRASS, TROUBLE, KEEPDOWN, SUBJUGATE**
oppressive **HOT, CLOSE, CRUEL, HARSH, HUMID, MUGGY, CRUSHING, STIFLING, TYRANNICAL**
oppressor **BULLY, TYRANT**
opprobrious **ABUSIVE, MALICIOUS, DEROGATORY, SCURRILOUS**
opprobrium **ODIUM, INFAMY, OBLOQUY**
oppugn **OPPOSE, DISPUTE, CRITICIZE, CONTROVERT**
Ops relative **ZEUS, CERES, SATURN, POSEIDON**
opt **PICK, GO FOR, CHOOSE, SELECT**
optical **OCULAR, VISUAL**
optical illusion **MIRAGE**
optical instrument **LENS, PRISM, ALIDADE, ERIOMETER, BINOCULAR, PERISCOPE, TELESCOPE, MICROSCOPE**
optimism **HOPE, CONFIDENCE**

optimist	DREAMER, IDEALIST, POLLYANNA	ordeal	TEST, CROSS, TRIAL, TORMENT, CRUCIBLE
optimistic	ROSY, UPBEAT, HOPEFUL, ROSEATE, SANGUINE	order	BID, LINE, FIAT, HEST, RANK, SALE, SORT, TELL, WRIT, ALINE, ARRAY, EDICT,
optimum	BEST, PRIME, CHOICE, FINEST		LODGE, SERIES, BEHEST, ENJOIN, EUTAXY, METHOD,
option	VOTE, CHOICE, ELECTIVE, ALTERNATIVE		SYSTEM, ARRANGE, COMMAND, SEQUENCE,
optional	ELECTIVE, VOLUNTARY	order, sacred	STABILITY JESUIT,
opulent	RICH, LAVISH, WEALTHY, LUXURIOUS		CARMELITE, FRANCISCAN, BENEDICTINE
opus	WORK, COMPOSITION	order of merit	AVIZ, BATH,
oracle	SEER, AUGUR, DELOS, SIBYL, DELPHI, SPHINX, DELPHOS		VASA, CROWN, SWORD, ALBERT, CHRIST, STOLAF, LEOPOLD, STLOUIS
oracular	VATIC, ORPHIC, PROPHETIC, SYBILLINE	orderly	AIDE, NEAT, TIDY, SPRUCE, LOGICAL, REGULAR,
oral	ALOUD, PAROL, VOCAL, PAROLE, SPOKEN, VERBAL, STOMATIC		OBEDIENT, METHODICAL
orally	OUT LOUD, VIVA VOCE	ordinal number	see p. 582
orange	MOCK, CHINO, HEDGE, NAVEL, OSAGE, MANDARIN, VALENCIA, TANGERINE	ordinance	LAW, CANON, EDICT, ASSIZE
Orange Bowl site	MIAMI	ordinary	USUAL, COMMON, NORMAL, AVERAGE, EVERYDAY; see TAVERN
orangutan	see APE	ordnance	GUNS, ARMS,
orate	TALK, SPEAK, ADDRESS, DECLAIM		ARMOR, WEAPONS, WEAPONRY, ARTILLERY
oration	SPEECH, ADDRESS, LECTURE	ordure	DUNG, FILTH, MANURE, EXCREMENT
orator	CATO, OTIS, BRYAN, HENRY, CICERO, LYSIAS, RHETOR, CUSHING, EVERETT, SPEAKER	ore	see MINERAL
		Oregon	see also p. 615
		Oregon city/town	BEND, MORO, VALE, BAKER, BURNS, SALEM, EUGENE, FOSSIL,
oratorio	ELIJAH, ST PAUL, MESSIAH, SEASONS		HEPPNER, MEDFORD, COQUILLE, PORTLAND
oratory	CHAPEL, CHANTRY	Oregon dam	OXBOW, MCNAY, OWYHEE
orb	EYE, GLOBE, PLANET, SPHERE	Oregon lake	CRUMP, GUANO,
orbit	PATH, AMBIT, CYCLE, DOMAIN, CIRCUIT		ALBERT, ALVORD, CRATER, HARNEY, OWYHEE, SILVER,
orbit point	APSE, APSIS, APOGEE, PERIGEE		SUMMER
orchard	TOPE, GROVE	Oregon mountain(s)	BLUE, HOOD, CASCADE, KLAMATH,
orchestra	PIT, BAND, PARQUET, ENSEMBLE, SYMPHONY, PHILHARMONIC		WALLOWA, SISKIYOU, THIELSEN, THREE SISTERS
orchestra section	BRASS, REEDS, TRAPS, WINDS, STRINGS, WOODWINDS, PERCUSSION; see p. 642	Oregon river	ROGUE, SNAKE, WALDO, OWYHEE, SILVER, UMPQUA, CROOKED, JOHNDAY, MALHEUR, NEHALEM, SILVIES, COLUMBIA, UMATILLA,
orchestrate	SCORE, ARRANGE		WILLAMETTE
orchid	DISA, FAHAM, SALEB, SALEP, SATYR, VANDA, DICHEA, POGONIA, EPIPHYTE	Oregon tribe	COOS, KUSAN, MODOC, YANAN, CAYUSE, CHINOOK, NEZPERCE
ordain	ENACT, FROCK, ORDER, DECREE, INVEST, APPOINT	Orestes friend	PYLADES

Orestes relative	ELECTRA, HERMIONE, AGAMEMNON, IPHIGENIA	origin	BUD, GERM, SEED, OUTSET, SOURCE, GENESIS, BEGINNING
organ	CALLIOPE	original	NEW, FIRST, FRESH, MCCOY, NOVEL, FONTAL, UNIQUE, PRISTINE
organ, body	see p. 502		
organ control	KNOB, STUD, PEDAL, PISTON, TABLET, COUPLER, DRAWKNOB	original sin	ADAM
		originally	ERST, FIRST(LY), AT FIRST, INITIALLY
organ division	ECHO, SOLO, ALTAR, CHOIR, GREAT, PEDAL, SWELL, CHANCEL, GALLERY, ANTIPHONAL	originate	(A)RISE, STEM, BEGIN, START, CREATE, INVENT
		originator	AUTHOR, FATHER, MOTHER, CREATOR, INVENTOR
organ part	BOX, PIPE, WIND, ACTION, PALLET, ROLLER, SLIDER, CONSOLE, SHUTTER, TRACKER	Orinoco tributary	ARO, META, APURE, CAURA, CARONI, VICHADA, GUAVIARE
organ stop	OBOE, SEXT, TERZ, GAMBA, NASAT, QUINT, VIOLA, DOLCAN, GEDEKT, MIXTUR, MONTRE, NASARD, SCHARF, TIERCE, AEOLINE, BASSOON, BOURDON, CELESTA, LARIGOT, MELODIA, MIXTURE, POSAUNE, RACKETT, SUBBASS, TERTIAN, TREMOLO, BOMBARDE, DIAPASON, DULCIANA, GEMSHORN, PRESTANT, REGISTER, KRUMMHORN, NACHTHORN, PRINCIPAL, UNDAMARIS, WALDFLOTE	oriole	PIROL, LORIOT, FIREBIRD, TROUPIAL
		oriole genus	CACICUS, ICTERUS
		Orion	HUNTER, ALGEBAR
		Orkney island	HOY, POMONA, ROUSAY, SANDAY, STRONSAY, RONALDSAY, SHAPINSAY
		Orleans heroine	JOAN(OFARC)
		ornament	EPI, BOSS, DECK, FRET, OUCH, STUD, DECOR, GUTTA, SPANG, AMULET, BEDECK, EMBOSS, FINIAL, SCROLL, EPAULET, ROSETTE, SPANGLE, EPAULETTE
organic	WHOLE, NATURAL, INHERENT, FUNDAMENTAL		
organism	BODY, ECAD, AMEBA, MONAD, MONAS, ZOOID, AMOEBA		
		ornamental	SHOWY, DAHLIA, ORNATE, DECORATIVE
organist	BACH, BIGGS, WALCHA	ornate	FANCY, SHOWY, FLORID, BAROQUE
organization	CLUB, CADRE, MORIM, SETUP, OUTFIT, SOCIETY	ornery	MEAN, TESTY, MULISH, STUBBORN
		ornithologist, famous	AUDUBON
organize	FORM, SETUP, SETOUT, ARRANGE, CLASSIFY, ESTABLISH	orotund	ROUND, POMPOUS, RESONANT, BOMBASTIC
		Orpah husband	CHILION
orgy	BASH, BINGE, SPREE, CAROUSAL	orphan	WAIF, STRAY, URCHIN
		orphan, famous	ANNIE
Orient	ASIA, EAST, LEVANT, FAR EAST	orphanage	ASYLUM
		Orpheus instrument	LYRE
orient	ADAPT, ADJUST, FAMILIARIZE	Orpheus relative	APOLLO, OEAGRUS, CALLIOPE, EURYDICE
oriental	ASIAN, EASTER, ORTIVE, EASTERN, LEVANTINE	ort	CRUMB, SCRAP
		orthodox	PROPER, CANONIC, ACCEPTED, MAINSTREAM
orientate	ADJUST, FAMILIARIZE		
orientation	COURSE, DIRECTION, ADJUSTMENT	Oscar winners	see p. 505
		Oscar category	EDITING
orifice	MAW, HOLE, LURA, PORE, MOUTH, STOMA, OPENING, OSTIOLE	oscillate	WAG, SWAY, WAVE, SWING, ALTERNATE, FLUCTUATE

oscine *see* SONGBIRD
osculate BUSS, KISS
osier WAND, SALLOW, WILLOW, DOGWOOD
Osiris relative NUT, SET, ATEF, ISIS, HORUS, ANUBIS
OSS successor CIA
ossuary URN, VAULT
ostensible ALLEGED, SEEMING, APPARENT
ostentation POMP, ECLAT, GLOSS, STRUT, PARADE, DISPLAY, SHOWINESS
ostentatious GAUDY, SHOWY, BRAZEN, FLAMBOYANT
ostracism EXILE, BARRING, BANISHMENT
ostracize BAR, SHUN, SNUB, BANISH, EXCLUDE
ostrich relative MOA, CASSOWARY
Ostrogoth *see* GOTH
Otello composer VERDI, ROSSINI
Othello character IAGO, BIANCA, CASSIO, EMILIA, MONTANO, RODERIGO, BRABANTIO, DESDEMONA
other NEW, ELSE, EXTRA, ADDED, ALTERNATE, DIFFERENT
otherwise ELSE, IFNOT
otic AURAL, AUDITORY
otiose IDLE, LAZY, FUTILE, USELESS, INDOLENT
otter PARAVANE; *see* MAMMALS, AQUATIC
otter-like LUTRINE
ottoman POUF, TURK, HASSOCK
Ottoman court PORTE
Ottoman governor BEY
ouch CLASP, BROOCH
Our Gang character PETE, DARLA
Our Mutual Friend character WEGG; *see* p. 629
Our Miss Brooks names EVE, GALE, GENE, ARDEN, CLINT, GORDON, OSGOOD, WALTER, CONKLIN, HARRIET
oust EJECT, EVICT, EXPEL, BOUNCE, DEPOSE, CASHIER
out UIT, AWAY, EXIT, ALIBI, FORTH, PASSE, EGRESS, ESCAPE, EXCUSE
out of date PASSE, STALE, DEMODE
out of place INAPT, UNSEEMLY

out of sorts MOODY, GRUMPY, PEEVED
out of the blue ABRUPTLY, SUDDENLY, UNEXPECTEDLY
out of the ordinary RARE, UNUSUAL
out of town AWAY
out-and-out RANK, SHEER, UTTER, ARRANT, ABSOLUTE, COMPLETE, DOWNRIGHT
outage BREAK, INTERVAL, BLACKOUT, BROWNOUT
outbreak RASH, EMEUTE, BOUTADE, ERUPTION
outbuilding BARN, SHED, GARAGE, OUTHOUSE
outburst GUST, FLARE, SPATE, STORM, FLAREUP, ERUPTION
outcast (Y)ETA, EXILE, HAGAR, LEPER, NOLAN, RONIN, PARIAH, ISHMAEL, CHANDALA
outclass BEST, EXCEL, OUTDO, SURPASS
outcome END, ISSUE, RESULT, UPSHOT, PRODUCT
outcry DIN, HUE, ROW, GAFF, YELP, CLAMOR, DIRDUM, HUBBUB, POTHER, UPROAR
outdated PASSE, DEMODE
outdo CAP, TOP, BEAT, BEST, EXCEL, SURPASS
outdoor OPENAIR, AL FRESCO
outer ECTAL, FOREIGN, EXTERIOR
outermost LAST, FINAL, EXTREME, FARTHEST
outfit KIT, RIG, GRAB, GEAR, SUIT, UNIT, GETUP, EQUIP, REGALIA, CAPARISON
outflank BYPASS, OUTWIT, THWART
outflow LOSS, EFFLUX, ESCAPE, HEMORRHAGE
outgo EXPENDITURE
outgoing FRIENDLY, SOCIABLE, EXTROVERT, GREGARIOUS
outgrowth RESULT, PRODUCT, OFFSHOOT
outhouse SHED, PRIVY, LATRINE
outing LARK, TRIP, JAUNT, EXCURSION
outlandish ALIEN, OUTRE, EXOTIC, STRANGE, BIZARRE
outlast OUTLIVE, OUTWEAR
outlaw BAN, RONIN, BANDIT, BRIGAND, PROHIBIT, PROSCRIBE, DESPERADO

outlay	COST, FUND, SPEND, EXPENSE	ovation	PRAISE, ACCLAIM, PLAUDIT, APPLAUSE
outlet	EXIT, VENT, STORE, EGRESS, SOCKET, BRANCH	oven	IMU, OON, UMU, KILN, LEER, LEHR, OAST, TILER, HIBACHI
outline	DRAW, LIMN, SHAPE, TRACE, SCHEMA, SKETCH, CONTOUR, PROFILE, SUMMARY, SILHOUETTE	over	OER, ATOP, DONE, ABOVE, AGAIN, ENDED, ACROSS, UNDULY, SURPLUS
outlive	SURVIVE	over and —	ABOVE
outlook	VIEW, SCOPE, STANCE, VISTA, PURVIEW	Over There composer	COHAN
		overabundance	EXCESS, SURPLUS, PLETHORA
outlying	REMOTE, DISTANT	overact	HAM, EMOTE, OUTDO
outmoded	DATED, PASSE, DESUETE	overacting	HISTRIONICS
outpost	FORT, PICKET, SENTRY, SETTLEMENT	overage	EXTRA, EXCESS, TOOOLD, SURPLUS
outpouring	FLOOD, SPATE, TORRENT	overall	LARGELY, GENERALLY, ONTHEWHOLE
output	CROP, YIELD, HARVEST, PRODUCTION	overalls	JEANS, LEVIS, DUNGAREES
outrage	ABUSE, AFFRONT, INJURY, INSULT, OFFENSE, ATROCITY	overbearing	BOSSY, ARROGANT, IMPERIOUS, DOMINEERING
outrageous	GROSS, FLAGRANT, SHAMEFUL, SHOCKING	overcast	SEW, GRAY, CLOUDY, DREARY, GLOOMY, LOWERING
outré	BIZARRE, ECCENTRIC, EXTRAVAGANT	overcharge	CHEAT, GOUGE, SCALP, STING, FLEECE, SWINDLE
outrigger	PRAU, PROA; see VESSEL		
outright	TOTAL, UTTER, ABSOLUTE	overcoat	BENJY, BENNY, CAPOT(E), RAGLAN, ULSTER, PALETOT, SPENCER, SURTOUT, BENJAMIN, BALMACAAN, GREATCOAT
outset	GETGO, START, BEGINNING, INCEPTION		
outshine	ECLIPSE, SURPASS		
outsider	ALIEN, STRANGER, FOREIGNER	overcome	BEAT, BEST, DEFEAT, MASTER, SUBDUE, TROUNCE
outskirts	(SU)BURBS, ENVIRONS	overconfident	BRASH, COCKSURE
outsmart	BEST, OUTFOX, OUTWIT	overcrowded	CONGESTED, GRIDLOCKED
outspoken	OPEN, BLUNT, FRANK, CANDID	overdo	EXCEED, EXHAUST, EXAGGERATE
outstanding	DUR, GREAT, OWING, UNPAID, TERRIFIC, EXCEPTIONAL	overdue	ARREAR, REMISS, UNPAID
		overeat	GORGE, STUFF, GLUTTONIZE, OVERINDULGE
outstretched	WIDE, PRONE		
outstrip	BEST, OUTDO, BETTER, SURPASS	overfill	SATE, BURST, STUFF
outward	ECTAD, VISIBLE, EXTRINSIC	overflow	DEBORD, SURPLUS; see FLOOD
outwit	FOIL, EUCHRE, OUTSMART	overhang	JUT, LOOM, EAVES, BEETLE
outwork	TENAIL, LUNETTE, RAVEUN	overhaul	REDO, REFIT, REPAIR, SERVICE, OVERTAKE, REFURBISH
oval	ELLIPTICAL, EGGSHAPED		
ovary	GONAD	overhead	ABOVE, ALOFT, COSTS, UPKEEP
ovary wall	EPICARP, ENDOCARP, PERICARP		
		overindulge	GLUT, SATE

overjoy	ELATE, DELIGHT
overlap	COINCIDE, IMBRICATE
overlay	LAP, CEIL, PAVE
overlook	MISS, OMIT, SKIP, IGNORE, REVIEW, SURVEY, CONDONE, NEGLECT
overlord	BAN, LIEGE, SUZERAIN
overly	TOO(MUCH), TOEXCESS
overpass	SPAN, BRIDGE, EXCEED, VIADUCT
overpower	DEFEAT, SUBDUE, CONQUER
overreach	CHEAT, OUTDO, OUTWIT, GO TOO FAR
override	NULLIFY, REVERSE
overrule	VETO, ANNUL, CANCEL, REVERSE, OVERRIDE, PULLRANK
overrun	FLOOD, INFEST, INVADE
overseas	ABROAD, FOREIGN
overseas broadcasting service	VOA
oversee	RUN, DIRECT, MANAGE, SUPERVISE
overseer	BOSS, CORK, BAILIFF, CAPORAL, MANAGER, STEWARD
overshadow	DIM, ECLIPSE, OBSCURE, DOMINATE, OUTWEIGH
overshoe	ARCTIC, GALOSH, PAITEN, RUBBER
oversight	ERROR, LAPSE, CONTROL, OMISSION, SUPERVISION
overstate	BLOWUP, OVERPLAY, EXAGGERATE
overt	OPEN, PUBLIC, BLATANT, EXPLICIT
overtake	PASS, CATCH(UP), OVERHAUL
overthrow	UPSET, DEPOSE, TOPPLE, UNSEAT, REVERSE
overtone	HINT, SUGGESTION, IMPLICATION
overture	BID, OFFER, ADVANCE, PRELUDE
overturn	ANNUL, UPEND, UPSET, CAPSIZE, REVERSE
overweening	ARROGANT, CONCEITED
overweight	FAT, OBESE
overwhelm	BEAT, CRUSH, DEFEAT, SWAMP, DELUGE
overwhelming	VAST, IRRESISTIBLE, OVERPOWERING
overwrought	TENSE, NERVOUS, STRESSED
Ovid birthplace	SULMO(NA)
Ovid work	AMORES, METAMORPHOSES
ovule, ovum	EGG, SEED, EMBRYO
owing	DUE, UNPAID, PAYABLE
owl	LULU, MOMO, RURU, MADGE, OWLET, PADGE, BOOBOOK, HOWLET, HULLET, MOPOKE, WOOLERT, MOREPOKE
Owl and the Pussycat author	LEAR
owl genus	BUBO, TYTO, KETUPA, NYCTEA
owl, young	OWLET
own	HAVE, HOLD, NANE, ADMIT, CONFESS, POSSESS
owner	HOLDER, LANDLORD, PROPRIETOR
ownership	TITLE, RIGHTS, TENURE, POSSESSION
ox	YAK, ANOA, BUCK, BUFF, BULL, CALF, DOGY, GAUR, MOIL, NEAT, OUSE, QUEY, TORO, URUS, ZEBU, BISON, BOBBY, BOSSY, CAURE, DOGIE, GAYAL, GYALL, STEER, BANTIN, BHARAL, BOVOID, BUFFLE, BURHEL, HUMLIE, NAHOOR, SARLAK, SARLYK, TAURUS, WISENT, AUROCHS, BANTENG, BUFFALO, BULLOCK, BURRHEL, TAURINE
ox genus	DOS, OVIBOS
oxen	KINE, NOWT
Oxford	OXON, BROGAN
Oxford fellow	DON
Oxford library	BODLEIAN
Oxford scholarship	RHODES
Oxford student	OXONIAN
oxide	CALX
oxidize	RUST, CALCINE, CORRODE
oxygen	OXID(E), OZONE
oxygen radical	OXYL
oyes, oyez	HEAR (YE)
oyster	SPAT, CHAMA, ANOMIA, CULTCH, HUITRE, SHARPER, SPONDYL
oyster bed material	CULCH, CU(L)TCH
oyster farm	PARK, CLAIRE
Oz	see WIZARD OF OZ
Oz station	HBO
Ozzie and Harriet names	RICK, DAVID, NELSON

P

P	PI, PEE, PAPA, PIANO
pace	RATE, STEP, TEMPO; *see* GAIT
pachyderm	HIPPO, RHINO, ELEPHANT
pacific	CALM, (E)IRENIC, PEACEFUL, TRANQUIL
Pacific battle site	GUAM, WAKE, SAIPAN, IWOJIMA
Pacific discoverer	BALBOA
Pacific island	YAP, GUAM, TRUK, WAKE, PALAU, MIDWAY, SAIPAN, TAHITI, ADMIRALTY; *see* p. 603
Pacific island group	COOK, SAMOA, AUSTRAL, GILBERT, LOYALTY, SOLOMON, CAROLINE, HAWAIIAN, MARIANAS, MARSHALL, MARQUESAS, MICRONESIA
Pacific islands language	BUGI, MORO, AKLAN, BATAK, BIKOL, MALAY, MAORI, BISAYA, CEBUAN, HANTIK, IGOROT, MANGAR, TAGALA, BISAYAN, CEBUANO, ILOCANO, TAGALOG, VISAYAN, ACHINESE, BALINESE, BUGINESE, JAVANESE, HAWAIIAN, MADURESE, MALAGASY, PAMPANGA, PAMPANGO, PAMPANGAN, SUNDANESE, HILIGAYNON, INDONESIAN, MELANESIAN, POLYNESIAN, SAMARLEYTE
pacifier	SOP, RING, FRIEND, NIPPLE, TEETHER, TEETHING RING
pacifist	DOVE, PEACENIK
pacify	*see* CALM
pack	RAM, WAD, CRAM, DECK, LADE, LOAD, ROLL, STOW, TAMP, BUNDLE, BURDEN, DEACON, FARDEL, STEEVE, SUMTER, COMPRESS, CONDENSE, KNAPSACK; *see* p. 523
pack animal	ASS, MULE, BURRO, CAMEL, LLAMA, DONKEY, JACKASS, SUMPTER
package	BOX, BALE, FADGE, CARTON, CEROON, PARCEL, ROBBIN, SEROON
packet	BOAT, SHIP; *see* PACKAGE
packing	LUTE, OAKUM, BUFFER, FILLER, GASKET, SPONGE, EXCELSIOR
packing material	GASKET, PEANUTS, EXCELSIOR, BUBBLE WRAP
packsaddle	APAREJO
pact	BOND, MISE, TREATY, BARGAIN, COMPACT, ENTENTE, COVENANT, CONCORDAT
pad	MAT, FILL, FLAT, ROOM, WASE, STUFF, TRAMP, DABBER, TABLET, CUSHION, NOTEBOOK
padding	DOWN, FELT, FILL, EXTRA, KAPOK, STRAW, COTTON, FILLER, STUFFING
paddle	*see* OAR
paddock	FIELD, ENCLOSURE
paddy wagon	BLACKMARIA
Paduan family	CARRARA
paean	ODE
pagan	ETHNIC, PAYNIM, HEATHEN, INFIDEL, IDOLATOR
page	CALL, FOLIO, RECTO, VERSO, RUBRIC, SUMMON, BELLHOP
pageant	FAIR, POMP, SHOW, MASQUE, PARADE, SPECTACLE
pageantry	POMP, SHOW, DISPLAY, CEREMONY, SPLENDOR, SPECTACLE
Pagliacci character	BEPPO, CANIO, NEDDA, TONIO, SILVIO
Pagliacci composer	LEONCAVALLO
pagoda	TA, PON, TAA, HOON
paid	HIRED, BRIBED, ONSTAFF, SALARIED
pail	COG, SOE, BOULK, COGUI, SKEEL, STOOP, STOUP, PIGGIN
pain	AIL, ACHE, PANG, AGONY, PYGLA, THROE, HASSLE, DISTRESS
pain description	ACHING, BURNING, CHRONIC, GNAWING, GRIPPING, THROBBING
painful	ACHY, SORE, IRKSOME, TORTUROUS, EXCRUCIATING
painkiller	COCA, TONIC, OPIATE, ANODYNE; *see* ANESTHETIC

painless NUMB(ING), UNFELT, EFFORTLESS
painlessness APONIA
painstaking LOVING, CAREFUL, DILIGENT, SCRUPULOUS
paint COAT, DAUB, DRAW, FARD, LIMN, FUCUS, ROUGE, STAIN, DEPICT, MAKEUP, PARGET, VENEER, MINIATE, PIGMENT, PORTRAY, STIPPLE, VARNISH
painter, famous see p. 543
painting OIL, PATA, MURAL, CANVAS, CARTOON, PICTURE, PORTRAIT, SEASCAPE, LANDSCAPE, CARICATURE
painting equipment BRUSH, EASEL, CANVAS, PALLET, ROLLER, PALETTE, SPATULA, TABORET, MAHLSTICK, MAULSTICK
painting medium OIL, GESSO, CASEIN, ACRYLIC, TEMPERA, ENCAUSTIC
painting method WASH, SECCO, FRESCO, COLLAGE, GOUACHE, IMPASTO, TEMPERA, GRISAILLE, CHIAROSCURO
painting style OP, POP, DADA, DECO, GENRE, NAIVE, CUBISM, ROCOCO, SESSHU, BAROQUE, CLASSIC, DADAISM, FAUVISM, IMPASTO, REALISM, ABSTRACT, FUTURISM, IDEALISM, GRISAILLE, MANNERISM, SYMBOLISM, MINIMALISM, ROMANESQUE, SURREALISM, POINTILLISM, ROMANTICISM, SUPREMATISM, PHOTOREALISM, CONCEPTUALISM, EXPRESSIONISM, IMPRESSIONISM, CONSTRUCTIVISM
pair DUO, TWO, DIAD, DUAD, DUET, DYAD, MATE, SPAN, TEAM, YOKE, BRACE, MARRY, COUPLE, COMBINE
paired TWIN, GEMEL, MATED, JUGATE, TEAMED, MATCHED
Pakistan, capital GUJRAT, LAHORE, MULTAN, QUETTA, ZIARAT, PESHAWAR
Pakistani SIKH, PATHAN
Pakistani canal NARA

Pakistani city/town WAH, BELA, KOTRI, PASNI, PIPRI, LAHOR(E), GWADAR, MARDAN, MULTAN, ORMARA, QUETTA, KARACHI, PESHAWAR, HYDERABAD, FAISALABAD, GUJRANWALA, RAWALPINDI
Pakistani clothing BURKA, BURQA, LUNGI
Pakistani language URDU, HINDI, SHINA, PASHTU, SINDHI, BENGALI, PUNJABI
Pakistani money ANNA, PICE, RUPEE
Pakistani mountain(s) HIMALAYA, KARAKORAM, TIRICHMIR
Pakistani mountain pass KHYBER, KARAKORAM
Pakistani people BALOCH, PASHTU, SINDHI, MUHAJIR, PUNJABI
Pakistani province SIND, PUNJAB, BALUCHISTAN
Pakistani river RAVI, SWAT, INDUS, CHENAB, JHELUM, KUNDAR, HYDASPES
Pakistani statesman AYUB, MIRZA, JINNAH
Pakistani woman BEGUM
pal CHUM, MATE, AMIGO, BUDDY, CRONY, CULLY, HOBNOB, HANGOUT
palace MANOR, COURT, CASTLE, ALCAZAR, CHATEAU, MANSION
paladin PEER, KNIGHT, CHAMPION, PROTAGONIST
Palal father UZAI
palanquin JAUN, KAGO, DOOLEE, LITTER
palanquin bearer HAMAL
palatable SAPID, TASTY, SAVORY, DELICIOUS, TOOTHSOME, APPETIZING
palate TASTE, UVULA, VELUM
Palau BELAU, PELEW
Palau, capital of KOROR, BABELTHUUP
Palau island KOROR, ANGAUR, ELIMALK, PELELIU, BABELTHUAP, URUKTHAPEL
Palau language TOBI, ANGAVR
Palau money DOLLAR
palaver CHAT, TALK, PARLEY, CHATTER, FLATTER
pale DIM, WAN, ASHY, ASHEN, MEALY, PASTY, DOUGHY,

PALLID, PALLOR, PASTEL,
SALLOW
paleface WHITE(MAN)
Palenque native MAYA
Palestine FRETS, CANAAN,
ISRAEL
Palestine city/town ACRE,
CANA, DION, GATH, DIBON,
EKRON, ENDOR, JOPPA,
LYDDA, TYRUS, BETHEL,
GADARA, GIBEAH, GILGAL,
HIPPOS, BEERSHEBA,
BETHLEHEM, CAPERNAUM,
JERUSALEM
Palestine district GAZA, HAIFA,
LYDDA, PERAEA, GALILEE,
SAMARIA, JERUSALEM
Palestine mountain EBAL,
NEBO, CARMEL, GILEAD
Palestine org. PLO, AL FATAH,
FEDAYEEN
Palestine (ancient) region EDOM,
MOAB, SYRIA, GESHUR,
GILEAD, PERAEA, GALILEE,
SAMARIA
Palestine river JABBOK,
JORDAN
palindrome EKE, EVE, TAT,
ANNA, BOOB, NOON, KAYAK,
MADAM, REFER, ROTOR,
HANNAH
palisade BAIL, FENCE, HURDIS,
ESPALIER
pall BORE, CLOY, GLUT, SATE,
CLOAK, GLOOM, WEARY,
DISGUST, SATIATE
Pallas ATHENA, MINERVA
pallet BED, HEAD, PATE, PAWL,
CLICK, LITTER, PALETTE,
MATTRESS, PLATFORM,
STRETCHER
palliate EASE, GLOZE, SALVE,
EXCUSE, SOFTEN, SOOTHE,
TEMPER, ASSUAGE, RELIEVE,
MITIGATE, ALLEVIATE,
EXTENUATE
palliative OPIATE, REMEDY,
BROMIDE, SEDATIVE
pallid WAN, GRAY, PALE,
ASHEN, SALLOW
palm LOOP, VOLA, FOIST,
KUDOS, THENAR, CONCEAL;
see PALM TREE
palm fiber DOH, BURI, EJOO,
DATIL, GOMUTI, RAFFIA
palm juice SURA
palm leaf OLA
palm liquor BENO, BINO, NIPA,
TUBA, VINO, TODDY

palm off FOB, FOIST
palm tree ENG, DOM, KOU,
ARAK, ATAP, BURI, BRAB,
COCO, DATE, DOUM, NIPA,
PAUM, SAGO, DOUM, ARECA,
ARENG, ASSAI, ATTAP,
BONGA, BONGO, BUNGA,
COCOA, COCOS, CYCAS,
DATIL, HOWEA, INAJA, JAGUA,
NIKAU, PALMA, RATAN,
SABAL, TODDY, TUCUM,
UNAMO, YAGUA, YARAY,
ARENGA, ASSAHY, GEBANG,
GOMUTI, GRIGRI, GRUGRU,
PACAYA, RAFFIA, RATTAN,
TUCUMA, CALAMUS,
COCONUT, PALMYRA, PIASABA,
PIASAVA, TALIPOT,
COCOANUT, DOOMPALM,
PIASSABA, PIASSAVA
Palmetto State SC, SOUTH
CAROLINA
palmistry CHIROGNOMY,
CHIROMANCY
palpable REAL, EVIDENT,
OBVIOUS, MANIFEST,
TANGIBLE
palpate FEEL
palpitate BEAT, PULSE, THROB,
QUIVER, PULSATE
palpitation BEAT, TIRL, PULSE,
THROB, PALMUS,
SALTATION
palsy PARALYZE, PARALYSIS,
VIBRATION
paltry MEAN, POOR, CHEAP,
PETTY, SMALL, SLIGHT,
TRIVIAL
pamper PET, HUMOR, SPOIL,
CODDLE, COSHER, COSSET,
FONDLE
pamphlet CHAP, TRACT,
BOOKLET, BROCHURE,
CHAPBOOK
Pan FAUNUS
pan CUT, RAP, RIB, SUMP,
BASIN, KNOCK, ROAST,
PIPKIN; see COOKING
panacea CURE, ELIXIR,
REMEDY, CUREALL,
NOSTRUM
panache FLAIR, VERVE,
APLOMB, SWAGGER
Panama DARIEN
Panama Canal city/town ANCON,
COLON, GATUN, BALBOA,
GAMBOA, CRISTOBAL
Panama Canal cut CULEBRA,
GAILLARD

Panama Canal engineer	panicky EDGY, FUNKY,
DELESSEPS	AFRAID, FEARFUL
Panama Canal locks GATUN,	panoply POMP, ARRAY,
MIRAFLORES, PEDRO	SHIELD, REGALIA
MIGUEL	panorama VIEW, SCAPE,
Panama, capital of PANAMA	VISTA, SCENERY
(CITY)	panpipe ANTARA, SYRINX
Panamanian city OCU, SONA,	Pan's lover ECHO, SYRINX
COLON, DAVID, CHITRE,	pant GASP, HUFF, PUFF,
PANAMA, TONOSI, SANTIAGO	YEARN
Panamanian island COIBA,	Pantagruel author RABELAIS
PEARL, CEBACO, PARIDA,	pantheon TOMB, TEMPLE
JICARON, CONTADORA	panther PARD, PUMA,
Panamanian measure CELEMIN	COUGAR, JAGUAR,
Panamanian money CENT,	LEOPARD
BALBOA, CENTESIMO	panties DRAWERS,
Panamanian national part DARIEN	UNDERPANTS
Panamanian neighbor COSTARICA	panting HYPERPNEA
Panamanian province COCLE,	pantomime SAVO, MIMIST,
COLON, DARIEN, HERRERA,	CHARADE
VERAGUAS	pantry AMBRY, EWERY,
Panamanian river CHEPO,	CLOSET, LARDER, SPENCE,
TUIRA, CHAGRES,	BUTTERY, CUPBOARD
SANPABLO, CHICAMOLA	pants JEANS, SLACKS, TIGHTS,
Panamanian tree COPA, YAYA,	BLOOMERS, BREECHES,
CA(U)TIVO	KNICKERS, TROUSERS,
pancake CREPE, FLAWN,	PLUSFOURS
FRAISE, FROISE, FRITTER,	pants material JEAN, CHINO,
HOTCAKE, SUZETTE,	DENIM, FLANNEL
FLAPJACK	pantywaist SISSY, MILKSOP,
pancreas SWEETBREAD	WEAKLING
pancreatic secretion INSULIN,	papal APOSTOLIC,
GLUCAGON	PONTIFICAL
panda WAH, BEARCAT	papal court CURIA
pandemic CARNAL, GENERAL,	papal palace VATICAN
PREVALENT, WIDESPREAD,	papal vestment *see* VESTMENT
COSMOPOLITAN	papal letter BREVE, BULL(A),
pandemonium DIN, RIOT,	ENCYCLICAL
CHAOS, NOISE, BEDLAM,	paper BOND, TAPA, CREPE,
TUMULT, UPROAR	ESSAY, KRAFT, MANILA,
pander PIMP, CATER,	PAPIER, PELURE, TISSUE,
PROCURER	VELLUM, PAPYRUS,
pane QUARREL, ROUNDEL	DOCUMENT
panegyric EULOGY, PRAISE,	paper clip inventor VAALER
TRIBUTE, ENCOMIUM	paper folding ORIGAMI
panel JURY, PANE, PLAQUE,	paper, imperfect CASSE, SALLE,
VENIRE	RETREE
panfry SAUTE	paper measure REAM, QUIRE,
pang ACHE, RACK, STAB,	BUNDLE
THROB, THROE, STITCH,	paper size CAP, DEMY, POST,
TWITCH, TWINGE	POTT, ATLAS, CROWN,
Pangloss's student CANDIDE	FOLIO, LEGAL, ROYAL,
panhandle BEG	BASTARD, EMPEROR,
Panhandle State WV(A), WEST	ELEPHANT, FOOLSCAP,
VIRGINIA	IMPERIAL
panhandler BUM, TRAMP,	paperwork BUMF
BEGGAR, MENDICANT	paprika PIMIENTO
panic FEAR, FRAY, FUNK,	Papua New Guinea, capital of
SCARE, FRIGHT, TERROR	PORTMORESBY

Papua New Guinea city/town   LAE, DARU, ARAWA, WABAG, WEWAK, BULOLO, GOROKA, MADANG, PORTMORESBY

Papua New Guinea island   BUKA, YELA, LIHIR, MANAM, MUYUA, HERMIT, KARKAR, MISIMA, MUSSAU, TAGULA, TULLIN, BUDIBUDI, KIRIWINA, NORMANBY, FERGUSSON, GOODENOUGH

Papua New Guinea language   MOTU, PIDGIN

Papua New Guinea money   KINA, TOEA

Papua New Guinea mountain   BALBI, BOSAVI, TALAWI, BANGETA, SUCKLING, THEFATHER, KNONGAIANG

Papua New Guinea river   FLY, TEDI, WAWOI, PURARI

papyrus   SEDGE, BIBLOS, BIBLUS, SCROLL, BULRUSH

par   EQUAL, NORMAL, AVERAGE, STANDARD

parable   TALE, FABLE, STORY, ALLEGORY, APOLOGUE

parachute   EJECT, JUMPOUT, PARAFOIL

parachute part   PACK, RISER, CANOPY, HARNESS, LIFTWEB, RIPCORD, UMBRELLA

paraclete   PLEADER, ADVOCATE

parade   ARRAY, MARCH, STRUT, FLAUNT, PAGEANT

paradigm   IDEAL, MODEL, EXAMPLE, PATTERN

paradise   EDEN, JODO, ZION, HEAVEN, UTOPIA, ELYSIUM, NIRVANA, SHANGRILA

Paradise Lost author   MILTON

paradiselike   EDENIC, ELYSIAN

paragon   TYPE, IDEAL, MODEL, EXEMPLAR, NONESUCH

paragraph   ITEM, CLAUSE, PILCROW, SECTION, PASSAGE

Paraguay, capital of   ASUNCION

Paraguayan city/town   ITA, YUTY, AYALA, JESUS, LUQUE, PILAR, ACAHAY, ARAQUA, YBYCUE, CAACUPE, CAAZAPA, ROSARIO, ASUNCION, PARAGUARI, FILADELFIA

Paraguayan lake   YPOA

Paraguayan language   GUARANI

Paraguayan measure   PIE, LINE, LINO, VARA, LEGUA, CORDEL, CUADRA

Paraguayan money   CENTIMO, GUARANI

Paraguayan neighbor   BRAZIL, BOLIVIA, ARGENTINA

Paraguayan region   CHACO, ITAPUA, CAAZAPA, CAAGUAZU, BOQUERON, CONCEPCION

Paraguayan river   APA, MELO, NEGRO, VERDE, ACARAY, PARANA, PARAGUAY, AQUIDABAN, PILCOMAYO

parakeet   BUDGIE, PARROT, BUDGERIGAR

parallel   EQUAL, MATCH, ANALOG, COUNTERPART

Parallel Lives author   PLUTARCH

parallelogram   DIAMOND, RHOMB(US), RHOMBOID, RECTANGLE

paralysis   PALSY, POLIO, PLEGIA, PTOSIS, PARESIS

paralyze   NUMB, STUN, CRIPPLE, DISABLE

paralyzed   NUMB, PALSIED, CRIPPLED

paramnesia   DEJA VU

paramount   CHIEF, LEADING, FOREMOST, PRINCIPAL

paramour   LEMAN, LOVER, SWAIN, MINION, MISTRESS

Parana tributary   IVAI, PARDO, TIETE, VERDE, SALADO

paranoid concern   PLOT

parapet   WALL, RAILING, BRATTICE

paraphernalia   GEAR, OUTFIT, EQUIPMENT, TRAPPINGS, BELONGINGS

paraphrase   RENDER(ING), RESTATE(MENT), REWORD(ING)

paraplegic   CRIPPLE, PARALYTIC

parasite   BINE, FLEA, MITE, PEGA, TRYP, APHID, LEECH, TOADY, FAWNER, REMORA, SPONGE

parasol   SUNSHADE, UMBRELLA

Parcae   see FATES

parcel   LOT, METE, PLAT, ALLOT, BUNDLE, PACKET, PACKAGE, (AP)PORTION

parch   DRY, SEAR, SCORCH, TORREFY, TORRIFY

parched	DRIED, THIRSTY, ANHYDROUS, DEHYDRATED
parchment	FOR(R)EL, VELLUM
parchment roll	PELL, SCROLL
pardon	MERCY, REMIT, ASSOIL, AMNESTY, CONDONE, FORGIVE, OVERLOOK
pardonable	VENIAL, EXCUSABLE
pare	CUT, PEEL, SKIVE, SCRAPE, WHITTLE
parent	DAM, SIRE, MATER, PATER, MOTHER, FATHER
parentage	BIRTH, DESCENT, LINEAGE, ANCESTRY
parental instinct	STORGE
parenthesis	EPISODE, INTERLUDE
parhelion	SUNDOG, MOCK SUN
pari —	PASSU
pariah	EXILE, LEPER, OUTCAST
Paris	LUTETIA, PARISII
Paris airport	ORLY, ROISSY, DEGAULLE, (LE) BOURGET
Paris bishop	DENIS
Paris cathedral	NOTRE DAME, SACRE COEUR
Pais museum	CLUNY, LOUVRE
Paris newspaper	SOIR, MONDE, TEMPS, FIGARO
Paris palace	ELYSEE, LOUVRE, TUILERIES, LUXEMBOURG
Paris relative	ENON, PRIAM, HECUBA, OENONE
Paris district	BOIS, CITE, PASSY, AUTEUIL, NEUILLY, LEFT BANK, RIGHT BANK, MONTMARTRE, MONTPARNASSE
Paris river	SEINE
Paris tower	EIFFEL
Paris slayer	PHILOCTETES
Paris suburb	ISSY, VITRY, CLICHY, DRANCY, SEVRES, NEUILLY, MONTREUIL
Paris university	SORBONNE
parish	DISTRICT, CONGREGATION
parish head	PASTOR, RECTOR
Parisian	GALLIC
park	GREEN, GARDEN, SQUARE, COMMON, PRATER, STADIUM
— Park	HYDE, REGO, CENTRAL
park, national	ZION, PLATE, ACADIA, ARCHES, DENALI, KATMAI, LASSEN, SHILOH, BIG

	BEND, GLACIER, OLYMPIC, REDWOOD, SAGUARO, SEQUOIA, ANTIETAM, BADLANDS, BISCAYNE, CARLSBAD, CHALMETE, COLONIAL, MANASSAS, PEA RIDGE, SARATOGA, WINDCAVE, YOSEMITE, HALEAKALA, MESA VERDE, JOSHUA TREE
parka	ANORAK, JACKET, PULLOVER
Parkinson's disease drug	LDOPA, LEVODOPA
parlance	IDIOM, SPEECH, DIALECT, LANGUAGE
parlay	BET, WAGER
parley	TALK, CONFER, POWWOW, PALAVER, PARLANCE, CONFERENCE
parliament	see ASSEMBLY
parliament report	HANSARD
parlor	DEN, SALA, SALO(O)N, LOCUTORY
parlor furniture	DIVAN, SETTEE, OTTOMAN, LOVESEAT
parochial	LOCAL, NARROW, INSULAR, REGIONAL, PROVINCIAL
parodist	APER, IMITATOR
parody	SATIRE, TRAVESTY, BURLESQUE
paroxysm	FIT, AGONY, SPASM, ATTACK, TREMOR, CONVULSION
parrot	KEA, ECHO, JAKO, KAKA, LORY, VASA, MACAW, MIMIC, POLLY, BUDGIE, KAKAPO, REPEAT, LORILET, ROSELLA, BUDGIGAR, COCKATOO, LORIKEET, LOVEBIRD, PARAKEET, POPINJAY
parrot genus	ARA
parry	FEND, WARD, FENCE, REPLY, DEFLECT
parse	ANALYZE
Parsee priest	MOBED
Parsec scripture	AVESTA
Parsifal character	KUNDRY, AMFORTAS, KLINGSOR
Parsifal composer	WAGNER
parsimonious	CLOSE, FRUGAL, STINGY, MISERLY
parsley	DILL, CICELY, LOVAGE, GARNISH
parson(age)	MANSE, RECTORY; see CLERGY

part ROLE, SOME, BREAK, CAMEO, LEAVE, PIECE, SEVER, SHARE, CLEAVE, DIVIDE, PARCEL, SECTOR, SUNDER, ELEMENT, PORTION, SECTION, SEGMENT, SEPARATE

part of speech NOUN, VERB, ADVERB, PRONOUN, ADJECTIVE, CONJUNCTION, PREPOSITION, INTERJECTION

partake EAT, SHARE, RECEIVE

Parthenon figure ATHENA, ELGIN MARBLES

Parthenon site ACROPOLIS

partial BIASED, HARMONIC, ONESIDED, OVERTONE, INCOMPLETE, PREJUDICED

partiality BIAS, FAVOR, LIKING, FONDNESS, PREJUDICE

participant PARTY, SHARER, CONTESTANT

participate SHARE, COMPETE, PARTAKE, TAKEPART

particle BIT, AFFIX, GRAIN, MESON, PALEA, MESOTRON, RAMENTUM; *see* ATOM, JOT

particular ODD, ITEM, FUSSY, DETAIL, UNIQUE, FINICAL, PRECISE

particularize DETAIL, ITEMIZE, SPECIFY, SPELLOUT

partisan MAQUI, BIASED, ZEALOT, ADHERENT, FOLLOWER, GUERRILLA

partition WALL, SEPTA, SCREEN, SEPTUM, DIVIDE(R)

partly INPART, SOMEWHAT

partner ALLY, MATE, PARD, WIFE, BUDDY, COHORT, SPOUSE, HUSBAND

partnership HUI, HOEY, CAHOOT(S), ALLIANCE

partridge KYAH, TITAR, CHUKAR, CHUKOR, REDLEG, SEESEE, FRANCOLIN

partridge, young CHEEPER

Partridge Family names DANNY, KEITH, TRACY, LAURIE, CHRIS(TOPHER), SHIRLEY

parturition LABOR, BIRTHING, DELIVERY, CHILDBIRTH

party TEA, BASH, GALA, PROM, SECT, STAG, CIRCLE, CLIQUE, SOCIAL, SOIREE, SHINDIG

party in power IN(CUMBENT)

party, kind of HEN, TEA, STAG, BRIDAL, PAJAMA, SOCIAL, SHOWER, SENDOFF, POLITICAL

party offering SLATE

party, political GOP, TORY, WHIG, UNION, REFORM, LIBERAL, LIBERTY, PEOPLES, AMERICAN, NATIONAL, SOCIALIST, DEMOCRATIC, REPUBLICAN

parvenu SNOB, CLIMBER, NOUVEAU, UPSTART

Pascal work PENSEES, PROVINCIALES

pasha DEH, AALI, DOWLAH

Pasiphaë's husband MINOS

pass COL, DIE, GAP, BYGO, COMP, FADE, GHAT, HAND, OMIT, SKIP, ADOPT, ELIDE, ENACT, GHAUT, LAPSE, REEVE, RELAY, DEFILE, ELAPSE, TICKET, SKITTER

pass, mountain *see p. 611*

pass the — BUCK

pass on DIE, CONVEY, IMPART, DECEASE

pass over OMIT, SKIP, EXCUSE, IGNORE, OVERLOOK

passable OK(AY), FAIR, SOSO, TOLERABLE, ACCEPTABLE

passage PATH, TEXT, TRIP, BYWAY, COURSE, CHANNEL, JOURNEY, PORTION, EXCERPT

passageway GAT, GUT, ADIT, DUCT, EXIT, HALL, ITER, AISLE, ALURE, CANAL, SLYPE, STOPE, STULM, ARCADE, CLAUSE, EGRESS, TRANSIT

passé OLD, PAST, DATED, OLD HAT, OBSOLETE, OUTMODED

passenger FARE, RIDER, COMMUTER

passing DEATH, CASUAL, MORTAL, CURSORY, FLEETING, MOMENTARY, TRANSIENT, TRANSITORY

passion FIRE, HEAT, LOVE, LUST, RAGE, ZEAL, ARDOR, FLAME, DESIRE, FERVOR, EMOTION, FEELING

passionate ARDENT, TORRID, AMOROUS, EMOTIVE, FERVENT, INTENSE, IRASCIBLE

passive IDLE, INERT, INACTIVE, QUIESCENT

Passover PASCH, SEDAR, SEDER, PASCHA

passport KEY, CONGE(E), DUSTU(C)K

password   KEY, PAROLE,
SHIBBOLETH
past   EX, AGO, GONE, OVER,
YORE, BEHIND, BEYOND,
BYGONE, GONEBY
pasta   ZITI, DITALI, MELONE,
RIGATI, FUSILLI, GNOCCHI,
MAFALDE, MEZZANI, PASTINA,
RAVIOLI, ROTELLE,
BUCATINI, LINGUINI,
SPAGHETTI; see NOODLES,
MACARONI
paste   HIT, PAP, BLOW, BOND,
GLUE, STRASS, MUCILAGE
pasteboard   BRISTOL
pastel   TINT, WOAD, CRAYON
paste-up   DUMMY, COLLAGE
Pasternak character   LARA,
YURY
Pasternak novel   DOCTOR
ZHIVAGO
pasteurize   STERILIZE
pastiche   JUMBLE, MEDLEY,
FARRAGO, PASTICCIO,
POTPOURRI
pastille   CACHOU, TABLET,
TROCHE, LOZENGE
pastime   PLAY, HOBBY, SPORT,
AMUSEMENT, DIVERSION
pastor   see CLERGY
pastoral   IDYL, RURAL, RUSTIC,
BUCOLIC, IDYLLIC
Pastoral Symphony composer
BEETHOVEN
Pastoral Symphony key   FMAJOR
pastry   FLAN, TART, CRUST,
TORTE, ECLAIR, STRUDEL,
NAPOLEON; see PIE, CAKE
pasture   ING, LEA, COLP, HEAF,
HOGA, AGIST, SHIELING
pasty   PIE, WAN, PALE,
DOUGHY, PALLID
pat   APT, DAB, FIT, TAP, GLIB,
CHUCK, CARESS
Patagonia country   CHILE,
ARGENTINA
Patagonia native   TEHUELCHE
Patagonia river   CHICO,
CHUBUT, DESEADO
patch   DARN, MEND, SPOT,
BODGE, CLOUT, PIECE
patchwork   CENTO, QUILT,
MEDLEY, MOSAIC,
MONTAGE
pate   HEAD, NOODLE
patella   ROTULA, KNEECAP,
KNEEPAN
paten   ARCA, DISC, HOST,
ARCAE

patent   BERAT, CLEAR, PLAIN,
TITLE, LICENSE, EVIDENT,
OBVIOUS
paternal   FATHERLY,
PATRIARCHAL
paternity   ORIGIN,
PARENTAGE, AUTHORSHIP,
FATHERHOOD
paternity text factor   DNA
paternoster   PRAYER, ROSARY
path   WAY, BERM, LANE,
LOCUS, ORBIT, TRAIL,
CASAUN, RODDIN(G)
pathfinder   GUIDE, SCOUT,
PIONEER
pathetic   SAD, MOVING,
TOUCHING, WRETCHED
Pathetique Sonata composer
BEETHOVEN
Pathetique Sonata key
CMINOR
Pathetique Symphony composer
TCHAIKOVSKY
Pathetique Symphony key
BMINOR
pathogen   GERM, VIRUS,
MICROBE, BACILLUS
pathological   MORBID
pathos   EMOTION,
POIGNANCY
patience   STOICISM,
FORTITUDE, ENDURANCE
patient   CASE, STOIC, INMATE,
SHUTIN, INVALID,
TOLERANT
patina   FILM, VERD, PATEN,
COATING, VERDIGRIS
patio   PIAZZA, TERRACE,
VERANDA
patois   CANT, ARGOT, GUMBO,
LINGO, JARGON, DIALECT
patriarch   ELDER, LEADER;
see p. 516
patrician   NOBLE, ELEGANT,
ARISTOCRAT
patrimony   ESTATE, LEGACY,
HERITAGE, BIRTHRIGHT
patriot   HALE, OTIS, ALLEN,
JINGO, PAUL REVERE,
CRISPUS ATTUCKS
patriotic group   DAR, SAR
patrol   SCOUT, SENTRY,
LOOKOUT, MONITOR
patrolman   COP, POLICE(MAN)
patron   ANGEL, BUYER, SAINT,
BACKER, CLIENT, SPONSOR,
ADVOCATE, CUSTOMER
patron saint   ELMO, IVES, LUKE,
OLAF, DENIS, GILES, JAMES,

PETER, ANTONY, FIACRE,
GEORGE, CRISPIN, FLORIAN,
PATRICK, NICHOLAS
patronage   EGIS, WING, AEGIS,
FAVOR, AUSPICES,
CLIENTELE
patronize   HUMOR, INDULGE,
SUPPORT, FREQUENT
patsy   SAP, DUPE, MARK,
VICTIM, FALLGUY
patter   RAP, YAK, CANT, PITCH,
SPIEL, CHATTER, RATATAT
pattern   MOLD, NORM, SETT,
TYPE, IDEAL, MODEL,
DAMIER, FORMAT, PARAGON,
STENCIL, TEMPLATE
paucity   LACK, DEARTH,
SCARCITY
Paul   SAUL
Paul's birthplace   TARSUS
Paul's companion   SILAS,
SOPATER
Paul's work   LETTER, EPISTLE
Paul Bunyan ox   BABE
paunch   POT, BELLY, RUMEN,
ABDOMEN
paunchy   FAT, PLUMP, PORTLY,
BLOATED, POTBELLIED
pauper   BEGGAR, INDIGENT,
MENDICANT
pause   LULL, REST, LETUP,
SELAH, TRUCE, C(A)ESURA,
RESPITE
pave   COAT, TILE, COVER,
COBBLE, ASPHALT, PREPARE
pavement   ROAD, ASPHALT,
ROADWAY, CONCRETE,
SIDEWALK
pavilion   TELD, TENT, KIOSK,
GAZEBO, MARQUEE,
BELVEDERE
paving material   TAR(MAC),
SETT, SLAB, TILE, PAVER,
BRICKS, CEMENT, ASPHALT,
MACADAM, CONCRETE,
FLAGSTONE
paw   PUD, FOOT, CLAW,
GAUM, HAND, MAUL,
MANUS, TOUCH, CLUTCH,
FATHER, FONDLE, HANDLE,
MOLEST, OLDMAN, FOREFOOT
pawl   COG, BOLT, CATCH,
DETENT, PALLET, RATCHET
pawn   DUPE, GAGE, HOCK,
TOOL, SPOUT, WAGER,
PIGNUS, PLEDGE, HOSTAGE
pawnbroker   UNCLE, SPOUT,
LENDER
pax   PEACE, FRIEND, TABLET

pay   FEE, TIP, ANTE, PONY,
QUIT, SOUD, WAGE, ATONE,
CLEAR, REMIT, SPEND,
DEFRAY, KICKIN, REWARD,
SALARY, SETTLE, STIPEND
payable   DUE, OWING, UNPAID
paymaster   BUXY, BAKSHI,
PURSER, CASHIER
payment   CRO, FEE, CENS, ERIC,
KIST, SCOT, ANNAT, ARLES,
HERIOT, LABOLA, REBATE,
HANDSEL, WERGILD
payola   BRIBE
PC competitor   MAC, SUN,
IMAC, APPLE
pea   DAL, TUR, DHAL, ARHAR,
CICER, DHOLL, PEASE,
PISUR, SENNA
peace   PAX, LISS, AMITY,
GRITH, IRENE, QUIET,
SHALOM, CONCORD,
HARMONY, NIRVANA
peace officer   *see* OFFICER
peace pipe   CALUMET
Peace Prize winner   *see p. 509*
peaceable   CALM, IRENIC,
PLACID, HENOTIC
peaceful   CALM, IRENIC,
SERENE, HALCYON, PACIFIC
peacemaker   MEDIATOR,
PACIFIER, PACIFIST,
ARBITRATOR
peach   RAT, PAVY, SING,
BEAUT, BETRAY, SNITCH,
SQUEAL
Peach State   GA, GEORGIA
peachy   NEAT, SOFT, FUZZY,
GREAT, PULPY, SWELL
peacock   MAO, PAON, PAVO,
PAWN, POSE, STRUT
peak   ALP, BEN, TOR, ACME,
APEX, CRAG, CUSP, CREST,
PITON, CLIMAX, SUMMIT,
ZENITH
peal   RING, TOLL, CHIME,
CLANG, RESOUND
peanut   MANI, GOOBER,
EARTHNUT
peanut product   OIL, BUTTER
Peanuts character   LUCY,
LINUS, PIGPEN
pear   BOSC, ANJOU, NOPAL,
PYRUS, COMICE, SECKEL,
SICKLE, BARTLETT, JARGONEL
pear drink   PERRY
pear, prickly   TUNA, NOPAL,
CACTUS, OPUNTIA
pearl   GEM, NACRE, ONION,
OLIVET

Pearl of Antilles	CUBA
pearl producer	NACRE,
	OYSTER, MOLLUSK
pearlweed	SAGINA
pearly	LUSTROUS, NACREOUS,
	OPALESCENT
pear-shaped	OBCONIC,
	PYRIFORM
Peary discovery	NORTHPOLE
peasant	TAO, CARL, LITI,
	PEON, RYOT, CEORL, CHURL,
	KULAK, RAYAT, COOLIE,
	COTTAR, COTTER, FELLAH,
	MUZHIK, TILLER, PAISANO
peashooter	PISTOL, BLOWGUN
peat	MOOR, TURF, TURBARY,
	SPHAGNUM
pebble(s)	JACK, SCREE, STONE,
	GRAVEL, CHUCKIE (STONE)
pebble game	CHUCKS
peccadillo	SIN, ERROR, FAULT,
	FAILING, OFFENSE
peccant	SINFUL, CORRUPT,
	SINNING
peccary	BOAR, JABALI,
	WARREE, TAGASSU
peck	DAB, NIP, KISS, KNIP,
	NIBBLE
peculate	STEAL, THIEVE,
	EMBEZZLE
peculiar	ODD, QUEER,
	UNUSUAL, BIZARRE,
	ECCENTRIC
peculiarity	TRAIT, ODDITY,
	FEATURE, ANOMALY
pecuniary	FISCAL, MONETARY,
	FINANCIAL
pedagogical	ACADEMIC,
	DIDACTIC, INSTRUCTIVE
pedagogue	TUTOR, TEACHER,
	EDUCATOR
pedagogy	TEACHING,
	TUTORING, EDUCATION
pedal	LEVER, CELESTE,
	TREADLE
pedant	TUTOR, SCHOLAR,
	TEACHER, DOGMATIST,
	EDUCATOR, DOCTRINAIRE
pedantic	BOOKISH, LITERAL,
	ACADEMIC, DIDACTIC,
	PEDESTRIAN
peddle	HAWK, SELL, TOUT,
	VEND, TRANT
peddler	HAWKER; see MERCHANT
pederasty	SODOMY
pedestal	BASE, GAINE, STAND,
	SUPPORT
pedestal part	DADO, ORLO,
	SOCLE, PLINTH, SURBASE

pedestrian	DULL, AFOOT, HIKER,
	ONFOOT, WALKER, PROSAIC
pedigree	LINE, RACE, STOCK,
	FAMILY, STRAIN, LINEAGE,
	ANCESTRY, DERIVATION
peduncle	STEM, SCAPE, STALK,
	STIPES
peek	PEEP, PEER, GLANCE
peel	BARE, BARK, FLAY, HARL,
	PARE, RIND, SHED, SKIN,
	SKIVE, EPICARP, UNDRESS
peep	SPY, KEEK, PEEK, PULE,
	SKEG, CHEEP, CHIRP,
	DEKKO, GLIMPSE
peep show	RAREE
peephole	EYELET, KEYHOLE
Peeping Tom	VOYEUR
peer	FERE, GAZE, PEEK, PEEP,
	FEERE, RIVAL; see NOBLE
Peer Gynt character	A(A)SE,
	KING, ANITRA
Peer Gynt relative	ASE,
	ANITRA, SOLVEIG
Peer Gynt writer	GRIEG, IBSEN
peerage	GENTRY, NOBILITY
peerage grades	DUKE, EARL,
	BARON, MARQUIS,
	MARQUESS, VISCOUNT
peeress	LADY, DUCHESS,
	BARONESS, MARQUISE
peerless	UNIQUE, MATCHLESS,
	UNEQUALED
peeve	IRK, VEX, ANNOY,
	GRATE, NETTLE, RANKLE,
	IRRITATE
peevish	CROSS, GRUFF,
	MOODY, TESTY, CRANKY,
	CRUSTY, IN A PET, TOUCHY
peg	HOB, LEG, NOB, TEE,
	KNAG, DOWEL, SPILL, STAKE,
	THOLE, SPIGOT, TRENAIL,
	TRUNNEL, TREENAIL
peignoir	GOWN, ROBE, DRESS,
	KIMONO, WRAPPER,
	NEGLIGEE, HOUSECOAT
Pegasus' mother	MEDUSA
pejorative	DISPARAGING
Peking	BEIPING
Peleg relative	REU, EBER
Peleus relative	AEACUS,
	THETIS, TELAMON,
	ACHILLES, ANTIGONE
pelican	KOAE, DARTER,
	SNAKEBIRD
Pelican State	LA, LOUISIANA
pellet	BALL, GOLI, PILL,
	BULLET, PALLION
pellmell	JUMBLED, HEADLONG,
	DISORDERLY, HELTERSKELTER

pellucid	**CLEAR, LIMPID, LUCENT**
Peloponnese	**MOREA**
Peloponnese subdivision	**ELIS, ACHAEA, ARCADIA, ARGOLIS, LACONIA, MESSENIA**
Peloponnesian War parties	**ATHENS, SPARTA**
pelota	*see* JAI ALAI
pelt	**FELL, HIDE, SKIN, STONE;** *see* FUR, LEATHER
pelvic	**ILIAC, PUBIC**
pen	**STY, COOP, COTE, JAIL, STIR, SWAN, YARD, HUTCH, KRAAL, QUILL, STYLE, CORRAL, INDITE, SCRIPT**
pen names	*see p. 557*
pen point	**NEB, NIB**
penal	**PUNITIVE**
penalize	**FINE, PUNISH**
penalty	**CAIN, FINE, FORFEIT, PUNISHMENT**
penance	**AMENDS, FASTING, ATONEMENT, CONTRITION**
penates	**LARES**
penchant	**YEN, BENT, FLAIR, TASTE, LIKING, LEANING**
pencil	**STYLUS**
pencil lead	**GRAPHITE**
pendant	**BOB, FOB, LOP, JAGG, LOCKET, EARRING, GIRANDOLE, LAVALIER(E)**
pending	**COMING, IMMINENT, IMPENDING**
pendulous	**HANGING, PENSILE, SWINGING, WAVERING**
Penelope relative	**ICARIUS, ULYSSES, ODYSSEUS, TELEMACHUS**
Penelope suitor	**ANTINOUS**
penetrable	**POROUS, PERVIOUS, PERMEABLE**
penetrate	**BORE, GORE, ENTER, IMBUE, IMPALE, INVADE, PIERCE**
penetrating	**KEEN, ACUTE, SHARP, ASTUTE, SUBTLE, PERCEPTIVE**
penguin	**GENTOO, JOHNNY**
peninsula	**ANN, ACTE, AKTI, EYRE, KOLA, KRIM, NECK, BANKS, GASPE, ITALY, KATAR, MALAY, MOREA, QATAR, SINAI, ARABIA, AVALON, BALKAN, BATAAN, BONDOC, CRIMEA, IBERIA, ISTRIA, JUTLAND, KOWLOON, MALACCA, LABRADOR, MELVILLE, KAMCHATKA**
penitence	**SORROW, REMORSE, CONTRITION**
penitent	**SORROW, CONTRITE, REMORSEFUL**
penitential period	**LENT**
penman	**CLERK, SCRIBE, WRITER, COPYIST**
penmanship	**HAND, SCRIPT, LONGHAND, HANDWRITING**
pennant	**FLAG, WHIP, BANNER, BURGEE, ENSIGN, PENCEL, PENNON, STREAMER**
penniless	**POOR, BROKE, NEEDY, BANKRUPT, INDIGENT**
Pennsylvania	*see also p. 615*
Pennsylvania city/town	**ERIE, YORK, MEDIA, BEAVER, BUTLER, EASTON, MERCER, WARREN, BEDFORD, INDIANA, LAPORTE, LEBANON, MILFORD, READING, SUNBURY, TOWANDA, CARLISLE, SCRANTON, TIONESTA, ALLENTOWN, LANCASTER, PITTSBURGH, PHILADELPHIA**
Pennsylvania Indian	**LENAPE, DELAWARE, IROQUOIS, ALGONQUIAN**
Pennsylvania lake	**ERIE, ARTHUR, GLENDALE**
Pennsylvania mountain(s)	**DAVIS, ARARAT, POCONO, ALLEGHENY, APPALACHIAN**
Pennsylvania river	**OHIO, TIOGA, BEAVER, LEHIGH, JUNIATA, DELAWARE, ALLEGHENY, SCHUYLKILL, MONONGAHELA, SUSQUEHANNA**
Pennsylvania school	**DREXEL, LEHIGH, TEMPLE, BUCKNELL, DUQUESNE, VILLANOVA**
penny	**CENT, GROAT, COPPER, SALTEE, RED CENT, FARTHING**
pension	**ANNUITY, STIPEND, SUBSIDY, ALLOWANCE**
pensive	**SAD, MOODY, MEDITATIVE, THOUGHTFUL**
pent (up)	**REPRESSED**
Pentateuch	**LAW, TORA(H);** *see p.515*
Pentacost	**WHITSUNDAY**
penthouse	**AERIE, PENTICE**
penurious	**MEAN, CLOSE, FRUGAL, STINGY, DESTITUTE**

penury	NEED, WANT, POVERTY, DESTITUTION
peon	HAND, PAWN, SERF, THRALL, LABORER, PEASANT
peony	PIN(E)Y, MOUTAN
people	MEN, MOB, CLAN, FOLK, ONES, RACE, FOLK, CROWD, DEMOS, GENTE, PLEBS, DAOINE, NATION, RABBLE
pep	VIM, DASH, ZEST, VERVE, VIGOR, ENERGY, GINGER
pepo	GOURD, MELON, SQUASH, PUMPKIN
pepper	ARA, AWA, BEAT, CAVA, IKMO, ITMO, KAVA, SIRI, BETEL, CHILE, CHILI, RIDDLE, STRAFE, CAYENNE, PAPRIKA, PIMENTO, KAVAKAVA
pepper variety	RED, BELL, BLACK, GREEN, WHITE, JALAPEÑO
peppery	HOT, FIERY, SHARP, SPICY, TESTY, PIQUANT, PUNGENT, SARCASTIC
peppy	BRISK, SPIRITED, VIVACIOUS
Pequod captain	AHAB
Pequod owner	PELEG, BILDAD
Pequod sailor	*see* **MOBY DICK**
per	BY, VIA, EACH, APIECE, THROUGH
per —	SE, DIEM, ANNUM
per ardua ad —	ASTRA
per capita	EACH, APIECE
per se	ALONE, AS SUCH, SOLELY
peradventure	MAYBE, PERHAPS, POSSIBLY
perambulate	WALK, STROLL
perceive	SEE, ESPY, HEAR, NOTE, SPOT, GRASP, SENSE, DESCRY, NOTICE, DISCERN
percentage	CUT, FEE, AGIO, DUTY, SHARE, SLICE, QUOTA, PORTION, ROYALTY
perceptible	TACTILE, VISIBLE, APPARENT, PALPABLE, DETECTIBLE
perception	EAR, ESP, TACT, GRASP, ACUITY, ACUMEN, NOESIS
perceptive	KEEN, ALERT, SHARP, ASTUTE, OBSERVANT
perch	ROD, SIT, JOOK, AERIE, ROOST
perch(-like fish)	*see p. 668*

perchance	MAYBE, COULDBE, PERHAPS, POSSIBLY,
percolate	BREW, DRIP, OOZE, PERK, SEEP, EXUDE, LEACH, FILTER, TRICKLE
percolator	BREWER, COFFEEPOT
percussion instrument	*see p. 642*
perdition	DOOM, HELL, RUIN, DOWNFALL, DAMNATION
Père Goriot author	BALZAC
peregrinate	ROAM, WANDER, JOURNEY
peregrine	ALIEN, FALCON, ROVING, FOREIGN, MIGRATORY
peremptory	FIRM, HARSH, DOGMATIC, RIGOROUS, ARBITRARY
perennial	YEARLY, LASTING, ENDURING, PERPETUAL
perfect	AOK, HONE, PURE, EXACT, IDEAL, MODEL, UTTER, REFINE, ACHIEVE, FLAWLESS, CONSUMMATE
Perfect Strangers names	BALKI, HARRY, LARRY, GORPLEY, JENNIFER, MARYANNE
perfection	IDEAL, MODEL, PURITY, PARAGON, CROWNING, EXCELLENCE, IMPECCABILITY
perfectionist	FUSSY, STRICT, STICKLER
perfectly	FULLY, QUITE, UTTERLY
perfidious	FALSE, DISLOYAL, FAITHLESS
perforate	BORE, DRILL, PRICK, PIERCE, RIDDLE, TREPAN, FENESTRATE
perforation	CUT, HOLE, PUNCH, ROULETTE
perforce	NECESSARILY, OFNECESSITY
perform	DO, ACT, PLAY, WORK, FINISH, RENDER, ACHIEVE, EXECUTE, DISCHARGE
perform surgery	CUT, LASE, OPERATE
performance	ACT, SHOW, REALIZATION, PRESENTATION, ACCOMPLISHMENT
performer	DOER, ACTOR, AGENT, SHINE, ARTIST, PLAYER, SINGER, ARTISTE

performers, group of CAST, TROUPE	permanently IN INK
perfume ATAR, MUSK, OTTO, AROMA, ATTAR, CENSE, PASTIL, SACHET, BOUQUET	permeable POROUS, PERVIOUS, PENETRABLE
	permeate IMBUE, DIFFUSE, PERVADE, INFILTRATE
perfume source ATAR, MUSK, ATTAR, IRONE, MYRRH, ORRIS, CASTOR, IONONE, SAFROL, BERGAMOT	permissible LICIT, ALLOWABLE, LEGITIMATE
	permission GRACE, LEAVE, ENTREE, CONSENT, LICENSE, SANCTION, AUTHORIZATION
perfunctory CARELESS, MECHANICAL	permissive LAX, SOFT, LENIENT, TOLERANT, INDULGENT
perhaps HAPLY, MAYBE, MAYHAP	permit LET, FIAT, VISA, ALLOW, EXEAT, GRANT, LEAVE, CEDULA, LICENSE, SANCTION, AUTHORIZE
Periander's wife MELISSA	
Pericles' city ATHENS	
Pericles' mistress ASPASIA	
peril RISK, DANGER, HAZARD, MENACE, JEOPARDY	permutation CHANGE, TRANSFORMATION
perimeter EDGE, BORDER, FRINGE, BOUNDARY	pernicious EVIL, FATAL, LETHAL, WICKED, HARMFUL, NOXIOUS
period AGE, DOT, EON, ERA, SPAN, TERM, TIME, CYCLE, EPOCH, STAGE, SYSTEM; see GEOLOGICAL	per(s)nickety FUSSY, FINICAL, FASTIDIOUS
	Peron's wife EVA, EVITA, ISABEL
periodic CYCLIC, ETESIAN, REGULAR, RECURRENT	perorate RANT, ORATE, RECAP, HARANGUE, SPEECHIFY, SUMMARIZE
periodical MAG, CYCLIC, REVIEW, WEEKLY, GAZETTE, JOURNAL, MONTHLY, MAGAZINE, SPORADIC, INTERMITTENT	perpendicular SINE, ERECT, PLUMB, STEEP, UPRIGHT, VERTICAL
peripatetic WALKER, ITINERANT, PEDESTRIAN, ARISTOTELIAN	perpetrate DO, COMMIT, EXECUTE
peripheral OUTER, DISTAL, EXTERNAL, OUTLYING	perpetual CHRONIC, ENDLESS, ETERNAL, LASTING, CONSTANT, CONTINUOUS
periphery EDGE, AMBIT, LIMIT, BORDER, BOUNDARY, PERIMETER	perpetuate PRESERVE, ETERNALIZE
periphrasis AMBAGE	perpetuity ETERNITY, INFINITY
perish DIE, END, DEPART, EXPIRE, PASSON, DECEASE	perplex ELUDE, STUMP, BAFFLE, CONFUSE, FLUMMOX, MYSTIFY, NONPLUS, BEWILDER
perishable CADUKE, BRITTLE, FRAGILE, EPHEMERAL, TRANSITORY	perplexing MAZY, BAFFLING, CONFOUNDING
peristyle COURT, COLONNADE	perquisite PERK, BONUS, BENEFIT, PRIVILEGE
periwinkle WINK, SHELL, SNAIL, VINCA, MUSSEL, MYRTLE, DOG(S)BANE	Perry Mason character PAUL DRAKE, DELLA STREET
perjure LIE, FORSWEAR	Perry Mason author ERLE STANLEY GARDNER
perjury, encourage SUBORN	
perk BOON, LIFT, BONUS, RAISE, BUBBLE, REWARD	persecute VEX, TEASE, HARASS, MOLEST, OPPRESS, TORTURE
perky GAY, PERT, SAUCY, JAUNTY, LIVELY, SPIRITED	persecution ABUSE, TORMENT, TORTURE, MOLESTATION
permanence CONSTANCY, ENDURANCE, DURABILITY	persecution complex PARANOIA
permanent FIXED, DURABLE, LASTING, PERPETUAL	Persephone CORA, KORE, PROSERPINA

Persephone relative   HADES,
PLUTO, DEMETER, ZAGREUS
Perseus relative   DANAE,
PERSEIS, ANDROMEDA
Perseus star   ALGOL
perseverance   PATIENCE,
TENACITY, DOGGEDNESS,
PERSISTENCE
persevere   GOON, ENDURE,
PERSIST, CONTINUE
Persia   IRAN
Persian   LUR, MEDE, IRANI; see
IRANIAN
Persian Gulf country   UAE,
IRAN, IRAQ, QATAR,
KUWAIT, BAHRAIN, CHALDEA,
SAUDI ARABIA
Persian rug   KALI, HERAT,
SARUK, SENNA, ANHALT,
SAROUK, ARDABIL, FERAHAN,
ISFAHAN, ISPAHAN,
TEHERAN, SERABAND
Persian ruler   SHAH, CYRUS,
DARIUS, SULTAN, XERXES
Persian title   AZAM
Persian Wars battles   PLATAEA,
SALAMIS, MARATHON,
THERMOPYLAE
persiflage   BANTER, JESTING,
BADINAGE, REPARTEE
persist   LAST, PLOD, ENDURE,
INSIST, KEEPON, PERSEVERE
persistence   TENACITY
persistent   DOGGED,
STUBBORN, INSISTENT,
TENACIOUS
person   MAN, ONE, PART,
ROLE, BEING, HUMAN,
WOMAN, SOMEBODY,
INDIVIDUAL
person, to a   ALL, BARNONE,
EVERYONE
persona non grata   UNDESIRABLE,
UNTOUCHABLE
personable   COMELY, GENIAL,
AMIABLE, CHARMING,
HANDSOME, SOCIABLE
personage   VIP, NIBS, STAR,
BIGWIG, NOTABLE,
CELEBRITY, DIGNITARY
personal   OWN, BODILY,
PRIVATE, CORPORAL,
INTIMATE, INDIVIDUAL
personal ad abbr.   MBF, MBM,
MWF, MWM, SJF, SJM, SWF,
SWM
personality   EGO, SELF, STAR,
NATURE, CELEBRITY,
CHARACTER

personify   EMBODY, TYPIFY,
PORTRAY, STANDFOR,
EXEMPLIFY, INCARNATE
personnel   CREW, CADRE,
HANDS, SQUAD, STAFF,
STABLE, TROUPE, WORKERS
perspective   VIEW, ANGLE,
STAND, VISTA, OUTLOOK,
PANORAMA, VIEWPOINT
perspicacious   KEEN, ACUTE,
OBSERVANT
perspicacity   ACUMEN,
INSIGHT
perspiration   DEW, SUDOR,
SWEAT, EGESTA,
HIDROSIS
persuade   COAX, URGE,
CAJOLE, ENTICE, INDUCE,
CONVINCE
persuasible   DOCILE,
AMENABLE
persuasion   PLEA, CREED,
FAITH, BELIEF, SUASION,
BRIBERY
persuasive   COGENT,
FORCEFUL, CONVINCING
pert   ARCH, BOLD, FLIP,
SASSY, SAUCY
pertain   RELATE, CONCERN,
BEAR (UP)ON
pertaining   APROPOS,
REGARDING
pertinacious   FIRM, DOGGED,
RESOLUTE, INSISTENT
pertinent   APT, FIT, ANENT,
GERMANE, RELEVANT
perturb   ALARM, WORRY,
HARASS, RUFFLE, DISQUIET
Peru, capital of   LIMA
peruse   CON, SCAN, STUDY,
SURVEY, SCRUTINIZE
Peruvian city/town   ICA, LIMA,
PUNO, CARAZ, CUZCO,
NAZCA, PISCO, PIURA, TACNA,
CALLAO, HUARAZ,
HUANUCO, IQUITOS,
AREQUIPA, CHICLAYO,
CHIMBOTE, TRUJILLO,
CAJAMARCA
Peruvian lake   TITICACA
Peruvian language   AYMARA,
QUECHUA
Peruvian measure   TOPO,
GALON
Peruvian money   SOL, LIBRA,
DINERO, PESETA
Peruvian mountain(s)   ANDES,
MISTI, HUASCAN,
COROPUNA, HUASCARAN

Peruvian neighbor   **CHILE,
BRAZIL, BOLIVIA, ECUADOR,
COLOMBIA**
Peruvian relic   **GUACO, HUACO**
Peruvian ruins   **CHANCHAN,
MACHUPICCHU**
Peruvian river   **ENE, ICA, NAPO,
PISCO, PURUS, TIGRE,
AMAZON, MORONA, YAGUAS,
YAVARI, MARANON,
PASTAZA, TAPICHE, UCAYALI,
APURIMAC, HUALLAGA,
PUTUMAYO, URUBAMBA**
pervade   **FILL, IMBRUE,
PERFUSE, PERMEATE**
pervasive   **PREVALENT,
SUFFUSIVE**
perverse   **BAD, SINFUL,
WICKED, WAYWARD,
CONTRARY, OBDURATE**
pervert   **WARP, TWIST,
DISTORT, CORRUPT,
DEPRAVE**
pesky   **VERY, VEXING,
IRKSOME, ANNOYING,
MISCHIEVOUS, TROUBLESOME**
pessimist   **CYNIC, GROUCH,
KILLJOY, WORRIER,
FATALIST**
pessimist,   *opp. of* **OPTIMIST**
pessimistic   **MOROSE,
CYNICAL, NEGATIVE,
FATALISTIC, DISCOURAGING**
pest   **NAG, BANE, CURSE,
BLIGHT, PLAGUE, SCOURGE,
NUISANCE**
pest control   **DCON, ORKIN**
pester   **NAG, ANNOY, TEASE,
BADGER, HARASS, HECTOR**
pesticide   **BHC, DDT, ALAR,
BORAX, ALDRIN, DIQUAT,
ARSENIC, BIOCIDE, CYANIDE,
AMITROLE, CREOSOTE,
NICOTINE, PYRETHRIN**
pestilence   **PLAGUE, MURRAIN,
SCOURGE, EPIDEMIC,
PANDEMIC**
pestle   **BRAY, PILUM, BEETLE,
MULLER, PISTIL**
pestle companion   **MORTAR**
pet   **CADE, NECK, SNIT, PIQUE,
CODDLE, COSSET, FONDLE**
petal   **LEAF**
petcock   **VALVE, FAUCET**
Peter and the Wolf character
SASHA, SONIA
peter out   **END, WANE, EXPIRE,
DWINDLE**
Peter Pan author   **BARRIE**

Peter Pan character   **HOOK,
NANA, SMEE, TINK, WENDY,
TINKERBELL, DARLING,
MICHAEL, TIGER LILY**
Peter the Great wife   **EUDOXIA**
petiole   **STEM, STALK, STIPE**
petition   **ASK, SUE, PLEA, SUIT,
APPEAL, REQUEST,
ENTREAT(Y)**
Petrarch's love   **LAURA**
petrel   **GONY, TITI, MOLLY,
NELLY, PRION, FORMEL,
FULMAR, GOONEY, TEETEE,
PINTADO, STINKER,
JOHNDOWN, ALBATROSS,
MALLEMUCK, MOLLEMUCK,
MOLLYHAWK**
petrify   **SCARE, OSSIFY,
HARDEN, TERRIFY,
PARALYZE, FOSSILIZE**
petrol   *see* **GAS**
petrolatum   **VASELINE**
petroleum derivative   **COKE,
PITCH, BUTANE, ASPHALT,
BENZINE, BITUMEN,
NAPHTHA, GASOLENE,
KEROSENE, PARAFFIN**
petroleum source   **SHALE**
Petruchio's wife   **KAT(IE)**
petticoat   **SLIP, CAMISOLE,
CRINOLINE**
Petticoat Junction names   **SAM,
KATE, BETTY JO, BRADLEY,
BILLIE JO, BOBBIE JO,
SHADYREST, HOOTERVILLE**
pettifogger   **TYRO, LAWYER,
SHYSTER, ATTORNEY,
QUIBBLER**
pettish   **CROSS, FRETFUL,
PEEVISH, PETULANT**
petty   **MEAN, MINOR, SMALL,
PALTRY, TRIVIAL, INFERIOR,
PICAYUNE**
petulance   **IRRITABILITY**
petulant   **CROSS, SHORT,
TESTY, FRETFUL, GROUCHY,
PEEVISH, IRRITABLE**
pew   **BENCH, STALL**
peyote   **CACTUS, MESCAL**
pH measures   **ACIDITY,
ALKALINITY**
Phaedra relative   **MINOS,
THESEUS**
phantasm, phantom   **GHOST,
EIDOLON, SPECTER,
ILLUSION**
Phantom of the Opera character
ERIK
pharaoh   *see* **EGYPTIAN**

Pharez relative	**TAMAR**
pharmacist	**DRUGGIST**
pharmacy	**DRUGSTORE**
pharynx	**THROAT, PASSAGE**
phase	**SIDE, ANGLE, FACET,**
	STAGE, ASPECT, INSTAR
pheasant	**CHIR, ARGUS,**
	CHEER, KALIJ, MONAL,
	HOAZIN, KALEEJ, MINAUL,
	MONAUL, MOONAL, PUKRAS,
	HOATZIN, KALEEGE,
	MOONAUL
Phideas statue	**ATHENA**
philander	**WOO, CHEAT,**
	DALLY, FLIST, LOVER,
	OPOSSUM, WALLABY,
	BANDICOOT
philanthropist	**ANGEL, DONOR,**
	SUPPORTER, BENEFACTOR
philanthory	**ALMS,**
	GENEROSITY
philatelic	*see* **STAMPS**
Philemon's wife	**BAUCIS**
philippic	**SCREED, TIRADE,**
	HARANGUE, JOBATION
Philippine archipelago	**SULU**
Philippine battle site	**BATAAN,**
	COREGIDOR
Philippine bay	**BALER, HONDA,**
	ORMOC, SUBIC, ILIGAN,
	BALAYAN, TAYABAS
Philippine city/town	**IBA, BOAC,**
	CEBU, DAET, JOLO, MATI,
	PILI, DAVAO, DIGOS,
	LAOAG, PASAY, PASIG,
	TAGUM, VIGAN,
	BUTUAN, ILOILO, MANILA,
	TANDAG, BACOLOD,
	CALOOCAN
Philippine guerrillas	**ABUSAYAF**
Philippine gulf	**DAVAO, LEYTE,**
	LINGAYEN
Philippine island	**CEBU, BATAN,**
	BOHOL, LEYTE, LUZON,
	PANAY, SAMAR, CUIJON,
	LUBANG, TABLAS, NEGROS,
	MASBATE, MINDORO,
	PALAWAN, MINDANAO,
	CORREGIDOR
Philippine lake	**TAAL, LANAO**
Philippine language	**PILIPINO;**
	see **PACIFIC ISLANDS**
Philippine leader	**ROXAS,**
	AQUINO, GARCIA, OSMENA,
	MARCOS, QUIRINO
Philippine measure	**LOAN,**
	BRAZA, CABAN, CHUPA,
	GANTA, SALOP, APATAN,
	BAUTA, QUINON
Philippine money	**PESO**
Philippine mountain	**APO, TAAL,**
	MAYON, PULOG, CANLAON,
	ARAYAT, ZAMBALES
Philippine president	**RAMOS,**
	ROXAS, AQUINO, GARCIA,
	LAUREL, MARCOS, OSMENA,
	QUEZON, QUIRINO
Philippine province	**ABRA, CEBU,**
	SULU, AKLAN, ALBAY, BOHOL,
	CAPIZ, DAVAO, LEYTE, RIZAL,
	AURORA, BATAAN, CAVITE,
	IFUGAO, ILOILO, LAGUNA,
	QUEZON, TARLAC, ANTIQUE,
	BALUCAN, BATANES,
	BENGUET, CAGAYAN, ISABELA,
	MASBATE, QUIRINO,
	ROMBLON
Philippine river	**AGNO, LANAO,**
	AGUSAN, CAGAYAN,
	MINDANAO
Philippine tree	**DAO, IBA, ACLE,**
	BOGO, IFIL, IPIL, ABILO,
	ALMON, ANILO, BAYOG,
	BAYOK, BETIS, DANLI, GUIJO,
	LAUAN, LIGAS, YACAL,
	ABILAO, ANILAO, ANILAU,
	DANGLIN
Philippine weight	**FARDO,**
	PICUL, PUNTO, LACHSA,
	QUILATE
Philippines, capital of	**MANILA**
Philistine	**BOOR, BARBARIAN**
Philistine city	**GATH, GAZA,**
	EKRON
philosopher	**CYNIC, DREAMER,**
	SKEPTIC, THINKER,
	THEORIST; *see p. 544*
philosopher's stone	**ELIXIR**
philosophy	**YOGA, DEISM,**
	CYNICS, EGOISM, MONISM,
	ATHEISM, ATOMISM,
	DUALISM, MARXISM,
	REALISM, SENSISM, SOPHISM,
	THOMISM, ELEATICS,
	FATALISM, HEDONISM,
	HUMANISM, IDEALISM,
	NIHILISM, PSYCHISM,
	SOMATISM, STOICISM,
	VITALISM, ANARCHISM,
	CASUISTRY, DIALECTIC,
	PLATONISM, EMPIRICISM,
	POSITIVISM, PRAGMATISM,
	EPICUREANISM,
	ANTHROPOSOPHY,
	SCHOLASTICISM,
	EXISTENTIALISM,
	UTILITARIANISM,
	TRANSCENDENTALISM

phlegmatic **CALM, COOL, DULL, INERT, WATERY, SLUGGISH, APATHETIC**
phloem **BARK, BAST, TISSUE**
phobia **FEAR, AGORA, DREAD, AVERSION**
Phoebe **MOON, DIANA, SELENE, ARTEMIS**
Phoebe daughter **LETO**
Phoebe on dice **FIVE**
Phoebus **SOL, SUN, APOLLO**
Phoenician city **TYRE, GEBAL, SIDON, BYBLOS, JUBAYL, BERYTUS**
Phoenician god(dess) *see p. 648*
Phoenician princess **EUROPA**
Phoenix **BENU**
phone *see* **TELEPHONE**
phonetic system **WA, ROMIC**
phonograph **PLAYER, VICTROLA, GRAMOPHONE**
phonograph part **NEEDLE, PREAMP, STYLUS, TONEARM, (TURN)TABLE**
phony *see* **FAKE**
photo(s) **MUG, PIC, PIX, SHOT, SNAP, STAT, SEPIA**
photocopy **STAT, XEROX**
photograph **GIF, JPG, JPEG, SHOT, SNAP(SHOT), PRINT, SEPIA, STILL, GLOSSY, PICTURE**
photographer **CAMERIST, CAMERAMAN, SHUTTERBUG**
photographer, famous **CAPA, ADAMS, ARBUS, ATGET, BRADY, LANGE, NADAR, TAMES, TALBOT, ABBOTT, FENTON, HANSEN, STRAND, WESTON, CAMERON, EMERSON, GARDNER, STEICHEN, STIEGLITZ**
photographic equipment **LENS, TIMER, CAMERA, FINDER, TRIPOD, SHUTTER, ENLARGER, FLASHGUN, FLASHBULB, FLASHCUBE**
photographic solution **BATH, FILM, HYPO, FIXER, TONER, REDUCER, DEVELOPER**
photography **PICTURES, SHOOTING**
phrase **CLAUSE, SAYING, SLOGAN, LOCUTION, UTTERANCE**
phraseology **DICTION, WORDING, EXPRESSION**
Phrygian god **MEN, ATTIS**
physic *see* **LAXATIVE**
physical **REAL, SOMAL,**

BODILY, SOMATIC, CORPOR(E)AL, MATERIAL, TANGIBLE
physical science **GEOLOGY, PHYSICS, ASTRONOMY, CHEMISTRY, MINERALOGY**
physical therapy **MASSAGE, EXERCISE**
physician **MD, DOC, CURER, LEECH, MEDIC, DOCTOR, MEDICO, SURGEON, INTERNIST**
physician, famous **ERB, MAYO, PARE, POTT, REED, RUSK, SALK, GALEN, HADEN, OSLER, PAGET, SABIN, SPOCK, CARREL, COLLES, DOOLEY, FINLAY, FINSEN, HALLER, HARVEY, JENNER, LISTER, MESMER, MORTON, PARRAN, PERERA, RHAZES;** *see* **NOBEL**
physicist, famous *see p. 545*
physics branch **OPTICS, STATICS, DYNAMICS, KINETICS, ACOUSTICS, MECHANICS**
physiognomy **MUG, FACE, PORTRAIT**
physique **BODY, BUILD, FRAME, SHAPE**
pi **MIXUP, JUMBLE, MIXTURE**
pianist, famous **ANDA, HESS, NERO, ARRAU, GOULD, KEMPF, ROSEN, BUSONI, CURZON, GARNER, ITURBI, LEVANT, SERIUN, CLIBURN, HOFMANN, RICHTER, SOLOMON, HOROWITZ, LHEVINNE, LIBERACE, PACHMANN, SZPILMAN**
piano **BABY, SOFT(LY), GRAND, SPINET, PIANOLA;** *see p. 642*
piazza **ARCADE, SQUARE, VERANDA**
picaresque **ROGUISH, EPISODIC**
Picasso **PABLO, PALOMA**
picayune *see* **PETTY**
Pichincha volcano city **QUITO**
pick **BEST, CULL, BEELE, ELITE, FLANG, GLEAN, PLUCK, NIBBLE, CHOOSE, OPT FOR, SELECT, CHOICE, PLECTRUM**
pick up **GET, LEARN, IMPROVE**
pickax **BEELE, GURLET, TUBBER, TWIBIL, MATTOCK**
picket **PALE, PENIN, STAKE, CORRAL, SENTRY, STRIKE, TETHER, PROTEST, WALKOUT, SENTINEL, PROTESTER**

pickle **FIX, JAM, ALEC, CORN, CURE, DILL, ACHAR, BRINE, SOUSE, GHERKIN**	**SALOMEY, NAPOLEON, PORKY PIG, MISS PIGGY**
pickpocket **DIP, WIRE, PRIG, DIPPER, CLYFAKER, CUTPURSE**	pig feed **SLOP**
	pig, neutered **BARROW**
	pig, young **ELT, GILT, GRICE, SHOAT, FARROW, PIGLET, TANTONY, SUCKLING**
Pickwick Papers author **DICKENS**	
picky **CHOOSY, PARTICULAR**	pigboat **SUBMARINE**
picky person **EATER**	pigeon **NUN, GOURA, TURBIT, FANTAIL, INFORMER;** see **DOVE**
picnic **LARK, SNAP, CINCH, JUNKET, OUTING, COOKOUT, CLAMBAKE**	
	— pigeon **CLAY**
Picnic author **INGE**	pigeon — **TOED**
pictorial **VIVID, GRAPHIC, ILLUSTRATED**	pigeon genus **COLUMBA**
	pigeon, young **PIPER, SQUAB, SQUEAKER**
picture **ICON, IMAGE, MURAL, CANVAS, DEPICT, FRESCO, EPITOME, MONTAGE, PROFILE, TABLEAU;** see **PHOTO**	
	pigeonhole **SLOT, NICHE, SHELVE, SECTION, CUBBY(HOLE)**
Picture of Dorian Gray author **WILDE**	pigheaded **BALKY, MULISH, STUBBORN, OBSTINATE**
picturesque **QUAINT, SCENIC, IDYLLIC, CHARMING**	pigment **TINT, COLOR(ANT), IMPASTO;** see p. 531
pidgin language **SABIR, JARGON, CHINOOK, DE MER**	pigment, absence of **ALBINISM, VITILIGO, LEUKODERMA**
	pigment-forming substance **DOPA**
pie **TART, PASTY, JUMBLE, PASTRY, COBBLER**	pigskin **FOOTBALL**
	pigtail **CUE, BRAID, PLAIT, QUEUE, COLETA**
pie filling **APPLE, MINCE, PECAN, PEACH, RAISIN, CHERRY, RHUBARB, MINCEMEAT**	
	pike **GAR, GED, ESOX, GEDD, JACK, LUCE, MUSKIE, ROBALO, ZANDER, ARAPAIMA, PICKEREL, SPONTOON**
piebald **PIED, PYOT, PINTO, CALICO**	
	piker **MISER, SCROOGE, TIGHTWAD, SKINFLINT**
piece **BIT, CHIP, PART, SLICE, CANTLE, COLLOP;** see **GUN**	
	pilaster **ANTA, PIER, ALETTE**
piece of cake **CINCH, WALKOVER**	Pilate's realm **JUDEA**
	Pilate's wife **PROCIA**
piece out **EKE, CANTLE**	pilchard **FUMADO, HERRING, PICHER, SARDINE**
piecemeal **SLOWLY, BIT BY BIT, GRADUALLY**	
	pile **NAP, HEAP, LOAD, REKE, RICK, HOARD, STACK**
Pied Piper river **WESER**	
Pied Piper town **HAMELIN**	pile driver **RAM, TUP, BEETLE, OLIVER, FISTUCA**
pier **COB, ANTA, COBB, PILASTER, BUTTRESS;** see **LANDING**	
	pile up **AMASS, HOARD**
	piles **HEMORRHOIDS**
pierce **GORE, STAB, GOUGE, GRIDE, LANCE, THIRL, IMPALE, PUNCTURE**	pilfer **COP, ROB, SNIG, FILCH, MOOCH, STEAL, SWIPE, THIEVE, SHOPLIFT**
piercing **KEEN, SHARP, BITING, SHRILL, CUTTING, INCISIVE**	pilgrim **ALDEN, HADJI, IHRAM, PALMER, MIGRANT, PIONEER**
piety **FAITH, DEVOTION, HOLINESS**	pilgrim destination **KUM, QUM, ROME, MECCA, JERUSALEM**
piffle **ROT, HOKUM, HOGWASH, NONSENSE**	Pilgrim settlement **PLYMOUTH**
	Pilgrim ship **MAYFLOWER**
pig **HOG, SOW, MOLD, SLOB, INGOT, SHOAT;** see **SWINE**	pilgrimage **HADJ, QUEST, CRUSADE**
pig, famous **PORKY, ARNOLD, BIG RED, LOUISA, WILBUR,**	pilgrim's garb **IHRAM**
	Pilgrim's Progress author **BUNYAN**

Pilgrim's Progress character
    DEMAS, CHRISTIAN
pill   DOSE, GOLI, BOLUS,
    DRAGEE, PELLET, TABLET,
    CAPSULE
pillage   see PLUNDER
pillar   LAT, JAMB, PIER, PROP,
    HERMA, NEWEL, SHAFT,
    STELE, OBELISK, PILASTER
pillar of —   FIRE, SMOKE,
    STRENGTH
Pillars of Hercules   ABILA,
    CALPE, GIBRALTAR,
    JEBELMUSA
pillory   CANG, JOUG, YOKE,
    BRANK, STOCK, TRONE,
    BRANKS, CANGUE
pillow   COD, PAD, BOLSTER,
    CUSHION, HEADREST
pillow filler   CEIBA, EIDER,
    KAPOK, FEATHERS
pilot   FLYER, GUIDE, STEER,
    AVIATOR, HELMSMAN
pilotless aircraft   DRONE,
    GLIDER
pimento   PEPPER, RELISH,
    PAPRIKA, ALLSPICE
pimp   PANDER(ER),
    FANCYMAN, PROCURER
pimple   BOIL, POCK, PLOOK,
    WHEAL, PAPULE, PUSTULE
pin   FID, NOG, ACUS, TIGE,
    AGLET, DOWEL, RIVET,
    THOLE, BROOCH, COTTER,
    FIBULA, PINTLE, SKEWER,
    SKITTLE
pinafore   TIER, APRON
pince-nez   LORGNON
pincer(s)   CLAW, CHELA,
    TONGS, FORCEPS, NIPPERS,
    TWEEZER(S)
pinch   NIP, DASH, CRAMP,
    PUGIL, TWEAK, ARREST,
    STRAIT, SQUEEZE
pinched   URLED, CHITTY
Pindar work   ODE
pine   FADE, FLAG, MOPE, YEARN
pine tree   IE, CHIL, CHIR, HALA,
    HUON, IEIE, MIRO, PINO,
    BUNYA, KAORI, KAURI,
MATAI, MATSU, OCOTE, PINON,
    VACOA, COWRIE, KAURIE,
    KAWRIE, TARWOOD,
    CHIRPINE, CHEERPINE
Pine Tree State   ME, MAINE
pineapple   NANA, PINA, PUYA,
    ANANA(S)
pinguid   FAT(TY), OILY,
    GREASY, UNCTUOUS

pinion   COG, GEAR, WING,
    PENNON, FEATHER,
    COGWHEEL
pinion partner   RACK
pink   PIERCE, RADICAL,
    SCALLOP; see p. 531
pink-slip   CAN, FIRE, SACK
pinnacle   EPI, ACME, APEX,
    PEAK, SERAC, SUMMIT,
    ZENITH
pinniped   SEAL, WALRUS
Pinocchio author   COLLODI
Pinocchio carver   GEPETTO
pinochle deck, card not in   TREY,
    DEUCE, CINQUE, QUATRE
pinochle deck, lowest card   NINE
pinochle term   DIX, BETE,
    MELD, KITTY, WIDOW
pinochle-like game   BEZIQUE
pinpoint   DOT, LOCATE,
    IDENTIFY
pins and needles   PARESTHESIA
pintado   CERO, CHINTZ,
    SIERRA, KINGFISH
pintail   DUCK, GROUSE
pinto   PIEBALD, MOTTLED
pinup   GIRLIE, CHEESECAKE
pioneer   FOUND, MINER,
    SAPPER, SETTLER,
    TRAILBLAZER
pious   GODLY, DEVOUT,
    SACRED, SAINTLY,
    RELIGIOUS
pip   ACE, HIT, ROUP, SEED, SPOT
pipe   HUB, TEE, FIFE, FLUE,
    MAIN, NUBB, REED, TUBE,
    BRIAR, BRIER, RISER, STRAW,
    DUDEEN, HOOKAH,
    CALUMET, CONDUIT,
    NARG(H)ILE
pipe smoke   TEWEL, HOOKAH,
    CALUMET, NARGILE
pipelike   TUBATE
pipe part   BOWL, HUBB, STEM,
    STUMMEL
piping   REEDY, SHRILL,
    TRIMMING
piquant   RACY, SHARP, SPICY,
    ZESTY, PUNGENT
pique   VEX, PEEVE, STING,
    EXCITE, NETTLE, PROVOKE
piquet term   PIC, CAPOT,
    REPIC, RUBICON, SINKING
piracy   COPYING, PLUNDER,
    ROBBERY, PLAGIARISM
pirate   XEBEC, SEARAT,
    BRIGAND, CORSAIR,
    PICAROON, PLAGIARIST,
    PRIVATEER, FREEBOOTER

pirate, famous	**HOOD, KIDD, ANSON, DRAKE, ROVER, MORGAN, VIKING, CORNISH, LAFITTE, BARBAROSSA, BLACKBEARD**
pirate flag	**JOLLY ROGER**
Pisa sight	**(LEANING)TOWER**
pistol	*see* **GUN**
piston	**VALVE, PLUNGER**
pit	**GAP, HOLE, MINE, POCK, SEED, SUMP, ABYSS, FOSSA, FOVEA, LACUNA, POTHOLE**
pitch	**KEY, SHY, TAR, CANT, CAST, CHIP, HURL, LINE, PLUG, REEL, TONE, FLING, TOSS, CURVE, LURCH, RESIN, SLOPE, SPIEL, TWIRL, PATTER, SLIDER, BITUMEN**
pitch, in baseball	**CURVE, SLIDER, SPITTER, BEANBALL, KNUCKLER, SPITBALL**
pitcher	*see* **JUG, BASEBALL**
pitcher motion	**WINDUP, DELIVERY**
piteous	**PATHETIC**
pitfall	**TRAP, SNARE, HAZARD**
pith	**JET, NUB, CORE, GIST, MEAT, PULP, MARROW**
pithy	**CORKY, MEATY, TERSE, CONCISE**
pitiable	**MEAN, PALTRY, TRAGIC, MISERABLE**
pitiful	**MEAN, DISMAL, PATHETIC, WRETCHED**
pitiless	**MEAN, CRUEL, RUTHLESS**
pittance	**BIT, TRIFLE**
pitted	**ETCHED, STONED, FOVEATE**
Pittsburgh museum	**WARHOL**
Pittsburgh team	**PIRATES, PENGUINS, STEELERS**
pituary gland hormone	**PROLACTIN**
pity	**RUE, RUTH, MERCY, CHARITY**
pivot	**AXIS, SLUE, TURN, HINGE, PINTLE, SWIVEL**
pixel	**DOT**
pixilated	**FEY, DOTTY, DRUNK, TIPSY**
pixy	*see* **ELF**
placard	**BILL, POST(ER), AFFICHE**
placate	**PACIFY, APPEASE, MOLLIFY**
place(s)	**JOB, SET, LIEU, LOCI, RANK, SEAT, SPOT, LOCUS, NICHE, POSIT, SCENE, SETIN,**

	SITUS, STEAD, VENUE, ASSIGN, LOCALE, STATUS
placebo	**TOADY, VESPERS, SUGAR PILL, SYCOPHANT**
placid	**CALM, QUIET, SUANT, SERENE, HALCYON, TRANQUIL**
plagiarism	**THEFT, PIRACY**
plagiarize	**CRIB, LIFT, PIRATE**
plague	**WANION, MURRAIN, SCOURGE;** *see* **PEST, PESTER**
plaice	**SOLE, FLOUNDER**
plaid	**MAUD, TARTAN**
plain	**BARE, CHOL, EVEN, MERE, VELD, WOLD, BLUNT, CAMPO, CLEAR, HEATH, LIANO, PAMPA, VELDT, WEALD, CHASTE, HOMELY, STEPPE, TUNDRA, EVIDENT, LOWLAND, OBVIOUS, PRAIRIE, SAVANNA**
Plains Indian	**OTO, CREE, CROW, IOWA, KIOWA, OSAGE, PONCA, SIOUX, DAKOTA, OJIBWA, PAWNEE, QUAPAW, SARCEE, WICHITA, CHEYENNE, COMANCHE, MISSOURI, BLACKFOOT**
plaint	**MOAN, GRIPE, LAMENT**
plaintiff	**SUER, SUITOR, ACCUSER, LITIGANT**
plaintive	**SAD, WISTFUL, MOURNFUL, MELANCHOLY**
plait	**PLY, MESH, PLAT, PLEX, BRAID, QUEUE, TRESS, PIGTAIL**
plan	**MAP, PLAT, PLOT, DRAFT, ETTLE, DESIGN, INTEND, SCHEMA, PROJECT**
plane	**FLAT, GRADE, LEVEL, SMOOTH, SURFACE;** *see* **AIRCRAFT**
planet	**MARS, EARTH, PLUTO, VENUS, SATURN, URANUS, JUPITER, MERCURY, NEPTUNE**
planetarium	**ORRERY**
plank	**DECK, BOARD, SLATE, TICKET**
plankton	**ALGA, KRILL**
plant(s)	**SOW, MILL, FLORA, INSERT, FACTORY;** *see p. 681*
plant, carnivorous	**SUNDEW, FLYTRAP, PINKFAN**
plant disease	**BLET, BUNT, CURL, ESCA, GALL, RUST, SMUT, ERGOT, SCALD, AECIUM, BLIGHT, FUNGUS, ERINOSE, STIFFEN**
plant fiber	*see p. 535*

plant, odorous RUE, MINT,
ANISE, BASIL, TANSY,
THYME, HYSSOP, YARROW,
BUGBANE, BURDOCK,
FIGWORT, HENBANE, MILFOIL,
ANGELICA, CAMOMILE,
MARJORAM, TARRAGON
plant, hydroelectric GURI,
ROSS, ASWAN, NUREK,
SWIFT, ASSUAN, BRATSK,
DALLES, FURNAS, HOOVER,
INGURI, BOULDER,
KUIBYSHEV, VOLGOGRAD;
see p. 613
plant, medicinal RUE, ALOE,
HERB, SENNA, TANSY,
URENA, ARNICA, IPECAC,
SIMPLE, SPURGE, BONESET,
GENTIAN, LOBELIA
plantation HOLT, FINCA,
VERBAL, BOWERY,
HACIENDA
plantation, type of COFFEE,
COTTON, RUBBER,
SUGARCANE
plantlike animal CORAL,
SPONGE, ZOOPHYTE
plasma WHEY, BLOOD
plaster DAUB, ADOBE, BESOT,
GESSO, GROUT, SMEAR,
PARGET, STUCCO
plaster of Paris YESO, GESSO,
GYPSUM, STUCCO, HYDRATE
plastered DRUNK
plastic BUNA, UREA, ALKYD,
FURAN, NYLON, VINYL,
CASEIN, FURANE, LIGNIN,
LUCITE, ACETATE, ACRYLIC,
FICTILE, FORMICA, NITRATE,
PLIABLE, POLYMER,
TERPENE, BAKELITE,
PHENOUC, RESINOID,
SYNTHETIC
Plastic — Band ONO
plate DOD, GRID, SLAB,
PATEN, SCUTE, DISCUS,
TAGGER
plateau MESA, PLAT, PUNA,
KAR(R)OO, PARAMO
platform BEMA, DAIS, KANG,
DOLLY, SOLEA, STAGE,
PERRON, PODIUM, PULPIT,
SOLLAR, SOLLER, ESTRADE,
ROSTRUM, TRIBUNE
Plath book ARIEL
platinum-like alloy WHITE GOLD
platitude ION, MENO, CLICHE,
TRUISM, BROMIDE,
TRITENESS

Plato work CRITO, PHAEDO,
REPUBLIC, SYMPOSIUM
Plato's idea EIDE, EIDOS
Plato's student ARISTOTLE
Plato's teacher SOCRATES
platoon leader LOOEY,
LIEUTENANT
Platoon director STONE
platter DISC, DISH, ASHET,
PLATE, SALVER, TRENCHER
plaudit CLAP(PING), PRAISE,
OVATION, APPLAUSE
plausible GLIB, AFFABLE,
POPULAR, CREDIBLE,
SPECIOUS
Plautus specialty COMEDY
play ACT, DRAMA, ENACT,
FARCE, SCOPE, SPIEL, SPORT,
COMEDY, MASQUE, MIRACLE,
MYSTERY, PAGEANT,
TRAGEDY
play (around) HORSE, FROLIC
play, famous WIZ, CATS, HAIR,
MAME, RENT, ANNIE, EVITA,
DANCIN, GEMINI, GREASE,
HARVEY, PIPPIN, CABARET,
CHICAGO, LIONKING,
OKLAHOMA, DEATHTRAP;
see also p. 512
play hooky TIB, SKIP
play part ACT, BIT, ACTI,
ACTV, ROLE, ACTII, ACTIV,
EXODE, SCENA, SCENE, ACTIII,
EXODOS, EXODUS, FINALE,
STANZA, WALKON, CURTAIN
playboy LOVER, GIGOLO,
GADABOUT
Playboy founder HEFNER
player(s) DUB, HAM, CAST,
DIVA, MIME, STAR, ACTOR,
SHINE, MUMMER, ACTRESS,
TROUPER, THESPIAN
playful MERRY, FRISKY,
SPORTIVE
playground equipment GYM,
SLIDE, SWING, TEETER,
CLIMBER, JUNGLEGYM
plaything TOY, PAWN,
BAUBLE, TRINKET
playwright see DRAMATIST
plaza MART, MARKET,
PIAZZA, SQUARE
plea NOLO, ABATER, APPEAL,
PRAYER, REQUEST,
DEMURRER, ENTREATY,
PETITION
plead BEG, SUE, ARGUE, PRESS,
ALLEGE, ENTREAT,
IMPLORE

pleasant   NICE, LEPID, GENIAL,
       AFFABLE, AMIABLE
Pleasant Island   NAURU
pleasantry   GAG, WIT, JEST,
    JOKE, BANTER, WITTICISM
please   SUIT, FANCY, ARRIDE,
       DELIGHT, GLADDEN,
       GRATIFY, INDULGE
pleased   GLAD, HAPPY,
       TICKLED, THRILLED,
       CONTENTED
pleasing   NICE, ROSEATE,
       ENGAGING, AGREEABLE
pleasure   JOY, WILL, WISH,
    LIKING, RELISH, DELIGHT,
    ECSTASY, ENJOYMENT
pleat   FOLD, TUCK, CRIMP,
    PLAIT, SHIRR, CREASE,
    GATHER, RUFFLE, PLICATE
pleated   PLISSE, PLICATE,
       SHIRRED
plebeian   COARSE, COMMON,
       VULGAR, ORDINARY
plebiscite   REFERENDUM
pledge   VAS, VOW, BOND,
    GAGE, OATH, PAWN, SWEAR,
    TOAST, TROTH, ENGAGE
Pleiades   MAIA, MEROPE,
    ALCYONE, CELAENO,
    ELECTRA, STEROPE, TAYGETA
Pleiades parent   ATLAS,
       PLEIONE
plenipotentiary   ABSOLUTE,
    UNLIMITED, AMBASSADOR
plenteous   COPIOUS, FLOWING,
    PROFUSE, ABUNDANT
plentiful   AMPLE, PROFUSE,
    ABUNDANT, PLENTIFUL
plenty   ENOW, LOADS,
    ENOUGH, LIBERTY,
    OPULENCE
pleonasm   EXCESS, NIMIETY,
    TAUTOLOGY, REDUNDANCY
pliable   WAXY, LITRE, PLIANT,
    SUPPLE, PLASTIC
pliers   CLAMP, WRENCH
plight   VOW, GAGE, PLEDGE,
    SCRAPE, DILEMMA
plinth   BASE, ORLO, SOCLE
PLO leader   ABBAS,
    (YASSER)ARAFAT
plod   SLOG, STEP, TRUDGE
plot   LOT, SITE, CABAL,
    SCHEME, CONSPIRE,
    SCENARIO
plover   OXEYE, PRINE, SANDY,
    SNIPE, STILT, TIRMA,
    CURLEW, DIKKOP, DRIVER,
    GODWIT, HAGDON, JACANA,

    MARLIN, TURNIX, WILLET,
    CAPELLA, COURSER,
    DOTTREL, DOWITCH,
    LAPWING, TATTLER,
    WIMBREL, DOTTEREL,
    KILLDEER, WHIMBREL,
    DOWITCHER
plover genus   LIMOSA, TOTANUS
plow   DIG, ROVE, TILL, TURN,
       FURROW
plow part   SOLE, SHARE, SLADE,
    COLTER, CLEVIS, SHEATH
plowed land   ERD, ARADO,
       FURROW
ploy   RUSE, MANEUVER,
       STRATEGY
pluck   GRIT, SAND, NERVE,
    SPUNK, STRUM, TWANG,
    VALOR, AVULSE, SNATCH,
       TWEEZE
plucky   GAME, BRAVE, SPUNKY
plug   NAG, TAP, WAD, BOTT,
    BUNG, CORK, QUID, BOOST,
    CAULK, SHIVE, SPILE, PLATER,
    TAMPON, STOPPER
plug-ugly   THUG, ROWDY,
    TOUGH, RUFFIAN
plum   SLA, AMRA, GAGE, JOBO,
    KAKI, SLOE, DRUPE, DUHAT,
    ISLAY, JAMAN, PRUNE,
    DAMSON, ORLEANS
plumage   DOWN, FEATHERS
plumb   MARK, ERECT, PROBE,
    SOUND, FATHOM, VERTICAL
plumber   FITTER
plumber's tool   SNAKE,
    WRENCH, PLUNGER
plume   DOWN, CREST, EGRET,
    PREEN, QUILL, AIGRET,
    FEATHER, PANACHE
plummet   DIVE, DROP, FALL,
       PLUNGE
plump   FAT, BUXOM, FUBSY,
    PUDGY, STOUT, CHUBBY,
    ROTUND
plunder   ROB, LOOT, PREY,
    SACK, BOOTY, RAVEN,
    RAVIN, REAVE, RIFLE, SPOIL,
    STRIP, MARAUD, PILFER,
    RAPINE, RAVAGE, RAVINE,
    PILLAGE, RANSACK
plunge   DIP, DIVE, DUNK,
       DOUSE
plurality   MAJORITY,
       MULTITUDE
plus   AND, ADDED, EXTRA,
       ADDITIONAL
plush   POSH, SWANKY,
       LUXURIOUS

Plutarch work	**LIVES, ETHICA,**
	MORALIA
Pluto	**DIS, HADES, ORCUS**
Pluto relative	**OPS, CERES,**
SATURN, DEMETER, JUPITER,	
NEPTUNE, PROSERPINA	
plutocrat	**MOGUL, NABOB, FAT**
CAT, TYCOON, MAGNATE,	
CAPITALIST	
ply	**BENT, FOLD, LAYER,**
PURSUE, PRACTICE,	
THICKNESS	
Plymouth Colony governor	
CARVER, WINSLOW,	
BRADFORD	
plywood layer	**VENEER**
Po	**PADUS, ERIDANUS**
Po city	**MILAN, PADUA,**
TURIN, TORINO, VERONA,	
BRESCIA	
Po tributary	**ADDA, DORA,**
OGUO, MINCIO, TANARO,	
TICINO	
poach	**FILCH, SHIRR, STEAL,**
PILFER, TRESPASS	
Pocahontas	**REBECCA**
Pocahontas father	**POWHATAN**
Pocahontas husband	**ROLFE**
pock	*see* PIMPLE
pocket	**FOB, SAC, LODE,**
POCHE, CAVITY, CULDESAC	
pocketbook	**PURSE, WALLET,**
NOTEBOOK	
pockmark	**PIT, SCAR**
poco	**LITTLE, SOMEWHAT**
pod(s)	**GAM, ARIL, BOLL, HULL,**
HUSK, OKRA, PIPI, BENDY,	
CAROB, POUCH, SHELL,	
SHUCK, ACHENE, COCOON,	
CAPSULE, HARICOT,	
SEEDCASE	
podium	**DAIS, FOOT,**
LECTERN, PLATFORM	
Poe love	**LENORE**
Poe work	**BELLS, RAVEN,**
LENORE, GOLDBUG,	
ULALUME, ANNABEL LEE	
poem	**DIT, LAI, LAY, ODE,**
DUAN, EPOS, IDYL, CANTO,	
ELEGY, EPODE, IDYLL, POESY,	
PSALM, RUNES, VERSE,	
AMHRAN, BALLAD, EPOPEE,	
ODELET, RONDEL, SONNET,	
BUCOLIC, CANZONE,	
ECLOGUE, GEORGIC,	
VIRELAY, RONDEAU, SESTINA,	
TRIOLET, VIRELAY,	
MADRIGAL, VILLANELLE;	
see EPIC, VERSE	

poem part	**CANTO, PASSUS,**
STANZA, STROPHE	
poet	**BARD, FILI, SCOP, ODIST,**
RIMER, SCALD, SKALD,	
MYRIST, METRIST, MINSTREL	
poet, inferior	**HACK,**
POETASTER, VERSIFIER	
poetic abbr.	**EEN, ERE**
poet laureate (England)	**KAY,**
PYE, ROWE, TATE, LEWIS,	
AUSTIN, CIBBER, DANIEL,	
DRYDEN, EUSDEN, HUGHES,	
JONSON, MOTION, WARTON,	
BERNARD, BRIDGES,	
CHAUCER, SKELTON,	
SOUTHEY, SPENSER,	
BETJEMAN, DAVENANT,	
SHADWELL, MASEFIELD,	
TENNYSON, WORDSWORTH	
poet laureate (US)	**DOVE, HASS,**
KUNITZ, PINSKY, STRAND,	
WARREN, WILBUR, BRODSKY,	
COLLINS, NEMEROV,	
VANDUYN	
poet, famous	*see p. 625*
poetry	**POESY, VERSE**
poetry collection	**GARLAND,**
ANTHOLOGY	
poetry, muse of	**ERATO,**
CALLIOPE	
pogrom	**CARNAGE, KILLING,**
MASSACRE, SLAUGHTER	
poi source	**TARO**
poignant	**KEEN, BITTER,**
MOVING, TOUCHING	
point	**ACE, DOT, END, JOT,**
ORD, TIP, BARB, GOAL,	
NODE, SPIT, CLEAT, PUNTA,	
PUNTO, CRITERION	
point of view	**ANGLE, SLANT,**
OPINION	
point-blank	**BLUNT, DIRECT,**
STRAIGHT	
pointed	**KEEN, TERSE, ACUATE,**
OGIVAL, CAUSTIC,	
TAPERED, INCISIVE	
pointer	**ROD, YAD, CLUE, DIAL,**
HAND, VANE, WAND,	
ARROW, FESCUE, GNOMON,	
GUNDOG, SETTER	
pointless	**INANE, SILLY,**
SENSELESS	
poise	**MIEN, HOVER, APLOMB,**
BALANCE, BEARING,	
CARRIAGE, COMPOSURE	
poison	**BIK, AKIA, ANTU,**
BANE, BIKH, BISH, HAYA,	
HEMP, HOLA, INEE, LOCO,	
UPAS, ATTER, SUMAC,	

TAINT, TOXIN, URALI,
URARE, URARI, VENOM,
CONINE, CURARE, CURARI,
DATURA, MESCAL, ARSENIC,
CYANIDE
poison antidote *see* ANTIDOTE
poisoning PY(A)EMIA,
LATHYRISM, BOTULISM,
ERGOTISM, PLUMBISM,
PTOMAINE, SEPTIC(A)EMIA
poisonous TOXIC, NOCUOUS,
MEPHITIC, VENOMOUS,
VIRULENT
poisonous plant UPAS, ERGOT,
CONIUM, DATURA,
ACONITE, HEMLOCK,
HENBANE, FOXGLOVE,
LARKSPUR, MANDRAKE,
MAYAPPLE, NUXVOMICA,
BELLADONNA, NIGHTSHADE
poisonous snake ASP, ADDER,
COBRA, KRAIT, VIPER,
RATTLER, COPPERHEAD,
FERDELANCE
poke JAB, JOG, GOAD, PROD,
NUDGE, DAWDLE, MEDDLE,
THRUST
poker ROD, POTE, STOKER
poker hand PAIR, TRIO, FLUSH,
STRAIGHT, FULL HOUSE
poker term BUG, CAT, DOG,
PAT, POT, SEE, ANTE,
DRAW, FULL, FOLD, HOLE,
PAIR, RUNT, STAY, STUD,
BLAZE, FLASH, FLUSH,
KITTY, RAISE, SKEET,
TIGER, KICKER, KILTER,
PELTER, PIGEON,
BOBTAIL
pokerface DEADPAN
pokeweed POCAN, SCORE,
GARGET
pokey DULL, SLOW, STIR,
DOWDY; *see* JAIL
Poland POLSKA, SARMATIA;
see also POLISH
Poland, capital of WARSAW
polar ICY, COLD, ARCTIC,
FRIGID, EXTREME,
ENDMOST, CONTRARY,
OPPOSITE
polarize SPLIT, OPPOSE
pole PEW, ROD, AXIS, MAST,
PUNT, UFER, CABER, QUANT,
SPRIT, STILT, TRILL
pole to pole AX(I)AL
polecat FITCH, SKUNK,
FERRET, FITCHET,
FOU(L)MART, ZORIL(LE)

polemic ROW, FEUD, QUARREL,
ARGUMENT, ALTERCATION,
CONTROVERSY
polemics DEBATE, DISPUTE
polestar GUIDE, MAGNET,
POLARIS, NORTHSTAR
police CID, FBI, MVD, NKVD,
OGPU, GUARD, SURETE,
GESTAPO, PROTECT,
CARABINIERI,
CONSTABULARY
Police hit ROXANNE
police officer MP, COP, BULL,
DICK, FUZZ, NARC, ZARP,
BOBBY, FIVEO, MATRON,
MOUNTY, PEELER, REDCAP,
MARSHAL, OFFICER, SHERIFF,
TROOPER, ZAPTIAH,
FLATFOOT, GENDARME,
CONSTABLE, DETECTIVE,
PATROLMAN
police officer, television KOJAK,
KELLER, COLUMBO,
WILLIAMS, MCGARRETT
police procedure DRAGNET,
LIETEST, PARAFFIN,
POLYGRAPH
police station TANA
policy PLAN, METHOD,
WISDOM, STRATEGY
polio vaccine inventor SALK,
SABIN
polish WAX, BUFF, GLAZE,
GRACE, SHEEN, SHINE,
BURNISH, FURBISH, LEVIGATE
Polish assembly SEJM
Polish city/town LODZ, PILA,
BREST, CHELM, KONIN,
PLOCK, RADOM, TORUN,
GDANSK, KRAKOW, POZNAN,
SLUPSK, TARNOW, WARSAW,
ZAMOSC, WROCLAW,
KATOWICE, SZCZECIM,
BIALYSTOK
Polish composer CHOPIN,
ZELENSKI, MONIUSZKO,
PADEREWSKI, PENDERECKI,
WIENIAWSKY
Polish dance MAZURKA,
POLONAISE
Polish general BOR, ANDERS
polish off EAT, END, KILL,
FINISH, CONSUME
Polish ruling house ANJOU,
PIAST
Polish measure CAL, MILA,
MORG, LINJA, MORGA,
OPOLE, SAZEN, STOPA,
TORUN, WIOKA, CWIERC,

LUBLIN, RORZEC, KWARTA,
LORIEC, GARNIEC
Polish money DUCAT, GROSZ,
MARKA, ZLOTY, FENNIG,
HALERZ
Polish mountain RYSY
Polish pianist CHOPIN,
PADEREWSKI, RUBINSTEIN
Polish river BUG, NER, BOBR,
GWDA, LYNA, ODER, PISA,
WKRA, NAREW, NOTEC,
WARTA, BARYCZ, LIWIEC,
NEISSE, PILICA, WIEPRZ,
BIEBRZA, PARSETA
Polish ruler JOHN, LOUIS,
BATORY, WALESA, MIESKO,
CASIMIR, MOSCICKI,
SIKORSKI, VADISLAV,
PILSUDSKY, SIGISMUND
Polish weight LUT, FUNT,
UNCYA, KAMIAN, SKRUPUL
polished SLEEK, GLOSSY,
URBANE, ELEGANT
polisher WAX, BUFF, EMERY,
RABAT, BUFFER, CROCUS,
PUMICE
polite CIVIL, URBANE,
GENTEEL, GRACIOUS,
WELLBRED, COURTEOUS
politic ASTUTE, CRAFTY,
CUNNING, DISCREET,
JUDICIOUS
political CIVIC, CIVIL, PUBLIC,
BUREAUCRATIC
political party see PARTY
political science CIVICS,
GOVERNMENT
politician HEELER, CONNIVER,
LAWMAKER, POLITICO
poll CROP, HEAD, PATE, VOTE,
COUNT, SKULL, BALLOT,
SURVEY, CANVASS,
TABULATE
pollen DUST, SPORE
pollinate FERTILIZE
pollster ROPER, GALLUP,
HARRIS
pollute SOIL, SULLY, TAINT,
BEFOUL, DEFILE,
CONTAMINATE
polluted DIRTY, IMPURE,
DEFILED, TAINTED,
UNCLEAN
Pollux relative LEDA, CASTOR
Pollyanna OPTIMIST
Polonius relative LAERTES,
OPHELIA
poltergeist GHOST, SPOOK,
SPIRIT, PHANTOM

poltroon MOUSE, COWARD,
CRAVEN, CAITIFF,
DASTARD
Polydorus relative CREON,
HECUBA
polygon see GEOMETRIC
Polynesian language MAORI,
SAMOAN, TONGAN,
HAWAIIAN, TAHITIAN; see
PACIFIC ISLANDS
Polynesian royalty ALII
polyp CYST, CORAL, HYDRA,
TUMOR, GROWTH,
GORGONIA
pomaceous fruit POME, APPLE,
HAWTHORN
pomade MAKEUP, POMATUM,
OINTMENT, BANDOLINE
pommel BEAT, KNOB, POUND,
PUNCH, STRIKE
pomp SHOW, FLOURISH,
DISPLAY, CEREMONY,
GRANDEUR, SPLENDOR,
PAGEANTRY
Pomp and Circumstance composer
ELGAR
Pompadour lover LOUISXV
pompano SAUREL, ALEWIFE,
CARANGOID
Pompeia's husband CAESAR
Pompeii mountain VESUVIUS
pomposity WIND, BOMBAST,
CONCEIT, FUSTIAN,
ARROGANCE
pompous VAIN, GASSY,
TUMID, TURGID,
BOMBASTIC, GRANDIOSE
Ponchielli opera LA GIOCONDA
poncho CLOAK, RUANA,
SLICKER, RAINCOAT
pond LUM, MERE, TARN,
LAGOON, LOCHAN
ponder MULL, PORE, THINK,
WEIGH, REFLECT, RUMINATE
ponderous HEAVY, BULKY,
LABORED, MASSIVE,
WEIGHTY
Ponte Vecchio river ARNO
pontiff POPE, BISHOP,
PONTIFEX
pontifical PAPAL, PAPIST,
EPISCOPAL
pontoon RAFT, BARGE, FLOAT
pony NAG, TAT, CAVY, CRIB,
DRAM, TATT, TROT, NAGGY,
PONEY, TATOO, WELSH,
EXMOOR, SHELTY, TANGUN,
TATTOO, SHELTIE
Pooh creator MILNE

pooh-pooh DERIDE, DISMISS, RIDICULE

pool DIB, DUB, POT, CARR, JEEL, LIDO, LINN, LLYN, MERE, POND, TARN, KITTY, LAGOON, PUDDLE; see BILLIARDS; see also SWIMMING

pool member GENE, STENO

pool player SHARK, RACKER

poop out TIRE, WEAKEN, FRAZZLE

poor NEEDY, SEELY, PALTRY, SHABBY, INDIGENT, INFERIOR, DESTITUTE, PENNILESS

poorhouse HOSPICE, ALMSHOUSE, WORKHOUSE

poorly ILL, SICK, AILING, UNWELL

pop DAD, BANG, COLA, SHOT, SLAP, SNAP, SODA, BURST, CRACK, SHOOT, SMACK, TONIC, FATHER, REPORT, EXPLODE

pop the question PROPOSE

pop up ARISE, OCCUR

Pope PAPACY, PONTIFF, PRIMATE

Popes LEO, JOHN, PAUL, PIUS, CONON, DONUS, FELIX, GAIUS, LANDO, LINUS, PETER, RATH, SOTER, URBAN, ADRIAN, AGATHO, ALBERT, ANGELO, FABIAN, JULIUS, LUCIUS, MARCUS, MARTIN, PHILIP, SIXTUS, VICTOR, ANTEROS, CLEMENT, DAMASUS, GREGORY, RYGINUS, MARINUS, MONTINT, PACELLI, PASCHAL, ROMANUS, SERGIUS, STEPHEN, URSINUS, ZOSIMUS, JOHNPAUL, RONCALLI

Pope, English ADRIAN

Popeye character BLUTO, OLIVE OYL, WIMPY

Popeye creator SEGAR

Popeye food SPINACH

poplar ASP, ABELE, ALAMO, ASPEN, BALSAM

poppy MAW, OPIUM, PAPAVER, CELANDINE, CHICALOTE, BLOODROOT, CREAMCUPS, SANGUINARIA

poppycock ROT, BOSH, BULL, BUNK, CRAP, BALONEY, HOGWASH, MALARKEY, NONSENSE

pops conductor KUNZEL, FIEDLER, LOCKHART, WILLIAMS

populace DEMOS, HOIPOLLOI, see PEOPLE

popular LIKED, COMMON, DEMOTIC, FAMILIAR, PLEBEIAN, VULGATE, ACCEPTED, ENCHORIAL, PREVALENT

popularity FAME, RENOWN

populate PEOPLE, TENANT, INHABIT

population FOLK, DWELLERS, CITIZENRY, INHABITANTS

populous CROWDED, SWARMING

pop-up AD, BANNER

porcelain KO, JU, MING, CHINA, DERBY, IMARI, MURRA, SPODE, SEVRES, CELADON, FAIENCE, LIMOGES, MEISSEN, GOMBROON; see POTTERY

porch STOA, LANAI, STOOP, PARVIS, PIAZZA, GALILEE, PORTICO, VERANDA(H)

porcupine(-like rodent) CAVY, DEGU, AGUTI, CAVIA, COYPU, PORKY, URSON, AGOUTI, AGOUTY, APEREA, COYPOU, NUTRIA, ECHIDNA, HEDGEHOG

pore(s) CON, READ, STOMA, STUDY, PERUSE, PONDER, FORAMEN, OSTIOLE, STOMATA

porgy TAI, SCUP, BREAM, PARGO, SPAROID

pork PIG, HOG, LARDO(O)N; see CUT

Porky's love PETUNIA

pornographic LEWD, DIRTY, SMUTTY, VULGAR, OBSCENE, PRURIENT, SALACIOUS

porpoise INIA, SEAHOG, DOLPHIN, HOGFISH

porridge POB, MUSH, POBS, SAMP, ATOLE, BROSE, GROUT, GRUEL, BURGOO, POLENTA, POTTAGE, STIRABOUT

port OPORTO, LARBOARD; see HARBOR, WINE

portable LAPTOP, MOBILE, MOVABLE, NOTEBOOK

portal GATE(WAY), DOOR(WAY), ENTRY, ACCESS, POSTERN, ENTRANCE

portend, portent   *see* **PRESAGE**
portentous   **MAJOR, AMAZING,**
    OMINOUS, STUNNING,
    MOMENTOUS
porter   **AKABO, HAMAL,**
  TAMEN, COOLIE, DARWAN,
  KHAMAL, REDCAP, BELLBOY,
  BELLMAN, CARGADOR; *see*
    BEER
Porter musical   **CANCAN,**
  JUBILEE, ROSALIE,
  GAYDIVORCE, KISSMEKATE
portfolio   **CDS, CASE, ALBUM,**
  BRIEFCASE, SECURITIES,
    INVESTMENTS
porthole   **PEEPHOLE,**
    EMBRASURE
Porthos friend   **ARAMIS**
Portia relative   **BASSANIO**
Portia's maid   **NERISSA**
Portia's suitor   **ARAGON,**
    MOROCCO
portico   **STOA, XYST, PORCH,**
  ARCADE, LOGGIA, PARVIS,
  PIAZZA, XYSTUS, NARTHEX
portion   **BIT, DOT, LOT, DOLE,**
  FATE, METE, PART, QUOTA,
    SHARE, RATION
portion out   **DEAL, DOLE,**
    METE, ALLOT
portly   **FAT, BULKY, HEAVY,**
  OBESE, STOUT, STOCKY,
    CORPULENT
portmanteau   **TRUNK, VALISE**
Portoferraio island   **ELBA**
portrait   **EFFIGY, SKETCH,**
  PICTURE, PAINTING
portray   **DRAW, LIMN, DEPICT**
Port Timor capital   **DILI**
Portugal   **LUSITANIA**
Portugal, capital of   **LISBON**
Portuguese city/town   **BEJA,**
  FARO, BRAGA, EVORA,
  LAGOS, PORTO, VISEU,
  AVEIRO, LEIRIA, LISBON,
  SAGRES, SINTRA, AMADORA,
  COIMBRE, SETUBAL,
  SANTAREM, PORTALEGRE
Portuguese colony   **GOA,**
    MACAO
Portuguese explorer   *see*
    EXPLORER
Portuguese island   **AZORES,**
  MADEIRA, TERCIERA
Portuguese measure   **PE, BOTA,**
  MEIO, PIPA, VARA, ALMUD,
  BRACA, FANGA, GEIRA,
  LEGOA, LINHA, MILHA, PALMO,
  ALMUDE, COVADO, OITAVA,

    QUARTO, FERRADO,
    SELAMIN
Portuguese money   **REI, EURO,**
  REIS, CONTO, DOBRA,
  DINERO, ESCUDO, TOSTAQ,
  CENTAVO, CRUSADO,
  MOIDORE, JOHANNES
Portuguese mountain   **FRIA,**
    ESTRELA
Portuguese river   **AVE, COA,**
  LIMA, MIRA, SADO, DOURO,
  MINHO, SABOR, TAGUS,
  VOUGA, ZEZERE, GUADIANA,
    SORRAIRA
Portuguese title   **DOM, DONA,**
  SENHOR, FIDALGO,
  SENHORA, SENHORITA
Portuguese weight   **GRAO;** *see*
    BRAZILIAN
pose   **ASK, SIT, MIEN, FEIGN,**
  MODEL, PUZZLE, POSTURE,
  ATTITUDE, PRETENSE
Poseidon   **NEPTUNE**
Poseidon relative   **ZEUS, ARION,**
  HADES, ORION, CRONUS,
  TRITON, ANTAEUS, PEGASUS
poser   **ENIGMA, RIDDLE,**
  SITTER, TEASER, IMPOSTOR
posh   **CHIC, RITZY, ELEGANT,**
    LUXURIOUS
posit   **PUT, SAY, SET, PLACE,**
  ASSERT, ASSUME, SITUATE,
    POSTULATE
position   **JOB, LIE, RANK, ROLE,**
  SITE, STAND, STANCE,
  STATUS, UBIETY, FOOTING,
  STATION, ATTITUDE,
  LOCATION, PLACEMENT
positive   **FIRM, PLUS, SURE,**
  ACTUAL, THETIC, CERTAIN,
  ABSOLUTE, DEFINITE,
    EMPHATIC
positive pole   **ANODE**
positive principal   **YANG**
positively   **TRULY, INDEED,**
  REALLY, EXACTLY
positivism   **COMTISM,**
  ASSURANCE, CERTAINTY,
    DOGMATISM
posse   **BAND, GANG,**
    VIGILANTES
possess   **OWN, HAVE, HOLD,**
  OCCUPY, CONTROL
possessed   **MAD, HEXED,**
  CRAZED, BEWITCHED
possession(s)   **ASSET, ESTATE,**
  MANUAL, SEISIN, WEALTH,
  CUSTODY, PROPERTY,
    OWNERSHIP

possessive **GREEDY, JEALOUS, SELFISH**
possible **FEASIBLE, PROBABLE, POTENTIAL**
possibly **HAPLY, MAYBE, PERHAPS**
possum in comics **POGO**
possum, play **FEIGN, PRETEND**
post **DAX, JOB, BITT, CAMP, DURN, JAMB, MAIL, NEWEL, STARE, COLUMN, PILLAR, BOLLARD, CAPSTAN, GARRISON**
post office machine **SCALE, SORTER, CANCELER**
postage stamp paper **PELURE**
poster **BILL, AFFICHE, PLACARD**
posterior **HIND, REAR, DORSAL, RETRAL, BUTTOCK(S)**
posterity **SEED, HEIRS, ISSUE, FUTURE, PROGENY**
postmark **CACHET, IMPRINT, INDICIA**
postmortem **AUTOPSY, INQUEST, NECROPSY**
postmortem conductor **CORONER, AUTOPSIST**
postpone **DEFER, DELAY, TABLE, PUTOFF, SHELVE, SUSPEND**
postponement **STAY, STOP, DELAY, RESPITE, RAINCHECK**
postscript **PS, ADDENDUM, FOOTNOTE, AFTERTHOUGHT**
postulant **CLAIMANT, CANDIDATE, PETITIONER**
postulate **AXIOM, CLAIM, POSIT, ASSUME, PREMISE**
posture **MIEN, POSE, STANCE, BEARING, ATTITUDE, CARRIAGE**
posy **FLOWER, BOUQUET, CORSAGE, NOSEGAY**
pot **PAN, DIXY, LOTA, OLLA, POOL, CROCK, CRUSE, KITTY, LOTAH, ALUDEL, KETTLE, PIPKIN**
pot part **BET, ANTE**
potable **PURE, CLEAN, DRINKABLE**
potage **OLIO, SOUP, BROTH, GUMBO**
potassium **ALUM, NITER, GROUGH, KALITE, POTASH, MURIATE**
potation **DRAFT, DRINK**

potato **YAM, CHAT, SPUD, TATER, TATIE, TUBER, BATATA**
potato chip **CRISP, RUFFLE**
potbellied **BLOATED, PAUNCHY**
potbelly **PAUNCH, BAYWINDOW, CORPORATION**
potboiler **PENNYDREADFUL**
potency **VIS, POWER, VIGOR, STRENGTH, AUTHORITY**
potent **ABLE, COGENT, MIGHTY, STRONG, VIRILE**
potentate **CZAR, KING, RAJAH, RULER, PRINCE, MONARCH**
potential **ERGAL, LATENT, POSSIBLE**
pothead **HEAD, ADDICT**
pother **ADO, FUSS, STIR, WORRY, BUSTLE, FLURRY, UPROAR**
potherb **MINT, CLARY, CHIVES, PARSLEY; see p. 685**
pothole **PIT, CAVE, KETTLE, MUDHOLE**
potion **BREW, DOSE, DRAFT, TONIC, ELIXIR, PHILTER, NEPENTHE**
potpourri **OLIO, STEW, GRABBAG, MIXTURE, HODGEPODGE**
Potsdam conference participant **ATTLEE, STALIN, TRUMAN**
potshot **SNIPE**
pottage **SOUP, STEW, BROSE, BREWIS, PORRIDGE**
potter's tool **KICK, PALLET, LATHE, THROW, WHEEL**
pottery **CHUN, RUAN, TING, TUNG, YUEH, DELFT, LEEDS, BASALT, CROUCH, JASPER, FAIENCE, GOMBROON, WEDGWOOD; see PORCELAIN**
pottery, pert. to **CERAMIC, FICTILE**
potty **JOHN, BATTY, KOOKY, NUTTY, SNOOTY, TOILET**
pouch **POD, SAC(K), BURSA, C(A)ECUM, POCKET, SPORRAN, SPLEUCHAN**
pouch-shaped **SACCATE**
poultice **PLASTER, DRESSING, CATAPLASM, APPLICATION**
poultry **see FOWL**
poultry disease **PIP, POX, ROUP, GAPES**
poultry worker **SEXER**

pounce	CLAW, SWEEP, TALON, ASSAULT
pound	HIT, PEN, SOV, BEAT, BLOW, BRAY, DRUB, QUID, TAMP, TUND, THROB, THUMP, BRUISE, CORRAL, KENNEL
pounding implement	GAVEL, HAMMER, MALLET, PESTLE
pour	FLOW, GUSH, RAIN, SPEW, TEEM, DECANT, JIRBLE, LIBATE
pout	FRET, MOPE, MOUE, SULK, GRIMACE
poverty	LACK, NEED, WANT, DEARTH, PENURY, PAUCITY, SCARCITY, INDIGENCE
powder	ABIR, DUST, TALC, PICRA, ROUGE, POUNCE, PUMICE
powdery	FINE, DUSTY, FRIABLE, GRANULATED
power	OD, VIS, DINT, MANA, ODYL, SWAY, FORCE, MIGHT, POTENCY, CAPACITY, STRENGTH, AUTHORITY
— power	NTH
powerful	POTENT, STRONG, DYNAMIC, PUISSANT
powerless	WEAK, IMPOTENT
Powhatan daughter	POCAHONTAS
powwow	INDABA, PARLEY, COUNCIL, MEETING
pox	ACNE, PUSTULE, SYPHILIS
practicable	UTILE, USABLE, USEFUL, FEASIBLE, OPERABLE, EXPEDIENT
practical	SOUND, UTILE, LOGICAL, SENSIBLE, WORKABLE, PRAGMATIC
practically	ALMOST, NEARLY, INEFFECT
practice	PLY, USE, DRILL, HABIT, USAGE, PRAXIS, WORKOUT, EXERCISE, REHEARSE
practitioner	MEDIC, DOCTOR, WORKER, SURGEON, OPERATOR
pragmatic	PRACTICAL
prairie	MESA, LLANO, PLAIN(S), MEADOW, PAMPAS, STEPPE, TUNDRA, SAVANNA, GRASSLAND
prairie schooner	ARK, COVERED WAGON
Prairie State	IL, NB, ILL, NEB(R), ILLINOIS, NEBRASKA

praise	LAUD, TOUT, ECLAT, ELOGE, EXALT, EXTOL, KUDOS, EULOGY
praiseworthy	LAUDABLE, EXEMPLARY
pram	BUGGY, STROLLER, PERAMBULATOR
prance	CAPER, FRISK, STRUT, CAVORT, GAMBOL
Prancer partner	DANCER
prank	DIDO, HOAX, JAPE, JEST, LARK, ANTIC, CAPER, CURVET, CANTRIP, CAPRICE, GAMBADO, ESCAPADE, MISCHIEF
prate	GAB, YAP, BLAB, BURN, BURR
prattle	BLAB, PRATE, BABBLE, DRIVEL, JABBER, MURMUR, CHATTER
pray	BEG, ORA, SUE, DAWN, APPEAL, BESEECH
prayer	AVE, BEAD, BENE, PLEA, SUIT, ALENU, CREDO, GRACE, MATIN, SALAT, LITANY, NOVENA, ORISON, VESPER, ROGATION
prayer book	ORDO, MISSAL, PORTAS, PRIMER, PORTASS, BREVIARY
prayer call	ADAN, AZAN, EZAN
prayer place	IDGAH
prayer rug	ASAN
prayer starter	NOW, OUR
prayer stick	BAHO, PAHO, PAJO, BAHOO
prayerful	HOLY, PIOUS, DEVOUT
praying figure	ORANT
preach	TEACH, EXHORT, LECTURE, ADVOCATE, MORALIZE, SERMONIZE, EVANGELIZE
preacher	*see* EVANGELIST, CLERGY
Preakness winner	ALSAB, CITATION, WHIRLAWAY; *see p. 711*
precarious	RISKY, UNSAFE, UNSURE, INSECURE, UNSTABLE
precaution	CARE, WARNING
precede	LEAD, FOREGO, FORERUN, ANTEDATE
precedence	LEAD, RANK, PRIORITY, SENIORITY
precedent	RULE, MODEL, PRIOR, FORMER, EXAMPLE
precedent setter	TEST CASE

preceding	PAST, BEFORE, FORMER, PREVIOUS, FOREGOING
precept(s)	CODE, RULE, CANON, DICTA, SUTRA, TENET, APHORISM
preceptor	TUTOR, TEACHER
precinct(s)	AREA, WARD, REGION, DISTRICT, ENVIRONS
precious	DEAR, RARE, COSTLY, WORTHY, BELOVED, VALUABLE, CHERISHED
precipice	CRAG, LINN, PALI, BLUFF, CLIFF, STEEP
precipitate	RASH, HEADY, ABRUPT, HASTEN, SUDDEN, BRINGON
precipitation	DEW, HAIL, MIST, RAIN, SNOW, SLEET
precipitous	RASH, HASTY, SHEER, STEEP, ABRUPT
precis	BRIEF, DIGEST, RESUME, SUMMARY, ABSTRACT, SYNOPSIS
precise	TIDY, EXACT, RIGID, FORMAL, PRISSY, STRICT, EXPLICIT
precision	ACCURACY
preclude	BAR, CHECK, ESTOP, HINDER, IMPEDE, INHIBIT, PREVENT
precocious	EARLY, ADVANCED, PREMATURE
preconceive	IDEATE, SCHEME
precursor	HERALD, FORBEAR, ANCESTOR, HARBINGER, FORERUNNER
predator	SHARK, BANDIT, LOOTER, RAIDER, USURER, PLUNDERER
predatory	PREYING, RAVENOUS, VORACIOUS
predecessor	ANCESTOR, PRECURSOR, ANTECEDENT
predestination	LOT, FATE, KARMA, DESTINY, ELECTION
predicament	FIX, JAM, PASS, SPOT, SCRAPE, STRAIT, DILEMMA, STRAITS
predicate	BASE, ASSERT
predict	BODE, AUGUR, WEIRD, DIVINE, FORECAST, FORETELL
prediction	FORECAST, PROPHECY
predilection	BIAS, TASTE, LIKING, LEANING, FONDNESS, PARTIALITY, PREFERENCE
predisposed	PRONE, BIASED, INCLINED
predominant	RULING, REGNANT, CONTROLLING
preeminent	NOTABLE, SUPREME, RENOWNED
preempt	COOPT, SEIZE, USURP, APPROPRIATE
preen	GROOM, PLUME, PRIMP, PRINK
prefabricated	NISSEN, PREFAB, QUONSET
preface	PROEM, START, PRELUDE, FOREWORD, PREAMBLE, PROLOGUE, FRONTISPIECE
prefect	DEAN, WALI
prefer	PICK, ELECT, FANCY, FAVOR, OFFER, CHOOSE, TENDER, PROFFER
preferable	BETTER, DESIRABLE
preferably	RATHER, SOONER
preference	PICK, CHOICE, PREDILECTION
prefixes	*see p. 691*
pregnable	VULNERABLE
pregnancy	CYESIS, FETATION, FERTILITY, GESTATION
pregnancy, false	PSEUDOCYESIS
pregnancy outside uterus	ECTOPIC
pregnant	GRAVID, WEIGHTY, EXPECTING, MOMENTOUS
prehistoric	PRIMAL, ANCIENT, ARCHAIC, PRIMEVAL, PRIMITIVE
prejudice	BIAS, HARM, BIGOTRY, PREDISPOSE, INTOLERANCE
prejudiced	BIASED, RACIST, PARTIAL, PARTISAN, INTOLERANT
prejudicial	HARMFUL, HURTFUL, DAMAGING, INJURIOUS, DETRIMENTAL
prelate	INGE, POPE, ABBOT, BISHOP, PONTIFF, PRIMATE, CARDINAL
preliminary	PRIOR, PREFACE, PRELUDE, PREFATORY, INTRODUCTORY
prelude	INTRO, PROEM, PRELUDE, OVERTURE
premature	RASH, EARLY, UNTIMELY, PRECIPITATE
premeditated	PLANNED, PREPENSE, DELIBERATE
premier	ARCH, CHIEF, FIRST, FOREMOST

premiere OPENING
premise BASIS, LEMMA, POSTULATE
premium FEE, AGIO, BONUS, PRIZE, BOUNTY
— premium AT A
premonition HUNCH, INKLING, PORTENT, FOREBODING
preoccupation FIXATION, OBSESSION
preoccupied LOST, RAPT, ABSORBED, ENGROSSED, ABSTRACTED
preoccupy ABSORB, OBSESS
preparation DRUG, PLAN, COMPOUND, TRAINING, EDUCATION, READINESS, CONCOCTION
prepare FIT, EDIT, GIRD, PAVE, ADAPT, EQUIP, REDACT
prepared FIT, SET, YARE, READY, PROCESSED, QUALIFIED
prepare for cooking DRESS, MARINATE
preposition AT, BY, IN, ON, TO, ERE, FOR, OUT, FROM, INTO, ONTO, UNTO, UPON, WITH, AFTER
prepossessing WINNING, APPEALING, ATTRACTIVE
preposterous ABSURD, RIDICULOUS
prerequisite MUST, NEED(ED), REQUIRED, REQUIREMENT
prerogative RIGHT, PRIVILEGE
presage BODE, OMEN, SIGN, AUGUR, TOKEN, AUGURY, HERALD, OSTENT, PORTEND, PORTENT
prescribe LIMIT, ORDER, ASSIGN, DIRECT, ORDAIN, OUTLAW, DICTATE
prescribed THETIC
prescription RX, RECIPE, FORMULA, MEDICINE
presence ATTENDANCE
present BOON, GIFT, GIVE, NONCE, TODAY, BESTOW, DONATE, TENDER
presentable FIT, PROPER, PASSABLE, SUITABLE
presentation SHOW, DEBUT, DISPLAY, EXHIBIT, OFFERING, PERFORMANCE, INTRODUCTION
presentiment HUNCH, INTUITION, FOREBODING

presently NOW, ANON, ENOW, SOON, SHORTLY
preservation method for food DRYING, CANNING, FREEZING, IRRADIATION, FERMENTATION, REFRIGERATION, PASTEURIZATION
preservative SALT, BRINE, NITRATE, VINEGAR
preserve CAN, JAM, TIN, CORN, CURE, KEEP, SALT, SMOKE, FREEZE, PICKLE, MAINTAIN, CONFITURE, MARMALADE
preside (over) LEAD, CHAIR, DIRECT
president PREX(Y)
president assassinated KENNEDY, LINCOLN, GARFIELD, MCKINLEY
presidential assassin BOOTH, OSWALD, GUITEAU, CZOLGOSZ
presidential information see p. 696
presidential initials GH, DDE, FDR, JFK, LBJ, RMN, RWR, GHWB
presidential nickname ABE, CAL, IKE, RON, JACK, JERRY, JIMMY, TEDDY, GEORGEW
presidents elected by a minority BUSH, POLK, ADAMS, HAYES, NIXON, TAYLOR, TRUMAN, WILSON, CLINTON, GARFIELD, LINCOLN, HARRISON, CLEVELAND
presidio FORT, CITADEL, GARRISON
press JAM, CRAM, IRON, TAMP, CROWD, SERRY, STAMP, WEDGE, SQUASH, SQUEEZE, FLATTEN; see PRINTING
press agent FLACK, PUBLICIST
pressing URGENT, CRUCIAL, EXIGENT
pressure PUSH, URGE, PRESS, COMPEL, DURESS, LEANON, STRAIN, STRESS, TENSION
pressure unit BARAD, BARIE, PASCAL
prestige FAME, ECLAT, RENOWN, DISTINCTION
presto QUICKLY
presume DARE, INFER, ASSUME, SUPPOSE, VENTURE
presumption GUESS, AUDACITY, TEMERITY, INFERENCE, EFFRONTERY

presumptive LIKELY, PROBABLY, SUPPOSED

presumptuous BRASH, CHEEKY, ARROGANT

pretend ACT, FAKE, FEIGN, ALLEGE, PROFESS, SIMULATE, DISSEMBLE

pretender SHAM, FAKE(R), FRAUD, QUACK, USURPER, ASPIRANT, CLAIMANT, IMPOSTOR, SCIOLIST

pretense(s) AIRS, RUSE, SHOW, FEINT, GUISE, EXCUSE, PRETEXT

pretentious ARTY, SIDY, TAWDRY, POMPOUS

pretentious person PSEUD

pretext ALIBI, EXCUSE

pretty FAIR, BONNY, COMELY, MIGNON(NE)

pretzel shape KNOT

prevail WIN, SWAY, OBTAIN, TRIUMPH

prevalent RIFE, EXTANT, RAMPANT, PANDEMIC, WIDESPREAD

prevaricate FIB, LIE, PALTER, EQUIVOCATE

prevent BAR, BALK, STOP, AVERT, DEBAR, DETER, ESTOP, THWART, PRECLUDE, FORESTALL

preview SAMPLE, TRYOUT, TRAILER, FORETASTE

previous PRIOR, FORMER, EARLIER, PRECEDING

prey GAME, PRIZE, RAVIN, QUARRY

prey on DUPE, VICTIMIZE

Priam relative PARIS, HECTOR, HECUBA, TROILUS, LAOMEDON, CASSANDRA

Priam's kingdom TROY

price FEE, TAB, COST, FARE, RATE, TOLL, QUOTE, VALUE, WORTH, CHARGE

priceless RARE, COSTLY, PRECIOUS, CHERISHED, INCALCULABLE

pricey DEAR, COSTLY, EXPENSIVE

prick GOAD, SPUR, URGE, STING, PIERCE, PUNCTURE

prickle BARB, BUR(R), SETA, SPINE, ACANTHA, ACULEUS, SPICULA

prickly SPINY, BARBED, THORNY, ECHINATE, TINGLING

pride VANITY, CONCEIT, VAINGLORY

Pride and Prejudice author AUSTEN

Pride and Prejudice character DARCY, BENNET, BINGLEY, COLLINS, WICKHAM, ELIZABETH

pride member LION

priest ELI, FRA, LAMA, MUST, PAPA, ABUNA, DRUID, MOBED, SARIP, FLAMEN, SHAMAN, CALCHAS, PANDITA; see CLERGY; see p. 516

priestess AUGE, ENTUM, VESTAL

priestly AARONIC, CLERICAL, HIERATIC, PASTORAL, SACERDOTAL

priesthood MAGI, SALII

prig PRUDE, PEDANT

prim DEMURE, FORMAL, MODEST, PRISSY, PRUDISH

prima — DONNA, FACIE

primal FIRST, ORIGINAL, PRIMEVAL

primary MAIN, FIRST, CHIEF, ORIGINAL, PRINCIPAL

primate BISHOP; see APE, MONKEY

prime TOP, AONE, BEST, PICK, CREAM, FIRST, CHOICE, FINEST, UNISON, PREPARE

primer MANUAL, READER, HANDBOOK

primeval OLD, EARLY, NATIVE, PRISTINE

primitive WILD, BASIC, CRUDE, ROUGH, ANCIENT, BARBARIC, ABORIGINAL

primp PREEN, PRINK, PRUNE

primrose GLAUX, OXLIP, COWSLIP, PRIMULA, AURICULA

prince RAS, EMIR, IMAM, KHAN, KNEZ, RANA, IMAUM, NAWAB, SAYID, SAYYID, SHARIF, DAUPHIN, GAEKWAR, ATHELING

Prince Edward Island (PEI) see also p. 614

PEI bay EGMONT, ORWELL, BEDEQUE, COLVILLE, MALPEQUE, TRACADIE, CASCUMPEQUE

PEI city/town ALMA, IONA, ELDON, TRYON, ALBANY, BALTIC, BURTON, CONWAY,

ORWELL, PEAKES, SOURIS,
WILMOT, BRISTOL, ELMIRA,
TIGNISH
PEI island HOG, BIRD,
LENNOX, COURTIN,
GOVERNORS
PEI river HAY, MILL, WEST,
GRAND, NORTH, TRYON,
MORELL, MURRAY, FORTUNE,
MIDGELL, TIGNISH,
PERCIVAL
Prince of Darkness SATAN
princeling SATRAP
princely NOBLE, REGAL,
LAVISH, GENEROUS
princess RANI, BEGUM, RANEE,
INFANTA, MAHARANI
Princess Ida character GAMA,
BLANCHE, HILARION
Princeton mascot TIGER
princewood CYP
principal ARCH, MAIN, CHIEF,
MAJOR, RECTOR, PREMIER,
PRIMARY, HEADMASTER
principality REALM, DOMAIN,
PRINCEDOM
principate ASIR
Principe, capital of SAOTOME
principle LAW, YIN, CODE,
RULE, YANG, BASIS, LOGOS,
PRANA, TENET, PNEUMA,
PRECEPT, DOCTRINE, see
MAXIM
prink PREEN, PRIMP, PRUNE,
DRESSUP
print STAMP, ETCHING,
PICTURE, PUBLISH
printer DAY(E), FUST, TORY,
TYPO, PRESS, SHORT,
CAXTON, JENSON, THOMAS,
NUTHEAD, PLANTIN,
BRADFORD, FRANKLIN,
PRESSMAN, GUTENBERG
printer's mark see
PROOFREADER'S MARK
printing press part BED, FRAME,
INKER, QUOIN, BRAYER,
PLATEN, REGLET, ROUNCE,
GRIPPER
printing tools and terms see p. 724
prior ELDER, FORMER,
EARLIER, ANTERIOR,
PREVIOUS
prior to ERE, BEFORE
priority RANK, SENIORITY,
PRECEDENCE
priory ABBEY, NUNNERY,
CLOISTER, MONASTERY
prism NICOL

prison see JAIL
prison camp GULAG, BELSEN,
DACHAU, STALAG,
AUSCHWITZ
prisoner INMATE, TERMER,
CAPTIVE, CONVICT,
HOSTAGE, JAILBIRD
prissy NICE, PRIM, FUSSY,
PRECISE
pristine NEW, PURE, FIRST,
FRESH, PRIME, ORIGINAL
privacy SECRECY, SOLITUDE,
ISOLATION, SECLUSION
private PFC, PVT, INNER,
SECRET, INTIMATE,
PERSONAL, CONFIDENTIAL
private eye PI, TEC, SHAMUS,
GUMSHOE, DETECTIVE,
INVESTIGATOR
privateer see PIRATE
privation LACK, LOSS, WANT,
PENURY, POVERTY
privilege FAVOR, RIGHT,
OCTROI, PATENT, CHARTER,
LICENSE, FRANCHISE
privileged EXEMPT, FAVORED
privy JAKES, PRIVY, STOOL,
CLOACA, TOILET,
OUTHOUSE
privy to IN ON, PARTY TO
prix — FIXE
prize PRY, TERN; see AWARD
pro FOR, SIDE
pro — RATA, FORMA,
TEMPORE
— pro nobis ORA
— pro quo QUID
pro tem ACTING, INTERIM,
TEMPORARY, PROVISIONAL
probability ODDS, CHANCE,
PROSPECT, LIKELIHOOD
probable BELIKE, LIKELY
probation TEST, TRIAL,
ORDEAL
probe SOUND, STYLET,
EXAMINE, INQUEST
probity VIRTUE, DECENCY,
HONESTY, INTEGRITY
problem NUT, CRUX, ISSUE,
POSER, ENIGMA, PUZZLE,
RIDDLE, DILEMMA, OBSTACLE
problematic MOOT, DUBIOUS
proboscis NEB, NOSE, SNOUT,
TRUNK, ANTUA
procedure WAY, PLAN,
METHOD, POLICY,
MANEUVER
proceed GOON, MOVE, WEND,
ISSUE, MARCH, PRESS

proceedings ACTA, ACTS, ACTION

proceeds NET, GAIN, YIELD, INCOME, PRODUCE, PROFITS

process COURSE, METHOD, PRACTICE, TUBERCLE, APPENDAGE

procession FILE, TRAIN, PARADE, CORTEGE, RETINUE

processional HYMN, MARCH

proclaim CRY, KNELL, VOICE, HERALD, DECLARE

proclamation FIAT, BAN(K)S, EDICT, UKASE, NOTICE

proclivity BENT, LEANING, TENDENCY, INCLINATION

Procne relative ITYS, TEREUS, PANDION, PHILOMELA

procrastinate DEFER, DELAY, STALL, PUTOFF, POSTPONE

procreate BEGET, BREED, PRODUCE, MULTIPLY

proctor AGENT, PROXY, MONITOR

procure BUY, GET, WIN, OBTAIN, SECURE, ACQUIRE

procurer PIMP, PANDER

prod EGG, GOAD, POKE, URGE, DRIVE, IMPEL, INCITE

prodigal LAVISH, COPIOUS, WASTREL, GENEROUS, PLENTEOUS

prodigious HUGE, VAST, AMAZING, IMMENSE, ENORMOUS, PHENOMENAL

prodigy MARVEL, MIRACLE, PORTENT

produce BEAR, BEGET, CAUSE, YIELD, APPORT, CREATE, INWORK, WORK UP, ENGENDER, GENERATE

product CROP, OPUS, FRUIT, YIELD, EFFECT, RESULT, OUTCOME

production YIELD, OUTPUT

productive RICH, FECUND, FERTILE, CREATIVE, FRUITFUL, PROLIFIC, FRUCTUOUS

profane NOA, FOUL, VILE, DEFILE, VULGAR, VIOLATE, IMPIOUS, BLASPHEME, DESECRATE

profanity CURSING, SWEARING, BLASPHEMY

profess AVOW, CLAIM, AFFIRM, ALLEGE, PURPORT

profession ART, JOB, CALL, LINE, CRAFT, TRADE,

AVOWAL, CAREER, METIER, CALLING, PURSUIT, VOCATION

professional PRO, EXPERT, MASTER, SKILLED, COMPETENT

professor DON, DOCENT, DOCTOR, TEACHER, EDUCATOR, PEDAGOGUE

proffer OFFER, SUBMIT, TENDER, PROPOSE

proficiency SKILL, MASTERLY, APTITUDE, COMPETENCE

proficient APT, ABLE, ADEPT, EXPERT, SKILLED, TRAINED

profile SHAPE, SKETCH, CONTOUR, OUTLINE, SILHOUETTE

profit(s) NET, BOOT, GAIN, VAIL, AVAIL, RETURN, BENEFIT, PROCEEDS

profit-taker PERNOR

profitable FAT, UTILE, PAYING, USEFUL, GAINFUL, LUCRATIVE, IN THE BLACK

profiteer EXPLOIT

profligate WANTON, WASTEFUL, DISSOLUTE

profound DEEP, SOLEMN, ABSTRUSE

profuse LUSH, LAVISH, PRODIGAL, PLENTIFUL

progenitor SIRE, PARENT, ANCESTOR

progeny KIDS, SEED, ISSUE, SCION, CHILDREN

prognosis OUTLOOK, FORECAST, DIAGNOSIS

prognosticate AUGUR, PREDICT, FORETELL, PROPHESY

program APP, CARD, PLAN, AGENDA, OUTLINE, PLAYBILL, SCHEDULE, SYLLABUS, APPLICATION

progress COURSE, GROWTH, STRIDE, ADVANCE, PROCEED, IMPROVE(MENT)

prohibit BAN, (DE)BAR, TABU, VETO, TABOO, FORBID, ENJOIN, EXCLUDE

prohibited TABU, TABOO, BANNED, ILLICIT

prohibition BAN, NONO, TABU, VETO, DONOT, TABOO, EMBARGO

prohibitionist DRY, TEMPERANT

prohibitive EXCESSIVE, EXORBITANT, RESTRICTIVE

project	JUT, IDEA, PLAN, PITCH, SCHEME, PROPOSAL, PROTRUDE
projectile	BALL, SHELL, BULLET, ROCKET, MISSILE, TORPEDO
projecting piece	ARM, JOG, RIM, BOSS, BRIM, EAVE, COIGN, SOCLE, FLANGE, TENDON
projection	CAM, EAR, HOB, BARB, HOBB, KNOP, LOBE, SNAG, BULGE, LEDGE, PRONG, SHELF, SOCLE
proletarian	WORKER, LABORER
proliferate	BREED, SPREAD, MULTIPLY
prolific	FECUND, FERTILE, FRUITFUL, PRODUCTIVE
prolix	WORDY, DIFFUSE, VERBOSE, DISCURSIVE
prolong	EXTEND, STRETCH, LENGTHEN, PROTRACT
prom	HOP, BALL, DANCE
promenade	MALL, PRADO, MARINA, PASEAR, ALAMEDA
Prometheus' gift	FIRE
prominence	JUT, FAME, NOTE, EMINENCE, DISTINCTION
prominent	CHIEF, FAMED, FAMOUS, EMINENT, JUTTING, SALIENT, OUTSTANDING
promiscuous	LAX, LOOSE, MIXED, IMMORAL, LICENTIOUS
promise	IOU, (A)VOW, NOTE, OATH, WORD, PAROLE, PLEDGE, GUARANTEE
Promised Land	ZION, CANAAN
promising	ROSY, BRIGHT, FAVORABLE, AUSPICIOUS
promissory note	IOU, CHIT, PLEDGE, TICKET
promontory	TOR, CAPE, NASE, NAZE, NESS, NOUP, SKAW, SPIT
promote	AID, ABET, BOOST, FOSTER, ADVANCE, FURTHER
promoter	AGENT, FLACK, LOBBYIST, IMPRESARIO
promotion	BUILDUP, FANFARE, CAMPAIGN, PUBLICITY
prompt(ly)	CUE, EGG, SOON, URGE, YARE, EARLY, QUICK, INDUCE, PRONTO, PUNCTUAL
prompter	CUER, TICKLER
promulgate	ISSUE, PROMOTE, PUBLISH, ANNOUNCE, ADVERTISE

prone	APT, FLAT, LIKELY, SUPINE, DISPOSED, INCLINED, PROSTRATE
prong	NIB, PEG, FANG, PUGH, TINE, TOOTH, ANTLER
pronged item	FORK, HORN, RAKE, SPEAR, TOOTH, ANTLER, TRIDENT
— pro nobis	ORA
pronoun	IT, HER, HIM, HIS, ONE, OUR, SHE, YOU, HERS, MINE, OURS, THAT, THEE, THEM, THEY, THIS, THOU, YOUR, THEIR, THESE, THINE, THOSE
pronounce	SAY, BURR, SLUR, JUDGE, SPEAK, UTTER, STRESS, ARTICULATE
pronounced	CLEAR, OBVIOUS, SALIENT, CONSPICUOUS
pronouncement	EDICT, NOTICE, RULING, JUDGMENT, SENTENCE
pronto	NOW, ATONCE, DIRECTLY
pronunciation	ACCENT, DICTION, ENUNCIATION
pronunciation mark	*see* MARK
proof	SAFE, REPRO, TRIAL, GALLEY, REVISE, EVIDENCE
proofreader's mark	BF, LC, LD, LF, SP, TR, WF, ROM, CAPS, DELE, ITAL, STET, CARET, SPACE
prop	GIB, HOLD, STAY, BRACE, RANGE, CRUTCH, BOLSTER
prop plane	CESSNA, FOKKER
propaganda	BALLYHOO, NEWSPEAK, PUBLICITY
propagate	BREED, SPREAD, SCATTER, DISPERSE, ENGENDER, PROCREATE
propel	OAR, PEG, DRIVE, IMPEL, SHOVE, LAUNCH
propeller	BLADE, ROTOR, SCREW
propensity	BENT, BIAS, TALENT, LEANING, APTITUDE
proper	DUE, FIT, FAIR, JUST, MEET, RIGHT, DECENT, SEEMLY, APROPOS, DECOROUS, SUITABLE
properly	DULY, APTLY, FEATLY
property	ALOD, DHAN, LAND, ASSET, GOODS, LANDS, ESTATE, WEALTH, CHATTEL, ALLODIUM, HOLDINGS
property, hold on	LIEN

property, receiver of	**ALIENEE**
prophecy	**AUGURY,**
	FORECAST, PREDICTION
prophesy	**FORETELL;** *see*
	PRESAGE
prophet	**SEER, AUGUR, VATES,**
	ORACLE; *see p. 517*
prophetess	**SIBYL, PYTHIA(N),**
	SEERESS, CASSANDRA,
	PYTHONESS
prophetic	**VATIC, MANTIC,**
	FATIDIC, VATICAL,
	ORACULAR, FATIDICAL
propinquity	**TIE, KINSHIP,**
	AFFINITY, NEARNESS,
	VICINITY, PROXIMITY
propitiate	**ATONE, PLACATE,**
	APPEASE
propitious	**LUCKY, HOPEFUL,**
	TIMELY, GRACIOUS,
	FAVORABLE, OPPORTUNE,
	AUSPICIOUS
proponent	**ALLY, BACKER,**
	SPONSOR, ADVOCATE,
	CHAMPION
proportion	**PART, RATE,**
	QUOTA, RATIO, SHARE
proportional	**INSCALE**
proposal	**BID, PLAN, OFFER,**
	MOTION, TENDER,
	OVERTURE, PROPOSITION
propose	**MOVE, MEAN, NAME,**
	INTEND, AFFIANCE,
	POPTHEQUESTION
proposition(s)	**PLAN, LEMMA,**
	OFFER, PORISM, THESES,
	THESIS, PREMISE, THEOREM,
	PROPOSAL
proprietor	**OWNER, PATROON**
propriety	**APTNESS, DECORUM**
propulsion	**DRIVE, THRUST,**
	IMPETUS
prosaic	**DULL, LITERAL,**
	MUNDANE, TEDIOUS
proscribe	**BAN, BANISH,**
	FORBID, OUTLAW,
	INTERDICT
prose	**ESSAY, NOVEL, STORY,**
	TRACT, FICTION, ROMANCE,
	TREATISE, NONFICTION
prosecute	**SUE, PRESS, CHARGE,**
	INTEND, ARRAIGN,
	CARRYON, LITIGATE
prosecutor	**DA, ATTORNEY**
proselyte	*see* **CONVERT**
Proserpina	**CORA, PERSEPHONE**
Proserpina's relative	**CERES,**
	PLUTO
prosody	**METRICS, SCANSION**
prospect	**HOPE, MINE, VISTA,**
	SEARCH, PROMISE
prospective	**COMING, FUTURE,**
	LIKELY, INTENDED
prospector	**MINER,**
	SOURDOUGH
prospectus	**BLURB, CATALOG,**
	BROCHURE, HANDBILL
prosper	**GROW, BATTEN,**
	THRIVE, BURGEON,
	FLOURISH
prosperity	**HAP, BOOM, SONS,**
	WEAL, SONSE, WEALTH,
	WELFARE
Prospero's daughter	**MIRANDA**
Prospero's servant	**ARIEL,**
	CALIBAN
prosperous	**FAT, RICH, LUCKY,**
	PALMY, WEALTHY, WELLOFF,
	AFFLUENT, THRIVING
prostitute	**TART, TRAMP,**
	TRULL, WHORE, CHIPPY,
	HARLOT, TROLLOP
prostitution, house of	**BROTHEL,**
	BORDELLO, CATHOUSE
prostrate	**BOW, FELL, FLAT,**
	PRONE, FALLEN, REPENT,
	SUPINE
protagonist	**HERO, STAR, RIVAL**
protect	**SAVE, GUARD,**
	ENCASE, HARBOR,
	SCREEN, SHIELD, SHELTER,
	HIDEAWAY
protect from chafing	**KECKLE**
protection	**LEE, EGIS, WING,**
	AEGIS, APRON, SHELTER
protection, means of	**MOAT,**
	ARMOR, QUILL, SPINE,
	HELMET, FIREWALL,
	CAMOUFLAGE
protection right	**MUND, GRITH**
protector	**PATRON, REGENT,**
	SHIELD, DEFENDER,
	GUARDIAN
protege(e)	**WARD, CLIENT,**
	DISCIPLE
protein	**ZEIN, ABRIN, MUCIN,**
	RICIN, CASEIN, FIBRIN,
	GLOBIN, GLUTIN, HISTON,
	ALBUMIN, GLIADIN,
	HISTONE, HORDEIN, PEPTIDE,
	PEPTONE, GLOBULIN,
	GLUTELIN, PROLAMIN
protest	**SITIN, ASSERT,**
	OBJECT, OUTCRY, SQUAWK,
	DISSENT, COMPLAIN(T)
Protestant	**MORMON, BAPTIST,**
	ANGLICAN, LUTHERAN,
	METHODIST

protocol   (COM)PACT, CUSTOMS, DECORUM, CONTRACT

prototype   DIE, MOLD, IDEAL, MODEL, EXAMPLE, EXEMPLAR, ORIGINAL

protozoan   MONAD, AMEBIC, LOBOSA, EUGLENA, PROTIST, STENTOR, HELIOZOA, ORBULINA, SUCTORIA

protract   DEFER, DELAY, EXTEND, PROLONG, STRETCH

protrude   JUT, BULGE, BEETLE, PROJECT

protuberance   JAG, NUB, HUMP, KNOB, KNOT, LOVE, NODE, UMBO, WART, GNARL, INION, KNURL, TORUS

protuberant   STRUT, CONVEX, TOROSE, TOROUS, BULGING

proud   VAIN, HAUGHTY, ARROGANT, BOASTFUL

prove   TRY, SHOW, TEST, CHECK, EVINCE, VERIFY, DERAIGN, DEMONSTRATE

provenance   ORIGIN, DERIVATION

provender   HAY, CORN, FEED, FOOD, OATS, GRAIN, FODDER, FORAGE, ROUGHAGE, PROVISION(S)

proverb   *see* MAXIM

provide   CATER, ENDOW, ENDUE, AFFORD, PURVEY, FURNISH

provided   IF, BODEN, SOBEIT, THOUGH

provident   FRUGAL, PRUDENT, THRIFTY

providential   LUCKY, FORTUNATE, OPPORTUNE, AUSPICIOUS

provider   DONOR, EARNER, BREADWINNER

province   REGION, SPHERE, DISTRICT, TERRITORY; *see p. 591, 614*

provincial   LOCAL, RUSTIC, NARROW

provision   FARE, FEED, FOOD, CATES, PROVISO, PLANNING, VICTUALS, CONDITION, STIPULATION

provisional   IFFY, INTERIM, TEMPORARY, TENTATIVE

provisioner   SUTLER, VICTUALER, VIVANDIER

provisions   CATES, ANNONA, LARDER

proviso   SALVO, CLAUSE, CONDITION, STIPULATION

provisory   IFFY, SUBJECT, CONDITIONAL

provocation   GOAD, CAUSE, AFFRONT, INCITEMENT

provocative   RACY, PIQUANT, SEDUCTIVE, TANTALIZING

provoke   IRE, VEX, BAIT, GOAD, RILE, ROIL, ANGER, ANNOY, PEEVE, PIQUE, NEEDLE, NETTLE

prow   BOW, BEAK, PROA, STEM

prowess   SKILL, VALOR, COURAGE, EXPERTISE

prowl   LURK, ROAM, ROVE, SKULK, SNEAK, STEAL

proximate   NEAR(BY), NEXT, CLOSE, ADJACENT, IMMEDIATE

proximity   NEARNESS, PROPINQUITY

proxy   AGENT, DEPUTY, DELEGATE

prude   PRIG, PRUNE, PURITAN, BLUENOSE

prudence   CARE, CAUTION, DISCRETION

prudent   SAGE, WISE, CHARY, CAREFUL, CAUTIOUS

prudish   COY, NICE, DEMURE, PRISSY

prune   CUT, LOP, CLIP, PARE, PLUM, SNED, SNIP, TRIM, PREEN, SHEAR

prurient   LEWD, NASTY, LUSTFUL

Prussia, capital of (former)   BERLIN

Prussian city   KIEL, ESSEN, AACHEN, BERLIN, BRESLAU, HANOVER, MUNSTER, STETTIN, FRANKFURT, DUSSELDORF

Prussian ruler   ALBERT, FREDERICK

pry   NOSE, PEEK, JIMMY, LEVER, PRIZE, SNOOP

prying   NOSY, CURIOUS, INQUISITIVE

Psalm(s)   LAUD(S), HALLEL, PRAISE, VENITE, CANTATE, CANTICLE, MISERERE

Psalm ending   SELAH

Psalmist   DAVID

psaltery   DULCIMER

pseudo   FAKE, SHAM, FALSE, PHONY, SPURIOUS

pseudonym **NOM, ALIAS, ANANYM, ANONYM, PENNAME, SOBRIQUET;** *see p. 557*

psoriasis **ECZEMA, DERMATITIS**

psyche **MIND, PNEUMA, SPIRIT**

Psyche's lover **CUPID**

psychiatrist **SHRINK, ANALYST, ALIENIST**

psychiatrist, famous **JUNG, RANK, REIK, WARD, ADLER, BINET, BRILL, FREUD, JAMES, JANET, WUNDT, BREUER, HORNEY, MESMER, CHARCOT**

psychic **MENTAL, TELEPATHIC**

psychic energy **LIBIDO**

Psycho set **MOTEL, SHOWER**

psychological **MENTAL, CEREBRAL**

psychologist **BINET, REICH, PAVLOV, PIAGET, WATSON**

psychosis **INSANITY**

psychotic **MAD, CRAZY, INSANE, SCHIZOID**

Ptah **APIS**

ptisan **TEA, TISANE, DECOCTION**

pub *see* **TAVERN**

pub game **DARTS, SKITTLES**

puberty **YOUTH, MATURITY, NUBILITY, ADOLESCENCE**

public **FREE, KUNG, OPEN, CIVIC, KNOWN, OVERT, COMMON**

publican **TAXER, TAXMAN, INNKEEPER, BARKEEP(ER)**

publication **BOOK, ISSUE, PAPER, EDITION, JOURNAL, MAGAZINE, NEWSPAPER**

publicist **(PRESS)AGENT**

publicity **NOTICE, BUILDUP, RECLAME, BALLYHOO, LIMELIGHT, NOTORIETY**

publicize **AIR, PLUG, PUFF, TOUT**

publish **AIR, EDIT, VENT, ISSUE, PRINT, BLAZON, DELATE, REVEAL, SPREAD**

publisher **OCHS, LUCE, FIELDS, HEARST, MERRIAM, SULZBERGER**

Puccini opera **EDGAR, MANON, TOSCA, (LA) BOHEME, TURANDOT, BUTTERFLY**

Puccini heroine **MIMI, TOSCA, MINNIE, BUTTERFLY, CIO CIO SAN;** *see individual operas*

puck **ELF, IMP, DISK, SPRITE, GOBLIN**

pucker **FOLD, TUCK, PLAIT, COCKLE, CREASE, GATHER, CRINKLE, WRINKLE**

pudding **HOY, DUFF, SAGO, BURGOO, JUNKET, CUSTARD**

pudding, kind of **PLUM, RICE, CARROT, INSTANT, VANILLA, CHOCOLATE, YORKSHIRE**

puddle **POOL, MUDDY, PLASH, WALLOW, PLASHET, LOBLOLLY**

pudgy **FAT, DUMPY, SQUAT, STOUT, CHUBBY, STOCKY**

Pueblo chamber **KIVA, ESTUFA**

Pueblo Indian **HOPI, MOKI, PIRO, TAOS, TANO, TEWA, ZUNI, ACOMA, KERES, MOQUI, LAGUNA, PICURI, ANASAZI**

Pueblo spirit **KACHINA**

puerile **YOUNG, FOOLISH, CHILDISH, JUVENILE, INFANTILE**

Puerto Rican city/town **PONCE, ARROYO, CAGUAS, ARECIBO, BAYAMON, SAN JUAN, MAYAGUEZ, TRUJILLO**

Puerto Rican forest **EL YUNQUE**

Puerto Rican governor **MUNOZ, ALBERTO, SANCHEZ, MAYAGUEZ**

Puerto Rico, capital of **SAN JUAN**

puff **PAD, BRAG, FLAM, RISE, WAFF, WISP, BLURB, ELATE, SWELL, BREATH**

puff up **BLOW, BLOAT, ELATE, SWELL, INFLATE**

puffer **LIJA, MOLA, BLOWER, CHAPIN, DIODON, MOLOID, TAMBOR, BOXFISH, BURFISH, COWFISH, CUCKOLD, OLDWIFE, BLUEGILL, BURRFISH, TRUNKFISH**

pugilist *see* **BOXER**

pugnacious **HOSTILE, BELLICOSE, COMBATIVE, BELLIGERENT, QUARRELSOME**

Pulitzer prize *see p. 510*

pull **TOW, TUG, DRAG, HALE, RUGG, SOOL, YANK, BOISE, PLUCK, WRENCH**

pulled, something **MUSCLE, TENDON, FASTONE**

pulley **WHEEL, SHEAVE, TACKLE**

Pullman **BERTH, COACH, SLEEPER**

pullover	SHIRT, SWEATER	Punic Wars belligerent	ROME,
pulp	PAP, PITH, RAPE, ULLA,		CARTHAGE
	CHYME, SLIMI, POMACE	Punic Wars general	SCIPIO
pulpit(s)	AMBO, BEMA,	Punic Wars site	ZAMA
	MIMBAR, ROSTRA, ROSTRUM	punish	CANE, DOCK, FINE,
pulsate	BEAT, THROB, QUIVER,		FLOG, FRAP, WHIP, SPANK,
	LIBRATE, PALPITATE		STRAP, AMERCE, AVENGE,
pulse	SEED, BEAT, ARSIS,		CHASTEN, CORRECT,
	THROB, THUMP, CADENCE,		SCOURGE, CHASTISE,
	SPHYGMUS		PENALIZE, CASTIGATE,
pulverize	BRAY, MILL, MULL,		DISCIPLINE
	CRUSH, GRIND, POUND,	punisher	CANER, WHIPPER
	POWDER, ATOMIZE	punishment	RAP, FINE,
puma	COUGAR, PANTHER,		WRACK, FERULE, PENALTY
	CATAMOUNT	punishment tool	ROD, RACK,
Puma rival	NIKE, REEBOK		STICK, FERULE, STOCKS,
pumice	BUFF, SCRUB		GARROTE, PILLORY
pummel	BEAT, DRUB, BASTE,	punishment, *pert. to*	PENAL
	POUND, BATTER, BELABOR	punitive	PENAL, PUNITORY,
pump	DRAW, QUIZ, HEART,		INFLICTIVE
	INFLATE	Punjab inhabitant	JAT, SIKH
pumpkin	PEPO, GOURD,	punk	HOODLUM; *see* TINDER
	MELON, SQUASH	punster	WAG, WIT, COMIC,
pun	GROANER, EQUIVOKE,		JOKER
	WORDPLAY, PARONOMASIA	punt	BET, KENT, KICK,
punch	JAB, BLOW, BORE, POKE,		QUANT, GAMBLE
	DOUSE, PASTE, STAMP,	puny	TINY, WEAK, FRAIL,
	MATTOIR, PRITCHEL		SLIGHT
Punch and Judy dog	TOBY	pupil	GLENE; *see* STUDENT
punch card debris	CHAD	puppet	DOLL, DUPE, PAWN,
punctilious	NICE, PRIM,		TOOL, DUMMY, KUKLA,
	EXACT, FUSSY, STRICT,		OLLIE, EFFIGY, KERMIT,
	PRECISE, SCRUPULOUS		MAMMET, MAUMET,
punctual	EARLY, ONTIME,		MARIONETTE
	PROMPT, TIMELY	puppy	CUB, DOG, FOP, TAD,
punctuate	MARK, POINT,		WHELP, UPSTART
	INTERRUPT	purchase	BUY, ORDER,
punctuation mark	DOT, DASH,		ACQUIRE, PROCURE
	BRACE, CARET, COLON,	purchaser	CLIENT, EMPTOR,
	COMMA, POINT, SLANT,		PATRON, SHOPPER,
	HYPHEN, PARENS, PERIOD,		CONSUMER, PROCURER
	QUOTES, BRACKET, LEADERS,	purdah	VEIL, SCREEN,
	SOLIDUS, VIRGULE, ELLIPSIS,		ZENANA, CURTAIN
	GUILLEMET, SEMICOLON,	pure	MERE, NEAT, PUTE,
	APOSTROPHE, PARENTHESIS		SHEER, CHASTE, SIMPLE,
puncture	JAB, PRICK, PIERCE,		VIRGIN, SAINTLY, VIRTUOUS
	PERFORATE	purgative	*see* LAXATIVE
pundit	SAGE, SAVANT,	purgatory	HELL, LIMBO,
	SCHOLAR, AUTHORITY		EREBUS, AFTERLIFE
pungent	TEZ, TART, SHARP,	purge	RID, FLUX, KILL, WASH,
	SPICY, TANGY, PIQUANT		ATONE, FLUSH, PHYSIC,
pungent seasoning	CURRY,		PURIFY, CLEANSE, ABSTERGE,
	GINGER, PEPPER, CAYENNE,		EXORCISE, ELIMINATION
	MUSTARD	purification	BAPTISM,
pungent vegetable	LEEK,		LUSTRUM, CATHARSIS
	ONION, GARLIC, SHALLOT,	purify	WASH, CLEAN, CLEAR,
	SCALLION		PURGE, FILTER, REFINE,
punic	PURPLE, PERFIDIOUS,		STRAIN, CLARIFY, CLEANSE,
	TREACHEROUS		DISTIL(L), SANCTIFY

Puritan **PILGRIM, ROUNDHEAD, SEPARATIST**

puritanical **STRICT, AUSTERE, PRUDISH**

purity **VIRTUE, CHASTITY, SANCTITY, CLEANNESS, INNOCENCE**

purl **RIB, EDDY, LOOP, REEL, PEARL, WHIRL, FRINGE, GURGLE, MURMUR, RIPPLE**

purlieu(s) **HAUNT, BOUNDS, LIMITS, LOCALE, MILIEU, HANGOUT, CONFINES, ENVIRONS, OUTSKIRTS**

purloin **ROB, FILCH, STEAL, PILFER**

purple **LILAC, MAUVE, REGAL, ROYAL, AMETHYST, LAVENDER**

purport **FECK, GIST, CLAIM, SENSE, TENOR, IMPORT, MEANING, INTENT(ION)**

purpose **AIM, END, GOAL, SAKE, ARTHA, INTENT, MEANING, INTENT(ION)**

purposeful, purposive **TELIC**

purse **BAG, KNIT, BURSE, POUCH, PRIZE, CLUTCH, PUCKER, HANDBAG, FINANCES, RETICULE**

purser **BURSAR, CASHIER**

pursuant **ACCORDING, FOLLOWING**

pursue **DOG, HUNT, TAIL, CHASE, HOUND, STALK, TRAIL, FOLLOW**

pursuit **HUNT, CHASE, QUEST, CAREER, VENTURE, ENDEAVOR**

pursy **PUDGY, PUFFY, STOUT**

purvey **CATER, SUPPLY, DELIVER, FURNISH, PROVIDE, PROVISION**

purview **KEN, GRASP, REACH, SCOPE**

pus **PYIN, BUTTER, SANIES, PURULENCE, SUPPURATION**

push **PING, PORR, PROD, URGE, BOOST, DRIVE, NUDGE, SHOVE, EFFORT, JOSTLE, PROPEL, THRUST**

push around **BOSS**

push off **LEAVE, DEPART**

push on **PROCEED, CONTINUE**

pushover **DUPE, LARK, SNAP, CINCH, SOFTIE, SUCKER**

pushy **BOSSY, DYNAMIC, FORCEFUL, INSOLENT, AGGRESSIVE**

pusillanimous **FAINT, TIMID, FEARFUL, COWARDLY**

pussy(cat) **TABBY, KITTEN**

pustule *see* **PIMPLE**

put **SET, PLACE, PLANT, STATE, WAGER, IMPOSE**

put a — on it **LID**

put aside **DAFF**

put away **BANK, CACHE, STORE**

put down **DEMEAN, HUMBLE, RECORD, DEGRADE, SUPPRESS**

put forth **EXERT, OFFER, PROPOSE, PROPOUND**

put in **ADD, ELECT, ENTER, INSERT, INSTALL, INTROMIT**

put it there **SHAKE**

put off **DOFF, HAFT, DEFER, STALL**

put on **ADD, DON, ADORN, FEIGN, STAGE, PRODUCE**

put on hold **DEFER, DELAY, SHELVE**

put one's finger on **PINDOWN**

put out **EMIT, FIRE, OUST, SACK, ANNOY, DOUSE, EJECT, EVICT, EXPEL, SNUFF, PUBLISH**

put right **AMEND, CORRECT**

put to flight **ROUT, FEEZE, ROUT(ED)**

put up **ANTE, POST, BUILD, ERECT**

put up with **BEAR, ABIDE, ENDURE, TOLERATE**

putative **ALLEGED, REPUTED, PRESUMED, SUPPOSED**

putdown **INSULT**

putrefy **ROT, DECAY, DECOMPOSE**

putrescent **ROTTEN, ROTTING, DECAYING**

putrid **FOUL, RANK, FETID, ROTTEN, CORRUPT, DECAYED, STINKING**

putter **IDLE, LOAF, DABBLE, TINKER, FRITTER**

putting area **GREEN**

puzzle(s) **CRUX, POSE, AMAZE, POSER, REBUS, BAFFLE, CRUCES, ENIGMA, RIDDLE, MYSTIFY, NONPLUS, TANGRAM**

puzzling **ODD, UNCLEAR, BAFFLING, ENIGMATIC, MYSTIFYING**

Pygmalion author **SHAW**

Pygmalion relative **DIDO, PAPHOS, GALATEA, METHARME**
Pygmalion statue **GALATEA**
pygmy **RUNT, ATOMY, MINIM,** *see* **DWARF**
Pylades' friend **ORESTES**
pylon **POLE, MAST, POST, GATEWAY**
Pylos relative **NESTOR**
pyramid **CONE, KHUFU, CHEOPS, KHAFRE, MENKAURE**
pyramid builder **IMHOTEP**
pyramid site **GIZA**
Pyramus' lover **THISBE**
pyre **BONFIRE**
pyromaniac **FIREBUG, ARSONIST**
pyrotechnics **FIREWORKS**
pyrrhic victory site **ASCULUM**
Pythagoras birthplace **SAMOS**
Pythias' friend **DAMON**
python **BOA, ANACONDA**

Q

Q **CUE, KAPPA, QUEEN, QUEBEC**
Qatar, capital of **DOHA**
Qatar city/town **JUH, DOHA, UMMBAB, UMMSAID, FUWAYRIT**
Qatar money **RIYAL**
Qatar neighbor **BAHRAIN, SAUDIARABIA**
QED word **ERAT, QUOD, DEMONSTRANDUM**
quack **FAKE(R), CROCUS, HUMBUG, IMPOSTOR, SANGRADO, CHARLATAN, MOUNTEBANK**
quack medicine **ELIXIR, NOSTRUM**
quadrangle **YARD, COURT, CAMPUS, SQUARE, TETRAGON, COURTYARD**
quadrant **ARC, HENRY, FOURTH**
quadrate **AGREE, SQUARE, QUARTER**
quadrille **DANCE, LANCERS**
quadrivium **MUSIC, GEOMETRY, ASTRONOMY, ARITHMETIC**
quadruped **BEAST, ANIMAL, MAMMAL**

quadruple **FOURFOLD**
quae — **VIDE**
quaff *see* **DRINK**
quaggy **MIRY, SOFT, BOGGY, FLABBY**
quagmire **BOG, FEN, MORASS, SLOUGH**
quail **IOWA, WILT, COLIN, COWER, WINCE, BLENCH, FLINCH, BOBWHITE, PARTRIDGE**
quail genus **COLINUS**
quail, young **CHEEPER**
quaint **ODD, DROLL, CURIOUS, UNUSUAL**
quake **SHAKE, QUIVER, SHIVER, TREMOR, TEMBLOR, TREMBLE**
Quaker **FOX, PENN, HICKS, FRIEND, WHITTIER**
quaking **ASPEN, TREMOR, TREPID**
qualification **SKILL, ABILITY, FITNESS, PROVISO, CONDITION, COMPETENCY, EXPERIENCE**
qualified **FIT, ABLE, CAPABLE, LIMITED, LICENSED, COMPETENT**
qualify **FIT, PASS, ADAPT, EQUIP, LIMIT, ENTITLE, PREPARE**
qualifying word **ADVERB, ADJECTIVE**
quality **AURA, GUNA, CLASS, GRADE, RAJAS, TAMAS, TRAIT, METTLE, SATTVA, STATUS, TIMBRE, CALIBER, FEATURE, PROPERTY, ATTRIBUTE, CHARACTERISTIC**
qualm **PANG, DEMUR, DOUBT, NAUSEA, REGRET, TWINGE, REMORSE, SCRUPLE, MISGIVING, COMPUNCTION**
quandary **FIX, STRAIT, DILEMMA, PREDICAMENT**
— qua non **SINE**
quantify **COUNT, MEASURE**
quantity **DOSE, SIZE, GRIST, AMOUNT, EXTENT, NUMBER, PORTION**
quantity, indefinite **ANY, MANY, SOME, HANDFUL, SEVERAL**
quantity, large **LOTS, RAFF, RAFT, SLEW, BUSHEL**
quantity, math **NABLA, SCALAR, TENSOR, VECTOR**

quantity, small BIT, DAB, DASH, LICK, WHIT, SCRUPLE, SMIDGEN, SCANTLING

quantum SUM, AMOUNT, PORTION, MAGNETON, PARTICLE

quarantine DETAIN, ISOLATE, SEPARATE, SETAPART, ISOLATION

quarrel ROW, FEUD, SPAT, TIFF, CLASH, BICKER, BRABBLE, DISPUTE, RUCTION, SQUABBLE, ALTERCATION; see FIGHT

quarrelsome FACTIOUS, CONTENTIOUS, ARGUMENTATIVE

quarry PIT, GAME, MINE, PREY, EXCAVATION

quart LITER, FOURTH, HEALTHY

quarter COIN, LODGE, MERCY, BILLET, CANTON, FOURTH, LODGING, TWO BITS, DISTRICT

— and quarter DRAW

quarter of a circle QUADRANT

quarter note CROTCHET

quarter of year RAITH

quarters DIGS, ABODE, ETAPE, BILLET, BIVOUAC, COMMONS

quartz ONYX, SARD, AGATE, CHERT, FLINT, PRASE, JASPER, CITRINE, AMETHYST; see p. 689

quash CASS, VOID, ANNUL, QUELL, CASSARE, SQUELCH, SUPPRESS

quasi AS IF, ALMOST, KIND OF, SORT OF

Quasimodo creater HUGO

Quasimodo rescued ESMERALDA

quaternion TETRAD

quaver SHAKE, TRILL, EIGHTH

quay see LANDING

queasy ILL, SICK, UNEASY, DOUBTFUL, NAUSEOUS

Quebec see also p. 614

Quebec city/town ALMA, HULL, GASPE, LAVAL, LEVIS, MAGOG, MINES, PERCE, PRICE, SOREL, TRACY, GRANBY, MAGPIE, MOISIE, QUEBEC, SALLUIT, GATINEAU, MONTREAL, LONGUEUIL

Quebec lake GOUIN, MINTO, KIPAWA, MAGPIE, SAKAMI, ST JEAN, ALBANEL, CABONGA, KIAMIKA, PLETIPI, MUSQUARO, NACHICUN

Quebec mountain CARTIER, TREMBLANT

Quebec patron saint ANNE

Quebec river BELL, NORD, YORK, GEORGE, MATANE, MOISIE, OTTAWA, KOKSOAK, ROMAINE, EASTMAIN, GATINEAU, SAGUENAY

queen ENA, MAB, ANNE, BESS, DIDO, HERA, MARY, SATI, BASTA, BEGUM, ELENA, MARIE, RANEE, BEEGUM, ORIANA, REGINA, ELEANOR, EMPRESS, VICTORIA

Queen —'s lace ANNE

Queen Bodicea people ICENI

queen of fairies MAB, TITANIA

Queen of Scots MARY

Queen of Sheba BALKIS

Queen of the Nile CLEO

queenly REGAL, ROYAL, REG(IN)AL

queer ODD, RUM, DROLL, FUNNY, WEIRD, QUAINT, BIZARRE, CURIOUS, UNUSUAL, ECCENTRIC

quell END, CALM, ALLAY, CRUSH, QUASH, QUIET, SPRING

quench SATE, ALLAY, DOUSE, SLAKE, PUTOUT, STIFLE, EXTINGUISH

querulous FRETFUL, PEEVISH, PETULANT

query ASK, INQUIRE

quest HUNT, PROBE, SEARCH, CRUSADE, MISSION, PURSUIT

question ASK, NUT, POSE, QUIZ, GRILL, ISSUE, POINT, POSER, QUERY

questionable MOOT, FISHY, SHADY, DUBIOUS, SUSPECT, SUSPICIOUS

questionnaire POLL, SURVEY, CANVASS

questionnaire question HGT, WGT, NAME, OTHER, ADDRESS

question word HOW, WHO, WHY, WHAT, WHEN, WHOM, WHERE, WHICH, WHOSE

quetzal TROGON

queue CUE, FILE, BRAID, PIGTAIL

quibble PUN, CARP, CAVIL, EVADE, SOPHISM

quick   FAST, LISH, LIVE, YARE, AGILE, ALIVE, FLEET, HASTY, RAPID, SWIFT, TOSTO, ACTIVE, PRESTO, PROMPT, SNAPPY

quick bread   SCONE, MUFFIN, POPOVER, BISCUIT

quicken   HURRY, SPEED, ROUSE, HASTEN, ANIMATE, ENERGIZE, ACCELERATE

quickly   ANON, CITO, APACE, PRESTO, PRONTO, INSTANTER

quicksand   SYRT, TRAP, MORASS, SYRTIS

quicksilver   AZOTH, MERCURY, HEAUTARIT

quick-witted   KEEN, ALERT, SHARP, SMART, NIMBLE

quid   CUD, FID, WAD, CHAW, CHEW

quid pro quo   EXCHANGE, TIT FOR TAT, SUBSTITUTE

quidnunc   SNOOP, GOSSIP

quiescent   LATENT, DORMANT, INACTIVE

quiet   MUM, PST, TST, TUT, CALM, HUSH, LULL, ALLAY, STILL, PACIFY, SMOOTH, PEACEFUL

quietude   EASE, PEACE, QUIET, SERENITY

quietus   DEATH, RELEASE, DISCHARGE

quill(s)   COP, PEN, REMEX, SPINA, SPINE, CALAMI, PINION

quilt   DUVET, EIDER, CADDOW, COMFORTER

quilt stuffing   DUVETY(E), (EIDER) DOWN

quincunx   — FIVE

quinine   LOJA, KINA, LOXA, QUINA

quintessence   CORE, GIST, PITH, ELIXIR

quintuplets   DIONNE, FISHER

quip   GIBE, CRACK, SALLY, BANTER, RETORT, WITTICISM

quirk   KINK, WHIM, TWIST, ODDITY, MANNERISM, IDIOSYNCRASY

quirky   ODD, KINKY, ECCENTRIC

quirt   WHIP, ROMAL

quisling   TRAITOR, COLLABORATOR

quit   RID, DROP, FREE, STOP, CEASE, LEAVE, YIELD, DESIST, GIVEUP, RESIGN, RETIRE, VACATE

quitclaim   RELEASE, QUITTANCE

quite   VERY, FULLY, TRULY, REALLY, WHOLLY, UTTERLY

quits   EVEN

quittance   CESSION, PAYMENT, RECEIPT

quitter   LOSER, COWARD, SHIRKER, WELSHER

quiver   SHAKE, THRILL, SHEATH, TREMOR, FLUTTER, HOLSTER, TREMBLE, VIBRATE

quivering   see QUAKING

Quixote   see DON QUIXOTE

quixotic   WILD, UTOPIAN, FANCIFUL, ROMANTIC, CHIVALROUS

quiz   ASK, EXAM, TEST, PROBE, QUESTION

quizzical   ODD, QUEER, COMICAL, UNUSUAL

Quo Vadis character   NERO, LYGIA, MARCUS, PERRONIUS

quod — demonstrandum   ERAT

quodlibet   DEBATE, MEDLEY, FANTASIA

quoin   NOOK, BLOCK, NICHE, WEDGE, CORNER

quoits   JUKSKEI

quoits term   HOB, MOT, TEE, SKEI, DISCUS

quondam   ONCE, PAST, FORMER, WHILOM, ONETIME, PREVIOUS

quorum   PLENUM, COMPANY, MAJORITY

quota   SHARE, RATION

quotation   CHRIA, CITAL, PRICE, EXCERPT, EXTRACT, CITATION, ESTIMATE

quote   CITE, PRICE, REFER, ADDUCE, RECITE, ABSTRACT

quotidian   DAILY, TRIVIAL, ORDINARY, RECURRING

quotient   RATIO, RESULT, FRACTION

R

R   RHO, RESH, ROMEO

R pronounced like "L"   LALLATION

— Ra   AMEN

Ra consort   MUT

Ra relative   MA, SHU

rabbet **SLOT, GROOVE, TONGUE, CHANNEL**
rabbi **GAON, AMORA, HAKAM, MASTER**
rabbinical **PASTORAL, AUTHORITARIAN**
rabbit *see* **HARE**
rabbit community **WARREN**
rabbit, invisible **POOKA, HARVEY**
rabbit, young **KIT, BUNNY, LEVERET**
rabble **MOB, SCUM, RAFF, CROWD, DREGS, RAGTAG, CANAILLE, RIFFRAFF, HOI POLLOI**
rabble-rouser **RAGTAG, RIOTER, INCITER, AGITATOR, DEMAGOGUE**
Rabelaisian **BAWDY, EARTHY**
rabid **MAD, RAGING, VIOLENT, ZEALOUS, FANATICAL, HYDROPHOBIC**
rabies **LYSSA, LYTTA, HYDROPHOBIA**
Rabin's assassin **AMIR**
raccoon(-like mammal) **COON, COATI, PANDA, NARICA, RACOON, TELEDU, TREE BEAR**
raccoon genus **NASAU**
race **HIE, CLAN, DASH, FOLK, LADE, LINE, BREED, DERBY, FLUME, RELAY, TRIBE, FAMILY, PEOPLE, SPRINT, STIRPS, CONTEST, LINEAGE, REGATTA, PEDIGREE**
race, *pert to* **ETHNIC**
racecourse **LAP, OVAL, RING, TURF, ASCOT, BOWIE, DOWNS, EPSOM, TRACK, HIALEAH, JAMAICA, PIMLICO, AQUEDUCT, SARATOGA**
racehorse **PACER, MAIDEN, MUDDER, PLATER, SLEEPER, TROTTER**
racehorses **ZEN, NOOR, ALSAB, ARMED, CIGAR, KELSO, OMAHA, PAVOT, SWALE, SWAPS, ACKACK, ALTHEA, BUSHER, FOREGO, GUNBOW, NASHUA, PONDER, STYMIE, TIZNOW, ASSAULT, MANOWAR, NEEDLES, SHUTOUT, TOMFOOL, AFFIRMED, ALLALONG, BIMELICH, CITATION, CHARRYBACK, CRALLEDON, DETERMINE, KAUAI KING, MONARCHOS, SIR BARTON,**

STAGEHAND, WHIRLAWAY, SECRETARIAT; *see* p. 711
racer **FLIER, MILER, HOTROD, RUNNER, ATHLETE, SPRINTER**
racetrack *see* **RACECOURSE**
raceway **TRACK, GROOVE, CHANNEL, RACECOURSE**
Rachel relative **LEAH, BRACK, JACOB, LABAN, JOSEPH, CHEEVER, BENJAMIN**
racing, car *see* **AUTOMOBILE RACING**
racing colors **SILKS**
racism **BIGOTRY, JIMCROW, PREJUDICE**
racist **BIGOT, KLANSMAN**
rack **GIN, FRAME, STAND, STRESS, TENSION, TORMENT**
racket **BAT, DIN, GAME, BABEL, NOISE, FRACAS, HUBBUB, PADDLE, RUMPUS, UPROAR**
racket, criminal **GRAFT, NUMBERS, EXTORTION, SHAKEDOWN, PROSTITUTION**
raconteur **NARRATOR, STORYTELLER**
racquetball term **PHOTON**
racy **SPICY, LIVELY, RISQUE, PIQUANT, SPIRITED**
Radames' love **AIDA**
radar term **PPI, BEEP, BLIP, LORAN, RACON, SCOPE, RADOME, SHORAN**
radiance **GLORY, LIGHT, LUSTER, SPLENDOR, REFULGENCE**
radiant **AGLOW, ASHINE, BRIGHT, GLOWING, LUMINOUS**
radiate **BEAM, CAST, EMIT, SHINE, DIFFUSE, TRANSMIT**
radiation **EMISSION, DIFFUSION, DISPERSAL**
radiation unit **RAD, ROENTGEN**
radiator **RAD, HEATER, TRANSMITTER**
radical **RED, REBEL, ULTRA, LEFTIST, LEFT WING;** *see* **ROOT**
radio **SET, CRYSTAL, WIRELESS**
radio term **ROGER, TENFOUR**
radioactive element **NITON, RADON, CURIUM, IONIUM, RADIUM, THORON, ACTINON, FERMIUM, THORIUM, URANIUM, ACTINIUM, ASTATINE, FRANCIUM, NOBELIUM**

radioactivity unit   DPM, DPS,
REM, REP, CURIE, HALFLIFE
radium discoverer   CURIE
radium emanation   NITON,
RADON
radius   RAY, RANGE, SPOKE,
SWEEP
radix   BASE, ROOT, ETYMON,
RADICLE
raffish   LOW, TAWDRY,
VULGAR
raffle   DRAW(ING), LOTTERY
raft   BUOY, MOKI, BALSA,
BARGE, FLOAT, PONTOON
rafter   BEAM, SPAR, VIGA,
TIMBER
rag   MOCK, TEASE, SHRED,
TATTER
rag doll   ANN, ANDY, MOPPET
ragamuffin   WAIF, BEGGAR,
ORPHAN
rage   FAD, IRE, BOIL, FUME,
FURY, RAMP, RANT, RAVE,
RESE, FUROR, STORM, VOGUE,
WRATH, FRENZY, BLUSTER,
TANTRUM, RAMPAGE
ragged   ROUGH, FRAYED,
SHABBY
Raggedy doll   ANN, ANDY
raging   RAMPANT, VIOLENT,
RAMPAGING
ragout   HASH, STEW, SALMI,
GOULASH, HARICOT,
MULLIGAN
Rahab relative   BOAZ, SALMON
raid   FORAY, ONSET, INROAD,
INVADE, MARAUD, RAZZIA,
SORTIE, ASSAULT
raider   RANGER, COMMANDO
rail   BAR, RANT, SORA, FENCE,
SCOLD, REVILE, SEPTUM
rail (bird)   COOT, CREX, KORA,
MOHO, SORA, WEKA, CRAKE,
MUDHEN, COULAN,
MOORHEN, TIKLING,
WATERCOCK
railed transport   EL, SLED,
TRAM, METRO, TRAIN,
SUBWAY
railing   FENCE, GRATE,
PARAPET
raillery   BANTER, PARODY,
SATIRE, BADINAGE,
RIDICULE
railroad   EL, TRAIN(S),
RAILWAY, MONORAIL,
TRAM(LINE)
railroad car   VAN, FLAT, TANK,
BUGGY, COACH, DINER,

BOXCAR, DINGHY, REEFER,
SMOKER, TENDER, CABOOSE,
FLATCAR, GONDOLA,
PULLMAN, RATTLER,
SLEEPER, WAGONLIT
railroad term   TIE, CROW,
FROG, SPUR, YARD, CHAIR,
FLARE, FUSEE, GAUGE, SHUNT,
GANTLET, SLEEPER,
CROSSTIE, HIGHBALL,
PEDESTAL, SEMAPHORE
railroader   RAIL, GUARD,
BRAKIE, PORTER, FIREMAN,
BAKEHEAD, ENGINEER,
YARDMAN, MOTORMAN,
CONDUCTOR
raiment   *see* CLOTHING
rain   DAB, HAIL, HYET, MIST,
POUR, SPIT, TEEM, BRASH,
MISLE, SLEET, SPATE, VIRGA,
BESTOW, FLURRY, MIZZLE,
ONDING, SEREIN, SHOWER,
DRIZZLE, TORRENT,
DOWNPOUR, PRECIPITATION
rain, *pert. to*   HYETAL, PLUVIAL
rainbow   ARC, IRIS, MOTLEY,
SPECTRUM, VARIEGATED
rainbow, *pert. to*   IRID(I)AL
raincheck   DELAY,
POSTPONE(MENT)
raincoat   MACK, PONCHO,
OILSKIN, SLICKER,
OILSKINS
rainfall   *see* RAIN
rain gauge   UDOMETER,
HYETOMETER
rainless   ARID
rainy   WET, MISLY, MISTY,
S(L)OPPY, SHOWERY,
PLUVIOUS
raise   EAN, GROW, HIKE, LIFT,
REAR, BOOST, BREED, ERECT,
HOIST, AROUSE, MUSTER,
STIRUP, COLLECT, ELEVATE
raised   EMBOSSED
raisin   PASA, LEXIA, CURRANT
raison d'être   MEANING,
PURPOSE
rajah's wife   RANI, RANEE
rake   COMB, ROUE, SLANT,
LEERER, PEPPER, SCRAPE,
STRAFE, ENFILADE,
LOTHARIO, LIBERTINE
rake-off   SKIM, TAKE, SHARE,
PROFIT, COMMISSION,
PERCENTAGE
rakish   NATTY, JAUNTY,
DASHING, DEBONAIR,
DISSOLUTE

rally   **MEET, ROUSE, MUSTER,**
REVIVE, RESURGE,
ASSEMBLY, PEPMEETING

rallying cry   **MOTTO, SLOGAN**

ram   **TUP, BUTT, TAMP, ARIES,**
STUFF, WETHER

Ramachandra wife   **SITA**

ram-headed god   **AMON,**
KHNUM

ramble   **GAD, ROVE, STRAY,**
STROLL, MEANDER,
SAUNTER

rambling   **WORDY, AIMLESS,**
TEDIOUS, UNSETTLED

rambunctious   **WILD, ROUGH,**
ROWDY, UNRULY, RESTIVE
BOISTEROUS, DISORDERLY

ramification   **ARM, SPUR,**
BRANCH, RESULT,
OFFSHOOT

ramjet   **ATHODYD**

ramp   **RAGE, REAR, APRON,**
CLIMB, PITCH, SLANT, SLOPE,
RUNWAY, INCLINE, ROADWAY

rampage   **FURY, RAGE, TEAR,**
FRACAS, FRENZY,
TANTRUM, OUTBREAK

rampant   **RIFE, EPIDEMIC,**
WIDESPREAD

rampart   **WALL, AGGER,**
REDAN, VALLUM, PARAPET,
RAVELIN

ramrod   **POKER, INFLEXIBLE**

ramshackle   **SHAKY, FLIMSY,**
RICKETY, RUNDOWN,
DELAPIDATED

ranch   **GRANGE, ESTANCIA,**
HACIENDA, PLANTATION

ranch hand   **COWBOY,**
COWPOKE, WRANGLER

rancid   **RANK, FETID, PUTRID,**
SMELLY

rancor   **GALL, SPITE, VENOM,**
MALICE, ILLWILL

random   **CASUAL, CHANCE,**
AIMLESS, DESULTORY,
HAPHAZARD, HIT OR MISS

randy   **HOT, BAWDY, CRUDE,**
HORNY, VULGAR, LUSTFUL

range   **ROW, AREA, RANK,**
ROAM, SPAN, DRIFT, GAMUT,
ORBIT, SCALE, SCOPE, STOVE,
SWEEP, SIERRA, COMPASS;
see MOUNTAIN

ranger   **WARDEN, SOLDIER,**
FORESTER

Rangoon   **YANGON**

Rangoon measure   **LAH, DAIN,**
TAUN

Rangoon state   **PEGU**

rank   **ROW, RATE, TIER, CASTE,**
GRADE, GROSS, UTTER,
ARRANT, DEGREE, RANCID,
STATUS, FLAGRANT,
POSITION, STANDING

rank and file   **GIS, RUCK,**
SOLDIERS

rank, military   **PFC, SGT,**
ADMIRAL, GENERAL,
PRIVATE, SERGEANT,
LIEUTENANT

rankle   **GALL, FESTER,**
IRRITATE

ransack   **LOOT, RIFLE, SEARCH,**
PILLAGE, RUMMAGE

ransom   **CLAIM, REDEEM,**
RESCUE

rant   **NAG, RAGE, RAIL, RAVE,**
TIRADE, BLUSTER,
HARANGUE

rap   **BOP, BOX, CHAT, CUFF,**
TUNK, BLAME, THUMP,
WHACK, THWACK, CONVERSE,
SENTENCE

rapacious   **GREEDY, GRASPING,**
RAVENOUS, PREDATORY,
VORACIOUS

rapacity   **GREED, AVARICE,**
VORACITY

rape   **COLE, PULP, NAVET,**
SEIZE, RAVISH, ASSAULT,
CABBAGE, PLUNDER, VIOLATE

rapid   **FAST, FLEET, HASTY,**
QUICK, SWIFT, SPEEDY

rapidity   **SPEED, CELERITY,**
VELOCITY

rapidly   **FAST, APACE, SKELP,**
POSTHASTE

rapids   **CHUTE, DELLS, DALLES,**
CATARACT

rapier   **EPEE, FOIL, TUCK,**
BILBO, BLADE, SABRE,
SWORD

rapine   **RAVIN, PILLAGE,**
PLUNDER

rapport   **ACCORD, CONCORD,**
HARMONY, AFFINITY,
EMPATHY

rapscallion   **KNAVE, ROGUE,**
SCAMP, RASCAL,
SCOUNDREL

rapt   **INTENT, ENGAGED,**
ABSORBED, ENGROSSED

raptor   **OWL, HAWK, EAGLE,**
FALCON, VULTURE

rapture   **JOY, BLISS, DELIGHT,**
ECSTASY, TRANSPORT

rara avis   **ONER, RARITY**

rare	ODD, SCANT, SCARCE, SPARSE, UNIQUE, UNCOMMON
rare-earth element	CERIUM, ERBIUM, HOLMIUM, TERBIUM, THORIUM, YTTRIUM, SCANDIUM; *see p. 521*
rarefied	THIN, REFINED
rarefy	REFINE, ATTENUATE
rarely	SELDOM, SPORADICALLY
rarity	FIND, CURIO, RELIC, GEASON, SCARCITY
rascal	CAD, IMP, YAP, KNAVE, ROGUE, SCAMP, VARLET, SCALAWAG, SCOUNDREL
rase	LEVEL, DESTROY
rash	POX, WILD, HASTY, HEADY, HIVES, UNWISE, WANTON, MEASLES, ROSEOLA, SCABIES, ERUPTION, RECKLESS; *see* SKIN
rasher	HAM, BACON, SLICE, COLLOP
rashness	FOLLY, HASTE, TEMERITY
rasp	RUB, FILE, CHAFE, GRATE, ABRADE, SCRAPE
raspberry	SASS, ACINUS, BLACKCAP
raspy	HUSKY, ROUGH, HOARSE, GRATING
rasse	CIVET
rat	LIAR, SCAB, SNEAK, SQUEAL, STOOL, GNAWER, VERMIN, TRAITOR, INFORMER
rat(-like rodent)	LOIR, MOLE, PACA, TANA, VOLE, WANT, GUNDI, LABBA, LEROT, METAD, MOUDY, MOUSE, MOUSY, RANNY, SHREW, ZEMMI, ZEMNI, ZOKOR, GERBIL, JERBOA, MOUSEY, MYGALE, RATTAN, RATTON, TELL ON, HAMSTER, LEMMING, MUSKRAT, POTOROO, SANDRAT, SONDELI
rat genus	MUS, GUS, SOREX, ZAPUS, GEOMYS, MYODES, MYOXUS, TUPAIA
Rat Pack member	DAVIS, BISHOP, MARTIN, LAWFORD, SINATRA
ratchet	*see* DETENT
rate	TAX, AGIO, CESS, BATTA, CHIDE, JUDGE, MERIT, SCOLD, VALUE, ASSESS, DEGREE, ESTEEM, APPRAISE, ESTIMATE
rather	ERI, SOONER, INSTEAD
ratify	OK(AY), BIND, PASS, SEAL, SIGN, APPROVE, ENDORSE, SANCTION
rating	MARK, RANK, CLASS, GRADE, SCORE
ratio	RATE, QUOTA, DEGREE, QUOTIENT, PROPORTION
ration	DOLE, METE, ALLOT, LIMIT, SHARE, DOLEOUT, ALLOWANCE
rational	SANE, LUCID, SOUND, LOGICAL
rationale	BASIS, MOTIVE, REASON, GROUNDS
rationalize	THOB, REASON, EXPLAIN
ratite	MOA, EMU, KIWI, RHEA, OSTRICH, CASSOWARY
ratrace	SCRAMBLE, STRUGGLE
rattan	CANE, PALM, SEGA, BAMBOO
rattle	JAR, RALE, CLACK, UPSET, MARACA, CLAPPER, CLATTER, CONFUSE, DISCONCERT
rattle on	YAK, BLAB
raucous	LOUD, HARSH, HOARSE, STRIDENT
ravage	RAZE, RUIN, SACK, HAVOC, DESPOIL, PILLAGE, DEVASTATE
rave	RAGE, RANT, TEAR, STORM, BABBLE
ravel	FRAY, UNDO, SLEAVE, INVOLVE, ENTANGLE, SEPARATE, UNTANGLE
Ravel work	BOLERO, DAPHNIS, LA VALSE
raveling	LINT
raven	CROW, GRIP, CORBIE, DEVOUR, PLUNDER
ravenous	GREEDY, HUNGRY, LUPINE, STARVED, RAPACIOUS, VORACIOUS, GLUTTONOUS
Raven author	POE
Raven character	LENORE
ravine	GAP, DALE, DELL, GILL, GULF, LINN, NALA, OMBE, WADI, WADY, CHINE, COOMB, DONGA, GORGE, GULCH, GULLY, NOTCH, ARROYO, CANYON, NULLAH
raving	INSANE, FRENZIED, DELIRIOUS
ravish	RAPE, CHARM, SEDUCE, DELIGHT, ENCHANT, VIOLATE, ENTHRALL,

	DEFLOWER, ENRAPTURE, TRANSPORT	— ready	OVEN
raw	DAMP, SORE, BAWDY,	Reagan Library location	SIMI
	BLEAK, GREEN, UNRIPE,		VALLEY, CALIFORNIA
	UNCOOKED	real	TRUE, PUCKA, PUKKA,
rawboned	BONY, GAUNT,		ACTUAL, INESSE, FACTUAL,
	LANKY, SLENDER		GENUINE, CONCRETE,
ray	BEAM, BETA, ALPHA,		AUTHENTIC
	ANODE, CANAL, GAMMA,	real estate	LAND(S), DOMAIN,
	GLEAM, LASER, COSMIC,		HOLDING, AL(L)ODIUM,
	LENARD, ACTINIC,		PROPERTY
	CATHODE	real thing(s)	ENTIA, MCCOY
ray(-like fish)	DORN, SKATE,	realistic	SOBER, VIVID,
	MANTA, ROKER, BATOID,		GRAPHIC, PRACTICAL
	OBISPO, BATFISH, COWNOSE,	reality	FACT, TRUTH, VERITY,
	FIDDLER, PRISTIS, TORPEDO,		ACTUALITY
	STINGRAY, DEVILFISH	realize	NET, EARN, GAIN,
ray genus	RAIA, RAJA, MOBULA		GRASP, ATTAIN, EFFECT,
ray, type of	BETA, GAMMA,		OBTAIN, ACHIEVE
	LASER	really	ARU, QUITE, TRULY,
rayon	ACETATE, VISCOSE,		INDEED
	CELANESE	realm	REICH, DOMAIN,
rays, *pert. to*	RADIAL		EMPIRE, SPHERE,
raze	LEVEL, WRECK,		DEMESNE, KINGDOM,
	DESTROY, DEMOLISH		BAILIWICK
razor	SHAVER	reap	CUT, MOW, GAIN,
razz	JEER, SASS, TEASE,		GARNER, GATHER, SICKLE,
	DERIDE, HECKLE		HARVEST
RBI leader, all-time	AARON	Reaper, Grim	DEATH
RCA founder	SARNOFF	Reaper, Grim, tool	SCYTHE
RCA mascot	NIPPER	reaping tool	SCYTHE, SICKLE,
re	ABOUT, ANENT		TWIBIL(L)
reach	GAIN, GRASP, RANGE,	rear(ing)	AFT, BACK, HIND,
	TOUCH, ARRIVE, ATTAIN,		RAMP, TUSH, BREED, ERECT,
	EXTENT, STRETCH		NURSE, RAISE, STEND, STERN,
reactance measure	OHM		PESADE, SUCKLE, ARRIERE,
reaction	RISE, TAXIS, REFLEX,		DERRIERE
	TROPISM, RESPONSE	rear, to the	(AB)AFT, ASTERN
reactionary	TORY, BIRCHER,	reason	WHY, NOUS, ARGUE,
	DIEHARD, RIGHTIST,		BASIS, CAUSE, LOGIC, SENSE,
	MISONEIST, RIGHTWING,		GROUND, MOTIVE, SANITY,
	CONSERVATIVE		APRIORI
read	CON, PORE, SCAN,	reason, deprive of	DEMENT
	STUDY, PERUSE, PRELECT,	reasonable	FAIR, JUST, SANE,
	CONSTRUE, DECIPHER,		SOUND, LOGICAL,
	INTERPRET		RATIONAL, SENSIBLE,
read, inability to	ALEXIA		EQUITABLE
reader	BOOK, LECTOR,	reasoning	LOGIC, THOUGHT,
	PRIMER, ANAGNOST		THINKING, RATIONALE
readily	EASILY, FREELY,	reassure	BOLSTER, COMFORT,
	WILLINGLY		SUPPORT
readiness	EASE, SKILL, GRAITH,	Reba names	VAN, JAKE, KYRA,
	ALACRITY, EAGERNESS		BROCK, MITCH, BARBRA,
reading	KRI, KERE, KERI,		JOANNA, CHEYENNE
	LECTION	rebate	DISCOUNT, KICKBACK,
reading disability	DYSLEXIA		DEDUCTION
ready	SET, PREP, RIPE, YARE,	Rebecah (Rebecca) relative	ESAU,
	ALERT, HANDY, MATURE,		JACOB
	WILLING	Rebekah relative	LEAH, ISAAC,
			RACHEL

rebel **DEFY, RISE, MUTINY, RESIST, REVOLT, MUTINEER**

rebellion **DORR, MUTINY, PUTSCH, REVOLT, SEDITION, UPRISING, REVOLUTION, INSURRECTION**

rebellious **UNRULY, DEFIANT, LAWLESS, REFRACTORY**

rebirth **RENEWAL, REVIVAL, UPSURGE, RENAISSANCE**

rebound **DAP, ECHO, CAROM, BOUNCE, RESILE, RICOCHET**

rebuff **SLAP, SNIB, SNUB, SPURN, CENSURE, HIGHHAT**

rebuke **SLAP, CHIDE, BERATE, CENSURE, REPROVE, UPBRAID, REPRIMAND**

rebut **OPPOSE, REFUTE, CONTRADICT**

rebuttal **RETORT, REJOINDER, CONFUTATION**

recalcitrant **REBEL, MULISH, UNRULY, WAYWARD, PERVERSE, RENITENT**

recall **MEMORY, REPEAL, REVOKE, SUMMON, RETRACT, REMEMBER**

recant **ABJURE, DISAVOW, RETRACT**

recap **SUMUP, CONCLUDE**

recapitulate **SUMUP, REPEAT, RESTATE, SUMMARIZE**

recapitulation **REPRISE, SUMMARY, ABSTRACT**

recapture **REGAIN, RETAKE, RECOVER**

recede **EBB, WANE, REGRESS, RETREAT**

receipt **INTAKE, RECIPE, VOUCHER, QUITTANCE, ACKNOWLEDGMENT**

receipts **GATE, TAKE, INCOME, PROCEEDS, BOX OFFICE**

receive **GET, OBTAIN, COME BY, TAKE (IN), ABSORB, ACCEPT, ACQUIRE**

receiver **FENCE, RADIO, BAILEE, TRUSTEE**

recent **NEO, NEW, LATE, NOVEL, MODERN, NEOTERIC**

recently **ANEW, LATELY, OFLATE, LATTERLY**

receptacle **BIN, BOX, CAN, POT, URN, CASE, FONT, PAIL, TRAY, BASIN, CRATE, ACERRA, BASKET, BUCKET, HAMPER, VESSEL**

reception **FETE, LEVEE, SALON, DURBAR, SOIREE, ACCUEIL**

receptive **OPEN, AMENABLE, RESPONSIVE**

recess **BAY, APSE, NOOK, NICHE, INTERVAL;** *see* **CUBICLE**

recession **SLUMP, DECLINE, SETBACK, DOWNTURN, SLOWDOWN, DEPRESSION**

recipe **METHOD, FORMULA, RECEIPT, BLUEPRINT, PRESCRIPTION**

recipient **HEIR, DONEE, PAYEE, ALIENEE**

reciprocal **JOINT, MUTUAL, SHARED**

reciprocate **REQUITE, EXCHANGE, RETALIATE, INTERCHANGE**

recital **STORY, ACCOUNT, CONCERT, MUSICALE, NARRATION**

recitation **READING, RECITAL, NARRATIVE**

recite **SCAN, QUOTE, RELATE, NARRATE, RECOUNT**

reckless **MAD, RASH, WILD, DARING, MADCAP, WANTON, RAMSTAM, CARELESS, HEEDLESS**

reckon **ARET, COUNT, GUESS, JUDGE, TALLY, THINK, IMPUTE, COMPUTE, SUPPOSE**

reckoning **TAB, COUNT, GUESS, TALLY, TOTAL, CALCULATION**

— reckoning **DEAD**

reclaim **RENEW, REDEEM, REFORM, RECOVER**

recline **LIE, LEAN, LOLL, COUCH, LOUNGE**

reclining **RECUMBENT**

recluse **MONK, LONER, HERMIT, ASCETIC, EREMITE, ANCHORET, SOLITARY**

recognition **NOTICE, GREETING, AWARENESS**

recognizance **BOND, PLEDGE**

recognize **ID, OWN, AVOW, ADMIT, GRANT, IDENTIFY, REALIZE**

recoil **SHY, KICK, COWER, QUAIL, WINCE, RESILE, SHRINK, KICKBACK, RICOCHET**

recollect **RECALL, REMEMBER**

recollection **RECALL, MEMORY, ANAMNESIS, REMEMBRANCE, REMINISCENCE**

recombinant letters **DNA**	recruit **BOOT, LEVY, DRAFT,**
recommend **TOUT, ADVISE,**	**RALLY, ENLIST, INDUCT,**
COUNSEL, SUGGEST	**MUSTER, ROOKIE, DRAFTEE,**
recommendation **PLUG, BOOST,**	**ENLISTEE, CONSCRIPT**
ENDORSEMENT,	rectifier **DIODE**
TESTIMONIAL	rectify **(A)MEND, REMEDY,**
recompense **PAY, WAGE,**	**SALVAGE;** see **CORRECT**
REPAY; see **REWARD**	rectitude **DECENCY, HONESTY,**
reconcile **ATONE, SQUARE,**	**INTEGRITY**
HARMONIZE	recto, opp. of **VERSO**
recondite **DARK, DEEP,**	rector see **CLERGY**
OCCULT, SECRET, OBSCURE,	rectory **MANSE, LIVING,**
ABSTRUSE, PROFOUND	**BENEFICE, PARSONAGE**
reconnaissance **RECCO, RECON,**	recumbent **LYING, PRONE,**
ESPIAL, SURVEY	**PROSTRATE**
reconnoiter **SPY, CASE, SCAN,**	recuperate **RALLY, REVIVE,**
SCOUT, SURVEY, EXPLORE	**RECOVER**
record **CD, LP, LOG, TAB,**	recur **REPEAT, RETURN,**
ACTA, DISC, DISK, FILE, LIST,	**REVERT, COME BACK,**
NOTE, ROLL, TAPE, DIARY,	**REAPPEAR**
ENTER, ENTRY, FASTI, OLDIE,	recuse **REJECT, CHALLENGE**
AGENDA, ANNALS, DOCKET,	red **SIENNA, CARMINE,**
ENROLL, MINUTE, BLOTTER,	**CRIMSON, SCARLET,**
DOSSIER, HANSARD, PLATTER,	**MAGENTA;** see p. 531
REGISTER	Red Book author **MAO**
record keeper **JOAH**	Red Cross founder **CLARA**
recorder **CLERK, FLUTE,**	**BARTON, HENRI DUNANT**
STENO, TAPER, NOTARY,	red-deer-like **ELAPHINE**
SCRIBE, COPYIST, HISTORIAN,	Red Desert **NEFUD, ANNAFUD**
REGISTRAR, SECRETARY	red dye root **CHAY(A), CHOY(A)**
recording **DISC, DISK, TAPE,**	red pigment **ROSET, BRAZIL,**
WIRE, PLATTER	**ASTACIN**
recording label **AM, BMG, CBS,**	red planet **MARS**
CRI, DGG, EMD, EMI, IMP,	redact **EDIT, DRAFT, REVISE**
RCA, VOX, WEA, ARGO, KOCH,	redcap **PORTER, CARRIER**
OPUS, SONY, ARSIS, CETRA,	redden **BLUSH, COLOR, FLUSH**
DELOS, DENON, JANUS, NAXOS,	reddish **PUCE, RUBY, RUST,**
WERGO, BRIDGE, FATBOY,	**RUFOUS, RUFESCENT**
GOTHIC, LEGEND, TELARC,	redeem **FREE, ATONE,**
CAEDMON, CAPITOL,	**RANSOM, RESCUE,**
CEDILLE, CHANDOS, CRYSTAL,	**DELIVER**
EVEREST, ODYSSEY, PACIFIC,	Redeemer **GOEL, SAVIOR,**
TITANIC, POLYGRAM,	**MESSIAH, SAVIOUR**
QUALITON, VANGUARD,	redhead **CARROTTOP**
LOISEAU LYRE	red-letter **IMPORTANT,**
recount **TELL, RECITE,**	**NOTEWORTHY**
RELATE, NARRATE	redo **REVAMP, REVISE**
recoup **RECOVER, GETBACK,**	redolence **ODOR, SCENT**
WINBACK	redolent **ODOROUS,**
recourse **REFUGE, RESORT**	**AROMATIC, FRAGRANT**
recover **HEAL, MEND, RALLY,**	redouble **ECHO, REPEAT,**
SALVE, RECOUP, RECLAIM,	**INCREASE**
RETRIEVE, RECUPERATE	redoubt **FORT, CITADEL,**
recovery **TROVER, SALVAGE**	**STRONGHOLD**
recreant **BASE, FALSE, CRAVEN,**	redoubtable **AWFUL, DREAD,**
APOSTATE, COWARDLY	**FEARSOME**
recreation **FUN, PLAY, SPORT,**	redress **AMENDS, REMEDY,**
PASTIME, AMUSEMENT,	**WAYOUT, CORRECT,**
DIVERSION	**DAMAGES**

redshirt ANARCHIST, COMMUNIST, REVOLUTIONARY

reduce CUT, DIET, PARE, REEF, SLIM, THIN, SLASH, DERATE, LESSEN, SHRINK, CURTAIL, DECREASE, DIMINISH

reduction DROP, FALL, CUTBACK, DECLINE, MEIOSIS, DECREASE, LESSENING

redundance, redundancy NIMIETY, SURFEIT, SURPLUS, PLEONASM, TAUTOLOGY

redundant SURPLUS, PLEONASTIC, SUPERFLUOUS

redwood SEQUOIA

Reebok rival PUMA, NIKE

reed OAT, STALK

reedy THIN, TINNY, PIPING, SHRILL

reed instrument see p. 642

reef BAR, CAY, KAY, KEY, ATOLL, LEDGE, SHOAL, SANDBAR

reefer COAT, JOINT, MIDDY, JACKET, MIDSHIPMAN

reek FUG, FUME, SMELL, STINK, STENCH

reel PIRN, SPIN, SWAY, LURCH, SPOOL, WHEEL, WHIRL, BOBBIN, TEETER, TOTTER, WAMBLE, STAGGER

reeve SLIP, PASSIN, THREAD, BAILIFF, STEWARD, OVERSEER

refectory MESS, FRATER, MESSHALL, DININGHALL

refer CITE, HARP, ADVERT, ALLUDE, ASCRIBE, CONSULT, PERTAIN

referee JUDGE, UMPIRE, ARBITER, OVERMAN

reference REGARD, MENTION, ALLUSION, CITATION, TESTIMONIAL, RECOMMENDATION

reference book ATLAS, MANUAL, ALMANAC, DIRECTORY, THESAURUS, DICTIONARY, ENCYCLOPEDIA

reference mark FIST, STAR, DAGGER, DIESIS, OBELUS, ASTERISK

referendum PLEBISCITE

refine POLISH, PURIFY, CLARIFY, IMPROVE

refined GENTEEL, CULTURED, POLISHED

refinement CLASS, POLISH, CULTURE, ELEGANCE, GENTILITY, IMPROVEMENT

reflect ECHO, MUSE, CHEWON, MIRROR, PONDER

reflection ECHO, SIGN, SLUR, GLARE, IMAGE, MUSING, LIKENESS, ASPERSION, DISCREDIT

reflective REFLEX, PENSIVE, MEDITATIVE, THOUGHTFUL

reflex IMPULSE, INSTINCT, REACTION

reflux EBB, RETURN, REFLUENCE

reform AMEND, BETTER, CHANGE, ALTERATION, IMPROVEMENT

reformatory PRISON, MAGDALENE

reformer CRUSADER, IMPROVER

refractor LENS, PRISM, TELESCOPE

refractory UNRULY, STUBBORN, INTRACTABLE

refrain BOB, CURB, FALA, LALA, DERRY, TRALA, BURDEN, CHORUS, DESIST, LUDDEN, ABSTAIN, FORBEAR

refresh AIR, FAN, COOL, PEPUP, RENEW, REVIVE, ENLIVEN

refreshing COOL, BALMY, BRICK, BRACING

refreshment SNACK, TONIC, STIMULANT, PICKMEUP

refrigerant ICE, FREON, ETHANE, AMMONIA, CRYOGEN

refrigerate COOL, CHILL, FREEZE, PRESERVE

refrigerator COOLER, ICEBOX, FREEZER

refuge ARK, HAVEN, ASYLUM, HARBOR, HOSPICE, SANCTUM, SHELTER

refugee EMIGRE, ESCAPEE, FUGITIVE

refulgent BRIGHT, RADIANT, SHINING, GLEAMING

refurbish DOUP, FIX UP, RENOVATE

refuse COT, POB, COOM, BALK, DENY, LEES, MARC, SCUM, SLAG, COOMB, DRAFF, DROSS, OFFAL, SCRAP, TRASH, RECUSE, SCORIA, RUBBISH

refute	REBUT, COUNTER, DISPROVE	rehabilitate	RECOVER, RESTORE, RECUPERATE, RECONDITION
regain	RECOUP, SALVAGE, GET BACK, RECOVER	rehash	GOOVER, REPEAT, REVIEW, REWORK
regal	ROYAL, KINGLY, QUEENLY, STATELY	rehearse	DRILL, RECITE, PRACTICE
regale	FETE, FEAST, BANQUET	rehearsal	TRIAL, RECITAL, PRACTICE, PROLUSION
regalia	FINERY, EMBLEMS, INSIGNIA	rehem	ALTER
Regan relative	LEAR, GONERIL, CORDELIA	Rehoboam relative	ZIZA, ABIJA
regard	DEEM, GAZE, ESTEEM, CONCERN, OBSERVE, RESPECT, CONSIDER	reign	RAJ, RULE, SWAY, TERM, GOVERN, REGIME
regarding	*see* CONCERNING	reign, *pert. to*	REGNAL, REGNANT
regardless	ANYHOW, ANYWAY, DESPITE, ATANYRATE, INANYCASE	reimburse	REPAY, REFUND, PAYBACK
regenerate	RENEW	rein	LEAD, CHECK, LEASH, CONTROL, RESTRAIN
regent	RULER, DEPUTY, GOVERNOR, INTERREX	rein in	CURB
regime	RULE, SYSTEM, ROUTINE	reincarnation	REBIRTH, RECREATION
regimen	DIET, RULE, DRILL, COURSE, METHOD, SYSTEM	reindeer, Santa's	COMET, CUPID, VIXEN, DANCER, DASHER, DONNER, BLITZEN, PRANCER, RUDOLPH
regiment	ALAI, POLK, PULK, COSSACK		
region	AREA, BELT, ZONE, CLIME, LOCALE, SECTOR, CLIMATE, PURLIEU, SECTION, VICINITY	Reiner	ROB, CARL, FRITZ
		reinforce	FORTIFY, BUTTRESS
		reinstate	REVEST, PUT BACK, RESTORE
regional	LOCAL, DISTRICT, TERRITORIAL	reiterate	*see* REPEAT
register	LIST, ENROLL, SIGNUP; *see* RECORD	reject	JILT, SPURN, DISOWN, REBUFF, REFUSE, DECLINE, REPULSE
register key	CASH, CHANGE, CHARGE, NO SALE, PAID OUT	rejoice	EXULT, GLORY, REVEL, DELIGHT, CELEBRATE
registrar	CLERK, ACTUARY, GREFFIER, RECORDER	rejoin	REPLY, RETORT, ANSWER, RESPOND, REUNITE
regnant	RULING, REIGNING	rejoinder	REPLY, ANSWER, RETORT, RESPONSE
regress	REVERT, RELAPSE	rejuvenate	RENEW, REVIVE, REFRESH, RESTORE
regret	RUE, REPENT, DEPLORE, REMORSE	relapse	REVERT, BACKSLIDE
regretful	SORRY, CONTRITE, REPENTANT	relate	TELL, REFER, DETAIL, RECITE, NARRATE, PERTAIN, RECOUNT
regular	EVEN, USUAL, NORMAL, STABLE, STEADY, ORDERLY, UNIFORM, CONSTANT, HABITUAL, CUSTOMARY	related	(A)KIN, ENATE, AGNATE, ENATIC, GERMAN, COGNATE, ENATIVE, GERMANE
regulate	FIX, RULE, ORDER, ADJUST, MANAGE, POLICE, CONTROL	relation	KIN, SIB, TIE, KITH, LINK, RATIO, REGARD, ACCOUNT
regulation	LAW, RULE, ORDER, RULING, DIRECTIVE	relationship	BOND, LINK, KINSHIP, RAPPORT, AFFINITY, COGNATION, CONNECTION
regulator	VALVE, GAUGE, MONITOR, GOVERNOR, WATCHDOG		
regurgitate	SPEW, VOMIT, RECITE, REPEAT	relative	EME, KIN, SIB, AUNT, ENATE, INLAW, NIECE,

AFFINE, AGNATE, PARENT,
KINDRED, KINSMAN, SIBLING
relative pronoun　　WHO, THAT,
WHAT, WHICH
relax(ing)　EASE, REST, LOOSEN,
RELENT, SOFTEN, UNBEND,
DETENTE, SLACKEN
relaxation　　REST, LETUP,
REPOSE, LEISURE, RESPITE,
MODERATION
relay　　RACE, AGENT, SERVO,
SHIFT, REMUDA, REMOUNT,
TRANSMIT
relay post　　DAUK, DAWK
release　FREE, UNDO, LETGO,
LOOSE, UNTIE, EXEMPT,
REMISE, PUBLISH, LIBERATE,
CATHARSIS, DISCHARGE
relegate　　EXILE, ASSIGN,
BANISH, CONSIGN
relent　　THAW, MODIFY,
SOFTEN
relentless　　HARSH, PITILESS,
INSISTENT, PERSISTENT
relevant　　APT, GERMAN,
APROPOS, FITTING,
GERMANE, APPOSITE,
PERTINENT, APPLICABLE
reliability　　CONSISTENCY
reliable　　SOLID, TESTED,
TRUSTY, STEADFAST,
CONSISTENT, DEPENDABLE
reliance　　FAITH, TRUST,
CREDENCE, DEPENDENCE
relic　　CURIO, TOKEN,
MEMENTO, VESTIGE
relief　AID, BAS, DOLE, FRET,
REMEDY, SOLACE, SUCCOR,
COMFORT, REDRESS, RELEASE
relieve　RID, CURE, EASE, FREE,
ALLAY, SOFTEN, SOOTHE,
COMFORT, LIGHTEN,
REPLACE, MITIGATE,
PALLIATE, ALLEVIATE
religion　　CULT, BAHAI, CREED,
FAITH, HINDU(ISM), ISLAM,
PIETY, SHINTO, TAOISM,
JAINISM, JUDAISM, SIKHISM,
BUDDHISM, CHRISTIANITY,
CONFUCIANISM,
PROTESTANTISM,
ROSICRUCIANISM,
ZOROASTRIANISM
religious　　GODLY, PIOUS,
DEVOUT, DUTIFUL,
FAITHFUL, ORTHODOX,
CANONICAL, SECTARIAN,
SPIRITUAL, GODFEARING,
SCRUPULOUS

religious denomination, Protestant
AMISH, MORMON, QUAKER,
UNITED, BAPTIST,
LUTHERAN, REFORMED,
EPISCOPAL, MENNONITE,
METHODIST, UNITARIAN,
PENTECOSTAL,
PRESBYTERIAN
religious leader　　*see p. 545*
religious order　BABISM, JESUIT,
MARIST, TEMPLAR,
DOMINICAN, FRANCISCAN
relinquish　CEDE, QUIT, DEMIT,
WAIVE, YIELD, RESIGN,
ABNEGATE
reliquary　　APSE, ARCA(E),
CHEST, CASKET, SHRINE,
MEMORIA
relish　DASH, TANG, ZEST,
ACHAR, GUSTO, SAVOR; *see*
CONDIMENT
reluctant　LO(A)TH, AVERSE,
HESITANT, UNWILLING
rely (on)　BANK, LEAN, COUNT,
TRUST, DEPEND
remain　STAY, WAIT, KEEPON,
LINGER, CONTINUE
remainder　　REAR, REST,
ARREAR, RESIDUE, UNITATE,
LEFTOVER, RESIDUUM
remains　LEES, DREGS, RUINS,
TRACES, CORPSE, CADAVER,
VESTIGES
remand　　RECALL, RETURN,
SEND BACK
remark　MOT, WORD, CRACK,
SALLY, NOTICE, COMMENT,
OBSERVE
remarkable　　UNCO, SIGNAL,
NOTABLE, UNUSUAL,
STRIKING, EXTRAORDINARY
Rembrandt painting　　TITUS,
LUCRETIA, ASCENSION,
ANDROMEDA
remedy　FIX, SOP, BALM, CURE,
TREAT, BALSAM, ELIXIR,
PHYSIC, CORRECT, CUREALL,
NOSTRUM, PANACEA,
PLACEBO, ANTIDOTE
remember　　RECALL, REMIND,
RECOLLECT, REMINISCE
remembrance　　TOKEN,
MEMORY, MEMENTO,
KEEPSAKE, REMINDER,
SOUVENIR
remind　　PROMPT
reminder　　CUE, MEMO,
PROMPT, MEMENTO,
TICKLER, SOUVENIR

reminiscent EVOCATIVE, SUGGESTIVE

remiss LAX, SLACK, DERELICT, DILATORY, NEGLIGENT

remit PAY, SEND, ABATE, RELAX, LESSEN, PARDON, FORGIVE

remnant END, ORT, RAG, REST, SHRED, ODDMENT, RESIDUE, FRAGMENT; see DREGS

remodel CHANGE, RESHAPE, RENOVATE, MODERNIZE

remonstrance PROOF, PROTEST, COMPLAINT, OBJECTION

remonstrate PLEAD, OBJECT, PROTEST

remorse GRIEF, GUILT, QUALMS, REGRET, SORROW

remorseful SORRY, RUEFUL, ASHAMED, CONTRITE

remorseless HARD, CRUEL, CALLOUS, PITILESS, RUTHLESS, MERCILESS, INEXORABLE

remote (A)FAR, ALIEN, ALOOF, FAROFF, DISTANT

removal OUSTER, DELETION, DEDUCTION, DISMISSAL

remove GUT, DELE, DOFF, OUST, ELOIN, CANCEL, DELETE, DEPOSE, DISBAR, EXCISE, ELOIGN(E), IMPEACH, ELIMINATE

remunerate PAY, REWARD, RECOMPENSE

remuneration FEE, PAY, WAGE(S), INCOME, REWARD, SALARY, EMOLUMENT, COMPENSATION

remunerative GAINFUL, LUCRATIVE, REWARDING

Remus brother ROMULUS

Renaissance, renascence REBIRTH, RENEWAL, REVIVAL

renal NEPHRI(TI)C

rend RIP, RIVE, TEAR, REAVE, SPLIT, WREST, CLEAVE

render DO, PAY, GIVE, RIVE, DEPICT, CLARIFY, DELIVER, FURNISH, PERFORM, PRESENT, HANDOVER, TRANSLATE

rendezvous DATE, TRYST, MEETING, ASSIGNATON

rendition VERSION, PERFORMANCE, TRANSLATION, INTERPRETATION

renegade RAT, REBEL, TRAITOR, APÓSTATE; see DESERTER

renege WELSH, BACKOUT, DISAVOW, GOBACKON

renew MEND, RESUME, REVIVE, REFRESH, RESTORE, REFURBISH

rennet CURDLE, KESLOP, PIPPIN

renounce DENY, RENAY, ABJURE, REJECT, RENEGE, ABDICATE, ABNEGATE

renovate REDO, REMODEL, RENOVATE, MODERNIZE, REFURBISH

renown NOTE, PRESTIGE; see FAME

renowned see FAMOUS

rent GAP, LET, RIP, HIRE, TEAR, TORN, LEASE, SPLIT, AVENGE, SCHISM, PAYMENT

rent-a — CAR, WRECK

renunciation DENIAL, WAIVER, REJECTION, ABDICATION, REPUDIATION

reorganization SHAKEUP, RESTRUCTURING

repair GO, IMP, DARN, (A)MEND, BETAKE, REMEDY, RESTORE

repairman FIXER, MENDER, COBBLER, MRFIXIT, MECHANIC, TECHNICIAN

reparable FIXABLE, MENDABLE

reparation AMENDS, DAMAGES, REDRESS, REPAIRS, ATONEMENT, INDEMNITY, COMPENSATION

repartee MOT, QUIP, SALLY, BANTER, RETORT, RIPOST(E), REJOINDER

repast MEAL, LUNCH, SNACK, TIFFIN, COLLATION, REFECTION

repatriate RETURN, SENDBACK

repay MEED, REFUND, REWARD, REQUITE, REIMBURSE, RECOMPENSE

repeal ANNUL, CANCEL, REVOKE, RESCIND, ABROGATE

repeat BIS, DIN(G), ECHO, HARP, RAME, SEGNO, ENCORE, ITERATE, REPRISE, REITERATE

repeatedly OFT, ANEW, OFTEN, AGAIN, FREQUENTLY

repel   PARRY, SPURN, REBUFF, REJECT, RESIST

repellent   VILE, REPULSIVE, REVOLTING, IMPERMEABLE

repent   RUE, GRIEVE, REGRET, CRAWLING, CREEPING

repentance   REGRET, REMORSE, ATTRITION, PENITENCE, CONTRITION

repercussion   ECHO, EFFECT, IMPACT, RESULT, UPSHOT, REACTION, AFTERMATH

repertoire, repertory   LIST, RANGE, STOCK, INVENTORY

repetition   ROTE, PLOCE, ENCORE, HARPING, MERISM, PALILIA, ANAPHORA

replace   SWAP, TRADE, CHANGE, RETURN, RESTORE, SUPPLANT, REINSTATE

replacement   LOCUM, ALTERNATE, SURROGATE

replenish   REFILL, TOPOFF, RESTOCK

replete   FULL, RIFE, SATED, GORGED, STUFFED

replevin   BOND, PLEDGE, TROVER

replica   COPY, MODEL, MOCKUP, FACSIMILE, REPRODUCTION

replicate   COPY, FOLD, REPEAT, DUPLICATE

replication   ECHO, FOLD, REPLY, ANSWER, IMITATION, DUPLICATION

reply   ANSWER, REJOIN, RETORT, RESPOND, COMEBACK, RESPONSE

report   POP, BANG, FAME, NEWS, TELL, BLAST, BRUIT, NOISE, ONDIT, RUMOR, STATE, CAHIER, GOSSIP, ACCOUNT, HANSARD, BULLETIN

reporter   *see* NEWSPERSON

repose   LAY, LIE, CALM, EASE, REST, RELAX, CONFIDE

repository   BOX, SAFE, CHEST, VAULT, MUSEUM

reprehend   BLAME, CHIDE, REBUKE, CENSURE, REPROVE

reprehensible   GUILTY, LIABLE, CULPABLE

represent   ENACT, DENOTE, DEPICT, EMBODY, PORTRAY, DESCRIBE, SPEAK FOR, PERSONATE

representation   SIGN, IMAGE, SYMBOL, ACCOUNT, VERSION, DEPICTION

representative   AGENT, ENVOY, PROXY, DEPUTY, FACTOR, LEGATE, NUNCIO, DELEGATE

repress   CURB, CHECK, CRUSH, QUELL, STIFLE, SUBDUE, SMOTHER

reprieve   STAY, DELAY, GRACE, RESPITE

reprimand   BAWL(OUT), SCOLD, REBUKE, REPROVE

reprint   REISSUE, REVISION

reprisal   MARQUE, PAYBACK, REVENGE, RETORSION, VENGEANCE, RETALIATION

reprise   BIS, ENCORE, REPEAT

reproach   RACA, RATE, BLAME, CHIDE, SCOLD, TAUNT, BERATE, CENSURE

reprobate   RAKE, ROUE, ROGUE, RASCAL, SINNER, DEGENERATE

reproduce   COPY, BREED, DUPLICATE, PROCREATE, REPLICATE

reproduction   COPY, FAKE, REPLICA, BREEDING, DUPLICATE, FACSIMILE

reproductive body   EGG, EDEA, GONAD, OVARY, SPERM, SPORE, GAMETE, TESTIS

reproof   BLAME, REBUKE, CRITICISM

reprove   FLAY, CHIDE, SCOLD, BERATE, CENSURE

reptile   HISSER, SAURIA, CRAWLER, CREEPER, DIAPSID, LORICATA, LORICATE, SQUAMATA; *see p. 671*

reptiles, *pert. to*   SAURIAN, OPHIDIAN, VIPERINE

republic   STATE, NATION, COUNTRY, DEMOCRACY

Republic author   PLATO

Republican Party   GOP, WHIG

Republican Party mascot   ELEPHANT

repudiate   DENY, DISOWN, RECANT, DISAVOW

repugnance   HATE, HATRED, DISGUST, REVULSION, ABHORRENCE

repugnant   VILE, GROSS, HATEFUL, OFFENSIVE, DISGUSTING

repulse   SNUB, DETER, REPEL, SPURN, REBUFF, SICKEN

repulsion   DISGUST, DISLIKE, AVERSION, DISTASTE, REJECTION

repulsive	UGLY, GROSS, ODIOUS, FULSOME, REVOLTING	reserved	SHY, COLD, KEPT, ALOOF, QUIET, DISTANT, RETICENT
reputable	UPRIGHT, RESPECTABLE	reservoir	SUMP, STORE, CENOTE, CISTERN
reputation	NAME, IZZAT, ESTEEM; see FAME	Reservoir Dogs name	BLUE, PENN, PINK, WHITE, KEITEL, BLONDE, ORANGE, BUSCEMI
repute	ODOR, ESTEEM, REGARD, STANDING	reset	(RE)BOOT, ALTER, SHELTER
reputed	KNOWN, ALLEGED, PUTATIVE, SUPPOSED	reside	LIVE, ABIDE, DWELL, EXIST, INHABIT
request	ASK, CALL, PLEA, APPEAL, DEMAND, ASK FOR, BESEECH, ROGATION	residence	PAD, DIGS, HOME, SEAT, ABODE, HOUSE, ADDRESS, DOMICILE
requiem	MASS, DIRGE, ELEGY, LAMENT	resident	CIT, ITE, INMATE, INTERN, TENANT, CITIZEN,
Requiem Mass word	DIES, IRAE		DENIZEN, INTERNE
requiescat in —	PACE	residual	EXTRA, SURPLUS,
require	NEED, FORCE, COMPEL, ENTAIL, OBLIGE, INVOLVE, NECESSITATE		LEFTOVER, REMAINING
		residue	ASH, SLAG, DREGS, LEES, WASTE, REMAINS, SEDIMENT
requirement	NEED, REQUISITE, NECESSITY	resign	QUIT, DEMIT, ABANDON, WALKOUT
requisite	NEED, VITAL, ESSENTIAL, NECESSARY	resignation	PATIENCE, DEMISSION, ABDICATION, ACCEPTANCE
requisition	SEIZE, DEMAND, REQUEST, SEIZURE, CALL UPON, APPROPRIATE	resiliency	RECOIL, REBOUND, BUOYANCY, ELASTICITY
requite	ATONE, REPAY, RETALIATE	resilient	HARDY, TOUGH, SUPPLE, BUOYANT, DURABLE, ELASTIC, TENSILE
reredos	SCREEN	resin	ALK, GUM, LAC, ALKYD,
reroute	DETOUR, REDIRECT		AMBER, ANIME, COPAL,
rerun	REPEAT, REPLAY, RESHOW		ELEMI, GUGAL, JALAP, KAURI, MYRRH, PITCH, BALSAM,
rescind	ANNUL, CANCEL, RECALL, REPEAL		DAMMAR, ESERIN, MASTIC, STORAX, BURMITE,
rescue	FREE, SAVE, LET GO, RANSOM, BAIL OUT, DELIVER, RECOVER, RELEASE		CAMBOGE, EXUDATE, GALIPOT, GAMBOGE, LADANUM, ELECTRUM,
research	STUDY, EXPLORE, INQUIRY		GALUPOT, LABDANUM, SANDARAC
resemblance	IMAGE, LIKENESS, SIMILARITY	resist	BUCK, DEFY, FEND, AVOID, FIGHT, ENDURE, OPPOSE, CONFRONT, WITHSTAND
resent	RANKLE, BEGRUDGE		
resentful	SORE, ANGRY, BITTER, INDIGNANT	resistance	FIGHT, DEFIANCE, IMMUNITY, STRUGGLE
resentment	ANGER, CHOLER, RANCOR, DUDGEON, UMBRAGE, BITTERNESS	resistance fighter	EDES, ELAS, MAQUI, REBEL, ACTIVIST, PARTISAN, GUERRILLA
reservation	ROOM, RIDER, SALVO, PROVISO, PROVISION, STIPULATION	resolute	FIRM, FIXED, DOGGED, STANCH, RESOLVED
reserve	HOJU, FUND, KEEP (BACK), HOARD, STASH, STOCK, STORE, RETAIN, BACKLOG, DIGNITY, EARMARK, NEST EGG, DISTANCE, SET ASIDE, STOCKPILE	resolve	END, ANSWER, DECIDE, SETTLE, WORKOUT, TENACITY, DETERMINATION

resonance TONE, MEANING, TIMBRE, SYNTONY, SONORITY, IMPORT(ANCE)

resonant DEEP, RICH, ECHOING, OROTUND, SONOROUS, IMPORTANT, RESOUNDING

resort SPA, USE, REFER, ASYLUM, CHOICE, OPTION

resort, famous PAU, ENNA, NICE, MIAMI, CANNES, RIVIERA, ACAPULCO

resound BOOM, ECHO, PEAL, RING, RESONATE, REVERBERATE

resource(s) CASH, FUNDS, MEANS, SHIFT, ASSETS, DEVICE, CAPITAL

resourceful CUNNING, CREATIVE, INGENIOUS, PRACTICAL

respect OBEY, HONOR, SENSE, VALUE, DETAIL, ESTEEM, FOLLOW, REGARD, REVERE

respectable DECENT, UPRIGHT, ADEQUATE, REPUTABLE

respectful CIVIL, POLITE, REVERENT, COURTEOUS

respective OWN, EACH, SEVERAL, SEPARATE, PARTICULAR

respiration EUPN(O)EA, DYSPN(O)EA, BREATHING

respirator PUFFER, INHALER, VENTILATOR

respiratory disease COLD, CROUP, ASTHMA, HAYFEVER, EMPHYSEMA, PNEUMONIA, SINUSITIS, BRONCHITIS

respiratory system LUNG(S), ALVEOLI, TRACHEA, BRONCHUS, BRONCHIOLE

respire EXHALE, INHALE, BREATHE

respite LULL; see INTERVAL

resplendent SHINING, DAZZLING, BRILLIANT

resplendent land SRI LANKA

respond ACT, FEEL, RISE, REACT, REPLY, ANSWER, REJOIN

response REPLY, ANSWER, RETORT, REACTION, REJOINDER

response to minister IDO

responsibility JOB, DUTY, ONUS, BLAME, LIABILITY

responsible (RE)LIABLE, ANSWERABLE, DEPENDABLE

responsive RECEPTIVE

rest LIE, SIT, EASE, LEAN, BREAK, PAUSE, PERCH, GAFFLE, REPOSE, SIESTA, C(A)ESURA, SURPLUS, BREATHER

restate REPEAT, REWORD, PARAPHRASE, REFORMULATE

restaurant SPA, CAFE, DINER, GRILL, BISTRO, BUFFET, EATERY, ONEARM, AUTOMAT, BEANERY, PIZZERIA

restaurant employee CHEF, COOK, BUSBOY, WAITER, MAITRED, WAITRESS

rested LEANT

restful QUIET, PEACEFUL, SOOTHING, TRANQUIL

resthouse see INN

resting ABED, LATENT, DORMANT

restive EDGY, BALKY, MULISH, UNEASY, UNRULY, FIDGETY, SKITTISH

restless UNEASY, NERVOUS, RESTIVE, AGITATED

restlessness ITCH, AGITATION

restoration REPAIR, RENEWAL, RENOVATION

restorative TONIC, BRACER, ANODYNE, CURATIVE, REMEDIAL

restore FIX, HEAL, STET, REPAIR, REVIVE, RENOVATE, REINSTATE

restrain CURB, REIN, STAY, CHECK, DETER, STINT, ENJOIN, TETHER

restraint CURB, REIN, CHECK, LEASH, LIMIT, CONTROL, RESERVE, DISCIPLINE

restrict CRAMP, LIMIT, CENSOR, COERCE, CONFINE

restricted INSULAR, EXCLUSIVE

restrictive STYPTIC, LIMITING, ASTRINGENT

restroom WC, JOHN, TOILET, LAVATORY

result FRUIT, EFFECT, ISSUE, UPSHOT, OUTCOME

resume RENEW, PICK UP, PRECIS, DOSSIER, SUMMARY, ABSTRACT, RECOMMENCE

resurrect REVIVE, RESTORE

resurrection EASTER, REBIRTH, RENEWAL, RESTORATION

resuscitate SAVE, REVIVE

resuscitation	RENEWAL, REVIVAL, RESTORATION
retail	SELL, VEND, TRADE, PEDDLE
retail outlet(s)	MALL, EMPORIA, EMPORIUM
retailer	DEALER, TRADER, VENDOR, SELLER, MERCHANT
retain	OWN, HAVE, HIRE, KEEP, SAVE, EMPLOY, PRESERVE
retainer	FEE, SUTLER, VASSAL, PAYMENT, ADHERENT, ATTENDANT
retaining wall	REVETMENT, EMBANKMENT
retake	REFILM, RECAPTURE
retaliate	REACT, REPAY, AVENGE, GET EVEN, REQUITE
retaliation	TALION, REVENGE, REPRISAL, VENGEANCE, RETRIBUTION
retard	SLOW, BRAKE, CHECK, DUNCE, STUNT; *see* DELAY
retch	GAG, KECK, HEAVE, VOMIT, THROWUP
retention	CUSTODY, MEMORY
reticence	MODESTY, RESERVE, SHYNESS, SILENCE
reticent	QUIET, SILENT, RESERVED, TACITURN
reticule	(HAND)BAG
retina part	ROD, CONE, FOVEA, MACULA
retinue	COURT, MEINY, POSSE, STAFF, SUITE, TRAIN, ESCORT, STABLE, CORTEGE, ENTOURAGE
retire	QUIT, LEAVE, RECEDE, TURNIN, RETREAT, WITHDRAW
retired	ABED, EMERITUS
retiring	SHY, MODEST, RESERVED, DIFFIDENT
retort	QUIP, VIAL, SALLY, RIPOST, ALEMBIC, RIPOSTE, REPARTEE, REJOIN(DER)
retouch	PATCH, DOCTOR
retract	UNSAY, ABJURE, DISOWN, RECANT, REVOKE, DISAVOW, WITHDRAW
retraction	PALINODE, WITHDRAWAL
retread	RECAP
retreat	DEN, LAIR, NEST, NOOK, STUDY, ASYLUM, RECEDE, CENACLE, RETIRAL, KATABASIS; *see* REFUGE
retrench	SAVE, LESSEN, REDUCE, CURTAIL, CUTBACK
retribution	REWARD, NEMESIS, PAYBACK, REVENGE, REPRISAL, VENGEANCE
retrieve	FETCH, REGAIN, RECLAIM, RECOVER, RESTORE
retriever	SETTER, POINTER
retroactive	BACK(WARD)
retrograde, retrogress	EBB, LAPSE, RECEDE, RELAPSE, RETREAT, REVERSE
retrospect	REVIEW, REFLECT
retrospective	REVIEW, EXHIBITION, RETROACTIVE
return(s)	RECUR, VOTES, YIELD, ANSWER, PROFIT, REVERT, RIPOST, RESTORE, REVENUE, RIPOSTE, EXCHANGE
Return of the Native author	HARDY
Return of the Native character	VYE, CLYM, EUSTACIA, THOMASIN
returning	REDIENT
Reuben relative	LEAH, LEVI, ISAAC, JACOB, JUDAH, LABAN, SIMEON
revamp	REDO, CHANGE, REVISE, OVERHAUL, RENOVATE, REORGANIZE
reveal	AIR, OPE, BARE, EXPOSE, IMPART, UNVEIL, DIVULGE
revealing	LOWCUT, SKIMPY, HELPFUL, INSTRUCTIVE, SEETHROUGH
reveille	DIAN, LEVET
revel	ROMP, ENJOY, PARTY, GAMBOL, CAROUSE
reveler	PARTIER, CORYBANT, DEBAUCHEE
revelry	ORGY, DEBAUCH, FESTIVITY, SATURNALIA
revenge	TALION, REQUITE, VENDETTA
revenue	NET, ANNAT, RENTAL, INCOME, PROFIT, ANNATES, EARNINGS, RECEIPTS
reverberate	ECHO, BOUNCE, REECHO, RESOUND
reverberating	REBOANT(IC)
revere	ADORE, HONOR, ADMIRE, RESPECT, WORSHIP, VENERATE
reverence	AWE, BOW, CURTSY, HOMAGE, RESPECT,

WORSHIP, ADORATION, VENERATION
reverie DREAM, MUSING, TRANCE, FANTASY
reversal SWAP, HITCH, UPSET, UTURN, PROBLEM, SETBACK, EXCHANGE, VOLTEFACE
reverse VERSO, REVOKE, SETBACK, OPPOSITE, TRANSPOSE
reversion RETURN, ATAVISM, ESCHEAT
revert (RE)LAPSE, ESCHEAT, REGRESS
review PAN, RAVE, PARADE, REVISE, SURVEY, INSPECT, JOURNAL, CRITIQUE, CRITICISM, CRITICIZE, EPICRISIS, HATCHET JOB
reviewer CRITIC, COMMENTATOR
revile RAIL, ABUSE, SCORN, DEBASE, INSULT, VILIFY, BELITTLE, VILIPEND
revise EDIT, ALTER, AMEND, REDACT, UPDATE, CORRECT, REWRITE
revival REBIRTH, RENEWAL, RECOVERY, RESUSCITATION
revival technique CPR
revive RALLY, RENEW, COMETO, PERKUP, WAKEUP, REMOUNT, RESTAGE, RESURGE
revocation REPEAL, ANNULMENT
revoke ADEEM, ANNUL, RENIG, CANCEL, RECANT, RENEGE, REPEAL, RESCIND
revolt RISE, REBEL, MUTINY, RISEUP, DISGUST, NAUSEATE, UPRISING
revolting HORRID, LOATHSOME, OFFENSIVE, REPULSIVE
revolution REV, RPM, COUP, GYRE, TURN, CYCLE, CHANGE, REVOLT, ROTATION, UPHEAVAL, UPRISING
Revolutionary War battles CAMDEN, COWPENS, TRENTON, MONMOUTH, SARATOGA, SAVANNAH, YORKTOWN, PRINCETON, BENNINGTON, BRANDYWINE, BUNKERHILL, CHARLESTON, GERMANTOWN, LONGISLAND, TICONDEROGA
Revolutionary War general GAGE,

HOWE, KNOX, CLARK, GATES, WAYNE, DEKALB, GREENE, MARION, CLINTON, LEARNED, BURGOYNE, SULLIVAN, TARLETON, DUPORTAIL, CORNWALLIS, HUNTINGDON, VON STEUBEN, WASHINGTON
revolutionist, revolutionary HALE, LENIN, MARAT, ANARCH, CASTRO, FENIAN, PESTEL, SETTIMO
revolve BIRL, PIRL, ROLL, SPIN, TURN, TWIRL, WHIRL, CIRCLE, GYRATE, ROTATE
revolver see GUN
revolving ORBY
revue SHOW, REVIEW, FOLLIES, CABARET, VAUDEVILLE
revulsion NAUSEA, DISGUST, AVERSION, DISTASTE
reward CUP, PAY, TIP, UTU, BONUS, PRIZE, ENRICH, GUERDON; see AWARD
reword, rewrite EDIT, RESTATE, REPHRASE
Rhapsody in Blue composer GERSHWIN
Rhapsody in Blue performer WHITEMAN
rhea EMU, OPS, NANDU, CYBELE, OSTRICH
Rhea relative GE, GAEA, HERA, ZEUS, HADES, CRONOS, URANUS, DEMETER, POSEIDON
rhetoric STYLE, ORATORY, LANGUAGE
rhetorical FORENSIC, BOMBASTIC
rhetorical device LITOTES, ANAPHORA
rheumatism GOUT, LUMBAGO; see ARTHRITIS
Rhine LEK, WAAL, IJESSEL, MERWEDE
Rhine city BONN, KOLN, BASEL, ESSEN, KLEVE, MAINZ, WORMS, COLOGNE, KOBLENZ, MANNHEIM, ROTTERDAM, DUSSELDORF
Rhine tributary AAR, ILL, AARE, ERFT, LAHN, MAIN, NAHE, RUHR, SIEG, LIPPE, NECKAR, MOSELLE
rhinoceros ABADA, BADAR, BORELE, REITLOA
rhinoceros, young CALF
rhinoplasty NOSEJOB

rhizome	ROOT, STEM, TUBER, STOLON, ROOTSTALK	ribbed	WALED, COSTATE
		ribbed fabric	REP, CORDS, CORDUROY
Rhoda names	IDA, JOE, JULIE, BRENDA, HARPER, KAVNER, VALERIE	ribbon	TIE, BAND, TENE, AWARD, COQUE, MEDAL, STRIP, CORDON, FILLET, LISERE, DECORATION
Rhode Island	see also p. 615		
Rhode Island city/town	ALTON, EXETER, HOXSIE, MANTON, NATICK, SLOCUM, BRISTOL, GALILEE, NEWPORT, TARKILN, WARWICK, CRANSTON, PAWTUCKET, PROVIDENCE, WOONSOCKET	ribs, pert. to	COSTAL, COSTATE
		rice	BORO, SELA, ARROZ, CHITS, DARAC, GRAIN, PADDY, PALAY, CEREAL
		rice dish	PILAF, PILAU, RISOTTO
Rhonde Island Indian	PEQUOT, NIANTIC, POKANOKET, NARRAGANSETT	rice drink	BASI, SAKE, ARRACK
		rice, type of	WILD, BROWN, WHITE, BASMATI
Rhode Island lake	CARR, BEACH, WALUM, TIOGUE, WORDEN, WATCHAUG	Rice U. player	OWL
		riceball	PINDA
Rhode Island island	HOG, DYER, HOPE, BLOCK, RHODE, PATIENCE, PRUDENCE, CONANICUT	rich	OOFY, VIVID, LOADED, FERTILE, OPULENT, WEALTHY, AFFLUENT, WELLTODO
Rhode Island reservoir	SLACK, BORDEN, PASCOAG, SCITUATE, WOONSOCKET	rich person	HAVE, DIVES, MIDAS, NABOB, NAWAB, PLUTO, TYCOON, CROESUS
Rhode Island river	WOOD, QUEEN, BEAVER, MOOSUP, WARREN, SEEKONK, TEN MILE, PAWTUXET, SAKONNET, CHEPACHET, PAWCATUCK, BARRINGTON, BLACKSTONE	rich person, famous	KEE, DELL, FORD, MARS, ALLEN, GATES, HUGHES, WALTON, ROWLING, CARNEGIE, PRITZKER, VANDERBILT, ROCKEFELLER
Rhodes statue	COLOSSUS	Richard I relative	JOHN, HENRY, ELEANOR
Rhodesia	see ZIMBABWE		
rhododendron	LAUREL, ROSEBAY	Richard II character	BAGOT, BUSHY, GAUNT, GREEN, HENRY, PERCY, SCROOP, SURREY, AUMERLE, LANGLEY, MOWBREY
Rhone city town	LYON, ARLES, AVIGNON, TARASCON		
Rhone tributary	ISERE, SAONE, DURANCE		
		Richelieu successor	MAZARIN
rhubarb	SCRAP, SETTO, HASSLE, PIEPLANT	riches	PELF, LUCRE, MONEY, ASSETS, WEALTH, FORTUNE, OPULENCE, PROPERTY, TREASURE(S)
rhyme	POEM, POESY, VERSE, CRAMBO, DOGGEREL		
rhyme scheme	ABAB, ABBA, ABABA, AABBA	richly	WELL, AMPLY, FULLY
		richness	DEPTH, POWER, LUXURY, WEALTH, FORTUNE, OPULENCE, AFFLUENCE, FERTILITY, INTENSITY
rhythm	BEAT, LILT, TIME, METRE, PULSE, SWING, CADENCE		
rhythmic	PACED, REGULAR, CADENCED, METRICAL, PERIODIC		
		rickets	RACHITIS
		rickets symptom	BOWLEGS, DEFORMITY, KNOCKKNEES
rhythmic accent	ICTUS		
rialto	MART, BRIDGE, MARKET, EXCHANGE	rickety	FRAIL, ROCKY, SHAKY, WOBBLY, RACHITIC, UNSTABLE
rib	KID, BEAM, JOSH, MOCK, COSTA, RIDGE, STRUT, TEASE		
		rickshaw	SAMLOR
		ricochet	SKIP, CAROM, BOUNCE, DEFLECT, REBOUND
ribald	LOW, LEWD, RUDE, BAWDY, COARSE, VULGAR		

rictus	GAPE, ORIFICE, RINGENT
rid	FREE, REAM, SHED, CLEAR, PURGE, RELIEVE
riddance	RELEASE, CLEARANCE, SEVERANCE
riddle	REE, SIFT, REBUS, SIEVE, PEPPER, LOGOGRIPH, PERFORATE; see PUZZLE
ride	BAIT, DOSA, TRIP, ANNOY, DRIVE, MOUNT, TEASE, HARASS, JOURNEY
ride, take for a	DECEIVE, HOODWINK
rider	FARE, CLAUSE, JOCKEY, CODICIL, ADDITION, PASSENGER, EQUESTRIAN
ridge(s)	BILO, GYRI, RAME, KEEL, OSAR, RAND, SPUR, WALE, WELT, ARETE, CREST, ESKER, LANDE, OESAR, PARMA, RAPHE, SERRA, SPINE, STRIA, CARINA, CUESTA, RIDEAU, SIERRA
riding	ATOP, DISTRICT
ridicule	GUY, PAN, TWIT, MOMUS, BANTER; see MOCK
ridiculous	INANE, ABSURD, FOOLISH, LUDICROUS
Rienzi composer	WAGNER
rife	COMMON, ENDEMIC, PROFUSE, TEEMING, PREVALENT, WIDESPREAD
riffraff	MOB, SCUM, TRASH, RABBLE, REFUSE, CANAILLE
rifle	STRIP, DESPOIL; see GUN
rifleman	YAGER, JA(E)GER, SNIPER, MARKSMAN
rift	GAP, FLAW, RENT, CLEFT, CRACK, SPLIT, BREACH, CREVICE, SCHISM, FISSURE, SEPARATION
rig	FIT, CART, GEAR, DRESS, EQUIP, ATTIRE, FITOUT, OUTFIT, TACKLE, CARRIAGE
rigging	GEAR, TACK, ROPES, ROPING, SUPPORTS
rigging part	MAST, ROPE, SAIL, SPAR, YARD, CHAIN, SHROUD
right	CLAIM, DROIT, RECTO, TITLE, DEXTER, DEXTRAL, FITTING, LICENSE, REDRESS, SUITABLE, PREROGATIVE
right-handed	DEXTRAL
Right —	BANK
right now	ATONCE, PRONTO, PROMPTLY, IMMEDIATELY
right of way	PASSAGE, EASEMENT

right turn	GEE
righteous	GOOD, JUST, MORAL, VIRTUOUS
righteousness	DHARMA, VIRTUE, DECENCY, RECTITUDE
rightful	DUE, FIT, FAIR, JUST, LAWFUL, FITTING
rightfully	DULY, FAIRLY, JUSTLY
rigid	SET, FIRM, HARD, TAUT, STIFF, SEVERE, STRICT, ADAMANT, AUSTERE, RIGOROUS
rigmarole	BLATHER, NONSENSE
Rigoletto character	BORSA, GILDA, CEPRANO, MARULLO
Rigoletto composer	VERDI
rigor	HARDSHIP, SEVERITY, HARSHNESS, STRICTNESS
rigorous	HARSH, STERN, STIFF, STRUT, SEVERE, STRICT, AUSTERE
rile	IRE, VEX, ROIL, ANGER, ENRAGE, IRRITATE
rill	BROOK, FURROW, STREAM, TRENCH, VALLEY, RIVULET
rim	LIP, EDGE, ORLE, BRINK, CHIMB, CHIME, CHINE, FELLY, SOMMA, VERGE, FELLOE, FLANGE
rime	(HOAR)FROST
Rinaldo's horse	BAYARD
rind	BARK, HULL, HUSK, PEEL, SKIN, CRUST, SHELL, CORTEX, EPICARP, EXOCARP
ring(s)	CALL, CRIC, HOOP, LOOP, PEAL, TOLL, ARENA, CLINK, KNELL, LUNET, PHONE, CIRCLE, GASKET, GINNAL, SIGNET, TERRET, TERRIT, CIRCLET, ANNULET, GROMMET
Ring character	ERDA, LOGE, MIME, EAGEN, WOTAN, FAFNER, FASOLT, FRICKA, HUNDING, ALBERICH, SIEGMUND, SIEGFRIED, SIEGLINDE, BRUNNHILDE
Ring composer	WAGNER
ring part	CHATON; see SETTING
ringer	QUOIT, DOUBLE, POSEUR, HORSESHOE, LOOKALIKE
ringleader	BOSS, CHIEF, CAPTAIN, INSTIGATOR

ringlet	CURL, LOCK, WAVE, TRESS
ringmaster	MC, EMCEE, DIRECTOR
ring-shaped	ANNULAR, CIRCINATE
rinse	DIP, DYE, LAVE, TINT, WASH, BATHE
Rio —	MUNI, BRAVO, NEGRO, GRANDE
Rio de —	ORO, JANEIRO
Rio de Janeiro beach	COPACABANA
Rio de Janeiro festival	CARNIVAL
Rio de Janeiro mountain	CORCOVADO, SURGARLOAF
riot	BRAWL, MELEE, EMEUTE, FRACAS, UPROAR, DISORDER
rioter	STONER, BRAWLER, PROTESTOR, DEMONSTRATOR
riotous	WILD, NOISY, UNRULY, LAWLESS, VIOLENT, HILARIOUS
rip	REND, RIVE, TEAR, SPLIT
rip into	ATTACK
rip off	CON, CHEAT, STEAL, FLEECE, SWINDLE, PLAGIARIZE
riparian	LITTORAL, RIVERINE
ripe(n)	AUGUST; see MATURE
riposte	QUIP, RETORT, THRUST, COMEBACK
ripping	FINE, SPLENDID, EXCELLENT
ripple	LAP, PURL, LUFF, WAVE, GURGLE, RIFFLE, WAVELET, UNDULATION
riptide	UNDERTOW
rise	HILL, LOOM, SOAR, GETUP, OCCUR, REBEL, SLOPE, STAND, APPEAR, ASCENT, REVOLT, REACTION
risibility	MIRTH
risible	DROLL, FUNNY, AMUSING, GELASTIC, LAUGHABLE
rising	MONTANT, ANABATIC, ASCENDANT
risk	DARE, SINK, PERIL, STAKE, CHANCE, DANGER, GAMBLE, HAZARD, MENACE, IMPERIL, VENTURE, JEOPARDY, ENDANGER
risky	DICEY, CHANCY, UNSAFE, PERILOUS
risque	RACY, SEXY, DARING, OFFCOLOR, SCABROUS
rissole	MEATBALL
rite(s)	PAX, CULT, FORM, HAKO, AGAPE, SACRA, ABDEST, LITANY, NOVENA, RITUAL, LITURGY, CEREMONY; see SACRAMENT
ritual	FORMAL, LITURGIC(AL), CEREMONIAL; see RITE
ritzy	POSH, TONY, SWISH, CLASSY, SWANK(Y), ELEGANT, LUXURIOUS
rival	FOE, GLEN, EQUAL, MATCH, EMULATE, OPPONENT, COMPETITOR
rivalry	OPPOSITION, COMPETITION
riven	RENT, TORN, SPLIT
river	REE, RIO, BAHR, ILOG, STREAM, WATERWAY, TRIBUTARY, WATERCOURSE; see p. 606
river, Biblical	ULAI, ARNON, DRACO, HABOR, JABBOK, JORDAN, KISHON, TIGRIS
river crossed by Caesar	RUBICON
river crossed by Washington	DELAWARE
river, Europe's longest	VOLA
river in Kubla Khan	ALPH
river mouth	BEAL, BOCA, LADE, DELTA, ESTUARY
river of song	OHIO, AFTON, VOLGA, DANUBE, SWANEE
river, pert. to a	AMNIC
river, underworld	STYX, LETHE, ACHERON, COCYTUS, PHLEGETHON
riverbank	RIPA, LEVEE, SHORE
riverbank, of a	LITTORAL, RIPARIAN
riverbed	WADI, WADY, CHANNEL
riverboat	BARGE, FERRY, PACKET, PULWAR, SAMPAN; see BOAT
rivers, longest	NILE, VOLGA, AMAZON, YELLOW, YANGTZE, MISSOURI, MISSISSIPPI
rivet	PIN, BOLT, FASTEN(ER)
Riviera city	NICE, GENOA, CANNES, MONACO, SAVONA, ANTIBES, PORTOFINO
rivulet	RILL, BROOK, CREEK, GULLY, ARROYO, RUNNEL, STREAM, RUN(D)LET
Rizpah relative	AIA(H), SAUL
RNA element	CODON
roach	CARP, REEFER, SUNFISH

road	RTE, VIA, WAY, DRUN, ITER, LANE, PATH, PIKE, AGGER, ROUTE, TARMAC, FREEWAY, HIGHWAY, PARKWAY, THRUWAY, AUTOBAHN, SPEEDWAY, EXPRESSWAY
road, *pert. to*	VIATIC(AL)
roadblock	BARRIER, BLOCKADE, BARRICADE, CHECKPOINT
roadhouse	INN, HOTEL, TAVERN
roadster	BUGGY, TRAMP, RUNABOUT
roam	*see* WANDER
roan	BAY
Roanoke Island message	CROATOAN
roar	BELLOW; *see* NOISE, CRY
Roaring Twenties dance	CHARLESTON
Roaring Twenties woman	FLAPPER
roast	PAN, BAKE, BROIL, BROWN, PARCH, TEASE, BANTER, CALCINE, BARBECUE, CRITICIZE
roasting tool	OVEN, SPIT, GRILL, BARBECUE
rob	CLIP, FLAY, LOOT, RAID, REAVE, RIFLE, STEAL, FLEECE, HOLDUP, DEPRIVE, PLUNDER, PURLOIN
robber	YEGG, THIEF, BANDIT, DACOIT, MUGGER, BRIGAND, CATELAN, FOOTPAD, LADRONE, RAPPAREE, PICKPOCKET, SHOPLIFTER
robbery	RAID, THEFT, HOLDUP, PIRACY, BREAKIN, DACOITY, STICKUP, BURGLARY
robe	GOWN, PALL, TOGA, SIMAR, TALAR, KIMONO; *see* DRESS
robe material	SATIN, TERRY
Robert —	(E) LEE
Roberta composer	KERN
robin	RUDDOCK, REDBREAST
Robin Hood friend	JOHN, (FRIAR) TUCK, WILL, ALLAN, MARIAN, SCARLET
Robin Williams role	GARP, HEYM, MORK, GENIE, PARRY, PATCH, ARMAND, DOUBTFIRE, EUPHEGENIA
Robinson Crusoe author	DEFOE
Robinson Crusoe man	FRIDAY
robot	GORT, GOLEM, HYMIE, ROBBY, ROSEY, TOBOR, AUTOMATON
robots, play about	RUR
robust	HALE, HARDY, LUSTY, SOUND, STOUT, WALLY, STURDY, HEALTHY, VIGOROUS
roc	SIMURG
Rochester's love	EYRE
rock	CRAG, LAVA, REEL, SIMA, SWAY, TUFA, TUFF, WHIN, CHALK, CHERT, CLINT, CRETA, SHALE, SHIST, SLATE, TALUS, ULURU, APLITE, BASALT, DACITE, GNEISS, MARBLE, SCHIST, SCYLLA, TOTTER, DIORITE, GRANITE, HAPLITE, LIMESTONE; *see* MINERAL, STONE
rock cavity	VUGG, VUGH, GEODE
rock fragment	BRASH, SPALL, DETRITUS
rock, igneous	TRAP, MAGMA, GABBRO, QUARTZ, BASALT, DIORITE, GRANITE, PICRITE, SYENITE, PORPHYRY, PEGMATITE, PHONOLITE, PERIDOT(ITE)
rock salt	EMOL, AMOLE, HALITE
rock type	IGNEOUS, METAMORPHIC, SEDIMENTARY
rock, volcanic	LAVA, WACKE, BASALT, LATITE, PERLITE
Rockefeller	ABBY, JOHN, DAVID, NELSON, WILLIAM, LAURANCE, WINTHROP
Rockefeller Center muralist	SERT
rocket	DART, CHEER, CLOAK, MUSTARD, REPRIMAND; *see* p. 742
rocket fuel	LOX, HYDRAZINE
rocket part	CONE, AGENA, RETRO, BOOSTER, CAPSULE, NOSECONE
rockfish	BASS, REINA, RASHER, TAMBOR, GROUPER, STRIPER, BOCACCIO
Rockford Files name	ANGEL, BEERY, ROCKY, BECKER, DENNIS, GARNER, MARGOLIN
Rockies peak	YALE, BROSS, EOLUS, EVANS, LOGAN, PIKES, ANTERO, CASTLE, ELBERT, ROBSON, LAPLATA, MAROON

Rockies range   TETON, UINTA, WASATCH

rocky   HARD, SHAKY, STONY, CRAGGY, RUGGED, WOBBLY, UNSTEADY

Rocky Horror Picture Show name   BRAD, CURRY, EDDIE, JANET, MAGENTA, MEATLOAF, RIFFRAFF, SARANDON

rococo   ORNATE, BAROQUE, ARABESQUE, DECORATIVE

rod   BAR, CUE, AXLE, CANE, POLE, SPIT, WAND, OSIER, PERCH, STAFF, FERULE, TOGGLE; see GUN

rodent   GNAWER; see p. 665

rodent, So. Amer.   CAVY, DEGU, MARA, PACA, COYPU, AGOUTI

rodeo   ROUNDUP

rodeo event   RIDING, ROPING, WRESTLING

roe   OVA, KELK, MILT, SPAWN, CAVIAR

roger   OK, OVER, RIGHT

Rogers   ROY, WILL, KENNY, GINGER

rogue   CAD, IMP, WAG, SCUM, KNAVE, SCAMP, PICARO, RASCAL, VARLET, CAITIFF, HELLION, SHARPER

roguish   SLY, ARCH, PAWKY, IMPISH, WICKED, MISCHIEVOUS

roil   IRK, VEX, RILE, WHIP, ANNOY, CHURN, MUDDY, AGITATE

roister   BRAG, REVEL, SPREE

Roland companion   OLIVER

Roland foe   GAN, GANO, GANELON, FERRAGUS

Roland's horn   OLIVANT

role   BIT, JOB, DUTY, LEAD, PART, HEAVY, OFFICE, WALKON, INGENUE, FUNCTION, CHARACTER

roll   BAP, BUN, ROB, WAD, BOLT, FURL, LIST, ROTA, TOSS, BAGEL, BIALY, SLATE, ROSTER, SCROLL, TATTOO, CAROTTE

rollback   CUTBACK, REDUCTION

roller   see WHEEL

rollicking   LIVELY, CAREFREE

Rolling Stones member   WOOD, JONES, WATTS, WYMAN, JAGGER, TAYLOR, RICHARDS

roly-poly   PUDGY, TUBBY, CHUBBY

Roman   LATIN, ITALIAN, QUIRITE

roman à —   CLEF

Roman assembly   COMITIA

Roman author   CATO, LIVY, OVID, LUCAN, PLINY, CICERO, HORACE, SENECA, SILIUS, VIRGIL, SALLUST

Roman court   ROTA

Roman games   LUDI

Roman general   SULLA, TITUS, DRUSUS, MARIUS, SCIPIO, AGRIPPA, CASSIUS, AGRICOLA, LUCULLUS, BELASARIUS

Roman gods and goddesses   see p. 646

Roman hill   CAELIAN, VIMINAL, AVENTINE, PALATINE, QUIRINAL, ESQUILINE, CAPITOLINE

Roman measure   PES, JUGA, URNA, ACTUS, CLIMA, CUBIT, UNCIA, CULEUS, DOLIUM, GRADUS, MODIUS, PALMUS, PASSUS, SALTUS, VERSUS, CYATHUS, DIGITUS

Roman money   AS, AES, SEMIS, DINDER, SOLIDUS, DENARIUS, SESTERCE

Roman numeral   see p. 585

Roman official   AEDILE, CONSUL, PRAETOR, TRIBUNE

Roman poet   OVID, CENNA, LUCAN, VERGIL, VIRGIL, JUVENAL, LUCRETIUS

Roman port   OSTIA

Roman, prominent   LEO, GETA, NERO, NUMA, OTHO, ANGUS, CARUS, GALBA, NERVA, SULLA, TITUS, AVITUS, CAESAR, DECIUS, GALLUS, JULIAN, JULIUS, PROBUS, SCIPIO, TRAJAN, TULLUS, CARINUS, HADRIAN, ROMULUS, SEVERUS, TACITUS, AUGUSTUS, CALIGULA, CLAUDIUS, COMMODUS, DOMITIAN, MACRINUS, PERTINAX, TIBERIUS, CARACALLA, TARQUINIUS

Roman weight   AS, BES, LIBRA, UNCIA, DUELLA, SEXTULA, SOLIDUS

Roman writer   LIVY, PLINY, VARRO, PLAUTUS, TERENCE, VEGETIUS

romance   WOO, GEST, TALE, COURT, FABLE, GESTE, AFFAIR, FICTION
Romance language   *see* ITALIC
romance-teller   ANTERI
Romania   DACIA
Romania, capital of   BUCHAREST
Romanian city/town   ARAD, DEVA, IASI, BACAU, SIBIU, ZALAU, BRAILA, BRASOV, GALATI, TULCEA, VASLUI, CRAIOVA, SLATINA, CONSTANTA, TIMISOARA
Romanian composer   ENESCO
Romanian money   BAN, LEI, LEU, LEY
Romanian mountain   MOLDOVEANU
Romanian native   MAGYAR
Romanian river   JIU, OLT, CEMA, PRUT, ARGES, MURES, SIRET, SOMES, TIMIS, PRAHOVA, IALOMITA
Romanian ruler   DOMN, CAROL, MAURER, ILIESCU, CEAUSESCU
romantic   DREAMY, LOVING, TENDER, IDEALISTIC, PASSIONATE
Romany   ROM, GIPSY, GYPSY
Rome conqueror   ALARIC, GAISERIC
Rome founder   REMUS, ROMULUS
Romeo and Juliet character   PARIS, ROMEO, JULIET, TYBALT, CAPULET, BENVOLIO, LAURENCE, MERCUTIO, MONTAGUE
romp   PLAY, CAPER, FRISK, CAVORT, FROLIC, GAMBOL
Romulus   QUIRINUS
Romulus relative   MARS, RHEA, REMUS
rood   CRUCIFIX; *see* CROSS
roof   HIP, CURB, FISH, HOWE, GABLE, PRAIT, PALATE, WARREN, GAMBREL, MANSARD, KINGPOST, QUEENPOST; *see* DOME
roof part   EAVE, CLEAT, JOIST, RIDGE, SPRAG, STRUT, TRUSS, FILLET, PURLIN, RAFTER, VALLEY
roofing   RAG, TILE, SLATE, THATCH, PANTILE, SHINGLE
rook   CROW, CHEAT, CASTLE, SWINDLE
rookie   NOVICE, RECRUIT, DRAFTEE, BEGINNER, NEWCOMER, GREENHORN
room   ALA, DEN, ODA, CELL, EWRY, LOFT, PLAT, SALA, ATRIA, EWERY, OECUS, PLAIT, SPACE, ATRIUM, CHAMBER, ROTUNDA
room and board   LODGING, PENSION
roomer   GUEST, LODGER, BOARDER
roomy   AIRY, AMPLE, LARGE, SPACIOUS
Roosevelt   FDR, SARA, TEDDY, DELANO, ELEANOR, FRANKLIN, THEODORE
Roosevelt Library location   HYDE PARK, NEW YORK
roost   SIT, NEST, LIGHT, PERCH, ALIGHT, GARRET
rooster   COCK, CAPON, BANTAM, CHANTICLEER
rooster, young   COCKEREL
root   BASE, EDDO, ETYM, GRUB, STEM, TARO, CAUSE, IMBED, ORRIS, RADIX, RIFLE, TUBER, WATAP, ETYMON, FIBRIL, MANIOC, ORIGIN, RADISH, RAMSON, SEARCH, SENEGA, CASSAVA, GINSENG, RADICAL, RHATANY; *see* CHEER
rooter   FAN, BUFF
rootlet   RADICEL, RADICLE
root for   HAIL, CHEER, ACCLAIM, APPLAUD
root, type of   YAM, BEET, CHAY, CHOY, EDDO, GABE, GABI, JUCA, KALO, TARO, YAMP, YUCA, CHAYA, CHOYA, RAMPS, TANIA, TANYA, YAMPA, ARALIA, CARDON, CARROT, CASAVA, GINGER, RADISH, TANIER, TANNIA, TANYAH, TURNIP, CARDOON, CASSAVA, PARSNIP, RAMPION, RHUBARB, SALSIFY
roots, have   RESIDE
rope   CORD, JEFF, LAZO, BIGHT, BRACE, LASSO, LONGE, REATA, REEVE, RIATA, LARIAT, TETHER, CORDAGE, LINGTOW, MARLINE
rope fiber   *see* FIBER
rope, nautical   FOX, GUY, TYE, FAST, LIFT, SPAN, STAY, TACK, VANG, WAPP, BRAIL, EARING, GASKET, HAWSER, RATLIN, SENNIT, SHROUD,

LANIARD, LANYARD, PAINTER, RATLINE, SNOTTER
Roseanne names DJ, DAN, JOHN, LECY, BECKY, HARRIS, JACKIE, LAURIE, DARLENE, GOODMAN, METCALF
Rosalind maid ADELE
Rosamunda's king ALBOIN
rosary BEADS, CHAPLET, BEADROLL
rosary bead AVE, GAUD(Y)
rose GUL, GEUM, ROSA, DRYAS, DEWDROP, RAMBLER, SPIRAEA, HAWTHORN
Rose Bowl site PASADENA
rose of Sharon ALTHEA
roseate ROSY, BRIGHT, OPTIMISTIC
Rosebud SLED
Rosetti DANTE, CHRISTINA
rosewood MOLOMPI
Rosh — HASHANA
rosolic acid AURIN(E)
Rossini opera BARBER, OTELLO, WILLIAMTELL
roster LIST, ROLL, ROTA, RECORD, REGISTER
rostrum DAIS, PROW, PULPIT, PODIUM, LECTERN, TRIBUNE, PLATFORM
rosy RUDDY, BRIGHT, FLUSHED, HOPEFUL, BLUSHING, PROMISING
rot RET, WROX, DECAY, SPOIL, PUTREFY
rotate *see* REVOLVE
rotating piece CAM, TOP, AXIS, AXLE, GIRO, REEL, ARBOR, ROTOR, WHEEL, BOBBIN, DASHER, MANDREL, SPINDLE, CAROUSEL, GIRANDOLE
rotation TURNING, GYRATION, REVOLUTION, ALTERNATION
rote MEMORY, ROUTINE, PRACTICE, REPETITION
rotgut BOOZE, WHISK(E)Y
rotisserie SPIT, GRILL, SKEWER, BARBECUE
rotor STATOR
rotten BAD, OFF, FOUL, RANK, FETID, PUTRID, CORRUPT, DECAYED, SPOILED, TAINTED
rotter CAD, CUR
rotund FAT, OBESE, PLUMP, ROUND, STOUT, CORPULENT
roué *see* RAKE

rouge BLUSH, RUDDLE
rough CURT, RUDE, BUMPY, CRUDE, GRUFF, HARSH, HILLY, COARSE, BUBBLY, RUGGED, UNEVEN
rough cloth DENIM, TERRY, DUFFEL
roughage BRAN, FIBER, CELLULOSE
roughen CHAP, FRAY, FRET, RASP, ABRADE, RUFFLE, COARSEN
roughly ABOUT, CIRCA, AROUND, RUDELY, BRUTALLY, UNEVENLY, VIOLENTLY
roughneck BOOR, GOON, THUG, BULLY
roughness FORCE, RIGOR, LIPPER, IRREGULARITY
roughshod, go or ride TRAMPLE
roulette term BAS, RED, NOIR, PAIR, BLACK, PASSE, ROUGE, IMPAIR, MILIEU
round ROTA, AMBIT, ORBED, CYCLE, SALVO, PERIOD, ROTULA, ROTUND, GLOBATE, GLOBOID, CIRCULAR, GLOBULAR, SPHERICAL
Round Table *see p. 659*
round up AMASS, CORRAL, GATHER, COLLECT
roundabout AMBAGE, DETOUR, DEVIOUS, CIRCUITOUS
rounded ROTUND, FUSIFORM, APPROXIMATE
roundly FULLY, UTTERLY
roundup RODEO, REVIEW, RUNDOWN, SUMMARY
roundworm ASCARID, NEMATODE, PARASITE
rouse STIR (UP), (A)WAKEN, BESTIR, EXCITE
rousing BRISK, MOVING, BRACING, STIRRING
Rousseau character EMILE, JULIE
Rousseau work DEVIN, EMILE, JULIE, CONFESSIONS
roustabout LUMPER, LABORER, DECKHAND, STEVEDORE
rout MOB, BEAT, RIOT, RUCK, PANIC, DEFEAT, FLIGHT, DEBACLE, STAMPEDE
route WAY, PATH, ROAD, COURSE, DIRECT(ION), ITINERARY
routine RUT, DULL, ROTA, ROTE, HABIT, WONT, USUAL,

	NORMAL, SYSTEM, REGULAR, TEDIOUS, SCHEDULE, CUSTOMARY
rove	*see* WANDER
rover	HOBO, NOMAD, ERRANT, PIRATE, DRIFTER, VAGRANT, WANDERER
row	OAR, RANK, TIER, FILE, LINE, SCULL; *see* FIGHT
rowboat	GIG, BANCA, CANOE, COBLE, SKIFF, CAIQUE, WHERRY, GONDOLA
rowdy	BHOY, THUG, HOOD(LUM), ROUGH, YAHOO, RUFFIAN, LARRIKIN, PLUGUGLY, HOOLIGAN
rowlock	THOLE, POPPET
Roxanne's lover	CYRANO
Roy Rogers's horse	TRIGGER
Roy Rogers's wife	(DALE) EVANS
royal	REGAL, AUGUST, KINGLY, QUEENLY, IMPERIAL, PRINCELY
royalist	TORY, MONARCHIST, IMPERIALIST
royalty	FEE, ALII, RIGHTS, PERCENTAGE
RSVP	SIL, VOUS, PLAIT, REPONDEZ
rub	BUFF, WIPE, FROT, CHAFE, GRATE, SHINE, ABRADE, SCRAPE, BURNISH
Rubaiyat author	OMAR KHAYYAM
Rubaiyat translator	FITZGERALD
rubber	GUM, PARA, BUTYL, CEARA, LATEX, CAUCHO, ERASER, GALOSH, EBONITE, ELASTIC, GUAYULE
rubber, synthetic	BUNA, BUTYLE, CARIFLEX, NEOPRENE
rubber type	CEARA, INDIA, CAUCHO, EBONITE, NITRILE, KOROSEAL, VULCANITE
rubbers	OVERSHOES, GALOSHES
rubbish	ROT, JUNK, GULCH, DROSS, SCREE, STENT, DEBRIS, NONSENSE; *see* REFUSE
rubble	RUINS, DEBRIS, WRECKAGE
rubdown	MASSAGE
rube	HICK, YOKEL, RUSTIC
rubella	RASH, MEASLES, RUBEOLA, ROSEOLA
rubicund	RED, ROSY, RUDDY, FLORID

Rubinstein	ANTON, ARTUR
rubric	TITLE, CAPTION, HEADING
ruby	SARD, BALAS, SARDIUS
ruck	FOLD, HEAP, SLEW, STACK, CREASE, PUCKER, WRINKLE
ruckus	ROW, RIOT, BRAWL, MELEE, RUMPUS, UPROAR, COMMOTION, DISTURBANCE
rudder	HELM, TILLER
ruddy	RED, ROSY, SANGUINE
rude	CRUDE, GRUFF, HARSH, ROUGH, COARSE, RUGGED, VULGAR, BOORISH, UNCIVIL, IMPOLITE, INSOLENT, OFFENSIVE
rudiment	ABC, GERM, SEED, BASIC, ANLAGE, EMBRYO, ELEMENT, BEGINNING
rudimentary	BASIC, SIMPLE, INCHOATE, EMBRYONIC, VESTIGIAL, ELEMENTARY
rue	RUTA, REGRET, DEPLORE
rueful	SORRY, REGRETFUL, APOLOGETIC
ruff	REE(VE), RUCHE, TRUMP, COLLAR, FRAISE, TIPPET
ruffer	NAPPER
ruffian	GOON, THUG, BRAVO, BULLY, ROWDY, TOUGH, HOODLUM, HOOLIGAN
ruffle	VEX, MUSS, ROOL, SHIR, CRIMP, FRILL, PLEAT, RUCHE, SHIRR, GATHER, PUCKER, AGITATE, DISTURB, FLOUNCE, GADROON
rufous	RUSTY, TAWNY, RED(DISH)
rug	MAT, RYA, MAUD, THROW, CARPET, RUNNER, TOUPEE, DRUGGET, COVERING
rug, type of	*see* p. 537
rugby	RUGGER, FOOTBALL
rugby term	TRY, MARK, CHIEF, FIVES, PITCH, SCRUM, TOUCH, DESPOT, NOSIDE, SHOGUN, TACKLE, TYRANT, HEELING, KNOCKON, SCRUMMAGE
rugged	HARSH, ROUGH, CRAGGY, JAGGED, UNEVEN
rugose	RIDGED, BULLATE, CORRUGATED
ruin	DOOM, FALL, UNDO, HAVOC, SPOIL, WRACK, WRECK(AGE), DEBRIS, DESTROY

— and ruin	**WRACK**
ruins	**DEBRIS, REMAINS**
rule	**LAW, CODE, NORM,**
	CANON, HABIT, PRECEPT,
	DOMINEER; *see* **REIGN**
rule out	**BAR, OMIT, FORBID,**
	DISCARD, EXCLUDE
Rule Britannia composer	**ARNE**
ruler	**CZAR, KING, SHAH,**
	TSAR, CALIF, MPRET, NEGUS,
	NIZAM, RAJAH, CALIPH,
	FERULE, KAISER, SACHEM,
	SULTAN, CZARINA, TSARINA,
	MONARCH, SULTANA
ruling	**ORDER, DECREE,**
	REGNANT, DECISION,
	REIGNING
Rumanian	*see* **ROMANIAN**
rum	**BAD, ROM(ANY), QUEER,**
	LIQUOR
rumble	**ROLL, GROWL,**
	FRACAS, THUNDER
rumen	**CUD, PAUNCH,**
	STOMACH
ruminant	**COW, YAK, DEER,**
	GOAT, BISON, CAMEL,
	LLAMA, SHEEP, ALPACA,
	GIRAFFE, ANTELOPE;
	see p. 660
ruminate	**CHEW, MULL,**
	PONDER, REFLECT,
	COGITATE
rummage	**DIG, COMB, POKE,**
	GROPE, SEARCH, RANSACK
rummy	**GIN, ODD, QUEER,**
	CANASTA, STRANGE
rumor	**FAMA, BRUIT, ONDIT,**
	FURPHY, GOSSIP, NORATE,
	REPORT, HEARSAY
rump	**ARSE, CROUP, BREECH,**
	BUTTOCKS
rumple	**MUSS, TOUSLE,**
	CRUMPLE, DISHEVEL
rumpus	**FUSS, STIR, TODO,**
	POTHER, RACKET, TUMULT,
	COMMOTION
rumpus room	**PLAYROOM**
run	**HIE, FLOW, LEAK, SCUD,**
	YARD, BROOK, ELOPE,
	INCUR, PANIC, RAVEL, SPATE,
	ELAPSE, HASTEN, SPRINT,
	OPERATE, ARPEGGIO
run across	**MEET, ENCOUNTER**
run aground	**MOOR, BEACH,**
	STRAND
run away	**BOLT, FLEE, ELOPE,**
	DECAMP, ESCAPE, ABSCOND
run in	**ARREST, INSERT,**
	INCLUDE

run of the mill	**SOSO, COMMON,**
	AVERAGE, ORDINARY
run smoothly	**HUM**
run through	**STAB, PIERCE,**
	THRUST
run up	**INCUR**
runaround	**EVASION, EXCUSE,**
	AVOIDANCE
runaway	**AWOL, TRUANT,**
	ESCAPEE, RAMPANT,
	FUGITIVE
rundown	**KNOCK, TIRED,**
	WEARY, SHABBY, ACCOUNT,
	PUTDOWN, DERELICT,
	DELAPIDATED
rung	**BAR, STEP, ROUND,**
	SPOKE, STAVE, CUDGEL,
	RUNDLE
run-in	**SPAT, TIFF, CLASH,**
	FIGHT, SCRAP, HASSLE,
	QUARREL
runnel	**BROOK, GROOVE,**
	RUNLET, CHANNEL, RIVULET
runner	**SKI, AGENT, BLADE,**
	MILER, RACER, SCARF,
	STOLO(N), COURIER,
	SMUGGLER, SPRINTER,
	MESSENGER
runt	**CHIT, DWARF, PYGMY,**
	BANTAM
runway	**RAMP, CHUTE, STRIP,**
	TRACK, TRAIL, TARMAC,
	CHANNEL, TROUGH, AIRSTRIP
rupture	**RIFT, BREAK, BURST,**
	CRACK, SPLIT, BREACH,
	HERNIA, FISSURE
rural	**RUSTIC, BUCOLIC,**
	GEORGIC, AGRARIAN,
	ARCADIAN, PASTORAL
ruse	**DODGE, TRICK, GAMBIT,**
	ARTIFICE, STRATAGEM
rush	**HIE, RUN, DASH, DIVE,**
	RACE, RESE, HASTE, HURRY,
	ONSET, SPATE, SPEED, SPURT,
	SURGE, HASTEN, HURTLE,
	PLUNGE, SCURRY,
	SCRIMMAGE
Russell's viper	**DABOIA**
Russia, capital of	**MOSCOW**
Russia(n)	**RED, SOVIET,**
	MUSCOVY
Russian city	**UFA, AZOV,**
	BAKU, KIEV, LVOV, OMSK,
	OREL, PARM, TULA, TURA,
	BREST, KAZAN, KURSK,
	MINSK, TYNDA, VILNA,
	MOSCOW, PALANA, SAMARA,
	SURGUT, TAMBOV,
	MURMANSK, NOVOSIBURSK

Russian composer **GLIERE,
BORODIN, PROKOFIEV,
STRAVINSKY, TCHAIKOVSKY**
Russian co-op **ARTEL**
Russian council **DUMA**
Russian farm **MIR**
Russian gulf **OB, RIGA,
ANADYR, FINLAND,
SAKHALIN**
Russian island **BELYY,
KARAGIN, VAYGACH,
SAKHALIN**
Russian lake **VYG, ARAL,
ELTON, ILMEN, ONEGA,
BAIKAL, LADOGA**
Russian language *see* **SLAVIC,
CAUCASIAN**
Russian measure **FUT, LOF,
DUIM, PASS, STOF, OSMIN,
STOOP, VERST, ARSHIN,
CHARKA, PALETZ, SAGENE,
TCHAST ARCHINE, GARNETZ,
TOTCHKA**
Russian money **ALTIN, KOPEK,
RUBLE, KOPECK, ROUBLE,
POLTINA, IMPERIAL**
Russian neighbor **CHINA,
LATVIA, NORWAY, BELARUS,
ESTONIA, FINLAND, GEORGIA,
UKRAINE, MONGOLIA,
AZERBAIJAN, KAZAKHSTAN**
Russian news agency **TASS**
Russian newspaper **PRAVDA**
Russian, prominent **IVAN,
LVOV, PAUL, BASIL, FEDOR,
LENIN, PETER, ALEXIS, STALIN,
MICHAEL, MOLOTOV,
ROMANOV, TROTSKY,
YELTSIN, BREZHNEV,
BULGANIN, KERENSKY,
MALENKOV, ANDROPOV,
NICHOLAS, ALEXANDER,
CATHERINE, CHERNENKO,
ELIZABETH, GORBACHEV,
KHRUSHCHEV**
Russian region **SIBERIA**
Russian river **OB, KET, TAZ,
UDA, AMGA, AMUR, LENA,
MAYA, MUNA, NEVA,
YANA, ALDAN, DVINA,
ISHIM, TOBOL, VOLGA,
ADYCHA, ANOBAR, BUREYA,
CHULYM, CHUNYA, IRTYSH,
KOLYMA, MARKHA, OLENEK,
SHILKA, USSURI, YENISEY,
PECHORA**
Russian ruler **CZAR, TSAR**
Russian secret police **KGB,
NKVD, OGPU**

Russian spacecraft **LUNA,
LUNIK, SOYUZ, COSMOS,
VOSTOK, YANTAR, SPUTNIK**
Russian weight **LOT, PUD,
DOLA, FUNT, POOD, KAMIAN**
Russian writer **GOGOL,
GORKY, TOLSTOY, CHEKHOV**
rust **OXIDE, AERUGO,
CORRODE, OXIDIZE,
VERDIGRIS, CORROSION**
Rustam relative **ZAL, SOHRAB,
RUDABAH**
rustic **BOOR, CARL, HICK,
RUBE, CARLE, RURAL,
SWAIN, YOKEL, SYLVAN,
YEOMAN, BUCOLIC,
PEASANT, AGRESTIC**
rustle **STEAL, SWISH,
SUSURRATE**
rustler **ABACTOR, ABIGEUS**
Rustum *see* **RUSTAM**
rusty **CORRODED**
rut **HEAT, TRACK, FURROW,
GROOVE**
ruth **PITY, GRIEF,
COMPASSION**
Ruth relative **BOAZ, OBED,
NAOMI, EILEEN, MAHLON**
ruthless **CRUEL, BRUTAL,
CALLOUS, PITILESS,
MERCILESS**
Rwanda, capital of **KIGALI**
Rwandan city/town **BUTARO,
KIGALI, GISENYI**
Rwandan language **FRENCH,
SWAHILI**
Rwandan money **FRANC**
Rwandan mountain **KARISIMBI**
Rwandan neighbor **ZAIRE,
UGANDA, BURUNDI,
TANZANIA**
Rwandan tribes **TWA, HUTU,
TUTSI**
rye **ERGOT, DARNEL;** *see*
CEREAL, GYPSY
Ryukyu island **AMAMI,
TOKARA, OKINAWA,
SAKISHIMA**

S

S **ESS, SIGMA, SIERRA**
S-shaped **SIGMATE, SIGMOID**
Sabbath **SUNDAY, SATURDAY**
sabbatical **REST, LEAVE, TIME
OFF, VACATION**
sabe **KNOW**

— Sabe **KEMO**
saber **(Y)ATAGHAN;** *see* **SWORD**
sable **FUR, SKUNK, SOBOL, LEMMING, MUSTELINE**
sabot **CLOG, DINGHY, PATTEN**
sabotage **DAMAGE, DISABLE, DISRUPT(ION), VANDALISM, SUBVERSION, INCAPACITATE**
Sabrina the Teenage Witch names **JOAN, HART, ROXIE, MORGAN, SCORCH, MELISSA**
sac **POD, CYST, ASCUS, BURSA, INDIAN, VENTER, SILIQUE, VESICLE**
saccharine **SWEET, SUGARY, SYRUPY**
saccharine source **TAR**
sachem **HEAD, CHIEF, SAGAMORE**
sachet **BAG, PAD, PACKET**
sack **BAG, FIRE, LOOT, PACK, GUNNY, POUCH, RAVAGE, DISMISS, PILLAGE, PLUNDER, DISCHARGE**
sacking **JUTE, GUNNY, BURLAP**
sacrament **MASS, RITE, BAPTISM, PENANCE, UNCTION, EUCHARIST, MATRIMONY, COMMUNION, CONFIRMATION**
sacred **HOLY, PIOUS, DIVINE, BLESSED, HALLOWED, INVIOLATE, SACROSANCT, CONSECRATED;** *see also* **HOLY**
Sacred College member **CARDINAL**
sacred, make **BLESS, HALLOW, SANCTIFY, CONSECRATE**
sacred object **ICON, ZOGO, RELIC**
sacred place **ALTIS, ABATON, HIERON, SHRINE**
sacred text **TORAH, AVESTA, GOSPEL, TALMUD, HAGGADA(H), MASORA(H), SCRIPTURE**
sacrifice **COST, LOSS, FORGO, GIVEUP, IMMOLATE, LIBATION, OBLATION, OFFERING**
sacrifice, human **SUTTEE**
sacrificial offering **LAMB, HIERA, VIRGIN, SPRAGION**
sacrificial rite **SOMA**
sacrilege **IMPIETY, BLASPHEMY, PROFANITY**
sacrilegious **IMPIOUS, PROFANE, BLASPHEMOUS**
sacristan **SEXTON**

sacristy **VESTRY**
sacrosanct **HOLY, DIVINE, SACRED, REVERED, HALLOWED, INVIOLABLE, UNTOUCHABLE**
sad **BAD, BLUE, MESTO, DISMAL, DOLENT, GLOOMY, TRISTE, DOLEFUL, UNHAPPY, DEJECTED, DOLOROUS, CHEERLESS**
sadden **ATTRIST, DEPRESS, COMPRESS, MAKE BLUE**
saddle **LOAD, BURDEN, APAREJO, PILLION, ENCUMBER**
saddle part **PAD, HORN, CINCH, GIRTH, MANTA, PANEL, SKIRT, CANTLE, CORONA, JOCKEY, LATIGO, PANNEL, POMMEL, GAMBADO, STIRRUP, SUBADERO**
saddle type **ENGLISH, WESTERN**
saddlebag **ALFORJA**
Sadducee, *opp. of* **PHARISEE**
sadism **CRUELTY, BRUTALITY**
sadistic **CRUEL, BRUTAL**
sadist **ABUSER, HURTER**
sadness **DOLOR, GRIEF, MISERY, PATHOS, SORROW**
safari **TREK, CARAVAN, EXPEDITION**
safe **CHEST, SOUND, VAULT, COFFER, SECURE, ANODYNE, HARMLESS, INNOCENT, PROTECTED, STRONGBOX**
safe place **HOME, HAVEN, ASYLUM, HARBOR, ISLAND, REFUGE, HOSPICE, SHELTER, SANCTUARY**
safe-conduct **PASS, COWLE, PASSPORT**
safecracker **YEGG, PETE(R)MAN**
safeguard **WATCH, DEFEND, SHIELD, PROTECT, PRESERVE**
safekeeping **CARE, (A)EGIS, CUSTODY, STORAGE, PROTECTION**
safety **SECURITY, PROTECTION**
safety pin **CLASP, FIBULA**
sag **HANG, SINK, WARP, WILT, DROOP, SLUMP, BUCKLE, SLOUCH, DECLINE**
saga **MYTH;** *see* **EPIC**
sagacious **WISE, ASTUTE, SAPIENT, PERCEPTIVE**
sagacity **ACUMEN, WISDOM, PRUDENCE**

sagamore	CHIEF, SACHEM
sage	HERB, YODA, SOLON, NESTOR; see SCHOLAR
Sagebrush State	NV, NEV(ADA)
sagittary	DARIC, ARCHER, CENTAUR
sail	JIB, LUG, KITE, LUFF, VELA, GLIDE, ROYAL, CRUISE, LATEEN, MIZZEN, SPANKER, TOPMAST, TOPGALLANT
sail part	TIE, BUNT, CLEW, FOOT, HEAD, IRON, LIFT, REEF, WHIP, YOKE, HORSE, LEECH, SHEET, EARING, CRINGLE, BUNTLINE
sailboat	see SHIP
sailcloth	DUCK, CANVAS
sailor	GOB, TAR, SALT, LASCAIL, MARINE, SEABEE, SEADOG, SEAMAN, MARINER, MATELOT
saint	ST, PIR, STE, DADU, HOLY, ROCH, ALBAN, ALVAR, ARHAT, CANONIZE; see PATRON
St. Andrew's cross	SALTIRE
St. Anthony's cross	TAU
St. Christopher	see ST KITTS
St. Elmo's fire	FUROLE, HELENA, CORPOSANT
St. Francis's birthplace	ASSISI
St. Kitts and Nevis, capital of	BASSETERRE
St. Louis Blues composer	HANDY
St. Lucia, capital of	CASTRIES
St. Nicholas	SANTA
St. Paul	see PAUL
St. Vincent, capital of	KINGSTOWN
St. Vitus' dance	CHOREA
saintly	HOLY, PURE, PIOUS
saints, list of	HAGIOLOGY
sake	END, GOOD, WINE, CAUSE, BEHALF, BENEFIT
Saki	MUNRO, YARKE
salaam	BOW, BEND, KOWTOW, GREETING
salacious	LEWD, SPICY, RIBALD, SCANDALOUS
salad	SLAW, GREENS, SALLET, LETTUCE
salad dressing	RANCH, CAESAR, ITALIAN, REMO(U)LADE, MAYONNAISE, VINAIGRETTE, THOUSAND ISLAND
salad ingredient	CRESS, GREEN, CELERY, ENDIVE, GREENS,

	TOMATO, CABBAGE, LETTUCE, PARSLEY, ROMAINE, WATERCRESS
salamander	ASK, EFT, OLM, NEWT, ASKER, SIREN, TWEEG, TRITON, AXOLOTL, CAUDATA, DOGFISH, PROTEUS, URODELA, AMPHIUMA, MUD DEVIL, MUD PUPPY, NECTURUS, TRITURUS, WATERDOG, HELLBENDER; see LIZARD
salary	FEE, PAY, SCREW, WAGES, STIPEND, EARNINGS, COMPENSATION
sale	DEAL, BARGAIN, SELLOUT; see AUCTION
sale, kind of	CASH, FIRE, YARD, WHITE, GARAGE, AUCTION, RUMMAGE, CLEARANCE, INVENTORY
salesperson	AGENT, CLERK, VENDOR, DRUMMER, PEDDLER, AUCTIONEER
salient	NOTABLE, STRIKING, PROMINENT
saline	BRACK, SALTY, MARINAL, BRACKISH
saliva	SPIT, DROOL, RHEUM, DRIVEL, SLAVER, SPUTUM, SPITTLE
saliva, pert. to	SIALIC
sallow	WAN, PALE, OSIER, PASTY, SICKLY, WILLOW
sally	JEST, JOKE, QUIP, RAID, ERUPT, FORAY, BANTER, SORTIE, RIPOSTE
salmagundi	OLIO, MEDLEY, MISTURE, POTPOURRI
salmon(-like fish)	AYU, GIB, LAX, CHUM, COHO, DORE, JACK, KELT, KETA, MASU, PENK, PIKE, PINK, CISCO, COHOE, HADDO, HOLIA, HUCHO, LENOK, SMELT, SUEUR, UMBRA, ALEVIN, BAGGIT, CAPLIN, CHIVEY, HUCHEN, INANGA, KIPPER, SAMLET, AULOPID, CAPELAN, CAPELIN, CHINOOK, GWYNIAD, HOUTING, ICEFISH, OOLACAN, QUINNAT, REDFISH, SKEGGER, SOCKEYE, UMBRINE, CAPELING, EULACHAN, GRAYLING, GRYNLARD, LOOSEJAW, PICKEREL, MUDMINNOW, VIPERFISH; see p. 668

see p. 668

Salmon relative **BOAZ**	Samoa money **TALA, DOLLAR**
salmon, young **PARR, SMOLT,**	samovar **URN, TEAPOT**
GRILSE	Samoyed language **TAVGI,**
Salome relative **JOHN, JAMES,**	**YURAK, KAMASIN, YENISEI**
HEROD(IAS), ZEBEDEE	sample **CORE, POLL, TEST,**
salon **HALL, SHOP, LEVEE,**	**MODEL, TASTE, SWATCH,**
PARLOR, SOIREE, ATELIER,	**PATTERN**
GALLERY, BALLROOM	sampler **DEMO, MODEL,**
saloon **BAR, DIVE, SEDAN;**	**TESTER**
see **TAVERN**	Samson and Delilah composer
salt **SAL, NACL, BORAX,**	**SAINTSAENS**
BRINE, HUMOR, SOUSE,	Samson deathplace **GAZA**
HALITE, OLEATE, PICKLE;	Samson's lover **DELILAH**
see **SAILOR**	Samuel relative **ABIA, JOEL,**
salt away **BANK, SAVE, INVEST**	**ZUPH, ABIAH, HANNAH**
salt factory **SALTERN, SALTERY**	Samuel's teacher **ELI**
salt lake **SINK**	Samuel's victim **AGAG**
salt, *pert. to* **RALOID, SALINE**	samurai **RONIN**
salt pond **LICK, CHOTT,**	San Francisco district **NOB**
SHOTT, SALINA	**HILL, CHINATOWN,**
saltpeter **NITER, NITRE**	**HAIGHT-ASHBURY**
salty **RACY, BRACK, BRINY,**	San Francisco team **GIANTS,**
SPICY, BRACKISH	**FORTYNINERS**
salubrious **HEALTHY,**	San Marino, capital of **SAN**
HYGIENIC, SALUTARY,	**MARINO**
WHOLESOME	sanatory **CURATIVE**
salutary **HEALTHY,**	Sancho Panza master **(DON)**
HEALTHFUL, WHOLESOME,	**QUIXOTE**
BENEFICIAL	Sancho Panza mule **DAPPLE**
salutation **AVE, RAIL, ALOH,**	sanctify **BLESS, HALLOW,**
TOAST, ACHARA, CURTSY,	**PURIFY, BEATIFY,**
SALAAM, SHALOM, WELCOME	**CONSECRATE**
salute **BOW, DIP, TIP, HAIL,**	sanctimonious **SMUG, PIOUS,**
GREET, SALVO, CURTSY,	**HYPOCRITICAL**
WELCOME	sanction **OK(AY), BAN, AMEN,**
salvage **SAVE, REDEEM,**	**FIAT, OKAY, ASSENT,**
RESCUE, RECLAIM, RECOVER	**FIRMAN, RATIFY, ENDORSE,**
salvation **RESCUE, RECOVERY,**	**AUTHORIZE, INJUNCTION**
REDEMPTION, DELIVERANCE	sanctity **PURITY, HOLINESS**
Salvation Army founder **BOOTH**	sanctuary **BEMA, FANE, NAOS,**
salve **BALM, NARD, ANOINT,**	**BAMAB, HAVEN, ADYTUM,**
CERATE, LOTION, POMADE,	**REFUGE, SHRINE, TEMPLE,**
SOOTHE, RELIEVE, UNGUENT,	**CHANCEL, SHELTER,**
OINTMENT	**HALIDOM(E)**
salver **TRAY, WAITER, PLATTER**	sanctum **DEN, STUDY,**
salvia **CHIA, SAGE, CLARY**	**ADYTUM, RETREAT**
salvo **SHOT, BURST, ROUND,**	sand **GRIT, PAAR, BEACH,**
SALUTE, VOLLEY, ROVISO,	**PLUCK, SPUNK, GRAVEL,**
BROADSIDE	**POLISH, SILICA, SMOOTH,**
Samaritan **HELPER, ASSYRIAN,**	**COURAGE**
ISRAELITE	sand hill(s) **AREG, DENE, DUNE**
sambuca flavoring **ANIS(E)**	sandal **ZORI, THONG, CALIGA,**
same **ILK, IDEM, ALIKE,**	**PAITEN, TALARIA, FLIPFLOP,**
DITTO, EQUAL, CONSTANT,	**GUARACKE, HUARACLIE,**
MATCHING, IDENTICAL,	**HUARACHO**
CONSISTENT	sandalwood **ALGUM, ALMUG,**
same old **RUT**	**SANTAL**
Samoa, capital of **APIA;** *see also*	sandbank, sandbar *see* **REEF**
AMERICAN SAMOA	sandpaper **SMOOTHE, ABRASIVE**

sandpiper **CLEE, KNOT, QUIS, RUFF, STIB, REEVE, STINT, TEREK, AVOCET, DUNLIN, OXLING, REDLEG, TEETER, BROWNIE, TATTLER, WOODHEN, PEETWEET, REDSHANK, WOODCOCK**

sandpiper genus **TRINGA**

sandstone **GRIT, PAAR, BEREA, WACKE, ARKOSE, PSAMMITE**

sandstorm **SAMUM, HABOOB, SAMIEL, SIMOOM**

sandwich **CRAM, INSERT**

sandwich type **BLT, CLUB, HERO, PITA, HO(A)GIE, REUBEN, GRINDER, POORBOY, TORPEDO, SUBMARINE**

Sandwich Islands discoverer **COOK**

sandy **GRITTY, ARENOSE, SABULOUS**

sane **LUCID, SOBER, SOUND, RATIONAL, SENSIBLE, REASONABLE**

Sanford and Son names **FOXX, FRED, REDD, BUBBA, DONNA, GRADY, WOODY, ESTHER, LAMONT, MELVIN**

sanforize **PRESHRINK**

sangfroid **CALM, COOL, POISE, APLOMB**

sanguinary **GORY, BLOODY**

sanguine **RUDDY, ARDENT, UPBEAT, BLOODY, POSITIVE, CONFIDENT**

sanitarium **CLINIC, RESORT, RETREAT, HOSPITAL**

sanitary **CLEAN, HYGIENIC**

sanitation worker **DUMPER, ENGINEER**

sanity **SENSE, REASON, JUDGMENT, NORMALCY**

sans **WITHOUT**

sans doute **SURE(LY), CERTAINLY**

sans souci **CAREFREE**

Sanskrit **PALI, URDU, HINDI, VEDIC, ORIYA, BIHARI, LAHNDA, NEPALI, ROMANY, SINDHI, BENGALI, KONRANI, MARATHI, PUNJABI, ASSAMESE, GUJARATI, PRAKRITS, SINGHALESE; see INDIC**

Santa — **FE, ANNA, ANITA, CLAUS, BARBARA**

São Salvador state **BAHIA**

São Tomé and Principe, capital of **SAO TOME**

São Tomé and Principe city/town **NEVES, SANTANA, SAO TOME, TRINIDAD**

São Tomé and Principe island **CAROCO**

São Tomé and Principe money **DOBRA**

sap **DIG, BENO, COSH, DUPE, FOOL, DRAIN, DUMMY, FLUID, JUICE, WEAKEN**

sapid **TASTY, SAVORY, TASTEFUL, FLAVORFUL**

sapience **WISDOM, SAGACITY**

— sapiens **HOMO**

sapient **SAGE, WISE, KNOWING**

sapling **YOUTH, SPROUT, PLANTLET, SEEDLING**

sapodilla **ACANA, CHICO, MAMEY, BUSTIC, MAMMEE, SAPOTA, SAPOTE**

sapor **GUSTO, SAVOR, TASTE**

Sapphira husband **ANANIAS**

Sappho's island **LESBOS**

sappy **SILLY, FATUOUS, FOOLISH**

Saracen **ARAB, MOOR, MOSLEM**

Sarah handmaid **HAGAR**

Sarah relative **ISAAC, ABRAHAM**

Sarah slave **HAGAR**

Sarai husband **ABRAM**

sarcasm **GIBE, IRONY, JEERS, SATIRE, CYNICISM**

sarcastic **ACID, IRONIC, CAUSTIC, MORDANT, IRONIC(AL), SATIRIC, VITRIOLIC**

sarcoma **TUMOR, CANCER, GROWTH, MALIGNANCY**

sarcophagus **TOMB, CASKET, COFFIN, COOLER**

sardine **BANG, PILCHARD**

Sardinia, capital of **CAGLIARI**

Sardinian city/town **NUORO, OLBIA, ALGHERO, SASSARI, CAGLIARI, CARBONIA, IGLESIAS**

Sardinian language **CATALAN**

Sardinian river **TIRSO, POSADA**

sardonic **CAUSTIC, IRONIC(AL), SARCASTIC**

sargasso **SEAWEED**

sarong **PAREUS**

Sarpedon relative **ZEUS, MINOS, EUROPA**

sarsaparilla **MEAD, SMILAX, GINSENG**

sartor **TAILOR**

Sartre play **NO EXIT**
sash **OBI, BAND, TOBE, FRAME, CASING, GIRDLE, CUMMERBUND**
sashay **SWAY, GLIDE**
Saskatchewan *see also p. 614*
Saskatchewan city/town **BROCK, CABRI, GOVAN, ITUNA, LEASK, OGEMA, OXBOW, PENSE, WAKAW, CLIMAX, DENZIL, REGINA, SEDLEY, WEEKES, BEAUVAL, NIPAWIN, TORQUAY, SASKATOON, MOOSEJAW**
Sasketchewan river **BOW, CREE, SWAN, BATTLE, BEAVER, GEIKIE, OLDMAN, REDDEER, CLEARWATER, ASSINIBOINE**
Sasquatch **BIGFOOT**
sassafras **SALOOP, ROOTBEER**
sassy **SAUCY, FEISTY, IMPUDENT**
Satan **ABADDON, AHRIMAN, APOLLYON, MEPHISTO; see DEVIL**
satanic **DEVILISH, DIABOLICAL**
satchel **BAG, ETUI, GRIP, VALISE**
sate **FILL, GLUT, SLAKE, QUENCH, SATISFY, SURFEIT**
satellite, artificial *see p. 742*
satellites of Jupiter **IO, PAN, HERA, LEDA, CARME, ELARA, HADES, METIS, THERE, EUROPA, HESTIA, SINOPE, ANANICE, DEMETER, HIMALIA, LYSITHEA, ADRASTEA, AMALTHEA, CALUSTO, GANYMEDE, PASIPHAE, POSEIDON**
satellites of Mars **DEIMOS, PHOBOS**
satellites of Neptune **NEREID, TRITON**
satellites of Saturn **RHEA, DIONE, JANUS, MIMAS, TITAN, PHOEBE, TETHYS, CALYPSO, IAPETUS, TELESTO, HYPERION, ENCELADUS**
satellites of Uranus **ARIEL, OBERON, MIRANDA, TITANIA, UMBRIEL**
satiate *see* **SATE**
satiny **SILKY, LUSTROUS, SENSUOUS**
satire **IRONY, SPOOF, PARODY, SENDUP, LAMPOON, RIDICULE, BURLESQUE**

satirical **WRY, IRONIC, CAUSTIC**
satirist **POPE, SWIFT, BUTLER, HORACE, LUCIAN, OLDHAM, BOILEAU, JUVENAL, MOLIERE, FIELDING, LUCILIUS, VOLTAIRE**
satirize **SPOOF, PARODY, SENDUP, LAMPOON, RIDICULE**
satisfaction **CRO, UTU, AMENDS, REDRESS, PLEASURE, CONTENT(MENT), COMPENSATION**
satisfy **FIT, PAY, FILL, MEET, SERVE, FULFIL(L), GRATIFY, CONVINCE**
satisfying **FILLING, PLEASING, FULFILLING, REWARDING**
saturate **SOP, SOAK, IMBUE, STEEP, DRENCH, SEETHE**
Saturday Night Live name **DUNN, ROCK, SANZ, CHASE, MYERS, PARDO, SHORT, CARVEY, CURTIN, CUSACK, FARLEY, KATTAN, MILLER, MORRIS, MURPHY, MURRAY, NEALON, NEWMAN, RADNER, AYKROYD, BELUSHI, CRYSTAL, HARTMAN, PARNELL, PISCOPO, SANDLER, SHANNON, MICHAELS**
Saturday night special **GUN, PIECE, ZIPGUN, HANDGUN, REVOLVER, AUTOMATIC**
Saturday source **SATURN**
Saturn relative **OPS, CYBELE, JUPITER**
Saturn satellite **RHEA, DIONE, JANUS, MIMAS, TITAN, PHOEBE, TETHYS, IAPETUS, JAPETUS, HYPERION, ENCELADUS**
saturnalia **ORGY, REVELRY**
saturnine **GLUM, GRAVE, GLOOMY, MOROSE**
satyr **FAUN, LECHER, PANISC, SILENUS**
sauce **DIP, GRAVY, FLAVOR, RELISH, SEASON, DRESSING, IMPUDENCE, INSOLENCE**
sauce, type of **SOY, ALEC, CHILI, CURRY, GARUM, MELBA, WHITE, CATSUP, GANSEL, MORNAY, KETCHUP, MARENGO, SOUBISE, SUPREME, TABASCO, TARTARE, VELOUTE, BARBECUE,**

BECHAMEL, MARINARA, MATELOTE, MEUNIERE, REMOLADE, BEARNAISE, MACEDOINE, REMOULADE, WORCESTER, BORDELAISE, HOLLANDAISE

sauce thickener   ROUX, FLOUR

saucer   BOWL, DISH, DISK, PLATE, DISCUS, FRISBEE

saucy   ARCH, FLIP, PERT, RUDE, BRASH, SASSY, FLIPPANT, IMPUDENT, INSOLENT

Saudi Arabia, capital of   RIAD, RIYADH

Saudi-Arabian   see also ARABIAN

Saudi-Arabian city   TAIF, AFIF, HOFUF, JIDDA, LAYLA, MECCA, TABUK, ZALIM, JEDDAH, JUBAIL, MISKAH, NAJRAN, RIYADH, SHARQA, MEDINA

Saudi-Arabian desert   SUBAY, MAZHUR, ANNAFUD, ALJAFURAH, RUBALKHALI

Saudi-Arabian money   POUND, QURSH, RIYAL, HALALA

Saudi-Arabian mountain   LAWZ, RADWA, SAWDA, DABBAGH

Saudi-Arabian neighbor   IRAQ, OMAN, EGYPT, QATAR, SUDAN, YEMEN, JORDAN, KUWAIT, BAHRAIN, ERITREA

Saudi-Arabian region   ASIR

Saudi-Arabian ruler   FARD, SAUD, FAISAL, RHALID, IBNSAUD

Saudi relative   NER, KISH, ABIEL, JONATHAN

Saul's herdsman   DOEG

Saul relative   NER, KISH, AZEL, ABIEL, MERAB, MICHAL, JONATHAN

Saul successor   DAVID

saunter   AMBLE, MOSEY, STROLL, LOITER, MEANDER

saurian   LIZARD, REPTILE, DINOSAUR, ALLIGATOR, CROCODILE

sausage   FRANK, WURST, HOTDOG, SALAMI, WIENER, BOLOGNA, PROSAGE, PUDDING, SAVELOW, CERVELAT

savage   FELL, FERAL, YAHOO, BRUTAL, FERINE, FIERCE, BESTIAL, BARBARIAN, BARBAROUS, FEROCIOUS

Savage Island   NIUE

savagery   WILDNESS, BARBARISM, BARBARITY, BRUTALITY

savannah   PLAIN, GRASSLAND

savant   SAGE, PANDIT, PUNDIT; see SCHOLAR

save   BUT, KEEP, HOARD, LAYBY, SPARE, STINT, STORE, EXCEPT(ING), REDEEM, RESCUE, SALVAGE, ECONOMIZE

Saved by the Bell names   AC, ZACK, LISA, KELLY, JESSIE, THEMAX, SCREECH

saving   ESTATE, EXCEPT, FRUGAL

savings   HOARD, MONEY, STASH, NESTEGG, RESERVES

savings plan   IRA, ROTH

savior   JESUS, CHRIST, RESCUER, REDEEMER, LIBERATOR

savoir-faire   SAVVY, FINESSE, EXPERTISE, COMPETENCE

savor   ENJOY, TASTE, FLAVOR, RELISH, APPRECIATE

savory   SAPID, SIPID, TASTY, YUMMY, FLAVOR(FUL), PIQUANT, TOOTHSOME

savvy   CRAFT, KNOWHOW

saw   CUT, RIB, RASP, ADAGE, EDGER, MAXIM, MOTTO, SERRA, COPING, SAYING, TREPAN, PROVERB

saw type   JIG, RIP, BUCK, HACK, HAND, TABLE, RADIAL, CIRCULAR, CROSSCUT

sawbones   SURGEON

sawbuck   TEN(SPOT)

sawdust   SHAVING(S)

sawhorse   (SAW)BUCK, TRESTLE

sawlike part(s)   SERRA(E)

Saxon ruler   ALFRED, EGBERT, EDWARD, HAROLD

Saxony, capital of   DRESDEN

say   AVER, MOUTH, SPEAK, STATE, UTTER, VOICE, RECITE, DECLARE, MENTION

saying(s)   DIT, MOT, REDE, LOGIA, AGRAPHA; see MAXIM

scab   FINK, CRUST, MANGE, ESCHAR, BLACKLEG, STRIKEBREAKER

scabbard   CASE, SHEATH, PILCHER

scabies   ITCH, MANGE, PSORA, PSORIASIS

scabrous FLAKY, GRIMY, MANGY, SCALY, KNOTTY, RISQUE, SCABBY, SCURFY, SQUALID, SALACIOUS

scads LOTS, TONS, OODLES

scaffold STAGE, GIBBET, RIGGER, GALLOWS, STAGING, PLATFORM

scalawag SCAMP, RASCAL, BLACKGUARD, SCAPEGRACE

scald BURN, SEAR, SCORCH

scale BRIX, GOUP, PALE, CLIMB, FLAKE, GAMUT, PALEA, PALET, PLATE, RATIO, TRONE, LAMINA, SQUAMA, BALANCE, LAMELLA, GRADUATION

scale, notes of DI, DO, FA, FI, LA, LE, LI, ME, MI, RA, RE, RI, SE, SI, TE, TI, UT, DOH, SOH, SOL, RAY, MESE, NETE, MESON, TRITE; see GUIDONIAN NOTE

scale, type of BEAM, SPRING, COUNTER, TORSION, PLATFORM, ELECTRONIC

scallion LEEK, (GREEN) ONION, SHALLOT

scallop PINK, QUIN, CRENA, WHELK, MUSSEL, MOLLUSK, PERIWINKLE, CRENELATION

scallop genus PECTEN

scalloped WAVY, CRENATE

scalp ROB, FLAY, PEEL, SKIN, CHEAT, GOUGE, STRIP, DEFEAT, FLEECE, EPICRANIUM, OVERCHARGE

scalpel BLADE, KNIFE, LANCET, BISTOURY

scaly FLAKY, MANGY, SCURFY, LEPROSE, SCUTATE, TEGULAR, SQUAMATE

scam CON, HOSE, CHEAT, DODGE, STING, RIPOFF

scamp IMP, RASCAL, SCALAWAG

scamper RUN, DART, DASH, HURRY, SCUTTLE

scan EYE, READ, SKIM, SURVEY, ANALYZE

scandal ODIUM, SHAME, GOSSIP, IGNOMINY

scandal, political ABSCAM, KOREAGATE, WATERGATE, IRAN CONTRA, TEAPOT DOME, WHITEWATER

scandalize DECRY, SHOCK, OFFEND

scandalmonger GOSSIP

scandalous INFAMOUS, SHAMEFUL, SHOCKING, OUTRAGEOUS

Scandinavian ROS, RUS, DANE, FINN, GEAT, LAPP, NORSE, SWEDE, VIKING, NORSEMAN

Scandinavian country NORWAY, SWEDEN, DENMARK, ICELAND

Scandinavian measure see p. 631

scant FEW, MEAGER, SKIMPY, SLIGHT, SPARSE

scanty MEASLY, SPARSE

scapegoat BUTT, TOOL, PATSY, VICTIM, FALLGUY

scapegrace ROUE, ROGUE, SCAMP, RASCAL, REPROBATE

scar ARR, PIT, CRAG, FLAW, MARK, POCK, CATFACE, CICATRIX

scarab AMULET, BEETLE

scarce(ly) VIX, RARE, BARELY, HARDLY

scarcity LACK, DEARTH, PAUCITY, SHORTAGE

scare ALARM, DAUNT, DETER, PANIC, FRIGHT, STARTLE, TERRIFY

scarecrow BOGLE, MALKIN, MAUKIN, MAWKIN, MAULKIN, STRAWMAN

scaremonger ALARMIST, TERRORIST

scarf BOA, TIE, ASCOT, BARBE, FANON, FICHU, NUBIA, ORALE, STOCK, STOLE, THROW, CRAVAT, BANDANA, DOPATTA, MUFFLER, BANDANNA, KERCHIEF, MANTILLA; see SHAWL

Scarface (AL)CAPONE

Scarlett O'Hara's home TARA; see GONE WITH THE WIND

scarlike ULOID

scary EERY, EERIE, CREEPY, SPOOKY, FRIGHTENING

scathe HARM, DAMAGE, INJURE, SCORCH, LAMBASTE

scathing BITING, CUTTING, SEARING, SARCASTIC

scatter SOW, TED, ROUT, SCOAD, STREW, DISPEL, LITTER

scatterbrained DAFT, DAFFY, DIZZY, EMPTYHEADED

scattered SEME, DIFFUSE, SPORADIC

scavenge HUNT, FORAGE, SEARCH

scavenger	HYENA, FORAGER; VULTURE
scenario	BOOK, TEXT, SETUP, SCRIPT, OUTLINE, LIBRETTO, SITUATION
scene	SITE, VIEW, SCAPE, VISTA, LOCALE, TABLEAU
scene of action	ARENA, SPHERE
scenery	DROPS, FLATS, VISTA, DIORAMA, PANORAMA
scenic	LOVELY, PRETTY, PICTURESQUE
scent	AURA, DRAG, FOIL, NOSE, TRAIL; see ODOR
scent container	VIAL
scented	OLENT, SPICY, RAMMISH, AROMATIC, PERFUMED, REDOLENT
scepter	ROD, MACE, STAFF, FERULA, TRIDENT, JEWELED
schedule	LIST, PLAN, SLATE, AGENDA, ARRANGE, PROGRAM, CALENDAR
schema	PLAN, DIAGRAM, OUTLINE
schematic	CHART, DIAGRAM, ANALYTICAL
scheme	PLAN, PLOT, CABAL, CHART, SYSTEM, PROJECT
scheming	WILY, CONNIVING, CALCULATING
Schicklgruber	HITLER
schism	RIFT, SPLIT, CLIQUE, DISCORD, FACTION
schlemiel	see OAF
schlep	LUG, DRAG, HAUL, JERK, TOTE, CARRY
schmaltz	CORN, MUSH, SLUSH, SENTIMENTALITY
Schnozzola	DURANTE
scholar	BHAT, DEMY, SAGE, PUPIL, ULEMA, PANDIT, PEDANT, PUNDIT, SAVANT, HARMONIST
scholarly	ERUDITE, LEARNED, ACADEMIC, STUDIOUS
scholarly writings	ANNALS
scholarship	AWARD, BURSE, BURSARY, STIPEND, ERUDITION, LEARNING, PEDANTRY, FELLOWSHIP
scholastic	ACADEMIC, PEDAGOGIC
school	GAM, POD, TOL, ELEM, PREP, SECT, ECOLE, LYCEE, SHOAL, LYCEUM, MANEGE, ACADEMY, COLLEGE, EDUCATE, INSTITUTE, UNIVERSITY
school grounds	QUAD, CAMPUS
school of thought	ISM
school official	DEAN, PROVOST, PRINCIPAL, REGISTRAR, SUPERINTENDENT
school, type of	HIGH, PREP, NIGHT, PUBLIC, SUMMER, COLLEGE, DANCING, PRIVATE, MILITARY, FINISHING, ELEMENTARY, VOCATIONAL, PREPARATORY
schoolbook	TEXT, PRIMER; READER
schoolgirl	COED
schoolmaster	PEDANT, DOMINIE, PROCTOR, SNAPPER, TEACHER, PEDAGOGUE, INSTRUCTOR
schooner	TERN; see BOAT
Schwarzenegger film	TWINS, PREDATOR, TRUE LIES, TERMINATOR, TOTAL RECALL
science	ART, OLOGY, SKILL, STUDY, TECHNICS, KNOWLEDGE
science fiction award	HUGO, NEBULA
science fiction writer	DICK, POHL, VERNE, ALDISS, ASIMOV, BUTLER, CLARKE, DELANY, LEGUIN, BALLARD, ELLISON, HERBERT, BRADBURY, HEINLEIN
scientific	PRECISE, SYSTEMATIC, METHODICAL
scientist	SAVANT, CHEMIST, BOTANIST, BIOLOGIST, PHYSICIST
scimitar	SABER, SWORD, RAPIER
scintilla	BIT, IOTA, WHIT, SPARK, TRACE
scintillate	FLASH, GLISTEN, GLITTER, SPARKLE
scintillating	BRIGHT, DAZZLING, SPARKLING
scion	BUD, SON, HEIR, GRAFT, SHOOT, SPRIG
scissors	CUTTER, NIPPER, SHEARS, CLIPPER
scoff	CARP, GIBE, GIRD, JEER, JIBE, RAIL, LAUGH, SNEER, TAUNT, DERIDE, DISDAIN, RIDICULE
scofflaw	CROOK, FELON
scold	JAW, NAG, CARP, FLAY, RAIL, RATE, REDD, CHIDE,

	HARPY, SHREW, REVILE, VIRAGO, HARANGUE
scolding	EARFUL, REPROACH, REPRIMAND
sconce	HUT, FORT, HEAD, SHED, SKULL, BRAINS, HELMET, SCREEN, BRACKET, BULWARK, FORTIFY, PROTECT, SHELTER
scone	FARL, SKON, FARLE, BISCUIT
scoop	BEAT, GOUGE, LADLE, SPOON, DIGOUT, DIPPER, DREDGE, SCRAPE, SHOVEL, TROWEL
scoot	HIE, RUN, DART, DASH, DECAMP, SCURRY
scope	AREA, SPAN, AMBIT, RANGE, SWEEP, EXTENT, SPHERE, LATITUDE
Scopes trial counsel	BRYAN, DARROW
Scopes trial venue	DAYTON
scorch	BURN, CHAR, SEAR, SERB, PARCH, SINGE, BLISTER
scorcher	HOTDAY
score	TD, ACE, HIT, RUN, TAB, DEBT, DOWN, GOAL, TICK, CHALK, NOTCH, POINT, TALLY, BASKET, GROOVE, SAFETY, TWENTY, ACCOUNT, HOME RUN, SCRATCH, TOUCHDOWN
scoria	see DROSS, LAVA
scorn	GECK, MOCK, SCOFF, SCOUT, SPURN, CONTEMN, DISDAIN, CONTEMPT, DERISION
scorpion	ONAGER, SCOURGE, CATAPULT; see ARACHNID
scorpion fish	BLOB, SKIL, POGGE, REINA, VIUVA, BESHOW, COTTID, TAMBOR, BERGYLT, CORSAIR, COTTOID, POACHER, SCULPIN, SKIPPER
Scot	TAX, GAEL, LEVY, KILTIE, SCOTCHMAN
scotch	CUT, GASH, CHOCK, CRUSH, SCORE, FRUGAL, STINGY
Scotland	ALBA, ECOSSE, SCOTIA, CALEDONIA
Scotland, capital of	EDINBURGH
Scott, Sir Walter locale	KELSO
Scott, Sir Walter work	ROBROY, ROKEBY, IVANHOE, MARMION, KENILWORTH
Scottish city/town	AYR, ALLOA, PERTH, TROON, DUNDEE, GLASGOW, LERWICK, PAISLEY, ABERDEEN, DUMFRIES, GREENOCK, KIRKWALL, STIRLING, EDINBURGH, INVERNESS
Scottish county	AYR, BUTE, FIFE, ROSS, ANGUS, BANFF, MORAY, NAIRN, PERTH, ARGYLL, ORKNEY, BERWICK, COMARTY, PEEBLES, RENFREW, SELKIRK, WIGTOWN, ZETLAND, ABERDEEN, DUMFRIES, ROXBURGH, STIRLING, DUNBARTON, INVERNESS
Scottish dialect	LALLANS
Scottish firth	TAY, LOCH, LORN(E), CLYDE, FORTH, MORAY, CROMARTY
Scottish inlet	LORN, CLYDE, FORTH, MORAY, SOLWAY
Scottish island	RUM, BUTE, IONA, JURA, MULL, RHUM, UIST, ARRAN, BARRA, ISLAY, LEWIS, TIREE, HARRIS, ORKNEY, SANDAY, WESTRAY, HEBRIDES, SHETLAND, STRONSAY
Scottish loch	AWE, NESS, SHIN, LOYAL, SUNAN, LINNHE, LOMOND, TUMMEL, KANNOCII
Scottish measure	BOLL, UPPY, FIRLOT, CHALDER
Scottish money	DEMY, LION, BODLE, GROAT, BAUBEE, BAWBEE
Scottish poet	DUNN, BURNS, BARBOUR, FERGUSSON, MACDIARMID
Scottish region	FIFE, BORDERS, CENTRAL, LOTHIAN, TAYSIDE, DUMFRIES, GRAMPIAN, LOWLAND, HIGHLAND
Scottish river	AYR, DEE, DON, ESK, TAY, AVON, DOON, ISLA, TYNE, ANNAN, ARDLE, CLYDE, FORTH, TWEED, ALMOND, CARRON, TEVIOT, YARROW
Scottish ruler	MARY, BRUCE, EDGAR, JAMES, BAUOL, DUNCAN, ROBERT, STUART, MACBETH, MALCOLM
Scottish weight	BOLL, DROP, TRONE

scoundrel CAD, CROOK, KNAVE, ROGUE, SCAMP, RASCAL, VARLET, VILLAIN, REPROBATE

scour RUB, SAND, FLUSH, PURGE, SCRUB, POLISH, CLEANSE

scourge BANE, FLAY, FLOG, LASH, WHIP, CURSE, PLAGUE, PUNISH, AFFLICTION

Scourge of God ATTILA

scout SPY, SPIER, EXPLORE, SPOTTER, RECONNOITER

scout prey TALENT

scout unit DEN, PACK, TROOP, PATROL

scow TUB, BARGE, LIGHTER, FLATBOAT, SAILBOAT

scowl LOUR, FROWN, (G)LOWER, GRIMACE

scrabble CRAWL, CREEP, DOODLE, SCRAWL, SCRATCH

scraggy BONY, LEAN, THIN, MEAGER, SCANTY

scram GIT, BOLT, SCAT, SHOO, BEAT IT, VAMO(O)SE, GET LOST, SKEDADDLE

scramble TEAR, CRAWL, JUMBLE, RAT RACE, SCUTTLE, STRUGGLE

scrap ORT, RAZE, MAMMOCK; see BIT, FIGHT

scrapbook BOOK, ALBUM, FOLDER

scrape RUB, GALL, MESS, RAKE, RASP, BRUSH, GRATE, GRAZE, SCOUR, SCUFF, ABRADE, DREDGE, SCRATCH, SCUFFLE

scrapings RASION, RASURE, RAMENTA, SHAVINGS

scrappy PATCHY, CONTRARY, PUGNACIOUS

scratch MAR, RIT, RASP, CHAFE, ERASE, DEFACE, REJECT, SCRAPE, SCRIBBLE

Scratch, Old DEVIL

scrawl DOODLE, SCRIBBLE

scrawny BONY, LEAN, PUNY, THIN, GAUNT, SKINNY, SCRAGGY

scream YARM, SHRIEK, SQUALL, SCREECH; see CRY

screed see DIATRIBE

screen HIDE, BLIND, PAVIS, SCRIM, SHADE, SHOJI, TATTY, BONNET, GRILLE, MOVIES, PURDAH, SHIELD, SHROUD, REREDOS, BLINDAGE, PARAVENT; see SIEVE

screw FIX, COIL, PROP, TURN, TWIST, ATTACH, FASTEN, JAILER, ROTATE, PROPELLER

screw thread WORM

screw (up) FOUL, MESS, BOTCH

screwball ODD(BALL), ZANY, WACKY, MADCAP, ECCENTRIC

screwy ODD, NUTS, CRAZY, NUTTY, WACKY, WEIRD

scribble JOT, DASH(OFF), WRITE, DOODLE, SCRAWL

scribbler HACK

scribe CLERK, NOTARY, WRITER, PENMAN, COPYIST, SCRIVENER, SECRETARY, AMANUENSIS

scrimmage FIGHT, TUSSLE, SCUFFLE, SKIRMISH

scrimp SAVE, SKIMP, STINT, ECONOMIZE

scrip LIST, WALLET, SATCHEL, CERTIFICATE

script BOOK, HAND, TEXT, LINES, RONDE, SERTA, LIBRETTO, LETTERING, HANDWRITING

scriptural SACRED, BIBLICAL, APOSTOLIC

scripture BOOK, VEDA, AGAMA, BIBLE, KORAN, SRUTI, SUTRA, TORAH, AVESTA, GEMARA, GRANTH, MASORA, MISHNA, PURANA, SMRITI, TALMUD, TANTRA, ALCORAN, HAGGADA, HALAKAH, MASORAH, MIDRASH, MISHNAH

scrivener see SCRIBE

scrod COD(FISH)

scroll LIST, ROLL, VOLUTE

Scrooge associate MARLEY, CRATCHIT

Scrooge word BAH, HUMBUG

scrounge EKE, CADGE, PILFER, SPONGE

scrub RUB, MEAN, ABORT, BRUSH, SCOUR, CANCEL, CLEANSE

scruff FILM, NAPE, NUBIA, NUQUE

scrunch CRUSH, CRUMPLE

scruple JOT, IOTA, DEMUR, DOUBT, QUALM, MISGIVING

scrupulous NICE, EXACT, FUSSY, HONEST, FINICAL, PRECISE, METICULOUS

scrutinize CON, EYE, PORE(OVER), SCAN, PROBE, DISSECT, INSPECT

scrutiny	SCAN, AUDIT, STUDY, REVIEW, SURVEY, INSPECTION
scuba diver	SEAL, FROGMAN, AQUANAUT
scuba gear	MARK, TANK, SNORKLE
scuff	SCRAPE, SCRATCH, SLIPPER, ABRASION
scuffle	FRAY, BRAWL, MELEE, TUSSLE, WRESTLE
scull	ROW, SHELL, PADDLE, PROPEL
sculptor	ARTIST, CARVER, MOLDER, MODELER
sculptor, famous	see p. 546
sculptor's equipment	BURIN, POINT, PUNCH, CHISEL, GRAVER, ROCKER, STYLET, CALIPER, GRADINE, SPATULA, ARMATURE
sculpture	BUST, GRAVE, RELIEF, STATUE(TTE), CARVING, FIGURINE, BAS RELIEF
sculpture, famous	PIETA, PHAROS, RUSHMORE
sculpture, pert. to	GLYPTIC(AL)
sculptured	CARVED, CARVEN, GRAVEN, MOLDED, GLYPHIC, CHISELED
scum	SKIM, ALGAE, SPUME, RIFFRAFF; see DROSS
scuppernong	WINE, GRAPE, MUSCADINE
scurf	SCUM, SCALE, FURFUR, DANDRUFF
scurfy	FLAKY, MANGY, SCABBY, LEPROSE, LEPIDOTE
scurrilous	COARSE, VULGAR, ABUSIVE
scurry	DART, DASH, HURRY, BUSTLE, SCAMPER, SCUTTLE
scurvy	LOW, MEAN, VILE, NASTY, CONTEMPTIBLE
scut	TAIL, MENIAL, ROUTINE
scuttle	HOD, SINK, SCOOP, SWAMP, BUCKET; see SCURRY
scuttlebutt	RUMOR, GOSSIP, HEARSAY
Scylla lover	MINOS
Scylla opposite	CHARYBDIS
Scylla relative	NISUS, CRATAIS, PHORCYS
scythe	CUT, HACK, SICKLE
Scythian people	ALANS
sea	DEEP, MAIN, MARE, BRINE, OCEAN, SWELL, BILLOW; see p. 612

sea arm	BAY, GULF, LAKE, FIORD, FIRTH, FRITH, LOUGH, ESTUARY
sea, of the	NAVAL, MARINE, OCEANIC, PELAGIC, MARITIME, NAUTICAL
sea cow	DUGONG, MANATEE
sea cucumber	TREPANG
sea lettuce	ALGA, NORI, ULVA, LAVER, AMANORI
sea robber	see PIRATE
sea serpent	ELOPS
sea slug genus	DOTO
sea snail	WHELK
sea snake	KERRIL
seabird	AUK, ERN, MEW, ERNE, GULL, SHAG, SKUA, TERN, NODDY, SCAUP, SOLAN, FULMAR, GANNET, PETREL, PUFFIN, SCOTER, CORMORANT
seaboard	COAST
sea-ear	ABALONE
seafarer	see SAILOR
seal	DIE, SHUT, STOP, BULLA, CLOSE, SIGIL, STAMP, CACHET, CLINCH, FASTEN, RATIFY, SETTLE, SIGNET, FINALIZE
seal genus	PHOCA, PHOCIDAE, PHOCINAE
seal, pert. to	PHOCINE
seal, young	PUP
sea lion, young	PUP
seals	WIG, SEAL, MATKA, OTARY, SWILE, URSAL, URSUK, USSUK, UTSUK, BEATER, DOTARD, JACKET, MAKLAK, MATKAH, OTARIA, PHOCID, FURSEAL, OTARIAN, OTARINE, PHOCOID, SADDLER, SEALION, SEALKIE
sealskin	SCULP
seam	BED, DART, JOIN, LODE, VEIN, LAYER, SUTURE, STRATUM
seaman	see SAILOR
seamark	BUOY, MEITH, BEACON, PHAROS, LIGHTHOUSE
seamen's chapel	BETHEL
seamless	WHOLE, INTEGRAL
seamstress	SEWER, STITCHER, SEMPSTRESS
seamy	SEEDY, SHADY, SORDID
séance	SESSION, SITTING
seaplane	AEROBOAT, HYDROPLANE
seaport	HARBOR

sear DRY, BURN, CHAR,
BRAND, PARCH, SINGE,
SCATHE, SCORCH, WITHER
search COMB, SEEK (OUT),
DELVE, DOWSE, FRISK,
GROPE, QUEST, FERRET,
FORAGE, PURSUIT,
RANSACK, RUMMAGE
search engine LYCOS, YAHOO,
EXCITE, GOOGLE, HOTBOT,
INFOSEEK
searching KEEN, SHARP,
PROBING, PENETRATING
seashore *see* SHORE
seasickness HEAVES, NAUSEA,
MALDEMER
season(s) AGE, AHET, CORN,
CURE, FALL, SALT, SELF,
HORAE, INURE, SPICE,
AUTUMN, FLAVOR, PEPPER,
SPRING, SUMMER, TEMPER,
WINTER; *see p. 718*
season, church LENT, ADVENT,
EASTER, TRINITY, EPIPHANY,
ASCENSION, CHRISTMAS,
PENTECOST
seasonable APT, TIMELY,
SUITABLE, OPPORTUNE
seasonal CYCLIC, REGULAR,
PERIODIC, RECURRING
seasoned TESTED, VETERAN,
HARDENED
seasoning BAY, SALT, CHIVE,
THYME, BURNET, CELERY,
GARLIC, LOVAGE, CARAWAY,
CHERVIL, COWSLIP,
DITTANY, FIGWORT,
OREGANO, PIGNOLI,
MARJORAM, ORIGANUM,
SERPOLET; *see* SPICE, HERB,
CONDIMENT
seat(s) PEW, SEE, SIT, BANC,
BASE, HOLD, POST, RUMP, TAKE,
TARA, ASANA, BENCH, CHAIR,
DICKY, PLACE, SELLA, STOOL,
CENTER, CURULE, HOWDAH,
PEWAGE, SEDILE, SETTEE,
SETTLE, SEDILIA,
WHEELCHAIR, HEADQUARTERS
seating section LOGE, TIER,
BALCONY, ORCHESTRA
seawall PIER, JETTY,
BREAKWATER
seaweed AGAR, CUVY, KELP,
LIMU, NORI, DULSE, FUCUS,
LAVER, VAREC, WRACK,
TANGLE, VARECH, AMANORI,
ROCKWEED, SARGASSO,
CARRAG(H)EEN

seaworm SAO, LURG
seaworthy SNUG, STURDY,
STA(U)NCH, WATERTIGHT
Seb relative SET, SHU, ISIS,
OSIRIS, TEFNUT
sebaceous OILY, FATTY
sec DRY, BRUT, MOMENT,
INSTANT
secede SPLIT, SEPARATE,
WITHDRAW
secessionist BOLTER,
APOSTATE, SEPARATIST
seclude CLOSET, IMMURE,
CONFINE, ISOLATE
secluded QUIET, REMOTE,
PRIVATE, ISOLATED,
SHELTERED
seclusion QUIET, PRIVACY,
SOLITUDE, ISOLATION
second ABET, BACK(UP), NEXT,
FLASH, JIFFY, TRICE,
MINUTE, MOMENT, SUPPORT
second thought(s) DOUBT(S),
MISGIVING(S)
secondary BYE, LESS, MINOR,
LESSER, RESULTANT
second-guess ANTICIPATE
secondhand USED, WORN,
CASTOFF, RECYCLED,
HANDMEDOWN
secondhand dealer RAGMAN,
JUNKMAN
second-rate INFERIOR,
MEDIOCRE
second-string RELIEF, RESERVE
secrecy PRIVACY,
CONFIDENTIALITY
secret(s) PRIVY, INNER,
COVERT, HIDDEN, LATENT,
MYSTIC, ARCANA, OCCULT,
FURTIVE, PRIVATE; *see*
MYSTERY
secret society KKK, EGBO,
MEDA, PORO, TONG,
MAF(F)IA, CAMORRA,
BLACKHAND, KU KLUX KLAN
secretary DESK, CLERK, STENO,
SCRIBE, ASSISTANT,
AMANUENSIS, ESCRITOIRE
secrete HIDE, MASK, OOZE,
STOW, CACHE, EXUDE,
STASH, SECERN, CONCEAL,
SQUIRREL
secretion GUM, SAP, BILE,
LAAP, LERP, MUSK, LAARP,
LATEX, MUCUS, SEBUM,
SWEAT, ENZYME, SALIVA,
CHALONE, HORMONE,
AUTACOID, ESTROGEN

secretive	CAGEY, CLOSE, EVASIVE, FURTIVE, GUARDED, CAUTIOUS, RETICENT		DIOCESE, DISCERN, IMAGINE, OBSERVE, UNDERSTAND
secretly	SUBROSA, ON THE SLY	seed	NUT, PIP, PIT, SOW, BENN, GERM, MET, OVULE,
sect	CAMP, CULT, MEDA, WING, PARTY, SCHOOL, FACTION, DIVISION		SEMEN, SPERM, SPORE, STONE, KERNEL, NUCULE, NUTLET, PIPPIN, PYRENE
sectarian	BIGOTED, PARTISAN, FACTIONAL	seed coat	BUR, ARIL, BURR, HULL, HUSK, TESTA,
section	LEG, AREA, LARP, PART, ZONE, PIECE, SLICE, STAGE, DIVIDE, SECTOR, QUARTER, SEGMENT	seedless (plant)	TEGMEN, TESTAE, TEGUMEN FERN, AGAMOUS
secular	LAY, LAIC(AL), CIVIL, EARTHLY, MUNDANE, WORLDLY, MATERIAL, TEMPORAL	seed, type of	TARE, ANISE, BENNE, CACAO, COCOA, CUMIN, PANGI, PINON, PULSE, SIEVA, SITAO, COWPEA, CUMMIN, FENNEL, KANARI,
secure	FIX, GET, FAST, MOOR, SAFE, SURE, BELAY, RIVET, ANCHOR, FASTEN, LOCK(ED), OBTAIN, STABLE, ACQUIRE, ASSURED, CONFIDENT		LEGUME, LENTIL, PEANUT, SESAME, CARAWAY, HARICOT, MUSTARD; see BEAN, NUT
security	BOND, GAGE, GRITH, STOCK, PLEDGE; see SURETY	seedy	SEAMY, TACKY, SHABBY, SLEAZY, SORDID, RUNDOWN, SQUALID
sedan	CAR, LIMO, CHAIR, LITTER, LIMOUSINE	seek	TRY, HUNT, PURSUE, ATTEMPT, REQUEST, ENDEAVOR
sedate	CALM, COOL, GRAVE, QUIET, SOBER, STAID, SERIOUS, TRANQUILIZE	seek aid from seeming	TURNTO LIKE, QUASI, LIKELY, OUTWARD, APPARENT
sedative	AMYTAL, OPIATE, ANODYNE, BROMIDE, CALMANT, DEMEROL, LUMINAL, BARBITAL, GOOFBALL, NARCOTIC, NEMBUTAL	seemly seep	FIT(ING), MEET, RIGHT, COMELY, PROPER, DECOROUS, APPROPRIATE OOZE, LEAK, DRAIN, EXUDE, LEACH, TRICKLE
sedentary	SITTING, INACTIVE, DESKBOUND	seer	SAGE, SIBYL, ORACLE, ARUSPEX, PROPHET, PSYCHIC, CLAIRVOYANT
sediment	LEES, MULM, SILT, DRAFF, DREGS, LOESS, MAGMA, MOTHER, SLUDGE, RESIDUE, SILTAGE	seesaw	FLAP, TILT, WAVER, TEETER, BASCULE, ALTERNATE, VACILLATE
sedition	MUTINY, REVOLT, RISING, TREASON	seethe	BOIL, STEW, STEEP, BUBBLE, SIMMER, FERMENT
seduce	LURE, TEMPT, ENTICE, DEBAUCH, PERSUADE	seething	ABOIL, ANGRY, FUMING
seducer	VAMP, SIREN, DON JUAN, ENTICER, CASANOVA, LOTHARIO	Segesta, king of segment	ACESTES ARC, PART, TORE, SLICE, BRANCH, SECTOR, SOMITE, TELSON, PORTION, DIVISION
seduction	ENTICEMENT, TEMPTATION	segmental	TORIC
seductive	ALLURING, CHARMING, TEMPTING, BEGUILING , ATTRACTIVE	segregate	SEVER, DIVIDE, ISOLATE, SEPARATE, SETAPART, QUARANTINE
sedulous	BUSY, DILIGENT, ASSIDUOUS, INDUSTRIOUS	segregation	JIM CROW, APARTHEID, QUARANTINE, DISCRIMINATION
see	EYE, GET, DATE, (E)SPY, MEET, SPOT, VIDE, GRASP, VISIT, DESCRY, NOTICE,	seine Seine	NET, TRAWL, SAGENE SEQUANA

Seine tributary **AUBE, EPTE, EURE, OISE, MARNE, YONNE**
Seinfeld names **COSMO, DAVID, JERRY, LARRY, ELAINE, GEORGE, KRAMER, WILHELM**
Seinfeld creator **DAVID, SEINFELD**
Seir relative **ARAN, TIMNA**
seize **NAB, GRAB, HENT, GRASP, REAVE, USURP, ARREST, COLLAR, CAPTURE, GARNISH, DISTRAIN, CONFISCATE**
seizure **FIT, ATTACK, STROKE, CAPTURE, PAROXYSM, CONVULSION, CONFISCATION**
Selassie **LION (OF JUDAH)**
seldom **HARDLY, RARELY, INFREQUENTLY**
select **OPT, CULL, PICK, WALE, CREAM, ELITE, CHOOSE**
selection **PICK, CHOICE, OPTION, PREFERENCE**
selective service **DRAFT**
Selene **LUNA, MOON, HECATE, ARTEMIS**
Selene love **ENDYMION**
Selene parent **THEA, HYPERION**
self **EGO, SOUL, SEITY, ENTITY**
self-centered **SELFISH, EGO(T)ISTIC(AL), EGOCENTRIC**
self-confident **SMUG, COCKY, POISED, ASSURED, COCKSURE**
self-confidence **POISE, APLOMB**
self-conscious **SHY, TIMID, DEMURE, AWKWARD**
self-contained **INDEPENDENT**
self-defense **JUDO, KARATE, JUJITSU**
self-determination **FREEWILL**
self-esteem **PRIDE, EGOISM, VANITY, CONCEIT**
self-explanatory **CLEAR, OBVIOUS**
self-governing **AUTONOMOUS**
self-important **VAIN, PROUD, POMPOUS, ARROGANT, EGOTISTICAL**
self-love **NARC(ISS)ISM**
self-possessed **COOL, POISED, STEADY, COMPOSED**
self-respect **PRIDE, CONFIDENCE**
self-righteous **SMUG, PHARISAIC**

self-satisfied **SMUG, COMPLACENT, UNASPIRING**
selfish **MEAN, STINGY, MISERLY, EGO(T)ISTIC(AL), SELFCENTERED**
sell **HAWK, VEND, SCALP, BETRAY, MARKET, PEDDLE, RETAIL, AUCTION**
sell short **BELITTLE, DENIGRATE, DOWNGRADE**
seller **AGENT, BROKER, COSTER, VENDOR, PEDDLER, MERCHANT, RETAILER**
sellout **HIT, SALE, SMASH, CLEARANCE**
selvage **EDGE, STRIP, BORDER**
semblance **AIR, COPY, MIEN, SHOW, FEINT, GUISE, IMAGE, LIKENESS, APPEARANCE**
Semele relative **INO, AGAVE, CADMUS, DIONYSUS, HARMONIA**
Semele's lover **ZEUS**
semester **TERM, PERIOD**
seminar **CLASS, SYMPOSIUM**
seminary **SCHOOL, ACADEMY, COLLEGE**
semicircular symbol **LUNETTE**
Seminole chief **OSCEOLA**
Semiramis husband **NINUS**
Semiramis kingdom **BABYLON**
Semite **JEW, ARAB, HEBREW, BABYLONIAN, PHOENICIAN**
Semitic language **GEEZ, NUZI, GMAT, MAHRI, PUNIC, TIGRE, ARABIC, GURAGE, HARARI, HEBREW, QARAWI, SYRIAC, ARAMAIC, AMHARIC, EDOMITE, MALTESE, MINABAN, MOABITE, SABAEAN, SOKOTRI, AKKADIAN, AMMONITE, ASSYRIAN, ETHIOPIC, LIHYANIC, MANDAEAN, SAFAITIC, SHKHAURI, TALMUDIC, THAMUDIC, TIGRINYA, UGARITIC, CANAANITE, HARRANIAN, PHOENICIAN**
semper — **IDEM, FIDELIS**
senate **CURIA, CHAMBER, COUNCIL, ASSEMBLY, LEGISLATURE**
Senate majority leader **BYRD, DOLE, LOTT, TAFT, BAKER, LODGE, BARKLEY, JOHNSON, MITCHELL**
senator **SOLON, LAWMAKER, LEGISLATOR, REPRESENTATIVE**

Senators, longest serving   BYRD, LONG, PELL, YOUNG, HAYDEN, WARREN, ALLISON, RUSSELL, STENNIS, THURMOND

send   EMIT, SHIP, REMIT, ROUTE, CONVEY, FORWARD, DISPATCH, TRANSMIT

send back   REMIT, REMAND, RETURN

send up   APE, MOCK, PARODY

send-off   FAREWELL

Seneca   CAYUGA, IROQUOIAN

Seneca student   NERO

Senegal, capital of   DAKAR

Senegalese city/town   DAKAR, KOLDA, LOUGA, MATAM, MEKHE, PODOR, THIES, DAGANA, MBOULI, KAOLACK

Senegalese language   *see* WEST-ATLANTIC

Senegalese people   FULA, DIOLA, SERER, WOLOF, MANDINKA, TOUCOULEUR

Senegalese river   FALEME, SENEGAL, CASAMANCE

senile   OLD, AGED, DOITED, FEEBLE, INFIRM, DODDERING

senility   DOTAGE, CADUCITY, SENESCENCE

senior   AINE, DEAN, ELDER, OLDER, SUPERIOR

senior citizen   RETIREE, OLDTIMER

senior event   PROM

seniority   RANK, STATUS, PRIORITY, PRECEDENCE

sensation   ECLAT, THRILL, EMOTION, FEELING, PERCEPTION

sensational   LURID, EXCITING, (MELO)DRAMATIC, STARTLING

sensationalism   MELODRAMATICS

sense   ESP, FEEL, FLAIR, SIGHT, SMELL, TASTE, TOUCH, ACUMEN, INTUIT(ION), HEARING

Sense and Sensibility author   AUSTEN

sense organ   EAR, EYE, NOSE, NERVE, FEELER, PALP(US), ANTENNA, RECEPTOR, TASTE BUD

senseless   MAD, INANE, ABSURD, FUTILE, STUPID, WANTON, FOOLISH, IRRATIONAL

sensible   SANE, WISE, AWARE, SOBER, ASTUTE, PALPABLE, RATIONAL, TANGIBLE, REASONABLE

sensitive   RAW, SORE, ALERT, AWARE, TENDER, TOUCHY, SENTIENT

sensitivity   ALLERGY, ERETHISM, SYMPATHY, AWARENESS

sensual   CARNAL, LYDIAN, SEXUAL, FEELING, FLESHLY, HEDONIC

sensualist   RAKE, SYBARITE, LIBERTINE

sensuous   LUSH, PASSIONATE, VOLUPTUOUS

sentence   RAP, DOOM, JAIL, TERM, CONFINE, CONVICT, IMPOUND, VERDICT, DECISION, JUDGMENT

sentence, analyze   PARSE, DIAGRAM

sentence part   VERB, CLAUSE, PHRASE, SUBJECT, PREDICATE

sententious   CURT, TERSE, LACONIC, JUDICIAL, SUCCINCT, MAGISTERIAL

sentient   ALERT, ALIVE, AWARE, FEELING, CONSCIOUS

sentiment   VIEW, EMOTION, FEELING, OPINION

sentimental   GUSHY, SAPPY, SOPPY, MAUDLIN, MAWKISH, ROMANTIC, EMOTIONAL

sentimentality   CORN, MUSH, BATHOS

sentinel   GUARD, VIGIL, PICKET, SENTRY, LOOKOUT, VEDETTE, WATCHDOG

sentry   GUARD, WATCH, BIVOUAC, SENTINEL

Seoul   KEIJO

separate   PART, SIFT, SORT, APART, SEVER, SPLIT, DETACH, DIVIDE, SECEDE, SECERN, SUNDER, ISOLATE, DISCRETE, DISTINCT, SEGREGATE

separately   APART

separation   SCHISM, BREAKUP, DIVORCE, PARTING, AVULSION, DIVORCE, APARTHEID

separatist   DISSENTER, NONCONFORMIST

septic   TOXIC, NOXIOUS, POISONOUS

Septimus Severus reign (AD193–211)
CC, CCI, CCV, CCX, CCII, CCIV,
CCIX, CCVI, CCXI
sepulcher   *see* TOMB
sepulchral   GLOOMY, FUNEREAL
sepulture   BURIAL,
INTERMENT; *see* TOMB
sequel   EFFECT, UPSHOT,
OUTCOME, FOLLOWUP,
AFTERMATH
sequence   SCALE, TIERCE; *see*
SERIES
sequential   SERIAL, IN ORDER
sequester   ENISLE, CONFINE,
ISOLATE, CLOISTER,
SETAPART, SEGREGATE
sequestered   ISOLATED,
SECLUDED, IMPOUNDED,
CLOISTERED
sequin   SPANGLE, ZECCHIN(O)
seraglio   HAREM, SERAI,
ZENANA
Serbia and Montenegro, capital of
BELGRADE
Serbia and Montenegro city/town
BAR, BOR, NIS, PEC, BRUS,
RUMA, BUDVA, SABAC,
VRSAC, LJUBIC, NIKSIC,
NOVISAD, PANCEVO,
PRIZREN, BELGRADE,
KRALJEVO, PRISTINA,
SUBOTICA, KRAGUJEVAC
Serbia and Montenegro money
PARA, DINAR, FLORIN,
PERPERA
Serbia and Montenegro neighbor
BOSNIA, ALBANIA, CROATIA,
HUNGARY, ROMANIA,
BULGARIA, MACEDONIA
Serbia and Montenegro river   IBAR,
SAVA, TARA, TISA, ZETA,
BEGEI, DRINA, RASKA, TIMOK,
DANUBE, MORACA,
MORAVA, NISAVA, KOLUBARA
Serbo-Croatian dance   KOLO
serenade   WOO, COURT,
NOCTURNE, SERENATA,
SHIVAREE, CHIRIVARI
serendipity   LUCK, ACCIDENT,
FORTUITY
serene   CALM, IRENIC, PLACID,
PEACEFUL, TRANQUIL
serenity   CALM(NESS), PEACE,
REPOSE, PLACIDITY
serf   ESNE, NEIF, HELOT, LITUS,
NEIFE, SLAVE, COLONA,
COLONUS; *see* BONDMAN
serfdom   BONDAGE, HELOTRY,
SLAVERY, SUBJUGATION

serial killer   KARL, KRAFT,
LOPEZ, LUDKE, BEHRAM,
COTTON, HARVEY, TOPPIN,
BARBOSA, BATHORY,
MUDGETT, GONZALES
sergeant   NCO, GUNNY, SARGE,
CHIAUS, NONCOM, TOPKICK
serial   EPISODIC
serially   SERIATIM
series   RUN, SET, CHAIN,
GAMUT, CATENA, FLIGHT,
STRING, SEQUENCE,
SUCCESSION
serious   GRIM, GRAVE, SOBER,
SOLEMN, EARNEST,
CRITICAL
sermon   TALK, HOMILY,
KHUTBAH, LECTURE,
REPROOF
sermonize   PREACH, MORALIZE
serpent   SEPT, APEPI, ELOPS; *see*
p. 671
serpent worship   OPHISM
serpentine   OPHITE, OPHIOID,
SINUOUS, WINDING,
OPHIDIAN
serrated   JAGGED, NOTCHED,
SCALLOPED, SAWTOOTHED
serried   DENSE, PACKED,
COMPACT, SERRATE
Serug relative   NAHOR
servant   BOY, GYP, MAN, BATA,
HIND, MATY, MOZA, MOZO,
PAGE, ALILA, GILLY, HAMAL,
VALET, BATMAN, BUTLER,
FERASH, FLUNKY, GARCON,
GILLIE, LACKEY, MENIAL,
POTBOY, POTMAN, EQUERRY,
GOSSOON; *see* MAID
serve   ACE, AID, KAE, HELP,
CATER, ASSIST, ATTEND,
ENLIST, FOLLOW
server   TRAY, SALVER,
WAITER, WAITRESS
service   AID, USE, DUTY, MASS,
RITE(S), STINT, DEVOIR,
REPAIR, SETTING, CEREMONY,
MAINTAIN, ASSISTANCE
service, military   ARMY, NAVY,
CORPS, GUARD, AIR FORCE,
COAST GUARD, NATIONAL
GUARD
serviceable   HANDY, UTILE,
USABLE, USEFUL,
FUNCTIONAL
serviceman/woman   GI, VET,
WAC, WAVE; *see* SAILOR,
SOLDIER, SPAR, WREN
serviette   NAPKIN

servile   **MEAN, ABJECT, MENIAL, FAWNING, SLAVISH**

serving   **PLATE, SLICE, HELPING, PORTION**

servitude   *see* **SLAVERY**

sesame   **TIL, BENE, BENI, TEEL, BENNE, BENNI, SEMSEM**

— sesame   **OPEN**

Sesame Street character   **ZOE, BERT, ELMO, ERNIE, OSCAR, GROVER, KERMIT, NOODLE, BIG BIRD**

Sesame Street creator   **COONEY, HENSON**

session   **TERM, PERIOD, HEARING, MEETING, SITTING, ASSEMBLY**

set   **FIX, GEL, BENT, FIRM, JELL, BATCH, FIXED, MOUNT, RIGID, CIRCLE, CLIQUE, HARDEN, COTERIE, SCENERY, ARRANGED, COLLECTION, DISPOSITION**

set about   **BEGIN, ENTERON, ISOLATE**

set apart   **ISOLATE, SEPARATE, SEGREGATE, SEQUESTER**

set aside   **DEFER, DISCARD, REJECT**

set down   **ALIT, WRITE, ALIGHT**

set free   **DELIVER, RELEASE, UNLOOSE, LIBERATE**

set in motion   **STIRRUP, ACTIVATE**

set off   **EXPLODE, DETONATE**

set on fire   **TIND, AROUSE, EXCITE, IGNITE, STRIKE, INSPIRE**

set out   **GO, MARK, ISSUE, LEAVE, DEPART, ENGAGE**

set right   **FIX, REPAIR, CORRECT**

set up   **ERECT, FOUND, APPOINT, INSTALL, ESTABLISH**

setback   **UPSET, RELAPSE, REVERSE, REVERSAL**

Seth relative   **EVE, ABEL, ADAM, CAIN, ENOS**

settee   **SOFA, BENCH, COUCH, DIVAN**

setting   **PAVE, BEZEL, MOUNT, SCENE, CHATON, MILIEU, LOCATION**

settle   **FIX, PAY, PUT, CALM, NEST, PLACE, QUIET, SQUAT, COLONIZE, DETERMINE, DISCHARGE, ESTABLISH**

settled   **ALIT, FIXED, VESTED**

settlement   **AWARD, COLONY, OUTPOST, PAYMENT, VILLAGE, JUDGMENT, SOLUTION, AGREEMENT, CLEARANCE, QUITTANCE**

settler   **BOOMER, SOONER, PIONEER, COLONIST**

set-to   **BOUT, BRAWL, FIGHT, QUARREL**

setup   **PLAN, LAYOUT, MAKEUP**

seven   **VII, HEPTAD, PLEIAD, SEPTET, SEPTUOR, SEPTETTE**

Seven Deadly Sins   *see* **SINS**

Seven Dwarfs   *see* **DWARF**

Seven Hills of Rome   **CAELIAN, VIMINAL, AVENTINE, PALATINE, QUIRINAL, EXQUILINE, CAPITOLINE**

Seven Sisters   *see* **PLEIADES**

Seven Sisters schools   **SMITH, VASSAR, BARNARD, BRYN MAWR, RADCLIFFE, WELLESLEY, (MOUNT) HOLYOKE**

Seven Wonders   **ZEUS, PHAROS, RHODES, EPHESUS, COLOSSUS, PYRAMIDS**

sever   **CUT, LOP, REND, RIVE, BREAK, DIVIDE, SUNDER**

several   **FEW, SOME, DIVERS, VARIOUS, MANIFOLD, DIFFERENT**

severe   **DOUR, GRIM, HARD, CRUEL, GRAVE, HARSH, SHARP, STRICT, AUSTERE, SERIOUS**

severity   **RIGOR, ASPERITY, FEROCITY, AUSTERITY, HARSHNESS**

Severn River (England)   **HAFREN, SABRINA**

Severn tributary   **USK, WYE, AVON**

sew   **HEM, FELL, TACK, STITCH, SUTURE**

sew up   **CLOSE, FINALIZE, MONOPOLIZE**

sewage   **OFFAL, WASTE, REFUSE, RUBBISH, DRAINAGE**

Seward's Folly   **ALASKA**

sewing machine inventor   **ELIAS HOWE**

sewing terms   **HEM, TAT, BIND, FELL, KNIT, PURL, RUIN, SEAM, TACK, WHIP, BASTE, QUILT, RENTER, CROCHET**

sex   **COITUS, GENDER, INTERCOURSE**

Sex and the City names MRBIG, SARAH, CARRIE, PARKER, JESSICA, MIRANDA, SAMANTHA, CHARLOTTE

sex appeal CHARM, CHARISMA

sexes, common to both UNISEX, EPICENE

sexism BIAS, BIGOTRY, PREJUDICE

sexless FRIGID, NEUTER, ASEXUAL, STERILE, IMPOTENT

sextant QUADRANT, ALTIMITER

sexton BEADLE, SHAMAS, SHAMES, VERGER, SHAMMASH, SACRISTAN

sexual GAMIC, CARNAL, EROTIC, LIBIDINOUS

sexually transmitted disease AIDS, HERPES, SYPHILIS, GONORRHEA

sexy HOT, LEWD, RACY, EROTIC, STEAMY, AMOROUS, LIBIDINOUS

Seychelles, capital of VICTORIA

Seychelles island MAHE, ASTOVE, COETIVY, LADIGUE, PRASLIN, ALPHONSE, FARQUHAR, DES ROCHES, SILHOUETTE

Seychelles language CREOLE, SESELWA

Seychelles money RUPEE

shabby MEAN, WORN, DINGY, DOWDY, MANGY, RATTY, SEEDY, TACKY, RAGGED, SCURVY, RUNDOWN

shabby woman DOWD, SLUT, DOWDY, FRUMP, SLAVEN, SLATTERN

shack HUT, SHED, HOVEL, SHANTY

shackle BOND, IRON, BILBO; see CHAIN

shad ALLIS, ALOSA, ALEWIFE

shade HUE, TINT, TINGE, UMBER, UMBRA, VISOR, NUANCE, PASTEL, SCREEN

shade tree ASH, ELM, LIN(DEN)

shaded walk MALL, ARBOR, ALAMEDA, CLOISTER

shadow SPY, CLOUD, SHADE, UMBER, UMBRA, REFLECTION; see GHOST, TRAIL

Shadow, The LAMONT, CRANSTON

shadowy DIM, FAINT, VAGUE, UNREAL, OBSCURE, IMAGINARY

shady DIM, DUSKY, FISHY, VAGUE, CLOUDY, UMBRAL, ILLICIT, QUESTIONABLE

shaft AXIS, FLUE, FUST, POLE, ARBOR, ARROW, SCAPE, SPIRE, STELE, THILL, COLUMN, PILLAR, SPINDLE

shag NAP, PILE, CORMORANT

shaggy BUSHY, HAIRY, NAPPY, HIRSUTE, UNKEMPT

shake JAR, AGUE, FLAP, JOLT, ROCK, WAVE, NIDGE, QUAKE, SHIVER, QUIVER, TREMOR, AGITATE, UNNERVE, VIBRATE, UNSETTLE

shakedown BLACKMAIL, EXTORTION

Shakespeare play HAMLET, MACBETH, OTHELLO, TEMPEST, PERICLES; see p. 628

Shakespeare relative ANNE, JOHN, EDMUND, HAMNET, JUDITH, SUSANNA

Shakespearean actor KEAN, WARD, BOOTH, BURTON, KEMBLE, BURBAGE, GARRICK, GIELGUD, OLIVIER, SIDDONS, SOTHERN, MODJESKA, BARRYMORE

Shakespearean character see p. 628 and individual plays

Shakespearean theater GLOBE

shaking AGUE, JITTERY

shaky WEAK, ROCKY, FLIMSY, WOBBLY, RICKETY, TENUOUS, UNSOUND, UNSTEADY

shallot ONION, SCALLION

shallow SHOAL, TRITE, FORDABLE, SUPERFICIAL

sham FAKE, HOAX, MOCK, BOGUS, FALSE, FEIGN, FRAUD, PHON(E)Y, PRETENSE

shaman OBEAH, PRIEST, MEDICINEMAN

Shamash consort AYA

shambles MESS, CHAOS, MUDDLE, ABATTOIR, DISORDER, SLAUGHTERHOUSE

shame FIE, ABASH, GUILT, HUMBLE, MORTIFY, CHAGRIN, DISGRACE, DISHONOR, EMBARRASSMENT

shamefaced SHY, BASHFUL, BLUSHING, EMBARRASSED

shameful	ARRANT, IGNOBLE, INDECENT, SHOCKING, SCANDALOUS, DISGRACEFUL
shameless	BRASH, BRAZEN, CHEEKY, IMPUDENT
Shammah relative	AGEE
shampoo	SOAP, WASH, LOMILOMI
shamrock	CLOVER
Shang dynasty	YIN
shanghai	KIDNAP, ABDUCT, CARRYOFF
Shangri-la	UTOPIA, PARADISE
shank(s)	GAM, LEG, CRUS, GAMB, SHIN, CRURA
shanty	HUT, SHED, HOVEL, HUTCH, SHACK
shape	CAST, FORM, MOLD, GUISE, MODEL, STATE, FIGURE, SCULPT, TAILLE, CONTOUR, FASHION, CONFIGURATION
shapeless	VAGUE, DEFORM, INCHOATE, AMORPHOUS
shapely	TRIM, LITHE, SVELTE, GRACEFUL, CURVACEOUS, PROPORTIONED
Shaphat relative	ELISHA
shard	PIECE, SHELL, FRAGMENT, POTSHERD
share	CUT, LOT, METE, PART, ALLOT, DIVVY, QUOTA, STAKE, MOIETY, RATION, DOLEOUT, PARTAKE, PORTION, ALLOTMENT
shark	GATA, HAYE, JAWS, MAKO, TOPE, PUPPY, RHINA, TOPER, GALEID, GALEUS, ISURUS, LAMNID, REQUIN, ACRODUS, DOGFISH, ISUROID, PLACOID, RATFISH, REQUIEM, SAWFISH, TIBURON, GREAT WHITE, HAMMERHEAD
shark, young	CUB, PUPPY
sharp	ACID, GLEG, HIGH, KEEN, ACERB, ACUTE, ACRID, ALERT, CHEAT, CLEAR, EDGED, SPIKY, QUICK, ACUATE, BARBED, MARKED, CAUSTIC, INTENSE, POINTED, VIGILANT
sharpen	EDGE, HONE, WHET, GRIND, STROP
sharpening device	HONE, STEEL, STONE, STRAP, STROP, GRINDER, ABRASIVE, WHETSTONE, GRINDSTONE

sharper	GYP, KITE, CHEAT, CROOK, CONMAN, SWINDLER
sharpness	EDGE, ACUITY, ALERTNESS
sharpshooter	SHOT, CRACK, JAGER, SNIPER, MARKSMAN, RIFLEMAN
shatter	BREAK, BURST, SMASH
shave	CUT, CROP, PARE, TRIM, GRAZE, PLANE, SKIVE, SLICE, SCRAPE, WHITTLE
shaver	BOY, IMP, LAD, RAZOR, YOUTH, URCHIN, YOUNGSTER
shavetail	LOOEY, LIEUTENANT
shaving	CHIP, FLAKE, SCALE, PARING, SLIVER, SAWDUST
shawl	MAUD, WRAP, LAMBA, MANTA, PAITU, TALIS, TALIT, PATTOO, TALITH, TALLIS, TALLIT, PAISLEY, TALLITH; see SCARF
Shawnee adoptee	BOONE
Shawnee chief	TECUMSEH, TECUMTHA
shay	BUGGY, CHAISE, CARRIAGE, STANHOPE
she	HER, FEMALE
Shea Stadium team	METS
sheaf	BALE, GERB, GAVEL, BUNDLE
shear	SHAVE, FLEECE; see CLIP
Shearer	MOIRA, NORMA
shearing tool	MOWER, CLIPPER, CROPPER, SCISSOR(S)
sheath	COT, CASE, OCREA, DRESS, SHOCK, THECA, CASING, SLEEVE, SPATHE, CAPSULE, SCABBARD
sheathe	COVER, ENCLOSE, ENVELOP
shebang	AFFAIR, MATTER, BUSINESS
shed	HUT, MEW, CAST, COTE, DOFF, EMIT, MOLT, HOVEL, MOULT, SHACK, HANGAR, LEANTO, SHANTY, SLOUGH, DISCARD, RADIATE, EXUVIATE
sheen	GLEAM, GLOSS, SHINE, LUSTER, POLISH
sheep	EWE, RAM, TEG, LAMB, AGNUS, WETHER, CARACUL, CHEVIOT, LAMBKIN; see p. 660
sheep disease	COE, GID, ROT, LOCO, SHAB, SHAKES, STURDY, ANTHRAX, SCRAPIE, STAGGERS, RINDERPEST

sheep genus	BOS, OVIS
sheep, young	HOG, LAMB, COSSET, LAMBKIN, YEARLING
sheepdog	COLLIE, SHELTY, SHELTIE
sheepfold	PEN, REE, COTE, KRAAL, REEVE
sheepish	COY, SHY, MEEK, TIMID, BASHFUL, ASHAMED
sheeplike	MEEK, OVINE
sheepskin	BOCK, BOND, ROAN, BASIL, SKIVER, DIPLOMA, PARCHMENT
sheepskin hat	KALPAK
sheepwalk	SLAIT
sheer	MERE, PURE, VEER, GAUZY, STEEP, UTTER, SWERVE, GOSSAMER, VERTICAL, TRANSPARENT
sheet	RAG, COAT, FILM, LEAF, PAGE, SAIL, LAYER, LINEN, BEDDING, EXPANSE, (NEWS)PAPER
sheeting	LINEN, SATIN, PERCALE
shelf	BERM(E), LEDGE, GRADIN, LEDGER, MANTEL, RETABLE, SANDBAR
shell	POD, BOAT, BOMB, BURR, CASE, HULL, HUSK, LIMA, SHOT, SKIN, BIELD, CONCH, HARPA, MUREX, SHUCK, CONCHA, GONKER, TUNICA, BOMBARD, GRENADE, CARAPACE, NAUTILUS, INTEGUMENT
shell money	PEAG, COWRY, PEAGE, SEWAN, COWRIE, SEAWAN, WAMPUM, SEAWANT
shellac(k)	LAC, BEAT, DRUB, RESIN, VARNISH
shellacking	BEATING, WHIPPING, THRASHING
Shelley poem	ADONAIS
shellfish	CLAM, CRAB, MUSSEL, OYSTER, SHRIMP, SCALLOP; see p. 680
shelter	LEE, COTE, ROOF, SHED, BIELD, SHEAL, SCREEN; see REFUGE
sheltered	ALEE
shelve	CARRY, DEFER, DELAY, STOCK, PUTOFF, SUSPEND, POSTPONE
Shem descendant	UZAL, SEMITE
Shem relative	HAM, LUD, ARAM, EBER, ELAM, NOAH, NAAMAH, JAPHETH

shenanigan(s)	CAPER, PRANK, TRICK, FROLIC, MISCHIEF
Sheol	HELL, HADES
shepherd	TEND, HERDER, PASTOR, CORYDON, DAPHNIS, THYRSIS, SHEEPDOG
shepherdess	AMARYLLIS
sherbet	ICE, SORBET
sheriff	REEVE, ELISOR, POLICE, SHRIEVE, CONSTABULARY
Sherlock Holmes author	DOYLE
Sherlock Holmes's friend	WATSON
Sherpa sighting	YETI
sherry	JEREZ, OLOROSO, AMONTILLADO
sherry-wine coating	FLOR
Sherwood Forest hero	ROBINHOOD
Shetlands measure	URE, MARKLAND
shibboleth	MOTTO, BYWORD, SLOGAN, PASSWORD, TESTWORD
shield	ECU, TARP, AEGIS, MULGA, PAVIS, PELTA, SCUTE, TARGE, SCUTUM, TARGET, BUCKLER, CLIPEUS, ROTELLA, ROUNDEL, HIELAMAN
shield-shaped	PELTATE, SCUTATE, CLYPEATE
shift	GANG, GYBE, JIBE, MOVE, VARY, VEER, CHANGE, DODGE, SHUNT, SWITCH, CHEMISE, DEVIATE, TRANSFER
shiftless	LAZY, NOGOOD, INDOLENT, GOODFORNOTHING
shifty	SLY, FOXY, CAGEY, SNEAKY, TRICKY, EVASIVE
shill	DECOY, PLANT, ACCOMPLICE
shilly-shally	DALLY, HEDGE, WAVER, DAWDLE
shimmer	GLOSS, SHEEN, JIGGLE, LUSTER, GLIMMER
shimmy	SHAKE, BOOGEY
shin	SHANK, CLIMB
shinbone	TIBIA
shindig	PARTY, AFFAIR, OUTING
shindy	ROW, RIOT, BRAWL, HUBBUB, RACKET, COMMOTION
shine	WAX, GLOW, EXCEL, GLEAM, GLOSS, LIGHT, LUSTER, POLISH, RADIATE, RADIATE, TWINKLE

shiner MOUSE, BLACKEYE
shingle(s) BOB, CLIP, FLIP,
SHIM, SIGN, ZONA,
BEACH, FACIA, SLATE,
HERPES, SIDING
shining LUCID, NITID, SUNNY,
BRIGHT, LUCENT, RADIANT,
LUMINOUS
Shinto deity power KAMI
ship SEND, CONSIGN,
FORWARD, DISPATCH; see
also WARSHIP, VESSEL
— ship AHOY
ship crew ABLE, HAND, MATE,
BUNGS, COOPER, PURSER,
STORER, YEOMAN, STEWARD
ship, famous *see p. 730*
ship, device for raising CAMEL,
CAISSON
ship officer BOSN, MATE, PIPES,
MASTER, PURSER, CAPTAIN,
SKIPPER, BOATSWAIN
ship, part of *see p. 729*
ship, sailing *see p. 728*
shipment LOT, LOAD, CARGO,
FREIGHT
shipshape NEAT, SNUG, TIDY,
TRIM, TIGHT, TIPTOP,
ORDERLY
shipworm BORER, TEREDO
shipwreck WASA, TITANIC,
MARY ROSE, ANDREA DORIA
shire COUNTY
shirk FUNK, DUCK, AVOID,
DODGE, EVADE, SOLDIER,
MALINGER, GOLDBRICK
shirker BUM, DODGER,
EVADER, LOAFER, TRUANT,
SLACKER, GOLDBRICK
shirr GATHER
shirt TOB, SARK, TOBE, BANIA,
DICKY, WAMUS, BANIAN,
BANYAN, CAMISA, CAMISE,
DICKEY, JERSEY, CHEMISE,
PULLOVER
shivaree SERENADE,
CHARIVARI
shiver GRUE, SHAKE, QUIVER,
SHUDDER, TREMBLE
shoal BAR, BANK, REEF,
DRAVE, HORDE, RIFFLE
shoal-water deposit CULM
shoat SHOTE, PIGLET
shock BLOW, JOLT, STUN,
APPAL, BRUNT, SCARE,
SEISM, APPALL, IMPACT,
REVOLT, SICKEN, TRAUMA,
DISGUST, STARTLE
shocked AGHAST, APPALLED

shocking GHASTLY,
OFFENSIVE, REPUGNANT,
OUTRAGEOUS, SCANDALOUS
shod CALCED
shoddy POOR, CHEAP, TACKY,
FLIMSY, SHABBY, INFERIOR
shoe(s) CACK, GETA, MULE,
PUMP, ROMEO, SABOT, SLING,
STOGA, STOGY, WEDGE,
ANKLET, BROGAN, BROGUE,
BUSKIN, CALIGA, CRAKOW,
GAITER, LOAFER, OXFORD,
SANDAL, SLIPON, STEPIN,
STOGIE, WEDGIE, BLUCHER,
CHOPINE, CRAKOWE, SNEAKER,
BALMORAL, COLONIAL,
FOOTGEAR, FOOTWEAR,
PLATFORM, POULAINE
shoe designer VIVIER,
PERUGIA, FERRAGAMO
shoe implement (SHOE)HORN,
BUFFER
shoe part FLAP, HEEL, LACE,
LAST, RAND, SOLE, VAMP,
WELT, AGLET, SHANK, THONG,
UPPER, EYELET, INSOLE,
INSTEP, LACING, TASSEL,
TOEBOY, TOECAP, TONGUE,
UPPERS
shoelace part A(I)GLET, POINT
shoeless UNSHOD
shoemaker SNOB, SUTOR,
BOTCHER, COBBLER, CRISPIN
shoemaker's equipment AWL,
LAST, TREE, ELS(H)IN,
LINGEL, LINGLE
shoemaker's saint CRISPIN
shoes S(C)HOON, TALARIA
shoes, repair COBBLE, REHEEL,
RESOLE
shogunate headquarters EDO
shoo GIT, SCAT, SCRAM, BEAT
IT, BE GONE
shoo-in CINCH, WINNER
shoot BAG, BUD, HIT, ROD,
UDO, BINE, CHIT, CION,
DART, FIRE, KILL, LIMB, TWIG,
GEMMA, SCION, SNIPE,
SPRIG, STOLO, TURIO, VIMEN,
PROPEL, RATOON, SPROUT,
STOLON, TILLER, TURION,
TWINGE
shooting match TIR, SHOOT,
SKEET
shooting star *see* METEOR
shoot-out GUNFIGHT
shooter TAW, ALLEY, ARCHER,
BOWMAN, MARBLE,
MARKSMAN, RIFLEMAN

shooting **GUNFIRE, DISCHARGE, DETONATION**

shooting star **BOLIDE, LEONID, FIREBALL, METEOR(OID)**

shop **MART, STORE, TRADE, BAZAAR, MARKET, ATELIER, FACTORY, TABERNA, BOUTIQUE, EMPORIUM**

shopping **BUYING, EMPTION, PURCHASE**

shopping center **MALL, PLAZA, MARKET**

shoptalk **SLANG, JARGON**

shore **BANK, PROP, RIPA, BEACH, BRACE, COAST, WARTH, RIVAGE, STRAND, SEASIDE, SUPPORT, BUTTRESS, COASTLINE**

shore bird **SORA, SNIPE, STILT, WADER, AVOCET, CURLEW; see RAIL, SANDPIPER, PLOVER**

short **LOW, SHY, CURT, RUDE, BRIEF, PUDGY, SMALL, TERSE, ABRUPT, SCANTY, STUBBY, CONCISE, LACKING, LACONIC, DIMINUTIVE**

shortcut **ROUTE, BYPASS, CUTOFF**

short-lived **FLEETING, FLITTING, EPHEMERAL, TRANSIENT, TRANSITORY**

short-story writer *see p. 626*

short-tempered **EDGY, TESTY**

short-winded **PURSE, WHEEZY**

shortage **LACK, NEED, DEARTH, DEFICIT, SCARCITY**

shortchange **CON, GYP, CHEAT**

shortcoming **FLAW, FAULT, DEFECT, FOIBLE, FAILING, DRAWBACK, WEAKNESS**

shorten **BOB, LOP, CLIP, CROP, DELE, DOCK, ELIDE, REDUCE, ABRIDGE, CURTAIL, CONDENSE, ABBREVIATE**

shortening **FAT, OIL, LARD, OLEO, SUET**

shortest route **BEELINE, CROW(FLIES)**

shortfall **LACK, DEFICIT, SHORTAGE**

shorthand **GREGG, PITMAN, STENOTYPE, SPEEDWRITING**

shorthand sign **PHONOGRAM**

shortly **ANON, SOON, PRONTO, ABRUPTLY**

shorts **BOXERS, BRIEFS, TRUNKS, DRAWERS, JOCKEYS**

shortsighted **MYOPIC, UNTHINKING**

Shoshonean **UTE, HOPI, KOSO, OTOE, P(A)IUTE, COMANCHE**

shot **TRY, BALL, DOSE, CRACK, DRINK, GUESS, KAPUT, PHOTO, BULLET, CHANCE, ATTEMPT, FLECKED, LANGREL, TRASHED, LANGRAGE, SNAPSHOT, DISCHARGE, INJECTION**

shoulder **BEAR, BERM, EDGE, CARRY, LEDGE, SHOVE, ASSUME, EPAULE, JOSTLE, TAKEON, SCAPULA**

shoulder part **DELTOID, HUMERUS, SCAPULA, ACROMION**

shoulder, of the **ALAR, SCAPULAR**

shout **CALL, ROAR, YELL; see CRY**

shove **JAR, JOG, BUNT, PUSH, ELBOW, NUDGE, JOSTLE, SHOULDER**

shovel **DIG, VAN, PEEL, SCOOP, SPADE, TROWEL, BACKHOE**

show **EXPO, PLAY, GUIDE, LEGIT, RAREE, TRACE, USHER, EVINCE, REVEAL, CONCERT, DISPLAY, EXPOSE, PROGRAM, PRETENSE, SEMBLANCE, SPECTACLE**

Show Boat captain **ANDY**

Show Boat writer **KERN, FERBER**

show off **FLAUNT**

show up **COME, APPEAR, ARRIVE**

showcase **CABINET, ETALAGE, VITRINE**

shower **BATH(E), SKEW, SPATE, SPRAY; see RAIN**

shower, kind of **BABY, BRIDAL**

showman, famous **ROSE(LEE), BARNUM, CARROLL, RINGLING, ZIEGFELD**

show-off **HOTSHOT, EXHIBITIONIST**

showpiece **MODEL, SAMPLE, CLASSIC, EXAMPLE**

showroom model **DEMO**

showy **ARTY, LOUD, GAUDY, FLASHY, FLORID, GARISH, VULGAR, FLAMBOYANT, OSTENTATIOUS**

shrapnel **SHARD, SHELL, FRAGMENT**

shred **BIT, RAG, CUTUP, GRATE, PIECE, SCRAP, TEARUP, FRAGMENT, SPLINTER**

shrew	ERD, KATE, HARPY, VIXEN, TARTAR, VIRAGO, XANTIPPE	shuffle	MIX, CHANGE, RIFFLE, SHAMBLE, REARRANGE
shrewd	SLY, ARCH, CAGY, FOXY, WILY, CANNY, PAWRY, ASTUTE, CUNNING, PRUDENT	shun	DUCK, SNUB, AVOID, DODGE, ELUDE, EVADE, ESCHEW, IGNORE
shrewish	BITCHY	shunt	VEER, SHIFT, DIVERT, SWITCH
shriek	CRY, HOWL, SCREAM, SCREECH	shush	HUSH, QUIET, SILENCE
shrift	ABSOLUTION	shut	CLOSE(D), SEAL(ED), CONFINE, ENCLOSE
shrike	DRONGO, LANIUS, MINIVET, TRILLER	shut in	PENT(UP), CONFINE, INVALID
shrill	PIPY, ACUTE, SKIRL, ARGUTE, PIPING, STRIDENT	shut out	EXCLUDE, OSTRACIZE
shrimp	RUNT, CARID, PRAWN, SHAVER, ARTEMIA, CARIDEAN, CARIDOID, CREVETEE	shut up	DAM, (S)HUSH, CLOSET, IMMURE, SILENCE, IMPRISON
shrimp genus	CARIDA	shutdown	CLOSURE, STOPPAGE
shrine	ARK, PIR, NAOS, TOMB, TOPE, ALTAR, STUPA, CHASSE, DAGOBA, DARGAH, DURGAH, FATIMA, SAMOAH, CHAITYA, LOURDES, MARTYRY, FERETORY, RELIQUARY	shuteye	SLEEP
		shutout	DEFEAT
		shutter	BLIND, SHADE, BLINDS, GRILLE, LOUVER, PERSIENNE
		shuttle	PIRN, SPOOL, BOBBIN, VACILLATE
		shuttlecock	BIRD
shrink	COWER, QUAIL, WIZEN, CRINGE, FLINCH, RECOIL, REDUCE, WITHER, SHRIVEL, CONTRACT; see PSYCHIATRIST	shuttle, space	ATLANTIS, COLUMBIA, DISCOVERY, CHALLENGER, ENTERPRISE
		shy	COY, JIB, MIM, BALK, SKIT, CHARY, SHORT, START, TIMID, DEMURE, MODEST, RECOIL, BASHFUL, LACKING, RESERVED, RETIRING, VERECUND, DIFFIDENT
shrinkage	LOSS, DECREASE, CONTRACTION		
shrive	ABSOLVE		
shrivel	CURL, WIZEN, SHRINK, WITHER		
		Shylock	USURER
Shropshire	SALOP	Shylock's daughter	JESSICA
Shropshire river	SEVERN	shyster	TRICKSTER, PETTIFOGGER
shroud	PALL, VEIL, CLOAK, COVER, SHEET, SCREEN, CEREMENT, WINDINGCLOTH	Siam	see THAILAND
		Siamese twin	ENG, CHANG
Shrove Tuesday	MARDIGRAS	Sibelius work	FINLANDIA, SWAN (OF TUONELA)
shrub(s)	TOD, ARIA, BUSH, CADE, GOAT, INGA, ITEA, PELU, WHIN, WHUN, ALDER, CHICO, ELDER, FURZE, GORSE, HENNA, LILAC, SALAL, SAVIN, SUMAC, URENA, ABELIA, BONSAI, FRUTEX, JASMIN, KOWHAI, LAUREL, BOSCAGE, LANTANA; see EVERGREEN, ACACIA, TREES	Siberian	VOGUL, SAMOYED
		Siberian city/town	OMSK, CHITA, TOMSK, BARNAUL, IRKUTSK, KEMEROVO
		Siberian lake	BAIKAL
		Siberian river	OB, AMUR, LENA, YANA, TOBOL, ANADYR, IRTISH, KOLYMA, ULANUDE, YENISEI, KHATANGA
		sibilant	PSST, HISSING
shrubbery	TOD, BRIER, GARDEN, BOSCAGE, COPPICE, THICKET	sibyl	WITCH, SORCERESS; see SEER
		Sicilian	SICANIAN, TRINACRIAN
shrug	COWER, SHIVER, SHRINK, GESTURE	Sicilian city/town	GELA, AVOLA, ALCAMO, BRONTE,
shuck	POD, HUSK, SHELL		
shudder	see SHIVER		

CEFALU, RAGUSA, CATANIA, MARSALA, MESSINA, PALERMO, TRAPANI, SIRACUSA, SYRACUSE
Sicilian island **EGADI, LIPARI, USTICA**
Sicilian river **SALSO**
Sicilian volcano **ETNA**
sick **ILL, ABED, AILING, UNWELL, UNSOUND, INDISPOSED**
sickbay **CLINIC, HOSPITAL, INFIRMARY**
sicken **AIL, REBEL, AFFLICT, FALL ILL, NAUSEATE**
sickening **GROSS, OFFENSIVE, DISGUSTING**
sickle **SIVE, SCYTHE**
sickle-shaped **FALCATE**
sickly **ILL, WAN, PALE, WEAK, AILING, INFIRM, UNWELL**
sickness *see* **DISEASE**
Siddhartha **BUDDHA, GAUTAMA**
side **RIM, EDGE, TEAM, AGREE, FACET, FLANK, LATUS, PARTY, ASPECT, BORDER, MARGIN, FACTION**
side by side, place **APPOSE**
side, *pert. to* **COSTAL, LATERAL**
sideboard **BUFFET, CABINET, CREDENZA, CUPBOARD**
sidekick **PAL, CHUM, MATE, BUDDY, PARTNER, COMPANION**
sideline **HOBBY, PASTIME, AVOCATION**
sidereal **ASTRAL, STARRY**
sideslip **YAW, SKID**
sidesplitting **FUNNY, HILARIOUS**
sidestep **AVOID, EVADE, SKIRT, BYPASS**
sidetrack **AVERT, SHUNT, DIVERT**
sidewalk **FOOTWAY, PATHWAY, WALKWAY, FOOTPATH, PAVEMENT, BOARDWALK**
sideways, sidewise **ASKEW, ASLANT, ASKANCE**
sidewinder **CROTALUS, RATTLESNAKE**
siding **SPUR, PANELING**
sidle **CANT, CRAB, SKEW, SKIRT**
siege **ATTACK, ASSAULT, BLOCKADE**

siege, lay **BESET, INVEST**
Siegfried **SIGURD**
Siegfried's mother **SIEGLINDE**
Siegfried's slayer **HAGEN**
Siegfried's sword **BALMUNG**
Sierra Leone, capital of **FREETOWN**
Sierra Leone city/town **BO, KOIDU, PEPEL, KABALA, KAMBIA, KENEMA, MAKENI, MOYAMBA, FREETOWN**
Sierra Leone island **SHERBRO**
Sierra Leone language **TEMNE;** *see* **MANDE**
Sierra Leone money **LEONE**
Sierra Leone neighbor **GUINEA, LIBERIA**
Sierra Leone river **JONG, MANO, SEWA, ROKEL, KOLENTE**
siesta **(CAT)NAP, REST, BREAK, RECESS, SNOOZE**
sieve **BOLT, LAUN, SIFT, TEMS, PUREE, BOLTER, RIDDLE, SIFTER, GRIZZLY;** *see* **STRAINER**
sift **LUE, REE, SIE, BOLT, TEMS, RIDDLE, SCREEN, WINNOW**
sifter **SIEVE, BOLTER, COLANDER, STRAINER**
sigh **SOB, GASP, MOAN, SOUF, SOUGH, BREATH**
sight **AIM, EYE, KEN, BEAD, ESPY, VIEW, SCENE, VISTA, VISION, GLIMPSE, SPECTACLE**
sight, come into **LOOM, APPEAR**
sight, *pert. to* **OCULAR, VISUAL**
sightless **BLIND, UNSEEING**
sightly **COMELY**
sightsee **TOUR, TRAVEL, OBSERVE**
sightseer **TOURIST, OBSERVER, RUBBERNECK**
Sigmund relative **SIGNY, SIGURD, HJORDIS, VOLSUNG**
sign **MARX, OMEN, PLUS, RUNE, SEIN, BADGE, MINUS, PRESA, SEGNO, TOKEN, PORTENT**
sign **INK, MARK, NEON, OMEN, TOKEN, TRACE, SYMBOL, GESTURE, INDICIA, PORTENT, SHINGLE, VESTIGE, SYMPTOM, ENTER INTO, INDICATION**
sign, *pert. to* **SEMIC**
sign off on **OK**
sign up **HIRE, EMPLOY, ENGAGE, ENLIST, ENROL(L)**

signal   CUE, PST, TAP, BUZZ, ALARM, FLARE, FUSEE, SIREN, BEACON, CURFEW, DENOTE, ENSIGN, HOWLER, MOTION, BLINKER, CHAMADE, FOGHORN, SEMAPHORE

signatory   (CO)SIGNER

signature   HAND, PARAPH, SCROLL, AUTOGRAPH, MANUSCRIPT

signboard   SHINGLE

signet   SEAL, SIGIL

significance   POINT, SENSE, VALUE, IMPORT, MOMENT, WEIGHT, GRAVITY, IMPORTANCE

significant   TELLING, NOTABLE, WEIGHTY, IMPORTANT, MOMENTOUS, MEANINGFUL

signify   BODE, MEAN, SHOW, IMPLY, DENOTE

signpost   KEY, SIGN, GUIDE

Sigurd relative   REGIN, GUDRUN, SIGMUND

Sigurd's victim   FAFNIR

Sikhism, five items   KARA, KESH, KACHH, KANGHA, KIRPAN

Sikkim, capital of   GANGTOK

silage   FODDER

Silas Marner author   ELIOT

Silas Marner character   EPPIE

silence   GAG, PAX, MUM, CALM, HUSH, LULL, MUTE, OYEZ, REST, TACE, PEACE, QUIET, APHONY, MUFFLE, STIFLE, REPRESS

silencer   GAG, MUTE, BAFFLE, MUFFLER

silent   MUM, GLUM, MUTE, TACET, TACIT, NOISELESS, SOUNDLESS

silhouette   SHADOW, CONTOUR, PROFILE, SHADOW, OUTLINE, PROFILE

silica   MICA, SAND, SILEX, QUARTZ

silicate   MICA, ESTER, CERITE, EPIDOTE, TREMOLITE

silk   ALMA, GIMP, GROS, MOFF, GREGE, MOIRE, PEKIN, ROMAL, RUMAL, SATIN, SURAH, TULLE, CAMACA; see p. 535

silk-screen print   SERIGRAPH

silk source   ERIA, COCOON, AILANTHUS

silken   SERIC, GLOSSY, SATINY, SMOOTH, ELEGANT

silk thread   BAVE, POIL, TRAM, FLOSS, TRAME, SLEAVE, TUSSAH, TUSSER, TUSSORI

silkworm   ERI, BOMBYX, TUSSAH, TUSSORE

silkworm disease   UJI

silky   SOFT, SLEEK, GLOSSY, SATINY, SMOOTH, LUSTROUS, SERICEOUS

sill   FRAME, LEDGE, SHELF

silly   DAFT, ANILE, DAFFY, INANE, KOOKY, ABSURD, ASININE, FATUOUS, FOOLISH, PUERILE

silo   BIN, CRIB, GRANARY

silt   DREGS, FINES, LOESS, ALLUVIUM, SEDIMENT

silver   AG, LUNA, COINS, SYCEE, ARGENT, SILLER, STERLING, ARGENTUM

silver alloy   BILLON

Silver Spoons names   ERIN, JOEL, KATE, HARRY, RICKY, EDWARD, STRATTON

Silver State   NV, NEV(ADA)

silversides   GUPPY, KILLY, PLATY, LUCINA, GRUNION, GULARIC, MAYFISH

silvery   SHINY, ARGENT(INE)

Simenon character   MAIGRET

Simeon relative   OHAD

simian   APE, MONKEY, PRIMATE

similar   AKIN, (A)LIKE, CLOSE, AGNATE, PARALLEL, ANALOGOUS, COMPARABLE

similarity   AFFINITY, ANALOGY, LIKENESS, RELATION, SEMBLANCE

simile   ANALOGY, METAPHOR, COMPARISON

similitude   IMAGE, LIKENESS, FACSIMILE, SEMBLANCE

simmer   COOK, FUME, STEW, BROOD, SEETHE, PARBOIL

simmer down   COOL, SUBSIDE

Simon Legree   TASKMASTER

Simon relative   JUDAS

simpatico   NICE, (CON)GENIAL

simper   MINCE, SMILE, SMIRK, TEEHEE

simple   EASY, MERE, SNAP, NAIVE, PLAIN, SILLY, HOMELY, ARTLESS

simple-minded   NAIVE, ARTLESS, CHILDLIKE

simpleton   DAW, BOOB, COOT, DUPE, GAUP, GOWK, GUMP, BOOBY, GOOSE, NITWIT

simplify **REDUCE, ABRIDGE, SHORTEN, BOIL DOWN**
simply **JUST, ONLY, EASILY, MERELY, PURELY, SOLELY, WHOLLY**
Simpsons names **APU, BART, LISA, MARGE, BARNEY, GRAMPA, KRUSTY, QUIMBY, WIGGUM, BOUVIER**
Simpsons creators **SIMON, BROOKS**
simulacrum **SHAM, IMAGE, EFFIGY, TRAVESTY, SEMBLANCE**
simulate **ACT, APE, FAKE, MOCK, SHAM, FEIGN, AFFECT, INVENT**
simulation **FEINT, ANALOGUE, PRETENSE**
simultaneous **COEXISTENT, COINCIDENT, CONCURRENT**
sin **ERR, EVIL, SLIP, VICE, ERROR, INIQUITY, TRESPASS, PECCADILLO, TRANSGRESS;** see **DEADLY**
Sinatra birthplace **HOBOKEN**
Sinatra wife **AVA, MIA**
Sinbad bird **ROC**
since **AS, AGO, YET, SITH, SYNE, HENCE, BECAUSE**
sincere **OPEN, FRANK, CANDID, HONEST, EARNEST, GENUINE, HEARTFELT**
Sinclair **LEWIS, UPTON**
Sinclair character **BUDD, CASS, LANNY, BABBITT, DOREMUS**
sine qua non **ESSENTIAL, INDISPENSABLE**
sinecure **PLUM, SNAP, CINCH, EASY JOB**
sinew(s) **THEWS, MUSCLE, STRENGTH**
sinewy **ROPY, WIRY, TOUGH, BRAWNY, MUSCULAR**
sinful **EVIL, WICKED, IMMORAL, PECCANT**
sing **HUM, LILT, TELL, CAROL, CHANT, CHIRP, CROON, JODEL, TROLL, YODEL, SQUEAL, WARBLE**
Singapore, capital of **SINGAPORE**
Singapore language **MALAY, TAMIL, CHINESE**
Singapore money **DOLLAR**
singer **ALMA, ALME, ALTO, BARD, BASS, DIVA, WAIT, ALMAH, ALMEH, MEZZO, TENOR, VOICE, CANTOR, MUSICO, CAROLER, CHANTER,**

CHORIST, CROONER, GLEEMAN, SOPRANO, WARBLER, YODELER, BARITONE, BARYTONE, CHANTEUR, MELODIST, MINSTREL, SONGSTER, VOCALIST, CHORISTER, CHANTEUSE, CONTRALTO; see MUSICIAN, SONGBIRD; see p. 643
singer, famous popular **COMO, JONES, LANZA, TORME, CROSBY, MARTIN, NEWTON, PARTON, TWITTY, JACKSON, MADONNA, MANILOW, PRESLEY, SINATRA, STREISAND**
single **ACE, ONE, LONE, MONO, ONLY, SOLO, UNAL, ALONE, UNWED, SOLITARY**
single-handed see **SINGLY**
single-minded **ONETRACK, STEADFAST**
singly **SOLO, ALONE, SOLELY, UNAIDED**
singular **ODD, QUEER, UNIQUE, CURIOUS, STRANGE, UNUSUAL, PECULIAR**
sinister **BAD, EVIL, LEFT, WICKED, OMINOUS, PORTENTOUS**
sinister, opp. to **DEXTER**
sink **DIP, EBB, SAG, SET, BOWL, FAIL, FALL, FLAG, WANE, BASIN, DROOP, DROWN, SLUMP, DOLINA, GODOWN, SUBMERGE**
sinker **DONUT, WEIGHT, DOUGHNUT**
sinless **PURE, PERFECT, INNOCENT, SPOTLESS, VIRTUOUS**
sinning **ERRANT, PECCANT**
sins, seven deadly **ENVY, LUST, RAGE, GREED, PRIDE, SLOTH, GLUTTONY**
sinuous **WAVY, SNAKY, CURVED, SPIRAL, DEVIOUS, WINDING, SERPENTINE**
sinus **ANTRA, ANTRUM, CAVITY**
Sioux tribe **CROW, IOWA, OTO(E), BRULE, OMAHA, OSAGE, PONCA, TETON, DAKOTA, LAKOTA, MANDAN, NAKOTA, OGLALA, SANTEE, ARIKARA, CATAWBA, TUTELOS, YANKTON, ARIKAREE, BLACKFOOT**

sip	SUCK, TASTE, SAMPLE, SAMPLING	size	AREA, BULK, GLAZE, AMOUNT, DEGREE, EXTENT, VOLUME, MEASURE, CAPACITY, MAGNITUDE
siphon	DRAW(OFF), PUMP, DRAIN, STRAW, EXTRACT		
sir	*see* TITLE	size up	EYE, CASE, JUDGE, ASSESS
sire	BEGET, FATHER, PROCREATE	sizing	GLUE, GLAZE, SEALER
siren	VAMP, CIRCE, NYMPH, LURLEI, LORELEI, ENCHANTRESS	sizzle	FRY, BURN, HISS, FRIZZ(LE)
		skate	RAY, SKID, GLIDE, SLIDE
sirocco	*see* WIND	skateboarding term	AIR, HIT,
sisal	*see* HEMP		FAKIE, ZONK, BURGER,
Sisera's killer	JAEL		INVERT, LAUNCH, (N)OLLIE,
sissy	WIMP, COWARD, CHICKEN, MILKSOP, WEAKLING		SWITCH, VARIAL, MCTWIST, WIPEOUT, HEELFLIP, WALLRIDE, ALLEYOOP, SWITCHBACK
sister	NUN, SIB, SIS, AUNT, NURSE, SOROR	skater, famous	*see p. 713*
Sister Carrie author	DREISER	skating term	AXEL, LUTZ,
sisterhood	SODALITY, SORORITY		CAMEL, WALTZ, MOHAWK, WALLEY, CHOCTAW,
Sistine Madonna painter	RAPHAEL		SALCHOW, TOELOOP, BUTTERFLY
sistrum	RATTLE	skedaddle	RUN, BLOW, BOLT,
Sisyphus relative	AEOLUS, MEROPE, CORINTH		FLEE, SCOOT, DECAMP
		skein	RAP, WEB, HANK, HASP, MESH, SLEAVE
sit	POSE, BROOD, PERCH, ROOST, HUNKER, CONVENE	skeleton	ATOMY, BONES,
site	POST, SPOT, SEAT, SCENE, LOCALE, LOCATION		CADRE, CORAL, FRAME, SPONGE; *see p. 500*
sitter	NURSE, AUPAIR	skeleton, disease of	RICKETS,
sitting	POSE, CLUTCH, SEANCE, SEDENT, ASTRIDE, SESSION		RACHITIS
		Skelton character	CLEM, FREDDIE
Sitting Bull opponent	CUSTER	skeptic	CYNIC, LUCIAN,
Sitting Bull son	CROWFOOT		PYRRHO, THOMAS,
Sitting Bull tribe	SIOUX		AGNOSTIC, APORETIC
situate	SET, PLACE, LOCATE, POSIT(ION)	skeptical	DUBIOUS, CYNICAL, AGNOSTIC, PYRRHONIC
situation	JOB, CASE, POST, SITE, STATE, PLIGHT, POSITION	skepticism	DOUBT, DISTRUST, DISBELIEF, AGNOTICISM
situp muscles	ABS	sketch	DRAW, LIMN, SKIT, DRAFT, DESIGN, DOODLE, SEND UP, DRAWING, OUTLINE, ESQUISSE, CARICATURE
Siva relative	UMA, DEVI, KALI, MAYA, SATI, DURGA, GAURI, AMBIKA, SKANDA, BHAVANI, PARVATI		
		sketchy	CRUDE, HASTY, ROUGH, SUPERFICIAL
six	HEXAD, SENARY, SESTET, SEXTET	skew	TWIST, SWERVE, DISTORT
Six, Les	AURIC, DUREY, MILHAUD, POULENC, HONEGGER, TAILLEFERRE	skewer	PIN, SPIT, TRUSS, BROACH, SKIVER, BROCHETTE
sixth sense	ESP, INTUITION	ski	RUNNER, SCHUSS, SNOWSHOE
sizable	BIG, HUGE, VAST, AMPLE, GREAT, HEFTY, LARGE, BULKY, GOODLY, IMMENSE, MASSIVE, GOODSIZED, SUBSTANTIAL, CONSIDERABLE	ski part	TIP, HEEL, SOLE, GAMBER, SHOVEL
		ski resort	ALTA, ASPEN, WHISTLER
		ski term	INRUN, MOGUL,

PISTE, SCHUSS, SLALOM,
CHRISTY, KLISTER, VORLAGE,
PASSGANG, SITZMARK,
SNOWPLOW, TELEMARK
skid SLEW, SLIP, SLUE, VEER,
SLIDE, SIDESLIP
skid row SLUM, BOWERY
skid row character HOBO,
BEGGAR, VAGRANT,
DERELICT
skier HESS, KJUS, KILLY,
MAHRE, MAIER, TOMBA,
AAMODT, ACCOLA, GREENE,
PROELL, THOENI, WENZEL,
ALPHAND, SCHRANZ,
GOETSCHL, KOSTELIC,
STENMARK, WALLISER,
SCHNEIDER, ZURBRIGGEN
skiff DINGHY, ROWBOAT
skill ART, GIFT, CRAFT,
TALENT, FINESSE,
KNOWHOW, DEXTERITY,
EXPERTISE, PROFICIENCY
skilled ABLE, DEFT, ADEPT,
HANDY, ADROIT, EXPERT,
DEXTEROUS, ACCOMPLISHED
skillet SPIDER; see COOKING
skillful ABLE, DEFT, ADEPT,
ADROIT, DAEDAL, HABILE,
SCIENT
skim DART, FLIT, SCAN,
SCUD, SCUM, GLIDE,
BROWSE
skimp MEAGER, SCANTY,
SCRIMP, NEGLECT,
ECONOMIZE
skimpy MEAGER, SCANT,
FRUGAL, STINGY
skin FUR, BARK, COAT, FELL,
FLAY, HIDE, PELT, BLYPE,
BLEED, CUTIS, DERMA, SCREW,
STRIP, CORIUM, FLEECE,
LAMINA, PATINA, PLATING,
COVERING, EPIDERMIS
skin, pert. to DERMAL,
DERMIC, CUTANEOUS
skin-deep CURSORY,
SHALLOW, SUPERFICIAL
skin disease ACNE, ITCH,
YAWS, FAVUS, HIVES, LUPUS,
MANGE, PINTA, PSORA, SCALL,
SCURF, TINEA, TUMOR,
ULCER, ARAKIS, CANCER,
ECZEMA, HERPES, LICHEN,
TETTER, LEPROSY, PURPURA,
PRURIGO, SCABIES, SERPIGO,
IMPETIGO, MILIARIA,
RINGWORM, VITILIGO,
PSORIASIS, ERYSIPELAS

skin inflammation BOIL,
PAPULE, PIMPLE, PUSTULE,
SHINGLES, CARBUNCLE
skinflint MISER, PIKER,
NIGGARD, SCROOGE,
TIGHTWAD
skink ADDA, ADDU
skinless APELLOUS
skinny DIRT, LANK, LEAN,
SLIM, THIN, SCRAGGY,
SKELETAL, EMACIATED
skip DAP, FLIT, JUMP, OMIT,
CAPER, ELIDE, SALTO,
SPRING, ABSCOND, RICOCHET
skip school TIB, SKIP,
PLAYHOOKY
skipper RAIS, REIS, PILOT,
SAURY, MASTER, CAPTAIN
skirmish TILT; see FIGHT
skirt EDGE, JUPE, MIDI, MINI,
SAYA, AVOID, DODGE,
EVADE, JUPON, PARBU, TUNIC,
BASQUE, BORDER, FRINGE,
PANIER, PEPLUM, DIRNDL,
PANNIER, CRINOLINE,
HOOPSKIRT, OVERSKIRT,
PETTICOAT
skit JIBE, PLAY, CAPER,
NUMBER, PARODY, SKETCH
skitter RUN, SKIP, SCAMPER
skittish SHY, JUMPY, FICKLE,
JITTERY, NERVOUS, RESTIVE,
TIMOROUS, CHANGEABLE
skittle(s) PIN, BOWLS,
NINEPINS
skivvy UNDIES, UNDERWEAR
skulduggery TRICKERY
skulk LURK, PROWL, SLINK,
SNEAK
skull HEAD, SCAP, MAZARD,
SCONCE, CRANIUM
skull bone ZYGOMA,
MAXILLA, SPHENOID,
PARIETAL, OCCIPITAL
skull part INION, BREGMA,
GONION, LAMBDA, NASION,
CRANIUM, DACRYON,
PTERION, CALVARIA,
BRAINPAN
skull, pert. to INIAL, CRANIAL
skullcap COIF, BEANIE, PILEUS,
CALOTTE, CHECHIA,
YARMULKE, ZUCCHETTO
skunk TELEDU, POLECAT,
MEPHITIS
sky COPE, TIEN, AZUR, LANGI,
VAULT, WELKIN
sky pilot PADRE, PARSON,
PRIEST, CHAPLAIN

skylark	FROLIC, CAVORT
skylight	DORMER, ABATJOUR
skyline	HORIZON
skyrocket	SOAR, SHOOT(UP)
skyscraper	TOWER, HIGHRISE
slab	BAR, HUNK, CHUNK, DALLE, SLICE, STELE, TABLET
slack	LAX, DUFF, IDLE, LAZE, LULL, LOOSE, FLABBY, REMISS, RELAXED
slacken	EASE, ABATE, LETUP, RELAX, LOOSEN
slacker	SPIV, IDLER, LOAFER, TRUANT, LAGGARD, SHIRKER
slacks	PANTS, TROUSERS
slag	see DROSS, LAVA
slake	SATE, ALLAY, QUENCH, SATISFY
slam	PAN, RAP, BANG, BASH, SHUT, VOLE, POUND, BATTER
slammer	JAIL, CLINK, PRISON
slander	DIS, MUD, SLUR, DECRY, LIBEL, SMEAR, DEFAME, MALIGN, REVILE, ASPERSE, CALUMNY, ROORBACK
slang	CANT, JIVE, ARGOT, FLASH, LINGO, JARGON, PATOIS, DIALECT
slant	BIAS, ANGLE; see SLOPE
slanted, slanting	AWRY, SKEW, ASKEW, SKEWY, RAKISH
slap	HIT, RAP, BIFF, BLOW, CUFF, SNUB, SWAT, SMACK, INSULT
slap-happy	SILLY, FOOLISH
slapdash	HASTY, SLOPPY, CARELESS, SHIPSHOD
slapstick	COMEDY, HORSEPLAY, BURLESQUE
slash	CUT, DAB, JAG(G), GASH, HACK, SLIT
slat(s)	LATH, STAVE, STRIP, BATTEN, LOUVER, SPLINE
slate	TILE, DOCKET, LINEUP, TABLET, TICKET, CHOICE; see LIST
slattern	HUSSY, TRAMP, HARLOT, SLOVEN, TROLLOP
slaughter	KILL, ROUT, SLAY, MURDER, POGROM, CARNAGE, KILLING, BUTCHER(Y), GENOCIDE, MASSACRE
slaughterhouse	ABATTOIR, BUTCHERY, KNACKERY, SHAMBLES
Slav	POLE, SERB, SORB, WEND, CROAT, CZECH, VENED, BULGAR, SLOVAK
slave	ARDU, DASI, ESNE, ALIPIN, MAROON, THRALL; see BONDMAN
slave driver	MARTINET, TASKMASTER, SIMON LEGREE
slave trader	MANGO
slaver	SPIT, DROOL, DRIVEL, TRADER, SLOBBER, SALIVATE
slavery	TOIL, CHAINS, BONDAGE, DRUDGERY, CAPTIVITY
Slavic language	CZECH, POLISH, SLOVAC, RUSSIAN, SERBIAN, SLOVENE, SORBIAN, WENDISH, POLABIAN, BULGARIAN, KASHUBIAN, UKRAINIAN, MACEDONIAN, BYELORUSSIAN
slavish	BASE, MEAN, VILE, ABJECT, MENIAL, FAWNING, SERVILE
slay	DOIN, KILL, MURDER, BUTCHER, MASSACRE, ASSASSINATE
slayer	KILLER, ASSASSIN, MURDERER
sleazy	LOW, BASE, CHEAP, TAWDRY, TRASHY
sled	LUGE, PUNG, HURDLE, SLEDGE, SLEIGH, COASTER, TRAVOIS; see VEHICLE
sledge	CLUB, MAUL, SLED, HAMMER, MALLET, SLEIGH, TRAVOIS(E)
sleek	NEAT, SLICK, GLASSY, GLOSSY, SMOOTH, GROOMED
sleep	NAP, NOD, REM, DOSS, DOZE, WINK, SOPOR, DROWSE, SIESTA, SNOOZE
sleepaway	CAMP
sleeper	TIE, BEAM, TRAIN, AMTRAK, PULLMAN
sleeping car	PULLMAN
sleeping place	BED, COT, BUNK, CRIB, BERTH, FUTON
sleeping sickness	NAGANA
sleepiness	SOMNOLENCE
sleeping bag	SACK
sleeping pill	SECONAL, VERONAL, BARBITAL, GOOFBALL
sleeping sickness term	TSETSE, SURAMIN, TRYPANOSOME

sleepless   **WAKEFUL, RESTLESS, VIGILANT**
sleepwalker   **SOMNAMBULIST**
sleepy   **DOZY, DROWSY, LANGUID, OSCITANT, LETHARGIC, SOMNOLENT**
sleet   **ICE, HAIL, GRAUPEL**
sleeve   **ARM, GIGOT, DOLMAN, BUSHING**
sleeveless garment   **ABA, CAPE, VEST, CLOAK, MANTLE**
sleigh   *see* **SLED**
sleight   **FEINT, SKILL, TRICKERY**
sleight of hand   **MAGIC, TRICK(ERY), LEGERDEMAIN**
sleight-of-hand artist   **SHARPER**
slender   **LANK, LEAN, SLIM, THIN, LITHE, REEDY, SVELT, SLIGHT**
slenderize   **DIET, SLIM, REDUCE**
sleuth   *see* **DETECTIVE**
slew   **LOTS, SLUE, SPATE, SWAMP, SLOUGH**
slice   **CUT, CHIP, COLP, GASH, HUNK, SLAB, LAYER, PIECE, SHAVE, SLASH, CANTLE, COLLOP, FLITCH, RASHER, PORTION**
slick   **OILY, SLEEK, SUAVE, CLEVER, SMOOTH, SLIPPERY**
slicker   **DUDE, PONCHO, OILCOAT, SHARPER, RAINCOAT**
slide   **SKID, SLIP, SLUE, CHUTE, COAST, GLIDE, LAWINE, AVALANCHE**
slight   **CUT, SLIM, SLUR, SNUB, FAINT, SCANT, SPURN, PINTSIZE**
slightly   **JUST, HARDLY, SOMEWHAT**
slim   **THIN, SCANT, SMALL, SPARE, MEAGER, SLIGHT, SVELTE**
slime   **MUD, MIRE, MUCK, OOZE, FILTH, MOTHER, SLUDGE, SEDIMENT**
slimy   **EELY, GREASY, VISCID, VISCOUS**
sling   **CAST, HURL, FLING, PITCH**
sling mud at   **ASPERSE**
slingshot   **CATAPULT**
slink   **LURK, CREEP, PROWL, SKULK, SNEAK, STEAL**
slinky   **SHIFTY, SNEAKY, FURTIVE, SINUOUS, STEALTHY**

slip(s)   **ERR, BULL, DOCK, SKYT, BONER, LAPSE, ERROR, GAFFE, GLIDE, ELAPSE, ERRATA, CUTTING, FAUX PAS, SOLECISM**
slipcase   **FOREL, (SLIP)COVER**
slipper   **MULE, ROMEO, BOOTEE, BOOTIE, CRAKOW, JULIET, PINSON, CHINELA, CHINELE, CRAXOWE, BABOUCHE**
slippery   **SLY, EELY, SLIMY, SHIFTY, ELUSIVE**
slipshod   **MESSY, SLOPPY, CARELESS, SLOVENLY**
slip-up   **ERROR, BOOBOO, MISTAKE, OVERSIGHT**
slit   **CUT, CARF, FENT, GASH, CLEFT, SLASH, SLICE**
slither   **SLIP, CRAWL, CREEP, GLIDE, SLIDE, SLINK**
sliver   **SHARD, SLICE, SHAVING, SPLINTER**
slob   **PIG, CLOD, LUMMOX, SLOVEN**
slobber   **DROOL, DRIVEL, SLAVER, SALIVATE**
slog   **PLOD, SLUG, TOIL, DRUDGE**
slogan   **MAXIM, MOTTO, SHIBBOLETH**
sloop   **DRAY, SLED, CUTTER, LONGBOAT, SAILBOAT**
slop   **MUCK, SLIME, SLOSH, SLUSH, SWILL, WASTE, REFUSE, GARBAGE, SPATTER**
slope   **TIP, BANK, BRAE, CANT, RADE, KEEL, RAKE, RAMP, RISE, TILT, BEVEL, SCRAP, SPLAY, TALUS, ESCARP, GLACIS, VERSANT, GRADIENT**
sloping   **ASLAN, OBLIQUE, PITCHED, INCLINED**
sloppy   **MESSY, UNTIDY, CARELESS, SLIPSHOD**
slosh   **SLOP, SPILL, SPLASH**
slot   **CUT, TRACK, TRAIL, GROOVE, KEYWAY**
slot machine   **BANDIT**
slot machine coin   **SLUG**
sloth   **AI, UNAU, BHALU, TORPOR, INERTIA, INDOLENCE**
sloth genus   **BRUTA**
slouch   **SAG, HULK, DROOP, SLUMP, DROOP(ING)**
slough   **BOG, MIRE, MOLT, SHED, BAYOU, INLET, MARSH, SWAMP**

Slovak city/town   NITRA,
KOSICE, LEVICE, MARTIN,
POPRAD, PRESOV, ZILINA,
BARDEJOV, BRATISLAVA
Slovak language   SLOVAK,
HUNGARIAN
Slovak measure   LAN, SAH,
JITRO, KOREC, LATRO,
LOKET, STRYCH
Slovak money   CROWN,
DUCAT, HALER, HELLER,
KORUNA, HALIEROV
Slovak neighbor   POLAND,
HUNGARY, UKRAINE,
CZECH REPUBLIC
Slovak president   BENES,
MECIAR, MASARYK,
NOVOTNY, SVOBODA,
DZURINDA, SCHUSTER
Slovak river   UZ, HRON, IPEL,
HOMAD, NITRA, ORAVA,
SLANA, TOPLA, MORAVA,
POPRAD, LABOREC, TORYSA
Slovakia, capital of   BRATISLAVA
sloven   SLOB, CLART
Slovenia, capital of   LJUBLJANA
Slovenian city/town   PTUJ,
KRANJ, KRSKO, TRZIC,
MARIBOR, LJUBLJANA
Slovenian lake   BLED
Slovenian money   TOLAR,
STOTIN
Slovenian mountain   TRIGLAV
Slovenian neighbor   ITALY,
AUSTRIA, CROATIA,
HUNGARY
Slovenian river   MURA, SAVA,
SOCA, DRAVA
slovenly   DIRTY, MESSY,
FROWZY, SLOPPY, UNTIDY,
UNKEMPT
slow   DULL, POKY, LARGO,
LENTO, SLACK, TARDY,
ADAGIO, RETARD, ANDANTE,
SLUGGISH, LARGHETTO
slow-witted person   DOLT,
DOPE, DUMMY, DUNCE,
DIMWIT
slowpoke   SLOTH, SNAIL,
DAWDLER, LAGGARD,
STRAGGLER
sludge   MUD, MIRE, OOZE,
SLAG, FILTH, SLUSH,
SEWAGE, SEDIMENT
slug   HIT, BASH, BELT, BLOW,
SWAT, LIMAX, SNAIL, TOKEN,
BULLET, ELYSIA, GEOPHILA
sluggard   DRONE, IDLER,
LOAFER

sluggish   DULL, LOGY, POKY,
DOPEY, INERT, LEADEN,
TORPID, LETHARGIC,
PHLEGMATIC
sluice   SOW, CLOW, GATE,
GOUT, GOWT, FLUME,
SASSE, SEWER
slum   GHETTO, TENEMENT
slumber   NAP, DOZE, SLEEP,
REPOSE
slump   SAG, SINK, WANE,
DROOP, SPRAWL, DECLINE
slur   ELIDE, SMEAR, STAIN,
SULLY, INSULT, STIGMA,
AFFRONT, SLANDER,
INNUENDO, DISCREDIT
slush   MIRE, POSH, SLOSH,
SLEECH
slut   DOXY, JADE, SLOB,
BITCH, HUSSY, QUEAN,
TROLLOP, SLATTERN
sly   ARCH, FOXY, SLEE, WILY,
CAGEY, SLOAN, ARTFUL,
ASTUTE, CRAFTY, SHREWD,
CUNNING
smack   HIT, BLOW, BUSS, KISS,
SLAP, GUSTO, SAVOR, SMITE,
TASTE, WHACK, STRIKE,
THWACK
small   LIL, WEE, PUNY, SNUG,
TINY, DINKY, ELFIN, MICRO,
PETIT, PETTY, TEENY,
BANTAM, MINUTE, PETITE
small amount   DRAM, PINCH,
MODICUM; see BIT, JOT
small arm   RIFLE, PISTOL,
CARBINE, REVOLVER
small fry   KID, CHILD,
YOUNGSTER
small person   RUNT, DWARF,
PYGMY, BANTAM, MIDGET,
SHRIMP
small-minded   MEAN, PETTY,
NARROW, INTOLERANT
smallpox   VARIOLA,
VARICELLA
Smallville name   KENT
smaragd   EMERALD
smart   CHIC, KEEN, POSH,
TRIG, BRISK, NATTY, STING,
CLEVER, CRAFTY, DAPPER,
SPRUCE, CUNNING,
DASHING, INTELLIGENT
smart one   NERD, ALECK,
BRAIN
smash   HIT, DASH, PASH,
BREAK, CRUSH, WRECK,
SHATTER
smash, opp. of   LOB

smashup	CRASH, WRECK, ACCIDENT, COLLISION
smattering	TINGE
smear	DAUB, DEFAME, MALIGN, SMUDGE, SLANDER; *see* STAIN
smell	NOSE, SENSE, SNIFF, WHIFF, DETECT, INHALE; *see* ODOR
smelly	*see* FETID
smelter	BLAST, FORGE, FURNACE
smelting waste	SLAG, DROSS
Smetana work	MOLDAU, BARTERED BRIDE
smidgeon	BIT, TAD, IOTA, MITE
smile	BEAM, GRIN, FLEER, SMIRK, SIMPER
smirch	BLOT, DIRTY, SMEAR, STAIN, SULLY, BLOTCH, MALIGN, SMUDGE
smirk	GRIN, LEER, SNEER, SIMPER
smite	HIT, CUFF, STRIKE, AFFLICT
smith	MIME, FORGE(R), TINKER, VULCAN
smithereens	BITS, PIECES, FRAGMENTS
smithy	FORGE, STITHY, BLACKSMITH
smitten	TAKEN, IN LOVE, ENAMORED, STRICKEN, AFFLICTED
smock	APRON, FROCK, CAMISE, GABERDINE
smog	MIST, SOOT, SMAZE, POLLUTION
smoke	CURE, FLOC, FUME, LUNT, PUFF, REEK, SMOG, CIGAR, SMAZE, LIGHTUP, CIGARETTE
smokeless powder	FILITE, CORDITE
smoker	STAG, MIXER, PARTY
smokestack	FLUE, FUNNEL, CHIMNEY
smoky	HAZY, FUMED, REEKY, SOOTY, FUMOSE
smolder	BURN, FUME, SMOKE
smooch	PET, BUSS, KISS, PECK, MAKE OUT
smooth	EVEN, GLIB, IRON, LENE, SAND, GLOSS, GRIND, LEVEL, PREEN, SLEEK, SLICK, SUAVE, GLASSY
smorgasbord	BUFFET

smother	CHOKE, DEADEN, STIFLE, REPRESS, STRANGLE, SUFFOCATE
smudge	BLOT, DIRT, SLUR, SMEAR, STAIN, BLACKEN
smug	TRIM, SPRUCE, SNOBBISH, STUCKUP, SATISFIED, CONCEITED
smuggle	RUN, BOOTLEG
smuggler	GUNRUNNER, RUMRUNNER, BOOTLEGGER
smut	ROT, SOOT, DIRT, MUCK, PORN(O), FILTH, GRIME, FUNGUS, MILDEW, INDECENCY, OBSCENITY
smutty	LEWD, VULGAR, OBSCENE, INDECENT
snack	BITE, NOSH, OREO, BEVER, CANAPE, MORSEL, NACHOS, TIFFIN
snafu	MESS, CHAOS, MIXUP, FOULUP, SCREWUP
snag	TEAR, HITCH, TOOTH
snail	CONE, WILK, CONUS, DRILL, HELIX, MITRA, OLIVA, PHYSA, THAIS, TURBO, WHELK, CERION, DODMAN, NATICA, WINKLE, RISSOID, VALVATA, VERTIGO, VITRINA, DOGWHELK, EARSNAIL, GEOPHILA, JANTHINA, NERITINA, SOLARIUM, TOPSHELL, PERIWINKLE
snail genus	NERITA, LYMNAEA, PURPURA
snake	ASP, BOA, ADDER, COBRA, PYTHON, RATTLER, REPTILE, SERPENT, ANACONDA, OPHIDIAN, RATSNAKE, KINGSNAKE; *see p. 671*
snake genus	NAJA, ELAPS, BOIDAE, CAUSUS, NATRIX, COLUBER, OPHIDIA, BUNGARUS, COLUBRID, CROTALUS, ELAPIDAE, ELAPINAE, SERPENTES
snake, *pert. to*	OPHIC
snakebite aid	GUACO, CEDRON
snake-haired woman	*see* GORGON
snake-like	APODAL, ANGUINE, SINUOUS, COLUBRINE
snaky	WAVY, ANGUINE, SINUOUS, WINDING, SERPENTINE
snap	NIP, PEP, POP, BARK, BITE, DASH, HIKE, KNAP, BREAK, COOKY, CRACK, FLICK,

FILLIP, WAFER, SIMPLE, FASTENER, SINECURE
snap up **SNUP**
snapdragon **FIGWORT**
snapper **SESI, TAMURE**
snappish **EDGY, CROSS, TESTY, UNCIVIL**
snappy **CHIC, COLD, BRISK, JAZZY, SHARP, SMART, FLASHY, STYLISH**
snapshot **SHOT, PHOTO, PRINT, PICTURE, POLAROID**
snare **GIN, NET, WEB, LURE, TRAP, BENET, DECOY, SPRINGE**
snarl **GIRN, GNAR, GNARL, HURR, GNARR, GROWL, TANGLE**
snatch **GET, NAB, GRAB, JERK, EREPT, FILCH, SWIPE, WREST, CLUTCH, KIDNAP, PILFER**
sneak **LURK, SKULK, SLINK, STEAL, WEASEL**
sneer *see* **MOCK**
sneeze **SNUFF, KERCHOO, STERNUTATION**
sneezing, causing **ERRHINE, PTARMIC**
snicker **KNIFE, LAUGH, GIGGLE, TITTER**
snicker — **SNEE**
snide **SLY, MEAN, NASTY, MALICIOUS, SARCASTIC**
sniff **NOSE, SCENT, SMELL, SNORT, DETECT**
snifter **NIP, SIP, SHOT, INHALER**
snigger **LAUGH, GIGGLE, CHUCKLE, SNICKER**
snip **CUT, CLIP, PIECE, SHEAR**
sniper **SHOOTER, AMBUSHER, MARKSMAN**
snippy **CURT, GRUFF, SURLY, SNOTTY, BRUSQUE**
snit **STEW, PIQUE, TIZZY, DITHER**
snitch **PEACH, STEAL, SWIPE, INFORM, PILFER, SQUEAL**
snivel **CRY, SNIFF, WHINE, SNUFFLE, WHIMPER**
snob **PRIG, SNOOT, BRAHMIN, ELITIST, PARVENU**
snobbish **POTTY, SNOOTY, SNOTTY, UPPISH, UPPITY, SUPERIOR**
snood **NET, SNELL, FILLET**
snoop **PRY, LURK, PROWL, SKULK**
snootiness **AIRS, CONCEIT**

snooty **VAIN, STUFFY, SNOBBISH**
snooze **NAP, DOZE, SLEEP, CATNAP, SIESTA**
snore **RALE, SNIFF, WHEEZE, RHONCUS, SAW LOGS, STERTOR**
snoring **STERTOR**
snorkeling site **REEF**
snort **NIP, SNUR, DRINK, LAUGH, SNIFF, SNUFF**
snot **MUCUS, PHLEGM**
snotty **RUDE, SURLY, MUCOID, INSOLENT**
snout **NEB, BEAK, NOSE, SERRA, MUZZLE, PROBOSCIS**
snouted creature **HOG, PIG, TAPIR, DESMAN, ECHIDNA, ANTEATER, AARDVARK, ELEPHANT**
snow **SNA, FIRN, NEVE, PASH, SLEET, COCAINE**
snow house **IGLOO**
snow vehicle **SLED(GE), SLEIGH, SNOCAT, SNOWMOBILE**
snowbird **ADDICT**
snowstorm **BLIZZARD**
snow-white **CHASTE**
snowy **NIVAL, BRUMAL, NIVEOUS**
snub **CUT, SCORN, IGNORE, REBUFF, SLIGHT, AFFRONT**
snuff **PINCH, SNIFF, SNORT, WHIFF, RAPPEE**
snuff out **KILL, DOUSE, EXTINGUISH**
snuffbox bean **CACOON**
snug **COSY, COZY, TAUT, TRIG, WARM**
snuggle **HUG, CUDDLE, NESTLE**
so **SAE, SIC, ERGO, THUS, TRUE, VERY, HENCE**
so be it! **AMEN**
so long **CIAO, TATA, SEEYA, GOODBY(E)**
soak **BOX, HIT, RET, SOG, SOP, SOUSE, STEEP, FLEECE**
soap **SAPO, SUDS, AMOLE, CASTILE, DETERGENT**
Soap names **MARY, TATE, JESSICA, CAMPBELL**
soap vine **GOGO**
soapbox speaker **QUACK, ORATOR, RANTER, AGITATOR, DEMAGOGUE**
soapstone **TALC**
soapy **SOFT, FOAMY, SOAVE, SLIPPERY, UNCTUOUS, SAPONACEOUS**

soar   FLY, RISE, SAIL, GLIDE, TOWER, ASCEND

sob   CRY, BAWL, MOAN, SIGH, WAIL, WEEP, YOOP

sober   SANE, GRAVE, QUIET, STAID, FRUGAL, SEDATE, SOLEMN, SOMBER, SERIOUS, MODERATE, TEMPERATE

sobriety   GRAVITY, MODERATION, TEMPERANCE

sobriquet   ALIAS, AGNAME, COGNOMEN, NICKNAME

so-called   ALLEGED, SUPPOSED

soccer   FOOTBALL; see p. 714

soccer player   HAMM, PELE, AKERS, FOUDY, LILLY, CRUYFF, PUSKAS, YASHIN, EUSEBIO, PLATINI, CHARLTON

sociable   GENIAL, AFFABLE, FRIENDLY, GREGARIOUS

social   BEE, TEA, CIVIC, CIVIL, PARTY, SOIREE, CONVIVIAL

social climber   SNOB, ADVENTURER

social connection   IN, NETWORK

social insect   ANT, BEE, WASP, VESPID, TERMITE

Socialist   DEBS, MARX, OWEN, SHAW, CABET, ENGELS, JAURES, THOMAS, FOURIER, PROUDHON, SUN YATSEN, SAINTSIMON

socialite   JETSETTER

socialize   HOBNOB, MINGLE, FRATERNIZE

society   ELITE, GENTRY, FOUR HUNDRED; see ASSOCIATION

Society Islands   MOOREA, TAHITI, BORABORA; see LEEWARD, WINDWARD

Society of Friends founder   FOX

sock(s)   BOP, BOX, HIT, BLOW, HOSE, ANKLET, WALLOP, STOCKING

socket   PAN, JACK, CAVITY, FITTING, MORTISE

sockeye   SALMON

Socrates' method   MAIEUTIC(S)

Socrates' poison   HEMLOCK

Socrates' pupil   PLATO, PHAEDO

Socrates' wife   XANTIPPE

sod   DIRT, PEAT, TURF, EARTH, GLEBE, SWARD

soda   POP, FIZZ, SELTZER

sodden   WET, SOGGY, POACHY, SOAKED

Sodi relative   GADDIEL

sodium   SAL(T), SODA, NITER, NITRE, TRONA, NATRON

Sodom kingdom   BERA

sodomy   BUGGERY, PEDERASTY

sofa   COUCH, DIVAN, SQUAB, CANAPE, DAYBED, SETTEE, SETTLE, LOVESEAT, DAVENPORT, CHESTERFIELD

soft   LOW, EASY, NASH, NESH, WAXY, WEAK, PAPPY, SILKY, PIANO, GENTLE, MELLOW, PLIANT, TENDER, SUBDUED, VELVETY

soft drink   ADE, POP, COKE, COLA, SODA, PEPSI, SODA POP

soft fabric   SILK, PANNE, SATIN, VELVET, CASHMERE

soft shoulder   BERM(E)

soft touch   (EASY) MARK, SUCKER, PUSHOVER

soften   BATE, EASE, MELT, MUTE, RELAX, YIELD, LENIFY, MELLOW, RELENT, TEMPER, MOLLIFY, MITIGATE; see MELT

softener   ALOE

softly   PIANO, GENTLY, FAINTLY

softness   LAXITY, PLIANCY, LENIENCE, WEAKNESS, MELLOWNESS

soft-pedal   MUTE, MODERATE, PLAY DOWN, TONE DOWN

soft-soap   SNOW, CAJOLE, BLARNEY, FLATTER(Y)

soft-spoken   SUAVE, GENTLE, AFFABLE

softy   SISSY, WEAKLING

soggy   WET, SOAKED, SODDEN

Sohrab relative   see RUSTAM

soigne   NEAT, TIDY, STYLISH, WELL GROOMED

soil   SOD, LOAM, MARL, DIRTY, GOMBO, HUMUS, LOESS, STAIN, DEFILE, PEDOCAL

soiled   DIRTY, GRUBBY

soirée   FETE, PARTY

— soit qui mal y pense   HONI

sojourn   REST, STAY, ABIDE, TARRY, VISIT, STOPOVER

sojourner   LODGER, BOARDER

solace   CALM, ALLAY, CHEER, RELIEF, SOOTHE, ASSUAGE, COMFORT, CONSOLE

solar disk   ATEN, ATON

solar eclipse phenomenon CORONA

solar year/lunar year differential EPACT

solarium PORCH, PARLOR, SUNROOM

solder FUSE, WELD, BRAZE, PATCH, ROSIN

soldier GI, ERK, ROK, VET, GUGU, KERN, SWAD, ANZAC, ASKAR, CADET, CROAT, JAGER, KERNE, NIZAM, POILU, REDIF, SEPOY, TOMMY, UHLAN, ATKINS, GALOOT, JAEGER, LANCER, ZOUAVE, DOGFACE, JARHEAD, PANDOUR, SADSACK, BUCKSKIN, DOUGHBOY; see MERCENARY

soldier, kind of FOOT, CAVALRY, INFANTRY, MERCENARY

soldiers ARRAY, TROOPS, MILITIA, MILITARY, RESERVES, ARMEDFORCES

sole LONE, MERE, ONLY, VOLA, SLADE, SINGLE, UNIQUE, SOLITARY; see FLOUNDER

sole, of the PLANTAR

solecism SLIP, ERROR, GAFFE, LAPSE, BLUNDER, BARBARISM

solely ONLY, MERELY, EXCLUSIVELY

solemn GRAVE, FORMAL, SOMBER, SERIOUS

solemnity RITE, GRAVITY, SOBRIETY, FORMALITY, OBSERVANCE

solemnize OBSERVE, PERFORM, CELEBRATE

solicit ASK, BEG, BID, MUM, PLEA, TOUT, URGE, COURT, PLEAD, CANVASS

solicitation ENTREATY, PETITION, PERSUASION

solicitor LAWYER, ADVOCATE, ATTORNEY, BARRISTER

solicitous EAGER, ANXIOUS, HEEDFUL, CONCERNED

solicitude CARE, HEED, WORRY, ANXIETY, CONCERN

solid FIRM, HARD, DENSE, MASSY, COMPACT; see GEOMETRIC

solidarity UNION, UNITY, COHESION

solidify OSSIFY, PETRIFY; see CONGEAL

solidity DENSITY, FIRMNESS, STABILITY

solitaire KLONDIKE, CANFIELD, PATIENCE

solitary (A)LONE, SINGLE, REMOTE

solitude PRIVACY, ISOLATION, LONELINESS

solo ARIA, SONG, ALONE, SCENA, SINGLE, UNAIDED

Solomon SAGE, WISE MAN, WISEACRE

Solomon island group RUSSELL, SHORTLAND, SANTA CRUZ, NEW GEORGIA

Solomon Islands FLORIDA, MALAITA, RENNELL, CHOISEUL, GUADALCANAL

Solomon Islands, capital of HONIARA

Solomon Islands city/town AOLA, AUKI, GIZO, BUALA, MUNDA, TAKWA, SAHALU, MALANGO

Solomon relative AMNON, DAVID, ABSALOM, MENELIK, ADONIJAH, REHOBOAM, BATHSHEBA

Solomon temple rebuilder HIRAM

solon SAGE, SENATOR, WISE MAN, LAWGIVER, LEGISLATOR

soluble DISPERSIBLE

solution KEY, CLUE, ANSWER, COLLOID, MIXTURE

solution strength TITER, TITRE

solve DECODE, UNFOLD, UNRAVEL, WORKOUT, DECIPHER

solvent WATER, CUMENE, GLYCOL, KETONE, PHENOL, ACETONE, ALCOHOL, ANILINE, BENZENE, DIOXANE, LIGROIN, FURFURAL, GLYCEROL

Somalia, capital of MOGADISHU

Somalian city/town EYL, HOBYO, MARKA, BERBERA, XAAFUUN, KISMAAYO, MOGADISHU

Somalian leader BARRE, AIDEED, HASSAN

Somalian measure CABA, JARAT, TABAL, JUCRART

Somalian money BESA, SOMALO, SHILLING

Somalian neighbor KENYA, YEMEN, DJIBOUTI, ETHIOPIA

Somalian river **EYL, JUBBA,**
JACEYL, SHABEELLE
somber **DARK, DIRE, FUSC,**
MURKY, DISMAL, GLOOMY
some **ANY, ONE, ABOUT, A BIT**
OF, CERTAIN, VARIOUS
somersault **FLIP**
something **PART, VERY,**
MATTER, ANYTHING,
EXTREMELY
sometime **ONCE, ERST,**
FORMER, ONEDAY,
SOMEDAY, ERSTWHILE,
OCCASIONAL
sometimes **ATTIMES,**
NOWANDTHEN,
OCCASIONALLY
somewhat **FAIRLY, PARTLY,**
RATHER, SLIGHTLY
somewhere **ELSE, SOMEPLACE**
somnambulist **SLEEPWALKER**
somnolence **LETHARGY,**
DROWSINESS, SLEEPINESS
somnolent **DROWSY, SLEEPY**
son **BAR, MAC, FILS, FITZ,**
HEIR, CADET, SCION,
ABSALOM, DAUPHIN,
PROGENY
son of **IBN, MAC, FITZ**
sonant **VOICED, SOUNDING**
sonar **ASDIC**
sonata section **CODA, RECAP,**
RONDO, THEME, MINUET,
SCHERZO, EXPOSITION,
DEVELOPMENT,
RECAPITULATION
son-in-law **GENER**
song **AIR, LAY, ODE, UTA,**
ARIA, DITE, FADO, GLEE,
HYMN, LEED, LIED, MASS,
MELE, NOEL, PEAN, TUNE,
BAROL, BLUES, CHANT,
DERRY, DIRGE, DITTY, DOINA,
ELEGY, LYRIC, MATIN, MELOS,
MOTET, PAEAN, PSALM,
THEME, ANTHEM, ARIOSO,
AUBADE, BALLAD, CHANTY,
CHAUNT, CHORAL, LIEDER,
STROUD, CANCION,
CANTATA, CANZONE,
CHANCON, CHANSON,
CHANTEY, CHORALE,
DESCANT, LULLABY,
WASSAIL, ANTIPHON,
CANTICLE, CAVATINA,
CORONACH, FOLK SONG,
MADRIGAL, PART SONG,
SERENADE; *see p. 643*
— song **FORA**

song and — **DANCE**
songbird **JAY, TIT, LARK,**
WREN, MAVIS, PIPIT, ROBIN,
VIREO, SINGER, BABBLER,
CATBIRD, COWBIRD,
GRACKLE, SKYLARK,
TANAGER, WAXWING,
NUTHATCH, THRASHER,
TITMOUSE, VOCALIST;
see p. 675
songbird genus **LOXIA,**
ANTHUS, OSCINE, CAPELLA,
MIMIDAE
song, kind of **SWAN**
songlike **LYRIC, MELIC,**
ARIOSE, CANTABILE
Song of the South character
REMUS
songster, songstress *see* **SINGER**
sonority **TIMBRE, RESONANCE**
sonorous **LOUD, ROTUND,**
BOOMING, RINGING,
VIBRANT, RESONANT
sonship **FILIETY**
soon **ANON, ENOW, TITE,**
EARLY, BETIME, PRONTO,
ERELONG, SHORTLY,
PROMPTLY
sooner **ERE(R), RATHER,**
OKLAHOMAN
Sooner State **OK, OKLAHOMA**
soot **COOM, DIRT, SMUT,**
SOTE, COLLY, GRIME,
BISTER, CARBON,
LAMPBLACK
soothe **CALM, EASE, LULL,**
ALLAY, SALVE, APPEASE,
ASSUAGE, COMFORT,
MOLLIFY, PLACATE, RELIEVE
soothing **DULCIT, ANODYNE,**
LENITIVE
soothsayer **SPAER, AUSPEX,**
DIVINE, ORACLE, PYTHON,
PALMIST, (H)ARUSPEX; *see*
ORACLE
sooty **BLACK, DIRTY, GRIMY,**
PITCH, BLACKENED
sop **DIP, SOAK, BRIBE, STEEP,**
MORSEL, ABSORB, SOAK UP,
SPONGE
Sophie's Choice name **KLINE,**
NATHAN, STINGO, STREEP
sophism **FALLACY**
sophist **CASUIST**
sophisticate **SPOIL, DEBASE,**
CORRUPT, COSMOPOLITAN
sophisticated **HEP, HIP, BLASE,**
COMPLEX, REFINED,
WORLDLY, CULTURED

sophistication	CULTURE, FINESSE, BREEDING, ELEGANCE, REFINEMENT, WORLDLINESS	sortilege	LOT, PROPHECY, DIVINATION; see MAGIC
sophistry	FALLACY, CASUISTRY	sorts, out of	ILL, CROSS, INDISPOSED
Sophocles character	ELECTRA, OEDIPUS	so-so	FAIR, OKAY, POOR, MEDIUM, MEDIOCRE, MIDDLING, PASSABLE, TOLERABLE
Sophocles play	AJAX, ELECTRA, ANTIGONE, OEDIPUS REX	sot	LUSH, WINO, BLOAT, RUMMY, SOUSE, TOPER, TIPPLER, DRUNKARD
sophomoric	CALLOW, CHILDISH, IMMATURE	sotto voce	SOFTLY, FAINTLY
sopor	STUPOR, LETHARGY	soubrette	MAID, COQUETTE
soporific	DULL, SLEEPY, SEDATIVE	soufflé	MOUSSE, MERINGUE
sopping	WET, SOAKED, DRENCHED	sough	SIGH
soppy	MUSHY, MAWKISH, SENTIMENTAL	soul	BA, AME, ATMA, CORE, MIND, PITH, ANIMA, ATMAN, HEART, PRANA, PNEUMA, PSYCHE, SPIRIT, JIVATMA, ESSENCE
soprano	TREBLE; see SINGER		
sora	RAIL, CRAKE, ORTOLAN	— and soul	BODY, HEART
sorcerer	see WIZARD	soulful	DEEPFELT, EMOTIONAL
sorceress	USHA, CIRCE, LAMIA, SIREN, WITCH	sound	FIRM, HALE, NOTE, SAFE, TONE, TRIG, AUDIO, INLET, NOISE, PLUMB, PUGET, SOLID, VALID, YAMPI, FATHOM, STRAIT, HEALTHY, RELIABLE, NOOTKA
sorcery	MAGIC, ALCHEMY, THEURGY, WIZARDRY, WITCHCRAFT; see MAGIC		
sorcery term	COVEN, CRAFT, ESBAT, GROVE, FAMULUS	sound, make	HEAL
sordid	LOW, BASE, MEAN, POOR, VILE, DIRTY, SEAMY, SQUALID	sound off	SPEAK OUT, HOLD FORTH
		sound, pert. to	SONIC, SONANT
sordino	MUTE	sounding	SONANT, RESONANT, SONOROUS
sore	CUT, RAW, ACHY, BUBA, SAIR, ANGRY, IRKED, ULCER, VEXED, WOUND, ACHING, LESION, PAINED, GRIEVED, INFLAMED, SENSITIVE	sounding device	SONAR, SONDE
		soundless	MUTE, SILENT, ASONANT
sorehead	LOSER, GRIPER, GROUCH, SOURPUSS	soundly	FULLY, FIRMLY, SOLIDLY, THOROUGHLY
sorghum	DARI, DURR, MILO, KAFIR, SORGO, IMPHEE, KAFFIR, SORGHO; see GRAIN	soundproof	QUIET, ACOUSTIC
		soup	BISK, STEW, BROTH, GUMBO, PUREE, BISQUE, BURGOO, POTAGE, CHOWDER, POTTAGE, BOUILLON, CONSOMME
sorority	SODALITY, SISTERHOOD		
sorrow	RUE, WOE, DOLOR, LAMENT, REMORSE	soup base	STOCK
sorrowful	SAD, UNHAPPY, DEJECTED	soup garnish	CHEESE, CRACKER, CROUTON, PARSLEY
sorry	LOW, SAD, BASE, MEAN, POOR, PALTRY, TRIVIAL, CONTRITE, PENITENT, REGRETFUL	soup, kind of	PEA, BEAN, LEEK, ONION, POTATO, TOMATO, SPLITPEA, MINESTRONE, VICHYSSOISE
sort	ILK, CULL, KIND, SIFT, TYPE, GRADE, NATURE, TRIAGE, VARIETY, CLASSIFY	soupçon	BIT, HINT, TRACE, SUSPICION
sorter	GRADER, STAPLER	sour	WRY, ACID, TART, ACERB, ACRID, ACIDIC, BLEEZE, ACETOSE
sortie	RAID, DRIVE, FORAY, SALLY, ATTACK, OFFENSIVE		

source	FONT, ROOT, TEXT, WELL, CAUSE, FOUNT, ORIGIN, SPRING, AUTHORITY, DERIVATION
sourdine	MUTE
sourpuss	BEAR, CRAB, GROUCH, SOREHEAD
Sousa	MARCHKING
souse	DUCK, DUNK, SOAK, DRENCH, PICKLE, DRUNKARD
soused	DRUNK, TIPSY, LOADED
soutane	TUNIC, CASSOCK
South	SUR, DIXIE, AUSTER
So. Africa, capital of	CAPETOWN, PRETORIA, BLOEMFONTEIN
So. African	BOER, AFRIKANER
So. African city/town	KATHU, DURBAN, GEORGE, SOWETO, UMTATA, WELKOM, LIMPOPO, SESHEGO, TEMBISA, PIPETOWN, PRETORIA, CAPETOWN, JOHANNESBURG
So. African desert	KALAHARI
So. African language	AFRIKAANS; see BANTU
So. African leader	SMUTS, DONGES, DEKLERK, HERTZOG, MANDELA, VORSTER
So. African measure	MUID, MOREN, SCHEPEL
So. African money	CENT, POND, RAND, FLORIN, DAALDER
So. African mountain	KAMIES, BOKKEVELD
So. African political group	ANC, BSP, PAC, INKATHA
So. African river	SAND, VAAL, BLYDE, MOLOPO, ORANGE, TUGELA, CALEDON, SUNDAYS, OLIFANTS
So. America, highest point	ACONCAGUA
So. America, largest city	SAOPAULO
So. America, largest country	BRAZIL
So. America, largest island	TIERRA DEL FUEGO
So. America, largest lake	TITICACA
So. America, longest river	AMAZON
So. America, lowest point	SALINASCHICAS

So. America, smallest country	SURINAME
So. American leader	MIRANDA, SAN MARTIN
So. American tree	COCA, CUCA, MORA, TOLU, VERA, BALSA, CACAO, CAROB, CEBIL, CEIBO, COUMA, HEVEA, SORVA, TENIO, UMIRI, UMIRY, BOMBAX, ASSEGAI
So. American tribe	see p. 732
So. Carolina, So. Dakota	see also p. 615
So. Carolina city/town	YORK, AIKEN, UNION, CAMDEN, CONWAY, DILLON, MARION, SALUDA, SUMTER, GAFFNEY, LAURENS, BEAUFORT, COLUMBIA, FLORENCE, CHARLESTON, SPARTANBURG
So. Carolina Indian	KUSSO, SIOUX, SANTEE, CATAWBA, NATCHEZ, CHEROKEE, WACCAMAW, CHICKAMAUGA
So. Carolina island	BULL, CAPE, JOHNS, CAPERS, EDISTO, MORRIS, MURPHY, PARRIS, HUNTING, SEABROOK, HILTONHEAD
So. Carolina lake	MARION, MURRAY, WATEREE, MOULTRIE
So. Carolina river	BLACK, COOPER, EDISTO, ENOREE, LUMBER, PEEDEE, SALUDA, SANTEE, LYNCHES, TUGALOO, WATEREE, CONGAREE, COMBAHEE, SAVANNAH, CHATTOOGA
So. Dakota city/town	BISON, CLARK, HAYTI, HURON, LEOLA, MURDO, ONIDA, SALEM, SELBY, CUSTER, KADOKA, PIERRE, WINNER, YANKTON, RAPIDCITY, SIOUXFALLS
So. Dakota Indian	SIOUX
So. Dakota lake	OAHE, SHARPE, WAUBAY, PRESTON
So. Dakota river	GRAND, JAMES, WHITE, MOREAU, CHEYENNE, MISSOURI
South Pacific character	LIAT, CABLE, EMILE, PINZA, TOZZI, BRAZZI, GAYNOR, LUTHER, NELLIE, STEWPOT
So. Pacific island	FIJI, SAMOA, TONGA, TAHITI
South Pole	see ANTARCTICA

South Sea island **BALI, FUJI,
SULU, SAMOA, TONGA,
TAHITI, SOCIETY,
PITCAIRN**
south wind **NOTUS, AUSTER**
Southeastern Conference **LSU,
AUBURN, ALABAMA,
FLORIDA, GEORGIA, OLEMISS,
ARKANSAS, KENTUCKY,
TENNESSEE**
southerly, southern **AUSTRAL**
southern France **MIDI**
southpaw **LEFTY**
souvenir **TEE, RELIC, TSHIRT,
MEMENTO, KEEPSAKE**
sovereign **QUID, SKIV,
IMPERIAL;** see **MONARCH**
sovereignty **SWAY, EMPERY,
DYNASTY, DOMINION,
HOME RULE**
soviet **COUNCIL;** see **RUSSIAN**
Soviet president **STALIN,
KALININ, MIKOYAN,
BREZHNEV, PODGORNY,
GORBACHEV, KRUSHCHEV**
Soviet Union, former **CCCP,
USSR;** see **RUSSIA**
sow **SOO, SEED, PLANT,
SCATTER;** see **SWINE**
soybean product **MISO, SUFU,
TOFU, TAHO, TAUSI,
TOKUA, TAHURE**
spa **AIN, EMS, SPA, BATH,
FONT, BADEN, BILIN,
BUXTON, GEYSER, RESORT,
SPRING, BALNEUM,
THERMAE, CASTALIA,
SARATOGA**
space **GAP, LORA, LORE,
ROOM, VOID, AREOLA,
AREOLE, EXTENT, HIATUS,
METOPE, EXPANSE**
space, *pert. to* **SPATIAL**
spacecraft **MARS, APOLLO,
COSMOS, GEMINI, PROTON,
RANGER, SKYLAB, VENERA,
VIKING, MARINER,
MERCURY, PEGASUS, PIONEER,
PROGNOZ, SPUTNIK,
VOSKHOD, VOYAGER,
ELEKTRON, EXPLORER,
PROGRESS, SPACELAB,
SURVEYOR, VANGUARD,
FRIENDSHIP;** see **ROCKET,
SATELLITE;** see p. 742
spacecraft launch site
**(CAPE)KENNEDY,
(CAPE)CANAVERAL,
COSMODROME**

spaced out **HIGH, STONED,
ZONKED, DRUGGED**
spaceman see **ASTRONAUT**
spacious **VAST, LARGE,
ROOMY, CAPACIOUS,
COMMODIOUS**
spade **DIG, LOY, CARD, SPUD,
SHOVEL**
spaghetti see **PASTA**
Spain see also **SPANISH**
Spain, capital of **MADRID**
Spain, Spaniard **DIEGO,
IBERIA(N), CASTILIAN**
Spain, language of **BASQUE,
CATALAN, GALICIAN**
span **ARCH, PAIR, TEAM,
YOKE, BRIDGE**
Spanish cellist **CASALS**
Spanish city/town **JAEN, LEON,
LUGO, VIGO, AVILA, CADIZ,
GIJON, PALMA, BILBAO,
BURGOS, LERIDA, MADRID,
MALAGA, MERIDA, MURCIA,
TOLEDO, CORDOBA,
GRANADA, SEGOVIA, SEVILLE,
ALICANTE, PAMPLONA,
VALENCIA, BARCELONA,
SARAGOSSA, GUADALAJARA**
Spanish dance **JOTA, BAILE,
PAVIN, TANGO, BOLERO,
CANARY, CARIOCA,
CACHUCHA, FANDANGO,
FLAMENCO, GUARACHA**
Spanish dialect **ASTURIAN,
ARAGONESE, CASTILIAN,
ANDALUSIAN**
Spanish dish **OLLA, TAPAS,
PAELLA, BACALAO,
CHORIZO, GAZPACHO**
Spanish explorer **BALBOA,
CORTES, DESOTO,
CORONADO, MAGELLAN**
Spanish hero **(EL) CID**
Spanish island **IBIZA, LOBOS,
CANARY, GOMERA, HIERRO,
CABRERA, MAJORCA,
MINORCA, BALEARIC**
Spanish kingdom **LEON,
ARAGON, CASTILE**
Spanish leader **AZANA,
AMADEO, FRANCO, JOSEPH,
PHILIP, ZAMORA, ALFONSO,
CHARLES, ISABELLA,
FERDINAND**
Spanish measure **BUTT, CODO,
COPA, DEDO, MOYO, VARA,
ALMUD, BRAZA, CAHIZ,
LEGUA, LINEA, MEDIO, PALMO,
SESMA, ARROBA, CUARTA,**

Spanish money	ESTADO, FANEGA, RACION, YUGADA, CANTARA, CELEMIN, ESTADEL, PULGADA
Spanish money	DURO, EURO, PESO, REAL, PESETA, ALFONSO, CENTIMO, PISTOLE
Spanish mountain(s)	ASTURIAN, MULHACEN, PYRENEES, MONTSERRAT
Spanish painter	DALI, GOYA, MIRO, SERT, MURILLO, PICASSO, VELASQUEZ
Spanish possession	CEUTA, BIZA, PALMA, GOMERA, HIERRO, CABRERA, MAJORCA, MELILLA, TENERIFE
Spanish region	ARAGON, CASTILE, ASTURIAS, LAMANCHA, VALENCIA, ANDALUSIA, CATALONIA
Spanish river	EBRO, MINO, DUERO, JUCAR, TAGUS, SEGURA, GUADIANA, GUADALQUIVIR
Spanish title	DON, SRA, DONA, SRTA, SENOR, SENORA
Spanish weight	ONZA, LIBRA, MARCO, TOMIN, ADARME, ARROBA, DINERO, OCHAVA
Spanish words	*see p. 565*
Spanish writer	ALEMAN, ENCINO, IBANEZ, ALARCON, CERVANTES
Spanish-American War battle	SANTIAGO, MANILA BAY, SAN JUAN HILL
spank	SMACK, PADDLE, PUNISH
spanner	WRENCH
spar	BOX, BOOM, GAFF, MAST, YARD, SPRIT; *see* FIGHT
spare	BARE, BONY, LEAN, SAVE, THIN, EXTRA, GAUNT, EXCESS, LENTEN, MEAGER, SCANTY, RESERVE
spare parts	GASH
spare time	LEISURE, VACATION
sparing	FRUGAL, HUMANE, SAVING, THRIFTY, MERCIFUL, TOLERANT
spark	ARC, WOO, BEAU, COURT, GLEAM, LOVER, SWAIN, TRACE, KINDLE, SCINTILLA
spark producer	FLINT
sparkle	FLASH, GLEAM, GLISTEN, GLITTER, CORUSCATE
sparkle, make	AERATE
sparkling	FIZZY, BUBBLY, LIVELY, DAZZLING
sparrow	DONEY, CHIPPY, CHIPPIE, DUNNOCK, RICEBIRD
sparse	FEW, MEAGER, SCANTY, SCARCE
Sparta	LACEDAEMON
spartan	BOLD, BRAVE, HARSH, STERN, STOIC(AL), HEROIC, AUSTERE
Spartan magistrate	EPHOR
Spartan ruler	AGIS, LEDA, LEONIDAS, MENELAUS, TYNDAREUS
spasm	FIT, TIC, CRAMP, ICTUS, THROE, CHOREA, CLONUS
spasmodic	JERKY, FITFUL, ERRATIC, IRREGULAR
spasms, series of	CLONUS
spat	ROW, TIFF, GAITER, DISPUTE
spate	RASH, FLOOD, DELUGE, FRESHET, DOWNPOUR
spatial	AREAL, DIMENSIONAL
spatter	SPRAY, SPLASH, SPECKLE, SPRINKLE
spatula	KNIFE, TROWEL, BLUNGER, SPREADER
spawn	OVA, ROE, EGGS, REDD, BEGET, PRODUCE
spay	GELD, NEUTER, CASTRATE, STERILIZE
speak	SAY, LISP, TALK, DRAWL, ORATE, UTTER, VOICE, ARTICULATE
speak for	DEFEND, UPHOLD, TESTIFY
speak, inability to	ALALIA, MUTISM, APHASIA
speak out	ASSERT, PROTEST
speakeasy	DIVE, JOINT
speaker	AUDIO, ORATOR, RHETOR, TALKER, WOOFER, LOCUTOR, TWEETER
speaker of languages	LINGUIST, POLYGLOT
spear	GIG, DART, FRAM, GAFF, GORE, PIKE, ACLYS, BLADE, LANCE, ONCIN, PILUM, SHAFT, SHOOT, VOUGE, ATLATL, ERAMEA, GIDGEE, GLAIVE, PICKLE, PIERCE, ASSAGAI, ASSEGAI, BAYONET, BOURDON, HARPOON, JAVELIN, LEISTER, TRIDENT, VERUTUM, GAVELOCK

spear thrower **ATLATL, WOMERA**
spear-shaped **HASTATE**
special **RARE, KHASS, UNIQUE, UNUSUAL, DISTINCT, PECULIAR, PARTICULAR**
special person **ONER**
specialist **EXPERT, AUTHORITY**
specialize **CONFINE, RESTRICT, CONCENTRATE**
specialty **AREA, LINE, FIELD, FORTE, MAJOR, METIER, TALENT, FEATURE, APTITUDE, STRENGTH, CONCENTRATION**
specie **CASH, COIN, MONEY**
species **CASH, COIN, MONEY, CURRENCY; see CLASS**
specific **EXACT, PRECISE, CONCRETE, DEFINITE, EXPLICIT, PARTICULAR**
specifically **TO WIT, NAMELY, EXPRESSLY**
specify **CITE, NAME, DETAIL, ITEMIZE, STIPULATE, DESIGNATE**
specimen **MODEL, SLIDE, COTYPE, SAMPLE, SWATCH, SYNTYPE**
specious **SEEMING, APPARENT, DECEPTIVE, PLAUSIBLE**
specious reasoning **IDOLISM, SOPHISM, AMPHIBOLY, SYLLOGISM, NON SEQUITUR**
speck **BIT, DOT, FLAW, IOTA, MOTE, FLECK, PARTICLE**
speckle **DOT, SPOT, SPECK, DAPPLE**
spectacle **SHOW, BYSEN, DRAMA, SCENE, PARADE, DISPLAY, PAGEANT, EXTRAVAGANZA**
spectacles *see* **EYEGLASSES**
spectacular **AMAZING, IMPRESSIVE, BREATHTAKING**
spectator **VIEWER, WATCHER, BEHOLDER, OBSERVER, ONLOOKER**
Spectator founder **STEELE**
specter **AURA, BOG(E)Y, GHOST, SHADE, SPOOK, SPIRIT, SPRITE, WRAITH, EIDOLON, PHANTOM, APPARITION**
spectral **EERY, EERIE, SPOOKY, GHOSTLY, SUPERNATURAL**
spectrum **GAMUT, RANGE, COMPASS, RAINBOW**

speculate **RISK, GUESS, CHANCE, GAMBLE, THEORIZE, CONJECTURE**
speculative **IFFY, RISKY, CHANCY, PENSIVE, THEORETICAL, CONJECTURAL**
speculator **GUYER, GAMBLER, SCALPER, THEORIST**
— Spee **GRAF**
speech **LINE, TALK, SPIEL, SERMON, TONGUE, DIALECT, LECTURE, OENOMEL, ORATION, PARLANCE, DISCOURSE, SOLILOQUY, UTTERANCE, DECLAMATION**
speech art **ORATORY, RHETORIC**
speech organ **LARYNX, TONGUE, VOICEBOX, VOCAL CHORD**
speech, part of **NOUN, VERB, ADVERB, PRONOUN, ADJECTIVE, CONJUNCTION, INTERJECTION, PREPOSITION**
speech problem **LISP, ALALIA, ALEXIA, ALOGIA, APHASIA, STAMMER, STUTTER, LALLATION, IMPEDIMENT**
speech sound **LENIS, FORTIS, SONANT, CADENCE, PHONEME, ALLOPHONE**
speech therapy subject **LISP, APHASIA, STAMMER, STUTTER, DYSPHEMIA, TONGUETIE, CLUTTERING**
speechify **ORATE, DECLAIM**
speechless **MUM, DUMB, MUTE, SURD, APHASIC, APHEMIC, APHONIC, VOICELESS, TONGUETIED**
speed **FLY, HIE, RUN, ZIP, PACE, RACE, TEAR, HASTE, TEMPO, HASTEN, VELOCITY**
speed unit **VELO**
speedily **FAST, AMAIN, APACE, EXPRESS, POSTHASTE**
speedway **TRACK, RACECOURSE**
speedy **FAST, QUICK, RAPID, SWIFT, PROMPT, EXPRESS**
spell **HEX, JYNX, TERM, TURN, CHARM, SHIFT, STINT, PERIOD, HOODOO, TRANCE, INTERVAL, INTERLUDE**
spellbind **CHARM, ENCHANT, ENTRANCE, FASCINATE**
speller, bad **CACOGRAPHER**
spelling — **BEE**

spelunker's site CAVE
spend PAY, GIVE, LAVISH,
PAYOUT, DISBURSE,
DISPENSE
spendthrift WASTER,
ROUNDER, WASTREL,
PRODIGAL, SQUANDERER
Spenser character UNA,
GLORIANA
Spenser work COMPLAINTS,
FAERIEQUEEN
spent WORN, TIRED, EFFETE,
FAGGED, CONSUMED,
EXHAUSTED
sperm GERM, MILT, SEED,
SEMEN, POLLEN, CACHALOT
spew EMIT, EJECT, EXPEL,
ISSUE, RETCH, SPURT,
VOMIT, DISGORGE
sphere ORB, ARENA, FIELD,
GLOBE, ORBIT, SCOPE,
DOMAIN, PLANET, RONDULE,
PROVINCE
spherical ROUND, ROTUND,
GLOBATE, GLOBOID,
GLOBOSE, GLOBOUS,
GLOBULAR
Sphinx ENIGMA, HAWKMOTH
Sphinx composition MAN, RAM,
HAWK, LION
Sphinx site GIZA, THEBES
spice DASH, MACE, MULL,
TANG, CLOVE, CUBEB,
GUSTO, CASSIA, NUTMEG,
SEASON, STACTE, ALLSPICE;
see HERB, SEASONING,
CONDIMENT
spice ball FAG(G)OT
Spice Girl BABY, EMMA, GERI,
POSH, GINGER, SPORTY,
MELANIE, VICTORIA
Spice Islands see MOLUCCAS
spick-and-span MINT, NEAT,
TRIM, CLEAN
spicule TOXA, OXEA, ACTINE
spicy RACY, FIERY, RISQUE,
PUNGENT, AROMATIC
spider COP, TRIVET, GRIDDLE,
SKILLET, ARACHNID
spider fluid ARANEIN
spider genus LYCOSA,
ARGIOPE, ATTIDAE,
PHOLCUS, ARANEIDA,
ULOBORUS
spiders ARAIN, ATTID,
ARRAND, KATIPO, MYGALE,
ARANEID, LYCOSID, MYGAUD,
PHOLCID, PHRYNID,
ATTERCOP, ETTERCAP,

LONGLEGS, ORBITELE,
SOLIFUGE, SOLPUGID,
THOMISID, ULOBORID,
WANDERER, TARANTULA,
BLACK WIDOW
spiel LINE, PITCH
spiffy NEAT, NIFTY, SMART,
CLASSY, CLEVER, SPRUCE
spigot PLUG, SPILE;
see FAUCET
spike DAG, EAR, GAD, BROB,
CHOB, LACE, TINE, SPICA,
ANTLER, IMPALE
spiked TINED, SPICATE
spile TAP, BUNG, PLUG,
SPOUT, SPIGOT
spill PEG, PIN, ROD, FALL,
PLUG, SHED, SLOP, TUMBLE,
OVERFLOW
Spillane hero MIKE HAMMER
spin BIRL, EDDY, REEL, RIDE,
TWIRL, WHIRL, ROTATE
Spin City names FOX, NIKKI,
SHEEN, STACEY, CAITLIN,
MICHAEL, CHARLIE, RANDALL,
FLAHERTY, LOCKLEAR
spinach ORACH, GREENS,
ORACHE
spinal RACHIAL, RACHIDIAN
spinal cord MYELON
spinal cord inflammation
MYELITIS, RACHITIS
spinal cord marrow NUCHA
spindle COP, AXIS, AXLE, HASP,
ARBOR, QUILL, MANDREL
spine AXIS, AXON, SETA,
ARETE, CHINE, QUILL,
THORN, CHAETA, NEEDLE,
RACHIS, VERTEBRA
spineless LIMP, WEAK, TIMID,
FEEBLE, LIMBER, COWARDLY,
FLEXIBLE, INVERTEBRATE
spinet PIANO, UPRIGHT,
VIRGINAL, HARPSICHORD
spine-tingling EERY, EERIE,
SCARY, CHILLING
spinning machine MULE,
JENNY, CHARK(H)A,
THROSTLE
spinning term FLYER, WHORL,
BOBBIN, ROVING, WHARVE,
DISTAFF, SPINDLE, TREADLE,
TRAVELER
spinning wheel inventor SPEYER
spinster MAIDEN, VIRGIN,
(OLD) MAID, BACHELORETTE
spiny HISPID, THORNY,
PRICKLY, SPINOSE,
ACICULAR, ACANTHOID

spiracle   AIRHOLE, BLOWHOLE
spiral(s)   HELIX, VOLUTE,
HELICAL, HELICES,
HELICOID, SCROLLED
spire   APEX, PEAK, CROWN,
SHAFT, STALK, FLECHE,
STEEPLE; see TOWER
spirit   AKH, FAY, JIN, BOKO,
ELAN, JINN, KUEI, SOUL,
ZEMI, AGIEL, ARIEL, DEMON,
DEVIL, GEIST, GENIE, GENII,
HUACA, JINNI, RELPY, LARES,
METAL, DAEMON, ELIXIR,
ESPRIT, JINNEE, KELPIE,
MANITO, MORALE, UNDINE,
YAKSHA, BANSHEE, KATCINA,
LEMURES, MANITOU; see
GHOST
spirited   EAGER, LUSTY,
LIVELY, SPUNKY
spiritless   COLD, DEAD, DULL,
DEJECTED, LIFELESS,
LISTLESS
spirits   MOOD, HUMOR; see
LIQUOR
spiritual   HOLY, SACRED,
RELIGIOUS, SUPERNATURAL
spiritual, opp. of   BODILY,
MUNDANE, CORPOREAL
spiritualism   WICCA,
OCCULTISM
spit   EMIT, HISS, RAIN, SHOAL,
AMBEER, IMPALE, PIERCE,
SALIVA, SKEWER,
EXPECTORATE
spithall   WAD, SINKER, SLIDER
spite   VENOM, GRUDGE,
MALICE, RANCOR, SPLEEN
spiteful   CATTY, HATEFUL,
HOSTILE, RANCOROUS,
VINDICTIVE
spitfire   VIRAGO, HELLCAT,
HOTHEAD
spitting image   TWIN, DOUBLE,
(DEAD) RINGER
spittle   SALIVA
spittoon   CUSPIDOR
splash   LAP, DAUB, PURL,
SWASH, SPARGE, SP(L)ATTER
splashy   SHOWY, BLASHY,
STRIKING, SENSATIONAL
splatter   DASH, SPLASH,
SPRINKLE
splay   EXPAND, EXTEND,
SPREAD, UNFOLD,
DISLOCATE
spleen   IRE, GALL, MILT,
ANGER, SPITE, MALICE,
MELANCHOLY

splendid   FINE, GRAND,
AUREATE, DAZZLING,
MAGNIFICENT
splendor   POMP, ECLAT, SHEEN,
LUSTER, GRANDEUR,
BRILLIANCE
splenetic   EDGY, TESTY,
CHOLERIC, PETULANT
splenic   MILTY, LIENAL
splice   WED, JOIN(T), UNITE
splint   CAST, LATH, SLAT,
BRACE, SUPPORT
splinter   SHARD, SPILL, SHIVER,
SLIVER, FLINDER, FRAGMENT
split   DUNT, TEAR, RIFT,
BURST, LEAVE, PEACH,
CLEAVE, DEPART, SCHISM,
SQUEAL; see SUNDER
split hairs   CAVIL, QUIBBLE
splotch   BLOT, STAIN, SPLASH
splurge   SPEND, SPLASH
spoil(s)   MAR, PET, ROT, LOOT,
MARD, SOUR, UNDO, BOOTY,
BOTCH, DECAY, TAINT,
CODDLE
spoiled   BAD, SOUR, MOLDY,
MUSTY, ROTTEN, CODDLED,
HUMORED, PAMPERED
spoils   LOOT, BOOTY, PRIZE,
TROPHY, PLUNDER
spoilsport   KILLJOY, SOURPUSS,
WET BLANKET
spoke   PIN, RUNG, RADIUS,
RUNDEL
spoked   RADIAL
spoken   ORAL, ALOUD, VOCAL,
PAROL(E), VIVAVOCE
spokesperson   AGENT, PROXY,
VOICE, MOUTHPIECE
spoliate   ROB, RAVAGE,
DESPOIL, DESTROY,
PLUNDER
sponge   BUM, MUMP, SOAK,
SWAB, ASCON, CADGE,
ERASE, MOOCH(ER), ASCULA,
LEUCON, BLOTTER,
DEADBEAT, PARASITE
sponge spicule   OXEA, TOXA,
ACTINE
spongy   POROUS, ELASTIC,
SQUISHY, ABSORBENT
sponsor   ANGEL, BACKER,
PATRON, SURETY,
BIGDADDY, GODFATHER
sponsorship   (A)EGIS, BACKING,
AUSPICES
spontaneous   FREE,
IMPROMPTU, IMPULSIVE,
VOLUNTARY

spoof	FOOL, HOAX, JOKE, PUTON, PARODY, LAMPOON, TRAVESTY	spot	JAM, PIP, ESPY, FLAW, SMUT, MACLE, NEVUS, PINCH, DETECT, MACULA, SMUTCH, TILAXA, OCELLI, OCELLUS, TROUBLE
spook	SPY, GHOST, SCARE, SPECTRE, STARTLE		
spooky	EERIE, WEIRD, UNCANNY, SPECTRAL	spotless	PURE, CLEAN, LOOSE, CHASTE, IMPECCABLE, IMMACULATE
spool	COP, PIRN, (UN)REEL, WHORL, BOBBIN, WHARVE		
		spotlight	BEAM, FOCUS, BEACON, ADVERTISE, EMPHASIZE, LIMELIGHT
spoon	DIP, PET, KISS, NECK, LADLE, SCOOP		
spoon out	DOLE, METE	spotted	PIED, PINTO, MACLED, NOTATE, DAPPLED, PIEBALD, SKEWBALD
spoon-fed	CODDLED, PAMPERED		
spoonful	DOSE, DOLLOP	spotty	PATCHY, UNEVEN
spoor	TRACE, TRACK, TRAIL	spousal	NUPTIAL, WEDLOCK, MATRIMONIAL
Sporades island	COO, CASO, LERO, SIMI, CHIOS, LIPSO, PATMO, SAMOS, TILOS, CALCHI, CALINO, IKARIA, LESBOS, NISIRO, SKYROS, SKIATHOS, SKOPELOS, SCARPANTO, ILIODHROMIA		
		spouse	MATE, CONSORT, PARTNER, see HUSBAND, WIFE
		spout	JET, GUSH, SPILE, FAUCET, NOZZLE
		sprain	PULL, TEAR, TWIST, WRICK, WRENCH
sporadic	FITFUL, DESULTORY, IRREGULAR, OCCASIONAL	sprawl	LIE, LOLL, CRAWL, LOUNGE, SLOUCH, SPREAD
spore(s)	GERM, SEED, SORI, SORUX, ZYGOTE	spray	FOAM, MIST, SCUD, SURF, TWIG, SPRIG, SPUME, LIPPER, ATOMIZE, NEBULIZE
spore case(s)	ASCI, ASCUS, THECA		
spore fruit	AECIA, TELIA, AECIUM, TELIUM	spread	FAN, TED, MEAL, OLEO, BRUIT, FEAST, RANCH, RIVET, SCOPE, STREW, DEPLOY, GOSSIP, NORATE, BANQUET, STRETCH
sporran	PURSE, POUCH		
sport	RUX, ROMP, WEAR, FROLIC, GAMBOL, PASTIME		
		spread out	FAN, FLARE, DEPLOY, DIFFUSE
sport field	GRID, OVAL, RINK, COURT, GREEN, LINKS, TRACK, COURSE, GROUND, DIAMOND, GRIDIRON; see ARENA	spree	BAT, JAG, BOUT, BUST, LARK, TOOT, BINGE, DRUNK, BENDER, FROLIC, CAROUSAL
		sprig	BRAD, HEIR, TWIG, SCION
sporting	FAIR, ATHLETIC, GAMBLING	sprightly	TID, PERT, AGILE, ALERT, BRISK, PEART, BLITHE
sporting event	BOUT, HUNT, RACE, MEET, MATCH, CONTEST	spring(s)	BOLT, COIL, JUMP, KELD, LEAP, SEEP, STEM, (A)RISE, BOUND, VAULT, RECOIL, RESILE, BOUNCE, ORIGIN, EMANATE; see SPA
sportive	GAT, MERRY, FRISKY, PLAYFUL, PRANKISH		
sports	see p. 702		
sportscaster	HILL, GOWDY, HEARN, GUMBEL, HODGES, MADDEN, SCULLY, COSELL, GIFFORD, DIERDORF, BRADSHAW, MICHAELS, MUSBURGER	spring, pert. to	FONTAL, VERNAL
		springboard	BATULE
		springlike	VERNAL
		springe	TRAP, SNARE
		springy	BOUNCY, ELASTIC, FLEXIBLE, RUBBERY
sportsman	HUNTER, GAMBLER, SHIKARI		
sportsmanship	FAIRNESS	sprinkle	DEG, SOW, SPRAY, MOTTLE, SPARGE, DREDGE, SCATTER
sporty	FAST, SHOWY, CASUAL, DRESSY, FLASHY, SNAZZY		

sprinkling	SEME, ASPERGES, ASPERSION
sprint	RUN, ZIP, DASH, RACE, RUSH, SPEED
sprinter	RACER, ATHLETE
sprite	see ELF, SPIRIT
sprout	BUD, CHIT, GROW, SCION, SHOOT, BURGEON, SAPLING, GERMINATE
spruce	AYAN, TRIG, TRIM, NATTY, PICEA, YEDDO, DAPPER
spry	AGILE, BRISK, QUICK, ACTIVE, LIVELY, NIMBLE
spud	TATER, POTATO
— spumante	ASTI
spume	FOAM, SCUM, FROTH
spun	WOVEN
spunk	GRIT, PUNK, PLUCK, SPARK, METTLE, COURAGE; see TINDER
spunky	GAME, BRAVE, TESTY, PLUCKY, SPIRITED
spur	GAFF, GOAD, URGE, ERGOT, PRICK, ROWEL, CALCAR, GRIFFE, INCITE
spurious	FAKE, FAKY, BOGUS, FALSE, PHONY
spurn	KICK, FLOUT, SCORN, REFUSE, REJECT
spurt	JET, GUSH, BURST, SPRAY, SQUIRT
sputter	SPEW, SPIT, BLURT, BABBLE, JABBER
sputum	SALIVA, SPIT(TLE)
spy	KEEK, KYKE, PEEK, PEER, AGENT, PINTO, SCOUT, SNOOP, INFORMER, OPERATIVE
spy, famous	ABEL, BOND, GOLD, HALE, (MATA)HARI, ANDRE, FUCHS, ARNOLD, CAVELL, SMILEY, SOBELL, ROSENBERG
spy org.	CIA, KGB, OSS, MOSSAD
squabble	ROW, SPAT, BICKER, HASSLE, DISPUTE, QUARREL
squad	BAND, CREW, TEAM, UNIT, PATROL, PLATOON
squadron	FLEET, ARMADA, FLOTILLA, ESCADRILLE
squalid	DIRTY, SEEDY, MANGY, NASTY, FILTHY, SORDID
squall	CRY, BAWL, GALE, GUST, WAIL; see WIND
squalor	DIRT, FILTH, MISERY, POVERTY
squama	ALULA, TEGULA, CALYPTER
squander	SPEND, WASTE, MISUSE, DISSIPATE
square	BOXY, EVEN, FAIR, FORUM, PLAZA, TALLY, COMMON, PIAZZA, STRAIGHT, RECTANGLE
— and square	FAIR
square dance	REEL, HOEDOWN, QUADRILLE
squash	PEPO, CRUSH, QUELL, CUSHAW, CYMLING, FLATTEN, PUMPKIN, SCALLOP, SQUELCH, ZUCCHINI
squat	DUMPY, FUBSY, PUDGY, CROUCH
squatter	CATCHER, SETTLER
squaw	WIFE, WOMAN, MAHALA, MAHALY
squawk	CRY, CALL, KICK, GRIPE, GROUSE, OBJECT, SCREAM, GRUMBLE, PROTEST, COMPLAIN
squeak	CRY, PEEP, CHEEP, CREAK, SQUEAL
squeal	CRY, BLAB, SING, PEACH, RAT (ON), INFORM, TATTLE, TELL ON
squeamish	HELO(E), QUEASY, FINICAL, NERVOUS, SKITTISH
squeeze	EKE, HUG, CRAM, CRUSH, WRING, EXACT, EXTORT, EXTRACT
squelch	KIBOSH, STEPON, STIFLE, THWART, SILENCE, SUPPRESS
squib	BLURB, COWARD, LAMPOON, SARCASM, FIREWORK
squid	CALAMAR, INKFISH, CALAMARY
squiggle	MARK, CURVE, DOODLE, GIGGLE, SCRAWL
squint	PEEK, PEER, BLINK
squire	BEAU, DONZEL, ESCORT, ARMIGER, GALLANT, CHAPERON, HENCHMAN, ATTENDANT
squirm	WORM, TWIST, WIGGLE, WRITHE, WRIGGLE
squirrel(-like rodent)	BUN, SCUG, BOBAC(K), SISEL, XERUS, BEAVER, CHIPPY, GOPHER, MARMOT, SUSLIK, TAGUAN, TALPID, ASSAPAN, CHIPPIE
squirrel genus	XERUS, TAMIAS

squirt **KID, TOT;** *see* **SPURT**
Sri Lanka, formerly **CEYLON**
Sri Lanka, capital of **COLOMBO**
Sri Lankan city/town **YALA,**
GALLE, KANDY, KOTTE,
MUTUR, JAFFNA, AMPARA,
BADULLA, COLOMBO,
NEGOMBO, DEHIWALA,
MORATUWA
Sri Lankan language **TAMIL,**
SINHALA
Sri Lankan measure **PARAH,**
AMUNAM
Sri Lankan money **CENT,**
TANG, RUPEE
Sri Lankan mountain **KNUCKLES**
Sri Lankan native **TODA,**
VEDDA(H)
Sri Lankan peninsula **JAFFNA**
Sri Lankan river **GAL, GIN,**
YAN, ARUW, KALA, MAHA,
DEDURU, MAHAWELI
S-shaped **SIGMATE, SIGMOLD**
stab **GORE, PINK, IMPALE,**
PIERCE, SKEWER,
THRUST
stability **FIRMNESS, SOLIDITY,**
CONSTANCY, PERMANENCE
stabilizer **GYRO, BALLAST**
stable **MEW, BARN, BYRE,**
FAST, FIRM, MEWS, SOLID,
STALL, SECURE, STEADY,
PADDOCK, CONSTANT
stable scene **CRECHE**
stableboy **MAFU**
stableman **GROOM, AVENER,**
OSTLER, CURRIER, HOSTLER
staccato, *opp. of* **LEGATO**
stack **FIX, MOW, FLUE, PILE,**
RICK, MOUND, CHIMNEY,
SCINTLE
stack, blow one's **ANGER, LOSE**
IT, FLARE UP
stacked **CURVACEOUS,**
VOLUPTUOUS
stadium **STANDS;** *see* **ARENA**
staff **ROD, MACE, ANKUS,**
BATON, CROOK, PEDUM,
SQUAD, VERGE, BASTON,
CUDGEL, CROSIER, RETINUE,
SCEPTER, THYRSUS,
CADUCEUS
staff of life **BREAD**
stag **BUCK, DEER, HART,**
MALE, POLLARD; *see* **DEER**
stage **DAIS, PHASE, DEGREE,**
PRESENT, PRODUCE,
ROSTRUM, PLATFORM,
SCAFFOLD; *see* **THEATER**

stage direction **EXIT, ASIDE,**
ENTER, MANET, EXEUNT,
SENNET
stage, early **GETGO, ONSET**
stage equipment **RAG, TAB,**
DROP, FLAT, FOOT, OLEO,
PROP, SPOT, CLOTH, FLOAT,
TEASER, CURTAIN, FLIPPER
stage names *see p. 557*
stage part **DOCK, GRID, LOFT,**
WING, APRON, FLIES, SKENE,
BOARDS, BRIDGE, SKENAI,
PAREDUS, RETURNS,
COULISSE, GRIDIRON,
PLATFORM, PROSCENIUM
stage whisper **ASIDE**
stagecoach **RIG, CONCORD,**
CONESTOGA
stagehand **GRIP, CHIPS, FLY**
MAN, GAFFER, JUICER, PIT
MAN, BEST BOY, CALL BOY,
SCENIST
stagger **REEL, STOT, SWAY,**
LURCH, FALTER, TOTTER,
WAMBLE, FLOUNDER,
ALTERNATE
staggering **AREE, STUNNING,**
ASTONISHING
stagnant **DEAD, DULL, INERT,**
STATIC, TORPID, DORMANT,
LISTLESS, SLUGGISH,
STATIONARY
stagnate **IDLE, FESTER,**
LANGUISH, VEGETATE
stagnation **STASIS**
stagy **AFFECTED,**
THEATRICAL,
MELODRAMATIC
staid **SOBER, SEDATE, STEADY**
stain **DYE, BLOT, SPOT, TINT,**
TASH, SULLY, TAINT,
SMIRCH, SMUDGE, SMUTCH,
STIGMA, BLEMISH, TARNISH,
DISHONOR, SAFRANIN
stair **STEP, STILE, TREAD**
stair term **RUN, POST, RISE,**
NEWEL, RISER, TREAD,
FLIGHT, NOSING, RUNDLE,
LANDING, RAILING,
BALUSTRADE
staircase **GRECE, FLIGHT,**
PERRON, STAIRS
stake **PEL, POT, ANTE, PALE,**
POST, CLAIM, SPILE, WAGER,
GAMBLE, IMPONE, PALING,
PICKET, FINANCE, INTEREST,
PALISADE
stakelike **PALAR**
stakeout **VIGIL, SURVEILLANCE**

stalag inmate	POW, PRISONER
stale	DRAB, DULL, BANAL, FUSTY, MUSTY, PASSE, TIRED, TRITE, EFFETE, RANCID, STAGNANT
stalemate	TIE, DRAW, PATT, IMPASSE, DEADLOCK, STANDOFF
Stalin daughter	SVETLANA, ALLILUYEVA
Stalinabad	DUSHANBE
stalk(s)	CULM, STEM, CHASE, SCAPE, STIPE, TRACK, CAULIS, FOLLOW, PURSUE, RATOON, PEDICEL, PEDICLE, PETIOLE
stall	PEW, CRIB, LOGE, QUIT, STOG, BERTH, BOOTH, CHOKE, DELAY, FLOOD, NICHE, HAMPER, HINDER, STABLE, CUBICLE
stallion	STUD, STEED, ENTIRE, MORGAN
Stallone nickname	SLY
stalwart	BOLD, BRAVE, TOUGH, ROBUST, STRONG, GALLANT, RESOLUTE, STEADFAST
stamen	STALK, ANTHER
stamina	GRIT, PLUCK, STRENGTH, ENDURANCE
stammer	ER, HAW, HEM, HALT, PAUSE, FAFFLE, FALTER, STUTTER
stamp	DIE, CHOP, SEAL, BRAND, SIGIL, CACHET, EMBOSS, PESTLE, IMPRINT
stamp alternative	METER
stamp out	CRUCH, ELIMINATE, ANNIHILATE
stampede	BOLT, DASH, ROUT, RUSH, PANIC, CHARGE, FLIGHT, RAMPAGE
stance	AIR, POSE, BEARING, POSTURE, POSITION
stanch	DAM, FIRM, LEAL, STEM, STOP, CHECK, QUELL, SUPPRESS
stanchion	BAR, PROP, STAY, SUPPORT
stand	BASE, RISE, ZARF, ABIDE, BOOTH, EASEL, STALL, CASTER, ENDURE, TEAPOY, TRIPOD, TRIVET, PODIUM, TABORET
stand by	BACK, WAIT, DEFEND, SUPPORT, MAINTAIN

stand for	MEAN, TAKE, BROOK, DENOTE, TOLERATE, REPRESENT
stand out	GLARE, ENDURE, OUTLAST, PROJECT
standard	PAR, NORM, TOUG, TYPE, UTUG, CANON, IDEAL, MODEL, NORMA, TITER, LABARUM; see FLAG
standardize	CALIBRATE, NORMALIZE
standby	COVER, STAPLE, MAINSTAY, ALTERNATE
standee	STRAPHANGER
stand-in	COVER, DEPUTY, SURROGATE, SUBSTITUTE
standing	RANK, ERECT, RATING, REPUTE, STATIC, STATUS, PRESTIGE
standoff	TIE, DRAW, IMPASSE, DEADLOCK, STALEMATE
standoffish	COOL, ALOOF, DISTANT, RESERVED, WITHDRAWN
standout	BEST, ONER, LEADER
standpoint	VIEW(POINT), OPINION, PERSPECTIVE
standstill	HALT, STOP, IMPASSE, DEADLOCK, CESSATION
stanza	STEV, ENVOY, STAVE, ALCAIC, DISTICH, STROPHE, RUBAIYAT
stanza type	OCTAVE, SESTET, SEXTAIN, TRIOLET, OCTONARY, QUATRAIN, HEXASTICH, HEPTASTICH, TETRASTICH
staple	LOCK, TOWN, TUBE, FIBER, STOCK, PILLAR, COMMODITY, NECESSITY
star	ACE, COR, NOVA, ASTER, CELEB, MACHO, ETOILE, STELLA, ASTERISK; see p. 740
star chamber	COURT, TRIBUNAL
star cluster	GALAXY, SPIRAL, ASTERISM, MILKY WAY, PLEIADES
Star of David	HEXAGRAM
star, *pert. to*	SIDEREAL, CELESTIAL
Star-Spangled Banner author	FRANCIS SCOTT KEY
Star Trek name	DATA, KIRK, SPOCK, UHURA
Star Trek creator	RODDENBERRY
star, type of	HOLE, DWARF, GIANT, PULSAR

Star Wars character	**HAN,**
EWOK, JEDI, LEIA, LUKE,	
SOLO, YODA, JABBA, HAN	
SOLO, BOBA FETT,	
CHEWBACCA, DARTH VADER,	
OBIWAN KENOBI, LUKE	
SKYWALKER	
starch	**AMYL, ARUM, SAGO,**
SALEP, AMYLUM, FARINA,	
MANIOC, AMIDINE, AMYLOSE,	
CASSAVA, STIFFEN,	
TAPIOCA, GLYCOGEN,	
ARROWROOT, CARBOHYDRATE	
starch source	**YAM, ARUM,**
CORN, SAGO, TARO, CANNA,	
WHEAT, MANIOC, CASSAVA,	
POTATO, COONTIE,	
CURCUMA, TAPIOCA	
star-crossed	**DOOMED, UNLUCKY**
stare	**BOOF, GAPE, GAWK,**
GAZE, OGLE, GLARE	
staring	**AGAPE**
stark	**MERE, BLEAK, SHEER,**
UTTER, BARREN, DESOLATE,	
DOWNRIGHT	
starlet	**ACTRESS, INGENUE**
starlike	**ASTRAL, STARRY,**
ASTROSE, STELLAR,	
SIDEREAL, STELLATE	
starling	**HUIA, MINO,**
MYNA(H), PASTOR	
starry	**ASTRAL, STELLAR,**
SIDEREAL, GLITTERY,	
GLITTERING	
stars	*see p. 740*
Stars and Stripes Forever composer	
SOUSA	
star-shaped	**ASTROSE,**
ASTEROID, STELLATE,	
ASTERIATED	
— and starts	**FITS**
start	**FIT, SHY, JERK, JUMP,**
BEGIN, FOUND, ONSET,	
ROUSE, SETUP, SHOCK,	
LAUNCH, ORIGIN, TWITCH,	
BEGINNING, ESTABLISH	
starting point	**GO, TEE, EDEN,**
GATE, SCRATCH, STEP ONE	
startle	**ALARM, SCARE, SHOCK,**
FRIGHTEN, SURPRISE	
starvation	**FAMINE, INEDIA**
starve	**DIET, FAST, PINE,**
FAMISH, HUNGER	
stash	**HIDE, STOW, CACHE,**
HOARD, SECRETE	
state	**AVER, AVOW, ETAT,**
MOOD, CLAIM, ESTRE,	
TUATH, ALLEGE, FETTLE,	
NATION, POLITY, STATUS	

state, U.S., information	*see p. 615*
statehood	**NATIONALITY**
statehouse	**CAPITOL**
stately	**GRAND, NOBLE,**
REGAL, AUGUST, FORMAL,	
COURTLY, IMPOSING,	
MAJESTIC, DIGNIFIED,	
GRANDIOSE	
statement	**BILL, EDICT,**
DICTUM, PRECIS, ACCOUNT,	
BULLETIN, CITATION,	
AFFIDAVIT, ASSERTION,	
TESTIMONY, DEPOSITION,	
DECLARATION	
stateroom	**CABIN**
statesman	**GENRO, SOLON,**
STATIST, DIPLOMAT,	
POLITICIAN	
statesman, famous	*see p. 546*
static	**FIXED, INERT, PASSIVE,**
INACTIVE, STATIONARY; *see*	
INTERFERENCE	
station	**POST, RANK, TANA,**
DEPOT, PLACE, TERMINAL,	
TERMINUS	
stationary	**FIXED, STILL, AT**
REST, STATIC, STABILE,	
IMMOBILE	
stationer	**BOOKSELLER**
stationery	**PEN, CARD, PAPER,**
PENCIL, ENVELOPE,	
PAPETERIE	
statistician	**ACTUARY**
statistics	**DATA, FIGURES**
statuary	**BUST, TORSO,**
SCULPTOR	
statue	**ICON, ORANT, TORSO,**
EFFIGY, XOANON,	
ACROLITH, FIGURINE	
Statue of Liberty sculptor	
BARTHOLDI	
statuesque	**TALL, SHAPELY,**
STATELY, GRACEFUL	
statuette	**FIGURINE**
stature	**RANK, HEIGHT,**
STANDING, IMPORTANCE	
status	**RANK, POSITION,**
STANDING, CONDITION	
statute	**ACT, LAW,**
ORDINANCE	
staunch	**FIRM, TRUE, LOYAL,**
SOLID, SOUND, STABLE,	
STEADY, FAITHFUL,	
WATERTIGHT	
stave	**LAG, BASH, RUNG, STAP**
stave off	**FEND, WARD, AVERT,**
PREVENT	
stay	**BAR, GUY, CURB, HALT,**
LAST, LIVE, PROP, STOP,	

TACK, WAIT, ABIDE, ALLAY, BRACE, CEASE, CHECK, DELAY, DWELL, TARRY, LINGER, REMAIN, RESIDE, SUPPORT, SUSPEND

staying power STAMINA, STRENGTH, ENDURANCE

staylace AGLET

stead LIEU, PLACE

steadfast FIXED, LOYAL, CONSTANT, RESOLUTE, UNWAVERING

steady BEAU, CALM, EVEN, FIXED, STABLE, CONSTANT, UNIFORM

steak CLUB, CHUCK, FILET, FLANK, ROUND, TBONE, MINUTE, NEW YORK, SIRLOIN

steak preparer CUBER

steal COP, NIM, ROB, BONE, CHOR, CRIB, GLOM, HOOK, LIFT, LOOT, FLICH, HEIST, PINCH, POACH, SWIPE, PILFER, RUSTLE, SNATCH, SNITCH, BARGAIN

stealthy SLY, DELINE, SECRET, SNEAKY, CUNNING, FURTIVE, CLANDESTINE, SURREPTITIOUS

steam GAS, OAM, BOIL, COOK, FUME, MIST, STUFA, VAPOR

steam turbine inventor PARSONS

steamboat PACKET

steamer LINER, BOILER, LAUNCH; *see* SHIP

steamroll BULLY, CRUSH, LEVEL, BULLDOZE

steamroller BULLDOZER

steamship *see* LINER, SHIP

steamy HOT, SEXY, FOGGY, LUSTY, MISTY, EROTIC, TORRID, LUSTFUL, PASSIONATE

steed MOUNT, CHARGER, PRANCER, STALLION

steel BLADE, INURE, SWORD, DAGGER, HARDEN, TEMPER, FORTIFY

Steele journal TATLER, SPECTATOR

steelyard SCALE, BALANCE

steep RET, SOP, BOWK, SOAK, IMBUE, SHEER, ABRUPT

steeple SPIRE, TOWER, BELFRY, TURRET, MINARET

steer YAW, COND, CONN, HELM, LUFF, GUIDE, PILOT; *see* CATTLE

steerage HOLD, CABIN, GUIDANCE, DIRECTION

steering mechanism HELM, WHEEL, RUDDER, TILLER

steersman COX, PILOT, COXSWAIN

stein MUG, FLAGON, TANKARD

Steinbeck novel GRAPESOFWRATH, OFMICEANDMEN

stellar ASTRAL, STARRY, LEADING, STARRING

stem AXIS, BASE, BINE, CANE, CORM, CULM, PROW, RISE, ARISE, SHAFT, STALK, STIPE, STRAW, TUBER, DERIVE, PEDICEL, PEDUNCLE; *see* ROOT

stench HOGO; *see* ODOR

Stendhal character SOREL

step(s) PAS, GAIT, PACE, GRADE, PHASE, STAIR, STILE, TREAD, CHASSE, GRADIN, STRIDE

step-in(s) MULE, SHOE, LOAFER, DRAWERS, SLIPPER, MOCCASIN

stepmother, like a NOVERCAL

steppe PLAIN, PASTURE, GRASSLAND

Steppenwolf author HESSE

stereotype LABEL, PIGEONHOLE

sterile ARID, GELD, BARREN, OTIOSE, ASEPTIC, USELESS, GERMFREE, IMPOTENT, SANITARY, FRUITLESS, INFERTILE

sterilize GELD, SPAY, NEUTER, PURIFY, DISINFECT

stern AFT, DOUR, GRIM, HALM, REAR, HARSH, AUSTERE

sternum BREASTBONE

steroid NANDROLONE, STANOZOLOL, OXANDROLONE

stevedore LADER, NAVVY, DOCKER, LOADER, LUMPER, PACKER, STOWER, DOCKMAN, LONGSHOREMAN

Stevenson character HYDE, JEKYLL, (LONG JOHN) SILVER

stew BOIL, COLL, FRET, FUME, HASH, OLIO, OLLA, SNIT, CURRY, BURGOO, DITHER, RAGOUT, SIMMER, GOULASH, HARICOT, POTTAGE, TERRINE, COUSCOUS, MULLIGAN,

BRUNSWICK, FRICASSEE,
BOURGUIGNON
steward REEVE, BUTLER,
FACTOR, BAILIFF, DAPIFER,
KHANSAMAH
stick(s) BAR, BAT, CUE, GAD,
BRIN, CANE, GLUE, POGO,
WAND, BATON, CAMAN,
FAGOT, PASTE, STILT,
STUMP, ADHERE, BAFFLE,
CLEAVE, COHERE, MUNDLE,
PUZZLE; see STAFF
stick in the mud FOGY, MIRE,
IDLER
stick out JUT, BULGE, BEETLE,
EXTRUDE, PROTRUDE
stick up ROB, HOLD UP,
ASSAULT
sticker BURR, SEAL, LABEL,
POSER, THORN
stickler PURIST, TAPIST,
QUIBBLER, PERFECTIONIST
stickum GLUE, GUNK, PASTE
stickup HEIST, HOLDUP,
ROBBERY
sticky GOOEY, GUMMY,
HUMID, MUGGY, TACKY,
SWEATY, VISCID, VISCOUS,
GLUTINOUS
stiff HOBO, FIRM, HARD,
PRIM, RIGID, TENSE, CORPSE,
FORMAL, WOODEN, STILTED
stiffen BRACE, STEEL,
HARDEN, TAUTEN
stiffness RIGOR, HARDNESS,
PRIMNESS, RIGIDITY
stifle DAMP, CHOKE, MUFFLE,
SCOTCH, REPRESS,
SUPPRESS, SUFFOCATE
stigma see STAIN
stigmatize MARK, SLUR,
BRAND, SHAME, DEFAME
stiletto DIRK, DAGGER, STYLET
still BUT, YET, CALM, COSH,
INERT, PLACID, RETORT,
WITHAL, ALEMBIC,
DISTILLERY, MOTIONLESS,
STATIONARY, NEVERTHELESS
stillborn DEAD, ABORTIVE,
LIFELESS
stillness CALM, HUSH, PEACE,
SILENCE, QUIETUDE
stilt AVOCET, CRUTCH
stilted RIGID, STIFF,
POMPOUS, PEDANTIC
stimulant TONIC, COFFEE,
THEINE, CAFFEIN,
AMMONIA, CAFFEINE
stimulate FAN, FIRE, GOAD,

SPUR, WHET, ELATE, ROUSE,
EXCITE, ANIMATE
stimulus GOAD, PROD, SPUR,
DRIVE, STING, MOTIVE,
INCENTIVE, INCITEMENT,
INDUCEMENT
sting BARB, BITE, DUPE, TRAP,
CHEAT, GOUGE, PRICK,
SETUP, SMART, WOUND,
NETTLE
stinger ANT, BEE, RAY, GNAT,
WASP, CORAL, HORNET,
SCORPION, STING RAY,
JELLYFISH, MANOFWAR
stinging NIPPY, CAUSTIC
stingy MEAN, CLOSE, TIGHT,
SCANTY, SKIMPY, MISERLY,
NIGGARDLY, PENURIOUS
stink see ODOR
stinker SKUNK, POLECAT
stint DUTY, TASK, CHORE,
SKIMP, SCRIMP, SKINCH
stipend ANN, FEE, PAY, WAGE,
ANNAT, SALARY, PENSION,
PREBEND, ALLOWANCE
stipple DOT, FLECK, DAPPLE,
MOTTLE, STREAK, SPECKLE
stipulate DEMAND, PROVIDE,
REQUIRE, SPECIFY,
INDICATE
stipulation CLAUSE, PROVISO,
AGREEMENT, CONDITION,
PROVISION, PREREQUISITE
stir ADO, FUSS, RILE, ROIL,
TODO, BUDGE, AROUSE,
INCITE; see JAIL
stirring MOVING, ROUSING,
THRILLING
stirrup STAPES, GAMBADO,
FOOTREST
stitch SEW, ACHE, DARN,
MEND, SEAM, TACK, TUCK,
BASTE, CRICK, QUILT,
FASTEN, SUTURE
stoat ERMINE, WEASEL
stock BUTT, FUND, RACE,
BREED, GOODS, HOARD,
STORE, TRUNK, STIRPS,
SUPPLY, CAPITAL, LINEAGE,
PLENISH, REPERTORY
stock exchange CURB, NYSE,
BOURSE, MARKET, NASDAQ
stock market event IPO
stock statistic LOW, HIGH,
OPEN, CLOSE
stock, take APPRAISE,
INVENTORY
stock type COMMON,
PREFERRED

stockade	PEN, BOMA, ETAPE, CORRAL, BULWARK
stockings	HOSE, NYLONS, HOSIERY
stockpile	CACHE, HOARD, STORE, RESERVE
stocky	STUB, DUMPY, PLUMP, SQUAT, CHUNKY
stodgy	DULL, STOLID, STUFFY, TEDIOUS
stoic	ZENO, SENECA, PATIENT, SPARTAN
stoicism	PATIENCE, AUSTERITY, FORTITUDE, STOLIDITY
stoke	FEED, FUEL, POKE, STIR, TEND
stoker	TEASER, FIREMAN
stole	SCARF, ORARION, FILCHED
stolen property	HAUL, LOOT, PELF, SWAG, MANNER, MAINOUR
stolid	DULL, HEAVY, OBTUSE, WOODEN, PHLEGMATIC
stomach	MAW, CRAW, BELLY, RUMEN, TRIPE, OMASUM, PAUNCH, VENTER, ABDOMEN, CRAVING, TOLERATE
stomachache	COLIC, GRIPE, BELLYACHE, TUMMYACHE
stomp	CLUMP, STAMP, TRAMPLE
stone	GEM, PIT, FLAG, SEED, TYMP, GEODE, HERMA, LAPIS, STEAN, STEEN, TABLE, ASHLAR, PEBBLE, CALLAIS, DORNICK, ROSETEA, LAPIDATE, LAPILLUS; see ROCK, MINERAL
Stone Age period	EOLITHIC, NEOLITHIC
stone heap	AHU, KARN, CAIRN(E)
stone, precious	LASK, OPAL, RUBY, BAHIA, DORJE, LASKE, RUBIN, VAJRA, ADAMAS, LASQUE, LIGURE, TABLET, ANTHRAX, BRIOLET, CATSEYE, DIAMOND, EMERALD, JACINTH, PRASINE, RUBELET, SMARAGD, HYACINTH, SAPPHIRE
stone, semiprecious	JADE, BERYL, LAPIS, MACLE, TOPAZ, GARNET, IOLITE, QUARTZ, SPINEL, ZIRCON, AXINITE, EUCLASE, GIRASOL, HYALITE, KUNZITE, OLIVINE,

	OVALINE, PERIDOT, TURCOIS, TURKOIS, AMETHYST, ESSONITE, GIRASOLE, MELANITE, NEPHRITE, SODALITE, TURQUOISE
stone, sharpening	HONE, WHET, OILSTONE
stone, woman turned to	NIOBE
stonecutter	MASON, CARVER, JADDER. LAPICIDE, LAPIDARY
stonecutter's tool	SAX, HAWK, SEAX, DROVE, GAVEL, BANKER, BROACH, CHISEL, BOASTER
stoned	HIGH, DOPED, DRUNK, SPACEY, ZONKED, DRUGGED, TURNED ON, SPACED OUT
stonelike	LITHOID
stonewall	EVADE, STALL, THWART, FRUSTRATE, FILIBUSTER
stoneware	GRES, POTTERY
stonework	MASONRY
stony	HARD, ROCKY, ADAMANT, CALLOUS, PETROUS, PITILESS
stooge	DUPE, FOIL, PAWN, TOOL, DUMMY, LACKEY
Stooges, Three	MOE, CURLY, LARRY, SHEMP
stool	SEAT, PRIVY, STUMP, TABOURET, FOOTSTOOL
stool pigeon	RAT, SPY, MARK, DECOY, INFORMER
stoop	BOW, BEND, DEIGN, PORCH, CROUCH, VERANDA(H)
stop	DAM, END, BALK, CONK, PLUG, QUIT, REST, STEM, WHOA, AVAST, BELAY, CLOSE, PAUSE, STALL, ARREST, DESIST; see ORGAN
stopcock	VALVE, FAUCET
stopgap	EXPEDIENT, MAKESHIFT, SUBSTITUTE
stoppage	GAP, JAM, HALT, STASIS, CLOTURE, EMBARGO, DISRUPTION, DISCONTINUANCE
stopper	TAP, WAD, BUNG, CORK, PLUG, SHIVE, SPILL, TAMPION
stopwatch	TIMER
storage	PRESERVATION
storage location	BIN, BANK, BARN, SHED, SILO, DEPOT, ARMORY, CELLAR, CLOSET,

LARDER, PANTRY, FREEZER,
GRANARY, CUPBOARD,
ELEVATOR, MAGAZINE,
RESERVOIR, WAREHOUSE
store   PX, COOP, MART, POST,
SAVE, SHOP, TOKO, AMASS,
CACHE, HOARD, STOCK,
GARNER, ENSILE, OUTLET,
SUPPLY, CANTEEN, GROCERY,
SUTLERY, BOUTIQUE,
WAREHOUSE
storehouse   BARN, GOLA, SILO,
DEPOT, ETAPE, ARSENAL,
GRANARY, MAGAZINE
storekeeper   GROCER,
MERCHANT
storeroom   VAULT, CELLAR,
CLOSET, LARDER, PANTRY,
BUTTERY
storied   FAMOUS, LEGENDARY,
CELEBRATED
stork   JABIRU, MAGUARI,
MARABOU, ADJUTANT
stork genus   CICONIA
storm   BLOW, BURA, FUME,
FURY, GALE, KONA, RAGE,
RANT, RAVE, BURAN, ORAGE,
ATTACK, SAMIEL, SIMOON,
KHAMSIN, SHAITAN, TEMPEST,
TORNADO, TYPHOON
stormy   WILD, ROUGH,
RAGING, VIOLENT,
INCLEMENT, TURBULENT,
TEMPESTUOUS
stormy petrel   ASSILAG
story   EPIC, GEST, ITEM, LORE,
REDE, SAGA, TALE, YARN,
CONTE, FABLE, GESTE, NOVEL,
LEGEND, ARTICLE, PARABLE,
ALLEGORY
storyteller   DISOUR, FABLER,
JESTER, RECITER,
RACONTEUR, ALLEGORIST
stout   FAT, BURLY, HUSKY,
PORTLY, STANCH, STOCKY;
see BEER
Stout (Rex) detective   (NERO)WOLFE
stouthearted   BOLD, BRAVE,
DAUNTLESS
stove   ETNA, OVEN, RANGE,
COOKER, HEATER, FURNACE
stovepipe   FLUE, SILK, TOPHAT
stow   CAN, CRAM, PACK,
STASH, STORE, STEEVE,
CONCEAL
stowage   PACKING, STORAGE
stowaway   ILLEGAL,
DEADBEAT
Stowe burial place   ANDOVER

Stowe character   TOPSY, UNCLE
TOM, LITTLE EVA,
SIMON LEGREE
straddle   RIDE, HEDGE,
MOUNT, BYPASS, BESTRIDE
strafe   RAKE, PEPPER, RIDDLE,
CENSURE
straggle   STRAY, TRAIL,
DAWDLE, WANDER
straggler   STRAY, ROAMER,
DRIFTER, RAMBLER,
WANDERER
straight   AROW, FAIR, JUST,
PURE, PLAIN, RIGHT,
DIRECT, HONEST, NONSTOP,
THROUGH, UNDILUTED
straight and —   NARROW
straight man   FOIL, STOOGE
straighten   ALIGN, ALINE,
UNCURL, RECTIFY
straightway   NOW, ANON, AT
ONCE, BEDENE
straightforward   OPEN, BLUNT,
FRANK, CANDID, DIRECT,
HONEST, SINCERE,
FORTHRIGHT
strain   TAX, LINE, TIRE, EXERT,
STOCK, EFFORT, FILTER,
PURIFY, LINEAGE, TENSION,
FILTRATE
strained   TAUT, TENSE,
FORCED, UPTIGHT
strainer   SILE, SIEVE, STRUM,
TAMIS, TAMMY, SCREEN,
PUSHKIN, COLANDER
strait   BASS, NECK, MENAI,
NARROW, TORRES,
CHANNEL, EVRIPOS,
MALACCA, MESSINA
MACKINAC, MAGELLAN,
GIBRALTAR
Strait of Messina rock   SCYLLA
straitjacket   RESTRAIN(ER)
straitlaced   DOUR, PRIM, STAID,
STRICT, PROPER,
PURITANICAL
straits   BIND, PINCH, CRUNCH,
PLIGHT, POVERTY,
DISTRESS, HARDSHIP
strand   PLY, BEACH, FIBER,
SHORE, THREAD
stranded   ALONE, BEACHED,
DESERTED
strange   ODD, RARE, UNCO,
FREMD, OUTRE, WEIRD,
EXOTIC, QUAINT,
FOREIGN, UNUSUAL,
PECULIAR, SINGULAR,
ECCENTRIC

stranger ALIEN, EMIGRE,
NEWCOMER, OUTSIDER,
FOREIGNER
strangle KILL, CHOKE, SCRAG,
GARROT, STIFLE, GARROTTE,
JUGULATE, THROTTLE,
SUFFOCATE
stranglehold GRIP, MONOPOLY
strangulate CHOKE, GARROTE,
SQUEEZE, THROTTLE,
CONSTRICT
strangulation GARROTE,
STRICTURE, CONSTRICTION
strap TIE, BAND, BELT, JESS,
LORA, REIM, REIN, LEASH,
THONG, HALTER, LATIGO,
THRASH
straphanger STANDEE,
COMMUTER
strapped BROKE, NEEDY,
SHORT
strapping HARDY, LUSTY,
ROBUST
strap-shaped LORATE, LIGULATE
strass GLASS, PASTE
stratagem COUP, PLOY, RUSE,
WILE, SCHEME, TACTIC,
TREPAN, ARTIFICE,
MANEUVER
strategy PLAN, SCHEME,
TACTIC(S), MANEUVER
Stratford river AVON
stratified LAYERED,
LAMINATED
stratum BED, SEAM, LAYER,
FOLIUM
Strauss opera SALOME,
ARIADNE, DONJUAN,
ELEKTRA, FLEDERMAUS
Stravinsky work RITE (OF
SPRING), FIREBIRD,
PETROUCHKA, PULCINELLA
straw CULM, REED, TUBE,
CHAFF, HAULM, FESCUE
straw vote *see* POLL
strawman DUMMY,
JACKSTRAW, SCARECROW
stray ERR, GAD, WAIF, DOGIE,
RAMBLE, DEVIATE, DIGRESS,
MAVERICK
streak ROE, RUN, LINE, VEIN,
SMEAR, STRIA, TRAIT,
STRIAE
streaky LINY, ROWY, LACED,
STRIATE
stream AAR, RIO, RUN, FLOW,
RILL, SIRE, BOURN, BROOK,
RIVER, ARROYO, RUNNEL,
SWALLET

streambed RUNWAY, CHANNEL
streamer FLAG, BANNER,
BURGEE, BUNTING,
PENNANT, HEADLINE
streamlined TRIM, SPEEDY,
EFFICIENT, SIMPLIFIED
street RIO, RUE, VIA, WAY,
LANE, ROAD, CALLE, DRIVE,
ARTERY, AVENUE,
CAUSEWAY, BOULEVARD
— Street EASY
street arab WAIF, GAMIN,
URCHIN
street musician BUSKER
street sign STOP, YIELD,
DETOUR, ONEWAY,
NOUTURN
streetcar TRAM, TROLL(E)Y
streetwalker WHORE, HARLOT,
HOOKER, PROSTITUTE
strength MAIN, FORCE,
MIGHT, POWER, VIGOR,
ENERGY, POTENCY
strengthen GIRD, PROP, BRACE,
HARDEN, FORTIFY,
TOUGHEN
strenuous HARD, TOUGH,
TIRING, ARDUOUS,
VIGOROUS, ENERGETIC
stress ARSIS, ICTUS, ACCENT,
STRAIN, TENSION,
EMPHASIS, PRESSURE,
EMPHASIZE
stretch EKE, LIE, SPAN, STENT,
STINT, TRACT, EXPAND,
EXTEND, SPREAD, DISTEND
stretched out CRANED,
PROLATE
stretcher FRAME, DOOLIE,
GURNEY, LITTER, (S)TENTER
strew SOW, SPREAD,
SCATTER, DISPERSE
stricken BESET, AFFLICTED
strict NICE, EXACT, RIGID,
STERN, SEVERE, AUSTERE,
EXACTING, RIGOROUS
strictness RIGOR, SEVERITY,
PRECISION
stricture CENSURE, STENOSIS,
CRITICISM
stride GAIT, PACE, STEP,
MARCH, ADVANCE,
PROGRESS
strident LOUD, HARSH,
SHRILL, BLARING, GRATING,
RAUCOUS
strife WAR, FEUD, STASIS,
DISCORD, CONFLICT,
STRUGGLE, CONTENTION

strike	BAT, RAP, BAFF, CONK, PELT, PUTT, SLAP, SLUG, SOCK, SWAT, WHAM, CLOUT, SMITE, WHACK, LARRUP, PELTER, POMMEL, BOYCOTT, WALKOUT		STOUT, TOUGH, BRAWNY, COGENT, MADURO, ROBUST, SINEWY, STURDY, VIRILE, HEALTHY, ATHLETIC, POWERFUL, PUISSANT
strike —	A POSE	strong point	FORTE
strike out	FAN, FAIL, DELE(TE), CANCEL, EXPUNGE	strong-arm man	GOON, THUG, BOUNCER
strike, type of	SITIN, HUNGER, WILDCAT, SYMPATHY, SLOWDOWN	strongbox	SAFE, VAULT, COFFER
		stronghold	see FORT
strikebreaker	see SCAB	strongly	AMAIN
striking	VIVID, STUNNING, ATTRACTIVE, IMPRESSIVE, REMARKABLE	strongman	ATLAS, TITAN, DESPOT, SAMPSON, TARZAN, SAMPSON, DICTATOR, HERCULES
string	ROW, SET, CORD, HANG, LACE, LINE, CHAIN, TWINE, CATGUT, THREAD	strophe	STANZA
		structure	FRAME, EDIFICE
string along	DUPE, FOOL, DECEIVE	struck	SMIT, INAWE
		structural	ORGANIC, TECTONIC, SKELETAL
string of beads	ROSARY, STRAND, CHAPLET, NECKLACE	structure	FORM, SHAPE, EDIFICE, BUILDING, COMPOSITION
stringed instrument	see p. 642	struggle	VIE, COPE, MELEE, PENIEL, STRIFE, CONFLICT, FLOUNDER
stringency	RIGOR, SEVERITY		
stringent	HARSH, SEVERE, STRICT, FORCEFUL, COMPELLING	strum	TIRL, PLUCK, THRUM, FINGER
stringy	ROPY, WIRY, SINEWY, FIBROUS, THREADY, VISCOUS	strumpet	HARLOT, PROSTITUTE
		strut	GAIT, BRACE, SASHAY, SUPPORT, SWAGGER
strip	BARE, FLAY, HADE, LATH, LIST, PEEL, SKIN, SLAT, SWATH, BATTEN, DIVEST, FILLET, FLENSE, SPLINE, STRAKE, DISROBE, UNDRESS	stub	END, BUTT, SNAG, GUARD, STUMP
		stubble	BEARD, STALKS, STUMPS, BRISTLES, REMNANTS, WHISKERS
stripe	BAR, BAND, KIND, LINE, MARK, TYPE, STREAK, CHEVRON	stubborn	TOUGH, DOGGED, MULISH, ORNERY, FROWARD, WILLFUL, OBDURATE, OBSTINATE
striped	VITTATE, STRIATED		
stripling	BOY, LAD, CHIEL, SPRIG, YOUTH		
stripper	ECDYSIAST	stubbornness	OBDURACY, TENACITY, PERSISTENCE, PERTINACITY
strive	TRY, VIE, LABOR, STRAIN, CONTEND, ENDEAVOR, STRUGGLE	stubby	SHORT, SQUAT, STOCKY, BRISTLY
stroke	FIT, PAT, PET, BAFF, BEAT, BOLT, COUP, FEAT, ICTUS, THROB, CARESS, FONDLE, SEIZURE, APOPLEXY, CONVULSION	stuck-up	VAIN, ALOOF, PROUD, SNOOTY, UPPISH, HAUGHTY, ARROGANT, SNOBBISH
		stud	PIN, PEG, BOSS, KNOB, NAIL, BREEDER, STALLION
stroll	ROVE, TURN, WALK, JAUNT, RAMBLE, MEANDER, SAUNTER, PROMENADE	student	COED, TYRO, AGGIE, CADET, ELEVÉ, PLEBE, PUPIL, ECOLIER, LEARNER, MONITOR, SCHOLAR, DISCIPLE
stroller	ROVER, WALKER, CARRIAGE		
strong	FERE, HALE, GAMY, BURLY, HARDY, LUSTY,	studied	PLANNED, WILLFUL, CALCULATED, DELIBERATE

studies **LEARNING, EDUCATION, SCHOOLING**

studio **APT, SALON, ATELIER, WORKSHOP, APARTMENT**

studio product **RELEASE**

studious **BOOKY, BOOKISH, DILIGENT, SCHOLARLY, INDUSTRIOUS**

study **CON, DEN, BONE, CRAM, PORE, READ, ETUDE, WEIGH, PERUSE, PONDER, EXAMINE**

study group **CLASS, SEMINAR**

stuff **JAM, PAD, RAM, WAD, CRAM, FILL, JUNK, PLUG, SATE, GORGE, THINGS, OVEREAT, SATIATE**

stuff and — **NONSENSE**

stuffed **FULL, PACKED, CRAMMED, REPLETE**

stuffing **WAD, FARCE, KAPOK, FILLING, DRESSING, SALPICON**

stuffy **CLOSE, MUSTY, SULTRY, AIRLESS**

stum **MUST, JUICE, RENEW**

stumble **ERR, SLIP, STOT, TRIP, BLUNDER, FLOUNDER**

stumbling block **SNAG, HURDLE, OBSTACLE, HINDRANCE**

stump **BUTT, SNAG, STUB, PUZZLE, ZUCKLE, PERPLEX, REMNANT**

stun **DAZE, FLOOR, SHOCK, ASTOUND, STARTLE**

stunning **LOVELY, GORGEOUS, DAZZLING, STRIKING, BEAUTIFUL, ATTRACTIVE, ASTONISHING**

stunt **FEAT, DWARF, TRICK, RETARD**

stupefy **DAZE, DOPE, MAZE, NUMB, STUN, BESOT, ASTOUND, ASTONISH**

stupendous **HUGE, VAST, AMAZING, AWESOME, IMMENSE, HUMONGOUS, MONSTROUS**

stupid **DUMB, DUNS, CRASS, DENSE, DOPEY, OBTUSE, GLAIKIT**

stupid person **ASS, OAF, CLOD, COOT, DODO, DOLT, LOON, LOUT, LOWN, MOKE, DUMMY, DUNCE, GOOSE, IDIOT, MORON, NINNY, NITWIT, DUMBBELL, BLOCKHEAD**

stupor **COMA, SOPOR, APATHY, TORPOR, TRANCE,** **LETHARGY, NARCOSIS, OSCITANCY**

sturdy **GID, HARDY, STOUT, WALLY, ROBUST**

sturgeon **HUSO, ELOPS, BELUGA, GANOID, HAUSEN, KALUGA, BELOUGA, STERLET, PADDLEFISH**

Sturm und — **DRANG**

stutter **FALTER, STAMMER, HESITATE**

Stuyvesant's estate **BOWERY**

sty **HAW, PEN, DUMP, HOVEL, PIGPEN, PIGSTY**

Stygian **DARK, GLOOMY, HADEAN, HELLISH, INFERNAL**

style **FAD, TON, CHIC, FORM, MODE, NAME, GENRE, VOGUE, DESIGN, MANNER, METHOD, FASHION, TECHNIQUE**

style, architectural **ROMAN, GOTHIC, ROCOCO, BAROQUE, SPANISH, BYZANTINE, ROMANESQUE, RENAISSANCE**

style, furniture **EMPIRE, RUSTIC, ARCADIAN, PROVINCIAL**

style, painting **GENRE, CUBISM, DADISM, FAUVISM, ABSTACT**

style, typography *see* **TYPE STYLE**

stylet **PROBE, DAGGER, LANCET, STILETTO**

stylish **CHIC, TONY, NOBBY, SMART, CLASSY, DRESSY, JAUNTY, MODISH, TRENDY, A LA MODE, ELEGANT, VOGUISH, FASHIONABLE**

stylish dresser **FOP, DUDE, TOFF, DANDY, SPARK, SWELL, SOCIALITE, CLOTHESHORSE**

stylus **PEN, NEEDLE, SCRIBER**

stymie **BALK, FOIL, BAFFLE, IMPEDE, THWART**

styptic **ALUM, AMADOU, ASTRINGENT**

Styx ferryman **CHARON**

suave **OILY, POLITE, SMOOTH, URBANE, GRACIOUS, COURTEOUS**

sub **HERO, HOAGIE, SANDWICH**

sub rosa **COVERTLY, INSECRET, SECRETLY**

subbase **PLINTH**

subconscious   ID, ANIMA, PSYCHE, SUBLIMINAL

subcontinent   INDIA, NEWGUINEA

subcontract   SUBLET, SUBLEASE, OUTSOURCE

subdivide   DISSECT, SPLIT(UP), PARCEL(OUT)

subdivision   PART, TRACT, SECTOR, SUBURB, CATEGORY

subdue   BEAT, CRUSH, QUELL, WORST, DEFEAT, MASTER, CONQUER, REPRESS, OVERCOME, OVERPOWER

subject   NOUN, TEXT, LIEGE, PRONE, THEME, TOPIC, VASSAL

subjection   YOKE, THRALL, DOMINATION, SUBJUGATION

subjective   BIASED, MENTAL, IMAGINED, INTERNAL, INTROSPECTIVE

subjugate   TAME, DEFEAT, SUBDUE, CONQUER, ENSLAVE, VANQUISH

sublimate   PURIFY, REFINE

sublime   LOFTY, NOBLE, EXALTED

submarine   HERO, UBOAT, HOAGIE, TURTLE, PIGBOAT, NAUTILUS, SANDWICH

submarine, atomic   SKATE, SARGO, TRITON, NAUTILUS

submerge   DIVE, SINK, DROWN, SWAMP, DELUGE, ENGULF, PLUNGE, IMMERSE, INUNDATE

submersible   UBOAT, SUBMARINE

submission   PATIENCE, OBEDIENCE, SURRENDER, COMPLIANCE, RESIGNATION

submissive   MEEK, TAME, DOCILE

submit   BOW, OBEY, REFER, STOOP, YIELD, COMPLY, GIVEIN, PROPOSE, SURRENDER

subordinate   AIDE, SECOND, HIRELING, MYRMIDON, SECONDARY

suborn   BRIBE, PAYOFF, CORRUPT, PERJURE

subpoena   WRIT, ORDER, SUMMONS, CITATION

subscribe   AGREE, ENROL(L), SIGNUP, CONDONE, SUPPORT, ADVOCATE, PURCHASE, SANCTION

subscription   DONATION, ENDORSEMENT

subsequent   LATER, ENSUING

subsequently   ANON, NEXT, LATER, AFTERWARDS, THEREAFTER

subservient   ABJECT, SERVILE, OBEISANT, GROVELING

subside   EBB, SINK, WANE, ABATE, DWINDLE

subsidiary   BRANCH, ANCILLARY, AUXILIARY, SECONDARY, SUCCURSAL, TRIBUTARY, PENSIONARY

subsidize   BACK, FINANCE, SPONSOR, UNDERWRITE

subsidy   AID, GRANT, FUNDING, PENSION, SUPPORT

subsist   FARE, LIVE, ABIDE, EXIST, CONTINUE

subsistence   BEING, UPKEEP, EXISTENCE, PROVISION, LIVELIHOOD

substance   GIST, PITH, MEANS, STUFF, WEALTH, ESSENCE, PURPORT, REALITY, MATERIAL

substandard   POOR, INFERIOR, MEDIOCRE

substantial   REAL, AMPLE, SOLID, SOUND, MASSIVE, ABUNDANT

substantially   MAINLY, BASICALLY, ESSENTIALLY

substantiate   PROVE, VERIFY, BOLSTER, CONFIRM, WARRANT

substantiation   PROOF, EVIDENCE, VERIFICATION

substantive   SOLID, CONCRETE

substitute   VICE, PROXY, SIT IN, DEPUTY, ERSATZ, STANDIN, SUPPLANT, SURROGATE

substitution   SWAP, TRADE, SWITCH, METONYMY, REPLACEMENT

subsume   INCLUDE

subterfuge   PLOY, RUSE, DODGE, SHIFT, TRICK, DEVICE, EVASION, PRETEXT, ARTIFICE, INTRIGUE

subterranean   BURIED, HIDDEN, NETHER, INFERNAL, UNDERGROUND

subtle   SLY, DEEP, NICE, THIN, WILY, ARTFUL, CUNNING, DEVIOUS, PROFOUND subtlety   ART, CRAFT, GUILE, FINESSE, QUILLET, DELICACY

subtract   *see* DEDUCT

suburb   LOWY, BARRIO, ENVIRON, BANLIEUE, FAUBOURG, OUTSKIRTS

subvention   AID, GRANT, RELIEF, SUBSIDY

subversion   MUTINY, REBELLION

subversive   RED, REBEL, RADICAL, DISSIDENT

subvert   RUIN, UPSET, REVOLT, CORRUPT, UNDERMINE

subway   BMT, IND, IRT, BART, TUBE, METRO, TUNNEL, RAILWAY, UNDERGROUND

succeed   WIN, ENSUE, GOFAR, FOLLOW, THRIVE, PROSPER, FLOURISH

succeeding   NEXT, FOLLOWING, SEQUENTIAL

success   HIT, SRO, LUCK, ARTHA, TRIUMPH, VICTORY, CONQUEST, PROSPERITY

successful   ONTOP, DOMINANT, EFFECTIVE, FORTUNATE, PROSPEROUS

successful person   COMER, NABOB, VICTOR, WINNER, CHAMPION

succession   SERIES, SEQUENCE

successive(ly)   AROW, SERIATE

successor   SCION, HEIR(ESS), FOLLOWER, (IN)HERITOR, REPLACEMENT

succinct   BRIEF, PITHY, TERSE, CONCISE, LACONIC

succor   AID, HELP, RELIEF, COMFORT, ASSIST(ANCE)

succubus   DEMON, FIEND, INCUBUS, DEMON(ESS), STRUMPET

succulent   LUSH, JUICY, TASTY, DELICIOUS

succumb   DIE, YIELD, GIVEIN, SUBMIT

succursal   BRANCH, AUXILIARY, SUBSIDIARY

such   SIC, LIKE, SIMILAR

suck   SIP, DRAW, LURE, PULL, BLEED, DRAIN, ABSORB, GUZZLE, INHALE, EXTRACT

sucker   BABY, DUPE, GULL, LEECH, PATSY, REMORA, SPROUT, FALL GUY, LOLLIPOP, PUSHOVER

suckle   REAR, NURSE, FOSTER, LACTATE, NOURISH, NURTURE, BREASTFEED

suckling   BABY, NEONATE, TODDLER, NURSLING, WEANLING

suction   SIPHONAGE

Sudan, capital of   KHARTOUM

Sudanese city/town   KAS, WAU, YEI, JUBA, AKUBU, AMADI, ATBARA, EDDAMER, ELOBEID, GEDAREF, KASSALA, MALAKAL, KHARTOUM, OMDURMAN

Sudanese lake   CHAD

Sudanese language   EFE, MADI, MORU, LENDU, NUBIAN; *see* GUR, MANDE

Sudanese money   DINAR

Sudanese native   PEUL

Sudanese neighbor   CAR, CHAD, EGYPT, KENYA, LIBYA, ZAIRE, UGANDA, ERITREA, ETHIOPIA

Sudanese river   GEL, JUR, LOL, SUE, BORO, GASH, NILE, SOBAT, ARRAHAD, ATBARA, BARAKA, ALJABAL

sudarium   NAPKIN, MANIPLE, HANDKERCHIEF

sudden   RASH, HASTY, ABRUPT, PRECIPITATE

suddenly   PRESTO, ABRUPTLY, UNEXPECTEDLY

Suddenly Susan names   JACK, LUIS, NANA, NATE, TODD, VICKI, BROOKE, SHIELDS, THEGATE

sudsy   FOAMY, BUBBLY, FROTHY

sue   WOO, COURT, APPEAL, ENTREAT, LITIGATE, PROSECUTE

suet   FAT, LARD, TALLOW

Suez Canal builder   LESSEPS

Suez Canal port   (PORT) SAID, SUEZ, ISMAILIA

suffer   AIL, LET, ACHE, BEAR, BIDE, CLEM, DREE, ALLOW, ENDURE, PERMIT, STARVE, UNDERGO, TOLERATE

sufferance   PATIENCE, ENDURANCE, TOLERATION

suffering   PAIN, ANGUISH, TORMENT, DISTRESS

suffice   DO, GETBY, SERVE, SATISFY

sufficiency   ADEQUACY, FULLNESS, ABUNDANCE, PROFUSION, REPLETION

sufficient   ENOW, AMPLE, ENOUGH, PLENTY, ADEQUATE

suffix	ENDING, POSTFIX, DESINENCE	suicide victim	COBAIN, MONROE, EASTMAN, HEMINGWAY
suffixes	*see p. 694*	suit	FIT, ADAPT, AGREE, HABIT, APPEAL, OUTFIT, PLEASE, PETITION, GABARDINE
suffocate	BURKE, CHOKE, STIFLE, SMOTHER, STRANGLE, ASPHYXIATE		
suffocating	STUFFY, AIRLESS, STIFLING	— suit	ZOOT
suffocation	CHOKING, STRANGULATION	suit (cards)	CUPS, CLUBS, WANDS, EAGLES, HEARTS, ROYALS, SPADES, SWORDS, DIAMONDS, PENTACLES
suffrage	VOTE, ELECT, BALLOT, CONSENT, OPINION, PRAYERS, FRANCHISE		
		suitable	APT, FIT, MEET, RIGHT, PROPER, FITTING, BECOMING, EXPEDIENT
suffragist	MILL, BROWN, BECKER, BRIGHT, ANTHONY, BLOOMER, STANTON	suitability	FITNESS, PROPRIETY, RIGHTNESS
		suitably	MEETLY, TIMELY
suffuse	WASH, BATHE, COLOR, IMBUE, TINGE, PERVADE	suitcase	*see* BAG
		suite	FLAT, ROOMS, ESCORT, SERIES, RETINUE
suffusion	GLOW, TINT, BLUSH, FLUSH, DIFFUSION	suiting	SERGE, FABRIC; *see p. 535*
Sufi disciple	MURID	suitor	BEAU, SUER, FLAME, SWAIN, WOOER
Sufistic concept	FANA		
sugar	GUR, OSE, CANE, GOOR, BIOSE, HEXOSE, KETOSE, PANELA, GLUCOSE, LACTOSE, MALTOSE, MANNOSE, PANOCHA, SUCROSE, DEXTROSE, FLATTERY, FRUCTOSE, ARABINOSE, SACCHAROSE	sulk	PET, MOPE, POUT, GROUCH, GRUMBLE
		sulky	BLUE, CROSS, IN A PET, MOROSE, SULLEN
		sullen	DOUR, GLUM, GRUFF, POUTY, SURLY, SULKY, TESTY, MOPING, MOROSE, BALEFUL
Sugar Bowl site	NEW ORLEANS	Sullivan collaborator	GILBERT
sugar cane disease	ILIAU	sully	SOIL, SMEAR, STAIN, TAINT, DEFILE, TARNISH, BESMIRCH
sugar daddy	ANGEL, PATRON		
sugar-molasses, mixture	MELADA		
sugar source	SAP, BEET, CANE, CORN, MILK, FRUIT, GRAPE, MAPLE	sulphurous	FIERY, HEATED, HELLISH, INFERNAL
		sultan	EMIR, IMAM, KHAN, MURAD, SELIM, CALIPH, SALADIN, PADISHAH, SULEIMAN
sugar substitute	ASPARTAME, CYCLAMATE, SACCHARIN		
sugary	SWEET, CANDIED, HONEYED	Sultan of Swat	(BABE) RUTH
suggest	HINT, IMPLY, SUBMIT, PROPOSE, INTIMATE, INSINUATE	sultanate	OMAN, MAURA, KUWAIT, MUSCAT
		sultan's residence	SERAI
suggestion	HINT, TRACE, ADVICE, PROPOSAL, INSINUATION	sultry	HOT, SEXY, CLOSE, FIERY, HUMID, MUGGY, EROTIC, STUFFY, TORRID, SENSUAL, TROPICAL, SWELTERING
suggestive	RISQUE, SYMBOLIC, INDICATIVE		
sui generis	RARE, UNIQUE, PECULIAR	sum	ADD, TOT(AL), AMOUNT, AGGREGATE
sui juris	SANE, COMPETENT, QUALIFIED	sum up	RECAP, SUMMATE, SUMMARIZE
suicidal	DEADLY, DEPRESSED, DESPONDENT	sumac	RHUS, YEARA, SUMACH
suicide	SUTTEE, SEPPUKU, FELODESE, RARAKIRI	Sumatran city/town	MEDAN, LANGSA, PADANG, PALEMBANG

Sumatran lake	TOBA
Sumatran mountain	DEMPO, LEUSER, KERINCI
Sumatran river	HARI, MUSI, ROKAN, ASAHAN, KAMPAR, INDRAGIRI
Sumerian dialect	EMESAL
summa — laude	CUM
summarily	CURTLY, SWIFTLY
summarize	RECAP, SUMUP, RECOUNT, RESTATE
summary	GIST, BRIEF, RECAP, DIGEST, PRECIS, RESUME, CONCISE, EPITOME, RUNDOWN, SYNOPSIS
summer	ETE, BEAM, (A)ESTIVAL, DOG DAYS, RADIATE
summer drink	JULEP, COOLER, SPRITZER
summerhouse	CASINO, COTTAGE
summery	WARM, SUNNY, (A)ESTIVAL, SUNSHINY, TROPICAL
summit(s)	CAP, DOD, TOP, ACME, APEX, KNAP, PEAK, CREST, APICES, ZENITH, PINNACLE
summit goal	PACT
summon(s)	BID, CALL, CITE, PAGE, SIST, VADY, WRIT, CLEPE, EVOKE, KNELL, BECKON, SUBPOENA
sump	PIT, WELL, DRAIN
sumptuous	LUXE, RICH, GRAND, DELUXE, LAVISH
sun	SOL, INTI, TITAN, HELIOS, PHOEBUS
sun deck	PORCH, TERRACE
sun god	*see p. 651*
sun term	ATEN, SPOT, APSIS, EPACT, UMBRA, CORONA, ECLIPTIC
Sun King	LOUIS (XIV)
sun, *pert. to*	SOLAR, HELIACAL
sunburnt skin	ADUST, BLYPE
Sunda island	ALOR, BALI, JAVA, TIMOR, BORNEO, SUMATRA, SULAWESI
Sundance's girl	ETTA
Sunday	HOLIDAY, SABBATH, LORDSDAY
Sunday best	FINERY, CLOTHES
sunder	REND, RIVE, TEAR, BREAK, SEVER, SPLIT, CLEAVE, DIVIDE, SEPARATE
sundial	HOROLOGE
sundial part	STYLE, GNOMON

sundog	GALL, PARHELION
sundries	NOTIONS, ODDSANDENDS
sundry	DIVERS, VARIOUS, MISCELLANEOUS
sunfish	MOLA, OPAH, BREAM, ROACH, CICHLID, CRAPPIE, BLUEGILL
sunflower	GUMWEED, MARIGOLD
Sunflower State	KS, KAN(SAS)
sunken fence	HAHA
sunless	DARK, SHADY, OVERCAST
sunny	WARM, PALMY, BRIGHT, CHEERY, CHEERFUL
sunrise	DAWN, SUNUP, AURORA
Sunrise at Campobello subject	FDR
sunroom(s)	PORCH, SOLARIA, SOLARIUM
sunset	DUSK, SUNDOWN, TWILIGHT, NIGHTFALL
sunshade	VISOR, AWNING, PARASOL
sunshine	CHEER, WARMTH, (DAY)LIGHT
Sunshine State	FL(A), FLORIDA
sunspot(s)	UMBRA, FACULA, MACULA, FRECKLE, PENUMBRA(E)
sunstroke	ICTUS, HELIOSIS
suntan lotion letters	SPF
Suomi	FINLAND
super	ACTOR, EXTRA
superannuated	AGED, ANILE, ANTIQUE, RETIRED, OBSOLETE, OUTDATED
superb	FINE, RICH, NOBLE, LORDLY, ELEGANT, STATELY, MAJESTIC, SPLENDID
supercilious	PROUD, SNOOTY, SNOTTY, HAUGHTY, ARROGANT, SNOBBISH
superficial	GLIB, HASTY, CASUAL, FLIMSY, SLIGHT, CURSORY, OUTWARD, PASSING, SHALLOW, SKETCHY, TRIVIAL, SKINDEEP
superfluous	EXTRA, DETROP, FUTILE, COPIOUS, EXCESSIVE, REDUNDANT
superfund organization	EPA
superhighway	FREEWAY, AUTOBAHN, SPEEDWAY, TURNPIKE, AUTOROUTE, AUTOSTRADA
superhuman	GODLY, DIVINE, GODLIKE, HERCULEAN

superimpose	COVER, OVERLAY
superintend	DIRECT, MANAGE, CONTROL, OVERSEE, SUPERVISE
superintendent	BOSS, CHIEF, FOREMAN, MANAGER, OVERSEER, SURVEYOR
superior	BOSS, BETTER, HIGHER, UTMOST, GREATER, TOPNOTCH, EXCELLENT, FIRSTRATE
superiority	EDGE, POWER, SUPREMACY
superiors	CHIEFS, BETTERS, LEADERS, MASTERS
superlative	ACME, ULTRA, SUPREME
Superman birthplace	KRYPTON
Superman characters	LARA, KALEL, LOIS LANE, CLARK KENT, JIMMY OLSEN
Superman portrayer	CAIN, REEVE
supermarket employee	CLERK, BAGGER, PRICER
supernal	DIVINE, ETHEREAL, HEAVENLY, CELESTIAL
supernatural	MAGIC, DIVINE, OCCULT, UNEARTHLY
supernatural power	MANA, NGAI, MAGIC, WAKAN, ORENDA
supernumerary	ACTOR, EXTRA, WALKON, STANDIN, FIGURANT
supersede	REPLACE, SUCCEED, SUPPLANT
superseded	OBSOLETE
supersensitive	THINSKINNED
supersonic sound	BOOM
superstition	FEAR, FREIT, BELIEF, PHOBIA, TRADITION
superstition, object of	FETICH, FETISH, LADDER, BLACK CAT, TALISMAN
superstitious	CREDULOUS
supervene	ENSUE, HAPPEN, EMANATE
supervise	DIRECT, GOVERN, MANAGE, OVERSEE
supervision	DIRECTION, SURVEILLANCE
supervisor	MANAGER, DIRECTOR, OVERSEER
supine	INERT, PRONE, PASSIVE, INACTIVE, PROSTRATE, RECUMBENT
supper	MEAL, DINNER

supplant	OUST, USURP, REPLACE, SUPERSEDE
supple	SOFT, AGILE, LITHE, LIMBER, PLIANT, LISSOME
supplement	ADD, EKE, ADJUNCT, APPENDIX
supplemental material	INDEX, TABLE, ADDENDA, GLOSSARY, ADDENDUM, APPENDIX
supplementary	ADDED, EXTRA, SECOND, ADDITIONAL
supplicant	BEGGAR, SUITOR, PLEADER, PETITIONER, WORSHIPPER
supplicate	BEG, PRAY, PLEAD, APPEAL, OBTEST, BESEECH, ENTREAT, PETITION, ROGATION
supplication	BID, PLEA, SUIT, ORISON, PRAYER, REQUEST, ENTREATY
supplier	PROVIDER, PURVEYOR
supplies	STOCK, STORES, PROVENDER, PROVISIONS
supply	CATER, EQUIP, RELAY, STOCK, ENDOW, BACKLOG, FURNISH, PROVIDE
supply ship	OILER, TENDER, VICTUALLER
support	FID, LEG, PEG, ABET, BACK, BASE, IBAR, PROP, STAY, BRACE, PILLAR, SECOND, TRIPOD, UNIPOD
support word	YEA
supporter	FAN, ALLY, DONOR, GIVER, BACKER, BEARER, PATRON, ROOTER, SECOND, ABETTOR, CARRIER, ADHERENT, ADVOCATE, FOLLOWER, PARTISAN
supportive	HELPFUL, REASSURING, SUSTAINING
suppose	WIS, TROW, WEEN, GUESS, OPINE, ASSUME, RECKON, IMAGINE, SURMISE
supposed	REPUTED, PUTATIVE, PRESUMED
supposition	THEORY, CONJECTURE, HYPOTHESIS
supposititious	FALSE, FEIGNED, PRETENDED, FICTITIOUS
suppository	PESSARY
suppress	BAN, CHECK, QUASH, QUELL, STIFLE, SMOTHER
suppression	INHIBITION, REPRESSION

suppurate   FESTER, RANKLE, PUTREFY, MATURATE

supremacy   MASTERY, DOMINION

supreme   CHIEF, FINAL, GREATEST, ULTIMATE

supreme being   GOD, ALLAH, DEITY, CREATOR

Supreme Court Justice   DAY, JAY, TAFT, BLAIR, BLACK, CHASE, CLARK, STONE, TANEY, WAITE, WHITE, BREYER, BURGER, BURTON, BYRNES, FORTAS, FULLER, HARLAN, HUGHES, MINTON, POWELL, SCALIA, SOUTER, THOMAS, VINSON, WARREN, WILSON, BRENNAN, CARDOZO, DOUGLAS, IREDELL, JACKSON, KENNEDY, OCONNOR, STEVENS, STEWART, BLACKMUN, BRANDEIS, GINSBURG, GOLDBERG, MARSHALL, RUTLEDGE, ELLSWORTH, REHNQUIST, WHITTAKER, FRANKFURTER

surcharge   TAX, BURDEN, IMPOST, (OVER)LOAD

surd   MUTE, DEADEN, DEFILE, STUPID, RADICAL, VOICELESS, IRRATIONAL

sure   FIRM, SAFE, SECURE, STABLE, CERTAIN

sure thing   CINCH, SHOOIN, CERTAINTY

surely   YES, INDEED, OFCOURSE, ABSOLUTELY, DEFINITELY

surety   VAS, BAIL, BOND, GAGE, HOSTAGE, MAINPRISE

surf   SEA, FOAM, SPRAY, SWELL, WAVES, ROLLERS, BREAKERS, WHITECAPS

surface   NAP, TAR, AREA, FACE(T), PAVE, NAPPE, VENEER, AIRFOIL, EXTERIOR, SUPERFICIAL

surfeit   see CLOY

surfeited   BLASE, SATED, REPLETE

surge   PUSH, RISE, ROLL, HEAVE, PITCH, SWELL, BILLOW

surgeon   MEDICO, DOCTOR, SAWBONES

surgery   BIOPSY, REMOVAL, SECTION, EXCISION, OPERATION

surgery, perform   CUT, LASE, OPERATE

surgical tools and terms   see p. 724

Suriname   DUTCHGUIANA

Suriname, capital of   PARAMARIBO

Surinamese city   JENNY, TEPOE, ALBINA, CORONIE, MEERZORG, PARAMARIBO

Surinamese language   DUTCH, TONGO, SRANAN, TAIUTAKI

Surinamese money   GUILDER

Surinamese river   LAWA, LUCIE, LITANI, PIKIEN, NICKERIE

surly   see SULLEN

surmise   GUESS, INFER, OPINE, THEORY, IMAGINE, PRESUME, SUSPECT, CONJECTURE

surmount   CAP, TOP, SCALE, MASTER, CONQUER, SURPASS, OVERCAME

surname   BYNAME, AGNOMEN, COGNOMEN, PATRONYMIC

surpass   CAP, TOP, BEST, EXCEL, OUTDO, ECLIPSE, OUTSTRIP

surplice   GOWN, COTTA, EPHOD

surplus   GLUT, EXTRA, SPARE, EXCESS, OVERAGE, RESERVE, RESIDUE, REMAINDER

surprise   AWE, DAZE, JOLT, AMAZE, ASTOUND, STARTLE, ASTONISH

surprised   AGAPE

surprising   UNEXPECTED, UNFORESEEN

surrender   CEDE, YIELD, REMISE, RESIGN, CESSION, DEDITION

surreptitious   COVERT, SECRET, FURTIVE, STEALTHY, UNDERCOVER, CLANDESTINE

surrogate   LOCUM, DEPUTY, REGENT, STANDIN

surround   GIRD, RING, BESET, INARM, AMBUSH, INVEST, ENCLOSE, ENVELOP

surrounding   MIDST, MILIEU, SETTING, ENVIRONMENT

surtax   DUTY, LEVY

surveillance   WATCH, PATROL, STAKEOUT, VIGILANCE, OBSERVATION

survey   MAP, PLOT, POLL, SCAN, REVIEW, CANVASS

survey choice   OTHER

surveying instrument   **ROD,
LEVEL, STADIA, ALIDADE,
CALIPER, TRANSIT, VERNIER**
surveyor   **ASSESSOR,
OVERSEER, ARPENTEUR**
surveyor's assistant   **RODMAN,
LINEMAN**
survival mechanism   **COPING**
survive   **LAST, LIVE (ON),
ENDURE, MAKE IT,
OUTLIVE**
Susa inhabitant   **ELAMITE**
Susan   **SUE, SUZY, SUSIE**
susceptible   **LIABLE, OPENTO,
SENSITIVE, RESPONSIVE**
suspect   **THINK, IMAGINE,
PRESUME, SURMISE**
suspend   **BAR, HALT, HANG,
STAY, DEFER, DISBAR,
ADJOURN, POSTPONE**
suspended   **HUNG, PENDENT,
PENSILE**
suspenders   **BRACES, GALLOWS,
GARTERS, HANGERS,
GALLUSES**
suspense   **DOUBT, ANXIETY,
ABEYANCE, UNCERTAINTY**
suspenseful   **TENSE,
HAZARDOUS**
suspension   **DELAY, PAUSE,
PENDENCY, STOPPAGE,
CESSATION**
suspicion   **FEAR, HINT, HUNCH,
TRACE, INKLING**
suspicious   **LEERY, DUBIOUS,
FEARFUL, PARANOID,
WATCHFUL, SKEPTICAL**
sustain   **CARRY, ENDURE,
RATIFY, NOURISH,
NURTURE, SUPPORT**
sustained   **(SOS)TENUTO**
sustenance   **FOOD, BREAD,
MANNA, UPKEEP, ALIMENT,
NUTRITION**
sutler   **TRADESMAN,
VICTUALLER**
suttee   **SUICIDE, IMMOLATION**
suture   **SEW, SEAM, RAPHE,
STITCH**
svelte   **SLIM, LITHE, LISSOM(E),
SLENDER, WILLOWY**
Svengali   **COAXER, RASPUTIN,
HYPNOTIST**
swab   **DAB, MOP, DAUB, QTIP,
WIPE, MALKIN, SPONGE**
swaddle   **BIND, TAPE, WRAP,
SWATHE**
swag   **HAUL, LOOT, SWAY,
BOOTY, LURCH**

swagger   **STRUT, PRANCE,
BLUSTER, FLOUNCE**
swain   **BEAU, LOVER, SUITOR,
GALLANT**
swale   **FEN, LATH, MOOR,
MARSH, PLANK, SHADE**
swallow   **EAT, BOLT, GULP,
ABSORB, INGEST, MARTIN,
MARTLET, HIRUNDINE**
swami   **FAKIR, MASTER,
PUNDIT, TEACHER**
swamp   **SLOO, SLUE, VLEI,
LOGAN, TAIGA, TERAI;**
see **MARSH**
swamped   **FLOODED,
SNOWEDUNDER**
swampy   **BOGGY, FENNY,
MARSHY, PALUDAL**
swan   **COB, PEN, ANSA,
CYGNET**
swan genus   **OLOR, CYGNUS**
Swan Lake role   **ODILE**
swan song   **END**
swan, young   **CYGNET**
swanky   **POSH, FANCY, PLUSH,
SHOWY, SMART, STYLISH**
swap   **TRADE, BARTER,
EXCHANGE**
sward   **SOD, LAWN, TURF,
GRASS, GREEN**
swarm   **BEVY, HIVE, NEST,
TEEM, CROWD, HORDE**
swarthy   **DUN, DARK, DUSKY**
swashbuckler   **BRAVO,
GASCON, RUFFIAN,
SLASHER**
swastika   **FYLFOT,
GAMMADION**
swat   **HIT, BLOW, CLIP, SLAP,
SLUG, CLOUT, WHACK,
STRIKE**
swatch   **SAMPLE**
swath   **BELT, TIER, QUEUE,
STRIP**
swathe   **BIND, WRAP,
BANDAGE, SWADDLE**
sway   **YAW, BIAS, REEL, ROCK,
ROLL, RULE, WAVER, LURCH,
POWER, DANGLE, FLUCTUATE**
Swaziland, capital of   **MBABANE**
Swaziland city town   **MPAKA,
BHUNYI, SITEKI, MBABANE,
MANZINI, PIGGSPEAK**
Swaziland language   **(SI)SWATI**
Swaziland money   **LILANGENI**
Swaziland neighbor
MOZAMBIQUE, SOUTH AFRICA
Swaziland river   **USUTU,
KOMATI, MBULUZI**

swear VOW, AVER, AVOW,
CURSE, AFFIRM, DEPONE,
DEPOSE, PLEDGE
sweat DRIP, OOZE, SEEP,
WORK, EXUDE, SUDOR,
EGESTA, LATHER, EXCRETE,
SWELTER, EXERCISE,
PERSPIRE, PERSPIRATION
sweater GANSEY, JERSEY,
SLIPON, CARDIGAN,
PULLOVER
sweaty CLAMMY, PERSPIRY,
TOILSOME
Sweden, capital of STOCKHOLM
Sweden, rulers of CARL, INGE,
JOHN, VASA, ADOLF, JOHAN,
OSCAR, SWEYN, BIRGER,
GUSTAF, GUSTAV, CHARLES,
SVERKER, ADOLPHUS,
GUSTAVUS, MARGARET,
CHRISTIAN, CHRISTINA,
FREDERICK
Swedish actress GARBO,
ULLMAN, BERGMAN
Swedish city/town LUND,
SAMA, GAVLE, MALMO,
OLAND, VISBY, KALMAR,
UPPSALA, GOTEBORG,
JOKKMOKK, STOCKHOLM
Swedish island FARO, ORNO,
GRASO, OLAND, GOTLAND
Swedish king ERIC, WASA,
OSCAR, BERNADOTTE
Swedish lake VANERN,
MALAREN, VATTERN,
HJALMAREN
Swedish measure AM, ALN,
POT, REP, TUM, FAMN,
FODER, KANNA, KAPPE, LINJE,
NYMIL, SPANN, TUNNA,
JUMFRU, KOLLAST, TUNLAND,
OXHUVUD
Swedish money ORE, DALER,
KRONA, RIGSDALER
Swedish Nightingale JENNY
LIND
Swedish sculptor MILLES
Swedish river DAL, UME, KLAR,
PITE, TORNE, INDALS,
MUONIO, VINDEL, LJUNGAN,
LJUSNAN, LULEALV,
ANGERMAN
Swedish weight ASS, ORT,
PUND, STEN, UNTZ,
NYLAST, LISPUND
sweep DRAG, DUST, RAKE,
SCAN, SKIM, BROOM,
BRUSH, RANGE, SWATH,
TRAIL

sweeping WIDE, BROAD,
TOTAL, RADICAL,
COMPREHENSIVE
sweepstakes LOTTO, RAFFLE,
LOTTERY
sweet HONEY, DULCET,
SYRUPY, SUGARY; see CANDY
sweet potato YAM, BATATA,
CAMOTE, OCARINA
sweetbread RIS, THYMUS,
PANCREAS
sweeten CANDY, GLAZE,
DULCIFY
sweetener SOP, SUGAR, SYRUP,
GLUCOSE, SPLENDA,
SUCARYL, SUCROSE,
ASPARTAME, CYCLAMATE,
INCENTIVE, SACCHARIN
sweetheart JO, GRA, BEAU, JILL,
LASS, FLAME, LEMAN, LOVER,
POPSY, FIANCE, LASSIE,
STEADY, SUITOR, FIANCEE,
VALENTINE
sweetmeat see CANDY
sweetness SAPOR
swell COOL, FOPO, DUDE,
GROW, PLIM, PUFF, RISE,
SNOB, SURF, WAVE, BLOAT,
BULGE, DANDY, GREAT,
HEAVE, NEATO, BILLOW,
DILATE, EXPAND, GROOVY,
BRUMMEL, DISTEND, INFLATE
swelling STY, WEN, BUBO,
GALL, LUMP, NODE, PUFF,
BLAIN, EDEMA, POLYP, VARIX,
GOITER, STRUMA, POLYPUS,
HEMATOMA
swelling reducer ICE, ASPIRIN
swelter ROAST, SWEAT,
PERSPIRE
sweltering MUGGY, SULTRY,
TORRID
swerve SHY, SKEW, VEER,
SHEER, CAREEN, DEVIATE
swift CRAN, FAST, FLIT,
FLEET, SWIFTLET
swift genus APUS
swiftly APACE
swig BELT, GULP, DRAFT,
DRINK
swill SLOP, SWIG, QUAFF,
REFUSE, GARBAGE
swim KICK, BATHE, FLOAT,
PADDLE, STROKE
swimmer FISH, DIVER, NAIAD,
MERMAN, MERMAID,
FROGMAN, NATATOR
swimmer's worry ORCA,
SHARK, MANOWAR

swimming	**NATANT**
swimming pool toy	**WORM,**
	NOODLE
swimsuit	*see* **BATHING SUIT**
swindle(r)	**CON, SKIN, BUNCO,**
COZEN, GRIFT, TREPAN; *see*	
	CHEAT
swine	**HOG, PIG, SOW, APER,**
BENE, BOAR, GALT, GILT,	
PORK, RUNT, SUID, YILT,	
DUROC, ESSEX, GRICE,	
PIGGY, SHOAT, SHOTE, SHOTT,	
SNORK, SUINA, COCHON,	
GUSSIE, JABALI, JAVALI,	
PIGGIE, PIGLET, PORKER,	
PORKET, TITMAN, GRUNTER,	
PECCARY, ROASTER,	
SNORKER, SUFFOLK, SUIDIAN	
swine feeding	**PANNAGE**
swine fever	**ROUGET**
swine genus	**SUS**
swine, *pert. to*	**PORCINE**
swing	**BAT, FLAP, HANG, JAZZ,**
JIVE, LILT, SLUE, SWAY,	
CAREEN, DANGLE, RHYTHM,	
SWITCH, BRANDISH	
swinging	**PENDULOUS**
swinish	**PORCINE, SUILLINE**
swipe	**LIFT, LEVER, STEAL,**
HANDLE, PILFER, STRIKE	
swirl	**CURL, EDDY, GORCE,**
GURGE, TWIST, WHORL	
Swiss, Switzerland	**LADIN,**
	SUISSE, HELVETIA
Swiss city/town	**ZUG, BERN,**
BIEL, BRIG, CHUR, SION,	
THUN, BASEL, STANS,	
ASCONA, GENEVA, GLARUS,	
SCHWYZ, ZURICH, LUCERNE,	
ZERMATT, FRIBOURG,	
LAUSANNE, MONTREUX,	
	NEUCHATEL
Swiss commune	**AUSA, VICH**
Swiss Family Robinson author	
	WYSS
Swiss game	**JASS**
Swiss language	**LADIN,**
	ROMANS(C)H
Swiss lake	**GENEVA, WALLEN,**
LUCERNE, CONSTANCE,	
	BRIENZERSEE
Swiss measure	**POT, AUNE,**
FUSS, IMMI, MUID, PIED,	
SAUM, ZOLL, LIEUE, MAASS,	
POUCE, SCHUH, STAAB,	
TOISE, PERCHE, SETIER,	
KLAFTER, VIERTEL	
Swiss money	**BATZ, FRANC,**
RAPPE, CENTIME	

Swiss mountain	**DOM, ALPS,**
JURA, JUNGFRAU,	
GLARNISCH, MATTERHORN	
Swiss neighbor	**ITALY, FRANCE,**
AUSTRIA, GERMANY	
Swiss patriot	**TELL**
Swiss river	**INN, AARE, EMME,**
THUR, RHINE, RHONE,	
SARINE, TICINO, EMMENTAL	
Swiss state	**CANTON**
switch	**TWIG, SHUNT, TOGGLE**
switch part	**FROG, ROCKER**
switch word	**ON, OFF,**
Switzerland, capital of	**BERN(E),**
	LAUSANNE
swivel	**TURN, PIVOT, SWING,**
	ROTATE
swollen	**PUFFY, TUMID,**
BOLLEN, EDEMIC, TOROSE,	
TURGID, TURGENT, VARICOSE	
swoon	**SWEB, FAINT, SYNCOPE**
swoop	**DIVE, PLUNGE,**
POUNCE, DESCEND,	
	DESCENT
sword	**GRAM, BLADE, STEEL**
sword, famous	**ASCALON,**
ASKELON, BALMUNG,	
	EXCALIBUR
sword part	**POMMEL**
swords, type of	**SAX, BOLO,**
CHIV, EPEE, FALX, FOIL, KRIS,	
PATA, SEAX, TUCK, BILBO,	
BRAND, CATAN, DIEGO,	
ESTOC, KUKRI, SABER,	
ANDREW, BANCAL, BARONG,	
DUSACK, FLORET, GLAIVE,	
KATANA, KHANDA,	
MACANA, PARANG, RAPIER,	
SPATHA, TOLEDO, VERDUN,	
WAITER, CUTLASS, ESPADON,	
ESTOQUE, FERRARA,	
MACHETE, SLASHER,	
YASHMAC, BASELARD,	
CLAYMORE, DAMASCUS,	
FALCHION, SCHLAGER,	
SCIMITAR, YATAGHAN,	
	SCHIAVONE
swordfish	**AUS, DORADO**
swordplay	**FENCING**
sword-shaped	**ENSATE,**
XIPHOID, ENSIFORM,	
	GLADIATE
swordsman, swordswoman	
	FENCER, EPEEIST
sworn statement	**AFFIDAVIT,**
TESTIMONY, DEPOSITION	
sybarite	**EPICURE, HEDONIST,**
BONVIVANT, SENSUALITY,	
	VOLUPTUARY

sycamore	PLANE, PLATAN(E)
sycophant	LEECH, TOADY, FLUNKY, YESMAN
syllable	MORA, ARSIS, MORAE, TONIC, PENULT, SONANT, THESIS, ULTIMA
syllabus	OUTLINE, PROGRAM, ABSTRACT, SYNOPSIS
syllogism	LOGIC, DEDUCTION, REASONING
syllogism part	PREMISE
sylph	FAIRY, GNOME, UNDINE, HUMMINGBIRD
sylvan	SHADY, WOODY, WOODED, BUCOLIC
symbol	SIGN, TOKEN, ASPECT, EMBLEM
symbolic	ICONIC, EMBLEMATIC, FIGURATIVE
symbolic figure	ZOA
symbolize	MEAN, IMPLY, FIGURE, TYPIFY, BETOKEN, SIGNIFY, STANDFOR
symmetrical	EQUAL, REGULAR, BALANCED, PARALLEL
symmetry	GRACE, BALANCE, HARMONY, PROPORTION, UNIFORMITY
sympathetic	KIND, TENDER, CONGENIAL, COMPASSIONATE
sympathetic, not	AVERSE
sympathize	PITY, CONDOLE, FEELFOR, EMPATHIZE, COMMISERATE
sympathy	PITY, RUTH, ACCORD, EMPATHY, AFFINITY, COMPASSION
symphony	BAND, ORCHESTRA, PHILHARMONIC
symphony movement	LARGO, FINALE, MENUET, MINUET, SCHERZO, MINUETTO
symposium	FEAST, FORUM, BANQUET, SEMINAR, COLLOQUY, GATHERING, CONFERENCE
symptom	SIGN, WARNING, PRODROME, SYNDROME, INDICATION
synagogue	SHUL; see TEMPLE
synagogue officer	PARNAS(S), SHAM(M)AS, SHAM(M)ASH
synchronize	JIBE, MESH, AGREE, MATCH, COINCIDE, HARMONIZE, COORDINATE
synchronous	COEVAL, COINCIDENT, SIMULTANEOUS
syncopation	JAZZ, RAGTIME
syncope	FAINT, SWOON, ELISION
syncretize	COMBINE, RECONCILE
syndicate	POOL, JUDGE, CARTEL, COMBINE, CONSORTIUM
syndrome	SIGNS, SYMPTOM(S)
synergistic	COACTIVE, CONCURRENT
synergy	CONCERT, COINCIDENCE
synod	COUNCIL, MEETING, ASSEMBLY
synopsis	GIST, DIGEST, RESUME, SUMMARY, ABSTRACT
synoptic gospel	LUKE, MARK, MATTHEW
syntax	ORDER, GRAMMAR, STRUCTURE
synthesis	BLEND, FUSION, MIXTURE
synthetic	MADE, ERSATZ, MANMADE, ARTIFICIAL; see FABRIC
syphilis	POX, LUES
syphilis test	HAHN
Syracuse founder	ARCHIAS
Syracuse tyrant	GELON, DIONYSIUS
Syria	ARAM
Syria, capital of	DAMASCUS
Syrian city/town	DAR, ALEP, DEIR, DUMA, HAMA, HOMS, HAMAH, RAQQA, SIDON, ALEPPO, JABLAL, MANBIJ, MASYAF, TADMUR, TARTUS, LATAKIA, PALMYRA, RASAFEH, ARRAQQAH, DAMASCUS
Syrian measure	MAKUK, GARAVA
Syrian money	POUND
Syrian mountain	CARMEL, HERMON, LEBANON, LIBANUS
Syrian neighbor	IRAQ, ISRAEL, JORDAN, TURKEY
Syrian president	ASSAD
Syrian river	ASI, BALIKH, KHABUR, ORONTES, EUPHRATES
Syrian weight	COLA
syringe	NEEDLE, INJECTOR
syrinx	PANPIPE
syrup	KARO, SAPA, MAPLE, ORGEAT, SORGHUM, TREACLE, MOLASSES

system	ISM, WAY, CODE, ORDER, METHOD, REGIME, ROUTINE, REGIMENT, PROCEDURE
systematic	ORDERLY, REGULAR, RATIONAL, METHODICAL, REGIMENTAL
systematize	ORDER, CLASSIFY, ORGANIZE, STANDARDIZE
syzygy	PAIR, DIPODY

T

T	TAU, TEE, TANGO
T-shaped	TAU
tab	LUG, PAN, TAG, BILL, CHIT, FLAP, LOOP, CHECK, LABEL, STRIP, CHARGE, TICKET, ACCOUNT
tabard	CAPE, CLOAK, JACKET, MANTLE
tabby	SILK, MOIRE, MOREEN, TAFFETA, BRINDLED; see CAT
tabernacle	PYX, SHUL, TENT, AMBRY, HILET, NICHE, CHURCH, MOSQUE, TEMPLE, SYNAGOGUE
tabes	ATROPHY, MARASMUS, PHTHISIS, EMACIATION, CONSUMPTION, TUBERCULOSIS
table	PYE, DESK, FARE, FOOD, MENU, PEND, DEFER, SHELVE, VANITY, COUNTER, CREDENCE, POSTPONE, POUDREUSE; see LIST, STAND
table game	POOL, PINGPONG, BILLIARDS
table payment	ANTE
tableau	ARRAY, SCENE, DIORAMA
tableland	MESA, PLAT, PUNA, KAROO, PLATEAU
tablet	PAD, BRED, PILL, SLAB, FACIA, SLATE, STELE, TROCHE, TESSERA
tableware	CUP, BOWL, DISH, FORK, GLASS, KNIFE, PLATE, SPOON, SAUCER, TUREEN, PLATTER
tabloid	LURID, PAPER, TABLET, SHOCKING
taboo	BAN, BAR, APU, NONO, PROHIBIT, VERBOTEN, FORBID(DEN), PROHIBITION
taboo, opp. to	NOA

tabor	DRUM, SNARE, ATABAL, TIMBREL, TABOURET
Tabor, Mt. site	ISRAEL
tabouret	SEAT, STOOL, TABLE
tabula —	RASA
tabulate	LIST, ARRAY, CHART, TALLY, FIGURE
tachometer reading	RPM(S)
tacit	MUTE, SILENT, UNSAID, IMPLIED, IMPLICIT, UNSPOKEN
taciturn	MUTE, BRIEF, QUIET, LACONIC, RETICENT, SATURNINE
tack	BEAT, BUSK, FARE, FOOD, JIBE, BASTE, ZIGZAG, SECURE; see NAIL
tackle	CAT, GUN, GEAR, LUFF, GRASP, JEERS, GARNET, OUTFIT, RUNNER, TAKE ON
tacky	DOWDY, SEEDY, SHABBY, SHODDY, STICKY, TAWDRY
Tacoma sound	PUGET
tact	FINESSE, DIPLOMACY
tactful	POLITE, DISCREET, DIPLOMATIC, CONSIDERATE
tactical	STRATEGIC
tactic(s)	PLOY, METHOD, POLICY, MANEUVER, STRATEGY
tactile	PALPABLE, TANGIBLE, TOUCHABLE
tactless	RUDE, BLUNT, GAUCHE, IMPOLITE, THOUGHTLESS
tad	TOT, TYKE, GAMIN, PEEWEE, URCHIN
tadpole	POLLIWOG
taffeta	SILK, GAUDY, TABBY, SAMITE
tag	TAIL, LABEL, A(I)GLET, APPEND
Tahiti, formerly	OTAHEITE
Tahiti capital	PAPEETE
tai —	CHI
tail	BUN, FUD, TAG, BUNT, CODA, HIND, SCUT, CAUDA, QUEUE, STALK, TRAIL, VERSO, FOLLOW, SHADOW, WREATH
tail, pert. to	CAUDAL, CAUDATE
tailing	SCRAP, WASTE, REFUSE, REJECT
tailless	ACAUDAL, ANUROUS
tail-loser	TADPOLE
tailor	FIT, SEW, DRAPER, SARTOR, SNYDER, CLOTHIER

tailor's equipment	**HAM,**
GOOSE, NEEDLE, THREAD,	
SADIRON, THIMBLE	
taint	**ROT, HOGO, STAIN,**
SULLY, INFECT, BLEMISH,	
POLLUTE, CONTAMINATE	
tainted	**BAD, RANCID, SPOILT,**
SPOILED	
Taiwan	**FORMOSA**
Taiwan, capital of	**TAIPEI**
Taiwan city/town	**ILAN, SUAO,**
CHIAI, NANTOU, TAINAN,	
TAIPEI, CHILUNG, TAITUNG,	
PANCHIAO, CHAOCHOU,	
FENGSHAN, SANCHUNG,	
TAICHUNG	
Taiwan island	**LANYU, LUTAO,**
MATSU, PENGHU, QUEMOY	
Taiwan money	**DOLLAR**
Taiwan mountain	**TZUKAO,**
YUSHAN	
Taiwan river	**TACHIA,**
KOOPING, TANSHUI	
Taj Mahal builder	**JAHAN,**
JEHAN	
Taj Mahal location	**AGRA**
Tajikistan, capital of	**DUSHANBE**
Tajikistan city/town	**KULOB,**
NORAK, KHORUGH,	
DUSHANBE, KHUDZHAND	
Tajikistan money	**RUBL,**
ROUBLE	
Tajikistan mountain	**LENIN,**
PAMIR, KARLMARX	
Tajikistan river	**PANI, VAKHSH,**
AMUDARYA	
take	**GET, NAB, WIN, GRAB,**
GRIP, PICK, ADOPT, CLASP,	
GRASP, SEIZE, STEAL, USURP,	
ACCEPT, ARREST, OBTAIN,	
OCCUPY, TAKEIN, PROCURE	
— and take	**GIVE**
take action	**PROCEED**
take advantage of	**ABUSE,**
EXPLOIT	
take away	**ADEEM, HEAVE,**
REVOKE	
take back	**ABJURE, RECALL,**
RECANT, RETRACT	
take by force	**GRAB, SEIZE,**
USURP, WREST, KIDNAP,	
SNATCH, CAPTURE	
take care	**HEED, MIND,**
BEWARE	
take for granted	**ASSUME,**
PRESUME	
take in	**REAP, ADOPT, CHEAT,**
DECEIVE	
take it easy	**REST, RELAX**

take off	**FLY, DOFF, FLEE,**
BEGIN, LEAVE, MIMIC,	
START, DETACH, DEPART,	
DETACH, PARODY, REMOVE	
take offense	**BRIDLE, RESENT**
take on	**HIRE, ADOPT, ANNEX,**
APPEND, ASSUME, EMPLOY,	
OPPOSE	
take out	**DELE, KILL, ELIDE,**
MURDER, EXPUNGE	
take over	**SEIZE, USURP,**
ASSUME, CAPTURE	
take over for	**RELIEVE**
take part	**SHARE, PARTICIPATE**
take place	**OCCUR, HAPPEN**
take place of	**SUPPLANT,**
SUPERSEDE	
take shape	**GEL, FORM, JELL,**
CRYSTALLIZE	
take stock	**ASSESS, SURVEY,**
APPRAISE, CONSIDER	
take turns	**ALTERNATE**
take up	**FILL, ADOPT, BEGIN,**
MOUNT, START, ACCEPT,	
OCCUPY	
taken aback	**STARTLED,**
SURPRISED, UNPREPARED	
takings	**NET, PROFITS,**
RECEIPTS, WINNINGS	
talc(um)	**MICA, POWDER,**
AGALITE, STEATITE,	
SOAPSTONE	
tale	**LAI, REDE, GESTE,**
LEGEND; *see* **STORY**	
Tale of Two Cities author	
DICKENS	
Tale of Two Cities character	
LUCIE, CARTON, DARNAY	
talent	**ART, DOWER, FLAIR,**
FORTE, KNACK, GENIUS,	
FACULTY	
talented	**ABLE, CLEVER,**
GIFTED, ENDOWED	
talisman	*see* **CHARM**
talk	**GAB, GAS, JAW, YAK,**
BLAB, BUKH, BUKK, CHAT,	
CHIN, KNAP, RANT, RAVE,	
SASS, CRACK, ORATE, PRATE,	
SPEAK, SPIEL, CONFER,	
GOSSIP, PARLEY, PATTER,	
SPEECH, YABBER, CHATTER,	
LECTURE, PALAVER,	
PRATTLE, CONVERSE,	
HARANGUE	
talk about	**DISCUSS**
talk back	**LIP, SASS, RETORT**
talk big	**BRAG, BOAST**
talk down	**BELITTLE,**
MINIMIZE, DISPARAGE	

talk down to **DEMEAN,**	tame **CALM, DULL, FLAT,**
PATRONIZE, CONDESCEND	**BREAK, BORING, DOCILE,**
talk, empty **GAS, BULL,**	**GENTLE, SUBDUE, INSIPID,**
HUMBUG, PATTER,	**TRAINED, DOMESTIC(ATED),**
HOGWASH, BUNCOMBE,	**(HOUSE)BROKEN**
CLAPTRAP	tamed **BROKEN, GENTLE,**
talk into **INDUCE, CONVINCE,**	**DOMESTICATED**
BRING (A)ROUND	Tamerlane birthplace
talk out of **DISSUADE**	**SAMARKAND**
talk show host **HALL, KING,**	Tamerlane descendant
LENO, PAAR, JONES, OPRAH,	**BABER**
CARSON, POVICH, RIVERA,	Taming of the Shrew character
RIVERS, DONAHUE,	**SLY, KATE, BIANCA, GREMIO,**
RAPHAEL, WINFREY,	**GRUMIO, BAPTISTA,**
WOOLERY, WILLIAMS	**HORTENSIO, KATHERINA**
talk to oneself **SOLILOQUIZE**	Tammany leader **TWEED,**
talkative **JAWY, GABBY,**	**SACHEM**
WORDY, CHATTY, PROLIX,	tamp **PUG, RAM, PACK,**
GARRULOUS, LOQUACIOUS	**POUND**
talkative person **JAY, GABBER,**	tamper **GAFF, ALTER,**
GASBAG, MAGPIE,	**CHANGE, MEDDLE, MODIFY,**
WINDBAG, CHATTERBOX	**MONKEY, TINKER, TRIFLE,**
talking point **TOPIC**	**INTERFERE**
tall **HIGH, LARGE, LOFTY,**	tampon **PLUG, SPONGE,**
ALPINE, TOWERING,	**PACKING, PADDING**
OUTLANDISH, EXAGGERATED	tan **DUN, TAW, BUFF, ECRU,**
tall order **CHORE**	**FLOG, ROSS, BEIGE, BROWN,**
tallith **SHAWL, MANTLE**	**KHAKI, TAWNY, BRONZE(D),**
tallow **FAT, OIL, SEBO, SUET,**	**TANNIN, THRASH**
SEBUM, STEAT, GREASE,	tanager **YENI, LINDO;** *see p. 675*
STEARIN	tandoori **(CLAY) OVEN**
tally **FIT, TAB, JIBE, AGREE,**	tang **NIP, BITE, ZEST, SAVOR,**
CHECK, COUNT, MATCH,	**TASTE, STING, FLAVOR,**
NOTCH, SCORE, RECORD,	**PIQUANCY, PUNGENCY**
SQUARE, ACCOUNT,	Tanganyika *see* **TANZANIA**
CHALKUP, CORRESPOND	tangent **ADJACENT, TOUCHING**
Talmai relative **MAACAH,**	tangible **REAL, SOLID,**
ABSALOM	**ACTUAL, TACTILE,**
Tamar relative **PHAREZ**	**CONCRETE, PALPABLE,**
Talmud part **GEMARA,**	**MATERIAL**
HAGGADA, HALAKHA,	Tangiers measure **KULA, MUDD**
MISHNAH	tangle **MAT, FOUL, KNOT,**
Talmudic **GEMARIC,**	**SHAG, SNAG, CATCH, SNARL,**
MISHNAIC, RABBINIC	**ENMESH, JUMBLE, MUDDLE,**
talon **CLAW, FANG, HEEL,**	**SLEAVE, EMBROIL,**
NAIL, OGEE, SPUR, STOCK,	**COMPLICATE, INTERTWINE**
HALLUX, POUNCE, ZIPPER	tangy **SHARP, ZESTY,**
talus **SCREE, SLOPE, ANKLE,**	**PIQUANT, PUNGENT**
DEBRIS, ASTRAGALUS,	tank **TUB, VAT, JAIL, BASIN,**
HUCKLEBONE	**OILER, CISTERN, VEHICLE,**
tam(-o'-shanter) **CAP, BERET**	**CONTAINER, RESERVOIR**
Tamar husband **ER, ONAN,**	tank, type of **BT, MARK,**
JUDAH	**JUMBO, TIGER, PANZER,**
tamarack **LARCH**	**STALIN, WILLIE, SHERMAN,**
tambour **DRUM, FRAME,**	**VICKERS, CROMWELL,**
TABORET, EMBROIDERY	**PERSHING, CENTURION**
tambourine **DRUM, RIKK,**	tankard **CUP, MUG, STEIN,**
TAAR, DAIRA, DAIRE,	**FLAGON, CHALICE**
TABOR, TIMBREL	tanker problem **SPILL**

Tannhauser composer **WAGNER**	tapir **(D)ANTA**
tanning need **BATE, KINO,**	tapster **BARMAN, BARKEEP,**
ALDER, FURAN, SUMAC,	**BARMAID, SKINKER**
CASHOO, LOTION, CATECHU,	tar **GOB, GOO, BREA, PITCH,**
SUNLAMP, QUEBRACHO	**RESIN, SMEAR, STAIN,**
tantalize **VEXT, TEASE, TEMPT,**	**DEFAME, MALTHA, SLUDGE,**
SEDUCE, PROVOKE,	**ASPHALT, BITUMEN,**
TORTURE, TITILLATE	**BLACKEN; see SAILOR**
Tantalus relative **ZEUS, NIOBE,**	taradiddle **FIB, LIE, BUNK,**
PELOPS	**NONSENSE**
tantamount **EQUAL,**	tardy **LATE, SLOW, SLACK,**
EQUIVALENT	**REMISS, BELATED,**
tantrum **(CAT)FIT, HUFF,**	**OVERDUE, DILATORY**
RAGE, CONNIPTION	tare **JOT, ATOM, WEED, WHIT,**
Tanzania, capital of **DODOMA**	**VETCH, WEIGHT**
Tanzanian city/town **WETE,**	target **AIM, END, BUTT, GOAL,**
KOANI, LINDI, MBEYA,	**MARK, QUARRY, BULLSEYE,**
MOSHI, TANGA, ARUSHA,	**OBJECTIVE**
DODOMA, IRINGA, KIGOMA,	Tarheel State **NC, NORTH**
MWANZA, MTWARA, SONGEA,	**CAROLINA**
TABORA, TUNDURU,	tariff **TAX, DUTY, LEVY, LIST,**
MOROGORO, DARESSALAAM	**RATE, IMPOST, CUSTOMS**
Tanzanian island **MAFIA,**	Tariff Act author **SMOOT,**
PEMBA, ZANZIBAR	**HAWLEY**
Tanzanian lake **NYASA,**	Tarkington character **SAM,**
RUKWA, NATRON,	**LOLA, WILLIE, AMBERSON**
MANYARA, VICTORIA	Tarkington work **PENROD,**
Tanzanian money **SHILLING**	**SEVENTEEN, ALICEADAMS**
Tanzanian mountain **RUNGWE,**	tarmac **RUNWAY**
KILIMANJARO	tarnish **SOIL, STAIN, SULLY,**
Tanzanian neighbor **KENYA,**	**TAINT, DEFAME, BLACKEN,**
ZAIRE, UGANDA, ZAMBIA,	**DISCOLOR**
MOZAMBIQUE	taro **MOD, GABE, GABI, TUBER**
Tanzanian people **GOMA,**	taro dish **POI**
BANTU, SUKUMA, WAGOGO,	tarot **see CARD**
SWAHILI, WABINGA	tarpaulin **TARP, CANVAS,**
Tanzanian river **WAMI,**	**OILCLOTH**
KAGERA, RUFIJI, RUVUMA,	tarpon **ELOPS, OXEYE, SABALO,**
PANGANI, MUHUWESI,	**TARPUM, BONEFISH**
KILOMBERO	Tarquin avenger **PORSENA**
Taoism founder **LAOTZU**	tarry **LAG, BIDE, STAY, WAIT,**
tap **PAT, RAP, DRAFT, KNOCK,**	**ABIDE, DALLY, DELAY,**
TOUCH, DECANT, OUTLET;	**DAWDLE, LINGER, LOITER,**
see SPIGOT, TAVERN	**SOJOURN**
tape, clear **ERASE**	tarsus **HOCK, ANKLE, SHANK**
taper **VCR, WANE, LESSEN,**	tart **ACID, FLAN, KEEN, SOUR,**
NARROW, DECREASE,	**ACERB, ACRID, HUSSY,**
DIMINISH; see CANDLE	**SAUCY, TRAMP, HARLOT,**
tapered **CONOID, SPIRED,**	**PASTRY, ACERBIC,**
TERETE	**STRUMPET, ACIDULOUS**
tapestry **RUG, ARRAS, TAPIS,**	tartan **SCOT, SHIP, CHECK,**
BAYEUX, CARPET, DORSAL,	**PLAID**
DOSSER, GOBELIN	tartar **ARGAL, ARGOL,**
tapeworm **T(A)ENIA, CESTODE,**	**TARTRE; see TATAR**
CESTOID, PARASITE	Tartarus **HELL, HADES**
taphouse **see TAVERN**	Tartuffe **HYPOCRITE,**
tapioca source **SALEP, CASAVA,**	**PRETENDER**
MANIOC, CASSAVA,	Tartuffe author **MOLIERE**
MANIHOT	Tarzan author **BURROUGHS**

Tarzan character   JANE, CHEETA
task   TASK, DUTY, ONUS,
    WORK, GRIND, LABOR,
    STINT, BURDEN, CHARGE,
    PENSUM, ASSIGNMENT
task, take to   SCOLD, REBUKE
taskmaster   BOSS, LEGREE,
    MARTINET, OVERSEER,
    SLAVEDRIVER
Tasmania, capital of   HOBART
Tasmanian city/town   DOVER,
    BURNIE, HOBART, STRAHAN,
    MARRAWAH, LAUNCESTON
Tasmanian mountain   OSSA
Tasmanian river   DEE, HUON,
    OUSE, CLYDE, DAVEY,
    LEVEN, TAMAR, DERWENT
tassel   TUFT, TERCEL, ZIZITH
taste   SIP, SUP, TRY, BENT,
    TANG, GUSTO, SAPOR,
    SAVOR, SNACK, TRACE,
    DEGUST, FLAVOR, LIKING,
    PALATE, SOUPCON,
    PENCHANT, PREFERENCE
tasteful   KEEN, SAPID, TASTY,
    DAINTY, SAVORY, ELEGANT,
    REFINED, DISCRIMINATING
tasteless   DULL, FLAT, BLAND,
    CRUDE, STALE, VAPID,
    GAUCHE, INSIPID
tasty   see SAVORY
Tatar   TURK, THIEF, VALET,
    BEGGAR, SAVAGE,
    MONGOL(IAN)
Tatler founder   STEELE
tatter   DAG, RAG, TAG, SCRAP,
    SHRED, FRAGMENT
tatterdemalion   BEGGAR,
    RAGAMUFFIN
tattered   TORN, FRAYED,
    RAGGED
tattle   BLAB, CHAT, TALK,
    PEACH, GOSSIP, INFORM,
    SNITCH, CHATTER
tattler   GOSSIP, INFORMER
tattoo   PRICK, SALVO, SIGNAL,
    VOLLEY, DRUMMING
tattooing   MOKO
taunt   GIBE, JEER, MOCK, TWIT,
    SCOFF, SNEER, NEEDLE,
    PROVOKE
taut   EDGY, SNUG, TRIG,
    RIGID, STIFF, TENSE, TIGHT,
    NERVOUS
tautology   PLEONASM,
    REDUNDANCE, REPETITION
tavern   BAR, INN, PUB, TAP,
    CAFE, KHAN, TAMBO,
    BISTRO, SALOON, BARROOM,

    CANTINA, TAPROOM,
    ALEHOUSE, ORDINARY,
    ROADHOUSE
tavern fare   ALE, BEER, BREAD,
    LAGER, STOUT, CHEESE,
    SAUSAGE
taw   MIB, VEX, LASH, LINE,
    WHIP, AGATE, ALLEY, STAKE,
    THONG, HARASS, MARBLE,
    RINGTAW, SHOOTER
tawdry   CHEAP, GAUDY,
    FLASHY, GARISH, SLEAZY,
    VULGAR
tawny   DUSKY, SWART,
    FULVOUS, RUBIATE
tax   CRO, FEE, CESS, DUTY,
    GELD, LEVY, SCAT, SCOT,
    SESS, TIRE, TOLL, LIKIN,
    RATAL, SCATT, STENT,
    TITHE, ABKARI, ANNALE,
    ASSESS, AVANIA, CUSTOM,
    EXCISE, HIDAGE, IMPOST,
    INCOME, OCTROI, TAILLE,
    TARIFF, ANNATES, SCUTAGE,
    TALLAGE, TRIBUTE
tax collector   IRS, OCTROI,
    CUSTOMS, ASSESSOR,
    REVENUER, COLLECTOR
tax evader   CAPONE
tax, type of   SALES, EXCISE,
    INCOME, CUSTOMS,
    ROADUSE, PROPERTY
taxable   DUTIABLE,
    ASSESSABLE
taxation   BLAME, CENSUS,
    ASSESSMENT, IMPOSITION
taxi   CAB, HACK, ARABA,
    HANSOM, JITNEY, DROSHKY
Taxi names   JIM, ALEX, ANDY,
    JUDD, KANE, TONY, BOBBY,
    CAROL, DANNY, DANZA,
    LATKA, LOUIE, NARDO, SIMKA,
    DEVITO, ELAINE, HENNER,
    HIRSCH, MARILU,
    KAUFMAN, IGNATOWSKI
taxing   TIRING, TRYING,
    ONEROUS, DEMANDING
taxonomic level   CLASS, GENUS,
    ORDER, FAMILY, PHYLUM,
    KINGDOM, SPECIES, SUBCLASS,
    INFRACLASS, SUPERCLASS,
    SUPERFAMILY, SUPERPHYLUM
Te —   DEUM
tea   CHA, KAT, QAT, TAY,
    CHAA, FAAM, KHAT, MATE,
    PECO, TCHA, TSIA, BOHEA,
    CONGO, DIRCA, HYSON,
    LEDUM, OOPAK, PEKOE,
    YERBA, CONGOU, KEEMUN,

	OOLONG, OOPACK, OSWEGO, PTISAN, TISANE, CAMBRIC, LAPSANG, SOUCHONG
tea brand	LIPTON, NESTEA, SALADA, TETLEY, BIGELOW
tea party participant	POURER
teacake	LUNN, SCON(E)
teach	FORM, REAR, TUTE, COACH, DRILL, EDIFY, TRAIN, TUTOR, PREACH, SCHOOL, EDUCATE, INSTRUCT
teacher	DON, RAB, REB, ALIM, GURU, PROF, MOLLA, MULLA, RABBI, TUTOR, DOCENT, MASTER, MENTOR, MOLLAH, MULLAH, PUNDIT, PEDAGOG, LECTURER, PREACHER, PRECEPTOR, PROFESSOR, INSTRUCTOR
teachers' org.	NEA
teaching	MORAL, DOCENT, PRECEPT, TUITION, GUIDANCE, TRAINING, TUTELAGE, SCHOOLING, TUTORSHIP, INSTRUCTION
teachings	PRECEPT, DOCTRINE
teakettle	WHISTLER
team	RIG, CREW, FIVE, GANG, NINE, PAIR, SEAN, YOKE, ELEVEN, STRING, TANDEM
teamster	CARTER, DRIVER, TRUCKER
teapot	SUK(E)Y, KETTLE, SAMOVAR
teapot cover	COS(E)Y, COZY
tear	JAG, RIP, BEAD, REND, RENT, BINGE, REAVE, SPEED, SHRED, SPLIT, SPREE, BENDER, TATTER, RAMPAGE, DIVULSE, LACERATE
— and tear	WEAR
tear down	RAZE, STRIKE, BULLDOZE, DEMOLISH, DISMANTLE
tearful	SAD, MOIST, CRYING, MAUDLIN, UNHAPPY, WEEPING, LACHRYMOSE
tearjerker	SOBSTORY
tearless	DRYEYED
tears, *rel. to*	LACRIMAL, LACHRYMAL
— of tears	VALE
tease	KID, RAG, RIB, VEX, COMB, JOSH, MOCK, RAZZ, RIDE, TARR, TWIT, TAUNT, BOTHER, HARASS, HECTOR, NEEDLE, PESTER, TITILLATE

teaser	AD, POKER, COMEON, STOKER
teat	DUG, PAP, TIT, UDDER, NIPPLE, MAMMILLA
teatime	AFT(ERNOON)
technical	SKILLED, SCIENTIFIC
technicality	DETAIL, NUANCE, LOOPHOLE, FORMALITY
technicality modifier	MERE
technician	EXPERT, MECHANIC
technique	ART, STYLE, METHOD, SYSTEM, PROCEDURE, METHODOLOGY
technology	CRAFT, SKILL, KNOWHOW
tedious	DRY, DULL, BORING, DREARY, HUMDRUM, IRKSOME, TIRESOME, MONOTONOUS
tedium	ENNUI, BOREDOM, MONOTONY
tee	HOB, PEG, JACK
tee off	ANGER, ANNOY, DRIVE, START, REPRIMAND
teed off	ANGRY, ANNOYED
teem	POUR, SWARM, ABOUND, MULTIPLY
teeming	FLOWING, REPLETE, ABUNDANT, PLENTIFUL
teenager	YOUTH, ADOLESCENT
teeny	WEE, TINY
teepee	HUT, LODGE, WIGWAM, WICKIUP
teeter	REEL, SWAY, WAVER, SEESAW, WOBBLE
teeth	*see* TOOTH
teeth, false	PLATE, DENTURE
teething	ERUPTION, DENTITION
teetotaler	DRY, NAZARITE, ABSTAINER
Teflon inventor	PLUNKETT
tegumen(t)	ARIL, SKIN, COATING, COVERING
Tel —	AVIV
Telamon relative	AJAX, AEACUS, PELEUS
telecast	TELEVISE
telegram	WIRE, CABLE, TELEX, MESSAGE, DAY LETTER
telegraph	CABLE, SIGNAL
telegraph inventor	VAIL, COOKE, MORSE, WHEATSTONE
telegraph part	BUG, KEY, ANVIL, TAPPER, TICKER, PORTARULE

telegraph signal   DAH, DIT,
DOT, DASH
telegraph speed unit   BAUD
telepathic   PSYCHIC
telephone   BUZZ, CALL, DIAL,
RING, PHONE
telephone inventor   BELL
telephone part   CORD, DIAL,
KEYPAD, RINGER, CRADLE,
RECEIVER, MOUTHPIECE
telephone term   DSL, TRUNK,
CENTRAL
telphone trio   ABC, DEF, GHI,
JKL, MNO, PRS, TUV, WXY
telescope   TUBE, GLASS,
HUBBLE, BINOCLE, SHORTEN
telescope part   LENS, MIRROR,
EYEPIECE, OBJECTIVE
telescope type   XRAY, RADIO,
OPTICAL, INFRARED,
ASTROLABE, REFLECTING
television   TV, HDTV, TELLY,
VIDEO
television award   EMMY
television channel   ABC, AMC,
BBC, CBC, CBS, CNN, HBO,
MTV, NBC, PBS, SHO, TBS, TNT,
USA, ESPN, CSPAN
television character   *see*
individual shows
television duo   AMOS & ANDY,
REN & STIMPEY, STARSKY &
HUTCH, LAVERNE & SHIRLEY
television show type   GAME,
LIVE, NEWS, QUIZ, SOAP,
TALK, DRAMA, PANEL, RERUN,
SERIAL, SITCOM, REALITY,
VARIETY, WESTERN,
DOCUDRAMA, MINISERIES
television term   UHF, VHF,
SCAN, SNOW, ADDER,
GHOST, MIXER, RELAY,
PICKUP, SCREEN, SIGNAL,
ENCODER, VIDICON,
ORTHICON, SCOPHONY,
TELECAST, TELEVISE,
KINESCOPE
tell   BID, OWN, URGE, IMPART,
INFORM, REVEAL, DIVULGE,
ANNOUNCE; *see* RELATE
Tell's home   URI
tell off   RATE, CHIDE, SCOLD,
REBUKE, LECTURE, CHASTISE
tell on   RAT, PEACH, BETRAY,
INFORM, SNITCH, SQUEAL,
TATTLE
teller   POTDAR, CAMBIST,
NARRATOR, REPORTER;
see CASHIER

telling   COGENT, EFFECTIVE
telltale   REVEALING,
MEANINGFUL
tellurian   HUMAN, TERRAN,
EARTHLY, TERRESTRIAL
temblor   QUAKE, TREMOR,
EARTHQUAKE
temerity   GALL, BRASS, CHEEK,
NERVE, DARING, AUDACITY
temper   PET, MOOD, NEAL,
HUMOR, ANNEAL, DANDER,
NATURE, SOFTEN, SPIRIT,
TANTRUM, MODERATE,
DISPOSITION
temperament   MOOD, GEMUT,
NATURE, DISPOSITION
temperamental   MOODY,
TESTY, TOUCHY, IRRITABLE
temperance   SOBRIETY,
RESTRAINT, MODERATION
temperate   COOL, MILD,
SOBER, MODERATE
temperature   HEAT, FEVER
temperature regulator
CRYOSTAT, THERMOSTAT
tempest   GALE, STORM,
SQUALL, TUMULT, TURMOIL,
TYPHOON, OUTBURST,
HURRICANE
Tempest character   ARIEL,
CALIBAN, GONZALO,
MIRANDA, PROSPERO,
TRINCULO
tempestuous   STORMY,
VIOLENT, TURBULENT
Templar   KNIGHT, CRUSADER,
BARRISTER
Templar (Simon) portrayer
MOORE
temple   SHA, TAA, VAT, WAT,
DEUL, FANE, MOSK, NOAS,
RATH, SHUL, CELLA, HUACA,
KIACK, KOVIL, RATHA,
MOSQUE, PAGODA, TEOCALLI,
SYNAGOGUE
temple part   NAOS, CELLA,
TORII, ADYTUM, PRONAOS,
SANCTUM
Temple (Shirley) role   HEIDI
Temple U. player   OWL
tempo   BEAT, PACE, RATE,
TAKT, SPEED, TACTUS; *see p. 641*
temporal   LAY, CIVIL, CARNAL,
EARTHLY, MUNDANE,
SECULAR, WORLDLY,
TEMPORARY, TRANSIENT,
TRANSITORY
temporary   BRIEF, ACTING,
INTERIM, PASSING,

STOPGAP, FLEETING, TRANSIENT, TRANSITORY, PROVISIONAL

temporize DELAY, HEDGE, STALL, STONEWALL, PROCRASTINATE

tempt *see* ENTICE

temptation BAIT, LURE, TRAP, ENTICEMENT, INDUCEMENT

tempter DEVIL, SATAN, CHARMER, SERPENT

tempting ALLURING, ENTICING, SEDUCTIVE, ATTRACTIVE, APPETIZING

temptress *see* SIREN

ten IO, DECA(D), DENARY, TENNER

Ten Commandments DECALOG(UE)

Ten Commandments proscriptions LYING, KILLING, ADULTERY, COVETING, STEALING, PROFANITY

ten thousand MYRIAD

ten-sided DECAGONAL

tenable VIABLE, CREDIBLE, PLAUSIBLE, DEFENSIBLE

tenacious DOGGED, STICKY, ADHESIVE, CONSTANT, RESOLUTE, STUBBORN, OBSTINATE, PERSISTENT

tenacity PLUCK, PATIENCE, OBSTINACY, PERSISTENCE

tenancy SOCAGE, TENURE, OCCUPANCY

tenant KMET, SAER, INMATE, LESSEE, RENTER, VASSAL, CROFTER, OCCUPANT, RESIDENT

tend CARE, LEAN, MIND, GUARD, SERVE, WATCH, MANAGE, WAITON, INCLINE, MINISTER

tendency BENT, BIAS, DRIFT, TENOR, TREND, LEANING, PENCHANT, PROPENSITY, DISPOSITION

tender BID, BOAT, KIND, SOFT, SORE, OFFER, YOUNG, GENTLE, LOVING, FRAGILE, PAINFUL, PROFFER, DELICATE, SENSITIVE

tenderfoot NOVICE, ROOKIE, RECRUIT, BEGINNER

tenderhearted SOFT, KINDLY, HUMANE, LOVING, COMPASSIONATE

tenderloin MEAT, FILET (MIGNON), STEAK

tending APT, LIABLE, LEANING, CONDUCIVE

tendon CORD, THEW, SINEW, LEADER, MUSCLE

tendril BINE, CURL, SPRIG, BRANCH, CAPREOL

tenement FLAT, SLUM, HOUSE, ROOKERY

tenet ISM, DOGMA, MAXIM, BELIEF, PRECEPT, DOCTRINE

Tennessee *see also p. 615*

Tennessee city/town ERIN, ALAMO, DOVER, ERWIN, PARIS, ATHENS, BENTON, CAMDEN, CELINA, DUNLAP, JASPER, RIPLEY, SELMER, SPARTA, BOLIVAR, LEBANON, MEMPHIS, PULASKI, ALTAMONT, GALLATIN, TAZEWELL, JONESBORO, KNOXVILLE, NASHVILLE, CHATTANOOGA

Tennessee lake BOONE, NORRIS, DOUGLAS, WATAUGA, CHEROKEE, KENTUCKY, PICKWICK, REELFOOT

Tennessee mountain GUYOT, CHILHOWEE

Tennessee river ELK, RED, DEER, DUCK, WOLF, EMORY, OCOEE, CLINCH, PIGEON, COLLINS, STONES, HATCHIE, HARPETH, HOLSTON, TELLICO, TENNESSEE, MISSISSIPPI

Tennessee tourist attraction DOLLYWOOD, GRACELAND, HERMITAGE

tennis players *see p. 714*

tennis term AD, ACE, BAT, BYE, CUT, LET, LOB, SET, CHOP, GAME, LOBB, LOVE, TOSS, VASS, ALLEY, COURT, DEUCE, DRIVE, FAULT, LINER, MATCH, RALLY, SLICE, SMASH, BISQUE, RACKET, STROKE, VOLLEY, DOUBLES, SINGLES, SERVICE

Tennyson character ENID, MAUD, ARDEN, ENOCH, ISOLT, ELAINE

tenon COG, COAK, TUSK

tenor GIST, MOOD, TONE, DRIFT, SENSE, TREND, IMPORT, MEANING, PURPORT; *see* SINGER

tense FLEX, AORIST, UNEASY, ANXIOUS, NERVOUS, (UP)TIGHT, STRAINED; *see* TAUT

tense, grammatical PAST, FUTURE, PERFECT, PRESENT, PRETERIT, PLUPERFECT
tensile DUCTILE, FLEXILE, PLASTIC, PLIABLE, FLEXIBLE
tension STRAIN, STRESS, TAUTNESS, TIGHTNESS
tent PAWL, TIPI, WITU, YURT, TEPEE, TUPEK, YURTA, BIGTOP, ENCAMP, PUP TENT, WIGWAM, KIBITKA, MARQUEE, PAVILION
tent dweller ARAB, GYPSY, KEDAR, NOMAD, YURUK, CAMPER, INDIAN, BEDOUIN, SCENITE
tent, kind of PUP, CIRCUS, OXYGEN
tent show CIRCUS
tentacle PALP, FEELER, ANTENNA
tentacled animal SQUID, OCTOPUS, CEPHALOPOD, CUTTLEFISH
tentative TRIAL, INTERIM, MAKESHIFT, TEMPORARY, CONDITIONAL, PROVISIONAL
tenth part DECI, TITHE, DENARY
tentmaker OMAR, KHAYYAM
tenuity RARITY, FINENESS
tenuous RARE, THIN, FLIMSY, SLENDER
tenure TERM, HOLDING, OCCUPANCY, INCUMBENCY
ten-year period DECADE, DECENNIAL, DECENNIUM
tepee TENT, LODGE, WIGWAM, WICKIUP
Terah relative HARAN, ABRAHAM
teratism FETUS, FREAK, MONSTROSITY
Tereus relative ITYS
tergiversate LIE, DUCK, EVADE, DODGE, HEDGE, PARRY, SIDESTEP, PREVARICATE
tergiversation EVASION, APOSTASY, SUBTERFUGE
term DUB, CALL, NAME, WORD, LIMIT, REGIME, TENURE, BOUND(ARY), SEMESTER, EXPRESSION
termagant see SHREW
terminal END, ANODE, DEPOT, FINAL, LIMIT, CATHODE
terminal info ETA
terminate END, HALT, STOP, ABATE, CEASE, CLOSE,

EXPIRE, FINISH, COMPLETE, CONCLUDE
termination END(ING), CLOSE, EXPIRY, FINISH, RESULT, CONCLUSION
terminology PHRASING, WORDING, NOMENCLATURE
terminus END, GOAL, DEPOT, LIMIT, STATION, BOUNDARY
termite ANAI, NASUTE, TERMES, WHITEANT
terms CONDITIONS, PROVISIONS, STIPULATIONS
tern RIP, RIXY, NOIO, NODDY, PEARL, SCRAY(E), STERNA, MEDRICK, SKIMMER
ternary TRIO, THIRD, TRIAD, TRIPLE
terra firma LAND, EARTH, DRY LAND
terrace BERM(E), TIER, PATIO, PORCH, BALCONY, GALLERY, PLATEAU, PORTICO
terra-cotta BROWN, POTTERY
terrain TURF, FIELD, GROUND, SPHERE
terrazzo MOSAIC
terrene EARTH(Y), MUNDANE, WORLDLY, TERRITORY
terrestrial GAEAL, EARTHLY, MUNDANE, TERRENE, WORLDLY, SECULAR, TEMPORAL
terrible BAD, DIRE, AWFUL, SEVERE, FEARFUL, DREADFUL, HORRIBLE, APPALLING
terribly VERY, AWFULLY, GREATLY
terrier FOX, BULL, SKYE, CAIRN, BOSTON, SCOTCH, AIREDALE; see p. 662
terrific SUPER(B), FAROUT, FABULOUS, SPLENDID
terrified AGHAST, SCARED, PETRIFIED
terrify COW, ALARM, APPAL, DAUNT, SCARE, APPALL, DISMAY, TERRORIZE, INTIMIDATE
terrifying SCARY, GRISLY, CHILLING, DREADFUL
territorial LOCAL, RURAL, REGIONAL
territory AREA, REALM, DOMAIN, ENCLAVE, TERRENE, BAILIWICK
terror FEAR, DREAD, PANIC, FRIGHT

terrorism	ANARCHY, TYRANNY, SABOTAGE		AUSTIN, DALLAS, DENTON, EL PASO, GOLIAD, JASPER,
terrorist	GOON, THUG, APACHE, ALARMIST, NIHILIST		LAMESA, LAREDO, ODESSA, QUANAH, SEGUIN, SONORA, ZAPATA, BASTROP,
terrorize	COW, BULLY, SCARE, COERCE, BROWBEAT, FRIGHTEN, THREATEN, INTIMIDATE		HOUSTON, BEAUMONT, FLOYDADA, ARLINGTON, FORT WORTH, GALVESTON, SAN ANTONIO, CORPUS
terse	see BRIEF		CHRISTI
tessellated	INLAID, MOSAIC	Texas Indian	TIGUA,
tessera	CUBE, TILE, SQUARE, TABLET, PASSWORD		ALABAMA, KICKAPOO, COUSHATTA
test	GRE, SAT, BOSE, EXAM, GSAT, KAHN, QUIZ, ASSAY, PROVE, TEMPT, TRIAL, DRYRUN, LITMUS, ORDEAL, TRYOUT, VERIFY, EXAMINE, WORK OUT, EXPERIMENT, EXAMINATION	Texas lake	KEMP, CADDO, CEDAR, LAVON, TOYAH, WORTH, MEDINA, TEXOMA, TRAVIS
		Texas mountain	LOCKE, ELEPHANT, CATHEDRAL, LIVERMORE
testament	WILL, COVENANT	Texas river	RED, CREEK,
testator	LEGATOR, WITNESS		PECOS, BRAZOS, NUECES,
tester	CIEL, CANOPY, ASSAYER, EXAMINER		SABINE, TRINITY, WASHITA, WICHITA, CANADIAN, COLORADO, RIO GRANDE
testicle, animal	DOWCET		
testify	AVER, AVOW, AFFIRM, DEPONE, DEPOSE	Texas school	LAMAR, BAYLOR
		Texas shrine	ALAMO
testimonial	TRIBUTE, EVIDENCE, REFERRAL, COMPLIMENT, RECOMMENDATION	Tex-Mex order	TACO, NACHO, FAJITAS, JALAPENO, QUESADILLA, CHIMICHANGA
		text	BOOK, TOPIC, VERSE, MATTER, PASSAGE, SUBJECT, WORDING
testimony	EVIDENCE, STATEMENT, DEPOSITION, ATTESTATION, DECLARATION		
		textbook	MANUAL, PRIMER, READER, LIBRETTO
testy	CROSS, ORNERY, TOUCHY, PEEVISH, PEPPERY, WASPISH, IRASCIBLE, IRRITABLE	textile	CLOTH, MATERIAL; see FABRIC
		texture	NAP, WEB, WALE, WOOF, GRAIN, WEAVE, FABRIC
tetanus	LOCKJAW, TRISMUS		
tetched	LOCO, WITLESS, DEMENTED	Thackeray character	BAGG, BUTE, BECKY, SHARP, ESMOND
tetchy	TOUCHY, PEEVISH, IRRITABLE, SENSITIVE	Thai	SHAN, SIAMESE
		Thai city/town	LAE, NAN, TRAT, TRANG, RAYONG, BANGKOK, BANPHAI, KALASIN, PATTAYA, PIIRAYAO, SISAKET, CHIANGMAI, UDONTHANI, NONTHABURI, PATHUMTHANI
tête-à-tête	CHAT, SOFA, MEETING, PRIVATE		
tether	TIE, ROPE, LEASH, LONGE, STAKE, FASTEN, LARIAT, PICKET, SECURE		
Tetragrammaton	ADONAI, ELOHIM, YAHWEH, JEHOVAH		
tetrarch	HEROD		
Teucer relative	AJAX	Thai language	LAO, AHOM, SHAN, CHUANG, KHAMTI, ZHUANG, SIAMESE
Teuton	GOTH, GERMAN		
Texas	see also p. 615		
Texas city/town	EDNA, GAIL, POST, ROBY, RUSK, VEGA, WACO, ALICE, BAIRD, HONDO, LLANO, MARFA, OZONA, PAMPA, PECOS, TULIO,	Thai measure	WA, KEN, NIU, RAI, SAT, SEN, SOK, WAH, YOT, KEUP, NGAN, TANG, KWIEN, TANAN

Thai money AT(T), BAHT, FUANG, TICAL, PYNUNG, SALUNG, SATANG	theater district RIALTO, BROADWAY
Thai people MON, THAI, KAREN, KHMER, MALAY, PHUAN	theater group BMI, ANTA, ASCAP, EQUITY, HABIMA
	theater sign SRO, MARQUEE
Thai river CHI, KOK, MUN, NAN, PING, WANG, PASAK, MEKONG, CHAOPHRAYA	theater term BOX, PIT, CYKE, LOGE, AISLE, CAVEA, FRONT, SCENE, STAGE, STALL, WINGS, CIRCLE, PODIUM, BALCONY, DIAZOMA, GALLERY, PARTERRE, CYCLORAMA
Thai weight PAI, BAHT, HAPH, KLAM, KLOM, CHANG, COYAN, FUANG, PICUL, TICAL, SALUNG, SOMPAY, TAMLUNG	
	theatrical SHOWY, STAGY, SCENIC, POMPOUS, DRAMATIC, HISTRIONIC
Thailand SIAM	Theban poet PINDAR
Thailand, capital of BANGKOK	Theban ruler CREON, OEDIPUS
Thais writer FRANCE, MASSENET	Theban soothsayer TIRESIAS
	Thebes founder CADMUS
Thalia MUSE, GRACE; see MUSES	theft FRAUD, LARCENY, LOOTING, ROBBERY, BURGLARY, STEALING, THIEVERY
Thames city LEA, OCK, ETON, PANG, BRENT, COLNE, HENLEY, LONDON, MEDWAY, OXFORD, READING, STAINES, GRAVESEND	
	thematic TOPICAL, PERIODIC
	theme TEMA, TEXT, ESSAY, MOTIF, TOPIC, STRAIN, SUBJECT, LEITMOTIF
Thames estuary NORE	Themis parent GAEA, URANUS
Thames tributary ISIS, CHURN, CHERWELL, EVENRUSH, WINDRUSH	then POI, ANON, NEXT, THUS, HENCE, THEREFORE, AFTER(WARDS)
than AS, OR, NOR, TILL, BESIDE, ORELSE	thence THUSLY, HEREAFTER
	Theodoric DIRK
thane BARON, CHIEF, KNIGHT, MACBETH, WARRIOR	theologian see p. 545
	theological DIVINE, CANONICAL, RELIGIOUS
thank BLAME, REQUITE	
thankful OBLIGED, BEHOLDEN, GRATEFUL	theology CREED, DOGMA, BELIEF, DOCTRINE, RELIGION
thankless IMPOLITE, UNGRATEFUL	theorem AXIOM, PREMISES, POSTULATE, HYPOTHESIS, PROPOSITION
thankless person INGRATE	
thanksgiving GRACE, PAEAN, PRAISE	theoretical TITULAR, ABSTRACT, ACADEMIC, PLATONIC, SPECULATIVE, HYPOTHETICAL
That Girl names ANN, DON, LOU, HELEN, MARLO, DECAMP, THOMAS, ANNMARIE, ROSEMARY	
	theory ISM, IDEA, GUESS, NOTION, DOCTRINE, CONJECTURE, (HYPO)THESIS, SUPPOSITION
that is IE, VIZ, IDEST, NAMELY	
thatcher's peg SCOB	
thatching palm NIPA	therapeutic plant ALOE
thaw MELT, SOFTEN, UNBEND, LIQUEFY, DISSOLVE	therapist COUE
	therapy CURE, REMEDY, TREATMENT
theater GAFF, ODEA, SWAN, ARENA, DRAMA, GLOBE, HOUSE, LEGIT, ODEON, ODEUM, OPERA, STAGE, FARNESE, BROADWAY, THEATRON	there AT, YON, THEN, TOWARD, YONDER
	thereabouts CLOSE, NEAR(BY), NEARLY, ROUGHLY
theater award OBIE, TONY, GOLDEN GLOBE; see p. 512	thereafter NEXT, LATER, SINCE, AFTERWARDS, SUBSEQUENTLY

thereby UPON, THROUGH
therefore SO, ARGO, ERGO,
ARGAL, HENCE, SINCE,
WHENCE, ACCORDINGLY
thermal unit BTU, DEGREE,
CALORIE
thermometer GLASS, MERCURY
thermometer, type of CELSIUS,
DIGITAL, REAUMUR,
CLINICAL, CRYOMETER,
CENTIGRADE, FAHRENHEIT
thesaurus ROGET, LEXICON,
TREASURY, STOREHOUSE
thesaurus abbr. ADV, SUB, PREP
Theseus relative AEGEUS
Theseus slayer CREON
thesis ESSAY, TOPIC, THEORY,
ARGUMENT, TREATISE,
MONOGRAPH, POSTULATE,
DISSERTATION
thesis, opp. of ARSIS
thespian see ACTOR
Thessaly king AEOLUS
Thessaly valley TEMPE
Thetis relative PELEUS,
ACHILLES
thews SINEWS, MUSCLES
thick FAT, DULL, CRASS,
DENSE, GROSS, SOLID,
STOUT, STUPID
thicken GEL, CLOT, CURDLE,
CONGEAL, CONDENSE,
SOLIDIFY, COAGULATE
thickener ROUX, FLOUR,
TAPIOCA
thicket TOD, BOSK, BUSH,
RONE, SHAW, BRAKE, COPSE,
JUNGLE, BOSCAGE, SPINNEY,
TUSSOCK
thick-headed DENSE, STUPID,
WITLESS, HEBETATE
thick-lipped BLOBBER,
LABROSE
thickness PLY, BODY, GIRTH,
LAYER, BREADTH, DENSITY,
STRATUM
thickset BEEFY, STOUT,
CHUBBY, CHUNKY, PORTLY,
STOCKY, HEAVYSET
thick-skinned CALLOUS,
HARDENED, UNFEELING
thief CHOR, PRIG, GANEF,
GANOF, GONOF, PIKER,
SANSI, KLEPTO, BURGLAR,
FILCHER, LURCHER
thievery FRAUD, GRAFT,
THEFT, ROBBERY, SWINDLE,
EMBEZZLEMENT
thigh, of the FEMORAL

thigh part HAM, HIP, FEMUR,
FLANK, SARTORIUS
thimblerig CON, GYP, FRAUD,
SHELLGAME
thin FINE, LANK, LEAN, RARE,
REEDY, SHEER, SPARE,
DILUTE, PAPERY, RAREFY,
SPARSE, TENUOUS,
DELICATE, HAIRLINE
Thin Man character ASTA,
NICK, NORA, CHARLES
thing(s) RES, CHOSE, CLANTH,
HOODUS, JINGUS, MATTER,
DINGBAT, KADIGAN;
see GADGET
think WIS, DEEM, MULL,
MUSE, TROW, WEEN, OPINE,
IDEATE, REASON, RECKON,
IMAGINE, REFLECT
think back RECALL,
REMEMBER, RECOLLECT
thinking LOGIC(AL), REASON,
PENSIVE, RATIONAL,
MEDITATIVE
thinker SAGE, SAVANT,
PHILOSOPHER,
INTELLECTUAL
Thinker sculptor RODIN
thinness RARITY, TENUITY
thinness symbol DIME, RAIL
third TIERCE, TERNARY
third estate PEOPLE, COMMONS,
COMMONALTY, BOURGEOISIE
Third Man author GREENE
Third Man director WELLES
third-rate POOR, COMMON,
INFERIOR
thirst DESIRE, CRAVING,
DRYNESS, POLYDIPSIA
thirst-producing DIPSETIC
thirsty (A)DRY, ARID,
PARCHED, DESICCATED
thirty, series of TRENTAL
this and that OLIO, MIXTURE,
HODGEPODGE
Thisbe's lover PYRAMUS
thistle BURR, KUSUM,
DINDLE, SAFFLOWER
thither YON(D), THERE,
YONDER
Thomas opera HAMLET,
MIGNON
thong LORA, RIEM, BRAIL,
KNOUT, QUIRT, ROMAL,
STRAP
Thor ZEUS, DONAR, DONNER,
JUPITER
Thor relative SIF, ULL, ODIN,
ULLR

thorn **ETH, BARB, BROD, STOB,**
BRIAR, BRIER, SPINE,
TORUN, NETTLE, BRAMBLE,
PRICKLE
thorn apple **HAW, METEL,**
DATURA
Thornfield Hall governess **EYRE**
thorny **SPINY, BRAMBLY,**
SPINATE, SPINOSE
thorough **FULL, TOTAL,**
ABSOLUTE, COMPLETE,
SWEEPING
thoroughbred **HORSE, NOBLE,**
HIGHBORN, PUREBRED,
BLUEBLOOD, PEDIGREED,
ARISTOCRAT
thoroughfare **WAY, ROAD,**
ARTERY, AVENUE, STREET,
FREEWAY, HIGHWAY,
TURNPIKE, BOULEVARD,
CONCOURSE
thoroughgoing **COMPLETE,**
EXHAUSTIVE
thoroughly **FULLY, INDETAIL,**
COMPLETELY
though **YET, WHILE, ALBEIT,**
EVENIF, DESPITE
thought **CARE, HEED, IDEA,**
INTENT, NOTION, REGARD,
CONCEPT, THINKING,
ATTENTION, EXPECTATION
thoughtful **KIND, HEEDFUL,**
MINDFUL, TACTFUL,
CONSIDERATE
thoughtless **RASH, HEEDLESS,**
RECKLESS, INCONSIDERATE
thousand **MIL(LE), GRAND,**
CHILIAD
thousand years **CHILIAD,**
MILLIAD, MILLENNIUM
Thrace people **EDONI**
thrall *see* **BONDMAN**
thrash **WALE, YARK, YERK,**
BLESS, WHALE, TROUNCE;
see **BEAT**
thread **CLEW, CLUE, CORD,**
DOUP, FILO, POIL, PURL,
TRAM, WARP, WEFT, WORM,
FIBER, FILUM, LISLE, REEVE,
TENOR, TWINE, STAMEN,
RETICLE
threadbare **SEEDY, STALE,**
TRITE, RAGGED, SHABBY,
WORN (OUT), TATTERED
threadlike **FILAR, FILATE,**
FILOSE, NEMALINE
threat **OMEN, DANGER,**
MENACE, WARNING,
COERCION, INTIMIDATION

threaten **COW, BULLY,**
HARASS, HECTOR, MENACE,
INTIMIDATE
threatening **DARK, AWFUL,**
BLACK, SULLEN, LOOMING,
OMINOUS, WARNING,
IMMINENT, MENACING,
MINATORY, SINISTER
three **TER, DREI, TERN, TRIO,**
LEASH, THRIN, TRIAD,
TIERCE
three B's **BACH, BRAHMS,**
BEETHOVEN
three R's **READING, WRITNG,**
(A)RITHMETIC
threefold **TRINE, TERNAL,**
TREBLE, TERNARY, TERNATE
three-letter group **TRIGRAM**
Three Musketeers author **DUMAS;**
see **MUSKETEER**
Three Stooges *see* **STOOGE**
three-wheeled vehicle **TRICYCLE**
Three's Company names **DON,**
JACK, JOHN, CINDY, JANET,
JOYCE, RALPH, TERRI, DEWITT,
KNOTTS, RITTER, SOMERS,
CHRISSY, TRIPPER
threnody **DIRGE, REQUIEM,**
CORONACH
thresh **BEAT, WINNOW,**
THRASH
thresher **FLAIL, COMBINE**
threshold **EVE, SILL, LIMEN,**
ENTRANCE
threw **CAST, FLUNG, HURLED,**
TOSSED, PITCHED
thrift **LABOR, SAVING,**
ECONOMY, FRUGALITY
thrifty **FRUGAL, SAVING,**
MISERLY, SPARING,
ECONOMICAL
thrill **KICK, STIR, TIRL,**
THROB, EXCITE, QUIVER,
TINGLE, TREMOR,
EXHILARATE
thriller **CHILLER, SHOCKER,**
WHODUNIT
thrive **WAX, BOOM, ADDLE,**
BATTEN, PROSPER,
SUCCEED, FLOURISH
throat **MAW, CRAG, HASS,**
GORGE, FAUCES, GULLET,
PHARYNX, WEASAND,
WINDPIPE
throat disease **CROUP,**
ANGINA, THRUSH,
TONSILLITIS
throat part **LARYNX,**
PHARYNX, TRACHEA,

VOICEBOX, ESOPHAGUS, EPIGLOTTIS

throat, *pert. to*   (JU)GULAR, GUTTURAL

throaty   GRUFF, HOARSE, GUTTURAL

throb   BEAT, PUMP, POUND, PULSE, THUMP, PULSATE, VIBRATE, PALPITATE, PULSATION

throbbing   ACHY, BEATING, PITAPAT, PULSING, PALPITANT

throe(s)   PANG, RACK, AGONY, SPASM

throne   DAIS, RULE, ASANA, CHAIR, DIVAN, GADDI, GADHI, REIGN, MUSNUD

throng   HOST, CROWD, HORDE, PRESS, MULTITUDE, ASSEMBLAGE

throttle   GAG, CHOKE, SCRAG, VALVE, STIFLE, STRANGLE, ACCELERATOR

through   BY, PER, VIA, DONE, OVER

throughout   ALLOVER, EVERYWHERE

throw   CAST, HURL, REST, TOSS, WRAP, FLING, HEAVE, PITCH

throw off   ELUDE, EVADE, LIE TO, MISLEAD, CONFUSE

throw out   BOOT, OUST, TOSS, EJECT, EXPEL, BOUNCE, REJECT, DISCARD

throw over   JILT, CANCEL, ABANDON

throw the —   BOOK

throw up   PUKE, SPEW, RETCH, VOMIT

throwing style   OVERARM, SIDEARM, UNDERARM

thrush   OMAO, KAMAO, MAVIS, OUSEL, OUZEL, ROBIN, SHAMA, VEERY, DIPPER, MISSEL, MISTLE, REDWING, BELLBIRD

thrush genus   TURDUS, CINCLUS

thrust   JAB, JUT, BUTT, DART, FOIN, MURE, STAB, TILT, IMPEL, LUNGE, ONSET, SHOVE, DARTLE, EXSERT

thug   GOON, HOOD, TOUGH, DACOIT, MUGGER, GORILLA, HOODLUM, HOOLIGAN, CUTTHROAT

thumb   DIGIT, POLLEX, THENAR

— and Thummim   URIM

thumbnail   SMALL, CONCISE

Thummin partner   URIM

thump   BEAT, THUD, TUNK, POUND, THROB, CUDGEL, POMMEL

thunder   BOOM, CLAP, PEAL, ROLL, RUMBLE, FULMINATE

thundering   BOOM(ING), TONITRUANT

thunderstruck   AGHAST, AMAZED, ASTONISHED

Thurber hero   (WALTER) MITTY

thurible   CENSER

Thursday source   THOR

thus   SIC, YET, ERGO, THEREFORE

thwart   *see* BAFFLE

thyroid disorder   GOITER

tiara   CROWN, DIADEM, CORONET

Tiber tributary   NERA

Tiberius I reign year (AD13–37) XV, XX, XIV, XIX, XVI, XXI, XXV, XXX, XVII, XXII, XXIV, XXIX, XXVI, XXXI, XXXV

Tibet, capital of   LHASA

Tibeto-Burmese language   LAI, MRU, BODO, GARO, NAGA, LIMBU, MURMI, KACHIN, LEPCHA, LUSHEI, NEWARI, BURMESE, TIBETAN

Tibeto-Burmese people   KAW, AKHA

tic   CRICK, SPASM, TWITCH, NEURALGIA

tick   MARK, ACARI, ARGAS, CHECK, PIQUE, ACARID, CREDIT, IXODID, TAMPAN, ACARIDA, ACARINA, ARGASID, IXODIAN, CARAPATO, IXODIDAE; *see* MITE

tick off   IRE, ANNOY, INCENSE

ticked off   MAD, IRATE, PISSED, TEEDOFF, INCENSED

ticker   CLOCK, HEART, WATCH, TAPPER

ticket   TAG, PASS, LABEL, SLATE, BALLOT, DOCKET, NOTICE, SUMMONS

tickle   AMUSE, EXCITE, TINGLE, DELIGHT, TITILLATE

tickler   POSER, PUZZLE, REMINDER

ticklish   RISKY, TOUCHY, CRITICAL, DELICATE, SENSITIVE

Ticonderoga name	KNOX,	tile work	KASI
GATES, ALLEN, ARNOLD,		till	CASH, FARM, PLOW,
BURGOYNE			UPTO, CULTIVATE
tidal flow	EBB, BORE, NEAP,	till compartment	ONES, TENS,
EAGRE, FLOOD		DIMES, FIVES, NICKELS,
tidbit	GOSSIP, MORSEL,	PENNIES, QUARTERS,
KICKSHAW		TWENTIES
tide	FLOW, NEAP, SURF, TIME,	tiller	HELM, FARMER,
FLOOD, SURGE		PLOWMAN
tidings	NEWS, GOSPEL,	tilt	TIP, CANT, HEEL, LEAN,
EVANGEL		LIST, JOUST, SLANT, CAREEN,
tidy	NEAT, REDO, TRIG, TRIM,	SEESAW, TOURNEY,
KEMPT, SPRUCE, ORDERLY,		TOURNAMENT
SHIPSHAPE, STRAIGHTEN		timber	LOG, BEAM, BIBB, BITT,
tie	BEAM, BIND, BOND, LASH,	LOGS, KEVEL, BATTEN,
MOOR, TACH, TECK, NEXUS,		CAMBER, STUMPAGE
TACHE, TRUSS, LIGATE,		timber rot	DOAT, DOTE
SLEEPER; see NECKWEAR		Timbuktu	STICKS,
tied	WED, EVEN, EQUAL,		BOONDOCKS
FIXED, BOUND, MARRIED		time	AGE, ELD, EON, ERA, EVE,
tier	BANK, RANK, DECK,	AEON, BEAT, DATE, YORE,
LAYER, LEVEL, STAGE, STORY		EPOCH, TEMPI, TEMPO,
tie-up	SNAG, DELAY,	TENSE, MOMENT, DURATION;
HOLDUP, STOPPAGE		see p. 717
tiff	FIT, ROW, SPAT, TEMPER,	time being	NONCE
BICKER, QUARREL,		Time Machine author	WELLS
ARGUMENT, SQUABBLE		Time Machine people	ELOI,
tiffin	TEA, LUNCH(EON),		MORLOCKS
SNACK, CONDOR		time, pert. to	ERAL, TEMPORAL
tiger	PUMA, COUGAR,	time period	see p. 717
JAGUAR, LEOPARD,		timeless	ETERNE, AGELESS,
SABERTOOTH		CLASSIC, ETERNAL,
tiger, young	WHELP		IMMORTAL
tight	DRUNK, TIPSY, LOADED,	timely	EARLY, PROMPT,
STINGY, MISERLY; see TAUT		PUNCTUAL, EXPEDIENT,
tighten	FRAP, LACE, CLAMP,	OPPORTUNE, AUSPICIOUS
SCREW, TAUTEN		timepiece	CLOCK, WATCH,
tightfisted	CHEAP, STINGY,	SUNDIAL, HOURGLASS
FRUGAL, MISERLY		timer	STOPWATCH
tightlipped	MUM, SILENT,	timetable	PLAN, AGENDA,
TACITURN, SECRETIVE		PROGRAM, BRADSHAW,
tights	LEOTARD		SCHEDULE
tightwad	see MISER	timeworn	AGED, DULL, WORN,
Tigris	DULA, HIDDEKEL		SHABBY, OUTOFDATE
Tigris City	KUT, ASHUR,	timid	SHY, ARGH, PAVID,
CALAH, MOSUL, NIMRUD,		TREPID, BASHFUL, CHICKEN,
BAGHDAD, NINEVEH,		RETIRING, SHEEPISH,
SELEUCIA		TIMOROUS
Tigris tributary	ZAB, DIYALA	timing	PACE, PACING
Tijuana Brass leader	(HERB)	timing device	STOPWATCH
ALPERT		Timna relative	AMALEK
tile	FAVI, BRICK, DALLE,	Timon of Athens character	
FAVUS, KASHI, SLATE,		TIMON, LUCIUS, PHRYNIA,
IMBREX, TEGULA, CERAMIC,		LUCULLUS, TIMANDRA
PANTILE, TESSERA		timorous	SHY, PAVID, TIMID,
tile material	CLAY, STONE,		AFRAID, FEARFUL
KAOLIN, RUBBER, ARGILLI,		timothy	HAY, GRASS
PLASTIC, CONCRETE,		tin	CAN, COAT, STANNUM,
PETUNTSE		PRESERVE

tin, *pert. to*	STANNIC, STANNOUS
Tin Pan Alley org.	BMI, ASCAP
tinamou	YUTU, MACUCA, YNAMBU
tincture	DYE, DASH, TINT, COLOR, SHADE, STAIN, TINGE, ELIXIR, SOUPCON, VESTIGE; *see p. 531*
tinder	PUNK, AMADOU
tine	FANG, SNAG, TYND, PRONG, SPIKE, ANTLER
tinfoil	TAIN
tinge	DYE, DASH, IMBUE, TAINT, TOUCH, TRACE
tingle	DIRL, THIRL, DINDLE, THRILL, PARESTHESIA
tinhorn	CHEAP, PIKER, TWOBIT, GAMBLER, SMALLTIME
tinker	TOY, MEND, CAIRD, REPAIR, TAMPER, TRIFLE, DABBLE, PUTTER
Tinker's teammate	EVERS, CHANCE
tinkle	TING, CHINK, DINGLE
tinsel	GAUDY, SHOWY, LITTER, SPANGLE
tint	DYE, HUE, COLOR, SHADE, STAIN, TINGE; *see p. 531*
tiny	WEE, SMALL, TEENY, ATOMIC, LITTLE, MIDGET, MINUTE, PETITE, MINIATURE, MINUSCULE, MICROSCOPIC
tip	CUE, END, APEX, HINT, KNAP, ADVICE, VERTEX; *see* GRATUITY, TILT
tip off	WARN
tip over	UPEND
tipple	BIB, SIP, DRINK, GUZZLE, IMBIBE
tippler	SOT, DRUNK, TOPER, BIBBER, SOAKER
tipster	TOUT(ER), INSIDER
tipsy	*see* DRUNK
tiptoe	LURK, CREEP, SNEAK
tiptop	FIT, BEST, SUPREME, SHIPSHAPE
tirade	RANT, SPATE; *see* DIATRIBE
tire	FAG, BORE, CLOY, JADE, PNEU, WEARY, STRAKE, RETREAD
tire part	RIM, SHOE, SIPE, TUBE, TREAD, CASING
tired	WORN, JADED, WEARY, FATIGUED, EXHAUSTED
tireless	UNTIRING, ENERGETIC, INDEFATIGABLE
tiresome	DRAB, DULL, BORING, DREARY, TEDIOUS, WEARISOME, MONOTONOUS
tiring	TRYING, ARDUOUS, DRAINING, WEARISOME, EXHAUSTING
Tirol	*see* TYROL
tissue	WEB, BAST, BREI, MESH, TELA, FIBER, FASCIA, PHLOEM, NETWORK
tissue, connecting	PONS, STROMA, TENDON, LIGAMENT
Titania's spouse	OBERON
Titans	*see p. 646*
Titans parents	GE, GAEA, URANUS
tithe	TAX, LEVY, TEIND, TENTH, TIEND
Tithonus relative	PRIAM, LAOMEDON
titillate	AMUSE, AROUSE, EXCITE, TICKLE, TURNON, STIMULATE
title	MR, MS, SR, AGA, ALI, AYA, BEY, DOM, MME, MRS, PAN, RAS, SIR, SRI, VON, AGHA, BABA, COJA, DAME, EARL, EMIR, GRAP, HERR, HOJA, KAUN, KHAN, LORD, MAAM, MISS, NAIK, NAME, PANI, SIDI, TERM, TUAN, AGBAR, DONNA, EMEER, GRAZI, MADAM, MOLLA, MULLA, NAWAB, PACHA, PASHA, PRINZ, SAYID, SHREE, BASHAW, PANOIT, SAIYID, SAYYID, SHERIF, CAPTION, HEADING, HUZOOR, SHEREFF; *see* NOBLE
titmouse	CHICKADEE; *see* SONGBIRD
titter	LAUGH, GIGGLE, SNICKER
tittle	DOT, JOT, IOTA, WHIT, SPECK, PARTICLE
titular	TOKEN, NOMINAL, HONORIFIC
Titus Andronicus character	TITUS, MARCUS, TAMORA, LAVINIA, PUBLIUS, BASSIANUS, SATURNINUS
tizzy	FUSS, SNIT, DITHER, LATHER, FLUSTER
to and —	FRO
to wit	NAMELY, SCILICET
toad	AGUA, BUFO, HYLA, PIPA, TOADY, ALYTES, ANURAN, ROPTOAD, PADDOCK, LINGUATA, TREETOAD

toadstool	*see* MUSHROOM
toady	FAWN(ER), FLUNKY, LACKEY, TRUCKLE, PARASITE, FLATTERER, SYCOPHANT
toast	DRY, HEAT, LEEP, BREDE, BROWN, MELBA, SALUD, SANTE, SKOAL, CHEERS, PROSIT, SALUTE, SIPPET, SLAINTE
toastmaster	MC, EMCEE
toasty	COZY, WARM
tobacco	CAM, CAPA, CHEW, CRAW, PLUG, QUID, SANA, SHAG, WEED, SCREW, SNUFF, BURLEY, RAPPEE, VUELTA, CAPORAL, LATAKIA, ORONOCO, PERIQUE, TURKISH, UPPOWOC
tobacco ash	DOTTEL, DOTTLE
Tobacco Road author	CALDWELL
Tobacco Road character	PEARL, JEETER
toboggan	SLED, GLIDE, COASTER
tocsin	BELL, GONG, ALARM
toddle	PADDLE, TOTTER, WADDLE, SAUNTER
to-do	ADO, FUSS, STIR
toe	DIGIT, SLANT, HALLUX, MINIMUS
toehold	GRIP, FOOTING
toff	DUDE, SWELL
toft	KNOLL, HILLOCK, MESSUAGE
tog(s)	*see* CLOTHING
toga	GOWN, ROBE, CLOAK
together	CALM, COOL, AS ONE, JOINTLY, IN TANDEM, COLLECTED
Togo, capital of	LOME
Togo city/town	KARA, LOME, BASSA, BLITTA, SOKODE, KPALIME
Togo language	EWE, MINA, KABYE, FRENCH, DAGOMBA; *see* KWA
Togo money	FRANC
Togo neighbor	BENIN, GHANA, NIGERIA, BURKINA FASO
Togo people	EWE, MINA, KABYE, DAGOMBA
Togo river	OTI, MONO, OGOU
toil	MOIL, SLOG, TASK, WORK, LABOR, SLAVE, DRUDGE, EFFORT, STRIVE, TRAVAIL, DRUDGERY
toilet	WC, CAN, LOO, POT, HEAD, JOHN, PRIVY, COMMODE, LATRINE, LAVATORY
toilet water	BAYRUM, COLOGNE, LAVENDER
toiletry item	COMB, SOAP, BRUSH, RAZOR, LOTION, POWDER, COLOGNE, COLDCREAM, COSMETICS, MOUTHWASH, DENTIFRICE, TOOTHPASTE
toilsome	ONEROUS, ARDUOUS, LABORIOUS, STRENUOUS
token	FARE, SIGN, SLUG, BADGE, SCRIP, EMBLEM, PLEDGE, KEEPSAKE
Tokyo	(Y)EDO, YEDDO
Tokyo Bay city	CHIBI, TOKYO, YOKOHAMA, YOKOSUKA
Tokyo district	GINZA, AKADAKA, YOSHIWARA
tolerable	SOSO, MIDDLING, PASSABLE
tolerably	FAIRLY, ENOUGH, MODERATELY
tolerance	MARGIN, LENITY, STAMINA, PATIENCE, ALLOWANCE
tolerate	BEAR, ABIDE, BROOK, STAND, ENDURE, SUFFER
Tolkien character	ENT, ORC, HOBBIT; *see* LORD OF THE RINGS
Tolkien territory	MORDOR
toll	DUE, FEE, TAX, DUTY, RATE, PEAL, RING, KNELL, CHIMINAGE
Tolstoy character	ANNA, KITTY, LEVIN, PIERRE, ROSTOV, NATASHA, VRONSKY
Tolstoy work	COSSACKS, WAR AND PEACE
Tom Sawyer author	MARK TWAIN, CLEMENS
Thom Sawyer character	HUCK FINN, BECKY, POLLY
tomahawk	AX(E), HATCHET
tomato	FRUIT, WOMAN
tomato sauce	CATSUP, KETCHUP
tomato type	ROMA
tomb	CIST, MOLE, CRYPT, TABUT, VAULT, BARROW, DOKHMA, MASTABA, OSSUARY, TUMULUS, CISTVAEN, CROMLECH; *see* SHRINE
tomboy	ROMP, HOIDEN, HOYDEN

tombstone	SLAB, CAIRN, STELA, STELE, MARKER, TABLET, HEADSTONE
tomcat	GIB
tomfoolery	PRANK, NONSENSE, PLEASANTRY
tomorrow	MANANA
tonality	TONE, MELODY, HARMONY
tone	HUE, KEY, TEAN, TINT, TUNE, PITCH, SHADE, SOUND, ACCENT, TIMBRE
toneless	ATONY
Tonga, capital of	NUKUALOFA
Tonga island	see FRIENDLY
Tonga money	PAANGA
tongs	CLAMP, FORCEPS, NIPPERS, PINCERS
tongue	TAB, CHIB, FLAP, NEAP, TANG, IDIOM, GLOSSA, LINGUA, CLAPPER
tongue part	DORSUM
tongue, *pert. to*	APICAL, GLOSSAL
tongue-lashing	REPROOF, REPRIMAND
tonguelike	GLOSSAL, LINGUAL
tongue-tied	MUM, SHY, DUMB, MUTE, SILENT, WORDLESS
tonic	ALOE, TANSY, BRACER, ELIXIR, FILLIP, PICKUP, BRACING, CHIRATA, MEDICINE, ROBORANT, INVIGORATING
tonsil	AMYGDALA
Tony winners, musical	CATS, NINE, RENT, ANNIE, EVITA, FOSSE, KISMET, RAISIN, CABARET, COMPANY, CONTACT, PASSION, REDHEAD, TITANIC, APPLAUSE, FIORELLO, PRODUCERS; see p. 512
Tony winners, play	DA, JB, ART, EQUUS, PROOF, BECKET, FENCES, LUTHER, SLEUTH, AMADEUS, CRUCIBLE, MARAT SADE; see p. 512
too	ALSO, VERY, OVERLY, BESIDES
tool(s)	DUPE, GEAR, MEANS, DEVICE, GADGET, MACHINE, UTENSIL, APPARATUS, IMPLEMENT, INSTRUMENT; see p. 719
tool used on bovines	TROCAR
toot	HONK, BLARE, BLAST, SPREE

tooth	COG, GAM, PEG, FANG, JAGG, TINE, TUSH, TUSK, IVORY, MOLAR, PRONG, CANINE, CUSPID, WISDOM, INCISOR, BICUSPID
tooth incrustation	PLAQUE, TARTAR
tooth part	GUM, NECK, PULP, ROOT, CROWN, NERVE, DENTIN, ENAMEL, CEMENTUM
toothache	ODONTALGIA
toothed	DENTATE, SERRATE
toothless	EDENTATE
toothlike part	COG, TINE, PRONG, DENTIL, DENTICLE
toothpaste	ZIRCATE, DENTIFRICE
toothsome	TASTY, YUMMY, DAINTY, SAVORY, LUSCIOUS, PALATABLE, APPETIZING
top	AI, ACE, CAP, COP, EPI, LID, LIP, ACME, APEX, PEAK, CHIEF, CREST, EXCEL, PRIME, APICAL, FINIAL, VERTEX, ZENITH, SURPASS, DOMINATE
Topaz author	URIS
topcoat	RAGLAN, REEFER, OVERCOAT
toper	SOT, SOAK, DRUNK, RUMMY, SOUSE
topic	ISSUE, THEME, HEADING, SUBJECT
topical	LOCAL
topkick	SARGE, SERGE(ANT)
topknot	TUFT, CREST, ONKOS, PANACHE
topminnow	GUPPY, MOLLY, MOLLIE, HELLERI, PUPFISH, RIVULUS, GAMBUSIA, KILLIFISH, SWORDTAIL
topmost	APICAL
topnotch	AONE, BEST, TOPS, EXCELLENT, FIRSTRATE
Topper names	LEO, NEIL, COSMO, GEORGE, MARION, CARROLL, HENRIETTA
topping	CRUST, ICING, LAYER, GARNISH
topple	TRIP, DEFEAT, TOTTER, TUMBLE, COLLAPSE, OVERTURN, OVERTHROW
tops	AONE, BEST, SUPER
topsoil	LOAM
topsy-turvy	CHAOTIC, CONFUSED, DISORDERLY, UPSIDEDOWN
tor	CRAG, HILL, KNOLL
torch	BURN, LINK, LUNT, IGNITE, MUSSAL, CRESSET, FLAMBEAU

torment	VEX, BAIT, BANE, PAIN, RACK, AGONY, ANNOY, HARRY, TEASE, HARASS, ORDEAL, PLAGUE, TORTURE, DISTRESS
torn	REFT, RENT, RIVEN, SPLIT, RAGGED, TATTERED
tornado	FUNNEL, CYCLONE, TWISTER, WHIRLWIND
Toronto	YORK, HOGTOWN
Toronto team	RAPTORS, BLUEJAYS, MAPLE LEAFS
torpedo	SHELL, GUNMAN, GANGSTER, SABOTAGE, ASSASSIN, BODYGUARD, PROJECTILE
torpedo part	FIN, RUDDER, TRIGGER, WARHEAD, EXPLOSIVE, PROPELLER
torpid	DULL, NUMB, INERT, LISTLESS, SLUGGISH, LETHARGIC, APATHETIC
torpor	SLOTH, APATHY, STUPOR, INERTIA, LANGUOR, LETHARGY
torque	TWIST, ENERGY, STRESS, TORSION
torrent	RUSH, FLOOD, SPATE, DELUGE, DOWNPOUR
torrential	COPIOUS, RUSHING, VIGOROUS, TURBULENT
torrid	HOT, ARID, ARDENT, SULTRY, TROPICAL, SCORCHING
torsion	STRESS, TORQUE, PRESSURE, TWISTING, CONTORTION
torso	BODY, TRUNK
tort	WRONG, DAMAGE, INJURY, MISDEED, OFFENSE, MISDEMEANOR
tortoise	*see* TURTLE
tortuous	SNAKY, SPIRAL, CROOKED, DEVIOUS, SINUOUS, WINDING, SERPENTINE
torture	FLAY, PAIN, RACK, AGONY, GARBLE, MARTYR, ANGUISH, TORMENT, STRAPPADO
Tory	DIEHARD, LOYALIST
Tosca character	MARIO, SCARPIA
Tosca writer	SARDOU, PUCCINI
toss	LOB, CAST, FLIP, TAVE, BANDY, FLING, PITCH, THROW, BUFFET
tosspot	SOT, SOUSE, TOPER, DRUNK, DRINKER
tot	TAD, ADDUP, CHILD, COUNT, TOTAL, TODDLER
total	ADD, SUM, GROSS, UTTER, WHOLE, ENTIRE, DESTROY, COMPLETE
totalitarian	FASCIST, ONE PARTY, ABSOLUTE, DESPOTIC, TYRANNICAL, DICTATORIAL
tote	ADD, HAUL, LOAD, SACK, CARRY, COUNT, SATCHEL
totem	PHYLE, EPONYM, MOIETY
totem pole	XAT
totter	REEL, ROCK, SHAKE, STAGGER
toucan	TOCO, ARACARI
touch	HIT, PAT, RUB, TAP, TIG, ABUT, DASH, FEEL, LOAN, PALP, GRAZE, TINGE, TRACE, AFFECT, CONTACT, IMPINGE
touch and go	RISKY, GAMBLE, UNSURE, UNCERTAIN
touch, *pert. to*	HAPTIC, TACTIC, TACTILE, TACTUAL
touchdown	GOAL, SCORE, LANDING
touching	RE, ABOUT, ANENT, MOVING, TANGENT, POIGNANT
touchstone	NORM, TEST, MEASURE, STANDARD, CRITERION
touchwood	*see* TINDER
touchy	SORE, RISKY, TESTY, CHANCY, PEEVISH, IRRITABLE, CANTANKEROUS
tough	FIRM, WIRY, BULLY, CHEWY, HARDY, ROWDY, WITHY, STURDY, HARDBOILED
toughen	INURE, STEEL, ANNEAL, TEMPER
toupee	*see* HAIRPIECE
tour	EYRE, TRIP, SHIFT, SAFARI, VOYAGE, CIRCUIT, JOURNEY
tour de force	FEAT, EXPLOIT, MAGNUM OPUS, MASTERPIECE
tourist	VISITER, VOYAGER, TRAVELER, SIGHTSEER
tournament, tourney	TILT, JOUST, MATCH, COMPETITION
tournament round	SEMIS, FINALS, PRELIMS

tourniquet BINDER, GARROT, BANDAGE, COMPRESS

tousle MUSS, RUFFLE, RUMPLE, DISHEVEL

tout LAUD, PLUG, VAUNT, PRAISE, TALKUP, PROMOTE

tow TUG, DRAG, DRAW, PULL, FLAX, HARDS, HURDS

toward ABOUT, ECTAD, ENTAD, FACING

towboat TUG, MULE, TUGBOAT

towel DRY, WIPE, DIAPER, NAPKIN

towel material TERRY

tower TOR, EDAR, MEAH, TOPE, BABEL, PYLON, STUPA, BELFRY, DONJON, GAZEBO, GOPURA, PAGODA, RONDEL, DIKARA, DIKHRA, TURRET, VIMANA, MINARET, SIKHARA, TORRION, MARTELLO, CAMPANILE; see SPIRE, WATCHTOWER

towering LOFTY, EMINENT, ELEVATED, MONUMENTAL

towhead BLOND

town(ship) BURG, DEME, STAD, VILL, BAYAN, BURGH, MACHI, STADT; see VILLAGE

town, of a CIVIC, URBAN, OPPIDAN

toxic VENOMOUS, POISONOUS

toxin VENOM, POISON

toy DOLL, PLAY, DALLY, FLIRT, BAUBLE, FONDLE, GEWGAW, PLAYTHING; see TRIFLE

trace COPY, DRAW, HINT, TANG, TINGE, ENGRAM, SKETCH, OUTLINE, SOUPCON, VESTIGE

trachea DUCT, WEASAND, WINDPIPE

track DOG, RUT, RAIL, SLOT, SPUR, TURF, WAKE, RAILS, SCENT, SPOOR, TRAIL, COURSE, FOLLOW

tracker TAIL, PUGGI, HUNTER

tract AREA, ESSAY, EXTENT, LEAFLET, PAMPHLET, TREATISE

tractable EASY, DOCILE, WILLING, OBEDIENT, MALLEABLE

traction GRIP, DRIVE, DRAWING, PULLING, ADHESION, FOOTHOLD

tractor CAT, RIG, MULE, SEMI, GRADER

trade DEAL, BANDY, BUSINESS; see BARTER, PROFESSION, SELL

trademark LOGO(TYPE), MARK, BRAND, COLOPHON

trader MONGER; see MERCHANT

tradesman DEALER, MERCHANT, SHOPKEEPER

trading post PX, CANTEEN

trading site PIT, MART; see MARKET, RIALTO, CANTEEN

tradition LORE, USAGE, BELIEF, CUSTOM, CULTURE, HERITAGE, PRACTICE

traditional ORAL, INHERITED, CUSTOMARY, LEGENDARY, CONVENTIONAL

traduce SLUR, LIBEL, DEFAME, MALIGN, SMEAR

Trafalgar victor NELSON

traffic TRADE, BARTER, BUSINESS, COMMERCE, DEALINGS

traffic cone BOLLARD

traffic jam (ROAD)BLOCK, GRIDLOCK

trafficker DEALER, TRADER, MERCHANT, RETAILER

tragedian ACTOR, THESPIAN

tragedy DRAMA, CALAMITY, DISASTER, AFFLICTION, CATASTROPHE

tragedy, muse of EUTERPE, MELPOMENE

tragic SAD, FATAL, PATHETIC, CALAMITOUS, DISASTROUS

trail DOG, HEEL, TAIL, HOUND, SPOOR, TRACE, FOLLOW, SHADOW; see TRACK

trailblazer SCOUT, PIONEER, EXPLORER, PATHFINDER

trailer VAN, CART, WAGON, PREVIEW

train TUBE, COACH, DRILL, FLIER, LOCAL, EXPRESS, FREIGHT, LIMITED, SHUTTLE, SPECIAL, INSTRUCT, MANIFEST, FREIGHTER, PASSENGER; see RETINUE

trainee PUPIL, NOVICE, NOVITIATE, APPRENTICE

trainer COACH, HANDLER, TEACHER, INSTRUCTOR

training DRILL, BREEDING, EXERCISE, EDUCATION

traipse GAD, TRAIL, TRAMP, WANDER

trait	**HABIT, CUSTOM, FEATURE, QUALITY, CHARACTERISTIC**
traitor	**RAT, JUDAS, LAVAL, ARNOLD, PAUKER, PETAIN, RAKOSI, BETRAYER, CHAMBERS, QUISLING, TURNCOAT**
traitorous	**FALSE, UNTRUE, DISLOYAL, FAITHLESS, TREASONOUS**
Trajan reign year (AD 98–117)	**CI, CV, CX, CII, CIV, CIX, CVI, CXI, CXV, XCIX**
trajectory	**ARC, PATH, CURVE**
tram	**CAR, WAGON, TROLLEY, STREETCAR**
trammel	**NET, HOBBLE**
tramp	**BUM, HIKE, HOBO, TRAIPSE, VAGRANT**
trample	**CHAMP, CRUSH, POACH, TREAD**
trance	**COMA, DAZE, LUPA, SOPOR, SPELL**
tranquil	**CALM, QUIET, STILL, PLACID, SERENE, COMPOSED, PEACEFUL**
tranquility	**CALM PEACE, QUIET, ATARAXY, SERENITY, STILLNESS**
tranquilize	**CALM, PACIFY, SEDATE, SOOTHE**
tranquilizer	**DOWNER, LIBRIUM, ATARAXIC, SEDATIVE**
transact	**TREAT, CARRYON, CONDUCT, PERFORM, NEGOTIATE**
transaction	**DEAL, SALE, AFFAIR, BUSINESS**
transcend	**TOP, PASS, EXCEL, ASCEND, EXCEED**
transcendental	**PRIMORDIAL**
Transcendentalist	**KANT, ALCOTT, FULLER, EMERSON, PEABODY, THOREAU**
transcribe	**COPY, WRITE, RECORD, REPRODUCE**
transcription	**COPY, APOGRAPH, RECORDING, REPRODUCTION**
transfer	**CEDE, DEED, DECAL, GRANT, CONVEY, DEMISE, DEPUTE**
transferer	**ALIENOR**
transfigure	**MUTATE, TRANSFORM**
transfix	**PIN, STAB, IMPALE, PIERCE**
transform	**ALTER, CHANGE, CONVERT, TRANSMUTE**
transformation	**CHANGE, SWITCH, ALTERATION, METASTASIS**
transfuse	**IMBUE, INFUSE, INJECT, INSTILL, PERMEATE**
transgress	**ERR, SIN, DISOBEY, INFRACT, VIOLATE, INFRINGE, OVERSTEP**
transgression	**SIN, CRIME, LAPSE, OFFENSE, TRESPASS, VIOLATION**
transgressor	**SINNER, CULPRIT, OFFENDER, VIOLATOR, DELINQUENT**
transient	**BRIEF, MORTAL, PASSING, FLEETING, EPHEMERAL, TEMPORARY, EVANESCENT**
transistor radio inventor	**SONY**
— transit gloria mundi	**SIC**
transit, mass	**BUS, TRAIN, JITNEY, SUBWAY, TROLLEY**
transition	**FALL, FLUX, RISE, CHANGE, PASSAGE**
transitory	**BRIEF, FLEET(ING), CADUKE, CADUCOUS, EPHEMERAL**
translate	**DECODE, RENDER, INTERPRET**
translation	**VERSION, RENDITION, ADAPTATION, PARAPHRASE**
translator	**EXEGETE, INTERPRETER**
translucent	**CLEAR, GLASSY, PELLUCID, TRANSPARENT**
transmit	**BEAM, MAIL, POST, SEND, WIRE, CONVEY, BROADCAST**
transmute	**CHANGE, CONVERT**
transom	**SLAT, TRAVE, LINTEL, LOUVER**
transparent	**CLEAR, LUCID, SHEER, LIMPID, HYALINE, OBVIOUS, DIAPHANOUS**
transpire	**OCCUR, BEFALL, HAPPEN, UNFOLD**
transplant	**GRAFT, UPROOT, REPLANT, RELOCATE**
transport	**CART, MOVE, TOTE, BLISS, CARRY, ECSTASY, CONVEY(OR), RAPTURE**
transportation	**CARRIAGE, CONVEYANCE**
transported	**RAPT, THRILLED, ENRAPTURED**

transpose SWAP, INVERT, SWITCH, REVERSE, EXCHANGE, INTERCHANGE

Transvaal, capital of PRETORIA

transverse OBLIQUE, CROSSING, INTERSECTING

trap GIN, NET, TIPE, WEIR, SNARE, AMBUSH, ENSNARE

trapdoor DROP, HATCH

trappings DUDS, GEAR, TRIM, REGALIA, EQUIPMENT, ADORNMENTS

trapshooting term SKEET, PIGEON

trash GOOK, JUNK, RAFT, SCUM, WASTE, REFUSE, GARBAGE, RUBBISH, NONSENSE, RIFFRAFF

trashy BASE, CHEAP, JUNKY, SHODDY, WORTHLESS

Trask brothers ARON, CALEB

trattoria stock VINO, PASTA, LASAGNA

trauma BLOW, SHOCK, WOUND, INJURY, ORDEAL

travail PAIN, TOIL, LABOR, DISTRESS, DRUDGERY, EXERTION

travel MOVE, RIDE, TOUR, TREK, TRIP, WEND, DRIVE, JOURNEY

travel, pert. to VIATIC

traveler RIDER, VIATOR, PILGRIM, TOURIST, WAYFARER, ITINERANT

traverse DENY, CROSS, OPPOSE, THWART, OBSTRUCT, FRUSTRATE

travertine LIMESTONE

travesty FARCE, FIASCO, PARODY, LAMPOON, MOCKERY, CARICATURE

Traviata character FLORA, ALFREDO, GERMONT, VIOLETTA

Traviata composer VERDI

travois SLED

trawl NET, FISH, ANGLE, SEINE, DRAGNET

tray HOD, TILL, SALVER, SERVER, COASTER

treacherous UNTRUE, DISLOYAL, DECEPTIVE, PERFIDIOUS, TRAITOROUS

treachery DECEIT, PERFIDY, TREASON, BETRAYAL

treacle REMEDY, MOLASSES

tread PAD, STEP, TIRE, VOLT, SNEAK, TRAMPLE

treadle LEVER, PEDAL, CHALAZA

treadmill WHEEL

treason PERFIDY, BETRAYAL, SEDITION

treasure ROON, CACHE, HOARD, TROVE, CHERISH, REMEMBER

Treasure Island author STEVENSON

Treasure Island character BEN, JIM, PEW

Treasure State MT, MONT(ANA)

treasurer BURSAR, FISCAL, PURSER, BOUCHER

treasury FISC, FISK, BURSE, VAULT, BURSARY, COFFERS

treasury agent(s) TMAN, TMEN

treat USE, CURE, DEAL, DOSE, HEAL, DOCTOR, PAYFOR, REGALE, DELIGHT, ENTERTAIN

treat badly MOCK, ABUSE, INSULT

treatise ESSAY, SUMMA, TRACT, THESIS, MONOGRAPH, DISSERTATION

treatment CARE, STUDY, USAGE, REMEDY, THERAPY, HANDLING, MANAGEMENT

treaty PACT, CONVENT, COVENANT, PROTOCOL

treaties, nuclear INF, CTBT, SALT, START

treble HIGH, ACUTE, SHRILL, TRIPLE, CHANTER, SOPRANO

tree POLE, POST, STAKE, WOODS, CORNER, TIMBER, BOSCAGE, GALLOWS, SAPLING, SEEDLING; see FOREST

tree, pert. to SYLVAN, ARBOREAL

tree, type of APA, IFE, INA, KOU, ULE, ACER, AKEE, BHEL, BREA, CHIA, DITA, DOON, RULE, ILEX, KAKI, KOSO, OHIA, RATA, TITI, ACKEE, ASANA, BALSA, CAROB, LEHUA, MALUS, MANIU, NARRA, NOGAL, OCHNA, PADUS, POLAK, SALAL, SIMAL, TOONA, UNONA, ALMOND, LINDEN, LOCUST, WALNUT, QUASSIA, SOLANUM, TAMARIX, WALLABA; see p. 682

treeless area WOLD, CAMPO, LLANO, PAMPAS, STEPPE, TUNDRA, SAVANNA treelike ARBOREAL, BRANCHED, DENDRITIC, ARBORESCENT

trek HIKE, WALK, TRAMP, TRUDGE

trellis ARBOR, GRATING, LATTICE, PERGOLA, ESPALIER

tremble QUAKE, SHAKE, DIDDER, DODDER, SHIVER, SHUDDER, VIBRATE

tremendous AWFUL, GIGANTIC, COLOSSAL, ENORMOUS, APPALLING

tremolo TRILL, QUAVER, VIBRATO

tremor QUAKE, SHAKE, SHIVER, TEMBLOR, (EARTH)QUAKE

tremulous ASPEN, TIMID, TREPID, QUAVERY

trench *see* DITCH

trench, deep-sea IZU, YAP, BONIN, TONGA, KERMADEC, MARIANAS

trenchant KEEN, ACUTE, SHARP, CUTTING, FORCEFUL, INCISIVE

trencher BOARD, KNIFE, PLATE, CARVER, PLATTER

trend BENT, FLOW, DRIFT, TENOR, STREAM, FASHION

trendy IN, HIP

trepidation FEAR, ALARM, PANIC, UNEASE, AGITATION

trespass ERR, SIN, POACH, INVADE, TROVER, INTRUDE, MISDEED, ENCROACH

tress CURL, LOCK, BRAID, PLAIT, RINGLET

trestle STOOL, BRIDGE, TRIPOD, VIADUCT, (SAW)HORSE

triad TRIO, TRINARY, TRINITY

trial WOE, CASE, SUIT, ASSIZE, ORDEAL, HEARING, INQUEST, INQUIRY, LAWSUIT, HARDSHIP, AFFLICTION; *see* TEST

trial and — ERROR

trial baloon KITE, TEST, FEELER

trial site VENUE

triangle GORE, TRIO, DELTA, TRIAD, GUSSET, OBTUSE, TRIGON, SCALENE

triangle, food MEAT, DAIRY, FRUIT, STARCH, SWEET, VEGETABLE

triangle, kind of LOVE, RIGHT, ETERNAL, SCALENE, ISOSCELES, EQUILATERAL

triangle part LEG, BASE, SIDE, HYPOTENUSE

triangular DELTOID, TRIGONAL, TRIGONOUS

tribe CLAN, GENS, RACE, GROUP, FAMILY, NATION, PEOPLE; *see* BIBLICAL TRIBES; *see* p. 730

tribesman YAHO

tribulation WOE, TRIAL, ORDEAL, MISERY, DISTRESS, HARDSHIP, AFFLICTION

tribunal BAR, FEME, ROTA, VEHM, BENCH, COURT, FORUM

tribune DAIS, PULPIT, THRONE, ROSTRUM, OFFICIAL, PLATFORM, MAGISTRATE

tributary FORK, RIVER, BRANCH, FEEDER, STREAM, OFFSHOOT

tribute CAUP, KAIN, KUDOS, EULOGY, HOMAGE, ACCLAIM, CARATCH; *see* TAX

trice FLASH, JIFFY, SECOND, INSTANT, TWINKLING

trick FOB, FUB, DIDO, DUPE, FEKE, FLAM, GAWD, GULL, HOAX, JAPE, JEST, NICK, RUSE, WILE, DODGE, STUNT, GAMBIT, TREPAN, FICELLE, FLIMFLAM, HOODWINK, ILLUSION, DECEPTION, SUBTERFUGE

trickery ART, FRAUD, DECEIT, DUPERY, SLEIGHT, ARTIFICE, DECEPTION, SUBTERFUGE

trickle FEW, DRIP, DROP, LEAK, SEEP

tricks won BOOK, NULL, SLAM, CAPOT, NULLO

trickster CHEAT, KNAVE, ROGUE, SCAMP, RASCAL

tricky SLY, FOXY, WILY, CAGEY, CRAFTY, TOUCHY, COMPLEX, SENSITIVE, INTRICATE

trident SPEAR, LEISTER

tried and true TRUSTY, RELIABLE, DEPENDABLE, TRUSTWORTHY

Trieste measure ORNA, ORNE

trifle GRY, TOY, DOIT, FICO, PIFF, PLAY, DALLY, FLIRT, NIGGLE, PALTER, BAGATELLE

trifoliate TERNATE

trig	NEAT, PRIM, TIDY, TRIM, SMART, SPRUCE
trigger	SPUR, IMPEL, ACTIVATE, INITIATE, MOTIVATE
trigonometric function	SINE, COSINE, SECANT, COSECANT, (CO)TANGENT
trilateral	THREESIDED
trill	ROLL, CHIRP, SHAKE, TRILLO, WARBLE, MORDENT, TIRALEE, TREMOLO, TWITTER, VIBRATO
trim	CUT, FIT, LOP, CLIP, DOCK, NEAT, PARE, PINK, TIDY, TRIG, ADORN, PREEN, PRUNE, SHAVE, SHEAR, SHRAG, REDUCE, SVELTE, ORDERED
trimmed	SNOD, SHORN, ADORNED
trimming(s)	GIMP, FLOTS, FRILL, RUCHE, BURLET, DEFEAT, BEATING, PIPING, RUFFLE, FLOUNCE, GUIPURE, RUCHING, FURBELOW, RICKRACK
trimming tool	ZAX, SHEARS, CLIPPER, SCISSORS, PINKINGSHEARS
Trinidad and Tobago, capital of	PORTOFSPAIN
Trinidad and Tobago city/town	ARIMA, AROUCA, SAN JUAN, SIPATIA, PLYMOUTH, TUNAPUNA
Trinidad and Tobago mountain	ARIPO, TAMANA
Trinidad and Tobago river	COWA, NAVET, CARONI, INNISS, ORTOIRE
trinity	THREE, TRIAD, TRINE
trinket	GAUD, BIJOU, TOKEN, BAUBLE, GEWGAW, BIBELOT
trio	TRIAD, TRINE, TRINITY, THREE(SOME)
trip	ERR, FALL, SLIP, TOUR, JAUNT, LURCH, JUNKET, VOYAGE, JOURNEY, STUMBLE, EXCURSION
triple	TRI, TRIO, TRIAD, TREBLE, TERNATE
Triple Crown winner	OMAHA, ASSAULT, CITATION, WHIRLAWAY, SECRETARIAT
triplet(s)	TRIN(E), TERCET, TREBLE
tripod	CAT, EASEL, STAND, SPIDER, TRIVET
tripper	CAM, PAWL, DETENT, ADDICT, JUNKIE
trireme	GALLEY
trismus	LOCKJAW, TETANUS
Tristram (Tristan) beloved	ISOLT, ISEULT, ISOLDE
Tristram Shandy author	STERNE
trite	DULL, HACK, BANAL, CORNY, INANE, STALE, JEJUNE, HACKNEYED
triton	EFT, NEWT, SNAIL, SALAMANDER
Triton relative	POSEIDON, AMPHITRITE
Triton trumpet	CONCH
triturate	BRAY, CRUSH, POUND, PULVERIZE
triumph	JOY, WIN, EXULT, GLORY, PREVAIL, REJOICE, SUCCESS, VICTORY, CONQUEST, CELEBRATION
triumphant	ONTOP, ELATED, FLUSHED, WINNING, DOMINANT, EXULTANT, JUBILANT, VICTORIOUS
triumvirate	TRIO, TROIKA, TRIARCHY
triumvirate member	CAESAR, POMPEY, CRASSUS
trivet	SPIDER, TRIPOD
trivial	PETTY, COMMON, PALTRY, NUGATORY, TRIFLING, FRIVOLOUS, INSIGNIFICANT
trivium	LOGIC, GRAMMAR, RHETORIC
troche	PASTIL, ROTULA, LOZENGE, PASTIL(L)E
troglodyte	APE, HERMIT, SAVAGE, CAVEMAN, GORILLA, RECLUSE, BARBARIAN, CHIMPANZEE
trogon	QUETZAL, TOCORORO
Troilus and Cressida character	AJAX, HELEN, PARIS, PRIAM, AENEAS, HECTOR, ANTENOR, ULYSSES, CASSANDRA
Troilus killer	ACHILLES
Troilus lover	CRESSIDA
Troilus relative	PARIS, PRIAM, APOLLO, HECTOR, HECUBA
Trojan	ILIAN, DARDAN, TEUCRIAN
Trojan hero	AJAX, ENEAS, PARIS, AENEAS, AGENOR, DARDAN, HECTOR, ULYSSES, ACHILLES, DIOMEDES, AGAMEMNON
Trojan horse builder	EPE(I)US

Trojan king	**PRIAM**	trot	**JOG, LOPE, PACE, PONY,**
Trojan War cause	**HELEN**		**AMBLE, DANCE**
troll	*see* **DWARF**	troth	**VOW, PLEDGE, PROMISE**
trolley	**TRAM, STREETCAR**	trots	**FLUX, RUNS, DIARRHEA,**
trollop	**HUSSY, TRAMP,**		**DYSENTERY**
	WHORE, SLATTERN,	troubadour	**BARD, POET,**
	STRUMPET		**JONGLEUR, MINSTREL**
trombone	**SACKBUT;** *see p. 642*	trouble(s)	**ADO, AIL, IRK, WOE,**
troop	**BAND, UNIT, WALK,**		**FASH, ILLS, ANNOY, HARRY,**
	GROUP, MARCH, PARTY,		**PAINS, TRIAL, WORRY,**
	SQUAD, COMPANY		**BOTHER, EFFORT, HARASS,**
trooper	**RCMP, MOUNTIE,**		**MOLEST, PUTOUT,**
	SOLDIER, POLICEMAN,		**HOTWATER, IRRITATE,**
	CAVALRYMAN,		**DIFFICULTY, INCOMMODE**
	INFANTRY(MAN)	troubled	**TURBID, ANXIOUS,**
troops	**MEN, ARMY, FORCES**		**WORRIED, DISTURBED,**
troops quarters	**BILLET,**		**DISTRAUGHT**
	CANTON, BIVOUAC,	troublemaker	**IMP, KNAVE,**
	BARRACKS		**ROGUE, GOSSIP, HELLION,**
troopship	**TRANSPORT**		**AGITATOR**
trope	**METAPHOR**	troubleshooter	**FIXER,**
trophy	**CUP, PALM, MEDAL,**		**OMBUDSMAN**
	PRIZE, SCALP, LAUREL; *see*	troublesome	**PESKY, TRYING,**
	AWARD		**ANNOYING, VEXATIOUS**
tropic	**LIMIT, CANCER,**	trough	**HOD, TUB, BOSH,**
	CIRCLE, BOUNDARY,		**TRUG, BASIN, GUTTER,**
	PARALLEL, CAPRICORN		**MANGER, STRAKE, FEEDBOX;**
tropical	**HOT, STEAMY,**		*see* **CHANNEL**
	SULTRY, TORRID,	trounce	**BEAT, FLOG, WHIP,**
	EQUATORIAL, SWELTERING		**WHOMP, DEFEAT, THRASH,**
tropical disease	**AGUE, BUBO,**		**CLOBBER, LAMBASTE**
	YAWS, SPRUE, DENGUE,	troupe	**BAND, GROUP, TROOP,**
	CHOLERA, MALARIA,		**COMPANY**
	MEASLES, BERIBERI,	trouper	**ACTOR, PLAYER,**
	PSILOSIS, AMEBIASIS,		**ACTRESS, THESPIAN,**
	DIPHTHERIA		**PERFORMER, ENTERTAINER**
tropical fish	**OPAH, GUASA,**	trousers	**CHAPS, JEANS, PANTS,**
	SARGO, ROBALO, SALEMA,		**SLOPS, TREWS, SLACKS,**
	MOJARRA		**PEGTOPS, BREECHES**
tropical tree	**AXEE, BITO, EBON,**	trousseau	**BUNDLE**
	GUAO, HURA, KOKO, MABA,	trout	**CHAR, KELT, CHARR,**
	MAHO, PALM, SIDA, ACAPU,		**LONGE, SEWEN, SEWIN,**
	ANATO, ANONA, ARJAN,		**SIWIN, SPROD, TOGUE,**
	ARJUN, BALSA, BARIA, BONGO,		**TROUT, TRUFF, QUASKY,**
	CEIBA, CHICO, DALLI,		**TAIMEN, OQUASSA**
	EBONY, GUAMA, GUAVA,	trowel	**DARBY, FLOAT, PLANE,**
	ICACO, ICICA, IXORA, KOKKO,		**SCOOP**
	LEHUA, MAHOE, MARIA,	Troy	**ILIUM, ILLION, WEIGHT**
	PACAY, QUIRA, ROBLE, SAMAN,	Troy founder	**ILUS**
	SERON, SIRIS, TREMA, URUCU,	Troy king	**PARIS, PRIAM**
	VITEX, ZAMAN, ZORRO,	Troy, story of	**ILIAD**
	ACAJOU, ANATTO, ANNONA,	Troy, *pert. to*	**ILIAC, ILIAN,**
	BANANA, BANYAN, BAOBAB,		**TROJAN**
	BRAZIL, CASHEW, COLIMA,	truant	**TRONE, LAGGARD,**
	KUMBUK, LEBBEK, PAPAYA,		**SHIRKER, TRIVANT,**
	SAPOTA, ZAMANG, ANNATTO,		**VAGRANT**
	AVOCADO, SANDBOX,	truce	**LULL, PAUSE, PEACE,**
	CINCHONA, TAMARIND,		**RESPITE, ARMISTICE,**
	TAMARISK		**CEASEFIRE**

Trucial States	*see* UNITED ARAB EMIRATES
truck	RIG, VAN, CART, DRAY, HAUL, SEMI, SHIP, CARRY, LORRY, TRADE, BARROW, BARTER, CAMION, ONETON, TWOTON, PICKUP, PUSHCART; *see p. 726*
truckle	FAWN, STOOP, TOADY, CRINGE, KOWTOW
truculent	MEAN, CRUEL, DEADLY, VITRIOLIC
trudge	WALK, HIKE, PACE, PLOD, SLOG, MARCH, TRAMP
true	FAIR, JUST, LEAL, VERY, EXACT, LOYAL, RIGHT, ACTUAL, TRUSTY, FACTUAL, GENUINE, GERMANE, PRECISE, ACCURATE, FAITHFUL, RIGHTFUL, AUTHENTIC, LEGITIMATE
— and true	TRIED
truffle	FUNGUS, EARTHNUT, TUCKAHOE
truism	FACT, ADAGE, AXIOM, MAXIM, MOTTO, SAYING, PLATITUDE
Truk	*see* CHUUK
truly	YEA, QUITE, SOOTH, INDEED, REALLY
Truman birthplace	LAMAR
Truman relative	BESS, MARGARET
Truman Doctrine recipient	GREECE, TURKEY
trump	TOP, POLT, RUFF, OUTDO, PEACH, SURPASS
trumpery	FRAUD, TRASH, DECEIT, PALTRY, RUBBISH, NONSENSE
trumpet	HORN, BUGLE, BUCCINA, CLARION; *see p. 642*
trumpet call	TAPS, SENNET, SINNET, TUCKET, CHAMADE, FANFARE, FLOURISH, REVEILLE
truncate	LOP, TRIM, ABRIDGE, CURTAIL, ABBREVIATE
truncheon	CLUB, BATON, (NIGHT)STICK
trundle	CART, HOOP, ROLL, RULL, CASTER, ROTATE, TRAVEL, CIRCLET, REVOLVE
trunk	BOX, BOLE, BOOT, CABER, CHEST, SNOUT, TORSO, LOCKER, THORAX, ABDOMEN, CONTAINER, PROBOSCIS
truss	TIE(UP), BEAM, BIND, PROP, BRACE, STRAP, STRUT, TETHER, SUPPORT

trust	HOPE, RELY, TROW, FAITH, STOCK, BELIEF, CARTEL, CHARGE, COMMIT, CREDIT, CONSIGN, CUSTODY, MANDATE, MONOPOLY, RELIANCE, CONFIDENCE
trust fund	WAKF, WAQF, WUKF
trustee	AGENT, WARDEN, GUARDIAN, CUSTODIAN
trustworthy	SAFE, TRUE, LOYAL, TRIED, PROVEN, STA(U)NCH, RELIABLE
trusty	CONVICT, PRISONER; *see* TRUSTWORTHY
truth	TAO, UNA, FACT, AXIOM, CANDOR, FEALTY, TRUISM, VERITY, REALITY, VERITAS
truth drug	PENTOTHAL
truthful	FRANK, CANDID, HONEST, SINCERE, UPFRONT, VERACIOUS, VERIDIC(AL)
truthfulness	CANDOR, HONESTY, OPENNESS, VERACITY, SINCERITY
try	TAX, HEAR, MELT, SEEK, SHOT, TEST, CHECK, CRACK, ESSAY, ETTLE, JUDGE, PROVE, REFINE, STRIVE, ATTEMPT, ENDEAVOR
trying	DULL, BORING, VEXING, IRKSOME, ANNOYING, IRRITATING, BOTHERSOME
tryout	TEST, TRIAL, AUDITION
tryst	DATE, MEETING, RENDEZVOUS, ASSIGNATION
tryst site	LOVE NEST, LOVERS LEAP
tsar	*see* CZAR
tse-tse fly disease	NAGANA
tub	KID, KIT, SOE, COWL, GAAL, GAWN, GYLE, KNAP, KNOP, KEEVE, PIGGIN, SICFEL, KEELER, HOGSHEAD; *see* VAT
tuba	HELICON, SAXHORN, BASSHORN, BOMBARDON; *see p. 642*
tubby	FAT, OBESE, PLUMP, PUDGY, CHUBBY, ROLYPOLY
tube	DUCT, HOSE, PIPE, PIPET, SIPPER, SUBWAY, BURETTE, CONDUIT, PIPETTE, SNORKEL
tuber	OCA, YAM, EDDO, TARO, TRUB, JALAP, SALEB, SALEP, POTATO, TRUFFLE
tuberculosis	TB, PTHISIS, CONSUMPTION

tuberculous	PHTHISIC, CONSUMPTIVE
Tubuai island	*see* AUSTRAL
tubular	TUBATE, TUBIFORM, FISTULOUS
tuck	HEM, LAP, FOLD, HIDE, PLEAT, RUCHE, GATHER, PUCKER
tucker out	FAG, TIRE, WEARY, EXHAUST
— and tuck	NIP
Tuesday source	TIU, TIV, TIW
tuft	COMA, HULU, CLUMP, CREST, CLUSTER
tufted	HAIRY, MOSSY, COMATE, COMOSE, SWARDY, CRESTED, C(A)ESPITOSE
tug	TOW, DRAG, DRAW, HAUL, JERK, PULL, YANK
tuition	FEE(S), BILL, COST, TUTELAGE, EDUCATION
tulle	LACE, NET(TING)
tumble	FALL, DROP, SPIN, TRIP, PITCH, STAGGER, SOMERSAULT
tumbler	GLASS, NEEDLE, ACROBAT, GYMNAST
tumbleweed	THISTLE, AMARANTH
tumescence	BULGE, SWELLING
tumid	TURGID, POMPOUS, SWOLLEN, INFLATED, BOMBASTIC, DISTENDED, TUMESCENT
tummy	*see* BELLY
tumor	OMA, WEN, YAW, CYST, MORO, PIAN, GUMMA, MYOMA, POLYP, CANCER, GLIOMA, GROWTH, LIPOMA, ANGIOMA, FIBROMA, NEUROMA, OSTEOMA, OSTEOME, SARCOMA, HEMATOMA, MELANOMA
tumult	DIN, RIOT, BABEL, CHAOS, LURRY, MELEE, UPROAR, FERMENT, TURMOIL, DISORDER, AGITATION
tumultuous	NOISY, RIOTOUS, AGITATED, TURBULENT, BOISTEROUS, DISORDERLY
tuna	PEAR, TUNNY, OPUNTIA
tundra	PLAIN(S), SAVANNAH
tune	AIR, ARIA, FADO, DITTY, ADJUST, JINGLE, MELODY, STRAIN, REGULATE
tune up	LUBE, TIME, (RE)OIL, GREASE
tuneful	SWEET, DULCET, LYRICAL, MELODIC, MELODIOUS
tuneless	OFFKEY, DISSONANT, CACOPHONOUS
tunesmith	COMPOSER, SONGWRITER
tungsten	WOLFRAM, CARBOLOY
Tungusic language	GOLDI, LAMUT, MANCHU, TUNGUS
tunic	ROBE, JAMA(H), TOGA, CHITON, KIRTLE, MANTLE, CASSOCK, VESTMENT
Tunisia, capital of	TUNIS
Tunisian city	DOUZ, SFAX, ELJEM, GABES, GAFSA, SUSAH, TUNIS, ARIANA, DOUGGA, MAHDIA, SAFAQIS, SOUSSE, TAWZAR, TOZEUR, BIZERTE
Tunisian gulf	GABES, TUNIS
Tunisian island	JERBA
Tunisian measure	SAA(H), UEBA, CAFIZ, WHIBA
Tunisian money	DINAR
Tunisian river	MEDJERDA
Tunisian ruler	BEY, DEY
Tunisian weight	ROTL, ARTEL, ICKIA, KANTAR
tunnel	BORE, TUBE, CENTS, TANNA, BURROW, NOOSAC, MOFFAT, SEVERN, ARLBERG, CASCADE, CHUNNEL, HOLLAND, LINCOLN, SIMPLON
tunnel term	ADIT, SHAFT, SLOPE, STOPE, RISING, HEADING, SINKING
tunnel vision cause	GLAUCOMA
tunneler	ANT, DIGGER, SAPPER, BURROWER
tupelo	LIME, NYSSA, DOGWOOD, PEPPERIDGE
Turandot role	LIU, PANG, PING, PONG, CALAF
turban	LUNG(Y)I, MANDIL, MUNDIL
turbid	RIL(E)Y, MURKY, ROILY, CLOUDY, OPAQUE, ROILED
turbine	MOTOR, ROTOR, ENGINE, PROPELLER
turbulence	CHAOS, TUMULT, AGITATION, CONFUSION, COMMOTION
turbulent	WILD, RAGING, STORMY, AGITATED, BLUSTERY
turf	SOD, AREA, LAWN, PEAT, DIVOT, GRASS, SWARD, TRACK, TERRITORY
turgid	TOROSE, BLOATED, SWOLLEN

Turk	TA(R)TAR, OSMANLI, OTTOMAN
turkey	TOM, BUST, FLOP, FAILURE, GOBBLER
— turkey	TALK
Turkey, capital of	ANKARA; see also TURKISH
turkeys, group of	RAFTER
turkey part	LEG, WING, SNOOD, WATTLE, WISHBONE, CARBUNCLE, DRUMSTICK
turkey, young	POULT
Turkic language	KAZAK, TATAR, UZBEK, YAKUT, KAZAKH, IURGIZ, UIGHUR, BASHKIR, CHUVASH, KIRGIUZ, TURKISH, TURKMEN, TURKOMAN
Turkic man	OGOR
Turkish city	VAN, AGRI, KARS, ORDU, TROY, URFA, ADANA, BURSA, IZMIR, KONYA, TRUVA, ANKARA, BODRUM, EDESSA, HARRAN, MERCIN, SAMSUN, ANTALYA, ISTANBUL, ESKISEHIR, GAZIANTEP
Turkish district	CAZA
Turkish government	PORTE
Turkish gulf	KERME, SAROS, ANTALYA, ISKENDERUN
Turkish island	BOZCA, ADALAR, BURGAZ, HEYBELI, MARMARA, BOZCAADA, PRINKIPO
Turkish lake	ACI, KUS, TUZ, VAN, BURDUR, ULABAT, AKSEHIR, EGRIDIR, BEYSEHIR
Turkish leader	BAYAR, INONU, KEMAL, SUNAY, DEMIREL
Turkish measure	PIK, HATT, KHAT, ZIRA, ALMUD, BERRI, DONUM, KILEH, ARSHIN, DJERIB, FORTIN, PARMAK
Turkish money	LIRA, PARA, ALTUN, ASPER, MAHBUB, SEQUIN, ALTILIK, BESHLIK, PLASTER, ZECCHINO
Turkish mountain	CILO, AKDAG, ALADAG, ARARAT, KACKAR, SUPHAN, ERICYAS
Turkish president	BAYAR, INONU, SUNAY, ATATURK
Turkish river	GOK, AKSU, ARAS, FRAT, GEDIZ, GOKSU, KIZIL, KOPRU, MURAT, YESIL, CEYHAN, ERGENE, KELKIT, SEYHAN, TIGRIS, YENICE,

	SAKARYA, MENDERES, EUPHRATES, KIZILIRMAK
Turkish sultan	CALIF, SELIM, CALIPH, PADISHAH
Turkish ruler	KHAN, CALIPH, SULTAN
Turkish title	AG(H)A, EMIR, PASHA
Turkish weight	OKA, OKE, RILE, ROTL, CEQUI, CHEKE, KERAT, IULEH, BATMAN, DIRHAM, KANTAR, MISKAL, YUSDRUM
Turkmenistan, capital of	ASHGABUT, ASHKHABAD
Turkmenistan city/town	KERKI, TEJEN, CHELEKEN, ASHKHABAD, CHARDZHOU, DASHHOWUZ
Turkmenistan desert	SUNDUKL
Turkmenistan money	MANAT
Turkmenistan river	ATREK, TEJEN, MORGHAB
turmoil	CHAOS, HURLY, BUSTLE, TUMULT, WELTER, DISORDER, COMMOTION
turn	UP, HAW, AIRT, BEND, BENT, GYRE, VEER, VERT, SLUE, SPIN, DRIFT, EVERT, HINGE, PIVOT, SHUNT, VERTE, VOLTI, WHIRL, DETOUR, GYRATE, REVERT, ROTATE, REVOLVE; see VEER
— and turn	TOSS
turn against	CROSS, BETRAY
turn aside	AVERT, PARRY
turn back	LOOP, REPEL, RETURN, REPULSE, RETREAT, BACKTRACK
turn down	VETO, SPURN, REJECT, DECLINE
turn in	BETRAY, RETIRE, DELIVER, GO TO BED, HIT THE SACK
turn inside out	EVERT
Turn of the Screw author	JAMES
turn off	EXIT, REPEL, DIVERT, DISGUST
turn on	AROUSE, BETRAY, EXCITE
turn over	CEDE, SPILL, UPEND, UPSET, CAPSIZE
turn up	COME, SHOW, APPEAR, ARRIVE
turnabout	SHIFT, REVERSAL, ABOUTFACE, VOLTEFACE
turnaround	FLIPFLOP, REVERSAL, ABOUTFACE, VOLTEFACE, IMPROVEMENT

turncoat	JUDAS, BOLTER, TRAITOR, APOSTATE, RENEGADE	tutor	TUTE, COACH, GUIDE, MENTOR, TEACHER, INSTRUCTOR
turndown	NO, VETO, REFUSAL, REJECTION	Tuvalu	ELLICE, LAGOON
turning point	CRUX, ELBOW, CRISIS, SOLSTICE	Tuvalu, capital of	FUNAFUTI
		Tuvalu island	NANUMEA, FUNAFUTI, NUKUFETAU, NUKULAILAI
turnip	BAGA, NEEP, SWEDE		
turnkey	SCREW, GAOLER, JAILER, KEEPER, WARDER	tuxedo	TUX, FORMAL, BLACKTIE
turnoff	EXIT, RAMP, DETOUR	TVA dam	BOONE, OCOEE, NORRIS, WILSON, CHATUGE, TELLICO, WATAUGA, WHEELER, CHEROKEE
turnout	RIG, GETUP, EQUIPAGE, ATTENDANCE		
turnover	PIE, TART, UPSET, PASTRY, SAMOSA		
		TV duel member	LENO, LETTERMAN
turnpike	HIGHWAY, THRUWAY, TOLL ROAD	TV host	PAAR, CARSON; see TALK SHOW HOST
turnstile	GATE, TIRL		
Turow (Scott) work	ONEL	TV shows, famous	see p. 535
turpentine	TURP, SOLVENT, CLEANER, GAL(L)IPOT	twaddle	ROT, BABBLE, DRIVEL, JARGON, CHATTER, FUSTIAN, PRATTLE, GIBBERISH
turpentine derivative	ROSIN, PINENE, TERPENE		
		tweak	JERK, PINCH, PLUCK, TWIST, TWITCH
turpentine resin	ALK, GALIPOT		
turpitude	BASENESS, VILENESS, DEPRAVITY	tweezers	PINCERS
		Twelfth Night	EPIPHANY
turret	TOWER, CUPOLA, BARBICAN, BARTIZAN	Twelfth Night character	TOBY, BELCH, CURIO, FESTE, MARIA, VIOLA, OLIVIA, ORSINO, ANTONIO, MALVOLIO
turtle	EMYD, ARRAU, COOTER, EMYDEA, GOPHER, JURARA, SLIDER, ATHECAE, PAINTED, SNAPPER, TURTLET, ARCHELON, EMYDIDAE, MATAMATA, TERRAPIN, TORTOISE, HAWKSBILL		
		twenty	XX, CORGE, SCORE
		twenty-fourth part	CARAT, KARAT
		twerp	SPRAT, SQUIRT
		twice	BIS, ENCORE
		twig	SLIP, LIMB, SCION, SHOOT, SPRIG, WITHE, BRANCH
turtle delicacy	CALIPEE, CALIPASH		
turtle genus	EMYS, CHELYS, CARETEA, CHELONE, TESTUDO, TRIGNYX, CHELONIA, CHELYDRA, EMYDINAE, TERRAPENE	twigs, made of	VIRGAL, WATTLED
		twilight	EVE, DUSK, GLOAM, EVENTIDE, GLOAMING
		twin	ENG, COPY, CHANG, GEMEL, DOUBLE, DIDYMOUS, IDENTICAL, DOPPELGANGER
Tuscan city	PISA, LUCCA, SIENA, AREZZO, FIRENZE, LIVORNO, FLORENCE		
Tuscan river	ARNO, ORCIA, OMBRONE	Twin Cities	ST PAUL, MINNEAPOLIS
tusk	FANG, HORN, IVORY, SCRIVELLO	twin crystal	MACLE
tussle	FIGHT, GRAPPLE, SCUFFLE, WRESTLE	twine	COIL, CORD, ROPE, HEMP, WIND, TWIST
tussock	TUFT, CLUMP, HUMMOCK, THICKET	twinge	PANG, STAB, CRICK, QUALM, SPASM, THROB, TINGLE, STITCH, TWITCH, SCRUPLE
tutelage	CARE, AEGIS, CHARGE, CUSTODY, AUSPICES, PROTECTION, INSTRUCTION		
		twinkle	WINK, GLEAM, GLINT, FLICKER, GLIMMER, GLITTER, SPARKLE
tutelary deity	LARES, PENATES		

twinkling	WINK, FLASH, MOMENT, INSTANT	tycoon	BARON, MOGUL, NABOB, SHOGUN, GRANDEE, MAGNATE, ENTREPRENEUR
twirl	SPIN, WHIRL, GYRATE, PIROUETTE	Tyndareus relative	LEDA
twist	FEAK, FOIL, KINK, SKEW, SLUB, WARP, GNARL, GRIND, WRICK, INTORT, SQUIRM, CONTORT	type	ILK, FONT, KIND, NORM, SORT, BRAND, BREED, CLASS, GENRE, MODEL, SPECIES
twisted	(A)WRY, SKEW, KINKY, TORSE, TORTILE, PERVERTED	type part	BODY, FACE, FEET, KERN, NECK, NICK, STEM, BEARD, SERIF, SHANK, GROOVE, COUNTER, SHOULDER
twister	see WHIRLWIND		
twit	RAG, RIB, JEER, JIBE, SCOFF, TEASE, RIDICULE	type size	PICA, RUBY, AGATE, CANON, ELITE, PEARL, MINION, PRIMER, BREVIER, DIAMOND, ENGLISH, PARAGON, EXCELSIOR, NONPAREIL
twitch	TIC, JERK, SPASM, TWEAK, FIDGET, TWINGE, VELLICATE		
twitter	CHIRP, TITTER, WARBLE, CHATTER, CHIRRUP	type style	ROMAN, ITALIC, SCRIPT, BOLD(FACE), LIGHT(FACE), MONOSPACE, TYPEWRITER
twixt	BETWEEN		
two	DUO, PAIR, BRACE, TWINS	typeface	PIE, HESS, NEWS, TIMES, AGATE, ARIAL, BEMBO, GOUDY, IONIC, ROMAN, RONDE, RUNIC, TIMES, VOGUE, BODONI, BULMER, CASLON, COCHIN, FUTURA, GOTHIC, ITALIC, MONACO, SCRIPT, STYMIE, CENTURY, CHICAGO, COURIER, CURSIVE, GENEVA, GRANJON, CLOISTER, GARAMOND, PALATINO, SANSERIF, HELVETICA
two-bit	CHEAP, TAWDRY, WORTHLESS		
two-edged	ANCIPITAL, ANCIPITOUS		
two-faced	FALSE, SHIFTY, DECEITFUL, INSINCERE, HYPOCRITICAL		
twofold	DUAL, TWIN, BINAL, BINARY		
two-footed	BIPED(AL)		
Two Gentlemen of Verona character	JULIA, SPEED, LAUNCE, SILVIA, THURIO, LUCETTA, PROTEUS		
		typesetter	PRINTER, COMPOSITOR, LINOTYPIST, MONOTYPIST
two-handed	BIMANOUS, AMBIDEXTROUS	typewriter inventor	SHOLES
two-legged	BIPED	typewriter, kind of	TELEX, MANUAL, ELECTRIC, ELECTRONIC, TELETYPE
two-month period	BIMESTER		
two-seater	TANDEM, ROADSTER	typewriter part	KEY, TAB, BAIL, SHIFT, PLATEN, ROLLER, SPACER, CARRIAGE, TABULATOR
two-sided	BILATERAL		
two-spot	DEUCE		
two-time	CHEAT (ON), BETRAY, DOUBLECROSS	typhoon	WIND, STORM, MONSOON, HURRICANE
two-timer	CHEAT, JUDAS, TRAITOR, BETRAYER, ADULTERER	typhoon name	NINA, RITA, RUBY, VERA, SALLY, SARAH; see HURRICANE
two-week period	FORTNIGHT	typical	TYPY, IDEAL, MODEL, USUAL, NORMAL, REGULAR, EXEMPLARY
two-wheeled carriage	GIG, CART, CALASH, HANSOM, CALECHE, TILBURY		
two-wheeled vehicle	TONGA, BICYCLE, SCOOTER	typify	EMBODY, EXEMPLIFY, SYMBOLIZE, EPITOMIZE
twofold	DUAL, BINAL, BINARY, DOUBLE, DUPLEX	typographical error	TYPO, ERRATUM
twosome	COUPLE	tyrannical	CRUEL, SEVERE, UNJUST, DESPOTIC, DICTATORIAL
2001 computer	HAL		

tyrannize	BULLY, OPPRESS, BROWBEAT, DOMINEER, INTIMIDATE
tyranny	TIGOR, CRUELTY, SEVERITY, DESPOTISM, OPPRESSION, DICTATORSHIP
tyrant	NERO, CAESAR, DESPOT, AUTOCRAT, DICTATOR, OPPRESSOR
Tyre royalty	DIDO, HIRAM
tyro	NOVICE, ROOKIE, AMATEUR, STUDENT, NEOPHYTE
Tyrolean city	ZAMS, PFUNDS, LANDECK, INNSBRUCK
Tyrolean river	INN, LECH, ADIGE
tzar	*see* CZAR

U

U	EU, HAIRPIN, UNIFORM, UPSILON
UAE	*see* UNITED ARAB EMIRATES
Ubangi	MAKUA, MOBANGI
Ubangi tributary	BOMU, UELE, KOTTO, MPOKO, OUAKA
ubiety	LOCATION, POSITION
ubiquitous	PERVASIVE, EVERYWHERE, OMNIPRESENT
U-boat	SUB(MARINE), PIGBOAT
udder	BAG, DUG, MAMMA
Uganda, capital of	KAMPALA
Ugandan city	ARUA, GULU, JINJA, MBALE, KASESE, MASAKA, MOROLO, NIMULE, SOROTI, TORORO, MASINDI, MBARARA
Ugandan lake	KYOGA, ALBERT, EDWARD, GEORGE, VICTORIA
Ugandan language	LUO, LUGANDA, SWAHILI
Ugandan leader	AMIN, OBOTE, MUSEVENI
Ugandan money	SHILLING
Ugandan mountain	ELGON, MOROTO, MORUNGOLE, MARGHERITA
Ugandan neighbor	KENYA, SUDAN, ZAIRE, RWANDA, TANZANIA
Ugandan people	ARAB, ASIAN, LANGO, PYGMY, ACHOLI, BAGANDA, EUROPEAN

Ugandan president	OBOTE, MUSEVENI
Ugandan river	NILE, ACHWA, PAGER, DOPETH, MUZIZI
Ugandan waterfall	OWEN, RIPON, KABALEGA
ugly	NASTY, PLAIN, HORRID, HOMELY, HIDEOUS, HOSTILE, DREADFUL, UNATTRACTIVE
ugly, render	MAR, DEFACE, UGLIFY, DISFIGURE
ukase	EDICT, DECREE
Ukraine, capital of	KIEV
Ukrainian city	KIEV, LVIV, LUTSK, YALTA, ODESSA, DONETSK, KHARKIV, LUNANSK, MARIUPO, TERNOPIL, CHERNOBYL, MIKOLAYIV, SIMFEROPOL, SEVASTOPOL, DNIPROPETROVSK
Ukrainian lake	LENIN
Ukrainian money	GRIVNA, GRYNIA, HRYVNA, SCHAGIV, KOPIYKA
Ukrainian mountain	KAMULA, HOVERLYA
Ukrainian neighbor	POLAND, RUSSIA, BELARUS, HUNGARY, MOLDOVA, ROMANIA, SLOVAKIA
Ukrainian president	KRAVCHUK
Ukrainian river	BUG, DESNA, INGUL, SLUCH, DONETS, PRIPET, ZBRUCH, DNIEPER, INGULETS, TELEREV, DNIESTER
ukulele	UKE, GUITAR
Ualume author	POE
Ulan Bator	URGA
ulcer	BOIL, SORE, CANKER, ABSCESS, ABTHOUS, CHANCRE
ulcerate	FESTER
ulterior	HIDDEN, LATENT, UNKNOWN, CONCEALED
ultimate	LAST, BASIC, FINAL, EVENTUAL, FARTHEST, DEFINITIVE, FUNDAMENTAL
ultimate object	ENDALL
ultimatum	DEMAND, EITHEROR, WARNING, CHALLENGE, LAST OFFER
ultra	MEGA, VERY, EXTREME, (E)SPECIALLY
ululate	BAY, CRY, HOWL, PULE, MEWL, WAIL, LAMENT
Ulysses	ODYSSEUS

Ulysses author	JOYCE, TENNYSON
Ulysses character	BLOOM, MOLLY, DEDALUS, LEOPOLD
Ulysses dog	ARGUS
Ulysses friend	MENTOR
Ulysses realm	ITHACA
Ulysses relative	LAERTES, PENELOPE, TELEMACHUS
umbilical cord	FUNICULUS, YOLKSTALK
umbrage	PIQUE, SHADOW, OFFENSE, INDIGNATION
umbrella	GAMP, CHUTE, SHADE, CHATYA, PARASOL, SUNSHADE
umbrella part	RIB
umbrella tree	WAHOO, MAGNOLIA
umlaut	DIERESIS
umpire	REF, UMP, JUDGE, ARBITER, DAYSMAN, REFEREE
U.N. agency	FAO, IDA, ILO, IMF, IMO, ITU, UPU, WHO, WMO, GATT, IAEA, IBRD, ICAO, IFAO, WIPO, UNRRA, UNESCO
U.N. official language	ARABIC, FRENCH, CHINESE, ENGLISH, RUSSIAN, SPANISH
U.N. president	ARCE, ESSY, KHAN, MAZA, EVATT, GANEV, KAVAN, MALIK, MARCO, MUNRO, NERVO, SALIM, SPAAK, THORN, ARANHA, BOLAND, BROOKS, CAPUTO, FLORIN, HAMBRO, HOLLAI, ISMAIL, LUSAKA, MOJSOV, NANVEN, ORTEGA, PANDIT, PINIES, RAHMAN, ROMULO, BENITES, CATALAN, ENTEZAM, FANFANI, GURIRAB, HOLKERI, ILLUECA, KITTANI, LIEVANO, MANESCU, OPERTTI, PEARSON, RASHEED, SHIHABI, WECHMAR, BELAUNDE, KLEFFENS, UDOVENKO, RODRIGUEZ, BOUTEFLIKA
U.N. Sec'y-General	LIE, ANNAN, (U)THANT, WALDHEIM, DECUELLAR, HAMMERSKJOLD
U.N. Security Council permanent members	UK, US, CHINA, FRANCE, RUSSIA

unabashed	COOL, BRASH, BRAZEN
unable	UNFIT, INCAPABLE
unaccented	ATONIC
unacceptable	INTOLERABLE, OBJECTIONABLE
unaccompanied	LONE, SOLO, ALONE, SOLITARY
unaccustomed	NEW, UNUSED, UNFAMILIAR
unadorned	BALD, BARE, NAKED, PLAIN, STARK, CHASTE, SIMPLE
unadulterated	NEAT, PURE
unaffected	NAIVE, SIMPLE, ARTLESS, NATURAL
unaided	SOLO, ALONE
unalloyed	PURE
unanimity	UNITY, ACCORD, HARMONY, AGREEMENT
unanimous	COMMON, UNDISPUTED
unapproachable	ALOOF, DISTANT, UNFRIENDLY, STANDOFFISH
unarmed	VULNERABLE, DEFENSELESS
unaspirated	LENE
unassuming	MEEK, HUMBLE, MODEST, RETIRING, UNPRETENTIOUS
unattached	FREE, SINGLE, VAGILE, UNMARRIED
unauthorized	ILLEGAL, ILLICIT, UNOFFICIAL
unavailing	IDLE, VAIN, FUTILE, USELESS
unavoidable	CERTAIN, INEVITABLE, INESCAPABLE
unaware	NAIVE, INNOCENT, OBLIVIOUS
unbalanced	MAD, BIASED, UNEVEN, DERANGED, DISTURBED, LOPSIDED, UNHINGED, UNSTABLE, INEQUITABLE
unbearable	AWFUL, ODIUS, INTOLERABLE
unbecoming	UGLY, PLAIN, UNFLATTERING
unbelievable	UNLIKELY, FANTASTIC, INCREDIBLE
unbeliever	GIAOUR, DOUBTER, SKEPTIC, AGNOSTIC; see HEATHEN, INFIDEL
unbend	FREE, THAW, RELAX, LOOSEN, STRAIGHTEN
unbending	SET, FIRM, FIXED, RIGID, DOGMATIC, INFLEXIBLE

unbiased FAIR, JUST, EQUITABLE, IMPARTIAL

unblemished PURE, CLEAR, PERFECT, FLAWLESS, SPOTLESS

unbounded INFINITE, LIMITLESS

unbreakable SOLID, TOUGH, STRONG, DURABLE, RESILIENT

unbridled UNRULY, RAMPANT, UNCHECKED, UNRESTRAINED

unbroken WILD, WHOLE, INTACT, STEADY, CONSTANT, CONTINUOUS

unburden FREE, DIVEST, RELEASE, RELIEVE

uncalled-for UNDUE, UNPROVOKED, UNNECESSARY

uncanny UNCO, EERIE, WEIRD, CREEPY

Uncas beloved CORA

unceasing ENDLESS, CONSTANT, PERPETUAL

unceremonious CURT, ABRUPT, BRUSQUE

uncertain SHAKY, VAGUE, UNSURE, DUBIOUS

uncertainty DOUBT, HESITATION, INSECURITY

unchanged ORIGINAL, PRISTINE

unchecked RIFE, LOOSE, RAMPANT, UNBRIDLED

uncivil RUDE, IMPOLITE

uncivilized CRUDE, COARSE, VULGAR, BARBARIC, PRIMITIVE

unclad NUDE, NAKED

uncle EAM, EME, OOM, SAM, YEME, DUTCH, NUNKA, NUNKS, NUNKY, REMUS

Uncle Remus author HARRIS

Uncle Remus offering TALE

Uncle Remus title BRER

Uncle Tom's Cabin author STOWE

Uncle Tom's cabin character ELIZA, TOPSY, (LITTLE) EVA, (SIMON) LEGREE

unclean TREF, VILE, DIRTY, TREFA, FILTHY, IMMUND, LEPROUS, TAINTED, POLLUTED

unclear DIM, VAGUE, BLURRED, INDISTINCT

uncloak EXPOSE, REVEAL, UNMASK

unclothe TIRL, STRIP, DIVEST

uncluttered NEAT, TIDY, ORDERLY

unco VERY, NOVEL, WEIRD, NOTABLE, STRANGE, UNCANNY, UNKNOWN

uncomfortable SORE, TIGHT, UNEASY, AWKWARD, PAINFUL, DIFFICULT

uncommitted FREE, NEUTRAL, UNATTACHED

uncommon ODD, RARE, EXOTIC, SPECIAL, UNUSUAL, SINGULAR

uncommunicative SILENT, RESERVED, RETICENT, TACITURN, SECRETIVE

uncompromising RIGID, INFLEXIBLE, UNBENDING

unconcerned ALOOF, BLASE, DETACHED, NONCHALANT, INDIFFERENT

unconditional FULL, TOTAL, ABSOLUTE, UNQUALIFIED

unconscionable WRONG, EXCESSIVE, UNETHICAL, EXORBITANT

unconscious OUT, ASLEEP, BLOTTO, REFLEX, UNAWARE, COMATOSE, LIFELESS, AUTOMATIC, INSENSIBLE

unconscious state COMA, FAINT, SWOON, TRANCE, SYNCOPE, NARCOSIS

unconstitutional ILLEGAL, UNLAWFUL

uncontrolled WILD, CHAOTIC, FRENETIC

unconventional ODD, OUTRE, QUIRKY, BOHEMIAN, ECCENTRIC

uncooked RAW

uncooperative CONTRARY, STUBBORN, DIFFICULT

uncouple UNDO, DETACH, SEPARATE, UNFASTEN

uncouth RUDE, CRUDE, COARSE, GAUCHE, VULGAR, BOORISH, UNCIVILIZED

uncouth person CAD, BOOR, LOUT, YAHOO, CODGER, GALOOT

uncover BARE, DENUDE, EXPOSE, REVEAL, UNEARTH

uncovered BARE, NUDE, NAKED, EXPOSED

unction OIL, UNGUENT, OINTMENT

unctuous	OILY, SMUG, SLEEK, SUAVE, GREASY, PINGUID	underline	MARK, STRESS, EMPHASIZE, HIGHLIGHT, UNDERSCORE
uncultivated	COARSE, FALLOW, VIRGIN, UNTILLED	underling	AIDE, SLAVE, MINION, INFERIOR, SUBALTERN
uncultured	RUDE, BOORISH, UNREFINED		
undamaged	SAFE, WHOLE, INTACT, UNHURT, UNHARMED	underlying	CORE, BASIC, CAUSAL, FUNDAMENTAL
		undermine	SAP, ERODE, WEAKEN, SUBVERT
undaunted	BOLD, FEARLESS, INTREPID	underneath	BASE, BELOW, BOTTOM
undecided	OPEN, UNSURE, INDOUBT, PENDING, UNCLEAR, AMBIVALENT, UNRESOLVED	undernourished	STARVED, FAMISHED
		underpin	BOLSTER, SUPPORT, BUTTRESS, CORROBORATE
undeductible	NET(T)	underrate	BELITTLE, UNDERVALUE
undefeated	CHAMPION, UNBEATEN		
undefiled	PURE, CHASTE	underscore	see UNDERLINE
undemonstrative	RESERVED, IMPASSIVE, PHLEGMATIC, RESTRAINED	undershirt(s)	VEST, JERSEY, SKIVVY, SINGLET
		undersong	TIERCE, REFRAIN
undeniable	TRUE, FACTUAL, IRREFUTABLE, INDISPUTABLE	understand	DIG, KEN, KNOW, TWIG, GETIT, GRASP, SAVVY, VALUE, TAKEIN, PERCEIVE, COMPREHEND
undeniably	INDEED, INCONTESTABLY		
under	SUB, ALOW, SOUS, BELOW, INFRA, NEATH, SOTTO, NETHER	understandable	CLEAR, SIMPLE, LOGICAL, REASONABLE
		understanding	KEN, DEAL, KIND, NOUS, PACT, GRASP, SENSE, ACCORD, EMPATHY, ENTENTE, SYMPATHY, AGREEMENT, KNOWLEDGE, THOUGHTFUL, SYMPATHETIC
underage	MINOR, JUVENILE		
underbrush	SCRUB, BUSHES, BOSCAGE		
undercooked	PINK, RARE, BLOODY		
underclothes	see UNDERWEAR		
undercover	COVERT, SECRET	understate	MINIMIZE, PLAYDOWN
undercover agent	SPY, MOLE, PLANT, OPERATIVE	understatement	IRONY, LITOTES, MODESTY
undercurrent	AIR, HINT, INNUENDO	understood	TACIT, SILENT, IMPLICIT, UNSPOKEN
underdog	ALSORAN, RUNNERUP	understudy	SUB, COVER, DOUBLE, SECOND, STANDIN, APPRENTICE, SUBSTITUTE
underdone	see UNDERCOOKED		
underestimate	MISJUDGE		
undergarment	SLIP, PANTY, SHIRT, TEDDY, CHEMISE, SINGLET	undertake	ACCEPT, ASSUME, PLEDGE, TACKLE, VOLUNTEER
		undertaker	CERER, EMBALMER, MORTICIAN
undergo	DREE, ENDURE, SUFFER, EXPERIENCE	undertaking	JOB, TASK, MISSION, PROJECT, VENTURE
undergraduate	FROSH, PLEBE, JUNIOR, FRESHMAN, SOPHOMORE	undertow	RIPTIDE
		undervalue	DISPRIZE, DEPRECIATE
underground	TRAIN, HIDDEN, SECRET, SUBWAY, ALTERNATIVE, RESISTANCE	underwater	MARINE, SUNKEN, UNDERSEA, SUBMARINE, SUBMERGED
undergrowth	BRUSH, SCRUB, BUSHES	underwater craft	SUB, UBOAT, PIGBOAT, SUBMARINE, BATHYSCAPHE, BATHYSPHERE
underhand(ed)	SLY, DERN, COVERT, SECRET, SNEAKY, CLANDESTINE		

underwear BRA, JUMP, SLIP, CYMAR, JUMPS, SIMAR, SMOCK, STAYS, TEDDY, BRIEFS, BUSTLE, CAMISA, CAMISE, CORSET, GIRDLE, UNDER, UNDIES, BANDEAU, CHEMISE, DESSOUS, DRAWERS, GSTRING, NIGHTIE, PANTIES, STAMMEL, STEPINS, CAMISOLE, CORSELET, KNICKERS, LINGERIE, SCANTIES, BRASSIERE, LOINCLOTH

underworld MOB, MAFIA, GANGLAND; *see* HADES, HELL

underwrite BACK, FUND, COVER, ENSURE, INSURE, ENDORSE, BANKROLL, GUARANTEE

underwriter ANGEL, BACKER, INSURER, SPONSOR

undeserving INDIGN, UNWORTHY

undesirable UNINVITED, UNWELCOME, OBJECTIONABLE

undeveloped BARREN, EMBRYO, LATENT, EMERGENT

undies *see* UNDERWEAR

undignified MEAN, UNSEEMLY, INDECOROUS

undiluted NEAT, PURE, STRAIGHT

undiminished WHOLE, UNABATED

undisciplined WILD, UNRULY, SAVAGE, CHAOTIC

undiscovered VIRGIN, UNDETECTED

undisguised OPEN, FRANK, OVERT, CANDID, BLATANT, UNCONCEALED

undisputed ACCEPTED, UNDENIABLE, ACKNOWLEDGED

undivided FULL, TOTAL, WHOLE, ENTIRE, INTACT, COMPLETE

undo OPEN, UNTIE, CANCEL, LOOSEN, UNFASTEN

undoing RUIN, DEFEAT, DOWNFALL

undomesticated WILD, FERAL, NATURAL, UNTAMED

undone RAW, RUINED, FINISHED, UNDERCOOKED

undoubtedly INDEED, SURELY, CERTAINLY

undress STRIP, DISROBE, DISHABILLE

undue TOOMUCH, EXCESSIVE, INORDINATE

undulate ROLL, WAVE, SWELL, RIPPLE, PULSATE

undulation WAVE, SWELL, RIPPLE, TREMOLO, PULSATION

unduly OVERLY, TOOMUCH, EXCESSIVELY

undying ABIDING, ENDLESS, ETERNAL, ENDURING, DEATHLESS

unearth DIGUP, EXHUME, EXPOSE, REVEAL, DISCLOSE, DISCOVER

unearthly EERIE, WEIRD, CREEPY, GHOSTLY, STRANGE

uneasiness QUALMS, UNREST, ANXIETY, MALAISE, DISQUIET, DISCOMFORT

uneasy EDGY, ON EDGE, ANXIOUS, NERVOUS, WORRIED, CONCERNED

uneasy, be STEW

uneducated ILLITERATE, UNLETTERED

unemotional COLD, DETACHED, IMPASSIVE, OBJECTIVE

unemployed IDLE, JOBLESS, LAIDOFF, AVAILABLE

unending ETERNAL, PERPETUAL, CONTINUOUS

unethusiastic COOL, TEPID, LUKEWARM, APATHETIC

unequal UNEVEN, UNFAIR, UNBALANCED

unequalled PEERLESS, MATCHLESS, NONPAREIL

unequivocal CLEAR, PLAIN, EXPLICIT, UNAMBIGUOUS

unerring SURE, CORRECT, ACCURATE

uneven ODD, EROSE, ROUGH, HUBBLY, PATCHY, RAGGED, SPOTTY, LOPSIDED, ONESIDED

uneventful DULL, BORING, HUMDRUM

unexcelled CHAMPION, UNBEATEN

unexceptional COMMON, ORDINARY

unexciting DULL, BORING, PROSAIC, TEDIOUS

unexpected SUDDEN, SURPRISING, UNFORESEEN

unfailing SURE, CERTAIN, RELIABLE, TRUSTWORTHY

unfair FOUL, WRONG, BIASED, UNJUST, PARTIAL, ONESIDED

unfair move FOUL, FULK

unfaithful FALSE, UNTRUE, DISLOYAL, ADULTEROUS, TRAITOROUS

unfaithfulness APISTIA, ADULTERY, TREACHERY, DISLOYALTY

unfamiliar NEW, ALIEN, EXOTIC, FOREIGN, STRANGE

unfasten UNDO, UNTIE, UNHOOK, UNLOCK

unfathomable DEEP, VAST, ARCANE, ENIGMATIC, INSCRUTABLE

unfavorable ILL, POOR, ADVERSE, HOSTILE, CONTRARY, CRITICAL

unfeeling COLD, NUMB, CRUEL, CALLOUS, PITILESS, HEARTLESS

unfettered FREE, LOOSE, UNCHAINED

unfinished CRUDE, ROUGH, PARTIAL, SKETCHY, INCOMPLETE

unfit INAPT, INEPT, FLABBY, UNQUALIFIED, UNSUITABLE, INCOMPETENT

unflappable CALM, COOL, COMPOSED, IMPERTURBABLE

unflattering BLUNT, UNBECOMING, UNATTRACTIVE

unfledged GREEN, YOUNG, CALLOW, IMMATURE

unflinching FIRM, RESOLUTE, UNWAVERING

unfold OPEN, DEPLOY, EVOLVE, REVEAL, UNFURL

unforeseen SUDDEN, UNEXPECTED

unforgettable MEMORABLE

unforgiving RUTHLESS, INTOLERANT, VINDICTIVE

unfortunate FATEFUL, HAPLESS, LUCKLESS

unfounded FALSE, UNTRUE, BASELESS, GROUNDLESS

unfrequented LONELY, ISOLATED, SECLUDED

unfriendly COLD, HOSTILE, INIMICAL, UNSOCIABLE

unfrock OUST, DEPOSE, DEGRADE, DISCHARGE

unfruitful VAIN, BARREN, STERILE, UNREWARDING

unfurl OPEN, UNFOLD

unfurnished BARE, EMPTY, VACANT

ungainly GAWKY, STIFF, CLUMSY, AWKWARD, UNGRACEFUL

ungodly WICKED, IMPIOUS, PROFANE

ungraceful GAWKY, CLUMSY, AWKWARD, UNGAINLY

ungracious RUDE, UNCIVIL, IMPOLITE

ungrateful HARSH, LISTLESS, THANKLESS, UNTHANKFUL

unguarded OPEN, CARELESS, INDISCREET

unguent BALM, NARD, CRATE, SALVE, CEROMA, CHRISM, POMADE

ungula see CLAW, HOOF

unhallowed UNHOLY, IMPIOUS, PROFANE, SECULAR

unhappy SAD, BLUE, DIRE, MOROSE, DEJECTED, WRETCHED, MISERABLE

unharmed SAFE, INTACT, UNHURT

unhealthy FRAIL, AILING, MORBID, SICKLY, UNWELL

unhesitating READY, PROMPT, CERTAIN

unhinged MAD, CRAZY, DERANGED

unhitch DETACH, RELEASE

unholy WICKED, IMPIOUS, PROFANE

unhorse THROW, UNSEAT

unhurried EASY, SLOW, CASUAL, LANGUID, LEISURELY

unicorn LIN, REEM, MONOCEROS

uniform EVEN, FLAT, FLOT, GARB, DRESS, EQUAL, HABIT, LIVERY, OUTFIT, STEADY, COSTUME

unify FUSE, MERGE, COMBINE, CONSOLIDATE

unimaginative DULL, BANAL, BLAND, TRITE, PROSAIC, UNINSPIRED

unimpeachable PERFECT, SPOTLESS, BLAMELESS

unimportant MINOR, PETTY, SLIGHT, TRIVIAL

uninformed UNAWARE, IGNORANT

uninhabited **VACANT, DESERTED, UNOCCUPIED**

unintelligible **INCOHERENT, INARTICULATE**

unintentional **ACCIDENTAL, INADVERTENT**

uninteresting **DRY, DULL, BORING**

uninterrupted **ENDLESS, NONSTOP, CONTINUAL, INCESSANT**

union **BLOC, BOND, ARTEL, GUILD, HANSE, LOCAL, FUSION, LEAGUE, MERGER, LIAISON, ALLIANCE, JUNCTION, MARRIAGE, COALITION, FEDERATION**

union (labor) **AFL, CIO, ELA, HUI, ILA, ITA, IWW, TWU, UAW, UMW, AFRA, ILGWU, AFLCIO**

Union of Soviet Socialist Republics **CCCP, USSR, RUSSIA**

unique **LONE, ONLY, SOLE, SINGLE, EXCLUSIVE, MATCHLESS**

unique person or thing **ONER**

unison **UNITY, ACCORD, HARMONY, AGREEMENT, UNANIMITY**

unit **ONE, ITEM, PART, GROUP, PIECE, TROOP, MODULE, DIVISION, DETACHMENT**

unit of measurement *see p. 631*

unite **MIX, WED, ALLY, FUSE, JOIN, KNIT, MELD, WELD, YOKE, BLEND, MERGE, RABET, COMBINE, FEDERATE**

United Arab Emirates **TRUCIAL OMAN, TRUCIAL COAST, TRUCIAL STATES**

United Arab Emirates, capital of **ABUDHABI**

United Arab Emirates city/town **AJMAN, ALAYN, DUBAI, KALBA, DUBAYY, WADHIL, ABUDHABI**

United Arab Emirates money **DIRHAM**

United Arab Emirates neighbor **IRAQ, OMAN, SAUDI ARABIA**

United Kingdom *see* **ENGLAND**

United Nations *see* **U.N.**

United States *see* **U.S.**

unitalicized **ROMAN**

Unitarianism founder **BIDDLE**

unity **FUSION, UNISON, CONCORD, HARMONY, AGREEMENT, SOLIDARITY**

universal **ASTRAL, COSMIC, GLOBAL, CATHOLIC, ECLECTIC, ECUMENIC, PANDEMIC, ECUMENIC(AL)**

universe **LOKA, WORLD, COSMOS, CREATION;** *see p. 740*

university **ACADEMY, INSTITUTE, IVORY TOWER;** *see* **COLLEGE;** *see p. 524*

university extension **EDU**

unjust **UNDUE, BIASED, UNFAIR, PARTIAL**

unkeeled **RATITE**

unkempt **MESSY, SHABBY, UNTIDY, RUMPLED, SCRUFFY, TOUSLED**

unkind **MEAN, CRUEL, CALLOUS, HEARTLESS**

unknown **ANON, IGNOTE, STRANGE, INCOGNITO, ANONYMOUS**

unlawful **CROOKED, ILLEGAL, ILLICIT, CRIMINAL, PROHIBITED**

unlearned **RUDE, BORREL, IGNORANT, UNTAUGHT, ILLITERATE**

unleash **RELEASE, SETFREE**

unleavened **AZYMOUS**

unleavened bread **HOST, AZYME, WAFER, MATZO(TH)**

unless **BUT, LEST, NISI, SAVE, EXCEPT**

unlettered **IGNORANT, UNEDUCATED**

unlikely **DOUBTFUL, IMPROBABLE, FARFETCHED**

unlimited **VAST, INFINITE, BOUNDLESS**

unload **DUMP, DROP(OFF), SELL, DELIVER, DISCHARGE**

unlock **OPE(N), SOLVE, DECODE, REVEAL**

unloose **UNDO, UNTIE, LET OUT, RELEASE, SET FREE**

unlucky **HAPLESS, INFAUST**

unman **WEAKEN, CASTRATE**

unmanageable **WILD, UNRULY**

unmanly **SISSY, EFFEMINATE**

unmarried **FREE, SOLE, UNWED, SINGLE, BACHELOR, CELIBATE, SPINSTER**

unmarried state **AGAMY, CELIBACY**

unmask **EXPOSE, REVEAL, UNCOVER**

unmentionables **UNDERWEAR**

unmerciful **COLD, CRUEL, UNFEELING**

unmistakable	CLEAR, OVERT, PLAIN, EVIDENT, OBVIOUS, APPARENT
unmitigated	PURE, SHEER, TOTAL, UTTER, UNADULTERATED
unmoved	COLD, INDIFFERENT, INSENSITIVE
unmoving	INERT, STILL, FROZEN, STATIC
unnatural	ODD, WEIRD, FORCED, UNCANNY, ABERRANT, ABNORMAL, PERVERTED, ARTIFICIAL
unnecessary	NEEDLESS, AVOIDABLE
unnerve	ALARM, SCARE, SHAKE, SHOCK, RATTLE, UNHINGE
unobtrusive	MODEST, DISCREET, INCONSPICUOUS
unoccupied	IDLE, EMPTY, VACANT
unofficial	CASUAL, PRIVATE, INFORMAL
unoriginal work	REHASH
unorthodox	ECCENTRIC, HERETICAL, NONCONFORMIST
unpaid	DUE, OWING
unpalatable	NASTY, INSIPID, INEDIBLE, UNSAVORY, TASTELESS
unpleasant	BAD, FOUL, NASTY, DISTASTEFUL
unplowed	LEA, FALLOW, UNTILLED
unplowed strip	RADE
unpolished	RUDE, CRUDE, ROUGH, COARSE
unprecedented	NEW, NOVEL, UNIQUE, UNPARALLELED
unpredictable	ERRATIC, WAYWARD
unprejudiced	FAIR, NEUTRAL, UNBIASED, IMPARTIAL
unpremeditated	CHANCE, UNPLANNED, ACCIDENTAL
unprepared	COLD, ADHOC, ADLIB, UNREADY, IMPROMPTU
unprepossessing	UGLY, PLAIN, HOMELY, UNATTRACTIVE
unpretentious	PLAIN, MODEST, SIMPLE, NATURAL
unprincipled	AMORAL, IMMORAL, UNETHICAL
unprocessed	RAW, CRUDE, WHOLE, NATURAL, ORGANIC

unproductive	BARREN, INFERTILE
unprofessional	LAY, LAICAL, AMATEUR, INEXPERT, UNETHICAL
unprofitable	SECK, BARREN, FUTILE, LOSING
unpropitious	MALIGN, ADVERSE
unqualified	TOTAL, UTTER, ABSOLUTE, UNSKILLED, UNTRAINED, INCOMPETENT
unquestionable	CERTAIN, ABSOLUTE, CONCLUSIVE
unravel	FEAZE, SOLVE, TEASE, UNTANGLE
unreadable	ILLEGIBLE, SCRIBBLED
unreal	FAKE, FALSE, ERSATZ, PHANTOM, FANTASTIC, IMAGINARY, ARTIFICIAL
unreasonable	UNFAIR, ILLOGICAL, IRRATIONAL
unrefined	RAW, CRASS, CRUDE, COARSE, EARTHY
unrelenting	ADAMANT, INEXORABLE, UNYIELDING
unreliable	FICKLE, ERRATIC, CAPRICIOUS, INACCURATE
unremitting	CHRONIC, CONSTANT, INCESSANT
unrequited	SCORNED
unreserved	OPEN, FRANK, TOTAL, UTTER, CANDID
unrest	FERMENT, DISQUIET, AGITATION
unrestrained	WILD, WANTON, ABANDONED, DISSOLUTE
unripe	RAW, GREEN, IMMATURE
unrivaled	PEERLESS, MATCHLESS, UNEQUALED, UNSURPASSED
unroll	OPEN, UNDO, UNFURL, UNWIND
unruffled	COOL, CALM, POISED, UNFAZED, COLLECTED
unruly	WILD, RESTIVE, FRACTIOUS, DISORDERLY
unsafe	RISKY, DANGEROUS
unsatisfactory	POOR, FAILING, WANTING
unsavory	NASTY, SEEDY, GROTTY, SLEAZY, OFFENSIVE
unscramble	CRACK, DECODE, SORTOUT, DECIPHER
unscrupulous	CORRUPT, RUTHLESS, UNETHICAL

unseat	OUST, DEPOST, REMOVE, DETHRONE, OVERTHROW	untalented	INEPT, MEDIOCRE, UNSKILLED
unseemly	UNDUE, IMPROPER, UNBECOMING	untamed	WILD, FERAL, FERINE
unseen	LATENT, INVISIBLE	untangle	COMB, BRUSH, UNRAVEL
unselfish	KIND, LIBERAL, GENEROUS, SELFLESS	untenable	FLAWED, UNSOUND, INDEFENSIBLE
unsettled	MOOT, TENSE, UPSET, TROUBLED, VARIABLE	unthinkable	INCREDIBLE, UNIMAGINABLE
unshaken	FIRM, SURE, STEADY, STEADFAST	unthinking	RASH, BLUNT, BRUTE, CARELESS
unsheathe	DRAW, PULL (OUT)	untidy	DOWDY, MESSY, SLOPPY, UNKEMPT, SLOVENLY
unsightly	UGLY, HIDEOUS, UNATTRACTIVE	untie	FREE, UNDO, LOOSE(N), UNBIND, UNKNOT, UNFASTEN
unskilled	RAW, INEPT, CLUMSY, AMATEUR, AWKWARD	until	HENT, TILL, WHEN, PENDING
unsolicited	UNWANTED, VOLUNTARY	untilled	LEA, FALLOW
unsophisticated	CRUDE, NAIVE, SIMPLE, ARTLESS, INNOCENT, PRIMITIVE	untimely	EARLY, PREMATURE, INOPPORTUNE
		untold	LEGION, MYRIAD, COUNTLESS
unsound	ILL, SICK, FRAIL, SHAKY, FAULTY, FLAWED, UNSAFE, SPECIOUS, UNSTABLE	untouchable	SAFE, LEPER, EXEMPT, PARIAH, BRAHMAN
unsparing	LAVISH, LIBERAL	untouched	VIRGIN, PRISTINE
unspeakable	VILE, WICKED, APPALLING	untoward	UNRULY, ADVERSE, UNLUCKY, UNFAVORABLE
unspoiled	PURE, FRESH, INTACT, NATURAL, WHOLESOME	untrained	GREEN, UNTAUGHT, UNTUTORED
unspoken	MUTE, TACIT, SILENT, APHONIC, IMPLIED	untrammeled	FREE, LOOSE
		untried	NEW, NOVEL, UNPROVEN, UNTESTED
unstable	FICKLE, LABILE, ASIATIC, ERRATIC	untrue	FALSE, NOTSO, WRONG, DISLOYAL, UNFAITHFUL
unsteady	SHAKY, WOBBLY, ERRATIC, RICKETY, INCONSTANT	untruth	FIB, LIE, TALE, CANARD, FICTION, FALSEHOOD
unstinting	LAVISH, GENEROUS	untutored	AMATEUR, ARTLESS, IGNORANT, UNTAUGHT
unsuccessful	FAILED, BOOTLESS, FRUITLESS, INEFFECTIVE		
unsuitable	INAPT, UNFIT, WRONG	unused	NEW, IDLE, VACANT, UNACCUSTOMED
unsupported	BRALESS, UNPROVEN	unusual	ODD, RARE, NOVEL, OUTRE, EXOTIC, CURIOUS, STRANGE
unsure	DOUBTFUL, HESITANT, UNCERTAIN	unusual thing	ONER, RARA AVIS, SUI GENERIS
unsurpassed	BEST, PEERLESS, MATCHLESS	unveil	BARE, EXPOSE, REVEAL, UNCOVER
unsuspecting	NAIVE, UNWARY, GULLIBLE	unvoiced	SURD, MUTED, TACIT, ELIDED, SILENT
unsweetened	DRY, SEC	unwarranted	UNDUE, BASELESS
unsympathetic	COLD, HARD, UNCARING, HEARTLESS	unwary	RASH, NAIVE, GULLIBLE, INNOCENT
untainted	PURE, CLEAN, INNOCENT, UNSULLIED	unwed	SINGLE

unwelcome	ANNOYING, NON GRATA, UNWANTED
unwell	ILL, SICK, AILING, POORLY
unwholesome	NASTY, NOXIOUS, UNHEALTHY
unwieldy	BULKY, HEAVY, CLUMSY, UNGAINLY, CUMBERSOME
unwilling	LO(A)TH, AVERSE, RELUCTANT
unwilling, be	NILL
unwind	REST, UNDO, CHILL, RELAX, LOOSEN
unwise	FOOLISH, UNSOUND, IMPOLITIC
unwitting	UNAWARE, IGNORANT, ACCIDENTAL
unwonted	RARE, INDIGN, UNUSED, UNACCUSTOMED
unworldly	NAIVE, WEIRD, ASTRAL, SPIRITUAL
unworthy	VILE, UNFIT, INDIGN, UNDESERVING
unwritten	ORAL, BLANK, TACIT, SPOKEN
unyielding	FAST, FIRM, GRIM, STANCH, ADAMANT
up	OVER, ABOVE, ALOFT, BOOST
up and coming	PROMISING
up to	UNTIL
up-and-comer	STARLET
Upanishad	ISHA
upbeat	ARSIS, CHEERY, POSITIVE
upbraid	TWIT, CHIDE, SCOLD, ACCUSE, BERATE, REBUKE, CENSURE
upbringing	NURTURE, REARING, BREEDING, EDUCATION
update	REVISE, REWIRE, MODERNIZE
upend	UPSET, TOPPLE
upgrade	SLOPE, BETTER, IMPROVE, INCLINE
upheaval	MAYHEM, REVOLT, DEBACLE, DISORDER
uphold	BACK, DEFEND, SUPPORT, SUSTAIN, CHAMPION
upholstery	DOSSAL, DOSSEL, GOBELIN
upholstery material	FRISE, SCRIM, LAMPAS, MOHAIR, MOREEN, VELURE, TABARET, VALANCE, VELOURS, MOQUETTE

upkeep	CARE, REPAIR, PENSION, RUNNING, MAINTENANCE
uplift device	BRA(SSIERE)
upon	BY, ON, EPI, SUR, ATOP, ONTO, OVER
upper	VAMP, BERTH, HIGHER, SUPERIOR
upper hand	EDGE, LEAD, MASTERY, ADVANTAGE
Upper Volta	*see* BURKINA FASO
uppermost	CHIEF, FIRST, PRINCIPAL
uppity	PROUD, HAUGHTY, ARROGANT, SNOBBISH
upright	FAIR, JUST, TRUE, ERECT, ON END, PIANO, SPINET, VERTICAL
uprising	COUP, (E)MEUTE, PUTSCH, REVOLT
uproar	ADO, DIN, RIOT, BABEL, HUBBUB, RACKET, RUCKUS
uproot	DIGUP, DISPLACE, DERACINATE
upset	SPILL, TOPPLE, CAPSIZE, DISTURB, TROUBLE, DISTRESS
upshot	END, RESULT, OUTCOME
upside down	UPENDED, INVERT(ED), TOPSYTURVY
upstage	SHOWUP
upstart	SNOB, MINION, PARVENU
upsurge	BOOM, GAIN, RISE, INCREASE
uptight	EDGY, TENSE
up-to-date	NEW, MODERN, CURRENT, TOPICAL
upward	ALOFT, UPHILL
Uranium exporter	NIGER, CANADA, NAMIBIA, AUSTRALIA, SOUTH AFRICA
Uranus relative	GE, GAEA, RHEA, SATURN, TITANS
urban	CITY, CIVIC, OPPIDAN, MUNICIPAL
urbane	SUAVE, SMOOTH, POLISHED
urbanize	CITIFY, POLISH, REFINE, GENTRIFY
urchin	IMP, TAD, ARAB, GAMIN, ECHINUS, MUDLARK
Urfa	EDESSA
urge	EGG, PLY, YEN, ABET, COAX, GOAD, LUST, PROD, SPUR, IMPEL, PLEAD, PRESS, EXHORT, ENTREAT, IMPORTUNE

urgency NEED, HURRY, PRESS, EXIGENCY

urgent RUSH, VITAL, PRESSING, INSISTANT

Uriah relative BATHSHEBA

urial SHA

Urim partner THUMMIM

urinary tract BLADDER, KIDNEYS, URETERS, URETHRA

urinate PEE, WET, PIDDLE, MICTURATE

urine PEE, PISS, WATER

Uris novel HAJ, MILA, QBVII, TOPAZ, EXODUS, TRINITY, BATTLECRY, ARMAGEDDON

URL ending COM, EDU, GOV, MIL, NET, ORG

urn JUG, POT, KIST, VASE, STEEN, VESSEL, PITCHER

urticaria RASH, HIVES, UREDO

Uruguay, capital of MONTEVIDEO

Uruguay city/town MELO, PANDO, SALTO, MINAS, ROCHA, SALTO, RIVERA, ARTIGAS, COLONIA, DURAZNO, MALDONADO, LASPIEDRAS, MONTEVIDEO

Uruguyan Indian CHARRUA

Uruguayan measure CUADRA, SUERTE

Uruguayan money PESO

Uruguayan mountain ANIMAS

Uruguayan river YI, CUAREIM, SANJOSE, SANLUIS, URUGUAY, YAGUARON, RIONEGRO, CEBOLLATI

urus TUR, AUROCHS

U.S., capital of WASHINGTON

U.S. measures *see* MEASURE

U.S. money CENT, DIME, MILL, EAGLE, PENNY, DOLLAR, NICKEL, QUARTER; *see p. 638*

U.S. mountain ELBERT, SHASTA, RAINIER, WHITNEY, MAUNAKEA, MAUNALOA, MCKINLEY, MITCHELL

U.S. presidential information *see p. 696*

U.S. region EAST (COAST), WEST (COAST), MIDWEST, SUN BELT, RUST BELT, DIXIELAND, SOUTHWEST, NEW ENGLAND

U.S. river *see p. 606*

U.S. state information *see p. 615*

usage USE, HABIT, CUSTOM, MANNER, CONTROL, PRACTICE, TREATMENT

use TAP, ACTON, APPLY, EXERT, INURE, WASTE, CUSTOM, EMPLOY, FUNCTION

use up DRAIN, SPEND, CONSUME, EXHAUST

used WORN, SPENT, PREOWNED, SECONDHAND

useful HANDY, OFUSE, UTILE, HELPFUL, EXPEDIENT, PRACTICAL, BENEFICIAL, FUNCTIONAL

usefulness AVAIL, VALUE, WORTH, PROFIT, UTILITY, EFFICACY

useless IDLE, NULL, VOID, FUTILE, OTIOSE, INUTILE

user BUYER, ADDICT, CONSUMER, EXPLOITER

U-shaped device CLEVIS

usher PAGE, GUIDE, ESCORT, CONDUCT, ACCOMPANY, ATTENDANT

usual RIFE, COMMON, NORMAL, WONTED, TYPICAL, FAMILIAR, HABITUAL, CUSTOMARY

usually MOSTLY, ASARULE, COMMONLY, NORMALLY, GENERALLY, TYPICALLY

usurer SHARK, SHYLOCK, LOAN SHARK

usurp GRAB, SEIZE, ASSUME

usurper TYRANT

usury INTEREST, LOANSHARKING

Utah *see also p. 615*

Utah city/town LOA, MOAB, OREM, HEBER, KANAB, LOGAN, MANTI, NEPHI, OGDEN, PRICE, PROVO, SANDY, TOOELE, VERNAL, SALT LAKE CITY

Utah Indian UTE, OURAY, PAIUTE, UINTAH

Utah lake BEAR, FISH, SWAN, UTAH, CLEAR, SEVIER, GREATSALT

Utah mountain NEBO, WAAS, ELLEN, KINGS, PEALE, DELANO, EMMONS, NAVAJO

Utah river BEAR, RAFT, GREEN, PRICE, WHITE, SEVIER, FREMONT, COLORADO

utensil TOOL, DEVICE, GADGET, IMPLEMENT, INSTRUMENT

utensil, kitchen FORK, TONG, KNIFE, LADLE, SCOOP, SIEVE, WHISK, BEATER, FUNNEL,

GRATER, SIFTER, SKIMMER, STRAINER
uterus WOMB, MATRIX
uterus part CERVIX, VAGINA, CARDINAL, ENDOMETRIUM
utility VALUE, WORTH, BENEFIT, SERVICE, EFFICACY, FUNCTION
utilize USE, AVAIL, EMPLOY, EXPLOIT
utmost NTH, BEST, FULL, EXTREME, SUPREME, FARTHEST
utopia HEAVEN, ARCADIA, PARADISE, SHANGRILA
Utopia author MORE
Utopian IDEAL, EDENIC, QUIXOTIC, IDEALISTIC
Utopian community AMANA, ICARIA, NAUVOO, ONEIDA, EPHRATA, BROOK FARM, NEW HARMONY
utter BID, SAY, RANK, VENT, SHEER, SPEAK, STARK, TOTAL, COMPLETE
utterance WORD, SOUND, DICTUM, REMARK, STATEMENT, EXPRESSION
uttered ORAL, SPOKEN
utterly FULLY, QUITE, STARK, WHOLLY, ENTIRELY
Uzbekistan, capital of TASHKENT
Uzbekistan city/town NUKUS, NAWOIY, BUKHARA, JIZZAKH, URGANCH, TASHKENT, ANDIZHAN, NAMANGAN, SAMARQAND
Uzbekistan money SAM
Uzbekistan neighbor KYRGYZSTAN, KAZAKHSTAN, TAJIKISTAN, AFGHANISTAN, TURKMENISTAN

V

V VAV, VEE, FIVE, VICTOR, UPSILON, VICTORY
vacancy GAP, JOB, POST, BLANK, SPACE, VACUUM, OPENING
vacant VOID, BLANK, EMPTY, DEVOID, HOLLOW, VACUOUS
vacate QUIT, ANNUL, LEAVE, GIVEUP, EVACUATE
vacation REST, LEAVE, RESPITE, HOLIDAY, FURLOUGH

vacation locale SEA, SPA, BEACH, RESORT, SEASIDE
vaccinate PROTECT, IMMUNIZE, INOCULATE
vaccination JAB, SHOT, PROTECTION, INOCULATION, IMMUNIZATION
vaccine SERUM, ANTIGEN, ANTIDOTE
— des vaches RANZ
vacillate REEL, WAVER, SEESAW, TEETER, WHIFFLE, HESITATE
vacuous IDLE, EMPTY, INANE, HOLLOW
vacuum VOID, SPACE, CAVITY, HOLLOW
vacuum, opp. of PLENUM
vacuum-packed AIRTIGHT
vacuum tube DIODE, OCTODE, TRIODE, ELECTRODE
vade mecum GUIDE, MANUAL, HANDBOOK
vagabond BUM, VAG, HOBO, LOREL, SHIRK, TRAMP, RODNEY, TRUANT, WAFFLE, VAGRANT; see WANDERER
vagary WHIM, FANCY, CAPRICE
vagrant SPIN, CAIRD; see VAGABOND
vague DIM, HAZY, FUZZY, DREAMY, DISTANT, UNCLEAR, OBSCURE, IMPRECISE, INDISTINCT
vain IDLE, SMUG, EMPTY, PROUD, VAPID, FUTILE, CONCEITED
vainglorious PROUD, BOASTFUL, INFLATED, CONCEITED
vainglory AIRS, PRIDE, VANITY, CONCEIT
vair fur MINIVER
valance PELMET, PALMETTE
vale ADIEU, FAREWELL; see VALLEY
valedictory ORATION, ADDRESS
valentine BELOVED, SWEETHEART
Valentine candy COCKLE
valet see SERVANT
valiant BOLD, BRAVE, WIGHT, HEROIC, INTREPID, STALWART

valid	LEGAL, SOUND, COGENT, DEJURE, OFFICIAL, SUITABLE
validate	STAMP, RATIFY, CERTIFY, CONFIRM, AUTHORIZE
validity	FORCE, WEIGHT, COGENCY, LEGALITY, AUTHORITY
valise	BAG, CASE, ETUI, GRIP, SATCHEL
Valjean pursuer	JAVERT
Valjean's theft	LOAF
Valkyrie	BRUNHILDE
valley	DALE, DELL, GHOR, GLEN, RILL, VAAL, VALE, WADI, WADY, ATRIO, COOMB, DHOON, GLADE, KLOOF, NEMEA, RILLE, SWALE, TEMPE, BOLSON, COULEE, DINGLE, HOLLOW, STRATH, GEHENNA
valor	NERVE, BRAVERY, COURAGE, HEROISM, CHIVALRY
valorous	BOLD, BRAVE, HEROIC, GALLANT, FEARLESS
valuable	DEAR, COSTLY, USEFUL, HELPFUL, PRECIOUS, EXPENSIVE
value	USE, RATE, PRIZE, WORTH, ASSESS, REGARD, CHERISH, RESPECT, APPRAISE, IMPORTANCE, DENOMINATION
valve	CUSP, DAMPER, POPPET, VENTIL, VALVULA; *see* FAUCET
vamoose	BLOW, LEAVE, SCRAM, BEAT IT, BUZZ OFF
vamp	FLIRT, ADLIB, UPPER, SEDUCE
vampire	BAT, GHOUL, LAMIA, LEECH, LILITH, DRACULA, PARASITE
vampire slayer	BUFFY
van	FORE, FRONT(LINE), LORRY, TRUCK
Van Gogh locale	ARLES
vandal	HUN, GOTH, TEUTON
vandalism	HARM, DAMAGE, SABOTAGE
vandalize	WRECK, DAMAGE, DEFACE, SABOTAGE
vane	ANEMOMETER, (WEATHER)COCK
vanguard	LEAD, FRONT(LINE), FOREFRONT
vanish	FADE, SINK, DIEOUT, EVANESCE, DISAPPEAR
vanity	AIRS, PRIDE, EGOISM, CONCEIT, EGOTISM, VAINGLORY
Vanity Fair author	THACKERAY
Vanity Fair character	BECKY SHARP
vanquish	BEAT, CRUSH, DEFEAT, CONQUER, OVERCOME
vantage point	COIGN(E)
Vanuatu	NEWHEBRIDES
Vanuatu, capital of	PORTVILA
Vanuatu city/town	LAOL, TOAK, NORSUP, ISANGEL, LOLTONG, NATAPAO, PORT OLRY, PORT VILA
Vanuatu island	MALO, ANIWA, EFATE, MAEWO, TANNA, AMBRIM, FUTUNA, MALAKULA
Vanuatu language	BISLAMA
Vanuatu money	VATU
vapid	BLAND, INANE, STALE, JEJUNE, INSIPID
vapor	ATMO, BRAG, FUME, HAZE, MIST, REEK, ROKE, BRUME, CLOUD, STEAM, BREATH, CONTRAIL
vaporize	SPRAY, STEAM, GASIFY, ATOMIZE
vaporizer	SPRAY, AEROSOL, ATOMIZER
vaquero	COWBOY
Varangians	ROS
variable	FICKLE, SHIFTY, UNEVEN, ERRATIC, MUTABLE, PROTEAN, ADJUSTABLE
variance	ODDS, CONFLICT, DIFFERENCE, DISCREPANCY
variant	CHOICE, OPTION, ALTERNATIVE
variation	SHADE, CHANGE, NUANCE, LECTION, DISPARITY
Variations on America composer	IVES
varicolored	MOTLEY, MOTTLED, RAINBOW, VARIEGATED
varicose	CIRSOID, DILATED, SWOLLEN
varied	MIXED, SUNDRY, DIVERSE, ASSORTED
variegated	PIED, SHOT, PINTO, CALICO, DAPPLE, MOTLEY
variety	KIND, SORT, TYPE, CLASS, GENUS, SPECIES
variety show host	PAAR,

	CARSON, LAROSA,
	GODFREY, SULLIVAN,
	LETTERMAN
variola	COWPOX, HORSEPOX,
	SMALLPOX
various	MANY, SUNDRY,
	DIVERSE, SEVERAL,
	NUMEROUS
varlet	CAD, PAGE, CHURL,
	KNAVE
varnish	TUNG, GLAZE, GLOSS,
JAPAN, ENAMEL, LACQUER,	
	SHELLAC(K)
varnish ingredient	LAC, KINO,
	COPAL, ELEMI, RESIN
varsity	TEAM, SENIOR,
	COLLEGIATE
vary	ALTER, CHANGE,
DEPART, DIFFER, DIVERGE	
vase	URN, ASKOS, DINOS,
	DIOTA, ECHEA, TAZZA,
DEINOS, PELIKE, SITULA,	
	AMPHORA, ECHEION,
	POTICHE
Vashti husband	AHASUERUS
vassal	LIEGE; see BONDMAN
vast	BIG, HUGE GREAT,
COSMIC, OCEANIC, IMMENSE	
vat	BAC, TUN, BECK, KEIR,
	KIER, KIVE, TANK, KEEVE,
	KIEVE, CISTERN
Vatican	VATICAN CITY
vaudeville	REVUE, VARIETY,
	CABARET, BURLESQUE
vault	ARCH, DOME, LEAP,
	SAFE, TOMB, BOUND, CRYPT,
	GRAVE, CURVET, SEPULCHER
vaulted	DOMED, ARCHED
vaunt	BRAG, CROW, BOAST,
	BLUSTER
VCR button	FWD, REC, REW,
	PLAY, PAUSE
vector	HOST, DRIVE, CARRIER,
	GRADIENT, TRANSMIT
vector, opp. of	SCALAR
Vedic dialect	PALI, SANSKRIT
veer	SHY, YAW, SKEW, SLUE,
	SWAY, TURN, SHEER, SHIFT,
	SWERVE
Vega constellation	LYRA
vegetable	PEA, SOY, BEAN,
	BEET, CORN, KALE, LEEK,
	OCRA, OKRA, OKRO, BENDY,
	CHARD, ONION, PEASE,
	ROOTS, SABZI, CARROT,
	LEGUME, POTATO,
	CABBAGE, HARICOT,
	LETTUCE, SOYBEAN,
	SPINACH

vegetable, erroneous	TOMATO
vegetarian	VEGAN
vegetate	IDLE, LOAF,
	KILLTIME, STAGNATE
vegetation	FLORA, VERDURE
vehemence	VIGOR, FERVOR,
	PASSION, VIOLENCE
vehement	HOT, KEEN, AMAIN,
	ARDENT, FERVENT
vehicle	FORM, AGENT, STYLE,
	MEDIUM, DILUENT,
	CONVEYANCE; see p. 726
veil	CAUL, MASK, PALL,
	VELUM, SHROUD, YASMAK,
	MUFFLER, YASHMAK
vein	CAVA, VENA, DRIFT,
	TENOR, DUCTUS, VENULA,
	ARTERIA, JUGULAR,
	VENACAVA; see LODE
velocity	PACE, RATE, HASTE,
	SPEED, RAPIDITY
velvet	GAIN, PANNE, PLUSH,
	PROFIT, VELOUR
venal	SORDID, CORRUPT,
	SELFISH
vend	SELL, ISSUE, PURVEY
vendetta	FEUD, GRUDGE,
	VENGEANCE
vendor	see MERCHANT
vendue	SALE, AUCTION
veneer	LAC, BURL, COVER,
	LAYER, ENAMEL, FACADE,
	FINISH, POLISH, OVERLAY
venerable	OLD, AGED, HOAR,
	SAGE, HOARY
Venerable monk	BEDE
venerate	ADORE, HALLOW,
	REVERE, IDOLIZE, WORSHIP
veneration	AWE, DULIA,
	ESTEEM, LATRIA, RESPECT
venereal disease	VD, CLAP,
	DOSE, HERPES, SYPHILIS,
	CHANCROID, GONORRHEA
Venetia (ancient) town	ATRIA,
	BRIXIA, MANTUA, VERONA,
	VICENTIA
Venetian blind	JALOUSIE
Venetian bridge	RIALTO
Venetian district	RIALTO
Venetian island	BURANO,
	MURANO, RIALTO,
	GIUDECCA, TORCELLO,
	SANMARCO, SANLAZZARO
Venetian magistrate	DOGE
Venetian money	BETSO, BEZZO
Venetian painter	TITIAN,
	TIEPOLO, VERONESE,
	TINTORETTO
Venetian resort	LIDO

Venezuela, capital of **CARACAS**
Venezuelan city/town **CORO,**
PETARE, ZARAZA,
CARORA, CUMANA, MERIDA,
BARINAS, CARACAS,
GUARICO, MATURIN,
TRUJILLO, TUCUPITA,
VALENCIA, BARCELONA,
MARACAIBO
Venezuelan island **COCHE,**
CUBAGUA, MARGARITA
Venezuelan lake **VALENCIA,**
MARACAIBO
Venezuelan language **ARAWAK,**
CARIBAN, CHIBCHA
Venezuelan leader **LEONI,**
CALDERA
Venezuelan money **REAL,**
MEDIO, FUERTE, BOLIVAR,
CENTIMO, MOROCOTA
Venezuelan mountain **DUIDA,**
VENAMO, BOLIVAR,
RORAIMA
Venezuelan people **CARIB,**
TIMOTE, WARRAU,
GOAJIRO, GUARAUNO
Venezuelan river **ARO, PAO,**
TUY, META, APURE, UNARE,
BARIMA, CARONI, CAURA,
ARAUCA, TOCUYO,
GUAINIA, ORINOCO,
GUAVIARE, RIONEGRO,
VENTUARI, CATATUMBO
vengeance **TALION, WANION,**
REPRISAL, RETALIATION
vengeful **BITTER, SPITEFUL,**
VINDICTIVE
venial **MINOR, TRIVIAL,**
EXCUSABLE, PARDONABLE
Venice *see* **VENETIAN**
venom **BANE, GALL, SPITE,**
TOXIN, MALICE, POISON
venomous **TOXIC, DEADLY,**
LETHAL, VIPERINE,
MALICIOUS, POISONOUS
venomous animal **COBRA,**
KRAIT, MAMBA, VIPER,
ADDER, TAIPAN, RATTLER,
RINGHALS, SCORPION,
STINGRAY, BOOMSLANG,
JELLYFISH, STONEFISH,
TARANTULA, BLACK WIDOW,
BUSHMASTER, CORAL
SNAKE, FERDELANCE,
TICPOLONGA, COPPERHEAD,
RATTLESNAKE
vent **BUNG, EMIT, FLUE, ISSUE,**
VOICE, EGRESS, OUTLET,
CHIMNEY, EXHAUST

ventilate **AIR (OUT), FAN,**
AERATE, FRESHEN
ventilation **AIRING, AERATION**
ventral **HEMAD, HEMAL,**
STERNAL
ventriloquist **PUPPETEER**
venture **DARE, RISK, FLING,**
FLYER, STAKE, HAZARD,
UNDERTAKING
venturesome **BOLD, BRAVE,**
HARDY, DARING, FEARLESS
venue **BOUT, SITE, MATCH,**
GROUND
Venus **ISHTAR, ASTARTE,**
DAYSTAR, APHRODITE
Venus, island of **MELOS**
Venus beloved **ADONIS**
Venus relative **AMOR, CUPID,**
DIONE, AENEAS, VULCAN
veracious **TRUE, HONEST,**
SINCERE, ACCURATE,
TRUTHFUL
veracity **TRUTH, HONESTY,**
ACCURACY, SINCERITY
veranda **PYAL, PATIO, LOGGIA;**
see **PORCH**
verb, auxiliary **BE, ARE, CAN,**
DID, HAD, HAS, MAY, WAS,
HAST, HAVE, MUST, WILL,
COULD, MIGHT, SHALL,
SHALT, WOULD, SHOULD
verbal **ORAL, VOCAL, SPOKEN**
verbalize **VOICE, EXPRESS,**
ARTICULATE
verbatim **EXACT(LY), LITERAL(LY)**
verbiage **PROLIXITY,**
WORDINESS
verbose **WINDY, WORDY,**
PROLIX, DIFFUSE, EFFUSIVE,
TALKATIVE
verboten **TABU, TABOO,**
FORBIDDEN
verdant **LUSH, GREEN, FERTILE**
Verdi character **AIDA, OSCAR;**
see also individual operas
Verdi opera **AIDA, BALLO,**
ERNANI, OTELLO, MACBETH,
NABUCCO, DON CARLO,
FALSTAFF, TRAVIATA,
RIGOLETTO, TROVATORE
verdict **DECREE, RULING,**
FINDING, DECISION,
JUDGMENT
verdigris **AERUGO, PATINA**
verdure **GREENS, FOLIAGE,**
GREENERY
verge **EDGE, TRIM, BRINK,**
MARGE, BORDER
Vergil *see* **VIRGIL**

verify TEST, AUDIT, PROVE, ATTEST, CONFIRM

verily YEA, AMEN, CERTES, INDEED, REALLY

veritable REAL, TRUE, ACTUAL, GENUINE

verity AXIOM, TRUTH, REALITY

vermin BUGS, LICE, MICE, PEST, SCUM, WEASEL, VARMINT

vermin, clear of DERAT

Vermont see also p. 615

Vermont city/town BARRE, CHELSEA, NEWPORT, RUTLAND, ST ALBANS, BENNINGTON, BURLINGTON, MIDDLEBURY, MONTPELIER

Vermont Indian ABENAKI, ALGONQUIN

Vermont lake CHAMPLAIN

Vermont mountain JAY, GORE, SNOW, BURKE, OKEMO, TABOR, BROMLEY, STRATTON, HAYSTACK, MANSFIELD, KILLINGTON

Vermont river WEST, WHITE, ASCUTNEY, HAYSTACK, LAMOILLE, METTAWEE, POULTNEY, WINOOSKI, CONNECTICUT

vernacular CANT, ARGOT, LINGO, DIALECT

vernal GREEN, SPRING, AESTIVAL

Verne character FOGG, NEMO

Verne submarine NAUTILUS

vernier NONIUS

versatile DEFT, MOBILE, TALENTED, ADAPTABLE

verse RANN, STICH; see POEM

versed ADEPT, SKILLED, FAMILIAR, PROFICIENT

—versa VICE

verse form IAMB, DACTYL, DIPODY, OCTAVE, PANTUN, ANAPEST, COUPLET, DIMETER, DISTICH, SESTINA, SPONDEE, TRISEME, TROCHEE, VIRELAY, ANAPAEST, QUATRAIN

versifier POET, RIMER, RHYMER, POETESS, POETASTER

version SIDE, REPORT, ACCOUNT, RENDITION, TRANSLATION

vertebrate AVIS, FISH, MAMMAL, REPTILE

vertex TOP, ACME, APEX, HEAD, CROWN, HEIGHT, SUMMIT, ZENITH, PINNACLE

vertical ERECT, PLUMB, UPRIGHT, PERPENDICULAR

vertically APEAK, UPRIGHT

vertiginous DIZZY, GIDDY, ROTARY, SPINNING

vertigo DINUS, MEGRIM, SCOTOMY, DIZZINESS

Vertigo name JUDY, MIDGE, (KIM) NOVAK, BARTON, ERNIES, SCOTTIE, (JAMES) STEWART

verve PEP, VIM, ZIP, BRIO, DASH, ELAN, ZEST, ARDOR, VIGOR, ENERGY

very SAME, UNCO, QUITE, ACTUAL, EVER SO, VASTLY, REALLY, AWFULLY, PRECISE

vesicle SAC, BLEB, CYST, BULLA, CAVITY, BLISTER, UTRICLE

Vespasian reign year (AD 69–79) LXX, LXXI, LXXV

vespers EVENSONG

vessel AMA, CUP, JAR, JUG, MUG, PAN, POT, TUB, TUN, URN, VAT, BOWL, CASK, ETNA, FONT, LOTA, OLLA, TANK, VASE, AMULA, BASIN, BOCAL, FLASK, GLASS, GOURD, LOTAH, STEIN, AFTABA, BOTTLE, CRATER, PATERA, DECANTER

vessels see p. 728

vest ENDOW, GILET, CLOTHE, UNDER, VESTEE, EMPOWER, WAISTCOAT, TATTERSALL

vestal PURE, CHASTE, SACRED

Vestal Virgin RHEA, TUCCIA, AEMILIA, CLAUDIA, URBINIA

vestibule HALL, ENTRY(WAY), FOYER, LOBBY

vestige RELIC, SHRED, TRACE, SHADOW, REMNANT, SURVIVAL

vestment, ecclesiastic ALB(A), COPE, COWL, AMICE, COTTA, EPHOD, FANON, FROCK, MITER, MITRE, ORALE, PHANO, RABAT, RABBI, SIMAR, STOCK, STOLE, ALMUCE, CASULA, CHIMER, GUIMPE, PILEUS, ROCHET, PLANET, TIPPET, VAKASS, BERETTA, BIRETTA, BUSKINS, CAPUCHE, CASSOCK, CHIMERE, CHRISOM, CHRYSOM,

CUCULLA, MANIPLE,
MOZETTA, ORARION,
ORARIUM, PALIUM, PLANETA,
SOUTANE, TUNICLE,
ZIMARRA, BERRETTA,
CAPUCHIN, CHASUBLE,
DALMATIC, MOZZETTA,
SCAPULAR, SURPLICE
vestry   CHAPEL, SACRISTY
vesture   ROBE, SEISIN, CLOTHE,
APPAREL, COSTUME,
ENVELOP
Vesuvius, city destroyed by
POMPEII,
HERCULANEUM
Vesuvius city   NAPLES
vetch   ERS, AKRA, TARE, FITCH
veteran   EXPERT, STAGER,
OLDHAND, TROUPER,
OLDTIMER
veterinarian   FARRIER
vetiver   BENA, CUSCUS
veto   DENY, QUASH, FORBID,
KIBOSH, NAYSAY
vex   IRK, CARK, FASH, GALL,
RILE, ROIL, HARRY, NETTLE,
DISTURB, TROUBLE
vexation   BANE, BOTHER,
PLAGUE, NUISANCE
vexatious   IRKSOME,
BOTHERSOME,
TROUBLESOME
via   BY, PER, USING,
BYWAYOF, THROUGH
viable   ALIVE, FEASIBLE,
POSSIBLE, PRACTICAL
viaduct   BRIDGE, TRESTLE,
OVERPASS
vial   CRUET, BEAKER, BOTTLE,
AMPOULE
viand(s)   *see* FOOD
vibrant   ALIVE, VITAL, VIVID,
BRILLIANT, PULSATING
vibrate   TIRL, DINDLE, JIGGLE,
JUDDER, QUAVER, QUIVER,
THRILL, TREMBLE
vibration   THROB, QUIVER,
TREMOR, TREMOLO,
FREMITUS
vicar   AGENT, DEPUTY; *see*
CLERGY
Vicar of Christ   POPE
vicarious   VIVID, PROXY,
EXPLICIT
vice   SIN, STEAD, JUNIOR,
PIACLE, INIQUITY,
SUBORDINATE
vice—   VERSA
Vice President (U.S.)   *see p. 696*

viceroy   NAWAB, EXARCH,
REGENT
Vichy premier   LAVAL
vicinity   AREA, ENVIRONS,
LOCALITY
vicious   BAD, EVIL, MEAN,
CRUEL, SINFUL, WICKED
vicissitude   CHANGE,
MUTABILITY
victim   DUPE, FISH, GOAT,
GULL, MARK, PREY, CULLY,
MARTYR, CATSPAW, FALLGUY
victimize   ABUSE, CHEAT, PICK
ON, PREY ON, PERSECUTE
victor   CHAMP, WINNER,
CONQUEROR
victorious   PALMARY,
TRIUMPHAL, SUCCESSFUL
victory   NIKE, PALM, ROUT,
LAUREL, SUCCESS,
TRIUMPH, CONQUEST
victory cry   ABU, ABOO
victual(s)   *see* FOOD
victualer   SUTLER, CATERER
— vide   QUAE
vie   COPE, RIVAL, STRIVE,
COMPETE, CONTEND
Vienna   WIEN
Viennese park   PRATER
vier   RIAL, ENTRANT
Vietnam, capital of   HANOI
Vietnamese city   HUE, VINH,
DALAT, HANOI, HOIAN,
CAMPHA, CANTHO, DANANG,
MOCBAI, PLAIKU, SAIGON,
NAMDINH, QUINOHN,
HAIPHONG
Vietnamese island   PHUQUOC,
CONSONSON, BACHLONGVI
Vietnamese leader   KY, DIEM,
DONG, MANH, MINH,
RHANU, THIEU
Vietnamese measure   LY, GON,
MAU, NGU, QUO, SAO, TAO,
SHITA, THUOC, TRUONG
Vietnamese money   XU, HAO,
DONG, PIASTER
Vietnamese mountain   LUONG,
FANSIPAN
Vietnamese neighbor   LAOS,
CHINA, CAMBODIA
Vietnamese people   CHAM,
KHMER
Vietnamese region   ANAM
Vietnamese river   CHU, RED,
BLACK, SESAN, MEKONG,
SONGBA, DONGNAI, SONGCAI
Vietnamese weight   TA, CAN,
BINH, DONG

Vietnam Memorial designer **LIN**
view **EYE, OGLE, SCENE, VISTA, OBJECT, EYESHOT, OPINION**
viewpoint **BELIEF, STANCE, OPINION, ATTITUDE**
vigil **EVE, WATCH, SURVEILLANCE**
vigilant **WARY, ALERT, AWAKE, WATCHFUL**
vigilante **NIGHTRIDER**
vignette **SQUIB, SKETCH, PICTURE, ORNAMENT**
vigor **VIR, STAMINA; see ENERGY, FORCE**
vigor, lack of **ANEMIA**
vigorous **HALE, HARDY, VITAL, ROBUST, ENERGETIC**
Viking **ERIC, LEIF, OLAF, ROLLO, ROVER, PIRATE**
Viking character **RUNE**
vile **LOW, BASE, MEAN, CHEAP, ABJECT, SORDID, VULGAR**
vilify **ABUSE, MALIGN, REVILE**
villa **ALDEA, DACHA, ESTATE, CHATEAU, MANSION**
village **GAV, REW, CRAL, KAIK, RAIK, MURA, STAD, VILL, CASAL, DESSA, KAIKA, KRAAL, BUSTEE, CASALE, PUEBLO, RANCHO, CLACHAN; see HAMLET**
villain **BOOR, HEAVY, KNAVE, ROGUE, BADDIE, LEGREE**
villainous **BAD, EVIL, MEAN, VILE, WICKED, ILL BRED, INFAMOUS**
villein **see SERF**
vim **PEP, ZIP, ELAN, ZEST, VIGOR, ENERGY**
vincit omnia — **VERITAS**
vindicate **CLEAR, ACQUIT, JUSTIFY, EXONERATE**
vindication **PROOF, EVIDENCE, EXONERATION, JUSTIFICATION**
vindictive **MEAN, BITTER, SPITEFUL, MALICIOUS, VENGEFUL**
vine **AKA, HOP, IVY, IYO, PEA, BINE, CIPO, GILO, ODEL, GRAPE, LIANA, COWAGE, LABLAB, CLIMBER, COWHAGE, CREEPER, WISTERIA**
vinegar **EISEL, ACETUM, ALEGAR, EISELL**
vinegar, *pert. to* **ACETIC**

vinegary **SOUR, ACETOSE**
vineyard **CLOS, COTE, CHATEAU**
vintage **AGE, ERA, OLD, PRIME, CLASSIC, ANTIQUE**
viol **REBEC, FIDDLE, VIELLE, QUINTON**
violate **RAPE, ABUSE, INJURE, RAVISH, INFRACT, ENCROACH, DESECRATE**
violation **ABUSE, BREACH, INTRUSION, INFRACTION, INFRINGEMENT**
violence **FURY, RAGE, FORCE, ASSAULT, FEROCITY, BRUTALITY**
violent **WILD, RABID, FIERCE, RAGING, RAVING, STORMY**
violet **PANSY, VIOLA, KISS ME, PENSEE; see p. 531**
violin **see p. 642**
violin bowing **SAUTE, UPBOW, DOWNBOW, PIZZICATO, SALTANDO**
violin maker **AMATI, CREMONA, GUARNERI, STRADIVARI**
violin part **NUT, NECK, WAIST, BRIDGE, BUTTON, PEG(BOX), SCROLL, CHINBOARD, TAILPIECE, FINGERBOARD**
violinist **AUER, NERO, BENNY, ELMAN, STERN, YSAYE, MUTTER, HEIFETZ, MENUHIN, PERLMAN, SZIGETI, GRUMIAUX, KREISLER, KREUTZER, MILSTEIN, OISTRAKH, PAGANINI**
VIP **BIG(WIG), BIGSHOT, CELEBRITY**
viper **HABU, BITIS, DABOIA, DABOYA, JESSUR, HOGNOSE, BONETAIL, CERASTES, JARARACA, LACHESIS, MOCCASIN, PIT VIPER, PUFF ADDER, FERDELANCE; see SNAKE**
viper genus **ECHIS, BOTHROPS**
virago **SHREW, VIXEN, AMAZON, HELLCAT**
Virgil birthplace **MANTUA**
Virgil hero(ine) **DIDO, (A)ENEAS**
Virgil poem **(A)ENEID**
virgin **PURE, PIETA, CHASTE, MAID(EN), VESTAL, MADONNA, UNTOUCHED**
Virgin Islands **PETER, NORMAN, ANEGADA, TORTOLA**

Virginia *see p. 615*
Virginia city/town WISE,
BLAND, LURAY, SALEM,
SURRY, GRUNDY, LOUISA,
SALUDA, SUSSEX, FAIRFAX,
NORFOLK, CULPEPER,
LEESBURG, MANASSAS,
RICHMOND, RUSTBURG,
DINWIDDIE, LYNCHBURG,
CHESAPEAKE, PORTSMOUTH
Virginia Indian UNAMI,
MONACAN, POWHATAN,
ANISTOHINI, CHICKAHOMINY,
RAPPAHANNOCK
Virginia lake ANNA, GASTON,
CLAYTOR, DRAMMOND,
PHILPOTT, BULESTONE
Virginia mountain ROGERS,
CUMBERLAND,
SHENANDOAH,
MASSANUTTEN
Virginia river DAN, JAMES,
MAURY, SMITH, CLINCH,
POWELL, BULLRUN, HOLSTON,
POTOMAC, RIVANNA,
ROANOKE, BANISTER,
MEHERRIN, NOTTOWAY,
PAMUNKEY, MATTAPONI,
APPOMATTOX, COW PASTURE,
SHENANDOAH
virginity PURITY,
MAIDENHOOD,
BACHELORHOOD,
SPINSTERHOOD
virgule COMMA, SOLIDUS
virile MACHO, MANLY,
POTENT, MASCULINE
virtual NEAR, IMPLICIT,
POTENTIAL
virtually ALMOST, NEARLY,
TOTALLY, IN EFFECT
virtue MERIT, QUALITY,
CHASTITY, GOODNESS
virtues, cardinal HOPE, FAITH,
CHARITY, JUSTICE,
PRUDENCE, FORTITUDE,
TEMPERANCE
virtuosity SKILL, TALENT,
ABILITY, KNOWHOW
virtuoso EXPERT, PRODIGY,
SKILLFUL
virtuous GOOD, MORAL,
UPRIGHT, RIGHTEOUS
virulence VENOM, RANCOR,
MALIGNANCY
virulent RABID, DEADLY,
NOXIOUS
virus GERM, VENOM,
VACCINE, PATHOGEN

virus, type of POX, TOGA,
ADENO, ARENA, RETRO,
HERPES, CORONA, PAPOVA,
PICOMA, RHABDO
visa PASS, PAPERS, PERMIT,
DOCUMENTS
visage ASPECT; *see* FACE
vis-a-vis DATE, ESCORT,
TOWARD, AGAINST,
ENCOUNTER
viscera GUTS, VITALS,
INNARDS
viscid GLUEY, GUMMY,
SYRUPY, STICKY, VISCOSE,
VISCOUS
viscous LIMY, ROPY, SIZY,
GLUEY, SLIMY, STICKY
vise CLAM, CLAMP, CLINCH,
GRIPPER
Vishnu incarnation RAMA,
BUDDHA, KALKIN, KRISHNA
Vishnu relative SRI, INDRA,
LAKSHMI, RURMINI
visible CLEAR, INVIEW,
PATENT, VISUAL, EVIDENT,
DISCERNIBLE
Visigoth *see* GOTH
Visigoth king ALARIC
vision DREAM, GHOST,
ESPIAL, PHANTOM
vision defect ANOPIA, MYOPIA,
DIPLOPIA, CATARACTS,
HYPEROPIA, ASTIGMATISM
visionary FEY, AIRY, IDEAL,
DREAMY, UNREAL,
FANTAST, UTOPIAN
visionary play RUR
visit GAM, SEE, CALL, STAY
(ON), HAUNT, SOJOURN
visitation ORDEAL, CALAMITY,
DISASTER, HARDSHIP,
AFFLICTION
visitor GUEST, CALLER,
COMPANY
visitor from afar ET
visor BRIM, SHADE, VIZARD,
EYESHADE, SUNSHADE
vista VIEW, SCENE, OUTLOOK,
SCENERY, PANORAMA
visual OCULAR, OPTICAL,
VISIBLE
visualize SEE, IDEAT,
IMAGINE, PICTURE
Vita Nuova author DANTE
vital ALIVE, LIVING, MORTAL,
ESSENTIAL, IMPORTANT
vital energy HORME
vitality SAP; *see* ENERGY
vitalize VIVIFY, ANIMATE

vitamin	PABA, BIOTIN, CITRIN, FLAVIN, NIACIN, ADERMIN, ANEURIN, CHOLINE, TORULIN, CAROTENE, THIAMINE, CALCIFEROL, PYRIDOXINE, RIBOFLAVIN, TOCOPHEROL
vitamin deficiency disease	SCURVY, RICKETS
vitamin source	EGG, FISH, MILK, YOLK, LIVER, YEAST, ALFALFA, CAROTENE
vitiate	VOID, SPOIL, TAINT, DEFILE, IMPAIR
vitreous	GLASSY, BRITTLE, HYALINE, TRANSPARENT
vitrify	BAKE, FUSE, GLAZE
vitriolic	SHARP, BITING, CAUSTIC
vitriols	SORY, SULFATE
vituperate	RAIL, ABUSE, SCOLD, BERATE, REVILE, STRAFE
vituperative	ABUSIVE, SCATHING, SLANDEROUS
vivacious	BREEZY, LIVELY, ANIMATED, CHEERFUL, ENERGETIC
vivacity	BRIO, DASH, ELAN; see ENERGY
viva voce	ORAL(LY)
vive le —	ROI
vivid	LIVE, CLEAR, LUCID, BRIGHT, GRAPHIC
vividness	RELIEF
— de vivre	JOIE
vixen	see FOX, VIRAGO
vocabulary	ARGOT, JARGON, LEXICON, GLOSSARY, WORDBOOK
vocal	ORAL, TONIC, SONANT, VERBAL, VOICED; see SONG
vocalist	SINGER, CROONER, SONGSTER, SONGSTRESS
vocalize	SING, UTTER, PHONATE
vocation	ART, WORK, CRAFT, TRADE, CAREER, METIER, OFFICE, CALLING, MISSION
— voce	VIVA, SOTTO
vociferous	LOUD, NOISY, VOCAL, BLATANT
vogue	TON, MODE, FAVOR, USAGE, CUSTOM, FASHION
voice	SAY, VOX, EMIT, VOCE, VOTE, SOUND, TONGUE; see SINGER

voice box	LARYNX
voice, *pert. to*	ORAL, VOCAL, PHONETIC
voiced	ORAL, ALOUD, TONIC, SONANT, VIBRANT
voiceless	MUTE, SURD, SILENT, ASONANT, SPIRATE
void	NUL(L), SPACE, VACANT, VACATE, VACUUM, INVALID; see ANNUL
— and void	NULL
volatile	BIRD, FICKLE, MUTABLE, UNSTABLE, HAZARDOUS
volcanic	FIERY, VIOLENT, VESUVIAN, EXPLOSIVE
volcanic ejection	MOYA, TUFF, BELCH, SALSE, PUMICE; see LAVA
volcanic rock	TUFF, WACK, TRASS, BASALT, LATITE, PUMICE, TAXITE, PERLITE, LAPILLUS, OBSIDIAN, RHYOLITE, TRACHYTE, TEPURITE, PROPYLITE, TALPATATE
volcano	see p. 611
Volga	RA, ETIL, ITIL
Volga city	GORKI, KAZAN, MOSCOW, SAMARA, SARATOV, VOLGOGRAD, STALINGRAD
Volga tributary	OKA, KAMA, SURA, MOLOGA, SAMARA
volition	WILL, OPTION, CONATION
volley	BURST, ROUND, SALVO, DISCHARGE
Voltaire	AROUET
Voltaire work	ZADIG, ZAIRE, ALZIRE, CANDIDE
volte face	TURN, PIVOT, REVERSAL, ABOUT FACE
voluble	GLIB, FLUENT, VERBOSE, TALKATIVE
volume	BULK, MASS, RANGE, CUBAGE, LOUDNESS; see BOOK
voluminous	BIG, AMPLE, LARGE, ROOMY, CAPACIOUS
voluntarily	FREELY, GLADLY, WILLINGLY
voluntary	CHOSEN, UNPAID, FANTASIA, CHARITABLE
volunteer	OFFER, DONATE, HELPER
Volunteer State	TN, TENN(ESSEE)

voluptuary	HEDONIST, SYBARITE, SENSUALIST		
voluptuous	SEXY, SENSUAL, SENSUOUS		W
vomit	KECK, PUKE, SPEW, BELCH, REJECT, THROWUP	W	WAW, WEN, WHISKEY
vomiting	EMESIS	wacky	FEY, MAD, ODD, CRAZY, SCREWY, MADCAP
Vonnegut novel	JAILBIRD, GALAPAGOS, SLAPSTICK, CATS CRADLE	wad	GOB, CHAW, CRAM, LUMP, STUFF, BUNDLE
voodoo	HEX, OBI, JINX, OBEAH, VODUN, WITCHCRAFT	waddle	WOBBLE, SHUFFLE
		waddy	CLUB, STICK, RUSTLER
		wade	FORD, SLOG, PLODGE, WALLOW
voodoo deity	ZOMBI	wadi	WASH, GULLY, OASIS, RAVINE, VALLEY, CHANNEL
voodoo spell	MOJO		
voracious	GREEDY, HUNGRY, EDACIOUS, RAVENOUS, INSATIABLE	wading bird	IBIS, RAIL, SORA, CRANE, EGRET, HERON, SNIPE, STORK, UMBER, AVOCET, CURLEW, JACANA, JABIRU, GRALLAE, FLAMINGO
vortex	EDDY, GYRE, MAELSTROM		
votary	FAN, NUN, MONK, DEVOTEE, BELIEVER	wafer	DISK, HOST, OBLEY, LAMINA, TROCHE
vote	AYE, NAY, NOD, YEA, POLL, ELECT, PROXY, STRAW, BALLOT, PLACET	waffle	CAKE, GUFF, DRIVEL, PRATTLE, VACILLATE
		waft	GUST, WAIF, CARRY, FLOAT, BREATH, BREEZE
voter(s)	ELECTOR, BALLOTER, ELECTORATE, CONSTITUENT	wag	WAVE, SHAKE, WIGGLE; see JOKER
vouch (for)	AVER, AFFIRM, ATTEST, SPONSOR, GUARANTEE	wage(s)	FEE, PAY, UTU, HIRE, BATTA, SALARY, STIPEND
		wage earner	WORKER, LABORER, EMPLOYEE, BREADWINNER
voucher	CHIT, NOTE, STUB		
vouchsafe	DEIGN, GRANT, STOOP, YIELD, BESTOW, CONCEDE	wager	RISK, HAZARD; see BET
		wages	PAY, INCOME, SALARY, STIPEND, EARNINGS, RECOMPENSE, COMPENSATION
vow	VUM, OATH, PLEDGE, PROMISE		
vowel mark	ACUTE, BREVE, CARON, GRAVE, TILDE, MACRON, OGONEK, UMLAUT, DI(A)ERESIS, CIRCUMFLEX	waggish	DROLL, MERRY, JOCULAR, ROGUISH, SPORTIVE
		Wagner opera	RING, RIENZI, TRISTAN, WALKURE, PARSIFAL, LOHENGRIN, SIEGFRIED
voyage	TREK, TRIP, CRUISE, SAFARI, VOYAGE, JOURNEY		
V-shaped item	WEDGE	Wagner relative	LISZT, MINNA, COSIMA, WIELAND, WOLFGANG
Vulcan relative	JUNO, MAIA, CACUS, CUPID, VENUS		
vulcanite	EBONITE	Wagnerian role	ELSA, ERDA, SENTA, ISOLDE, RIENZI, TRISTAN; see RING
vulcanize	CURE		
vulgar	LOW, MEAN, RUDE, COARSE, BOORISH	wagon	CART, TRAM, WAIN, ARABA, TELEGA, TUMBREL
vulnerable	LIABLE, SUSCEPTIBLE	wagon part	NEAP, POLE, BLADE, THILL, CLEVIS
vulpine	FOXY, WILY, CRAFTY, TRICKY, CUNNING		
vulture	URUBU, ATRATA, CONDOR, BUZZARD, GRIFFON	waif	ARAB, GAMIN, STRAY, URCHIN, MUDLARK, FOUNDLING

wail	HOWL, KEEN, WAUL, MOURN, LAMENT, ULULATE
wainscot	PANEL, WALLBOARD
waist	GIRTH, BODICE, HALTER, MIDRIFF; see BLOUSE
waistband	OBI, BELT, SASH, GIRDLE, CINCTURE
waistcoat	VEST, GILET, JACKET
waistline	GIRTH
wait	BIDE, STAY, TARRY, LINGER
wait on	TEND, CATER, SERVE
waiter/waitress	CARHOP, GARCON, SALVER, SERVER, HOSTESS, STEWARD, ATTENDANT
waive	ABEY, CEDE, DEFER, FOREGO, RENOUNCE, RELINQUISH
wake	STIR, AWAKE, ROUSE, VIGIL, WAKEN, WATCH, TRACK, AROUSE, AWAKEN, KINDLE
wakeful	ALERT, VIGILANT, WATCHFUL, INSOMNIAC
Walden author	THOREAU
Waldorf salad ingredient	WALNUT
wale	RIB, WELT, WHEAL
Wales	CYMRU, CAMBRIA; see also WELSH
Wales, capital of	CARDIFF
walk	HIKE, LIMP, MALL, PACE, PAUP, PLOD, SLOG, STEP, STOA, AMBLE, MARCH, MINCE, STRUT, TRAMP, LUMBER, STROLL, WADDLE, ALAMEDA, LAMBETH, SAUNTER, SWAGGER
walkaway	ROUT, VICTORY
walker	HIKER, PACER, TREKKER, AMULANT, STROLLER, PEDESTRIAN
walking	ONFOOT
walking stick	CANE, KEBBY, STAFF, WADDY, MALAGA, RATTAN, MALACCA
walkway	PATH, ALLEY, CATWALL, PASSAGE, SIDEWALK
wall	MUR(E), BERM, DIKE, LEVEE, SEPTA, SPINA, ESCARP, PARIES, SEPTUM, BARRIER, PARAPET, RAMPART
wall covering	ARRAS, PAINT, PAPER, TAPESTRY
wall piece	DADO, PANEL, TEMPLET, TEMPLATE, WAINSCOT

Wall Street transaction	BUY, IPO, LBO, PUT, CALL, SELL, TRADE
wallboard	WAINSCOT, GYPSUM (BOARD)
walled city	BURG
wallet	PURSE, SCRIP, FOLDER, BILLFOLD, POCKETBOOK
walleye	ALEWIFE, LEUCOMA, STRABISMUS
wallop	HIT, LAM, BEAT, BLOW, SMITE
wallow	REVEL, GROVEL, WELTER, MUDHOLE, LUXURIATE
walnut	BANNUT; see NUT
walrus	MORSE, SEACOW, UNICORN, WALTRON, ODOBENUS
walrus genus	BRUTA
Waltons creator/source	HAMNER
Waltons name	IKE, ERIN, JASON, JENNY, WAITE, OLIVIA, JOHNBOY, ELIZABETH
waltz	ZIP, BREEZE
waltz king	STRAUSS
wampum	BEADS, PEAG(E), MONEY, SE(A)WAN, ROANOKE
wan	ASHY, PALE, ASHEN, WAXEN, PALLID, SALLOW, SICKLY
wand	ROD, MACE, BATON, WITHE, WATTLE, SCEPTER, CADUCEUS
wand-shaped	VIRGATE
wander	ERR, GAD, HAAK, HAIR, HAKE, MILL, MOON, ROAM, ROVE, RANGE, STRAY, DIGRESS, MEANDER
wanderer	WAIF, GYPSY, NOMAD, ROVER, STRAY, PALMER, VIATOR, BEDOUIN, MIGRANT, SCENITE, ITINERANT; see VAGABOND
wandering	ERRANT, TRUANT, NOMADIC, ODYSSEY, BOHEMIAN, VAGABOND
wane	EBB, FADE, ABATE, SUBSIDE, DECREASE, DIMINISH
wangle	GET, OBTAIN, FINAGLE, WHEEDLE
want	LACK, MISS, NEED, CRAVE, YEARN, DEARTH, PENURY, POVERTY, SHORTAGE
wanted person	OUTLAW, ESCAPEE

wanting   SANS, MINUS, SHORT,
    WITHOUT, DEFECTIVE,
    IMPERFECT
wanton   LEWD, WILD, LOOSE,
    LUSTFUL, NEEDLESS,
    IMMORAL, GRATUITOUS
wapiti   *see* DEER
war(fare)   BOER, GULF, WEER,
    CIVIL, FIGHT, JEHAD, JIHAD,
    PUNIC, WORLD, BALKAN,
    GALLIC, KOREAN, STRIFE,
    CRIMEAN, CRUSADE,
    SAMNITE, VIETNAM,
    CONFLICT, HOSTILITY
War and Peace author   TOLSTOY
War and Peace character   PIERRE,
    ROSTOV, NATASHA,
    BEZUKHOV, BOLKONSKY
war god(dess)   TYR, ARES, ENYO,
    MARS; *see p. 653*
war group   ARMADA
war participant   COMBATANT,
    ANTAGONIST, BELLIGERENT;
    see WARRIOR, SOLDIER
war, *pert. to*   MARTIAL
war injury   LIMP
war, religious   JIHAD, CRUSADE
warble   TRILL, YODEL; *see* SING
warbler   HOODIE, MUFFET,
    CREEPER, WHITETHROAT; *see*
    also SONGBIRD
warbler genus   SYLVIA,
    SEIURUS
war cry   ABOO, ALALA,
    AMORT, WHOOP, BANZAI,
    WARISON, GERONIMO
ward   FEND, AVERT, REPEL,
    PARRY, CUSTODY,
    PROTEGE(E)
warden   GUARD, JAILER,
    RANGER, GUARDIAN,
    CUSTODIAN
warden, type of   FIRE, GAME,
    FOREST, PRISON, AIRRAID
warder   GUARD, KEEPER,
    TURNKEY, CUSTODIAN
wardrobe   CHEST, PRESS,
    ATTIRE, CLOSET, ARMOIRE,
    CLOTHES, TROUSSEAU
wardship   CARE, CUSTODY,
    RESPONSIBILITY
warehouse   HONG, DEPOT,
    ETAPE, BODEGA, GODOWN,
    ARSENAL, ENTREPOT
wares   GOODS, STUFF,
    PRODUCTS, MERCHANDISE
warfare   COMBAT, STRIFE,
    CONFLICT, FIGHTING,
    HOSTILITIES

war-horse   STEED, CLICHE,
    CHARGER, VETERAN
warlike   ODINIC, MARTIAL,
    MILITANT, BELLICOSE,
    COMBATIVE, AGGRESSIVE,
    BELLIGERENT
warlock   *see* WITCH,
    MAGICIAN
warm   BEER, COZY, HEAT,
    SNUG, KIND(LY), BALMY,
    CALID, TEPID, ARDENT,
    LOVING, REHEAT, TENDER,
    LUKEWARM, TEMPERATE,
    AFFECTIONATE
warm-blooded   ARDENT,
    FERVENT, PASSIONATE
warm-hearted   KIND, LOVING,
    AFFECTIONATE
warmer   STOVE, HEATER,
    HOTPLATE
warmonger   HAWK, JINGO,
    WARLORD, DEMAGOGUE,
    MILITARIST
warn   FLAG, ADVISE, SIGNAL,
    CAUTION, PREVISE,
    ADMONISH
warning   OMEN, ALARM,
    ALERT, SNARL, CAVEAT,
    PORTENT
warp   BIAS, CRAM, SILT,
    BUCKLE, CONTORT,
    DISTORT
warp term   ABB, DENT, LOOM,
    REED, LEASE, RAVEL,
    THRUM, EVENER, RADDLE,
    ROLLER, STAMEN
warplane   *see* AIRCRAFT
warrant(s)   WRIT, BERAT,
    MERIT, ASSURE, PLEVIN,
    DESERVE, JUSTIFY,
    GUARANTEE
warranty   PLEDGE, CONTRACT,
    GUARANTEE
warren   HUTCH, RABBITRY
warrior   TOA, GAZI, IMPI,
    SINGH, SPAHI, AMAZON,
    SANNUP, COSSACK, HESSIAN,
    SAMURAI; *see* SOLDIER
warship   LST, RAM, SUB,
    BOYER, SCOUT, UBOAT,
    ANDREW, CARACK, CHASER,
    PTBOAT, CARRACK,
    CARRIER, CORSAIR, CRUISER,
    FLATTOP, FRIGATE,
    GUNBOAT, LANTCHA,
    MONITOR, SNORKEL,
    CORVETTE, FIRESHIP,
    FLAGSHIP, GALLEASS,
    GALLIASS, IRONCLAD,

MANOFWAR, BOMBARDER,
DESTROYER, EAGLEBOAT,
FIRSTRATE, MINELAYER,
SUBMARINE

wart   LUMP, MOLE, WEN,
TUMOR, GROWTH, VERRUCA

warts, covered with   VERRUCOSE

wary   CAG(E)Y, CANNY,
CHARY, CAUTIOUS
SUSPICIOUS

wash   LAVE, LOSH, SWAB,
BATHE, ELUTE, LEACH,
RINSE, SWILL, ARROYO,
COULEE, LAUNDER

washed out   PALE, FADED,
BLEACHED

washed up   BEAT, RUINED,
THROUGH

washer   GASKET, SCRUBBER

washing   ELUTION, LAVATION,
LAUNDRY

washings   ELUATE

Washington (state)   see also p. 615

Washington city/town   KELSO,
PASCO, ASOTIN, COLFAX,
TACOMA, YAKIMA, EPHRATA,
EVERETT, OLYMPIA,
PROSSER, SEATTLE, SPOKANE,
CHEHALIS

Washington DC designer   LENFANT

Washington DC memorial
LINCOLN, JEFFERSON

Washington DC river   POTOMAC

Washington DC section
GEORGETOWN

Washington DC team   BULLETS,
REDSKINS, SENATORS

Washington Indian   HOH, SAUK,
LUMMI, MAKAH, SAMISH,
SKAGIT, YAKAMA, COWLITZ,
(S)KLALLAM, TULALIP,
NOOKSACK, PUYALLUP,
QUILEUTE, QUINAULT,
SUIATTLE, NISQUALLY,
SHOKOMISH, SUQUAMISH,
SNOQUALMIE

Washington island   CAMANO,
WHIDBEY, SANJUAN

Washington lake   ANNE, ROSS,
BAKER, BANKS, GORGE,
GREEN, MOSES, SLIDE,
CHELAN, DIABLO, RIDLEY,
WILLOW, BERDEEN, SHANNON,
TRAPPER, WHATCOM,
DOUBTFUL, HOZOMEEN,
THORNTON, ROOSEVELT

Washington mountain   DOME,
GOAT, HOCK, JACK, LIME,
BACON, BAKER, BEEBE,

LOGAN, SPRAT, TOWER,
CRATER, DEVILS, DIABLO,
BALLARD, BONANZA,
DESPAIR, OLYMPUS, PRAIRIE,
PROPHET, PYRAMID,
RAINIER, REDOUBT, SHUKSAN,
TRIUMPH, WHATCOM,
ELDORADO, STHELENS,
WINTHROP, LIBERTYBELL

Washington mountain range   BLUE,
ROCKY, ENTIAT, SADDLE,
CASCADE, OLYMPIC,
WENATCHEE

Washington river   SNAKE,
METHOW, NACHES, SKAGIT,
YAKIMA, COWLITZ, SANPOLI,
SPOKANE, TOUCHET,
CHEHALIS, COLUMBIA,
NOOKSACK, NISQUALLY,
WENATCHEE

washout   DUD, BOB, FLOP,
FIASCO, FAILURE

washroom   BATHROOM,
LAVATORY, RESTROOM

washstand   COMMODE

wasp   BIKE, MASON, SPHEX,
WAPSE, WHAMP, WOPSE,
DAUBER, DIGGER, HORNET,
VESPID, CYNIPID, EUMENID,
MASARID, MUDWASP,
MUTILLA, VESPINA,
ACULEATA, SANDWASP

waspish   TESTY, SNAPPISH,
IRRITABLE

wasp genus   VESPA, BEMBEX,
BEMBIX, TIPHIA, EUMENES

wassail   SPREE, TOAST,
GUZZLE, CAROUSE,
REVELRY, CELEBRATION

waste   GNAW, IDLE, LOSS,
SADD, SCUM, SUDD, CHAFF,
DECAY, DREGS, DROSS,
GURRY, BARREN, REFUSE,
ATROPHY, FRITTER,
GARBAGE, EFFLUVIUM

waste fiber   NOIL, FLOSS

Waste Land author.   TS ELIOT

waste silk   KNUB, FRISON

waste time   IDLE, LOAF,
DAWDLE, FIDDLE, LOITER,
PUTTER, FRIBBLE, SOLDIER

wasted   THIN, TIRED, USELESS,
WORN OUT, EMACIATED

wasteful   LAVISH, WASTREL,
PRODIGAL, PROFLIGATE

wasteland   MOOR, HEATH,
DESERT, WASTREL

wastrel   BUM, PRODIGAL,
SPENDTHRIFT

watch **EYE, SEE, SPY, GLOM, MIND, TEND, GUARD, VIGIL, DIGITAL, ANALOG(UE)**

watch part **BAND, CASE, DIAL, HAND, PAWL, STEM, STUD, BEZEL, CLICK, CROWN, JEWEL, DETENT, PALLET, CRYSTAL**

watchdog **GARM, BANDOG, MASTIFF, CERBERUS**

watcher **GUARD, LOOKOUT, WITNESS, OBSERVER**

watchful **ALERT, AWAKE, CAUTIOUS, VIGILANT**

watchman **ARGUS, GUARD, SENTRY, SERENO, VEDETTE, CHOKIDAR**

watchtower **TURRET, ATALAYA, LOOKOUT, MIRADOR, BARBICAN**

watchword **MOTTO, SLOGAN, PASSWORD, SHIBBOLETH, BATTLE CRY**

water **EAU, AQUA, BROO, EAUX, RAIN, BRINE, HTWOO, DILUTE, HYDROL, IRRIGATE, SPRINKLE**

Water Bearer **AQUARIUS**

water, body of **BAY, SEA, COVE, GULF, LAKE, LOCH, MERE, POND, POOL, TARN, BAYOU, BROOK, CANAL, CREEK, INLET, LOUGH, OCEAN, RIVER, SOUND, HARBOR, LAGOON, STREAM**

water bird **ERN, COOT, GULL, IBIS, LOON, RAIL, SWAN, TERN, BRANT, CRANE, EGRET, HERON, OUSEL, STILT, AVOCET, JACANA, SLATCH, PELICAN**

water boy **BHISTI, BHEESTY, BHEESTIE**

water buffalo **ARNA, ARNEE, CARABAO**

water chestnut **LING, TRAPA, CALTROP**

Water Lilies painter **MONET**

water, living in **LOTIC, AQUATIC, LENITIC**

water passage *see* **PASSAGE**

water pipe **HOOKAH, NARGHILE, NARGILEH**

water spirit **ARIEL, NIXIE, KELPIE, SPRITE, UNDINE**

water surface **RYME**

watercolor **GOUACHE, TEMPERA, AQUARELLE**

watercourse **RIA, FLUX, KHOR, LADE, RACE, BROOK, CREEK,** **GULLY, NULLA, RIVER, NULLAH, RAVINE, STREAM**

watercress **EKER**

waterfall **LINN, CHUTE, SAULT, CASCADE;** *see p.* 612

Watergate figure **DEAN, NIXON, SIRICA, ERLICHMAN, HALDERMAN**

watering device **CAN, HOSE, PUMP, SPRAY, NOZZLE, HYDRANT, SPRINKLER**

watering place **BATH, SPA, WELL, OASIS;** *see* **SPRING**

waterless **DRY, ARID, ANHYDROUS**

Waterloo victor **WELLINGTON**

waterproof **SEALED, HERMETIC, LEAKPROOF, WATERTIGHT, IMPERMEABLE**

waterproofing material **CANVAS, RUBBER, PLASTIC, MACINTOSH**

water-raising device **WHIM, WHIN, NORIA, SWEEP, TABUT, SHADUF, TABOOT, SHADOOF**

waters, dead **STYX**

watershed **BASIN, CRISIS, DIVIDE**

watertight box **CAISSON, COFFERDAM**

watertight, make **CAULK**

waterway **CANAL, RIVER, STRAIT, STREAM, CHANNEL**

waterwheel **NORIA, SAKIA, PADDLE, SAKIEH, TURBINE**

watery **WET, THIN, WEAK, MOIST, RUNNY, SOGGY, WASHY, DILUTE(D), SEROUS, AQUEOUS**

wattle **GILL, DEWLAP, LAPPET**

wattle tree **BOREE, MYALL**

wave **FLY, WAFT, BECKON, COMBER, RIPPLE, ROLLER, BREAKER;** *see* **BILLOW**

waver **SWAY, FALTER, QUIVER, TEETER, HESITATE, VACILLATE**

waves, make **CRIMP, REBEL, DISSENT, ROCK THE BOAT**

wavy **ONDY, UNDE, UNDY, CRISP, NEBULE, REPAND, UNDATE, UNDOSE**

wax **CERE, CODE, GROW, PELA, CERIN, CEROMA, CERESIN**

wax, *pert. to* **CERAL**

wax catcher **BOBECHE**

waxen **WAN, PALE, PASTY, SALLOW, SICKLY**

way **TAO, VIA, ITER, LANE, MODE, ROAD, WONT, HABIT, MEANS, ROUTE, METHOD, TACTIC**

way out **EXIT, EGRESS, MODERN**

waybill **MANIFEST**

wayfarer **VIATOR, TRAVELER, ITINERANT**

waylay **STOP, ACCOST, AMBUSH, INTERCEPT**

Wayne, John, nickname **DUKE**

wayside rest **PARAO**

wayward **ERRANT, UNRULY, WANTON, DEFIANT, ERRATIC, WILLFUL, CAPRICIOUS**

WB sitcom **REBA**

weak **WAN, FLAT, PUNY, FAINT, FRAIL, DEBILE, EFFETE, FEEBLE, INFIRM, FLACCID, FRAGILE, DECREPIT, VULNERABLE**

weak-minded **STUPID, IDIOTIC, MORONIC, IMBECILE**

weaken **SAP, DILUTE, LABEFY, VITIATE, ENERVATE, ENFEEBLE**

weakening **FADY, FADING, FAILING**

weakling **SOP, WIMP, PULER, SISSY, SOFTIE, CRYBABY, PANTYWAIST**

weakness **ATONY, DEFECT, FOIBLE, ACRATIA, FRAILTY, FONDNESS**

wealth **PELF, LUCRE, ASSETS, MAMMON, CAPITAL, FORTUNE, OPULENCE, AFFLUENCE**

wealth, land of **OPHIR**

wealthy **LUSH, FLUSH, HEELED, MONEYED, OPULENT; see RICH**

weapon **ARM(E), ARMS; see p. 502**

weaponry **ORDNANCE**

wear **DON, USE, FRAY, CHAFE, ERODE, ABRADE, CORRODE**

wear and — **TEAR**

weariness **ENNUI, TEDIUM, FATIGUE, BOREDOM, LASSITUDE**

wearisome **DREE, DULL, BORING, DREARY, DREICH, TEDIOUS, TIRESOME**

weary **FAG, BORE, JADE, TIRE, TIRED, TUCKER, DRAINED, WORNOUT, EXHAUSTED**

weasel(-like mammals) **FOIN, MINK, PATE, VARE, BROCK, FITCH, HURON, OTTER, PAHMI, PEKAN, RATEL, SABLE, SKUNK, STOAT, TAYRA, ZORIL, BADGER, BAUSON, BRAIRO, ERMINE, FERRET, FISHER, GALERA, GRISON, MARTEN, WEASEL, FITCHET, GLUTTON, MINIVER, POLECAT, SANDPIG, ZORILLA, BRAIREAU, CARCAJOU, KOLINSKY, MUISHOND**

weasel genus **GULO, LATAX, LUTRA, MELES, MARTES, MYDAUS, ENHYDRA, ICTONYX, MUSTELA, TAXIDEA, MEPHITIS**

weather **CLIME, ERODE, ENDURE, SEASON, CLIMATE, SURVIVE, WEARAWAY, WITHSTAND**

weather term **FOG, HOT, ICY, THI, WET, COLD, FAIR, GALE, HAIL, RAIN, SMOG, SNOW, WARM, CHILL, FOGGY, FROST, GUSTY, HUMID, SLEET, SMAZE, THERM, WINDY, CHILLY, CLOUDY, DEGREE, ISOBAR, STORMY, DROUGHT, HUMIDITY, ISOTHERM, OVERCAST**

weathercock **FANE, VANE, GIROUETTE**

weathered **WORN, FADED, TOUGH, ERODED, TANNED, BLEACHED, WINDSWEPT**

weatherglass **BAROMETER**

weatherman **FORECASTER, METEOROLOGIST**

weave **MAT, KNIT, LOOM, BRAID, PLAIT, FLASH, PLEACH, ENTWINE**

weaver **WEBSTER**

weaverbird **NUN, BAYA, TAHA, VEUVE, OXBIRD, WHIDAH, WHYDAR, WAXBILL**

weaverbird genus **QUELEA**

weaving term **COP, LAY, UNI, HECK, SLEY, WOOF, LATHE, LEASE, LISSE, RAVEL, BOBBIN, LAPETT; see LOOM**

web **NET, MESH, TELA, TRAP, TISSUE, NETWORK, GOSSAMER, INTERNET**

Web address ending *see URL*

web, *pert. to* **TELAR(Y), RETIARY**

Web portal **AOL, MSN, YAHOO**

webbed **PALMATE**
web-footed bird **DUCK, LOON, SWAN, GOOSE, AVOCET, GANNET, PELICAN, PENGUIN, ALBATROSS, CORMORANT**
weblike **TELAR**
Weber opera **OBERON, EURYANTHE, (DER) FREISCHUTZ**
wed **JOIN, MATE, WIVE, MARRY, MERGE, UNITE, ESPOUSE**
wedding **HYMEN, ESPOUSAL, MARRIAGE, NUPTIALS**
wedding anniversary *see p. 718*
wedding announcement **BAN(N)S**
wedding party member **MATRON, BESTMAN, RINGBOY, SPONSOR, GROOMSMAN, BRIDESMAID, FLOWERGIRL, RINGBEARER**
wedding words **IDO**
wedge **CAM, JAM, FROE, FROW, GLUT, GORE, SHIM, CHOCK, COIGN, QUOIN, SPRAG, COTTER, CUNEUS, GUSSET**
wedge-shaped **CUNEATE**
wedlock **MARRIAGE, MATRIMONY**
Wednesday **HUMPDAY, MIDWEEK**
Wednesday source **WODEN**
wee **TINY, SMALL, LITTLE, MINUTE, ITSYBITSY, MINUSCULE**
weed **HOE, CULL, DOCK, PEST, TARE, COUCH, JIMSON, QUITCH, SPURRY, CRARLOCK, DANDELION**
weedkiller **ROUNDUP, PARAQUAT, HERBICIDE**
weeds **CRAPE. VEILS, MOURNING**
week **OUK, SENNET, HEBDOMAD, SENNIGHT**
weekday **FERIA**
weekly **RAG, PAPER, HEBDOMADAL, PERIODICAL**
weeks, two **FORTNIGHT**
weenie **HOTDOG, FRANK(FURTER)**
weep **ORE, SOB, BAWL, BOHO(O), BOOHOO, LAMENT, BLUBBER; see CRY**
weeping statue **NIOBE**
weepy **SEEPY, TEARFUL**
weevil **KIS, BOLL, BORER; see BEETLE**
weft **WOFT, WOOF**

weigh **TELL, COUNT, PONDER, CONSIDER**
weigh down **LOAD, BESET, SADDEN, DEPRESS, OPPRESS, ENCUMBER, OVERLOAD**
weighing device *see* **SCALE**
weight **BOB, TOD, HEFT, LOAD, NAIL, PARI, TRON, TROY, CLOVE, PEISE, TRONE, VALUE;** *see p. 636*
weight allowance **TRET**
weight, metric **TON, GRAM, KILO, QUINTAL, KILOGRAM, MILLIGRAM**
weight, pert. to **BARIC**
weight, U.S. & British *(for other countries see specific entry)* **CWT, KEG, KIP, TON, DRAM, CARAT, OUNCE, POUND, BARREL, CENTAL;** *see p. 636*
weight system **TROY, METRIC, AVOIRDUPOIS**
weightless **LIGHT, FEATHERY**
weighty **GRAVE, HEAVY, SERIOUS, IMPORTANT**
weir **DAM, TRAP, GARTH**
weird **ODO, EERY, UNCO, EERIE, SPOOKY, UNCANNY, ELDRITCH, UNEARTHLY**
weirdo **NUT, KOOK, SCREWBALL**
welcome **HAIL, ASKIN, GREET, ACCEPT, ACCOIL, SALUTE, EMBRACE, RECEIVE**
Welcome Back, Kotter names **GABE, JUAN, JULIE, ARNOLD, HOTZIE, KAPLAN, VINNIE, FREDDIE, BOOMBOOM, BUCHANAN, TRAVOLTA**
weld **SEAM, JOINT, SOLDER**
welding material **SOLDER, THERMIT(E)**
welfare **WEAL, BENEFIT, WELLBEING**
welfare org. **CARE, YMCA, YWCA, RED CROSS, SALVATION ARMY**
welkin **SKY, VAULT, HEAVEN, FIRMAMENT**
well **AIN, PIT, BIEN, GUSH, FONT, HALE, SUMP, SHAFT, SOUND, SPRING, FOUNTAIN**
well curb **PUTEAL**
well lining **STEEN**
well said **TOUCHE**
well-being **GOOD, HEALTH, WELFARE**
wellborn **NOBLE**
well-bred **POLITE, GENTEEL, REFINED, EDUCATED**

well-done EUGE, BRAVO, BULLY, OVERCOOKED
well-founded SOUND, VALID
well-groomed NEAT, TRIG, DAPPER, SOIGNE, SPRUCE
well-heeled RICH, MONEYED, WELL OFF, AFFLUENT, PROSPEROUS
well-known NOTED, FAMOUS, FAMILIAR, RENOWNED
well-off RICH, WEALTHY, AFFLUENT, PROSPEROUS
well-read VERSED, LEARNED, LITERATE
Welsh CHEAT, CYMRY, KYMRY, TAFFY, CYMRIC, KYMRIC, RENEGE, SWINDLE, CAMBRIAN; see also WALES
Welsh city/town MOLD, BANGOR, CARDIFF, NEWPORT, RHONDDA, SWANSEA, HAWARDEN, PEMBROKE
Welsh dog CORGI
Welsh island ANGLESEY
Welsh people CYMRY
Welsh rabbit RAREBIT
Welsh river DEE, WYE, TEME, CONWY, TEIFI, CONWAY, SEVERN
Welsh saint DAVID
welt LASH, WALE, STRIP, RIDGE, SWELLING
wen CYST, MOLE, CLYER, TALPA
wench DELL, DOXY, HUSSY; see also MAID
wend PASS, SORB, JOURNEY, MEANDER
Wendat BEAR, CORD, DEER, ROCK, HURON, WYANDOT
werewolf TURNSKIN, LOUPGAROU, LYCANTHROPE
West African tree AXEE, ODUM, ACKEE, IROKO
West-Atlantic language GOLA, KISSI, LIMBA, SERER, TEMNE, WOLOF, BALANTE
West Australia, capital of PERTH
West Indian music CALYPSO
West Indian tree MABI, ACANA, GENIE, GINEP, YACCA, BALATA, PIMENTO, ALLSPICE; see INDIAN
West Indies island CUBA, NEVIS, CAYMAN, NASSAU, TOBAGO, ANTIGUA, BAHAMAS, BARBUDA, JAMAICA,

STKITTS, ANTILLES, DOMINICA
West Point mascot MULE
West Point motto DUTY, HONOR, COUNTRY
West Pointer PLEB, CADET, PLEBE, YEARLING
West Side Story character ICE, RIFF, TONY, ANITA, CHINO, MARIA, ACTION, KRUPKE, BERNARDO
West Virginia see also p. 615
West Virginia city/town CLAY, LOGAN, WAYNE, WELCH, HAMLIN, KEYSER, RIPLEY, ROMNEY, WESTON, BECKLEY, FAIRMONT, WHEELING, PRINCETON, CHARLESTON, HUNTINGTON
West Virginia lake SUTTON, TYGART, BLUESTONE
West Virginia mountain SPRUCEKNOB
West Virginia river ELK, NEW, OHIO, CHEAT, CACAPON, KANAWHA, POTOMAC, TUGFORK, BIGSANDY, GUYANDOTTE
western OATER, HESPERIAN, OCCIDENTAL
Western Samoa see SAMOA
wet DIP, RET, SOP, WAT, ASOP, DAMP, DANK, SOAK(ED), MOIST(EN), SOPPING
wet blanket KILLJOY, SPOILSPORT
wetback PEON, BRACERO
wether RAM, EUNUCH
wetlands BOG, SWAMPS, MARSHES
whack HIT, BEAT, BELT, SLAP, SMACK
whale FLOG, THRASH
whale(s) ORC, SEI, CETE, ORCA, KRENG, OTARY, POGGY, SCRAG, SPERM, BALEEN, BELUGA, BLOWER, FINNER, GIBBAR, KILLER, BOWHEAD, FINBACK, FINFISH, GRAMPUS, MARSOON, RIPSACK, RORQUAL, SPOUTER, ZIPHIAN, BALAENID, CACHALOT, HUMPBACK, MOBY DICK, MUTILATE, LEVIATHAN
whale genus HUSE, HUSO, BALAENA, ORCINUS, ZALOPHUS
whale hunter AHAB

whale sound MEW, BARK, SONG, CLICK, WHINE, SQUEAL, CHIRRUP, WHISTLE
whale, young CALF
whalebone BALEEN
whalebone carving SCRIMSHAW
whales, *pert. to* CETIC, CETACEAN
whammy HEX, JINX, CURSE, EVILEYE
wharf *see* LANDING
what HOW, WHICH, PARDON
what? HUH, COME AGAIN
whatever ATANYRATE
whatnot OMNIUM, CABINET, ETAGERE
wheat SUJI, SUJEE, DURUM, EMMER, SPELT, EINKORN, POULARD
wheat disease BUNT, RUST, SMUT, ERGOT
Wheatley relative PETERS
wheedle COG, COAX, CAJOLE, WANGLE, INVEIGLE, PERSUADE
wheel(s) DISK, HELM, ROLL, ROTA, SPIN, NORIA, ROWEL, CASTER, GYRATE, PULLEY, ROTATE, SHEAVE, SPROCKET
wheel part CAM, HOB, HUB, RIM, AXLE, NAVE, TIRE, ARBOR, FELLY, SPOKE, FLANGE, STRAKE
Wheel of Fortune name (PAT)SAJAK, (VANNA)WHITE
wheeler-dealer SCHEMER, GO GETTER, OPERATOR
wheels CAR, AUTO(MOBILE)
wheeze GAG, GASP, PUFF, RALE
whelk WELT, WALE, MUREX, SNAIL, PAPULE, PIMPLE, MOLLUSK, PUSTULE, GASTROPOD
whelp LAD, PUP(PY), YOUTH
when TIME, WHILE, WHEREAS
where WHITHER, LOCATION, WHEREABOUTS
whereas SINCE, WHILE, SEEING, INASMUCH
wherefore WHY, HENCE, BECAUSE
whereupon WHEN, AT WHICH
wherewithal CASH, FUNDS, MEANS, MONEY, RESOURCES
wherry BARGE, SCULL, LIGHTER, ROWBOAT
whet HONE, GRIND, (A)ROUSE, KINDLE, SHARPEN

whether IF, EITHER, INCASE
whether — OR NOT
whetstone RIP, BUHR, HONE
whey SERA, SERUM, WHIG
whiff GUST, PUFF, WAFT, SMELL
while AS, YET, WHEN, ALBEIT, DAWDLE, DURING, WHEREAS
whilom ONCE, QUONDAM, FORMER(LY), ERST(WHILE)
whim FAD, TOY, KINK, FREAK, HUMOR, NOTION, CAPRICE, IMPULSE
whimper KEEN, WHINE; *see* CRY
whimsical QUIRKY, FANCIFUL, CAPRICIOUS
whimsy FANCY, HUMOR, NOTION, VAGARY, CAPRICE
whine MEWL, MOAN, PULE, YIRN, WHIMPER, COMPLAIN
whinny FURZY, HINNY, NEIGH
whip TAN, CROP, FLAY, FLOG, LACE, LASH, PLET, WALE, AZOTE, FLAIL, KNOUT, QUIRT, CHICOTE, KURBASH, SJAMBOK; *see* BEAT
whip mark WALE, WEAL, STRIPE
whip up CHURN, PREPARE
whiplash FALY, FLOG, THONG, INJURY, THRASH
whippersnapper SQUIRT, UPSTART
whipping boy SCAPEGOAT
whipsocket SNEAD
whirl EDDY, GYRE, REEL, SPIN, GYRATE
whirligig ROTOR, CAROUSEL
whirlpool EDDY, WEEL, WIEL, GURGE, SWIRL, VORTEX, MAELSTROM
whirlwind EDDY, CYCLONE, TORNADO, TWISTER
whirlybird CHOPPER, AUTOGYRO, HELICOPTER
whisk BEAT, WHIP, BROOM, BRUSH, FLUFF (UP)
whiskers HAIR, BEARD, CHOPS, GOATEE, VIBRISSA, MUSTACHE, SIDEBURN(S)
whiskey BOOZE, HOOCH, POTEEN, ROTGUT, BOOTLEG, POTHEEN, FIREWATER, MOONSHINE; *see* LIQUOR
whisper HINT, SIGH, ASIDE, TUTEL, MURMUR, BREATHE
whist term MORT, SLAM, SOLO, VOLE, GRAND, MISERE

whistle	CALL, FUTE, PIPE, TOOT, SIREN, TOOTLE, CATCALL
whit	DOIT; see BIT
white	WAN, ASHY, BAWN, FAIR, ASHEN, LABAN, CHALKY, COLORLESS
White Cliffs location	DOVER
White House designer	HOBAN
White House marriages	ADAMS, CLEVELAND
white man	BUCKRA, GRINGO, CACHILA, PALEFACE
white-bread	BLAND
white-collar employee	CLERK
white-sale fabric	PERCALE
whitefish	CISCO, POWAN, POLLAN, POLLEN, INCONNU, LAVARET, VENDACE, TULLIBEE
whiten	BLANCH, BLEACH, ETIOLATE
whitewash	CLEAR, GLOSS, PARGET, CONCEAL
whiting	COD, HAKE, CHALK, POLLACK, WALLEYE, DRUMFISH, MENHADEN, WEAKFISH
Whittier heroine	MAUD, MOLL(Y)
whittle	CUT, DOCK, PARE, CARVE, ERODE, SHAPE, SHAVE, SLICE, DEDUCT, REDUCE, FASHION
whiz	ACE, HUM, PIRR, WHIR, EXPERT, PRODIGY
Who's the Boss? names	MONA, TONY, DANZA, ANGELA, JONATHAN, SAMANTHA
whoa	STOP, HOLLA
whodunit	MYSTERY, THRILLER
whole	FULL, TOTO, SOUND, TOTAL, UNCUT, ENTIRE, INTACT, COMPLETE, ENTIRETY, TOTALITY, UNBROKEN
wholehearted	TOTAL, SINCERE, HEARTFELT
wholesale	BULK, GROSS, MASSIVE
wholesaler	BROKER, JOBBER, MIDDLEMAN, DISTRIBUTOR
wholesome	GOOD, HEALTHY, NUTRITIOUS, NOURISHING
wholly	FULLY, TOTALLY, UTTERLY, ENTIRELY, COMPLETELY
whoop	HOOT, YELL; see CRY

whooping cough	CHINCOUGH, PERTUSSIS
whopper	LIE, GIANT, STORY, WHALE
whore	BAWD, HARLOT, STRUMPET, PROSTITUTE
whorehouse	BROTHEL
whorl	SWIRL, SPIRAL, VOLUTE, VORTEX
wick	SNAST, SNUFF, TAPER, SNASTE
wicked	see EVIL
wicker	BURI, CANE, RUSH, TWIG, OSIER, STRAW, WITHE, WOVEN, RAFFIA, RATTAN, WILLOW
wickerwork	RA(T)TAN
wicket	ARCH, GATE, HOOP, STUMP, INNING, WINDOW
wickiup	HUT, LODGE, TE(E)PEE, SHANTY
wide	VAST, AMPLE, BROAD, LARGE, ROOMY, SPACIOUS
— and wide	FAR
widely	BROADLY, GENERALLY
widen	DILATE, EXPAND, AMPLIFY, ENLARGE
widespread	RIFE, COMMON, GENERAL, RAMPANT, PREVALENT
widgeon	see DUCK
widow	SKAT, RELICT, SUTTEE, BEREAVE
widow's share	MITE, T(I)ERCE
width	SPAN, BREADTH, LATITUDE
wield	PLY, USE, EXERT, BRANDISH, EXERCISE
wiener	HOTDOG, REDHOT, FRANK(FURTER)
wife	MRS, RIB, FEME, FERE, FRAU, FROW, UXOR, BRIDE, FEMME, SQUAW, MATRON, MISSUS, OLDLADY; see SPOUSE
wife's property	DOS
wifely	UXORIAL
wig	MAT, RUG, BUSBY, DIVOT, DOILY, JASEY, PERUKE, TOUPEE, PERIWIG, RAMIL(L)IE
wiggle	WAG, SHAKE, TWIST, SQUIRM, WANGLE, WOBBLE, WRIGGLE
wigwam	TIPI, TE(E)PEE, WICKIUP
wild	MAD, GAGA, CRAZY, FERAL, RABID, FERINE, MADCAP, SAVAGE, STORMY,

	UNRULY, NATURAL,
	UNTAMED, UNBROKEN
Wild Duck playwright	IBSEN
Wild West show	RODEO
wildcat	BALU; *see* CAT
wilderness	WILDS, DESERT,
	JUNGLE, BACKWOODS,
	BOONDOCKS, WASTELAND
wildfire	ERYSIPELAS
wildlife preserve	WETLAND,
	SANCTUARY
wile	ART, LURE, RUSE, TRICK,
	DECEIT, ARTIFICE
will	WISH, BEHEST, DESIRE,
	CONATION, VELLEITY,
	VOLITION, TESTAMENT
will beneficiary	DEVISEE
will maker	DEVISOR
willful	WAYWARD,
	STUBBORN, OBSTINATE
William Tell composer	ROSSINI
willies	CREEPS, JITTERS,
	NERVOUSNESS
willing	BAIN, KEEN, LIEF,
	EAGER, READY, PLIANT,
	DISPOSED, INCLINED,
	AGREEABLE
willingly	FAIN, LIEF, GLADLY,
	READILY
willingness	DESIRE, CONSENT,
	ALACRITY, EAGERNESS,
	ENTHUSIASM
willow	ITEA, EDDER, OSIER,
	SALIX, WITHY
willowy	LITHE, LISSOM,
	SVELTE, SLENDER
will-power	DRIVE, RESOLVE,
	RESOLUTION,
	DETERMINATION
willy-nilly	ANYHOW,
	REGARDLESS
Wilson's thrush	VEERY
wilt	FADE, COWER, DROOP,
	WITHER, SHRIVEL
wily	SLY, FOXY, CLEVER,
	CRAFTY, SHIFTY, SUBTLE,
	CUNNING
wimble	AUGER, GIMLET
wimp	WEAKLING
wimple	GORGET, WIMLUNGE
win	GET, EARN, GAIN,
	GARNER, PREVAIL, SUCCEED,
	TRIUMPH, VICTORY
wince	SHY, START, FLINCH,
	CRINGE, RECOIL
winch	CRANK, HOIST,
	WINDLASS
wind (air)	AFER, BISE, BORA,
	FOHN, GALE, GUST, KONA,

	PUNA, PUNO, FOEHN, LESTE,
	NOTUS, SIROC, TRADE,
	AUSTER, BOREAS, BREATH,
	BUSTER, DUSTER, FLATUS,
	FLURRY, KAMSIN, SAMIEL,
	SARSAR, SHAMAL, SHIMAL,
	SIMOOM, SIMOON, SOLANO,
	ZEPHYR, CYCLONE, ETESIAN,
	GREGALE, KHAMSIN, MISTRAL,
	MONSOON, PAMPERO,
	SIROCCO, TEMPEST
wind (twist)	BEND, COIL,
	CURL, SNAKE, TWINE, TWIST
wind indicator	COCK, CONE,
	SOCK, VANE, SLEEVE
wind instrument	HORN, OBOE,
	FLUTE, BASSOON, TRUMPET,
	CLARINET, TROMBONE; *see*
	p. 642
wind instrument part	KEY(WORK),
	BELL, COIL, LILL,
	MOUTHPIECE
wind up	EXCITE
windbag	BRAGGART,
	CHATTERER
windborne	AEOLIAN
winded	GASPING, PUFFING,
	BREATHLESS
windfall	BOON, BONUS, PRIZE,
	BONANZA, FORTUNE
winding	MAZY, SNAKY,
	SPIRAL, AMBAGE,
	TORTUOUS
winding sheet	SHROUD,
	CEREMENT
winding way	TRAIL
windjammer	SHIP, BUGLER,
	BANDSMAN
windlass	REEL, WHIM, WHIN,
	CRANK, WINCH, CAPSTAN
windless	CALM, AIRLESS
windmill fighter	(DON)QUIXOTE
windmill part	AWE, CAP, CURB,
	SAIL, VANE
window	SASH, ORIEL, OXEYE,
	DORMER, LUCARNE,
	ROUNDEL, TRANSOM,
	SKYLIGHT
window dressing	TRIM, DISPLAY
window part	CAME, PANE,
	SASH, SILL, MUNTIN,
	LEADING, MULLION,
	TRANSOM
window setter	GLAZIER
windpipe	TRACHEA,
	WEASAND
windrow	SWATH, FURROW
windshield option	TINT,
	WIPER, DEICER

windstorm BLOW, GALE,
BURA(N), SQUALL,
TORNADO, TWISTER,
TYPHOON
windup END, CLOSE, FINALE,
FINIS(H), CLOSURE,
CONCLUSION
Windward Islands BEQUIA,
CANOUAN, GRENADA,
STLUCIA, MUSTIQUE,
CARRIACOU, STVINCENT,
MARTINIQUE
windy AIRY, BLOWY, GABBY,
GASSY, GUSTY, STORMY,
VERBOSE, BOASTFUL,
TALKATIVE
Windy City CHICAGO
wine CRU, RED, SEC, VIN,
BRUT, CUIT, CUTE, DOUX,
MUST, GRAVE, WHITE,
NATURAL; see p. 563
wine and — DINE
wine cask TUN, BOSS, BUTT,
PIPI, PUNCHEON
wine deposit LEES, ARGAL,
ARGOL, GRIFFE, TARTAR
wine disorder CASSE
wine drink see DRINK
wine, pert. to VINIC, VINOUS
wine, spiced NEGUS, BISHOP,
SANGAREE, HIPPOCRAS
wine steward SOMMELIER
wine term DRY, SEC, BRUT,
BODY, SEVE, VINT, FLINTY,
BOUQUET
wine with honey MULSE
wineglass TULIP, RUMMER
winemaker GALLO, ROSSI
winemaking OENOLOGY
winemaking area ASTI, NAPA,
LOIRE, RHONE, LATIUM,
SONOMA, VERONA, MARSALA,
TUSCANY, BORDEAUX,
BURGUNDY, PIEDMONT,
RIESLING, SYLVANER,
CHAMPAGNE
wing ALA, ELL, ALAE, ALULA,
ANNEX, PENNA, PINNA,
ALETTE, PINION, ELYTRON,
TEGMINA, TEGUMEN
wing part FLAP, FLANK,
AILERON
wing, pert. to ALAR
winged AILE, ALAR, ALATE,
PENNATE
winged deity EROS, NIKE,
CUPID
winged figure IDOLON,
IDOLUM, EIDOLON

winged fruit SAMARA
winged horse PEGASUS
wing-footed ALIPED
wingless APTERAL,
DEALATE(D)
Wings names JOE, ROY, FAYE,
BRIAN, HELEN, LOWELL,
HACKETT
wink BAT, BLINK, SIGNAL,
SQUINT, FLICKER, NICTATE
winner CHAMP(ION), VICTOR,
SUCCESS, SURE THING
Winnie the Pooh author MILNE
Winnie the Pooh character ROO,
OWL, POOH, KANGA,
(CHRISTOPHER) ROBIN,
PIGLET, TIGGER, EEYORE,
HEFFALUMP
winning AHEAD, LEADING,
CHARMING, ENGAGING,
OUTFRONT, ATTRACTIVE
winnow FAN, SIFT, SCATTER,
SEPARATE
winsome GAY, LIVELY,
LOVABLE, CHARMING,
ENGAGING
winter CHILL, FROST, ICINESS,
HIBERNATE
winter wear FLANNEL
Winter's Tale character DION,
MOPSA, DORCAS, EMILIA,
CAMILLO, LEONTES, FLORIZEL,
PAULINA, PERDITA,
HERMIONE
wintry ARCTIC, BOREAL,
BRUMAL, HIEMAL, HYEMAL,
HIBERNAL
wipe MOP, RUB, SWAB, CLEAN,
CLEAR, ERASE, EFFACE
wipe out KILL, ERASE,
REMOVE, ELIMINATE,
ERADICATE, EXTERMINATE
wire CORD, LEAD, LINE, LITZ,
CABLE, CIRCUIT, RETICLE
wireless RADIO
wiry LEAN, THIN, STIFF,
TOUGH, SINEWY, BRISTLY
Wisconsin see also p. 615
Wisconsin city/town ALMA,
ANTIGO, JUNEAU, RACINE,
WAUSAU, BARABOO,
ELKHORN, KENOSHA, KESHENA,
MADISON, OSHKOSH,
PORTAGE, VIROQUA,
APPLETON, GREENBAY,
LACROSSE, WAUKESHA,
EAUCLAIRE, FONDDULAC,
MANITOWOC, MILWAUKEE,
SHEBOYGAN, JANESVILLE

Wisconsin Indian ONEIDA, HOCHUNK, CHIPPEWA, MENOMINEE, POTAWATOMI

Wisconsin lake DUBAY, GREEN, WILLOW, CHIPPEWA, PUCKAWAY, WINNEBAGO, KOSHKONONG

Wisconsin mountain RIB

Wisconsin river FOX, ROCK, WOLF, BLACK, SUGAR, OCONTO, YELLOW, STCROIX, CHIPPEWA, FLAMBEAU, KICKAPOO, PESHTIGO, MENOMINEE, WISCONSIN, PECATONICA, MISSISSIPPI

Wisconsin school LAWRENCE, MARQUETTE, NORTHLAND

wisdom WIT, LORE, ACUMEN, GNOSIS, INSIGHT, LEARNING, PRUDENCE, INTELLIGENCE

wise SAGE, SAVVY, SHREWD, ERUDITE, KNOWING, LEARNED, SAPIENT, JUDICIOUS, SAGACIOUS

wise guy JOKER, SMARTALECK

wise man MAGI, SAGE, MAGUS, SOLON, WITAN, GASPAR, MENTOR, NESTOR, PANDIT, SAVANT, MAHATMA, SOLOMON

wiseacre SAGE, KNOWITALL, SMARTALECK

wisecrack GAG, GIBE, JEST, JOKE, RETORT

wish HOPE, LONG, PINE, WANT, FANCY, DESIRE, ASPIRATION

wishbone FURCULA, FURCULUM, CROSSARM

wishful EAGER, HOPEFUL, LONGING, DESIROUS

wishy-washy WEAK, INSIPID, SPINELESS, INDECISIVE

wisp CURL, TAIT, TATE, TUFT, WASE, TRESS

wispy THIN, FRAIL, FLIMSY, SLIGHT

wisteria FUJI

wistful PENSIVE, REFLECTIVE

wit WAG, HUMOR, IRONY, ESPRIT, CUNNING, SARCASM, HUMORIST

witch HAG, HEX, BRUJA, CIRCE, CRONE, ENDOR, HECAT, LAMIA, BELDAM, DUESSA, HECATE, LILITH, ACRASIA, BELDAME, CARLINE, WARLOCK

witch city ENDOR, SALEM

witch doctor BRUJO, GOOFER, SHAMAN, WIZARD

witch, TV ENDORA, SAMANTHA

witchcraft *see* SORCERY, MAGIC

with BY, CUM, CHEZ, PLUS, AMONG, USING, THROUGH

withal ALSO, STILL, BESIDES

withdraw QUIT, WEAN, LEAVE, DEPART, REMOVE, RETIRE, SECEDE, EXTRACT, RETREAT, RETRACT

withdrawn SHY, RESERVED, ISOLATED, RETIRING, SECLUDED

withe TWIG, OSIER, BRANCH, WICKER

wither BURN, FADE, SERE, WILT, BLAST, WIZEN, SHRIVEL

withered SERE, WIZENED

withering SCORNFUL, SARCASTIC

withhold DENY, KEEP, DETAIN, REFUSE, RESERVE

within BEN, INLY, INNER, INTERNAL

without EX, SANS, SINE, MINUS, LACKING, OUTSIDE

without delay APACE, ATONCE, FORTHWITH, IMMEDIATELY

without equal ALONE, UNIQUE

withstand DENY, STAND, ENDURE, RESIST, SURVIVE

witless DULL, DUMB, SILLY, STUPID, FOOLISH, CLUELESS

witness SEE, SIGN, TESTE, ATTEST, TESTIFY, OBSERVE, DEPONENT, ONLOOKER

witticism *see* JOKE

witty DROLL, CLEVER, AMUSING, HUMOROUS

wizard *see* MAGICIAN

Wizard of Oz actor LAHR, BURKE, HALEY, BOLGER, MORGAN, GARLAND, HAMILTON

Wizard of Oz author BAUM

Wizard of Oz character EM, PIP, TOTO, HENRY, GLINDA, TINMAN, DOROTHY, SCARECROW

wizardy MAGIC, SKILL, SORCERY, WITCHCRAFT

wizen BURN, SEAR, DRYUP, WITHER, SHRIVEL

WKRP in Cincinnati character
ART, LES, ANDY, HERB, LONI,
SIMS, FEVER, VENUS, BAILEY,
BIGGUY, GORDON, HOWARD,
JOHNNY, TRAVIS,
HESSEMAN, JENNIFER

WKRP in Cincinnati creator
HUGH, WILSON

wobble   REEL, SHAKE, WAVER,
TEETER, TOTTER, WADDLE,
STAGGER

wobbly   SHAKY, RICKETY,
UNSTEADY

Wodehouse character   JEEVES

Woden   ODIN

woe   BANE, BLUES, DOLOR,
GRIEF, MISERY, DESPAIR,
TROUBLE

woebegone   SAD, DOLEFUL,
PITIFUL, DESOLATE

woeful   SAD, TRISTE,
MOURNFUL, MELANCHOLY

wolf   HURE, LOBO, CHANCO,
COYOTE, THOOID; see DOG

wolf genus   CANIS

wolfish   LUPINE, THOOID,
RAVENOUS

Wolverine State   MI,
MICH(IGAN)

woman   SHE, BINT, PERI, BELLE,
HOURI, MENAD, VIXEN,
MAENAD, PARAMOUR; see
HAG, MADAM, WIFE, FEMALE

woman hater   MISOGYNIST

woman, loose   BAWD, TART,
HUSSY, QUEAN, QUEEN,
TRULL, WENCH, WHORE,
TROLLOP, STRUMPET

woman, military   WAC, WAF,
WAVE

woman, slang   HEN, BABE,
DAME, BROAD, FRAIL, SKIRT,
SQUAW, FLOSSY, HEIFER,
TOOTSY

woman, young   BABE, GIRL,
LASS, MISS, MAIDEN,
DEMOISELLE

woman chaser   see WOMANIZER

womanhood   FEMININITY,
MULIEBRITY

womanish   WEAK, FEMININE,
EFFEMINATE

womanizer   RAKE, ROUE, WOLF,
CASANOVA, LOTHARIO,
LADYKILLER

womb   WAME, BELLY, MATRIX,
UTERUS, VENTER

women's rights movement
FEMINISM, LIB(ERATION)

wonder   AWE, DOUBT,
MARVEL, QUESTION,
SURPRISE, AMAZEMENT

Wonder State   AR, ARK(ANSAS)

Wonder Years names   JACK,
KAREN, KEVIN, NORMA,
WAYNE, ARNOLD, WINNIE

wonderful   GREAT, SUPERB,
AMAZING, COLOSSAL,
TERRIFIC

Wonderland   see ALICE

wont   HABIT, USAGE,
CUSTOM, ROUTINE

woo   see COURT

wood(s)   ASH, ELM, GUM, LOG,
OAK, YEW, LANA, BALSA,
BIRCH, BOARD, CAHUY,
CEDAR, COPSE, EBONY, KOKRA,
MAPLE, NARRA, XYLEM,
ALERCE, CHERRY, LUMBER,
TIMBER, WALNUT, CHESTNUT,
MAHOGANY, ROSEWOOD,
SYCAMORE; see FOREST, GOLF

wood, bend in   SNY

wood, hard   ASH, ELM, OAK,
ASPEN, BIRCH, EBONY,
MAPLE, NARRA, LOCUST,
MOLAVE, WALNUT, WILLOW,
HICKORY, MAHOGANY,
ROSEWOOD, GRENADILLA

wood measure   CORD, FATHOM

wood, piece of   DEAL, LATH,
SLAT, BOARD, PLANK,
SPRAG, STAVE, BILLET

wood, soft   FIR, PINE, CEDAR,
SPRUCE, HEMLOCK,
REDWOOD

woodchuck   MARMOT, WEJACK

woodcutter   LOGGER, SAWYER,
LUMBERJACK

wooded   BOSKY, SYLVAN

wooden   RIGID, STIFF, TREEN,
STOLID, XYLOID, DEADPAN,
LIFELESS, LIGNEOUS

woodland   WOOD(S), FOREST,
SYLVA(N)

woodpecker   IYNX, KATE,
PICULE, YAFFLE, FLICKER,
LOGCOCK, PICULET,
WITWALL, WRYNECK

woodpecker genus   JYNX, PICI,
YUNX

woodsman   HUNTER, LOGGER,
RANGER, TRAPPER,
FORESTER, LUMBERJACK

woodwind   OBOE, FLUTE,
CLARINET, BASSOON; see p. 642

woodwork   MOLDING,
PANELING

woodworking tool ADZ, AWL, ADZE, FROE, FROW, PLANE, CHISEL

woody TREEN, SYLVAN, XYLOID, LIGNEUS

Woody Allen wife ROSEN, LASSER, SOON YI

woof ABB, WEFT, TEXTURE

wool DOWN, FRIB, GARE, HAIR, YARN, TATE, FLOCK, FLEECE, FLOCCUS; see p. 535

wool cluster NEP

wool measure HEER

wool package FADGE

wool variety ALPACA, ANGORA, MERINO, VIRGIN, CHALLIS

woolen fabric REPP, BEIGE, CASHA, LODEN, MUNGO, TWEED, BEAVER, CAMLET, DUFFLE, FRIEZE, HODDEN, JERSEY, MELTON, MERINO, TARTAN, VELOUR, CHALLIE, CHALLIS, DELAINE, DOESKIN, ETAMINE, STAMMEL, WORSTED, PETERSHAM, LANDSDOWNE

woolly FLEECY, LANATE, LANOSE, PERONATE

woozy TIPSY, GROGGY, MUDDLED, CONFUSED, BEFUDDLED

word NEWS, TERM, LOGOS, PAROL, RHEMA, PAROLE, PLEDGE, ANAGRAM, PROMISE, TIDINGS, UTTERANCE

word for word VERBAL, LITERAL, TEXTUAL, VERBATIM

word game REBUS, BOGGLE, GHOSTS, RIDDLE, ANAGRAM, CHARADE, HANGMAN, ACROSTIC, SCRABBLE, GEOGRAPHY, CONUNDRUM, CROSSWORD, GUGGENHEIM, PALINDROME

word inventor COINER, NEOLOGIST

word misuse SOLECISM, MALAPROPISM

word of God LOGOS

word of honor OATH, PAROLE, PROMISE

word part SYL, SYLLABLE

word puzzle REBUS, ANAGRAM, CRYPTIC ACROSTIC, CROSSWORD, WORD SEARCH

word root ETYMON

word processor EDITOR

wordbook LEXICON, GLOSSARY, LIBRETTO, THESAURUS, VOCABULARY

wordiness VERBIAGE, PROLIXITY, VERBOSITY

wording DICTION, PHRASING

wordless MUTE, TACIT, AMAZED, SILENT

words TEXT, LYRICS, DISPUTE, ARGUMENT, LANGUAGE

wordy WINDY, PROLIX, DIFFUSE, TEDIOUS, VERBOSE, TALKATIVE

work FAG, JOB, PLY, MOIL, OPUS, TOIL, CHARE, CHORE, ERGON, GRIND, LABOR, SLAVE, STINT, POTTER, TRAVAIL

work group CREW, GANG, TEAM, SQUAD, DETAIL

work out SOLVE, TRAIN, DEVELOP, EXERCISE

work unit ERG(ON), KILERG

work up ROUSE, EXCITE, FOMENT, DEVELOP, ELABORATE

workable DOABLE, FEASIBLE, OPERABLE, PRACTICAL

workaday PLAIN, HUMDRUM, ROUTINE, ORDINARY, EVERYDAY, QUOTIDIAN

workaholic GRIND, ERGOPHILE, TASKMASTER

workbook TEXT, MANUAL, PRIMER

worked up FIRED, RILED, INFLAMED

worker ARRY, CREW, DOER, HAND, PEON, ROTO, VOLK, CAGER, COOLIE, TOILER, YEOMAN, ARTISAN, LABORER, OPERANT, OPERATOR, CRAFTSMAN, TECHNICIAN

worker, migratory HOBO, OKIE, PEON, BRACERO, FLOATER, WETBACK

workers FORCE, LABOR, STAFF, PERSONNEL

workhorse HACK, DRUDGE, TOILER, PLODDER

workhouse ASYLUM, ALMSHOUSE

working ON, ACTIVE, RUNNING, FUNCTIONAL, OPERATIONAL

workmanlike EXPERT, SKILLED, PROFESSIONAL

workroom	DEN, LAB, MILL, SHOP, PLANT, STUDY, STUDIO, ATELIER	worm track	NEREITE
		worms, can of	PROBLEM, TROUBLE, HEADACHE
works	PLANT, OEUVRE, FACTORY, MACHINERY	wormwood	MOXA, CHAGRIN, ABSINTHE, TARRAGON
workshop	LAB, MILL, PLANT, STUDIO, ATELIER, FACTORY	wormy	LOUSY, ROTTEN
		worn	OLD, USED, EROSE, JADED, SPENT, EFFETE, FRAYED, MAGGED, SHABBY, ABRADED, ATTRITE, TATTERED
worktable	DESK, BENCH
work up	IRK, (A)ROUSE, UPSET, EXCITE
world	LOKA, EARTH, GLOBE, COSMOS, MANKIND, UNIVERSE	worn out	BEAT, SHOT, JADED, SENT, TIRED, WEARY, BUSHED, POOPED, DECREPIT, EXHAUSTED
World War I battle	ARRAS, MARNE, SOMME, YPRES, AMIENS, ASIAGO, VERDUN, ARGONNE, CAMBRAI, CORONEL, JUTLAND, CAPORETTO, CHARLEROI, FALKLANDS, DOGGERBANK, TANNENBERG, CHATEAU THIERRY, VITTORIO VENETO	worried	BESET, VEXED, ANXIOUS, TROUBLED, CONCERNED
		worrisome	IRKSOME, TROUBLESOME
		worry	RUX, CARE, FRAB, FRET, STEW, CONCERN, LOOKOUT, DISTRESS; *see* VEX
		worsen	DECAY, DECLINE, PEJORATE, AGGRAVATE, DETERIORATE
World War I group	AEF, BEF, AMEX
World War II area	CBI, ETO, MTO	worship	PUJA, PRAY, ADORE, DULIA, HOMAGE, LATRIA, REVERE, RITUAL, IDOLIZE, VENERATE
World War II battle	BULGE, KURSK, LEYTE, LOMBOK, MIDWAY, TOBRUK, BRITAIN, IWO JIMA, JAVA SEA, SAVO SEA, CORAL SEA, EL ALAMEIN, GUADACANAL, STALINGRAD	worshipper(s)	FLOCK, ADORER, PRAYER, CONGREGATION
		worshipful	PIOUS, DEVOUT, RELIGIOUS
World War II conference	CAIRO	worst	BEAT, BEST, ROUT, DEFEAT
World War II landing	D DAY
World War II landing site	ORAN	worsted cloth	SERGE, ETAMINE, GABARDINE
worldly	LAY, LAIC, CARNAL, MORTAL, MUNDANE, SECULAR	worth	MERIT, VALUE, IMPORT, MEANING
world-shattering	NEW, RADICAL, INNOVATIVE	worthless	RIP, BAFF, RACA, LOSEL, PALTRY, TRASHY, NUGATORY
World's Fair sites	GHENT, OSAKA, PARIS, LONDON, VIENNA, CHICAGO, NEW YORK, SEATTLE, BRUSSELS, MONTREAL, VANCOUVER	worthwhile	USEFUL, GAINFUL, VALUABLE, BENEFICIAL
		worthy	HONEST, UPRIGHT, LAUDABLE, VALUABLE, DESERVING, MERITORIOUS
worldwide	*see* UNIVERSAL	would be	HOPEFUL, ASPIRING
worm	LOA, NAID, NAIS, NEMA, WORM, APODA, BORER, FLUKE, LEECH, ANOPLA, APODAN, CADDIS, ENOPLA, EUNICE, NEREIS, PALOLO, PEDATA, PLOIMA, SEAFAN, SYLLID, ANNELID, ASCARID, ASCARIS, PINWORM, ANNELIDA; *see p. 679*	wound	CUT, HURT, PAIN, SORE, STAB, VULN, INJURY, LESION, OFFEND, TRAUMA
		wrack and —	RUIN
		wraith	GHOST, SPIRIT, SPECTRE, APPARITION
worm, to	INCH, CRAWL, CREEP, SINUATE	wrangle	ROW, SPAR, SPAT, BICKER, HAGGLE, HASSLE, DISPUTE, SQUABBLE

wrangler	COWBOY, HAFTER, HERDER, HERDSMAN, STOCKMAN
wrap	LAP, FURL, STOLE, SWATHE, SWADDLE; see SHAWL, CLOAK
wrapper	BINDER, TILLOT, VESTURE, ENVELOPE
wrapping material	LEAF, CLOTH, PAPER, KRAFT, MATTING, CELLOPHANE
wrasse	BOLLAN, CUNNER, TAPIRO, CHOGSET, HOGFISH
wrath	see ANGER
wreak	EXACT, PUNISH, INFLICT, OPPRESS
wreath	LEI, ORLE, TORSE, INFULA, CIRCLET; see GARLAND
wreathe	COIL, WIND, TWIST, ENTWINE, ENVELOP, GARLAND, ENCIRCLE
wreck	RAZE, RUIN, BREAK, SMASH, CRACKUP, SHATTER
wreckage	DEBRIS, JETSAM, FLOTSAM
wrench	JERK, YANK, TWIST, MONKEY, SPRAIN, SPANNER, STILLSON
wrest	GRAB, JERK, REND, YANK, PLUCK, TWIST, WRING, ELICIT, EXTORT, SNATCH
wrestle	TUSSLE, GRAPPLE; see FIGHT
wrestler	MATMAN, MAULER, GRAPPLER
wrestling	SUMO
wrestling term	PIN, CHIP, FALL, HANK, HIPE, HYPE, LOCK, MARE, CLICK, HITCH, NELSON, BACKHEEL, CHANCERY, HEADLOCK, SCISSORS, TAKEDOWN, GRAPEVINE
wretch	WORM, KNAVE, ROGUE, RASCAL, CAITIFF, VILLAIN
wretched	SAD, MEAN, ABJECT, DISMAL, WOEFUL, FORLORN, PITIFUL, UNHAPPY, MISERABLE
wriggle	DODGE, SHIMMY, SQUIRM, WANGLE, WIGGLE
wriggler	WORM
wriggling	EELY
Wrigley Field team	CUBS
wring	TWIST, WREST, WRENCH, EXTRACT, SQUEEZE

wrinkle	FOLD, RUCK, RUGA, SEAM, ANGLE, RUGAE, PIMPLE, FURROW, PUCKER, CRINKLE, CRUMPLE, SHRIVEL
wrinkled	RUGOSE, RUGOUS
wrist	JOINT, CARPUS
wrist guard	BRACE
wrist injury	SPRAIN, FRACTURE
writ	AIEL, CAPE, BREVE, TALES, CAPIAS, ELEGIT, VENIRE, PRECIPE, PROCESS, SUMMONS, MANDAMUS, PRAECIPE, SUBPOENA
write	PEN, NOTE, FRAME, INDITE, NOTATE, SCRAWL, SCRIVE
write up	REPORT, SKETCH
writer	CLERK, PENMAN, PROSER, SCRIBE, COPYIST; see AUTHOR, POET, NOVELIST, DRAMATIST
writhe	TWIST, SQUIRM, CONTORT
writing	TEXT, PROSE, SCRIPT, LETTERING, INSCRIPTION, LITERATURE
writing instrument	NIB, PEN, BRUSH, CHALK, PLUME, QUILL, STYLE, PENCIL, STYLUS, SNORKEL, BALLPOINT
writing system	KANJI, LATIN, ROMAN, HANGUL, CHINESE, LINEAR A, LINEAR B, AKKADIAN, SUMERIAN, CUNEIFORM PICTORIAL, HIEROGLYPHIC
wrong(s)	BAD, EVIL, HARM, MALA, TORT, ABUSE, AMISS, MALUM, DAMAGE, INJURE, OFFEND, IMMORAL, ERRONEOUS, INCORRECT
wrongdoer	CROOK, FELON, THIEF, KILLER, OUTLAW, SINNER, CULPRIT, CRIMINAL, HOODLUM, CRIMINAL, OFFENDER, MALEFACTOR
wrongful	UNFAIR, UNJUST, ILLEGAL, IMPROPER, UNLAWFUL
wrongheaded	RASH, UNWISE, FOOLISH, STUBBORN, MISGUIDED
wrongly	FALSELY, SINFULLY, IMPROPERLY, MISTAKENLY, ERRONEOUSLY
wroth	ANGRY, CROSS, IRATE

wrought	SHAPED, FASHIONED
wry	DRY, ASKEW, IRONIC, TWISTED, CONTRARY, PERVERSE, SARDONIC, DISTORTED
wryneck	WEET, LOXIA, WHIPLASH, TORTICOLLIS
Wuthering Heights author	BRONTE
Wuthering Heights character	CATHY, EDGAR, NELLY, HARETON, LOCKWOOD, HEATHCLIFF
Wyandot	*see* WENDAT
Wycliffe disciple	LOLLARD
Wyoming	*see also p. 615*
Wyoming city/state	CODY, LUSK, BASIN, DIXON, CASPER, SAVERY, LARAMIE, RAWLINS, WORLAND, CHEYENNE, GILLETTE, SHERIDAN, SUNDANCE
Wyoming Indian	UTE, CROW, ARAPAHO, SHOSHONE
Wyoming mountain	HUNT, CLOUD, GREEN, LEIDY, CROSBY, HOLMES, ISABEL, NEEDLE, BURWELL, DEADMAN, FORTRESS, WASHBURN, GANNETT, WYOMING, TEAPOTDOME
Wyoming mountain range	GREEN, ROCKY, TETON, BIGHORN, LARAMIE, SEMINOE, WYOMING, ABSAROKA, SALT RIVER, RATTLESNAKE
Wyoming river	BEAR, GREEN, SNAKE, BITTER, NOWOOD, PLATTE, POWDER, BIGHORN, LARAMIE, CHEYENNE, NIOBRARA, SHOSHONE, SWEETWATER, YELLOWSTONE

X

X	EX, XI, CHI, TEN, MARK, XRAY, CROSS, SIGNATURE
Xanadu river	ALPH
Xanthippe	SCOLD, SHREW, VIRAGO, TERMAGANT
Xanthippe's husband	SOCRATES
Xerxes relative	ATOSSA, DARIUS, ESTHER
X ray	EXAMINE, ROENTGEN, TOMOGRAPH, PHOTOGRAPH
X-ray inventor	RO(E)NTGEN

X-shaped	XED, CHIASMAL, CRUCIATE
xylophone	SARON, GAMELAN, MARIMBA, GAMELANG, GIGELIRA, STICCADO, VIBRAHARP

Y

Y('s)	WYE, YOK, WIES, YODH, YANKEE, UPSILON
yabber	TALK, CHATTER
yacht	*see* VESSEL
yacht basin	MARINA
yahoo	LOUT, BRUTE, SAVAGE
Yahweh	GOD, YHVH, YHWH, JEHOVAH
yak	OX, SARLAK, SARLYK
yak crossbreed	DZO, ZUM, ZOBO
Yale	ELI
Yalta conference member	STALIN, CHURCHILL, ROOSEVELT
Yale major	DRAMA
yam	HOI, UBE, UBI, UVE, UVI, KAAWI
yammer	HOWL, WAIL, YELL, SHOUT, WHIMPER, COMPLAIN
yang, *opp. of*	YIN
Yangtze River	CHANG, JINSHA
Yangtze River city	WUHU, BATANG, NANKING, YICHANG, CHONGQING
Yangtze tributary	WU, HAN, MIN, YALONG, JIALING
yank	JERK, TWIST
Yankee	AMERICAN, NORTHERNER
yap	NAG, YIP, TALK, JABBER, SQUAWK; *see* CRY
yard	QUAD, SPAR, GARTH, PATIO
yardage	LENGTH, DISTANCE
yardstick	RULER, MEASURE, STANDARD, BENCHMARK, CRITERION
yarn	ABB, FIB, FOX, GARN, KNOP, SHAP, SLUB, TALE, INKLE, THRUM, CREWEL, SPINEL, THREAD; *see* STORY, FIBER
yarn count	TYPP
yarn measure	COP, LEA, RAP, CLEW, CLUE, HANK, HEER, SKEIN
yaw	GANE, GAPE, JIBE, TACK,

	VEER, LURCH, STEER, SWERVE
yawl	DANDY, KETCH, SAILBOAT, JOLLYBOAT
yawn	GAPE, YAUP, YAWP, OSCITATE
yawning	GAPING, CAVERNOUS
yawp	CRY, YAP, BAWL, GAPE, HOWL, WAIL, YAWN
yaws	FRAMB(O)ESIA
yearling	KID, LAMB, NEWBORN
year	ANNO, HAAB
year type	LEAP, LUNAR, SOLAR, FISCAL, CALENDAR, SIDEREAL, TROPICAL
yearbook	ANNUAL, ALMANAC
Yearling author	RAWLINGS
yearly	ANNUAL, ETESIAN, PERANNUM
yearly payment	ANNAT, TITHE
yearn	ACHE, FLAG, PINE, COVET, CRAVE, HANKER
yearning	YEN, WISH, DESIRE, HUNGER, THIRST, LONGING
yeast	LOB, BARM, BEES, KOJI, SOTS, LEAVEN, ANAMITE, FERMENT
yegg	THIEF, ROBBER, BURGLER, SAFECRACKER
yell	GOWL, HOWL, YOWL; see CRY
yellow	AZO, BUFF, GOLD, AMBER, GREGE, OCHER, AFRAID, CRAVEN, GOLDEN, MELINE, QUINCE, CHICKEN, CITRINE, SAFFRON, PRIMROSE; see p. 531
yellow ocher	SIL
Yellow Sea arm	BOHAI
yellowish	SALLOW, XANTHIC, LUTESCENT; see p. 531
yelp	YAP, YIP, KIYI, YAUP, YAWP, YOUP
Yemen, capital of	SANAA
Yemen city	ADEN, HAYS, QANA, RADA, RIDA, ABYAN, AMRAN, MARIB, MINAR, MOCHA, NISAB, SALIF, SANAA, SAYUN, TAIZZ, TARIM, ZABID, DHAMAR, SAYHUT, SHAQRA, SIRWAH, SHIHARA
Yemen money	FILS, RIAL, DINAR, RIYAL
Yemen neighbor	OMAN, ERITREA, SAUDI ARABIA
yen	URGE, TASTE, DESIRE,

	HUNGER, LIKING, CRAVING, YEARNING
yeoman	SQUIRE, DECKHAND, MYRMIDON, ASSISTANT
yes	AY, OK, AYE, YEA, YEP, OKAY, YEAH, AGREED
yet	BUT, SOFAR, STILL, THOUGH, BESIDES, HOWEVER
yeti	MONSTER, SNOWMAN
yew	TREE, CONIFER, HEMLOCK
yew genus	TAXUS
Yiddish author	DIK, AS(C)H, LEYB, GORDIN, NISTER, PERETS, PINSKI, SINGER, ALEICHEM, SCHWARTZ
yield	BOW, NET, BEND, CEDE, GIVE, WAIVE, COMPLY, RETURN, FURNISH, PRODUCE
yielding	DOCILE, PLIANT, ELASTIC, ACQUIESCENT
yodel	SING, WARBLE
yoga	HATHA, JNANA, KARMA, BHAKTI
yoga trance	DHYANA, DHARANA, SAMADHI
yogi	FAKIR, JNANI, SWAMI, YOGIN; see ASCETIC
Yogi —	BEAR, BERRA
Yogi Bear character	BOOBOO
yoke	TIE, CANG, JOIN, LINK, TEAM, BANG(H)Y, CANGUE, COUPLE, INSPAN, HARNESS, SERVITUDE
yoke part	BOW, RIEM, SKEY, OXBOW, RIEMPIE
yokel	OAF, HICK, RUBE, YAHOO, RUSTIC, BUMPKIN
yolk	YELLOW, VITELLUS
Yom —	KIPPUR
yore	ELD, LONGAGO, WAYBACK
Yorkshire city	LEEDS
Yorkshire river	ESK, URE, NIDD, OUSE, DERWENT
young	NEW, RAW, FRESH, GREEN, PUERILE, TEENAGE, IMMATURE, JUVENILE, YOUTHFUL, ADOLESCENT
young animal(s)	see also specific animal CUB, KID, KIT, PUP, CALF, COLT, FOAL, GILT, JOEY, STOT, BROOD, FILLY, PUPPY, SHOAT, WHELP, LITTER, SUCKLING, YEARLING

young bird *see also specific bird*
EYAS, CHICK, POULT, EAGLET,
CHEEPER, FLAPPER, NESTLING,
SQUEAKER, FLEDGLING
young fish *see also specific fish*
FRY, FINGERLING
youngster   KID, LAD, TAD, TOT,
TEEN, TIKE, TYKE, CHILD,
MINOR, YOUTH, SHAVER,
URCHIN, GOSSOON,
TEENAGER
youth   LAD, TEEN, CHIEL,
MINOR, SHAVER, INFANCY,
PUBERTY, MINORITY,
TEENAGER, CHILDHOOD,
PUERILITY, STRIPLING,
YOUNGSTER, ADOLESCENCE
youthful   BOYISH, CALLOW,
NEANIC, GIRLISH, PUERILE
Yseult   *see* ISOLDE
Yucatan people   MAYA
yucca   PITA, DATE
Yugoslav language   *see* SLAVIC
Yugoslav measure   OKA, RIP,
AKOV, RALO, DONUM,
KHVAT, LANAZ, PALAZ,
STOPA, RALICA, MOTYKA
Yugoslav money   PARA, DINAR
Yugoslav premier   BROZ, TITO
Yugoslav weight   TOVAR,
WAGON, DRAMMA,
SATLIJK
Yugoslavia   *see* SERBIA AND
MONTENEGRO, CROATIA,
SLOVENIA, MACEDONIA,
BOSNIA AND HERZEGOVINA
Yukon Territory   *see also p. 614*
Yukon Territory city/town   ELSA,
MAYO, SNAG, MINTO,
DAWSON, DONJEK, MACRAE,
TESLIN, TAKHINI,
CARCROSS, CERMACKS,
WHITEHORSE
Yukon Territory lake   MAYO,
KLUANE, FRANCES, AISHIHIK
Yukon Territory mountain   KEELE,
LOGAN, SELOUS, BURGESS,
LUCANIA, CAMPBELL
Yukon Territory mountain range
ROCKY, SELWYN, CASSIAR,
OGILVIE, STELIAS,
RICHARDSON
Yukon Territory river   COAL,
HART, PEEL, EAGLE, FIRTH,
LEWES, LIARD, PELLY,
SNAKE, WHITE, YUKON,
HYLAND, TESLIN, NISLING,
KLONDIKE, MACMILLAN,
PORCUPINE

yule   CHRISTMAS
yummy   TASTY, LUSCIOUS,
DELICIOUS, DELECTABLE

Z

Z   ZED, ZETA, ZULU, ZAYIN,
IZZARD
Zaire   *see* CONGO (Dem. Rep.)
Zaire, formerly   BELGIAN
CONGO, CONGO FREE STATE
Zaire, capital of   KINSHASA
Zaire city/town   BENI, BOMA,
GEMENA, KITWIT, BUTEMBO,
KABINDA, KANANGA,
KOLWEZI, KINSHASA,
MBANDAKA, GANDAJIKA,
MBUJIMAYI, LUBUMBASHI
Zaire falls   INGA,
LIVINGSTONE
Zaire lake   KIVU, MWERU,
ALBERT, EDWARD,
TANGANYIKA
Zaire money   ZAIRE
Zaire mountain range   CRYSTAL,
MITUMBA, VIRUNGA,
RUWENZORI
Zaire neighbor   CAR, CONGO,
SUDAN, ANGOLA, RWANDA,
ZAMBIA, UGANDA, BURUNDI
Zaire president   MOBUTO
Zaire river   RUKI, UELE,
CONGO, KASAI, LINDI, LOILE,
LUVUA, WAMBA, ZAIRE,
LOMAMI, LUKUGA, UBANGI,
ARUWIMI, LUALABA, LUKENIE,
LULONGA, SALONGA,
SANKURU, TSHUAPA, ITIMBIRI
Zal relative   *see* RUSTAM
Zambezi tributary   CHOBE,
KAFUE, SHIRE, LUANGWA,
SANYATI
Zambia, capital of   LUSAKA
Zambian city/town   CHOMA,
KABWE, KITWE, MANSA,
MONGU, MONZE, NDOLA,
KSAMA, LUSAKA, CHIPATA,
SENAUGA
Zambian lake   MWERU,
BANGWEULU, TANGANYIKA
Zambian language   *see* BANTU
Zambian money   KWACHA
Zambian mountain   SUNZU,
MAHONI
Zambian people   LOZI, BEMBA,
LUNDA, NGONI, TONGA,
KAONDE, LUVALE, NYANJA

Zambian river **KAFUE,**	zigzag **YAW, TACK, WIND,**
ZAMBEZI, LUANGWA,	**FORKED, CRANK(LE),**
KAMBONDO	**CROOKED, MEANDER**
zany **FOOL, CRAZY, WACKY,**	Zillah relative **LEMECH,**
MADCAP, SCREWY	**NAAMAH**
Zanzibar weight **GISLA**	zilch *see* **ZERO**
zap **END, KAYO, KILL, BLAST**	Zilpah relative **GAD, ASHER,**
zeal **ELAN, ZEST, ARDOR,**	**JACOB**
GUSTO, VERVE, FERVOR,	Zimbabwe, capital of **HARARE**
RELISH	Zimbabwe city/town **GWERU,**
zealot **PARTISAN,**	**HARARE, HWANGE,**
ENTHUSIAST; *see* **FAN,**	**KADOMA, KARIBA, MUTARE,**
FANATIC	**KEWKWE, MASHAVA,**
zealotry **DEVOTION,**	**BULAWAYO, MASVINGO,**
FANATICISM	**CHITUNGWIZA**
zealous **AVID, EAGER,**	Zimbabwe falls **VICTORIA**
ARDENT, FERVID, EARNEST,	Zimbabwe, formerly **RHODESIA**
FERVENT	Zimbabwe leader **MUGABE**
Zebedee relative **JOHN, JAMES**	Zimbabwe money **DOLLAR**
zebra **DAUW, QUAGGA,**	Zimbabwe mountain **BINGA,**
ZEBRASS, ZEBROID, ZEBRULA	**INYANGANI**
zebra crossbreed **ZOBO**	Zimbabwe neighbor **ZAMBIA,**
zebra, young **FOAL**	**BOTSWANA, MOZAMBIQUE,**
Zechariah relative **ABI,**	**SOUTH AFRICA**
ELIZABETH	Zimbabwe river **SABI, TULI,**
Zen **CHAN**	**LUNDI, LIMPOPO, MWENEZI,**
Zen goal **SATORI**	**SANYATI, ZAMBEZO**
Zen technique **KOAN, MONDO,**	zinc **BLENDE, SPELTER,**
SATORI	**TUTENAG**
zenith **TOP, ACME, APEX,**	zing **PEP, VIM, DASH, ELAN,**
PEAK, HEYDAY, SUMMIT,	**ZEST, PUNCH, VIGOR,**
PINNACLE	**ENERGY, VITALITY**
zenith, opposite of **NADIR**	Zionism founder **HERZL**
Zeno follower **CYNIC, STOIC**	zip **PEP, TANG, VIGOR, STINGO**
zephyr **WAFT, WIND, DRAFT,**	zipper **TALON, CLOSURE,**
BREATH, BREEZE	**FASTENER**
zeppelin **BLIMP, AIRSHIP,**	Zipporah relative **MOSES,**
DIRIGIBLE	**ELIEZER, GERSHOM**
Zeresh husband **HAMAN**	zippy **FAST, RAPID, SWIFT,**
zero **NIL, ZIP, ZILCH,**	**ZESTY, FRISKY, LIVELY,**
NOUGHT, NOTHING	**SNAPPY, ZESTFUL**
Zeruah relative **JEROBOAM**	zircon **AZORITE, JACINTH,**
Zerubbabel son **OHEL**	**JARGOON**
Zeruiah relative **JOAB, ASAHEL,**	zither-like instrument **ASOR,**
ABISHAI	**KOTO, VINA, CITHARA**
zest **BITE, TANG, GUSTO,**	zodiac signs *see p. 741*
TASTE, RELISH, PIQUANCY;	zodiacal situation **HAYZ**
see **ZEAL**	Zola novel **NANA, REVE,**
zestful **KEEN, ZIPPY, LIVELY,**	**TERRE, WRITE, DEBACLE,**
PIQUANT, ENERGETIC,	**GERMINAL**
ENTHUSIASTIC	Zola, officer defended by
Zeus epithet **AMMON, SOTER,**	**DREYFUS**
TELEIOS	zombie **ROBOT, ANDROID**
Zeus relative *see pp. 646, 654*	zone **AREA, BELT, CLIME,**
Zhivago love **LARA**	**TRACT, REGION, SECTOR,**
Zibiah relative **JOASH,**	**DISTRICT**
AHAZIAH	zonked **HIGH, DOPED,**
ziggurat **TOWER, TEMPLE,**	**STONED, WASTED,**
PYRAMID	**DRUGGED**

zoo	**VIVARIUM, MENAGERIE**
zoom	**ZIP, WHIZ, ROCKET**
Zoroastrian	**YEMA, PARSI,**
	PARSEE, MASDAIST
Zoroastrian scripture	**AVESTA**
zoster	**SHINGLES**

Zulu language	**BANTU**
Zulu warrior	**IMPI**
Zuni	**PUEBLO**
Zuni cities	**(SEVEN CITIES OF)**
	CIBOLA

SECTION II
Categories

ABBREVIATIONS AND ACRONYMS

AA Alcoholics Anonymous
AB bachelor of arts, Alberta
AC alternating current; account; air conditioning
AD anno Domini; active duty
AE aged (Lat.)
AK Alaska
AL Alabama; American League
AM ante meridiem; amplitude modulation; master of arts
AP Associated Press
AR Arkansas
AS American Samoa; Anglo-Saxon
AV Authorized Version (of the Bible); audiovisual; average; avenue
AZ Arizona
BA Bachelor of Arts
BC before Christ; British Columbia
BD bachelor of divinity; board
BF boldface (type)
BN battalion
BS bachelor of science
BT baronet
BU bushel
BV Blessed Virgin (Mary)
BX base exchange
CA California; Central America; Coast Artillery; chartered accountant
CB citizens band; Companion of the Bath
CC carbon copy; cubic centimeters
CD cord
CE Common (or Christian) Era; civil engineer
CF compare; center fielder
CG centigram
CH China; Chinese; church; chapter
CK check
CL centiliter(s)
CM centimeter
CO Colorado; conscientious objector; commanding officer; company; county
CP communist party
CR credit; creditor
CT cent(s); carat
CU cubic
CZ Canal Zone (Panama)
DA district attorney
DB decibel
DC direct current; District of Columbia
DD doctor of divinity
DE Delaware
DL deciliter; deciliters
DM decimeter; decimeters; deutsche mark
DO ditto
DP displaced person
DR doctor; debit; debtor; dram
DZ dozen; dozens
ED editor(ial)
EE electrical engineer
EG for example (Lat., exempli gratia); Egypt(ian)
EP extended play
EU European Union
EX Exodus
EZ Ezra
FB fullback
FF and following (pages)
FL flourished
FM frequency modulation
FN footnote
FR father; French
FT feet; foot; fort
FY fiscal year
GA Georgia
GB gigabyte; Great Britain
GI general (or government) issue; a private soldier
GK Greek
GM gram; grams
GR grain; gross
GU Guam
HA hectare
HB halfback
HI Hawai(ian Islands)
HJ here lies (Lat., hic jacet)
HM His Majesty; Her Majesty
HP horsepower
HQ headquarters
HR House of Representatives; hour; hours
HS high school
HT height
HZ hertz
IA Iowa
IC integrated circuit
ID Idaho; id est (Lat., that is)
IE that is (Lat., id est)
IL Illinois
IN inch; inches
IO input/output
IQ intelligence quotient
IS island(s); Isaiah; intermediate school
IT Italian; italic (type)
IV intravenous
JD doctor of laws (Lat., juris doctor)
JG junior grade
JP justice of the peace
JR junior
JV junior varsity

KB	kilobyte		Miss/Mrs.; manuscript		computer; politically correct;
KC	King's Counsel; Knights of Columbus; kilocycle(s); koruna (Czech currency)	**MT**	Montana; mountain		piece; percent; postcard
KG	knight of the Order of the Garter; keg(s); kilogram(s)	**NA**	North America; not applicable; not available	**PD**	police department; paid
		NB	Nebraska; New Brunswick; note well (Lat., nota bene)	**PE**	Prince Edward Island
KM	kilometer			**PG**	parental guidance recommended (a motion picture rating)
KO	knockout	**NC**	North Carolina;		
KP	kitchen police		no charge		
KT	Knight Templar; knight	**ND**	North Dakota	**PH**	a measure of acidity or alkalinity
		NE	northeast; New England		
KW	kilowatt(s)	**NF**	Newfoundland and Labrador	**PI**	Philippine islands; private investigator
KY	Kentucky				
LA	Louisiana	**NG**	no good	**PK**	peck
LB	pound	**NH**	New Hampshire	**PL**	plural
LC	landing craft; lower case (type)	**NL**	National League; New Latin	**PM**	post meridiem; prime minister; postmaster
LF	left field				
LI	Long Island	**NO**	north; northern; number	**PO**	post office; purchase order
LL	Late Latin				
LP	long play	**NP**	no protest; notary public	**PP**	pages; parcel post
LS	landing ship			**PQ**	Province of Quebec
LT	lieutenant	**NS**	new style; Nova Scotia		
MA	Massachusetts; master of arts	**NT**	New Testament; Northwest Territories	**PR**	Puerto Rico; public relations; pair
MB	megabyte; Manitoba			**PS**	postscript (Lat., post scriptum); Psalm(s)
MC	master of ceremonies; member of Congress	**NU**	Nunavut		
		NV	Nevada	**PT**	part; pint; point; part-time
		NZ	New Zealand		
MD	Maryland; Doctor of Medicine (Lat., medicinae doctor)	**OB**	he (she) died (Lat., obiit)	**PX**	post exchange
		OD	overdose; Officer of the Day; overdraft; olive drab (uniforms); overdrawn	**QB**	quarterback
				QC	Quebec
ME	Maine; Middle English; Methodist Episcopal; mechanical engineer			**QT**	quart
				QV	which see (Lat., quod vide)
		OE	Old English		
MF	Middle French	**OF**	Old French	**RC**	Red Cross; Reserve Corps; Roman Catholic
MI	mile	**OH**	Ohio		
ML	milliliter	**OK**	Oklahoma	**RD**	rural delivery
MM	millimeter; Messieurs	**ON**	Old Norse; Ontario	**RF**	radio frequency; right field
				RI	Rhode Island
MN	Minnesota	**OP**	opus	**RM**	ream (paper); room
MO	Missouri; money order; mode of operation (Lat., modus operandi); month(s)	**OR**	Oregon; operating room		
		OS	operating system	**RN**	registered nurse
		OT	Old Testament	**RR**	railroad
		OX	Oxford	**RT**	right
		OZ	ounce(s)	**RV**	recreational vehicle
MP	military police; member of parliament	**PA**	Pennsylvania; public address; purchasing agent; press agent	**RX**	medical prescription
MR	mister			**RY**	railway
MS	Mississippi; master of science;	**PC**	personal	**SA**	South Africa; South America;

	corporation; sex appeal	**VT**	Vermont; verb transitive	**ADM**	admiral
SC	South Carolina; science; small capital letters (type)	**WI**	Wisconsin; West Indies	**ADP**	automatic data processing
		WK	week; work	**ADT**	atlantic daylight time
SD	South Dakota	**WM**	William	**ADV**	adverb
SE	southeast	**WO**	warrant officer; without	**AEC**	Atomic Energy Commission
SF	science fiction	**WV**	West Virginia	**AEF**	American Expeditionary Force
SI	Staten Island	**WW**	world war		
SJ	Society of Jesus (Jesuits)	**WY**	Wyoming	**AFB**	air force base
SK	Saskatchewan	**XL**	extra large	**AFC**	automatic frequency control; American Football Conference
SO	south; southern	**XP**	Christ		
SP	shore patrol; Spain; Spaniard; Spanish	**XT**	Christ		
		YD	yard		
		YR	year(s)	**AFL**	American Federation of Labor
SQ	square	**YT**	Yukon Territory		
SR	senior; senor; sister			**AFR**	Africa, African
		AAA	American Automobile Association	**AFT**	American Federation of Teachers
SS	saints; steamship; Social Security; shortstop				
		AAU	Amateur Athletic Union	**AGT**	agent
ST	saint; street	**ABA**	American Bar Association; American Boxing Association; American Basketball Association	**AID**	Agency for International Development
SW	southwest				
TA	teaching assistant			**AKA**	also known as; alias
TB	tuberculosis				
TD	touchdown			**AKC**	American Kennel Club
TM	transcendental meditation				
		ABC	American Broadcasting Company; Argentina, Brazil, and Chile	**ALA**	Alabama
TN	Tennessee; trade name			**ALP**	American Labor Party
TP	township			**AMA**	American Medical Association
TR	troop				
TT	Trust Territories			**AMB**	ambassador
TV	television			**AME**	American Methodist Episcopal
TX	Texas	**ABD**	all but dissertation; abdomen		
UC	upper case letters (type)	**ABM**	antiballistic missile	**AMG**	allied military government
UL	Underwriters Laboratories	**ABR**	abridgment	**AMP**	ampere; amperage
		ABS	able-bodied seaman; absent		
UN	United Nations			**AMT**	amount
UP	United Press International	**ACF**	Administration for Children and Families	**APB**	all points bulletin
				APO	army post office
US	United States (of America)			**APR**	annual percentage rate; April
		ADA	Americans for Democratic Action; American Dental Association; Americans with Disabilities Act		
UT	Utah			**APT**	apartment
VA	Virginia; Veterans' Administration			**ARC**	American (National) Red Cross
VC	Victoria Cross; Vietcong; video recorder				
				ARK	Arkansas
VD	venereal disease	**ADC**	Aid to Dependent Children	**ARM**	adjustable rate mortgage
VI	Virgin Islands; verb intransitive	**ADD**	attention deficit disorder	**ARR**	arrangement
				ART	article
VP	vice-president	**ADJ**	adjective; adjutant	**ASC**	American Society of Cinematographers
VS	veterinary surgeon; versus				

AST	Alaska Standard Time	BRO	brother	CEL	Celsius
ASV	American Standard Version	BPS	bits per second	CEO	chief executive officer
		BRO	bros; brother(s)		
ATC	air traffic control	BSA	Boy Scouts of America	CFL	Canadian Football League
ATF	Bureau of Alcohol, Tobacco, and Firearms	BSC	bachelor of science	CFM	cubic feet per minute
		BSH	bushel; bushels	CFO	chief financial officer
ATL	Atlantic	BTU	British thermal unit	CFS	cubic feet per second
ATM	automated teller machine	BVM	Blessed Virgin Mary	CGS	centimeter gram second
ATT	attorney	BWI	British West Indies	CHE	chemical engineer
ATV	all-terrain vehicle	BYO	bring your own	CHM	chairman
AUG	August	CAA	Civil Aeronautics Authority	CHR	Christian
AUS	Australia			CIA	Central Intelligence Agency
AUX	auxiliary	CAB	Civil Aeronautics Board		
AVE	avenue	CAD	computer-aided design	CID	Criminal Investigation Department
AVG	average				
BBA	bachelor of business administration	CAL	California	CIE	company (Fr., compagnie)
		CAM	computer-aided manufacturing		
BBB	Better Business Bureau	CAN	Canada; Canadian	CIO	Congress of Industrial Organizations
BBC	British Broadcasting Corporation	CAP	capital(ized)		
		CAR	carat	CIS	Commonwealth of Independent States (12 members of former Soviet Union)
BBL	barrels	CAT	computerized axial tomography		
BBS	bulletin board system				
BCE	before Common (or Christian) Era	CBC	Canadian Broadcasting Corporation	CIT	cited; citation
				CLI	cost-of-living index
BEF	British Expeditionary Force or Forces	CBI	China, Burma, and India	CLU	Civil Liberties Union
		CBO	Congressional Budget Office	COD	cash on delivery
BFA	bachelor of fine arts			COL	Colonel; Columbia; Colorado; Colombia
BHP	brake horsepower	CBS	Columbia Broadcasting System		
BIA	Bureau of Indian Affairs	CBT	Chicago Board of Trade	COM	commander; commodore; commerce
BIB	Bible; Biblical	CBX	computerized branch exchange	COO	chief operating officer
BID	twice a day (in prescription)				
BIO	biography	CCC	Civilian Conservation Corps; Commodity Credit Corporation	COR	Corinthians
BLG	building			CPA	certified public accountant
BLT	bacon, lettuce, and tomato (sandwich)			CPI	consumer price index
		CDC	Centers for Disease Control and Prevention	CPL	corporal
BMI	Broadcast Music, Inc.			CPO	chief petty officer
BOP	Federal Bureau of Prisons	CDR	commander	CPR	cardiopulmonary resuscitation
		CDT	central daylight time		
BOR	borough				
BOT	botany	CEA	Council of Economic Advisors	CPU	central processing unit
BPD	barrels per day				
BRB	be right back				

CRC	Civil Rights Commission		mittee		toxicated
CRT	cathode-ray tube	DNR	do not resuscitate	DWT	pennyweight
CSA	Confederate States of America	DNS	domain name service	ECA	Economic Cooperation Administration
CST	central standard time	DOA	dead on arrival	ECG	electrocardiogram
CTS	cents	DOC	doctor; Department of Commerce	EDP	electronic data processing
CWO	chief warrant officer	DOD	Department of Defense	EDT	eastern daylight time
CWT	hundredweight	DOE	Department of Energy	EDW	Edward
CYO	Catholic Youth Organization	DOJ	Department of Justice	EEC	European Economic Community
DAR	Daughters of the American Revolution	DOL	Department of Labor	EEG	electroencephalogram
DAT	digital audio tape	DOS	disk operating system; Department of State	EEO	Equal Employment Opportunity
DAV	Disabled American Veterans	DOT	Department of Transportation	EFT	electronic funds transfer
DBA	doing business as	DOZ	dozen; dozens	EKG	electrocardiogram
DBL	double	DPH	doctor of philosophy	EMB	embassy
DCM	Distinguished Conduct Medal	DPI	dots per inch	ENC	enclosure
DDS	doctor of dental surgery	DPL	denied persons list	ENE	east-northeast
DDT	dichlorodiphenyltrichloroethane (an insecticide)	DPT	department; diphtheria, pertussis, and tetanus	ENG	England; English
				ENS	ensign
				EOE	equal opportunity employer
DEA	Drug Enforcement Administration	DPW	Department of Public Works	EPA	Environmental Protection Agency
DEC	December	DSC	doctor of science; Distinguished Service Cross	EPH	Ephesians
DEG	degree			ERA	earned-run average; Equal Rights Amendment
DEL	Delaware				
DEM	Democratic; Democrat	DSL	digital subscriber line	ESA	Economic Stability Administration
DEN	Denmark	DSM	Distinguished Service Medal		
DEW	distant early warning	DSO	Distinguished Service Order	ESE	east-southeast
DFC	Distinguished Flying Cross	DST	daylight saving time	ESL	English as a second language
DFM	Distinguished Flying Medal	DTP	desktop publishing; diptheria, tetanus, and pertussis	ESP	extrasensory perception; especially
DIR	director				
DKR	Danish kroner			ESQ	esquire
DMD	Doctor of Dental Medicine	DTS	delirium tremens	EST	eastern standard time; Estonia; established; estimate(d)
DMV	Department of Motor Vehicles	DUI	driving under the influence (of alcohol, drugs, etc.)	ETA	estimated time of arrival
DMZ	demilitarized zone				
DNA	deoxyribonucleic acid	DVM	doctor of veterinary medicine	ETC	et cetera (and so forth)
DNC	Democratic National Committee	DWI	driving while intoxicated	ETH	Ethiopia
				ETO	European the-

	ater of operations	FWS	Fish and Wildlife Service		tion, and Welfare
ETV	educational television	FYI	for your information	HGT	height
EVA	extravehicular activity	GAL	Galatians; gallon; gallons	HHS	Department of Health and Human Services
FAA	Federal Aviation Administration	GAO	General Accounting Office	HIV	human immunodeficiency virus
FAM	Free and Accepted Masons	GAR	Grand Army of the Republic	HMO	health maintenance organization
FAO	Food and Agriculture Organization	GDP	gross domestic product	HMS	His (Her) Majesty's Ship
FAQ	frequently asked question	GED	general equivalency diploma	HON	the honorable
FBI	Federal Bureau of Investigation	GEN	Genesis; general	HOS	Hosea
FCA	Farm Credit Administration	GEO	George	HOV	high-occupancy vehicle
FCC	Federal Communications Commission	GER	German; Germany; gerund	HRA	Health Resources Administration
FDA	Food and Drug Administration	GHQ	general headquarters	HRH	His (Her) Royal Highness
FEA	Federal Energy Administration	GIF	graphics interchange format	HRS	hours
FEB	February	GMT	Greenwich mean time	HST	Hawaiian standard time
FED	federal	GNP	gross national product	HTS	heights
FEM	feminine; female	GOP	Grand Old Party (Republican party)	HUD	Department of Housing and Urban Development
FET	Federal excise tax	GOV	governor	HWY	highway
FFF	very loud (music)	GPA	grade point average	ICC	Interstate Commerce Commission
FFV	First Families of Virginia	GPM	graduated payment mortgage	ICU	intensive care unit
FHA	Federal Housing Administration	GPO	Government Printing Office	IHC	Jesus
FIG	figuratively	GPS	Global Positioning System	IHS	Jesus
FIN	Finland; Finnish	GPU	(formerly) Soviet Secret Police	ILA	International Longshoremen's Association
FLA	Florida	GRE	Graduate Record Examination	ILO	International Labor Organization
FOB	free on board				
FOE	Fraternal Order of Eagles; Fraternal Order of Elks	GSA	Girl Scouts of America; General Services Administration	IMF	International Monetary Fund
FPC	Federal Power Commission	GUI	graphical user interface	IMO	in my opinion
FPO	fleet post office	HAB	Habakkuk	INC	incorporated
FRB	Federal Reserve Board	HAG	Haggai	IND	Indiana
FRI	Friday	HBO	Home Box Office	INF	infinitive
FTC	Federal Trade Commission	HCP	handicap	INS	International News Service; Immigration and Naturalization Service
FTP	file transfer protocol	HDW	hardware		
		HEB	Hebrew(s)		
FWD	forward; four-wheel drive	HEW	Department of Health, Education,	IOC	International Olympic Com-

	mittee	**JUN**	June	**MAD**	mutual assured
IOU	I owe you	**KAN**	Kansas		destruction (nu-
IPA	International	**KAS**	Kansas		clear war)
	Phonetic Al-	**KGB**	the intelligence	**MAJ**	major
	phabet		agency of the	**MAN**	Manitoba
IRA	individual re-		former Soviet	**MAP**	modified Ameri-
	tirement		Union		can plan
	account; Irish	**KIA**	killed in action	**MAR**	March
	Republican	**KJV**	King James	**MAX**	maximum
	Army		Version	**MBA**	master of busi-
IRC	internet relay	**KKK**	Ku Klux Klan		ness administra-
	chat; Interna-	**KWH**	kilowatt-hour		tration
	tional Red Cross	**LAB**	Labrador	**MDT**	mountain day-
IRE	Ireland	**LAM**	Lamentations		light time
IRO	International	**LAN**	local area	**MED**	medicine
	Refugee Organi-		network	**MET**	metropolitan
	zation	**LAT**	Latin; latitude	**MEX**	Mexican
IRR	irregular	**LAV**	lavatory	**MFD**	manufactured
IRS	Internal Reve-	**LBO**	leveraged	**MFG**	manufacturing
	nue Service		buyout	**MFN**	most favored
ISL	island	**LBS**	pounds		nation
ISO	International	**LCD**	liquid crystal	**MFR**	manufacturer
	Standardization		display	**MGR**	manager; mon-
	Organization	**LCI**	landing craft in-		signor
ISP	internet service		fantry	**MHG**	Middle High
	provider	**LCP**	landing craft		German
ISR	Israel		personnel	**MHZ**	megahertz
ITA	International	**LDS**	Latter-day	**MIA**	missing in
	Trade Adminis-		Saints		action
	tration	**LED**	light-emitting	**MIC**	Micah
ITC	U.S.		diode	**MIL**	military
	International	**LEM**	lunar excursion	**MIN**	mineral; miner-
	Trade Com-		module		alogy
	mission	**LEV**	Leviticus	**MLG**	Middle Low
ITO	International	**LGK**	Late Greek		German
	Trade Organi-	**LLB**	bachelor of laws	**MME**	madame
	zation		(Lat., legum bac-	**MMR**	measles,
IUD	intrauterine		calaureus)		mumps, and ru-
	device	**LLD**	doctor of laws		bella
IWW	Industrial Work-	**LNG**	liquefied natu-	**MON**	Monday
	ers of the World		ral gas	**MPG**	miles per gallon
JAG	judge advocate	**LOC**	Library of Con-	**MPH**	miles per hour
	general		gress	**MRS**	mistress
JAN	January	**LOG**	logarithm	**MRV**	multiple re-
JAP	Japan; Japanese	**LOL**	laughing out		entry vehicle
JAS	James		loud	**MSA**	Metropolitan
JCS	joint chiefs of	**LPG**	liquefied petro-		Statistical Area
	staff		leum gas	**MSG**	monosodium
JCT	junction	**LPN**	licensed practi-		glutamate
JDL	Jewish Defense		cal nurse	**MSS**	manuscripts
	League	**LSD**	lysergic acid di-	**MST**	mountain stan-
JHS	junior high		ethylamide (a		dard time
	school		hallucinogenic	**MTS**	mountains
JNO	John		drug)	**MVD**	Soviet Ministry
JOS	Joseph; Josiah	**LSI**	landing ship in-		of Internal Af-
JPG	joint		fantry		fairs
	photographic	**LST**	landing ship	**MVP**	most valuable
	(experts) group		tank		player
JUL	July	**LTD**	limited	**NAB**	National Asso-

ciation of Broadcasters

NAH Nahum

NAM National Association of Manufacturers

NBA National Basketball Association

NBC National Broadcasting Company

NBS National Bureau of Standards

NCO noncommissioned officer

NEA National Educational Association; National Endowment for the Arts

NEB Nebraska

NEG negative

NEH Nehemiah; National Endowment for the Humanities

NET National Educational Television

NEV Nevada

NFL National Football League

NHL National Hockey League

NHS National Health Service

NIT National Invitational Tournament

NNE north-northeast

NNW north-northwest

NOM nominative

NOR Norwegian; Norway

NOV November

NOW National Organization for Women

NPR National Public Radio

NRA National Recovery Administration; National Rifle Association

NRC Nuclear Regulatory Commission

NSA National Student Association; National Security Agency

NSC National Security Council

NSF National Science Foundation

NTA sodium-nitrilotriacetate

NUM Numbers

NWT Northwest Territories

NYC New York City

OAS Organization of American States

OAU Organization of African Unity

OBE officer of the Order of the British Empire

OBJ objective; object

OBO or best offer

OBS obsolete

OCD Office of Community Development

OCR optical character recognition

OCS officer candidate school; Office of Community Services

OCT October

OED Oxford English Dictionary

OEM original equipment manufacturer

OEO Office of Economic Opportunity

OES Order of the Eastern Star

OFF officer; office

OMB Office of Management and Budget

ONT Ontario

OOB off-off-Broadway

OPA Office of Price Administration

ORE Oregon

OSS Office of Strategic Services

OTB off-track betting

OTC one-stop inclusive tour charter; over the

counter

OTS officers' training school

OWI Office of War Information

OZS ounces

PAC political action committee; Pacific

PAL Police Athletic League

PAN Panama

PAR paragraph; parallel

PBA Professional Bowlers Association

PBS Public Broadcasting Service

PBX private branch (telephone) exchange

PCB polychlorinated biphenyl (a poisonous industrial chemical)

PCP phencyclidine (a hallucinogenic drug)

PCT percent

PDA personal digital assistant

PDQ pretty damn quick

PDT Pacific daylight time

PEI Prince Edward Island

PEN International Association of Poets, Playwrights, Editors, Essayists, and Novelists

PFC private first class

PGA Professional Golfers' Association

PHB bachelor of philosophy

PHD doctor of philosophy (Lat., philosophiae doctor)

PIM personal information manager

PIN personal identification number

PIX	pictures		(Lat., requiescat		flex (camera)
PKG	package(s)		in pace)	SOP	soprano
PLO	Palestine Libera-	RIT	ritardando	SOS	a radio distress
	tion Organi-	RMS	rooms		signal
	zation	RNA	ribonucleic acid	SQQ	and the follow-
PMS	premenstrual	ROM	read-only mem-		ing ones
	syndrome		ory; Roman;	SRA	senora
POE	port of entry		Romans	SRO	standing room
POL	Poland; Polish	RPM	revolutions per		only
POS	possessive;		minute	SSA	Social Security
	point of sale;	RSV	Revised Stan-		Administration
	point of service		dard Version (of	SSE	south-southeast
POW	prisoner of war		the Bible); respi-	SSN	Social Security
PPD	postpaid		ratory synctial		number
PPO	preferred pro-		virus	SSR	Soviet Socialist
	vider organi-	RTE	route		Republic
	zation	RUM	Rumania; Ru-	SSS	Selective Ser-
PPS	post		manian		vice System
	postscriptum	RUS	Russia; Russian	SST	supersonic
PSA	Psalms	RWY	railway		transport
PST	Pacific standard	SAC	Strategic Air	SSW	south-southwest
	time		Command	STE	saint (female)
PTA	Parent-Teacher	SAE	self-addressed	SUF	suffix
	Association		envelope	SUN	Sunday
PTO	please turn over	SAG	Screen Actors	SYM	symphony
	(the page)		Guild	SYR	Syria
PVC	polyvinyl	SAM	Samuel; surface-	SYS	system
	chloride		to-air missile	TBA	to be announced
PVT	private	SAR	Sons of the	TBS	tablespoon;
PWA	Public Works		American		Turner Broad-
	Administration		Revolution		casting System
QED	which was to be	SAT	Scholastic Apti-	TEL	telephone; tele-
	demonstrated		tude Test; Satur-		vision; telegram
	(Lat., quod erat		day; Saturn	TEX	Texas
	demon-	SBA	Small Business	TFR	terrain-
	strandum)		Administration		following radar
QMC	quartermaster	SCH	school	THC	tetrahydrocan-
	corps	SCI	science		nabinol (the
QTY	quantity	SDA	Students for		principal chem-
QUE	Quebec		Democratic Ac-		ical in mari-
RAF	Royal Air Force		tion; Seventh-		juana)
RAM	random access		Day Adventist	THD	doctor of the-
	memory	SDI	Strategic De-		ology
RBI	run(s) batted in		fense Initiative	THI	temperature-
RDA	recommended	SDS	Students for a		humidity index
	daily allowance		Democratic	THU	Thursday
REA	Rural Electrifi-		Society	TIM	Timothy
	cation Admin-	SEC	Securities and	TIX	tickets
	istration		Exchange	TKO	technical
REM	rapid eye		Commission		knockout
	movement	SEN	senate	TLC	tender loving
REP	Republican; rep-	SEQ	the following		care
	resentative		(Lat., sequentes)	TNT	trinitrotoluene
RET	retired	SGD	signed		(explosive)
REV	Revelation; rev-	SGT	sergeant	TSA	Transportation
	erend	SIB	Siberia; Siberian		Security Ad-
RFD	rural free de-	SIC	Sicily; Sicilian		ministration
	livery	SIG	signor	TSP	teaspoon
RIP	rest in peace	SLR	single-lens re-	TUE	Tuesday

TVA	Tennessee Valley Authority	**VHA**	Veterans Health Administration	**ACCT**	account; accountant
TWP	township	**VHF**	very high frequency	**ACDC**	alternating current, direct current; bisexual
UAE	United Arab Emirates	**VHS**	video home system		
UAR	United Arab Republic	**VIP**	very important person	**ACLU**	American Civil Liberties Union
UAW	United Automobile Workers; United Aircraft Workers; United Agricultural Implements Workers	**VIZ**	namely (Lat., videlicet)	**ACTH**	adrenocorticotropic hormone
		VMD	doctor of veterinary medicine		
		VOA	Voice of America	**ADVT**	advertisement
				AERO	aeronautical; aeronautics
UDC	United Daughters of the Confederacy	**VOL**	volume		
		WAC	Women's Army Corps	**AFAM**	Ancient Free and Accepted Masons
UFO	unidentified flying object	**WAF**	Women in the Air Force		
UFW	United Farm Workers	**WAN**	wide area network	**AFDC**	Aid to Families with Dependent Children
UHF	ultrahigh frequency	**WBA**	World Boxing Association		
UKR	Ukraine	**WBC**	World Boxing Council; white blood cells	**AGCY**	agency
ULT	last month			**AGLA**	Thou art powerful and eternal, Lord (Heb., Athah gobon leolam, Adonai), an exorcism word
UMW	United Mine Workers	**WED**	Wednesday		
UPC	Universal Product Code	**WHA**	World Hockey Association		
UPI	United Press International	**WHO**	World Health Organization	**AIDS**	acquired immune deficiency syndrome
UPS	United Parcel Service	**WIS**	Wisconsin		
URL	uniform resource locator	**WNW**	west-northwest		
		WPA	Works Progress Administration	**ALAS**	Alaska
URU	Uruguay	**WPB**	War Production Board	**ALTA**	Alberta
USA	Union of South Africa; United States Army; United States of America			**AMER**	America; American
		WPM	words per minute	**AMEX**	American Stock Exchange; American Express
		WSW	west-southwest		
		WTO	World Trade Organization		
USN	United States Navy	**WVA**	West Virginia		
USO	United Service Organizations	**WWW**	world wide web	**ANAT**	anatomical; anatomy
		WYO	Wyoming	**ANON**	anonymous
USP	United States Pharmacopeia	**YDS**	yards	**ANSI**	American National Standards Institute
		YRS	years		
USS	United States ship	**YUC**	Yucatan		
USU	usually	**ZIP**	zone improvement plan	**ANTA**	American National Theater and Academy
VAT	value-added tax	**ZPG**	zero population growth		
VCR	videocassette recorder			**APOC**	Apocalypse
VDT	video display terminal	**AARP**	American Association of Retired Persons	**ARCH**	Archbishop; architect; archaic
VET	veteran; veterinarian			**ARIZ**	Arizona
VFW	Veterans of Foreign Wars	**ABBR**	abbreviation	**ARVN**	Army of the Republic of
		ACAD	academy		

	Vietnam		ganization for	**ELIZ**	Elizabeth;
ASAP	as soon as possible		Nuclear Research		Elizabethan
				ENGR	engineer
ASSN	association	**CERT**	certificate;	**ESQR**	esquire
ASST	assistant		certify	**ESTH**	Esther
ATNO	atomic number	**CETA**	Comprehensive	**ETAL**	and others (Lat., et alii)
ATTN	attention		Employment and Training Act	**EXCH**	exchange
ATTY	attorney			**EXOD**	Exodus
ATWT	atomic weight			**EXPR**	expressive
AUST	Austria; Austrian	**CFTC**	Commodity Futures Trading Commission	**EXTN**	extension
				EZEK	Ezekiel
AVDP	avoirdupois			**FDIC**	Federal Deposit Insurance Corporation
AWOL	absent without leave	**CHAS**	Charles		
BAPT	Baptist	**CHEM**	chemistry; chemical; chemist	**FEPA**	Fair Employment Practices Act
BART	baronet; Bay Area Rapid Transit				
		CINC	commander in chief	**FEPC**	Federal Employment Practices Commission
BELG	Belgian; Belgium	**CMDR**	commander		
BENJ	Benjamin	**COLA**	cost-of-living adjustment; cost-of-living allowance	**FICA**	Federal Insurance Contributions Act (Social Security)
BESS	several NASA satellites				
BGEN	brigadier general				
BIOL	biology	**COLO**	Colorado		
BLDG	building	**COMP**	comparative	**FIDO**	Freaks, Irregulars, Defects, Oddities
BLIT	bachelor of letters	**COMR**	commissioner		
		CONG	congregational; congress; congressional	**FIFA**	Federation internationale de football association
BLVD	boulevard				
BMOC	big man on campus				
BPOE	Benevolent and Protective Order of Elks	**CONJ**	conjunction		
		CONN	Connecticut	**FIFO**	first in, first out
		CONT	continued		
		CORE	Congress of Racial Equality	**FLEM**	Flemish
BRAZ	Brazil; Brazilian			**FNMA**	Federal National Mortgage Association (Fannie Mae)
BRIG	brigadier	**CORP**	corporal; corporation		
BRIT	British				
BROS	brother(s)	**DEPT**	department		
BULG	Bulgaria; Bulgarian	**DEUT**	Deuteronomy		
		DIAG	diagram	**FOIA**	Freedom of Information Act
BYOB	bring your own bottle	**DIAL**	dialect(ical)		
		DIST	district	**FREQ**	frequency
CAPT	captain	**ECCL**	Ecclesiastes	**FRNT**	front
CARE	Cooperative for American Relief Everywhere	**ECOM**	electronic computer-originated mail	**GAAP**	generally accepted accounting principles
CATV	community antenna television	**ECON**	economics		
		ECUA	Ecuador	**GATT**	General Agreement on Tariffs and Trade
CCTV	closed-circuit television	**EEOC**	Equal Employment Opportunity Commission		
CENT	centigrade; centimeter; century			**GENL**	general
		EFTA	European Free Trade Association	**GENT**	gentleman
CERN	European Or-			**GEOG**	geographic; geography

GEOL	geological; geology		vices digital network		Archives and Records Administration
GEOM	geometrical; geometry	**JATO**	jet-assisted takeoff	**NASA**	National Aeronautics and Space Administration
GIGO	garbage in, garbage out	**JEEP**	general purpose vehicle		
GOES	geostationary operational environmental satellite	**JOBS**	job opportunities in the business sector	**NASL**	North American Soccer League
GOVT	government	**JOSH**	Joshua	**NATL**	national
GRAM	grammar	**JPEG**	joint photographic experts group	**NATO**	North Atlantic Treaty Organization
GRBR	Great Britain				
HDBK	handbook				
HDTV	high-definition television	**JUDG**	Judges	**NAUT**	nautical
		KANS	Kansas	**NCAA**	National Collegiate Athletic Association
HIST	historical	**KILO**	kilogram(s); kilometer(s)		
HTML	hypertext markup language				
		LIFO	last in, first out	**NCHS**	National Center for Health Statistics
HTTP	hypertext transfer protocol	**LONG**	longitude		
		LOOM	Loyal Order of Moose	**NCID**	National Center for Infectious Diseases
HUAC	House Un-American Activities Committee	**LPGA**	Ladies Professional Golf Association		
				NDAK	North Dakota
		MACC	Maccabees	**NDIC**	National Drug Intelligence Center
HVAC	heating, ventilating, and air-conditioning	**MADD**	mothers against drunk driving		
				NEBR	Nebraska
		MASC	masculine	**NETH**	Netherlands
IBID	in the same place (Lat., ibidem)	**MASH**	mobile army surgical hospital	**NIRA**	National Industrial Recovery Act
ICBM	intercontinental ballistic missile	**MATH**	mathematics	**NKVD**	the former Soviet Secret Police
		MDSE	merchandise		
		MECH	mechanics		
IMIT	imitative	**MEMO**	memorandum	**NLRB**	National Labor Relations Board
INCL	inclusive; including	**MICH**	Michigan		
		MIME	multipurpose internet mail extensions	**NMEX**	New Mexico
INRI	Iesus Nazarenus Rex Iudaeorum (Jesus of Nazareth, King of the Jews)			**NTSB**	National Transportation Safety Board
		MINN	Minnesota		
		MIRV	multiple independently targeted re-entry vehicle		
INST	the present month			**NTWT**	net weight
INTL	international	**MISC**	miscellaneous	**NYSE**	New York Stock Exchange
IOOF	Independent Order of Odd Fellows	**MISS**	Mississippi		
		MLLE	mademoiselle	**OBAD**	Obadiah
		MOMA	Museum of Modern Art (New York)	**OKLA**	Oklahoma
IRBM	intermediate-range ballistic missile			**OPEC**	Organization of Petroleum Exporting Countries
		MONT	Montana		
		MSGR	monsignor		
ISBN	International Standard Book Number	**MSGT**	master sergeant	**ORCH**	orchestra
				OREG	Oregon
		MYTH	mythology	**ORIG**	original(ly)
ISDN	integrated services digital	**NARA**	National	**OSHA**	Occupational

	Safety and Health Administration	**SALT**	Russian Strategic Arms Limitation Talks; Strategic Arms Limitation Treaty		and landing (aircraft)
OXON	Oxford (Lat., Oxoniensis)			**SUBJ**	subject; subjunctive
				SUFF	suffix
PADJ	participial adjective			**SUND**	Sunday
		SALV	Salvador; Salvator	**SUPT**	superintendent
PARA	Paraguay				
PART	participle	**SAML**	Samuel	**SWAT**	Special Weapons and Tactics
PATH	Port Authority Trans-Hudson	**SARS**	severe acute respiratory syndrome		
PAYT	payment			**SWED**	Sweden; Swedish
PENN	Pennsylvania	**SASE**	self-addressed stamped envelope	**SWIT**	Switzerland
PERS	Persia; Persian			**SWTZ**	Switzerland
PERT	pertaining			**TBSP**	tablespoon
PHAR	pharmaceutical; pharmacopoeia; pharmacy	**SASK**	Saskatchewan	**TENN**	Tennessee
		SCOT	Scottish; Scotland	**TGIF**	thank God it's Friday
		SDAK	South Dakota	**THEO**	Theodore; Theodosia
PHIL	Philemon; Philip; Philippians; Philippine	**SECY**	secretary		
		SEPT	September	**THOS**	Thomas
		SEQQ	the following ones (Lat., sequentia)	**TINA**	there is no alternative
PKWY	parkway			**TUES**	Tuesday
PORT	Portugal; Portuguese	**SGML**	standard generalized markup language	**TYPP**	thousand yards per pound (of yarn)
PREF	prefix				
PREP	preposition; preparatory	**SHAK**	Shakespeare	**UNCF**	United Negro College Fund
PRET	preterit	**SIDS**	sudden infant death syndrome	**USAF**	United States Air Force
PROF	professor				
PROM	programmable read-only memory	**SING**	singular	**USCG**	United States Coast Guard
		SLAV	Slavic; Slavonian	**USDA**	United States Department of Agriculture
PRON	pronoun				
PROT	Protestant	**SOPH**	sophomore		
PROV	Proverbs; province	**SPAR**	Coast Guard Women's Reserve	**USES**	United States Employment Service
PROX	next (Lat., proximo)	**SPCA**	Society for Prevention of Cruelty to Animals		
RCAF	Royal Canadian Air Force			**USIA**	United States Information Agency
RCMP	Royal Canadian Mounted Police	**SPCC**	Society for Prevention of Cruelty to Children	**USMA**	United States Military Academy
ROBT	Robert				
ROFL	rolling on floor laughing	**SPQR**	the senate and the Roman people (Lat., senatus populusque Romanus)	**USMC**	United States Marine Corps
ROTC	Reserve Officers' Training Corps			**USNA**	United States Naval Academy
RRSP	Registered Retirement Savings Plan	**SRTA**	señorita	**USNR**	United States Naval Reserve
		SSGT	staff sergeant		
RSVP	please reply (Fr., repondez s'il vous plait)	**STAT**	immediately (Lat., statim)	**USOC**	United States Olympic Committee
RUSS	Russia;	**STOL**	short takeoff	**USPO**	United States Patent Office

USPS	United States Postal Service		Association
USSR	Union of Soviet Socialist Republics	YWHA	Young Women's Hebrew Association
USTA	United States Tennis Association	ZECH	Zechariah
		ZEPH	Zephaniah
		ZOOL	zoological; zoology
VERT	vertical		
VTOL	vertical take-off and landing (aircraft)	ADMIN	administration
WAAC	Women's Auxiliary Army Corps	AFTRA	American Federation of Television and Radio Artists
WAAF	Women's Auxiliary Air Force		
WASH	Washington	ARITH	arithmetic; arithmetical
WASP	Women's Air Force Service Pilots; white Anglo-Saxon Protestant	ASCAP	American Society of Composers, Authors, and Publishers
WATS	Wide-Area Telecommunications Service	ASCII	American Standard Code for Information Interchange
WCTU	Women's Christian Temperance Union	ASEAN	Association of Southeast Asian Nations
WHAM	winning the hearts and minds of the people	ASPCA	American Society for the Prevention of Cruelty to Animals
WISC	Wisconsin		
WORM	write once-read many		
WRAC	Women's Royal Army Corps	ASSOC	associate; association
WRAF	Women's Royal Air Force	ASSYR	Assyrian
		AUSTL	Australia
		BASIC	Beginner's All-purpose Symbolic Instruction Code
WRNS	Women's Royal Naval Service		
XING	crossing		
XMAS	Christmas	CDROM	compact disk read-only memory
YHWH	Yahweh		
YMCA	Young Men's Christian Association		
YMHA	Young Men's Hebrew Association	CENTO	Central Treaty Organization
		CHRON	Chronicles
YWCA	Young Women's Christian	COBOL	Common Business

	Oriented Language
CODEC	coder/decoder
CONTR	contract; contralto
CREEP	Committee to Re-Elect the President
CSPAN	Cable Satellite Public Affairs Network
CZECH	Czechoslovakia
DLITT	doctor of letters
EMAIL	electronic mail
EPCOT	Experimental Prototype Community of Tomorrow
EPROM	erasable programmable read-only memory
ETSEQ	and the following (Lat., et sequens)
FUBAR	fouled-up beyond recognition
GULAG	Soviet Labor Camp
HDQRS	headquarters
ILGWU	International Ladies' Garment Workers' Union
LASER	light amplification by stimulated emission of radiation
LIEUT	lieutenant
LITTD	doctor of literature
LORAN	long-range navigation
MASER	microwave amplification by stimulated emission of

	radiation	**SEATO**	Southeast			Federation
MEDIT	Mediter-		Asia Treaty			of Labor
	ranean		Organi-			and Con-
MODEM	modulator;		zation			gress of In-
	demodulator	**SHAEF**	Supreme			dustrial
NAACP	National As-		Headquar-			Organiza-
	sociation for		ters Allied			tions
	the		Expedition-	**AMVETS**	American
	Advance-		ary Forces		Veterans
	ment of Col-	**SHAPE**	Supreme		of World
	ored People		Headquar-		War II,
NAFTA	North		ters Allied		Korea, and
	American		Powers in		Vietnam
	Free Trade		Europe	**ARCHIT**	architect;
	Agreement	**SNAFU**	situation		archi-
NARAD	Navy Re-		normal, all		tecture
	search and		fouled up	**ASTRON**	astronomy
	Devel-	**SONAR**	sound navi-	**BICYEA**	Best Ice
	opment		gation		Cream
NIMBY	not in my		ranging		You Ever
	backyard	**START**	strategic		Ate
NORAD	North		arms reduc-	**BOMFOG**	Brother-
	American		tion talks		hood of
	Air Defense	**SWITZ**	Switzerland		Man, Fa-
	Command	**TCPIP**	transmission		therhood
OBGYN	obstetrics		control pro-		of God
	gynecology		tocol/in-		(blather)
OPCIT	in the work		ternet	**CADCAM**	computer-
	cited (Lat.,		protocol		aided
	opere citato)	**THURS**	Thursday		design/
OXFAM	Oxford	**TIROS**	television		computer-
	Committee		and infrared		aided man-
	for Famine		observation		ufacturing
	Relief		satellite	**CINCUS**	com-
PAREN	parentheses	**TREAS**	treasurer;		mander-in-
PERUV	Peruvian		treasury		chief U.S.
PHARM	pharmaceuti-	**UNRRA**	United Na-		fleet
	cal;		tions Relief	**COLLOQ**	colloquial
	pharmaco-		and Reha-	**COMSAT**	Communi-
	poeia;		bilitation		cations
	pharmacy		Administra-		Satellite
PHILA	Philadelphia		tion		Corp.
PLUPF	pluperfect	**VENEZ**	Venezuela	**INTERJ**	inter-
PLUTO	pipeline	**VISTA**	Volunteers		jection
	under the		in Service to	**MESSRS**	messieurs
	ocean		America	**NASCAR**	National
POTUS	President of	**WAVES**	Women Ac-		Associa-
	the United		cepted for		tion for
	States		Volunteer		Stock Car
RADAR	radio		Emergency		Auto
	detecting		Service (U.		Racing
	and ranging		S. Navy)	**NASDAQ**	National
SCAND	Scandi-				Associa-
	navian	**ABSCAM**	Abdul En-		tion of
SCUBA	self-		terprises		Securities
	contained		SCAM		Dealers
	underwater	**AFGHAN**	Afghan-		Auto-
	breathing		istan		mated
	apparatus	**AFLCIO**	American		Quotation

PATHOL	pathology	tional, So-
PHOTOG	photog-raphy	cial, and Cultural
PROTEM	for the time being	Organization
PTBOAT	patrol torpedo boat	UNICEF United Nations Interna-tional Children's Emergency Fund
QANTAS	Queensland and Northern Territory Aerial Services	
SUPERL	superlative	
UNESCO	United Nations Educa-	UNIVAC Universal Automatic Computer

YIPPIE	Youth International Party member
YUPPIE	young urban professional
BENELUX	Belgium, Netherlands, Luxembourg Economic Union
WYSIWYG	what you see is what you get

AIRPORT AND AIRLINE CODES
AIRPORTS

ABJ	Abidjan, Ivory Coast (Port-Bouet)
ABQ	Albuquerque, NM
ABV	Abuja, Nigeria
ABZ	Aberdeen, United Kingdom (Dyce)
ACA	Acapulco, Mexico (Alvarez)
ACC	Accra, Ghana (Kotoka)
ADB	Izmir, Turkey (Menderes)
ADD	Addis Ababa, Ethiopia (Bole)
ADJ	Amman, Jordan
ADL	Adelaide, Australia
AEP	Buenos Aires, Argentina (Newbery)
AHO	Alghero, Sardinia (Fertilia)
AKL	Auckland, New Zealand
AKR	Akron, OH (Fulton)
ALA	Almaty, Kazakhstan
ALG	Algiers, Algeria (Boumediene)
ALP	Aleppo, Syria (Nejrab)
ALY	Alexandria,

	Egypt
AMM	Amman, Jordan (Queen Alia)
AMS	Amsterdam, Netherlands (Schipol)
ANC	Anchorage, AK (Stevens)
ANK	Ankara, Turkey (Etimesgut)
ANR	Antwerp, Belgium (Deurne)
ANU	St. John's Antigua & Barbuda (Bird)
APA	Denver, CO (Centennial)
APW	Apia, Samoa (Faleolo)
AQP	Arequipa, Peru (Ballon)
ARN	Stockholm, Sweden (Arlanda)
ASB	Ashgabat, Turkmenistan
ASK	Yamoussoukro, Ivory Coast
ASM	Asmara, Eritrea (Yohannes IV)
ASU	Asuncion, Paraguay (Silvio Pettirossi)
ATH	Athens, Greece (Eleftherios Venizelos)

ATL	Atlanta, GA (William Hartsfield)
AUA	Oranjestad, Aruba (Queen Beatrix)
AUH	Abu Dhabi, United Arab Emirates (Nadia)
AUS	Austin, TX (Bergstrom)
AXA	The Valley, Anguilla (Wall Blake)
AXH	Houston, TX (Southwest)
AZI	Abu Dhabi, United Arab Emirates (Bettina)
AZP	Mexico City, Mexico (Atizapan)
BAH	Manama, Bahrain
BAK	Baku, Azerbaijan (Bina)
BAQ	Barranquilla, Colombia (Ernesto Cortissoz)
BBR	Basse-Terre, Guadeloupe (Baillif)
BBU	Bucharest, Romania (Baneasa)
BCN	Barcelona, Spain

	(El Prat)		Sweden		sia (Soekarno-Hatta)
BDA	Hamilton, Bermuda (Kindley)		(Bromma)	CGN	Cologne, Germany (Konrad Adenauer)
BDO	Bandung, Indonesia (Husein Sastranegara)	BNA	Nashville, TN
BNJ	Bonn, Germany (Hangelar)
BOG	Bogota, Colombia (Eldorado)	CGX	Chicago, IL (Meigs)
BEG	Belgrade, Serbia and Montenegro (Surcin)	BOM	Mumbai, India (Sahar)	CHC	Christchurch, New Zealand
BOS	Boston, MA (Logan)	CIA	Rome, Italy (Ciampino)
BEN	Benghazi, Libya (Benina)
BER	Berlin, Germany	BRN	Bern, Switzerland (Bern-Belp)	CKG	Chongqing, China
BEY	Beirut, Lebanon
BFI	Seattle, WA (Boeing)	BRU	Brussels, Belgium	CKY	Conakry, Guinea (G'bessia)
BFL	Bakersfield, CA (Meadows)	BSB	Brasilia, Brazil
BSL	Basel, Switzerland (EuroAirport)	CLE	Cleveland, OH (Hopkins)
BFN	Bloemfontein, South Africa
BFS	Belfast, United Kingdom	BSR	Basra, Iraq	CLO	Cali, Colombia (Alfonso Bonilla Aragon)
BTR	Baton Rouge, LA (Ryan)
BGF	Bangui, Central African Republic (M'Poko)	BTS	Bratislava, Slovakia (Ivanka)	CLT	Charlotte, NC (Douglas)
CMB	Colombo, Sri Lanka (Bandaranaika)
BGI	Bridgetown, Barbados (Grantley Adams)	BUD	Budapest, Hungary (Ferihegy)
BUF	Buffalo, NY	CMN	Casablanca, Morocco (Mohamed V)
BGO	Bergen, Norway (Flesland)	BUH	Bucharest, Romania
BGW	Baghdad, Iraq (Al Muthana)	BWI	Baltimore, MD	CNF	Belo Horizonte, Brazil (Tancredo Neves-Confins)
BWN	Bandar Seri Begwan, Brunei
BHD	Belfast, United Kingdom	BXO	Bissau, Guinea-Bissau (Bissallanca)	COO	Cotonou, Benin (Cadjehoun)
BHM	Birmingham, AL
BHX	Birmingham, United Kingdom (Elmdon)	COS	Colorado Springs, CO
BZE	Belize City, Belize (Philip Goldson)	CPH	Copenhagen, Denmark (Kastrup)
BHZ	Belo Horizonte, Brazil
BZV	Brazzaville, Congo (Maya Maya)	CPT	Cape Town, South Africa (D. F. Malan)
BIR	Biratnagar, Nepal
BJL	Banjul, Gambia (Yundum)	CAG	Cagliari, Sardinia (Elmas)	CRK	Luzon, Philippines (Clark)
BJM	Bujumbura, Burundi	CAI	Cairo, Egypt
CAN	Guangzhou, China (Baiyun)	CRP	Corpus Christi, TX
BJS	Beijing, China
BJY	Belgrade, Serbia and Montenegro (Batajnica)	CAS	Casablanca, Morocco (Mohammed V)	CUK	Sao Paulo, Brazil (Cumbica)
CUN	Cancun, Mexico
BKA	Moscow, Russia (Bykovo)	CBR	Canberra, Australia	CWL	Cardiff, United Kingdom
BKK	Bangkok, Thailand	CCU	Calcutta, India (Dum Dum)	CZM	Cozumel, Mexico
BKO	Bamako, Mali (Senou)	CDG	Paris, France (Charles de Gaulle)	DAC	Dhaka, Bangladesh (Zia)
BLR	Bangalore, India
BLZ	Blantyre, Malawi (Chileka)	CGH	Sao Paulo, Brazil (Congonhas)	DAM	Damascus, Syria
DAR	Dar es Salaam, Tanzania
BMA	Stockholm,	CGK	Jakarta, Indone-	DCA	Washington,

	DC (Reagan)
DCF	Roseau, Dominica (Cane)
DEL	Delhi, India (Indira Ghandi)
DEN	Denver, CO
DFA	Abu Dhabi, United Arab Emirates
DFW	Dallas/Fort Worth, TX
DIL	Dili, East Timor (Comoro)
DKR	Dakar, Senegal (Yoff)
DLA	Douala, Cameroon
DME	Moscow, Russia (Domodemovo)
DND	Dundee, United Kingdom (Riverside)
DNK	Dnipropetrovsk, Ukraine
DOD	Dodoma, Tanzania
DOH	Doha, Qatar
DOM	Roseau, Dominica (Melville Hall)
DRS	Dresden, Germany
DSM	Des Moines, IA
DUB	Dublin, Ireland
DUR	Durban, South Africa (Louis Botha)
DUS	Dusseldorf, Germany (Rhein-Ruhr)
DVO	Davao City, Philippines (Francisco Bangoy)
DYU	Dushanbe, Tajikistan
DZA	Mamoutzou, Mayotte (Pamandzi)
EAP	Basel, Switzerland (EuroAirport)
EBB	Kampala, Uganda (Entebbe)
EDI	Edinburgh, United Kingdom (Turnhouse)

ELP	El Paso, TX
EOH	Medellin, Colombia
ESB	Ankara, Turkey (Esenboga)
ESS	Essen, Germany (Mulheim)
EVN	Yerevan, Armenia (Zvartnots)
EWR	Newark, NJ
EZE	Buenos Aires, Argentina (Ezeiza)
FAI	Fairbanks, AK
FAT	Fresno, CA (Yosemite)
FBM	Lubumbashi, Democratic Republic of the Congo (Luano)
FCO	Rome, Italy (Fiumicino)
FDF	Fort-de-France, Martinique (Le Lamentin)
FGI	Apia, Samoa (Fabali Si)
FIH	Kinshasa, Democratic Republic of the Congo (N'Djili)
FNA	Freetown, Sierra Leone (Lungi)
FNJ	Pyongyang, North Korea (Sunan)
FRA	Frankfurt, Germany (Rhein-Main)
FRU	Bishkek, Kyrgyzstan
FSP	St. Pierre, St. Pierre & Miquelon
FUN	Fongafale, Tuvalu (Funafuti)
FWA	Fort Wayne, IN
GBE	Gaborone, Botswana (Sir Seretse Khama)
GCJ	Johannesburg, South Africa (Grand Central)
GDL	Guadalajara, Mexico (Miguel Higaldo y Costilla)
GDN	Gdansk, Poland (Rebiechowo)

GEO	Georgetown, Guyana (Timehri)
GIB	Gibraltar, Gibraltar (North Front)
GIG	Rio de Janeiro, Brazil (Galeao)
GNO	St. George's, Grenada (Pointes Salines)
GOH	Nuuk, Greenland (Godthab)
GOJ	Nizhniy Novgorod, Russia (Sormavo)
GOT	Goteborg, Sweden (Landvetter)
GRU	Sao Paulo, Brazil (Guarulhos)
GSE	Goteborg, Sweden (Save)
GSO	Greensboro, NC (Piedmont Triad)
GUA	Guatemala City, Guatemala (La Aurora)
GVA	Geneva, Switzerland (Cointrin)
GYE	Guayaquil, Ecuador (Simon Bolivar)
GZM	Gozo, Malta
HAG	The Hague, Netherlands
HAH	Moroni, Comoros (Hahaya)
HAV	Havana, Cuba (Jose Marti)
HEL	Helsinki, Finland (Vantaa)
HEM	Helsinki, Finland (Malmi)
HEX	Santo Domingo, Dominican Republic (Herrera)
HFA	Haifa, Israel (U. Michaeli)
HGS	Freetown, Sierra Leone (Hastings)
HIR	Honiara, Solomon Islands (Henderson)
HKG	Hong Kong, China (Chek Lap Kok)
HLP	Jakarta, Indone-

	sia (Halim Per-danakusuma)		(Borispol)	LCK	Columbus, OH (Rickenbacker)
HND	Tokyo, Japan (Haneda)	KEF	Reykjavik, Iceland (Keflavik/Leifur Eriksson)	LCY	London, United Kingdom
HNL	Honolulu, HI	KGL	Kigali, Rwanda (Gregoire Kayi-banda/Ka-nombe)	LED	St. Petersburg, Russia (Pul-kovo-2)
HOU	Houston, TX (Hobby)				
HPR	Pretoria, South Africa (Central)	KHH	Kaohsiung, Taiwan	LEX	Lexington, KY (Blue Grass)
HRK	Kharkov, Ukraine	KHI	Karachi, Pakistan (Quaid-e-Azam)	LFW	Lome, Togo (Tokoin)
HYD	Hyderabad, India			LGA	New York, NY (LaGuardia)
IAD	Washington, DC (Dulles)	KIN	Kingston, Jamaica (Norman Manley)	LGB	Long Beach, CA (Daugherty)
IAH	Houston, TX (George Bush)	KIV	Chisinau, Moldova	LGW	London, United Kingdom (Gatwick)
IBA	Ibadan, Nigeria				
ICN	Inchon, South Korea	KIX	Osaka, Japan (Kansai)	LHE	Lahore, Pakistan
ICT	Wichita, KS (Mid-Continent)	KLA	Kampala, Uganda	LHR	London, United Kingdom (Heathrow)
IEV	Kiev, Ukraine (Zhulyany)	KRK	Krakow, Poland (John Paul II/Balice)	LIL	Lille, France (Lesquin)
IFN	Isfahan, Iran			LIM	Lima, Peru (Jorge Chavez)
IND	Indianapolis, IN	KRT	Khartoum, Sudan		
INU	Yaren, Nauru (Nauru Island)			LIN	Milan, Italy (Linate)
ISB	Islamabad, Pakistan (Chaklala)	KSC	Kosice, Slovakia (Barca)	LIS	Lisbon, Portugal (Portela de Sacavem)
		KTM	Kathmandu, Nepal (Tribhuvan)		
IST	Istanbul, Turkey (Ataturk-Yesilkov)			LIT	Little Rock, AR (Adams)
		KTP	Kingston, Jamaica (Tinson)	LJU	Ljubljana, Slovenia (Brnik)
ITM	Osaka, Japan (Itami)	KTW	Katowice, Poland (Pyrzowice)		
IZM	Izmir, Turkey (A. Menderes)	KTZ	Hong Kong, China	LLW	Lilongwe, Malawi (Kamuzu)
JAX	Jacksonville, FL			LOS	Lagos, Nigeria (Murtala Muhammed)
JED	Jeddah, Saudi Arabia (King Abdul Aziz)	KUL	Kuala Lumpur, Malaysia (Subang)		
		KUN	Kaunas, Lithuania	LPB	La Paz, Bolivia (Kennedy)
JFK	New York, NY (Kennedy)			LPL	Liverpool, United Kingdom (Speke)
JIB	Djibouti, Djibouti (Ambouli)	KWI	Kuwait City, Kuwait		
JKT	Jakarta, Indonesia	LAD	Luanda, Angola (Belas)	LTQ	Le Touquet, France (Paris-Plage)
JMY	Freetown, Sierra Leone (Manny Yoko)	LAS	Las Vegas, NV (McCarran)		
				LUK	Cincinnati, OH (Lunken)
JNB	Johannesburg, South Africa	LAX	Los Angeles, CA		
		LBA	Leeds, United Kingdom	LUX	Luxembourg, Luxembourg (Findel)
JNU	Juneau, AK	LBG	Paris, France (Le Bourget)		
JRS	Jerusalem, Israel (Atarot)			LVS	Las Vegas, NV
		LBH	Sydney, Australia (Palm Beach)	LYN	Lyon, France (Bron)
KBL	Kabul, Afghanistan (Khwaja Rawash)	LBV	Libreville, Gabon (Leon M'Ba)	LYP	Faisalabad, Pakistan
KBP	Kiev, Ukraine			LYS	Lyon, France

	(Saint-Exupery)
MAA	Chennai, India (Meenambakkam/Chennai)
MAD	Madrid, Spain (Barajas)
MAJ	Majuro, Marshall Islands
MAN	Manchester, United Kingdom (Ringway)
MBA	Mombasa, Kenya (Moi)
MCI	Kansas City, MO
MCT	Muscat, Oman (Seeb)
MDE	Medellin, Colombia (Olaya Herrera)
MDL	Mandalay, Myanmar
MDW	Chicago, IL (Midway)
MEB	Melbourne, Australia (Essendon)
MEL	Melbourne, Australia (Tullamarine)
MEM	Memphis, TN
MEX	Mexico City, Mexico (Benito Juarez)
MFM	Macao, Macau
MGA	Managua, Nicaragua (Augusto Cesar Sandino)
MGJ	Montgomery, NY (Orange County)
MGM	Montgomery, AL (Dannelly)
MGQ	Mogadishu, Somalia (Petrella)
MIA	Miami, FL
MIL	Milan, Italy
MKE	Milwaukee, WI (General Mitchell)
MLA	Malta, Malta (Luqa)
MLE	Male, Maldives
MLE	Omaha, NE (Millard)
MLW	Monrovia, Liberia (Spriggs Payne)
MMA	Malmo, Sweden

MMX	Malmo, Sweden (Sturup)
MNL	Manila, Philippines (Ninoy Aquino)
MPM	Maputo, Mozambique (Mavalane)
MPN	Stanley, Falkland Islands (Mount Pleasant)
MQC	Miquelon, St. Pierre & Miquelon
MRS	Marseille, France (Marignane-Provence)
MRU	Plaine Magnien, Mauritius (Sir Seewoosagur Ramgoolam)
MSP	Minneapolis-St. Paul, MN (Wold/Chamberlain)
MSQ	Minsk, Belarus (Velikydvor)
MSU	Maseru, Lesotho (Moshoeshoe I)
MSY	New Orleans, LA (Louis Armstrong)
MTY	Monterrey, Mexico (Mariana Escobedo)
MWC	Milwaukee, WI (Lawrence Timmerman)
MXP	Milan, Italy (Malpensa)
NAP	Naples, Italy (Capodichino)
NAS	Nassau, Bahamas
NBO	Nairobi, Kenya (Jomo Kenyatta)
NDJ	N'Djamena, Chad
NGO	Nagoya, Japan (Komaki)
NIC	Nicosia, Cyprus
NIM	Niamey, Niger
NKC	Nouakchott, Mauritania
NKG	Nanjing, China (Loukou)
NLO	Kinshasa, Democratic Republic

	of the Congo (N'Dolo)
NMK	Nicosia, Cyprus (Makarios)
NRT	Tokyo, Japan (Narita)
NTR	Monterrey, Mexico (del Norte)
NVR	Novgorod, Russia
OAK	Oakland, CA
OKC	Oklahoma City, OK (Will Rogers)
OKD	Sapporo, Japan (Okadama)
OMA	Omaha, NE (Eppley)
OMS	Omsk, Russia
OPO	Oporto, Portugal (Pedras Rubras)
ORD	Chicago, IL (O'Hare)
ORF	Norfolk, VA
ORG	Paramaribo, Suriname (Zorg en Hoop)
OSL	Oslo, Norway
OSM	Mosul, Iraq
OTP	Bucharest, Romania (Otopeni)
OUA	Ouagadougou, Burkina Faso
OVB	Novosibirsk, Russia (Tolmachevo)
PAP	Port-au-Prince, Haiti
PBC	Puebla, Mexico (Hermanos Serdan)
PBH	Thimphu, Bhutan (Paro)
PBM	Paramaribo, Suriname (Johan Adolf Pengel)
PDX	Portland, OR
PEK	Beijing, China
PHL	Philadelphia, PA
PHX	Phoenix, AZ (Sky Harbor)
PID	Paradise Island, Bahamas
PIE	St. Petersburg, FL
PIT	Pittsburgh, PA
PKV	Pskov, Russia
PLU	Belo Horizonte, Brazil (Pam-

	pulha)
PMO	Palermo, Sicily (Punta Raisi)
PNH	Phnom Penh, Cambodia (Pochentong)
PNI	Palikir, Micronesia (Pohnpei)
POM	Port Moresby, Papua New Guinea (Jacksons)
POS	Port of Spain, Trinidad and Tobago (Piarco)
POZ	Poznan, Poland (Lawica)
PPG	Pago Pago, American Samoa
PRG	Prague, Czech Republic (Ruzyne)
PRY	Pretoria, South Africa (Wonderboom)
PSY	Stanley, Falkland Islands
PTY	Panama City, Panama (General Omar Torrijos Herrara)
PVG	Shanghai, China (Pudong)
PVR	Puerto Vallarta, Mexico (Gustavo D. Ordaz)
PWM	Portland, ME
QFV	Bergen, Norway (Harbor Pier)
QHS	Hims, Syria
QJC	Thimphu, Bhutan
QJX	Bangkok, Thailand (Nong Khai)
QKV	Osaka, Japan (Sakai)
QLS	Lausanne, Switzerland (La Blecherette)
QMN	Mbabane, Swaziland (Manzini)
QMP	Macao, Macao
QNQ	Malmo, Sweden
QPG	Singapore, Singapore (Paya Lebar)
QPP	Berlin, Germany
QRA	Johannesburg,

	South Africa (Rand/Germiston)
QUF	Tallinn, Estonia (Pirita Harbour)
QVU	Vaduz, Liechtenstein
QYI	The Hague, Netherlands
QYY	Bialystok, Poland (Krywlany)
RAI	Praia, Cape Verde
RAK	Marrakech, Morocco (Menara)
RBA	Rabat, Morocco (Sale)
RBD	Dallas, TX (Redbird)
RDU	Raleigh-Durham, NC
REK	Reykjavik, Iceland
RGN	Rangoon, Myanmar (Mingaladon)
RIO	Rio de Janeiro, Brazil
RIX	Riga, Latvia (Spilve)
RKE	Copenhagen, Denmark (Roskilde)
RML	Colombo, Sri Lanka
RNV	Cleveland, MS
ROB	Monrovia, Liberia (Roberts)
ROC	Rochester, NY
ROM	Rome, Italy
ROR	Koror, Palau (Babelthuap)
RSC	Riga, Latvia (Skulte)
RSE	Sydney, Australia (Aurose Bay)
RTM	Rotterdam, Netherlands
RUH	Riyadh, Saudi Arabia (King Khalid)
RUN	Saint-Denis, Reunion (Gillot)
RVH	St. Petersburg, Russia (Rshevka)
SAI	San Marino, San Marino
SAL	San Salvador, El

	Salvador (Cuscatlan)
SAN	San Diego, CA (Lindbergh)
SAO	Sao Paulo, Brazil
SAW	Istanbul, Turkey (Sabiha Gokcen)
SCK	Stockton, CA
SCL	Santiago, Chile (Arturo Merino Benitez)
SDA	Baghdad, Iraq
SDF	Louisville, KY (Standiford)
SDL	Scottsdale, AZ
SDQ	Santo Domingo, Dominican Republic (de las Americas)
SDU	Rio de Janeiro, Brazil (Santos Dumont)
SDV	Tel Aviv, Israel (Sde Dov Hoz)
SEA	Seattle, WA
SEL	Seoul, South Korea (Kimpo)
SEZ	Victoria, Seychelles (Pointe Larue)
SFO	San Francisco, CA
SGL	Manila, Philippines
SGT	Stuttgart, AR
SHA	Shanghai, China (Hongqiao)
SHE	Shenyang, China
SIN	Singapore, Singapore (Changi)
SJC	San Jose, CA
SJJ	Sarajevo, Bosnia and Herzegovina (Butmir)
SJO	San Jose, Costa Rica (Juan Santamaria)
SKB	Basseterre, St. Kitts and Nevis (Golden Rock)
SKP	Skopje, Macedonia
SLU	Castries, St. Lucia (Vigie)
SMF	Sacramento, CA
SOF	Sofia, Bulgaria (Vrajdebna)

SPK	Sapporo, Japan (Chitose)	
SPL	Amsterdam, Netherlands (Schipol)	
SRE	Sucre, Bolivia (Jauna Azurduy de Padilla)	
SSG	Malabo, Equatorial Guinea	
STI	Santiago, Dominican Republic (Cibao)	
STO	Stockholm, Sweden (Ska-Edeby)	
SUB	Surabaya, Indonesia (Juanda)	
SUS	St. Louis, MO (Spirit of St. Louis)	
SUV	Suva, Fiji (Nausori)	
SVD	Kingstown, St. Vincent and the Grenadines (Arnos Vale/E.T. Joshua)	
SVO	Moscow, Russia (Sheremetyevo)	
SWK	Milan, Italy (Segrate)	
SYD	Sydney, Australia (Kingsford Smith)	
SZB	Kuala Lumpur, Malaysia (Peninsular General)	
SZG	Salzburg, Austria (Mozart)	
TAE	Taegu, South Korea	
TBS	Tbilisi, Georgia (Novoalexeyevka)	
TBU	Nuku'Alofa, Tonga (Fua' Amotu)	
TDZ	Toledo, OH (Metcalf)	
TGU	Tegucigalpa, Honduras (Toncontin)	
THF	Berlin, Germany (Tempelhof)	
THR	Teheran, Iran (Mehrabad)	
TIA	Tirana, Albania	
TIJ	(Rinas) Tijuana, Mexico (General Abelardo Rodriguez)	
TIP	Tripoli, Libya (Idris)	
TLL	Tallinn, Estonia (Ulemiste)	
TLV	Tel Aviv, Israel (Ben Gurion)	
TMS	Sao Tome, Sao Tome and Principe	
TNR	Antananarivo, Madagascar (Ivato)	
TPA	Tampa, FL	
TPE	Taipei, Taiwan (Chiang Kai-Shek)	
TRN	Turin, Italy (Caselle)	
TRW	Tarawa, Kiribati (Bonriki)	
TSA	Taipei, Taiwan (Sung Shan)	
TSE	Astana, Kazakhstan	
TSN	Tianjin, China (Zhangguizhuang)	
TUL	Tulsa, OK	
TUN	Tunis, Tunisia (Carthage)	
TUS	Tucson, AZ	
TWY	Tawa, Tibet, China	
TXG	Taichung, Taiwan	
TXL	Berlin, Germany (Tegel)	
UIO	Quito, Ecuador (Mariscal Sucre)	
UKY	Kyoto, Japan	
ULC	Santiago, Chile (Los Cerrillos)	
ULN	Ulan Bator, Mongolia (Buyant-Ukhaa)	
VCP	Sao Paulo, Brazil (Viracopos)	
VIE	Vienna, Austria	
VKO	Moscow, Russia (Vnukovo)	
VLC	Valencia, Spain	
VNO	Vilnius, Lithuania	
VNY	Los Angeles, CA (Van Nuys)	
VTE	Vientiane, Laos (Wattay)	
VXX	Mexico City, Mexico (Sertel)	
WAW	Warsaw, Poland (Okecie)	
WDH	Windhoek, Namibia (J. G. Strijdom)	
WGA	Mesa, AZ (Williams)	
WHP	Los Angeles, CA (Whiteman)	
WIL	Nairobi, Kenya (Wilson)	
WLG	Wellington, New Zealand	
XMM	Monte Carlo, Monaco	
XSP	Singapore, Singapore (Seletar)	
XXB	Manchester, United Kingdom (Woodford)	
YAO	Yaounde, Cameroon (Nsimalen)	
YEG	Edmonton, Canada	
YGF	Cape Town, South Africa (Youngsfield)	
YHU	Montreal, Canada (St.-Hubert)	
YMX	Montreal, Canada (Mirabel)	
YND	Ottawa, Canada (Gatineau)	
YOW	Ottawa, Canada (Macdonald-Cartier)	
YRO	Ottawa, Canada (Rockliffe)	
YUL	Montreal, Canada (Dorval)	
YVA	Moroni, Comoros (Hahaya/Iconi)	
YVR	Vancouver, Canada	
YWG	Winnipeg, Canada	
YXD	Edmonton, Canada	
YXU	London, Canada	
YYC	Calgary, Canada	
YYZ	Toronto, Canada (Lester B. Pearson)	
ZAG	Zagreb, Croatia	

		ZHY	Geneva,		zania (Kisauni)
	(Pleso)		Switzerland	**ZRH**	Zurich, Switzer-
ZAM	Zamboanga,	**ZLQ**	Zurich,		land (Zurich-
	Philippines		Switzerland		Kloten)
ZDJ	Bern,	**ZNZ**	Zanzibar, Tan-		
	Switzerland				

AIRLINES

Aer Lingus	EI	Finnair	AY
Aeroflot	SU	Hawaiian Airlines	HA
Aerolineas Argentinas	AR	Iberia	IB
Air Canada	AC	JAL (Japan Airlines)	JL
Air France	AF	KLM (Royal Dutch Airlines)	KL
Air India	AI	Korean Air	KE
Air Jamaica	JM	LOT (Polish Airlines)	LO
Alaska Airlines	AS	Lufthansa	LH
Alitalia	AZ	Mexicana	MX
Aloha Airlines	AQ	Northwest Airlines	NW
America West	HP	Olympic Airways	OA
American Airlines	AA	Qantas	QF
American Trans Air	TZ	Sabena	SN
Austrian Airlines	OS	SAS	SK
Bahamasair	UP	**Singapore Airlines**	**SQ**
British Airways	BA	Southwest Airlines	WN
Cathay Pacific	CX	Swissair	SR
Continental Airlines	CO	TAP (Air Portugal)	TP
Croatia Airlines	OU	Trans World Airlines	TW
Czech Airlines	OK	United Airlines	UA
Delta Airlines	DL	US Airways	US
Egypt Air	MS	Varig	RG
El Al Israel	LY	Virgin Atlantic Airways	VS

ANATOMY—PARTS OF THE BODY

HEAD, NECK, TRUNK, LIMBS

ARM	CHAP	MANO	CANAL
EAR	CHIN	NAIL	CAPUT
EYE	CRUS	NAPE	CHEEK
GUM	CUSP	NECK	CHEST
HIP	DERM	NOSE	CILIA
JAW	DUCT	PALM	CROWN
LEG	FACE	PONS	CUTIS
LID	FIST	ROOT	DERMA
LIP	FOOT	RUMP	DIGIT
ORA	GYRI	SHIN	ELBOW
ORB	HAIR	SKIN	FRONS
TOE	HAND	SOLE	GLAND
	HEAD	TUBE	GROIN
ARCH	HEEL	UVEA	GYRUS
BACK	IRIS	VEIN	INION
BILE	JOWL	VOLA	JOINT
BONE	KNEE		LYMPH
BREE	LENS	ANKLE	MANUS
BUMP	LIMB	BELLY	MOUTH
BUST	LOBE	BLOOD	NARES
CALF	LOIN	BOSOM	NERVE
CELL	LOOF	BRAIN	NUCHA

INDEX	AXILLA	PAUNCH	METOPON
NUQUE	BASION	PLANTA	NOSTRIL
ORGAN	BREAST	POLLEX	OCCIPUT
OXTER	BREGMA	RETINA	PAPILLA
PELMA	CERVIX	RICTUS	TOENAIL
PENIS	CORIUM	SCRUFF	
PINNA	CORNEA	TEMPLE	ANTINION
PUPIL	CORTEX	THENAR	BRACHIUM
RUGAE	DACTYL	THORAX	CALLOSUM
SCALA	DORSUM	THROAT	CALVARIA
SERUM	EYELID	TONGUE	CEREBRUM
SHANK	FACIES	TRAGUS	FOREHEAD
SINUS	FINGER	TRIGON	OLFACTOR
THIGH	GULLET	VERTEX	OMPHALOS
THUMB	HAUNCH		PHILTRUM
TORSO	LABIUM	ABDOMEN	PLECTRUM
TRUNK	LOBULE	AURICLE	SHOULDER
UVULA	LUNULA	EARDRUM	SINCIPUT
VELUM	LUNULE	ENDERON	UNDERLIP
WAIST	MARROW	EYEBALL	UPPERLIP
WRIST	MEATUS	EYEBROW	
	MEDIUS	EYELASH	EPIDERMIS
ANTRUM	MENTUM	FOREARM	
ARMPIT	OCULUS	GINGIVA	
ARTERY	PALATE	LOBULUS	

BONES

OS	TIBIA	CRANIUM	EYETOOTH
	TOOTH	DENTINE	HEELBONE
HIP	VOMER	ETHMOID	LACERTUS
RIB		FRONTAL	LACRIMAL
	BICEPS	GRINDER	PHALANGE
DENS	CANINE	HAMATUM	SCAPHOID
FANG	CARPUS	HIPBONE	SHINBONE
OSSA	COCCYX	HUMERUS	SIDEBONE
ULNA	CUBOID	INCISOR	SPHENOID
	CUSPID	ISCHIUM	TEMPORAL
AMBON	CUTTER	JAWBONE	UNCIFORM
ANCON	DENTAL	JUGULUM	VERTEBRA
ANKLE	DENTIN	KNEECAP	
ANVIL	DIPLOE	KNUCKLE	CALCANEUM
BLADE	FIBULA	MALLEUS	CARTILAGE
CAPUT	HALLUX	MASTOID	CHEEKBONE
COSTA	INSTEP	MAXILLA	CUNEIFORM
FEMUR	LUMBAR	OSSELET	LACHRYMAL
HYOID	MAGNUM	OSSICLE	OCCIPITAL
ILIUM	PELVIS	OTOLITH	TRICUSPID
INCUS	RACHIS	PATELLA	VERTEBRAE
MALAR	RADIUS	PHALANX	
MEROS	ROTULA	SCAPULA	
MOLAR	SACRUM	SCIATIC	
NASAL	SPLINT	STERNUM	
PUBIS	STAPES	TRICEPS	
RAMUS	TARSUS	WORMIAN	
SKULL	ZYGOMA		
SPINE		BACKBONE	
TALUS	BONELET	BICUSPID	
TEETH	COCHLEA	CLAVICLE	

ORGANS AND GLANDS

COR	METRA	URETER	BRONCHUS
	OVARY	UTERUS	DUODENUM
GALL	VALVE	VISCUS	ENTRAILS
LUNG			PANCREAS
NEER	ATRIUM	BLADDER	PLACENTA
NEIR	BOWELS	ENTERON	PROSTATE
TEAT	CAECUM	FIMBRIA	TONSILLA
WOMB	CARDIA	JEJUNUM	WINDPIPE
	CARPUS	OMENTUM	
BOWEL	KIDNEY	PAROTID	DIAPHRAGM
CALYX	LARYNX	PHARYNX	ENDOCRINE
CECUM	MATRIX	PYLORUS	ESOPHAGUS
COLON	NIPPLE	SIGMOID	INTESTINE
GLANS	PLEURA	STOMACH	LYMPHATIC
HEART	PLEXUS	THYROID	PITUITARY
HEPAR	RECTUM	TRACHEA	VENTRICLE
ILEUM	SPLEEN	VISCERA	
LIVER	THYMUS		
MAMMA	TONSIL	APPENDIX	

ARTERIES, MUSCLES, JOINTS, NERVES, VEINS

CAVA	WRIST	DELTOID	MENTALIS
COXA		DILATOR	MUSCULUS
DURA	ARTERY	ERECTOR	PALMARIS
GENU	DUCTUS	GLUTEUS	PECTORAL
KNEE	FLEXOR	ILIACUS	PERONEUS
TELA	MYELON	JUGULAR	RISORIUS
VEIN	RECTUS	LEVATOR	SCALENUS
VENA	SOLEUS	MIDRIFF	SERRATUS
	TAENIA	NASALIS	SPINALIS
AORTA	TENDON		SPLENIUS
CHORD	TENSOR	ABDUCTOR	VENA CAVA
PSOAS	VASTUS	ADDUCTOR	
SINEW	VENULA	EXTENSOR	LABYRINTH
SPALD		GANGLION	SARTORIUS
TENDO	ARTERIA	LIGAMENT	SPHINCTER
TENIA	ARTHRON	MAMMILLA	TRAPEZIUS
TERES	CANINUS	MANDIBLE	
VAGUS	CAROTID	MASSETTE	

ARMS AND ARMOR

ARMS

CANNON AND GUN

*Indicates gun

DAG*	IRON*	DRAKE	CULVER
GAT	KRAG*	LUGER*	DRAGON*
ROD*	ROER*	MAXIM*	FALCON
	STEN	MINIE*	FOWLER
BREN*		MOYEN	HEATER*
COLT*	ASPIC	RIFLE*	JEZAIL*
HAIK*	BAKER	BARKER*	JINGAL*
HAKE*	BARIL*	BERTHA	LICORN

MAUSER*	BAZOOKA	SHOTGUN*	CARRONADE
MINNIE	BOMBARD	TEREBRA	DERRINGER*
MORTAR	BULLDOG*	UNICORN	HARQUEBUS
MUSKET*	CARBINE*		VEUGLAIRE
PISTOL*	DUNGEON*	CULVERIN	ZUMBOORUK
POMPOM	GATLING*	FIRELOCK*	
ROSCOE*	HACKBUT	HOWITZER	HARQUEBUSE*
TREPAN	LANTAKA	PISTOLET*	SERPENTINE
TUPERA*	LOMBARD	TROMBONE*	
	MOYENNE		BLUNDERBUSS*
BASTARD	ROBINET	AUTOMATIC*	

SWORD AND DAGGER

*Indicates dagger

SAX	CATAN	MACANA	YASHMAC
	DIEGO	PARANG	
BOLO	ESTOC	RAPIER	BASELARD
CHIV	KATAR*	SPATHA	CLAYMORE
CRIS*	KUKRI	STYLET*	DAMASCUS
DIRK*	SABER	TOLEDO	FALCHION
EPEE	SKEAN*	VERDUN	SCILAGER
FALX		WAFTER	SCIMITAR
FOIL	ANDREW		STILETTO*
KRIS	ANLACE*	BAYONET*	YATAGHAN
PATA	BANCAL	CUTLASS	
SEAX	SARONG	ESPADON	EXCALIBUR
TURK	BODKIN*	ESTOGUE	SCHIAVONE
	CREESE*	FERRARA	
BALAS*	DUSACK	KHANJAR*	MISERICORDE*
BILBO	FLORET	MACHETE	SNICKERSNEE*
BOWIE	GLAIVE	PONIARD*	
BRAND	KHANDA	SLASHER	

CLUB

KIRI	STICK	MULLAH	TRUNCHEON
MACE		TAIAHA	
MERE	WADDY		KNOBKERRIE
PATU		BLUDGEON	MAQUAHUITL
POLT	CUDGEL		POGAMOGGAN
	LIBBET	BLACKJACK	
BILLY	MACANA	BOOMERANG	MORGENSTERN
STAFF	MARREE	SHILLALAH	

AX

BILL	ONCIN	BOUCHER	FRANCISC
CELT	FASCES	HALBERD	LOCHABER
	MACANA	TWIBILL	PARTISAN
HACHE	POLEAX		TOMAHAWK

BOW AND ARROW

*Indicates arrow

BOLT*	VIRE*	LONGBOW	CROSSBOW
DART*	ROVER*	QUARREL	MANGONEL
REED*	SHAFT*	ARBALEST	SUMPITAN*
ROOD	ONAGER	BALLISTA	TREBUCHET
SELF*	SUMPIT*	CATAPULT	

MISSILE

BALL	SLUG	BULLET	TORPEDO
BOLA	GRAPE	DUMDUM	SHRAPNEL
BOLT	KILEY	PELLET	BOOMERANG
BOMB	SHAFT	WOMERA	PROJECTILE
DART	SHELL	GRENADE	
SHOT	ATLATL	OUTCAST	

SPEAR

DART	PILUM	ASSAGAI	TRIDENT
FRAM	SHAFT	BAYONET	VERUTUM
PIKE	VOUGE	BOURDON	
		HARPOON	GAVELOCK
ACLYS	ATLATL	JAVELIN	
LANCE	GIDGEE	LEISTER	
ONCIN	GLAIVE		

ARMOR
FULL SUIT

BARD	BARDE	JAZERANT	BRIGANDINE
MAIL	CUIRASS	PLACCATE	CATAPHRACT
WEED	PANOPLY		

BODY

TACE	CORIUM	LAMBOYS	PLASTRON
	LORICA	SURCOAT	
ACTON	TASSET		BRAGUETTE
CULET	TONLET	DEMISUIT	ECREVISSE
TASSE		DOSSIERE	HABERGEON
	BROIGNE	GAMBESON	MAMELIERE
BYRNIE	HAUBERK	PANSIERE	

HEAD AND NECK

COIF	CASQUE	BASINET	CABASSET
HELM	GALERA	GALERUM	GORGERIN
	GORGET	GALERUS	
ARMET	HEAUME	VENTAIL	COIFFETTE
GALEA	HELMET		
VISOR	MORION	AVENTAIL	CERVELIERE
	SALLET	BURGONET	MENTONIERE
BEAVER	SECRET		

SHOULDER TO HAND

ARMLET	BRASSART	CUBITIERE	REREBRACE
AILETTE	GAUNTLET	EPAULIERE	PASSEGARDE
ROUNDEL	PAULDRON	GARDEBRAS	
BRASSARD	VAMBRACE		

THIGH TO FOOT

JAMB	CUISSE	JAMBEAU	SOLLERET
CUISH	GREAVE	PALLETTE	GENOUILLERE
JAMBE	CHAUSSE	SABBATON	

AWARDS
ACADEMY AWARDS

Year	Picture	Actor	Actress	Director
1927–28	Wings	Emil Jannings	Janet Gaynor	Frank Borzage
1928–29	Broadway Melody	Warner Baxter	Mary Pickford	Frank Lloyd
1929–30	All Quiet on the Western Front	George Arliss	Norma Shearer	Lewis Milestone
1930–31	Cimarron	Lionel Barrymore	Marie Dressler	Norman Taurog
1931–32	Grand Hotel	Fredric March	Helen Hayes	Frank Borzage
		Wallace Beery		
1932–33	Cavalcade	Charles Laughton	Katharine Hepburn	Frank Lloyd
1934	It Happened One Night	Clark Gable	Claudette Colbert	Frank Capra
1935	Mutiny on the Bounty	Victor McLaglen	Bette Davis	John Ford
1936	The Great Ziegfeld	Paul Muni	Luise Rainer	Frank Capra
1937	Life of Emile Zola	Spencer Tracy	Luise Rainer	Leo McCarey
1938	You Can't Take It With You	Spencer Tracy	Bette Davis	Frank Capra
1939	Gone With the Wind	Robert Donat	Vivien Leigh	Victor Fleming
1940	Rebecca	James Stewart	Ginger Rogers	John Ford
1941	How Green Was My Valley	Gary Cooper	Joan Fontaine	John Ford
1942	Mrs. Miniver	James Cagney	Greer Garson	William Wyler
1943	Casablanca	Paul Lukas	Jennifer Jones	Michael Curtiz
1944	Going My Way	Bing Crosby	Ingrid Bergman	Leo McCarey
1945	The Lost Weekend	Ray Milland	Joan Crawford	Billy Wilder
1946	The Best Years of Our Lives	Fredric March	Olivia de Havilland	William Wyler
1947	Gentleman's Agreement	Ronald Colman	Loretta Young	Elia Kazan
1948	Hamlet	Laurence Olivier	Jane Wyman	John Huston
1949	All the King's Men	Broderick Crawford	Olivia de Havilland	Joseph L. Mankiewicz
1950	All About Eve	Jose Ferrer	Judy Holliday	Joseph L. Mankiewicz
1951	An American in Paris	Humphrey Bogart	Vivien Leigh	George Stevens
1952	The Greatest Show on Earth	Gary Cooper	Shirley Booth	John Ford
1953	From Here to Eternity	William Holden	Audrey Hepburn	Fred Zimmerman
1954	On the Waterfront	Marlon Brando	Grace Kelly	Elia Kazan

1955	Marty	Ernest Borgnine	Anna Magnani	Delbert Mann
1956	Around the World in 80 Days	Yul Brynner	Ingrid Bergman	George Stevens
1957	The Bridge on the River Kwai	Alec Guinness	Joanne Woodward	David Lean
1958	Gigi	David Niven	Susan Hayward	Vincente Minnelli
1959	Ben-Hur	Charlton Heston	Simone Signoret	William Wyler
1960	The Apartment	Burt Lancaster	Elizabeth Taylor	Billy Wilder
1961	West Side Story	Maximilian Schell	Sophia Loren	Jerome Robbins, Robert Wise
1962	Lawrence of Arabia	Gregory Peck	Anne Bancroft	David Lean
1963	Tom Jones	Sidney Poitier	Patricia Neal	Tony Richardson
1964	My Fair Lady	Rex Harrison	Julie Andrews	George Cukor
1965	The Sound of Music	Lee Marvin	Julie Christie	Robert Wise
1966	A Man for All Seasons	Paul Scofield	Elizabeth Taylor	Fred Zinnemann
1967	In the Heat of the Night	Rod Steiger	Katharine Hepburn	Mike Nichols
1968	Oliver!	Cliff Robertson	Katharine Hepburn/Barbra Streisand	Sir Carol Reed
1969	Midnight Cowboy	John Wayne	Maggie Smith	John Schlesinger
1970	Patton	George C. Scott	Glenda Jackson	Franklin Schaffner
1971	The French Connection	Gene Hackman	Jane Fonda	William Friedkin
1972	The Godfather	Marlon Brando	Liza Minnelli	Bob Fosse
1973	The Sting	Jack Lemmon	Glenda Jackson	George Roy Hill
1974	The Godfather Part II	Art Carney	Ellen Burstyn	Francis Ford Coppola
1975	One Flew Over the Cuckoo's Nest	Jack Nicholson	Louise Fletcher	Milos Forman
1976	Rocky	Peter Finch	Faye Dunaway	John G. Avildsen
1977	Annie Hall	Richard Dreyfuss	Diane Keaton	Woody Allen
1978	The Deer Hunter	Jon Voight	Jane Fonda	Michael Cimino
1979	Kramer vs. Kramer	Dustin Hoffman	Sally Field	Robert Benton
1980	Ordinary People	Robert DeNiro	Sissy Spacek	Robert Redford
1981	Chariots of Fire	Henry Fonda	Katharine Hepburn	Warren Beatty
1982	Gandhi	Ben Kingsley	Meryl Streep	Richard Attenborough

1983	Terms of Endearment	Robert Duvall	Shirley MacLaine	James L. Brooks
1984	Amadeus	F. Murray Abraham	Sally Field	Milos Forman
1985	Out of Africa	William Hurt	Geraldine Page	Sydney Pollack
1986	Platoon	Paul Newman	Marlee Matlin	Oliver Stone
1987	The Last Emperor	Michael Douglas	Cher	Bernardo Bertolucci
1988	Rain Man	Dustin Hoffman	Jodie Foster	Barry Levinson
1989	Driving Miss Daisy	Daniel Day-Lewis	Jessica Tandy	Oliver Stone
1990	Dances with Wolves	Jeremy Irons	Kathy Bates	Kevin Costner
1991	The Silence of the Lambs	Anthony Hopkins	Jodie Foster	Jonathan Demme
1992	Unforgiven	Al Pacino	Emma Thompson	Clint Eastwood
1993	Schindler's List	Tom Hanks	Holly Hunter	Steven Spielberg
1994	Forrest Gump	Tom Hanks	Jessica Lange	Robert Zemeckis
1995	Braveheart	Nicolas Cage	Susan Sarandon	Mel Gibson
1996	The English Patient	Geoffey Rush	Frances McDormand	Anthony Minghella
1997	Titanic	Jack Nicholson	Helen Hunt	James Cameron
1998	Shakespeare in Love	Roberto Benigni	Gwyneth Paltrow	Steven Spielberg
1999	American Beauty	Kevin Spacey	Hilary Swank	Sam Mendes
2000	Gladiator	Russell Crowe	Julia Roberts	Steven Sodebergh
2001	A Beautiful Mind	Denzel Washington	Halle Berry	Ron Howard
2002	Chicago	Adrien Brody	Nicole Kidman	Roman Polanski
2003	The Return of the King	Sean Penn	Charlize Theron	Peter Jackson

MISS AMERICA

1921	Margaret **GORMAN**	1941	Rosemary **LAPLANCHE**
1922–23	Mary **CAMPBELL**	1942	Jo-Carroll **DENNISON**
1924	Ruth **MALCOLMSON**	1943	Jean **BARTEL**
1925	Fay **LAMPHIER**	1944	Venus **RAMEY**
1926	Norma **SMALLWOOD**	1945	Bess **MEYERSON**
1927	Lois **DELANDER**	1946	Marilyn **BUFORD**
1928–32	(no award)	1947	Barbara **WALKER**
1933	Marion **BERGERON**	1948	BeBe **SHOPP**
1934	(no award)	1949	Jacque **MERCER**
1935	Henrietta **LEAVER**	1950	(no award)
1936	Rose **COYLE**	1951	Yolande **BETBEZE**
1937	Bette **COOPER**	1952	Colleen **HUTCHINS**
1938	Marilyn **MESEKE**	1953	Neva **LANGLEY**
1939	Patricia **DONNELLY**	1954	Evelyn **AY**
1940	Frances **BURKE**	1955	Lee **MERIWETHER**

1956	Sharon **RITCHIE**	1982	Elizabeth **WARD**
1957	Marian **MANNING**	1983	Debra **MAFFETT**
1958	Marilyn **VANDERBUR**	1984	Vanessa **WILLIAMS**
1959	Mary Ann **MOBLEY**		(resigned)
1960	Lynda **MEAD**		Suzette **CHARLES**
1961	Nancy **FLEMING**	1985	Sharlene **WELLS**
1962	Maria **FLETCHER**	1986	Susan **AKIN**
1963	Jacquelyn **MAYER**	1987	Kellye **CASH**
1964	Donna **AXUM**	1988	Kaye Lani Rae **RAFKO**
1965	Vonda **VANDYKE**	1989	Gretchen **CARLSON**
1966	Deborah **BRYANT**	1990	Debbye **TURNER**
1967	Jane **JAYROE**	1991	Marjorie **VINCENT**
1968	Debra **BARNES**	1992	Carolyn **SAPP**
1969	Judith **FORD**	1993	Leanza **CORNETT**
1970	Pamela **ELDRED**	1994	Kimberly **AIKEN**
1971	Phyllis **GEORGE**	1995	Heather **WHITESTONE**
1972	Laurel Lea **SCHAEFER**	1996	Shawntel **SMITH**
1973	Terry **MEEUWSEN**	1997	Tara **HOLLAND**
1974	Rebecca **KING**	1998	Kate **SHINDLE**
1975	Shirley **COTHRAN**	1999	Nicole **JOHNSON**
1976	Tawny **GODIN**	2000	Heather **FRENCH**
1977	Dorothy **BENHAM**	2001	Angela **BARAQUIO**
1978	Susan **PERKINS**	2002	Katie **HARMAN**
1979	Kylene **BARKER**	2003	Erika **HAROLD**
1980	Cheryl **PREWITT**	2004	Ericka **DUNLAP**
1981	Susan **POWELL**		

NOBEL PRIZE
CHEMISTRY

AGRE	**ALDER**	**CALVIN**	**SANGER**
CECH	**HUBER**	**HARDEN**	**SUMNER**
CRAM	**KARLE**	**HEEGER**	**TANAKA**
CURL	**KROTO**	**HEVESY**	**WALKER**
FENN	**LIBBY**	**KARRER**	**WERNER**
HAHN	**NATTA**	**LELOIR**	**WITTIG**
HOFF	**POPLE**	**MARCUS**	**ZEWAIL**
KLUG	**PREGL**	**MARTIN**	
KOHN	**SODDY**	**MICHEL**	**CRUTZEN**
KUHN	**SYNGE**	**MOLINA**	**KNOWLES**
LEHN	**TAUBE**	**MULLIS**	**OSTWALD**
OLAH		**NERNST**	**PAULING**
SKOU		**NOYORI**	**POLANYI**
TODD	**ALTMAN**	**PERUTZ**	**ROWLAND**
UREY	**BAEYER**	**RAMSAY**	**SMALLEY**

ECONOMICS

SEN	**OHLIN**	**MERTON**	**SCHOLES**
NASH	**SIMON**	**MILLER**	**SCHULTZ**
ARROW	**SMITH**	**MYRDAL**	**STIGLER**
COASE	**SOLOW**	**SELTEN**	**VICKREY**
ENGLE	**STONE**	**SPENCE**	
FOGEL	**TOBIN**		**HARSANYI**
HICKS		**AKERLOF**	**KAHNEMAN**
KLEIN	**ALLAIS**	**GRANGER**	**MIRRLEES**
LEWIS	**BECKER**	**HECKMAN**	**STIGLITZ**
LUCAS	**DEBREU**	**KUZNETS**	
NORTH	**FRISCH**	**MUNDELL**	**SAMUELSON**

LITERATURE

FO	HESSE	ONEILL	ROLLAND
OE	HEYSE	SARTRE	SIEFERT
	LEWIS	TAGORE	SOYINKA
PAZ	SACHS	UNDSET	WALCOTT
	WHITE		
BOLL	YEATS	BECKETT	FAULKNER
BUCK		BERGSON	GORDIMER
CELA	ANDRIC	BRODSKY	XINGJIAN
GIDE	BELLOW	CANETTI	CHURCHILL
MANN	DUGARD	COETZEE	HEMINGWAY
SHAW	ELYTIS	GOLDING	PASTERNAK
	EUCKEN	KERTESZ	SHOLOKHOV
AGNON	FRANCE	KIPLING	STEINBECK
BUNIN	HAMSUN	MAHFOUZ	
CAMUS	HEANEY	MARQUEZ	LAGERKVIST
ELIOT	JENSEN	MAURIAC	
GRASS	NERUDA	NAIPAUL	

MEDICINE

DAM	HENCH	ADRIAN	PAVLOV
	HUBEL	BARANY	PORTER
CORI	JACOB	BEADLE	RICHET
DALE	JERNE	BEKESY	SPERRY
HESS	KREBS	BISHOP	THOMAS
HILL	KROGH	BLOBEL	VARMUS
HUNT	LEWIS	BORDET	WATSON
KATZ	LOEWI	BURNET	WELLER
KOCH	LURIA	CARREL	WIESEL
ROSS	LWOFF	CLAUDE	
ROUS	LYNEN	DOMAGK	BRENNER
VANE	MINOT	ECCLES	DOHERTY
	MONIZ	ENDERS	FISCHER
ARBER	MONOD	FINSEN	FLEMING
BLACK	MURAD	FLOREY	HOPKINS
BLOCH	NEHER	GASSER	HORVITZ
BOVET	NURSE	GILMAN	IGNARRO
BROWN	OCHOA	HUXLEY	ROBERTS
CHAIN	SHARP	KANDEL	RODBELL
COHEN	SMITH	KOCHER	SAKMANN
CRICK	SNELL	KOSSEL	SULSTON
DOISY	TATUM	MORGAN	
ELION	TEMIN	MULLER	ERLANGER
GOLGI	YALOW	MURPHY	MEYERHOF
		MURRAY	MILSTEIN

PEACE

IRC	KING	BAJER	PASSY
KYI	MOTT	BALCH	PERES
ORR	PIRE	BEGIN	RABIN
THO	ROOT	DAWES	SADAT
	SATO	EBADI	
BELO	TUTU	FRIED	ADDAMS
HULL		GOBAT	ANGELL
HUME	ANNAN	LAMAS	ARAFAT
JUNG	ASSER	LANGE	BRANDT
			BRIAND

BUNCHE	MENCHU	WALESA	SANCHEZ
BUTLER	MONETA	WIESEL	THERESA
CARTER	MYRDAL	WILSON	TRIMBLE
CASSIN	NANSEN		
CREMER	QUIDDE	MANDELA	ESQUIVEL
DUNANT	UNICEF	ROTBLAT	SAKHAROV

PHYSICS

CHU	DALEN	FOWLER	CHARPAK
LEE	DAVIS	FRANCK	CORNELL
	DIRAC	GLASER	DEHMELT
BOHR	FERMI	JENSEN	KENDALL
BORN	FITCH	LANDAU	KOSHIBA
HESS	FRANK	LENARD	LEGGETT
LAUE	GABOR	PERRIN	MARCONI
PAUL	HERTZ	PLANCK	STORMER
PERL	HOOFT	POWELL	VELTMAN
RABI	HULSE	RAMSAY	
RYLE	KILBY	REINES	EINSTEIN
TAMM	KUSCH	ROHRER	GIACCONI
TING	MAYER	RUBBIA	GINZBURG
TSUI	PAULI	TAYLOR	KETTERLE
WIEN	RAMAN	TOWNES	KLITZING
YANG	RUSKA	WALTON	LAUGHLIN
	SEGRE	WIEMAN	OSHEROFF
BASOV	SHULL	WIGNER	PHILLIPS
BETHE	STARK	WILSON	ROENTGEN
BLOCH	STERN	YUKAWA	
BOTHE		ZEEMAN	ABRIKOSOV
BRAGG	BARKLA		
BRAUN	BINNIG	ALFEROV	
CURIE	CRONIN	BEDNORZ	

PULITZER PRIZE
DRAMA

BOCK	MAMET	LARSON	SACKLER
CRUZ	MOSEL	MILLER	SAROYAN
GALE	PARKS	NORMAN	SHEPARD
INGE	SIMON	ONEILL	WEIDMAN
RICE	VOGEL	WILDER	
UHRY		WILSON	ANDERSON
	ABBOTT	ZINDEL	GOODRICH
AKINS	COBURN		HAMLISCH
ALBEE	CROUSE	BURROWS	KINGSLEY
CHASE	FULLER	GORDONE	MACLEISH
DAVIS	GILROY	HACKETT	SHERWOOD
EDSON	HENLEY	HARNICK	SONDHEIM
FOOTE	HOWARD	KUSHNER	WILLIAMS
GREEN	HUGHES	LINDSAY	
KELLY	KLEBAN	LOESSER	
KRAMM	LAPINE	PATRICK	MARGULIES

FICTION

LEE	FORD	DAVIS	POOLE
	GRAU	DRURY	RUSSO
AGEE	ROTH	LEWIS	TOOLE
BUCK	WOUK	LURIE	TYLER

WELTY	MILLER	CHEEVER	HIJUELOS
	PORTER	COZZENS	MARQUAND
BARNES	PROULX	GLASGOW	MCMURTRY
BELLOW	SHAARA	GUTHRIE	MICHENER
BUTLER	SMILEY	LAFARGE	MITCHELL
CATHER	STYRON	MALAMUD	MORRISON
CHABON	TAYLOR	MOMADAY	RAWLINGS
FERBER	UPDIKE	RICHTER	SINCLAIR
FLAVIN	WALKER	SHIELDS	STAFFORD
HERSEY	WARREN	STEGNER	
KANTOR	WILDER	WHARTON	EUGENIDES
LAHIRI	WILSON		STEINBECK
MAILER		FAULKNER	

POETRY

DOVE	BROOKS	ASHBERY	MCGINLEY
DUNN	COFFIN	HILLYER	MEREDITH
TATE	DENNIS	JUSTICE	ROBINSON
	DILLON	KINNELL	SANDBURG
AIKEN	GRAHAM	MERRILL	SCHUYLER
AUDEN	HOWARD	MUELLER	TEASDALE
BACON	KUNITZ	MULDOON	VANDOREN
BENET	LEVINE	NEMEROV	WIDDEMER
DUGAN	LOWELL	ROETHKY	WILLIAMS
FROST	MERWIN	SHAPIRO	
GLUCK	MILLAY	SIMPSON	SNODGRASS
HECHT	OLIVER	STEVENS	WURDEMANN
KIZER	SEXTON	VANDUYN	
KUMIN	SNYDER	VIERECK	KOMUNYAKAA
MOORE	SPEYER		ZATURENSKA
OPPEN	STRAND		
PLATH	TAYLOR	BERRYMAN	
SIMIC	WARREN	EBERHART	
	WILBUR	FLETCHER	
BISHOP	WRIGHT	MACLEISH	

MUSIC

RAN	RANDS	ARGENTO	KIRCHNER
	ROREM	BASSETT	MARSALIS
HUSA	ROUSE	COPLAND	PETERSON
IVES		MARTINO	REYNOLDS
JOIO	ALBERT	MENOTTI	SCHULLER
TOCH	BARBER	SCHUMAN	SESSIONS
WARD	BOLCOM	SOWERBY	SPRATIAN
	CARTER	THOMSON	WUORINEN
ADAMS	HANSON	WERNICK	
BRANT	KERNIS	ZWILICH	CORIGLIANO
CRUMB	PISTON		DAVIDOVSKY
GOULD	PORTER	COLGRASS	DELTREDICI
KUBIK	POWELL	DRUCKMAN	LAMONTAINE
MOORE	WAGNER	HARBISON	SCHWANTNER
PERLE	WALKER		

GRAMMY AWARDS
LIFETIME ACHIEVEMENT AND LEGEND AWARDS*

**both awards

LEE, Peggy	BERLIN, Irving	MANCINI, Henry
WHO, The	CARTER, Benny	ORBISON, Roy
	CARUSO, Enrico	PRESLEY, Elvis
CASH, Johnny*	CASALS, Pablo	REDDING, Otis
COLE, Nat "King"	CROSBY, Bing	RICHARD, Little
COMO, Perry	DOMINO, Fats	ROBESON, Paul
GAYE, Marvin	EVERLY Bros.	SEGOVIA, Andres
JOEL, Billy*	HERMAN, Woody	SINATRA, Frank**
JOHN, Elton*	HOOKER, John Lee	VAUGHAN, Sarah
KING, B. B.	LENNON, John	
MONK, Thelonious	MARLEY, Bob	ANDERSON, Marian
	MATHIS, Johnny	COLTRANE, John
ACUFF, Roy	MILLER, Glenn	FRANKLIN, Aretha**
BASIE, Count	MILLER, Mitch	HOROWITZ, Vladimir
BERRY, Chuck	MINGUS, Charlie	MAYFIELD, Curtis**
BLAND, Bobby "Blue"	MONROE, Bill	MINNELLI, Liza*
BROWN, James	NELSON, Willie*	MITCHELL, Joni
CLINE, Patsy	PARKER, Charlie	PETERSON, Oscar
COOKE, Sam	PUENTE, Tito	ROBINSON, Smokey**
DAVIS, Miles	SEEGER, Pete	WILLIAMS, Sr., Hank
DAVIS, Jr., Sammy	WALLER, Fats	
DYLAN, Bob	WATERS, Muddy	ARMSTRONG, Louis
EVANS, Bill	WEBBER, Andrew	BEACHBOYS
GREEN, Al	Lloyd*	BELAFONTE, Harry
HOLLY, Buddy	WONDER, Stevie	BERNSTEIN, Leonard
HORNE, Lena		ELLINGTON, Duke
JAMES, Etta	ASTAIRE, Fred	GILLESPIE, Dizzy
JONES, Quincy*	BEEGEES*	GRAPPELLI, Stephane
MILLS Brothers	BENNETT, Tony	MCCARTNEY, Paul
PRICE, Leontyne	BRUBECK, Dave	PAVAROTTI, Luciano*
SMITH, Bessie	CHARLES, Ray	STREISAND, Barbra**
SOLTI, Sir Georg	CLOONEY, Rosemary	TOSCANINI, Arturo
STERN, Isaac	DIDDLEY, Bo	
TATUM, Art	GARLAND, Judy	FITZGERALD, Ella
TORME, Mel	GOODMAN, Benny	RUBINSTEIN, Artur
WELLS, Kitty	GUTHRIE, Woody	STRAVINSKY, Igor
ZAPPA, Frank	HEIFETZ, Jascha	
	HENDRIX, Jimi	ROLLING STONES
ATKINS, Chet	HOLIDAY, Billie	SIMON &
	JACKSON, Mahalia	GARFUNKEL
	JACKSON, Michael*	

TONY AWARDS
1st line, best play; 2nd line, best musical

Year	Play/Musical	Author/Composer
1948	Mister Roberts	Thomas Heggen
1949	Death of a Salesman	Arthur Miller
	Kiss Me Kate	Cole Porter
1950	The Cocktail Party	T.S. Eliot
	South Pacific	Richard Rodgers
1951	The Rose Tattoo	Tennessee Williams

	Guys and Dolls	Frank Loesser
1952	The Fourposter	Jan de Hartog
	The King and I	Richard Rodgers
1953	The Crucible	Arthur Miller
	Wonderful Town	Leonard Bernstein
1954	The Teahouse of the August Moon	John Patrick
	Kismet	Alexander Borodin
1955	The Desperate Hours	Joseph Hayes
	The Pajama Game	Richard Adler, Jerry Ross
1956	The Diary of Anne Frank	Frances Goodrich, Albert Hackett
	Damn Yankees	Richard Adler, Jerry Ross
1957	Long Day's Journey Into Night	Eugene O'Neill
	My Fair Lady	Frederick Loewe
1958	Sunrise at Campobello	Dore Schary
	The Music Man	Meredith Willson
1959	J.B.	Archibald MacLeish
	Redhead	Albert Hague
1960	The Miracle Worker	William Gibson
	Fiorello!	Jerry Bock
	The Sound of Music	Richard Rodgers
1961	Becket	Jean Anouilh
	Bye, Bye Birdie	Charles Strouse
1962	A Man for All Seasons	Robert Bolt
	How to Succeed in Business Without Really Trying	Frank Loesser
1963	Who's Afraid of Virginia Wolf?	Edward Albee
	A Funny Thing Happened on the Way to the Forum	Stephen Sondheim
1964	Luther	John Osborne
	Hello, Dolly!	Jerry Herman
1965	The Subject Was Roses	Frank Gilroy
	Fiddler on the Roof	Jerry Bock
1966	Marat/Sade	Peter Weiss
	Man of La Mancha	Mitch Leigh
1967	The Homecoming	Harold Pinter
	Cabaret	John Kander
1968	Rosencrantz and Guildenstern Are Dead	Tom Stoppard
	Hallelujah, Baby!	Jule Styne
1969	The Great White Hope	Howard Sackler
	1776	Sherman Edwards
1970	Borstal Boy	Frank McMahon
	Applause	Charles Strouse
1971	Sleuth	Anthony Shaffer
	Company	Stephen Sondheim
1972	Sticks and Bones	David Rabe
	Two Gentlemen of Verona	Galt MacDermot
1973	That Championship Season	Jason Miller
	A Little Night Music	Stephen Sondheim
1974	The River Niger	Joseph A. Walker
	Raisin	Judd Woldin
1975	Equus	Peter Shaffer
	The Wiz	Charles Smalls
1976	Travesties	Tom Stoppard
	A Chorus Line	Marvin Hamlisch
1977	The Shadow Box	Michael Cristofer
	Annie	Charles Strouse
1978	Da	Hugh Leonard

	Ain't Misbehavin'	Eubie Blake
1979	The Elephant Man	Bernard Pomerance
	Sweeney Todd	Stephen Sondheim
1980	Children of a Lesser God	Mark Medoff
	Evita	Andrew Lloyd Webber
1981	Amadeus	Peter Shaffer
	42nd Street	Harry Warren
1982	The Life and Adventures of Nicholas Nickelby	David Edgar
	Nine	Maury Yeston
1983	Torch Song Trilogy	Harvey Fierstein
	Cats	Andrew Lloyd Webber
1984	The Real Thing	Tom Stoppard
	La Cage aux Folles	Jerry Herman
1985	Biloxi Blues	Neil Simon
	Big River	Roger Miller
1986	I'm Not Rappaport	Herb Gardner
	The Mystery of Edwin Drood	Rupert Holmes
1987	Fences	August Wilson
	Les Miserables	Claude-Michel Schoenberg
1988	M. Butterfly	David Henry Hwang
	Phantom of the Opera	Andrew Lloyd Webber
1989	The Heidi Chronicles	Wendy Wasserstein
	Jerome Robbins' Broadway	(various)
1990	The Grapes of Wrath	John Steinbeck
	City of Angels	Cy Coleman
1991	Lost in Yonkers	Neil Simon
	The Will Rogers Follies	Cy Coleman
1992	Dancing at Lughnasa	Brian Friel
	Crazy for You	George Gershwin
1993	Angels in America: Millennium Approaches	Tony Kushner
	Kiss of the Spider Woman	John Kander
1994	Angels in America: Perestroika	Tony Kushner
	Passion	Stephen Sondheim
1995	Love! Valour! Compassion!	Tony Richardson
	Sunset Boulevard	Andrew Lloyd Webber
1996	Master Class	Terrence McNally
	Rent	Jonathan Larson
1997	The Last Night of Ballyhoo	Alfred Uhry
	Titanic	Maury Yeston
1998	Art	Yasmina Reza
	The Lion King	Elton John, Tim Rice, Jay Rifkin
1999	Side Man	Warren Leight
	Fosse	(various)
2000	Copenhagen	Michael Frayn
	Contact	(various)
2001	Proof	David Auburn
	The Producers	Mel Brooks
2002	Edward Albee's The Goat or Who Is Sylvia?	Edward Albee
	Thoroughly Modern Millie	Jeanine Tesori
2003	Take Me Out	Richard Greenberg
	Hairspray	(various)

THE BIBLE
BOOKS OF THE OLD TESTAMENT

King James Version	*Abbr.*	*Douay Version*	*Abbr.*
1. GENESIS	GEN	GENESIS	GEN
2. EXODUS	EX(OD)	EXODUS	EX(OD)
3. LEVITICUS	LEVI(IT)	LEVITICUS	LEVI(IT)
4. NUMBERS	NUM(B)	NUMBERS	NUM(B)
5. DEUTERONOMY	DEUT	DEUTERONOMY	DEUT
6. JOSHUA	JOS(H)	JOSUE	JOS
7. JUDGES	JUD(G)	JUDGES	JUD(G)
8. RUTH		RUTH	
9. SAMUEL I	SAM(L)	KINGS I	KI, KGS
10. SAMUEL II	SAM(L)	KINGS II	KI, KGS
11. KINGS I	KI, KGS	KINGS III	KI, KGS
12. KINGS II	KI, KGS	KINGS IV	KI, KGS
13. CHRONICLES I	CHRON	PARALIPOMENON I	PAR
14. CHRONICLES II	CHRON	PARALIPOMENON II	PAR
15. EZRA	EZ(R)	ESDRAS I	ESD
16. NEHEMIAH	NEH	ESDRAS II	ESD
17. ESTHER	ES(TH)	ESTHER	ES(TH)
18. JOB		JOB	
19. PSALMS	PS(A)	PSALMS	PS(A)
20. PROVERBS	PROV	PROVERBS	PROV
21. ECCLESIASTES	ECCL(ES)	ECCLESIASTES	ECCL(ES)
22. SONG OF SOLOMON	S OF SOL	CANTICLE OF CANTICLES	CANT
23. ISAIAH	IS(A)	ISAIAS	IS(A)
24. JEREMIAH	JER	JEREMIAS	JER
25. LAMENTATIONS	LAM	LAMENTATIONS	LAM
26. EZEKIEL	EZEK	EZECHIEL	EZECH
27. DANIEL	DAN(L)	DANIEL	DAN(L)
28. HOSEA	HOS	OSEE	
29. JOEL	JL, JO	JOEL	JL, JO
30. AMOS		AMOS	
31. OBADIAH	OB(AD)	ABDIAS	
32. JONAH		JONAS	
33. MICAH	MIC	MICHEAS	MICH
34. NAHUM	NAH	NAHUM	NAH
35. HABAKKUK	HAB	HABACUC	HAB
36. ZEPHANIAH	ZEPH	SOPHONIAS	SOPH
37. HAGGAI	HAG	AGGEUS	AGG
38. ZECHARIAH	ZECH	ZACHARIAS	ZACH
39. MALACHI	MAL	MALACHIAS	MAL

THE APOCRYPHA
*Indicates books in Douay Version

TOBIT	WISDOM*
BARUCH*	SUSANNA
ESDRAS I, II	MACHABEES I, II*
ESDRAS III, IV	ECCLESIASTICUS*
ESTHER*	BEL AND THE DRAGON
JUDITH*	PRAYER OF MANASSES
SIRACH	SUSANNA AND THE ELDERS
TOBIAS	SONG OF THE THREE CHILDREN

BIBLICAL NAMES

AHI	IVAH	AHLAB	LYCIA
BUZ	LAEL	ALVAN	MARLI
EVE	LEAH	BEZER	REAIA
ABBA	MARA	CUSHI	REUEL
ABDA	NAUM	ETRAM	SARID
ADAM	OBIL	HADAD	SHEAL
AIAH	ORAL	HADID	SILAS
BELA	OREN	HAGGI	SIRAM
ERAN	PUAH	HAMUL	TALAH
ESLI	REBA	ISHOD	TIRIA
EZER	SERA	ISHUI	UPHAZ
EZRI	SHOA	JAPHO	URIEL
HORI	SUAH	JARAD	ZABAD
IDDO	UCAL	JERAH	ZAHAM
IRAM	ADLAI	KEDAR	ZELAH
ISUI	AHBAN		

BIBLICAL RULERS

OG	BALAK	ZEBAH	SHINAB
ASA	CYRUS	ZIMRI	SISERA
GOG	DAVID	ABIJAH	UZZIAH
PUL	HAMOR	ACHISH	AHAZIAH
TOU	HEROD	ARETAS	AMAZIAH
AGAG	HIRAM	BAASHA	JOHORAM
ARAB	HOHAM	CAESAR	MENAHEM
AHAZ	JABIN	DARIUS	PEKAIAH
AMON	JOASH	HAZAEL	SHALLUM
BERA	HOBAB	HEZION	SHISHAK
DOEG	JORAM	HOSHEA	SOLOMON
ELAH	MESHA	JOAHAZ	ATHALIAH
JEHU	NADAB	JOSIAH	HEZEKIAH
NERO	PEKAH	JOSUAH	HYRCANUS
OMRI	PIRAM	JOTHAM	JEROBOAM
OREB	REKEM	LEMUEL	REHOBOAM
REBA	REZIN	NAHASH	SHESHONK
SAUL	REZON	NECHOR	ZEDEKIAH
AHIRA	SIHON	SARGON	

PRIESTS

ELI	ELIJAH	ELEAZAR	ELIASHIB
IRA	JADDUA	HILIXAR	JEHOIADA
EZRA	JOIADA	JOHANAN	AHIMELECH
AARON	JOSHUA	JOIAKIM	ZEPHANIAH
ANNAS	SAMUEL	SERAIAH	
URIAH	ALCIMUS	ABIATHAR	
ZADOK	ANANIAS	CAIAPHAS	

PATRIARCHS

DAN	ENOS	NOAH	ISAAC
GAD	ESAU	SETH	JACOB
HAM	HETH	SHEM	JARED
REU	IRAD	SIRE	JUDAH
CAIN	LEVI	ASRER	KENAN
EBER	NASI	ENOCH	NAHOR

PATER	JOKTAN	ISHMAEL	MAHALEEL
PELEG	JOSEPH	JAPHETH	MEHUJAEL
SERUG	LAMECH	ZEBULUN	NAPHTALI
TERAH	REUBEN	ARPHAXAD	METHUSAEL
CAINAN	SIMEON	BENJAMIN	METHUSELAH
CANAAN	ABRAHAM	ISSACHAR	

PROPHETS

AMOS	JONAH	ELISHA	OBADIAH
JEHU	MICAH	HAGGAI	JEREMIAH
JOEL	MOSES	ISAIAH	HABAKKUK
LEHI	NAHUM	NATHAN	ZECHARIAH
ODED	DANIEL	SAMUEL	ZEPHANIAH
HOSEA	ELIJAH	MALACHI	

QUEENS, QUEEN-MOTHERS

ABI	ZIBIAH	JERUSHA	NEHUSHTA
AZUBAH	AHINOAM	JEZEBEL	TAHPENES
ESTHER	BERNICE	MAACHAH	BATHSHEBA
NAAMAH	CANDACE	ZEBUDAH	JECHOLIAH
VASHTI	HAMUTAL	ATHALIAH	JEOHADDAM
ZERUAH	JEDIDAH	DRUSILLA	

JUDGES

ELI	TOLA	GIDEON	OTHNIEL
EHUD	ABDON	SAMSON	SHAMGAR
ELON	BARAK	SAMUEL	JEPHTHAH
JAIR	IBZAN	DEBORAH	ABIMELECH

WOMEN CHURCH WORKERS

LOIS	RHODA	PERSIS	SYNTYCHE
CHLOE	APPHIA	CLAUDIA	TRYPHENA
JULIA	DORCAS	EUODIAS	TRYPHOSA
LYDIA	EUNICE	SUSANNA	PRISCILLA
PHEBE	JOANNA	SAPPHIRA	

APOSTLES AND DISCIPLES

JOHN	brother of James
JUDE	
LEVI	= MATTHEW
JAMES	brother of John
JUDAS	= JUDE
JUDAS	ISCARIOT
PETER	brother of Andrew
SIMON	= PETER
SIMON	the Canaanite or the Zealot
ANDREW	brother of Peter
CEPHAS	= PETER
PHILIP	
THOMAS	DIDYMUS
MATTHEW	
MATTHIAS	Judas' successor
THADDAEUS	= JUDE
BARTHOLOMEW	Nathanael

BIBLICAL PLACES
TOWNS

DAN	BEREA	ASHDOD	TARSUS
LUZ	CALAH	BETHEL	ANTIOCH
NOB	DEBIR	CYRENE	ASCALON
ONO	DERBE	DOTHAN	BABYLON
CANA	ELATH	EMMAUS	BEEROTH
ETAM	ENDOR	GADARA	BETHANY
GATH	ERECH	GIBEAH	CORINTH
GAZA	GEBAL	HEBRON	EPHESUS
IVAH	GERAR	IBLEAM	JERICHO
MAON	GOLAN	KENATH	MEGIDDA
MARI	HAZOR	LIBNAH	NINEVEH
MYRA	JEBUS	MEDEBA	ASHKALON
TYRE	JOPPA	MIGDOL	CAESAREA
ZOAR	PERGA	PAPHOS	NAZARETH
ACCAD	RESEN	PISHON	TIBERIAS
ARDER	SIDOM	RIBLAH	BETHLEHEM
BABEL	SODOM	SARDIS	
BARIS	TROAS	SHILOH	

BIBLICAL SITES, MOUNTAINS, LANDS
SITES

UR	AENON	ATHLIT	MIZPAH
LUD	GEZER	BASHAN	SHARON
TOB	HALAH	BOZRAH	BAALBEK
ARAM	MOREH	ENGEDI	CALVARY
EDEN	NEGEB	HINNOM	GALILEE
ELAH	OPHIR	KADESH	GEHENNA
ELIM	PAHAN	KIDRON	SHITTIM
NAIN	SIRAH	LAGASH	BETHESDA
SHUR	AJALON	MASSAH	

MOUNTAINS

HOR	SEIR	SENIR	CARMEL
EBAL	ZION	SINAI	HERMON
NEBO	HOREB	TABOR	PISGAH
PEOR	MIZAR	ARARAT	THANACH

LANDS

NOD	SABA	MYSIA	CANAAN
EDOM	EDREI	PELLA	GOSHEN
ELAM	EKRON	SUMER	TADMOR
MOAB	JUDAH	ZOBAH	LEBANON

TRIBES OF ISRAEL

Sons of Jacob	Mother	Sons of Jacob	Mother
DAN	Bilhah	REUBEN	Leah
GAD	Zilpah	SIMEON	Leah
LEVI	Leah	ZEBULON	Leah
ASHER	Zilpah	BENJAMIN	Rachel
JUDAH	Leah	ISSACHAR	Leah
JOSEPH	Rachel	NAPHTALI	Bilhah

TRIBES

DAN	EMIMS	REUBEN	RODANIM
GAD	JUDAH	SEMITE	SABAEAN
KIR	LUBIM	SIMBON	ZEBULUN
LUD	MEDES	SINITE	BENJAMIN
CUSH	MINNI	AMORITE	GADARINE
EDOM	ANAKIM	DINAITE	ISSACRAR
LEVI	ARKITE	DODANIM	MIRARITE
MOAB	HAMITE	EDOMITE	NAPHTALI
PHUT	HIVITE	HITTITE	NAZARITE
SHOA	HORITE	MINAEAN	CANAANITE
UZAL	JOSEPH	MITANNI	SAMARITAN
ASHER	KENITE	MOABITE	SHELANITE
DUMAH	LEVITE	REPHAIM	

BOOKS OF THE NEW TESTAMENT

	Abbr.		Abbr.
MATTHEW	MAT	TIMOTHY I	TIM
MARK		TIMOTHY II	TIM
LUKE		TITUS	TIT
JOHN		PHILEMON	PHIL(EM)
THE ACTS	ACTS	HEBREWS	HEB(R)
ROMANS	ROM	JAMES	JA(S)
CORINTHIANS I	COR	PETER I	PET
CORINTHIANS II	COR	PETER II	PET
GALATIANS	GAL	JOHN I	
EPHESIANS	EPH(ES)	JOHN II	
PHILIPPIANS	PHIL	JOHN III	
COLOSSIANS	COL(OSS)	JUDE	
THESSALONIANS I	THESS	REVELATION	REV
THESSALONIANS II	THESS		

Note: All names as given above are also used in the Douay Version with the exception of Revelation, therein named APOCALYPSE (APOC)

FAMILY RELATIONS

Father	Offspring	Father	Offspring
ELI	Hophni, Phinehas	ESAU	Korah, Anah
HAM	Cush, Phut	JONA	Peter
JOB	Jemima, Kezia	KISH	Saul
NER	Abner	LEVI	Gershon, Jochebed
NUN	Joshua	NOAH	Ham, Shem, Japheth
ADAM	Abel, Cain, Seth	OBED	Jesse
AHAB	Athaliah	SAUL	Jonathan, Merab, Michal
AHAZ	Helekiah	SEIR	Timna
AMON	Josiah	SETH	Enos
ARAM	Mash	SHEM	Aram, Eber
BOAZ	Obed	SODI	Gaddiel
BUZI	Ezekiel	AARON	Nadab, Adihu, Eleazar,
CAIN	Enoch		Ithamar
CUSH	Nimrod	ABIEL	Kish, Ner
EBER	Peleg, Joktan	AMRAM	Aaron, Moses, Miriam
ELON	Bashemath, Adah	ASHER	Ara

Father	Offspring	Mother	Offspring
BEERI	Judith	ABI	Hezekiah
CALEB	Achsah	EVE	Abel, Cain, Seth
DAVID	Solomon, Tamar, Absalom,	ADAH	Jabal, Jubal
	Amnon, Adonijah,	ANNA	Mary
	Ithream, Maacah	JAEL	Shua
ELIAM	Bathsheba	LEAH	Levi, Dinah, Judah, Reuben,
ENOCH	Methuselah, Irad		Simeon, Zebulun, Issachar
HARAN	Lot, Milcah, Ischa	LOIS	Eunice
HEBER	Shuah	MARY	Jesus, James, Joses
HEROD	Antipas	RUTH	Obed
ISAAC	Jacob, Esau	ABIAH	Ashur
ITHRA	Amasa	EGLAH	Ithream
JACOB	Dan, Gad, Levi, Asher,	HAGAR	Ishmael
	Dinah, Judah, Joseph, Reuben,	NAOMI	Mahlon, Chilion
	Simeon, Zebulun, Benjamin,	RAHAB	Boaz
	Issachar, Naphtali	SARAH	Isaac
JAMES	Jude	TAMAR	Pharez
JARED	Enoch	TIMNA	Amalek
JESSE	David, Abigail	ABITAL	Shephatiah
JOASH	Gideon	BILHAH	Dan, Naphtali
JONAS	Peter	EUNICE	Timothy
JUDAH	Er	HANNAH	Samuel
LABAN	Leah, Rachel	JUDITH	Korah
MOSES	Gershom, Eliezer	MAACAH	Asa, Absalom, Abijah
NAHOR	Terah, Maacah, Huz	MILCAH	Haran, Rebekah, Huz
SERUG	Nahor	NAAMAH	Rehoboam
SIMON	Judas	RACHEL	Joseph, Benjamin
TERAH	Haran, Abraham	SALOME	James, John
ADAIAH	Jedidah	TALMAI	Maachah, Absalom
GILEAD	Jephthah	ZERUAH	Jeroboam
JETHRO	Zipporah	ZIBIAH	Joash
JOKTAN	Obal, Ebal	ZILLAH	Naamah
JOSEPH	Manasseh, Ephraim, Jesus,	ZILPAH	Gad, Asher
	James, Jude	ABIGAIL	Amasa
LAMECH	Noah, Naamah, Jabal,	AHINOAM	Jonathan, Amnon,
	Jubal, Tubalcain		Merab, Michal
MACHIR	Gilead	HAMUTAL	Zedekiah
MANOAH	Samson	JEDIDAH	Josiah
PHAREZ	Tamar	JEZEBEL	Athaliah, Jehoram
SALMON	Boaz	REBECAH	Esau, Jacob
SAMUEL	Abiah	REBEKAH	Leah, Rachel
TALMAI	Maacah	ZERUIAH	Joab, Asahel, Abishai
ABRAHAM	Isaac, Ishmael	ATHALIAH	Ahaziah
ABSALOM	Maacah	JOCHEBED	Moses, Aaron, Miriam
DIBLAIM	Gomer	ZIPPORAH	Gershom, Eliezer
ELKANAH	Samuel	BATHSHEBA	Solomon
ETHBAAL	Jezebel		
ISHMAEL	Massa	Wife	Husband
SHAPHAT	Elisha	ABI	Ahaz
SOLOMON	Rehoboam	ADAH	Lamech, Esau
ZEBEDEE	James, John	ANAH	Esau
ALPHAEUS	James	JAEL	Heber
HERODIAS	Salome	LEAH	Jacob
JEREMIAH	Hamutal	MARY	Joseph, Cleophas
REHOBOAM	Abija	RUTH	Mahion, Boaz
ZECHARIAH	Abi	ABIAH	Hezron
METHUSELAH	Lamech	EGLAH	David

Wife	Husband	Wife	Husband
EPHAH	Caleb	VASHTI	Ahasuerus
GOMER	Hosea	ZERESH	Haman
HAGAR	Abraham	ZIBIAH	Ahaziah
HELAH	Ashur	ZILLAH	Lemech
MERAB	Adriel	ZILPAH	Jacob
NAOMI	Elimelech	ABIGAIL	Nabal, David, Ithra
ORPAH	Chilion	ABIHAIL	Rehoboam
RAHAB	Salmon	AHINOAM	Saul, David
SARAH	Abraham	ASENATH	Joseph
SARAI	Abram	CLAUDIA	Pilate
TAMAR	Er, Onan, Judah	DEBORAH	Lapidoth
ABITAL	David	HAGGITH	David
AZUBAH	Asa, Caleb	HAMUTAL	Josiah
BILHAH	Jacob	JEDIDAH	Amon
ESTHER	Ahasuerus	JEZEBEL	Ahab
HANNAH	Elkanah	KETURAH	Abraham
JUDITH	Esau	REBEKAH	Isaac
MAACAH	David, Rehoboam	ELISHEBA	Aaron
MICHAL	Phalti, David	HADASSAH	= ESTHER
MILCAH	Nahor	HERODIAS	Herod
MIRIAM	Hur	JOCHEBED	Amram
RACHEL	Jacob	SAPPHIRA	Ananias
RIZPAH	Saul	ZIPPORAH	Moses
SALOME	Zebedee	BASHEMATH	Esau
		BATHSHEBA	Uriah, David

CHEMICAL ELEMENTS

Element	No.	Symbol	Type[1]	Group	Source
TIN	50	Sn	M		cassiterite
GOLD	79	Au	M		sylvanite
IRON	26	Fe	M		hematite
LEAD	82	Pb	M		galena
NEON	10	Ne	G		atmosphere
ZINC	30	Zn	M		sphalerite
ARGON	18	Ar or A	G		atmosphere
BORON	5	B	N		borax
*RADON	86	Rn	G		radium
XENON	54	Xe	G		atmosphere
BARIUM	56	Ba	M	alkaline-earth	barite
CARBON	6	C	N		graphite
CERIUM	58	Ce	M	lanthanide	monazite
CESIUM	55	Cs	M		pollucite
COBALT	27	Co	M		smaltite
COPPER	29	Cu	M		cuprite
*CURIUM	96	Cm	M	actinide	plutonium
*DUBNIUM					= HAHNIUM
ERBIUM	68	Er	M	lanthanide	gadolinite
HELIUM	2	He	G	natural	gas
INDIUM	49	In	M		sphalerite
IODINE	53	I	N	halogen	Chile saltpeter
NICKEL	28	Ni	M		nickelite
OSMIUM	76	Os	M		iridosmine
OXYGEN	8	O	G		atmosphere
*RADIUM	88	Ra	M	alkaline-earth	pitchblende

Element	No.	Symbol	Type¹	Group	Source
SILVER	47	Ag	M		argentite
SODIUM	11	Na	M		Chile saltpeter
SULFUR	16	S	N		limestone
ARSENIC	33	As	M		orpiment
BISMUTH	83	Bi	M		bismite
BOHRIUM	107	Bh	M	actinide	synthetic
BROMINE	35	Br	N	halogen	sea water
CADMIUM	48	Cd	M	zinc	ores
CALCIUM	20	Ca	M	alkaline-earth	gypsum
FERMIUM	100	Fm	M	actinide	plutonium
GALLIUM	31	Ga	M		bauxite
HAFNIUM	72	Hf	M		zircon
*HAHNIUM	105	Hn	M	actinide	synthetic
HASSIUM	108	Hs	M	actinide	synthetic
HOLMIUM	67	Ho	M	lanthanide	gadolinite
IRIDIUM	77	Ir	M		iridosmine
KRYPTON	36	Kr	G		atmosphere
LITHIUM	3	Li	M		spodumene
MERCURY	80	Hg	M		cinnabar
NIOBIUM	41	Nb	M		columbite
RHENIUM	75	Re	M		molybdenite
RHODIUM	45	Rh	M	platinum	ores
SILICON	14	Si	N		silica
SULPHUR					= SULFUR
TERBIUM	65	Tb	M	lanthanide	monazite
THORIUM	90	Th	M	actinide	thorite
THULIUM	69	Tm	M	lanthanide	rare earth
URANIUM	92	U	M	actinide	pitchblende
WOLFRAM		W			= TUNGSTEN
YTTRIUM	39	Y	M		rare earth
*ACTINIUM	89	Ac	M	actinide	pitchblende
ALUMINUM	13	Al	M		bauxite
ANTIMONY	51	Sb	M		stibnite
ASTATINE	85	At	N	halogen	bismuth
CHLORINE	17	Cl	N	halogen	salt
CHROMIUM	24	Cr	M		chromite
EUROPIUM	63	Eu	M	lanthanide	monazite
FLUORINE	9	F	N	halogen	fluorite
*FRANCIUM	87	Fr	M		actinium
HYDROGEN	1	H	G		atmosphere
LUTETIUM	71	Lu	M	lanthanide	rare earth
NITROGEN	7	N	N	sodium	nitrate
*NOBELIUM	102	No	M	actinide	curium
PLATINUM	78	Pt	M		alluvial
*POLONIUM	84	Po	M		pitchblende
RUBIDIUM	37	Rb	M		pollucite
SAMARIUM	62	Sm	M	lanthanide	monazite
SCANDIUM	21	Sc	M		monazite
SELENIUM	34	Se	N		clausthalite
TANTALUM	73	Ta	M		tantalite
THALLIUM	81	Tl	M		crookesite
TITANIUM	22	Ti	M		rutile
TUNGSTEN	74	W	M		scheelite
VANADIUM	23	V	M		vanadinite
AMERICIUM	95	Am	M	actinide	uranium
*BERKELIUM	97	Bk	M	actinide	americium
BERYLLIUM	4	Be	M	alkaline-earth	beryl

Element	No.	Symbol	Type[1]	Group	Source
COLUMBIUM		Cb			= NIOBIUM
GERMANIUM	32	Ge	M		germanite
LANTHANUM	57	La	M		rare earth
MAGNESIUM	12	Mg	M	alkaline-earth	magnesite
MANGANESE	25	Mn	M		pyrolusite
NEODYMIUM	60	Nd	M	lanthanide	monazite
*NEPTUNIUM	93	Np	M	actinide	uranium
PALLADIUM	46	Pd	M	gold	ores
*PLUTONIUM	94	Pu	M	actinide	pitchblende
POTASSIUM	19	K	M	potassium	chloride
RUTHENIUM	44	Ru	M		iridosmine
STRONTIUM	38	Sr	M	alkaline-earth	celestite
TELLURIUM	52	Te	M		sylvanite
YTTERBIUM	70	Yb	M	lanthanide	rare earth
ZIRCONIUM	40	Zr	M		zircon
DYSPROSIUM	66	Dy	M	lanthanide	rare earth
GADOLINIUM	64	Gd	M	lanthanide	gadolinite
LAWRENCIUM	103	Lw	M	actinide	synthetic
*MEDELEVIUM	101	Md or Mv	M	actinide	einsteinium
MEITNERIUM	109	Mt	M	actinide	synthetic
MOLYBDENUM	42	Mo	M		molybdenite
PHOSPHORUS	15	P	N		apatite
*PROMETHIUM	61	Pro	M	lanthanide	rare earth
*SEABORGIUM	106	Sg	M	actinide	
TECHNETIUM	43	Tc	M		uranium
*CALIFORNIUM	98	Cf	M	actinide	curium
*EINSTEINIUM	99	Es or E	M	actinide	plutonium
PRASEODYMIUM	59	Pr	M	lanthanide	rare earth
PROTACTINIUM	91	Pa	M	actinide	uranium
*RUTHERFORDIUM	104	Rf	M	actinide	synthetic

*radioactive element
[1]M = metallic, N = nonmetallic, G = gaseous

COLLECTIVE NOUNS

CAN	worms	DRAY	squirrels
CRY	hounds, actors	DULE	doves
DEN	thieves	FALL	woodcock
GAM	whales	GANG	elks
MOB	kangaroos	HAND	bananas
NYE	pheasants	HERD	elephants, horses
POD	whales, seals	HILL	beans, ruffs
RAG	colts	HOST	angels, sparrows
RUN	poultry	HUSK	hares
		KNOT	toads
ARMY	caterpillars, herring	LEAP	leopards
BALE	turtles	MUTE	hounds
BAND	gorillas	NEST	pheasants, vipers, wasps
BEVY	clams, oysters, swans, partridges	NIDE	pheasants
		PACK	hounds, wolves
CAST	hawks, bread	PAIR	horses
CETE	badgers	PASS	asses
DOSE	salts	PEEP	chickens
DOWN	hares	ROPE	pearls

SPAN	mules	SWARM	bees, eels
STUD	mares	TROOP	kangaroos, monkeys
TEAM	ducks, horses, oxen	WATCH	nightingales
TRIP	goats	WEDGE	swans
WALK	snipes		
WING	plovers	BARREL	monkeys
YOKE	oxen	CLUTCH	chicks
		COLONY	ants
BRACE	ducks	DECEIT	lapwings
BROOD	chicks	FLIGHT	birds, stairs
BUNCH	grapes	GAGGLE	geese
CATCH	fish	HARRAS	horses
CHARM	finches	KINDLE	kittens
CLOUD	gnats	LITTER	pigs
COVEN	witches	MURDER	crows
COVER	coots	MUSTER	peacocks
COVEY	partridge, quail	PASSEL	brats
CRASH	rhinoceroses	PENCIL	lines
DRIFT	swine	PLAGUE	locusts
DROVE	cattle, sheep	RAFTER	turkeys
FLOCK	geese, sheep	SCHOOL	fish
GRIST	bees	SLEUTH	bears
HORDE	gnats	SPRING	teal
HOVER	trout	STRING	ponies
LABOR	moles	TISSUE	lies
LEASH	foxes, greyhounds	VOLERY	birds
MONTH	Sundays		
PARTY	jays	CLOWDER	cats
PRIDE	lions	CLUSTER	cats
ROUND	drinks	CLUTTER	cats
ROUTE	wolves	COLLEGE	cardinals
SEDGE	cranes	DESCENT	woodpeckers
SHEAF	wheat	SOUNDER	boars, swine
SHOAL	fish	TIDINGS	magpies
SHOCK	corn		
SIEGE	cranes	CONGERIES	witches
SKEIN	geese	MUTATION	thrushes
SKULK	foxes, friars	PADDLING	ducks
SLATE	candidates	RICHNESS	martens
SLOTH	bears		
SMACK	jellyfish	EXALTATION	larks
SORDE	mallards	CONGREGATION	plovers

COLLEGES, NICKNAMES AND TEAMS
COLLEGES

COE	RICE	EMORY	DEPAUL
MIT	UCLA	LORAS	DEPAUW
NYU	YALE	PRATT	DREXEL
USC	BATES	RIDER	FURMAN
VMI	BEREA	SMITH	GANNON
VPI	BROWN	TUFTS	HARPUR
CASE	CLARK	AUSTIN	HOBART
DREW	COLBY	BAYLOR	HOWARD
DUKE	DRAKE	BUTLER	HUNTER
FENN	DRURY	CALVIN	LEHIGH

LOYOLA	XAVIER	COLGATE	OBERLIN
MCGILL	ADELPHI	CORNELL	PARSONS
MERCER	AMHERST	DENISON	RUTGERS
MORGAN	ANDREWS	FORDHAM	SIMMONS
OLIVET	ANTIOCH	GONZAGA	STETSON
POMONA	BARNARD	GOUCHER	STEVENS
PURDUE	BENTLEY	HAMPTON	STJOHNS
TEMPLE	BETHANY	HARVARD	SUFFOLK
TULANE	BOWDOIN	HOFSTRA	TRINITY
UPSALA	BRADLEY	LASALLE	WILLIAM
VASSAR	CHAPMAN	MCMURRY	YESHIVA
WAGNER	CITADEL	NEWCOMB	

COLLEGE NICKNAMES

DONS	MULES	TITANS	PIRATES
ELIS	AGGIES	UCLANS	QUAKERS
EPHS	AZTECS	BADGERS	ROCKETS
NAVY	BIGRED	BEAVERS	SOONERS
OWLS	BISONS	BENGALS	SPIDERS
RAMS	BRAVES	BOBCATS	TARTANS
TARS	BRUINS	BONNIES	TROJANS
UTES	CADETS	BRONCOS	VANDALS
VOLS	EAGLES	BULLETS	VIKINGS
ZIPS	EPHMEN	COUGARS	VIOLETS
BEARS	FLYERS	COWBOYS	BEARCATS
BULLS	FRIARS	DRAGONS	BUCKEYES
DUKES	GATORS	FALCONS	BULLDOGS
FORDS	ILLINI	GOPHERS	COLONELS
HAWKS	JUMBOS	HUSKIES	HOOSIERS
HOYAS	REBELS	INDIANS	KINGSMEN
IRISH	REDMEN	KEYDETS	TARHEELS
LIONS	SAXONS	LARRIES	WOLFPACK
LOBOS	TIGERS	MAROONS	WOLVERINES

COLLEGE TEAMS

Nickname	College/Team	State
AGGIES	California-Davis	CA
	New Mexico State	NM
	North Carolina A&T	NC
	Texas A&M	TX
	Utah State	UT
ANTEATERS	California-Irvine	CA
AZTECS	San Diego State	CA
BADGERS	Wisconsin-Madison	WI
BANANA SLUGS	California-Santa Cruz	CA
BEACONS	Massachusetts-Boston	MA
BEARCATS	Cincinnati	OH
BEARKATS	Sam Houston State	TX
BEARS	Baylor	TX
	Brown	RI
	Mercer	GA
	Morgan State	MD
	SW Missouri State	MO
BEAVERS	City College of New York	NY
	Maine-Farmington	ME
	Oregon State	OR

Nickname	College/Team	State
BENGALS	Idaho State	ID
BIG GREEN	Dartmouth	NH
BIG RED	Cornell	NY
BISON	Bucknell	PA
	Howard	DC
	North Dakota State	ND
BLACK BEARS	Maine-Orono	ME
BLACK KNIGHTS	Army	NY
BLACKBIRDS	Long Island	NY
BLAZERS	Bard	NY
BLOODHOUNDS	John Jay	NY
BLUE DEMONS	DePaul	IL
BLUE DEVILS	Duke	NC
BLUEJAYS	Johns Hopkins	MD
BLUE RAIDERS	Middle Tennessee State	TN
BOBCATS	Bates	ME
	Montana State	MT
	Ohio	OH
	SW Texas State	TX
BOILERMAKERS	Purdue	IN
BOMBERS	Ithaca	NY
BREWERS	Vassar	NY
BRONCOS	Boise State	IA
	Santa Clara	CA
	Western Michigan	MI
BRUINS	California-Los Angeles (UCLA)	CA
BUCCANEERS	Beloit	WI
	East Tennessee State	TN
BUCKEYES	Ohio State	OH
BUFFALOES	Colorado-Boulder	CO
BULLDOGS	Alabama A&M	AL
	Butler	IN
	California State-Fresno	CA
	Citadel	SC
	Fresno State	CA
	Georgia	GA
	Louisiana Tech	LA
	Mississippi State	MS
	North Carolina-Asheville	NC
	Samford	AL
	South Carolina State	SC
	Yale	CT
BULLS	South Florida	FL
CADETS	Army	NY
CANNONEERS	Pratt Institute	NY
CARDINALS	Ball State	IN
	Louisville	KY
	Stanford	CA
	Wesleyan	CT
CATAMOUNTS	Vermont	VT
	Western Carolina	NC
CAVALIERS	Virginia	VA
CHIEFTAINS	Seattle	WA
CHIPPEWAS	Central Michigan	MI
COBBERS	Concordia	MN
COLONELS	Eastern Kentucky	KY
	Nicholls State	LA

Nickname	College/Team	State
COMMODORES	Vanderbilt	TN
CORNHUSKERS	Nebraska-Lincoln	NE
COUGARS	Brigham Young (BYU)	UT
	Chicago State	IL
	Houston	TX
	Washington State	WA
COWBOYS	McNeese State	LA
	Oklahoma State	OK
	Wyoming	WY
COYOTES	South Dakota	SD
CRIMSON	Harvard	MA
CRIMSONTIDE	Alabama-Tuscaloosa	AL
CRUSADERS	Holy Cross	MA
	Susquehanna	PA
CYCLONES	Iowa State	IA
DELTADEVILS	Mississippi Valley	MS
DEMONDEACONS	Wake Forest	NC
DEMONS	Northwestern State	LA
DONS	San Francisco	CA
DRAGONS	Drexel	PA
	Moorhead State	MT
DUCKS	Oregon	OR
	Duquesne	PA
	James Madison	VA
DUTCHMEN	Union	NY
EAGLES	Boston College	MA
	Eastern Michigan	MI
	Eastern Washington	WA
	Emory	GA
	Georgia Southern	GA
	Morehead State	KY
ELIS	Yale	CT
ENGINEERS	Massachusetts Institute of Technology (MIT)	MA
	Rensselaer Institute of Technology	NY
EPHS	Williams	MA
EXPLORERS	LaSalle	PA
FALCONS	Air Force	CO
	Bowling Green	OH
FIGHTIN' BLUE HENS	Delaware	DE
FIGHTING GAMECOCKS	South Carolina	SC
FIGHTING ILLINI	Illinois-Champaign	IL
FIGHTING IRISH	Notre Dame	IN
FIGHTING SIOUX	North Dakota	ND
FIGHTING TIGERS	Louisiana State (LSU)	LA
FLAMES	Illinois-Chicago	IL
	Liberty	VA
FLYING DUTCHMEN	Hofstra	NY
FRIARS	Providence	RI
GATORS	Florida	FL
	San Francisco State	CA
GAUCHOS	California-Santa Barbara	CA
GENERALS	Washington & Lee	VA
GOBBLERS	Virginia Tech	VA
GOLDEN BEARS	California-Berkeley	CA
GOLDEN EAGLES	California State-Los Angeles	CA
	Southern Mississippi	MS
	Tennessee Tech	TN

Nickname	College/Team	State
GOLDEN FLASHES	Kent State	OH
GOLDEN GOPHERS	Minnesota-Minneapolis	MN
GOLDEN HURRICANE	Tulsa	OK
GOLDEN KNIGHTS	Clarkson	NY
GOLDEN LIONS	Arkansas-Pine Bluff	AR
GOLDEN TIGERS	Tuskegee	AL
GREEN WAVE	Tulane	LA
GREYHOUNDS	Moravian	PA
GRIFFINS	Reed	OR
GRIZZLIES	Montana	MT
HATTERS	Stetson	FL
HAWKEYES	Iowa	IA
HAWKS	Monmouth	NJ
HIGHLANDERS	California-Riverside	CA
	Radford	VA
HILLTOPPERS	Western Kentucky	KY
HOKIES	Virginia Tech	VA
HOOSIERS	Indiana	IN
HORNED FROGS	Texas Christian (TCU)	TX
HORNETS	Alabama State	AL
	California State-Sacramento	CA
	Delaware State	DE
	Kalamazoo	MI
HOYAS	Georgetown	DC
HURRICANES	Miami	FL
HUSKIES	Connecticut	CT
	Northeastern	MA
	Northern Illinois	IL
	Washington	WA
INDIANS	Arkansas State	AR
	Louisiana-Monroe	LA
	SE Missouri State	MO
JACKRABBITS	South Dakota State	SD
JASPERS	Manhattan	NY
JAYHAWKS	Kansas	KS
JUDGES	Brandeis	MA
JUMBOS	Tufts	MA
KANGAROOS	Missouri-Kansas City	MO
KEYDETS	Virginia Military Institute (VMI)	VA
KNIGHTS	Queens	NY
KOHAWKS	Coe	IA
LAKERS	Roosevelt	IL
LEATHERNECKS	Western Illinois	IL
LEOPARDS	Lafayette	PA
LIONS	Columbia	NY
	Emerson	MA
LITTLE QUAKERS	Swarthmore	PA
LOBOS	New Mexico	NM
LONGHORNS	Texas-Austin	TX
LORD JEFFS	Amherst	MA
LORDS	Kenyon	OH
LUMBERJACKS	Northern Arizona	AZ
	Stephen F. Austin	TX
LYONS	Mount Holyoke	MA
	Wheaton	MA
MACCABEES	Yeshiva	NY
MAROONS	Chicago	IL
	Roanoke	VA

Nickname	College/Team	State
MAVERICKS	Nebraska-Omaha	NE
MAWRTERS	Bryn Mawr	PA
MEAN GREEN EAGLES	North Texas	TX
MIDSHIPMEN	Navy	MD
MINERS	Texas-El Paso (UTEP)	TX
MINUTEMEN	Massachusetts-Amherst	MA
MOCS	Tennessee-Chattanooga	TN
MOUNTAINEERS	West Virginia	WV
MOUNTAIN HAWKS	Lehigh	PA
MUSKETEERS	Xavier	OH
MUSTANGS	Southern Methodist (SMU)	TX
NANOOKS	Alaska-Fairbanks	AK
NITTANY LIONS	Penn State	PA
ORANGEMEN	Syracuse	NY
OWLS	Rice	TX
	Temple	PA
PALADINS	Furman	SC
PANTHERS	Adelphi	NY
	Eastern Illinois	IL
	Northern Iowa	IA
	Pittsburgh	PA
	Wisconsin-Milwaukee	WI
PENGUINS	Youngstown State	OH
PHOENIX	Wisconsin-Green Bay	WI
PILOTS	Portland	OR
PIONEERS	Denver	CO
	Smith	NY
PIRATES	East Carolina	NC
	Seton Hall	NJ
POLAR BEARS	Bowdoin College	ME
PRESIDENTS	Washington & Jefferson	PA
QUAKERS	Pennsylvania	PA
RACERS	Murray State	KY
RAGIN' CAJUNS	Louisiana-Lafayette	LA
RAINBOWS	Hawaii	HI
RAMBLERS	Loyola	IL
RAMS	Colorado State	CO
	Fordham	NY
	Rhode Island	RI
RATTLERS	Florida A&M	FL
RAZORBACKS	Arkansas-Fayetteville	AR
REBELS	Mississippi	MS
RED RAIDERS	Colgate	NY
	Texas Tech	TX
RED WAVE	Haverford	PA
REDBIRDS	Illinois State	IL
REDHAWKS	Miami	OH
RIVERMEN	Missouri-St. Louis	MO
ROADRUNNERS	California State-Bakersfield	CA
	Texas-San Antonio	TX
ROCKETS	Toledo	OH
ROYALS	Scranton	PA
RUNNIN' REBELS	Nevada-Las Vegas (UNLV)	NV
SALUKIS	Southern Illinois	IL
SCARLET KNIGHTS	Rutgers	NJ
SEAWOLVES	Alaska-Anchorage	AK
SEMINOLES	Florida State	FL

Nickname	College/Team	State
SETTLERS	Pace	NY
SKYHAWKS	Tennessee-Martin	TN
SOARING EAGLES	Elmira	NY
SOONERS	Oklahoma	OK
SPARTANS	Case Western	OH
	Dubuque	IA
	Michigan State	MI
	Norfolk State	VA
	North Carolina-Greensboro	NC
	San Jose State	CA
	Tampa	FL
SPIDERS	Richmond	VA
STATESMEN	Hobart	NY
SUN DEVILS	Arizona State	AZ
SYCAMORES	Indiana State	IN
TAR HEELS	North Carolina-Chapel Hill	NC
TARTANS	Carnegie Mellon	PA
TARTARS	Wayne State	MI
TERRAPINS	Maryland-College Park	MD
TERRIERS	Boston	MA
THOROBREDS	Kentucky State	KY
THOROUGHBREDS	Skidmore	NY
THUNDERING HERD	Marshall	WV
TIGERS	Auburn	AL
	Clemson	SC
	DePauw	IN
	Grambling State	LA
	Jackson State	MS
	Memphis State	TN
	Missouri-Columbia	MO
	Morehouse	GA
	Princeton	NJ
	Tennessee State	TN
	Texas Southern	TX
	Towson State	MD
TITANS	California State-Fullerton	CA
	Detroit	MI
	Illinois Wesleyan	IL
	Oral Roberts	OK
TRIBE	William & Mary	VA
TRITONS	California-San Diego	CA
TROJANS	Arkansas-Little Rock	AR
	Southern California (USC)	CA
	Troy State	AL
	Virginia State	VA
UTES	Utah	UT
VANDALS	Idaho	ID
VIKINGS	Cleveland State	OH
	Lawrence	WI
	Portland State	OR
VOLUNTEERS	Tennessee	TN
WARRIORS	Marquette	WI
WAVES	Pepperdine	CA
WEEVILS	Arkansas-Monticello	AR
WHITE MULES	Colby	ME
WILDCATS	Arizona	AZ
	Kansas State	KS

Nickname	College/Team	State
	Kentucky	KY
	New Hampshire	NH
	Northwestern	IL
	Villanova	PA
	Weber State	UT
WOLF PACK	Nevada-Reno	NV
WOLFPACK	North Carolina State	NC
WOLVERINES	Michigan-Ann Arbor	MI
YELLOW JACKETS	Georgia Tech	GA
	Randolph-Macon	VA
	Rochester Institute of Technology	NY
YEOMEN	Oberlin	OH
ZIPS	Akron	OH

COLORS

ASH	gray	GULL	gray	ALOMA	yellow/red
BAT	gray	HEBE	red	AMBER	yellow/red
BAY	brown	HOAR	gray	ASHEN	gray
DOE	red/yellow	HOPI	brown	AZTEC	yellow/red
DUN	red/yellow	INDE	indigo blue	AZURE	blue
FOX	brown	IRON	gray	BAPHE	red
IVY	green	JADE	green	BEIGE	red/yellow
JET	black	LAKE	red	BERYL	blue/green
OAK	brown	LAKY	red	BLOND	yellow/red
RAT	yellow	LAMA	brown	BLUET	blue
RED		LAVA	yellow/red	BRICK	red/yellow
SKY	blue	LEAD	gray	BROWN	
TAN	red/yellow	LIME	yellow/red	CACAO	red/yellow
TEA	yellow/green	MESA	brown	CADET	blue
BARK	red/yellow	MILK	white	CAMEL	brown
BICE	blue/green	MOSS	green	CAMEO	(varies)
BLUE		MUSK	yellow/red	CEDAR	yellow/red
BOLE	red/yellow	NAVY	blue	CEDRE	green
BRAN	red/yellow	NILE	blue/green	CHING	blue
BUFF	yellow/red	NUDE	red/yellow	COCOA	brown
CLAY	yellow/red	OPAL	(varies)	CONGO	brown
CORK	brown	PINK		CORAL	red
CORN	red/yellow	PLUM	blue/red	CREAM	red/yellow
CUBA	brown	PUCE	red	DELFT	blue
CYAN	blue	PURI	yellow	DURRY	yellow
DEER	brown	ROAN	yellow/red	EBONY	black
DORE	yellow	ROSE	red	EMAIL	green/blue
DOVE	blue/gray	RUBY	red	EMBER	yellow/red
DRAB	brown	RUST	red/yellow	FAIRY	green
DUNE	red/yellow	SAGE	green	FLAME	red
DUSK	blue/red	SAND	red/yellow	FLESH	red/yellow
DUST	red/yellow	SAXE	blue	GREEN	
ECRU	red/yellow	SEAL	brown	GYPSY	brown
FAON	brown	SIAM	brown	HAZEL	brown
FAWN	brown	TEAK	brown	HENNA	brown
FLAX	red/yellow	WINE	red	HOARY	gray
FLEA	red	ZINC	blue/red	IVORY	white/yellow
GOLD		ACIER	gray	KHAKI	brown
GOYA	red	ACORN	red/yellow	LEMON	yellow
GRAY		AGATE	red/ycllow	LILAC	blue/red

LIVER	brown	CARROT	red/yellow	SALMON	red/yellow
MAIZE	yellow/red	CASTOR	red/yellow	SEASAN	red/yellow
MAPLE	red/yellow	CERISE	red	SEVRES	blue
MAUVE	blue/red	CHERRY	red	SHRIMP	red
MELON	red/yellow	CITRON	yellow	SIENNA	brown
METAL	gray/blue	CLARET	red	SIERRA	red
MOCHA	brown	COBALT	green/blue	SILVER	gray
MOUSE	gray	COCHIN	brown	SORREL	brown
MUMMY	brown	COFFEE	brown	STUCCO	red/yellow
NEGRO	brown	CONDOR	brown	SULFUR	yellow
NIKKO	blue	COPPER	brown	SULTAN	red
OCHER	yellow	CYANIC	blue	TIFFIN	brown
OLIVE	gray	DAHLIA	blue/red	TITIAN	red
PABLO	brown	DAMASK	red	TOMATO	red
PANSY	blue/red	DAMSON	blue/red	TUSCAN	red
PEACH	red/yellow	ERMINE	white	TYRIAN	blue/red
PEARL	gray/blue	ESKIMO	brown	VESTAL	red/blue
PERSE	blue	EVEQUE	blue/red	VIOLET	
PLOMB	gray	FALLOW	yellow	WALNUT	brown
POPPY	red	FUSTIC	yellow/red	YELLOW	
PRUNE	blue/red	GARNET	red	ZENITH	blue
PUTTY	yellow/red	HATHOR	blue	ADMIRAL	blue
RAVEN	black	HAVANA	brown	ANEMONE	red/blue
ROUGE	red	HUNTER	green	ANNATTO	red/yellow
SABLE	black	INDIGO	red/blue	ANTIQUE	red/yellow
SEDGE	brown	JASPER	yellow/green	APRICOT	red/yellow
SEPIA	brown	LIERRE	green	ARDOISE	red/blue
SIENA	red	MADDER	blue/red	BEGONIA	red
SIRUP	red/yellow	MALLOW	blue/red	BISCUIT	red/yellow
SLATE	blue/red	MANILA	yellow/red	BITUMEN	brown
SMALT	blue	MARINE	blue	CALDRON	red
SNUFF	brown	MAROON	brown	CARAIBE	brown
SPRAY	blue/green	MASCOT	blue/red	CARMINE	red
STEEL	gray	MASTIC	yellow/red	CELADON	green
STRAW	red/yellow	MIKADO	red/yellow	CELESTE	blue
SUDAN	red/yellow	MIMOSA	yellow	CHAMOIS	red/yellow
SUEDE	brown	MINIUM	red	CITRINE	yellow
TAUPE	yellow	MODENA	blue/red	CORBEAU	green
TAWNY	brown	MOUSSE	green	CRIMSON	red
TENNE	brown	MURREY	red	EMERALD	
TIVER	red	MYRTLE	green		yellow/green
TOTEM	red/yellow	NUTRIA	red/yellow	FEUILLE	brown
TWINE	red/yellow	ONDINE	yellow/green	FILBERT	brown
UMBER	brown	ORANGE		FIREFLY	yellow/red
VENUS	green	ORCHID	blue/red	FUCHSIA	red
ACACIA	yellow	ORIENT	blue	GAMBOGE	red/yellow
ACAJOU	brown	ORIOLE	red/yellow	GLAIEUL	red
AFGHAN	yellow/red	PAWNEE	red/yellow	GOBELIN	blue
ALESAN	red/yellow	PENSEE	blue/red	GRANITE	red
ARGENT	white	PONGEE	yellow/red	GRIZZLE	gray
AUBURN	red	PURPLE		HEATHER	blue/red
AUTUMN	red/yellow	PURREE	yellow	JONQUIL	yellow
BEAVER	brown	QUAKER	gray	LEATHER	red/yellow
BISTER	brown	RADDLE	red	LOBSTER	red/yellow
BISTRE	brown	RAISIN	blue/red	LOGWOOD	blue
BRONZE	brown	RESEDA	green	MAGENTA	red/blue
CANARY	yellow	RUBRIC	red	MALABAR	brown
CANDID	white	RUDDLE	red/yellow	MASCARA	red
CANNON	yellow/gray	RUSSET	brown	MATELOT	blue

MERMAID	yellow/green
MESANGE	green/blue
MUSTARD	red/yellow
NACARAT	red
OAKWOOD	brown
OLDWOOD	red
OPHELIA	red/blue
OXBLOOD	yellow/red
PEACOCK	blue
PERIDOT	green
PIMENTO	red
PONCEAU	red
PRAIRIE	yellow/red
PRALINE	brown
PRASINE	green
ROSEATE	red
SAFFRON	yellow
SCARLET	red
SERPENT	green/yellow
SUBFUSC	brown
TANBARK	brown
TEAROSE	yellow/red
THISTLE	blue/red
TILLEUL	green

TOBACCO	brown
TUSSORE	red
ABSINTHE	green
ALDERNEY	red/yellow
ALGERIAN	brown
BISMARCK	red/yellow
BORDEAUX	red
BRUNDORE	black/green
CAFENOIR	brown
CAPUCINE	yellow
CARDINAL	red
CERULEAN	blue
CHASSEUR	green
CHAUDRON	brown
CHESTNUT	brown
CINNABAR	red
CREVETTE	red
EMINENCE	blue/red
FUCHSINE	red
GENDARME	blue
GERANIUM	yellow/red
GLOWWORM	green/yellow
GUNMETAL	gray
HYACINTH	blue/red

LAVENDER	blue/red
MAHOGANY	brown
MANDARIN	red/orange
MARIGOLD	orange
MAUVETTE	blue/red
MAZARIN	blue
MOSSROSE	red
MULBERRY	red
MUSHROOM	brown
NOISETTE	brown
PALMETTO	yellow/green
PARAKEET	green
PERROCHE	green
PRIMROSE	red/yellow
RAWUMBER	brown
ROSEWOOD	red/yellow
SAPPHIRE	blue
SAUTERNE	red/yellow
SHAMROCK	green
TERRAPIN	brown
VIRIDIAN	yellow/green
WEDGWOOD	blue
WISTERIA	blue/red

DISEASES AND ACHES

POX	BULLA	RAMEX	CALIGO
STY	CAUMA	RHEUM	CANCER
TIC	CHILL	SHOCK	CANKER
UTA	COLIC	SPASM	CHILLS
	COUGH	SPRUE	CHOREA
ACNE	CROUP	TABES	COMEDO
AGUE	DINUS	TINEA	CORYZA
BLEB	EDEMA	TUMOR	COWPOX
BUBA	FAINT	ULCER	CRAMPS
BUBO	FAVUS	ULCUS	DENGUE
COLD	FEVER	UREDO	DROPSY
COMA	GLEET		ECZEMA
CYST	HIVES	ABASIA	EMESIS
GOUT	INOMA	ABULIA	GLIOMA
ITCH	KAKKE	AINHUM	GOITER
LATA	LEPRA	ALALIA	GRIPPE
PICA	LUPUS	ALBUGO	HERNIA
PUNA	LYSSA	ALEXIA	HERPES
RASH	MANGE	ALPHOS	HYDROA
VETA	MANIA	ANEMIA	IRITIS
YAWS	MUMPS	ANEPIA	LIPOMA
ZONA	MYOMA	ANGINA	MACULA
	NENTA	ANOPIA	MEGRIM
AGRIA	NGANA	APHTHA	MYOPIA
AGROM	PALSY	ASONIA	NAUSEA
ATAXY	PILES	ASTHMA	OMITIS
BENDS	POLIO	ATAXIA	OTITIS
BLAIN	POLYP	BRUISE	PALMUS
BUBAS	PSORA	BUNION	PESTIS

PLAGUE	COLITIS	TORMINA	HOOKWORM
PIOSIS	EARACHE	TOXEMIA	HYSTERIA
QUINSY	EMPYEMA	TRISMUS	IMPETIGO
RABIES	FIBROMA	TYPHOID	INSANITY
SCURVY	FISTULA	UVEITIS	INSOMNIA
SEPSIS	HICCUPS	VARIOLA	JAUNDICE
SPRAIN	ICTERUS	VERTIGO	LEUKEMIA
STRUMA	ILEITIS	WRYNECK	LORDOSIS
SYCOMA	LEPROSY		MELANOMA
TETANY	LINITIS	ACIDOSIS	MIGRAINE
TETTER	LOCKJAW	ADENOIDS	MYELITIS
THRUSH	LUMBAGO	AKINESIA	MYOSITIS
TUSSIS	MADNESS	ALASTRIM	MYXODEMA
TYPHUS	MALARIA	ALLERGIA	NECROSIS
ULITIS	MEASLES	ALOPECIA	NEURITIS
UREMIA	MOROSIS	BERIBERI	NEUROSIS
ZOSTER	MYCOSIS	BOTULISM	OBTUSION
	OSTEOMA	BURSITIS	PARANOIA
	OSTEOME	CARDITIS	PARAPHIA
ABSCESS	OSTITIS	CATARACT	PELLAGRA
ACHOLIA	OTALGIA	COPHOSIS	PHLEGMON
ADIPOMA	PARESIS	CORONARY	PHTHISIS
ALGESIA	PINKEYE	DEAFNESS	PINWORMS
ALLERGY	PODAGRA	DEMENTIA	PLEURISY
AMENTIA	POLYPUS	DIABETES	PRURITUS
AMNESIA	PRURIGO	DIARRHEA	PYORRHEA
ANAPHIA	PURPURA	DIPLOPIA	RACHITIS
ANGIOMA	RENITIS	DISCITIS	RHINITIS
ANOPSIA	RICKETS	DIURESIS	RINGWORM
APHAGIA	ROSEOLA	EMBOLIUM	SCIATICA
APHASIA	RUBELLA	EPILEPSY	SHINGLES
APHONIA	RUPTURE	ERYTHEMA	SMALLPOX
APHORIA	SARCOMA	EXANTHEM	STENOSIS
ASTASIA	SCABIES	FRACTURE	SYPHILIS
ATROPHY	SPASMUS	GANGRENE	TAPEWORM
BLISTER	STREMMA	GLAUCOMA	TOXAEMIA
CAISSON	SYCOSIS	HEADACHE	TRACHOMA
CATARRH	TERTIAN	HEMATOMA	VITILIGO
CHOLERA	TETANIA		
	TETANUS		

ENTERTAINMENT

FAMOUS MOVIES

AI	TRON	SHREK	STRADA
ET	ZULU	THING	TOPPER
FLY	AKIRA	ALIENS	ALADDIN
KES	ALFIE	AMELIE	AMADEUS
	ALIEN	BENHUR	BULLITT
BLOW	FARGO	BLOWUP	CAMILLE
DR NO	GHOST	CARRIE	DIEHARD
GIGI	GIANT	GREASE	JEZEBEL
IRIS	LAURA	HARVEY	MOROCCO
JAWS	MARTY	MATRIX	NETWORK
MASH	ORDET	PATTON	PLATOON
OMEN	ROCKY	PICNIC	ROXANNE
REDS	SHANE	PSYCHO	SABRINA

SERVANT	AIRPLANE	RASHOMON	NINOTCHKA
SUNRISE	CASTAWAY	STARWARS	NOTORIOUS
TITANIC	CHOCOLAT		STAGECOACH
TOOTSIE	DUCKSOUP	ANNIEHALL	TAXIDRIVER
TRAFFIC	FANTASIA	CHINATOWN	UNFORGIVEN
TWISTER	GODZILLA	CASABLANCA	INTOLERANCE
VERTIGO	HANNIBAL	EASYRIDER	
WITNESS	HIGHNOON	LOVESTORY	
	KINGKONG	NASHVILLE	

FAMOUS TV SHOWS

ED	ARNIE	BENSON	SPENCER
ER	BABES	BEULAH	TABITHA
	BETTE	CHEERS	VALERIE
ALF	COACH	CYBILL	WEBSTER
FAY	COSBY	FTROOP	WORKING
FLO	ELLEN	GIDGET	YESDEAR
INK	GRADY	GLORIA	
ROC	HAZEL	GRINDL	BROTHERS
ZOE	JENNY	INLAWS	CLUELESS
	JESSE	KOTTER	HENNESEY
ABBY	JULIA	MAGGIE	LOVEBOAT
AMEN	KOJAK	MARGIE	MISTERED
DUET	MAUDE	MARTIN	MUNSTERS
FISH	MOLLY	MICKEY	ROSEANNE
HYPE	NANCY	MOESHA	SEINFELD
MAMA	NANNY	NURSES	SIMPSONS
MORK	NIKKI	ROPERS	SPINCITY
NORM	PEARL	SCRUBS	SZYSZNYK
REBA	RHODA	SPARKS	THATGIRL
SIBS	SALLY	TOPPER	
SOAP	SIMON	TYCOON	
	SUSIE		BEWITCHED
TAXI	TAINA	BLOSSOM	DINOSAURS
THEA	TAMMY	FRASIER	HAPPYDAYS
TICK	TIIROB	FRIENDS	ODDCOUPLE
WKRP	TITUS	NEWHART	
	WINGS	PARKERS	GIRLFRIENDS
		PHYLLIS	JEFFERSONS
ALICE		SABRINA	
ANGEL	ARLISS		
ANGIE	BECKER	SANFORD	TOASTOFTHETOWN

FABRICS AND FIBERS

*Indicates cordage

MAT	BAST*	GROS	LACE
NET	BATT	HEMP*	LAME
RAS	COIR	HUCK	LAWN
REP	CREA	HUSI	LENO
SAK	CRIN	IKAT	LINT
TAT	DRAB	IMBE*	MACO
WEB	DUCK	IXLE*	MAUD
	ERUC*	JEAN	MESH
ACCA	FELT	JUSI	MOFF
ADAD*	FERU*	JUTE*	MUGA
ALMA	FLAX*	KELT	MULL
BAFT	GIMP	KEMP	PILE

PIMA	RUMAL	KERSEY	COATING
PINA	SAKEL	LAMPAS	DOESKIN
PITA*	SALLO	LINAGA*	DRUGGET
REPP	SATIN	LINENE	DUVETYN
RHEA*	SCRIM	LINSEY	EPINGLE
SABA	SERGE	MADRAS	ESPARTO
SANA*	SHELA	MALINE	ESTAMIN
SILK	SISAL*	MELTON	ETAMINE
SUNN*	SUEDE	MERINO	FILASSE
SUSI	SURAH	MOHAIR	FLANNEL
TAPA	SURAT	MOREEN	FOULARD
TASH	SWISS	MUSLIN	FUSTIAN
TASS	TABBY	NANKIN	GALATEA
TATE	TAMIS	OXFORD	GINGHAM
TRAM	TARSE	PEELER	HABUTAI
WOOL	TERAP*	PENANG	HOLLAND
	TERRY	POPLIN	JACONET
ABACA*	TOILE	RADIUM	MIXTURE
ADATI	TULLE	RAFFIA*	MOGADOR
ATLAS	TWEED	RATINE	NANKEEN
BAIZE	TWILL	SALLOO	ORGANDY
BATIK	TWIST*	SAMITE	ORGANZA
BEIGE	UNION	SATEEN	OTTOMAN
CADIS	VICHY	SAXONY	PAISLEY
CHINE	VOILE	SELING	PERCALE
CRAPE	WIGAN	SHELAH	SATINET
CRASH		STAPLE*	SILESIA
CREPE	ALACHA	TAMISE	STAMMEL
DATIL*	ALPACA	TANJIB	SUITING
DENIM	AMBARY*	TARTAN	TABARET
DOREA	ANGORA	THREAD*	TABINET
DORIA	ARMURE	TILLOT	TAFFETA
DRILL	BATTIK	TISSUE	TEXTILE
FILET	BEAVER	TOBINE	TICKING
FLOSS	BOUCLE	TRICOT	TIFFANY
GAUZE	BROCHE	TUSSAH	VEILING
GULIX	BURLAP*	TUSSEH	VELOURS
GUNNY	CADDIS	VELOUR	WOOLLEN
ISTLE*	CALICO	VELURE	WORSTED
IXTLE*	CAMACA	VELVET	
KAPOK	CAMLET	VICUNA	BARATHEA
KASHA	CANVAS	WADMAL	BIRDSEYE
KHAKI	CHINTZ	WOOLEN	BROCATEL
LACIS	COTTON	YACHAN	CASHMERE
LAINE	COUTIL	ZANANA	CHAMBRAY
LINEN	COVERT	ZENANA	CHENILLE
LISLE	CRETON	ZEPHYR	CORDUROY
LLAMA	DAMASK		COUTELLE
MANTA	DIMITY	ALACHAH	COUTILLE
MOIRE	DOMETT	ALLOVER	CRETONNE
MUNGO	DOWLAS	BATISTE	DOMESTIC
OLONA*	EPONGE	BROCADE	DUNGAREE
PANNE	ETOILE	BUCKRAM	DUVETINE
PEKIN	FAILLE	BUNTING	ESTAMENE
PIQUE	FLEECE	CAMBRIC	HOMESPUN
PLAID	FRIEZE	CHALLIS	JACQUARD
PLUSH	FRISCA	CHAMOIS	LUSTRINE
RAMIE	GLORIA	CHEVIOT	MILANESE
ROMAL	GURRAH	CHIFFON	MOGADORE

MOLESKIN	TARLATAN	COTTONADE	MESSALINE
NAINSOOK	TARLETAN	EIDERDOWN	ORGANZINE
OILCLOTH	VALENCIA	GABARDINE	PARAMATTA
OSNABURG	WHIPCORD	GEORGETTE	PERCALINE
PRUNELLA	ZIBELINE	GRENADINE	SATINETTE
SARSENET		GROSGRAIN	SHARKSKIN
SHANTUNG	ALBATROSS	HAIRCLOTH	TRICOTINE
SHEETING	ASTRAKHAN	HUCKABACK	VELVETEEN
SHIRTING	BENGALINE	LONGCLOTH	
TAPESTRY	CASSIMERE	MATELASSE	

MAN-MADE FABRICS AND FIBERS

ARNEL	ARALAC	FORTREL	REVOLITE
DYNEL	DACRON	GORETEX	REXENITE
FIBRO	DYNELO	SARELON	
KODEL	LASTEX	SPANDEX	FIBERGLAS
LYCRA	TYCORA	TREVIRA	FIBREGLAS
NYLON	VICARA		POLYESTER
ORLON	VINYON	CAPROLAN	POLYFIBRE
RAYON		CELANESE	
VELON	ACETATE	FIBREFAX	CHEMSTRAND
	ACRILAN	FORTISAN	

RUGS AND CARPETS

AGRA	SUMAK	TADRIZ	DAGESTAN
BAKU	TAPET	WILTON	FERAGHAN
KUBA	TEKKE		GHIORDES
	USHAK	BERGAMA	KABISTAN
CHILA	YOMUD	BERGAMO	KARABAGH
HERAT	YORUK	BOKHARA	LESGHIAN
KAZAK		DERBEND	SERABEND
KILIM	AFGHAN	DRUGGET	
KULAH	GELEEM	FERAHAN	ANATOLIAN
LADIK	HERATI	GIORDES	AXMINSTER
MECCA	KASHAN	GUENDJE	BROADLOOM
MELAS	KIRMAN	HAMADAN	CAUCASIAN
MELES	MOGHAN	INGRAIN	KHOROSSAN
MOSUL	NAMMAD	ISFAHAN	KURDISTAN
NAMDA	OUSHAK	SHIRVAN	SAMARKAND
NUMDA	RUNNER		
SARUK	SAROUK	AKHISSAR	
SENNA	SHIRAZ	BRUSSELS	

FAMOUS NAMES

(see also LITERATURE, p. 624)

ARCHITECTS

LIN	LOOS	WANK	HOBAN
PEI	MEAD	WREN	JONES
ADAM	MIES	AALTO	MCKIM
HOOD	NASH	BACON	MELER
HUNT	POPE	COSTA	MILLS
JAHN	POST	GAUDI(YCORNET)	MOORE
KAHN	ROOT	GEHRY	OBATA

PELLI	SMIRKE	LESCAZE	PALLADIO
PUGIN	UPJOHN	LUTYENS	PIRANESI
ROCHE	URBAHN	MAYBECK	SAARINEN
SOANE	WAGNER	OLMSTED	SKIDMORE
STEIN	WALKER	PEREIRA	SULLIVAN
STONE	WALTER	PORTMAN	VANBRUGH
WHITE	WRIGHT	RUDOLPH	YAMASAKI
BREUER	ALBERTI	VENTURI	BELLUSCHI
CHANIN	BEHRENS	WURSTER	BORROMINI
EIFFEL	BERLAGE	BRAMANTE	CORBUSIER
FULLER	BERNINI	BULFINCH	JEFFERSON
GIOTTO	BURNHAM	BUNSHAFT	LABROUSTE
GRAVES	DAVINCI	CHAMBERS	MACKINTOSH
JENNEY	GARNIER	HARDOUIN	MENDELSOHN
KLENZE	GROPIUS	HARRISON	RICHARDSON
LEDOUX	HALPRIN	HASTINGS	STRICKLAND
NEUTRA	KOHNSON	HOFFMANN	LECORBUSIER
PAXTON	LAFARGE	LEONARDO	BRUNELLESCHI
ROGERS	LATROBE	NIEMEYER	MICHELANGELO

ASTRONOMERS

BODE	HEWISH	GALILEO	SHOEMAKER
HALE	HUBBLE	LAPLACE	WOLSZCZAN
OORT	KEPLER	PENZIAS	COPERNICUS
BRAHE	KUIPER	PTOLOMY	HIPPARCHUS
HOYLE	LOWELL	SHAPLEY	SCHIAPARELLI
JEANS	NEWTON	WHIPPLE	
SAGAN	PIAZZI	HERSCHEL	
HALLEY	CASSINI	TOMBAUGH	

BIOLOGISTS, NATURALISTS

(see also p. 509)

TULL	DARWIN	BORLAUG	LINNAEUS
COHEN	MENDEL	BURBANK	VONFRISCH
SACHS	MILLER	DEVRIES	LEEWENHOEK
CARVER	AUDUBON	LAMARCK	THEOPHRASTUS
CUVIER	BATESON	WALLACE	

CHEMISTS

(see also p. 508)

DAVY	BECHER	HODGKIN	ARRHENIUS
HOFF	COUPER	OSTWALD	BOLTZMANN
UREY	DALTON	PASTEUR	CANIZZARO
BOYLE	KEKULE	PAULING	CAVENDISH
CURIE	LIEBIG	SEABORG	LAVOISIER
KUHNE	PROUST	AVOGADRO	MENDELEEV
NOBEL	BUCHNER	LANGMUIR	PRIESTLEY
SODDY	CROOKES	MILLIKAN	
STAHL	FISCHER	NEWLANDS	

CARTOONISTS

FOX	LOW	BECK	GRAY
KEY	REA	CAPP	HART
LEE	ARNO	DING	KANE

KING	KEANE	DISNEY	FRELENG
NAST	KELLY	FISHER	HOGARTH
SZEP	KIRBY	FOSTER	KETCHAM
ADAMS	KOREN	HARVEY	MAULDIN
BARKS	LANTZ	LARSON	MONTANA
BOOTH	MINGO	LEVINE	PROHIAS
BUELL	MYERS	MARTIN	RAYMOND
CHAST	OPPER	MOORES	SHUSTER
CRANE	SEGAR	MULLIN	THURBER
CRUMB	STEIG	PETERS	TRUDEAU
DAVIS	STONE	SCHULZ	GOLDBERG
DIRKS	YOUNG	SIEGEL	GROENING
DITKO	ADDAMS	SOGLOW	HERBLOCK
GOULD	CANIFF	WALKER	MACNELLY
HATLO	CONRAD	WILSON	OLIPHANT
JUDGE	DEBECK	FEIFFER	

CHOREOGRAPHERS

FELD	SHAWN	HORTON	VESTRIS
HOLM	THARP	IVANOV	WEIDMAN
KURT	TUDOR	PETIPA	CHAMPION
PAGE	ARPINO	TAYLOR	NIJINSKY
AILEY	ASHTON	TETLEY	NIKOLAIS
FOSSE	BEJART	WIGMAN	MACMILLAN
JONES	BLASIS	DEMILLE	BALANCHINE
KELLY	CRANKO	JOFFREY	CUNNINGHAM
LIFAR	DUNHAM	MASSINE	
LIMON	FOKINE	NOVERRE	
PETIT	GRAHAM	ROBBINS	

COMEDIANS

MAY	BRICE	FIELDS	GLEASON
BALL	BURNS	KEATON	GROUCHO
BARR	CHASE	KOVACS	HACKETT
COCA	COHEN	LAUREL	NEWHART
HOPE	HARDY	LITTLE	RICKLES
KAYE	LEWIS	MARTIN	SKELTON
LAHR	LLOYD	RADNER	VANDYKE
MARX	PITTS	TOMLIN	COSTELLO
SAHL	PRYOR	WILSON	ROSEANNE
WYNN	SALES	AYKROYD	FERNANDEL
ALLEN	ABBOTT	BELUSHI	
BENNY	CAESAR	BUTTONS	
BORGE	DRAPER	CHAPLIN	

COMPOSERS

ABT	IVES	BIZET	GREEN
ARNE	KERN	BLAKE	GRIEG
BACH	LALO	BLOCH	GROFE
BERG	ROME	COHAN	GUIDO
BOCK	WOLF	DINDY	HANDY
CAGE	ADLER	DUKAS	HAYDN
DUKE	ARLEN	ELGAR	HOLST
FAIN	AUBER	FRIML	IBERT
FOSS	BALFE	GLUCK	LEHAR

LISZT	COWARD	BABBITT	PURCELL
LOEWE	DELIUS	BELLINI	RODGERS
LULLY	DVORAK	BERLIOZ	ROMBERG
RAVEL	FOSTER	BORODIN	ROSSINI
REGER	FRANCK	BRITTEN	SMETANA
ROREM	GOUNOD	COPLAND	STRAUSS
SOUSA	HANDEL	CORELLI	VIVALDI
STYNE	JOPLIN	DEBUSSY	YOUMANS
VERDI	LENNON	DEFALLA	GERSHWIN
WEBER	MAHLER	DELIBES	MASCAGNI
WEILL	MOZART	HERBERT	MASSENET
BARBER	PORTER	JOSQUIN	SCHUBERT
BARTOK	ROGERS	LOESSER	SIBELIUS
BERLIN	SCHUTZ	MANCINI	SONDHEIM
BOULEZ	TAYLOR	MENOTTI	SULLIVAN
BRAHMS	WAGNER	MILHAUD	TELEMANN
CARTER	WEBERN	POULENC	BACHARACH
CHOPIN	ALBENIZ	PUCCINI	BERNSTEIN

DANCERS

ALME	HORTON	JAMISON	KIRKLAND
BRUHN	PERROT	MARKOVA	MAKAROVA
DOLIN	PETIPA	MARTINS	MITCHELL
GRISI	ROGERS	MASSINE	NIJINSKA
JONES	TETLEY	NUREYEV	NIJINSKY
KELLY	VALOIS	PAVLOVA	ROBINSON
LIFAR	WIGMAN	RAMBERT	TAGLIONI
LIMON	ZORINA	SHEARER	VILLELLA
RASCH	ASTAIRE	STDENIS	KARSAVINA
SALLE	BUJONES	ULANOVA	TALLCHIEF
SHAWN	CAMARGO	VESTRIS	CUNNINGHAM
ALONSO	CERRITO	WEIDMAN	BARYSHNIKOV
BOLGER	EISSLER	DAMBOISE	PLISETSKAYA
CASTLE	FARRELL	DANILOVA	YOUSKEVITCH
DUNCAN	FONTEYN	EGLEVSKY	
GRAHAM	GREGORY	HUMPHREY	

DIRECTORS

(see also p. 505)

LEE	BUNUEL	BERGMAN	LUBITSCH
OZU	DESICA	CHAPLIN	SCORSESE
RAY	GODARD	COPPOLA	TRUFFAUT
COEN	MURNAU	DEMILLE	ALMODOVAR
FORD	OPHULS	FELLINI	ANTONIONI
LANG	POWELL	KUBRICK	HITCHCOCK
LEAN	RENOIR	SEMBENE	SPIELBERG
CAPRA	WELLES	GRIFFITH	EISENSTEIN
HAWKS	WILDER	KUROSAWA	FASSBINDER

DISCOVERERS

OHM	LEIF	DAVYS	FREUD
DAVY	SALK	DEWAR	GABOR
ERIC	BINET	FERMI	HENRY
KOCH	CURIE	FIELD	HERTZ

SABIN	KEPLER	EHRLICH	PASTEUR
SIMON	MENDEL	FARADAY	WAKSMAN
DALTON	NEWTON	FLEMING	COLUMBUS
DARWIN	PAVLOV	GALILEI	EINSTEIN
DOMAGK	PLANCK	GALILEO	HERSCHEL
EUCLID	WALLIS	HUYGENS	LINNAEUS
HARVEY	BANTING	KENDALL	THOMPSON
JENNER	CARLSON	MOSELEY	DESCARTES

ENTREPRENEURS

FORD	GATES	DISNEY	CANDLER
JOBS	GETTY	DUPONT	COLGATE
KROC	HONDA	FISHER	EASTMAN
WARD	KRUPP	HAMMER	KELLOGG
ARDEN	SEARS	HUGHES	CARNEGIE
ASTOR	SLOAN	MORGAN	SINCLAIR
BUSCH	ARMOUR	MORITA	VANDERBILT
FIELD	CONRAN	BRANSON	ROCKEFELLER

EXPLORERS

RAE	SCOTT	DESOTO	PIZARRO
LEIF	SMITH	DEVACA	RALEIGH
BYRD	ULLOA	ESPEJO	CABRILLO
PIKE	AMADAS	HUDSON	CARDENAS
CABOT	BALBOA	PINEDA	CAVELIER
CLARK	BARLOW	PINZON	COLUMBUS
DRAKE	BERING	WILKES	MAGELLAN
HEDIN	CABRAL	ALARCON	VESPUCCI
LEWIS	CORTES	CARTIER	CHAMPLAIN
LOGAN	DAGAMA	ERICSON	FROBISHER
ONATE	DELEON	JOLLIET	MACKENZIE
PERRY	DELONG	MENDOZA	MARQUETTE
PONCE	DENIZA	NICOLET	MARQUETTE

HISTORIANS

LOT	CANTU	DAUNOU	CARLYLE
BEDE	NEPOS	FROUDE	LELEWEL
HUME	PARIS	GIBBON	PSELLUS
KNOX	PLINY	MIGNET	SALLUST
LIVY	RANKE	MOTLEY	TACITUS
MORE	RENAN	OSGOOD	TOYNBEE
STOW	SEGUR	STUBBS	HERODOTUS
ADAMS	SKENE	WILSON	
BACON	STEIN	BOSSUET	
BEARD	CAMDEN	BOSWELL	

INVENTORS

HOE	IVES	WATT	MORSE
BELL	LAND	YALE	NOBEL
BENZ	LONG	BAIRD	ORAIN
COLT	OTIS	COOKE	TESLA
DAVY	SWAN	FITCH	BUNSEN
HOWE	TAIT	HYATT	DIESEL

DURYEA	RUMSEY	GATLING	DEFOREST
EDISON	SPERRY	GODDARD	FRANKLIN
FOKKER	WANKEL	LAENNEC	GILLETTE
FULTON	WRIGHT	MARCONI	GOODYEAR
GEIGER	BABBAGE	PULLMAN	LANGMUIR
KEPLER	BRAILLE	REAUMUR	MERCATOR
LENOIR	CARRIER	SIEMENS	ROENTGEN
LESTER	CURTISS	SPRAGUE	SIKORSKY
MALZEL	DAIMLER	WHITNEY	WATERMAN
MERCER	DAVINCI	BERLINER	GUTENBERG
NEWTON	EASTMAN	BESSEMER	
NIPKOW	FARADAY	BUSHNELL	
PASCAL	FLEMING	DAGUERRE	

JOURNALISTS

BLY	HERSH	HOPPER	MENCKEN
BOX	KRAFT	KURALT	PARSONS
CAEN	KROCK	MURROW	PEARSON
DANA	NOYES	PAULEY	TARBELL
HOWE	ROYKO	POVICH	WALLACE
LUCE	SMITH	RATHER	BOUDINOT
OCHS	SWOPE	RESTON	BRINKLEY
PYLE	WHITE	RUNYON	BRISBANE
REED	BIERCE	SAWYER	CRONKITE
REID	BOWLES	SHIRER	LIEBLING
RICE	BROKAW	SWAYZE	LIPPMANN
RIIS	CHILDS	THOMAS	REASONER
SNOW	COSELL	FLEESON	SEVAREID
WEED	CURTIS	GREELEY	THOMPSON
ADAMS	FINLEY	GUNTHER	WINCHELL
ALSOP	GODKIN	HEATTER	WOODWARD
BROUN	GRAHAM	HUNTLEY	BERNSTEIN
DAVIS	HARVEY	KEMPTON	
EVANS	HEARST	LANDERS	
GRADY	HERSEY	MCCLURE	

MATHEMATICIANS

HERO	KELVIN	CREMONA	EINSTEIN
BOOLE	MOBIUS	EUDOXUS	BERNOULLI
EULER	NAPIER	HUYGENS	DESCARTES
GAUSS	NEWTON	HYPATIA	TARTAGLIA
VIETA	PAPPUS	LAPLACE	WHITEHEAD
ALTUSI	PASCAL	LEIBNIZ	ARCHIMEDES
CANTOR	WIENER	PTOLEMY	PYTHAGORAS
CAUCHY	ALHAZEN	RUSSELL	
EUCLID	ALKASHI	VERNIER	
FERMAT	CARROLL	ALBIRUNI	

MILITARY LEADERS

COX	HAIG	BANKS	EARLY
LEE	HOWE	BRAGG	GRANT
NEY	KNOX	BUELL	JONES
ORD	PIKE	CLARK	LEAHY
CLAY	SAXE	DAYAN	MEADE
FOCH	SIMS	DEWEY	MILNE
GAGE	ALLEN	DRAKE	MURAT

PERRY	PATTON	HOUSTON	MARSHALL
WOLFE	PETAIN	JACKSON	MONTCALM
ABRAMS	PICKEN	SHERMAN	MITCHELL
ARNOLD	PUTNAM	TIRPITZ	NAPOLEON
CAESAR	RAEDER	BLUECHER	PERSHING
CUSTER	ROMMEL	BURGOYNE	SCHUYLER
GORDON	SPAATZ	BURNSIDE	SHERIDAN
HALSEY	STUART	CROCKETT	STILWELL
HODGES	SUMTER	FARRAGUT	ALEXANDER
JOFFRE	ZHUKOV	HANNIBAL	HOCHIMINH
MOLTKE	BRADLEY	JELLICOE	MACARTHUR
NELSON	DECATUR	JOHNSTON	EISENHOWER
NIMITZ	FORREST	LAWRENCE	WASHINGTON

OPERA SINGERS

ALDA	CALLAS	FERRIER	DERESZKE
BORI	CARUSO	FLEMING	FLAGSTAD
LIND	DELUCA	HAMPSON	LABLACHE
PONS	DESSAY	JERITZA	MALIBRAN
PREY	FARRAR	LEHMANN	MELCHIOR
AMATO	GARDEN	MILANOV	PONSELLE
CALVE	GRAHAM	NILSSON	RETHBERG
EAMES	HEMPEL	NORDICA	SEMBRICH
GIGLI	KANAWA	RYSANEK	TEKANAWA
GOBBI	KIPNIS	STEVENS	TROYANOS
GRISI	PEERCE	TEBALDI	WELITSCH
KRAUS	SCHORR	TIBBETT	FARINELLI
MELBA	SCOTTO	TRAUBEL	MCCORMACK
PASTA	STEBER	VIARDOT	PAVAROTTI
PATTI	TUCKER	VICKERS	SUTHERLAND
PEARS	WARREN	ANDERSON	TAGLIAVINI
PINZA	DESTINN	BJORLING	TETRAZZINI
SAYAO	DOMINGO	CARRERAS	

PAINTERS

(see also Sculptors)

ARP	BACON	KLIMT	WYETH
RAY	BLAKE	KLINE	ALBERS
CARR	BOSCH	LEGER	ANDREA
COLE	COROT	LIPPI	BENTON
DALI	CURRY	LOUIS	BRAQUE
DORE	DAVID	MANET	CATLIN
DOVE	DAVIS	MARIN	CHURCH
DUFY	DEGAS	MONET	COPLEY
GOYA	DURER	MOSES	DAVIES
GRIS	ENSOR	MUNCH	DEMUTH
HALS	ERNST	PEALE	EAKINS
KENT	GORKY	RYDER	GIOTTO
KLEE	GRECO	SARTO	HARING
MARC	GROSZ	SEGAL	HASSAM
MIRO	HENRI	SHAHN	HOLZER
PAIK	HICKS	STEEN	HOPPER
RENI	HOMER	SULLY	INGRES
WEST	JOHNS	VINCI	INNESS
WOOD	KAHLO	WATTS	LEBRUN

MILLET	CASSATT	SHEELER	CONSTABLE
MOREAU	CEZANNE	UCCELLO	CORREGGIO
NEWMAN	CHAGALL	UTRILLO	DEKOONING
OROZCO	CHARDIN	VANDYCK	DELACROIX
PISANO	CHIRICO	VANEYCK	DONATELLO
RENOIR	COURBET	VANGOGH	FEININGER
RIBERA	DAUMIER	VERMEER	FRAGONARD
RIVERA	DAVINCI	WATTEAU	GERICAULT
RIVERS	DUCHAMP	ANGELICO	GIORGIONE
ROTHKO	ELGRECO	BECKMANN	GRUNEWALD
RUBENS	GAUGUIN	BOCCIONI	KANDINSKY
SEURAT	HOFMANN	CARRACCI	KOKOSCHKA
SISLEY	HOGARTH	GHIBERTI	REINHARDT
STELLA	HOLBEIN	LEONARDO	REMBRANDT
STUART	INDIANA	MAGRITTE	REMINGTON
TAMAYO	LORRAIN	MALEVICH	SIQUEIROS
TANGUY	MAILLOL	MANTEGNA	VELAZQUEZ
TATLIN	MATISSE	MONDRIAN	BOTTICELLI
TITIAN	MORISOT	PISSARRO	CARAVAGGIO
TURNER	MURILLO	REYNOLDS	MOTHERWELL
WARHOL	OKEEFFE	ROCKWELL	TINTORETTO
BELLINI	PARRISH	ROSSETTI	PRENDERGAST
BELLOWS	PICASSO	ROUSSEAU	GAINSBOROUGH
BERNINI	POLLOCK	RUYSDAEL	LICHTENSTEIN
BONHEUR	POUSSIN	TRUMBULL	RAUSCHENBERG
BONNARD	RAPHAEL	VERONESE	VANDERWEYDEN
BOUCHER	ROUAULT	VUILLARD	TOULOUSELAUTREC
BRUEGEL	SARGENT	WHISTLER	
	SCHIELE	ZURBARAN	

PHILOSOPHERS

AYER	QUINE	BENTHAM	VOLTAIRE
HUME	RAWLS	BERGSON	ALGHAZALI
JOAD	ROYCE	DERRIDA	ARISTOTLE
KANT	SMITH	DIDEROT	AUGUSTINE
MARX	ANSELM	HUSSERL	DESCARTES
MILL	AUSTIN	JASPERS	EPICTETUS
MORE	BECKET	LEIBNIZ	HEIDEGGER
MOTI	BUDDHA	RUSSELL	LUCRETIUS
RYLE	ENGELS	SPENCER	NIETZSCHE
ZENO	FICHTE	SPINOZA	SANTAYANA
ADLER	HERDER	TILLICH	WHITEHEAD
BACON	HOBBES	UNAMUNO	ANAXAGORAS
BARTH	HUXLEY	AVERROES	ANAXIMENES
BRUNO	LAOTZE	AVICENNA	DEMOCRITUS
BUBER	MARCEL	BEAUVOIR	EMPEDOCLES
CAMUS	NOZICK	BERKELEY	HERACLITUS
COMTE	PASCAL	BOETHIUS	MAIMONIDES
DEWEY	PEIRCE	DIOGENES	PARMENIDES
EDMAN	PROUST	EPICURUS	PYTHAGORAS
HEGEL	SARTRE	FOUCAULT	ANAXIMANDER
JAMES	SCOTUS	MARITAIN	KIERKEGAARD
LOCKE	SENECA	PLOTINUS	MACHIAVELLI
MOORE	THALES	ROUSSEAU	MONTESQUIEU
OCCAM	ABELARD	SOCRATES	SCHOPENHAUER
PLATO	AQUINAS	SPENGLER	WITTGENSTEIN

PHYSICIANS AND MEDICAL RESEARCHERS

(see also p. 509)

JUNG	SABIN	BANTING	FRANKLIN
KOCH	BOWMAN	BERNARD	SYDENHAM
ROSS	DARWIN	EHRLICH	BLACKWELL
SALK	HARVEY	FLEMING	HIPPOCRATES
BROCA	JENNER	PASTEUR	ERASISTRATUS
CRICK	PAVLOV	WILKINS	
FREUD	STOKES	AVICENNA	
GALEN	WATSON	FLOURENS	

PHYSICISTS

(see also p. 510)

OHM	JOULE	ALVAREZ	GELLMANN
ABBE	ROSSI	CELSIUS	GRIMALDI
BOHR	TESLA	DOPPLER	ROENTGEN
HAHN	VOLTA	FARADAY	BECQUEREL
MACH	AMPERE	FEYNMAN	DEBROGLIE
BOYLE	BUNSEN	MAXWELL	FAHRENHEIT
CURIE	KELVIN	CHADWICK	RUTHERFORD
DYSON	NEWTON	CORIOLIS	TORRICELLI
ERMAN	PLANCK	EINSTEIN	JOLIOTCURIE
FERMI	TELLER	FOUCAULT	SCHRODINGER
HERTZ	WILSON	FRANKLIN	

RELIGIOUS LEADERS

BAB	SMITH	SUNDAY	ZWINGLI
FOX	YOUNG	WESLEY	CHANNING
HUS	ABBOTT	WOLSEY	GARRISON
ARND	ANSELM	AQUINAS	IGNATIUS
EDDY	BECKET	BEECHER	MOHAMMED
HUSS	BIDDLE	BRUNNER	MUHAMMAD
INGE	BOEHME	CRANMER	TALMADGE
KNOX	BUDDHA	EDWARDS	WILLIAMS
ADLER	CALVIN	FALWELL	WYCLIFFE
BARTH	COTTON	NIEBUHR	MCPHERSON
BOOTH	GRAHAM	ROBERTS	BONHOEFFER
BUBER	LAOTZU	RUSSELL	SCHWEITZER
JESUS	LOYOLA	SEABURY	
MOODY	LUTHER	TILLICH	
PEALE	MATHER	TYNDALL	

SCULPTORS

(see also Painters)

ARP	SMITH	ROBBIA	MAILLOL
BALL	WATTS	ZORACH	NOGUCHI
GABO	CALDER	BERNINI	PEVSNER
MIRO	CANOVA	BORGLUM	PHIDIAS
DEGAS	FRENCH	CELLINI	PICASSO
MOORE	GIOTTO	CORNELL	ZADKINE
MYRON	MILLES	DAVINCI	BAILLACH
RODIN	PISANO	EPSTEIN	BRANCUSI

DAVIDSON	KOLLWITZ	OLDENBURG	VERROCCHIO
DUBUFFET	LIPCHITZ	SANSOVINO	MICHELANGELO
GIRARDON	NEVELSON	GIACOMETTI	SAINTGAUDENS
GRIBERTI	DONATELLO	MODIGLIANI	
HEPWORTH	MESTROVIC	PRAXITELES	

STATESMEN

DAY	LODGE	PELHAM	WALPOLE
FOX	MARAT	ACHESON	ADENAUER
ITO	NENNI	ASQUITH	BISMARCK
EDEN	NITYI	BALDWIN	BREZHNEV
BLOM	SMUTS	BALFOUR	BURHARIN
CATO	SPAAK	BULLITY	CROMWELL
CLAY	THANT	CALHOUN	DISRAELI
FISH	TISZA	CLAYTON	DOLLFUSS
GREY	ATYLEE	COLBERT	GAMBETTA
MEIR	BRIAND	HERRIOT	HAMILTON
PEEL	BUELOW	KELLOGG	LITVINOV
PITY	BUNCHE	KOSSUTH	MIRABEAU
ROOT	CAVOUR	LANSING	POTEMKIN
TITO	CICERO	MASARYK	RATHENAU
TOJO	CURZON	MAZARIN	STANHOPE
BENES	DANTON	PULASKI	BENGURION
BEVIN	DULLES	REYNAUD	CHURCHILL
CABOT	ERHARD	SALAZAR	GORBACHEV
CIANO	FOUCHE	STANLEY	KISSINGER
DAWES	GEORGE	STIMSON	PILSUDSKI
HENRY	HORTHY	TROTZKY	RICHELIEU
	HUGHES		ROOSEVELT
	LYTYON		

FAMOUS TRIOS

AGLAIA, EUPHROSYNE, THALIA (Graces)
ALECTO, TISIPHONE, MEGAERA (Furies/Erinyes/Eumenides)
AMO, AMAS, AMAT
ATHOS, ARAMIS, PORTHOS
BACH, BEETHOVEN, BRAHMS
CALM, COOL, COLLECTED
CAME, SAW, CONQUERED
CLOTHO, ATROPOS, LACHESIS
FAITH, HOPE, CHARITY
FATHER, SON, HOLY GHOST
PETER, PAUL, AND MARY
NINA, PINTA, SANTA MARIA
READING, WRITING, ARITHMETIC
TOM, DICK, HARRY
VENI, VIDI, VICI

FIRST AND LAST NAMES

Derek, Diddley	BO	Abbott	BUD	Ameche	DON
Kaline	AL	Abner	LIL	Anais	NIN
Jolson	AL	Acuff	ROY	Ang	LEE
Pacino	AL	Alastair	SIM	Angelico	FRA
Sharpton	AL	Aldo	RAY	Annabel	LEE
Simpson	OJ	Alfonso	DON	Arden	EVE
Yo-Yo	MA	Allen	MEL	Auerbach	RED

Aykroyd	DAN	Guevara	CHE	Torme	MEL
Ayres	LEW	Hammarskjold	DAG	Trygve	LIE
Baba	ALI	Hirobumi	ITO	Turner	NAT
Baer	MAX	Hodges	GIL	Turpin	BEN
Basinger	KIM	Hogan	BEN	Ulmann	LIV
Beatty	NED	Houston	SAM	Uncle	SAM
Beerbohm	MAX	Hur	BEN	Vermeer	JAN
Beiderbecke	BIX	Hus	JAN	Vigoda	ABE
Ben	HUR	Iacocca	LEE	Wallach	ELI
Benatar	PAT	Irving	AMY	Whitney	ELI
Blakey	ART	Jan	HUS	Wray	FAY
Blanc	MEL	Janis	IAN	Yat-sen	SUN
Blas	GIL	Jonson	BEN	Young	GIG
Bloch	RAY	Khan	AGA, ALI	Yutang	LIN
Bobby	ORR	Knotts	DON		
Bolger	RAY	Kroc	RAY	Aaron	BURR, HANK
Bon Jovi	JON	Landers	ANN	Acheson	DEAN
Bradbury	RAY	Lee	ANG	Adam	BEDE
Brooks	MEL	Leno	JAY	Adams	JOHN, EDIE,
Brynner	YUL	Linkletter	ART		MAUD
Buchwald	ART	Louis	JOE	Addams	JANE
Bush	JEB	Lowell	AMY	Adolph	OCHS
Buttons	RED	Lupino	IDA	Alan	ALDA, LADD
Caesar	SYD	Man	RAY	Alban	BERG
Caldwell	ZOE	Marquis	DON	Alden	JOHN
Calloway	CAB	Masaryk	JAN	Alexander	HAIG, POPE
Carney	ART	Maya	LIN	Alfred	LUNT
Carson	KIT	Mel	OTT	Alger	HISS
Chaney	LON	Myrna	LOY	Ali	KHAN
Charisse	CYD	Neal	DOW	Allen	FRED
Claiborne	LIZ	Novak	KIM	Allyson	JUNE
Clancy	TOM	Ott	MEL	Aly	KHAN
Cliburn	VAN	Paine	TOM	Ambler	ERIC
Coltrane	CHI	Peerce	JAN	Anderson	LONI
Deighton	LEN	Peron	EVA	Andersson	BIBI
DeLuise	DOM	Piniella	LOU	Andre	GIDE
DiMaggio	DOM, JOE	Planck	MAX	Andrew	SHUE
Doris	DAY	Rather	DAN	Angelou	MAYA
Dorothy	DIX	Ray	MAN	Anita	LOOS
Durocher	LEO, LIP	Rayburn	SAM	Anka	PAUL
Duryea	DAN	Rockefeller	JAY	Anna	HELD
Eddie	FOY	Rogers	ROY	Anthony	EDEN
Elaine	MAY	Rohmer	SAX	Antony	MARK
Erwin	STU	Rose	AXL	Arkin	ALAN
Everly	DON	Ruby	DEE	Arlene	DAHL
Farrow	MIA	Rutledge	ANN	Armstrong	NEIL
Ferrer	MEL	Ryan	MEG	Arnaz	DESI
Fortas	ABE	Sandra	DEE	Arsenio	HALL
Francis Scott	KEY	Saud	IBN	Artemus	WARD
Gabor	EVA	Sawyer	TOM	Arthur	ASHE
Gardner	AVA	Schmeling	MAX	Asa	GRAY
Garfunkle	ART	Silvers	SID	Ashcroft	JOHN
Gazzara	BEN	Snead	SAM	Atkins	CHET
Gehrig	LOU	Starr	KAY	Austen	JANE
Gershwin	IRA	Stevens	CAT	Autry	GENE
Gorcey	LEO	Stout	REX	Babe	RUTH
Gould	JAY	Sumac	YMA	Baez	JOAN
Gray	ASA	Tatum	ART	Bagnold	ENID
Greenfield	MEG	Tolstoy	LEO	Baldwin	ALEC

Barrymore	**DREW, JOHN**	
Bartok	**BELA**	
Bates	**ALAN**	
Bede	**ADAM**	
Bellow	**SAUL**	
Bennett	**CERF**	
Benny	**JACK**	
Bernard	**SHAW**	
Berra	**YOGI**	
Bert	**LAHR**	
Billy	**ROSE**	
Bismarck	**OTTO**	
Bjorn	**BORG**	
Blitzer	**WOLF**	
Blum	**LEON**	
Bogarde	**DIRK**	
Boleyn	**ANNE**	
Bombeck	**ERMA**	
Bonheur	**ROS**	
Boros	**JEFF**	
Bradley	**OMAR**	
Bridges	**BEAU, JEFF, WARD**	
Bronte	**ANNE**	
Brooks	**ADAMS**	
Broz	**TITO**	
Brummel	**BEAU**	
Buffalo Bill	**CODY**	
Burl	**IVES**	
Calve	**EMMA**	
Cannon	**DYAN**	
Captain	**AHAB, NEMO**	
Carl	**JUNG**	
Carnegie	**DALE**	
Cassius	**CLAY**	
Catherine	**PARR**	
Cezanne	**PAUL**	
Chagall	**MARC**	
Chaka	**KHAN**	
Chaplin	**OONA**	
Charlie	**ROSE**	
Chase	**ILKA**	
Chico	**MARX**	
Chomsky	**NOAM**	
Chris	**ROCK**	
Christian	**DIOR**	
Christie	**ANNA**	
Clapton	**ERIC**	
Clark	**MARK**	
Conde	**NAST**	
Condoleezza	**RICE**	
Connie	**MACK**	
Cooper	**GARY**	
Courtney	**LOVE**	
Crockett	**DAVY**	
Cronyn	**HUME**	
Crosby	**BING**	
Coward	**NOEL**	
Craig	**RICE**	
Dalton	**ABBY**	
Daniels	**BEBE**	
Danza	**TONY**	
David	**HUME**	
Dean	**RUSK**	
Dee	**RUBY**	
De La Roche	**MAZO**	
Dench	**JUDI**	
Descartes	**RENE**	
Dewey	**JOHN**	
Diamond	**NEIL**	
Diana	**DORS, RIGG**	
Didrickson	**BABE**	
Dinesen	**ISAK**	
Disney	**WALT**	
"Dizzy"	**DEAN**	
Domino	**FATS**	
Donahue	**PHIL, TROY**	
Dorian	**GRAY**	
Dorothy	**GISH**	
Dove	**RITA**	
Dow	**NEAL**	
Drury	**LANE**	
Dudevant	**SAND**	
Dunaway	**FAYE**	
Eartha	**KITT**	
Edith	**PIAF**	
Edouard	**LALO**	
Eleanora	**DUSE**	
Elias	**HOWE**	
Elihu	**ROOT, YALE**	
Elizabeth	**DOLE**	
Ella	**LAMB**	
Ellington	**DUKE**	
Elliot	**CASS**	
Elmer	**RICE**	
Elton	**JOHN**	
Emile	**ZOLA**	
Emily	**POST**	
En-Lai	**CHOU, ZHOU**	
Eric	**IDLE**	
Erica	**JONG**	
Eriksson	**LEIF**	
Ernie	**PYLE**	
Estrada	**ERIK**	
Eubank	**WEEB**	
Eugene	**DEBS, ARAM**	
Evans	**DALE**	
Everett	**CHAD**	
Eyre	**JANE**	
Fay	**WRAY**	
Ferber	**EDNA**	
Ferrer	**JOSE**	
Flanders	**MOLL**	
Foch	**NINA**	
Foxx	**REDD**	
Frances	**ALDA**	
Franchot	**TONE**	
Frans	**HALS**	
Franz	**BOAS**	
Fritz	**LANG**	
Gagarin	**YURI**	
Gardner	**ERLE**	
Garr	**TERI**	
George	**SAND**	
Geste	**BEAU**	
Getz	**STAN**	
Gil	**BLAS**	
Gingrich	**NEWT**	
Gluck	**ALMA**	
Golda	**MEIR**	
Goldberg	**RUBE**	
Goldie	**HAWN**	
Gomer	**PYLE**	
Gordon	**GALE**	
Goriot	**PERE**	
Grant	**CARY, WOOD**	
Gregory	**PECK**	
Grey	**ZANE**	
Griffin	**MERV**	
Griffith	**ANDY, HUGH**	
Guido	**RENI**	
Guthrie	**ARLO**	
Haley	**ALEX**	
Hamsun	**KNUT**	
Harlow	**JEAN**	
Harold	**UREY**	
Harpo	**MARX**	
Harrison	**FORD**	
Hart	**MOSS**	
Harte	**BRET**	
Hayworth	**RITA**	
Heche	**ANNE**	
Hefner	**HUGH**	
Held	**ANNA**	
Helmer	**NORA**	
Helmut	**JAHN**	
Hendrix	**JIMI**	
Henry	**CLAY, FORD**	
Hershiser	**OREL**	
Heyerdahl	**THOR**	
Hopkins	**MARK**	
Horace	**MANN**	
Horne	**LENA**	
Huey	**LONG**	
Hugo	**WOLF**	
Huntley	**CHET**	
Ibn	**SAUD**	
Idle	**ERIC**	
Ilsa	**LUND**	
Immanuel	**KANT**	
Imogene	**COCA**	
Italo	**TAJO**	
Iturbi	**JOSE**	
Ives	**BURL**	
Jacob	**RIIS**	
James	**ETTA**	

Jane	**EYRE, GREY**	Millett	**KATE**	Sholem	**ASCH**
Janet	**RENO**	Moffo	**ANNA**	Sibelius	**JEAN**
Jenny	**LIND**	Mondrian	**PIET**	Silitoe	**ALAN**
Jerome	**KERN**	Montez	**LOLA**	Simon	**NEIL**
Joan	**BAEZ**	Moore	**DEMI**	Siskel	**GENE**
Joel	**COEN**	Moss	**HART**	Slaughter	**ENOS**
Johnny	**CASH, DEPP**	Mostel	**ZERO**	Smith	**ADAM**
Jonas	**SALK**	Muni	**PAUL**	Sommer	**ELKE**
Jones	**ETTA**	Musial	**STAN**	Sorvino	**MIRA**
Jung	**CARL**	Nash	**BEAU**	Speaker	**TRIS**
Kalman	**IMRE**	Nastase	**ILIE**	Squire	**CASS**
Karenina	**ANNA**	Nathan	**HALE**	Stan	**GETZ**
Karl	**MARX**	Neuwirth	**BEBE**	Steve	**JOBS**
Kazan	**ELIA**	Nicolas	**CAGE**	Stevens	**RISE**
Khachaturian	**ARAM**	Niels	**BOHR**	Stokes	**CARL**
Khayyam	**OMAR**	Nina	**FOCH**	Storm	**GALE**
Kingsley	**AMIS**	O'Casey	**SEAN**	Strauss	**LEVI**
Klee	**PAUL**	Ogden	**NASH**	Stravinsky	**IGOR**
Knievel	**EVEL**	Orson	**BEAN**	Syngman	**RHEE**
Kreuger	**IVAR**	Pacelli	**PIUS**	Tanguy	**YVES**
Krupa	**GENE**	Parker	**BIRD, FESS**	Teri	**GARR**
Lahr	**BERT**	Parks	**ROSA**	The Red	**ERIC**
Lancaster	**BURT**	Paul	**ANKA, KLEE,**	Theda	**BARA**
Lardner	**RING**		**MUNI**	Thomas	**ARNE, MANN**
Laurel	**STAN**	Pavlova	**ANNA**	Tilden	**BILL**
Lawrence	**WELK**	Perot	**ROSS**	Tipper	**GORE**
Lazarus	**EMMA**	Perry	**COMO**	Tito	**BROZ**
Leon	**BLUM**	Peter	**ARNO**	Trent	**LOTT**
Levesque	**RENE**	Phileas	**FOGG**	Trotsky	**LEON**
Lillian	**GISH**	Pinza	**EZIO**	Tunney	**GENE**
Lily	**PONS**	Pons	**LILY**	Turing	**ALAN**
Limbaugh	**RUSH**	Porter	**COLE**	Tweed	**BOSS**
Lin	**MAYA**	Pound	**EZRA**	Ty	**COBB**
Locke	**JOHN**	Purviance	**EDNA**	Tyler	**ANNE, JOHN**
Lollobrigida	**GINA**	Raoul	**DUFY**	Uriah	**HEEP**
Long	**HUEY**	Ray	**KROC**	Vannevar	**BUSH**
Loretta	**SWIT**	Redd	**FOXX**	Vincent van	**GOGH**
Louis	**RIEL**	Rita	**DOVE**	Virginia	**DARE**
Lucille	**BALL**	Roberts	**ORAL**	Waller	**FATS**
Lucrezia	**BORI**	Robeson	**PAUL**	Walter	**REED**
Ludwig	**EMIL**	Rockwell	**KENT**	Warburg	**OTTO**
Lugosi	**BELA**	Roger	**MUDD**	Warhol	**ANDY**
Lund	**ILSA**	Rogers	**WILL**	Warren	**EARL**
Ma	**YOYO**	Rowlands	**GENA**	Waugh	**ALEC**
"Mad Dog"	**COLL**	Royko	**MIKE**	Webster	**NOAH**
Magritte	**RENE**	Rusk	**DEAN**	Weill	**KURT**
Mamie	**DOUD**	Ruth	**BABE**	Westheimer	**RUTH**
Marco	**POLO**	Saarinen	**EERO**	Whiteman	**PAUL**
Margaret	**ROSE**	Sagan	**CARL**	Wiesel	**ELIE**
Marquette	**PERE**	Sally	**LUNN, RIDE**	Wiley	**POST**
Marx	**KARL**	Salvador	**DALI**	Willard	**EMMA**
Mary	**TODD**	Sam	**NUNN**	Wilson	**FLIP**
Mata	**HARI**	Satie	**ERIK**	Zane	**GREY**
Max	**BAER**	Schipa	**TITO**	Zebulon	**PIKE**
Maxwell	**ELSA**	Schulberg	**BUDD**	Zeppo	**MARX**
Meara	**ANNE**	Scott	**BAIO, DRED**		
Meg	**RYAN**	Sevareid	**ERIC**	Abdul	**PAULA**
Meitner	**LISE**	Shalom	**ASCH**	Abigail	**SMITH,**
Merrill	**DINA**	Sheedy	**ALLY**		**ADAMS**

Enoch **ARDEN**	Gorme **EYDIE**	Julia **CHILD**
Enrico **FERMI**	Grable **BETTY**	June **HAVOC**
Errol **FLYNN**	Graham **BILLY**	Kadar **JANOS**
Ethan **ALLEN, FROME**	Green **HETTY**	Kafka **FRANZ**
Eudora **WELTY**	Gregory **HINES**	Kahlo **FRIDA**
Eva **CURIE, GABOR,**	Greta **GARBO**	Karan **DONNA**
PERON	Gretzky **WAYNE**	Karel **CAPEK**
Eva Marie **SAINT**	Grofe **FERDE**	Kay **STARR**
Evelyn **WAUGH**	Guitry **SACHA**	Kazantzakis **NIKOS**
Evert **CHRIS**	Gustav **KLIMT**	Keaton **DIANE**
Evita **PERON**	Hals **FRANS**	Kefauver **ESTES**
Eydie **GORME**	Hank **AARON**	Keller **HELEN**
Ezra **POUND**	Hanks **NANCY**	Khan **CHAKA**
Farlay **MOWAT**	Hannah **DARYL**	Kim **NOVAK**
Farr **JAMIE**	Harold **ICKES**	Kirstie **ALLEY**
Ferde **GROFE**	Hasso **SIGNE**	Koussevitzky **SERGE**
Fernand **LEGER**	Hayes **HELEN**	Kovacs **ERNIE**
Fibber **MCGEE**	Hedren **TIPPI**	Kreisler **FRITZ**
Field **CYRUS**	Heep **URIAH**	Kurt **WEILL**
Fields **TOTIE**	Heinrich **HEINE**	Lagerlof **SELMA**
Fisher **AVERY**	Helen **HAYES**	Lane **DRURY**
Flynn **ERROL**	Helms **JESSE**	Lanza **MARIO**
Fonda **HENRY**	Henrik **IBSEN**	Lauder **ESTEE**
Ford **BETTY, EDSEL,**	Hetty **GREEN**	Lauper **CYNDI**
HENRY	Hieronymus **BOSCH**	Lawes **LEWIS**
Forman **MILOS**	Hines **FATHA**	Legree **SIMON**
Foster **JODIE**	Hiss **ALGER**	Lehar **FRANZ**
Francis **BACON,**	Hitler **ADOLF**	Lehmann **LOTTE**
DRAKE	Holly **BUDDY**	Leinsdorf **ERICH**
Franck **CESAR**	Horatio **ALGER**	Lena **HORNE**
Frank **CAPRA, ZAPPA**	Houdini **HARRY**	Lescaut **MANON**
Frankfurter **FELIX**	Howe **ELIAS**	Levant **OSCAR**
Franz **KAFKA, LEHAR,**	Ian **JANIS**	Lewis **LAWES**
LISZT	Ianos **KADAR**	Lil **ABNER**
Frida **KAHLO**	Ichabod **CRANE**	Liszt **FRANZ**
Frome **ETHAN**	Ilka **CHASE**	Lonigan **STUDS**
Fulton **SHEEN**	Isaac **STERN**	Loos **ANITA**
Gabler **HEDDA**	Jackson **JESSE**	Lorna **DOONE**
Gabor **JOLIE, MAGDA**	James **JESSE, JOYCE**	Lott **TRENT**
Gantry **ELMER**	Jawahanal **NEHRU**	Loy **MYRNA**
Garbo **GRETA**	Jay **GOULD**	Lunn **SALLY**
Garson **GREER**	Jean P. **MARAT**	MacDowell **ANDIE**
Gaynor **JANET, MITZI**	Jeff **BOROS**	Maksim **GORKI**
Gene **AUTRY**	Jefferson **DAVIS**	Mamet **DAVID**
Georg **SOLTI**	Jesse **HELMS, JAMES**	Manuel de **FALLA**
George **LLOYD**	John **ADAMS, ALDEN,**	Marie **CURIE**
Georges **BIZET**	**BROWN, DEWEY,**	Mario **CUOMO,**
Gertrude **STEIN**	**ELTON, SMITH,**	**LANZA**
Gherman **TITOV**	**TYLER**	Marner **SILAS**
Gide **ANDRE**	John Philip **SOUSA**	Marx **CHICO, HARPO,**
Giordano **BRUNO**	Jonathan **SWIFT**	**ZEPPO**
Giuseppe **VERDI**	Jong **ERICA**	Maude **ADAMS**
Glenn **CLOSE**	Joplin **JANIS, SCOTT**	Maurice **RAVEL**
Glynis **JOHNS**	Jose **GRECO**	Maurois **ANDRE**
Goldoni **CARLO**	Joyce **JAMES**	Maxim **GORKI**
Gomez **LEFTY**	Juan **PERON**	McDonald **AUDRA**
Goodman **BENNY**	Jubal **EARLY**	Medgar **EVERS**
Gorbachev **RAISA**	Judi **DENCH**	Meir **GOLDA**
Gorky **MAXIM**	Jules **VERNE**	Mel **ALLEN, TORME**

Menachem	**BEGIN**	Rickover	**HYMAN**	Trudeau	**GARRY**
Meriwether	**LEWIS**	Riis	**JACOB**	Truman	**HARRY**
Merman	**ETHEL**	Ringo	**STARR**	Tully	**ALICE**
Midler	**BETTE**	Rivera	**DIEGO**	Tycho	**BRAHE**
Mike	**ROYKO**	Roberts	**COKIE**	Varden	**DOLLY**
Miller	**GLENN**	Rockne	**KNUTE**	Victor	**BORGE**
Milton	**BERLE**	Roger	**EBERT**	Virginia	**WOOLF**
Minh	**HOCHI**	Root	**ELIHU**	Vladimir	**LENIN**
Minuit	**PETER**	Rosa	**PARKS**	Walter	**BRUNO**
Mitchell	**MARIA**	Rose	**BILLY**	Walton	**IZAAK**
Monroe	**JAMES**	Rosenblum	**MAXIE**	Waters	**ETHEL**
Morini	**ERICA**	Ross	**PEROT**	Welles	**ORSON**
Moshe	**DAYAN**	Rothschild	**MEYER**	Werner von	**BRAUN**
Murphey	**AUDIE**	Rommel	**ERWIN**	Wharton	**EDITH**
Nader	**RALPH**	Rubinstein	**ANTON,**	Wilde	**OSCAR**
Nancy	**HANKS**			William Butler	**YEATS**
Nash	**OGDEN**	Rudolf	**FRIML**	Winfrey	**OPRAH**
Nasser	**GAMAL**	Runyon	**DAMON**	Winger	**DEBRA**
Nation	**CARRY**	Sadat	**ANWAR**	Winona	**RYDER**
Nero	**WOLFE**	Salk	**JONAS**	Winslow	**HOMER**
Newton	**ISAAC**	Salmon	**CHASE**	Wood	**GRANT**
Nikola	**TESLA**	Sam	**UNCLE**	Xavier	**CUGAT**
Nikolai	**LENIN**	Samuel **MORSE, PEPYS**		Yale	**EUHU**
Nin	**ANAIS**	Sancho	**PANZA**	Yogi	**BERRA**
Odilon	**REDON**	Sharon	**ARIEL**	Zola	**EMILE**
Oksana	**BAIUL**	Sharp	**BECKY**	Zimbalist	**EFREM**
Onegin	**EUGEN**	Shaw	**ARTIE**	Zsa Zsa	**GABOR**
Orlando	**LASSO**	Shire	**TANIA**		
Oscar	**WILDE**	Shore	**DINAH**	Abe	**FORTAS,**
Pancho	**VILLA**	Sidney	**LUMET**		**VIGODA**
Parton	**DOLLY**	Sigmund	**FREUD**	Adams	**BROOKS**
Pasternak	**BORIS**	Signe	**HASSO**	Adenauer	**KONRAD**
Pasteur	**LOUIS**	Simon	**CARLY**	Adolphe	**MENJOU**
Patrick	**HENRY**	Sinclair **LEWIS, UPTON**		Alan	**TURING**
Paula	**ABDUL**	Sklodowska	**CURIE**	Albee	**EDWARD**
Pauling	**LINUS**	Sojourner	**TRUTH**	Albertus	**MAGNUS**
Peron	**EVITA**	Solti	**GEORG**	Aldous	**HUXLEY**
Perry	**MASON**	Sonja	**HENIE**	Alexis	**CARREL**
Petula	**CLARK**	Spacek	**SISSY**	Ambrose	**BIERCE**
Philo	**VANCE**	Standish	**MILES**	Anatole	**FRANCE**
Piaf	**EDITH**	Starr	**RINGO**	Andrew Lloyd	**WEBBER**
Picasso	**PABLO**	Stengel	**CASEY**	Andy	**WARHOL**
Pierre	**CURIE**	Stephen	**CRANE**	Angelo	**GIOTTO**
Pirandello	**LUIGI**	Stern	**ISAAC**	Anjelica	**HUSTON**
Polo	**MARCO**	Stevenson	**ADLAI**	Anne	**BOLEYN**
Post	**EMILY**	Streep	**MERYL**	Anthony	**SUSANB**
Powell	**COLIN**	Sunday	**BILLY**	Antonin	**DVORAK,**
Priscilla	**ALDEN**	Tajo	**ITALO**		**SCALIA**
Pyle **ERNIE, GOMER**		Tamburlaine	**TIMUR**	Ariel	**SHARON**
Radner	**GILDA**	Tania	**SHIRE**	Armand	**HAMMER**
Rainer	**RILKE**	Tarkington	**BOOTH**	Arrhenius	**SVANTE**
Ralph	**NADER**	Templar	**SIMON**	Asch	**SHOLEM**
Rathbone	**BASIL**	Thatcher	**BECKY**	Ashe	**ARTHUR**
Reni	**GUIDO**	Theodore	**BIKEL**	Assante	**ARMAND**
Reno	**JANET**	Thomas	**DYLAN,**	Bacall	**LAUREN**
Rex	**STOUT**	**HARDY, MOORE,**		Baiul	**OKSANA**
Rhodes	**CECIL**		**WOLFE**	Balzac	**HONORE**
Rice **CRAIG, ELMER**		Tom	**PAINE**	Barenboim	**DANIEL**
Rickenbacker	**EDDIE**	Torquato	**TASSO**	Barrymore	**LIONEL**

Hercule	**POIROT**	Mann	**HORACE,**	Ryder	**WINONA**
Hernando	**CORTES,**		**THOMAS**	Sax	**ROHMER**
	DESOTO	Mantle	**MICKEY**	Schweitzer	**ALBERT**
Hilton	**CONRAD**	Marcel	**PROUST**	Shostakovich	**DMITRI**
Honore	**BALZAC**	Margaret	**ATWOOD**	Sigrid	**UNDSET**
Horatio	**NELSON**	Marilyn	**MONROE**	Silas	**MARNER**
Howard	**COSELL,**	Marin	**CHEECH**	Simon	**LEGREE**
	HUGHES	Marlon	**BRANDO**	Sissy	**SPACEK**
Hugh	**HEFNER**	Martha	**CUSTIS,**	Skelton	**MARTHA**
Hughes	**HOWARD**		**GRAHAM**	Spengler	**OSWALD**
Hugo	**VICTOR**	Martin	**LUTHER**	Spinoza	**BARUCH**
Hume	**CRONYN**	Mascagni	**PIETRO**	Stalin	**JOSEPH**
Humphrey	**BOGART,**	May	**ELAINE**	Strachey	**LYTTON**
	HUBERT	Melville	**HERMAN**	Streisand	**BARBRA**
Huxley	**ALDOUS**	Mendel	**GREGOR**	Sumner	**WELLES**
Ignazio	**SILONE**	Menuhin	**YEHUDI**	Tebaldi	**RENATA**
Imre	**KALMAN**	Meryl	**STREEP**	Thomas	**HOBBES**
Indira	**GANDHI**	Mia	**FARROW**	Thornton	**WILDER**
Irene	**CASTLE**	Mickey	**MANTLE**	Tippi	**HEDREN**
Irving	**BERLIN**	Milquetoast	**CASPAR**	Todd	**DOLLEY**
Isaac	**NEWTON**	Mohandas	**GANDHI**	Toqueville	**ALEXIS**
Izaak	**WALTON**	Mowat	**FARLAY**	Toscanini	**ARTURO**
Isadora	**DUNCAN**	Muhammud	**ELIJAH**	Truman	**CAPOTE**
Jack	**LONDON**	Munch	**EDVARD**	Trump	**DONALD**
Jackson	**ANDREW**	Murdoch	**RUPERT**	Ulapova	**GALINA**
Jacqueline	**BISSET**	Mussolini	**BENITO**	Undset	**SIGRID**
Jane	**ADDAMS,**	Myrdal	**GUNNAR**	Urey	**HAROLD**
	AUSTEN	Nanette	**FABRAY**	Van Buren	**MARTIN**
Janis	**JOPLIN**	Nat	**TURNER**	Vecelli	**TITIAN**
Jean	**HARLOW**	Nilsson	**BIRGIT**	Vernon	**CASTLE**
Jim	**NABORS**	Noel	**COWARD**	Villa	**PANCHO**
Johannes	**BRAHMS,**	Nora	**HELMER**	Waksman	**SELMAN**
	KEPLER	Norman	**MAILER**	Wallace	**DEWITT**
Johns	**GLYNIS**	Norris	**CHUCK**	Walt	**DISNEY**
Johnson	**ANDREW,**	Ochs	**ADOLPH**	Washington	**BOOKER,**
	LYNDON	O'Henry	**PORTER**		**DENZEL**
Jose	**ITURBI**	Orson	**WELLES**	Waugh	**EVELYN**
Josef	**STALIN**	Orville	**WRIGHT**	Webster	**DANIEL**
Julius	**CAESAR**	Pablo	**CASALS**	Welty	**EUDORA**
Katie	**COURIC**	Paganini	**NICOLO**	Will	**ROGERS**
Keaton	**BUSTER**	Panza	**SANCHO**	William	**SAFIRE**
Kelly	**EMMETT**	Pascal	**BLAISE**	Willy	**BRANDT**
Kern	**JEROME**	Pere	**GORIOT**	Winchell	**WALTER**
Klein	**CALVIN**	Phineas	**BARNUM**	Wolfe	**THOMAS**
Knut	**HAMSUN**	Ponce	**DELEON**	Wright	**WILBUR**
Knute	**ROCKNE**	Priscilla	**MULLEN**	Wyeth	**ANDREW**
Kodaly	**ZOLTAN**	Proust	**MARCEL**	Yasir	**ARAFAT**
Lauren	**BACALL**	Pulitzer	**JOSEPH**	Yeager	**CHUCK**
LeMay	**CURTIS**	Ralph	**BUNCHE**	Yves	**TANGUY**
Lloyd	**GEORGE**	Reagan	**RONALD**	Zanuck	**DARRYL**
Lombroso	**CESARE**	Redon	**ODILON**	Zoltan	**KODALY**
Lorenzo de	**MEDICI**	Richard	**WAGNER**		
Lucrezia	**BORGIA**	Robert	**DENIRO**	Aleksei	**KOSYGIN**
Ludwig	**ERHARD**	Robinson	**CRUSOE,**	Amelia	**EARHART**
Lumet	**SIDNEY**		**JACKIE**	Andrew	**JACKSON,**
Lupin	**ARSENE**	Rolland	**ROMAIN**		**JOHNSON**
Mack	**CONNIE**	Ronald	**REAGAN**	Anna	**PAVLOVA**
Mahler	**GUSTAV**	Rudy	**VALLEE**	Arthur	**CHESTER**
Mailer	**NORMAN**	Rustin	**BAYARD**	Attlee	**CLEMENT**

Baldwin **STANLEY**	Gogol **NIKOLAI**	Primo **CARNERA**
Barnum **PHINEAS**	Gorbachev **MIKHAIL**	Priscilla **MULLINS**
Baryshnikov **MIKHAIL**	Grant **ULYSSES**	Prosper **MERIMEE**
Benvenuto **CELLINI**	Guglielmo **MARCONI**	Rabin **YITZHAK**
Bergen **CANDICE**	Gwyneth **PALTROW**	Red **BUTTONS**
Bierce **AMBROSE**	Hall **ARSENIO**	Rembrandt **VANRIJN**
Bo **DIDDLEY**	Henri **BERGSON**	Rhee **SYNGMAN**
Brecht **BERTOLT**	Homer **WINSLOW**	Ring **LARDNER**
Caldwell **ERSKINE**	Hoover **HERBERT**	Roosevelt **ELEANOR**
Carlo **GOLDONI**	Horace **GREELEY**	Rosa **BONHEUR**
Carmichael **STOKELY**	Hull **CORDELL**	Rupert **MURDOCH**
Carroll **DODGSON**	Isak **DINESEN**	Russell **LILLIAN**
Casey **STENGEL**	Jesse **VENTURA**	Safire **WILLIAM**
Chamberlain **NEVILLE**	Judd **WYNONNA**	Scalia **ANTONIN**
Chet **HUNTLEY**	Kemal **ATATURK**	Seurat **GEORGES**
Chubby **CHECKER**	Khan **GENGHIS**	Simon **BOLIVAR,**
Cullen **COUNTEE**	Laurence **OLIVIER**	**TEMPLAR**
Dewitt **WALLACE**	Leger **FERNAND**	Smith **ABIGAIL**
Dietrich **MARLENE**	Leif **ERIKSSON**	Stepin **FETCHIT**
Diller **PHYLLIS**	Leon **TROTSKY**	Susan **ANTHONY**
Dionne **ANNETTE**	Leonardo **DAVINCI**	Taylor **ZACHARY**
Dodgson **CARROLL**	Lillian **RUSSELL**	Titov **GHERMAN**
Dolly **MADISON**	Louis **PASTEUR**	Van Buren **ABIGAIL**
Donizetti **GAETANO**	Luther **BURBANK**	Van Gogh **VINCENT**
Dorothy **SAYERS**	Macchiavelli **NICCOLO**	Victor **HERBERT**
Dukakis **MICHAEL,**	Manet **EDOUARD**	von Braun **WERNHER**
OLYMPIA	Marc **CHAGALL**	Walter **GROPIUS,**
Dvorak **ANTONIN**	Marcel **DUCHAMP**	**RALEIGH**
Eden **ANTHONY**	March **FREDRIC**	Ward **ARTEMUS**
Eldridge **CLEAVER**	Mark **ANTHONY**	Warren **HARDING**
Ellen **BURSTYN**	Mark Twain **CLEMENS**	Wendell **WILLKIE**
Fabray **NANETTE**	Noam **CHOMSKY**	Willkie **WENDELL**
Fillmore **MILLARD**	O'Keeffe **GEORGIA**	Young **BRIGHAM**
Flagstad **KIRSTEN**	Omar **BRADLEY**	Yuri **GAGARIN**
Fonda **BRIDGET**	Pablo **PICASSO**	Ziegfeld **FLORENZ**
France **ANATOLE**	Paltrow **GWYNETH**	
Galina **ULANOVA**	Parsons **LOUELLA**	Bebe **NEUWIRTH**
Georgia **OKEEFFE**	Pike **ZEBULON**	Florenz **ZIEGFELD**
Giacomo **PUCCINI**	Pissarro **CAMILLE**	Johnson **LADYBIRD**
Gian-Carlo **MENOTTI**	Pius **PACELLI**	Hughes **LANGSTON**
Gish **DOROTHY,**	Pollock **JACKSON**	Marshall **THURGOOD**
LILLIAN		Tone **FRANCHOT**

MIDDLE NAMES

Abd—Krim	**EL**	Francis—Coppola	**FORD**
Chiang—Shek	**KAI**	Henry—Beecher	**WARD**
John—Passos	**DOS**	James—Polk	**KNOX**
Katherine—Porter	**ANN**	Jean—Sartre	**PAUL**
Louisa—Alcott	**MAY**	John—Getty	**PAUL**
Mao—Tung	**TSE**	John—Jones	**PAUL**
Mary—Evans	**ANN**	Julia—Howe	**WARD**
Nasr—Din	**ED**	Peter—Hayes	**LIND**
Sun—Sen	**YAT**	Thomas—Benton	**HART**
		Thomas — Edison	**ALVA**
Chester—Arthur	**ALAN**	William—Benet	**ROSE**
Claudia—Taylor	**ALTA**		
Ermanno—Ferrari	**WOLF**	Arthur—Doyle	**CONAN**

Arthur—Sulzberger	**HAYES**	Nicholas—Butler	**MURRAY**
Charles—Hughes	**EVANS**	Nicolas—Korsakov	**RIMSKY**
Clare—Luce	**BOOTH**	Paul—White	**DUDLEY**
Coretta—King	**SCOTT**	Percy—Shelley	**BYSSHE**
David—George	**LLOYD**	Richard—Sears	**WARREN**
Dwight—Eisenhower	**DAVID**	Ronald—Reagan	**WILSON**
Edgar—Poe	**ALLAN**	Samuel—Coleridge	**TAYLOR**
Erich—Remarque	**MARIA**	Steven—Cleveland	**GROVER**
Francis—Key	**SCOTT**	William—Bryant	**CULLEN**
Frank—Wright	**LLOYD**	William—Porter	**SYDNEY**
Harlan—Stone	**FISKE**	William—Taft	**HOWARD**
Helen—Moody	**WILLS**	William—Yeats	**BUTLER**
Henry—Lodge	**CABOT**		
Henry—Thoreau	**DAVID**	Adam—Powell	**CLAYTON**
Herbert—Hoover	**CLARK**	Alvah — Roebuck	**GRAHAM**
James—Garfield	**ABRAM**	Dante—Rossetti	**GABRIEL**
John—Astor	**JACOB**	Elizabeth—Browning	**BARRETT**
John—Garner	**NANCE**	Erle—Gardner	**STANLEY**
Joyce—Oates	**CAROL**	Gerald—Ford	**RUDOLPH**
Mary—Eddy	**BAKER**	George—Walker Bush	**HERBERT**
Peter—Tchaikovsky	**ILICH**	George—Shaw	**BERNARD**
Ralph—Emerson	**WALDO**	Harriet—Stowe	**BEECHER**
Richard—Lee	**HENRY**	Hubert—Humphrey	**HORATIO**
Walt—Disney	**ELIAS**	John—Curry	**STEUART**
William—Harrison	**HENRY**	John—Rockefeller	**DAVISON**
		John—Swayze	**CAMERON**
Alexander—Bell	**GRAHAM**	Marcus—Cicero	**TULLIUS**
Anne—Lindbergh	**MORROW**	Mary—Rinehart	**ROBERTS**
Charles—Reilly	**NELSON**	Norman—Peale	**VINCENT**
Edward—Lytton	**BULWER**	Oliver—Holmes	**WENDELL**
Franklin—Roosevelt	**DELANO**	Pierre—Trudeau	**ELLIOTT**
Franz—Haydn	**JOSEPH**	Richard—Nixon	**MILHOUS**
Gaius—Caesar	**JULIUS**	Sarah — Parker	**JESSICA**
George Herbert—Bush	**WALKER**	Thomas—Eliot	**STEARNS**
Herbert—Wells	**GEORGE**	Ulysses—Grant	**SIMPSON**
Howard—Hughes	**ROBARD**	Wolfgang—Mozart	**AMADEUS**
James—Johnson	**WELDON**		
John—Adams	**QUINCY**	James—Cooper	**FENIMORE**
John—Booth	**WILKES**	Johann—Goethe	**WOLFGANG**
John—Coolidge	**CALVIN**	John—Morgan	**PIERPONT**
John—Dulles	**FOSTER**	John—North	**RINGLING**
John—Mill	**STUART**	Richard—Sheridan	**BRINSLEY**
John—Sousa	**PHILIP**	William—Bryan	**JENNINGS**
Leslie—Hope	**TOWNS**	William—Hearst	**RANDOLPH**
Lyndon—Johnson	**BAINES**	William—Sherman	**TECUMSEH**
Mamie—Doud	**GENEVA**		
Martin—King	**LUTHER**	George—Custer	**ARMSTRONG**

UNUSED FIRST OR LAST NAMES

Fidel Castro—	**RUZ**	—Rupert Murdoch	**KEITH**
—Calvin Coolidge	**JOHN**	—Alistair Cooke	**ALFRED**
—Beatrix Potter	**HELEN**	—Andy Williams	**HOWARD**
—Corazon Aquino	**MARIA**	—Annie Oakley—	**PHOEBE, MOSES**
—Debra Winger	**MARIE**	Bela Lugosi—	**BLASKO**
—Dionne Warwick	**MARIE**	—Dashiell Hammett	**SAMUEL**
—Ingmar Bergman	**ERNST**	—Gregory Peck	**ELDRED**
—Norma Shearer	**EDITH**	Joe Louis—	**BARROW**
—Paul McCartney	**JAMES**	—Louis Armstrong	**DANIEL**

—Montgomery Clift	**EDWARD**	—Oliver Hardy	**NORVELL**
—Oliver Reed	**ROBERT**	—Ryan O'Neal	**PATRICK**
—Clark Gable	**WILLIAM**	—Steve McQueen	**TERENCE**
—Faye Dunaway	**DOROTHY**	—Jane Russell	**ERNESTINE**

PEN NAMES AND PSEUDONYMS

Pen Name	*Real Name*	*Pen Name*	*Real Name*
BOZ	Charles Dickens	**ALICE TOKLAS**	Gertrude Stein
SARI	Anne Elizabeth Fleur	**ARTEMUS WARD**	Charles Farrar
OUIDA	Marie Louse de la Ramee		Browne
OHENRY	William SydneyPorter	**GEORGE ELIOT**	Mary Ann Evans
STENDHAL	Marie-Henri Beyle	**JOHN LECARRE**	David Cornwell
VOLTAIRE	Francois-Marie de Arouet	**PABLO NERUDA**	Neftali Ricardo
ELIA LAMB	Charles Lamb		Reyes Basoalto
MARK TWAIN	Samuel Clemens	**TONI MORRISON**	Chloe Anthony
SSVANDINE	Willard Huntington		Wofford
	Wright	**GEORGE ORWELL**	Eric Blair
NANCY BOYD	Edna St. Vincent	**LEWIS CARROLL**	Charles Lutwidge
	Millay		Dodgson
CURRER BELL	Charlotte Bronte	**ANATOLE FRANCE**	Jacques
GEORGE SAND	Armandine Lucile		Anatole Francois Thibault
	Dupon Dudevant	**PETROLEUM V NASBY**	David
PIERRE LOTI	Julien Viaud		Russ Locke

ORIGINAL NAMES OF CELEBRITIES
BY STAGE NAME

Stage Name	*Given Name*
ANT, Adam	Stuart Goddard
DAY, Doris	Doris von Kappelhoff
DEE, Sandra	Alexandra Zuck
LEE, Peggy	Norma Egstrom
POP, Iggy	James Jewel Osterburg
ALDA, Alan	Alphonso D'Abruzzo
CAGE, Nicolas	Nicolas Coppola
CHER	Cherilyn Sarkisian
FOXX, Redd	John Sanford
JOHN, Elton	Reginald Dwight
JUDD, Wynonna	Christina Ciminella
KHAN, Chaka	Yvette Stevens
ROSE, Axl	William Bailey
RYAN, Mcg	Margaret Hyra
WOOD, Natalie	Natasha Gurdin
AIMEE, Anouk	Francoise Sorya
ALLEN, Woody	Allen Konigsberg
BENNY, Jack	Benjamin Kubelsky
BERRY, Chuck	Charles Edward Anderson
BLAKE, Robert	Michael Gubitosi
BORGE, Victor	Borge Rosenbaum
BURNS, George	Nathan Birnbaum
CAINE, Michael	Maurice Micklewhite
DAVIS, Bette	Ruth Davis
DEREK, Bo	Cathleen Collins
DYLAN, Bob	Robert Zimmerman
GARBO, Greta	Greta Gustafsson

Stage Name	Given Name
GRANT, Cary	Archibald Leach
JONES, Tom	Thomas Woodward
LANZA, Mario	Alfredo Cocozza
LEIGH, Janet	Jeanette Morrison
LEWIS, Jerry	Joseph Levitch
LOREN, Sophia	Sophia Scicoloni
LORRE, Peter	Laszlo Lowenstein
MOORE, Garry	Thomas Morfit
PARKS, Bert	Bert Jacobson
SATIE, Eric	Alfred Leslie
SHEEN, Charlie	Carlos Estevez
SHEEN, Martin	Ramon Estevez
SILLS, Beverly	Belle Silverman
STARR, Ringo	Richard Starkey
WAYNE, John	Marion Morrison
WYMAN, Jane	Sarah Jane Fulks
BACALL, Lauren	Betty Joan Perske
BARDOT, Brigitte	Camille Javal
BROOKS, Albert	Albert Einstein
COOPER, Alice	Vincent Furnier
COOPER, Gary	Frank Cooper
COSELL, Howard	Howard Cohen
CRUISE, Tom	Thomas Mapother IV
CURTIS, Tony	Bernard Schwartz
DENVER, John	Henry John Deutschendorf
EMINEM	Marshall Mathers
FIELDS, W. C.	William Claude Dukenfield
GARNER, James	James Baumgardner
HOLDEN, William	William Beedle
HOPPER, Hedda	Elda Furry
HUDSON, Rock	Roy Scherer, Jr.
HUNTER, Kim	Janet Cole
KEATON, Diane	Diane Hall
KEATON, Michael	Michael Douglas
LAUREL, Stan	Arthur Jefferson
MALDEN, Karl	Mladen Sulilovich
MARTIN, Dean	Dino Crocetti
MARTIN, Tony	Alvin Morris
MERMAN, Ethel	Ethel Zimmerman
MONROE, Marilyn	Norma Jean Mortenson, Norma Jean Baker
MOSTEL, Zero	Samuel Joel Mostel
OBRIAN, Hugh	Hugh Krampke
RAMONE, Joey	Jeffrey Hyman
RIVERS, Joan	Joan Sandra Molinsky
ROGERS, Ginger	Virginia McMath
ROGERS, Roy	Leonard Slye
ROONEY, Mickey	Joe Yule, Jr.
SHARIF, Omar	Michael Shalhoub
THOMAS, Danny	Amos Jacobs
TUCKER, Sophie	Sophia Kalish
TWITTY, Conway	Harold Jenkins
WILDER, Gene	Jerome Silberman
ALLYSON, June	Ella Gaisman
ANDREWS, Julie	Julia Wells

Stage Name	Given Name
ASTAIRE, Fred	Frederick Austerlitz
BENATAR, Pat	Patricia Andrejewski
BENNETT, Tony	Anthony Benedetto
BURSTYN, Ellen	Edna Rae Gillooly
BUTTONS, Red	Aaron Chwatt
DIDDLEY, Bo	Elias Bates
DOUGLAS, Kirk	Issur Danielovitch
GARLAND, Judy	Frances Gumm
GRANGER, Stewart	James Stewart
HOUDINI, Harry	Ehrich Weiss
ICECUBE	O'Shea Jackson
JOURDAN, Louis	Louis Gendre
LOMBARD, Carole	Jane Peters
MONTAND, Yves	Ivo Levi
PALANCE, Jack	Walter Palanuik
RANDALL, Tony	Leonard Rosenberg
SOTHERN, Ann	Harriette Lake
STEVENS, Connie	Concetta Ingolia
WINTERS, Shelley	Shirley Schrift
BABYFACE	Kenneth Edmonds
CHARISSE, Cyd	Tula Ellis Finkles
CRAWFORD, Joan	Lucille LeSueur
GOLDBERG, Whoopi	Caryn Johnson
HAYWORTH, Rita	Margarita Cansino
LAWRENCE, Steve	Sidney Leibowitz
MACLAINE, Shirley	Shirley Beaty
MEATLOAF	Marvin Lee Aday
PICKFORD, Mary	Gladys Smith
STANWYCK, Barbara	Ruby Stevens
FAIRBANKS, Douglas	Douglas Ullman
MANSFIELD, Jayne	Vera Jane Palmer

BY GIVEN NAME

Given Name	Stage Name
ADAY, Marvin Lee	Meat Loaf
COLE, Janet	Kim Hunter
GUMM, Frances	Judy Garland
HALL, Diane	Diane Keaton
HYRA, Margaret	Meg Ryan
LAKE, Harriette	Ann Southern
LEVI, Ivo	Yves Montand
SLYE, Leonard	Roy Rogers
YULE, Joe, Jr.	Mickey Rooney
ZUCK, Alexandra	Sandra Dee
BAKER, Norma Jean	Marilyn Monroe
BATES, Elias	Bo Diddley
BEATY, Shirley	Shirley MacLaine
COHEN, Howard	Howard Cosell
DAVIS, Ruth	Betty Davis
FULKS, Sarah Jane	Jane Wyman
FURRY, Elda	Hedda Hopper
HYMAN, Jeffrey	Joey Ramone
JAVAL, Camille	Brigitte Bardot

Given Name	Stage Name
LEACH, Archibald	Cary Grant
SMITH, Gladys	Mary Pickford
SORYA, Francoise	Anouk Aimee
WEISS, Ehrich	Harry Houdini
WELLS, Julia	Julie Andrews
BAILEY, William	Axl Rose
BEEDLE, William	William Holden
CHWATT, Aaron	Red Buttons
COOPER, Frank	Gary Cooper
DWIGHT, Reginald	Elton John
GENDRE, Louis	Louis Jourdan
GURDIN, Natasha	Natalie Wood
JACOBS, Amos	Danny Thomas
KALISH, Sophia	Sophie Tucker
LESLIE, Alfred	Eric Satie
MCMATH, Virginia	Ginger Rogers
MORFIT, Thomas	Garry Moore
MORRIS, Alvin	Tony Martin
MOSTEL, Samuel Joel	Zero Mostel
PALMER, Vera Jane	Jayne Mansfield
PERSKE, Betty Joan	Lauren Bacall
PETERS, Jane	Carole Lombard
ULLMAN, Douglas	Douglas Fairbanks
CANSINO, Margarita	Rita Hayworth
COCOZZA, Alfredo	Mario Lanza
COLLINS, Cathleen	Bo Derek
COPPOLA, Nicolas	Nicolas Cage
DOUGLAS, Michael	Michael Keaton
EDMONDS, Kenneth	Babyface
EGSTROM, Norma	Peggy Lee
ESTEVEZ, Carlos	Charlie Sheen
ESTEVEZ, Ramon	Martin Sheen
FINKLES, Tula Ellis	Cyd Charisse
FURNIER, Vincent	Alice Cooper
GAISMAN, Ella	June Allyson
GODDARD, Stuart	Adam Ant
INGOLIA, Concetta	Connie Stevens
JACKSON, O'Shea	Ice Cube
JENKINS, Harold	Conway Twitty
JOHNSON, Caryn	Whoopi Goldberg
KRAMPKE, Hugh	Hugh O'Brian
LESUEUR, Lucille	Joan Crawford
LEVITCH, Joseph	Jerry Lewis
MATHERS, Marshall	Eminem
SANFORD, John	Redd Foxx
SCHERER, Roy Jr.	Rock Hudson
SCHRIFT, Shirley	Shelly Winters
STARKEY, Richard	Ringo Starr
STEVENS, Ruby	Barbara Stanwyck
STEVENS, Yvette	Chaka Khan
STEWART, James	Stewart Granger
ANDERSON, Charles Edward	Chuck Berry
BIRNBAUM, Nathan	George Burns
CROCETTI, Dino	Dean Martin

Given Name	Stage Name
DABRUZZO, Alphonso	Alan Alda
EINSTEIN, Albert	Albert Brooks
GILLOOLY, Edna Rae	Ellen Burstyn
GUBITOSI, Michael	Robert Blake
JACOBSON, Bert	Bert Parks
KUBELSKY, Benjamin	Jack Benny
MAPOTHER, Thomas IV	Tom Cruise
MOLINSKY, Joan Sandra	Joan Rivers
MORRISON, Jeanette	Janet Leigh
MORRISON, Marion	John Wayne
SCHWARTZ, Bernard	Tony Curtis
PALANUIK, Walter	Jack Palance
SHALHOUB, Michael	Omar Sharif
WOODWARD, Thomas	Tom Jones
BENEDETTO, Anthony	Tony Bennett
CIMINELLA, Christina	Wynonna Judd
JEFFERSON, Arthur	Stan Laurel
LEIBOWITZ, Sidney	Steve Lawrence
MORTENSON, Norma Jean	Marilyn Monroe
OSTERBURG, James Jewel	Iggy Pop
ROSENBAUM, Borge	Victor Borge
ROSENBERG, Leonard	Tony Randall
SARKISIAN, Cherilyn	Cher
SCICOLONI, Sophia	Sophia Loren
SILBERMAN, Jerome	Gene Wilder
SILVERMAN, Belle	Beverly Sills
ZIMMERMAN, Ethel	Ethel Merman
ZIMMERMAN, Robert	Bob Dylan
AUSTERLITZ, Frederick	Fred Astaire
DUKENFIELD, William Claude	W.C. Fields
GUSTAFSSON, Greta	Greta Garbo
KONIGSBERG, Allen	Woody Allen
LOWENSTEIN, Laszlo	Peter Lorre
SULILOVICH, Malden	Karl Malden
ANDREJEWSKI, Patricia	Pat Benatar
BAUMGARDNER, James	James Garner
MICKLEWHITE, Maurice	Michael Caine
DANIELOVITCH, Issur	Kirk Douglas
DEUTSCHENDORF, Henry John	John Denver
VONKAPPELHOFF, Doris	Doris Day

FOOD AND DRINK
MENU AND COOKING TERMS

CUT	BREE	MELT	STEW
DIP	CHOP	PARE	STIR
FRY	CUBE	ROLL	WHIP
MIX	DUST	ROUX	
	FRIT	SEAR	ASPIC
BAKE	HASH	SHIR	AUJUS
BEAT	LARD	SIFT	BASTE
BOIL	MASH	SOAK	BLEND

BROIL	PUREE	FLAMBE	GARNISH
BRUSH	ROAST	FOLDIN	PARBOIL
CHILL	SAUTE	FRAPPE	PREHEAT
COUPE	SCALD	GIBLET	RAREBIT
CREAM	SCORE	MORTAR	RISSOLE
CREPE	SHIRR	OMELET	SCALLOP
CURRY	SIEVE	PANFRY	SPATULA
DOUGH	STALK	PESTLE	VINTAGE
FILET	STEAM	REDUCE	
FLAKE	STEEP	SIMMER	APERITIF
FROST	STOCK	SKEWER	AUBEURRE
GLACE	TOAST	SPONGE	AUGRATIN
GLAZE	TRUSS	TIDBIT	BARBECUE
GRATE			BOUILLON
GRILL	BATTER	ALAKING	DEVILLED
GRIND	BLANCH	ALAMODE	FLAMANDE
KNEAD	BRAISE	BOUQUET	JULIENNE
MINCE	CANAPE	CHOWDER	MARINADE
PASTE	CREOLE	FILLING	MARINATE
PATTY	DREDGE	FLAMAND	PANBROIL
POACH	FILLET	FONDANT	STUFFING

MENU ITEMS AND DISHES

AME	PIZZE	TONGUE	CHOPSUEY
BAP	SALAD	TRIFLE	CHOWCHOW
BUN	SALMI		COQUILLE
JAM	SCONE	ABAISSE	CROSTADA
KAI	STEAK	BEIGNET	DUMPLING
PIE	TORTE	BLINTZE	FLAPJACK
POI	WAFER	BRIOCHE	FRICANDO
		CASSATA	KEDGEREE
AGAR	BISQUE	COMPOTE	MARZIPAN
BABA	BLINIS	CROUTON	MEATBALL
CAKE	BONBON	CUPCAKE	MERINGUE
CHOU	BORSCH	DESSERT	MIREPOIS
FLAN	BORSHT	GARBORE	MIREPOIX
PATE	BOUDIN	GNOCCHI	NAPOLEON
SABA	CATSUP	KETCHUP	SANDWICH
SOUP	COLLOP	LASAGNE	SHASHLIK
TART	CUSCUS	PANCAKE	TORTILLA
	CUTLET	PARFAIT	
ASADO	ECLAIR	PEASOUP	
BOMBE	ENTREE	POLENTA	ANTIPASTO
BROSE	FONDUE	POPOVER	CREAMPUFF
BROTH	GATEAU	PRALINE	CROQUETTE
CABOB	HAGGIS	PUDDING	FRICANDEL
CANIN	KNODEL	RAVIOLI	FRICASSEE
GRAVY	KUCHEN	RISOTTO	FROGSLEGS
GUMBO	MOUSSE	RISSOLE	HAMBURGER
KABOB	MUFFIN	SAVARIN	MADRILENE
LACTO	NOUGAT	SHERBET	SALLYLUNN
PASTA	PANADA	SOUFFLE	SCHNITZEL
PILAF	PANADE	SPUMONI	SPAGHETTI
PILAU	PASTRY	TIMBALE	STIRABOUT
PILAW	POSOLE	ZAKUSKA	TOURNEDOS
PIZZA	SUNDAE		VOLAUVENT
	TAMALE	AGARAGAR	

SAUCES

SOY	GANSEL	TARTARE	MEUNIERE
	MORNAY	VELOUTE	
ALEC			BEARNAISE
CHILI	MARENGO	BARBECUE	REMOULADE
CURRY	SOUBISE	BECHAMEL	WORCESTER
GARUM	SUPREME	MARINARA	
MELBA	TABASCO	MATELOTE	

HERBS, SPICES, FLAVORINGS

BAY	DULSE	ALKANET	SHALLOT
RUE	ONION	ANCHUSA	VANILLA
SOY	SUMAC	BITTERS	VERBENA
	TANSY	BONESET	ACHILLEA
BALM	THYME	BUGLOSS	ALLSPICE
DILL		CALUMET	ANGELICA
FILE	BORAGE	CANELLA	BERGAMOT
FORB	BURNET	CARAWAY	CAPSICUM
LEEK	CASSIA	CAYENNE	CARDAMOM
MACE	CATNIP	CHERVIL	CHARLOCK
MINT	CELERY	COMFREY	CINNAMON
SAGE	CICELY	COWSLIP	COLEWORT
SALT	COMINO	DITTANY	COSTMARY
	FENNEL	FIGWORT	ESCHALOT
ANISE	GARLIC	GINSENG	ESTRAGON
BASIL	GINGER	JUNIPER	FINOCCHI
BENNE	HYSSOP	LAURIER	GALANGAL
BROOM	LOVAGE	MILFOIL	LAVENDER
CAPER	NUTMEG	MUGWORT	MARIGOLD
CHILI	PEPPER	MUSTARD	MARJORAM
CHIVE	PERSIL	OREGANO	ORIGANUM
CIBOL	ROCKET	PAPAVER	ROQUETTE
CLARY	SAVORY	PAPRIKA	ROSEMARY
CLOVE	SESAME	PARSLEY	SAMPHIRE
COCOA	SORREL	PARSNIP	SERPOLET
CUBES	SUMACH	PIGNOLI	TARRAGON
CUMIN		PIMENTO	TURMERIC
CURRY	ALECOST	SAFFRON	VERONICA

WINES

AHR	ANJOU	TAVEL	BARSAC
AYL	BADEN	TINTA	BEAUNE
	BLANC	TOKAY	CANARY
ASTI	BYRRH	TRIER	CHINON
BUAL	CAPRI	XERES	CLARET
GIRO	CORVO	YQUEM	GRAVES
HOCK	FIXIN	ZUCCO	LILLET
NAHE	MACON		MALAGA
PORT	MEDOC	ALBANA	MASDEU
ROSE	PFALZ	ALBANO	MONICA
SACK	PICON	ALELLA	MUSCAT
SAKE	PLONK	ALSACE	PATRAS
SARI	RIOJA	ARBOIS	PERNOD
SEKT	ROUGE	AUSONE	PINEAU
	SOAVE	BAROLO	RUFINA

SAUMUR	FLEURIE	SERCIAL	DUBONNET
SHERRY	INFERNO	SEYSSEL	FRASCATI
SPANNA	MADEIRA	VERDISO	GRENACHE
VOLNAY	MALMSEY	VESUVIO	MUSCADET
YVORNE	MARGAUX	VINGRIS	MUSCATEL
	MARSALA	VOUVRAY	PIESPORT
BANYULS	MAYWINE		RHEINGAU
CALDARO	MOSCATO	ALEATICO	RIESLING
CATAWBA	MOSELLE	ALSATIAN	RUBYPORT
CHABLIS	OLOROSO	BORDEAUX	SANCERRE
CHIANTI	ORVIETO	BURGUNDY	SAUTERNE
CREMANT	PASSITO	CABERNET	SYLVANER
DAGORED	POMEROL	CALVADOS	TOURAINE
EPERNAY	POMMARD	CHABLAIS	VERMOUTH
FALERNO	REDWINE	COLDDUCK	
FLANREN	SEEWEIN	CORONATA	

CORDIALS AND SPIRITS

ALE	ARROPE	AQUAVIT	PRUNELLE
GIN	BANANA	BACARDI	SCHNAPPS
RUM	BARACK	BITTERS	TIAMARIA
RYE	BRANDY	BOURBON	VIOLETIE
	CASSIS	CURACAO	
BEER	CHERRY	DAMIANA	APPLEJACK
BEND	COGNAC	NOYEAUX	BOCACHICA
BOCK	FRAISE	PARFAIT	COINTREAU
MEAD	GENEPI	QUETSCH	FRAMBOISE
MOKA	KALUHA	RASPAIL	MANDARINE
	KIRSCH	SLOEGIN	METHEGLIN
CACAO	KUMISS	TEQUILA	MIRABELLE
KEFIR	KUMMEL	VANILLE	SLIVOVITZ
LAGER	MASTIC	WHISKEY	
NOYAU	MENTHE		APRICOTINE
PEACH	PORTER	ABSINTHE	BLACKBERRY
PISCO	PULQUE	ADVOCAAT	CHARTREUSE
POMBE	SCOTCH	ANISETTE	CORNWHISKY
SNAPS	SNAPPS	ARMAGNAC	FIORDEALPI
STOUT	STREGA	CALVADOS	GOLDWASSER
VODKA	TAFFIA	CLEANRUM	MARASCHINO
	WHISKY	CORFINIO	
ANANAS	YVETTE	DRAMBUIE	
ARRACK		NEARBEER	

COCKTAILS AND MIXED DRINKS

BS	SLING	ROBROY	DAIQUIRI
	SMASH	ROYALE	HIGHBALL
FIZZ	TODDY	ZOMBIE	HOTTODDY
FLIP			PINKLADY
GROG	BISHOP	BACARDI	SANGAREE
PURL	CHASER	COBBLER	SPRITZER
SOUR	COOLER	COLLINS	
	EGGNOG	MARTINI	ALEXANDER
BRONX	FRAPPE	SIDECAR	CUBALIBRE
DAISY	GIBSON	STINGER	LAMBSWOOL
JULEP	GIMLET	SWIZZLE	MANHATTAN
NEGUS	POSSET	WASSAIL	MARGARITA
PUNCH	RICKEY		PISCOSOUR

FOREIGN WORDS
ALPHABETICAL BY FOREIGN WORD
SPANISH

ACA	hither, here	CADA	each	POCO	few, little
AHI	there	CAJA	box, cash	REJA	grate, grille, lattice
AJO	garlic	CAMA	bed		
AMO	master, owner	CAPA	cape	RICO	rich
ANO	year	CARA	face, facade	ROJO	red
ASI	thus	CARO	dear	ROPA	clothes, drygoods
DAR	give	CASA	home, house		
DEL	of the	CERA	wax	ROTO	broken, ragged
HOY	today	CIMA	peak, summit, top	SALA	hall, living room, parlor
IDA	departure				
LEY	law	CODO	elbow	SANO	healthy, sound
MAS	more	COMO	as, how?, like, why	SITO	located, situated
MUY	very				
OJO	eye	COSA	thing	SOGA	cord, rope
OLE	bravo	DAMA	lady, mistress	SOLO	only
ORO	gold	DEDO	finger, toe	TAJO	cut
OSO	bear	DIOS	God	TODO	all, every, whole
POR	because of, by, for, through	EDAD	age		
		ELLO	it	TORO	bull
REY	king	ENTE	being	TRAS	after, behind
RIA	estuary, inlet	ESTE	east	VACA	cow
RIO	river	FRIO	cold	VEGA	meadow, plain
RON	rum	GATO	cat, jack		
SER	to be	HABA	bean, kernel	ACASO	chance, maybe, perhaps
SUR	south	HIJA	daughter		
TIA	aunt	HIJO	child, son		
TIO	uncle	JEFE	chief	ACERA	sidewalk
VER	see	JUEZ	judge	ADIOS	good-bye
VEZ	time, turn	LADO	direction, room, side	ALDEA	village
				AMIGA	friend
ABAD	abbot	LAGO	lake	AMIGO	friend
ACTO	event, lawsuit	LOMA	hill	ANIMO	soul, spirit, will
AGUA	water	MALO	bad, evil, poor		
ALBO	white	MANO	hand	ANTES	before, formerly
ALLA	there	MESA	table		
ALLI	there	MONO	monkey	ATRAS	back, behind
ALMA	soul	NINA	girl, young	BAHIA	bay
ALMO	sweetheart	NINO	boy, child, young	BARBA	beard, chin
ALTO	high, loud			BARCA	boat
AMAR	to love	OBRA	construction, repair, work	BARCO	boat
AQUI	here			BELLO	beautiful
ASAR	to annoy, roast	OCIO	idleness, leisure, pastime	CABRA	goat
ASNO	ass, donkey			CALDO	broth
ASTA	horn, mast, spear			CALOR	heat, warmth
		OIDO	ear	CANON	canyon
AYER	yesterday	ONDA	wave	CARNE	meat
AZUL	blue	PASO	gait, pace, step	CARTA	letter
BAJO	low, short, under	PATO	drake, duck	CHICA	girl, child, lass
		PAVO	turkey		
BANO	bath	PELO	hair, nap	CHICO	boy, child, little, small
BESO	kiss	PEON	laborer		
BOCA	mouth	PERO	but	CHITO	hush
BOLA	ball	PICO	beak, point	CIELO	heaven, sky

CUICO	cop	NEGRO	black		stream
DIOSA	goddess	NOCHE	night	BARATO	cheap
DOLER	to ache, to grieve, to hurt	NORTE	north	BLANCO	white
		NUEVO	new	BODEGA	wine cellar, grocery store
		OESTE	west		
DONDE	where	PADRE	father	CABEZA	head
DUENA	landlady	PAMPA	prairie	CALIDO	warm
DUENO	landlord, master	PERRO	dog	CAMBIO	change, exchange rate
		PLATA	silver		
ENANO	little	PLATO	plate		
ESTAR	to be	POBRE	poor	CAMISA	shirt
ESTIO	summer	PRESO	convict, prisoner	CIUDAD	city
FALDA	dress, foothill, skirt			COCINA	kitchen
		RATON	mouse	COMIDA	dinner, food, meal
FINCA	plantation, property, real estate	REATA	lasso		
		RECIO	strong	CORREO	mail, post office
		REINA	queen		
FONDA	inn, restaurant	SENAL	landmark, mark, sign, token, trace	CUANDO	when
				DUENO	chaperon
FRESA	strawberry			ESPOSA	wife
FUEGO	fire	SENOR	gentleman, master, mister, sir	ESPOSO	husband
GALLO	cock, rooster			GITANO	gypsy, tricky
GENTE	folks, people, troops	SILLA	chair	GRANDE	large
		TABLA	table	GUERRA	conflict, war
HABLA	language	TANTO	so much	HOMBRE	man
HASTA	until	TARDE	afternoon, evening, late	INGLES	English
HUEVO	egg			LADRON	robber, thief
JUEGO	game, play	TENER	to have	MANANA	morning
LETRA	letter	TESTA	head	PAGADO	paid
LUEGO	soon, then	TOMAR	to have	PALOMA	dove, pigeon
MADRE	mother	UNICO	only	PASADO	past
MATAR	kill	VELOZ	agile, quick	POSADA	inn
MERCA	purchase	ZORRO	fox	PRENSA	press
MONJA	nun			RESERO	cowboy, herdsman
MOSCA	fly	ABADIA	abbey		
MUJER	woman	ALERTA	watchword	SENORA	lady, madam, Mrs.
NADAR	to float, to swim	ALTEZA	Highness		
		ALTURA	height		
NAVIO	ship, vessel	ARROYO	creek,	TARDIO	late

FRENCH

AME	soul	DOS	back	MAL	evil, ill(ness), sick(ness)
AMI	friend	DUC	duke		
ANE	ass, donkey	EAU	water	MER	sea
BAL	ball (dance)	EST	east, is	MUR	wall
BAS	low, stocking	ETE	summer	NEE	born
BLE	corn, wheat	FER	iron	NEZ	nose
BON	good	FEU	fire, heat	NOM	fame, name, noun
CAS	case, circumstance, event	FIL	thread		
		FOI	credit, faith, honor	NON	no
				OIE	goose
COL	mountain pass, neck	FOU	fool(ish)	OUI	yes
		GRE	wish, liking, will	PEU	few, little
COU	neck	ICI	here	PIS	worse
CRU	crude, raw, vineyard	ILE	island	PLI	fold, wrinkle, habit
		JEU	game, sport		
DES	since	JUS	gravy, juice	RIZ	rice
DIT	said, spoken	LIS	lily	ROI	king

SEC	dry	**EGAL**	equal	**PRET**	ready
SEL	salt	**ETAT**	state	**PRIX**	cost, price,
SUD	south	**ETRE**	be(ing)		prize
SUR	on, over, upon,	**FAIM**	hunger	**PUIS**	then
	sure	**FAIT**	deed	**RECU**	receipt
SUS	upon	**FAUX**	false	**REVE**	dream
TEL	such	**FILS**	son	**RIEN**	nothing
TIR	fire, shooting	**FLIC**	cop	**RIRE**	laugh
UNI	level, united	**FOIS**	time	**ROTI**	roast
VIF	lively	**GANT**	glove	**ROUX**	red
VIN	wine	**GARE**	beware, station	**SANS**	without
		GENS	people	**SCIE**	saw
ABAS	down with	**GRAS**	fat	**SEUL**	alone
ABBE	abbot	**GRIS**	gray	**SOIE**	silk
ABRI	dugout, shelter	**HAUT**	high	**SOIF**	thirst
ACTE	act	**HEIN**	exclamation	**SOIN**	care
AIGU	sharp	**HIER**	yesterday	**SOIR**	evening
AILE	wing(ed)	**HORS**	out	**SOIT**	agreed!
AINE	elder	**IDEE**	idea	**SOUS**	under
AISE	comfort, ease	**IVRE**	drunk	**TANT**	so much
AMER	bitter	**JEUX**	games	**TARD**	late
AMIE	friend	**JOUR**	day	**TETE**	head
ANGE	angel	**JUGE**	judge	**TOIT**	roof
ANSE	handle	**JUPE**	petticoat, skirt	**TOUS**	all, every
ARME	weapon	**LAIT**	milk	**TOUT**	all, any, every,
AUBE	dawn	**LIER**	tie		whole
AVEC	with	**LIRE**	read	**TRES**	very
AVIS	opinion,	**LORS**	then	**VELO**	bicycle
	warning	**LOUP**	half mask, wolf	**VERT**	green
AZUR	blue	**MAIN**	hand	**VITE**	quick
BAIN	bath	**MAIS**	but	**VOIR**	see
BANC	bench	**MARI**	husband	**VRAI**	true
BEBE	baby	**MERE**	mother	**YEUX**	eyes
BETE	beast, stupid	**MIDI**	noon		
BIEN	well	**MIEL**	honey	**ACHAT**	purchase
BLEU	blue	**MONT**	mountain	**ADIEU**	farewell
BOIS	wood	**MOUE**	grimace	**AIMER**	to love
BRAS	arm	**NEUF**	new	**AINSI**	thus
BRUN	brown	**NOIR**	black	**ALLEE**	avenue
CHER	dear, expensive	**NORD**	north	**ALLER**	to go
CHEZ	among, at	**NUIT**	night	**ALORS**	then
	home with,	**OBUS**	shell	**AMANT**	lover
	with, in	**OEIL**	eye	**AMOUR**	love
CHOU	cabbage	**OEUF**	egg	**APRES**	after
CHUT	hush!	**ONDE**	wave	**ARBRE**	tree
CIEL	heaven, sky	**OSER**	to dare	**ARGOT**	slang
CLOU	nail	**OTER**	to doff, to	**ARRET**	arrest, pause
COUT	cost		remove	**ASSEZ**	enough
CUIR	leather	**PAIN**	bread	**AUSSI**	also
DANS	in	**PAIX**	peace	**AUTRE**	other
DEFI	defiance	**PAYS**	country, land,	**AVANT**	before,
DEJA	already		nation		forward
DELA	beyond	**PEAU**	skin	**AVARE**	miser
DIEU	God	**PERE**	father	**AVION**	airplane
DORE	gilded, gilt,	**PEUR**	fear	**AVOIR**	have
	golden	**PIED**	foot	**BAGUE**	ring
DOUX	gentle, soft,	**PIRE**	worse	**BIERE**	beer
	sweet	**PONT**	bridge	**BLANC**	white
DRAP	cloth	**PRES**	almost, near	**BOEUF**	beef

BOIRE	to drink	**MOINS**	less	**AMENDE**	penalty, reparation
BONNE	maid, nurse	**MONDE**	world		
BRUIT	fame, noise, reputation	**MUSEE**	museum	**AMITIE**	friendship
		NEIGE	snow	**AUTOUR**	around
CARRE	square	**NEUVE**	new	**AVENIR**	future
CHAUD	hot, warm	**NUAGE**	cloud	**BAISER**	to kiss
CHERE	dear	**ONCLE**	uncle	**BAISSE**	fall of stocks
CHERI	dear	**ORAGE**	storm	**BERGER**	shepherd
CHIEN	dog	**OUEST**	west	**BEURRE**	butter
COMME	like	**OUTRE**	bizarre	**BOURSE**	stock exchange
COMTE	count, earl	**PARMI**	amid		
DETTE	debt, obligation	**PEINE**	pain, penalty, trouble	**CACHOT**	dungeon, prison
DOIGT	finger	**PETIT**	small	**CADEAU**	gift
DROIT	law, right, straight	**PLAGE**	beach	**CAHIER**	blank book, copy book
		PLEIN	full		
ECOLE	school	**PLUIE**	rain	**CAREME**	Lent
ELEVE	pupil	**POCHE**	pocket	**CARNET**	notebook
EMAIL	enamel	**POIDS**	weight	**CHAISE**	chair
ENCRE	ink	**POILU**	soldier	**CHEVAL**	horse
ENFER	hell	**POIRE**	pear	**CLOCHE**	bell
ENFIN	finally	**POSTE**	mail	**DABORD**	at first
ENTRE	among, between	**POULE**	chicken	**DETROP**	too much, superfluous
		PRISE	capture		
ETAGE	floor	**QUAND**	when	**DIABLE**	devil
FAUTE	error, fault, lack	**REINE**	queen	**DOUANE**	customs
		RENTE	annuity, income	**ECRIRE**	write
FILLE	daughter			**EGLISE**	church
FLEUR	flower	**REPAS**	meal	**ENCORE**	again
FRAIS	fresh	**REVER**	to dream	**ENFANT**	child
FRERE	brother	**RICHE**	rich	**ETOILE**	star
FROID	cold	**ROSEE**	dew	**FAUSSE**	false
GAFFE	blunder	**ROUGE**	red	**FIACRE**	carriage
GRAND	large	**SALLE**	hall, room	**FRAISE**	strawberry
HELAS	alas	**SALUT**	cheers, greeting, safety	**GAREDE**	beware
HEURE	hour			**GATEAU**	cake
HIVER	winter			**GAUCHE**	awkward, clumsy, left
HOMME	man	**SANTE**	health		
JAIME	I love	**SAVON**	soap	**GUERRE**	war
JAUNE	yellow	**SELON**	according	**HAUSSE**	rise of prices
JEUNE	young	**SOEUR**	sister	**LANGUE**	language, tongue
JOLIE	pretty	**SOMME**	sum		
LACHE	coward(ly)	**SORTE**	kind, manner, sort	**MAISON**	home, house
LAPIN	rabbit			**MARIEE**	bride
LEGER	light, slight	**TABLE**	table	**MEUBLE**	furniture
LIVRE	book	**TANTE**	aunt	**MOEURS**	customs
LOUER	to hire, to rent	**TASSE**	cup	**MONTRE**	watch
		TENIR	to hold, to possess	**MOUCHE**	fly
LOURD	heavy			**MOUTON**	sheep
LYCEE	school	**TERRE**	earth, land, world	**NAVIRE**	ship
MAIRE	mayor			**NOMBRE**	number
MAMAN	mamma	**TOMBE**	grave	**OCTROI**	concession, toll
MARIE	bridegroom	**VACHE**	cow		
MARIN	marine, sailor	**VERRE**	glass	**OUVERT**	open
MATIN	morning	**VOICI**	here	**PAREIL**	equal
MELER	to mix	**VOILA**	there!	**PARLER**	to speak
MERCI	thanks			**PATOIS**	dialect, lingo
METRO	subway	**AFFAME**	hungry	**PAUVRE**	poor
MIEUX	better	**AGNEAU**	lamb	**PENSEE**	thought

ROUSSE	red		groomed		bureau,
SAISON	season	SOLDAT	soldier		safety,
SAVOIR	to know, to	SOLEIL	sun		security
	understand	SOURIS	mouse	TRENTE	thirty
SOIGNE	well	SURETE	police		

ITALIAN

AVO	grandfather	MANO	hand	CARTA	paper
BUE	ox	MELA	apple	CASSA	chest
CON	with	NASO	nose	CIELO	heaven, sky
DIO	God	NAVE	ship	CITTA	city, town
ETA	age	NERO	black	CONTO	account
GIU	below, down	NORD	north	CORSA	course, race
IVI	there	ODIO	hatred	CORSO	street
MAI	always, ever,	OGGI	today	DETTO	said
	never	OGNI	each, every	DONNA	lady
OCA	goose, simpleton	PELO	hair	DONNE	women
ORA	duration, hour,	POCO	few, little, thin	DUOMO	cathedral
	now, time	POMO	apple	ESTRO	ardor
OVE	where	RIVA	shore	FATTO	done
PIU	many, more	SALA	hall	FERIA	holiday
QUA	here	SEDE	seat	FERRO	iron
QUI	here	SERA	afternoon,	FESTA	feast, holiday
SUD	south		evening, night	FORCA	fork
ZIA	aunt	SETE	thirst	FORZA	force, power,
ZIO	uncle	SITO	situated		strength
		UOMO	husband, man	FRATE	monk
AGRO	sour	UOVO	egg	GAMBA	leg
ALBA	dawn	VEDO	I see	GATTA	cat
ARTE	art	VERO	real, true	GROSS	large
ASSI	much	VISO	face	ISOLA	isle
ATTO	act, deed	VOCE	voice	LADRO	thief
BENE	well			LEGGE	law
BERE	to drink, to	ABITO	dress	LEGNO	wood
	swallow	ACQUA	water	LESSO	boiled
CAPO	head	ADDIO	farewell,	LETTO	bed
CARA	dear		good-bye	MADRE	mother
CARO	dear	ALTRO	other	MENTE	mind
CERA	wax	AMARE	to love	MOLTO	many, much,
CIMA	mountain peak,	AMICA	friend		very
	summit	AMICO	friend	MONDO	world
CODA	end, tail	AMORE	love	NOTTE	night
COSA	matter, thing	ANIMA	soul, spirit	OVEST	west
COSI	so, thus	ASINO	ass, donkey	PADRE	father
DONO	gift, talent	ASTRO	star	PALLA	ball
DOPO	after	AVERE	to get, to	PASTA	dough
ECCO	lo!		have	PASTO	meal
ESTE	east	BABBO	dad	PELLE	skin
FEDE	confidence,	BACIO	kiss	PONTE	bridge
	faith	BARBA	beard	PORTA	door, gate
GELO	frost, ice	BASTA	enough	PORTO	harbor
GESU	Jesus	BIRRA	beer	PREGO	please
GIRO	tour	BOCCA	mouth	PUNTO	not at all
GITA	tour	BOLLO	stamp	RETTO	straight
IERI	yesterday	BUONO	good	RICCO	rich
LAGO	lake	CAFFE	cafe	ROSSO	red
LATO	side	CALLE	street	SALSA	sauce
LUME	light	CAMPO	camp, field	SARTO	tailor

SCUSA	excuse	**ALLORA**	then	**FIGLIO**	son
SEDIA	chair	**AMANTE**	lover	**GIORNO**	day
SEGNO	sign	**ANCORA**	yet	**GRANDE**	large
SENZA	without	**APERTO**	open	**GRAZIE**	thanks
SONNO	sleep	**AVANTI**	forward	**GROSSO**	large
SOTTO	under	**BIANCO**	white	**MARITO**	husband
SPADA	sword	**CANALE**	canal	**MONETA**	money
SPOSA	bride, spouse	**CASALE**	hamlet,	**NIENTE**	nothing
SPOSO	spouse		village	**POVERO**	poor
TANTO	so much	**CHIAVE**	key	**QUANDO**	when, how
TARDO	late	**DACAPO**	again, from		much
TERGO	back		the	**REGINA**	queen
TESTA	head		beginning	**SCARPA**	shoe
TORRE	tower	**DENARO**	money	**SIGNOR**	gentleman
TORTO	twisted,	**DESTRO**	right	**STELLA**	star
	wrong	**DOGANA**	custom	**STESSO**	same, self
TUTTI	all		house	**STRADA**	road
TUTTO	all	**DOMANI**	tomorrow	**TAVOLA**	table
		ESSERE	to be	**VALUTA**	value
ADESSO	now	**ESTERO**	foreign		
ALBERO	tree	**FIGLIA**	daughter		

GERMAN

AAL	eel	**ALTE**	age, old	**FEIN**	elegant, fine
ABT	abbot	**ARZT**	doctor	**FLUG**	flight
ACH	alas	**AUGE**	eye	**FRAU**	lady, wife,
AHN	ancestor	**AULA**	hall		woman
ALS	as, than	**BART**	beard	**FREI**	free
ARM	poor	**BAUM**	tree	**FRUH**	early
AUF	of, on, upon	**BEIN**	to lag	**GABE**	gift
AUS	from, of, out of	**BETT**	bed	**GANZ**	all
BEI	about, among, at,	**BIER**	beer	**GAST**	visitor
	with	**BILD**	figure, image,	**GELD**	cash, coin,
EIS	ice		picture		money
ENG	narrow	**BLAU**	blue	**GERN**	gladly,
IST	is	**BLUT**	blood		willingly
KUH	cow	**BROT**	bread	**GOTT**	God, lord
MIT	with	**BUCH**	book	**GRAF**	count, earl,
NAH	near	**BUND**	band, bundle,		nobleman
NEU	new		league	**HAAR**	hair
NIE	never	**DAME**	lady, woman	**HALS**	neck
OHR	ear	**DANN**	then	**HAUS**	house,
OST	east	**DENN**	for, than, then		residence
SUD	south	**DIEB**	thief	**HEIM**	home
TAL	valley	**DING**	thing	**HERR**	gentleman,
TOR	gate	**DOCH**	still, yet		lord, mister, sir
TOT	dead	**DORF**	village	**HERZ**	heart
UHR	clock, watch	**DORT**	there, yonder	**HIER**	here
UND	and	**ECHT**	genuine, pure,	**HOCH**	high, tall, viva
VON	from; of		real		(salute)
VOR	before	**EDEL**	noble	**HUHN**	chicken
WEG	path, way	**EHER**	first	**HUND**	dog
WIE	how	**ENTE**	duck	**JEDE**	every
ZUG	train	**ERDE**	earth	**JENE**	that
		ESEL	ass	**KALT**	cold
ABER	but	**ETWA**	about, nearly,	**KLUG**	clever
ADEL	nobility		perhaps	**LIED**	air, song, tune
ALLE	all	**FAUL**	dirty, foul, lazy	**LUFT**	air

MANN	man	**ALLES**	everything	**PROST**	cheers!
MEER	sea	**ANDER**	different, else	**REGEN**	rain
MEHR	more	**ANGST**	fear	**REICH**	empire, rich
MORD	murder	**APFEL**	apple	**SEELE**	soul
NACH	after, behind	**BEIDE**	both	**SONNE**	sun
NEIN	no	**BESEN**	broom	**SPIEL**	game, play
NEUE	new	**BITTE**	please, request	**STAAT**	state
NOCH	besides, yet			**STADT**	city, town
NORD	north	**BLITZ**	lightning	**STAHL**	steel
OBEN	above, top	**BRAUT**	bride	**STUHL**	chair
OBER	upper	**BRIEF**	letter	**SUDEN**	south
OBST	fruit	**DAHER**	hence	**TAFEL**	table
ODER	or	**DAMEN**	ladies	**TANTE**	aunt
OHNE	without	**DANKE**	thanks	**TISCH**	table
PAAR	couple, pair	**DURCH**	across, through	**UNTEN**	below, beneath
RAUM	room, space				
REDE	language, speech	**DURST**	thirst	**UNTER**	below, beneath
		EINST	once		
RUHE	calm, peace, repose, rest	**EISEN**	iron	**VATER**	father
		ESSEN	to eat	**WAGEN**	carriage, to dare
RUHM	glory	**GABEL**	fork		
SAAL	hall, room	**GASSE**	alley, lane, path, street	**WARUM**	why
SEHR	greatly, much, very			**WENIG**	few, little
SEIN	be(ing)	**GATTE**	husband, spouse		
SIEG	triumph, victory	**GEBEN**	to give	**ARBEIT**	labor, toil, work
		GEHEN	to go, to move, to walk		
SINN	mind			**BILLIG**	cheap
SOHN	son			**BRUDER**	brother
SPAT	late	**GEIST**	mind, soul, spirit	**EINMAL**	once
TIEF	deep			**FRAUEN**	ladies
TURM	tower	**HABEN**	to have	**GATTEN**	wife
UBER	above, over	**HAFEN**	harbor, haven	**GLOCKE**	bell
UFER	bank, shore	**HEUTE**	today	**HERREN**	gentleman
VIEL	many, much	**IMMER**	always	**HIMMEL**	heaven, sky
VOLK	nation, people, race	**INSEL**	island	**LOFFEL**	spoon
		JAGER	hunter	**MESSER**	knife
VOLL	full	**KLEIN**	little, small	**MITTAG**	noon
WAHR	genuine, real, true	**KREUZ**	cross	**MORGEN**	morning, tomorrow
		KRIEG	strife, war		
WEIB	wife, woman	**LEDER**	leather	**MUTTER**	mother
WEIL	because	**LESEN**	to read	**NORDEN**	north
WEIT	distant, far, wide	**LEUTE**	people, persons	**PROSIT**	cheers!
				SCHNEE	snow
WELT	humanity, society, world	**LIEBE**	affection, love	**SCHULE**	school
		NACHT	night	**SELBST**	self
WENN	if, when	**NEBEN**	beside	**SOLDAT**	soldier
WEST	west	**NEUER**	new	**TELLER**	plate
WIRT	host	**NEUES**	new	**WESTEN**	west
WOHL	well	**NICHT**	not	**WIEDER**	again
		ONKEL	uncle	**WISSEN**	to know, knowledge
ABEND	evening	**OSTEN**	east, Orient		
		PREIS	cost, prize		

LATIN

AES	copper	**ARX**	citadel, fortress	**CUM**	with
AMO	I love	**AUT**	either, or	**DEA**	goddess
ARA	altar, pyre	**BIS**	twice	**DEI**	gods
ARS	art, trade	**COR**	heart	**DUX**	leader

EST	is
FAS	lawful, divine law
HEU	alas
IBI	there
IRA	anger, wrath
JUS	law
LAC	milk
LEX	law
MOS	custom, will
NON	not
ORA	edge, shore, pray
PAX	peace
PES	foot
QUA	as
RES	thing
REX	king
SED	but
TER	three times
UBI	where
VAE	alas
VAS	pledge, vessel
VIR	husband, man
VIS	force, power, strength
ACTU	thing done
ACUS	needle, pin
AGER	field
AGNI	lambs
AGRI	fields
ALIA	other
ALII	others
ALTA	high
AMAS	you love
AMAT	he loves
ANNO	in the year
ANTE	before
AQUA	water
AVES	birds
AVIS	bird
AVUS	grandfather
BENE	well
BONA	property
CAVE	beware
CENA	dinner, supper
CITO	soon
DIEM	day
DIES	day(s)
DIXI	I have spoken
ECCE	behold!, lo!
EHEU	alas
ERAT	was
ESSE	be(ing)
GENU	knee
HORA	hour
IBID	at the same place
IDEM	same

ITER	road
LANA	wool
LAUS	praise
MARE	sea
MENS	mind
MONS	mountain
NEMO	nobody
NISI	except, unless
NOTA	note, observe!
NUNC	now
OVUM	egg
PARS	part
PONS	bridge
POST	after
PUER	boy, child
RATA	proportion, share
REUS	culprit, defendant
SINE	without
SORS	lot, prophecy
SPES	hope
TACE	hush!
TOTO	in all
URBS	city
UXOR	wife
VADE	go away!
VIDE	see!
VITA	life
VOLA	palm (hand)
ABBAS	abbot
ACIES	battle line, keenness
ACTES	edge
ACTUS	thing done
AEGER	sick
AGNUS	lamb
ALIUD	another thing
ALIUS	other
AMICA	friend
ANIMA	air, wind, soul
ANNUS	year
ANTEA	before
ASTRA	stars
AURUM	gold
BEATA	blessed, happy
BONUM	good
CALIX	cup, goblet
CAUDA	tail
CIBUS	fodder, food
CIRCA	about
COENA	supper
COPIA	abundance, plenty
CULPA	error, fault, negligence

DIVUS	divine
DOLUS	deceit, fraud
FIDES	confidence, faith, trust
FILIA	daughter
FRONS	brow, forehead
GALEA	helmet
IDEST	that is
IGNIS	fire
INTRA	within
JANUA	door
JUXTA	nearby
LATUS	broad, wide, side
LENIS	gentle, smooth, soft
LIBER	book
LOCUS	place
MALUM	evil
MALUS	bad, wicked
MANET	it remains
MISSA	Mass, the
MODUS	form, method
NEFAS	sinful, unlawful
NIHIL	nothing
NOMEN	name
OBSTA	resist!
OMNIA	all
OMNIS	all
OTIUM	ease, leisure
PECUS	cattle, flock, herd
PORTA	door, gate
QUARE	why
QUOAD	as far as
REGES	kings
RETRO	backward, behind
RITUS	rite, usage
SANUS	healthy, sound
SOLUS	alone, only
SUPER	above, over, upon, more
TERRA	earth, ground, land
TOTUM	all
TRANS	across, over
VENIA	pardon
VINUM	sour, wine
ACHAIA	Greece
AESTAS	summer
ALITER	otherwise
AMICUS	friend
BEATUS	blessed, happy

BELLUM	war	**IGITUR**	therefore	**PRIMUM**	first
CIRCUM	around	**ITERUM**	again	**PRIMUS**	first
DEXTER	right	**LAPSUS**	error,	**REGINA**	queen
DOCTUS	learned, well		gliding,	**REGNUM**	authority,
	informed		sliding		kingdom,
EMPTIO	buying	**MAGNUS**	great		tyranny
FEMINA	woman	**PARTIM**	partly	**SEMPER**	always
FERRUM	iron	**PATRIA**	fatherland	**SERVUS**	servant,
FILIUS	son	**PISCES**	fishes		slave
FURTUM	theft	**PISCIS**	fish	**SORTES**	lots

ALPHABETICAL BY DEFINITION
SPANISH

aunt	**TIA**	bath	**BANO**	grille	**REJA**
be, to	**SER**	beak	**PICO**	hair	**PELO**
bear	**OSO**	bean	**HABA**	hall	**SALA**
because of	**POR**	bed	**CAMA**	hand	**MANO**
bravo	**OLE**	behind	**TRAS**	healthy	**SANO**
by	**POR**	being	**ENTE**	here	**AQUI**
departure	**IDA**	blue	**AZUL**	high	**ALTO**
estuary	**RIA**	box	**CAJA**	hill	**LOMA**
eye	**OJO**	boy	**NINO**	home	**CASA**
for	**POR**	broken	**ROTO**	horn	**ASTA**
garlic	**AJO**	bull	**TORO**	house	**CASA**
give	**DAR**	but	**PERO**	how?	**COMO**
gold	**ORO**	cape	**CAPA**	idleness	**OCIO**
here	**ACA**	cash	**CAJA**	it	**ELLO**
hither	**ACA**	cat	**GATO**	jack	**GATO**
inlet	**RIA**	chief	**JEFE**	judge	**JUEZ**
king	**REY**	child	**NINO, HIJO**	kernel	**HABA**
law	**LEY**	clothes	**ROPA**	kiss	**BESO**
master	**AMO**	cold	**FRIO**	laborer	**PEON**
more	**MAS**	construction	**OBRA**	lady	**DAMA**
of the	**DEL**	cord	**SOGA**	lake	**LAGO**
owner	**AMO**	cow	**VACA**	lattice	**REJA**
river	**RIO**	cut	**TAJO**	lawsuit	**ACTO**
rum	**RON**	daughter	**HIJA**	leisure	**OCIO**
see	**VER**	dear	**CARO**	like	**COMO**
south	**SUR**	direction	**LADO**	little	**POCO**
there	**AHI**	donkey	**ASNO**	living room	**SALA**
through	**POR**	drake	**PATO**	located	**SITO**
thus	**ASI**	drygoods	**ROPA**	loud	**ALTO**
time	**VEZ**	duck	**PATO**	love, to	**AMAR**
today	**HOY**	each	**CADA**	low	**BAJO**
turn	**VEZ**	ear	**OIDO**	mast	**ASTA**
uncle	**TIO**	east	**ESTE**	meadow	**VEGA**
very	**MUY**	elbow	**CODO**	mistress	**DAMA**
year	**ANO**	event	**ACTO**	monkey	**MONO**
		every	**TODO**	mouth	**BOCA**
abbot	**ABAD**	evil	**MALO**	nap	**PELO**
after	**TRAS**	facade	**CARA**	only	**SOLO**
age	**EDAD**	face	**CARA**	pace	**PASO**
all	**TODO**	few	**POCO**	parlor	**SALA**
annoy, to	**ASAR**	finger	**DEDO**	pastime	**OCIO**
as	**COMO**	gait	**PASO**	peak	**CIMA**
ass	**ASNO**	girl	**NINA**	peak	**PICO**
bad	**MALO**	God	**DIOS**	plain	**VEGA**
ball	**BOLA**	grate	**REJA**	point	**PICO**

poor	**MALO**	egg	**HUEVO**	queen	**REINA**
ragged	**ROTO**	evening	**TARDE**	quick	**VELOZ**
red	**ROJO**	father	**PADRE**	real estate	**FINCA**
repairs	**OBRA**	fire	**FIJEGO**	restaurant	**FONDA**
rich	**RICO**	float, to	**NADAR**	rooster	**GALLO**
roast, to	**ASAR**	fly	**MOSCA**	ship	**NAVIO**
room	**LADO**	folks	**GENTE**	sidewalk	**ACERA**
rope	**SOGA**	foothill	**FALDA**	sign	**SENAL**
short	**BAJO**	formerly	**ANTES**	silver	**PLATA**
side	**LADO**	fox	**ZORRO**	sir	**SENOR**
situated	**SITO**	friend **AMIGA, AMIGO**		skirt	**FALDA**
son	**HIJO**	game	**JUEGO**	sky	**CIELO**
soul	**ALMA**	gentleman	**SENOR**	small	**CHICO**
sound	**SANO**	girl	**CHICA**	so much	**TANTO**
spear	**ASTA**	goat	**CABRA**	soon	**LUEGO**
step	**PASO**	goddess	**DIOSA**	soul	**ANIMO**
summit	**CIMA**	good-bye	**ADIOS**	spirit	**ANIMO**
sweetheart	**ALMO**	grieve, to	**DOLER**	strawberry	**FRESA**
table	**MESA**	have, to	**TENER,**	strong	**RECIO**
there	**ALLA, ALLI**		**TOMAR**	summer	**ESTIO**
thing	**COSA**	head	**TESTA**	swim, to	**NADAR**
toe	**DEDO**	heat	**CALOR**	table	**TABLA**
top	**CIMA**	heaven	**CIELO**	then	**LUEGO**
turkey	**PAVO**	hurt, to	**DOLER**	token	**SENAL**
under	**BAJO**	hush	**CHITO**	trace	**SENAL**
water	**AGUA**	inn	**FONDA**	troops	**GENTE**
wave	**ONDA**	kill, to	**MATAR**	until	**HASTA**
wax	**CERA**	landlady	**DUENA**	vessel	**NAVIO**
white	**ALBO**	landlord	**DUENO**	village	**ALDEA**
whole	**TODO**	landmark	**SENAL**	warmth	**CALOR**
why	**COMO**	language	**HABLA**	west	**OESTE**
work	**OBRA**	lass	**CHICA**	where	**DONDE**
yesterday	**AYER**	lasso	**REATA**	will	**ANIMO**
young	**NINO**	late	**TARDE**	woman	**MUJER**
		letter **CARTA, LETRA**			
ache, to	**DOLER**	little **CHICO, ENANO**		abbey	**ABADIA**
afternoon	**TARDE**	mark	**SENAL**	cellar	**BODEGA**
agile	**VELOZ**	master	**SENOR,**	change	**CAMBIO**
back	**ATRAS**		**DUENO**	chaperon	**DUENA**
bay	**BAHIA**	maybe	**ACASO**	cheap	**BARATO**
be, to	**ESTAR**	meat	**CARNE**	city	**CIUDAD**
beard	**BARBA**	mister	**SENOR**	conflict	**GUERRA**
beautiful	**BELLO**	mother	**MADRE**	cowboy	**RESERO**
before	**ANTES**	mouse	**RATON**	creek	**ARROYO**
behind	**ATRAS**	new	**NUEVO**	dinner	**COMIDA**
black	**NEGRO**	night	**NOCHE**	dove	**PALOMA**
boat	**BARCA, BARCO**	north	**NORTE**	English	**INGLES**
broth	**CALDO**	nun	**MONJA**	exchange rate	**CAMBIO**
boy	**CHICO**	only	**UNICO**	food	**COMIDA**
canyon	**CANON**	people	**GENTE**	grocery store	**BODEGA**
chair	**SILLA**	perhaps	**ACASO**	gypsy	**GITANO**
chance	**ACASO**	plantation	**FINCA**	head	**CABEZA**
child	**CHICA, CHICO**	plate	**PLATO**	height	**ALTURA**
chin	**BARBA**	play	**JUEGO**	herdsman	**RESERO**
cock	**GALLO**	poor	**POBRE**	Highness	**ALTEZA**
convict	**PRESO**	prairie	**PAMPA**	husband	**ESPOSO**
cop	**CUICO**	prisoner	**PRESO**	inn	**POSADA**
dog	**PERRO**	property	**FINCA**	kitchen	**COCINA**
dress	**FALDA**	purchase	**MERCA**	lady	**SENORA**

large	GRANDE	past	PASADO	vessel	NAVIO
late	TARDIO	pigeon	PALOMA	war	GUERRA
madam	SENORA	post office	CORREO	warm	CALIDO
mail	CORREO	press	PRENSA	watchword	ALERTA
man	HOMBRE	robber	LADRON	when	CUANDO
meal	COMIDA	shirt	CAMISA	white	BLANCO
morning	MANANA	stream	ARROYO	wife	ESPOSA
Mrs.	SENORA	thief	LADRON	will	ANIMO
paid	PAGADO	tricky	GITANO	wine cellar	BODEGA

FRENCH

ass	ANE	nose	NEZ	beast	BETE
back	DOS	noun	NOM	be(ing)	ETRE
ball (dance)	BAL	on, over	SUR	bench	BANC
born	NEE	raw	CRU	beware	GARE
case	CAS	rice	RIZ	beyond	DELA
circumstance	CAS	said	DIT	bicycle	VELO
corn	BLE	salt	SEL	bitter	AMER
credit	FOI	sea	MER	black	NOIR
crude	CRU	shooting	TIR	blue	AZUR, BLEU
donkey	ANE	sick(ness)	MAL	bread	PAIN
dry	SEC	since	DES	bridge	PONT
duke	DUC	soul	AME	brown	BRUN
east	EST	south	SUD	but	MAIS
event	CAS	spoken	DIT	cabbage	CHOU
evil	MAL	sport	JEU	care	SOIN
faith	FOI	stocking	BAS	cloth	DRAP
fame	NOM	such	TEL	comfort	AISE
few	PEU	summer	ETE	cop	FLIC
fire	FEU, TIR	sure	SUR	cost	COUT, PRIX
fold	PLI	thread	FIL	country	PAYS
fool(ish)	FOU	united	UNI	dare	OSER
friend	AMI	upon	SUR, SUS	dawn	AUBE
game	JEU	vineyard	CRU	day	JOUR
good	BON	wall	MUR	dear	CHER
goose	OIE	water	EAU	deed	FAIT
gravy	JUS	wheat	BLE	defiance	DEFI
habit	PLI	will	GRE	doff	OTER
heat	FEU	wine	VIN	down with	ABAS
here	ICI	wish	GRE	dream	REVE
honor	FOI	worse	PIS	drunk	IVRE
ill	MAL	wrinkle	PLI	dugout	ABRI
illness	MAL	yes	OUI	ease	AISE
iron	FER			egg	OEUF
is	EST	abbot	ABBE	elder	AINE
island	ILE	act	ACTE	equal	EGAL
juice	JUS	agreed	SOIT	evening	SOIR
king	ROI	all	TOUS, TOUT	every	TOUS, TOUT
level	UNI	almost	PRES	exclamation	HEIN
liking	GRE	alone	SEUL	expensive	CHER
lily	LIS	already	DEJA	eye	OEIL
little	PEU	among	CHEZ	eyes	YEUX
lively	VIF	angel	ANGE	false	FAUX
low	BAS	any	TOUT	fat	GRAS
mountain pass	COL	arm	BRAS	father	PERE
name	NOM	at home with	CHEZ	fear	PEUR
neck	COL, COU	baby	BEBE	foot	PIED
no	NON	bath	BAIN	friend	AMIE

games	**JEUX**	silk	**SOIE**	coward(ly)	**LACHE**
gentle	**DOUX**	skin	**PEAU**	cup	**TASSE**
gilded	**DORE**	skirt	**JUPE**	daughter	**FILLE**
gilt	**DORE**	sky	**CIEL**	dear	**CHERE, CHERI**
glove	**GANT**	soft	**DOUX**	debt	**DETTE**
God	**DIEU**	so much	**TANT**	dew	**ROSEE**
golden	**DORE**	son	**FILS**	dog	**CHIEN**
gray	**GRIS**	state	**ETAT**	dream, to	**REVER**
green	**VERT**	station	**GARE**	drink, to	**BOIRE**
grimace	**MOUE**	stupid	**BETE**	earl	**COMTE**
half mask	**LOUP**	sweet	**DOUX**	earth	**TERRE**
hand	**MAIN**	then	**LORS, PUIS**	enamel	**EMAIL**
handle	**ANSE**	thirst	**SOIF**	enough	**ASSEZ**
head	**TETE**	tie	**LIER**	error	**FAUTE**
heaven	**CIEL**	time	**FOIS**	fame	**BRUIT**
high	**HAUT**	true	**VRAI**	farewell	**ADIEU**
honey	**MIEL**	under	**SOUS**	fault	**FAUTE**
hunger	**FAIM**	very	**TILES**	finally	**ENFIN**
husband	**MARI**	warning	**AVIS**	finger	**DOIGT**
hush!	**CHUT**	wave	**ONDE**	floor	**ETAGE**
idea	**IDEE**	weapon	**ARME**	flower	**FLEUR**
in	**CHEZ, DANS**	well	**BIEN**	forward	**AVANT**
judge	**JUGE**	whole	**TOUT**	fresh	**FRAIS**
land	**PAYS**	wing(ed)	**AILE**	full	**PLEIN**
late	**TARD**	with	**AVEC, CHEZ**	glass	**VERRE**
laugh	**RIRE**	without	**SANS**	go	**ALLER**
leather	**CUIR**	wolf	**LOUP**	grave	**TOMBE**
milk	**LAIT**	wood	**BOIS**	greeting	**SALUT**
mother	**MERE**	worse	**PIRE**	hall	**SALLE**
mountain	**MONT**	yesterday	**HIER**	have	**AVOIR**
nail	**CLOU**	according	**SELON**	health	**SANTE**
nation	**PAYS**	after	**APRES**	heavy	**LOURD**
near	**PRES**	airplane	**AVION**	hell	**ENFER**
new	**NEUF**	alas	**HELAS**	here	**VOICI**
night	**NUIT**	also	**AUSSI**	hire	**LOUER**
noon	**MIDI**	amid	**PARMI**	hold	**TENIR**
north	**NORD**	among	**ENTRE**	hot	**CHAUD**
nothing	**RIEN**	annuity	**RENTE**	hour	**HEURE**
opinion	**AVIS**	arrest	**ARRET**	I love	**JAIME**
out	**HORS**	aunt	**TANTE**	income	**RENTE**
peace	**PAIX**	avenue	**ALLEE**	ink	**ENCRE**
people	**GENS**	beach	**PLACE**	kind	**SORTE**
petticoat	**JUPE**	beef	**BOEUF**	lack	**FAUTE**
pretty	**JOU**	beer	**BIERE**	land	**TERRE**
price	**PRIX**	before	**AVANT**	large	**GRAND**
prize	**PRIX**	better	**MIEUX**	law	**DROIT**
quick	**VITE**	between	**ENTRE**	less	**MOINS**
read	**LIRE**	bizarre	**OUTRE**	light	**LEGER**
ready	**FRET**	blunder	**GAFFE**	like	**COMME**
receipt	**RECU**	book	**LIVRE**	love	**AMOUR**
red	**ROUX**	bridegroom	**MARIE**	love, to	**AIMER**
remove	**OTER**	brother	**FRERE**	lover	**AMANT**
roast	**ROTI**	capture	**PRISE**	maid	**BONNE**
roof	**TOIT**	cheers	**SALUT**	mail	**POSTE**
saw	**SCIE**	chicken	**POULE**	mamma	**MAMAN**
see	**VOIR**	cloud	**NUAGE**	man	**HOMME**
sharp	**AIGU**	cold	**FROID**	manner	**SORTE**
shell	**OBUS**	count	**COMTE**	marine	**MARIN**
shelter	**ABRI**	cow	**VACHE**	mayor	**MAIRE**

meal	**REPAS**	thanks	**MERCI**	home	**MAISON**
miser	**AVARE**	then	**ALORS**	horse	**CHEVAL**
mix	**MELER**	there!	**VOILA**	house	**MAISON**
morning	**MATIN**	thus	**AINSI**	hungry	**AFFAME**
museum	**MUSEE**	tree	**ARBRE**	kiss	**BAISER**
new	**NEUVE**	trouble	**PEINE**	know	**SAVOIR**
noise	**BRUIT**	uncle	**ONCLE**	lamb	**AGNEAU**
nurse	**BONNE**	warm	**CHAUD**	language	**LANGUE**
obligation	**DETTE**	weight	**POIDS**	left	**GAUCHE**
other	**AUTRE**	west	**OUEST**	Lent	**CAREME**
pain	**PEINE**	when	**QUAND**	lingo	**PATOIS**
pause	**ARRET**	white	**BLANC**	mouse	**SOURIS**
pear	**POIRE**	winter	**HIVER**	notebook	**CARNET**
penalty	**PEINE**	world	**MONDE, TERRE**	number	**NOMBRE**
pocket	**POCHE**	yellow	**JAUNE**	open	**OUVERT**
possess	**TENIR**	young	**JEUNE**	penalty	**AMENDE**
pupil	**ELEVE**			police bureau	**SURETE**
purchase	**ACHAT**	again	**ENCORE**	poor	**PAUVRE**
queen	**REINE**	around	**AUTOUR**	prison	**CACHOT**
rabbit	**LAPIN**	at first	**DABORD**	red	**ROUSSE**
rain	**PLUIE**	awkward	**GAUCHE**	reparation	**AMENDE**
red	**ROUGE**	bell	**CLOCHE**	rise of prices	**HAUSSE**
rent, to	**LOUER**	beware	**GAREDE**	safety	**SURETE**
reputation	**BRUIT**	blank book	**CAHIER**	season	**SAISON**
rich	**RICHE**	bride	**MARJEE**	security	**SURETE**
right	**DROIT**	butter	**BEURRE**	sheep	**MOUTON**
ring	**BAGUE**	cake	**GATEAU**	shepherd	**BERGER**
room	**SALLE**	carriage	**FIACRE**	ship	**NAVIRE**
safety	**SALUT**	chair	**CHAISE**	soldier	**SOLDAT**
sailor	**MARIN**	child	**ENFANT**	speak	**PARLER**
school	**ECOLE, LYCEE**	church	**EGLISE**	star	**ETOILE**
sister	**SOEUR**	clumsy	**GAUCHE**	stock exchange	**BOURSE**
slang	**ARGOT**	concession	**OCTROI**	strawberry	**FRAISE**
slight	**LEGER**	copybook	**CAHIER**	sun	**SOLEIL**
small	**PETIT**	customs	**DOUANE, MOEURS**	superfluous	**DETROP**
snow	**NEIGE**	devil	**DIABLE**	thirty	**TRENTE**
soap	**SAVON**	dialect	**PATOIS**	thought	**PENSEE**
soldier	**POILU**	dungeon	**CACHOT**	toll	**OCTROI**
sort	**SORTE**	equal	**PAREIL**	tongue	**LANGUE**
square	**CARRE**	fall of stocks	**BAISSE**	too much	**DETROP**
storm	**ORAGE**	false	**FAUSSE**	understand	**SAVOIR**
straight	**DROIT**	fly	**MOUCHE**	war	**GUERRE**
subway	**METRO**	friendship	**AMITIE**	watch	**MONTRE**
sum	**SOMME**	furniture	**MEUBLE**	well groomed	**SOIGNE**
table	**TABLE**	future	**AVENIR**	write	**ECRIRE**
		gilt	**CADEAU**		

ITALIAN

against	**CON**	here	**QUA, QUI**	uncle	**ZIO**
age	**ETA**	hour	**ORA**	where	**OVE**
always	**MAI**	many	**PIU**	with	**CON**
aunt	**ZIA**	more	**PIU**		
below	**GIU**	never	**MAI**	act	**ATTO**
down	**GIU**	now	**ORA**	after	**DOPO**
duration	**ORA**	ox	**BUE**	afternoon	**SERA**
ever	**MAI**	simpleton	**OCA**	apple	**MELA, POMO**
God	**DIO**	south	**SUD**	art	**ARTE**
goose	**OCA**	there	**IVI**	black	**NERO**
grandfather	**AVO**	time	**ORA**	confidence	**FEDE**

dawn	**ALBA**	account	**CONTO**	much	**ASSAI, MOLTO**
dear	**CARA, CARO**	all	**TUTTI, TUTTO**	night	**NOTTE**
deed	**ATTO**	ardor	**ESTRO**	not at all	**PUNTO**
drink, to	**BERE**	ass	**ASINO**	other	**ALTRO**
each	**OGNI**	back	**TERGO**	paper	**CARTA**
east	**ESTE**	ball	**PALLA**	please	**PREGO**
egg	**UOVO**	beard	**BARBA**	power	**FORZA**
end	**CODA**	bed	**LETTO**	race	**CORSA**
evening	**SERA**	beer	**BIRRA**	red	**ROSSO**
every	**OGNI**	boiled	**LESSO**	rich	**RICCO**
face	**VISO**	bride	**SPOSA**	said	**DETTO**
faith	**FEDE**	bridge	**PONTE**	sauce	**SALSA**
few	**POCO**	cafe	**CAFFE**	sign	**SEGNO**
frost	**GELO**	camp	**CAMPO**	skin	**PELLE**
gift	**DONO**	cat	**GATTA**	sky	**CIELO**
hair	**PELO**	cathedral	**DUOMO**	sleep	**SONNO**
hall	**SALA**	chair	**SEDIA**	so much	**TANTO**
hand	**MANO**	chest	**CASSA**	soul	**ANIMA**
hatred	**ODIO**	city	**CITTA**	spirit	**ANIMA**
head	**CAPO**	course	**CORSA**	spouse	**SPOSA, SPOSO**
husband	**UOMO**	dad	**BABBO**	stamp	**BOLLO**
ice	**GELO**	done	**FATTO**	star	**ASTRO**
I see	**VEDO**	donkey	**ASINO**	straight	**RETTO**
Jesus	**GESU**	door	**PORTA**	street	**CALLE, CORSO**
lake	**LAGO**	dough	**PASTA**	strength	**FORZA**
light	**LUME**	dress	**ABITO**	sword	**SPADA**
little	**POCO**	enough	**BASTA**	tailor	**SARTO**
lo!	**ECCO**	excuse	**SCUSA**	thief	**LADRO**
man	**UOMO**	farewell	**ADDIO**	tower	**TORRE**
matter	**COSA**	father	**PADRE**	town	**CITTA**
mountain peak	**CIMA**	feast	**FESTA**	twisted	**TORTO**
much	**ASSI**	field	**CAMPO**	under	**SOTTO**
night	**SERA**	force	**FORZA**	very	**MOLTO**
north	**NORD**	fork	**FORCA**	water	**ACQUA**
nose	**NASO**	friend	**AMICA, AMICO**	west	**OVEST**
real	**VERO**	gate	**PORTA**	without	**SENZA**
seat	**SEDE**	get, to	**AVERE**	women	**DONNE**
ship	**NAVE**	good	**BUONO**	wood	**LEGNO**
shore	**RIVA**	good-bye	**ADDIO**	world	**MONDO**
side	**LATO**	harbor	**PORTO**	wrong	**TORTO**
situated	**SITO**	have, to	**AVERE**		
so	**COSI**	head	**TESTA**	again	**DACAPO**
sour	**AGRO**	heaven	**CIELO**	be(ing)	**ESSERE**
summit	**CIMA**	holiday	**FERIA, FESTA**	canal	**CANALE**
swallow, to	**BERE**	iron	**FERRO**	custom house	**DOGANA**
tail	**CODA**	isle	**ISOLA**	daughter	**FIGLIA**
talent	**DONO**	kiss	**BACIO**	day	**GIORNO**
thin	**POCO**	lady	**DONNA**	foreign	**ESTERO**
thing	**COSA**	late	**TARDO**	forward	**AVANTI**
thirst	**SETE**	law	**LEGGE**	from the beginning	
thus	**COSI**	leg	**GAMBA**		**DACAPO**
today	**OGGI**	love	**AMORE**	gentleman	**SIGNOR**
tour	**GIRO, GITA**	love, to	**AMARE**	hamlet	**CASALE**
true	**VERO**	many	**MOLTO**	how much	**QUANTO**
voice	**VOCE**	meal	**PASTO**	husband	**MARITO**
wax	**CERA**	mind	**MENTE**	key	**CHIAVE**
well	**BENE**	monk	**FRATE**	large	**GROSSO,**
yesterday	**IERI**	mother	**MADRE**		**GRANDE**
		mouth	**BOCCA**	lover	**AMANTE**

money	DENARO,	road	STRADA	then	ALLORA
	MONETA	same	STESSO	tomorrow	DOMANI
nothing	NIENTE	self	STESSO	tree	ALBERO
now	ADESSO	shoe	SCARPA	value	VALUTA
open	APERTO	son	FIGLIO	village	CASALE
poor	POVERO	star	STELLA	when	QUANDO
queen	REGINA	table	TAVOLA	white	BIANCO
right	DESTRO	thanks	GRAZIE	yet	ANCORA

GERMAN

abbot	ABT	because	WEIL	greatly	SEHR
about	BEI	bed	BETT	hair	HAAR
alas	ACH	beer	BIER	hall	AULA, SAAL
among	BEI	behind	NACH	heart	HERZ
ancestor	AM	be(ing)	SEIN	here	HIER
and	UND	besides	NOCH	high	HOCH
as	ALS	blood	BLUT	home	HEIM
at	BEI	blue	BLAU	host	WIRT
before	VOR	book	BUCH	house	HAUS
clock	UHR	bread	BROT	humanity	WELT
cow	KUH	bundle	BUND	if	WENN
dead	TOT	but	ABER	image	BILD
ear	OHR	calm	RUHE	lady	DAME, FRAU
east	OST	cash	GELD	language	REDE
eel	AAL	chicken	HUHN	late	SPAT
from	AUS, VON	clever	KLUG	lazy	FAUL
gate	TOR	coin	GELD	league	BUND
how	WIE	cold	KALT	leg	BEIN
ice	EIS	count	GRAF	lord	GOTT, HERR
is	IST	couple	PAAR	man	MANN
narrow	ENG	deep	TIEF	many	VIEL
near	NAH	dirty	FAUL	mind	SINN
never	NIE	distant	WEIT	mister	HERR
new	NEU	doctor	ARZT	money	GELD
of	AUF, AUS, VON	dog	HUND	more	MEHR
on	AUF	duck	ENTE	much	SEHR, VIEL
out of	AUS	earl	GRAF	murder	MORD
path	WEG	early	FRUH	nation	VOLK
poor	ARM	earth	ERDE	nearly	ETWA
south	SUD	elegant	FEIN	neck	HALS
than	ALS	every	JEDE	new	NEUE
train	ZUG	eye	AUGE	no	NEIN
upon	ALE	far	WEIT	nobility	ADEL
valley	TAL	figure	BILD	noble	EDEL
watch	UHR	fine	FEIN	nobleman	GRAF
way	WEG	first	EHER	north	NORD
with	BEI, MIT	flight	FLUG	old	ALTE
		for	DENN	or	ODER
about	ETWA	foul	FAUL	over	UBER
above	OBEN, UBER	free	FREI	pair	PAAR
after	NACH	fruit	OBST	peace	RUHE
age	ALTE	full	VOLL	people	VOLK
air	LIED, LUFT	gentleman	HERR	perhaps	ETWA
all	ALLE, GANZ	genuine ECHT,	WAHR	picture	BILD
ass	ESEL	gift	GABE	pure	ECHT
band	BUND	gladly	GERN	race	VOLK
bank	UFER	glory	RUHM	real	ECHT, WAHR
beard	BART	God	GOTT	repose	RUHE

residence	**HAUS**	both	**BEIDE**	read, to	**LESEN**
rest	**RUHE**	bride	**BRAUT**	request	**BITTE**
room	**RAUM, SAAL**	broom	**BESEN**	rich	**REICH**
sea	**MEER**	carriage	**WAGEN**	small	**KLEIN**
shore	**UFER**	chair	**STUHL**	soul	**GEIST, SEELE**
sir	**HERR**	cheers!	**FROST**	south	**SUDEN**
society	**WELT**	city	**STADT**	spirit	**GEIST**
son	**SOHN**	cost	**PREIS**	spouse	**GATTE**
song	**LIED**	cross	**KREUZ**	state	**STAAT**
space	**RAUM**	dare, to	**WAGEN**	steel	**STAHL**
speech	**REDE**	different	**ANDER**	street	**GASSE**
still	**DOCH**	east	**OSTEN**	strife	**KRIEG**
tall	**HOCH**	eat, to	**ESSEN**	sun	**SONNE**
than	**DENN**	else	**ANDER**	table	**TAFEL, TISCH**
that	**JENE**	empire	**REICH**	thanks	**DANKE**
then	**DANN, DENN**	evening	**ABEND**	thirst	**DURST**
there	**DORT**	everything	**ALLES**	through	**DURCH**
thief	**DIEB**	father	**VATER**	today	**HEUTE**
thing	**DING**	fear	**ANGST**	town	**STADT**
top	**OBEN**	few	**WENIG**	uncle	**ONKEL**
tower	**TURM**	fork	**GABEL**	walk, to	**GEHEN**
tree	**BAUM**	game	**SPIEL**	war	**KRIEG**
triumph	**SIEG**	give, to	**GEBEN**	why	**WARUM**
true	**WAHR**	go, to	**GEHEN**		
tune	**LIED**	arbor	**HAFEN**	again	**WIEDER**
upper	**OBER**	have, to	**HABEN**	bell	**GLOCKE**
very	**SEHR**	haven	**HAFEN**	brother	**BRUDER**
victory	**SIEG**	hence	**DAHER**	cheap	**BILLIG**
village	**DORF**	hunter	**JAGER**	cheers!	**PROSIT**
visitor	**GAST**	husband	**GATTE**	gentlemen	**HERREN**
viva (salute)	**HOCH**	iron	**EISEN**	heaven	**HIMMEL**
well	**WOHL**	island	**INSEL**	knife	**MESSER**
west	**WEST**	ladies	**DAMEN**	to know, knowledge	
when	**WENN**	lane	**GASSE**		**WISSEN**
wide	**WEIT**	leather	**LEDER**	labor	**ARBEIT**
wife	**FRAU, WEIB**	letter	**BRIEF**	ladies	**FRAUEN**
willingly	**GERN**	lightning	**BLITZ**	morning	**MORGEN**
without	**OHNE**	little	**KLEIN, WENIG**	mother	**MUTTER**
woman	**DAME, FRAU,**	love	**LIEBE**	noon	**MITTAG**
	WEIB	mind	**GEIST**	north	**NORDEN**
world	**WELT**	move, to	**GEHEN**	once	**EINMAL**
yet	**DOCH, NOCH**	new	**NEUER, NEUES**	plate	**TELLER**
yonder	**DORT**	night	**NACHT**	school	**SCHULE**
		not	**NICHT**	self	**SELEST**
across	**DURCH**	once	**EINST**	sky	**HIMMEL**
affection	**LIEBE**	orient	**OSTEN**	snow	**SCHNEE**
alley	**GASSE**	path	**GASSE**	soldier	**SOLDAT**
always	**IMMER**	people	**LEUTE**	spoon	**LOFFEL**
apple	**APFEL**	persons	**LEUTE**	toil	**ARBEIT**
aunt	**TANTE**	play	**SPIEL**	tomorrow	**MORGEN**
below	**UNTER**	please	**BITTE**	west	**WESTEN**
beneath	**UNTEN**	price	**PREIS**	wife	**GATTIN**
beside	**NEBEN**	rain	**REGEN**	work	**ARBEIT**

LATIN

alas	**HEU, VAE**	art	**ARS**	but	**SED**
altar	**ARA**	as	**QUA**	citadel	**ARX**
anger	**IRA**	bronze	**AES**	copper	**AES**

custom	MOS	field	AGER	another thing	ALIUD
divine law	PAS	fields	AGRI	as far as	QUOAD
edge	ORA	go away!	VADE	backward	RETRO
either	AUT	grandfather	AVUS	bad	MALUS
foot	PES	he loves	AMAT	battle line	ACIES
force	VIS	high	ALTA	before	ANTEA
fortress	ARX	hope	SPES	behind	RETRO
goddess	DEA	hour	HORA	blessed	BEATA
gods	DEI	hush!	TACE	book	LIBER
heart	COR	I have spoken	DIXI	broad	LAWS
husband	VIR	in all	TOTO	brow	FRONS
I love	AMO	in the year	ANNO	cattle	PECUS
is	EST	knee	GENU	confidence	FIDES
king	REX	lambs	AGNI	cup	CALIX
law	JUS, LEX	life	VITA	daughter	FILIA
lawful	FAS	lo!	ECCE	deceit	DOLUS
leader	DUX	lot	SORS	divine	DIVUS
man	VIR	mind	MENS	door	JANUA, PORTA
milk	LAC	mountain	MONS	earth	TERRA
not	NON	needle	ACUS	ease	OTIUM
or	AUT	nobody	NEMO	edge	ACTES
peace	PAX	note	NOTA	error	CULPA
pledge	VAS	now	NUNC	evil	MALUM
power	VIS	observe!	NOTA	faith	FIDES
pray	ORA	other	ALIA	fault	CULPA
pyre	ARA	others	ALII	fire	IGNIS
shore	ORA	palm (hand)	VOLA	flock	PECUS
strength	VIS	part	PARS	fodder	CIBUS
there	IBI	pin	ACUS	food	CIBUS
thing	RES	praise	LAUS	forehead	FRONS
three times	TER	property	BONA	form	MODUS
trade	ARS	prophecy	SORS	fraud	DOLUS
twice	BIS	proportion	RATA	friend	AMICA
vessel	VAS	road	ITER	gate	PORTA
where	UBI	same	IDEM	gentle	LENIS
will	MOS	sea	MARE	goblet	CALIX
with	CUM	see!	VIDE	gold	AURUM
wrath	IRA	share	RATA	good	BONUM
		soon	CITO	ground	TERRA
after	POST	supper	CENA	happy	BEATA
alas	EHEU	thing done	ACTU	healthy	SANUS
at the same place	IBID	unless	NISI	helmet	GALEA
before	ANTE	was	ERAT	herd	PECUS
behold!	ECCE	water	AQUA	keenness	ACIES
be(ing)	ESSE	well	BENE	kings	REGES
beware	CAVE	wife	UXOR	lamb	AGNUS
bird	AVIS	without	SINE	land	TERRA
birds	AVES	wool	LANA	leisure	OTIUM
boy	PUER	you love	AMAS	Mass, the	MISSA
bridge	PONS			method	MODUS
child	PUER	abbot	ABBAS	more	SUPER
city	URBS	about	CIRCA	name	NOMEN
culprit	REUS	above	SUPER	nearby	JUXTA
day	DIEM	abundance	COPIA	negligence	CULPA
day(s)	DIES	across	TRANS	nothing	NIHIL
defendant	REUS	air	ANIMA	only	SOLUS
dinner	CENA	all	OMNIA, OMNIS, TOTUM	other	ALIUS
egg	OVUM			over	SUPER, TRANS
except	NISI	alone	SOLUS	pardon	VENIA

place	LOCUS	usage	RITUS	Greece	ACHAIA
plenty	COPIA	why	QUARE	happy	BEATUS
remains, it	MANET	wicked	MALUS	iron	FERRUM
resist!	OBSTA	wide	LATUS	kingdom	REGNUM
rite	RITUS	wind	ANIMA	learned	DOCTUS
sick	AEGER	wine	VINUM	lots	SORTES
side	LATUS	within	INTRA	otherwise	ALITER
sinful	NEFAS	year	ANNUS	partly	PARTIM
smooth	LENIS			queen	REGINA
soft	LENIS	again	ITERUM	right	DEXTER
soul	ANIMA	always	SEMPER	servant	SERVUS
sound	SANUS	around	CIRCUM	slave	SERVUS
sour	VINUM	authority	REGNUM	sliding	LAPSUS
stars	ASTRA	blessed	BEATUS	son	FILIUS
supper	COENA	buying	EMPTIO	summer	AESTAS
tail	CAUDA	error	LAPSUS	theft	FURTUM
that is	IDEST	fatherland	PATRIA	therefore	IGITUR
thing done	ACTUS	first	PRIMUM, PRIMUS	tyranny	REGNUM
trust	FIDES	fish	PISCIS	war	BELLUM
unlawful	NEFAS	fishes	PISCES	well informed	DOCTUS
upon	SUPER	friend	AMICUS	woman	FEMINA
		gliding	LAPSUS		
		great	MAGNUS		

ARTICLES, PRONOUNS, POSSESSIVES, AND NUMERALS IN FIVE LANGUAGES

ARTICLES

Spanish	French	Italian	German	
EL	AU	I	DAS	EINEN
LA	DU	IL	DEM	EINER
LO	LA	LA	DEN	EINES
UN	LE	LE	DER	
LAS	UN	LO	DES	
LOS	AUX	UN	DIE	
UNA	DES	GLI	EIN	
UNAS	LES	UNA	EINE	
UNOS	UNE	UNO	EINEM	

PRONOUNS AND POSSESSIVES

*Indicates possessive pronouns or adjectives

Spanish

EL	TU*	NOS	ELLA
LA	YO	QUE	ELLO
LE	ESA	SUS*	ESAS
LO	ESE	TAL	ESOS
ME	ESO	TUS*	ESTA
MI*	LAS	UNA	ESTE
OS	LES	UNO	ESTO
SE	LOS	VOS	MIOS*
SU*	MIA*	ALGO	NADA
TE	MIO*	CADA	SUYA*
TI	MIS*	CUAL	SUYO*

TUYA	ESTAS	ALGUNA	NINGUNO
TUYO	ESTOS	ALGUNO	NUESTRA*
UNAS	NADIE	CUALES	NUESTRO*
UNOS	QUIEN	NINGUN	QUIENES
ALGUN	SUYAS*	ALGUIEN	USTEDES
AQUEL	SUYOS*	ALGUNAS	VUESTRA*
CUYAS	TALES	ALGUNOS	VUESTRO*
CUYOS	TUYAS*	AQUELLA	VOSOTRAS
ELLAS	TUYOS*	AQUELLO	VOSOTROS
ELLOS	USTED	NINGUNA	

French

Y	LES	ELLE	SIENS*
CA	LUI	LEUR	TELLE
CE	MES*	MIEN*	TIENS*
EN	MOI	NOUS	VOTRE*
IL	MON	QUEL	AUCUNE
JE	NOS*	QUOI	AUTRUI
LA	NUL	RIEN	CELLES
LE	QUE	SIEN*	CHACUN
MA	QUI	TELS	LEQUEL
ME	SES*	TIEN*	MIENNE*
ON	SOI	VOUS	NOTRES*
OU	SON*	AUCUN	QUELLE
SA	TEL	CELLE	SIENNE*
SE	TES*	CELUI	TELLES
TA	TOI	CETFE	TIENNE*
TE	TON*	ELLES	VOTRES*
TU	VOS*	LEURS*	CHACUNE
CES	CECI	MIENS*	MIENNES*
CET	CELA	NOTRE*	QUELLES
EUX	CEUX	NULLE	SIENNES*
ILS	DONT	QUELS	TIENNES*

Italian

CI	MIA*	SUOI*	NOSTRO*
IO	MIE*	TALE	OGNUNA
LA	MIO*	TALI	OGNUNO
LE	NOI	TUOI	QUEGLI
LI	SUA*	COLEI	QUELLA
LO	SUE*	COLUI	QUELLE
ME	SUO*	NIUNO	QUELLI
MI	TAL	NULLA	QUELLO
NE	TUA*	QUALE	QUESTA
SE	TUE*	QUALI	QUESTE
SI	TUO*	ALCUNA	QUESTI
TE	VOI	ALCUNE	QUESTO
TI	EGLI	ALCUNI	VOSTRA*
TU	ELLA	ALCUNO	VOSTRE*
VI	ESSA	ALTRUI	VOSTRI*
CHE	ESSE	COLORO	VOSTRO*
CHI	ESSI	COSTEI	COSTORO
CIO	ESSO	COSTUI	NESSUNA
CUI	LORO*	NIENTE	NESSUNO
GLI	MIEI*	NOSTRA*	QUALCHE
LEI	QUAL	NOSTRE*	
LUI	QUEL	NOSTRI*	

German

DU	EUER*	JEDEM	KEINEM
ER	EURE*	JEDEN	KEINEN
ES	IHRE*	JEDER	KEINER
DAS	JEDE	JEDES	KEINES
DEM	JENE	JENEM	MEINEM*
DEN	KEIN	JENEN	MEINEN*
DER	MICH	JENER	MEINER*
DIE	MEIN*	JENES	MEINES*
ICH	SEIN*	KLEIN	NICHTS
IHM	SICH	MEINE*	SEINEM*
IHN	DEINE*	SEINE*	SEINEN*
IHR*	DENEN	UNSER*	SEINER*
MAN	DEREN	DEINEM*	SEINES*
MIR	DERER	DEINEN*	UNSERE*
SIE	DIESE	DEINER*	WELCHE
UNS	ETWAS	DEINES*	WESSEN
WAS	EUERE*	DESSEN	JEMANDS
WEM	EUREM*	DIESEM	NIEMAND
WEN	EUREN*	DIESEN	UNSEREM*
WER	EURER*	DIESER	UNSEREN*
WES	EURES*	DIESES	UNSERER*
WIR	IHNEN	EUEREM*	UNSERES*
DEIN*	IHREM*	EUEREN*	WELCHEM
DICH	IHREN*	EUERER*	WELCHEN
DIES	IHRER*	EUERES*	WELCHER
EUCH	IHRES*	JEMAND	WELCHES

Latin

EA	NOS	ISTO	TUAS*
EI	QUA	MEAE*	TUIS*
EO	QUI	MEAM*	TUUM*
HI	QUO	MEAS*	TUUS*
ID	SUA*	MEIS*	CUIUS
IS	SUI*	MEOS*	EADEM
ME	SUO*	MEUM*	EARUM
SE	TOS	MEUS*	EIDEM
TE	TUA*	MIHI	EODEM
TU	TUI*	QUAE	EORUM
CUI	TUO*	QUAM	HARUM
EAE	VOS	QUAS	HORUM
EAM	EIUS	QUEM	HUIUS
EAS	HAEC	QUID	ILLAE
EGO	HANC	QUIS	ILLAM
EIS	HUIC	QUOD	ILLAS
EOS	HUNC	QUOS	ILLIS
EUM	IDEM	SIBI	ILLOS
HAC	ILLA	SUAE*	ILLUD
HAE	ILLE	SUAM*	ILLUM
HAS	ILLI	SUAS*	IPSAE
HIC	ILLO	SUIS*	IPSAM
HIS	IPSA	SUOS*	IPSAS
HOC	IPSE	SUUM*	IPSIS
HOS	IPSO	SUUS*	IPSOS
MEA*	ISTA	TIBI	IPSUM
MEI*	ISTE	TUAE*	ISTAE
MEO*	ISTI	TUAM*	ISTAM

ISTAS	MEARUM*	ALIQUAE	QUAEDAM
ISTIS	MEORUM*	ALIQUAM	QUAEQUE
ISTOS	NOSTER*	ALIQUAS	QUANDAM
ISTUD	NOSTRA*	ALIQUEM	QUASDAM
ISTUM	NOSTRI*	ALIQUID	QUASQUE
NOBIS	NOSTRO*	ALIQUIS	QUEMQUE
VOBIS	QUADAM	ALIQUOD	QUENDAM
ALICUI	QUARUM	ALIQUOS	QUIDDAM
ALIQUA	QUIBUS	CUIQUAM	QUIDQUE
ALIQUI	QUIDAM	EIUSDEM	QUISQUE
ALIQUO	QUIQUE	ILLARUM	QUOQUAM
CUIDAM	QUOQUE	ILLORUM	QUOSDAM
CUIQUE	QUOQUO	IPSARUM	QUOSQUE
EAEDEM	QUORUM	IPSORUM	VESTRAE*
EANDEM	SUARUM*	ISTARUM	VESTRAM*
EASDEM	SUORUM*	ISTORUM	VESTRAS*
EISDEM	TUARUM*	NOSTRAE*	VESTRIS*
EOSDEM	TUORUM*	NOSTRAM*	VESTROS*
EUNDEM	VESTER*	NOSTRAS*	VESTRUM*
ILLIUS	VESTRA*	NOSTRIS*	
IPSIUS	VESTRI*	NOSTROS*	
ISTIUS	VESTRO*	NOSTRUM*	

NUMERALS

	Spanish	French	Italian	German	Latin
1	UNO	UN	UN	EIN	UNUS
2	DOS	DEUX	DUE	ZWEI	DUO
3	TRES	TROIS	TRE	DREI	TRES
4	CUATRO	QUATRE	QUATTRO	VIER	QUATTUOR
5	CINCO	CINQ	CINQUE	FUNF	QUINQUE
6	SEIS	SIX	SEI	SECHS	SEX
7	SIETE	SEPT	SETTE	SIEBEN	SEPTEM
8	OCHO	HUIT	OTTO	ACHT	OCTO
9	NUEVE	NEUF	NOVE	NEUN	NOVEM
10	DIEZ	DIX	DIECI	ZEHN	DECEM
11	ONCE	ONZE	UNDICI	ELF	UNDECIM
12	DOCE	DOUZE	DODICI	ZWOLF	DUODECIM
20	VEINTE	VINGT	VENTI	ZWANZIG	VIGINTI
30	TREINTA	TRENTE	TRENTA	DREISSIG	TRIGINTA
40	CUA-RENTA	QUARANTE	QUARANTA	VIERZIG	QUADRA-GINTA
50	CIN-CUENTA	CINQUANTE	CINQUANTA	FUNFZIG	QUINQUA-GINTA
60	SESENTA	SOIXANTE	SESSANTA	SECHZIG	SEXAGINTA
70	SETENTA	SOIXANTE-DIX	SETTANTA	SIEBZIG	SEPTUA-GINTA
80	OCHENTA	QUATRE-VINGT	OTTANTA	ACHTZIG	OCTOGINTA
90	NOVENTA	QUATRE-VINGT-DIX	NOVANTA	NEUNZIG	NONAGINTA
100	CIENTO	CENT	CENTO	HUNDERT	CENTUM
1000	MIL	MILLE	MILLE	TAUSEND	MILLE

GAMES

GO	MACAO	BELOTTE	PINOCHLE
	MONTE	BEZIQUE	POPE JOAN
CAT	OHELL	BOLIVIA	PYRAMIDS
GIN	OMBRE	CANASTA	ROULETTE
HEI	PEDRO	CASSINO	ROUNDERS
LOO	PITCH	CROQUET	SCRABBLE
NAP	POKER	HANGMAN	SIXTYSIX
PAM	RUMMY	LOWBALL	SKITTLES
PIG	SALVO	MARBLES	SLAPJACK
RUM	SAMBA	MUGGINS	TUG OF WAR
TAG	SHOGI	OLDMAID	
UNO	STOPS	PACHISI	ACEYDEUCY
	STUSS	PALLONE	BADMINTON
BRAG	TAROT	PLAFOND	BAGATELLE
DICE	WHIST	SEVENUP	BILLIARDS
FARO		SNOOKER	BLACKJACK
FROG	BOCCIE	TENPINS	FORTYFIVE
GOLF	BOSTON		HOPSCOTCH
JASS	BRIDGE		PARCHEESI
KENO	CRAMBO	ANAGRAMS	SOLITAIRE
LUDO	ECARTE	BACCARAT	TEAKETTLE
MILL	EIGHTS	CHARADES	TIT TAT TOE
PICO	EUCHRE	CHECKERS	TWENTYONE
POOL	FANTAN	CHOUETTE	WATERBALL
SKAT	GHOSTS	CONQUIAN	
SOLO	GOBANG	CRAPETTE	
VINT	GOFISH	CRIBBAGE	BACKGAMMON
	HAMMER	DOMINOES	BATTLESHIP
	HAZARD	DRAUGHTS	CATEGORIES
BANDY	HEARTS	I DOUBT IT	HORSESHOES
BINGO	MEMORY	JACKPOTS	PANGUINGUE
CATCH	MERELS	LACROSSE	POST OFFICE
CHESS	PIQUET	LEAPFROG	TETHERBALL
CINCH	POCHEN	MAHJONGG	
CRAPS	QUOITS	MICHIGAN	CHEMIN DE FER
DARTS	ROUNCE	MONOPOLY	HIDE AND SEEK
FARGO	SHINNY	NAPOLEON	RUSSIAN BANK
FIVES	SLOUGH	OKLAHOMA	TIDDLYWINKS
HALMA	TIVOLI	PALLMALL	
JACKS	AUTHORS	PATIENCE	CONSEQUENCES
LOTTO	BARBUDI	PINGPONG	SHUFFLEBOARD

GEOGRAPHY

COUNTRIES AND CAPITALS

CAR	Bangui	IRAN	Teh(e)ran
UAE	Abu Dhabi	IRAQ	Baghdad
UAR	= EGYPT	LAOS	Vientiane
		MALI	Bamako
CHAD	N'Djamena	OMAN	Muscat
CUBA	Havana	PERU	Lima
FIJI	Suva	SIAM	= THAILAND
IRAK	= IRAQ	TOGO	Lome

BENIN	Porto-Novo	PANAMA	Panama (City)
BURMA	Yangon (Rangoon)	POLAND	Warsaw
CHILE	Santiago	RUSSIA	Moscow
CHINA	Beijing (Peking)	RWANDA	Kigali
CHINA (Republic)	= TAIWAN	SERBIA	Belgrade
CONGO (Republic)	Brazzaville	SWEDEN	Stockholm
CONGO (Democratic Republic)		TOBAGO	= Trinidad and Tobago
	Kinshasa	TAIWAN	Taipei
CZECH	= CZECHREPUBLIC	TURKEY	Ankara
EGYPT	Cairo	TUVALU	Funafuti
GABON	Libreville	UGANDA	Kampala
GHANA	Accra	ZAMBIA	Lusaka
HAITI	Port-au-Prince		
INDIA	New Delhi	ALBANIA	Tirana
ITALY	Rome	ALGERIA	Algiers (El Djazair)
JAPAN	Tokyo	ANDORRA	Andorra la Vella
KENYA	Nairobi	ANTIGUA	St. John's
KOREA, NORTH	Pyongyang	ARMENIA	Yerevan
KOREA, SOUTH	Seoul	AUSTRIA	Vienna
LIBYA	Tripoli	BAHAMAS	Nassau
MALTA	Valletta	BAHRAIN	Manama
NAURU	Yaren	BARBUDA	St. John's
NEPAL	Kathmandu	BELARUS	Minsk
NIGER	Niamey	BELGIUM	Brussels
PALAU	Koror (Babelthuup)	BERMUDA	Hamilton
PAPUA	Port Moresby	BOLIVIA	La Paz, Sucre
QATAR	Doha	BRITAIN	London
SAMOA	Apia	BURUNDI	Bujumbura
SPAIN	Madrid	COMOROS	Moroni
SUDAN	Khartoum	CROATIA	Zagreb
SYRIA	Damascus	DAHOMEY	= BENIN
TONGA	Nuku'alofa	DENMARK	Copenhagen
WALES	Cardiff	ECUADOR	Quito
YEMEN	Sana'a	ENGLAND	London
ZAIRE	= CONGO (Dem. Rep.)	ERITREA	Asmara
		ESTONIA	Tallinn
ANGOLA	Luanda	FINLAND	Helsinki
BELIZE	Belmopan	GEORGIA	Tbilisi
BHUTAN	Tashi-chho (Thimphu)	GERMANY	Berlin
BOSNIA	Sarajevo	GRENADA	St. George's
BRAZIL	Brasilia	HOLLAND	= NETHERLANDS
BRUNEI	Bandar Seri Begawan	HUNGARY	Budapest
CANADA	Ottawa	ICELAND	Reykjavik
CEYLON	= SRI LANKA	IRELAND	Dublin
CYPRUS	Nicosia	JAMAICA	Kingston
FRANCE	Paris	LEBANON	Beirut
GAMBIA	Banjul	LESOTHO	Maseru
GREECE	Athens	LIBERIA	Monrovia
GUINEA	Conakry	MALDIVE (ISLANDS)	= MALDIVES
GUINEA (Equatorial)	Malabo	MOLDOVA	Kishinev
GUYANA	Georgetown	MOROCCO	Rabat
ISRAEL	Jerusalem	MYANMAR	Yangon (Rangoon)
JORDAN	Amman	NIGERIA	Abuja
KUWAIT	Kuwait (City)	ROMANIA	Bucharest
LATVIA	Riga	SAOTOME	Sao Tome
MALAWI	Lilongwe	SENEGAL	Dakar
MEXICO	Mexico City	SOLOMON (ISLANDS)	Honiara
MONACO	Monaco(-ville)	SOMALIA	Mogadishu
NORWAY	Oslo	STKITTS (AND NEVIS)	Basseterre

TRUCIAL (STATES)	= UAE	MAURITIUS	Port Louis
TUNISIA	Tunis	NICARAGUA	Managua
UKRAINE	Kiev	SANMARINO	San Marino
URUGUAY	Montevideo	SINGAPORE	Singapore
VANUATU	Vila	SWAZILAND	Mbabane
VATICAN	Vatican City	VENEZUELA	Caracas
VIETNAM	Hanoi		
		AZERBAIJAN	Bakir
BARBADOS	Bridgetown	BANGLADESH	Dacca (Dhaka)
BOTSWANA	Gaborone	ELSALVADOR	San Salvador
BULGARIA	Sofia	IVORYCOAST	Abidjan
CAMBODIA	Phnom Penh		(Yamoussoukro)
CAMEROON	Yaounde	KAZAKHSTAN	Astana (Akmo'a)
COLOMBIA	Bogota	KYRGYZSTAN	Bishkek
DJIBOUTI	Djibouti	LUXEMBOURG	Luxembourg(-ville)
DOMINICA	Roseau	MADAGASCAR	Antananarivo
ETHIOPIA	Addis Ababa	MAURITANIA	Nouakchott
HONDURAS	Tegucigalpa	MICRONESIA	Palikir
KIRIBATI	(South) Tarawa	MOZAMBIQUE	Maputo
MALAGASY	= MADAGASCAR	NEWZEALAND	Wellington
MALAYSIA	Kuala Lumpur	SAINTLUCIA	Castries
MALDIVES	Male	SEYCHELLES	Victoria
MARSHALL (ISLANDS)	Majuro	TANGANYIKA	= TANZANIA
MONGOLIA	Ulan Bator (Ulaan	UPPERVOLTA	= BURKINAFASO
	Baatar)	UZBEKISTAN	Tashkent
PAKISTAN	Islamabad	YUGOSLAVIA	= SERBIA
PARAGUAY	Asuncion		
PORTUGAL	Lisbon	AFGHANISTAN	Kabul
PRINCIPE	Sao Tome	BURKINAFASO	Ouagadougou
RHODESIA	= ZIMBABWE	MONTENEGRO	Belgrade
SCOTLAND	Edinburgh	NETHERLANDS	Amsterdam (The
SLOVAKIA	Bratislava		Hague)
SLOVENIA	Dushanbe	PHILIPPINES	Manila
SRILANKA	Colombo	SAUDIARABIA	Riad (Riyadh)
SURINAME	Paramaribo	SIERRALEONE	Freetown
TANZANIA	Dar-es-Salaam	SOUTHAFRICA	Capetown, Pretoria,
THAILAND	Bangkok		Bloemfontein
TRINIDAD (and Tobago)	Port-of-	SWITZERLAND	Bern(e), Lausanne
	Spain		
ZIMBABWE	Harare	GREATBRITAIN	London
		GUINEABISSAU	Bissau
ARGENTINA	Buenos Aires	HERZEGOVINA	Sarajevo
AUSTRALIA	Canberra	SAINTVINCENT	Kingstown
CAPEVERDE	Praia	UNITEDSTATES	Washington
COSTARICA	San Jose	TURKMENISTAN	Ashgabut
DOMINICAN (REPUBLIC)	Santo	WESTERNSAMOA	= SAMOA
	Domingo		
EASTTIMOR	Dili	CZECHREPUBLIC	Prague (Praha)
GREENLAND		LIECHTENSTEIN	Vaduz
	= KALAALLITNUNAAT	STCHRISTOPHER	= STKITTS
GUATEMALA	Guatemala City	UNITEDKINGDOM	London
INDONESIA	(D)jakarta		
KAMPUCHEA	= CAMBODIA	KALAALLITNUNAAT	Nuuk
LITHUANIA	Vilnius		(Gothab)
MACEDONIA	Skopje	NORTHERNIRELAND	Belfast

OTHER COUNTRIES OF EUROPE, ANCIENT AND MODERN
FORMER INDEPENDENT COUNTRIES OF MEDIEVAL AND MODERN TIMES

LEON	SICILY	LIVONIA	PIEDMONT
BADEN	VENICE	MORAVIA	RUTHENIA
GENOA	ARMENIA	NAVARRE	CIRCASSIA
HESSE	BATAVIA	PRUSSIA	DARMSTADT
PARMA	BAVARIA	SILESIA	OLDENBERG
PSKOV	BOHEMIA	TUSCANY	POMERANIA
SAVOY	CASTILE	VENETIA	SCHLESWIG
ARAGON	ESTONIA	ANATOLIA	WALLACHIA
MODENA	GALICIA	ESTHONIA	BESSARABIA
NAPLES	GEORGIA	HANNOVER	WESTPHALIA
NASSAU	GRANADA	HOLSTEIN	MECKLENBERG
SAXONY	HANOVER	LOMBARDY	MESOPOTAMIA

ANCIENT COUNTRIES OF BRITISH ISLES

KENT	MERCIA	DANELAW	PECTLAND
ESSEX	SCOTIA	IRELAND	EASTANGLIA
WALES	SUSSEX	DALRIADA	NORTHUMBRIA
ANGLIA	WESSEX	HIBERNIA	

COUNTRIES, REGIONS, AND CITIES OF ANCIENT ROMAN TIMES

GAUL	ALBANIA	PICENUM	HIBERNIA
DACIA	BAETICA	POMPEII	MASSILIA
GADES	BELGICA	SALONAE	PANNONIA
HIPPO	BRITAIN	SAMNIUM	SARDINIA
NARBO	CORDUBA	SCANDLA	SARGOSSA
UTICA	CORSICA	TOLETUM	SARMATIA
APULIA	ETRURIA	VENETIA	AQUITANIA
ARABIA	GALICIA	BRUTTIUM	BRITANNIA
GALLIA	GERMANY	CAESAREA	CALEDONIA
IBERIA	LIGURIA	CALABRIA	ILLYRICUM
ISTRIA	LUCANIA	CAMPANIA	LONDINIUM
LATIUM	LUTETIA	CARTHAGE	LUSITANIA
MOESIA	MESSANA	DALMATIA	PALESTINE
RAETIA	NORICUM	EBORACUM	MAURETANIA
SICILY	NUMIDIA	GERMANLA	
UMBRIA	ODESSUS	HELVETIA	

ANCIENT GREEK AND EASTERN STATES AND CITIES

COS	ELIS	AEGAE	ILIUM
IOS	ELON	AENIS	IONIA
	GAZA	AENUS	IPSUS
ACTE	ICUS	ARGOS	ISSUS
ARIA	LATO	ASINE	LAMIA
CEOS	PISA	BARCA	LEROS
CIUS	SIND	CARIA	LIBYA
CYME	SOLI	CHIOS	LYDIA
DIAM	SUSA	DELOS	MALIS
DURA	TEOS	DORIS	MEDIA
ELAM	TYRE	GOLGI	MELOS

MYSIA	MYLASA	DECELEA	ECBATANA
NAXOS	MYRINE	ELEUSIS	ERYTHRAE
NEMEA	PAPHOS	EPHESUS	GANDHARA
PAROS	PARIUM	ERETRIA	GEDROSIA
PELLA	PATALA	GANDARA	HYRCANIA
PYDNA	PATRAE	GORDIUM	LAPETHUS
PYLOS	PERSIA	GORTYNA	MAGNESIA
RAGAE	PHASIS	IALYSUS	MARATHON
SAMOS	PHERAE	IDALIUM	MARGIANA
SIDON	PONTUS	LACONIA	MESSENIA
SYENE	PRIENE	LARISSA	MYTILENE
SYRIA	RHODES	LEUCTRA	OLYNTHUS
TEGEA	SAGALA	MACEDON	PELUSIUM
TELOS	SARDES	MARONEA	PERGAMUM
TEMPE	SCIONE	MEMPHIS	PHASELIS
TENOS	SCYROS	MESSENE	PHILIPPI
THERA	SESTUS	METHONE	PRIANSUS
TROAS	SICYON	MILETUS	SELENCIA
TYANA	SINOPE	MYCENAE	SERIPHOS
ZIDON	SKUDRA	MYCONOS	SITHONIA
	SMYRNA	NISIBIS	SOGDIANA
	SPARTA	NISYROS	TAMASSUS
ABDERA	TARSUS	OLYMPIA	THESSALY
ABYDUS	TAXILA	PAEONLA	TRAPEZUM
ACRAEA	THASOS	PAGASAE	ZARIASPA
AMASIA	THEBES	PALLENE	
ANAPHE	THRACE	PALMYRA	ACARNANIA
ANCORE	TIRYNS	PARTHIA	ARACHOSIA
ANCYRA	TYRONE	PHOCAEA	BABYLONIA
ANDROS	ZEUGMA	PHRYGIA	BUCEPHALA
APAMEA		PIRAEUS	CALCHEDON
ARBELA	AETOLIA	PISIDIA	CARPATHOS
ATHENS	AMATHUS	PRAESUS	CHAERONEA
ATTICA	AMORGOS	SALAMIS	CHORASMIA
CARDIA	AMYCLAE	SAMARIA	CTESIPHON
CAUNUS	ANTIOCH	SCYTHIA	DASCYLIUM
CITIUM	ARCADIA	SIPHNOS	DOLOPIANS
CNIDUS	ARGOLIS	STAGIRA	DRANGIANA
CORONE	ARMENIA	SUSIANA	EPIDAURUS
CUNAXA	ARSINOE	TANAGRA	JERUSALEM
CURIUM	ASSYRIA	TENEDOS	MARACANDA
CYRENE	BABYLON	THERMUM	MESAMBRIA
DELPHI	BACTRIA	TRALLAS	NAUCRATIS
DODONA	BISITUN	TROEZEN	NICOMEDIA
EPIRUS	BOEOTIA	XANTHUS	PHARSALUS
EUBOEA	CALYDON		PHOENICIA
HYDREA	CAMIRUS		PTOLOMAIS
ICARIA	CERYNIA	ACANTHUS	THAPSACUS
IMBROS	CHALCIS	AMBRACIA	
ITHACA	CILICIA	AMPHISSA	
LEMNOS	CIMILOS	BERENICE	ALEXANDRIA
LESBOS	CLEONAE	BITHYNIA	CAPPADOCIA
LEUCAS	CNOSSUS	CALYMNOS	CHALCIDICE
LINDUS	CORCYRA	CARMANIA	PERSEPOLIS
LISSUS	CORINTH	CARPASIA	SAMOTHRACE
LOCRIS	CYDONIA	COLOPHON	
MEGARA	CYNURIA	DAMASCUS	THERMOPYLAE
	CYTHERA		

DEPARTMENTS, COMMUNES, PROVINCES, STATES, DISTRICTS, REGIONS, COUNTIES, CANTONS, COLONIES, POSSESSIONS

AIN	France	RAND	South Africa
AKI	Japan	REWA	India
ANS	Belgium	RIFF	Morocco
AYR	Scotland	RUHR	Germany
EDE	Netherlands	SAAR	France
ELY	England	SIND	India
EPE	Netherlands	SULU	Philippines
GOA	India	SWAT	Pakistan
MOL	Belgium	VAUD	Switzerland
PAU	France	VICH	Spain
RIF	Morocco	VIMY	France
URI	Switzerland		
VAR	France	AALST	Belgium
ZUG	Switzerland	AARAU	Switzerland
		ACQUI	Italy
BAGO	Philippines	ADIRA	Italy
BAIA	Brazil	AGRIA	Italy
BIEL	Switzerland	AKYAB	Myanmar
BIRR	Ireland	ALAVA	Spain
BOGO	Philippines	ALBAY	Philippines
BUTE	Scotland	ALGAU	Germany
CHUR	Switzerland	ALORA	Spain
COMO	Italy	ALOST	Belgium
DOAB	India	ALWAR	India
ELIS	Greece	ALWUR	India
ENNA	Italy	AMAPA	Brazil
ESTE	Italy	AMARA	Iran
EURE	France	ANGRI	Italy
FANO	Italy	ANGUL	India
FARS	Iran	ANGUS	Scotland
FIFE	Scotland	ANJOU	France
GAZA	Israel	ANNAM	Vietnam
GEEL	Belgium	AONIA	Greece
GHOR	Afghanistan	ARGAO	Philippines
HAUD	Ethiopia	ARLON	Belgium
ISSY	France	ASOLO	Italy
JAEN	Spain	ASSAM	India
JIND	India	ASSEN	Netherlands
KAFA	Ethiopia	ASWAN	Egypt
KENT	England	AUBIN	France
LAON	France	AUTUN	France
LARA	Venezuela	AVILA	Spain
LEON	Spain	BADEN	Germany
LUGO	Italy, Spain	BAENA	Spain
MAYO	Ireland	BAHIA	Brazil
MONS	Belgium	BALKH	Afghanistan
NAGA	Philippines	BAMRA	India
NEJD	Saudi Arabia	BANAT	Romania; Bosnia and
OUDH	India		Herzegovina
PARA	Brazil	BANFF	Canada
PEGU	Myanmar	BEHAR	India

BENIN	Nigeria	MASSA	Italy
BERAR	India	MEATH	Ireland
BERKS	England	MEDOC	France
BIHAR	India	MONZA	Italy
BLYTH	England	NAIRN	Scotland
BORNU	Nigeria	NATAL	South Africa
BOURG	France	NEGEB	Israel
BRAGA	Portugal	NEGEV	Israel
BREDA	Netherlands	NUBIA	Sudan
BUCKS	England	PAVIA	Italy
CAPIZ	Philippines	PERAK	Malaysia
CAPRI	Italy	PIAUI	Brazil
CAVAN	Ireland	POOLE	England
CEARA	Brazil	SAVOY	France
CHACO	South America	SIENA	Italy
CHLAI	China	SINDH	India
CLARE	Ireland	SLIGO	Ireland
COORG	India	SORIA	Spain
CUNEO	Italy	TERNI	Italy
DELFT	Netherlands	TIGRE	Ethiopia
DERBY	England	TIROL	Austria
DEVON	England	TYROL	Austria
DORIS	Greece	UDINE	Italy
ESSEX	England	WALES	United Kingdom
EUPEN	Belgium	WILTS	England
EUTIN	Germany		
EVERE	Belgium	AARGAU	Switzerland
EVORA	Portugal	ACADIA	Canada
FORLI	Italy	ACHAEA	Greece
GALLS	Ethiopia	ALCAMO	Italy
GANDO	Nigeria	ALCIRA	Spain
GOLAS	Brazil	ALIAGA	Philippines
GOUDA	Netherlands	ALLGAU	Germany
HANTS	England	ALMELO	Netherlands
HEJAZ	Saudi Arabia	ALPHEN	Netherlands
HERAT	Afghanistan	ALSACE	France
HESSE	Germany	AMRARA	Ethiopia
HONAN	China	ANCASH	Peru
HOPEH	China	ANDRIA	Italy
HOPEI	China	ANGELN	Germany
HUNAN	China	ANGOLA	Portugal
HUNZA	India	ANHALT	Germany
HUPEH	China	ANTRIM	Ireland
IMOLA	Italy	AOMORI	Japan
IONIA	Greece	APULIA	Italy
JEHOL	China	ARAGON	Spain
JHIND	India	ARAKAN	Myanmar
KAFFA	Ethiopia	ARAUCO	Chile
KALAT	Pakistan	ARCADY	Greece
KANSU	China	AREZZO	Italy
KEDAH	Malaysia	ARMAGH	Ireland
KERRY	Ireland	ASHTON	England
KIRIN	China	ASSISI	Italy
KUTCH	India	ATHOLE	Scotland
LECCE	Italy	ATTICA	Greece
LIPPE	Germany	BAYBAY	Philippines
LOUTH	Ireland	BENGAL	India
LUCCA	Italy	BOSNIA	Bosnia and Herzegovina
LUXOR	Egypt	BRUGGE	Belgium

CARCAR	Philippines	UMBRIA	Italy
CHAHAR	China	VALAIS	Switzerland
CHIHLI	China	VENDEE	France
COCHIN	India	YUNNAN	China
CORATO	Italy		
DORSET	England	ALBERTA	Canada
EMILIA	Italy	ALMADEN	Spain
EMPOLI	Italy	ALMANSA	Spain
FUKIEN	China	ANDENNE	Belgium
FULHAM	England	ARCADIA	Greece
GILGIT	India	ASHANTI	Ghana
GLARUS	Switzerland	BAVARIA	Germany
GUIANA	South America	BOEOTIA	Greece
HAZARA	Pakistan	BOHEMIA	Czech Republic
KARROO	South Africa	BRABANT	Belgium
KUWAIT	Asia	CASTILE	Spain
LATIUM	Italy	CHELSEA	England
MODENA	Italy	CROATIA	Croatia
OAXACA	Mexico	DURANGO	Mexico
OLDHAM	England	GALICIA	Poland, Spain
ORISSA	India	GASCONY	France
PAHANG	Malaysia	GWALIOR	India
PAMIRS	Asia	HOLBORN	England
PANJAB	India	JALISCO	Mexico
PERLIS	Malaysia	KARELIA	Russia
PRIPET	Russia	LAMBETH	England
PUNJAB	India	LAPLAND	Sweden
RAGUSA	Italy	LIVONIA	Latvia
SAXONY	Germany	MASURIA	Poland
SERBIA	Serbia and Montenegro	MORAVIA	Czech Republic
SHANSI	China	MORELOS	Mexico
SHARON	Israel	NAVARRA	Spain
SHENSI	China	ORIENTE	Cuba
SIKKIM	India	RIVIERA	France
SONORA	Mexico	SARAWAK	Indonesia
STYRIA	Austria	SIBERIA	Asia
SURREY	England	SINALAO	Mexico
SUSSEX	England	SITSANG	China (Tibet)
SWABIA	Germany	SURINAM	South America
TERUEL	Spain	TABASCO	Mexico
THRACE	Greece	TESCHEN	Poland
		THURGAU	Switzerland

CITIES—UNITED STATES AND TERRITORIES

*Indicates state capital

ADA	OH	ARMA	KS	EDNA	TX
AJO	AZ	AYER	MA	ELKO	NV
AVA	MO	AZLE	TX	ELMA	NY
ELY	MN	BATH	ME	ELOY	AZ
OLA	AR	BEND	OR	ENID	OK
OPP	AL	BREA	CA	ERIE	PA
ROY	UT	BUHL	ID	GARY	IN
RYE	NY	CARY	NC	HAYS	KS
WAR	WV	CODY	WY	HILO	HI
		DALE	PA	HOLT	MI
ALEA	HI	DORA	AL	HOPE	AR
ALMA	MI	DUNN	NC	HUGO	MN, OK
ARCO	ID	DUPO	IL	HULL	MA

IOLA	KS	CARMI	IL	ORONO	ME
IRMO	SC	CASEY	IL	OSSEO	MN
KENT	OH	CAYCE	SC	OWEGO	NY
KUNA	ID	CHICO	CA	PAMPA	TX
LEHI	UT	CHINO	CA	PAOLA	KS
LIMA	OH	CLARE	MI	PAOLI	PA
LODI	NJ	CLUTE	TX	PARIS	KY
LYNN	MA	CLYDE	OH	PARMA	OH
MART	TX	COCOA	FL	PASCO	WA
MAUD	OK	COLBY	KS	PEARL	MS
MENA	AR	CORRY	PA	PECOS	TX
MESA	AZ	CREWE	VA	PEIUN	IL
MILO	ME	CUERO	TX	PELLA	IA
MORA	MN	DANIA	HI	PHARR	TX
NAPA	CA	DEPEW	NY	PIQUA	OH
NIXA	MO	DERRY	NH	PLANO	TX
NOVI	MI	DIXON	IL	PRATT	KS
OMAK	WA	DONNA	TX	PROVO	UT
OREM	UT	DOVER*	DE	PRYOR	OK
PANA	IL	EATON	OH	RATON	NM
RENO	NV	EDINA	MN	RAYNE	LA
RUSK	TX	ELDON	MO	RIFLE	CO
RUTH	NV	ELGIN	IL	RIPON	WI
RYAN	OK	ENNIS	TX	ROLFE	LA
SACO	ME	ERWIN	TN	ROLLA	MO
SPUR	TX	EWING	NJ	ROTAN	TX
TAMA	IA	FARGO	ND	SALEM*	OR
TROY	MI, NY	FLINT	MI	SANDY	UT
WACO	TX	FLORA	IL	SAYRE	PA
WARE	MA	GALAX	VA	SELMA	AL
WEIR	KS	GALVA	IL	STOWE	PA, VT
WRAY	CO	GREER	SC	TAMPA	FL
YORK	PA	HAVRE	MT	TEMPE	AZ
YUMA	AZ	HOBBS	NM	TOMAH	WI
ZION	IL	HOUMA	LA	TULSA	OK
		ILION	NY	TYLER	TX
AIKEN	SC	IONIA	MI	UKIAH	CA
AKRON	OH	IRWIN	PA	UTICA	NY
ALAMO	TX	ISLIP	NY	VISTA	CA
ALBIA	IA	JESUP	GA	WAHOO	NE
ALCOA	TN	KAPAA	HI	WAYNE	NJ
ALICE	TX	KEENE	NH	WELCH	WV
ALTON	IL	KELSO	WA	WIXOM	MI
ANOKA	MN	LADUE	MO	WYLIE	TX
ASPEN	CO	LAMAR	CO	WYNNE	AR
BARRE	VT	LIHUE	HI	XENIA	OH
BEREA	OH	LOGAN	UT	YREKA	CA
BIXBY	OK	MACON	GA	YULEE	FL
BLAIR	NE	MIAMI	FL		
BOISE*	ID	MINGO	OH	ADRIAN	MI
BOONE	LA	MINOT	ND	AGAWAM	MA
BOWIE	MD	NAMPA	ID	ALBANY*	NY
BRONX	NY	NILES	IL	ALGONA	LA
BRYAN	TX	NYACK	NY	ANTIGO	WI
BUTTE	MT	OCALA	FL	ARVADA	CA
CAIRO	GA, IL	OGDEN	UT	AUBURN	NY
CAMAS	WA	OLNEY	IL	AURORA	CO, IL
CANEY	KS	OMAHA	NE	AUSTIN*	TX
CAREY	OH	ONAWA	IA	BANGOR	ME

BARTOW	FL	EMMAUS	PA	MONSON	MA
BELOIT	WI	EPPING	NH	MUNCIE	IN
BENTON	AR	EUCLID	OH	NASHUA	NH
BETHEL	PA	EUGENE	OR	NATICK	MA
BILOXI	MS	EULESS	TX	NEWARK	NJ
BLAINE	MN	EUNICE	LA	NEWTON	MA
BONHAM	TX	EUREKA	CA	NORMAN	OK
BORGER	TX	EUSTIS	FL	NUTLEY	NJ
BOSTON*	MA	EXETER	NH	ODESSA	TX
BREWER	ME	FRESNO	CA	OLATHE	ID
BUFORD	GA	GALENA	IL	ORANGE	CA
BUNKIE	LA	GALION	OH	OWOSSO	MI
BURNET	TX	GERING	NE	OXWARD	CA
CAMDEN	NJ	GIRARD	OH	PALMER	MA
CANTON	MI, OH	GOLDEN	CO	PAWPAW	MI
CASPER	WY	GORHAM	ME	PAXTON	IL
CELINA	OH	GRETNA	LA	PAYSON	UT
CICERO	IL	GROTON	CT	PEORIA	IL
CLOVIS	NM	HAMDEN	CT	PIERRE	AZ
COHOES	NY	HARLAN	KY	PIERRE*	SD
COLTON	CA	HELENA*	MT	POMONA	CA
CONROE	TX	HINTON	WV	PUEBLO	CO
CONWAY	AR	HOBART	IN	PUTNAM	CT
CORBIN	KY	IDABEL	OK	QUEENS	NY
CORONA	CA	IRVINE	CA	QUINCY	MA
COSCOB	CT	IRVING	TX	RACINE	WI
COVINA	CA	ITHACA	NY	RAHWAY	NJ
CRESCO	IA	JASPER	AL	RANGER	TX
CUDAHY	WI	JOLIET	IL	RENOVO	PA
DALLAS	TX	JOPLIN	MO	RENTON	WA
DALTON	GA	JUNEAU*	AK	RESTON	VA
DARIEN	CT	KEARNY	NJ	REVERE	MA
DAWSON	GA	KENTON	OH	SALINA	KS
DAYTON	OH	KEOKUK	IA	SAVAGE	MN
DEKALB	IL	KOKOMO	IN	SCOTIA	NY
DELAND	FL	LAREDO	TX	SEGUIN	TX
DELANO	CA	LAUREL	MS	SENECA	SC
DEMING	NM	LAWTON	OK	SEWARD	AK, NE
DENTON	TX	LAYTON	VT	SHARON	PA
DENVER*	CO	LEMARS	IA	SHELBY	NC
DEPERE	WI	LENNOX	CA	SIDNEY	OH
DESOTO	MO	LENOIR	NC	SKOKIE	IL
DEXTER	MO	LINDEN	NJ	SLATON	TX
DILLON	SC	LOMITA	CA	SNYDER	TX
DOLTON	IL	LORAIN	OH	SOLVAY	NY
DOWNEY	CA	LOWELL	MA	SONORA	AZ, CA
DRACUT	MA	MACOMB	IL	SPARKS	NV
DUBOIS	PA	MADERA	CA	STAMPS	AR
DULUTH	MN	MALDEN	MA	STEGER	IL
DURHAM	NC	MARION	IN, OH	STPAUL*	MN
EASTON	PA	MCADOO	PA	STROUD	OK
ECORSE	MI	MCCOMB	MS	SUMTER	SC
EDMOND	OK	MENTOR	OH	TACOMA	WA
ELDORA	LA	MERCED	CA	TAYLOR	MI
ELKTON	MD	MILTON	MA	THROOP	PA
ELMIRA	NY	MOBILE	AL	TIFFIN	OH
ELRENO	OK	MOLINE	IL	TIFTON	GA
ELWOOD	IN	MONACA	PA	TIGARD	OR
ELYRIA	OH	MONROE	LA	TIPTON	IN

TOLEDO	OH	CONCORD*	NH	KEWANEE	IL
TOWSON	MD	COOSBAY	OR	KEY WEST	FL
TOPEKA*	KS	CORDELE	GA	KILGORE	TX
TUCSON	AZ	CORINTH	MS	KILLEEN	TX
TULARE	CA	CORNING	NY	KINSTON	NC
TUPELO	MS	COTULLA	TX	KITTERY	ME
UPLAND	CA	CRAFTON	PA	LACONIA	NH
URBANA	IL	CROWLEY	LA	LANSING*	MI
VERNAL	UT	CULLMAN	AL	LAPORTE	IN
VERNON	TX	DECATUR	IL	LARAMIE	WY
VINITA	OK	DECORAH	IA	LASALLE	IL
VIOLET	LA	DELPHOS	OH	LATROBE	PA
WALDEN	NY	DENISON	TX	LIBERAL	KS
WARREN	MI, OH	DETROIT	MI	LINCOLN*	NE
WAUSAU	WI	DICKSON	PA	LIVONIA	MI
WEISER	ID	DORMONT	PA	LUBBOCK	TX
WINONA	MN	DOUGLAS	AZ	LYNWOOD	CA
WOBURN	MA	DUBUQUE	IA	MADISON*	WI
YAKIMA	WA	DUNDALK	MD	MANKATO	MN
YEADON	PA	DUNEDIN	FL	MATTOON	IL
		DUNMORE	PA	MAYWOOD	IL
ABILENE	KS, TX	DURANGO	CO	MCALLEN	TX
ALAMEDA	CA	EDMONDS	WA	MEDFORD	MA, OR
ALTOONA	PA	ELKCITY	OK	MEMPHIS	TN
AMHERST	MA	ELKHART	IN	MENASHA	WI
ANAHEIM	CA	ELMONTE	CA	MIDLAND	TX
ANDOVER	MA	ENFIELD	CT	MILFORD	CT
ANSONIA	CT	EVERETT	MA	MINEOLA	NY
ARDMORE	PA	FARRELL	PA	MISSION	TX
ASHLAND	KY	FINDLAY	OH	MOBERLY	MO
ATLANTA*	GA	FONTANA	CA	MODESTO	CA
ATTALLA	AL	FORTLEE	NJ	MORENCI	AZ
AUGUSTA	GA	FRIDLEY	MN	MULLINS	SC
AUGUSTA*	ME	GADSDEN	AL	NATCHEZ	MS
BASTROP	LA	GAFFNEY	SC	NEEDHAM	MA
BAYCITY	MI	GARDENA	CA	NEWPORT	RI
BAYONNE	NJ	GARLAND	TX	NOGALES	AZ
BEDFORD	OH	GARRETT	IN	NORFOLK	VA
BELMONT	MA	GENESEO	IL	NORWALK	CA, CT
BENICIA	CA	GLENCOE	IL	NORWOOD	OH
BERKLEY	MI	GRAFTON	WV	OAKLAND	CA
BETHANY	OK	GREELEY	CO	OAKPARK	IL
BEVERLY	MA	GRESHAM	OR	OILCITY	PA
BOONTON	NJ	GUTHRIE	OK	OKOLONA	KY
BOULDER	CO	HAGATNA	Guam	OLD TOWN	ME
BOZEMAN	MT	HAMMOND	IN	OLYMPIA*	WA
BRISTOL	CT	HAMPTON	VA	ONTARIO	CA
BUFFALO	NY	HIALEAH	FL	ORLANDO	FL
BURBANK	CA	HIBBING	MN	OSHKOSH	WI
CAMERON	TX	HINGHAM	MA	OTTUMWA	IA
CAMILLA	GA	HOBOKEN	NJ	PADUCAH	KY
CHATHAM	NJ	HOLYOKE	MA	PARAMUS	NJ
CHELSEA	MA	HORNELL	NY	PARSONS	KS
CHESTER	PA	HOUSTON	TX	PASSAIC	NJ
CHEVIOT	OH	INKSTER	MI	PHOENIX*	AZ
CHICAGO	IL	IRONTON	OH	PONTIAC	MI
CLAYTON	MO	JACKSON*	MS	PULASKI	VA
CLIFTON	NJ	KEARNEY	NJ	QUITMAN	GA
CLINTON	LA	KENOSHA	WI	RALEIGH*	NC

RARITAN	NJ	BRAINERD	MN	OSSINING	NY
READING	PA	BROCKTON	MA	PALMDALE	CA
REDDING	CA	BROOKLYN	NY	PALOALTO	CA
ROANOKE	VA	BRYNMAWR	PA	PARADISE	NY
ROSELLE	NJ	CADILLAC	MI	PASADENA	CA, TX
RUTLAND	VT	CALDWELL	ID	PATERSON	NJ
SAGINAW	MI	CALEXICO	CA	PLYMOUTH	MA, MN
SALINAS	CA	CARLISLE	PA	PRESCOTT	AZ
SANFORD	NC	CARLSBAD	NM	RICHMOND*	VA
SAN JOSE	CA	CARTERET	NJ	ROCKFORD	IL
SAN JUAN*	PR	CHANDLER	AZ	ROCKHILL	SC
SANTA FE*	NM	CHEYENNE*	WY	SANDIEGO	CA
SAPULPA	OK	CHICOPEE	MA	SANDUSKY	OH
SEATTLE	WA	COLUMBIA	MD, MS	SANMATEO	CA
SEDALIA	MO	COLUMBIA*	SC	SANTAANA	CA
SHAWNEE	OK	COLUMBUS	GA, OH	SARASOTA	FL
SPENCER	MA	CORTLAND	NY	SAVANNAH	GA
SPOKANE	WA	CRANSTON	RI	SCRANTON	PA
STURGIS	MI	DALYCITY	CA	STAMFORD	CT
SUFFOLK	VA	DANVILLE	IL, VA	STAUNTON	VA
SUNAPEE	NH	DEARBORN	MI	STOCKTON	CA
TARBORO	NC	DEERPARK	OH	STTHOMAS	VI
TARRANT	AL	EDINBURG	TX	SYRACUSE	NY
TAUNTON	MA	EVANSTON	IL	TALLULAH	LA
TEANECK	NJ	EVERETT	WA	TORRANCE	CA
TENAFLY	NJ	FAIRMONT	WV	TUSKEGEE	AL
TERRELL	TX	FREDONIA	NY	VALDOSTA	GA
TRENTON*	NJ	FREEMONT	CA	VINELAND	NJ
VALLEJO	CA	GASTONIA	NC	WAHPETON	ND
VANWERT	OH	GLENDALE	AZ, CA	WATERLOO	IA
VENTURA	CA	GREENEAY	WI	WAUKEGAN	IL
VISALIA	CA	GULFPORT	MS	WAUKESHA	WI
WAIPAHU	HI	HAMILTON	OH	WESTPORT	CT
WALTHAM	MA	HANNIBAL	MO	WHEELING	WV
WAREHAM	MA	HARTFORD*	CT	WHITTIER	CA
WARWICK	RI	HASTINGS	NE	WILMETTE	IL
WEBSTER	MA	HAZLETON	PA	WOODBURY	NJ
WEIRTON	WV	HONOLULU*	HI	YARMOUTH	MA
WESLACO	TX	IOWACITY	IA	YUBACITY	CA
WHEATON	IL	KANKAKEE	IL		
WICHITA	KS	LACROSSE	WI	ANNAPOLIS*	MD, TX
WINDBER	PA	LAKEWOOD	CO, NJ	ARLINGTON	VA
WINSTED	CT	LASVEGAS	NV	ASHEVILLE	NC
WOOSTER	OH	LAWRENCE	MA	ASHTABULA	OH
YANKTON	SD	LEWISTON	ME	BALTIMORE	MD
YONKERS	NY	LOCKPORT	NY	BARBERTON	OH
		MARIETTA	GA	BELVEDERE	CA
AMARILLO	TX	MISSOULA	MT	BETHLEHEM	PA
ANN ARBOR	MI	MONTEREY	CA	BIDDEFORD	ME
ANNISTON	AL	MUKILTEO	WA	BRADENTON	FL
APPLETON	WI	MUSKEGON	MI	BRAINTREE	MA
BEAUMONT	TX	MUSKOGEE	OK	BREMERTON	WA
BELLEVUE	NE, WA	MESQUITE	TX	BRUNSWICK	GA
BERKELEY	CA	METAIRIE	LA	CAMBRIDGE	MA
BESSEMER	AL	MOREHEAD	KY	CAPECORAL	FL
BETHESDA	MD	NEWBURGH	NY	CARROLTON	TX
BILLINGS	MT	NEWHAVEN	CT	CARSONCITY*	NV
BISMARCK	ND	OAKRIDGE	TN	CHAMPAIGN	IL
BOGALUSA	LA	OKMULGEE	OK	CHARLOTTE	NC

CLEVELAND	OH	KALAMAZOO	MI	WORCESTER	MA
COSTAMESA	CA	KNOXVILLE	TN		
COVINGTON	KY	LAFAYETTE	LA	BATONROUGE*	LA
DESMOINES*	LA	LANCASTER	PA	CHARLESTON*	WV
EAUCLAIRE	WI	LEVITTOWN	NY, PA	HARRISBURG*	PA
ELIZABETH	NJ	LEXINGTON	KY	LITTLEROCK*	AR
ENGLEWOOD	NJ	LONGBEACH	CA	MONTGOMERY*	AL
ESCONDIDO	CA	LYNCHBURG	VA	MONTPELIER*	VT
FALLRIVER	MA	MANHATTAN	KS, NY	PROVIDENCE*	RI
FAIRBANKS	AK	NASHVILLE*	TN	SACRAMENTO*	CA
FLAGSTAFF	AZ	PENSACOLA	FL		
FONDDULAC	WI	RIVERSIDE	CA	SPRINGFIELD*	IL
FORTDODGE	IA	ROCHESTER	NY	TALLAHASSEE*	FL
FRANKFORT*	KY	SALISBURY	NC		
FULLERTON	CA	SANANGELO	TX	INDIANAPOLIS*	IN
GALESBURG	IL	SANTAROSA	CA		
GALVESTON	TX	SHEBOYGAN	WI	OKLAHOMACITY*	OK
GRAPEVINE	TX	SOUTHBEND	IN		
HAMTRAMCK	MA	SOUTHGATE	CA	SALTLAKECITY*	UT
HAVERHILL	MA	TEXARKANA	AK		
HENDERSON	NV	UNIONCITY	NJ	JEFFERSONCITY*	MO
HILLSBORO	OR	WATERBURY	CT		
HOLLYWOOD	CA	WESTALLIS	WI	CHARLOTTEAMALIE	
JOHNSTOWN	PA	WESTPOINT	NY		VI

FOREIGN CITIES

City	Country				
		SPA	Belgium	BERN	Switzerland
ABA	Nigeria	TSU	Japan	BIDA	Nigeria
ABO	Finland	UBE	Japan	BIEL	Switzerland
AIX	France	UFA	Russia	BISK	Russia
AUE	Germany	ULM	Germany	BLED	Slovenia
AVA	Myanmar			BONE	Algeria
BAM	Iran	ACRE	Israel	BONN	Germany
BOR	Russia, Serbia and	ADEN	Yemen	BRNO	Czech Republic
	Montenegro	ADUA	Ethiopia	BUDA	Hungary
DAX	France	AGAR	India	BUEA	Cameroon
DIR	Pakistan	AGEN	France	BUGA	Colombia
EDE	Nigeria	AGRA	India	BUNA	Papua New
EDO	Japan	AIUD	Romania		Guinea
EMS	Germany	ALBI	France	BURG	Germany
FES	Morocco	ALES	France	CAEN	France
FEZ	Morocco	ALEY	Lebanon	CALI	Colombia
HOF	Germany	AMOL	Iran	CEBU	Philippines
HUE	Vietnam	AMOY	China	CHEB	Czech Republic
ICA	Peru	AMUL	Iran	CHUR	Switzerland
IRI	South Korea	ANSI	China	CLUJ	Romania
ITA	Paraguay	APAM	Mexico	COBH	Ireland
IWO	Nigeria	APIA	Western Samoa	CORK	Ireland
KEM	Russia	APRA	Guam	CORO	Venezuela
KUM	Iran	ARAD	Romania	DHAR	India
LAE	Papua New Guinea	ASCH	Germany	DILI	East Timor
LEH	India	AYAN	India	DOHA	Qatar
NIS	Serbia and	BAGE	Brazil	EGER	Hungary
	Montenegro	BAJA	Hungary	ETAH	Greenland
OYO	Nigeria	BAKU	Azerbaijan	FUYU	China
QUM	Iran	BALE	Switzerland	GAYA	India
SAN	Mali	BARI	Italy	GAZA	Israel
		BATH	England	GENT	Belgium

GERA	Germany	PARA	Brazil	ARICA	Chile
GIZA	Egypt	PEGU	Myanmar	ARIES	France
GRAZ	Austria	PERM	Russia	ARRAH	India
GYOR	Hungary	PILA	Poland	ARRAS	France
HAMM	Germany	PISA	Italy	ASHIO	Japan
HILO	Hawaii	POLA	Croatia	ATAMI	Japan
HOFU	Japan	PORI	Finland	AVILA	Spain
HOKO	South Korea	PRAG	Czech Republic	AVOLA	Italy
HOMS	Libya, Syria	PULA	Croatia	BABUL	Iran
HULL	England	PUNO	Peru	BACAU	Romania
HUTT	New Zealand	RIAD	Saudi Arabia	BADEN	Austria
IASI	Romania	RIGA	Latvia	BAHIA	Brazil
IFNI	Morocco	RIVA	Italy	BALLY	India
IPIN	China	ROME	Italy	BALTA	Ukraine
IPOH	Malaysia	SAIS	Egypt	BASEL	Switzerland
IRUN	Spain	SANA	Yemen	BASRA	Iraq
JAEN	Spain	SENS	France	BATUM	Georgia
JENA	Germany	SETE	France	BAURU	Brazil
KANO	Nigeria	SIAN	China	BEIRA	Portugal
KHOI	Iran	STLO	France	BEKES	Hungary
KIEL	Germany	SUEZ	Egypt	BELEM	Brazil
KIEV	Ukraine	SUMY	Ukraine	BEPPU	Japan
KOBE	Japan	SUSA	Iran	BERNE	Switzerland
KOFU	Japan	SUVA	Fiji	BIHAR	India
KURE	Japan	TARA	Ireland	BLOIS	France
LABE	Guinea	TULA	Russia	BOGOR	Indonesia
LIDO	Italy	URFA	Turkey	BREST	France
LIMA	Peru	VIGO	Spain	BULAN	Philippines
LINZ	Austria	VILA	Scotland	BUNDI	India
LODI	Italy	WIEN	Austria	BURSA	Turkey
LODZ	Poland	WUHU	China	BYTOV	Poland
LOME	Togo	YAFA	Israel	CADIZ	Spain
LOTA	Chile			CAIRO	Egypt
LVOV	Ukraine	ACCRA	Ghana	CANEA	Greece
LWOW	Ukraine	ADANA	Turkey	CAPUA	Italy
LYON	France	ADONI	India	CAVAN	Ireland
MALE	Maldive Islands	ADOWA	Ethiopia	CEARA	Brazil
METZ	France	ADUWA	Ethiopia	CELLE	Germany
MITO	Japan	AGANA	Guam	CEUTA	Morocco
MOJI	Japan	AHLEN	Germany	CHIBA	Japan
MONS	Belgium	AHWAZ	Iran	CHITA	Russia
NAHA	Japan	AIGUN	China	CLEVE	Germany
NARA	Japan	AKITA	Japan	COLON	Panama
NAWA	Syria	AKOLA	India	COWES	England
NICE	France	AKURE	Nigeria	DACCA	Pakistan
NISH	Serbia and	ALLOA	Scotland	DAKAR	Senegal
	Montenegro	AMARA	Iraq	DATIA	India
NUUK	Kalaallit Nunaat	AMBON	Indonesia	DAVAO	Philippines
	(Greenland)	AMBUR	India	DAVOS	Switzerland
OBAN	Scotland	AMMAN	Jordan	DELHI	India
OITA	Japan	ANAPA	Russia	DERNA	Libya
OMSK	Russia	ANCON	Panama	DHAKA	Bangladesh
ORAN	Algeria	ANCUD	Chile	DIJON	France
OREL	Russia	ANGOL	Chile	DOORN	Netherlands
ORLY	France	ANGUL	India	DOUAI	France
ORSK	Russia	ANZIO	Italy	ELCHE	Spain
OSLO	Norway	APAPA	Nigeria	EMDEN	Germany
OTSU	Japan	ARBIL	Iran	ERLAU	Hungary
OULU	Finland	ARCOT	India	ESSEN	Germany

FIUME	Croatia	MALMO	Sweden	SIENA	Italy
FUSAN	South Korea	MASAN	North Korea	SIMLA	India
GALLE	Sri Lanka	MECCA	Saudi Arabia	SOFIA	Bulgaria
GATUN	Panama	MEDAN	Indonesia	SPLIT	Croatia
GENOA	Italy	MEMEL	Lithuania	SUCRE	Bolivia
GHENT	Belgium	MILAN	Italy	SURAT	India
GIJON	Spain	MINSK	Belarus	SUWON	South Korea
GOMEL	Belarus	MOSUL	Iraq	TAEGU	South Korea
GORKY	Russia	NAMPO	North Korea	TANTA	Egypt
GOTHA	Germany	NAMUR	Belgium	TOKAY	Hungary
GREIZ	Germany	NANCY	France	TOKYO	Japan
HAGEN	Germany	NATAL	Brazil	TOMSK	Russia
HAIFA	Israel	NIGEL	South Africa	TOURS	France
HALLE	Germany	NIMES	France	TRANI	Italy
HAMAR	Norway	OGAKI	Japan	TRENT	Italy
HANDA	Japan	OMURA	Japan	TRIER	Germany
HANOI	Vietnam	OMUTA	Japan	TUNIS	Tunisia
HARAR	Ethiopia	OPOLE	Poland	TURIN	Italy
HERAT	Afghanistan	ORURO	Bolivia	TURKU	Finland
HERNE	Germany	ORYOL	Russia	VAASA	Finland
HOMEL	Belarus	OSAKA	Japan	VADUZ	Liechtenstein
HORTA	Portugal	OSTIA	Italy	VARNA	Bulgaria
HUBLI	India	OTARU	Japan	VICHY	France
IJEBU	Nigeria	PADUA	Italy	VILNA	Lithuania
ISCHL	Austria	PALMA	Spain	VISBY	Sweden
ITAMI	Japan	PALOS	Spain	WILNA	Lithuania
IZMIR	Turkey	PARIS	France	WORMS	Germany
IZMIT	Turkey	PARMA	Italy	WUHAN	China
JAFFA	Israel	PASAY	Philippines	WUWEI	China
JEDDA	Saudi Arabia	PATAN	Nepal	YALTA	Ukraine
JEREZ	Spain	PATNA	India	YAREN	Nauru
JIDDA	Saudi Arabia	PENKI	China	ZOMBA	Malawi
KABUL	Afghanistan	PENZA	Russia		
KANDY	Sri Lanka	PERAK	Malaysia	AACHEN	Germany
KASUR	Pakistan	PERTH	Australia	AARHUS	Denmark
KAZAN	Russia	PINSK	Belarus	ABADAN	Iran
KEIJO	South Korea	PLZEN	Czech Republic	ABUKIR	Egypt
KERCH	Ukraine	PODOR	Senegal	AEGION	Greece
KHIVA	Uzbekistan	PONCE	Puerto Rico	AEGIUM	Greece
KIMPO	South Korea	POONA	Afghanistan	AGADES	Nigeria
KIROV	Russia	POSEN	Poland	AGADIR	Morocco
KIRYU	Japan	PRAHA	Czech Republic	AKASHI	Japan
KOCHI	Japan	PRAIA	Cape Verde	ALATYR	Russia
KONIA	Turkey	PUSAN	South Korea	ALBURY	Australia
KONYA	Turkey	QUITO	Ecuador	ALEPPO	Syria
KOVNO	Lithuania	RABAT	Morocco	ALLADA	Benin
KOWNO	Lithuania	RADOM	Poland	ALTONA	Germany
KYOTO	Japan	REIMS	France	ALTORF	Switzerland
LAGOS	Nigeria	RESHT	Iran	AMALFI	Italy
LAHTI	Finland	REVAL	Estonia	AMBALA	India
LANUS	Argentina	ROUEN	France	AMBATO	Ecuador
LAPAZ	Bolivia	SAGAR	India	AMIENS	France
LEEDS	England	SAKAI	Japan	ANCONA	Italy
LHASA	China (Tibet)	SALTA	Argentina	ANGERS	France
LIEGE	Belgium	SEDAN	France	ANGKOR	Cambodia
LILLE	France	SEOUL	South Korea	ANKARA	Turkey
LOMAS	Argentina	SHASI	China	ANNECY	France
LUTSK	Poland	SHOKA	Taiwan	ANSHAN	China
MAINZ	Germany	SIDON	Lebanon	AOMORI	Japan

APATIN	Croatia	DOUALA	Cameroon	LUBECK	Germany
APOLDA	Germany	DUBLIN	Ireland	LUBLIN	Poland
ARCOLE	Italy	DUMDUM	India	LUGANO	Switzerland
ARNHEM	Netherlands	DUNDEE	Scotland	LUSAKA	Zambia
ASMARA	Eritrea	DURBAN	South Africa	MACEIO	Brazil
ASTANA	Kazakhstan	EDESSA	Greece	MADRAS	India
ASTARA	Azerbaijan	ERFURT	Germany	MADRID	Spain
ATHENS	Greece	ERIVAN	Armenia	MADURA	India
BAGUIO	Philippines	EXETER	England	MALABO	Equatorial
BALBOA	Panama	FUSHUN	China		Guinea
BAMAKO	Mali	GALATI	Romania	MALAGA	Spain
BANDAR	Brunei	GDYNIA	Poland	MALANG	Indonesia
BANDRA	India	GENEVA	Switzerland	MANAMA	Bahrain
BANGUI	Central	GONDAR	Ethiopia	MANAUS	Brazil
	African Republic	GOSLAR	Germany	MANTUA	Italy
BANJUL	Gambia	GRASSE	France	MAPUTO	Mozambique
BARMEN	Germany	GRODNO	Belarus	MASERU	Lesotho
BARODA	India	GROZNY	Russia	MEDINA	Saudi Arabia
BASTIA	France	GUNTUR	India	MENTON	France
BATUMI	Georgia	HAMELN	Germany	MERIDA	Mexico
BEIRUT	Lebanon	HANKOW	China	MESHED	Iran
BEJAIA	Algeria	HARARE	Zimbabwe	MINDEN	Germany
BENONI	South Africa	HARBIN	China	MINHOW	China
BERGEN	Norway	HARRAR	Ethiopia	MODENA	Italy
BHOPAL	India	HAVANA	Cuba	MONACO	Monaco
BILBAO	Spain	HIMEJI	Japan	MORONI	Comoros
BINGEN	Germany	HOBART	Australia	MOSCOW	Russia
BISSAU	Guinea-Bissau	HOHHOT	China (Inner	MUKDEN	China
BOCHUM	Germany		Mongolia)	MULTAN	Pakistan
BOGOTA	Colombia	IBADAN	Nigeria	MUMBAI	India
BOLTON	England	ILOILO	Philippines	MUNICH	Germany
BOMBAY	India	ILORIN	Nigeria	MURCIA	Spain
BOUGIE	Algeria	IMPRAL	India	MUSCAT	Oman
BRAILA	Romania	INCHON	South Korea	MYSORE	India
BRASOV	Romania	INDORE	India	NAGANO	Japan
BREMEN	Germany	JAIPUR	India	NAGOYA	Japan
BRIONI	Switzerland	JALAPA	Mexico	NAGPUR	India
BRUNEI	Brunei	JOHORE	Malaysia	NANTES	France
BURGAS	Bulgaria	KALUGA	Russia	NAPLES	Italy
CAGUAS	Puerto Rico	KANPUR	India	NARVIK	Norway
CALAIS	France	KAOLAN	China	NASSAU	Bahamas
CALLAO	Peru	KASHAN	Iran	NIAMEY	Niger
CAMBAY	India	KASSEL	Germany	NINGPO	China
CANNES	France	KAUNAS	Lithuania	NOUMEA	New
CANTON	China	KAZVIN	Iran		Caledonia
CASSEL	Germany	KEDIRI	Indonesia	NUMAZU	Greece
CAVITE	Philippines	KHULNA	Bangladesh	ODENSE	Denmark
CAXIAS	Brazil	KIGALI	Rwanda	ODESSA	Ukraine
CEGLED	Hungary	KIGALI	Rwanda	OPORTO	Portugal
CHAPRA	India	KUNSAN	South Korea	ORADEA	Romania
CHOLON	Vietnam	KUWAIT	Kuwait	OREBRO	Sweden
CHOSHI	Japan	LAHORE	Pakistan	ORENSE	Spain
COLMAR	France	LEIDEN	Netherlands	OSTEND	Belgium
CRACOW	Poland	LEMANS	France	OTTAWA	Canada
CUCUTA	Colombia	LERIDA	Spain	OVIEDO	Spain
DAIREN	China	LEYDEN	Netherlands	OXFORD	England
DANZIG	Poland	LIDICE	Czech Republic	PADANG	Indonesia
DELPHI	Greece	LISBON	Portugal	PASSAU	Germany
DODONA	Greece	LUANDA	Angola	PATRAS	Greece

PEKING	China	ALGIERS	Algeria	KALININ	Russia
PILSEN	Czech Republic	ALLEPPI	India	KAMPALA	Uganda
PLAUEN	Germany	ALMAATA	Kazakhstan	KARACHI	Pakistan
POTOSI	Bolivia	ANDORRA	France	KHARKOV	Ukraine
POZNAN	Poland	ANTIBES	France	KOLKATA	India
PRAGUE	Czech	ANTIGUA	Guatemala	KOWLOON	China
	Republic	ANTWERP	Belgium	LAPLATA	Argentina
QUEBEC	Canada	ARACAJU	Brazil	LATAKIA	Syria
QUETTA	Pakistan	AVIGNON	France	LEGHORN	Italy
RAGUSA	Croatia	BAGHDAD	Iraq	LEHAVRE	France
RAIPUR	India	BANDUNG	Indonesia	LEIPZIG	Germany
RAMPUR	India	BANGKOK	Thailand	LIMOGES	France
RECIFE	Brazil	BATAVIA	Indonesia	LOCARNO	Switzerland
RENNES	France	BEIJING	China	LUCERNE	Switzerland
RIJEKA	Croatia	BELFAST	Ireland	MADEIRA	Portugal
RIMINI	Italy	BENARES	India	MANAGUA	Nicaragua
RIYADH	Saudi Arabia	BENGASI	Libya	MARSALA	Italy
ROSEAU	Dominica	BERBERA	Somalia	MASHHAD	Iran
ROSTOV	Russia	BERGAMO	Italy	MBABANE	Swaziland
SAIGON	Vietnam	BISHKEK	Kyrgystan	MESSINA	Italy
SANTOS	Brazil	BIZERTE	Tunisia	MOMBASA	Kenya
SASEBO	Japan	BOLOGNA	Italy	NAIROBI	Kenya
SENDAI	Japan	BRESCIA	Italy	NANKING	China
SEVRES	France	BRESLAU	Poland	NICOSIA	Cyprus
SPARTA	Greece	BRISTOL	England	NITEROI	Brazil
STRESA	Italy	CALGARY	Canada	PALERMO	Italy
SUZUKA	Japan	CALICUT	India	PAPEETE	Tahiti
SYDNEY	Australia	CARACAS	Venezuela	POLTAVA	Ukraine
TABRIZ	Iran	CARDIFF	Wales	POTSDAM	Germany
TAIPEI	Taiwan	CATANIA	Italy	PUNAKHA	Bhutan
TALIEN	China	CAYENNE	French	RANGOON	Burma
TARAWA	Kiribati		Guiana	RAPALLO	Italy
TEHRAN	Iran	CHENGTU	China	RAVENNA	Italy
TETUAN	Morocco	CHENNAI	India	ROSARIO	Argentina
THEBES	Greece	COLOGNE	Germany	ROSTOCK	Germany
TILSIT	Russia	COLOMBO	Sri Lanka	SALERNO	Italy
TIRANA	Albania	CONAKRY	Guinea	SANJOSE	Costa Rica
TOBRUK	Libya	CORDOBA	Argentina	SANTAFE	Argentina
TOLEDO	Spain	CORDOVA	Spain	SAPPORO	Japan
TOULON	France	COTONOU	Benin	SARATOV	Russia
TOYAMA	Japan	CREMONA	Italy	SEVILLA	Spain
TRALEE	Ireland	DRESDEN	Germany	SEVILLE	Spain
TSINAN	China	DUNKIRK	France	SIALKOT	Pakistan
UPSALA	Sweden	ESFAHAN	Iran	STALINO	Ukraine
URUMQI	China	FERRARA	Italy	STETTIN	Poland
	(Xinjiang)	GANGTOK	India	TALLINN	Estonia
VENICE	Italy		(Sikkim)	TAMPICO	Mexico
VERDUN	France	GLASGOW	Scotland	TANGIER	Morocco
VERONA	Italy	GODTHAB	Kalaallit	TARANTO	Italy
VIENNA	Austria		Nunaat (Greenland)	TBILISI	Georgia
VYBORG	Russia	GRANADA	Spain	TEHERAN	Iran
WARSAW	Poland	HAARLEM	Netherlands	TELAVIV	Israel
YAHATA	Japan	HAMBURG	Germany	THIMPHU	Bhutan
YANGKU	China	HANOVER	Germany	TIANJIN	China
YAWATA	Japan	HANYANG	China	TILBURG	Netherlands
ZAGREB	Croatia	ISFAHAN	Iran	TORONTO	Canada
ZURICH	Switzerland	ISPAHAN	Iran	TORREON	Mexico
		IVANOVO	Russia	TRIESTE	Italy
ABIDJAN	Ivory Coast	JAKARTA	Indonesia	TRIPOLI	Libya

TUCUMAN	Argentina	DJIBOUTI	Djibouti	SURABAJA	Indonesia
UTRECHT	Netherlands	DUISBURG	Germany	TASHKENT	Uzbekistan
VILNIUS	Lithuania	FORTLAMY	Chad	VALLETTA	Malta
WINDSOR	Canada	FREETOWN	Sierra	YOKOHAMA	Japan
WROCLAW	Poland		Leone		
YAOUNDE	Cameroon	GABORONE	Botswana	AMSTERDAM	
YEREVAN	Armenia	GOTEBORG	Sweden		Netherlands
		HANGCHOW	China	BANGALORE	India
ABUDHABI	United	HELSINKI	Finland	BUCHAREST	Romania
	Arab Emirates	KHARTOUM	Sudan	BUJUMBURA	Burundi
ADELAIDE	Australia	KINGSTON	Jamaica	CHONGQING	China
ASUNCION	Paraguay	LILONGWE	Malawi	GUANGZHOU	China
AUCKLAND	New	MANNHEIM	Germany	JERUSALEM	Israel
	Zealand	MEDELLIN	Colombia	KATHMANDU	Nepal
BATHURST	Gambia	MONROVIA	Liberia	MOGADISHU	Somalia
BELMOPAN	Belize	MONTREAL	Canada	PHNOMPENH	
BENGHAZI	Libya	NAGASAKI	Japan		Cambodia
BRASILIA	Brazil	NDJAMENA	Chad	PORTONOVO	Benin
BRISBANE	Australia	NEWDELHI	India	PYONGYANG	North
BRUSSELS	Belgium	PNOMPENH	Cambodia		Korea
BUDAPEST	Hungary	PRETORIA	South	REYKJAVIK	Iceland
CALCUTTA	India		Africa	SANMARINO	San
CANBERRA	Australia	SALONIKA	Greece		Marino
CAPETOWN	South	SANTIAGO	Chile	STOCKHOLM	Sweden
	Africa	SAOPAULO	Brazil	STUTTGART	Germany
DAMASCUS	Syria	SARAJEVO	Bosnia and	TASHICHHO	Bhutan
DJAKARTA	Indonesia		Herzegovina	ULANBATOR	Mongolia
		SHENYANG	China	VIENTIANE	Laos

ISLANDS

RE	Atlantic	UAP	Pacific	COOK	Pacific
WE	Pacific (France)	UEA	Pacific	CORN	Caribbean
		VIS	Croatia	CRES	Adriatic
ALS	North Sea	WEII	Indonesia	CUBA	Caribbean
API	Pacific	YAP	Pacific	CUYO	Philippines
ARU	Pacific (Indonesia)	YEU	France	DALL	Bering
CAT	Atlantic	ZEA	Greece	EBON	Pacific
COS	Greece			EFAT	Pacific
EPI	Pacific	ADAK	Bering Sea	ELBA	Mediterranean
FYN	North Sea	AERO	North Sea		(Italy)
HOG	North America	ALOR	Indian Ocean	FANO	Denmark
HOY	Scotland	ANAA	Pacific	FARO	Baltic
IKI	Japan	APEU	Atlantic	FIJI	Pacific
IOS	Greece	ARAN	Ireland	FOGO	Atlantic
IZU	Japan	ARBE	Adriatic	FOHR	North Sea
KAI	Indonesia	AROE	Indonesia	GIZO	Pacific
KEI	Indonesia	ARUN	Bering	GOZO	Mediterranean
KOS	Greece	ATIU	Pacific	GUAM	Pacific (US)
KRK	Adriatic (Croatia)	ATKA	Bering	HERM	England
LAU	Pacific	ATTU	Bering	HVAR	Croatia
MAN	England	AVES	Caribbean	IONA	Scotland
OBI	Indonesia	BALI	Indonesia	JAVA	Indian Ocean
OKI	Japan	BATU	Indonesia	JAWA	Indian Ocean
PAG	Adriatic (Croatia)	BIAK	Pacific	JOLO	Philippines
RAB	Adriatic (Croatia)	BUKA	Pacific	KAIS	Iran
REY	Panama	BURU	Indian Ocean	KEOS	Greece
RUM	Scotland	BUTE	Atlantic	KURE	Pacific
SAL	Atlantic	CEBU	Philippines	LAUT	Indonesia

LEON	Spain	BANDA	Indian Ocean	LEYTE	Philippines
LETI	Indonesia	BANKA	Indian Ocean	LOBOS	Atlantic
LIFU	Pacific	BANKS	Arctic (Canada)	LUZON	Philippines
MAHE	Indian Ocean	BATAN	Pacific	MACAO	China
MAUI	Pacific		(Philippines)	MAKIN	Pacific
MILO	Greece	BICOL	Pacific	MALTA	Mediterranean
MOEN	Denmark		(Philippines)	MANUA	Pacific
MONA	Caribbean	BIOCO	Atlantic	MELOS	Greece
MUHU	Baltic		(Equatorial Guinea)	MISOL	Pacific
MULL	Scotland	BLOCK	Atlantic (US)	NAURU	Pacific
NIAS	Indonesia	BOHOL	Pacific	NAXOS	Greece
NIUE	Pacific		(Philippines)	NDENI	Pacific
OAHU	Pacific	BONIN	Pacific	NEVIS	Caribbean
ORRS	Caribbean	BYLOT	Arctic	OLAND	Baltic
OSEL	Estonia	CALDY	Wales	PAGAI	Indonesia
OTEA	New Zealand	CAPRI	Italy	PALAU	Pacific
PAGI	Indonesia		(Mediterranean)	PANAY	Philippines
PAXO	Greece	CERAM	East Indies	PAPUA	Pacific
PICO	Atlantic		(Indonesia)	PAROS	Greece
PLUM	Pacific	CHEJU	South Korea	PARRY	Arctic
QAIS	Iran	CHIOS	Greece	PAXOI	Greece
RAPA	Pacific	CIOVO	Mediterranean	PAXOS	Greece
RODI	Mediterranean	COATS	Arctic (Canada)	PELEE	Canada
ROSS	Indian Ocean,	COCOS	Indian Ocean	PELEW	Pacific
	Pacific	CORFU	Mediterranean	PEMBA	Indian Ocean
ROTI	Indonesia		(Greece)		(Tanzania)
SADO	Japan	CRETE	Mediterranean	PSARA	Greece
SARK	England		(Greece)	QISHM	Iran
SAVO	Pacific	DAMAR	Indian Ocean	QUAIS	Iran
SAVU	Indonesia	DELOS	Greece	RAOUL	Pacific
SCIO	Greece	DEVON	Arctic	ROCAS	Brazil
SKYE	Atlantic		(Nunavut)	RUGEN	Baltic
SULA	Indonesia	DISKO	Arctic	SAMAR	Philippines
SULU	Philippines		(Greenland)	SAMOA	Pacific (US;
SYLT	North Sea	DOMEL	Indian Ocean		Samoa)
SYRA	Greece	DUCIE	Pacific	SAMOS	Greece
TANA	Pacific	EFATE	Pacific	SANGI	Indonesia
TRUK	Pacific	ELLIS	Pacific	SERAM	East Indies
UIST	Scotland	EXUMA	Atlantic		(Indonesia)
UNST	Scotland	FAROE	Atlantic	SOLTA	Croatia
UVEA	Pacific		(Denmark)	SPICE	Pacific
VATE	Pacific	FAYAL	Atlantic	SUMBA	East Indies
WAKE	Pacific	FOULA	Atlantic		(Indonesia)
		GOUGH	Atlantic	SUNDA	Indian Ocean
ABACO	Caribbean	HITRA	North Sea	SYROS	Greece
ALAND	Baltic (Finland)	HONDO	Japan	TANNA	Pacific
ALOFI	Pacific	HOSTE	Pacific (Chile)	TENOS	Greece
ALSEN	North Sea	ISLAY	Scotland	THERA	Greece
AMAMI	Japan	IVIZA	Mediterranean	TIMOR	East Indies
AMLIA	Bering	JAPAN	Pacific		(Indonesia)
AMMIN	China	KASOS	Mediterranean	TONGA	Pacific
AMRUM	North Sea	KAUAI	Pacific	UMNAK	Bering
ARRAN	Scotland	KISHM	Iran	UPOLU	Pacific
ARROE	Indonesia	KISKA	Bering	WAKDE	Indian Ocean,
ARUBA	Caribbean	KUNIE	Pacific		Pacific
	(Netherlands)	KURIL	Pacific	WHITE	Arctic
BABAR	Indonesia	LANAI	Pacific	WIGHT	England
BAKER	North America	LEROS	Greece	ZANTE	Greece
BALUT	Pacific	LETTI	Indonesia		

AALAND Baltic	**KODIAC** Pacific (US)	**ANDAMAN** Indian
ACHILL Atlantic	**KOMODO** Indonesia	Ocean (India)
AEGEAN Mediterranean	**KYOSAI** South Korea	**ANTIGUA** Caribbean
AEGINA Mediterranean	**KYUSHU** Japan	**AUSTRAL** Pacific
AGATTU Pacific	**LABUAN** Indonesia	**BAHREIN** Persian Gulf
ALABAT Pacific	**LANTAR** Thailand	**BARANOF** Pacific
AMAGER Denmark	**LEMNOS** Greece	**BARENTS** Arctic
AMBRIM Pacific	**LESBOS** Greece	**BERKNER** Antarctica
AMELIA Atlantic	**LEUCAS** Greece	**BERMUDA** Atlantic
AMUKTA Bering	**LIPARI** Italy	**CAVIANA** Atlantic
ANDROS Atlantic,	**LOMBOK** Indonesia	(Paraguay, Brazil)
Mediterranean	**MACTAN** Philippines	**CAYENNE** South
ANGAUR Pacific	**MADURA** East Indies	America
AZORES Atlantic	(Indonesia)	**CELEBES** Indonesia
(Portugal)	**MALDEN** Pacific	**CHANNEL** Atlantic
BAFFIN Arctic (Canada)	**MANSEL** Arctic	(UK)
BAHAMA Atlantic	(Canada)	**CHATHAM** Pacific
BANGKA East Indies	**MARAJO** Brazil	**CORSICA** Mediterranean
(Indonesia)	**MIDWAY** Pacific	**CURACAO** Caribbean
BINTAN Indonesia	**NEGROS** Philippines	**DIOMEDE** Bering
BORDEN Arctic	**ORKNEY** Atlantic (UK)	(Russia)
(Canada)	**PARRIS** North America	**FAEROES** Atlantic
BORNEO East Indies	**PENANG** Indonesia	**FALSTER** Denmark
(Indonesia, Brunei,	**POMONA** Scotland	**FORMOSA** Taiwan
Malaysia)	**PONAPE** Pacific	**GILBERT** Pacific
BOUVET Atlantic	**RHODES** Mediterranean	**GOTLAND** Baltic
BURIAS Philippines	(Greece)	(Sweden)
CAMANO North	**RIESCO** Pacific (Chile)	**ICELAND** Atlantic
America	**ROTUMA** Atlantic	**IRELAND** Atlantic
CANARY Atlantic	**SAISHU** South Korea	**IWOJIMA** Pacific
(Spain)	**SANDAY** Scotland	**JAMAICA** Caribbean
CANDIA Mediterranean	**SAREMA** Estonia	**KOLGUEV** Arctic
CARMEN Atlantic,	**SAVAII** Pacific	**LAALAND** Denmark
Mexico	**SCARBA** Atlantic	**LOFOTEN** Arctic
CAYMAN Caribbean	**SCILLY** England	**LOLLAND** Denmark
CERIGO Mediterranean	**SHEMYA** Bering	**MADEIRA** Atlantic
CEYLON Indian Ocean	**SIBUTU** Philippines	**MAJORCA**
CHILOE Pacific (Chile)	**SICILY** Mediterranean	Mediterranean
CYPRUS Mediterranean	(Italy)	**MARAJO** Atlantic
EASTER Pacific (Chile)	**TAHITI** Pacific (France)	(Brazil)
ELLICE Pacific	**TAIWAN** Pacific	**MARIANA** Pacific
EUDOEA Mediterranean	**TANAGA** Bering	**MINDORO** Philippines
(Greece)	**THASOS** Greece	**MINORCA**
FLORES East Indies	**TINIAN** Pacific	Mediterranean
(Indonesia)	**TOBAGO** Caribbean	**MOLUCCA** Pacific
FUTUNA Pacific	**TORTUE** Caribbean	**NICOBAR** Indian
GARUPA Atlantic	**TRAILL** Arctic	Ocean
(Paraguay, Brazil)	(Greenland)	**NUNIVAK** Pacific (US)
GILLIS Arctic	**TUBUAI** Pacific	**OKINAWA** Pacific
GOMERA Atlantic	**TULAGI** Pacific	**PALAWAN** Philippines
GRAHAM Pacific (US)	**UNIMAK** Bering	**REUNION** Indian
HAINAN Pacific	**USEDOM** Baltic	Ocean (France)
(China)	**VIRGIN** Caribbean	**SALAMIS** Greece
HAWAII Pacific (US)	(US, UK)	**SEMICHI** Bering
HONSHU Japan		**SUMATRA** East Indies
INAGUA Atlantic	**ACKLINS** Atlantic	(Indonesia)
ITURUP Arctic (Russia)	**AGALEGA** Indian	**SUMBAWA** East Indies
JERSEY Atlantic	Ocean	(Indonesia)
KANAGA Bering	**AMAKUSA** Japan	**TERNATE** Indonesia

TORTOLA	Caribbean	MOLUCCAS East	ELLESMERE Arctic
TORTUGA Caribbean	Indies (Indonesia)	(Canada)
VANUATU Pacific	SAKHALIN Pacific	GALAPAGOS Pacific
WRANGEL Arctic	(Russia)	(Ecuador)
(Russia)	SARDINIA	GREENLAND Atlantic
	Mediterranean (Italy)	(Denmark)
ADELAIDE Antarctica	SHETLAND Atlantic	HALMAHERA East
AKIMISKI Arctic	(UK)	Indies (Indonesia)
(Canada)	SOMERSET Arctic	KANGAROO Pacific
ALEUTIAN Bering (US)	(Canada)	(Australia)
AMCHITKA Bering	SRILANKA Indian	KERGUELEN Indian
ANTILLES Caribbean	Ocean	Ocean
BALEARES	STHELENA Atlantic	KUPREANOF Pacific
Mediterranean (Spain)	(UK)	(US)
BARBADOS Caribbean	SVALBARD Arctic	MARQUESAS Pacific
BATHURST Arctic	(Norway)	(France)
(Canada)	TASMANIA Pacific	MILNELAND Arctic
BERMUDAS Atlantic	(Australia)	(Greenland)
BORNHOLM Baltic	TENERIFE Atlantic	NANTUCKET Atlantic
(Denmark)	TRINIDAD Caribbean	(US)
CAROLINE Pacific	UNALASKA Bering	ROOSEVELT Ant-
CYCLADES	VICTORIA Arctic	arctica
Mediterranean	ZANZIBAR Indian	
DOMINICA Caribbean	Ocean (Tanzania)	GUADELOUPE
FALKLAND Atlantic		Caribbean (France)
(UK)	ADMIRALTY Pacific	HISPANIOLA Caribbean
GOTTLAND Baltic	(US)	(Haiti, Dominican Rep.)
GUERNSEY England	ALEXANDER	MADAGASCAR Indian
HEBRIDES Atlantic	Antarctica	Ocean
(UK)	ANTICOSTI Atlantic	MARTINIQUE
HOKKAIDO Japan	(Canada)	Caribbean (France)
HONGKONG Pacific	ASCENSION Atlantic	MICRONESIA Pacific
(China)	(US)	NEWBRITAIN East
KOTELNYY Arctic	BALEARICS	Indies (Papua New
(Russia)	Mediterranean (Spain)	Guinea)
MARIANAS Pacific	BOLSHEVIK Arctic	NEWIRELAND East
MARSHALL Pacific	(Russia)	Indies (Papua New
(Australia)	CAPEVERDE Atlantic	Guinea)
MELVILLE Arctic	CHICHAGOF Pacific	NEWZEALAND Pacific
(Canada)	(US)	SEYCHELLES Indian
MINDANAO Philippines	CHRISTMAS Pacific	Ocean
	(Kiribati)	YOSSUDARSA East
		Indies (Indonesia)

RIVERS OF THE UNITED STATES

DAN	VA	WIND	WY	LIARD	AK
ELK	TN, WV			LLANO	TX
FOX	WI	ALSEK	AK	MACON	LA
NEW	VA	BLACK	AR, MO	MIAMI	OH
RED	OK	BRONX	NY	NEUSE	NC
		CACHE	AR	OSAGE	KS, MO
EAST	NY	CEDAR	IA, MN	PEARL	MS
GILA	NM	COOSA	AL, GA	PECOS	NM, TX
IOWA	IA	FLINT	GA	ROGUE	OR
KERN	CA	GRAND	MI, MO, SD	SNAKE	MN, Northwest
LOUP	NE	GREEN	CO, IL, IN, KY,	WHITE	AR, CO, SD,
MILK	MT		WY, UT		TX, UT
OHIO	Midwest	JAMES	= DAKOTA	YAQUI	NM
ROCK	IL, WI	JAMES	VA	YAZOO	MS

YUKON	AK	
BARREN	KY	
BEAVER	PA	
BRAZOS	TX	
CAHABA	AL	
CLINCH	TN	
COPPER	AK	
DAKOTA	ND	
HUDSON	NY	
KANSAS	KS	
MOHAWK	NY	
NECHES	TX	
NEOSHO	KS, OK	
NOATAK	AK	
NUECES	TX	
OCONEE	GA	
OWYHEE	ID, OR	
PEEDEE	NC, SC	
PLATTE	IA, MO, NE	
POWDER	MT, OR, WY	
SABINE	LA, TX	
SALMON	ID	
SANTEE	SC	
SCIOTO	OH	
STJOHN	ME	
TANANA	AK	
TONGUE	MT, WY	
WABASH	ID, IL	
ALABAMA	AL	
BIGHORN	MT, WY	
CAHAWBA = CAHABA		
DOLORES	CO, UT	
GENESEE	NY, PA	
HOLSTON	TN	

JOHNDAY	OR	
KANAWHA	WV	
KLAMATH	OR	
KOYUKUK	AK	
LARAMIE	CO, WY	
LICKING	KY	
POTOMAC	Mid-Atlantic	
ROANOKE	NC, VA	
SANJUAN	Southwest	
STCROIX	MN, WI	
STJOHNS	FL	
SUSITNA	AK	
SUWANEE	FL, GA	
TRINITY	CA, TX	
WASHITA	OK, TX	
WASHITA = OUACHITA		
ALTAMAHA	GA	
ARKANSAS	Southwest	
BIGBLACK	MS	
CANADIAN	Southwest	
CAPEFEAR	NC	
CHEYENNE	SD	
CHIPPEWA	WI	
CIMARRON	NM, OK	
COLORADO	Southwest	
COLUMBIA	Northwest	
COLVILLE	AK	
DELAWARE	Mid-Atlantic	
GUNNISON	CO	
HUMBOLDT	NV	
ILLINOIS	IL	
KENNEBEC	ME	
KENTUCKY	KY	
MISSOURI	Central	
NIOBRARA	NE, WY	

OUACHITA	AR, LA	
RIOBRAVO = RIOGRANDE		
RIOPECOS = PECOS		
SAVANNAH	GA, SC	
ALLEGHENY	PA	
DESCHUTES	OR	
DESMOINES	IA	
KUSKOKWIM	AK	
MERRIMACK	MA, NH	
MINNESOTA	MN	
MUSKINGUM	OH	
PENOBSCOT	ME	
PORCUPINE	AK	
RIOGRANDE	Southwest	
SMOKYHILL	CO, KS	
STFRANCIS	AR, MO	
TENNESSEE	South	
TOMBIGBEE	AL, MS	
WISCONSIN	WI	
CUMBERLAND	KY, TN	
REPUBLICAN	KS, NE	
SACRAMENTO	CA	
SANJOAQUIN	CA	
WILLAMETTE	OR	
MISSISSIPPI	Central	
SUSQUEHANNA	MD, NY, PA	
YELLOWSTONE	MT, ND, WY	
TALLAHATCHIE	MS	

FOREIGN RIVERS

AA	Algeria	COI	China	LEE	Ireland
BO	Chile	DAL	Sweden	LOA	Chile
OB	Russia	DEE	UK	LOT	France
OM	Russia	DON	Russia	LYS	Belgium
PO	Italy	EMS	Germany	MIN	China
SI	China	EXE	England	MUN	Thailand
WU	China	FLY	Papua New Guinea	MUR	Austria
XI	China	HAB	Pakistan	NAB	Germany
		HAN	China	NAN	Thailand
AAR	Switzerland	HSI	China	OKA	Russia
AIN	France	ICA	Peru	OLT	Romania
AMU	Central Asia	ILI	China	OMO	Ethiopia
APA	Paraguay	ILL	Austria, France	PEI	China
ARO	Venezuela	INN	Germany	RUR	Germany
BOW	Canada	JIU	Romania	SAN	Poland
BUG	Poland	JUR	Egypt	SYR	Central Asia
CAM	England	KAN	China	TAY	Scotland
CHU	Kyrgyzstan, Kazakhstan	KEM	Russia	TZU	China

UFA	Russia	IBAR	Gabon	RAMU	Papua New
UME	Sweden	ILEK	Russia		Guinea
UNA	Croatia, Bosnia	IPEL	Slovakia	RAVI	India
	and Herzegovina	ISAR	Germany	REMS	Germany
URE	England	ISER	Czech Republic	RENO	Italy
USK	Wales, England	IVAI	Brazil	RIET	South Africa
VAH	Slovakia	JARI	Brazil	ROER	Germany
VAR	France	JUBA	Africa	RUHR	Germany
WEI	China	KAMA	Russia	SAAR	France
		KARA	Turkmenistan	SADO	Portugal
AARE	Switzerland	KEMI	Finland	SAMA	Peru
ABRA	Philippines	KLAR	Norway	SAVA	Slovenia, Croatia,
ADDA	Italy	KOSI	India		Bosnia, Serbia
AGNO	Philippines	KUPA	Slovenia, Croatia	SEIM	Ukraine
AIRE	England, France	KURA	Turkey, Georgia,	SEJM	Ukraine
AKSU	Turkey		Azerbaijan	SPEY	Liechtenstein
ALLE	Germany	KUSI	India	STYR	Ukraine
ALMA	Ukraine	KWEI	China	SULA	Ukraine
ALTA	Norway	LAHN	Germany	SURA	Russia
AMGA	Iran	LENA	Russia	SWAN	Australia
AMUR	Asia	LIAO	China	SWAT	Pakistan
ANUJ	Russia	LOIR	France	TAJO	Spain
ARAS	Turkey	LULE	Sweden	TANA	Kenya, Norway
ARDA	Bulgaria	LUNI	India	TARN	France
ARNO	Italy	LWAN	China	TEJO	Spain
ARTA	Greece	MAAS	Netherlands	TISA	Ukraine, Hungary
ATHI	Kenya	MALI	Myanmar	TOMO	Colombia
AUBE	France	MAND	Iran	TURA	Kazakhstan,
AUDE	France	MAYA	Ukraine		Russia
AVON	England	MAYO	Mexico	TYNE	England
AVRE	France	META	Colombia	UELE	Africa
BANN	Ireland	MONO	Togo	URAL	Kazakhstan,
BENI	Bolivia	MSTA	Russia		Russia
BOBR	Poland	MUSI	Indonesia	VAAL	South Africa
CHER	France	NAAB	Germany	VAKH	Russia
CLUJ	Romania	NAPO	Ecuador	WAAL	Netherlands
CRNA	Macedonia	NASS	Canada	YALU	Korea, China
DALY	Australia	NERA	Italy	YANA	Russia
DOCE	Brazil	NEVA	Russia	YSER	France
DOON	Scotland	NILE	Africa	YUAN	China
DRAU	Austria	NMAI	Myanmar		
DRIN	Albania	NORE	Ireland	ABUNA	Bolivia
DUNA	Europe	NYSA	Poland	ADIGE	Italy
EBRO	Spain	ODER	Poland	ADOUR	France
EDER	Germany	OHRE	Germany, Czech	AGOUT	France
EGER	Germany, Czech		Republic	AGUAN	Honduras
	Republic	OISE	France	AISNE	France
ELBE	Germany	ONON	Russia	AKABA	Mongolia
EMBA	Russia	ORNE	France	AKOBO	Ethiopia
EMME	Switzerland	OUSE	England	ALDAN	Russia
ENNS	Austria	OXUS	Central Asia	ALLER	Germany
ERNE	Ireland	PARA	Brazil	ALLIA	Italy
ESLA	Spain	PARU	Brazil	ALUTA	Romania
EURE	France	PING	Thailand	AMECA	Mexico
GEBA	Africa	PITE	Sweden	ANCRE	France
GERS	France	PRUT	Romania	ANGAT	Philippines
HRON	Slovakia	RAAB	Austria	ANNAN	Scotland
HWAI	China	RABA	Austria	APURE	Venezuela
HWEI	China			AQABA	Jordan

ARAKS	Turkey	KAJAN	Guatemala	SHASI	China
ARGES	Romania	KARUN	Iran	SIANG	China
ARGOS	Greece	KASAI	Africa	SIRET	Romania
ARGUN	China, Russia	KATUN	Kazakhstan	SOBAT	Ethiopia
ATRAK	Iran	KHETA	Russia	SOMES	Hungary
ATREK	Iran	KLONG	Thailand	SOSVA	Kazakhstan
ATUEL	Argentina	KOBDO	Mongolia	SPREE	Germany
BAXOY	Sudan	KUBAN	Russia	STOUR	England
BANAS	India	LAGAN	Sweden	SURMA	India
BENIN	Nigeria	LALIN	China	SYNYA	Kazakhstan
BENUE	Africa	LEMPA	El Salvador	TAGUS	Romania
BETWA	India	LIARD	Canada	TAPTI	India
BHIMA	India	LINDI	Congo	TARIM	China
BOSNA	Bosnia and	LIPPE	Germany	TEREK	Georgia, Russia
	Herzegovina	LOIRE	France	TIBER	Italy
BOYNE	Ireland	LULUA	Democratic	TIETE	Brazil
BYTOM	Poland		Republic of the Congo	TIGRE	Ecuador
CAMPO	Cameroon	MARNE	France	TIMIS	Romania, Serbia
CAUCA	Colombia	MEUSE	France		and Montenegro
CAURA	Venezuela	MEZEN	Russia	TISTA	India
CHANG	China	MINHO	Spain	TISZA	Ukraine,
CHARI	Africa	MOSEL	Germany		Hungary
CHETA	Russia	MUTAN	China	TOBOL	Kazakhstan
CLYDE	Scotland	NAMOI	Australia	TORNE	Finland
CONGO	Africa	NEMAN	Belarus,	TRAUN	Austria
CUITO	Africa		Lithuania	TRENT	England,
DESNA	Ukraine	NEGRO	Argentina		Canada
DNEPR	Russia, Belarus,	NERIS	Poland	VENTA	Latvia
	Ukraine	NIGER	Africa	VESLE	France
DOUBS	France	NONNI	China	VISLA	Poland
DOURO	Italy	NOTEC	Poland	WARTA	Poland
DRAVA	Europe	OGLIO	Italy	WESER	Germany
DRAVE	Europe	OGOKI	Canada	WISLA	Poland
DULCE	Argentina	OGOWE	Gabon	XINGU	Brazil
DVINA	Russia, Latvia,	ORTON	Peru		
	Belarus	OSKOL	Russia	ABAKAN	Russia
EIDER	Germany	PALAR	India	AFRINE	Turkey
ETSCH	Italy	PARDO	Brazil	AGUSAN	Philippines
ETSIN	China	PATIA	Colombia	ALBANY	Canada
FARAH	Afghanistan	PEACE	Canada	AMAZON	Brazil
FULDA	Germany	PERAK	Malaysia	ANGARA	Russia
GANGA	India	PIAVE	Italy	ARAGON	Spain
GAUYA	Latvia	PIBOR	Sudan	ARAUCA	Colombia
GOGRA	India	PIURA	Peru	ARIEGE	France
GUDEN	Denmark	PURUS	Peru	ATBARA	Sudan
GUMAL	Pakistan	RAPTI	Nepal	BAFING	Sudan
HAVEL	Germany	REGEN	Germany	BALIKH	Turkey
HUANG	China	REUSS	Switzerland	BARCOO	Australia
ILLER	Germany	RHEIN	Germany	BARITO	Indonesia
INDRE	Colombia	RHINE	Europe	BEAVER	Canada
INDUS	Pakistan	RHONE	France	BELAYA	Russia
IRIKI	Brazil	ROPER	Australia	BIOBIO	Chile
ISERE	France	SAALE	Germany	BRENTA	Italy
ISHIM	Russia	SANGA	Congo	CARONI	Venezuela
ISKER	Bulgaria	SAONE	France	CARROT	Canada
JACUL	Brazil	SARRE	France	CHUBUT	Argentina
JUMNA	India	SEINE	France	CHULYM	Russia
JUTAL	Brazil	SENNE	Belgium	DANUBE	Europe
KAFUE	Africa	SHARI	Africa	DAWSON	Australia

DELICE	Turkey	ORKHON	Mongolia	MADEIRA	Brazil
DNESTR	Ukraine,	PAHANG	Malaysia	MARITSA	Turkey
	Moldova	PARANA	Brazil	MORGHAB	
DONETS	Russia,	PATUCA	Honduras		Afghanistan,
	Ukraine	PECORA	Russia		Turkmenistan
ENISEI	Russia	PENNER	India	MOSELLE	France
FRASER	Canada	PINEGA	Russia	NARBADA	India
GALANA	Kenya	PREGEL	Poland, Russia	NARMADA	India
GAMBIA	Guinea, The	PRIPET	Ukraine,	ORINOCO	Venezuela
	Gambia		Belarus	PECHORA	Russia
GANDAK	Nepal	RAJANG	Indonesia	SALWEEN	Burma
GANGES	India	SALADO	Argentina	SELENGA	Russia
GILGIT	India	SALWIN	Myanmar	SENEGAL	West Africa
HAILAR	China, Russia	SAMARA	Russia	SHANNON	Ireland
HAWASH	Ethiopia	SEVERN	Wales,	SITTANG	Burma
HINGOL	Pakistan		England	SONGHUA	China
IGUACU	Brazil	SONORA	Mexico	SUNGARI	China
INGURI	Georgia	SOURIS	Canada	UCAYALI	Peru
IRTISH	Asia	STRUMA	Bulgaria	URUGUAY	Brazil,
IRTYSH	Asia	SUTLEJ	India		Argentina, Uruguay
JAPURA	Colombia	THAMES	England	VISTULA	Poland
JISERA	Czech Republic	THEISS	Ukraine,	YANGTZE	China
JORDAN	Middle East		Hungary	YENISEI	Russia
KHILOK	Russia	TICINO	Switzerland	YENISEY	Russia
KOLYMA	Russia	TIGRIS	Turkey	ZAMBESI	Africa
KOMATI	South Africa	TUGELA	South Africa	ZAMBEZI	Africa
KURUME	Japan	UAUPES	Colombia		
LIMMAT	Switzerland	UBANGI	Democratic	AMUDARYA	Central
LOANGE	Congo	Republic of the Congo			Asia
LOPORI	Democratic	VIENNE	France	ARAGUAIA	Brazil
Republic of the Congo		VLTAVA	Czech	GODAVARI	India
MADIDI	Bolivia		Republic	HAMILTON	Canada
MAMORE	Bolivia	YALUNG	China	OBIRTYSH	Asia
MEKONG	Asia	YAMUNA	India	OKAVANGO	Africa
MODDER	South Africa	YAPURA	Colombia	PARAGUAY	Brazil,
MOISIE	Canada	YELLOW	China		Paraguay, Argentina
MOLDAU	Czech			PUTUMAYO	Peru
	Republic	ABITIBI	Canada	RIONEGRO	Argentina
MOLOGA	Russia	ALBERGA	Australia	SYRDARYA	Central
MOSCOW	Russia	BERMEJO	South		Asia
MOSKVA	Russia		America		
MURGAB	Afghanistan,		Australia	ATHABASCA	Canada
	Turkmenistan	DARLING	Australia	EUPHRATES	Asia
MURRAY	Australia	DNIEPER	Russia,	IRRAWADDY	India
NECKAR	Germany		Belarus, Ukraine	MACKENZIE	Canada
NEISSE	Poland	GARONNE	France	MAGDALENA	
NELSON	Canada	GLENELG	Australia		Colombia
OLDMAN	Canada	KRISHNA	India	PILCOMAYO	Bolivia,
OLENEK	Russia	KUBANGO	Africa		Paraguay, Argentina
OMOLON	Russia	LIMPOPO	Africa	RIOGRANDE	Mexico
ORANGE	South Africa	LUALABA	Democratic	TOCANTINS	Brazil
		Republic of the Congo			

MOUNTAINS, RANGES, PASSES

ABU	ANDES	ANADIR	VOSGES
API	ARBER	ANTERO	ZAGROS
APO	ATHOS	ARARAT	ALBERES
DOM	ATLAS	ARDOST	ANTHONY
ERZ	BAKER	ARKONA	BERNINA
HOR	BLANC	BAIKAL	BRENNER
IDA	BOLAN	BANDAI	DAPSANG
OMI	BROMO	BLANCA	ELBORUS
OSO	CACHI	BURZIL	EVEREST
TAI	CENIS	CARMEL	FORAKER
ADAM	CORNO	CARNIC	HELICON
AGUA	DICTE	CHUMBI	HUBBARD
AJAX	EIFEL	DARYAL	MAMISON
ALAI	EIGER	DONNER	MUZTAGH
BACO	ELGON	DONREK	NILGIRI
BEAR	EOLUS	EKBERT	OROHENA
CISA	EVANS	ELBRUS	PALOMAR
COOK	GIOVI	ELBRUZ	RAINIER
DUAR	GUMAL	EREBUS	ROCKIES
FUTA	GUYOT	FREJUS	SEMENOV
HARZ	HATYA	GRAIAN	SHAVANO
HENG	HEKLA	GUNTUR	SIMPLON
HOOD	HOREB	HERMON	STELIAS
IJEN	HUILA	KAILAS	SUDETEN
JURA	IDJEN	KAZBEK	VIRGUNA
KIBO	LEONE	KHYBER	CAUCASUS
MERU	LOGAN	KOLIMA	COROPUNA
MIDI	LONGS	KUNLUN	DEMAVEND
MUIR	MAIPO	MAKALU	FUJIYAMA
NEBO	MAYON	MERAPI	HIMALYA
OETA	NECOI	OLIVET	ILLIMANI
OMEI	OZARK	ORTLER	JUNGFRAU
OSSA	POTRO	PELION	MCKINLEY
RIGI	PULAR	POCONO	PYRENEES
TAAL	RATON	ROBSON	WRANGELL
TAIF	SIPKA	SAHAMA	ACONCAGUA
TODI	SIANI	SEGURA	ANNAPURNA
URAL	TABOR	SHASTA	APPENINES
VISO	TAHAN	SHIPKA	DOLOMITES
ALDAN	ALADAG	TACANA	NANDADEVI
ALLEN	ALATAU	TAUNUS	PIKESPEAK
ALTAI	ALUBLA	TOLIMA	TUPUNGATO
ALTAR	ALWAND	TRISUL	CHIMBORAZO
ALTYN	AMPATO	ULAWUN	MATTERHORN

VOLCANOES

ASO	NASU	ASKJA	KELUT
AWU	NYOS	AZUMA	KISKA
OKU	POAS	BALBI	MANAM
USU	RUIZ	BATUR	MAYON
ETNA	SIAU	FUEGO	OKMOK
FOGO	TAAL	GEDEH	OSIMA
FUJI	AETNA	HEKLA	PAGAN
GEDE	ASAMA	IRAZU	PASTO

PELEE	HUDSON	PURACE	LAASCAR
RAUNG	IZALCO	RABAUL	LANGILA
YASUR	KARKAR	SANGAY	LIAIMA
AJUSCO	KATMAI	SEGUAM	OMETEPE
AKUTAN	KRAFLA	SEMERU	REDOUBT
ALCEDO	LASCAR	SHASTA	TAMBORA
AMBRYM	LASSEN	SLAMET	TRIDENT
ANTUCO	LLAIMA	TACANA	KARTHALA
ARAYAT	LOPEVI	TELICA	KRAKATOA
ARENAL	MARAPI	TIATIA	KRAKATAU
BIGBEN	MASAYA	TOLIMA	MAUNALOA
CHOKAI	MAZAMA	ATITLAN	PINATUBO
COLIMA	MERAPI	CHICHON	RINDJANI
DOINYO	ONTAKE	ERTAALE	VESUVIUS
DOMUYO	OSORNO	GARELOI	
DUKONO	PACAYA	ILIAMNA	
EREBUS	PAVLOF	KILAUEA	

LAKES, SEAS

RED	ATLIN	ONEGA	PEIPUS
REE	ATTER	PETEN	RUDOLF
SEG	BAKER	POOPO	SAGAMI
VAN	BALAH	PSKOV	SALTON
ZEE	BELOE	TAHOE	SCOTIA
ZUG	BLACK	TAUPO	SIMCOE
ARAL	CADDO	TSANA	TASMAN
AZOV	CHANY	TUMBA	VANERN
BAFA	CHINA	URMIA	ANDAMAN
BAHR	CORAL	WHITE	ARABIAN
BIWA	ELTON	ACHKEL	ARAFURA
CHAD	ENARE	AEGEAN	ATITLAN
COMO	GARDA	ALAKUL	BALATON
DEAD	GARRY	ALBANO	BALKASH
DEBO	HURON	ALBERT	BARENTS
ERIE	ILMEN	ANNECY	CASPIAN
ISEO	INARI	APOPKA	DUBAWNT
KARA	JAPAN	BABINE	NIPIGON
KIVU	JUNIN	BAIKAL	ONTARIO
MEAD	KYOGA	BALTIC	TORRENS
ROSS	LANAO	BERING	ADRIATIC
SULU	LEMAN	DONNER	BEAUFORT
TAAL	MERIN	IONIAN	BISMARCK
TANA	MINTO	IZABAL	CARIBBEAN
THUN	MIRIM	KHANKA	MANITOBA
ABAYA	MWERU	LADOGA	MICHIGAN
AMMER	NIRIZ	LAPTEV	SUPERIOR
AMPER	NORTH	MAGADI	TITICACA
ASNEN	NYASA	ONEIDA	MEDITERRANEAN

WATERFALLS

JOG	AKAKA	KEGON	ELSALO
LIN	ANGEL	SAULT	FINCHA
LYN	BOWEN	SEVEN	GUAIRA
FOSS	DELLA	TOWER	HANDOL
FRUA	DETTI	TULLY	HELENA
LINN	FORCE	VETTI	HOWICK
TWIN	GLASS	AGOYAN	IGUAZU

KRIMML	YUDAKI	NIAGARA	VICTORIA
MARINA	CASCADE	PANTHER	WALLAMAN
NARADA	CAUVERY	PASSAIC	YOSEMITE
RIBBON	FEATHER	RHAIADR	GIESSBACH
SIMMEN	GASTEIN	RUACANA	HORSESHOE
SKYKJE	GLOMACH	CATARACT	MINNEHAHA
TUGELA	GOLLING	CUQUENAN	STAUBBACH
VERNAL	HANDEGG	GAVARNIE	BRIDALVEIL
VETTIS	IGUASSU	SHOSHONE	CUMBERLAND
VORING	KALAMBO	TAKAKKAW	

DESERTS

ERG	ARUNTA	ALHAMAD	SONORAN
REG	GIBSON	ANNAFUD	COLORADO
GOBI	DAHAMA	ARABIAN	KALAHARI
THAR	LIBYAN	ATACAMA	KIZILKUM
DAHNA	MOJAVE	KARAKUM	KYZYLKUM
NAMIB	NUBIAN	PAINTED	VIZCAINO
NEFUD	SAHARA	QARAQUM	PATAGONIA
SHAMO	SYRIAN	SECHURA	DEATHVALLEY

BRIDGES

EADS	LONDON	SEVERIN	HELLGATE
ELSA	MAPIMI	STJOHNS	LONGVIEW
FORTH	MTHOPE	VECCHIO	MACKINAC
MERIC	QUEBEC	WESTEND	MIRABEAU
SANDO	RIALTO	ARRABIDA	TRANSBAY
SIGHS	BAYONNE	BROOKLYN	WATERLOO
STORY	BIRECIK	BURDEKIN	GOLDENGATE
TOWER	NARROWS	CORNWALL	TRIBOROUGH
HOBART	OAKLAND	DEERISLE	VERRAZANO
HOWRAH	RAINBOW	FORTPITT	WHITESTONE

DAMS

GURI	CONTRA	WISHON	SANLUIS
MICA	COUGAR	ATATURK	TARBELA
OAHE	DEGRAY	BRIONES	TRINITY
ASWAN	FRIANT	CACHUMA	TUCURUI
ERTAN	GRANBY	CARTERS	WATAUGA
GATUN	HOOVER	CASITAS	BLUEMESA
GORKY	INGURI	CHIRKEY	COGSWELL
KEBAN	KARIBA	CICEROZ	DWORSHAK
NUREK	KISHAU	COCHITI	FORTPECK
ROGUN	KUROBE	CONCHAS	GARDINER
SWIFT	MANGLA	CURNERA	GARRISON
TANDA	MCNARY	ELCAJON	KAKHOVKA
TEHRI	NAVAJO	FONTANA	KINGSLEY
WYMAN	SAKUMA	HIRAKUD	KREMASTA
ASSUAN	SHASTA	LUZZONE	MERRIMAN
BEKHME	SULTAN	PACTOLA	MRATINJE
BHAKRA	VAIONT	PAHLEVI	OROVILLE
BUFORD	WINSOR	SANFORD	PINEFLAT

CANADA AT A GLANCE

Province	Date*	Abbr.	Capital
1 Alberta	1905	AB, Alta.	Edmonton
2 British Columbia	1871	BC, B.C.	Victoria
3 Manitoba	1870	MB, Man.	Winnipeg
4 New Brunswick	1867	NB, N.B.	Fredericton
5 Newfoundland	1949	NF, Nfld., Newf.	St. John's
6 Nova Scotia	1867	NS, N.S.	Halifax
7 Ontario[1]	1867	ON, Ont.	Toronto
8 Prince Edward Island[2]	1873	PE, P.E.I.	Charlottetown
9 Quebec[3]	1867	QC, PQ, Que.	Quebec
10 Saskatchewan	1905	SK, Sask.	Regina

Territory	Abbr.	Capital
11 Yukon	YT, Y.T.	Whitehorse
12 Northwest Territories	NT, N.W.T.	Yellowknife
13 Nunavut	NU	Iqaluit

*Date of entry of province into Confederation
[1]Largest province in area
[2]Smallest province in area and population
[3]Largest province in population

PRIME MINISTERS

Name	Party	Term	Birthplace	Occupation
MACDONALD, Sir John Alexander	Cons.	1867–73	Glasgow, Scotland	Lawyer
MACKENZIE, Alexander	Liberal	1873–78	Pertshire, Scotland	
(MACDONALD, Sir JA)		1878–91		
ABBOTT, Sir John Joseph Caldwell	Cons.	1891–92	St. Andrews, PQ	Lawyer
THOMPSON, Sir John Sparrow David	Cons.	1892–94	Halifax, NS	Lawyer
BOWELL, Sir Mackenzie	Cons.	1894–96	Rickinghall, England	Editor
TUPPER, Sir Charles	Cons.	1896	Amherst, NS	Doctor
LAURIER, Sir Wilfrid	Liberal	1896–1911	St. Lin, PQ	Lawyer
BORDEN, Sir Robert Laird	Cons.-Unionist	1911–20	Grand Pre, NS	Civil servant
MEIGHEN, Arthur	Cons.-Unionist	1920–21	Perth, Ont.	Lawyer
KING, William Lyon Mackenzie	Liberal	1921–26	Kitchener, ON	Civil servant
(MEIGHEN, Arthur)		1926		
(KING, W.L. Mackenzie)		1926–30		
BENNETT, Richard Bedford	Cons.	1930–35	Hopewell, NB	Lawyer
(KING, W.L. Mackenzie)		1935–48		
STLAURENT, Louis Stephen	Liberal	1948–57	PQ	Lawyer
DIEFENBAKER, John George	Prog. Cons.	1957–63	Grey Co., ON	Lawyer

Name	Party	Term	Birthplace	Occupation
PEARSON, Lester Bowles	Liberal	1963–68	Toronto, ON	Historian
TRUDEAU, Pierre Elliot	Liberal	1968–79	Montreal, PQ	Lawyer
CLARK, Joe	Prog. Cons.	1979–80	High River, AB	Lawyer
(TRUDEAU, Pierre Elliot)		1980–84		
TURNER John Napier	Liberal	1984	Richmond, England	Lawyer
MULRONEY, Martin Brian	Prog. Cons.	1984–1993	Baie Comeau, PQ	Lawyer
CAMPBELL, Kim (Avril Phaedra)	Prog. Cons.	1993	Port Alberni, BC	Lawyer
CHRETIEN, (Joseph-Jacques) Jean	Liberal	1993–2003	Shawinigan, PQ	Lawyer
MARTIN, Paul Edgar	Liberal	2003–	Windsor, ON	Lawyer

THE UNITED STATES AT A GLANCE

	State	No.*	Abbr.	Capital
1	ALABAMA	22	AL, Ala.	Montgomery
2	ALASKA[1]	49	AK, Alas.	Juneau
3	ARIZONA	48	AZ, Ariz.	Phoenix
4	ARKANSAS	25	AR, Ark.	Little Rock
5	CALIFORNIA[2]	31	CA, Cal(if).	Sacramento
6	COLORADO	38	CO, Col(o).	Denver
7	CONNECTICUT	5	CT, Conn.	Hartford
8	DELAWARE	1	DE, Del.	Dover
9	FLORIDA	27	FL, Fla.	Tallahassee
10	GEORGIA	4	GA, Ga.	Atlanta
11	HAWAII	50	HI, Haw.	Honolulu
12	IDAHO	43	ID, Id.	Boise
13	ILLINOIS	21	IL, Ill.	Springfield
14	INDIANA	19	IN, Ind.	Indianapolis
15	IOWA	29	IA, Ia.	Des Moines
16	KANSAS	34	KS, Kan(s).	Topeka
17	KENTUCKY	15	KY, Ky.	Frankfort
18	LOUISIANA	18	LA, La	Baton Rouge
19	MAINE	23	ME, Me.	Augusta
20	MARYLAND	7	MD, Md.	Annapolis
21	MASSACHUSETTS	6	MA, Mass.	Boston
22	MICHIGAN	26	MI, Mich.	Lansing
23	MINNESOTA	32	MN, Minn.	St. Paul
24	MISSISSIPPI	20	MS, Miss.	Jackson
25	MISSOURI	24	MO, Mo.	Jefferson City
26	MONTANA	41	MT, Mont.	Helena
27	NEBRASKA	37	NE, Neb(r).	Lincoln
28	NEVADA	36	NV, Nev.	Carson City
29	NEW HAMPSHIRE	9	NH, N.H.	Concord
30	NEW JERSEY	3	NJ, N.J.	Trenton
31	NEW MEXICO	47	NM, N.M.	Santa Fe
32	NEW YORK	11	NY, N.Y.	Albany
33	NORTH CAROLINA	12	NC, N.C.	Raleigh
34	NORTH DAKOTA	39	ND, N.D.	Bismarck
35	OHIO	17	OH, O.	Columbus

	State	No.*	Abbr.	Capital
36	OKLAHOMA	46	OK, Okla.	Oklahoma City
37	OREGON	33	OR, Ore.	Salem
38	PENNSYLVANIA	2	PA, Penn(a).	Harrisburg
39	RHODE ISLAND[3]	13	RI, R.I.	Providence
40	SOUTH CAROLINA	8	SC, S.C.	Columbia
41	SOUTH DAKOTA	40	SD, S.D.	Pierre
42	TENNESSEE	16	TN, Tenn.	Nashville
43	TEXAS	28	TX, Tex.	Austin
44	UTAH	45	UT, Ut.	Salt Lake City
45	VERMONT	14	VT, Vt.	Montpelier
46	VIRGINIA	10	VA, Va.	Richmond
47	WASHINGTON	42	WA, Wash.	Olympia
48	WEST VIRGINIA	35	WV, W.Va.	Charleston
49	WISCONSIN	30	WI, Wis(c).	Madison
50	WYOMING	44	WY, Wyo.	Cheyenne
---	DISTRICT OF COLUMBIA		DC	Washington

*Order of admission into the Union; 1–13 Original States
[1]Largest in area, smallest in population
[2]Largest in population
[3]Smallest in area

	State Nickname	State Motto
1	Heart of Dixie, Cotton, Camellia State	We Dare Defend Our Rights
2	The Last Frontier	North to the Future
3	Grand Canyon, Sunset Land	Ditat Deus: God Enriches
4	Natural, Razorback	Regnat Populus: The People Rule
5	Golden, Grape	Eureka: I Have Found It
6	Centennial, Rover	Nil Sine Numine: Nothing without Providence
7	Constitution, Nutmeg	Qui Transtulit Sustinet: He who transplanted still sustains
8	First, Diamond	Liberty and Independence
9	Sunshine, Everglade	In God We Trust
10	Empire State of the South, Peach	Wisdom, Justice, Moderation
11	Aloha	The Life of the Land is Perpetuated In Righteousness
12	Gem, Gem of the Mountains	Esto Perpetua: Exist Forever
13	Prairie, Sucker State	State Sovereignty, National Union
14	Hoosier, Carnation	Crossroads of America
15	Hawkeye, Beautiful Land	Our Liberties We Prize, And Our Rights We Will Maintain
16	Sunflower, Jayhawk	Ad Astra Per Aspera: To The Stars Through Difficulties
17	Bluegrass	United We Stand, Divided We Fall
18	Pelican, Sugar, Creole	Union, Justice, Confidence
19	Pine Tree, Lumber	Dirigo: I Direct
20	Old Line, Free	Fatti Maschili, Parole Femine: Strong Deeds, Gentle Words
21	Bay, Old Colony	Ense Petit Placidam Sub Libertate Quietem: By the Sword We Seek Peace, but Peace Only Under Liberty
22	Great Lakes, Wolverine	Si Quaeris Peninsulam Amoenam, Circumspice: If You Seek a Pleasant Peninsula Look About You

	State Nickname	State Motto
23	North Star, Gopher	L'Etoile du Nord: Star of the North
24	Magnolia, Bayou	Virtute et Armis: By Valor and Arms
25	Show Me, Bullion	Salus Populi Suprema Lex Esto: The Welfare of the People Shall Be the Supreme Law
26	Treasure, Bonanza	Oro y Plata: Gold and Silver
27	Cornhusker, Beef	Equality Before the Law
28	Sagebrush, Silver, Battle-Born	All for Our Country
29	Granite, White Mountain	Live Free or Die
30	Garden	Liberty and Prosperity
31	Land of Enchantment, Sunshine	Crescit Eundo: It Grows as it Goes
32	Empire	Excelsior: Ever Upward
33	Tar Heel, Old North	Esse Quam Videri: To be Rather Than To Seem
34	Peace Garden, Sioux, Flickertail	Liberty and Union, Now and Forever, One and Inseparable
35	Buckeye	With God All Things Are Possible
36	Sooner	Labor Omnia Vincit: Labor Conquers All Things
37	Beaver, Webfoot	She Flies With Her Own Wings
38	Keystone, Quaker, Steel	Virtue, Liberty, and Independence
39	Little Rhody, Ocean	Hope
40	Palmetto	Dum Spiro, Spero: While I Breathe, I Hope
41	Coyote, Mount Rushmore	Under God, The People Rule
42	Volunteer, Big Bend	Agriculture and Commerce
43	Lone Star, Beef	Friendship
44	Beehive, Mormon	Industry
45	Green Mountain	Freedom and Unity
46	Old Dominion, Cavalier	Sic Semper Tyrannis: Thus Always to Tyrants
47	Evergreen, Chinook	Alki: Bye and Bye
48	Mountain, Panhandle	Montani Semper Liberi: Mountaineers Are Always Free
49	Badger, Cheese	Forward
50	Equality, Cowboy	Equal Rights
DC		Justitia Omnibus: Justice for All

	State Flower	State Tree	State Bird
1	Camelia	Southern pine	Yellowhammer
2	Forget-me-not	Sitka spruce	Willow ptarmigan
3	Saguaro cactus	Paloverde	Cactus wren
4	Apple blossom	Pine	Mockingbird
5	Golden poppy	Calif. Redwood	Calif. valley quail
6	Columbine	Blue spruce	Lark bunting
7	Mountain laurel	White oak	American robin
8	Peach blossom	American holly	Blue hen chicken
9	Orange blossom	Sabal palmetto palm	Mockingbird
10	Cherokee rose	Live oak	Brown thrasher
11	Hibiscus	Candlenut	Hawaiian goose
12	Syringa	White pine	Mountain bluebird
13	Butterfly violet	White oak	Cardinal
14	Peony	Tulip poplar	Cardinal
15	Wild rose	Oak	Eastern goldfinch
16	Sunflower	Cottonwood	Western meadowlark
17	Goldenrod	Kentucky coffee tree	Cardinal
18	Magnolia	Cypress	Eastern brown pelican
19	Pine cone & tassel	Eastern white pine	Chickadee

	State Flower	State Tree	State Bird
20	Black-eyed Susan	White oak	Baltimore oriole
21	Mayflower	American elm	Chickadee
22	Apple blossom	White pine	Robin
23	Lady's slipper	Red pine	Common loon
24	Magnolia	Magnolia	Mockingbird
25	Hawthorn	Dogwood	Bluebird
26	Bitterroot	Ponderosa pine	Western meadowlark
27	Goldenrod	Cottonwood	Western meadowlark
28	Sagebrush	Single-leaf piñon	Mountain bluebird
29	Purple lilac	White birch	Purple finch
30	Purple violet	Red oak	Eastern goldfinch
31	Yucca	Piñon, pinyon	Roadrunner
32	Rose	Sugar maple	Bluebird
33	Dogwood	Pine	Cardinal
34	Wild prairie rose	American elm	Western meadowlark
35	Scarlet carnation	Buckeye	Cardinal
36	Mistletoe	Redbug	Scissor-tailed flycatcher
37	Oregon grape	Douglas fir	Western meadowlark
38	Mountain laurel	Hemlock	Ruffed grouse
39	Violet	Red maple	Rhode Island red
40	Carolina jessamine	Palmetto	Carolina wren
41	Pasque flower	Black Hills spruce	Ringnecked pheasant
42	Iris	Tulip poplar	Mockingbird
43	Bluebonnet	Pecan	Mockingbird
44	Sego lily	Blue spruce	Seagull
45	Red clover	Sugar maple	Hermit thrush
46	American dogwood	Dogwood	Cardinal
47	Western rhododendron	Western hemlock	Willow goldfinch
48	Big rhododendron	Sugar maple	Cardinal
49	Wood violet	Sugar maple	Robin
50	Indian paintbrush	Cottonwood	Meadowlark
DC	American beauty rose	Scarlet oak	Wood thrush

NB.: Refer to p. 615 for state numbers

OUTLYING U.S. AREAS

Name	Capital	Motto
AMERICAN SAMOA	Pago Pago	Samoa Muamua le Atua (In Samoa, God is First)
GUAM	Hagatna	Where America's Day Begins
NORTHERN MARIANA	Saipan	
PUERTO RICO	San Juan	Joannes Est Nomen Eius (John is his name)
VIRGIN ISLANDS	Charlotte Amalie	

Name	Flower	Bird	Tree
AMERICAN SAMOA	Paogo (Ula-fala)		
GUAM	Puti Tai Nobio (Bougainvillea)	Toto (Fruit dove)	Ifit (Intsiabijuga)
NORTHERN MARIANA	Pumeria	Marianas Fruit Dove	Flame Tree
PUERTO RICO	Maga, Hibiscus	Reinita	Ceiba
VIRGIN ISLANDS	Yellow elder (Ginger Thomas)	Yellow breast	

HERALDRY

BEARINGS

CHARGE ORDINARY AND SUB-ORDINARY
*Indicates roundels

BAR	BENDY	CANTON	BORDURE
BEND	CHIEF	CLOSET	CHEVRON
COST	CROSS	COTISE	ENDORSE
FESS	FESSE	FILLET	FLANCHE
FRET	FILET	GARTER	QUARTER
GOLP*	FUSIL	MASCLE	ROUNDEL*
GORE	GEMEL	OGRESS*	SALTIER
GUZE*	GOLPE	ORANGE*	SALTIRE
HURT*	GYRON	PALLET	TORTEAU*
ORLE	LABEL	PELLET*	BARRULET
PALE	PLATE*	RIBAND	DANCEE
PALL	POMEY*	RUSTRE	SALTOREL
PILE	SCARP	SCARPE	TRESSURE
SYKE*	BEZANT*	VIROLE*	CHEVRONEL
BATON	BILLET	ANNULET*	SHAKEFORK

CROSS(LIKE)

CRUX	ANCREE	POTENT	PATONCE
PATY	BOTONE	AVELLAN	SALTIRE
URDE	BOTONY	BOTONEE	CERCELEE
URDY	CLECHE	CERCELE	CRUSILEE
FLORY	FITCHE	CRUSILE	FOURCHEE
POMME	FLEURY	FITCHEE	SARCELLE
URDEE	MOLINE	FOURCHE	

CREATURES

GRAY	badger	TALBOT	hound
LOUP	wolf	WYVERN	dragon
ALAND	mastiff	ENFIELD	fox-wolf
BROCK	badger	GRIFFON	lion-eagle
HARPY	woman-bird	GRYPHON	= GRIFFON
GRICE	young boar	LIONCEL	little lion
TYGER	tiger	MARTLET	bird
WYVER	dragon	MUSIMON	goat-ram
ALANDT	mastiff	ALLERION	eagle
BAGWYN	antelope-horse	OPENICUS	lion-dragon
CANNET	duck	POPINJAY	parrot
CHOUGH	raven	SANGLIER	wild boar

POSITIONS OF CREATURES

ASSIS	sitting	JESSANT	lying over
JACENT	lying over	PASSANT	walking
NATANT	swimming	RAMPANT	reared up
SEJANT	sitting	ROUSANT	rising
VOLANT	flying	SALIENT	leaping
VORANT	eating	STATANT	standing
COURANT	running	URINANT	diving
DORMANT	lying down	COUCHANT	lying
FLOTANT	floating	HAURIANT	diving
FORCENE	rearing	HAURIENT	diving
ISSUANT	partly visible	TRIPPANT	tripping

OBJECTS

VOL	two wings	TORSE	sheath
BREY	barnacle	GOUTTE	drop
SEAX	scimitar	MANCHE	sleeve
SYKE	fountain	MULLET	star
WEEL	fishtrap	TIRRET	manacle
BATON	staff	BOTEROL	sheath end
GERBE	sheaf	ESCROLL	scroll
LAVER	colter	ESTOILE	star
PHEON	arrowhead	LYMPHAD	boat

TINCTURES

OR	gold	TENNE	orange
VERT	green	ARGENT	silver
AZURE	blue	MURREY	dark red
GULES	red	PURPURE	purple
SABLE	black		

LINES OF PARTITION

NOWY	URDY	POTENTY	EMBATTLED
ONDE	WAVY	INDENTED	ENGRAILED
UNDE	NEBULY	INVECTED	RAYONNANT
UNDY	RAGULY	DANCETTY	DOVETAILED

FURS

PEAN	VAIR	ERMINE	POTENT

CADENCY
LINE OF SUCCESSION

LABEL	heir	ANNULET	5th son
CRESCENT	2nd son	FLEURDELIS	6th son
MULLET	3rd son	ROSE	7th son
MARTLET	4th son	MOLINE	8th son

OTHER TERMS

AILE	winged	TIERCE	in 3 parts
ENTE	grafted	TREFLE	three-lobed
PALY	divided vertically	APPAUME	showing palm
SEME	sprinkled, strewn	COMPONE	= GOBONY
VULN	to wound	EMBOWED	bent
BARRY	with horizontal bars	ENFILED	passed through
CLOUE	nail-studded	FRACTED	broken
GUTTE	semé of drops	IMBRUED	blood-stained
GUTTY	= GUTTE	MASCULY	lozenged
NOWED	knotted	UNGULED	hoofed
ROMPU	broken	ADDORSED	back to back
ACCOLE	side by side	AFFRONTE	face to face
CHECKY	checkered	AVERSANT	showing back
COUPED	cut off	CABOSHED	showing head
DEXTER	right side (of wearer)	DEBRUISE	cover partly
GOBONY	divided into squares	ENGOULED	partly swallowed
GRINED	maned	SANGLANT	bleeding
GUSSET	abatement	SINISTER	left side (of wearer)

LANGUAGE
LANGUAGE FAMILIES AND GROUPS

ARYAN	TURKIC	GERMANIC	AUSTRALIAN
BANTU	URALIC	HELLENIC	FINNOUGRIC
GREEK		KANARESE	INDONESIAN
INDIC	ARAMAIC	MONGOLIC	MELANESIAN
MUNDA	CHUVASH	MONKHMER	POLYNESIAN
TAMIL	HAMITIC	SLAVONIC	
TATAR	IRANIAN	TEUTONIC	HYPERBOREAN
YAKUT	MALAYAN		INDOCHINESE
	ROMANCE	BRYTHONIC	INDOIRANIAN
ALTAIC	ROMANIC	CANAANITE	MICRONESIAN
ARABIC	SEMITIC	CAUCASIAN	SINOTIBETAN
BALTIC		DRAVIDIAN	
CELTIC	AKKADIAN	INDOARYAN	INDOEUROPEAN
ITALIC	ALBANIAN	MONGOLIAN	INDOGERMANIC
PAPUAN	ARMENIAN	TASMANIAN	SCANDINAVIAN
SLAVIC	CUSHITIC		
TELUGU	ETHIOPIC	ANDAMANESE	

AMERICAN INDIAN LANGUAGE FAMILIES

(See page 730; names of languages and tribes are often the same)

COOS	WASHO	CADDOAN	ARAWAKAN
EYAK	WIYOT	CARIBAN	IROQUOIAN
POMO	YUCHI	CHINOOK	TSIMSHIAN
YUKI	YUMAN	KERESAN	ALGONQUIAN
ZUNI	YUROK	TLINGIT	ARAUCANIAN
HAIDA	AYMARA	ACHOMAWI	ATHAPASCAN
KAROK	MIXTEC	KOOTENAI	UTOAZTECAN
KIOWA	SHASTA	PENUTIAN	ESKIMOALEUT
MAYAN	SIOUAN	SALISHAN	NATCHEZ-
OTOMI	TANOAN	WAKASHAN	MUSKOGEAN

LANGUAGES

WA	BUGI	TAAL	DUTCH
WU	EFIK	THAI	FANTI
	ERSE	TINO	GALLA
EWE	FULA	TODA	GANDA
GEG	GARO	TOSK	GONDI
IBO	GEEZ	TULU	GREEK
KUI	KAMI	TUPI	HAKKA
LAI	KOMI	URDU	HAUSA
LAO	LAPP	XOSA	IRISH
MIN	LUBA	ZULU	KAREN
MRU	MANX		KHOND
TAI	MAYA	ATTIC	KOINE
TWI	MOLE	BATAK	LATIN
	MORO	BIKOL	LIMBU
AINU	NAGA	CARIB	MAKUA
AMOY	PALA	CROAT	MALAY
AVAR	PALI	CZECH	MALTO
BHIL	RONG	DAYAK	MAORI
BODO	SHAN	DORIC	MOSSI

MUONG	MANGAR	LAPPISH	KASHMIRI
MURMI	MINOAN	LATVIAN	KHERWARI
ORAON	NAVAJO	LEONESE	KIMBUNDU
ORIYA	NEPALI	LETTISH	LESGHIAN
OSCAN	NEWARI	LINGALA	LIVONIAN
PAMIR	OSTYAK	LOMBARD	MADURESE
PARSI	PAHARI	MARATHI	MALAGASY
PUNIC	PASHTO	MOABITE	MANDARIN
SABIR	PIDGIN	NAHUATL	MANDINGO
SHINA	POLISH	OSSETIC	PAMPANGO
SOTHO	PUSHTU	PAHLAVI	PHRYGIAN
TAGAL	ROMANY	PERMIAN	ROMANIAN
TAINO	RUANDA	PERSIAN	RUMANIAN
TAMIL	SAMOAN	PRAKRIT	SANSKRIT
TATAR	SINDHI	PUNJABI	SUMATRAN
TIGRE	SLOVAC	QUECHUA	SUMERIAN
UGRIC	SOMALI	QUICHUA	TAHITIAN
UZBEK	SYRIAC	ROMANSH	THRACIAN
VEDIC	TADJIK	RUSSIAN	TURKOMAN
VOGUL	TAGALA	SANTALI	UKRANIAN
WELSH	TAJIKI	SERBIAN	
XHOSA	TELUGU	SIAMESE	
	TONGAN	SLOVENE	AFRIKAANS
AEOLIC	TSWANA	SORBIAN	ALEMANNIC
AFGHAN	TUAREG	SPANISH	BULGARIAN
ARABIC	TUSCAN	SWABIAN	CAMBODIAN
ARAWAK	UIGHUR	SWAHILI	CANTONESE
AYMARA	VISAYA	SWEDISH	CHEREMISS
BASQUE	VOTYAK	TAGALOG	HOTTENTOT
BERBER	YORUBA	TIBETAN	ICELANDIC
BIHARI		TURKISH	KAMCHADAL
BISAYA	AEOLIAN	TURKMEN	KASHUBIAN
BRETON	AMHARIC	UMBRIAN	MALAYALAM
CELTIC	ARAMAIC	VISAYAN	NAVARRESE
COPTIC	AVESTAN	WENDISH	NORWEGIAN
CREOLE	BALUCHI	YENISEI	PROVENCAL
CRETAN	BASHKIR	YIDDISH	RUTHENIAN
CYMRIC	BENGALI	YUKAGIR	SARDINIAN
DANISH	BURMESE		SINHALESE
FRENCH	CATALAN	AKKADIAN	SUNDANESE
GAELIC	CEBUANO	ALBANIAN	TOCHARIAN
GALCHA	CHIBCHA	ANNAMESE	TOKHARIAN
GERMAN	CHINESE	ARMENIAN	UKRAINIAN
GOTHIC	CHUVASH	ASSAMESE	
HARARI	CORNISH	BALINESE	ANDALUSIAN
HEBREW	CYPRIAN	BAVARIAN	CIRCASSIAN
IGOROT	ENGLISH	BOEOTIAN	CORINTHIAN
IONIAN	FAROESE	ESTONIAN	HINDUSTANI
KACHIN	FINNISH	FRANKISH	LITHUANIAN
KAFIRI	FLEMISH	GALICIAN	PHOENICIAN
KAZAKH	FRISIAN	GEORGIAN	PORTUGUESE
KELTIC	GAULISH	GOIDELIC	RAJASTHANI
KODAGU	GUARANI	GUJARATI	SINGHALESE
KOREAN	HITTITE	HAWAIIAN	VIETNAMESE
KYMRIC	ILOCANO	ILLYRIAN	
LEPCHA	IRANIAN	JAPANESE	AZARBAIJANI
LYDIAN	ITALIAN	JAVANESE	AZERBAIJANI
MAGYAR	KHALKHA	KANARESE	BYELORUSSIAN
	KIRGHIZ		
	KURDISH		

ALPHABETS
ENGLISH

A	1	LX	24	PEE	16
E	5	WY	25	TEE	20
I	9	BEE	2	VEE	22
O	15	CEE	3	WYE	25
U	21	CUE	17	ZED	26
AR	18	DEE	4	ZEE	26
EF	6	ESS	19	AITCH	8
EL	12	GEE	7	DOUBLEU	23
EM	13	JAY	10		
EN	14	KAY	11		

ARABIC

BA	2	AYN	18	THA	4
FA	20	JIM	5	WAW	27
HA	6, 26	KAF	22	ZAY	11
RA	10	KHA	7	ALIF	1
TA	3,16	LAM	23	DHAL	9
YA	28	MIM	24	SHIN	13
ZA	17	NUN	25	GHAYN	19
DAD	15	SAD	14		
DAL	8	SIN	12		

GREEK

MU	12	RHO	17	KAPPA	10
NU	13	TAU	19	OMEGA	24
PI	16	BETA	2	SIGMA	18
XI	14	IOTA	9	THETA	8
CHI	22	ZETA	6	LAMBDA	11
ETA	7	ALPHA	1	EPSILON	5
PHI	21	DELTA	4	OMICRON	15
PSI	23	GAMMA	3	UPSILON	20

HEBREW

HE	5	ALEF	1	SHIN	22
PE	17	AYIN	16	TETH	9
AIN	16	BETH	2	YODH	10
MEM	13	CAPH	11	ALEPH	1
NUN	14	ELEF	1	CHETH	8
SIN	21	KAPH	11	GIMEL	3
TAV	23	KOPH	19	ZAYIN	7
TAW	23	QOPH	19	DALETH	4
VAU	6	RESH	20	LAMEDH	12
WAW	6	SADE	18	SAMEKH	15

LITERATURE
AUTHORS

LEE	STAEL	PROUST	ANDERSON
PAZ	STEIN	SINGER	ANNUNZIO
	STOWE	STERNE	BENCHLEY
AGEE	SWIFT	STYRON	BRADBURY
AMIS	TWAIN	TAGORE	CHANDLER
ASCH	TYLER	UPDIKE	CHRISTIE
BUCK	VERNE	WALKER	DOCTOROW
FORD	WAUGH	WARREN	FAULKNER
GIDE	WELLS	WRIGHT	FIELDING
GREY	WELTY		FLAUBERT
HUGO	WHITE	BALDWIN	FORESTER
JONG	WOLFE	BELLAMY	GORDIMER
MANN	WOOLF	BURGESS	HEINLEIN
RAND	WYLIE	CALVINO	KENEALLY
ROTH	ZWEIG	CARROLL	KOSINSKI
SAND		CHEEVER	LAGERLOF
WOUK	ALCOTT	CLAVELL	LAWRENCE
ZOLA	ALGREN	CLEMENS	MELVILLE
	ASIMOV	COLETTE	MEREDITH
AIKEN	ATWOOD	DICKENS	MICHENER
AUDEN	AUSTEN	DINESEN	MITCHELL
BARTH	BALZAC	DREISER	MORRISON
BENET	BARRIE	DURRELL	RABELAIS
CAMUS	BELLOC	FORSTER	SALINGER
CAPEK	BELLOW	FUENTES	SINCLAIR
CRANE	BIERCE	GOLDING	STENDHAL
DEFOE	BORGES	HAMMETT	TROLLOPE
DOYLE	BRETON	HOWELLS	TURGENEV
DUMAS	BRONTE	HURSTON	VONNEGUT
ELIOT	CAPOTE	KEROUAC	
GOGOL	CATHER	KIPLING	CERVANTES
GORKY	CONRAD	LARDNER	DOS PASSOS
GRASS	COOPER	LEACOCK	HAWTHORNE
GREER	DAUDET	LESSING	HEMINGWAY
HARDY	DAVIES	MALAMUD	MCCULLERS
HARTE	FERBER	MALRAUX	MOOREHEAD
HENRY	GOETHE	MAUGHAM	PASTERNAK
HESSE	GUZMAN	MAURIAC	STEINBECK
JAMES	HELLER	NABOKOV	STEVENSON
JOYCE	HERSEY	NAIPAUL	THACKERAY
KAFKA	HOLMES	PYNCHON	
LEWIS	IRVING	RICHLER	FITZGERALD
LOWRY	KRANTZ	ROLLAND	MCCULLOUGH
MILNE	LESAGE	RUSHDIE	
MUNRO	LONDON	SAROYAN	DOSTOYEVSKY
OATES	MAILER	SHELLEY	SOLZHENITSYN
OHARA	MALOUF	THOREAU	
PATON	MILLER	TOLSTOI	GARCIA-
SCOTT	ORWELL	TOLSTOY	MARQUEZ
SHUTE	PORTER	WHARTON	

POETS

GAY	HEINE	MILLAY	MASTERS
KEY	HESSE	MILTON	MERRILL
POE	IBSEN	MUSSET	MISTRAL
	JOYCE	NERUDA	NEMEROV
DOVE	KEATS	OLIVER	PUSHKIN
GRAY	KIZER	PARKER	RIMBAUD
NASH	MOORE	PINDAR	ROETHKE
OVID	PLATH	SEXTON	RONSARD
POPE	POUND	SAPPHO	ROSTAND
TATE	RILEY	STRAND	SHELLEY
	RILKE	TAGORE	SPENSER
AIKEN	SCOTT	THOMAS	STEVENS
AUDEN	SIMIC	VILLON	WHITMAN
BACON	TASSO	VIRGIL	
BATES	WILDE	WILBUR	
BENET	YEATS		ANNUNZIO
BLAKE		ARIOSTO	BROWNING
BURNS	ARNOLD	ASHBERY	CUMMINGS
BYRON	BISHOP	CHAUCER	MALLARME
CRANE	BRECHT	EMERSON	MELVILLE
DANTE	BROOKS	GAUTIER	MEREDITH
DONNE	COWPER	GILBERT	PETRARCH
DUGAN	DRYDEN	HERRICK	ROSSETTI
ELIOT	GOETHE	HILLYER	SANDBURG
FROST	HOLMES	HOUSMAN	SCHILLER
GLUCK	HORACE	JEFFERS	STENDHAL
GUEST	HUGHES	JUSTICE	TEASDALE
HARDY	JONSON	KHAYYAM	TENNYSON
HARTE	KILMER	KIPLING	VOLTAIRE
HECHT	LEVINE	LINDSAY	WHITTIER
	LOWELL	MARLOWE	

DRAMATISTS

GAY	GUARE	MOLINA	HELLMAN
KYD	IBSEN	MOLNAR	KAUFMAN
	LEWIS	OCASEY	MARLOWE
ASCH	MAMET	ONEILL	MOLIERE
HARE	ODETS	PINTER	OSBORNE
HART	SIMON	RACINE	PLAUTUS
HUGO	SYNGE	SARTRE	ROSTAND
INGE	WILDE	SENECA	SAROYAN
RABE	YEATS	STEELE	SHEPARD
RICE	ZWEIG	WILDER	TERENCE
SHAW		WILSON	WEBSTER
	BARRIE	ZINDEL	
ALBEE	BRECHT		ANDERSON
AUDEN	COWARD	ANOUILH	ANNUNZIO
BARRY	DEKKER	BAGNOLD	BEAUMONT
BEHAN	DRYDEN	BECKETT	CALDERON
CAPEK	FERBER	BUCHNER	FLETCHER
DUMAS	GOETHE	CHEKHOV	SCHILLER
ELIOT	HENLEY	GILBERT	SHERIDAN
GENET	HUGHES	GOLDONI	SHERWOOD
GOGOL	JONSON	IONESCO	STOPPARD
GORKY	MILLER	JEFFERS	TOURNEUR

VOLTAIRE	CORNEILLE	SOPHOCLES	GARCIALORCA
WILLIAMS	EURIPIDES		SHAKESPEARE
	GIRAUDOUX	PIRANDELLO	WASSERSTEIN
AESCHYLUS	GOLDSMITH	STRINDBERG	
CHAYEFSKY	MIDDLETON		ARISTOPHANES

SHORT-STORY WRITERS, ESSAYISTS

SAND	KAFKA	PARKER	KIPLING
	PAINE	PORTER	LARDNER
ALGER	STEAD	RUNYON	MALAMUD
BABEL	STEIN	SINGER	PUSHKIN
CAPER	WOOLF	TAGORE	
DOYLE			ALEICHEM
GOGOL	BIERCE	BENNETT	ANDERSEN
GORKI	BUNYAN	BOSWELL	ROUSSEAU
GRIMM	FRANCE	CHEEVER	TURGENEV
HARTE	HUDSON	CHEKHOV	(DE)MAUPASSANT
HENRY	IRVING	EMERSON	

FAMOUS BOOKS

KIM	NIGHT	DRACULA	MOBYDICK
USA	SOBIG	HERLAND	PETERPAN
THEM	CARRIE	LORDJIM	STRANGER
TOWN	HERZOG	ODYSSEY	HIROSHIMA
BIBLE	HOBBIT	PROPHET	NATIVESON
FIXER	JUNGLE	REIVERS	ONTHEROAD
ILIAD	LOLITA	ULYSSES	PYGMALION
KORAN	PRINCE	BIGSLEEP	ARROWSMITH
LOVER	BELOVED	IRONWEED	

FICTIONAL CHARACTERS
AMERICAN LITERATURE

EVA	ARTIE	GATSBY	PREWITT
JIM	AUGIE	JESSUP	REBECCA
RIP	BRETT	LAPHAM	SELLERS
TOM	CANTY	LEGREE	WAPSHOT
	ELMER	LENNIE	ZENOBIA
AHAB	HOLLY	MUNROE	HOLGRAVE
ANNA	HORNE	PRYNNE	INJUNJOE
BESS	OHARA	SAWYER	MCTEAGUE
BROM	PUTTY	SHELBY	QUEEQUEG
BUDD	POLLY	SNOPES	REDROVER
CORA	PORGY	VENNER	SCARLETT
DICK	STARK	WILKES	STARBUCK
DRED	STUDS	WINKLE	THATCHER
DUER	TOPSY		UNCLETOM
FINN	TOZER	AGAPIDA	
MOBY	TRAUM	ANTONIA	
OMOO	UNCAS	BABBITT	DODSWORTH
PREW	ASHLEY	DOREMUS	SNODGRASS
SLIM	AYLMER	HAWKEYE	TOMSAWYER
	BUMPPO	LONIGAN	
APLEY	GANTRY	MELANIE	ARROWSMITH

LITERATURE OF GREAT BRITAIN AND IRELAND

AGG	KULU	TINTO	MELEMA
BHO	LAWS	TORRE	MOWGLI
DAN	LYON	TROIL	ROMOLA
DHU	MEON	TRYAN	ROWENA
FAG	MOLL	VINCY	SEXTON
JIM	NIBS	WAMBA	ZEPHON
KIM	RIMA		
LEW	TUCK	ABDIEL	ADONAIS
MEG	WAGG	ARIOCH	ALASTOR
PEW		ASHTON	BELINDA
UMA	AISSA	ATOSSA	BLUDYER
UNA	AKELA	BEETLE	CRAWLEY
WAT	ARDEN	BESSEE	DERONDA
	ARGAN	BINNIE	DINMONT
ABEL	BALOO	BOLTON	FENELLA
AMAL	BARDI	BOURKE	GIZELLE
BECK	BLANE	CRUSOE	HARLETH
BEDE	BONEY	DECOUD	IVANHOE
CASS	BRACY	DEEVER	LATIMER
COAN	BRECK	DOBBIN	LORDJIM
COKE	BULBO	ESMOND	LYDGATE
ENID	DEANS	FLORAC	MATILDA
EYRE	EDGAR	FRIDAY	RODRIGO
GANN	FOKER	GRAEME	SHAFTON
GARM	GARTH	HELDAR	SHANDON
GUNN	GLEGG	JACQUE	SHIRLEY
HATT	SHAWE	JEKYLL	SWEENEY
HOOK	SILAS	LARSEN	TRAVERS
HYDE	SNOW	MAISIE	URFRIED
IPPS	SORTI	MARLOW	WILLEMS
JANE	TESSA	MARNER	ZOPHIEL

LITERATURE OF CONTINENTAL EUROPE

ASE	LELIE	FROLLO	GRANDET
BLY	MITYA	GABLER	HERNANI
	ORGON	GORIOT	ISIDORE
ANNA	SONIA	HELMER	KATUSHA
GOTZ	STIVA	JAVERT	LEANDRE
GYNT	TARAS	MARION	MANDERS
NEMO	VANYA	MARSAY	MARTINE
NORA	WERLE	MIGNON	MEISTER
PEER		SHATOV	MYSHKIN
PERE	ALVING	TRILBY	POPINOT
PONS	ANITRA		PORTHOS
	ARAMIS	ALCESTE	RESTAUD
AOUDA	ARISTE	ALOADIN	SOLVEIG
ARGAN	ASHLEY	ALYOSHA	VALJEAN
ATHOS	BELINE	ANSELME	VAUTRIN
BAGOT	BUNGAY	ARVALAN	VRONSKI
BRAND	CATHOS	CAMILLE	WERTHER
BULBA	COLLIN	CLEANTE	WILHELM
EYOLF	DANTES	COSETTE	
FAUST	EGMONT	DORANTE	ATHANAEL
HEDDA	ESPARD	GERONTE	BERGERET
HULAT	FEDORA	GOBSECK	CHRYSALE

DELORMES	KARENINA	TARTUFFE	KARAMAZOV
FLORINDA	LADURLAD		QUASIMODO
GORGIBUS	NASTASIA	CHICHIKOV	
GRETCHEN	RODERICK	DARTAGNAN	
HARPAGON	SHIGALOV	ESMERALDA	

SHAKESPEARE

NYM	ROBIN	WOLSEY	SAMPSON
SAY	ROMEO		SHALLOW
	RUGBY	AEMILIA	SHYLOCK
ADAM	SNOUT	ANTONIO	SIMPCOX
CADE	SOSIA	BEROWNE	SLENDER
DAVY	SPEED	BERTRAM	SOLINUS
DION	TIMON	CALIBAN	TEMPEST
HERO	TITUS	CAMILLO	THESEUS
IAGO		CAPULET	TITANIA
IDEN	ADRIAN	CLAUDIO	TROILUS
IRAS	AEGEON	CONRADE	TYRRELL
JAMY	ALONSO	CRANMER	URSWICK
JOHN	ANGELO	DUMAINE	VALERIA
LEAR	ANTONY	ESCALUS	VARRIUS
LUCE	BANQUO	ESCANES	
PETO	BIANCA	FLEANCE	ABHORSON
PUCK	BOLEYN	GATESBY	ANNEPAGE
ROSS	BOTTOM	GONERIL	BAPTISTA
SNUG	CAESAR	GONZALO	BARDOLPH
VAUX	CAPHIS	GREGORY	BASSANO
	CLOTEN	HORATIO	BELARIUS
ANGUS	DORCAS	HOTSPUR	BENEDICK
ARIEL	DROMIO	IACHIMO	BENVOLIO
BAGOT	DUNCAN	JESSICA	BERNARDO
BIRON	FABIAN	LARTIUS	BORACHIO
BOYET	FENTON	LAVACHE	CAMPEIUS
BUSHY	GREMIO	LAVINIA	CAPUCIUS
CAIUS	GRUMIO	LEONATO	CLAUDIUS
CELIA	HAMLET	LEONTES	COMINIUS
CORIN	JULIET	LUCETTA	CORDELIA
CURAN	JULIUS	LUCIANA	CRESSIDA
CURIO	LAUNCE	MACBETH	DOGBERRY
EGEUS	LENNOX	MACDUFF	DONPEDRO
ELBOW	MUTIUS	MALCOLM	EGLAMOUR
FESTE	OBERON	MARCADE	FALSTAFF
FLUTE	ORSINO	MARCIUS	FASTOLFE
FROTH	PISTOL	MIRANDA	FLUELLEN
GOBBO	POMPEY	MONTANO	GADSHILL
GOFFE	PORTIA	MOWBRAY	GARDINER
GOWER	RUMOUR	NERISSA	GARGRAVE
HENRY	SCROOP	OPHELIA	GRATIANO
JULIA	SEYTON	ORLANDO	HARCOURT
LAFEU	SILVIA	OTHELLO	LAURENCE
LOVEL	SIWARD	PAULINA	LODOVICO
LUCIO	TALBOT	PERDITA	LYSANDER
MELUN	TAMORA	PHRYNIA	MENTEITH
MOPSA	THAISA	PISANIO	MERCUTIO
OSRIC	THURIO	PROTEUS	MONTAGUE
PHEBE	TRANIO	PUBLIUS	PANTHINO
PINCH	TYBALT	RICHARD	PAROLLES
REGAN	VERGES	SALANIO	PERICLES

PHILOTUS	VIOLENTA	BRABANTIO	GUIDERIUS
POLONIUS	VIRGILIA	CAITHNESS	MARCELLUS
PROSPERO	VOLUMNIA	CLEOPATRA	ROTHERHAM
RATCLIFF		CORNELIUS	SEBASTIAN
REIGNIER	APEMANTUS	CYMBELINE	TOBYBELCH
RODERIGO	ARVIRAGUS	DESDEMONA	VALENTINE
SALARINO	BALTHASAR	DONALBAIN	VENTIDIUS
STEPHANO	BASSIANUS	ERPINGHAM	VINCENTIO
TRINCULO	BOURCHIER	GLENDOWER	VOLTEMAND

DICKENS

AMY	BATES	DOMBEY	PLUMMER
BET	BETSY	DORRIT	PODSNAP
CLY	BEVAN	HARMON	SCROOGE
PIP	CHOKE	JARLEY	SLOWBOY
TOX	CLARE	LAMMLE	SLUMKEY
	FAGIN	MAYLIE	SNAGSBY
BAPS	KROOK	MERDLE	SNUBBIN
BRAY	MIGGS	NIPPER	SPENLOW
DORA	NANCY	OLIVER	STRYVER
FANG	NOGGS	REDLAW	TINYTIM
FIPS	QUILP	SLEARY	TROTTER
FOGG	RUDGE	TAPLEY	
GAMP	SIKES	WARDLE	BAGSTOCK
HEEP	SMIKE		CHADBAND
JOWL	TWIST	BAILLIE	CRATCHIT
KAGS		BLIMBER	CRUMMLES
MELL	BAILEY	BROWDIE	CRUNCHER
NELL	BARKIS	DEFARGE	HAVISHAM
OMER	BOFFIN	ESTELLA	HORTENSE
PEPS	BUCKET	JAGGERS	LIRRIPER
POTT	BUMBLE	JEDDLER	
PRIG	BUZFUZ	JELLYBY	MAGWITCH
TIGG	CARKER	MANETTE	MICAWBER
VECK	CARTON	MOWCHER	NICKLEBY
WEGG	DARNAY	NADGETT	
	DARTLE	NUBBLES	PEGGOTTY
BALOO	DODSON	PIPCHIN	SKIMPOLE

CHARACTERS IN ARABIAN NIGHTS

AGIB	HAROUN	BADOURA	BARMECIDE
AMINE	SINBAD	HOUSSAIN	SCHACABAC
GANEM	ALADDIN	MORGIANA	
FATIMA	ALIBABA	SHARIAH	

SLEUTHS IN LITERATURE & TV

SAM	MASON	VANCE	SHAYNE
CHAN	MCKEE	WOLFE	THANET
COOL	MORAN	CARTER	WIMSEY
FELL	MORSE	HAMMER	CHARLES
MAYO	NORTH	HOLMES	DALZIEL
MOTO	PASCO	HORNET	FREEMAN
BROWN	QUEEN	JUSTUS	MACLAIN
DUPIN	SAINT	MARPLE	MAIGRET
JONES	SALEM	POIROT	MARLOWE
LUPIN	SPADE	PORTER	MERLINI

RAFFLES	WEXFORD	WESTLAKE	ELLERY QUEEN
TEMPLAR	FUMANCHU	DALGLEISH	GREEN HORNET
VALCOUR	ROCKFORD	MERRIVALE	

UNUSUAL FIRST NAMES IN LITERATURE

CLEM	MANON	PEYTON	PHILEAS
DINE	MATEO	SANCHO	WILKINS
EDEN	NIKKI	SOAMES	ZULEIKA
GYPO	PHILO	YANERY	ALGERNON
MOIT	RHETT	FLORIAN	EMMELINE
AGGIS	TANIS	HERCULE	FANCOURT
BINGO	URIAH	ICHABOD	SCARLETT
COSMO	ARSENE	KIMBALL	TRISTRAM
DISKO	BIGGER	MINIVER	WACKFORD
GAVIN	CLOVIS	MYCROFT	
LORNA	PENROD	PEACHEY	

NAMES IN NURSERY RHYMES

DAW	MOREY	PORGIE	DAMETROT
DUN	POLLY	SPRATT	ETTICOAT
COLE	PUNCH	TONSEY	FLINDERS
JILL	SIMON	TUCKER	KINGCOLE
JUDY	TAFFY	WARLEY	TOMTHUMB
POLT	BOGGEN	WILLIE	BETTYBLUE
ROSE	BOPEEP	WINKIE	DANDYPRAT
TROT	FOSTER	BLUEBEN	MCDIDDLER
WREN	GRIGGS	BOLDERO	REDBREAST
COLIN	GRUNDY	FAUSTUS	TOMMYTROT
GILES	HORNER	HUBBARD	
JENNY	JENNIE	SHAFTOE	
KITTY	MUFFET	TERENCE	

ANIMALS IN LITERATURE

JIP	PHAO	BAYARD	XANTHUS
MEG	RAMA	DAPPLE	RABICANO
APIS	RANN	FLOPIT	SLEIPNIR
BABE	TOBY	KATMIR	BLACKBESS
BIMI	TYLO	LASSIE	BOATSWAIN
BRAN	ARGUS	RAKUSH	BRIGADORE
CHIL	BAMBI	ROLAND	CAVALCADE
EGAN	BEVIS	WINNIE	FERDINAND
GHAO	OJALI	ALBORAK	GUNPOWDER
GRIP	FADDA	BAJARDO	MARCHHARE
MANG	GRANT	BAVIECA	MEHITABEL
MOTI	JUMBO	PEGASUS	ROSINANTE
MYSA	OSCAR	RABIGAN	BLACKBEAUTY
NANA	RUKSH	REDWULL	

MEASURES AND WEIGHTS
LINEAR MEASURES

Algeria	TERMIN		ABDAT		HASTA
Arabia	BARID	Egypt, ancient	KHET		GEERAH
	FARSAKH		THEB		UNGLEE
	FARSANG		CUBIT	Indonesia	KILAN
	MARHALA		SCHENE		TJENKAL
Arabia, ancient	CABDA		CHORYOS	Iran	GUZ
	MILLE	Estonia	ELLE		MOU
	QASAB		LIIN		ZAR
	ASSBAA		SULD		MANSION
	GHALVA		TOLL	Ireland	BANDLE
Argentina	VARA		FADEN		FATHMUR
	BRAZA		SAGENE	Italy	CANNA
	LEGUA	Ethiopia	TAT		PALMO
Austria	FUSS	France	LIEUE		PUNTO
	LINIE		LIGNE		MIGLIO
	MEILE		PERCHE		BRACCIO
	PUNKI	Germany	FUSS	Japan	BU
	KLAFTER		STAB		JO
Belgium	AUNE		ZOLL		MO
	PIED		KETTE		RI
	PERCHE		STRICH		BOO
Brazil	PE		KLAFTER		CHO
	VARA	Greece	PIK		RIN
	BRACA		GRAMME		SUN
	LEGOA		PALAME		HIRO
	MILHA		STADION		SHAKU
	PALMO	Greece, ancient	BEMA	Java	PAAL
	PASSO		POUS	Mexico	VARA
	COVADO		PYGON		LEGUA
Chile	VARA		DICHAS		LINEA
	LEGUA		ACAENA		PULGADA
	LINEA		ORGYIA	Norway	FOT
	CUADRA		STADIUM		ALEN
China	LI	Hebrew	EZBA	Paraguay	PIE
	TU		REED		VARA
	FEN		CUBIT		LEGUA
	CHIH	Holland	EL		CORDEL
	CHANG		DUIM		CUADRA
Cyprus	PIK		VOET	Poland	CAL
Czech Republic	SAH		ROEDE		MILA
	LATRO		STREEP		LINJA
	LOKEAT	Honduras	VARA		SAZEN
Denmark	FOD		MILLA		STOPA
	MIL		TERCIA		LOKIEC
	ALEN	Iceland	FET	Portugal	PE
	FAVN		ALIN		VARA
	RODE		LIMA		BRACA
	LINJE	India	GUZ		LEGOA
	TOMME		JOW		LINHA
	LANDMIL		KOS(S)		MILHA
Dominican Republic			HATH		PALMO
	ONA		JAOB		COVADO
Ecuador	CUADRA		COVID	Rangoon	LAN
Egypt	PIK		CROSA		DAIN

	TAUN		PALMO		KEN
Rome, ancient	PES		SESMA		NIU
	ACTUS		CUARTA		SEN
	CUBIT		PULGADA		SOK
	UNCIA	Sweden	ALN		YOT
	GRADUS		FOT		KEUP
	PALMUS		REF	Turkey	PIK
	PASSUS		TUM		HATT
	DIGITUS		FAMN		KHAT
Russia	FUT		LINJE		ZIRA
	DUIM		NYMIL		BERRI
	VERST	Switzerland	AUNE		ARSHIN
	ARSHIN		FUSS		PARMAK
	PALETZ		PIED		LY
	SAGENE		ZOLL	Vietnam	GON
	TOTCHKA		LIEUE		NGU
	VERCHOK		POUCE		THUOC
Spain	CODO		SCHUH		TRUONG
	DEDO		STAAB	Yugoslavia (former)	RIP
	VARA		TOISE		KHVAT
	BRAZA		PERCHE		PALAZ
	LEGUA	Thailand	KLAFTER		STOPA
			WA(H)		

U.S. COMMON LINEAR AND METRIC EQUIVALENTS

		1 INCH	= 2.54 cm.
12 in.	=	1 FOOT	= .3048 m.
3 ft.	=	1 YARD	= .9144 m.
5-1/2 yd.	=	1 ROD	= 5.029 m.
40 rd.	=	1 FURLONG	= 200.15 m.
8 fur.	=	1 MILE	= 1.6093 km.
3 mi.	=	1 LEAGUE	= 4.8279 km.

METRIC MEASURES AND EQUIVALENTS

KILOMETER	= 1000 m.	= .62 mi.
HECTOMETER	= 100 m.	= 3937 in.
DECAMETER	= 10 m.	= 393.7 in.
METER	= 1 m.	= 39.37 in.
DECIMETER	= 0.1 m.	= 3.937 in.
CENTIMETER	= 0.01 m.	= .3937 in.
MILLIMETER	= 0.001 m.	= .03937 in.

U.S. AND U.K. UNCOMMON LINEAR MEASURES

CUT	300 yd.	LINK	7.92 in.	OUNCE	1/64 in.
ELL	45 in.	NAIL	2.25 in.	PERCH	5.5 yd.
LEA	120 yd.	PACE	30 in.	PRIME	1 in.
BOLT	40 yd.	PALM	3-4 in.	SKEIN	360 ft.
HAND	4 in.	POLE	5.5 yd.	FATHOM	6 ft.
HANK	840 yd.	ROOD	7 yd.	SECOND	1/12 in.
HEER	600 yd.	SPAN	9 in.	THREAD	1.5 yd.
IRON	1/48 in.	CHAIN	22 yd.		
LINE	1/12 in.	DIGIT	.75 in.		

SURFACE MEASURES

Arabia, ancient			YOKE		UNCIO
	FEDDAN	Iceland	FERFET		SALTUS
	QASABA		FERALIN		VERSUS
Argentina	QUADRA		FERMILA	Somalia	JARAT
	MANZANA	India	BEGA		JUCHART
Austria	JOCH		BIGHA	South Africa	MORGEN
Brazil	CUARTA	Indonesia	BOUW	Spain	YUGADA
	TAREFA	Iraq	MISHARA		CELEMIN
Bulgaria	LEKHA	Italy	TAVOLA		ESTADEL
Chile	CUADRA	Japan	BU	Sweden	TUNLAND
China	MU		GO	Thailand	RAI
	KISH		SE		NGAN
	CHING		CHO	Turkey	DONUM
Cuba	TAREA		TAN		DJERIB
	CORDEL		TSUBO	United Kingdom	
Czech Republic	LAN	Libya	JABIA		CHAIN
	JITRO	Mexico	LABOR		COVER
	KOREC		SITIO		JUGUM
	STRYCH	Nicaragua	SUERTE		VIRGATE
Denmark	ALBUM		ESTAJAL	United States	ACRE
Dominican Republic			MANZANA		BLOCK
	TAREA	Norway	MA(A)L		CHAIN
Egypt	SAHME	Paraguay	LINE		LABOR
	AURURE		LINO	Uruguay	CUADRA
	FEDDAN	Peru	TOPO		SUERTE
Estonia	TUN	Philippines	LOAN	Vietnam	MAU
Finland	TUNLAND		BRAZA		QUO
France	ARPENT		BALITA		SAO
Germany	MORGEN		QUINON	Yugoslavia (former)	
Greece	ACAENA	Poland	MORG(A)		RALO
	STREMMA		WIOKA		DONUM
Holland	BUNDER	Portugal	GEIRA		LANAZ
Hungary	HOLD		FERRADO		RALICA
	JOCH	Rome, ancient	CLIMA		MOTYKA
			JUGA		

U.S. SQUARE MEASURES AND METRIC EQUIVALENTS

160 sq. rds.	= 1 ACRE	= .0407 ha.
640 acres	= 1 SQ. MILE	= 259 ha.
36 sq. ml.	= 1 TOWNSHIP	

METRIC MEASURES AND EQUIVALENTS

HECTARE	= 10,000 sq. m.	= 2.471 acres
ARE	= 100 sq. m.	= 119.6 sq. yd.
CENTIARE	= 1 sq. m.	= 1,550 sq. in.

LIQUID MEASURES

Arabia	CUDDY		FERK		FRASCO
	ZUDDA		KIST	Austria	FASS
	NUSFIAH		CAFIZ		MASS
Arabia, ancient	DEN		CAPHITE		HALBE
	SAA	Argentina	GALON		PFIFF

Brazil	PIPA		LOG	Russia	FASS
	ALMUD		BATH		STO(O)F
	TONEL	Holland	AAM		CHARKA
Burma, former	BYEE		AUM		TCHAST
	SEIT		KAN		BOTCHKA
China	KO		STOOP	Somalia	CABA
	QUEI		MAATJE	Spain	BUTT
	SHIH		MUTSJE		COPA
Cyprus	OKA	Iceland	POTTUR		MOYO
	CASS		OLTUNNA		ARROBA
	KOUZA	India	DRONA		CANTARA
	KARTOS		MUSHTI	Sweden	AM
Denmark	POT	Indonesia	TAKAR		KANNA
	OLTONDE	Japan	GO		KAPPE
	VIERTEL		TO		JUMFRU
Egypt	RO(U)B		SHO		OXHUVUD
	ROBHAN		KOKU	Switzerland	POT
	MALOUAH		SHAKU		IMMI
Ethiopia	CUBA	Latvia	KANNE		SAUM
	KUBA		STOOF		MAASS
Finland	KANNU	Libya	BOZZE		SETIER
	TUNNA		MATTARO	Tangier	KULA
France	POT	Mexico	BARIL	Thailand	KWIEN
	PINTE		JARRA		TANAN
	CHOPINE	Peru	GALON	Trieste	ORNA
	POISSON	Philippines	CHUPA		ORNE
Germany	AAM		GANTA	United Kingdom	PIN
	FASS		APATAN		PIPE
	EIMER	Poland	CWIERC		FIRKIN
	FUDER		KWARTA		RUNLET
	KANNE		GARNIEC	United States	TUN
	MAASS	Portugal	BOTA		BUTT
Greece	BARILE		MEIO		DRAM
	COTULA		PIPA		DRUM
	KOILON		ALMUD(E)		PIPE
Greece, ancient	CHOUS		OITAVA		MINIM
	AMPHORA	Rome, ancient	URNA	Vietnam	TAO
Hebrew	CAB		CULEUS		SHITA
	KIN		DOLIUM	Yugoslavia (former)	OKA
	KOR		CYATHUS		AKOV

U.S. LIQUID MEASURES AND METRIC EQUIVALENTS

16 fl. oz.	= 1 PINT	= 0.4732 l.
4 gills	= 1 PINT	= 0.4732 l.
2 pt.	= 1 QUART	= 0.9463 l.
4 qt.	= 1 GALLON	= 3.7853 l.
31-1/2 gal.	= 1 BARREL	
2 bbl.	= 1 HOGSHEAD	

METRIC MEASURES AND EQUIVALENTS

KILOLITER	= 1000 l.	= 264.2 gal.
HECTOLITER	= 100 l.	= 26.42 gal.
DECALITER	= 10 l.	= 2.642 gal.
LITER	= 1 l.	= 1.057 qt.
DECILITER	= 0.1 l.	= 0.211 pt.
CENTILITER	= 0.01 l.	= 0.338 fl. oz.

DRY MEASURES

Algeria	**TARRI**	Germany	**KANNE**	Russia	**LOF**
Arabia	**TEMAN**		**MASSEL**		**OSMIN**
Argentina	**FENEGA**		**SCHEFFEL**		**GARNETZ**
	LASTRE	Greece	**BACHEL**	Scotland	**BOLL**
Austria	**MUTH**	Hebrew	**CAB**		**LIPPY**
	METZE		**KAB**		**FIRLOT**
	ACHTEL		**KOR**		**CHALDER**
	BECHER		**EPHA(H)**	Somalia	**TABLA**
	VIERTEL		**OMER**	South Africa	**MUID**
Brazil	**MOIO**		**SEAH**		**SCHEPEL**
	FANGA		**HOMER**	Spain	**ALMUD**
	QUARTO	Holland	**KOP**		**CAHIZ**
Bulgaria	**KRINA**		**ZAK**		**MEDIO**
Burma, former	**TENG**		**MUDDE**		**FANEGA**
Calcutta	**KUNK**		**SCHEPEL**		**RACION**
	RAIK	Hungary	**METZE**	Sweden	**FODER**
Ceylon (former)	**PARAH**	India	**GARCE**		**SPANN**
	AMUNAM	Indonesia	**GANTANG**		**TUNNA**
Channel Islands	**CABOT**	Italy	**STAIO**		**KOLLAST**
Chile	**FANEGA**		**MOGGIO**	Switzerland	**MUID**
China	**HO**		**RUBBIO**		**VIERTEL**
	HU	Japan	**TO**	Syria	**MAKUK**
	PU		**SHO**		**GARAVA**
	TOU		**KOKU**	Tangier	**MUDD**
	SHENG	Latvia	**KULMET**	Thailand	**SAT**
Costa Rica	**FANEGA**	Malta	**SALM(A)**		**TANG**
	CAJUELA	Mexico	**CARGA**		**TANAN**
Cyprus	**MEDIMNO**		**FANEGA**	Tunisia	**SAA(H)**
Denmark	**TONDE**	Norway	**SKIEPPE**		**UEBA**
	ACHTEL	Philippines	**CABAN**		**CAFIZ**
Egypt	**ARDEB**		**CHUPA**		**WHIBA**
	FARDE		**BANTA**	Turkey	**ALMUD**
	KILAH		**APATAN**		**KILEH**
	KEDDAH	Poland	**KORZEC**		**FORTIN**
	DARIBAH	Portugal	**MEIO**	United Kingdom	
Egypt, ancient	**ARTABA**		**FANGA**		**COOM(B)**
France	**MINOT**		**QUARTO**	United States	**CORD**
	HEMINE		**SELAMIN**		**BASKET**
		Rome, ancient	**MODIUS**		

U.S. DRY MEASURES AND METRIC EQUIVALENTS

2 pints	= 1 QUART	= 1.101 l.
8 qt.	= 1 PECK	= 8.809 l.
4 pk.	= 1 BUSHEL	= 35.24 l.
105 qt.	= 1 BARREL	

METRIC MEASURES AND EQUIVALENTS

KILOLITER	= 1.308 cu. yd.
HECTOLITER	= 2.838 bu.
DECALITER	= 1.135 pk.
LITER	= 0.9081 qt.
STERE	= KILOLITER

WEIGHTS

Country	Unit	Country	Unit	Country	Unit
Algeria	UCKIA		PICUL		LITRA
Arabia	BAHAR	Columbia	SACO		DRAMME
	CHEKI		CARGA		OBULUS
	KELLA		LIBRA		STATER
	MAUND		QUILATE		DRACHMA
	TOMAN		QUINTAL	Greece, ancient	
	MISKAL	Costa Rica	CAJA		DIOBOL
	BOKARD	Cyprus	CAJA		CHALCON
Arabia, ancient	ROTL		OKA	Guinea	AKEY
	NASCH		MOOSA		PISO
	NEVAT	Denmark	ES		UZAN
	OCQUE		LOD		BENDA
	OUKIA		ORT		SERON
Argentina	LIBRA		VOG	Hebrew	MINA
	QUINTAL		MARK		BEKA(H)
Austria	MARK		PUND		REBA(H)
	SAUM		UNZE		SHEKEL
	UNZE		KVINT	Holland	ONS
	DENAT		CENTNER		LOOD
	KARCH		LISPUND		POND
	STEIN		QUINTIN		GREIN
	PFUND	Egypt	OKA		KORREL
	PFENNIG		OKE		WICHTJE
	CENTNER		HEML	India	SER
Belgium	LIVRE		OKIA		DHAN
	CHARGE		ROTL		PALA
	CHARIOT		KERAT		PICE
Brazil	ONCA		UCKIA		RAT(T)I
	LIBRA		KANTAR		TOLA
	ARROBA		QUINTAL		ADPAO
	OITAVA	Egypt, ancient	KAT		BAHAR
	ARRATEL		KET		MAUND
	QUILATE		KHAR		CHITTAK
	QUINTAL		DEBEN	Indonesia	TJI
Bulgaria	OKA		OKEIH		HOEN
	OKE	Estonia	NAEL		TALI
	TOVAR		PUUD		WANG
Burma, former	MOO	Ethiopia	KASM		PICUL
	VIS(S)		NATY		REAAL
	KYAT		OKET		KOJANG
	TICAL		ALADA		KULACK
	ABUCCO		NETER	Iran	ZAR
	PIEKTHA		WAKEA		DRAM
Calcutta	DHAN		WOGIET		DUNG
	PANK	France	GROS		SANG
China	LI		MARC		ABBAS
	FEN		ONCE		DINAR
	HAO		LIVRE		BATMAN
	KIN		TONNE		GANDUM
	TAN	Germany	LOT		KARWAR
	YIN		PFUND		NAKHOD
	CHIN		STEIN		ABBASSI
	MACE		CENTNER	Italy	ONCIA
	SHIH	Greece	MNA		DENARO
	TAEL		OKA		GANDUM
	CATTY		MINA		LIBBRA

	OTTAVA	Rome	AS		SALUNG
Japan	MO		BES		SOMPAY
	FUN		LIBRA		TAMLUNG
	KIN		UNCIA	Tunisia	UCKIA
	RIN		DUELLA	Turkey	OKA
	SHI		SEXTULA		OKE
	KATI		SOLIDUS		KILE(H)
	KWAN	Russia	LOT		CEQUI
	NIYO		PUD		CHEKE
	MOMME		DOLA		KERAT
	PICUL		FUNT		BATMAN
Mexico	ONZA		POOD		DIRHAM
	CARGA		KAMIAN		KANTAR
	LIBRA	Scotland	BOLL		MISKAL
	MARCO		DROP		YUSDRUM
	ADARME	Spain	ONZA	United Kingdom	KIP
	ARROBA		LIBRA		KEEL
	OCHAVA		MARCO		BARGE
	TERCIO		TOMIN		CLOVE
	QUINTAL		ADARME		FAGOT
Morocco	ROTL		ARROBA		STONE
	GERBE	Sweden	DINERO		CENTAL
	KINDAR		ASS		FIRKIN
Norway	LOD		ORT		POCKET
	MARK		PUND	United States	KEG
	PUND		STEN		KIP
Philippines	FARDO		UNTZ		BARREL
	PICUL		NYLAST		CENTAL
	PUNTO	Syria	LISPUND	Vietnam	TA
	LACHSA	Thailand	COLA		CAN
	QUILATE		PAI		BIHN
Poland	LUT		BAHT		DONG
	FUNT		HAPH		
	UNCYA		KLAM	Yugoslavia (former)	
	KAMIAN		KLOM		TOVAR
	SKRUPUL		CHANG		WAGON
Portugal (see Brazil)			COYAN		DRAMMA
	GRAO		FUANG		STALIJK
			PICUL		GISAL
			TICUL	Zanzibar	

U.S. WEIGHTS AND METRIC EQUIVALENTS

*Hundredweight

3.086 grains	= 1 CARAT	= 200 mg.
27 11/32 gr.	= 1 DRAM	= 1.772 g.
16 dr.	= 1 OUNCE	= 28.35 g.
16 oz.	= 1 POUND	= .4536 kg.
20 cwts.	= 1 CWT.*	= 45.36 kg.
20 cwts.	= 1 TON	= .9072 M.T.

METRIC WEIGHTS AND EQUIVALENTS

Metric TON	= 2204.6 lb.
QUINTAL	= 220.46 lb.
KILO(GRAM)	= 2.2046 lb.
GRAM	= 15,432 gr.
MILLIGRAM	= .0154 gr.

MONEY AND COINS
ANCIENT AND MODERN

Abyssinian	**BESA**	
	GIRSH	
	TALARI	
Afghanistan	**PUL**	
	ABBASI	
	AMANIA	
	AFGHANI	
Albania	**LEK**	
	FRANC	
	QINTAR	
Anglo-Saxon	**ORA**	
	SCEAT	
Angola	**LWEI**	
	ESCUDO	
	MACUTA	
	ANGOLAR	
	CENTAVO	
Arabian	**TALARI**	
Argentina	**PESO**	
	CENTAVO	
Austria	**DUCAT**	
	KRONE	
	FLORIN	
	GULDEN	
	HELLER	
	GROSCHEN	
	SCHILLING	
Belgium	**BELGA**	
	FRANC	
	CENTIME	
Biblical	**BEKA(H)**	
	MITE	
	SHEKEL	
	TALENT	
Bolivia	**CENTAVO**	
	BOLIVIANO	
Brazil	**REIS**	
	CONTO	
	MILREIS	
	MOIDORE	
	CRUZEIRO	
Bulgaria	**LEV**	
	LEW	
	DINAR	
	STOTINKA	
Burma (former)	**PYA**	
	KYAT	
Ceylon (former)	**CENT**	
	TANG	
	RUPEE	
Chile	**PESO**	
	COLON	
	LIBRA	

	CONDOR	
	ESCUDO	
	CENTAVO	
China	**LI**	
	PU	
	FEN	
	CASH	
	CENT	
	TAEL	
	TIAO	
	YUAN	
	LIANG	
Colombia	**PESO**	
	REAL	
	CONDOR	
	CENTAVO	
Costa Rica	**COLON**	
	CENTIMO	
Czechoslovakia		
(former)	**DUCAT**	
	HALER	
	KRONE	
	HELLER	
	KORUNA	
Denmark	**ORA**	
	ORE	
	KRONE	
	SKILLING	
Dutch	*see* HOLLAND	
Dutch East Indies	**BONK**	
	DOIT	
	DUIT	
Ecuador	**SUCRE**	
	CONDOR	
	CENTAVO	
Egypt	**GIRSH**	
	POUND	
	RIVAL	
	PIASTER	
	MILLIEME	
El Salvador	**COLON**	
	CENTAVO	
Estonia	**SENT**	
	KROON	
	ESTMARK	
Ethiopia	**BESA**	
	GIRSH	
	TALARI	
	ASHRAFI	
Finland	**PENNI**	
	MARKKA	
France	**ECU**	

	SOL	
	SOU	
	AGNEL	
	FRANC	
	LIARD	
	LOUIS	
	OBOLE	
	BESANT	
	CENTIME	
	PISTOLE	
	SOLIDUS	
	NAPOLEON	
Gambia	**BUTUT**	
Genoa	**JANE**	
German East Africa		
	PESA	
	RUPIE	
Germany	**GROT**	
	MARK	
	KRONE	
	TALER	
	THALER	
	PFENNIG	
	BLAFFERT	
Greece	**OBOL**	
	LEPTON	
	STATER	
	DRACHMA	
Guatemala	**PESO**	
	QUETZAL	
Haiti	**FRANC**	
	GOU	
	ROE	
Hebrew	**GERAH**	
	SHEKEL	
Holland	**DOIT**	
	OORD	
	FLORIN	
	GULDEN	
	STIVER	
	DAALDER	
	GUILDER	
Honduras	**CENTAVO**	
	LEMPIRA	
Hungary	**GARA**	
	PENGO	
	FILLER	
Iceland	**AURAR**	
	EYRIR	
	KRONA	
India	**DAM**	
	LAC	
	PIE	

Country		Country		Country	
	ANNA		PATACA		BANI
	DAWM	Malaya	TRA	Russia	ALTIN
	FELS		TRAH		KOPEK
	HOON	Mexico	PESO		RUBLE
	LAKH		AZTECA		CHERVONETS
	PICE		CUARTO	Saudi Arabia	POUND
	TARA		CENTAVO		RIVAL
	CRORE	Mongolia	TUGRIK	Somalia	BESA
	MOHUR	Montenegro	PARA		SOMALO
	RUPEE		FLORIN	South Africa	CENT
	PAGODA		PERPERA		POND
Indonesia	RUPIAH	Morocco	OKIA		RAND
Iran	PUL		RIAL		FLORIN
	KRAN		DIRHAM		DAALDER
	POUL	Nepal	MOHAR	Spain	PESO
	RIAL		RUPEE		REAL
	DARIC	Nicaragua	CENTAVO		DOBLA
	DINAR		CORDOBA		PESETA
	MOHUR	Norway	ORE		ALFONSO
	SHAHI		KRONE		CENTIMO
	TOMAN	Oman	GAJ		PISTOLE
	ASHRAFI		GOZ	Sweden	ORE
	PAHLEVI		GHAZI		KRONA
Iraq	DINAR		BAIZA		RIGSDALER
Ireland	RAP		MAHMUDI	Switzerland	BATZ
	PENCE	Pakistan	ANNA		FRANC
	PENNY		PICE		RAPPE
	POUND		RUPEE		CENTIME
	SHILLING	Panama	CENT	Thailand	AT
Israel	POUND		BALBOA		ATT
	PRUTA	Paraguay	GUARANI		BAHT
Italy	LIRA	Peru	SOL		CATTY
	LIRE		LIBRA		FUANG
	TARI		DINERO		TICAL
	SCUDO	Poland	DUCAT		PYNUNG
	SOLDO		GROSZ		SALUNG
	TESTON(E)		MARKA		SATANG
Japan	BU		ZLOTY	Tunisia	DINAR
	RIN		FENNIG	Turkey	LIRA
	SEN		HALERZ		PARA
	YEN	Portugal	REI		ALTUN
	OBAN		CONTO		ASPER
	ICHIBU		DOBRA		MAHBUB
	ITZEBU		DINERO		SEQUIN
Korea	WON		ESCUDO		ALTILIK
	HWAN		TOSTAO		BESHLIK
Laos	AT		CRUSADO		PIASTER
	ATT		JOHANNES		ZECCHINO
	KIP	Rome, ancient	AS	Ukraine	GRIVNA
Latvia	LAT		AES		SCHAGIV
	RUBLIS		SEMIS	United Kingdom	
	SANTIMS		DINDER		ANGEL
	KAPEIKA		SOLIDUS		BODLE
Lithuania	LIT		DENARIUS		CROWN
	MARKA		SESTERCE		DRAKE
	CENTAS	Rumania	BAN		GROAT
	FENNIG		LEI		PENNY
	OSTMARK		LEU		PLACK
Macao	AVO		LEY		POUND

	United States			
BAWBEE		CENT		BOLIVAR
FLORIN		DIME		CENTIMO
GUINEA		MILL		MOROCOTA
CAROLUS		EAGLE	Venice	BETSO
JACOBUS		PENNY		BEZZO
UNICORN		DOLLAR		DONG
ATCHISON		NICKEL	Vietnam	PIASTER
FARTHING		QUARTER		
SHILLING	Venezuela	REAL	Yugoslavia (former)	
HALFCROWN		MEDIO		PARA
SOVEREIGN		FUERTE		DINAR

SLANG TERMS

BIT	12-1/2¢	QUID	pound	TANNER	sixpence
BOB	shilling	DEUCE	$2	TENNER	$10, £10
FIN	$5	FIVER	$5, £5	CENTURY	$100, £100
RED	penny	GRAND	$1,000	SAWBUCK	$10
PLUM	£100,000	MONKEY	£500	TWOBITS	quarter

DENOMINATIONS AND PORTRAITS

Portrait	Amount	Back of Bill
CHASE	$10,000	
GRANT	$50	U.S. Capitol
WILSON	$100,000	
JACKSON	$20	White House
LINCOLN	$5	Lincoln Memorial
MADISON	$5,000	
FRANKLIN	$100	Independence Hall
HAMILTON	$10	U.S. Treasury
MCKINLEY	$500	
CLEVELAND	$1,000	
JEFFERSON	$2	Signers of Declaration
WASHINGTON	$1	Great Seal of U.S.

MUSIC
MUSICAL TERMS

ALT	MODE	DUPLE	NEUME
BUS	MOLL	EPODE	PAUSE
BAR	NOTE	FUSEE	PEDAL
DOT	RAGA	GAMUT	PIENA
DUR	REST	GRACE	PIENO
JUG	ROOT	GUIDA	PITCH
KEY	SLUR	KLANG	PRESA
PES	TAKT	LONGA	SCALE
TER	TONE	MAJOR	SCORE
TIE		MAXIM	SHAKE
	ANCUS	METER	SHARP
CLEF	BRACE	MINIM	SOLFA
FLAT	BREVE	MINOR	SPACE
FUSA	CHORD	MOTIF	STAFF
HOLD	CLOSE	NEUMA	STAVE

TEMPO	PHRASE	INCIPIT	VIBRATO
TONIC	PLAGAL	KEYNOTE	
TRIAD	PNEUMA	MEASURE	ARPEGGIO
TRILL	QUAVER	MEDIANT	BASICSET
TROPE	RELISH	MELISMA	CAMBIATA
VIRGA	RENVOI	MORDENT	CLIMACUS
	RHYTHM	NATURAL	CROTCHET
BURDEN	SERIAL	ORISCUS	DIAPASON
CLIVIS	TACTUS	PODATUS	DOMINANT
DEGREE	TIERCE	PRESSUS	DYNAMICS
DITONE	TIMBRE	PUNCTUM	HALFNOTE
DORIAN	TRIPLE	PUNCTUS	HARMONIC
ENCORE	UNISON	RIPIENO	INTERVAL
GROUND		ROULADE	LIGATURE
HOCKET	AEOLIAN	SALICUS	MODALITY
IONIAN	BARLINE	SIXFOUR	NOTATION
LYDIAN	CADENCE	SOLFEGE	OSTINATO
MELODY	CLUSTER	SYNCOPE	PHRYGIAN
MOTIVE	FERMATA	TREMOLO	QUILISMA
OCTAVE	HARMONY	TRIPLET	SEMIFUSA
PARODY	HEMIOLA	TRITONE	SEMITONE

NOTES OF THE SCALE

*Guido's scale

DI	RI	SOL	ALAMIRE*
DO	SE	RAY	CESOLFA*
FA	SI	BEMI*	DELASOL*
FI	TE	BEFA*	DESOLRE*
LA	TI	MESE	GAMMAUT*
LE	UT*	NETE	CESOLFAUT*
LI		ELAMI*	DELASOLRE*
ME	ARE*	MESON	GESOLREUT*
MI	DOH	TRITE	
RA	ELA*	CEFAUT*	
RE	SOH	FEFAUT*	

MUSICAL DIRECTIONS

VIF	MESTO	PRESTO	DETACHE
PIU	MOLTO	RUBATO	DOLENTE
RIT	MOSSO	SUBITO	GIOCOSO
	OSSIA	TENUTO	GIOIOSO
ADUE	PIANO	VELOCE	LANGSAM
ARCO	SECCO	VIVACE	LEBHAFT
FINE	SEGUE		MARCATO
LENT	TACET	AGITATO	MARTELE
LOCO	TARDO	ALLEGRO	MORENDO
MENO		ALSEGNO	PORTATO
MOTO	ADAGIO	AMABILE	STRETTO
ZART	ARIOSO	AMOROSO	
	ATEMPO	ANDANTE	ABATTUTA
ANIME	BELEBT	ANIMATO	COLLARCO
DOLCE	COMODO	ATTACCA	COLLEGNO
FORTE	DACAPO		CONANIMA
GRAVE	GIUSTO	CALANDO	CONFUOCO
INNIG	MASSIG	CONBRIO	DALSEGNO
LARGO	MUNTER	CONMOTO	GRAZIOSO

LEGGIERO	MODERATO	SPIANATO	SULTASTO
MAESTOSO	PIUMOSSO	SPICCATO	TRECORDE
MARZIALE	RITENUTO	STACCATO	UNACORDA

MUSICAL INSTRUMENTS
STRING

	GORAH	GUITAR	SABBEKA
DEL	GOURA	KISSAR	SAMBUKE
GUE	GRAND	KITTAR	SAMISEN
KIT	GUDOK	REBECK	SARANGI
UKE	GUIGE	RIBIBE	SARINDA
ARPA	GUMBE	SANCHO	THEORBO
ASOR	GUMBY	SANTIR	UKULELE
BINA	GUSLA	SATTAR	UPRIGHT
CRUT	JAMON	SPINET	VIHUELA
GIGA	KITAR	TYMPAN	
GORA	NABLA	URHEEN	ARCHLUTE
HARP	NANGA	VIELLE	AUTOHARP
KOTO	NEBEL	VIOLIN	BARITONE
LUTE	PIANO	ZITHER	BELLHARP
LYRE	REBAB		CLAVICIN
ROTE	REBEC	BANDORE	CLAVIOLA
RUAN	SAROD	CEMBALO	DULCIMER
TURR	SITAR	CHROTTA	JEWSHARP
VINA	STRAD	CITHARA	MANDOLIN
VIOL	TARAU	CITTERN	PIANETTE
	TIPLE	CLAVIOL	POCHETTE
AMATI	VIOLA	CLAVIER	PSALTERY
BANJO	VOYAL	CREMONA	VIRGINAL
CANUN	VOYOL	GITTERN	ZIMBALON
CELLO		KANTELE	
CROOD	CATGUT	MANDOLA	BALALAIKA
CROWD	CHELYS	PANDORA	MONOCHORD
CRWTH	CITOLE	PANDORE	
GAMBA	FIDDLE	PIANINO	
GEIGE	GOUSLE	PIANOLA	

WIND

	BUGLE	SYRINX	PICCOLO
NEI	CHENG	TRIGON	RACKETT
OAT	CODON	TROMBA	SACKBUT
ALTO	CORNO		SAXHORN
BEME	FLUTE	ALTHORN	SERPENT
BEEN	KAZOO	ANKLONG	SHOPHAR
FIFE	ORGAN	ANKLUNG	TRUMPET
FUYE	REGAL	BAGPIPE	
HORN	SHAWM	BASSOON	BARITONE
LURE	SHENG	BUCCINA	CALLIOPE
OBOE	TRUMP	CLARION	CLARINET
PIPE	ZINKE	DIAULOS	CROMORNE
REED		HAUTBOY	MELODEON
SANG	ATABAL	HELICON	NEHILOTH
TCHE	CLARIN	MUSETTE	PANPIPES
TUBA	CORNET	OCARINA	POSTHORN
ZINK	LITUUS	PANPIPE	RECORDER
	POMMER	PIBCORN	SOURDINE
AULOS	SHOFAR	PIBGORN	TROMBONE

PERCUSSION

ZEL	PIANO	TYMPAN	TYMPANO
	PUNGI		UPRIGHT
DRUM	SARON	BOMBARD	
GONG	TABOR	CELESTA	CARILLON
RIKK	TOMBE	CLAVIAL	CASTANET
TAAR	ZANZE	CYMBALS	CLAPPERS
TOPH		MANDORE	CROTALUM
	CYMBAL	MARIMBA	MELODION
BELLS	KETTLE	PIANINO	PIANETTE
BONES	MARACA	PIANOLA	TABOURIN
BONGO	NAGARA	SISTRUM	TRIANGLE
CHIME	RAPPEL	TABORET	ZAMBOMBA
DAIRA	TABRET	TIMBREL	XYLOPHONE
DRONE	TAMTAM	TIMPANI	
GRAND	TIMBAL	TIMPANO	

MUSICIANS AND MUSICAL PARTS

*indicates musical parts

DUO	AULETE	GAMBIST	GRIDDLER
	BUGLER	GLEEMAN	LUTANIST
ALTO*	CANTOR	HARPIST	MELODIST
BAND	CHORUS	HORNIST	MINSTREL
BARD	CORNET	KAPELLE	ORGANIST
BASS*	HARPER	MAESTRO	SONGSTER
SOLO	LEADER	PIANIST	STRUMMER
TRIO	LUTIST	QUARTET	THRUMMER
WAIT	LYRIST	QUINTET	TWANGLER
	MUSICO	SOPRANO*	VIRTUOSO
	OBOIST	SOLOIST	VOCALIST
BASSO*	SEPTET	VIOLIST	
CANTO*	SEXTET	WARBLER	CHORISTER
CHOIR	SINGER	YODELER	CHANTEUSE
FIFER	VIOLER		CONDUCTOR
LUTER			CONTRALTO*
MEZZO*	CAROLER	BARITONE*	CORNETIST
NONET	CHANTER	BARYTONE*	ORCHESTRA
OCTET	CELLIST	COMPOSER	TIMPANIST
PIPER	CROONER	CYMBALER	TRUMPETER
TENOR*	DRUMMER	DUETTIST	VIOLINIST
VOICE	FIDDLER	FLAUTIST	
	FLUTIST		

MUSICAL FORMS AND DANCES
FORMS

AIR	KOLO	TEMA	DITTY
LAY	LEED	TRIO	DOINA
ODE	LIED	TUNE	ELEGY
	MASS		ETUDE
ARIA	NOEL	CANON	FUGUE
CODA	OPUS	CAROL	MARCH
DUET	RAGA	CHANT	MELOS
FADO	SHAG*	CUECA	MOTET
GLEE	SIVA	DERRY	OCTET
HYMN	SONG	DIRGE	OPERA

PAEAN	VERSET	QUINTET	MADRIGAL
REVUE		RAGTIME	NOCTURNE
ROUND	BRAVURA	RECITAL	NOTTURNO
SUITE	CADENZA	REQUIEM	OPERETTA
STUCK	CANTATA	ROMANCE	ORATORIO
THEME	CANZONE	SCHERZO	OVERTURE
TROLL	CHANSON	SESTOLE	PARLANDO
	CHORALE	TOCCATA	PARTSONG
ANTHEM	CONCERT	WASSAIL	PASTORAL
ARIOSO	DESCANT		RHAPSODY
AUBADE	FANFARE	ANTIPHON	SERENADE
BALLAD	LAVOLTA	BERCEUSE	SERENATA
CHAUNT	LULLABY	CANTICLE	SESTOLET
CHORAL	MUSETTE	CAVATINA	SONATINA
MINUET	MUSICAL	CONCERTO	SYMPHONY
POLSKA	PARTITA	CORONACH	TONEPOEM
SEPTET	PIBROCH	DUETTINO	
SEXTET	PRELUDE	FANTASIA	
SONATA	QUARTET	FOLKSONG	

DANCES

HAY	PAVAN	SHIMMY	ROMAIKA
HOP	POLKA	TRESCA	SARDANA
JIG	RONDO		SHUFFLE
	RUMBA	AURESCA	TWOSTEP
FRUG	SALSA	BOURREE	
HAKA	SAMBA	CANTICO	ANGLAISE
HORA	TANGO	CHACCON	BUNNYHOP
HULA	TWIST	CHACONA	BUNNYHUG
JOTA	VALSE	COURANT	CACHUCHA
JUBA	VOLTA	CZARDAS	CAKEWALK
KOLO	WALTZ	FORLANA	CHACONNE
POLO		FOXTROT	COTILLON
REEL	BALLET	FURIANT	COURANTE
SHAG	BOLERO	FURLANA	FANDANGO
SIVA	BRANLE	GAVOTTA	GALLIARD
	CANCAN	GAVOTTE	HABANERA
BOREE	CEBELL	HALLING	HORNPIPE
CONGA	DREHER	HOEDOWN	HULAHULA
CUECA	HORMOS	LANCERS	LANCIERS
FLING	MAXIXE	LAVOLTA	MATELOTE
GALOP	MORRIS	MAZURKA	RIGADOON
GAVOT	NAUTCH	MERENGUE	SARABAND
GIGUE	POLSKA	MORISCO	
LINDY	REDOWA	ONESTEP	
MAMBA	RHUMBA	RAGTIME	

OPERAS, OPERETTAS, MUSICALS

AIDA	NORMA	CONSUL	OTELLO
LULU	OHKAY	EILEEN	RIENZI
MONA	SADKO	ERNANI	SALOME
RING	SALLY	JEWESS	
SARI	SUNNY	LOUISE	THECID
ZAZA	THAIS	MARTHA	UNDINE
	TOSCA	MIGNON	ALCESTE
FAUST		MIKADO	ELEKTRA
LAKME	ARMIDE	NATOMA	FIDELIO
MANON	CARMEN	OBERON	FIREFLY

JUBILEE	PROPHET	ARABELLA	PARSIFAL
KATINKA	ROBERTA	CAROUSEL	PATIENCE
MARINKA	VANESSA	COPPELIA	SHOWBOAT
MAZEPPA	VOLPONE	IOLANTHE	SHOWGIRL
MAYTIME	WALKURE	LABOHEME	TURANDOT
NEWMOON	WOZZECK	OKLAHOMA	

MYTHOLOGY
GODS AND GODDESSES LISTED BY CULTURE
GREEK
GODS

PAN	fields, herds	PONTUS	sea
ZAN	= ZEUS	POTHOS	= EROS
ARES	war	TITANS	
EROS	love		ancestors of gods; see p. 646
ZEUS	chief	URANUS	heaven
CHAOS	first god	ALASTOR	avenger
COMUS	joy, mirth	ANTEROS	Eros' foe
HADES	underworld	OCEANUS	waters
HYMEN	marriage	PHAETON	= HELIOS (son of)
MOMUS	ridicule	PHOEBUS	= APOLLO
AEOLUS	winds	PRIAPUS	life power
APOLLO	youth, sun	PROTEUS	sea
BOREAS	north wind	SILENUS	woods
CABIRI	earth gods	DIONYSUS	wine, drama
CRONUS	Titan: crops	ENYALIUS	war
HELIOS	sun	HYPERION	sun
HERMES	herds, science, herald	MORPHEUS	sleep
HYPNOS	sleep	POSEIDON	sea
KRONOS	= CRONUS	THANATOS	death
NEREUS	sea	ASCLEPIUS	medicine
		HEPHAESTUS	fire

GODDESSES

GE	earth	BAUBO	sensuality
ARA	vengeance	COTYS	vegetation
ATE	discord, infatuation	DIONE	Titan: earth
EOS	dawn	ERATO	Muse: poetry
NYX	night	HERSE	dew
CLIO	Muse: history	HORAE	seasons
DICE	= DIKE	IRENE	Hora: peace
DIKE	Hora: justice	MANES	dead spirits
ENYO	war	MOIRA	fate
ERIS	discord	MUSES	arts
GAEA	= GE	TYCHE	fortune
GAIA	= GE	AGLAIA	Grace: brilliance
HEBE	youth	ATHENA	peace, arts
HERA	queen	BENDIS	= ARTEMIS
HORA	one of Horae	CLOTHO	Fate: spinner
IRIS	rainbow messenger	EIRENE	= IRENE
KORE	= PERSEPHONE	GRACES	gods' helpers
NIKE	victory	HECATE	moon, magic
RHEA	gods' mother	HESTIA	hearth
UPIS	childbirth	HYGEIA	health
ATTIS	vegetation	MOIRAI	Fates

PALLAS	= ATHENA	DEMETER		agriculture
PHOBOS	fear	EUNOMIA		Hora: law
SELENA	= SELENE	EUTERPE		Muse: music
SELENE	moon	HYGIEIA		health
SEMELE	earth	NEMESIS		retribution
THALIA	Grace: bloom	CALLIOPE		Muse: eloquence
THEMIS	Titan: earth, law	LACHESIS		Fate: disposer of lots
URANIA	Muse: astronomy	POLYMNIA		Muse: sacred song
ANTHEIA	flowers	APHRODITE		love, beauty
ARTEMIS	nature, moon	MELPOMENE		Muse: tragedy
ASTARTE	= ARTEMIS	MNEMOSYNE		Titan: memory
ATROPOS	Fate: thread	AMPHITRITE		sea
CHLORIS	flowers	EUPHROSYNE		Grace: joy
COTYTTO	= COTYS	PERSEPHONE		queen of underworld

TITANS
GODS

ZEUS	CREUS	OCEANUS	PROMETHEUS
ATLAS	CRONUS	HYPERION	
COEUS	IAPETUS	EPIMETHEUS	

GODDESSES

LETO	DIONE	TETHYS	MNEMOSYNE
MAIA	THEIA	THEMIS	
RHEA	PHOEBE	EURYNOME	

WIVES AND LOVERS OF ZEUS

IO	AEGLE	EUROPA	DEMETER
HERA	DANAE	SEMELE	CALLISTO
LEDA	DIONE	THEMIS	EURYNOME
LETO	METIS	ALCMENE	MNEMOSYNE
MAIA	AEGINA	ANTIOPE	

ROMAN
GODS

DIS	= Gk. PLUTO	CAELUS		sky
SOL	= Gk. HELIOS	FAUNUS		= Gk. PAN
AMOR	= Gk. EROS	SATURN		= Gk. CRONUS
JOVE	= Gk. ZEUS	SOMNUS		= Gk. HYPNOS
MARS	= Gk. ARES	VULCAN		fire
MORS	= Gk. THANATOS	BACCHUS		wine
CACUS	fire	JUPITER		= Gk. ZEUS
CUPID	= Gk. EROS	MERCURY		= Gk. HERMES
JANUS	gates	NEPTUNE		= Gk. POSEIDON
LARES	house gods	PENATES		household
LIBER	= BACCHUS	MULCIBER		= Gk. VULCAN
ORCUS	= Gk. HADES	QUIRINUS		war
PICUS	agriculture	SILVANUS		woods
PLUTO	= Gk. HADES	VERTUMNUS		season

GODDESSES

OPS	= Gk. RHEA	DIAN		= DIANA
PAX	= Gk. IRENE	JUNO		= Gk. HERA
CACA	fire	LUNA		moon

MAIA	Vulcan's mate	ANNONA	crops
NONA	= Gk. **CLOTHO**	AURORA	= Gk. **EOS**
SPES	hope	DECUMA	= Gk. **LACHESIS**
CERES	= Gk. **DEMETER**	LUCINA	childbirth
DIANA	= Gk. **ARTEMIS**	MATUTA	dawn, birth
EPONA	horses	PARCAE	Fates
FAUNA	fertility	POMONA	fruit
FIDES	faith	TELLUS	earth
FLORA	flowers	TRIVIA	= **DIANA**
MORTA	= Gk. **ATROPOS**	VACUNA	hunting
PALES	herds	BELLONA	war
SALUS	= Gk. **HYGIEA**	FERONIA	fountain
TERRA	earth	FORTUNA	fortune
VENUS	= Gk. **APHRODITE**	MINERVA	= Gk. **ATHENA**
VESTA	= Gk. **HESTIA**	JUVENTAS	= Gk. **HEBE**
AESTAS	summer	LIBITINA	burials
		PROSERPINA	queen of underworld

EGYPTIAN

GODS

NU	chaos	APUAT	old chief god
RA	sun, first god (black bull)	HORUS	day (hawk head)
RE	= **RA**	KHNUM	builder (ram head)
SU	= **SHU**	MENTU	sun, war (falcon head)
BES	evil averter, pleasure	SEBEK	evil (crocodile head)
GEB	= **KEB**	SEKER	= **SOKARI**
KEB	earth	THOTH	wisdom, magic (ibis head)
MIN	procreation	ANUBIS	judge of dead (jackal head)
SEB	= **KEB**	DHOUTI	= **THOTH**
SET	war, evil	KHENSU	= **KHONSU**
SHU	atmosphere	KHINEMU	= **KHNUM**
TEM	sun, creator	KHONSU	Ra triad member
TUM	= **TEM**	MNEVIS	= **RA**
AMEN	gods' father	OSIRIS	underworld (judge of dead)
ATEN	solar disk	SOKARI	night, sun (falcon head)
ATMU	= **TEM**	HERSHEF	= **OSIRIS**
ATUM	= **TEM**	IMHOTEP	learning
HAPI	Nile	KHEPERA	morning sun, creator
KHEM	= **MIN**		(beetle)
MENT	= **MENTU**	KHEPERI	= **KHEPERA**
PTAH	world shaper	SERAPIS	= **OSIRIS**
SETH	= **SET**	SOKARIS	= **SOKARI**
AMMON	= **AMEN**	HARMACHIS	rising sun

GODDESSES

MA	= **MAAT**	SATI	queen of gods
MUT	Ra triad member	AMENT	gods' mother
NUT	heavens	ATHOR	= **HATHOR**
ANTA	war	PACHT	= **SEKHET**
APET	maternity (hippo body)	HATHOR	love, joy (cow head)
BAST	"Lady of Life" (lion head)	SEKHET	sun heat (cat head)
BUTO	serpent	SESHAT	learning (lion head)
ISIS	fertility	SPHINX	wisdom
MAAT	truth, law	NEPHTHYS	dead ritual

ASSYRIAN, BABYLONIAN, PERSIAN, PHOENICIAN
GODS

EA	water, arts: triad member	GIRRU	fire
ZU	storm	MAZDA	= ORMAZD
ANU	heavens: triad member	NUSKU	fire, light
BEL	earth: triad member	SAMAS	= SHAMASH
EAR	= EA	SIRIS	liquor
HEA	= EA	AMESHA	= SPENTA
SIN	moon, wisdom	ANSHAR	gods' father
UTU	sun	ARIMAN	evil
ADAD	wind	BABBAR	sun
ADDA	= ADAD	ESHMUN	healing
ADDU	= ADAD	KISHAR	lower, world
APSU	chaos	MARDUK	chief, sun
ASUR	= ASHUR	MOLOCH	sacrifice
BAAL	fertility	NANNAR	= SIN
ENKI	= EA	NERGAL	sun; pest
ENZU	= SIN	OANNES	wisdom
IRRA	war	ORMAZD	creator, chief
NABU	wisdom	RAMMAN	= ADAD
NEBO	= NABU	RIMMON	= ADAD
UTUG	= UTU	SPENTA	Ormazd aid
AHURA	= ORMAZD	TAMMUZ	vegetation
ASHUR	chief, power	AHRIMAN	= ARIMAN
DAGAN	earth	MITHRAS	light, truth
DAGON	fish, fields	MINURTA	sun
ELLIL	= BEL	SHAMASH	sun, order
ENLIL	= BEL	NINGIRSU	war, fields

GODDESSES

ERUA	mother goddess	ALLATU	underworld
GULA	healing	BELILI	lower word
NAMA	= ARURU	INNINA	= ISHTAR
NINA	watery deep	ISHTAR	earth, war, love
ANATH	war	NINGAL	sun
ARURU	mother: earth	ANAHITA	earth
ISTAR	= ISHTAR	ASTARTE	love, moon
NANAI	earth	DAMKINA	earth
NINNI	= ISHTAR	ERESHKIGAL	= ALLATU
NINTU	= ARURU		

CELTIC, IRISH, BRITISH, WELSH, GAULISH
GODS

LER	sea	NUDD	sun
LUG	light, sun	ANGUS	love, beauty
BELI	= BELENUS	ARAWN	Annwn's lord
BRAN	the blessed	BALOR	Fomorian giant
BRES	god king	DAGDA	chief
ESUS	vegetation	DOMNU	a Fomorian
GWYN	underworld	DYLAN	waves
LLEU	= LLEW	LLUDD	= NUDD
LLEW	sun	MIDER	underworld
LLYR	sea	NUADA	= NUDD
LUGH	= LUG	NUADU	= NUDD

PWYLL	dead	OGMIUS	eloquence
AENGUS	an Angus	BELENUS	sun
ELATHA	a Fomorian	CAMULUS	war
HAFGAN	chief	GWYDION	sky, arts, magic
NODENS	= NODONS	PRYDERI	underworld
NODONS	sun	DIANCECHT	medicine
OENGUS	an Angus		

GODDESSES

ANA	mother goddess	BRIGIT	Mary of the Gael; fire
DON	= DANA	BRANWEN	sea
BADB	= BODB	MORRIGU	war
BODB	battle	BELISAMA	beauty
DANA	fertility, ancestress	ARIANRHOD	rivers
EPONA	horses, mules	BRIGANTIA	mother goddess

NORSE-TEUTONIC
GODS

AS	Aesir (singular)	AEGIR	sea
ER	= TIU	AESIR	chief gods
TY	= TIU	ALCIS	twin gods
VE	world creator, Odin's brother	BALDR	= BALDUR
EAR	= TIU	BRAGE	= BRAGI
LOK	= LOKI	BRAGI	poetry
TIU	sky, war	DONAR	thunder
TIW	= TIU	HODER	= HOTH
TYR	= TIU	HOTHR	= HOTH
ULL	bow skill, beauty	LODUR	= LOTRUR
ZIO	= TIU	NJORD	fertility
ASES	= AESIR	VANIR	early race of gods: crops,
BURI	father of gods		fertility
FREY	fertility	WODAN	= ODIN
HLER	= AEGIR	WODEN	= ODIN
HOTH	night, blind Balder slayer	WOTAN	= ODIN
LOKE	= LOKI	BALDER	= BALDUR
LOKI	discord	BALDUR	peace
ODIN	chief, war, wisdom;	HOENIR	creator of first human
	slays Ymir	LOTHUR	weather, crops
THOR	thunder, serpent slayer	NJORTH	= NJORD
VALI	Ragnarok survivor	VITHAR	Fenrir slayer
VANS	= VANIR	FORSETI	justice
VILI	world creator; Odin's brother	VIDHARR	= VITHAR
		HEIMDALL	Asgard guardian

GODDESSES

EIR	healing	URTH	= NORN
HEL	dead, underworld	WURD	= NORN
RAN	sea	FREYA	beauty, love
SIF	home	FRIGG	sky marriage, Friday source
URD	= NORN	SKULD	= NORN
ERDA	earth	GEFJON	= FRIGG
FREA	= FRIGG	HERTHA	= NERTHUS
FRIA	= FRIGG	ASYNJUR	Aesirs' aid
HELA	= HEL	NERTHUS	peace
NORN	fate, destiny	VERTHANDI	= NORN
SAGA	sorcery		

HINDU (VEDIC)
GODS

KA	unknown god	MITRA	sun
AGNI	fire	RUDRA	storm
AKAL	Immortal one	SHIVA	= SIVA
CIVA	= SIVA	SURYA	sun
DEVA	= DEWA	ASVINS	dawn: twins
DEWA	angel	BRAHMA	creator
KALI	"the black one"	GANESA	wisdom
KAMA	love (parrot)	KALIKA	= KALI
RAMA	Vishnu avatar	KUBERA	wealth
SIVA	supreme, destroyer, arts;	PUSHAN	roads, cattle
	miracles	SKANDA	war
SOMA	ritual liquor	VARUNA	cosmic order
VASU	= VISHNU	VISHNU	supreme, preserver
VAYU	wind	GANESHA	= GANESA
YAMA	judge of dead	HANUMAN	monkey king
BHAGA	love, wealth	PARVATI	"mountaineer"
DYAUS	sky, dawn, fire	SAVITAR	sun
GAURI	"the brilliant"	BALARAMA	= RAMA
INDRA	thunder	PARJANYA	rain
KALKI	Vishnu avatar	TRIMURTI	trinity
MARUT	storm	KARTIKEYA	= SKANDA

GODDESSES

SRI	beauty	USHAS	dawn
UMA	splendor	BRAHMI	speech
VAC	speech	CHANDI	"the fierce"
DEVI	mother goddess	SHAXTI	mother goddess
SHRI	= SRI	BRAVANI	= DEVI
USAS	= USHAS	CHANDRA	moon
VACH	= VAC	LAKSHMI	= SRI
DURGA	"the inaccessible" (on tiger)	ANNAPURNA	plenty
SHREE	= SRI	SARASVATI	= SHAKTI

MAYA AND AZTEC

CHAC	rain god	XOLOTL	coyote god
INTI	sun god	ITZAMNA	creator god
TOHIL	fire god	MICTLAN	underworld: Aztec
AHPUCH	god of death	CENTEOTL	corn god
IXCHEL	fertility goddess	KULULKAN	creator: Mayan
TLALOC	rain god	OMETEOTL	supreme creator

MISCELLANEOUS
GODS

ATAU	god: Polynesian	AMITA	= AMIDA
CHAC	— MOL: rain	EBISU	happiness: Japanese
JOSS	home: Chinese	DOTEI	happiness: Japanese
KANE	chief: Hawaiian	TINIA	= Gk. ZEUS: Etruscan
MAUI	chief culture hero: Polynesian	WENTI	literature: Chinese
TANE	forests: Hawaiian	BENTEN	happiness: Japanese
TIKI	man creator: Polynesian	JUMULA	heavens: Finnish
ALLAH	supreme being	TAAROA	chief: Polynesian
AMIDA	Jodo deity: Japanese	DAIKOKU	happiness: Japanese

HURAKAN	thunder: Quiche	BISHAMON	happiness: Japanese
JUROJIN	happiness: Japanese	MANABUSH	creator: Algonquian
KANALOA	leading: Hawaiian		(Great Hare)
KWANNON	mercy: Chinese	TANGAROA	chief: Polynesian
MANITOU	great spirit	SVANTOVIT	chief: Slavic

GODDESSES

MAMA	fertility: Peruvian	SEDNA	culture: Eskimo
PELE	fire, volcano: Hawaiian	TANIT	moon: Carthage
TARI	earth: Khond	TANITH	= TANIT
ALLAT	mother goddess	PERCHTA	earth, spinning: German

GODS AND GODDESSES
LISTED BY SPECIALTIES
*Indicates goddesses

CHIEF GODS, GODS' ANCESTORS, CREATORS, MOTHER GODDESSES

AS	ERUA*	ALLAT*	HAFGAN
EA	HERA*	AMENT*	INNINA*
BA	HLER	APUAT	ISHTAR*
RE	JOVE	ARURU*	MARDUK
VE	JUNO*	ASHUR	ORMAZD
ANA*	KANE	CHAOS	SATURN
ANU	MAUI	DAGDA	SHAKTI*
BEL	ODIN	ELLIL	VISHNU
HEA	PTAH	ENLIL	TAAROA
OPS*	RAMA	ISTAR*	BHAVANI*
ASES	RHEA*	MAZDA	JUPITER
ATMU	SATI*	NINNI*	KANALOA
ATUM	SIVA	NINTU*	KUKULKAN
BRES	VASU	NINURTA*	MANABUSH
BURI	VILI	VANIR	TANGAROA
CIVA	ZEUS	WODAN	
DEVI*	AHURA	WODEN	
ENKI	ALLAH	WOTAN	
		BRAHMA	

SUN, LIGHT, FIRE, SKY

ER	AMEN	NUSKU	NINGAL*
BA	AMON	SAMAS	NODENS
RE	ATEN	SURYA	SEKHET*
TY	BELI	USHAS*	URANUS
ANU	LLEU	VESTA*	VULCAN
EOS*	LLEW	APOLLO	BELENUS
NUT*	NUDD	AURORA*	KHEPERA
SHU	PELE*	BABBAR	MITHRAS
SOL	UTUG	CAELUS	NINURTA
TEM	DYAUS	GEFJON*	PHAETON
TIU	FRIGG*	HELIOS	PHOEBUS
TIW	GIRRU	HESTIA*	SAVITAR
TUM	LLUDD	JUMALA	SHAMASH
TYR	MITRA	MARDUK	SOKARIS
UTU	NUADA	MATUTA*	HYPERION
AGNI	NUADU	NERGAL	HARMACHIS

EARTH, FERTILITY,
WOODS, HUNTING, FIELDS, NATURE

GE*	GAIA*	FLORA*	POMONA*
BEL	ISIS*	ISTAR*	PUSHAN
DON*	MAMA*	NINTU*	SATURN
GEB	NAMA*	NJORD	SEMELE*
KEB	TANE	PALES*	TELLUS*
OPS*	TARI*	PICUS	VACUNA*
PAN	VANS	TERRA*	ANTHEIA*
SEB	ATTIS*	VANIR	ARTEMIS*
BAAL	ARURU*	ANNONA*	CHLORIS*
DANA*	CERES*	BENDIS*	DEMETER*
DANU*	COTYS*	CABIRI	PERCHTA*
ERDA*	DAGON	CRONUS	SILENUS
ESUS	DIANA*	CYBELE*	SILVANUS
FREY	DIONE*	ISHTAR*	CENTEOTL
GAEA*	FAUNA*	LOTHUR	

UNDERWORLD, DEATH,
SLEEP, NIGHT, MAGIC, MOON

DIS	YAMA	ANUBIS	ARTEMIS*
HEL*	DIANA*	BELILI*	ASTARTE*
NOX*	HADES	BENDIS*	CHANDRA
NYX*	HODER	HECATE*	GWYDION
SIN	HOTHR	HYPNOS	HERSHEF
ENZU	MANES	KALIKA*	MICTLAN
GWYN	MIDER	KISHAR	PRYDERI
HELA*	ORCUS	NANNAR	SERAPIS
HOTH	PLUTO	OSIRIS	SOKARIS
KALI*	PWYLL	SELENA*	LIBITINA*
KORE*	SEKER	SELENE*	MORPHEUS
LUNA*	TANIT*	SOKARI	NEPHTHYS*
MORS	THOTH	SOMNUS	THANATOS
SAGA*	ALLATU*	TANITH*	

FAITH, HOPE, FATE, HOME, HAPPINESS

URD*	COMUS	VESTA*	DAIKOKU
JOSS	EBISU	CLOTHO*	FORTUNA*
NONA*	FIDES*	HATHOR*	JUROJIN
NORN*	HOTEI	HESTIA*	PENATES
SPES*	LARES	KUBERA	BISHAMON
URTH*	MOIRA*	MOIRAI*	LACHESIS*
WURD	MORTA*	PARCAE*	ANNAPURNA*
WYRD*	TYCHE*	ATROPOS*	

MEDICINE, HEALTH, ARTS, SCIENCE, WISDOM

EA	ODIN	WENTI	SPHINX*
EIR*	SIVA	ATHENA*	BELENUS
HEA	VACH*	BRAHMI*	GANESHA
SIN	BRAGE	DHOUTI	IMHOTEP
VAC*	BRAGI	ESHMUN	MERCURY
BELI	HYGEA*	HERMES	MINERVA*
CIVA	MUSES*	HYGIEA*	DIONYSUS
ENKI	SALUS*	GANESA	ASCLEPIUS
GULA*	SEDNA*	NANNAR	DIANCECHT
NABU	SHIVA	OGMIUS	
NEBO	THOTH	SESHAT*	

WAR, DISCORD, VENGEANCE, EVIL

ER	BADB*	SETH	NERGAL
TY	BODB*	ANATH*	PHOBOS
ARA*	ENYO*	ANATU*	SKANDA
ATE*	ERIS*	ISTAR*	ALASTOR
EAR	FURY*	MENTU	BELLONA*
TIU	IRRA	SEBEK	CAMULUS
TIW	LOKE	WODAN	MORRIGU*
TYR	LOKI	WODEN	NEMESIS*
ZIO	MARS	WOTAN	ENYALIUS
ANTA*	MENT	ARIMAN	NINGIRSU
ARES	ODIN	ISHTAR*	QUIRINUS

SEA, SEASON, WIND, WEATHER

EA	LEIR	INDRA	BRANWEN*
ZU	LLYR	MARUT	CHACMOL
HEA	NINA*	RUDRA	HURAKAN
LER	THOR	AEOLUS	NEPTUNE
RAN*	VAYU	AESTAS*	OCEANUS
ADAD	AEGIR	BOREAS	PROTEUS
ADDA	DONAR	LOTHUR	BELISAMA*
ADDU	DYLAN	NEREUS	PARJANYA
ENIU	EURUS	PONTUS	POSEIDON
HAPI	HERSE*	RAMMAN	VERTUMNUS
IRIS*	HORAE*	TLALOC	AMPHITRITE

BEAUTY, LOVE, YOUTH, JOY, MARRIAGE, BIRTH

BES	SHRI*	PARCA*	POTHOS
SRI*	ULLR	SHREE*	THALIA*
ULL	UPIS*	VENUS*	ASTARTE*
UMA*	ANGUS	AENGUS	LAKSHMI*
AMOR	BHAGA	AGLAIA*	JUVENTAS*
APET*	COMUS	GEFJON*	APHRODITE*
BAST*	CUPID	GRACES*	ARIANRHOD
EROS	FREYA*	HATHOR*	
HEBE*	FRIGG*	LUCINA*	
KAMA	HYMEN	MATUTA*	

JUSTICE, PEACE, LAW, TRUTH

PAX*	BALDR	BALDUR	FORSETI
DICE*	IRENE*	EIRENE*	MITHRAS
DIKE*	ATHENA*	HERTHA*	NERTHUS*
MAAT*	BALDER	THEMIS*	

FAMILY RELATIONS

Father	Offspring	Father	Offspring
EA	Nina	BANA	Usha
RA	Shu, Maat	FINN	Ossian
ANU	Nanai	ILUS	Laomedon
BEL	Ninurta	LLYR	Bran, Branwen, Manawyddan
GEB	Osiris, Set, Nephthys, Isis	LOKI	Hel, Fenris (wolf),
SIN	Ishtar		Midgard (serpent)
AMEN	Khonsu	MARS	Romulus, Remus
AMON	Bast	ODIN	Balder, Vali (Vale), Vithar
APSU	Mummu	SIVA	Skanda, Ganesha
ARES	Cycnus, Phobos, Alcippe	THOR	Ull

Father	Offspring	Father	Offspring
VAYU	Hanuman	URANUS	Rhea, Themis, Cronus
WADE	Wayland	CECROPS	Herse
ZEUS	Ate, Ares, Eris, Hebe, Kore,	CEPHEUS	Andromeda
	Helen, Irene, Muses, Aeacus,	DELLING	Dag
	Apollo, Athena, Graces, Hermes,	EURYTUS	Iole
	Amphion, Artemis, Epaphus,	GWYDION	Dylan
	Dionysus, Hercules, Sarpedon,	HIMAVAT	Devi, Parvati, Shakti
	Aphrodite, Persephone,	JAPETUS	Atlas, Prometheus
	Hephaestus	ICARIUS	Penelope, Erigone
AESON	Jason	LAERTES	Ulysses
ATLAS	Hyades, Pleiades	OCEANUS	Styx, Doris
BELUS	Ninus, Danaus	OEDIPUS	Ismene
CHAOS	Nyx	PANDION	Procne
COEUS	Leto	PHORCYS	Gorgons, Graeae
CREON	Jocasta, Haemon	SIGMUND	Sigurd
CREUS	Pallas	TELAMON	Ajax
DAGDA	Aengus, Brigit	THAUMUS	Harpies
HOGNI	Hild	THESEUS	Hippolytus
INDRA	Arjuna	ULYSSES	Telemachus
IPHIS	Evadne	ANCHISES	Aeneas
LAIUS	Oedipus	DAEDALUS	Icarus
LLUDD	Gwynn	HYPERION	Eos, Helios
MINOS	Ariadne, Phaedra	LAOMEDON	Priam
PRIAM	Paris, Hector, Helenus,	POSEIDON	Otus, Zetes, Peias,
	Troilus, Polydorus, Polyxena,		Triton, Antaeus, Aloeus
	Deiphobus, Cassandra	SISYPHUS	Glaucus
ACHEUS	Telamon	TANTALUS	Niobe, Pelops
AEACUS	Telamon, Peleus	TITHONUS	Laomedon, Memnon
AEETES	Medea	TYNDAEUS	Diomed
AEGEUS	Theseus	AGAMEMNON	Electra, Orestes
AGENOR	Cadmus, Europa	DEUCALION	Hellen
APOLLO	Asclepius, Ion, Hymen	SCAMANDAR	Teucer
ATREUS	Menelaus, Agamemnon		
BALDER	Forseti	Mother	Offspring
BOREAS	Calais	GE	Uranus, Titans
BRAHMA	Daksha	IO	Epaphus
CADMUS	Ino, Semele	EOS	Memnon
CRONUS	Zeus, Hades, Hestia,	INO	Melicertes, Palaemon
	Poseidon, Hera, Demeter	NUT	Osiris, Set, Nephthys, Isis
DEVAKI	Krishna	NYX	Thanatos
ELATHA	Bres	OPS	= RHEA
EREBUS	Charon	CETO	Gorgons, Graeae
HELIOS	Circe	ENYO	Ares
HELLEN	Aeolus, Dorus	GAEA	Erechtheus, Cronus, Pontus,
HERMES	Pan, Silenus		Phoebe, Anteus, Themis
IASION	Plutus	HERA	Ares, Hebe, Ens, Hephaestus
NEREUS	Amphitrite, Nereids	ISIS	Horus
NJORTH	Frey	LEDA	Helen, Castor, Pollux
OILEUS	Ajax	LETO	Artemis, Apollo
OSIRIS	Horns, Anubis	MAIA	Hermes
PALLAS	Nike	NOTT	Dag
PELEUS	Achilles	RHEA	Zeus, Hades, Hera, Poseidon,
PELIAS	Alcestis, Acastus		Hestia, Demeter
PELOPS	Atreus	STYX	Nike
PENEUS	Daphne	ADITI	Aditya
RUSTUM	Sohrab	AEGLE	Graces
SATURN	= CRONUS	CERES	= DEMETER
SIGURD	Swanhild	DANAE	Perseus

Mother	Offspring
DIONE	Aphrodite
DORIS	Nereids
FRIGG	Balder
METIS	Zeus
NIOBE	Argus
SIGYN	Hel
THEIA	Eos
VENUS	Cupid
AEGINA	Aeacus
AETHRA	Hyades
CANACE	Aloeus
CREUSA	Ion
CYBELE	Zeus
EUROPA	Minos, Sarpedon
HECUBA	Paris, Helenus, Hector, Troilus, Polydorus, Polyxena, Deiphobus, Cassandra
LATONA	= LETO
PHOEBE	Leto
SEMELE	Dionysus
TETHYS	Styx
THEMIS	Astraea, Irene, Prometheus
THETIS	Achilles
URANIA	Hymen
ALCMENE	Hercules
ANTIOPE	Amphion
CLYMENE	Atlas
CORONIS	Asclepius
DEMETER	Persephone, Plotos
ELECTRA	Dardanus, Harpies
EURYBIA	Pallas
JOCASTA	Oedipus
PARVATI	Ganesha
PLEIONE	Pleiades
CALLIOPE	Orpheus
CALLISTO	Arcas
MNEMOSYNE	Muses
AMPHITRITE	Triton
RHEASYLVIA	Remus, Romulus
CLYTEMNESTRA	Electra, Orestes

Husband (Lover)	Wife (Lover)
EA	Damkina
ANA	Anatum
BEL	Belit
GEB	Nut
LER	Aoife
SET	Nephthys
SHU	Tefnut
AMEN	Mut
APSU	Tiarnat
ATLI	Gudrun
BAAL	Baalat(h)
BRES	Brigit
CEYX	Halcyone
EROS	Psyche
FREY	Gerth (Gerd)
HLER	Ran

Husband (Lover)	Wife (Lover)
IDAS	Marpessa
LOKI	Sigyn
NUDD	Morriu
ODIN	Frigg = Frea = Fria; Rind(r)
PTAH	Sekhet
RAMA	Sita
SIVA	Devi, Shakti, Parvati
THOR	Sif
ZEUS	see page 646
AEGIR	Ran
ATLAS	Pleione, Aethra
ATTIS	Cybele
BRAGE	Ithun(n) = Idun
DAGDA	Boann
CONOR	Deirdre, Medb
HADES	Kore = Cora
JASON	Creusa, Medea
KINGU	Tiamat
LAIUS	Jocasta
LYCUS	Dirce
MINOS	Pasiphae
NOISE	Deirdre
NINUS	Semiramis
ORION	Eos
PARIS	Oenone, Helen
PHAON	Sappho
PRIAM	Hecuba
PWYLL	Rhiannon
ADONIS	Aphrodite
AENEAS	Creusa, Dido, Lavinia
AILILL	Medb
APOLLO	Creusa, Urania, Cassandra
ATREUS	Aerope
BALDER	Nanna
BRAHMA	Brahmi, Sarasvati
CADMUS	Harmonia
CRONUS	Rhea
GUNNAR	Brunhild
HAEMON	Antigone
HECTOR	Andromache
MARDUK	Sarpanitu, Zirbanit, Erua
NEREUS	Doris
NERGAL	Allatu
NJORTH	Thjazi
OENEUS	Althaea
OSIRIS	Isis
PALLAS	Styx
PELOPS	Hippodamia
PONTUS	Gaea
RAVANA	Sita
SIGURD	Gudrun
TAMMUZ	Ishtar
TEREUS	Procne
URANUS	Gaea
VARUNA	Aditi
VISHNU	Lakshmi
VULCAN	Mala
ADMETUS	Alcestis

Husband (Lover)	Wife (Lover)	Husband (Lover)	Wife (Lover)
AMPHION	Niobe	ENDYMION	Selene
ATHAMAS	Ino	HERCULES	Hebe, Auge, Deianira
ATHAMUS	Nephele	HYPERION	Theia
GUNTHER	Brunhild	MENELAUS	Helen
GWYDION	Arianrhod	MELEAGER	Atalanta
IAPETUS	Clymene	MILANION	Atalanta
LEANDER	Hero	PHILEMON	Baucis
NINURTA	Gula	POSEIDON	Cancace, Amphitrite,
ORPHEUS	Eurydice		Gaea
PERSEUS	Andromeda	TITHONUS	Eos
PROCRIS	Cephalus	DEIPHOBUS	Helen
SHAMASH	Ai – Aya	DEUCALION	Pyrrha
THESEUS	Antiope, Ariadne, Phaedra	NARCISSUS	Echo
TROILUS	Cressida	SIEGFRIED	Kriemhild
ULYSSES	Penelope	TYNDAREUS	Leda
ASTRAEUS	Eos	AMPRITRYON	Alcmene
CEPANEUS	Evadne	EPIMETHEUS	Pandora
CEPHALUS	Eos	HEPHAESTUS	Charis
DIARMEIT	Brainne	HIPPOMENES	Atalanta

TERMS AND NAMES
GREEK AND ROMAN

IO	became heifer	NAIAD	sea nymph
KER	doom spirit	NAPEA	wood nymph
AJAX	hero-suicide	NIOBE	became stone
ARGO	Jason ship	OREAD	mountain nymph
DIDO	Carthaginian queen	ORION	hunter
FAUN	wood deity	PARIS	apple awarder; slew Achilles
IDAS	Castor slayer	PHAON	Lesbos boatman
ILUS	Troy founder	PRIAM	Troy king
NUMA	—POMPILIUS, king	REMUS	Romulus' brother
OTUS	giant	SATYR	man-horse
AEAEA	Circe's isle	SINON	deceived Troy
AEGIS	Zeus' shield	SIREN	bird-woman lure
ALTIS	sacred grove	SYBIL	seeress
ARGOS	sacred city	AENEAS	Troy war hero
ARGUS	Io guard: monster	ANANKE	ultimate fate
ARION	poet saved by fish; horse	ANCILE	sacred shield
ATLAS	heaven supporter	AUGEAS	Elis king (stables)
AULIS	Iphigenia place	BAUCIS	Zeus' host
CIRCE	sorceress	CHARON	Styx boatman
DRYAD	wood nymph	CREUSA	slain by Medea
GYGES	magic ring king	DANAUS	Lynceus foe
HARPY	bird-woman	DAPHNE	became tree
HELEN	Troy war cause	DELPHI	oracle site
HELLE	fell into sea	DODONA	oracle seat
HYADS	nymphs	EGERIA	well nymph
HYDRA	9-head monster	EREBUS	dark site
ILIUM	Troy	EUROPA	abducted by bull
IXION	wheel-bound king	GEMINI	Castor, Pollux
JASON	gets Golden Fleece	GORGON	monster
LAMIA	vampire	IOLAUS	Hercules' pal
LINUS	poet: lacerated	MAENAD	Nymph; Dionysus
MEDEA	sorceress; Jason aide		attendant
MIDAS	ass-eared king	MEDUSA	slain by Perseus
MINOS	king-judge	NAPAEA	wood nymph
MORMO	bugbear	NEREID	sea nymph

NESSUS	slain Centaur
PELIAS	Iolcus king
SPHINX	winged-lion woman slain by Oedipus
TRITON	sea demigod
TURNUS	Aeneas' rival
TYPHON	monster
ACTAEON	became stag
AGANICE	witch
ALOADAE	giants
ARACHNE	became spider
AVERNUS	inferno
BRISEIS	Achilles' captive
CALCHAS	Greek seer
CALYPSO	nymph (Ulysses)
CECROPS	Athens founder
CENTAUR	man-horse
CHIMERA	monster slain by Bellerophon
CYCLOPS	one-eyed giant
CYTHERA	Aphrodite isle
ELEUSIS	mysteries site
ERINYES	avenging spirits
GALATEA	Pygmalion statue
GLAUCUS	Argo helmsman
HELICON	sacred mountain
INACHUS	Argos king
LAOCOON	priest warner
LEMURES	night spirits
LYNCEUS	slew Danaus
MARSYAS	lost Apollo duel
OEDIPUS	Thebes king; slew father
OLYMPUS	sacred mountain
ORESTES	slew mother
PANDORA	box opener
PEGASUS	winged horse
ROMULUS	slew Remus
THESEUS	slew Minotaur
ULYSSES	Ithaca king
ACHILLES	Hector slayer; Patroclus pal
AGANIPPE	Muses' fountain
AMBROSIA	celestial food
ANTIGONE	buried alive
ATALANTA	huntress; picks golden apples
BRIAREUS	100-hand monster
CALLISTO	huntress; became boar
CERBERUS	Hades watchdog
DAEDALUS	aze-wing maker
GANYMEDE	gods' cupbearer
HELIADES	became trees
HERACLES	hero, strong
HERCULES	hero, man
MELAMPUS	seer
MINOTAUR	man-beast slain by Theseus
MYRMIDON	Achilles' ally
NAUSICAA	Ulysses' friend
PLEIADES	became stars
SISYPHUS	stone roller
TANTALUS	starving king
TIRESIAS	blind seer
TITHONUS	became butterfly
TIPHOEUS	100-head monster

HINDU AND VEDIC

AHI	sky serpent
ATMA	= ATMAN
BANA	100-arm giant
KALI	evil genius: Agni's tongue
KETU	Rahu's tail
MANU	wise ancestor
MERU	holy mountain
NAGA	semihuman serpent
RAHU	dragon: swallows sun
SURA	angel
YUGA	age of world
ASURA	evil spirit
ATMAN	universal ego
HANSA	Asvin's swan, goose
GANGA	holy river
KALPA	aeon
NANDI	Siva's bull
PITRI	semi-divine ancestor
PRANA	life breath
RISHI	holy sage
SESHA	= SHESHA
ARJUNA	gets Krishna revelation
AMRITA	life elixir
ANANTA	infinity
AVATAR	incarnation
BHRUGI	gods' messenger
DAITYA	evil spirit
DASYUS	evil demons
GARUDA	man-bird Vishnu bearer
NARAKA	hell
PATALA	underworld series
RIBHUS	artisans of the gods
SHESHA	serpent king
SVARGA	Indra's paradise
VASUIU	Naga king
VRITRA	dragon slain by Indra
YADAVA	Krishna's race
APSARAS	nymph, dancer
NIRVANA	reunion with Brahma
PURUSHA	male principle
SRADDHA	ancestor rite
AIRAVATA	Indra's elephant
LOKAPALA	world guardian
MAHADEVA	Siva title
NATARAJA	Siva; cosmic dancer
RAKSHASA	goblins
RAMAYANA	sanskrit epic
TVASHTAR	divine artificer

NORSE

ASK	first man	VOLVA	seeress
DIS	female spirit	ALVISS	dwarf
DAG	day; see NATT	ASGARD	god's abode
LIF	human survivor	ITHUNN	= ITHUN
NIX	water sprite	JOTUNN	= JOTUN
ASKR	= ASK	REGINN	= REGIN
AUI	slain king	SIGURD	Volsunga saga hero
EGIL"Tell story" hero; Voland brother	VOLUND	inventive smith
GARM	Hel's dog slays Tyr	ANDVARI	ring guardian
GERI	Odin's wolf	ALFHEIM	Frey's home
GRAM	Sigurd sword	BIFROST	rainbow bridge
NATTT	= NOTT: night	BALMUNG	Sigurd's sword
SURT	fire demon: Frey's slayer	MIDGARD	man's abode: earth
WADE	= WATT: storm giant	NAGLFAR	giant's ship
YMIR	"rime cold giant"	NIFLHEL	Hel's region
EGILL	= EGIL	VALHALL	Odin's hall of heroes
EMBLA	first woman	VINGOLF	Asgard hall
ETZEL	= ATLI	WAYLAND	= VOLUND
FREKI	Odin's wolf	ALBERICH	Nibelung dwarf
GIMLE	home of blessed	BRUNHILD	strong queen
GJOLL	Hel's icy river	DRAUPNIR	Odin's ring
HAGEN	Sigurd slayer; slain by	HRIMFAXI	Nott's horse
	Kriemhild	IRMINSUL	sacred trees
HOGNI	Hethin foe	MJOLLNIR	Thor's hammer
HYMIR	sea giant	NIBELUNG dwarf guarding treasure
ITHUN keeps golden apples of youth	NIFLHEIM	Hel's region
JOTUN	giant	RAGNAROK	"twilight of gods";
MIMIR	well-guarding giant		Aesir giants fight
REGIN	Sigurd's evil tutor	SLEIPNER	Odin's steed
SURTR	= SURT	TARNHELM	cap making invisible
TROLL	giant; dwarf	VALKYRIE	Odin's messenger
		YGGDRASIL	world tree

EGYPTIAN

AB	will, heart	ATUM	= RA
BA	soul (bird-man)	BAST	cat-goddess
KA	body	BENU	sacred heron
RA	sun-god	DUAT	underworld
AKH	spirit of man	HAPI	genius of Amenti
GEB	earth-god	HATI	= AB
NUN	chaos	ISIS	nature-goddess (cow-head)
NUT	sky-goddess	PTAH	thinker
SET	god of evil	AMSET	genius of Amenti
SHU	air-god	APEPI	great serpent
AANI	ape: dog-head	HORUS	solar deity (falcon-head)
AARU	abode of dead	KHNUM	ram-god
AMON	chief god	TAURT	hippo-head
ANKH	sacred cross	THOTH	ibis, patron of arts
APIS	sacred bull	AMENTI	abode of dead
ATOM	= RA	OPHOIS	war-god

BABYLONIAN

ROC	giant bird	AHURA	benign genie
AZHI	—DAHAKA: dragon	ARALU	underworld
DEVA	= DEAVA: demon	BELUS	king
YIMA	king of man	ETANA	eagle rider
ADAPA	first man	HAOMA	sacred liquor

IGIGI	heavenly; spirits	SIMORG	= ROC
KINGU	slain by Marduk	FEROHER	disk symbol
MUMMU	Apsu's agent	JAMSHID	pen king
ALOROS	king	NAMTARU	Hades messenger
ALULIM	= ALOROS	SIMORGH	= ROC
ENGUDI	wild man: Gilgamesh pal	FRAVASHI	spiritual guardian
ENUKKI	gods' servants	GILGAMESH	epic hero
RUSTAM	= RUSTUM: hero		

CELTIC

LUD	king	FIANNA	Fenian heroes
MIL	= MILEDH	LUGNAS	harvest feast
CROM	—DUBH'S SUNDAY: feast	MILEDH	Irish ancestor
MEDB	Queen of Connault	OSSIAN	hero
SHEE	= SIDHE: fairy fort, folk	TUATHA	—DE DANNAN: gods
DRUID	sage, conjurer	BANSHEE	warning spirit
FOMOR	sea robber; evil power	BELTANE	Mayday rite
KELPY	water spirit	MORGAIN	fairy: sister of Arthur
POOKA	marsh goblin	SAMRAIN	feast of dead
AILILL	king	FIRBOLGS	Fomor foes
ANNWFN	= ANNWN: Eden	TALIESIN	bard
AVALON	Arthur abode	LEPRECHAUN	tricky old man

MONSTERS

OGRE	man-eater	TYPHON	flaming 100-headed
ARGUS	100-eyed	CENTAUR	half-man, half-horse
HARPY	predatory, winged dragon	CHIMERA	lion-goat; flame-spewing
HYDRA	9-headed serpent	GRIFFIN	lion-eagle: gold guardian
LAMIA	woman-serpent	LAMASSU	bull with human head
SATYR	goat-man	PEGASUS	winged horse
BAGWYN	antelope-goat-horse	PISTRIX	sea monster
DRAGON	winged lizard	UNICORN	animal composite: 1 horn
GERYON	3 bodies, winged	VAMPIRE	undead creature
GORGON	snake-haired woman	BASILISK	dragon with fatal breath
KRAKEN	sea monster	MINOTAUR	youth-eating man-bull
SCYLLA	6-headed dog with 12 feet	BUCENTAUR	ox-man
SILENI	part man, part horse: satyr	CHARYBDIS	woman turned to
SPHINX	winged lion-woman; riddle		whirlpool
	poser	MANTICORE	horned lion-man
		SAGITTARY	Trojan ally

ROUND TABLE KNIGHTS AND RELATIONS

BORS	Lancelot's cousin	MORGAN	Arthur's sister
KAY	Arthur's foster brother	GERAINT	Enid's husband
BORT	= BOHORT: Lancelot's	GALAHAD	Sir —: son of Lancelot
	nephew	MORDRED	= MODRED
BALAN	brother of Balm	MORGAIN	= MORGAN
BALIN	brother of Balan	PELLEAS	lover of Ettarre
ARTHUR	son of Uther, Igraine	TRISTAN	= TRISTRAM
	(Igera)	BEDIVERE	took Arthur's body to
ELAINE	Lancelot's love (Lily Maid)		Avalon
GARETH	nephew of Arthur	LANCELOT	son of Ban
GAWAIN	son of Morgain, Lancelot	PERCIVAL	= PARSIFAL: Grail seeker
ISOLDE	= ISEULT: beloved of	TRISTRAM	Iseult's lover slain by
	Tristram; wife of Mark		Mark
MERLIN	magician, wizard	GUINEVER	Arthur's wife
MODRED	Arthur's slayer slain by	GUINEVERE	= GUINEVER
	him		

NATURAL HISTORY

*indicates genus

MAMMALS
EXTINCT

QUAGGA	ALLOCYON	HAPLOMYS	THYLACINE
AUROCHS	BLUEBUCK	NIMRAVUS	CORYPHODON
MAMMOTH	CAMELOPS	SCAPANUS	MEGATHERIUM
MOROPUS	DINICTIS	INDARCTUS	TRETRETRETRE
SEAMINK	EOHIPPUS	ONDATRINI	

OXEN, SHEEP, GOAT FAMILY (BOVIDAE)

ZO	GAUR	ANGUS	TAKIN
	GOUR	ARGAL	THAVE
BOB	HAPI	ARNEE	URIAL
BOS*	HOGG	AUDAD	VACHE
EWE	IBEX	BEDEN	WOOLY
KEB	JAAL	BILLY	YAKIN
KEY	KAIL	BISON	
KID	KINE	BOBBY	AGNEAU
KYL	KRAS	BOSSY	ANKOLI
MUG	LAMB	BRAWN	AOUDAD
MUL	LONK	BRAXY	ARGALI
NOT	MOIL	CAPRA*	AUROCS
OWE	MUGS	CAURE	BANTIN
PET	MULL	CRONE	BARHAL
PUR	NATA	CRONY	BARWAL
QUE	NEAT	CUSHA	BHARAL
RAM	NOTT	DEVON	BIDENT
SHA	OUSE	DOGIE	BOVOID
TEG	OVIS*	DUMBA	BRAMAN
TIP	OXEN	FLOCK	BRAMIN
TUP	QUEY	GAYAL	BUFFLE
TUR	REEM	GEMSE	BULKIN
URE	RUNT	GORAL	BURHEL
YAK	SHIP	GYALL	CABREE
YOE	SOCK	HEDER	CABRIT
ZOH	TAGG	JAELA	CALVER
	TAHR	JAGLA	CANNER
ANOA	TAIR	KAAMA	CAPRID
APIS	TEAP	KERRY	CATALO
ARNA	TEGG	KHAMA	CHAMAL
ARNI	TEHR	KIDDY	CHASER
ARUI	THAR	MOLLY	COSSET
AVER	TORO	NANNY	COTSOL
BOSS	TOUP	NIATA	CREANE
BUCK	UDAD	PASAN	CRUMMY
BUFF	UROY	PESAH	DEXTER
BULL	VEAL	PODDY	DINMAN
BUSS	ZEBU	SANGA	DOODIE
CADE	ZENU	SANGU	DUGHAM
CALF	ZOBO	SLINK	EVICKE
CAUR	ZOBU	SOOKY	EWETEG
CUSH		STEER	EXMOOR
DOGY	AGNUS	STIRK	GIMMER
DOWN	AMMON	SUCKY	HAWKEY

HAWKIE	MOOLLY	SUCKER	BUFFALO
HEIFER	MOUTON	SUSSEX	BULLOCK
HIEDER	MUFLON	TAURUS	CARACUL
HOGGET	MULLEY	THEAVE	CHEVIOT
HOGGIE	MUSKOX	TUSKER	CHILVER
HOGREL	MUSMON	VEALER	CRACKER
HUMLIE	MUTTON	WASTER	DELAINE
JERSEY	NAHOOR	WEAVER	DISHLEY
JHARAL	NAYAUR	WEDDER	EANLING
KIDDIE	OORIAL	WETHER	GRASSER
KIDLET	OVIBOS*	WISENT	KARAKUL
LAMBER	OXFORD	WOLLIE	LAMBKIN
LAMBIE	PASANG	WOOLLY	LINCOLN
MAILLE	PASENG		MOUFLON
MAZAMA	PAULAR	AUROCHS	MUFFLON
MAZAME	PAULIE	BERENDO	ROSELLA
MERINO	PESACH	BIGHORN	SINGLER
MOILEY	PUTTER	BLEATER	SLINKER
MOOLEY	ROMNEY	BRAHMAN	TAURINE
	SARLAK	BRAHMIN	
	SHEDER		

ANTELOPE FAMILY (ANTILOCAPRIDAE)

AHO	ARIEL	SEROW	MAZAMA
DOE	BEIRA	TAKIN	MAZAME
DZO	BEISA	TIANG	NAKONG
GNU	BONGO	YAKIN	NILGAI
GOA	BUBAL		NILGAU
KID	CAAMA	BAGWYN	OUREBI
KOB	DOODY	BUBALE	OZANNA*
NIL	ELAND	CABREE	PALLAH
	ETAAC	CABRIT	PASANG
ADMI	GAZEL	CHUKER	PASENG
ASSE	GEMSE	DIGDIG	PYGARG
BISA	GORAL	DIKDIK	RHEBOC
BUCK	GUIBA	DUIKER	RHEBOK
CORA	IZARD	DUYKER	SAKEEN
DAMA	KOBUS*	DZEREN	SHAMMY
GEMS	KORIN	DZERIN	SHAMOY
GNOO	LICHI	DZERON	
GUIB	MHORR	GOORAL	BERENDO
KOBA	MUGGS	GRIMME	BLAUBOK
KUDU	NAGOR	IMPALA	BLESBOK
MOHR	NUNNI	IMPOFO	BUBALIS
ORIX	OREAS	IZZARD	CHAMOIS
ORYX	ORIAS	KAINSI	CHIKARA
POKU	ORIBI	KOKOON	CONGONI
PUKU	PALLA	KOODOO	GAZELLA*
TOPI	PEELE	KOUDOU	GEMSBOK
TORA	SABLE	LECAMA	IMPALLA
	SAIGA	LECHEE	REDBUCK
	SASIN	LECHWE	SASSABI
ADDAX	SERAU		SASSABY
	SERAW		

SWINE FAMILY (SUIDAE)

BEN	HOG	SUS*	BOAR
BOR	PIG		FARE
ELT	SEW	APER	GALT
FAR	SOW	BENE	GILT

KRAS	GRICE	FARROW	GRUNTER
PORK	PIGGY	GUSSIE	PECCARY
SHOT	SHEAT	JAVALI	PORCINE
SLIP	SHOAT	PIGGIE	ROASTER
SUID	SHOTE	PIGLET	SNORKER
YELT	SNORK	PORKER	SOUNDER
YILT	SUINA	PORKET	SUFFOLK
		PORKIN	SUIDIAN
BONAV	BARROW	SUCKER	TANTANY
DUROC	BONIVE	TITMAN	TANTONY
ESSEX	COCHON		WARTHOG

DOG FAMILY (CANIDAE)

CUR	CANUS	CHANCO	SIGRIM
GIP	COLLY	COCKER	SIWASH
GYP	COOLY	COLFOX	SLEUTH
JIP	DABUH	COLLIE	SOMMER
MUT	DHOLE	COLPEO	SUNDOG
POM	DINGO	CORSAC	TALBOT
PUG	DOGGY	COYOTE	TANGUE
PUP	DUMBY	CUSSER	TANREC
RUG	ENTRY	DOGGIE	TARRIE
TOD	FEIST	FENNEC	TENREC
TOY	FYSTE	FENRIP	THOOID
WAP	GUARA	HUNTER	TOLLER
YAP	HOUND	HYAENA	TOWSER
	HUSKY	ISGRIM	TUFTER
ALAN	HYENA	ISGRIN	VULPES
ALCO	KIOTE	JACKAL	YAPPER
BICK	LYOME	JOWLER	YAUPER
CHOW	MASTY	KABERU	YAWPER
CYON*	MATIN	KELPIE	YELPER
DANE	MERLE	KOLSUN	
DIEB	PIDOG	KOULAN	BASTARD
FIST	POOCH	KRATIM	BULLDOG
GREW	PUPPY	LAPDOG	CHARLIE
HUND	RACHE	LOWRIE	CHARLEY
LEAM	RATCH	LUCERN	COURSER
LIME	SHOCK	LYCAON	GRIFFON
LOBO	SWIFT	MASTIS	HARRIER
LYAM	TRASY	MESSAN	MASTIFF
LYME	VIXEN	MESSET	MONGREL
MUTT	ZERDA	MESSIN	POINTER
PEKE	ZORRO	MOONER	SAMOYED
PULI		MOPPET	SCOTTIE
RACH	AGUARA	MOPSIE	TERRIER
SKYE	ALAUNT	POODLE	WHIPPET
THOS*	BAGMAN	RANGER	YAPSTER
TYKE	BANDOG	RATTER	
WAPP	BARBET	RENARD	AIREDALE
	BARKER	RUNNER	DOBERMAN
BAWTY	BASSET	SALUKI	FOXHOUND
BITCH	BAWTIE	SAMOED	LABRADOR
BOXER	BEAGLE	SAMOID	MALAMUTE
BRACH	BOWWOW	SCOTTY	PEKINESE
CAAMA	BRATCH	SEIZER	SAMOYEDE
CALEB	BRIARD	SETTER	SHEPHERD
CANID	BUFFER	SHAKAL	SPRINGER

CHIHUAHUA	GREYHOUND	YORKSHIRE	ROTTWEILER
DACHSHUND	LHASAAPSO		WEIMARANER
DALMATION	SCHNAUZER	BLOODHOUND	
GREATDANE	STBERNARD	POMERANIAN	

CAT FAMILY (FELIDAE)

CIT	CHAUS	YOUSE	OCELOT
GIB	CHITA	YOUZE	PAGUMA
KIT	CIVET	ZIBET	PAJERO
LEO	FEUD		PAPION
PUS	FELIS	ANGOLA	PARDAL
TAB	FITCH	ANGORA	POIANA
TOM	FOSSA	BOBCAT	PURRER
	GALET	BONDAR	PUSSIE
	GENET	CHETAH	SERVAL
BALU	KITTY	COUGAR	THOMAS
EYRA	MANUL	GIBCAT	TIBERT
KITT	MEWER	JAGUAR	TOMCAT
LION	MOGGY	KITTEN	ZIBETH
PARD	OUNCE	KITTIE	
PUMA	PISHU	KITTIE	
PUSS	PUSSY	LIBARD	CARACAL
SHER	QUEEN	LIONEL	CHEETAH
SHIR	RASSE	LIONET	GUEPARD
TIGE	SIMBA	MARGAY	LEOPARD
TIKE	SIVET	MEWLER	LIONCEL
	TABBY	MOUSER	LIONESS
	TIGER	MUSANG	PANTHER
BERBE	TILER	NEUTER	TIGRESS
CHATI	TOMMY		

HORSE, ASS, ZEBRA (EQUIDAE)

ASS	FOAL	STUD	JENNY
BAY	FUSS	TATT	KIANG
COB	GOER	TATU	KULAN
CUT	GOUR	TURK	KYANG
DUN	GRAS	YABU	LOPER
FUS	GRAY	YAUD	MILER
GEE	GREY	YAWD	MOREL
GRI	GROG	ZAIN	MOUNT
GRY	HACK		NAGGY
HAN	HOSS	ARABY	NEDDY
JAB	JADE	BIDET	PACER
JEE	KOHL	BRONC	PINTO
JOB	MOKE	BURRO	PIPER
NAG	MULE	CAPLE	PONEY
PAT	NAIG	CAPUL	RACER
POT	PONY	COBBE	ROGUE
RAW	PROD	CUDDY	RUNSY
RIG	PUCA	DICKY	SHIER
RIP	QUAD	DUMMY	SHIRE
TAT	RACE	EQUID	SHYER
TIT	RACK	EQUUS*	SHYRE
YAD	RIDE	FAVEL	SKAIT
	ROAN	FILLY	SKATE
ARAB	RUCK	HAIRY	SOMER
BARB	SCUT	HARAS	STEED
COBB	SIRE	HINNY	STIFF
COLT	STOT	HOBBY	TACKY

TATOO	ENTIRE	PELTER	BOBTAIL
WALER	EQUINE	PLATER	BRONCHO
WELSH	EXMOOR	PLOUGH	CAVALLO
WIDGE	FENCER	POLEYN	CHARGER
YABOO	FILLER	QUAGGA	CLIPPER
ZEBRA	GALYAK	REMUDA	COACHER
	GANGER	RINGER	COURSER
ALEZAN	GARRAN	ROADER	DRAFTER
AMBLER	GARRON	ROARER	FLEMISH
AMEZEH	GEEGEE	ROUNCY	GELDING
BANKER	GILLIE	RUNNER	HACKNEY
BAYARD	GILLOT	SAVAGE	JACKASS
BOLTER	GIRLIE	SHELTY	MONTURE
BRONCO	GLEYDE	SORREL	MUDLARK
BRUMBY	GRASNI	STAGER	MUSTANG
BUSSER	HACKNY	STONER	NEIGHER
CABBER	HARACE	TACKEY	PACOLET
CASTER	HUNTER	TANGAN	PIEBALD
CAYUSE	JENNET	TANGLE	PRANCER
CHEVAL	KEFFEL	TANGUM	SADDLER
COOSER	KIYANG	TANGUN	SHAFTER
CREAMY	KUMRAH	TARPAN	SHELTIE
CUDDIE	LADINO	TATTOO	SLEDDER
CURTAL	LEADER	TRACER	SPANKER
DAPPLE	MAIDEN	TURKEY	SUMPTER
DICKEY	MORGAN	VANNER	WHEELER
BOBBIN	HACKER	WEAVER	ZEBRASS
DONKEY	NAIGIE		ZEBRULA
DRIVER	ONAGER	ARABIAN	
	ORLOFF	BARBARY	

CAMEL, LLAMA (CAMELIDAE)

LAMA	DELOUL	OKAPIA*	GIRAFFA*
OUNT	HAGEEN	SERAPH	GIRAFFE
PACO	HAGEIN	VICUNA	GUANACO
GEMUL	HYGEEN	VIGONE	
OKAPI	MEHARA	VIGUNA	
ALPACA	MEHARI	CAMELUS*	

DEER, MOOSE (CERVIDAE)

DAE	PITA	PUDUA	RASCAL
DOE	PITO	RATWA	SAMBAR
ELK	PUDU	ROYAL	SAMBOO
ROE	REIN	SABIR	SAMBUR
	RUSA	SOWRE	SORREL
ALCE	SHOU	SPADO	TARAND
AXIS	SHOW	SURRE	THAMIN
DAUW	SIKA		VENADE
FAWN	SPAY	CERVID	VENSON
HART	STAG	CERVUS	WAPITI
HIND		CHITAL	
HINE	ALCES*	GUEMAC	
LOSH	KAKAR	GUEMUL	BROCKET
MAHA	KAKUR	HANGUL	CARIBOU
MORT	LOSHE	HAVIER	CERVINE
MUSK	MARAL	HEARST	CERVOID
NAPU	MOOSE	KIDANG	MOSCHUS*
OLEN	MUIST	MUNJAK	VENISON

RAT FAMILY (RODENTIA)

BUN	CAVIA*	ZOKOR	RABBIT
TAN	CONEY		RATTEN
WAT	COYPU	AGOUTI	RATTAN
	CUTTY	AGOUTY	ROTTAN
BAUD	DAMAN	APEREA	ROTTON
BAWD	DASSY	BOBACK	SUSLIK
CAVY	GANAM	CHIPPY	TAGUAN
CONY	GUNDI	COYPOU	TALPID
DEGU	HIRAX	CRABER	TAMIAS*
GLIS	HYRAX	CURURO	TAPETI
HARE	LABBA	DASSIE	TUPAIA*
LOIR	LEPUS	GEOMYS*	WABBER
MOLE	LEROT	GERBIL	WARNER
PACA	METAD	GNAWER	
PIKA	MOUDY	GOPHER	ASSAPAN
TANA	MOUSE	JERBOA	BELGIAN
TAWN	MOUSY	JUMPER	CHIPPIE
TUAN	PORKY	MALKIN	FLEMISH
TUZA	RANNY	MARMOT	HAMSTER
UTIA	RATON	MAUKIN	LEMMING
VOLE	SHREW	MOUSEY	LEPORID
WANT	SISEL	MYGALE	LEVERET
WATT	SOREX*	MYODES*	MUSKRAT
WONT	TALPA	MYOXUS*	PEDETES
	URSON	NUTRIA	POTOROO
	XERUS*	OARLAP	RATHARE
AGUTI	ZAPUS*	OARLOP	SANDRAT
BOBAC	ZEMMI	PARKER	SLEEPER
BUNNY	ZEMNI	POLISH	SONDELI

PRIMATES

APE	WAAG	PAPIO	CHACMA
KRA	WANA	PATAS	COAITA
LAR	WAWA	PIGMY	COLUGO
PAN	ZATI	PONGO	COUXIA
PUG		POTTO	COUXIO
SAI	ACARI	PYGMY	DOGAPE
	AOTUS*	QUATA	GALAGO
AANI	ARABA	RESUS	GIBBON
BRUH	AVAHI	SAJOU	GRIVET
DOUC	CEBID	SATYR	GUENON
HOMO	CEBUS*	SIFAC	HAPALE*
KAHA	DREEL	SIMIA*	HOGAPE
LORI	DRILL	TOQUE	HOWLER
MAHA	INDRI	UNGKA	INDRIS*
MAKI	JACKO	WAWAH	LANGUR
MIAS	JOCKO	YARKE	MACACA*
MICO	KAHUA		MACACO
MONA	KOKAM	ADAPID	MACHIN
MONK	LEMUR	ADAPIS*	MAIMON
MONO	LORIS	APELET	MARTIN
SAKI	MACAC	ATELES*	MOHOLI
SIME	MAGOT	AYEAYE	MORMON
TITI	MIDAS*	BABOON	NCHEGA
TOTA	MUNGA	BANDAR	NISNAS
VARI	ORANG	CAMPER	OURANG

PIGMEW	SIMPAI	COLOBIN	OUAKARI
PINCHE	TEETEE	COLOBUS*	ROLOWAY
RHESUS	VERVET	GUARIBA	SAIMIRI*
RILAWA	WAUWAU	HOOLOCK	SAPAJOU
SAGOIN	WEEPER	LEMURID	SIAMANG
SAMIRI	WISTIT	MACACUS*	STENTOR
SEACAT	WOUWOU	MACAQUE	TAMARIN
SIFAKA	YARKEE	NASALIS*	TARSIER
SIMIAN		NOSEAPE	WISTITI

MARSUPIALS

JOEY	TUNGO	DASYURE	MACROPUS*
ARIEL	YAPOK	KAPOUNE	TARSIPES*
BILBI		MARMOSA*	WALLAROO
	BOOMAH	MULGARA	BANDICOOT
COALA	BOOMER	OPOSSUM	DIDELPHIS*
FLIER	CUSCUS	WALLABY	PADEMELON
FLYER	JERBOA		PETAURIST
KOALA	MONCAT		PHALANGER
QUICA	MONGAN	ANTEATER	PHILANDER
SELVA	NUMBAT	COESCOES	THYLACINE
SILVA	POSSUM	DASYURUS*	
TAPOA	WOMBAT	FORESTER	
THILL	YAPOCK	KANGAROO	

WEASELS, BEAVERS, RACCOONS

DAS	OTTER	FERRET	FITCHET
	PAHMI	FICHAT	FITCHEW
COON	PANDA	FISHER	GLUTTON
FOIN	PEKAN	GALERA	GORKHUS
GULO*	RATEL	GRISON	ICTONYX*
MINK	SABLE	LASSET	MINIVER
PATE	SKUNK	MAPACH	MUSTELA*
VAIR	SOBOL	MARTEN	POLECAT
VARE	STOAT	MARTES*	RACCOON
	TAXUS	MYDAUS*	SANDPIG
BRARO	TAYRA	NARICA	TAXIDEA*
BROCK	TEJON	QUIQUE	ZORILLA
COATI	ZORIL	RACOON	ZORRINO
FITCH		SEAAPE	
HURON	BADGER	TELEDU	BRAIREAU
LATAX*	BAUSON	WEASEL	CARCAJOU
LUTRA*	BEAVER		KOLINSKY
MELES*	BRAIRO	CHINCHA	MEPHITIS*
NASUA*	BRELAW	CHINCHE	MUISHOND
MORSE	ERMINE	ENHYDRA*	ZORRILLO

AQUATIC MAMMALS
WHALE

ORC	SCRAG	BOWHEAD	SPOUTER
CETE	BALEEN	FINBACK	ZIPHIAN
HUSE*	BELUGA	FINFISH	BALAENID
HUSO*	BLOWER	GRAMPUS	CACHALOT
ORCA	FINNER	MARSOON	HUMPBACK
KRENG	GIBBAR	ORCINUS*	MUTILATE
OTARY	KILLER	RIPSACK	ZALOPHUS*
POGGY	BALAENA*	RORQUAL	

WALRUS

BRUTA*	UNICORN	ODOBENUS
MORSE	WALTRON	

DOLPHIN

INIA*	PALACH	NARWHAL	NARWHALE
SUSU	PORPUS	PELLOCK	PHOCAENA*
UNIE	SOOSOO	PULLOCK	PORPOISE
BOUTO	TURSIO	SNUFFER	TURSIOPS*
DORADO	DELPHIN	GAIRFISH	

SEAL

WIG	UTSUK	OTARIAN	PELAGIAN
SEAL	BEATER	OTARINE	PHOCIDAE*
MATKA	JACKET	PHOCOID	PHOCINAE*
PHOCA*	MAKLAK	SADDLER	SEACATCH
SWILE	MATKAH	SEALKIE	SEECATCH
URSAL	OTARIA	IIARPSEAL	SEALCHIE
URSUK	PHOCID	OTARIINE	
USSUK	FURSEAL	OTARIOID	

OTHERS

DUGONG	SEACOW	MANATEE	PINNIPED
MANATI	YUNGAN	SEALION	SIRENIAN
RYTINA	COWFISH	HALICORE	

OTHER MAMMALS

AI	BRUTA	ASWAIL	DASYPUS
BAT	DANTA	BOLITA	ECHIDNA
APAR	HATHI	BORELE	ECHINUS
BEAR	HATTY	DOTARD	ELEPHAS*
MUSS	JUMBO	JACKET	GRIZZLY
PEBA	MAKNA	MAKHNA	ICEBEAR
PEVA	MANID	MANGUE	LOXODON
TATU	MANIS	MATACO	SUNBEAR
UNAU	MUNGO	MATICO	TAMANDU*
URVA	POYOU	MONGOE	TATOUAY
ABADA	RHINO	NODIAK	TOXODON*
APARA	ROGUE	OLDMAN	
BHALU	SLOTH	PELUDO	
BRUIN	TATOU	ANTBEAR	

CRUSTACEANS

DAD	CARID	ZOOEA	PUNGAR
UCA	ERYON		PUNGER
	HIPPA	BUSTER	SHRIMP
CRAB	MAIAN	CANCER	SLATER
MAIA	MYSID	CARIDA*	SOWBUG
MAYA	MYSIS*	HOMARD	SPRITE
ZOEA	PRAWN	ISOPOD	SQUILL
	RACER	MYSOID	YABBER
ACORN	YABBI	PANDLE	YABBIE
ALIMA	YABBY	PARTAN	
AYUYU	ZOAEA	PEELER	ANATIFA

ANOMURA*	INACHID	ANATIFAE	FROGCRAB
ARTEMIA	LIMULID	BARNACLE	GRAPSOID
ASELLUS	LIMULUS*	BLUECRAB	INACHOID
ASTACUS*	LOBSTER	CAMBARUS*	KINGCRAB
BALANID	MACRURA*	CARIDEAN	LADYCRAB
BUCKLER	MUDCRAB	CARIDOID	LANDCRAB
BUCKLUM	MYSIDAE*	COPEPODA	LERNAEAN
BURSTER	OCIPODE*	CRABFISH	LIMULOID
CAMARON	ONISCUS*	CRAWFISH	OCHIDORE
CRAWDAD	PANFISH	CRAYFISH	OCYPODAN
CUMACEA*	PEACRAB	CREVETTE	PILLWORM
FIDDLER	PILLBUG	CUMACEAN	PORTUNUS*
GRAPSUS*	SHEDDER	EPICARID	RANINIAN
GRIBBLE	SQUILLA		

ARACHNIDS

BUG	CARTER	ARGASID	ACARAPIS*
FAG	CHEGOE	ARGIOPE*	ARANEIDA*
KED	CHEGRE	ATTIDAE*	ARCTISCA
	CHIGGA	BDELLID	ATTERCOP
MITE	CHIGOE	CHIGGER	CARAPATO
TICK	CHIGRE	CHIGGRE	FACEMITE
	ENIGUA	DEMODEX	GAMAPATO
ACARI	GIGGER	EGGMITE	IXODIDAE*
ARAIN	IXODID	IXODIAN	LONGLEGS
ARGAS	KATIPO	JAYHAWK	ORBITELE
ATTID	LEPTUS	LYCOSID	PEDIPALP
BICHO	LYCOSA*	MYGALID	SANDWORM
LOPPE	MYGALE	OCTOPOD	SCORPION
NANCY	REDBUG	PHOLCID	SOLIFUGE
NIGUA	SPIDER	PHOLCUS*	SOLPUGID
PIQUE	TAMPAN	PHRYNID	THOMISID
SCREW	WEAVER	POKOMOO	ULOBORID
SCROW		RETIARY	ULOBORUS*
	ACARIDA*	SANDBOY	WANDERER
ACARID	ACARINA*	SPIDGER	
ACARUS*	AGALENA*	SPINDER	TARANTULA
ACERAE*	ALACRAN	SPINNER	
ANANSI	ANNANCY	STINGER	
ARRAND	ARANEID		

FISH

AKU	IDE	BANG	CHAR
AWA	IHI	BARB	CHUB
AYU	KOI	BASS	CHUM
BAR	LAX	BLAY	COHO
BIB	LOB	BLOB	CONY
COB	MAH	BOCE	COOK
COD	ORF	BOGA	CUSK
DAB	RAY	BOHO	DACE
EEL	RUD	BRET	DORE
FIN	SMY	BRIT	DORN
FRY	SUN	BUTT	DRUM
GAG	TAI	CAJI	ESOX
GAR		CARP	FUGU
GED	ALEC	CAXI	GADE
HAG	AMIA	CERO	GATA

GEDD	SCUP	FLUKE	SCROD
GOBY	SESI	FRIAR	SEWEN
GRIG	SHAD	GADID	SEWIN
HAAK	SIER	GADUS*	SHARK
HAGG	SILE	GAPER	SKATE
HAIK	SISI	GIBEL	SLINK
HAKE	SKIL	GOBIO*	SMELT
HAKU	SNIG	GOODY	SMOLT
HAYE	SOLE	GRUNT	SMOOK
HIKU	SPET	GUASA	SMOUT
HIND	SPOT	GUPPY	SPRAG
HUCH	TANG	HADDO	SPRAT
HUSO	TINK	HILSA	SPROD
HUSS	TOPE	HITCH	SQUAT
JACK	TORO	HOUND	SULEA
JOCU	TUNA	HUCHO	SUNNY
KELT	ULUA	HURSE	SWORD
KETA	WAHA	JUREL	TECON
KIYI	WELS	KANAE	TENCH
LANT	ZANT	KILLY	TOGUE
LIJA		LAKER	TONNY
LUNG	ABOMA	LAMIA	TOPER
LORO	ACARA	LAUIA	TORSK
LOTA*	AGUJA	LOACH	TROUT
LOTO	ALLIS	LONGE	TRUBU
LUCE	ALOSA*	LOOTA	TRUFF
MADO	ALOSE	LUCET	TUNNY
MAKO	ANGEL	MANTA	ULKEN
MAPO	APODA	MARAY	UMBRA
MASU	BAGRE	MATIE	VIEJA
MERO	BALAO	MIDGE	VIUVA
MOKI	BARRY	MINIM	WAHOO
MOLA	BARSE	MINNY	WHIFF
MORT	BECCO	MOLET	WHITY
OPAH	BETTA	MORAY	WIRRA
ORFE	BLEAK	MUGIL*	WITCH
PARR	BLOAT	MURRY	XUREL
PEGA	BOGUE	MUSKY	
PENK	BOHOO	OXEYE	ACOUPA
PETO	BOLTI	PARGO	AGUAJI
PIKE	BOLTY	PATAO	AGUJON
PINK	BREAM	PERCA*	ALAIHI
POGY	BRILL	PERCH	ALEVIN
POLE	BULTI	PIRAI	ALLICE
POOR	CHARR	POGGE	ANABAS
POUT	CHIRO	POGGY	ANGLER
PRIM	CHOPA	PORGY	APOGON
QUAB	CISCO	POWAN	ARCHER
RAAD	COBIA	RAIAI*	ATINGA
RAUN	CRAVO	REINA	BAGGIE
RENA	DICKY	RHINA	BAGGIT
ROCK	DORAB	ROACH	BALLAN
ROUD	DORAD	ROKER	BALLAO
RUDD	DORAS*	RONCO	BARBEL
RUFF	DROUD	ROVET	BATOID
SAMA	ELOPS	SARGO	BECUNA
SAPO	ELVER	SARPO	BELONE*
SCAD	FLAIR	SAURY	BELUGA
SCAR	FLATH	SCAMP	BERVIE

BESHOW	GARVIE	PIRAYA	VENDIS
BESUGO	GASCON	PLAICE	VOLIER
BICHIR	GERRES	POLLAN	WACHNA
BLENNY	GOBIID	POPEYE	WALLER
BLOWER	GOLDNY	PORGEE	WARSAW
BONACI	GORAMY	PUFFER	WEEVER
BONETA	GRILSE	PUNECA	WIRRAH
BONITA	GRUBBY	QUASKY	WOOHOO
BONITO	GUNDIE	RAMPER	WRASSE
BOOHOO	GUNNEL	REDEYE	ZANDER
BOWFIN	HADDIE	REDFIN	ZINGEL
BRASSE	HAMLET	REMORA	
BUNKER	HAPUKU	REQUIN	ABADEJO
BURBOT	HASSAR	ROBALO	ACHIGAN
BUTTER	HEPPER	RONCHO	ACRODUS
CANDIL	HILSAH	ROMERO	ALEWIFE
CAPLIN	HUCHEN	RUNNER	ALFIONA
CARANX*	HUSSAR	SABALO	ANADROM
CARAPO	INANGA	SALELE	ANCHOVY
CARIBE	INIOME	SALEMA	ASPREDO
CHANOS*	INIOMI*	SALMON	BACALAO
CHAPIN	ISURUS	SAMLET	BARBUDO
CHEBOG	JERKIN	SANDER	BARFISH
CHERNA	JOHNNY	SARGUS	BATFISH
CHERNE	KELING	SAUGER	BEARDIE
CHEVIN	KIPPER	SAUQUI	BERGALL
CHIVEY	LAITHE	SAUREL	BERGYLT
COCUYO	LAMNID	SAVOLA	BERYCID
COELHO	LAUNCE	SCARUS	BIGHEAD
CONGER	LAWYER	SENNET	BLOATER
COTORO	LOOTAH	SEPHEN	BLUECAP
COTTID	MAHSIR	SHANNY	BONEDOG
CREOLE	MAHSUR	SHINER	BOWBACK
CROCUS	MAIGER	SIERRA	BOXFISH
CUBERA	MAIGRE	SKELLY	BUGFISH
CUCHIA	MARLIN	SLIMER	BUGHEAD
CUCUYO	MEAGER	SMOOTH	BURFISH
CUNNER	MEAGRE	SPARID	BURRITO
DARTER	MENNOM	SUCKER	CANDIRU
DARZEE	MENNON	TAILER	CAPELIN
DENTEX	MINNOW	TAIMEN	CATFISH
DIABLO	MOLOID	TAMBOR	CAVALLA
DIODON*	MORGAY	TAMURE	CAVALLY
DIPNOI*	MULLET	TANDAN	CHALACO
DOCMAC	MULLID	TARPON	CHALDER
DOCTOR	MULVEL	TARPUM	CHOGSET
DORADO	MURENA	TAUTOG	CHROMID
ELLECK	MURRAY	TESTAR	CICHLID
ELLOPS	MUSKIE	TETARD	CLUPEID
ESPADA	MYKISS	TINKER	CODFISH
FAUSEN	MYXINE*	TINOSA	CORSAIR
FINNAC	MYZONT	TOMCOD	COTTOID
FLATHE	NATIVE	TULIPE	COWFISH
FLIOMA	NONNAT	TURBOT	CRAPPIE
GADOID	OBISPO	TWAITE	CRAPPLE
GALEID	PAGRUS*	ULCHEN	CROAKER
GALEUS*	PARROT	ULICON	CUCKOLD
GANOID	PERCID	ULIKAN	CYCLOID
GARMON	PICUDA	ULIKON	DIPNOAN

DOGFISH	HAGFISH	OOLAKAN	SKIPPER
DOLPHIN	HALIBUT	OQUASSA	SLINKER
EELPOUT	HARMOOT	PEGADOR	SNAPPER
EGGFISH	HARMOUT	PEGASID	SOCKEYE
ELLFISH	HERRING	PEGASUS	SPARADA
ESCOLAR	HOGFISH	PICAREL	SPAROID
ESPADON	HOMILYN	PIGFISH	SQUETTE
ESSLING	ICEFISH	PINFISH	STERLET
FATHEAD	INCONNU	PINHEAD	SUNFISH
FIDDLER	ISUROID	PINTADO	SURGEON
FLAPPER	JEWFISH	PIRHANA	TAMBOUR
FOXFISH	JUGULAR	PLACOID	TELEOST
GARFISH	KEELING	POISSON	TIBURON
GARLOPA	KILLING	POLLACK	TOMTATE
GARPIKE	LABROID	POLLOCK	TOPKNOT
GEELBEC	LAMPERN	POMFRET	TORPEDO
GHOSTER	LAMPRET	POMPANO	TOTUAVA
GILLING	LAMPREY	PRISTIS*	TREVALI
GOBIOID	LAVARET	QUINNAT	TRIGGER
GOGGLER	LONGJAW	RATTAIL	TURFISH
GOLDNEY	LOPHIID	REDFISH	UMBRANA
GOURAMI	MACHETE	REQUIEM	UMBRINE
GRAMPUS	MAHSEER	ROCKEEL	VENDACE
GRINDER	MAYFISH	ROVETTO	VIAJACA
GROUPER	MOJARRA	SANDEEL	VOLADIR
GRUNION	MONARRA	SARDINE	WALLEYE
GUAPENA	MOONEYE	SAWFISH	WAREHOU
GUAVINA	MORWONG	SCEGGER	WHAPUKA
GUDGEON	MUDFISH	SCULPIN	WHAPUKU
GULARIS	MURAENA*	SEABASS	WHITING
GURNARD	OARFISH	SERRANO	WIDEGAB
GWINIAD	OCHIGAN	SILLAGO	WIDEGAP
GWYNIAD	OLDWIFE	SILURID	XIPHIAS*
HADDOCK	OOLACAN	SKEGGER	XYPIIIAS*

REPTILES

ASP	TEJU	GEKKO*	BOIDAE*
BOA	URAN	GUANO	BONGAR
BOM		KRAIT	CAIMAN
DAB	ABOMA	MAMBA	CAUSUS*
GOA	ADDER	NAKOO	CAYMAN
NAG	AGAMA*	RACER	CHELYS*
UTA*	ANOLE	SCINK	CHITAL
	ANOLI	SKINK	COODLE
ADDA	ARRAU	SNECK	COOTER
BOID	ASPIC	SWIFT	DABOIA
CROC	BITIS	TIGER	DABOYA
DABB	CARET	TOKAY	DIPSAS
DUBB	COBRA	TWEEG	DRAGON
EMYD	CRIBO	VARAN	ELAPID
EMYS*	DHABB	VIPER	EMYDEA
GILA	DHOBB		GAVIAL
IBID	DHUBB	AGAMID	GOPHER
IBIT	DRACO*	AMEIVA*	HARDIM
NAGA	ECHIS*	ANGUID	HISSER
NAJA*	ELAPS*	ANGUIS*	IGUANA
NAKO	GATOR	ANOLIS*	ILYSIA
SEPS	GECKO	ARBALO	JACARE

JESSUR	GEKKOTA*	ANGUIDAE	PITVIPER
JURARA	HAGWORM	ARCHELON	RATSNAKE
KARAIT	HOGNOSE	BASILISK	RINGHALS
KERRIL	IGUANIA*	BONETAIL	SAUROPOD
LACERT	IGUANID	BOTHROPS*	SCORPION
LEGUAN	JUNIATA	BUNGARUM	SHAGTAIL
LIZARD	LACERTA*	BUNGARUS*	SLOWWORM
MABUYA*	LAGARTO	CASCAVEL	SQUAMATA*
MOLOCH	LANGAHA	CERASTES	TERRAPIN
MUGGAR	LOGHEAD	CHELONIA	TORTOISE
MUGGER	MEHELYA*	CHELYDRA*	VIPERINE
MUGGUR	MONITOR	COLUBRID*	WATERDOG
NATRIX*	OPHIDIA*	CROTALUS*	WHIPTAIL
PYTHON	PRESTER	CUNECTES*	ZONUROID
SAURIA*	PYGOPUS*	EGGEATER	
SLIDER	RATTLER	ELAPIDAE*	ALLIGATOR
PEIOID	SANDBOA	ELAPINAE*	BLINDWORM
WLAPHE*	SAURIAN	EMYDIDAE	CHAMELEON
WORRAL	SCINCID	EMYDINAE*	CHUNKHEAD
YACARE	SCINCUS	FLAPJACK	COACHWHIP
ZONURE	SERPENT	GAVIALIS*	COLUBRINA
	SNAPPER	GEKKONID	CORNSNAKE
ANOLIAN	TARENTE	HAWKBILL	EPICRATES
ATHECAE	TEIIDAE*	HELODERM	GALLIWASP
ATHERIS	TESTUDO*	IGUANOID	HELODERMA
BOKADAM	TORTUGA	JARARACA	HETERODON
CAMOODI	TREEBOA	LACERATE*	IGUANODON
CARETTA*	TRIONYX*	LACHESIS	KINGCOBRA
CHEECHA	TUATARA	LORICATA*	KINGSNAKE
CHELONE*	TUCKTOO	LORICATE	MILKSNAKE
COLUBER*	TURTLET	LYGOSOMA*	MOLESNAKE
CRAWLER	VARANUS*	MATAMATA	PUFFADDER
CREEPER	VIPERID	MICRURUS	ROUGHTAIL
CULEBRA	ZONURID*	MOCCASIN	SERPENTES*
DIAPSID	ZONURUS*	MOKAMOKA	TERRAPENE*
ELAPINE		MOSASAUR	TREESNAKE
EUMECES*	AGAMIDAE	OPHIDIAN	WARTSNAKE
GEITJIE	ANACONDA	PELUSIOS*	WHIPSNAKE

EXTINCT

TANIUS	CERATOPS	KOTASAUR	BRONTOSAURUS
ALCODON	CLAOSAUR	SINOSAUR	PARASAUR-
TARCHIA	COELURUS	CARDIODON	OLOPHUS
TROODON	DEINODON	DICTONIUS	TYRANNO-
ALIWALIA	DINOSAUR	TALARURUS	SAURUSREX
ALLOSAUR	EORAPTOR	ANKYLOSAUR	
ASTRODON	FULENGIA	PLESIOSAUR	
BAROSAUR	GALTONIA	TRICERATOPS	

AMPHIBIANS

ASK	BUFO	RANA	ASKER
ESK	EVAT	TAED	EFFET
EFT	EVET	TAID	FROSH
OLM	FROG	TOAD	FROSK
PAD	HYLA	TODE	PADDO
TAG	NEWT	TOOD	PADDY
	PIPA		PADOW
AGUA	PODE	ANURA	PIPAL

RONCO	TRITON	HYLIDAE	GANGEREL
SIREN		PADDOCK	LINGUATA
TOADY	AGLOSSA	PODDOCK	MUDPUDDY
TWEEG	AXOLOTL	PROTEUS	NECTURUS
	CAUDATA	QUILKIN	TREETOAD
ALYTES	CAUDATE	TADPOLE	TRITURUS
ANURAN	COSTATA	URODELA	
CRAPON	CRAPAUD		HELLBENDER
MUDDER	CROAKER	AMPHIUMA	SALAMANDER
PADDOW	DOGFISH	BULLFROG	
PEEPER	GANGREL	CAECILIA	
TOGGLE	HOPTOAD	FERREIRO	

BIRDS
EXTINCT

MOA	AKEPA	DYATRIMA	TERATORNIS
DODO	KIOEA	HEATHHEN	PTERODACTYL
HUIA	AKIALOA	PROTOAVIS	ARCHEOPTERYX
MAMO	DIORNIS	PTEROSAUR	

PREY, HUNTING, GAME

IO*	UTUM	FORMEL	BUZZARD
		FULMAR	CACICUS*
ERN	AREND	GENTLE	CHEEPER
GOB	ARGUS*	GORHEN	COLINUS*
IOA	ASTUR	GROUSE	FLAPPER
IWA	BESRA	HOOTER	FLOPPER
OWL	BUTEO*	HOUTOU	FRIGATE
	CHEER	HOWLET	GALEENY
AURA	COLIN	HULLET	GOSHAWK
BUBO*	EAGLE	JAEGER	HARRIER
CHIL	FALCO*	KEELIE	KALEEGE
CHIR	GANGA	KETUPA*	KALLEGE
ERNE	GLEDE	LANNER	KESTREL
EYAS	HARPY	MERLIN	PANDION*
GLED	HOBBY	MEROPS*	PINTADO
HAWK	MADGE	MILVUS*	PUDDOCK
KAHU	MONAL	MOPOKE	PUTTOCK
KEET	OWLET	MUCARO	SAKERET
KITE	PADGE	NYCTEA*	SHAHEEN
KUKU	QUAIL	OSPREY	STANNEL
KYAH	SAKER	PIPIRI	TINAMOU
LOWA	URUBU	RAPTOR	VULTURE
LULU		SEESEE	WOODHEN
MOMO	ALCEDO*	SHAHIN	WOOLERT
OTIS*	AQUILA*	SHIKRA	
PAPA	AZIOLA	TERCEL	BOBWHITE
PERN	CHILLA	TURNIX	CARACARA
PISK	CHUKAR		GUACHARO
QUIS	CHUKOR	AESALON	MANOFWAR
RYPE	CONDOR	BOOBOOK	MOREPORK
TESA	ELANET	BULLBAT	PHEASANT
TYTO*	FANNER	BUSTARD	WOODCOCK

SHORE, WADING, DIVING

AUK	KIP	PEN	ALCA*
COB	MEW	QUA	ALLE*

ANAS*	DILLY	DARTER	COURLAN
APUS*	DIVER	DIPPER	COURSER
CHEN*	DRAKE	DOPPER	DOVEKIE
CLEE	EGRET	DUIKER	DOWITCH
COBB	EIDER	DUNLIN	DUNBIRD
COOT	GAVIA*	GANNET	DUNNOCK
DARR	GONEY	GARROT	FINFOOT
DOGY	GOOSE	GAVIAE*	GADWALL
DUCK	GORMA	GENTOO	GOLIATH
FALK	GUARA	GODWIT	GRALLAE*
FUTE	HARLE	GOONEY	GRAYLAG
GONY	HERLE	GORMAW	ICEGULL
GRUS	HERON	GUNNER	JACAMAR
GULL	IMBER	HAGDON	JACKSAW
HERN	LARID	JABIRU	KAMICHI
IBIS	MOLLY	JACANA	LAPWING
KNOT	MURRE	JAEGER	LIMPKIN
KOKO	NELLY	KIALEE	MALLARD
KORA	NODDY	KICKUP	MALMOCK
KULM	OMBER	KIRMEW	MARABOU
LOON	OXEYE	KITTLE	MOORHEN
LOWN	PEARL	KOTUKU	OLDWIFE
MALL	PEWEE	KULANG	PELICAN
NOIO	PEWIT	LUNGIE	PENGUIN
OLOR*	PRINE	MACUCA	PIMLICO
PIRR	PRION	MARLIN	PINTAIL
RAIL	QUAWK	MARROT	POCHARD
RIXY	REEVE	MUDHEN	PODITTI
RUFF	RODGE	NARECA*	PYGOPOD*
SHAG	ROTCH	PETREL	RANTOCK
SKUA	SANDY	PLOTUS*	SAWBILL
SMEE	SCAUP	PLOVER	SCAMELL
SMEW	SCRAY	PUFFIN	SKIMMER
SOCO	SHOOI	QUANDY	SQUACCO
SORA	SKIRR	ROTCHE	TARROCK
SULA	SKITE	SCOTER	TATTLER
SWAN	SKURR	SICSAC	TOTANUS*
TEAL	SNIPE	SIMBIL	TWISTER
TERN	SOLAN	STERNA*	WAYBILL
TITI	STILT	STRANY	WHOOPER
URIA*	STINT	TEASER	WIDGEON
WAEG	STORK	TEETEE	
	TIRMA	TEETER	ADJUTANT
	UMBER	TRINGA*	BALDPATE
AIAIA	WABBY	WILLET	BOATBILL
AJAJA	WAVEY	YOCKEL	DABCHICK
ALLAN	WHILK	ZUISIN	DOTTEREL
ANNET			FLAMINGO
ANSER*	AUKLET		GARGANEY
ARDEA*	AVOCET	ANHINGA*	JOHNDOWN
ARRIE	BANTAM	ASSILAG	KILLDEER
BOOBY	BONXIE	BIGFOOT	OLDSQUAW
BRANT	CANARD	BITTERN	PEETWEET
BUNTY	CHAUNA*	BROWNIE	SCREAMER
CHAJA	CHOUGH	CANETON	SHOEBILL
CRAKE	CHUNGA*	CAPELLA	SHOVELER
CRANE	CURLEW	CICONIA*	UMBRETTE
CUTTY	CYGNET	CINCLUS*	WHIMBREL
	CYGNUS*		

SONGBIRDS

ANI	JOREE	OLOMAO	MINIVET
ANO	JUNCO	ORIOLE	ORTALUS*
DAW	KAMAO	OSCINE*	ORTOLAN
IAO	LINDO	OXBIRD	PIRANGA*
KAE	MAVIS	PALOLA	REDPOLL
TUE	MERLE	ROLLER	REDWING
TUI	OUSEL	SHRIKE	RUDDOCK
	OUZEL	SIALIA*	SCOLDER
	PIPIT	SISKIN	SEIURUS*
BRAN	PIROL	SOARER	SKYLARK
CHAT	ROBIN	SYLVIA*	TANAGER
CROW	SERIN	THRUSH	TIMALIA*
FINK	SHAMA	TOWHEE	TITLARK
HIAT	SPINK	TURDUS*	WAGTAIL
KALA	TWITE	VERDIN	WARBLER
KATE	VEERY	WINNEL	WIMBREL
LARK	VIREO		
MERL			
MIRO	ANTHUS	BABBLER	BELLBIRD
MOHO	BULBUL	BUNTING	BLUEBIRD
MORO	BUNYAII	BUSHTIT	BOBOLINK
OMAO	BURION	CAPELLA	CARDINAL
PAPE	CANARY	CARIAMA	CHIPCHAP
POPE	CITRIL	CATBIRD	CHIPCHOP
WREN	CORBIE	CHEWINK	GROSBEAK
YENI	DRONGO	CHIRPER	HAWFINCH
TUTU	GREENY	COWBIRD	LAZYBIRD
	HOODIE	ICTERUS*	LONGSPUR
	KOKAKO	JACKDAW	PHILOMEL
AMMER	LANIUS*	KINGLET	PINCPINC
AMSEL	LINNET	KIROMBO	REDSTART
CUTTY	LORIOT	MAYBIRD	SNOWBIRD
DAYAL	MERUCA*	MIMIDAE*	THRASHER
HOODY	MOCKER	MIMINAE*	TITMOUSE
IRENA*	MUFFET		WHINCHAT

TROPICAL, PARROTS

OO	QUIT	MUNIA*	MOTMOT
	RAYA	PIPRA*	PARROT
ARA	RURU	PITTA*	PICULE*
KEA	TAHA	SARUS	PIPILE*
POE	TIWI	SYLPH	QUELEA*
	TOCK	TURCO	TOUCAN
ANNA	TOCO	VEUVE	TROGON
COLY	TODY		WELLAT
CRAX*		ARGALA	WHIDAH
GUAN	AGAMI	BARBET	WHYDAH
JACU	ARARA	BECARD	YETAPU
JYNX*	BREVE	BROLGA	YNAMBU
KAKA	CAGIT	CONURE	
KOAE	DAYAL	DIKKOP	ARACARI
LORO	GALAH	HOAZIN	COLIBRI
LORY	HANNA	HOMRAI	CORELLA
LUPE	LOURI	KAKAPO	GANGANG
MAKO	LOWAN	LEIPOA*	JACOBIN
PEHO	LOXIA*	LIMOSA*	KIROMBO
PICI*	MACAW	MANUAO	LORILET

MANAKIN	ROSELLA	CURASSOW	LYREBIRD
NAMAQUA	SERIEMA	HORNBILL	PARAKEET
POEBIRD	SIRGANG	KINGTODY	POPINJAY
QUETZAL	SUNBIRD	LORIKEET	TOCORORO
RASORES*	TOURACO	LOVEBIRD	

FLIGHTLESS

EMU	KAGU	NANDU	APTERYX
IHI	KIWI		OSTRICH
MOA	RHEA	MOORUP	NOTORNIS*
ROC	WEKA	RATITE	
DODO		TAKAHE	
EMEU	DIDUS*		

OTHER BIRDS

GOR	CAPON	GORBIT	DORKING
HEN	COOEE	GORLIN	FANTAIL
JAY	COOEY	HOOPOE	FLICKER
MAG	GOURA*	HOUDAN	GOBBLER
MAO	HECCO	HUMMER	GRACKLE
NUN	HUCCO	JERKIN	HIRUNDO*
OII	KOKIL	KOKILA	LEGHORN
PIE	MALEO	MAOMAO	LOGCOCK
TIT	MORUS	MARTIN	MARTLET
	MYNAH	NESTER	MEGAPOD
AVES	PIPER	PASTOR	PEACOCK
AVIS	POTOO	PEEPER	PICULET
BAYA	RALPH	PEEWIT	PUFFLEG
CHAB	RAVEN	PHOEBE	SNOWCAP
COLK	SPICK	PIGEON	SPARROW
DOVE	SQUAE	PULLET	STINKER
GORB	STARN	PULLUS	SWALLOW
GRIG	SWIFT	REDLEG	TOMFOOL
HUIA	TARIN	SAPPHO	WARRIOR
KOEL	TERIN	SULTAN	WAXWING
MAGG	UPUPA	SWELLY	WITWALL
MITU		TIKLIN	
MYNA	BATARA	TURBIT	BOATTAIL
NENE	BRAHMA	TURKEY	COCKATOO
PAVO*	CHEBEC	TYRANT	COQUETTE
PAWN	CHIPPY	WITTOL	KINGBIRD
PICA	COUCAL	YAFFLE	KIWIKIWI
ROOK	CUCKOO	YELPER	NIGHTJAR
STIB	CUSHAT		POORWILL
WAMP	DACELO	ANTBIRD	RAINBIRD
WEET	DRIVER	CHICKEN	RINGDOVE
	FUFFIT	COLUMBA*	STARLING
	GORBAL	CREEPER	WHEATEAR
BIDDY	GORBET	CUCULUS*	

INSECTS
BUGS AND SUCKING INSECTS

BUG	LERP	APHID	CICAD
NIT	NEPA*	APHIS*	CIMEX
	PELA	BICHO	DORRE
AFIS		BORER	EMESA
LAAP	ANASA*	CHINK	LOUSE

NEPID	COCCID	THRIPS	LYREMAN
PUNEE	COREID	TINGIS*	NEPIDAE*
PUNIE	CORIXA*		PSYLLID
SCALE	DIMERA*	ADELGES*	PUCERON
THRIP	DORBUG	APHIDID	PUNAISE
	ICERYA*	BOATBUG	RANATRA*
ALTICA*	JARFLY	BOATMAN	
BEDBUG	JASSID	CHERMES*	HOGLOUSE
BLIGHT	JUGATE	CICADID	MEALYBUG
BUGGER	PSYLLA*	CIMICID	PLANTBUG
CHINCH	PUNESE	CORSAIR	TAPEWORM
CHINTZ	PUNICE	CRAWLER	WATERBUG
CICADA	SKATER	DIMERAN	WHEELBUG
CIGALA	TAENIA*	LACEBUG	
CIGALE	TETRIX*	LEAFBUG	
CIXIID	TETTIX*	LYGAEID	

GRASSHOPPERS

CAGN	STICK	MANTIS	GRYLLID
DRUM		PHASMA	GRYLLUS*
GRIG	BLATTA*		KATYDID
WETA	CHANGA	BLATTID	KNOCKER
	EARWIG	CATYDID	MANTOID
BRUKE	EMPUSA	CRACKET	PROPHET
RACER	LOCUST	CRICKET	
ROACH	MANTID	DRUMMER	STICKBUG

BUTTERFLIES AND MOTHS

ERI	SWIFT	PROGNE	CRININE
PUG	TINEA*	PRUNER	CUTWORM
WIT	WHITE	PSYCHE	DANAINE
	WITCH	QUAKER	DELTOID
CLEW	ZEBRA	RISPER	DIURNAL
ERIA		RUSTIC	DRINKER
HAWK	APOLLO	SPHINX	EMPEROR
MAUL	ARCTIA*	THECLA*	ERMELIN
MOCH	BAGONG	TINEAN	ERMILIN
MOTE	BOGONG	TINEID	EURYMUS*
MOTH	CANKER	TURNUS	FIGWORM
SLUG	CODLIN	TUSSAH	FOOTMAN
WERI	COLIAS*	TUSSEH	HOPMOTH
WHIT	COPPER	TUSSER	JUGATAE*
	COSSID	URSULA	JUNONIA
ARGUS	DAGGER	VIOLET	MONARCH
AWETO	DANAID	WOUBIT	PSYCHID
COMMA	ERMINE	YELLOW	PUGMOTH
EGGER	GRAPTA*		PYRALID
ELFIN	HERALD	ADMIRAL	PYRALIS*
ERUCA	HUMMER	AGROTIS*	TINEOID
GHOST	IDALIA	ARCTIID	TORTRIX
IMAGO	IOMOTH	ATTACUS*	TUSSOCK
MICRO	LAPPET	AURELIA	TUSSORE
NYMPH	MILLER	BAGWORM	URANIID
OOBIT	MOODER	BEEMOTH	VANESSA
OUBIT	MORPHO*	BUDWORM	VICEROY
PISKY	NYMPHA	CODLING	WAXMOTH
PLUME	PIERIS*	CRAMBID	WEBWORM
SATYR	PLUSIA*	CRAMBUS	YAMAMAI

ARMYWORM	GREYLING	KNOTHORN	SPANWORM
BOLLWORM	HAWKMOTH	LUNAMOTH	WANDERER
FORESTER	HESPERID	PLUTELLA	
GLOWWORM	INCHWORM	SILKWORM	

FLIES AND MOSQUITOES

BOT	OXBOT	MUSCAE*	EARTICK
FAG	OXFLY	MUSCID	FURCULA
FLY	PERLA	NITTER	GALLFLY
GAD	PHORA*	PALMER	GLOWFLY
KEB	PULEX*	PERLID	GOUTFLY
KED	PUNKY	PHORID	GRANNOM
LOP	SALLY	PODURA	GRAYFLY
MAD	WHAME	PUNKIE	GREYFLY
	ZEBUB	SALLIE	HORNFLY
BOTT		SAWFLY	HUZZARD
CLEG	ASILID	SEROOT	MADDOCK
FLEA	ASILUS*	TIPULA*	MORPION
GLEG	BEEFLY	TORCEL	PULICID
KADE	BLOWER	TSETSE	TIPULID
KIVU	BOTFLY	UJIFLY	WIGGLER
MAWK	BREEZE	WABBLE	
TICK	CEPHID*	WARBLE	APPLEFLY
ZIMB	COOTIE	WORMIL	BEELOUSE
	CRICKE		BIRDTRICK
AEDES*	DAYFLY	BATTICK	BLACKFLY
CLEGG	FLEIGH	BLOWFLY	CRANEFLY
CRIKE	GADBEE	BLUEFLY	DOGLOUSE
CRUMB	GADFLY	CEPHOID	FRUITFLY
CULEX*	GENTIL	CHALCID	HORNTAIL
DRAKE	GENTLE	COLLIER	HOUSEFLY
FLECH	GORFLY	CONOPID	MOSQUITO
FLECK	LEPTID	CORNFLY	ONIONFLY
MAGOT	LEPTUS	CREEPER	PANORPID
MAITH	MAGGOT	CULICID	PEARSLUG
MATHE	MAITHE	DIOPSIS*	STONEFLY
MUSCA	MIDGET	DOLPHIN	TATUKIRA

BEETLES

DOR	LYCID	PIERID	FIDDLER
	MELOE	PTINID	FIREFLY
BOUD	SAGRA*	PTINUS*	GIRDLER
DOAR		SAWYER	GIRINID
DORE	BEETLE	SCARAB	GOLDBUG
DORR	CHAFER	SILPHA*	GYRINID
GOGA	CLERID	WEAVER	GYRINUS*
GOGO	CLERUS*	WEEVIL	HUMBUZZ
IPID	CUCUYO		JUNEBUG
POPE	ELATER	ADELOPS*	LADYBUG
TURK	GOLACH	AGRILUS*	LADYFLY
UANG	GOLOCH	BILLBUG	LAMPFLY
	IPIDAE*	BUZZARD	LUCANID
AMARA*	LAMIID	CADELLE	LUCANUS*
CLOCK	LARIID	CARABID	PTINOID
FIDIA	LYCTID	CARABUS	ROSEBUG
GOGGA	LYCTUS*	CUCUJID	TUMBLER
HISPA	MELOID	DARDAOL	VEDALIA*
LARIA*	PICUDO	ELATRID	

CURCULIO	HARDBACK	RUTILIAN	WIREWORM
GRAYBACK	LADYBIRD	SEARCHER	
GREYBACK	RUTELIAN	SQUEAKER	

WASPS, ANTS, BEES

ANT	MASON	DIGGER	DEBORAH
BEE	MAXIM	DINGAR	DESERET
DUN	MIDGE	DRIVER	EMMETTE
	MINIM	DRONEL	ERGATES
ANAI	NURSE	DRONER	EUMENES*
ANAY	QUEEN	DRONET	EUMENID
APIS*	SAUBA	ECITON*	FORAGER
ATTA*	SLAVE	HORNET	FORMICA*
BIKE	SPHEX	LASIUS*	FORMICE
CRAB	STOUT	NASUTE	KOOTCHA
COON	VESPA*	NEUTER	MASARID
COUN	WAPSE	PONERA*	MELISSA
GNAT	WHAMP	REDANT	MUDWASP
GYNE	WOPSE	TERMES*	MUTILLA
HIVE		TIPHIA*	PISMIRE
KING	AMAZON	VESPID	REPLETE
SMUT	APIDAE*	WORKER	TERMITE
STUT	APINAE*		TRIGONA*
WAPS	BEMBEX*	ANDRENA	VESPINA
WASP	BEMBIX*	ANTLING	
WOPS	BOMBUS*	ANTLION	ACULEATA
	BOMBYX*	APODAE*	ANGELITO
	BUMBEE	ARMYANT	HONEYBEE
DRONE	BUMBLE	BULLDOG	SANDWASP
EMMET	BUMMIE	BUMBLER	SAUBAANT
KARBI	CARDER	BUMMLER	WAXMAKER
KELEP	DAUBER	CYNIPID	WHITEANT

OTHER INSECTS

VEI	CADDIS	CINURAN*	FIREBRAT
	CINURA*	CODWORM	LACEWING
VERI	DOBSON	LEPISMA*	MILLEPED
	DRAGON	PSOCINE	MYRIAPOD
CADEW	PSOCID	TERMITE	PAUROPOD
CADIS	SHINER		
SEDGE		CHILOPOD	
TAINT	CADDICE	DIPLOPOD	

LOW (MARINE) LIFE, WORMS AND LARVAE

ERI	NAID	HYDRA	APODAN
ESS	NEMA	LARVA	CADDIS
LOA	SALP	LEECH	CRANIA
MAD	TURK	MATHE	ENOPLA
	WORM	MONAD	EPHYRA
BOLL		POLYP	EUNICE
BOUD	AMEBA	REDIA	FUNGIA
ERIA	APODA	SALPA	GENTIL
GILL	ARTER	TINEA	GENTLE
GRUB	BORER	VELUM	HOPPER
LURG	CORAL		LEPTUS
MAUK	ERUCA	AMOEBA	LOBOSA
MAWK	FLUKE	ANOPLA	LOOPER

MAGGOT	ASCARID	SANGSUE	HELIOZOA
MEDUSA	ASCARIS	SEAMOSS	HELMINTH
NEREIS	BRYOZOA	SERPULA	INFUSORY
PALOLO	CADELLE	STENTOR	NEMATODA
PEDATA	CARBORA	SUNSTAR	NEMATODE
PLAICE	CILIATA	TAGTAIL	NEMATOID
PLOIMA	CRINOID	TREPANG	ORBULINA
SEAFAN	DISCINA	TUSSORE	PHORONIS
SYLLID	ENOPLAN	VELELLA	PROTISTA
TEREDO	EUNICID	VESTLET	RETEPORA
TORCEL	FILARIA		RETEPORE
TUSSAH	FLYBLOW	ACALEPHE	ROTIFERA
TUSSEH	GORDIUS	ANNELIDA	SABELLID
TUSSER	LINGULA	ANNELOID	SEAMOUSE
WABBLE	LIPOPOD	ANNULATA	SHIPWORM
WEEVIL	OCULINA	ANNULATE	STARFISH
WORMIL	PINWORM	BDELLOID	SUCTORIA
	PLANULA	CERCARIA	TORNARIA
	PLUTEUS	CLEPSINE	TUBEWORM
	PORPITA	COMATULA	TOBICOLA
ACALEPH	PROTIST	CURCULIO	TUBIPORA
ACTINIA	ROTIFER	GORGONIA	TUBIPORE
AMEBULA	SABELLA		
ANNELID	SAGITTA		

MOLLUSKS

MYA	MUREX	CHITON	TEREDO
TUN	NACRE	CLIONE	TETHYS
	NAIAD	COCKLE	TRITON
CLAM	OLIVA	CONKER	UMBONE
CONE	ORMER	COTUIT	VOLUTA
LEDA	PEARL	COWRIE	VOLUTE
LIMA	PHYSA	DODMAN	WINKLE
NAID	PINNA	DOLIUM	
PIPI	POLYP	ELYSIA	ABALONE
PUPA	POULP	GWEDUC	ABALONI
QUIN	QUARL	HUITRE	ASTARTE
SLUG	SHELL	HYALEA	AURELIA
SPAT	SNAIL	JINGLE	BIVALVE
UMBO	SQUID	LIMPET	BLUBBER
UNIO	SQUIN	LIMPIN	CALAMAR
	THAIS	MACTRA	COQUINA
AWABI	TROCA	MUCKET	DECAPOD
BULLA	TURBO	MOUGAT	ETHERIA
CHAMA	UHLLO	MOUKET	FLIDDER
CHANK	VARIX	MUSCLE	GEODUCK
COHOG	VASUM	MUSSEL	GLAUCUS
CONCH	VENUS	NATICA	GOEDUCK
CONUS	WHELK	NUCULA	INKFISH
COPIS	WHORL	OYSTER	LIMNAEA
COWRY		PALOUR	MEDUSAN
DORIS	AEOLID	PECTEN	MYTILID
DRILL	AEOLIS	PHOLAS	MYTILUS
HARPA	ANOMIA	POULPE	NUCULID
HELIX	BYSSUS	PURPLE	OCTOPUS
JELLY	CARVEL	PYRULA	OOTHECA
LIMAX	CASSIS	QUAHOG	PANDORA
MITRA	CERION	STROMB	POLYPOD

POLYPUS	SPONDYL	VITRINA	JANTHINA
PURPURA	SUNFISH		MELANIAN
QUAHAUG	TELLINA	APLYSIAS	NAUTILUS
QUOHAUG	TEREBRA	ARKSHELL	NERETINA
RISSOID	TOHEROA	BULLNOSE	OPERCULA
SCALLOP	TOXIFER	CALAMARY	SOLARIUM
SCUTTLE	TROCHID	CASSIDID	STROBILA
SCYLLAE	TROCHUS	DITREMID	STROMBUS
SEPIOID	UNIONID	DEERHORN	TOPSHELL
SERPULA	VALVATA	DOGWHELK	UNIVALVE
SHARPER	VARICES	EARSHELL	VELUTINA
SLOBBER	VELIGER	EARSNAIL	VERMETID
SPIRULA	VERTIGO	GEOPHILA	VERMETUS

PLANTS
FLOWERS

BIK	GLAD	WOAD	CRAZY
GOB	HAGI	YAGE	CROCI
GUL	HEMP	YAJE	CUMAY
LIN	HOCK	YARR	CUMBU
LIS	HOYA	YUCA	DAFFY
LYS	IMBY		DAGGA
MAW	INGA	ABACA	DAISY
MAY	IRID	ABAKA	DALEA
MEU	IRIS	ABAMA	DATIL
MEW	IXIA	AGATI	DILLY
MUM	KIKU	AGAVE	DRYAS
NIL	LILY	ALTEA	DWALE
PHU	LISS	AMOLE	ERICA
PUA	LOTE	ANIBA	FAHAM
RUE	LUCE	ANILA	FURZE
SAK	LUCY	ASPIC	GANJA
SAN	MOXA	ASTER	GAURA
SEG	MAMA	ATEES	GILIA
	PINK	AVENS	GILLY
ALOE	PINY	BADAN	GLAUX
ANIL	POKE	BEHEN	GORSE
ASSI	POOA	BESOM	GOWAN
ATES	POSY	BHANG	GUACO
ATIS	PRIM	BLOBS	HELIO
ATTA	RINE	BLUET	HENNA
BELA	ROSA	BOCCA	HIPPO
BETA	ROSE	BOOTS	HOLLY
BIKH	RUTA	BRIDE	HOSTA
BISH	SAMH	BUCKY	HUBAM
BIXA	SANA	BUGLE	HULDI
BLOB	SANG	CAJUN	ILIMA
BOLT	SARA	CALLA	INULA
BUDA	SEGG	CAMAS	IREOS
CARL	SERI	CAMPE	IZOTA
CHES	SNOW	CARDO	JOWAR
DISA	SUNN	CARLE	JUVIA
FAAM	ULEX	CASSY	KEIRI
FLAG	WADE	CATHA	KEITA
FLAX	WABI	CEBIL	KOALI
FLIX	WELD	CHEIR	KUSUM
FUJI	WHIN	CHENA	LAYIA
GEUM	WINK	CRAIN	LEDUM

LILAC	SCOKE	DAHLIA	BOXWOOD
LINUM	SEDGE	FUNKIA	CAMPION
LOTOS	SEDUM	IBERIS	COWSLIP
LOTUS	SISAL	INDIGO	COXCOMB
LUPIS	SIZAL	KISSME	DEWDROP
MACAN	SOTOL	LUPINE	DOGBANE
MALVA	SULLA	LYCIUM	FLYTRAP
MENDY	TENAI	MADDER	FREEZIA
MESEM	TUCKY	MALLEE	FUCHSIA
MILLA	TULIP	MALLOW	GENTIAN
MILLY	VANDA	MIMOSA	GERBERA
MURGA	VINCA	NALITA	HEATHER
MURVA	VIOLA	ORCHID	HEMLOCK
NANCY	WOCAS	POMPOM	HENBANE
ORACH	WOKAS	PRIVET	HONESTY
ORPIN	YUCCA	RESEDA	IPOMOEA
ORYZA	YULAN	SMILAX	JASMINE
OXEYE		SORREL	JONQUIL
OXLIP	ADONIS	SPIREA	JUNIPER
PANSY	ALSIKE	STOCKS	LOBELIA
PEONY	ALTHEA	TEASEL	PAPAVER
PHLOX	ANILLA	THRIFT	PETUNIA
PINEY	CASSIA	VIOLET	PRIMULA
POCAN	CLOVER	ZINNIA	RAMBLER
POOAH	COLEUS		SOLANUM
POPPY	COLIMA	ACONITE	SPIRAEA
PROSE	CORNUS	ALTHAEA	SYRINGA
RUBIA	COSMOS	ANEMONE	THISTLE
SARSA	CROCUS	BEGONIA	VERBENA

TREES AND SHRUBS

* Noted for Fruit, Sap, Useful Bark

IE	DOM	TAY	AULA
KI	DUM	TEA*	AULU*
TI	EBO	TIL*	AUSU*
	ELB*	TOA	AUTE*
AAL	ELM	TUA	AUZU*
ACH	FEG	TUI	BAGO
AGA	FIR	TUN	BAKU*
AIK	GAB*	UGH	BANG
AKE	GUM*	ULE	BARU
AMA	HAU	YEW	BIJA
APA	HAW*		BIRK
ARN	HOP*	ACER	BITI
ASH	IBA*	ACLE	BITO
ASP	IFE	AKEE	BOBO
ATA	IVA	AKIA	BOGO
AVE*	JAK*	ALEM*	BOLA
AWA*	KAT*	AMLA	BRAB
BAY	KIO*	AMLI	BREA
BEL*	KOA	AMRA	BROM
BEX*	KOU	ANAM	BURI
BOX	LIM	ANDA	BURR
BUR	NIM	ARAK*	CADE*
CHE*	NYM	ARAR	CAJU*
CYP	OAK	ASAK	CEBA
DAO*	SAJ	ATAP*	CHAA*
DAR	SAL	ATLE	CHAW*

CHIA*	MABI*	TOON	ARJAN
CHIL	MAJO*	TORO	ARTAR
CHIR	MAKO	TORU	ARUSA*
COCA*	MIRO	TSIA*	ASANA
COCO*	MOJO	TULU	ASOKA
COLA*	MORA	TUNG	ASPEN
COPA	MYXA*	TUNO*	ASSAI
CORK*	NABK	TUNU	ATTAP
CUCA*	NABO	TUTU*	BABUL
CUYA	NAGA	TUUI	BACAO
DALI	NAIO*	TUWI	BAHAN
DHAK	NEEM*	ULME	BALAO
DILO	NIOG*	ULMO	BALAU
DITA	NIPA*	UPAS*	BALSA
DOON*	NUBK	VERA	BALZA
DOUM*	ODUM*	WABE	BANAK
DUKU*	OHIA	WABI	BARIA
EBOE	OLER	WHAU	BAROI
EBON	PALM	YATE	BATIS
EJOO*	PAUM	YAYA*	BAYOK
GAUB	PELU		BEALA
GOAI	PILI*	AALLI	BELAH
GUAO	PINE	ABELE	BELAR
HALA	PINO	ABETO	BETIS
HINO*	PIXY	ABIES	BIABO
HOLM	POON	ABILO	BILLA
HULE	PUKA	ABURA	BIRCH
HUON	PUNA	ACANA	BIRMA
HURA	RATA*	ACAPU	BOGUM*
ICHO*	RHUS	ACOMA*	BOKOM
IEIE	RIMU	ADJAB*	BOLDO*
IFIL	ROKA*	AEGLE*	BOLDU*
ILEX*	SADR	AFARA	BONGA*
IPIL	SAGO*	AGLET*	BONGO
IROK	SAIN	AGOHO	BOREE
ITEA	SALE	AGOJO	BUBBY*
JACA	SAUF	AJARI	BULAK*
JARA	SAUL	ALAMO	BUMBO*
JHOW*	SHEA*	ALANI	BUNYA
JUTE*	SHOQ	ALDER	BURAO
KAAT*	SIDA	ALGUM	BUXUS
KAIL	SIPO	ALISO	CACAO*
KAIO*	SOLA	ALLER	CAJOU
KAKI*	SUGI	ALMON	CAOBA
KARI*	SUNT	ALMUG	CAROB
KARO	SUPA*	ALNUS	CEDAR
KHAT*	TALA	ALPIN	CEIBE*
KIKI*	TAPA	AMAGA	CEIBO
KINO*	TARA	AMAPA	CHICO
KIRI	TAWA	AMATE	CLOVE*
KOKO*	TCHA*	AMBAY	COCOS
KOPI	TCHE*	ANABO	COOBA
KOZO*	TEAK	ANANA	COUMA*
LAMA	TECA	ANATO*	COYOL
LIAR	TEEL*	ANJAN	CURUA
LIND	TEIL	ANONA*	CYPRE
LING	THEA*	ARACA	DADAP
LINN	TITI*	ARECA	DALLI
MABA	TOOA	ARENG	DANLI

DAROO	LITHI	QUIRA	VITEX
DATIL	MABEE	RAFIA	WAHOO
DHAVA*	MAHOE	RATAN	WAMPI*
DIRCA	MAHUA*	RAULI	WICKY
DOMBA	MAHWA*	RETEM*	WILGA
DRAGO	MAIRE	RHAMN	WITCH
DUALI	MAJOE*	ROBLE	WITHY
DURIO*	MALOO	ROBUR	XYLIA
EBANO	MALUS*	ROHAN*	YACAL
EBONY	MAMET*	ROHUN*	YACCA
ELDER	MANGI	ROWAN*	YAGUA
FAGUS	MANIU	ROWEN	YARAI
GARAD*	MAPAU	RUBUS*	YEARA
GENIP*	MAPLE	SABAL	YEDDO
GIDIA	MAPOU	SALAL*	YOCCO*
GINEP*	MAQUI	SALIX	ZAMAN
GINKO*	MARIA	SAMAN	ZANTE
GOKAN	MATAI	SAPIN	ZILLA*
GOUMI*	MATSU	SASSY	ZORRO
GUAVA*	MATTI*	SAVIN*	
GUIJO	MELIA	SCRAG	ACACIA
HAKEA	MESUA*	SEESU	ACAJOU*
HAZEL*	MUDAR	SERON	ALMOND*
HEOAK	MULGA	SHOLA	ANILAO
HEVEA*	MYALL	SIMAI	BALSAM
HINAU*	NABAX	SIRIS	BANYAN
HOWEA	NARAS*	SISSU	BOMBAX*
ICACO*	NARRA	SORVA*	BRAZIL*
ICICA	NEBUK	SPRUG	CACHOU*
INAJA	NIEPA	SUMAC	CASHEW*
IROKO	NIKAU	TABOG	CASHIO*
IXORA	NIOTA	TAPPA	CODLIN*
JAQUA	NJAVE*	TARFA	GEMUTI
JIQUE	NOGAL*	TAXUS	GINGKO*
JIQUI	NONDA*	TECUM	GOMUTI
JOCUM	NURSE	TENIO	GRIGRI*
JUNCO	NYSSA*	TERAP	GRUGRU
KAPOR*	OADAL	THIEF	LAUREL
KAPUR*	OCHNA	THUJA*	LICHEE*
KARRI*	OCOTE*	TIKUR*	LINDEN
KAURI	ODOOM	TILIA	LITCHI*
KAURY*	OSIER	TIMBO	MISTLE
KEENA*	PACAY*	TINGI*	NUTMEG*
KHAIR*	PADUS*	TOONA	POPLAR
KHAYA	PALAS	TOWAI	RATTAN
KIAKI	PALMA	TOYON	TUPELO*
KIKAR*	PAVIA	TREMA*	WALNUT*
KOKAN	PECAN*	TSUGA	WILLOW
KOKIO	PENDA	TUART	
KONGU	PICEA	TUCUM	ARBUTUS
LANSA*	PINON*	ULMUS	AVOCADO*
LARCH	PIPAL*	UMIRI	CASCARA*
LARIX	PIPUL*	UNAMO	CATECHU
LAWAN	POLAK	UNONA*	COCONUT*
LEHUA	POOLI	URENA*	CONIFER
LICCA	POONA	URUCU*	DOGWOOD
LICHI*	PULAS	UVITO	HICKORY
LIGAS*	PYRUS*	VACOA	LINWOOD
LINGO	QUINA*	VEREK	PIASAVA

PIMENTO*	QUERCUS	SEQUOIA	TARWOOD
PLATANE	REDWOOD	SOLANUM*	TURTOSA
QUASSIA*	SANDBOX	TAMARIX	

CACTI, MOSSES, FUNGI

BLEO	DUGAL	PITAU	FUMAGO
BUNT	EKAHA	PONGA	LICHEN
CEPE	ERGOT	PONGO	MILDEW
FERN	FILIX	PONJA	NARDOO
MOLD	FOMES	PORIA	ZYTHIA
MOSS	FUNGO	TODEA	
MYXO	HYPHO	ULUHI	AMANITA
PUFF	IRPEX	UREDO	BLEWITS
PULU	MEESE	USNEA	BOLETUS
RUST	MNIUM	VALSA	CARDONA
SMUT	MOREL	VERPA	PARELLA
WEKI	MORIL	WHEKI	PARELLE
	MOULD	YEAST	STEREUM
BANGA	MUCOR		STINKER
BRAKE	MUSCI	AGARIC	TORTULA
BRYUM	NARDU	AMADOU	TRUFFLE
CACTI	NOPAL	ARCHIL	WOODSIA
CYCAS	PHOMA	CAEOMA	

EDIBLE FRUITS AND VEGETABLES, GRAINS AND HERBS

BON	ANAY	CIVE	JAVA
COS	ANET	COLE	JOBO
DAL	ANGO	CORN	JUCA
FEI	ANIS	COUS	KAIL
FIG	ANSU	COYO	KALE
HAW	ANTA	CRAB	KALO
HIP	ANZU	CRAP	KAVA
HOI	ARUM	CUKE	KAWA
KEY	ARVA	DATE	KERS
MUG	BAGA	DHAL	KIKI
NEP	BAHO	DILL	KING
NIP	BALM	DUKE	LEEK
NUT	BEAN	EDDO	LIMA
OAT	BEET	EKER	LIME
OCA	BEHN	FABA	LINT
PEA	BENE	FARD	MAND
RYE	BENI	FICO	MANI
SLA	BIGG	FIGO	MATE
SOY	BIWA	FLAT	MEUM
TOM	BOLE	FUJI	MINT
TUR	BORO	GABE	MOLY
UBE	BOSC	GABI	MUSA
UBI	BUNK	GAGE	NAPE
UME	BUYO	GEAN	NEEP
URD	CALE	GITH	NEPE
UVE	CANE	GOBO	NOOP
WOT	CEPA	GUAR	OCRA
YAM	CHAT	HABA	OKRA
	CHIT	HEVI	OLAX
AIPI	CHOU	IIING	OLEA
AMMI	CHOW	IKMO	PADI

PAGA	AKPEK	CUMIN	OHELO
PAHO	AMINI	CUPAY	OLENA
PAJO	ANANA	DHOLL	OLIVE
PALA	ANDRE	DOORA	ONION
PAPA	ANISE	DRIAS	OOPAK
PASA	ANJOU	DUHAT	OSAGE
PAUN	ANNIS	DURRA	OUABE
PAVY	ANONA	DURUM	PADDY
PECO	APIUM	EMMER	PAGLE
PEPO	APPLE	ERUCA	PANGI
PINA	ARARU	ERYUM	PAPAW
PITA	ARHAR	ETROG	PAVIE
PITO	ARROZ	FABES	PEACH
PLUM	ARZAN	FARDH	PEKOE
POHA	ARZUN	FICUS	PHACA
POME	AVENA	GOBBE	PINDA
RAGI	BADAM	GOURD	PINTO
RAMS	BAHOO	GRAPE	PISUM
RAPE	BASIL	GUAVA	PRUNE
RASP	BAUNO	GUBBO	PULSE
RIBE	BELLE	GUMBO	PUSSY
RICE	BENDY	HAVER	QUASH
RIMA	BENNE	HEDGE	RADIS
ROME	BENNI	HYSON	RAGEE
SABA	BENNY	INGAN	RAGGI
SAGE	BETEL	ISLAY	RAGGY
SEGO	BICHY	JAMAN	RAMPS
SIRI	BIGAS	JAMBO	RHOEO
SITH	BOHEA	JAMBU	RIBES
SIUM	BREBA	JAMUN	RUNCH
SIVE	BROMA	JAWAR	RURAL
SKAG	BUGLE	JINKS	SABZI
SKEG	CAFFE	KAFIR	SAIDI
SLOE	CAMAS	KAMAS	SALAD
SNAP	CANEL	KANGA	SALEB
SOIA	CARUM	KAROU	SALEP
SOJA	CEDRA	LEMON	SANAI
SORB	CHAIS	LEXIA	SARAH
SOYA	CHARD	LOOFA	SCRAB
SPUD	CHAYA	LUFFA	SHARD
SUJI	CHILE	MAIZE	SHIVE
TARE	CHILI	MANGO	SIEVA
TARO	CHINO	MAYES	SIRIH
TEFF	CHITS	MEBOS	SITAO
TIFF	CHIVE	MELON	SITHE
TRUB	CHOCO	METEL	SOLNE
TUNA	CHOKO	MILLO	SPELT
WORT	CHOUX	MOCHA	SPRUE
YAMP	CIBOL	MOLKA	SUJEE
YAVA	CICER	MOREL	SWEDE
YUCA	CLARY	MORON	TANIA
	CLING	MORUS	TATER
ADLAI	COCCO	MUNGO	TATIE
ADLAY	COCOA	MYRRH	TERFA
AIPIM	COLZA	NAVET	THYME
AJAVA	COPEI	NAVEW	TIROR
AJUGA	CRESS	NGAIO	TOKAY
AKALA	CROUT	NOGAL	TONKA
AKELA	CUBEB	OCHRO	TRIGO

TRUFF	CITRUS	PIPPIN	HARICOT
TUGUI	COFFEA	POMELO	KUMQUAT
TULSI	COLANE	POTATO	LETTUCE
VITIS	COLEUS	RADISH	MUSTARD
WHEAT	CUSHAW	RAISIN	OXHEART
YAMPA	DOUCIN	RENNET	PAPRIKA
YERBA	DURIAN	RUSSET	PARSLEY
YUCCA	ENDIVE	SALVIA	PARSNIP
	ESOPUS	SAVORY	PIMENTO
ALLIUM	FENNEL	SORREL	POMMELO
ARALIA	GARLIC	SQUASH	POPCORN
ATIMON	GINGER	TOMATO	POTHERS
BANANA	GOOBER	TURNIP	PUMPKIN
BAOBAB	HYSSOP		RAMPION
BARLEY	KANARI	APRICOT	RHUBARB
BATATA	LEGUME	AVOCADO	RICINUS
BORAGE	LENTIL	CABBAGE	ROMAINE
CAMMAS	LOQUAT	CARAWAY	SALSIFY
CARROT	MARRON	CARDOON	SCALLOP
CASABA	MEDLAR	CASSABA	SHALLOT
CASSIS	MUSKAT	CATAWBA	SOLANUM
CATNIP	OOLONG	CAYENNE	SOYBEAN
CELERY	ORANGE	CHERVIL	SPINACH
CEREAL	PAPAYA	CHICORY	TANGELO
CHILLI	PAWPAW	COCONUT	TAPIOCA
CHIVES	PEANUT	COLLARD	TARAGON
CITRON	PEPPER	CURRANT	WINESAP
	PICKLE	GRANATE	

GRASSES, VINES, WEEDS, OTHER HERBS

AJI	WAD	DURA	MUNG
AKA	ZEA	DURR	MUNJ
BEN		FUCI	NARD
BON	AGAR	GERS	NETI
BUN	AIRA	GILL	NITO
BUR	AKRA	GILO	NORI
DOD	ALFA	GOGO	ODAL
ERS	ALGA	GRIG	ODEL
GIT	AMIL	GUMI	OOZE
HAY	ARUM	HEII	PILI
HEY	BENA	HOLA	POLY
IFE	BOHO	HOVE	RAIT
IVE	BOJO	ICHU	RAND
IVY	CAPA	IVIN	REED
IYO	CHAY	JILL	REEK
JIL	CHOY	JITI	REIK
KEX	COCO	JOAR	REIT
ORE	COIX	JUAR	RESH
PIA	CUSH	KASA	RHEA
POA	CUVY	KELP	RHIA
RAG	DARI	KESH	RISP
RAY	DESI	KODA	RUSA
REA	DISS	KUSA	RUSH
RIX	DION	LASA	SASA
SEG	DODD	LIMU	SION
TOD	DOOB	LOCO	TANG
UDO	DOUB	MILO	TATH
URE	DREW	MOHA	TUIE

ULVA	DRAWK	PIPES	VIGNA
ULUA	DRIFT	PLUSH	VIJAO
WAAR	DRINN	PYXIE	VRAIC
	DULSE	QUILA	WRACK
AARON	DURBA	RAMEE	XYRID
ABRUS	DUTRA	RAMIE	XYRIS
ABUTA	EAVER	RAUPO	
ACUAN	FITCH	REESK	ACANTH
ADOXA	FUCUS	REREE	AGARUM
ADRUE	FUNDI	REXEN	AMYRIS
AGSAM	GALAX	RHEUM	AXWORT
AKEBI	GLAGA	ROOSA	BAMBOO
AKEKI	GOOMA	RUMEX	BORAGE
ALGAE	GRAMA	SABIA	BRYONY
ALGAL	HALFA	SEAVE	CATKIN
ANKEE	HICHU	SEDGE	CURARE
APIOS	HIRSE	SEGRA	CUSCUS
ARDOO	IVORY	SENNA	DARNEL
AWINI	JALAP	SEQUA	DATURA
BARID	JEETE	SIRKI	FESCUE
BATAD	KAINI	SLAKE	LICHEN
BATAK	KLOPS	SLOKE	NARDUS
BRIZA	KODRO	SORGO	QUITCH
BROME	KUSHA	SPART	REDTOP
BUAZE	KUTCH	SPIRE	TWITCH
CACUR	LAVER	SPRAT	URTICA
CAJAN	LEMNA	SPRET	YARROW
CALLA	LIANA	SPRIT	
CANNA	LIANE	SPROT	ALFALFA
CAREX	LIMON	STARR	CATTAIL
CAROA	LOASA	STIPA	ESPARTO
CARUA	MANNA	TACCA	FIGWORT
CHARA	MARAM	TASCA	GINSENG
CHESS	MATTA	TASCO	LUCERNE
CHUFA	MUNJA	TAMUS	MATWEED
CLITE	NEELE	TANSY	OREWEED
CLOTE	NONDO	TIBEY	RAGWEED
COGON	OLONA	TIMBO	SEATANG
COUCH	ORYZA	TRAPA	SEAWEED
CREAT	OSHAC	TYPHA	SORGHUM
CUTCH	OTATE	URALI	TIMOTHY
DASYA	PALAY	URARE	TOCUSSO
DIOON	PANAX	URARI	TUSSOCK
DONAX	PANIC	VAREC	VETIVER
DRABA	PICHI	VETCH	
	PILEA	VICIA	
	PIPER		

BOTANICAL TERMS

ARIL	CALYX	PINNA	CARPEL
AXIL	CLEFT	RAPHE	CORYMB
CYME	DRUPE	SEPAL	CYMOSE
NODE	EROSE	SINUS	HISPID
POME	HILUM	SPIKE	MIDRIB
SPUR	LATEX	STOMA	NODOSE
	LOBED	UMBEL	NUTLET
AMENT	OVATE	WHORL	PILOSE
BERRY	OVOID		PISTIL
BLADE	OVULE	ADNATE	POLLEN
BRACT	PETAL	ANTHER	RACEME

RACHIS	CAUDATE	HYALINE	SEPTATE
REPAND	CILIATE	INCISED	SERRATE
RETUSE	CLAVATE	LABIATE	SESSILE
RUGOSE	CONNATE	LEAFLET	SPICATE
SAMARA	CORDATE	OBOVATE	SPINOSE
SECUND	COROLLA	OBOVOID	SPINULE
SPATHE	CRENATE	PALMATE	STIPULE
STAMEN	CUNEATE	PANICLE	SULCATE
STIGMA	DENTATE	PEDICEL	SYNCARP
STOLON	EXOCARP	PELTATE	TERNATE
TERETE	FALCATE	PETIOLE	THYRSUS
	FOLIATE	PILCATE	VALVATE
ATHESIS	GLOBOSE	PINNATE	VEINLET
BACCATE	HABITAT	PLUMOSE	VILLOUS
CAPSULE	HASTATE	RADICLE	VIRGATE

MINERALS AND STONES

* Indicates gemstones

ICE	CRETA	GNEISS	BAUCITE
JET*	EARTH	GRAVEL	BAUXITE
ORE	ELVAN	GYPSUM	BEEKITE
WAD	EMERY	HELITE	BIOTITE
	FLINT	HELVIN	BITUMEN
ALUM	GESSO	HUMITE	BOGIRON
AUGE	GLASS	JARCON	BORNITE
BORT	LAPIS	JASPER*	BURMITE*
CLAY	NITER	KAINIT	CALCITE
COAL	NITRE	KAOLIN	CALLAIS
KNAR	OCHER	LATITE	CELSIAN
LAVA	OCHRE	MARBLE	CITEINE*
LIME	PRASE*	MORLOP	CRYSTAL
MICA	SHALE	ORMULU	CUPRITE
ONYX*	SLATE	PEBBLE	CYANITE
PACO	SMALT	PINITA	DANAITE
ROCK	STEEL	PLASMA*	DESMINE
SALT	STONE	POTASH	DIORITE
SAND	TABLE	POTASS	DRYBONE
SARD*	TALUS	PYRITE*	EDENITE
SIMA	TOPHE	PYROPE*	EPIDOTE
SODA	TRONA	RUBINE	FAHLERZ
TALC	YESSO	RUTILE	FAHLORE
TIZA		SALITE	FELSPAR
TOPH	ACMITE	SCHIST	GAHNITE
TUFA	ALBITE	SILICA	GEDRITE
TUFF	ANNITE	SINTER	GLIMMER
URAO	APLITE	SMIRIS	GRANITE
WADD	AUGITE	SPHENE	HELVINE
YESO	BARITE	STRASS	HESSITE
	BASALT		ICESPAR
	BLENDE	ALTAITE	ILVAITE
AGATE*	CEMENT	ALUNITE	INYOITE
AMBER*	CERUSE	AMALGAM	JADEITE
ARGIL	DACITE	ANATASE	JARGOON
ARITE	DIPYRE	APATITE	KAINITE
BOART	DOMITE	ASPHALT	KAOLINE
BORAX	EMERIL	AZURITE	KERNITE
CHERT	GALENA	BARYTES	KYANITE
CLINT			

LAURITE	ADULARIA	EMBOLITE	PICOTITE
MARTITE	AIKINITE	ENARGITE	PISANITE
ORTHITE	ALLANITE	EPSOMITE	PLUMBAGO
ORTHOSE	ANDESINE	FAYALITE	PREHNITE
PETZIDE	ANKERITE	FELDSPAR	PYROXENE
PLASTER	ASBESTOS	FLUORIDE	ROCKMILK
PYRITES	AUTUNITE	GALENITE	ROCKSALT
RASPITE	BORACITE	GANISTER	ROSELITE*
REALGAR	BRONZITE	GIBBSITE	SANIDINE
SAHLITE	BROOKITE	GOETHITE	SARDONYX*
SENAITE	CALAMINE	GRAPHITE	SELENITE
SYLVITE	CHLORITE	HEMATITE*	SERICITE
THORITE	CHROMITE	IDOCRASE	SIDERITE
THULITE	CINNABAR	ILMENITE	SMALTINE
TILEORE	CORUNDUM	JAROSITE	SMALTITE
TURGITE	CROCOITE	LAZULITE	STANNITE
ULEXITE	CRYOLITE	LAZURITE	STEATITE
URALITE	DANALITE	LIMONITE	STIBNITE
WOLFRAM	DATOLITE	MEIONITE	STILBITE
WOODTIN	DIALLAGE	MESITINE	SUNSTONE*
ZEOLITE	DIASPORE	MIMETITE	TENORITE
ZINCITE	DIOPSIDE	NOSELITE	TITANITE
ZOISITE	DOLOMITE	OBSIDIAN*	TROILITE
ZUNYITE	ELECTRUM	ORPIMENT	YENTNITE
	ELEOLITE	ORANGITE	WURTZITE
ACHROITE		PERTHITE	

PRECIOUS STONES

LASK	RUBIN	ANTHRAX	PRASINE
OPAL	VAJRA	BRIOLET	RUBELET
RUBY	ADAMAS	CATSEYE	SMARAGD
BAHIA	LASQUE	DIAMOND	HYACINTH
DORJE	LIGURE	EMERALD	SAPPHIRE
LASKE	TABLET	JACINTH	

SEMIPRECIOUS STONES

JADE	SPINEL	OLIVINE	FIREOPAL
BERYL	ZIRCON	OVALINE	GIRASOLE
MACLE	AXINITE	PERIDOT	MELANITE
TOPAZ	EUCLASE	TURCOIS	NEPHRITE
GARNET	GIRASOL	TURKOIS	SODALITE
IOLITE	HYALITE	AMETHYST	TURQUOIS
QUARTZ	KUNZITE	ESSONITE	

FAMOUS DIAMONDS

HOPE	HORNBY	REGENT	TENNANT
PITT	KOLLUR	CHAPADA	TIFFANY
MATAN	NASSAK	DEBEERS	CULLINAN
DUDLEY	ORLOFF	EUGENIE	KOHINOOR
DUTOIT	PIGOTT	STEWART	

ALLOYS

LAY	TULA	MOKUM	ALNICO
PIG	BIDRI	STEEL	ALUMEL
AICH	BRASS	TERNE	BIDERY
ASEM	CALIN	VIDRY	BIDREE
NIEL	INVAR	ALBATA	BILLON

BRONZE	SOLDER	ELINVAR	CARBOLOY
CERMET	TAMBAC	INCONEL	ELECTRUM
GARBLE	TEMPER	MIXTURE	HYPERNIK
LATTEN	TOMBAC	PAKTONG	NICHROME
NIELLO	AMALGAM	RHEOTAN	PACKTONG
OROIDE	BABBITT	SPELTER	STELLITE
ORMOLU	BIDDERY	TOMBACK	DURALUMIN
PEWTER	DURIRON	TUTENAG	

PREFIXES AND SUFFIXES
(COMBINING FORMS)
PREFIXES

AB	away from	CRY	freezing	TRI	three		
AC	= AD	DEC	ten	UNI	one		
AD	to(ward)	DIA	through; apart	URO	tail		
AF	= AD	DIF	= DIS	XER	dry		
AG	= AD	DIS	not; apart				
AL	= AD	DYS	poor condition	ACRO	high		
AN	upward; not	ECT	external	AERO	gas, air		
AP	= AD	END	internal	ALLO	different, another		
BE	all around; excessively	EPI	on; over; among	AMBI	both		
BI	two, twice	EXA	quintillionfold	ANTI	against		
CO	joint action	EXO	outside	AREO	Mars		
DE	off; down; wholly	GEO	earth	ARTO	bread		
DI	two	GYN	female	ATTO	quintillionth part		
EC	= EX	HEM	blood	AURI	gold, ear		
EO	early	HOL	complete	AUTO	self		
EU	well	HYL	wood	BARO	weight		
EX	out (of)	ISO	alike, identical	CACO	bad		
HY	arch	MAC	son of	CATA	away		
IL	not	MAL	bad	CELE	swelling		
IM	not	MIS	bad; wrong; not	CERA	horn, wax		
LY	loose	MYC	fungus	CETO	whale		
NE	= NEO	MYO	muscle	CHIL	lip		
OB	to(ward), against	NEO	new	CHOL	bile		
OO	egg	NON	not	DOPR	dung		
PY	pus	ORI	mouth	CARP	fruit		
UN	not; back	ORO	mountain	CRYO	cold		
ZA	very	OTO	ear	CYCL	circular		
ZO	animal	OVI	egg	CYMO	wave		
		OXA	oxygen	CYST	bladder, sac		
		OXY	oxygen; sharp	DECA	ten		
AER	aviation	PED	feet	DECI	1/10		
ANA	up; back; again	PEL	mud, clay	DEKA	tenfold		
ANO	upward	PIL	hair	DEMI	half		
APO	from; away	PRE	before	DEMO	populace		
AZO	nitrogen	PYO	pus	DICH	asunder		
BIN	twice	PYR	fire; heat	DINO	dreadful		
BIO	life	SYN	with; at the same time	DIPL	double		
BIS	twice	TEL	end	DYNA	power		
CAC	bad	TOX	poisonous	ECTO	outside		
CIS	on this side	TRE	town	ENDO	within		
COM	with; jointly						

ENNE	nine	NONA	ninth	VENO	vein
ENTO	inner	NOSO	disease	VINI	wine
EQUI	equal	NUCI	nut	XENO	foreign
EURY	broad	NUDI	bare	XERO	wax, dry
FITZ	son of	NYCT	night	XYLO	wood
GAMO	union	OCTA	eight	ZYGO	yoke; pair
GIGA	billionfold	OCTO	eight	ZYMO	fermentation
GONO	sex organs	OENO	wine		
GYNO	female	OLEO	oil	ACETO	acid
GYRO	gyrating	OLIG	few	ADENO	gland
HAEM	blood	OMNI	all	AMPHI	around
HAGI	saint	OSTE	bone	AMYLO	starch
HALI	sea, salt	PARA	near; beyond;	ANDRO	man
HECT	hundred		abnormal	ANEMO	wind
HELI	sun, spiral	PARI	equal	ANGIO	vessel
HEMI	half	PEDI	foot	ANGLO	English
HEMO	blood	PEDO	children	ANISO	unequal
HEXA	six	PERI	lungs, air	ANTHO	flower
HOLO	whole	PETA	quadrillionfold	ARCH	chief
HOMO	same	PHAG	eating	ASTRO	star
HYLO	wood	PHEN	benzene deriv.	AVANT	before
HYPO	below	PHIL	liking	BRADY	slow
ICOS	twenty	PHON	sound; voice	BREVI	short
IDEO	re: ideas	PICO	trillionth part	CALCI	lime
IDIO	personal	PILI	hair	CARDI	heart
INDO	Indian	PLAT	flat	CARPO	fruit
IODO	iodine	POLY	much, many	CENTI	1/100
KILO	thousand(fold)	PRAE	before	CHILO	lip
LACT	milk	PYRO	fire; heat	CHIRO	hand
LANI	wool	RATA	down; away	CHOLE	gall; bile
LEPT	fine	RENI	kidney	CHOLO	gall; bile
LEVO	left	REMI	oar	CHROM	color
LIPO	fat	RHEO	flow	CHRON	time
LITE	mineral; fossil	RHIN	nose	CHYLO	lymph
LITH	stone	SAUR	lizard	CIRRO	curl
LOCO	re: a place	SAXI	rock	COELE	cavity
LOGO	word; speech	SCIO	sky	COENO	recent
LUNI	moon	SEBI	tallow	COPRO	dung
LYTE	stone	SEMI	half	COSMO	universe
MANI	hand	SEPT	seven	COSTO	rib
MANU	hand	SERO	thin; body fluid	CUPRI	copper
MARI	sea	SINO	Chinese	CYANO	blue
MEDI	middle	SOLI	alone	CYCLO	circular
MEGA	great,	STAT	stationary	DENTI	tooth
	millionfold	STOM	mouth	DERMA	skin
MELA	black	TAXO	arrangement	DEUTO	second
MENO	month	TELE	far off; complete	DICHO	in 2 parts
MESO	middle	TELO	end	DIPLO	double
META	along; after	TENE	ribbon	ETHNO	race; people
MISO	hate	TERA	trillionfold	FEBRI	fever
MONO	single	THEO	of God, gods	FEMTO	quadrillionth
MUCO	mucous	THIO	brimstone		part
MYCO	fungus	TOPO	place	FERRO	iron
MYEL	marrow; spine	TOXO	poisonous	FIBRO	fiber
NANO	billionth part	TRIS	thrice	GALLO	Gallic, French
NASO	nose	TRIT	third	GLOSS	tongue
NECR	corpse	VARI	diverse	GRANI	grain
NEMA	thread	VASO	blood vessel	GRECO	Greek
NEMO	glade	VENI	vein	GYNEO	woman

HAEMO	blood	PATRI	father	CHROMO	color
HAGIO	sacred	PENNI	feather	CHRONO	time
HAPLO	single	PETRO	stone	CONTRA	against
HECTO	hundred(fold)	PHENO	benzene	CRYPTO	hidden
HELIO	sun		derivative	DACRYO	tears
HIPPO	horse	PHILO	loving	DENDRO	tree
HEPTA	seven	PHONO	sound	DEXTRO	right
HIERO	sacred	PHREN	diaphragm	DODECA	twelve
HISTO	tissue	PHYCO	seaweed	ECHINO	spiny
HOMEO	similar	PHYLL	leaf	ENTERO	intestine
HYALO	glass	PHYLO	tribe	ENTOMO	insect
HYDRO	water	PHYTO	plant	FRANCO	French
HYGRO	water	PICRO	bitter	GALACT	milk
HYPER	over; beyond	PISCI	fish	GASTRO	stomach
HYPNO	sleep	PLANI	plane	GRAPHO	drawing,
HYPSO	height	PLATY	broad		writing
ICONO	image-like	PLURI	several	HELICO	spiral
INFRA	below	PROTO	first	HEMATO	blood
INTER	among	PTERO	wing, feather	HEPATO	liver
INTRA	within	RECTI	straight	HETERO	other
INTRO	within	RETRO	behind	ICHNO	footprint
IRIDO	rainbow	RHIZO	root	INFERO	below
JUXTA	near; together	RHODO	rose; red	KERATO	horn, horny
KARYO	cell nucleus	RUSSO	Russian	KINETO	moving
KERAT	cornea, hard	SACRO	holy; sacrum	MEGALO	very large
	tissue	SAPRO	rotten	MELANO	black
LACTO	milk	SARCO	flesh	NEMATO	thread
LEPTO	slender	SAURO	lizard	NEPHRO	kidney
LEUKO	white	SCAPI	shaft	OBTUSI	blunt
LIGNO	wood	SPIRO	breath; spiral	ODONTO	teeth
LITHO	stones	SPORO	seed	PHRENO	diaphragm
LUTEO	yellow	STENO	little	PHYSIO	nature
MACRO	large	STYLO	sharp	PLEURO	side
MAGNI	large	TACHY	rapid	PNEUMO	lung
MATRI	mother	TAUTO	same	PRETER	beyond
METRO	measure	TETRA	four	PSUEDO	false
MEZZO	intermediate	TRANS	across	PSYCHO	of mind
MICRO	very small,	TURBO	turbine-driven	SANGUI	blood
	1/1,000,000	TURCO	Turkish	SCHIZO	split
MILLI	1/1,000	UTERO	womb	SCLERO	hard
MORPH	form	VERMI	worm	SESQUI	1-½
MULTI	many	YOCTO	septillionth	SOMATO	body
MYELO	marrow		part	SPHENO	wedge-shaped
MYRIA	many	YOTTA	septillionfold	SPLENO	spleen
MYTHO	myth	ZEPTO	sextillionth part	STEREO	firm
NECRO	corpse	ZETTA	sextillionfold	STETHO	chest
NEPHO	cloud			SUBTER	underneath
NEPHR	kidney	ACTINO	of rays	TRICHO	hair
NEURO	nerve	ADRENO	adrenal gland	TROPHO	nutrition
NOCTI	night	ANTERO	front	VARICO	enlarged vein
OCULO	eye	ARTHRO	joint	VENTRO	belly
ODONT	tooth	ARTERIO	artery	VESICO	bladder
OLIGO	few	AUSTRO	Austrian	XANTHO	yellow
ORTHO	straight	BRACHY	short		
OSTEO	bone	CARDIO	heart	BRONCHO	windpipe
PAEDO	child	CENTRI	central	CEPHALO	head
PALEO	remote	CERATO	horn; cornea	CEREBRO	brain
PANTO	all	CHAETO	hair	CERVICO	neck
PATHO	disease	CHALCO	copper; brass	CHONDRO	cartilage

DACTYLO	digit	ERYTHRO	red	THROMBO	blood clot
DERMATO	skin	FIBRINO	threadlike	TRACHEO	windpipe
DEUTERO	secondary	GALACTO	milky	CHROMATO	color

SUFFIXES

AC	relating to	IZE	treat; act on
AL	like	KIN	diminutive
CY	quality	LET	diminutive
ED	past tense	OCK	diminutive
EL	diminutive	OID	resembling
EN	made of	OLE	chemical compound
ER	doer	OMA	tumor
ET	diminutive	OPY	eye defect
FY	become, make	ORY	pert. to
IC	adjective	OSE	full of; sugar
IN	diminutive	OTE	resident
LE	diminutive	OUS	full of; like
LY	like	RIC	district
MO	numerical	ULE	diminutive
OL	chemical derivative	URE	act, result of
RY	= ERY	ZOA	animal
SY	diminutive		
TH	numerical	ACEA	of the nature
TY	quality; tens	ASIS	state; like
YL	radical form	ATIC	of the kind
		CENE	recent; new
ACY	quality	CIDE	murder
ANE	relating to	CRAT	ruler
ARD	one who is too	CULE	diminutive
ARY	relating to	CYTE	hollow vessel
BLE	able	DERA	neck types
DOM	domain	DERM	skin
EAE	classifying suffix	DIOL	chem. compound
ENT	adjective ending	EMLA	blood
ERY	condition; state	ENCE	quality
EST	superlative	ENNE	fem. ending
ETH	numerical	ENOL	chem. compound
FIC	adjective ending	ESCE	verb ending
FID	divided	ETTE	diminutive
GEN	producing agent	FUGE	flight
GON	geom. figures	GAMY	union
IAL	adjective ending	GENY	origin
ICS	activity area	GLOT	tongued
IDE	chemical compound	GONY	origin
INE	feminine noun	GYNE	female
ING	noun-forming	GYNY	female
INI	order	IBLE	able
ISE	cause to be	ICAL	adjective ending
ISH	belonging to	IOUS	adjective ending
ISM	doctrine	ITIS	inflammation
IST	believer	ITOL	alcohol(ic)
ITA	diminutive	KINS	diminutive
ITE	native; product; believer; fossil; salt; rock	LING	diminutive
		LITE	mineral, rock
ITY	condition	LITH	stone
IVE	tendency	LOGY	science

MENT	action	OIDEA	class name
MONY	state	OLOGY	science
NOMY	study	OPSIS	sight
ODUS	toothed	OSITY	noun ending
OLIC	chemical compound	PATHY	suffering
OPIA	eye defect	PHAGE	eating
OSID	sugar	PHAGY	eating
OSIS	process	PHANE	resembling
OTIC	of ear	PHANY	appearance
PEDE	feet	PHASY	speech
PHIL	liking	PHILE	loving
PHYL	leaf	PHOBE	fear
PODA	foot	PHONE	sound
PODE	foot	PHORE	bearer
RHEA	discharge	PHYTE	plant
SAUR	lizard	PLAST	structure
SION	action; result	PLASY	formation
STAT	stationary	PLEGY	paralysis
STER	occupation	PLOID	number form
TEEN	plus ten	POLIS	city
TENE	ribbon	RRHEA	discharge
TION	action; result	SCOPY	science; viewing
TOMY	cutting	SOPHY	knowledge
TRIX	fem. agent	TIOUS	adjective ending
TUDE	noun ending	TROPE	turning
URET	chem. ending	TROPY	turning
URGY	working of	ULENT	full of
URIA	urine disease	ULOSE	marked by
VORE	eating	ULOUS	full of
XION	action; result		
ZOIC	animal	AGOGUE	leading
		BILITY	ability
AEMIA	blood	CARPAL	fruit
ALGIA	pain	CHROIC	color
ARCHY	ruling	CRATIC	ruling
ATION	result of being	FEROUS	bearing; yielding
ATIVE	relative to	GAMOUS	uniting
ATORY	produced by	GRAPHY	science
CIDAL	to kill	GYNOUS	female
COELE	body cavity	ISTICS	science of
CRACY	rule	LITHIC	stone
EDRAL	faced	MYCETE	fungus
ESQUE	like	ODYNIA	pain
GENIC	of origin	OLATRY	worship of
GONIO	angle	PAROUS	giving birth
HEMIA	blood	PATHIC	disease, feeling
IASIS	morbid state	PHAGIA	eating
IATRY	treatment	PHASIA	speech
ICLAN	practitioner	PHILIA	loving
ILITY	noun ending	PHOBIA	fear
ISTIC	adjective ending	PHONIA	voice
ITION	action; result	PLASIA	formation
LATRY	worship	PLEGIA	paralysis
LETTE	diminutive	PODIUM	leg
LYSIS	disintegration	PODOUS	feet
MANCY	divination	RRHAGE	abnormal flow
METRY	measurement	THERMY	heat
		VOROUS	eating

PRESIDENTIAL INFORMATION

	Name	Year of Inaug.	Party	Vice-Pres.
1	**WASHINGTON**, George	1789	Fed.	**ADAMS**
2	**ADAMS**, John	1797	Fed.	**JEFFERSON**
3	**JEFFERSON**, Thomas	1801	Dem.-Rep.	**BURR, CLINTON**
4	**MADISON**, James	1809	Dem.-Rep.	**CLINTON, GERRY**
5	**MONROE**, James	1817	Dem.-Rep.	**TOMPKINS**
6	**ADAMS**, John Quincy	1825	Ind.	**CALHOUN**
7	**JACKSON**, Andrew	1829	Dem.-Rep.	**CALHOUN, VAN BUREN**
8	**VAN BUREN**, Martin	1837	Dem.-Rep.	**JOHNSON**
9	**HARRISON**, William Henry	1841	Whig	**TYLER**
10	**TYLER**, John	1841	Whig	
11	**POLK**, James Knox	1845	Dem.	**DALLAS**
12	**TAYLOR**, Zachary	1849	Whig	**FILLMORE**
13	**FILLMORE**, Millard	1850	Whig	
14	**PIERCE**, Franklin	1853	Dem.	**KING**
15	**BUCHANAN**, James	1857	Dem.	**BRECKENRIDGE**
16	**LINCOLN**, Abraham	1861	Rep.	**HAMLIN, JOHNSON**
17	**JOHNSON**, Andrew	1865	Dem.	
18	**GRANT**, Ulysses Simpson	1869	Rep.	**COLFAX, WILSON**
19	**HAYES**, Rutherford Birchard	1877	Rep.	**WHEELER**
20	**GARFIELD**, James Abram	1881	Rep.	**ARTHUR**
21	**ARTHUR**, Chester Alan	1881	Rep.	
22	**CLEVELAND**, Stephen Grover	1885	Dem.	**HENDRICKS**
23	**HARRISON**, Benjamin	1889	Rep.	**MORTON**
24	**CLEVELAND**, Stephen Grover	1893	Dem.	**STEVENSON**
25	**MCKINLEY**, William	1897	Rep.	**HOBART, ROOSEVELT**
26	**ROOSEVELT**, Theodore	1901	Rep.	**FAIRBANKS**
27	**TAFT**, William Howard	1909	Rep.	**SHERMAN**
28	**WILSON**, Thomas Woodrow	1913	Dem.	**MARSHALL**
29	**HARDING**, Warren Gamaliel	1921	Rep.	**COOLIDGE**
30	**COOLIDGE**, John Calvin	1923	Rep.	**DAWES**
31	**HOOVER**, Herbert Clark	1929	Rep.	**CURTIS**
32	**ROOSEVELT**, Franklin Delano	1933	Dem.	**GARNER, WALLACE, TRUMAN**
33	**TRUMAN**, Harry S	1945	Dem.	**BARKLEY**
34	**EISENHOWER**, Dwight David	1953	Rep.	**NIXON**
35	**KENNEDY**, John Fitzgerald	1961	Dem.	**JOHNSON**
36	**JOHNSON**, Lyndon Baines	1963	Dem.	**HUMPHREY**
37	**NIXON**, Richard Milhous	1969	Rep.	**AGNEW, FORD**
38	**FORD**, Gerald Rudolph	1974	Rep.	**ROCKEFELLER**
39	**CARTER**, James Earl, Jr.	1977	Dem.	**MONDALE**
40	**REAGAN**, Ronald Wilson	1981	Rep.	**BUSH**
41	**BUSH**, George Herbert Walker	1989	Rep.	**QUAYLE**
42	**CLINTON**, Bill	1993	Dem.	**GORE**
43	**BUSH**, George Walker	2001	Rep.	**CHENEY**

	Sec'y of State	*Def. Cand.*
1	Jefferson, Randolph, Pickering	
2	Pickering, Marshall	Jefferson
3	Madison	Burr, Pinckney
4	Smith, Monroe	Pinckney, Clinton
5	Adams	King, Adams
6	Clay	Jackson, Clay, Crawford
7	Van Buren, Livingston, McLane, Forsyth	Adams, Clay
8	Forsyth	Harrison
9	Webster	Van Buren
10	Webster, Upshur, Calhoun	
11	Calhoun, Buchanan	Clay
12	Buchanan, Clayton	Cass
13	Clayton, Webster, Everett	
14	Marcy	Scott
15	Marcy, Cass, Black	Fremont
16	Black, Seward	Douglas, Breckenridge, Bell, McClellan
17	Seward	
18	Washburne, Fish	Seymour, Greeley
19	Fish, Evarts	Tilden
20	Evarts, Blaine	Hancock
21	Blaine, Frelinghuysen	
22	Frelinghuysen, Bayard	Blaine
23	Bayard, Blaine, Foster	Cleveland
24	Gresham, Olney	Harrison, Weaver
25	Olney, Sherman, Day, Hay	Bryan
26	Hay, Root, Bacon	Parker
27	Bacon, Knox	Bryan
28	Knox, Bryan, Lansing, Colby	Roosevelt, Taft, Hughes
29	Hughes	Cox
30	Hughes, Kellogg	Davis, Lafollette
31	Kellogg, Stimson	Smith
32	Hull, Stettinius	Hoover, Landon, Willkie, Dewey
33	Stettinius, Byrnes, Marshall, Acheson	Dewey
34	Dulles, Herter	Stevenson
35	Rusk	Nixon
36	Rusk	Goldwater
37	Rogers, Kissinger	Humphrey, Wallace, McGovern
38	Kissinger	
39	Vance	Ford
40	Haig, Shultz	Carter, Mondale
41	Baker, Eagleburger	Dukakis
42	Christopher, Albright	Bush, Dole
43	Powell	Gore

Name	Birthplace	Age*	Profession
1 WASHINGTON	Wakefield, VA	57	Farmer
2 ADAMS	Braintree, MA	61	Lawyer
3 JEFFERSON	Shadwell, VA	57	Farmer
4 MADISON	Port Conway, VA	57	Lawyer
5 MONROE	Westmoreland County, VA	58	Lawyer
6 ADAMS	Braintree, MA	57	Lawyer
7 JACKSON	Waxhaw, SC	61	Lawyer
8 VAN BUREN	Kinderhook, NY	54	Lawyer
9 HARRISON	Berkeley, VA	68	Officer
10 TYLER	Greenway, VA	51	Lawyer
11 POLK	Mecklenburg County, NC	49	Lawyer
12 TAYLOR	Orange County, VA	64	Officer
13 FILLMORE	Cayuga County, NY	50	Wool carder, lawyer
14 PIERCE	Hillsboro, NH	48	Lawyer
15 BUCHANAN	Mercersburg, PA	64	Lawyer
16 LINCOLN	Hardin County, KY	52	Storekeeper, postmaster, lawyer
17 JOHNSON	Raleigh, NC	56	Tailor
18 GRANT	Point Pleasant, OH	46	Lawyer
19 HAYES	Delaware, OH	54	Officer
20 GARFIELD	Orange, OH	49	Bargeman, teacher
21 ARTHUR	Fairfield, VT	50	Teacher
22 CLEVELAND	Caldwell, NJ	47	Teacher, lawyer
23 HARRISON	North Bend, OH	55	Lawyer
24 CLEVELAND	Caidwell, NJ	55	Lawyer
25 MCKINLEY	Niles, OH	54	Lawyer
26 ROOSEVELT	New York, NY	42	Police commissioner
27 TAFT	Cincinnati, OH	51	Lawyer
28 WILSON	Staunton, VA	56	Teacher
29 HARDING	Corsica, OH	55	Publisher
30 COOLIDGE	Plymouth, VT	51	Lawyer
31 HOOVER	West Branch, IA	54	Engineer
32 ROOSEVELT	Hyde Park, NY	51	Lawyer
33 TRUMAN	Lamar, MO	60	Storekeeper
34 EISENHOWER	Denison, TX	62	Officer
35 KENNEDY	Brookline, MA	43	Author
36 JOHNSON	Stonewall, TX	55	Teacher
37 NIXON	Yorba Linda, CA	56	Lawyer
38 FORD	Omaha, NB	61	Lawyer
39 CARTER	Plains, GA	52	Engineer
40 REAGAN	Tampico, IL	69	Actor
41 BUSH, G.H.W.	Milton, MA	64	Businessman
42 CLINTON	Hope, AR	46	Lawyer
43 BUSH, G.W.	New Haven, CT	54	Businessman

*at inauguration

*Sec'y of Defense**	*Attorney General*
1 Knox, Pickering, McHenry	Randolph, Bradford, Lee
2 McHenry, Dexter	Lee
3 Dearborn	Lincoln, Breckenridge, Rodney
4 Eustis, Armstrong, Monroe, Crawford	Rodney, Pinkney, Rush
5 Calhoun	Rush, Wirt
6 Barbour, Porter	Wirt
7 Eaton, Cass, Butler	Berrien, Taney, Butler
8 Poinsett	Butler, Grundy, Gilpin
9 Bell	Crittenden
10 Bell, Spencer, Porter, Wilkins	Crittenden, Legare, Nelson
11 Marcy	Mason, Clifford, Toucey
12 Crawford	Johnson
13 Conrad	Crittenden
14 Davis	Cushing
15 Floyd, Holt	Black, Stanton
16 Cameron, Stanton	Bates, Speed
17 Stanton, Schofield	Speed, Stanbery, Evarts
18 Rawlins, Sherman, Belknap, Taft, Cameron	Hoar, Akerman, Williams, Pierrepont, Taft
19 McCrary, Ramsey	Devens
20 Lincoln	MacVeagh
21 Lincoln	Brewster
22 Endicott	Garland
23 Proctor, Elkins	Miller
24 Lamont	Olney, Harmon
25 Alger, Root	McKenna, Griggs, Knox
26 Root, Taft, Wright	Knox, Moody, Bonaparte
27 Dickinson, Stimson	Wickersham
28 Garrison, Baker	McReynolds, Gregory, Palmer
29 Weeks	Daugherty
30 Weeks, Davis	Daugherty, Stone, Sargent
31 Good, Hurley	Mitchell
32 Dern, Woodring, Stimson	Cummings, Murphy, Jackson, Biddle
33 Patterson, Royall, Forrestal, Johnson, Marshall, Lovett	Clark, McGrath
34 Wilson, McElroy, Gates	Brownell, Rogers
35 McNamara	Kennedy
36 McNamara, Clifford	Kennedy, Katzenbach, Clark
37 Laird, Richardson, Schlesinger	Mitchell, Kleindienst, Richardson, Saxbe
38 Schlesinger, Rumsfeld	Saxbe, Levi
39 Brown	Bell, Civiletti
40 Weinberger, Carlucci	Smith, Meese, Thornburgh
41 Cheney	Thornburgh, Barr
42 Aspin, Perry, Cohen	Reno
43 Rumsfeld	Ashcroft

* before 1947, Secretary of War

	Nickname	*Wife's Name*
1	Old Fox, Atlas of Independence, Father of His Country	CUSTIS, Martha Dandridge
2	Duke of Baintree, Atlas of	SMITH, Abigail
3	Long Tom, Sage of Monticello, Man of the People	SKELTON, Martha Wayles
4	Father of the Constitution	TODD, Dorothea (Dolley) Payne
5	Last Cocked Hat, Era of Good Feeling President	KORTWRIGHT, Elizabeth
6	Accidental President, Old Man Eloquent	JOHNSON, Luisa Catherine
7	Old Hickory, Sharp Knife	ROBARDS, Rachel Donelson
8	Red Fox of Kinderhook, Little Magician	HOES, Hannah
9	Hero of Tippecanoe, Old Tip(pecanoe)	SYMMES, Anna Tuthill
10	His Accidency	CHRISTIAN, Letitia (1)
		GARDINER, Julia (2)
11	Young Hickory	CHILDRESS, Sarah
12	Old Rough and Ready	SMITH, Margaret Mackall
13	American Louis Philippe	POWERS, Abigail (1)
		MCINTOSH, Caroline Carmichael (2)
14	Handsome Frank, Young Hickory of the Granite Hills	APPLETON, Jane Means
15	Old Buck, Ten-cent Jimmy	
16	Old Abe, Railsplitter, Great Emancipator	TODD, Mary
17	Sir Veto, King Andy	MCCARDLE, Eliza
18	Silent Man, Old Three-Stars, Hero of Appomattox	DENT, Julia
19	Old Eight to Seven, President de facto, Dark Horse President, His Fraudulency	WEBB, Lucy Ware
20	Canal Boy, the Preacher	RUDOLPH, Lucretia
21	Elegant Arthur, The Gentleman Boss	HERNDON, Ellen (Nell) Lewis
22	Old Veto, Stuffed Prophet, Big Steve, Uncle Jumbo	FOLSOM, Frances
23	Little Ben, Kid Gloves Harrison	SCOTT, Caroline Lavinia (1)
		DIMMICK, Mary Scott Lord (2)
24	Perpetual Candidate	FOLSOM, Frances
25	Stocking-foot Orator, Idol of Ohio	SAXTON, Ida
26	Bull Moose, Rough Rider, Trust-Buster, TR, Teddy	LEE, Alice Hathaway (1)
		CAROW, Edith Kermit (2)
27	Wobbly Willie	HERRON, Helen
28	Woody, Schoolmaster in Politics	AXSON, Ellen Louise (1)
		GALT, Edith Bolling (2)
29		DEWOLFE, Florence (Fossie) Mabel Kling
30	Silent Cal	GOODHUE, Grace Anna
31		HENRY, Lou
32	FDR, New Dealer	ROOSEVELT, Anna Eleanor
33	Give 'Em Hell Harry	WALLACE, Elizabeth (Bess) Virginia
34	Ike	DOUD, Mary (Mamie) Geneva
35	JFK, Jack	BOUVIER, Jacqueline Lee
36	LBJ	TAYLOR, Claudia (Lady Bird) Alta
37	Tricky Dick	RYAN, Thelma (Patricia) Catherine Patricia

Nickname	Wife's Name
38 Jerry	**WARREN**, Elizabeth (Betty) Ann Bloomer
39 Jimmy	**SMITH**, Eleanor Rosalynn
40 The Gipper, Dutch, The Great Communicator	**DAVIS**, Anne (Nancy) Frances Robbins
41 Poppy	**PIERCE**, Barbara
42 Bubba, Bill	**RODHAM**, Hillary
43 W	**WELCH**, Laura

SOUNDS AND CRIES

*Indicates those of animals

BAY*	JUKE*	CHIRP*	TWANG
BOO	LISP	CHUCK*	TWEET*
CAW*	MEWL*	CLANG	VOICE
CRY	MOAN	CLANK	WHACK
DIN	PEAL	CLICK	WHANG
HUM*	PEEP*	CLINK	WHINE*
KEY	PING	CLOOP	WHIRR
LOW*	PUFF	CLUCK*	WHOOP
MEW*	PURL	CLUMP	WOOSH
MOO*	RALE	CLUNK	
POP	RING	COOEE	ACCENT
POW	ROAR*	COOEY	ALARUM
RAP	ROLL	CRACK	BELLOW*
SOB	SIGH	CREAK	BOOHOO
TAP*	SING*	CRUMP	BOWWOW*
YAP*	SLAM	DRONE	BUBBLE
ZIP	TALK	FLUMP	CACKLE*
	TANG	GLUCK	CANARY
BANG	THUD	GRIDE	CLAMOR
BARK*	TICK	GROAN	CRUNCH
BARR*	TINK	GROWL*	FIZZLE
BELL*	TOLL	GRUNT*	GAGGLE*
BIRR	TONE	HALLO	GOBBLE*
BLAT*	TOOT	HOLLO	GUGGLE
BONG	TUCK	KNELL	GURGLE
BOOM	TUNE	LARUM	HALLOA
BRAY*	WHAM	MIAOU*	HALLOO
BUST	YARR	MIAOW*	HUBBUB
CALL	YAUP	MUSIC	JANGLE
CHUG	YAWL	NEIGH*	JINGLE
CLAP	YAWP	NOISE	MELODY
CLOP	YELL	PLASH	MUFFLE
CRAW*	YELP*	PLUMP	MURMUR
CROW*	YOHO	QUACK*	MUTTER
DING		SHOUT	NICKER
ECHO	ALARM	SKIRL	OUTCRY
FIZZ	BINGO	SMACK	PATTER
FLOP	BLARE	SNARL*	PLAINT
GLUG	BLAST	SNORE	RATTLE
GOWL	BLEAT*	SNORT*	REPORT
HISS*	BINGO	SOUGH	RUSTLE
HONK*	CHEEP*	SWISH	SCREAM
HOWL*	CHINK*	TRILL	SCROOP
JUCK*	CHIRM*	TROAT	SHRIEK

SHRILL	TIMBRE	CADENCE	SCREECH
SIZZLE	TINGLE	CHATTER	SONANCY
SPEECH	TINKLE	CHIRRUP	SQUELCH
SPLASH	UPROAR	CLANGOR	SIRIDOR
SQUALL*	WHEEZE	CLATTER	TALLYHO*
SQUAWK*	WHINNY*	DUBADUB	TIRALEE*
SQUEAK*	WHOOSH	GRUMBLE	TRUMPET*
SQUEAL*	YOICKS	PITAPAT	TWITTER
SQUISH		RATATAT	WHIMPER
TATTOO	BLATTER	RUBADUB	WHISTLE

EXCLAMATIONS AND OATHS

AH	HIC	ALAS	WHEW
BO	HIP	ARAH	
EH	HOI	ARRA	ALACK
HA	HOO	ARRHA	ARRHA
HI	HOY	BOOH	BEDAD
MY	HUH	CHUT	BEGAD
OH	ODS	DANG	BLIMY
OW	OHO	DRAT	FAUGH
UM	OUF	EGAD	HELLO
	PAH	EHEU	HEUCH
	PEW	EVOE	HEUGH
ACH	POH	GOSH	HURRA
AHA	PST	HECK	HUZZA
AUH	PUE	HEIN	LAWKS
BAH	SOH	HOCH	PSHAW
BAM	TCH	HUSH	UHHUH
BAW	TCK	LAWK	ZOOKS
BOH	TST	NUTS	ZOWIE
FIE	TUT	OONS	
FOH	UGH	OUCH	
GEE	WEE	OUGH	CRIKEY
GRR	WHY	PHEW	CRIPES
HAH	WOW	PHUT	HURRAH
HAW		PISH	HURROO
HEM		PSHA	OCHONE
HEP	AHEM	SOOK	SBLOOD
HEU	AHEY	TUSH	
HEY	AITH	WHAM	ZOUNDS

SPORTS

GOLF	DISCUS	BATBALL	SNOOKER
JUDO	DIVING	BOWLING	TENPINS
POLO	HOCKEY	CRICKET	TILTING
POOL	KARATE	CROQUET	
	PELOTA	CURLING	BASEBALL
BANDY	QUOITS	FENCING	BOLOBALL
BOWLS	RACING	FISHING	FOOTBALL
CATCH	SHINNY	HUNTING	HANDBALL
DARTS	SKIING	JAIALAI	HURDLING
FIVES	SOCCER	JOGGING	LACROSSE
RUGBY	SQUASH	PALLONE	NINEPINS
TRACK	TENNIS	RUNNING	PALLMALL
		SHOTPUT	PINGPONG
BOXING	ARCHERY	SKATING	ROUNDERS

SKITTLES   BILLIARDS   DECKTENNIS   BALLOONBALL
SOFTBALL   ICEHOCKEY   GYMNASTICS   TABLETENNIS
SOLOBALL   STICKBALL   HORSESHOES
SWIMMING   WATERBALL   ICESKATING
TUGOFWAR   WATERPOLO   LAWNTENNIS
            WRESTLING   VOLLEYBALL
BADMINTON   BASKETBALL

AUTO RACING
INDIANAPOLIS 500 WINNERS

Year	Winner	Year	Winner
1911	Ray Harroun	1959	Rodger Ward
1912	Joe Dawson	1960	Jim Rathmann
1913	Jules Goux	1961	A.J. Foyt Jr.
1914	Rene Thomas	1962	Rodger Ward
1915	Ralph DePalma	1963	Parnelli Jones
1916	Dario Resta	1964	A.J. Foyt Jr.
1917–18	(not held)	1965	Jim Clark
1919	Howdy Wilcox	1966	Graham Hill
1920	Gaston Chevrolet	1967	A.J. Foyt Jr
1921	Tommy Milton	1968	Bobby Unser
1922	Jimmy Murphy	1969	Mario Andretti
1923	Tommy Milton	1970	Al Unser
1924	L.L. Corum-Joe Boyer	1971	Al Unser
1925	Peter DePaolo	1972	Mark Donohue
1926	Frank Lockhart	1973	Gordon Johncock
1927	George Souders	1974	Johnny Rutherford
1928	Louis Meyer	1975	Bobby Unser
1929	Ray Keech	1976	Johnny Rutherford
1930	Billy Arnold	1977	A.J. Foyt Jr.
1931	Louis Schneider	1978	Al Unser
1932	Fred Frame	1979	Rick Mears
1933	Louis Meyer	1980	Johnny Rutherford
1934	Bill Cummings	1981	Bobby Unser
1935	Kelly Petillo	1982	Gordon Johncock
1936	Louis Meyer	1983	Tom Sneva
1937	Wilbur Shaw	1984	Rick Mears
1938	Floyd Roberts	1985	Danny Sullivan
1939	Wilbur Shaw	1986	Bobby Rahal
1940	Wilbur Shaw	1987	Al Unser
1941	Floyd Davis-Mauri Rose	1988	Rick Mears
1942–5	(not held)	1989	Emerson Fittipaldi
1946	George Robson	1990	Arie Luyendyk
1947	Mauri Rose	1991	Rick Mears
1948	Mauri Rose	1992	Al Unser Jr.
1949	Bill Holland	1993	Emerson Fittipaldi
1950	Johnnie Parsons	1994	Al Unser Jr.
1951	Lee Wallard	1995	Jacques Villeneuve
1952	Troy Ruttman	1996	Buddy Lazier
1953	Bill Vukovich	1997	Arie Luyendyk
1954	Bill Vukovich	1998	Eddie Cheever Jr.
1955	Bob Sweikert	1999	Kenny Brack
1956	Pat Flaherty	2000	Juan Montoya
1957	Sam Hanks	2001	Helio Castroneves
1958	Jimmy Bryan	2002	Helio Castroneves
		2003	Gil de Ferran

BASEBALL
FAMOUS PLAYERS

*Indicates in the Hall of Fame

COBB*	LYONS*	MANTLE*	BOUDREAU*
DEAN*	MARIS	MANUSH*	BULKELEY*
FISK*	PEREZ*	MUSIAL*	CHADWICK*
FORD*	PLANK*	SCHALK*	CLARKSON*
FOXX*	RIXEY*	SISLER*	COCHRANE*
MAYS*	ROUSH*	SNIDER*	CRAWFORD*
MIZE*	TERRY*	TINKER*	CUMMINGS*
RICE*	VANCE*	WAGNER*	DIMAGGIO*
RUTH*	WALSH*	WRIGHT*	DRYSDALE*
WARD*	WANER*		HAMILTON*
	WHEAT*	APPLING*	HARTNETT*
	WILLS	BURKETT*	HEILMANN*
A'ARON*	YOUNG*	CHESBRO*	JENNINGS*
ANSON*		COLLINS*	ROBINSON*
BAKER*		HORNSBY*	SPALDING*
BANKS*	BENDER*	HUBBELL*	WILLIAMS*
BERRA*	CARTER*	HUGGINS*	
BROWN*	CHANCE*	JOHNSON*	
CAREY*	CLARKE*	MOLITOR*	ALEXANDER*
DUFFY*	DICKEY*	NICHOLS*	ECKERSLEY*
EVERS*	FELLER*	OROURKE*	GEHRINGER*
EWING*	FRISCH*	PENNOCK*	GREENBERG*
FABER*	GALVIN*	RIZZUTO*	KILLEBREW*
FLICK*	GEHRIG*	SIMMONS*	MATHEWSON*
GROVE*	GRIMES*	SPEAKER*	MCGINNITY*
KEEFE*	KALINE*	TRAYNOR*	RADBOURNE*
KELLY*	KEELER*	WADDELL*	
KINER*	KOUFAX*	WALLACE*	CAMPANELLA*
	LAJOIE*		

MANAGERS AND EXECUTIVES

DARK	TORRE	RIGNEY	BOUDREAU*
HOUK	VEECK*	YAWKEY*	COCHRANE*
MACK*		ZIMMER	COMISKEY*
MELE	ALSTON*		DUROCHER*
	BARROW*	DRESSEN	GRIFFITH*
FRICK*	CRONIN*	HUGGINS*	MCCARTHY*
GRIMM	ECKERT	JOHNSON*	MURTAUGH
HANEY	HARRIS*	MCPHAIL*	MCKECHNIE*
KEANE	LANDIS*	OMALLEY*	
LOPEZ*	MARTIN	STENGEL*	
PRICK	MCGRAW*		HUTCHINSON
TERRY*	RICKEY*	ANDERSON*	SOUTHWORTH

CY YOUNG WINNERS

1956	Don Newcombe	1964	Dean Chance
1957	Warren Spahn	1965	Sandy Koufax
1958	Bob Turley	1966	Sandy Koufax
1959	Early Wynn	1967	Mike McCormick, Jim
1960	Vernon Law		Lonborg
1961	Whitey Ford	1968	Bob Gibson, Denny McLain
1962	Don Drysdale	1969	Tom Seaver, Denny McLain,
1963	Sandy Koufax		Mike Cuellar

1970	Bob Gibson, Jim Perry	1988	Orel Hershiser, Frank Viola
1971	Ferguson Jenkins, Vida Blue	1989	Mark Davis, Bret Saberhagen
1972	Steve Carlton, Gaylord Perry	1990	Doug Drabek, Bob Welch
1973	Tom Seaver, Jim Palmer	1991	Tom Glavine, Roger Clemens
1974	Mike Marshall, Jim "Catfish" Hunter	1992	Greg Maddux, Dennis Eckersley
1975	Tom Seaver, Jim Palmer	1993	Greg Maddux, Jack McDowell
1976	Randy Jones, Jim Palmer		
1977	Steve Carlton, Sparky Lyle	1994	Greg Maddux, David Cone
1978	Gaylord Perry, Ron Guidry	1995	Greg Maddux, Randy Johnson
1979	Bruce Sutter, Mike Flanagan		
1980	Steve Carlton, Steve Stone	1996	John Smoltz, Pat Hentgen
1981	Fernando Valenzuela, Rollie Fingers	1997	Pedro Martinez, Roger Clemens
1982	Steve Carlton, Pete Vuckovich	1998	Tom Glavine, Roger Clemens
1983	John Denny, LaMarr Hoyt	1999	Randy Johnson, Pedro Martinez
1984	Rick Sutcliffe, Willie Hernandez	2000	Randy Johnson, Pedro Martinez
1985	Dwight Gooden, Bret Saberhagen	2001	Randy Johnson, Roger Clemens
1986	Mike Scott, Roger Clemens	2002	Randy Johnson, Barry Zito
1987	Steve Bedrosian, Roger Clemens	2003	Eric Gagne, Roy Halladay

MOST VALUABLE PLAYER—NATIONAL LEAGUE

1931	Frank Frisch	1962	Maury Wills
1932	Chuck Klein	1963	Sandy Koufax
1933	Carl Hubbell	1964	Ken Boyer
1934	Dizzy Dean	1965	Willie Mays
1935	Gabby Hartnett	1966	Roberto Clemente
1936	Carl Hubbell	1967	Orlando Cepeda
1937	Joe Medwick	1968	Bob Gibson
1938	Ernie Lombardi	1969	Willie McCovey
1939	Bucky Walters	1970	Johnny Bench
1940	Frank McCormick	1971	Joe Torre
1941	Dolph Camilli	1972	Johnny Bench
1942	Mort Cooper	1973	Pete Rose
1943	Stan Musial	1974	Steve Garvey
1944	Martin Marion	1975	Joe Morgan
1945	Phil Cavarretta	1976	Joe Morgan
1946	Stan Musial	1977	George Foster
1947	Bob Elliott	1978	Dave Parker
1948	Stan Musial	1979	Willie Stargell, Keith Hernandez
1949	Jackie Robinson		
1950	Jim Konstanty	1980	Mike Schmidt
1951	Roy Campanella	1981	Mike Schmidt
1952	Hank Sauer	1982	Dale Murphy
1953	Roy Campanella	1983	Dale Murphy
1954	Willie Mays	1984	Ryne Sandberg
1955	Roy Campanella	1985	Willie McGee
1956	Don Newcombe	1986	Mike Schmidt
1957	Hank Aaron	1987	Andre Dawson
1958	Ernie Banks	1988	Kirk Gibson
1959	Ernie Banks	1989	Kevin Mitchell
1960	Dick Groat	1990	Barry Bonds
1961	Frank Robinson	1991	Terry Pendleton

1992	Barry Bonds	1998	Sammy Sosa
1993	Barry Bonds	1999	Chipper Jones
1994	Jeff Bagwell	2000	Jeff Kent
1995	Barry Larkin	2001	Barry Bonds
1996	Ken Caminiti	2002	Barry Bonds
1997	Larry Walker	2003	Barry Bonds

MOST VALUABLE PLAYER—AMERICAN LEAGUE

1931	Lefty Grove	1967	Carl Yastrzemski
1932	Jimmie Foxx	1968	Denny McLain
1933	Jimmie Foxx	1969	Harmon Killebrew
1934	Mickey Cochrane	1970	John "Boog" Powell
1935	Hank Greenberg	1971	Vida Blue
1936	Lou Gehrig	1972	Dick Allen
1937	Charley Gehringer	1973	Reggie Jackson
1938	Jimmie Foxx	1974	Jeff Burroughs
1939	Joe DiMaggio	1975	Fred Lynn
1940	Hank Greenberg	1976	Thurman Munson
1941	Joe DiMaggio	1977	Rod Carew
1942	Joe Gordon	1978	Jim Rice
1943	Spud Chandler	1979	Don Baylor
1944	Hal Newhouser	1980	George Brett
1945	Hal Newhouser	1981	Rollie Fingers
1946	Ted Williams	1982	Robin Yount
1947	Joe DiMaggio	1983	Cal Ripken Jr.
1948	Lou Boudreau	1984	Willie Hernandez
1949	Ted Williams	1985	Don Mattingly
1950	Phil Rizzuto	1986	Roger Clemente
1951	Yogi Berra	1987	George Bell
1952	Bobby Shantz	1988	Jose Canseco
1953	Al Rosen	1989	Robin Yount
1954	Yogi Berra	1990	Rickey Henderson
1955	Yogi Berra	1991	Cal Ripken Jr.
1956	Mickey Mantle	1992	Dennis Eckersley
1957	Mickey Mantle	1993	Frank Thomas
1958	Jackie Jensen	1994	Frank Thomas
1959	Nellie Fox	1995	Mo Vaughn
1960	Roger Maris	1996	Juan Gonzalez
1961	Roger Maris	1997	Ken Griffey Jr.
1962	Mickey Mantle	1998	Juan Gonzales
1963	Elston Howard	1999	Ivan Rodriguez
1964	Brooks Robinson	2000	Jason Giambi
1965	Zoilo Versalles	2001	Ichiro Suzuki
1966	Frank Robinson	2002	Miguel Tejada
		2003	Alex Rodriguez

TEAMS
NATIONAL LEAGUE

CUBS	ASTROS	BREWERS	ROCKIES
METS	BRAVES	DODGERS	PHILLIES
REDS	GIANTS	MARLINS	CARDINALS
EXPOS	PADRES	PIRATES	

AMERICAN LEAGUE

TWINS	TIGERS	YANKEES	WHITESOX
ANGELS	INDIANS	BLUEJAYS	ATHLETICS
REDSOX	ORIOLES	MARINERS	
ROYALS	RANGERS	SENATORS	

BASKETBALL
FAMOUS PLAYERS

*Indicates in the Hall of Fame

DRJ*	LUCAS*	LESLIE	JOHNSON*
BIRD*	NEAL	MALONE*	MCGUIRE*
GOLA*	PRICE	MCADOO*	RUSSELL*
REED*	SMITH	MILLER*	SHARMAN*
WEST*	BAYLOR*	MURPHY*	SWOOPES
ALLEN	COOPER*	PETTIT*	GRIFFITH
BARRY*	COWENS*	PIERCE	HAVLICEK*
BELOV*	ERVING*	SKILES	HORNACEK
COUSY*	GERVIN*	BELLAMY*	MARAVICH*
FULKS*	JABBAR	BRADLEY*	HOLDSCLAW
HAYES*	JORDAN	FRAZIER*	ROBERTSON*
JONES*	LANIER*	IVERSON	CHAMBERLAIN*

TEAMS

SOL	HAWKS	SPARKS	RAPTORS
FIRE	KINGS	STARZZ	ROCKERS
FIVE	MAGIC	BLAZERS	ROCKETS
HEAT	SHOCK	BULLETS	WIZARDS
JAZZ	SPURS	CELTICS	CLIPPERS
LYNX	STING	HORNETS	MONARCHS
MAVS	STORM	LIBERTY	WARRIORS
NETS	COMETS	MERCURY	CAVALIERS
SUNS	KNICKS	MIRACLE	GRIZZLIES
BUCKS	LAKERS	MYSTICS	MAVERICKS
BULLS	PACERS	NUGGETS	SUPERSONICS
FEVER	SONICS	PISTONS	TIMBERWOLVES

NBA MOST VALUABLE PLAYER

1956	Bob Pettit	1980	Kareem Abdul-Jabbar
1957	Bob Cousy	1981	Julius Erving
1958	Bill Russell	1982	Moses Malone
1959	Bob Pettit	1983	Moses Malone
1960	Wilt Chamberlain	1984	Larry Bird
1961	Bill Russell	1985	Larry Bird
1962	Bill Russell	1986	Larry Bird
1963	Bill Russell	1987	Magic Johnson
1964	Oscar Robertson	1988	Michael Jordan
1965	Bill Russell	1989	Magic Johnson
1966	Wilt Chamberlain	1990	Magic Johnson
1967	Wilt Chamberlain	1991	Michael Jordan
1968	Wilt Chamberlain	1992	Michael Jordan
1969	Wes Unseld	1993	Charles Barkley
1970	Willis Reed	1994	Hakeem Olajuwon
1971	Lew Alcindor	1995	David Robinson
1972	Kareem Abdul-Jabbar	1996	Michael Jordan
1973	Dave Cowens	1997	Karl Malone
1974	Kareem Abdul-Jabbar	1998	Michael Jordan
1975	Bob McAdoo	1999	Karl Malone
1976	Kareem Abdul-Jabbar	2000	Shaquille O'Neal
1977	Kareem Abdul-Jabbar	2001	Allen Iverson
1978	Bill Walton	2002	Tim Duncan
1979	Moses Malone	2003	Tim Duncan

WNBA MOST VALUABLE PLAYER

1997	Cynthia Cooper	2001	Lisa Leslie
1998	Cynthia Cooper	2002	Sheryl Swoopes
1999	Yolanda Griffith	2003	Lauren Jackson
2000	Sheryl Swoopes		

BOXING
FAMOUS BOXERS

ALI	JOPPY	TUNNEY	WALCOTT
	LEWIS	BARKLEY	WILLARD
BAER	LOUIS	CARNERA	
BOWE	TYSON	CHARLES	BRADDOCK
BYRD		CORBETT	GRAZIANO
CLAY	GIRARD	DEMPSEY	MARCIANO
HART	HOLMES	DOUGLAS	ROBINSON
HILL	LISTON	FOREMAN	SULLIVAN
TATE	MCCALL	FRAZIER	HOLYFIELD
RUIZ	MOORER	FULLMER	JEFFERIES
	NORTON	GRIFFIN	JOHANSSON
BURNS	RAHMAN	JOHNSON	PATTERSON
DOKES	SPINKS	LALONDE	SCHMELING
DURAN	TORRES	LAMOTTA	
ELLIS	TRILLO	LEONARD	FITZSIMMONS
JONES	TUCKER	SHARKEY	

FOOTBALL
FAMOUS PLAYERS

*Indicates in the Pro Football Hall of Fame

OJ	ELWAY	BRODIE	PAYTON*
	FAULK	CARTER	ROCKNE
GIP	FAVRE	CSONKA*	RODNEY
RAY*	FOUTS*	DAWSON*	ROZIER
	GUYON*	DORAIS	RYPIEN
BAHR	HALAS*	DUDLEY*	STRONG*
BELL*	HEALY	FRIDGE	TAYLOR*
CARR*	HENRY*	GIPPER	THORPE*
DENT	JONES*	GRAHAM*	TITTLE*
HEIN*	LAYNE*	GRANGE*	TURNER*
MARA*	LEWIS	HARRIS*	UNITAS*
OWEN*	LYMAN*	HERBER*	WALKER*
PAGE*	NEALE*	HESTON	WARNER
RICE	SCOTT	HEWITT*	ZUPPKE
SIMS	SIMMS	HINKLE*	
SIPE	SMITH*	HOWARD	BATTLES*
	STAGG	HOWLEY	CONERLY
ALLEN*	STARR*	HUGHES	EDWARDS*
BAUGH*	SWANN*	HUTSON*	FOREMAN
BLOOD	WHITE*	ISBELL	GABRIEL
BRADY	YOUNG	LITTLE*	HORNUNG*
BROWN*		MARINO	HORWEEN
BUREN	AIKMAN	MCAFEE*	HUBBARD
CLARK*	ALBERT	NESSER	LAMBEAU*
DAVIS*	BLANDA*	NEVERS*	LEEMANS*

LUCKMAN*	RIGGINS*	ANDERSON	STAUBACH*
MAYNARD*	SIMPSON*	BRADSHAW*	THEISMANN
MCNALLY*	STABLER	CAMPBELL*	BILETNIKOFF*
MONTANA*	STANTON	PLUNKETT	
MOSELEY	TRAFTON*		

COACHES

FRY	HALAS*	FLORES	OSBORNE
	HAYES*	JORDAN*	PATERNO
HULA	HOLTZ	LANDRY*	SEIFERT
KNOX	JAMES	MADDEN	SNAVELY
KUSH	JONES*	MAJORS	SWEENEY
LEVY*	NEELY	NEHLEN	SWITZER
MORA	ROYAL	REEVES*	VERMEIL
NOLL	STAGG	VAUGHT	WOODSON
OWEN*	STRAM	WARNER	
YOST	WALSH*		ANDERSON
	WELSH	BILLICK	HOLMGREN
BIBLE		EDWARDS*	LOMBARDI*
BROWN*	BOWDEN	GILLMAN*	PARCELLS
DITKA*	BRYANT	HEISMAN	SHANAHAN
DOBIE	COOPER	JOHNSON*	
GIBBS*	DOOLEY	LAMBEAU*	BELICHICK
GRANT*	EWBANK*	MCGUGIN	CLAIBORNE

NFL MOST VALUABLE PLAYER

1957	Jim Brown	1982	Mark Moseley
1958	Gino Marchetti	1983	Joe Theismann
1959	Charley Conerly	1984	Dan Marino
1960	Norm Van Brocklin, Joe	1985	Marcus Allen
	Shmidt	1986	Lawrence Taylor
1961	Paul Hornung	1987	John Elway
1962	Jim Taylor	1988	Boomer Esiason
1963	Y.S. Tittle	1989	Joe Montana
1964	Johnny Unitas	1990	Joe Montana
1965	Jim Brown	1991	Thurman Thomas
1966	Bart Starr	1992	Steve Young
1967	Johnny Unitas	1993	Emmitt Smith
1968	Earl Morrall	1994	Steve Young
1969	Roman Gabriel	1995	Brett Favre
1970	John Brodie	1996	Brett Favre
1971	Alan Page	1997	Brett Favre, Barry Sanders
1972	Larry Brown	1998	Terrell Davis
1973	O.J. Simpson	1999	Kurt Warner
1974	Ken Stabler	2000	Marshall Faulk
1975	Fran Tarkenton	2001	Kurt Warner
1976	Bert Jones	2002	Rich Gannon
1977	Walter Payton	2003	Peyton Manning, Steve
1978	Terry Bradshaw		McNair
1979	Earl Campbell		
1980	Brian Sipe		
1981	Ken Anderson		

HEISMAN TROPHY WINNERS

CROW	CANNON	BELLINO	JANOWICZ
HART	CROUCH	CASSADY	KAZMAIER
SIMS	DETMER	DAWKINS	PLUNKETT
WARD	FLUTIE	DORSETT	SINKWICH
WARE	GEORGE	GARRETT	SPURRIER
	HARMON	GRIFFIN	STAUBACH
ALLEN	HOWARD	HORNUNG	TORRETTA
BAKER	HUARTE	HORVATH	WILLIAMS
BEBAN	LUJACK	JACKSON	WUERFFEL
BROWN	KELLEY	KINNICK	
DAVIS	OBRIEN	LATTNER	BERWANGER
DAYNE	PALMER	SANDERS	BLANCHARD
FRANK	ROGERS	SIMPSON	
OWENS	ROZIER	VESSELS	
SMITH	SALAAM	WOODSON	
WHITE	WALKER		
	WEINKE	BERTELLI	
AMECHE		CAMPBELL	

GOLF
FAMOUS GOLFERS
*Masters winner

ELS	COODY*	GOALBY*	GULDAHL*
	DUVAL	HARMON*	INKSTER
BEEM	FALDO*	KEISER*	LITTLER
BERG	FLOYD*	LANGER*	NICHOLS
BOLT	HAGEN	LEHMAN	SANDERS
FORD*	HOGAN*	OMEARA*	SARAZEN*
KING	JONES	OUIMET	SHEEHAN
KITE	PAVIN	NELSON*	STADLER*
LYLE*	PRICE	NORMAN	STRANGE
MIZE*	RAWLS	PALMER*	TREVINO
TEER	SINGH*	PICARD*	VENTURI
TOMS	SMITH*	PLAYER*	WOOSNAM*
WALL*	SNEAD*	SUTTON	WORSHAM
WEBB	STACY	VARDON	ZOELLER*
WEIR*	SUGGS	WATSON*	
WOOD*	WOODS*	WRIGHT	CRENSHAW*
		YANCEY	NICKLAUS*
AARON*	ARCHER*		OLAZABAL*
BEARD	BREWER*	BRADLEY	ZAHARIAS
BOROS	CASPER*	COUPLES*	MIDDLECOFF*
BURKE*	DUBBER	DEMARET*	BALLESTEROS*

HOCKEY
FAMOUS PLAYERS

ORR	HULL	KELLY	DRYDEN
ROY	JAGR	KURRI	DURNAN
	LACH	MOORE	HARVEY
			ICEMAN
BURE			IGINLA
COOK	BOSSY	CLARKE	IGINLA
HOWE	HASEK	COFFEY	MIKITA

PARENT	GRETZKY	PRONGER	LIDSTROM
PILOTE	LAFLEUR	RICHARD	MACINNIS
PLANTE	LEMIEUX	SELANNE	NICHOLLS
POTVIN	LINDSAY		TROTTIER
ROCKET	MOGILNY	BELLVEAU	
WILSON		ESPOSITO	GEOFFRION

TEAMS

JETS	DEVILS	WHALERS	ISLANDERS
WILD	FLAMES		LIGHTNING
	FLYERS	CAPITALS	PREDATORS
BLUES	OILERS	PANTHERS	THRASHERS
DUCKS	SABRES	PENGUINS	
KINGS	SHARKS	REDWINGS	BLACKHAWKS
LEAFS		SENATORS	HURRICANES
STARS	CANUCKS		MAPLELEAFS
	COYOTES	AVALANCHE	BLUEJACKETS
BRUINS	RANGERS	CANADIENS	

HORSE RACING
FAMOUS RACEHORSES

ZEV	GUNBOW	BIMELICH	CANDYSPOTS
	NASHUA	CITATION	COUNTFLEET
MOOR	PONDER	CARRYBACK	DEVILDIVER
ALSAB	STYMIE	CHALLEDON	GALLANTFOX
ARMED		DETERMINE	ROUNDTABLE
KELSO	ASSAULT	FUNNYCIDE	SEABISCUIT
OMAHA	MANOWAR	KAUAIKING	WARADMIRAL
PAVOT	NEEDLES	SIRBARTON	FIRSTFIDDLER
SWAPS	SHUTOUT	STAGEHAND	SWORDDANCER
	TOMFOOL	WHIRLAWAY	COUNTERPOINT
BUSHER		BUCKPASSER	NATIVEDANCER

TRIPLE CROWN WINNERS

1919	Sir Barton	1946	Assault
1930	Gallant Fox	1948	Citation
1935	Omaha	1973	Secretariat
1937	War Admiral	1977	Seattle Slew
1941	Whirlaway	1978	Affirmed
1943	Count Fleet		

KENTUCKY DERBY WINNERS

1875	Aristides	1887	Montrose
1876	Vagrant	1888	Macbeth II
1877	Baden Baden	1889	Spokane
1878	Day Star	1890	Riley
1879	Lord Murphy	1891	Kingman
1880	Fonso	1892	Azra
1881	Hindoo	1893	Lookout
1882	Apollo	1894	Chant
1883	Leonatus	1895	Halma
1884	Buchanan	1896	Ben Brush
1885	Joe Cotton	1897	Typhoon II
1886	Ben Ali	1898	Plaudit

1899	Manuel	1951	Count Turf
1900	Lieut. Gibson	1952	Hill Gail
1901	His Eminence	1953	Dark Star
1902	Alan-a-Dale	1954	Determine
1903	Judge Himes	1955	Swaps
1904	Elwood	1956	Needles
1905	Agile	1957	Iron Liege
1906	Sir Huon	1958	Tim Tam
1907	Pink Star	1959	Tomy Lee
1908	Stone Street	1960	Venetian Way
1909	Wintergreen	1961	Carry Back
1910	Donau	1962	Decidedly
1911	Meridian	1963	Chateaugay
1912	Worth	1964	Northern Dancer
1913	Donerail	1965	Lucky Debonair
1914	Old Rosebud	1966	Kauai King
1915	Regret	1967	Proud Citation
1916	George Smith	1968	Dancer's Image
1917	Omar Khayyam	1969	Majestic Prince
1918	Exterminator	1970	Dust Commander
1919	Sir Barton	1971	Canonero II
1920	Paul Jones	1972	Riva Ridge
1921	Behave Yourself	1973	Secretariat
1922	Morvich	1974	Cannonade
1923	Zev	1975	Foolish Pleasure
1924	Black Gold	1976	Bold Forbes
1925	Flying Ebony	1977	Seattle Slew
1926	Bubbling Over	1978	Affirmed
1927	Whiskery	1979	Spectacular Bid
1928	Reigh Count	1980	Genuine Risk
1929	Clyde Van Dusen	1981	Pleasant Colony
1930	Gallant Fox	1982	Gato del Sol
1931	Twenty Grand	1983	Sunny's Halo
1932	Burgoo King	1984	Swale
1933	Brokers Tip	1985	Spend a Buck
1934	Cavalcade	1986	Ferdinand
1935	Omaha	1987	Alysheba
1936	Bold Venture	1988	Winning Colors
1937	War Admiral	1989	Sunday Silence
1938	Lawrin	1990	Unbridled
1939	Johnstown	1991	Strike the Gold
1940	Gallahadion	1992	Lil E. Tee
1941	Whirlaway	1993	Sea Hero
1942	Shut Out	1994	Go for Gin
1943	Count Fleet	1995	Thunder Gulch
1944	Pensive	1996	Grindstone
1945	Hoop, Jr.	1997	Silver Charm
1946	Assault	1998	Real Quiet
1947	Jet Pilot	1999	Charismatic
1948	Citation	2000	Fusaichi Pegasus
1949	Ponder	2001	Monarchos
1950	Middleground	2002	War Emblem
		2003	Funny Cide

OLYMPICS
OLYMPIC SITES
SUMMER OLYMPIC GAMES

1896	Athens, Greece	1952	Helsinki, Finland
1900	Paris, France	1956	Melbourne, Australia
1904	St. Louis, MO	1960	Rome, Italy
1908	London, England	1964	Tokyo, Japan
1912	Stockholm, Sweden	1968	Mexico City, Mexico
1916	(not held)	1972	Munich, West Germany
1920	Antwerp, Belgium	1976	Montreal, Canada
1924	Paris, France	1980	Moscow, USSR
1928	Amsterdam, Netherlands	1984	Los Angeles, CA
1932	Los Angeles, CA	1988	Seoul, South Korea
1936	Berlin, Germany	1992	Barcelona, Spain
1940	(not held)	1996	Atlanta, GA
1944	(not held)	2000	Sydney, Australia
1948	London, England	2004	(Athens, Greece)
		2008	(Beijing, China)

WINTER OLYMPIC GAMES

1924	Chamonix, France	1964	Innsbruck, Austria
1928	St. Moritz, Switzerland	1968	Grenoble, France
1932	Lake Placid, NY	1972	Sapporo, Japan
1936	Garmisch-Partenkirchen, Germany	1976	Innsbruck, Austria
		1980	Lake Placid, NY
1940	(not held)	1984	Sarajevo, Yugoslavia
1944	(not held)	1988	Calgary, Alberta
1948	St. Moritz, Switzerland	1992	Albertville, France
1952	Oslo, Norway	1994	Lillehammer, Norway
1956	Cortina d'Ampezzo, Italy	1998	Nagano, Japan
1960	Squaw Valley, CA	2002	Salt Lake City, UT
		2006	(Turin, Italy)

SKATING
FAMOUS SKATERS

LU	BAIUL	HANLON	TICKNER
	BOBEK	NEPELA	TRENARY
ITO	BUSCH	SCHUBA	YAGUDIN
CHIN	DAVIS	STOJKO	
HOYT	HEISS	THOMAS	ALBRIGHT
KWAN	ORSER		DIJKSTRA
LITZ	WEISS	BOITANO	ELDREDGE
LORD	ZAYAK	FLEMING	HAMILTON
LYNN		GALINDO	KERRIGAN
OWEN	BOWMAN	HARDING	LIPINSKI
SATO	BUTTON	JENKINS	YAMAGUCHI
WITT	DANZER	PURSLEY	
WOOD	ERRATH	SEYFERT	
	GOEBEL	SHELLEY	
ALLEN	HAMILL	SUMNERS	

SOCCER
WORLD CUP

Year	Winner	Loser
1930	URUGUAY	ARGENTINA
1934	ITALY	CZECHOSLOVAKIA
1938	ITALY	HUNGARY
1942	*Not played*	
1946	*Not played*	
1950	URUGUAY	BRAZIL
1954	WESTGERMANY	HUNGARY
1958	BRAZIL	SWEDEN
1962	BRAZIL	CZECHOSLOVAKIA
1966	ENGLAND	WESTGERMANY
1970	BRAZIL	ITALY
1974	WESTGERMANY	NETHERLANDS
1978	ARGENTINA	NETHERLANDS
1982	ITALY	WESTGERMANY
1986	ARGENTINA	WESTGERMANY
1990	WESTGERMANY	ARGENTINA
1994	BRAZIL	ITALY
1998	FRANCE	BRAZIL
2002	BRAZIL	GERMANY

TENNIS
TENNIS CHAMPIONS

FRY	MOODY	KRAMER	NUTHALL
	OSUNA	LARNED	OSBORNE
ARTH	PERRY	LARSEN	RALSTON
ASHE	RIGGS	LIZANA	SAMPRAS
BETZ	ROCHE	MARBLE	SANTANA
BORG	SEARS	MULLOY	SEDGMAN
GRAF	SELES	MURRAY	SHRIVER
HARD	SMITH	PARKER	TALBERT
HART	VILAS	PAXWAX	TRABERT
HOAD	VINES	RAFTER	VICARIO
HUNT	WILLS	RICHEY	WALLACH
KING		SEGURA	
LUTZ	AGASSI	SEIXAS	BRUGUERA
MOYA	AUSTIN	STOLLE	CAPRIATI
NOAH	BECKER	SUKOVA	CONNOLLY
WADE	BOWREY	SUSMAN	GONZALES
WARD	BROUGH	SUTTON	ROSEWALL
WILLS	BROWNE	TILDEN	SABATINI
	CASALS	WRIGHT	WILANDER
BUDGE	COCHET		WILLIAMS
BUENO	COOPER	ALLISON	
COOKE	DROBNY	BARTZEN	GOOLAGONG
COSTA	DUPONT	BASSETE	BJURSTEDT
COURT	EBBERN	CONNORS	HOTCHKISS
EVERT	FRASER	EMERSON	PASARELLE
EALES	GIBSON	KUERTEN	SCHROEDER
KODES	GIMENO	LACOSTE	
KRIEK	HEWITT	LENGLEN	MCLOUGHLIN
LAVER	HINGIS	MALLORY	NAVRATILOVA
LENDL	JACOBS	MCENROE	
LLOYD	JAEGER	NASTASE	

WIMBLEDON—MEN'S

1950	Budge Patty	1977	Bjorn Borg
1951	Dick Savitt	1978	Bjorn Borg
1952	Frank Sedgman	1979	Bjorn Borg
1953	Vic Seixas	1980	Bjorn Borg
1954	Jaroslav Drobny	1981	John McEnroe
1955	Tony Trabert	1982	Jimmy Connors
1956	Lew Hoad	1983	John McEnroe
1957	Lew Hoad	1984	John McEnroe
1958	Ashley Cooper	1985	Boris Becker
1959	Alex Olmedo	1986	Boris Becker
1960	Neale Fraser	1987	Pat Cash
1961	Rod Laver	1988	Stefan Edberg
1962	Rod Laver	1989	Boris Becker
1963	Chuck McKinley	1990	Stefan Edberg
1964	Roy Emerson	1991	Michael Stich
1965	Roy Emerson	1992	Andre Agassi
1966	Manuel Santana	1993	Pete Sampras
1967	John Newcombe	1994	Pete Sampras
1968	Rod Laver	1995	Pete Sampras
1969	Rod Laver	1996	Richard Krajicek
1970	John Newcombe	1997	Pete Sampras
1971	John Newcombe	1998	Pete Sampras
1972	Stan Smith	1999	Pete Sampras
1973	Jan Kodes	2000	Pete Sampras
1974	Jimmy Connors	2001	Goran Ivanisevic
1975	Arthur Ashe	2002	Lleyton Hewitt
1976	Bjorn Borg	2003	Roger Federer

WIMBLEDON—WOMEN'S

1950	Louise Brough	1977	Virginia Wade
1951	Doris Hart	1978	Martina Navratilova
1952	Maureen Connolly	1979	Martina Navratilova
1953	Maureen Connolly	1980	Evonne Goolagong
1954	Maureen Connolly	1981	Chris Evert Lloyd
1955	Louise Brough	1982	Martina Navratilova
1956	Shirley Fry	1983	Martina Navratilova
1957	Althea Gibson	1984	Martina Navratilova
1958	Althea Gibson	1985	Martina Navratilova
1959	Maria Bueno	1986	Martina Navratilova
1960	Maria Bueno	1987	Martina Navratilova
1961	Angela Mortimer	1988	Steffi Graf
1962	Karen Hantze-Susman	1989	Steffi Graf
1963	Margaret Smith	1990	Martina Navratilova
1964	Maria Bueno	1991	Steffi Graf
1965	Margaret Smith	1992	Steffi Graf
1966	Billie Jean King	1993	Steffi Graf
1967	Billie Jean King	1994	Conchita Martinez
1968	Billie Jean King	1995	Steffi Graf
1969	Ann Haydon-Jones	1996	Steffi Graf
1970	Margaret Smith Court	1997	Martina Hingis
1971	Evonne Goolagong	1998	Jana Novotna
1972	Billie Jean King	1999	Lindsay Davenport
1973	Billie Jean King	2000	Venus Williams
1974	Chris Evert	2001	Venus Williams
1975	Billie Jean King	2002	Serena Williams
1976	Chris Evert	2003	Serena Williams

U.S. OPEN—MEN'S

1950	Arthur Larsen	1977	Guillermo Villas
1951	Frank Sedgman	1978	Jimmy Connors
1952	Frank Sedgman	1979	John McEnroe
1953	Tony Trabert	1980	John McEnroe
1954	Victor Seixas	1981	John McEnroe
1955	Tony Trabert	1982	Jimmy Connors
1956	Ken Rosewall	1983	Jimmy Connors
1957	Malcolm Anderson	1984	John McEnroe
1958	Ashley Cooper	1985	Ivan Lendl
1959	Neale Fraser	1986	Ivan Lendl
1960	Neale Fraser	1987	Ivan Lendl
1961	Roy Emerson	1988	Mats Wilander
1962	Rod Laver	1989	Boris Becker
1963	Rafael Osuna	1990	Pete Sampras
1964	Roy Emerson	1991	Stefan Edberg
1965	Manuel Santana	1992	Stefan Edberg
1966	Fred Stolle	1993	Pete Sampras
1967	John Newcombe	1994	Andre Agassi
1968	Arthur Ashe	1995	Pete Sampras
1969	Rod Laver	1996	Pete Sampras
1970	Ken Rosewall	1997	Patrick Rafter
1971	Stan Smith	1998	Patrick Rafter
1972	Ilie Nastase	1999	Andre Agassi
1973	John Newcombe	2000	Marat Safin
1974	Jimmy Connors	2001	Lleyton Hewitt
1975	Manuel Orantes	2002	Pete Sampras
1976	Jimmy Connors	2003	Andy Roddick

U.S. OPEN—WOMEN'S

1950	Margaret Osborne duPont	1977	Chris Evert
1951	Maureen Connolly	1978	Chris Evert
1952	Maureen Connolly	1979	Tracy Austin
1953	Maureen Connolly	1980	Chris Evert Lloyd
1954	Doris Hart	1981	Tracy Austin
1955	Doris Hart	1982	Chris Evert Lloyd
1956	Shirley Fry	1983	Martina Navratilova
1957	Althea Gibson	1984	Martina Navratilova
1958	Althea Gibson	1985	Hana Mandlikova
1959	Maria Bueno	1986	Martina Navratilova
1960	Darlene Hard	1987	Martina Navratilova
1961	Darlene Hard	1988	Steffi Graf
1962	Margaret Smith	1989	Steffi Graf
1963	Maria Bueno	1990	Gabriela Sabatini
1964	Maria Bueno	1991	Monica Seles
1965	Margaret Smith	1992	Monica Seles
1966	Maria Bueno	1993	Steffi Graf
1967	Billie Jean King	1994	Arantxa Sanchez Vicario
1968	Virginia Wade	1995	Steffi Graf
1969	Margaret Smith Court	1996	Steffi Graf
1970	Margaret Smith Court	1997	Martina Hingis
1971	Billie Jean King	1998	Lindsay Davenport
1972	Billie Jean King	1999	Serena Williams
1973	Margaret Smith Court	2000	Venus Williams
1974	Billie Jean King	2001	Venus Williams
1975	Chris Evert	2002	Serena Williams
1976	Chris Evert	2003	Justine Henin-Hardenne

TIME DIVISIONS— CALENDARS

No. of Month	Jewish	Islamic	Hindu
1	TISHRI, ETHANIM	MUHARRAM	BAISAKH
2	HESHVAN, BUL	SAFAR	JETH
3	KISLEY	RABIA 1	ASARH
4	TEBET(H), TEVET	RABIA 2	SA(RA)WAN
5	SHEBAT, SHEVAT	JUMADA 1	BHADON
6	ADAR	JUMADA 2	ASIN, KUAR
7	NISAN, ABIB	RAJAB	KA(R)TIK
8	IYAR, ZIF	SHABAN	AGHAN
9	SIVAN	RAMADAN	PUS
10	TAMMUZ	SHAWWAL	MAGH
11	AB, AV	DULRAADA	PHA(L)GUN
12	ELUL	DULHEGGIA	CHAIT

No. of Month	French Revolutionary	Egyptian	Roman
1	VENDEMIAIRE (vintage)	THOTH	MARTIUS
2	BRUMAIRE (fog)	PAOPHI	APRILIS
3	FRIMAIRE (sleet)	HATHOR	MAIUS
4	NIVOSE (snow)	CHOIAK	JUNIUS
5	PLUVIOSE (rain)	TYBI	JULIUS; QUINCTILIS
6	VENTOSE (wind)	MECHIR	AUGUSTUS; SEXTILIS
7	GERMINAL (seed)	PHAMENOTH	SEPTEMBER
8	FLOREAL (blossom)	PHARMUTHI	OCTOBER
9	PRAIRIAL (pasture)	PACHONS	NOVEMBRIS, NOVEMBER
10	MESSIDOR (harvest)	PAYNI	DECEMBER
11	THERMIDOR (heat)	APAR	JANUARIUS
12	FRUCTIDOR (fruit)	MESORE	FEBRUARIUS

No. of Month	French	Spanish	German	Italian
1	JANVIER	ENERO	JANUAR	GENNAIO
2	FEVRIER	FEBRERO	FEBRUAR	FEBBRAIO
3	MARS	MARZO	MARZ	MARZO
4	AVRIL	ABRIL	APRIL	APRILE
5	MAI	MAYO	MAI	MAGGIO
6	JUIN	JUNIO	JUNI	GIUGNO
7	JUILLET	JULIO	JULI	LUGLIO
8	AOUT	AGOSTO	AUGUST	AUGUSTO
9.	SEPTEMBRE	SEPTIEMBRE	SEPTEMBER	SETTEMBRE
10	OCTOBRE	OCTUBRE	OKTOBER	OTOBRE
11	NOVEMBRE	NOVIEMBRE	NOVEMBER	NOVEMBRE
12	DECEMBRE	DICIEMBRE	DEZEMBER	DICEMBRE

SEASONS, DAYS, AND OTHER TERMS

English	French	Spanish	German	Italian	Russian
Spring	PRINTEMPS	PRIMAVERA	FRU(E)HLING	PRIMAVERA	VYESNA
Summer	ETE	VERANO	SOMMER	ESTATE	LYETO
Fall	AUTOMNE	OTONO	HERBST	AUTUNNO	OSEN
Winter	HIVER	INVIERNO	WINTER	INVERNO	ZIMA
Monday	LUNDI	LUNES	MONTAG	LUNEDI	VOSKRESENYE
Tuesday	MARDI	MARTES	DIENSTAG	MARTEDI	PONEDELNIK
Wednesday	MERCREDI	MIERCOLES	MITWOCH	MERCOLEDI	VTORNIK
Thursday	JEUDI	JUEVES	DONNERSTAG	GIOVEDI	SREDA
Friday	VENDREDI	VIERNES	FREITAG	VENERDI	CHETVERG
Saturday	SAMEDI	SABADO	SONNABEND	SABATO	PYATNITSA
Sunday	DIMANCHE	DOMINGO	SONNTAG	DOMENICA	SUBBOTA
Year	ANNEE	ANO	JAHR	ANNO	GOT
Month	MOIS	MES	MONAT	MESE	MYESATS
Week	SEMAINE	SEMANA	WOCHE	SETTIMANA	NYEDYELYA
Day	JOUR	DIA	TAG	GIORNO	DYEN
Hour	HEURE	HORA	STUNDE	ORA	CHAS
Time	TEMPS	TIEMPO	ZEIT	TEMPO	VREMYA

Latin

Time	**TEMPUS;** pl. **TEMPORA**	7th day of March, May, July, October,
Year	**ANNUS; ANNO**	5th day of other months, **NONES;**
Month	**MENSIS**	**NONAS; NONIS**
Day	**DIES; DIE**	15th day of March, May, July, October,
Hour	**HORA**	13th day of other months, **IDI-**
First day of month **CALENDS;**		**BUS, IDES, IDUS**
KALENDS, CALENDIS		Day before, **PRIDIE**

BIRTHSTONES

ONYX	July	AMETHYST	Feb.
OPAL	Oct.	ROZIRCON	Oct.
RUBY	July, Dec.	SAPPHIRE	April, Sept.
AGATE	May, June	SARDONYX	Aug.
BERYL	Oct.	CARNELIAN	Aug.
PEARL	June	MOONSTONE	June
TOPAZ	Nov.	TURQUOISE	July, Dec.
GARNET	Jan.	BLOODSTONE	March
JASPER	March	AQUAMARINE	March, Oct.
ZIRCON	Dec.	TOURMALINE	Oct.
DIAMOND	April	CHRYSOLITE	Sept.
EMERALD	May, June	ALEXANDRITE	June
PERIDOT	Aug.		

WEDDING ANNIVERSARIES

TIN	10	CHINA	9, 20	COTTON	2
GOLD	50	CORAL	35	SILVER	25
IRON	6	IVORY	14	CRYSTAL	15
LACE	13	LINEN	4	DIAMOND	60
RUBY	40	PAPER	1	EMERALD	55
SILK	4, 12	PEARL	30	LEATHER	3
WOOD	5	STEEL	11	POTTERY	9
WOOL	7	BRONZE	8	SAPPHIRE	45

TOOLS, INSTRUMENTS, IMPLEMENTS (AND PARTS)

SHAPING, POLISHING, SEPARATING

BOB	DARBY	WHISP	LASTER
DOD	EDGER	WIPER	MALKIN
MOP	FLUTE		MANGLE
RIP	GOOSE	BADGER	MILLER
RUB	GRAIL	BEADER	MOLDER
ZAX	HOWEL	CAPPER	NAPPER
	JOLLY	CARDEN	PALLET
BUFF	LATHE	CARLET	PLANER
BUNT	PAVER	CHUTER	POMMEL
CARD	PLANE	COMBER	PONTIL
COMB	PRINT	CURVER	PUTOIS
FILE	PRUNT	DABBER	RABBET
HARL	PUNTY	DAUBER	RAMROD
HONE	PUPPY	DUSTER	REAMER
LAUN	QUIRK	EVENER	REBATE
MILL	QUIRL	FINNER	ROUTER
PEEN	RABAT	FLAKER	RUFFER
RAPE	RICER	FLANCH	SANDER
RASP	RIFLE	FLANGE	SCREED
RESP	SABER	FLUTER	SCRIVE
RISP	SABLE	FORMER	SHAPER
SLIP	SABRE	GLAZER	SLOPER
SPAT	SIEVE	GOFFER	SMOOTH
SWAB	SIZER	GRADER	SOOTER
WISP	SLICK	GRATER	STRAIK
	SNIPE	HARROW	SWEDGE
	STEEP	HEMMER	TASTER
BROOM	STROP	HICKEY	TENTER
BRUSH	STRUM	IRONER	VELURE
CONER	SWAGE	JOLLEY	WAGWAG
CRIMP	WAXER		WINNOW
	WHISK		

LIFTING, LEVERING, PRYING

BAR	LIFT	JAMES	WINZE
FID	LOOT	JEMMY	
GIN	PALE	JIMMY	BAILER
GYN	PEAL	LADLE	BURTON
PRY	PEEL	LEASH	COUPER
TUG	PUMP	LEWIS	DIPPER
	WIND	PEAVY	DREDGE
BAIT	WINK	PEDAL	FORCER
BEAM		PINCH	GAFFLE
CRAB	BETTY	PRIZE	GAGGER
CROW	CRANE	QUOIN	GARNET
DART	DAVIT	STANG	GARROT
DRAG	DIDLE	SWAPE	GUNTER
GAFF	FILCH	SWEEP	HEAVER
GRAB	FLIRT	SWELL	KIBBLE
HAKE	GRIFF	SWIPE	LADKIN
HOCK	GRIPE	WEDGE	LADLER
JACK	HELVE	WINCH	LEAPER

LIFTER	PEAVEY	RIPPLE	TACKLE
LOWDER	PULLER	SEEDER	TILLER
OPENER	PUMPER	STONER	WRENCH

GRIPPING, HOLDING, CONNECTING

CAT	CLOG	POLE	CHEEK
DAG	COAK	RACK	CHIMB
DOG	COPE	RAKE	CHIME
DOP	COPS	REST	CHINE
EAR	CRIB	RODE	CHOCK
GAB	CROC	ROSE	CHUCK
GAG	CURB	RUNG	CHURN
GIB	DALE	SCAB	CHUTE
GIG	DOPP	SCOB	CLAMP
GUY	DRIP	SEAL	CLASP
HOD	DUCT	SEAT	CLAUT
KEP	DULL	SIME	CLEAT
LUG	FANG	SKID	CLEEK
NOG	FLAN	SNAP	CLICK
NUT	FORM	SOAM	CLINK
PEG	FROG	SOGA	COPSE
POT	GATE	SPAD	CRAMP
RIB	GAWN	SPAN	CREEL
SOW	GIMP	SPIT	CROME
TAB	GIRD	STAY	CROOK
TEE	GRID	STUB	DANDI
TEW	GYVE	STUD	DANDY
TIE	HACK	TACK	DOWEL
TOO	HANK	TONG	DRAIL
TUB	HASP	TRAP	DWANG
TUN	HAWK	TUBE	EASEL
TYE	HEAD	VIAL	FLASK
WAD	HECK	VICE	FLOAT
	HOOD	VISE	FLUME
ANSA	HOOK	YARD	FRAIL
BAIL	HORN	YOKE	FRAME
BEAK	KEEP		GIRSE
BIRN	KEIR	ANGLE	GIRTH
BOLT	KIER	ANVIL	GLAND
BOND	KILP	APRON	GOMER
BOOM	KING	APURN	GRATE
BOOT	KNAG	ARIES	GRILL
BOSS	KNOB	ARROW	GROPE
BRAD	KNOP	BANGY	GUIGE
BRAG	LAST	BASIN	HEART
BROB	LATH	BASON	HERSE
BUCK	LEAP	BIPOD	HONDA
BUNG	LILL	BLOCK	HORSE
CAGE	LINK	BOCAL	HOUND
CALM	LULL	BOWER	IRONS
CAME	LUTE	BRACE	JINNY
CASE	MAIL	BRANK	JOUGS
CAST	MOLD	CAMEL	KEDGE
CAUL	NAIL	CAVEL	KEEVE
CHUG	NOCK	CAVIL	KEVEL
CLEP	PAWL	CHAIR	KNOSP
CLEW	PECK	CHASE	LACER
CLIP	PIPE	CHECK	LINER

LONGE	TAMMY	COLLET	LOCKER
LUNET	TEEST	CONVOY	MATRIX
MOULD	THIEF	COTTER	MOOTER
NEDDY	THOLE	CRADLE	MORTAR
NIBBY	THONG	CRANCE	MUSROL
NOOSE	TONGS	CRUTCH	MUZZLE
OILER	TRAMP	DASHER	NORMAN
OLONA	TRAWL	DETENT	OLIVET
ORRIS	ULLER	DOGTIE	PACKER
PERCH	WADDY	DROGUE	POPPET
PIPET	WITHE	DUBBEH	RABBLE
PITON	WRIST	ETALON	RACKAN
PIVOT	WYTHE	EXAMEN	RUNDLE
PREEN		EYEBAR	RYPECK
RAKER	AMPULE	EYELET	SAGENE
RIBET	ANCHOR	FASCET	SCATCH
ROOVE	AXTREE	FETTER	SCAVEL
ROUGH	BANGHY	FEUTER	SEALER
SARPE	BEARER	FEWTER	SHEATH
SEINE	BEATER	FIBULA	SINKER
SETUP	BECKET	FILLER	SKEWER
SHAFT	BOWPIN	FRETTE	SOCKET
SHAPE	BRANCH	FUNNEL	SPIDER
SHIVE	BRIDLE	GIMMER	SPIGOT
SHORE	BROACH	GIMMOR	SPIKER
SKEET	BROOCH	GIRDER	STAPLE
SNARE	BUCCAN	GRILLE	STEADY
SNARL	BUCKET	GROMET	STRAKE
SPANG	BUCKLE	GUSSET	TACKET
SPEED	BULLET	HANGER	TAPLET
SPELK	BUTTON	HANGLE	TERRET
SPELL	CABLET	HILLER	TINGLE
SPIKE	CANGUE	HOLDER	TOGGEL
SPILE	CANNEL	HOPPER	TOGGLE
SPILL	CANOPY	HURTER	TUBULE
SPOKE	CAPLIN	JANKER	TUNNER
SPOUT	CARCAN	KEDGER	TURKIS
SPANG	CASING	KEEPER	TURRET
SPRIG	CATENA	LAGGEN	UPHROE
SQUIB	CHAFER	LAGGIN	VERVEL
STALL	CHESIL	LIKNON	VIROLE
STAVE	CLEVIS	LIMBER	WASHER
TAMIS	CLINCH	LINPIN	WELDER
	CLUTCH		ZIPPER
	COLLAR		

CUTTING, STRIKING, POUNDING

AX	HOB	SAX	COCK
SY	HOE	SEX	DAHO
	HOG	SUL	EAWT
ADZ	LEA	SYE	FROE
AXE	LIP	TUP	FROW
BIT	LOY	ULU	MACE
DAB	NIP		MALL
DAN	PEW	ADZE	MASH
DIG	PIC	BEAR	MAUL
FID	RAB	BENT	MEAK
GAD	RAM	BROD	MELL
GUN	SAW	CELT	MERE

MOGO	PRESS	EOLITH	POLEAX
MOON	RAZOR	FASCES	PRIEST
NIPS	REEST	FOLDER	PRUNER
PLEW	RIMER	FORFEX	PUDDLE
PLOW	ROWEL	FRAISE	RAMMER
POLT	SCOOP	FROWER	RANCER
SEAR	SHARE	FULLER	RANDER
SETT	SHARP	GOUGER	RAPPER
SNIP	SHAUL	GRAVER	RASPER
SOCK	SHAVE	GWEEON	RIMMER
SPUD	SHEEL	HACKER	RIPPER
SUCK	SHOOL	HAMMER	RIPSAW
SULL	SLANE	HEADER	RUTTER
TAMP	SLICE	HOGGER	SAPPER
	SLING	HUGGER	SCORER
	SPADE	JAGGER	SCUTCH
ADDIS	SPOON	JOGGER	SCYTHE
BLADE	STAMP	JOINER	SHAVER
BRIAR	STYLE	LABRYS	SHEARS
BRUZZ	THROE	LANCET	SHOVEL
BURIN	WAGON	LIPPER	SICKLE
CROZE		MACHET	SKIVER
DOLLY	ADDUCE	MAIDEN	SLATER
DRIFT	BARLOW	MALLET	SLEDGE
FACER	BEAMER	MARTEL	SLICER
FLAIL	BEETLE	MASHER	SPADER
FRAZE	BENDER	MEADER	STADDA
GAVEL	BINDER	MEALER	STYLET
GOUGE	BLADER	METATE	SULLOW
HACHE	BUNTER	MINCER	TAMPER
HARDY	BUSTER	MUCKLE	TEASEL
HOBBY	CARVER	NIBBER	THIXLE
JERRY	CATLIN	NIDGET	THRAIL
KNIFE	CHASER	NIPPER	TILTER
KNURL	CHISEL	OLIVER	TOOLER
LANCE	CHONTA	PAVIOR	TREPAN
LARRY	CLEAVE	PEELER	TREVET
LATHE	COLTER	PESTLE	TRIVAT
LEWIS	COUTEL	PICKAX	TRIVET
MADGE	CUTTER	PIOLET	TUBBAL
MATAX	CUTTLE	PLEWCH	TUBBER
PARER	DAMSEL	PLEWGH	TUSKAR
PEGGY	DAPPER	PLIERS	TWIBIL
PILUM	DIGGER	PLOUGH	VEINER
PLEWE	DIPPER	PODGER	WEEDER
PLIER	DOCTOR		
	DREDGE		

MOVING, REVOLVING, FLEXIBLE

AWE	POY	CRIC	PALM
CAM	PUY	DISC	PIRN
COG	RAX	DRUM	PLET
FAN	TOM	FLAP	PLUG
FLY	VAN	GEAR	REEL
FUR		HAIR	RING
JIB	AXIS	HARR	ROLL
KEY	AXLE	LEAF	ROPE
LAP	BEAD	LILY	ROVE
OAR	CONE	LITZ	TRIG

VANE	RATCH	BARREL	LASKET
VIOL	REATA	BEDKEY	LEADER
VIRL	RIATA	BILOPE	LIGGER
WHIP	ROMAL	BOBBIN	LINGEL
WING	SCULL	CANNON	LINGLE
WORM	SKEIF	CASTER	MULLER
	SKIVE	CHABUK	NORSEL
AZOTE	SNELL	CHAMAR	NOSSEL
BAGUE	SPOOL	CHOWRY	PADDLE
BEVEL	STILE	COILER	PANTER
CABLE	SWEPE	CURLER	PINION
CANON	SWING	CURPEL	PULLEY
CLACK	SWISH	CURPLE	RABAND
CODER	THROW	CURSOR	RADDLE
CRANK	TOMMY	DAMPER	RAFFLE
DITAL	TRACE	DERAIL	RATLIN
FELLY	TROLL	DOFFER	RATTLE
FLIER	TRULL	DRIVEN	RIGGER
FLYER	TWIST	DRIVER	ROBAND
GEMEL	VALVE	ENARME	RODING
GUIDE	VERGE	FAUCET	ROLLER
HEALD	VOYAL	FERULA	ROWLET
HINGE	VOYOL	FERULE	RUDDER
IDLER	WANTY	FLIGHT	RUNNER
INDEX	WAVER	FUSEAU	SHEAVE
JENNY	WHANG	GIMBAL	SHIVER
KNOUT	WHEEP	GIMMAL	SWIVEL
LASSO	WHIRL	GUIDER	TAPFER
LATCH	WIDDY	HEDDLE	TETHER
LEVER	WINCE	HINGLE	TORQUE
PILOT	WITHY	HORRAL	TURNER
PLETE	WOODY	KILHIG	VERREL
QUIRT	WREST	LAINER	WINDER
		LARIAT	

PIERCING, BORING

AWL	TING	NOBBY	CURATE
TAP		PIKEL	DIBBER
	ANKUS	PIKLE	DIBBLE
BROG	AUGER	PRICK	ELSHIN
CALK	BLUNT	PRONG	FERRET
FORK	BORER	SOWEL	FIZGAG
GOAD	BRAND	SPEAR	FRAMEA
MOLL	CORER	STING	GIMLET
NILL	DRILL	STRAW	GRAINS
PICK	ELBOW	TRIER	JUMPER
PIKE	ELSIN	VALET	NAUGER
POTE	ELSON		PECKER
PROG	FLUKE	BIDENT	PROBER
PUGH	FURCA	BODKIN	RIPPON
PYKE	GRAIN	BORREL	SCRIBE
SPUR	GRAIP	CALKER	STYLUS
TANG	LATHE	CALKIN	TWISEL
TINE	MORNE	CROTCH	WIMBLE

PRINTING TOOLS AND TERMS

EM	ROLL	STICK	OFFCUT
EN	RULE	TITLE	OFFSET
PI	SLIP	TOKEN	PICKUP
	SLUG		PLATEN
	SLUR		POSTER
BED	SORT	ACCENT	REGLET
CUT	STEM	BATTER	REVISE
FAT	STET	BEARER	ROLLER
FLY	TAKE	BODKIN	ROUNCE
JOB	TYPE	BRAYER	SETOFF
LAY		CANCEL	THIRTY
LOW		CASTER	TYMPAN
OUT	ALLEY	CERIPH	
PIE	BELLY	CHAPEL	
SUB	BLOCK	CLICHE	BASTARD
	BOXIN	COCKUP	CLICKER
	BRACE	DABBER	COLLATE
BANK	CARET	DAGGER	COMPOSE
BITE	CHASE	DELETE	COUNTER
BODY	COLON	DIESIS	FRISKET
CASE	COMMA	DOCTOR	GAGEPIN
COPY	CUTIN	DOUBLE	GRIPPER
DELE	DUMMY	EMBOSS	HEADING
DRAG	DWELL	FINGER	HELLBOX
DRAW	FRAME	GALLEY	IMPRINT
FACE	HORSE	IMPOSE	JOBWORK
FEET	INSET	INDENT	JUSTIFY
FIST	PLATE	ITALIC	MEASURE
FONT	POINT	LEADER	MORTISE
FORM	PROOF	LETTER	MOVABLE
KERN	QUOIN	LOCKUP	OPENING
LEAD	RUNIN	MACKLE	OVERLAY
LEAN	SERIF	MAKEUP	OVERRUN
LINE	SETUP	MARGIN	PACKING
NICK	SHAKE	MATRIX	PINMARK
QUAD	SHANK	MATTER	PLANNER
RACK	SHEET	NIPPER	QUADRAT
RISE	STAND		REPRINT

SURGICAL TOOLS AND TERMS

BUR	SWATH	SUTURE	EJECTOR
		SWATHE	FORCEPS
HYPO	BILABE	TAMPON	LEVATOR
SPUD	BOUGIE	TREPAN	MANDREL
SWAB	CATLIN	TROCAR	MANDRIN
	DOSSIL	TWEEZE	PIPETTE
AMPUL	GARROT	VELTIS	PLEDGET
CLAMP	GORGET	XYSTER	PLESSOR
FLEAM	LANCET		PLUGGER
LANCE	MATRIX	ABLATOR	PLUNGER
PROBE	NEEDLE	AMPOULE	SCALPEL
SETON	PROBER	AMPULLA	SPATULA
SNARE	SCALER	CANNULA	SYRINGE
STAFF	SPLINT	CATLING	TRACTOR
STUPE	STILET	CAUTERY	TRILABE
STYLE	STYLET	CURETTE	TROCHAIR

BISTOURY	ELEVATOR	TENACULA	TEREBELLA
CATHETER	EXPLORER		
CROTCHET	FORCIPES	EXCAVATOR	
DENTAGRA	SPECULUM	EXTRACTOR	
ECRASEUR	SQUEEZER	PERCUSSOR	

OTHERS

BOW	WICK	STILT	FINDER
CAP	WIRE	STOCK	FINGER
DIE		STONE	FLITCH
HUB	BOWET	STOVE	GADGET
JET	BRAKE	STRAP	HEATER
JIG	BRICK	TABLE	JIGGER
LOG	CHAIN	TEWEL	JIMJAM
PEN	CHUMP	TOLLY	KIPPIN
PIN	CODON	TORCH	LADDER
ROD	COVER	TUNER	LATHEE
SET	CROSS	TYPER	LINGOE
TIP	CROWN	VESTA	LOOPER
TOW	DEVIL		MAGNET
	DIODE		MARKER
	DIPSY	ABACUS	MODDLE
BALL	DUMMY	ALINER	NEEDLE
BAND	FUSEE	ANCONY	NIPPLE
BELL	FUZEE	AUDION	NONIUS
BULB	GADGE	BALLOW	NOZZLE
BUOY	GAUGE	BASTON	PENCIL
COIL	GUARD	BATULE	POOLER
CORD	HATCH	BLOWER	POPPER
CUFF	HELIX	BONNET	PRIMER
DENT	INKER	BOTTOM	PROKER
DIAL	LATHI	BRIDGE	PUSHER
DROP	LEVEL	BUMPER	REEDER
FACE	LINGO	BUNSEN	RICKER
FLUE	LOUPE	BURNER	RIDGER
FRET	MATCH	CANDLE	RIFFLE
FUSE	METER	CENTER	ROCKER
FUZE	METRE	CENTRE	ROOKER
GAGE	MIXER	CIERGE	ROUSER
HAAF	NICOL	CRAYON	SADDLE
HOSE	NORMA	CUPPER	SCREEN
IRON	PEDUM	CUTOFF	SERVER
LAMP	PEISE	CUTOUT	SETTER
LENS	PLUMB	DENTIN	SHAKER
LINE	POINT	DEVICE	SPACER
LOCK	POKER	DIACLE	SPLINE
LOOM	POUND	DIMMER	SPRING
LOOP	PUNCH	DIPSEY	STOKER
MIKE	QUILL	DIPSIE	SUCKER
RAIL	RANGE	DISCUS	SWITCH
RULE	RULER	DONKEY	TEDDER
SHOE	SCALE	DOTTER	THIVEL
SLAB	SCREW	DOUTER	TONGUE
SLUG	SHADE	DYNAMO	TROWEL
STOP	SHELL	ENGINE	TUYERE
TRIP	SIGHT	FEEDER	TWITCH
WAND	STAFF	FEELER	WEIGHT
WARP	STAKE	FILTER	WORKER
	STICK		

TRANSPORTATION
VEHICLES
MAN OR ANIMAL OPERATED

FLY	HURLY	BICYCLE	CAPECART
GIG	JERRY	BOUNDER	CARRIOLE
RIG	JUTKA	BRITZKA	CARROZZA
RUT	RATHA	CAISSON	CHARETTE
	SADOO	CALECHE	CLARENCE
ARBA	STAGE	CARAVAN	CURRICLE
BIGA	SULKY	CARIOLE	DEARBORN
BIKE	TONGA	CAROCHE	DEMOCRAT
BUTT	WAGON	CARRETA	DORMEUSE
BYKE		CHARIOT	DROSCHKE
CART	BARROW	CONCORD	EQUIPAGE
CHAY	BERLIN	CROYDON	HANDCART
DRAG	CALASH	DOGCART	MORPHREY
DRAY	CALESA	DOSADOS	ORDINARY
DUKE	CHAISE	DROSHKY	PUSHCART
EKKA	CHARET	FOURGON	QUADRIGA
GOAT	CISIUM	GONDOLA	RICKSHAW
HACK	DENNET	GROWLER	ROCKAWAY
LUGE	DROSKY	HACKERY	RUNABOUT
MAIL	ESSEDA	HACKNEY	SOCIABLE
PLOW	ESSEDE	KIBITKA	STANHOPE
PRAM	FIACRE	MORFREY	TARANTAS
PUTT	GHARRI	PHAETON	TRICYCLE
RATH	GHARRY	RICKSHA	VICTORIA
SADO	GOCART	SCOOTER	
SHAY	HANSOM	TALLYHO	BUCKBOARD
TEAM	HEARSE	TARTANA	CABRIOLET
TODE	HERDIC	TILBURY	CARROMATA
TRAP	JINGLE	TRUCKLE	CHARIOTEE
WAIN	JINKER	TUMBLER	CONESTOGA
	KOSONG	TUMBREL	DILIGENCE
ARABA	LANDAU	TUMBRIL	STRETCHER
BANDY	LIMBER	TURNOUT	TARANTASS
BRAKE	RECKLA	UNICORN	WAGONETTE
BREAK	SAFETY	VETTURA	
BRETT	SHOFUL	VISAVIS	FOURINHAND
CYCLE	SPIDER	VOITURE	GERMANTOWN
DANDY	SURREY	VOLANTE	JINRICKSHA
DILLY	TANDEM		JINRIKISHA
DOLLY	TELEGA	BAROUCHE	VELOCIPEDE
ESSED	TROIKA	BRANCARD	VOITURETTE
GURRY		BROUGHAM	WHEELCHAIR

AUTOMOBILES

RV	AUTO	TRAM	SEDAN
	DRAG	WYNN	TRUCK
ATV	HACK		
BUS	JEEP	COACH	CAMION
SUV	TANK	COUPE	HEARSE
VAN	TAXI	LORRY	HUMMER

JALOPY	MINIVAN	COUPELET	CHARABANC
JIGGER	OMNIBUS	DUMPCART	LANDAULET
JITNEY	SCOOTER	MOTORBUS	LIMOUSINE
LANDAU	SIDECAR	MOTORCAB	
PICKUP	TAXICAB	MOTORCAR	AUTOMOBILE
TOURER	TORPEDO	ROADSTER	BLACKMARIA
	TRACTOR	RUNABOUT	MOTORCYCLE
AUTOBUS	TRAILER	SUBURBAN	CONVERTIBLE
BERLINE	TRAMCAR		STATIONWAGON
FLIVVER	TROLLEY	AMBULANCE	
JALLOPY	VOITURE	CABRIOLET	

ON RUNNERS

BOB	PULKA	PALKEE	SNOWSHOE
SKI	SKATE	SLEDGE	TOBOGGAN
	TRAIN	SLEIGH	TRAVOISE
PULK			
PUNG	CUTTER	BOBSLED	BOBSLEIGH
SLED	HURDLE	COASTER	
	JAMPAN	GODEVIL	
PALKI	JUMPER	TRAVOIS	

PORTABLE

JUAN	DOOLEY	TOMJON	MUNCHEEL
KAGO	DOOLIE	TONJON	PALANKEEN
	HOWDAH		PALANQUIN
DANDI	KURUMA	CACOLET	STRETCHER
DANDY	LITTER	NORIMON	
DOOLI	TELEGA	SKILIFT	
SEDAN			

RAILROAD

HOG	WAGON	CABOOSE	BRAKEVAN
	BOXCAR	CARAVAN	CABLECAR
MULE	DINKEY	CLUBCAR	DAYCOACH
	DONKEY	EXPRESS	ELEVATED
COACH	ENGINE	FLATCAR	WAGONLIT
DINER	HELPER	GIRAFFE	
DINKY	JOPPER	GONDOLA	HOPPERCAR
DOLLY	SMOKER	LIMITED	PARLORCAR
DUMMY	SUBWAY	PULLMAN	LOCOMOTIVE
LOCAL	TENDER	SLEEPER	
MOGUL	WAGGON	SPEEDER	
TRAIN		TANKCAR	

PARTS OF VEHICLES

BOX	TIRE	WHEEL	RUMBLE
CAM	TUBE	WIPER	SADDLE
FAN			SPRING
RIM	BRAKE	BONNET	
	MOTOR	BUMPER	BATTERY
AXLE	PEDAL	CLUTCH	CHASSIS
GEAR	REINS	ENGINE	EXHAUST
HOOD	SHAFT	INTAKE	MAGNETO
PLUG	SPOKE	PILLAR	MUFFLER
SHOE	THILL	PISTON	STARTER

TONNEAU	IGNITION	SPROCKET	HANDLEBAR
	MUDGUARD	THROTTLE	SPARKPLUG
CYLINDER	OILGAUGE		
FLYWHEEL	RADIATOR	GEARSHIFT	

SHIPS

SAILING VESSELS

CAT	PINKY	LANCHA	HAGBOAT
GIG	PRAAM	LORCHA	ICEBOAT
HOY	RASEE	LUGGER	PATAMAR
	RAZEE	MISTIC	PIRAGUA
BARK	SETEE	PRAHAM	POLACCA
BRIG	SHARP	PULWAR	POLACRE
BUSS	SLOOP	SAILER	POOKAUN
DHOW	SMACK	SAMBUK	SEASLED
DONI	TJALK	SAMPAN	SHALLOP
JUNK	XEBEC	SANDAL	SHARPIE
KOFF	YANKY	SCAFFY	SKAFFIE
PINK	ZABRA	SETTEE	TARTANE
PRAM		SHIBAR	
SAIC	ARGOSY	SKAFFY	BALINGER
SAIL	BAIDAR	TARTAN	BALLAHOO
SNOW	BARQUE	TOSHER	BALLAHOU
TODE	BAWLEY	TRANKY	BILANDER
TOUP	BILALO		BILLYBOY
TROW	BOLIAH	BAGGALA	DAHABEAH
YAWL	BORLEY	BIRLING	ICEYACHT
ZULU	BOUTRE	BIRLINN	MACKINAC
	CAIQUE	BUMBOAT	MACKINAW
BARGE	CANGIA	CARAVEL	PATTAMAR
BATEL	CARVEL	CATBOAT	PATTIMAR
BOLIA	DINGHY	CLIPPER	SCHOONER
CASCO	DOGGER	FELUCCA	TONGKANG
DANDY	DROMON	FLYBOAT	
DHONI	GALIOT	FOYBOAT	
DRAKE	GAYYOU	FRIGATE	CARAVELLE
FOIST	HOGGIE	GAIASSA	MUMBLEBEE
KETCH	HOLCAD	GALLEON	SNEAKBOAT
	HOOKER	GALLIOT	TRABACOLO

ENGINE-DRIVEN VESSELS

TUG	PADDLE	DROGHER	LIGHTSHIP
	PONTIN	LIGHTER	MOTORBOAT
AVISO	PUFFER	PINNACE	PILOTBOAT
OILER	TENDER	STEAMER	POWERBOAT
OOLAK		TOWBOAT	SPEEDBOAT
QBOAT	CANALER		STEAMBOAT
SHOUT	COASTER	CANALLER	STEAMSHIP
	COLLIER	INDIAMAN	
DROGER	DREDGER	CABLESHIP	
LAUNCH	DRIFTER	GUARDSHIP	

WARSHIPS

LST	UBOAT	PTBOAT	FLATTOP
RAM	ANDREW	CARRACK	GUNBOAT
BOYER	CARACK	CORSAIR	LANTCHA
SCOUT	CHASER	CRUISER	MONITOR

SNORKEL	FLAGSHIP	MANOFWAR	FIRSTRATE
WARSHIP	GALLEASS	BOMBARDER	MINELAYER
CORVETTE	GALLIASS	DESTROYER	SUBMARINE
FIRESHIP	IRONCLAD	EAGLEBOAT	

OARED VESSELS

BAC	BUNGO	CAYUCO	CURRANE
BUM	CANOE	CORIAL	DROMOND
COG	COBLE	DINGEY	FOUROAR
GIG	DINGY	DUGOUT	GONDOLA
	DONGA	GALLEY	JANGADA
ACON	DUNGA	GOUPHA	LAKATOI
DINK	FLOAT	JANGAR	MASOOLA
DORY	FUNNY	KUPHAR	PAIROAR
GUFA	GOOFA	LERRET	PIROGUE
KUFA	JOLLY	NUGGAR	SCULLER
MULE	KAYAK	OOMIAK	SKIPPET
OARS	KELEK	OUMIAC	TRIREME
PAHI	MOSES	PITPAN	UNIREME
PLAT	PRAHU	PUNGEY	
PRAH	PUNGY	RANDAN	BIDARKEE
PRAO	SCULL	ROBROY	BULLBOAT
PRAU	SHELL	SEXERN	COCKBOAT
PROA	SKIFF	TORPID	DUCKBOAT
PUNT	UMIAK	UMIACK	GUNDALOW
RAFT	VINTA	WHERRY	LONGBOAT
SCOW	WAAPA		
WAKA		ALMADIA	BIRCHBARK
	BAIDAK	ALMADIE	BUCENTAUR
ACCON	BALLAM	BIDARKA	CATAMARAN
BALSA	BAROTO	BUCKEYE	OUTRIGGER
BANCA	BATEAU	CASCARA	TOOTHPICK
BARIS	BIREME	CORACLE	
BIDAR	BUGEYE	CURRACH	
BIRCH	CAYUCA	CURRAGH	

GENERAL

TOW	FERRY	SEALER	FLOTILLA
	FLEET	SLAVER	LIFEBOAT
BOAT	LINER	TANKER	
HULK	PRORE	TONNER	CANALBOAT
KEEL	RACER	VESSEL	FERRYBOAT
MAIL	YACHT	WHALER	FREIGHTER
MARD			PRIVATEER
MARN	ARMADA	PONTOON	TRANSPORT
NAVY	CUTTER	VEDETTE	WHALESHIP
	MARINE		
CRAFT	PACKET	DERELICT	

PARTS OF SHIPS

AFT	SNY	DECK	HULL
BOW	BACK	DOCK	JACK
BOX	BEAK	GAFF	KEEL
FID	BIBB	HEAD	LOOF
NEF	BITT	HELM	MAST
RIB	BOOM	HOLD	NOSE
RUN	BRIG	HULK	POLE

POOP	KEVEL	BOLLARD	SPANKER
PORT	ORLOP	BULWARK	SPIRKET
PROW	SNAPE	BUMPKIN	TOPMAST
RAIL	SPRIT	COUNTER	YARDARM
SKAG	STERN	FORETOP	
SKEG	WAIST	FUTTOCK	BEAKHEAD
SPAR		GANGWAY	BOWSPRIT
SPIR	BRIDGE	GUNWALE	BULLSEYE
STEM	BUNKER	JIBSTAY	CASEMATE
YARD	CANVAS	KEELSON	CUTWATER
	GALLEY	KILLICK	FOREFOOT
BILGE	GUNNEL	KNUCKLE	FOREJACK
BOWER	ISLAND	MAINTOP	FOREMAST
CABIN	RUDDER	SCUPPER	FOREYARD
DAVIT	STEEVE	SCUTTLE	MAINMAST
HATCH	STRAKE	SNORKEL	PORTHOLE
HAWSE	TILLER		WATERWAY

FAMOUS SHIPS

ARGO	TAINUI	TITANIC	SAVANNAH
FRAM	OREGON		TAKITUNU
GJOA		BISMARCK	YORKTOWN
NINA	ARIZONA	BONHOMME	
	HOROUTA	CLERMONT	LUSITANIA
AOTEA	MATATUA	ENDEAVOR	MAYFLOWER
ARAWA	MONITOR	GRAFSPEE	
MAINE	OLYMPIA	HALFMOON	BIRKENHEAD
PINTA	PELICAN	HARTFORD	SANTAMARIA
	REVENGE	MERRIMAC	
BOUNTY	SQUALUS	MISSOURI	

TRIBES, PEOPLE, NATIVES

NORTH OF MEXICO

LO	ERIE	TATU	HAIDA
	HANO	TEWA	HURON
AHT	HARE	TIOU	KANSA
AUK	HOHE	UTAH	KASKA
FOX	HOPI	WACO	KERES
HOH	HUPA	YANA	KIOWA
ITA	IONI	YUIT	KOROA
KAW	IOWA	YUKI	KWAPA
OFO	KASO	YUMA	LIPAN
OTO	LOUP	ZUNI	MAIDU
REE	MOKI		MAKAH
SAC	MONO	ACOMA	MIAMI
SIA	NOZI	ALEUT	MINGO
UTE	OTOE	ATNAH	MODOC
WEA	PIMA	BANAK	MOQUI
	PIRO	BLOOD	NAMBE
ADAI	POMO	BRULE	OMAHA
ATRA	SAUK	CADDO	OSAGE
COOS	SERI	CHAUI	OZARK
CREE	TAKU	COMOX	PECOS
CROW	TANO	CONOY	PIUTE
DENE	TAOS	CREEK	PONCA

SARSI	NAVAHO	CHUMASH	YONKALA
SIOUX	NAVAJO	CHUMAWI	
SITKA	NAUSET	CLALLAM	ALGONKIN
SKIDI	NEVOME	CLATSOP	APALACHI
SOOKE	NIPMUC	COLCINE	ARIKAREE
TETON	NIPMUK	DHEGIHA	ARIVAIPA
TIGUA	NOOTKA	ESSELEN	ATFALATI
TINNE	OGLALA	HELLELT	CAHUILLA
TONTO	ONEIDA	HIDATSA	CHEROKEE
TWANA	OTTAWA	HUCHNOM	CHEYENNE
UCHEE	PAIUTE	KITAMAT	CHIMAKUM
UINTA	PAKAWA	KITLOPE	CHIPPEWA
UNAMI	PAPAGO	KLAMATH	COLVILLE
WAPPO	PATWIN	KOASATI	COMANCHE
WASCO	PAWNEE	KOPRINO	COWICHAN
WASHO	PEORIA	KUTCHIN	COWICHIN
WIYAT	PEQUOT	KUTENAI	COYOTERO
WIYOT	PERICU	LLANERO	DELAWARE
YAMEL	PIEGAN	LUISENO	DIEGUENO
YAMIL	PUEBLO	MAHICAN	FLATHEAD
YAZOO	QUAPAW	MOHEGAN	HITCHITI
YUCHI	SALINA	MOHICAN	HUNKPAPA
YUROK	SALISH	MONACHI	ILLINOIS
	SAMISH	MONTAUK	IROQUOIS
	SANTEE	NANAIMO	KENIPSIM
ABNAKI	SEKANE	NATCHEZ	KICKAPOO
AGAWAM	SEKANI	NIANTIC	KIKATSIK
AHTENA	SENECA	NIPMUCK	KLASKINO
APACHE	SLAVEY	OJIBWAY	KLIKITAT
ATUAMI	SPOKAN	PUJUNAN	KWAKIUTL
BABINE	SUTAIO	SANETCH	MALECITE
BILOXI	TAGISH	SANPOIL	MASKEGON
CAHITA	TENINO	SANSARC	MENOMINI
CALUSA	TOLOWA	SERRANO	MIMDRENO
CAYUGA	TONGAS	SHASTAN	NESPELIM
CAYUSE	TUNICA	SHAWNEE	NEZPERCE
CHATOT	TUTELO	SHUSWAP	NOTTOWAY
COCOPA	UMPQUA	SIKSIKA	OKINAGAN
COOSUK	WALAPI	STIKINE	ONONDAGA
DAKOTA	WIKENO	TAHLTAN	PANAMINT
DOGRIB	WINTUN	TAKELMA	POWHATAN
EYEISH	YAKIMA	TEPEHUA	QUERECHO
FARAON	YAMASI	TIMICUA	QUILEUTE
HAIDAH	YOKUTS	TLINGIT	SAHAPTIN
HAINAI		TONKAWA	SEMINOLE
HAISLA	ALIBAMU	TULALIP	SHOSHONI
INNUIT	AMERIND	TUTUTNI	SIHASAPA
ISLETA	ANDARKO	WAICURI	SISSETON
KOSIMO	ARAPAHO	WAILAKI	SNONOWAS
KUCHIN	ARIKARA	WALAPAI	SOUHEGAN
LENAPE	BANNOCK	WAMESIT	TLAKLUIT
MANDAN	BEOTHUK	WISHOSK	TUSKEGEE
MAYEYE	CAHOKIA	WISHRAM	UMATILLA
MICMAC	CARRIZO	WYANDOT	UNALASKA
MOHAVE	CATAWBA	YAKUTAT	WAHPETON
MOHAWK	CHEHALI	YAMHILL	YAMASSEE
MOLALA	CHILCAT	YANKTON	YONKALLA
NAHANE	CHINOOK	YAVAPAI	
NASHUA	CHIWERE		
	CHOCTAW		

MEXICO-CENTRAL AMERICA

MAM	NAHUA	MIXTEC	OTOMACA
BOTO	OLIVE	NEVOME	OTOMACO
CHOL	OPATA	OTOMAC	PIRANDA
CUNA	OTOMI	PAKAWA	POKOMAM
ITZA	PETEN	PAPAGO	TARASCO
JOVA	PINTO	PERICU	TEPANEC
MAYA	PIPIL	SABUJA	TEPEHUA
MAYO	SMOOS	SERIAN	TIRRIBI
MIXE	TAINO	SUERRE	TZENTAL
PAME	XINCA	TARASC	TZOTZIL
PIMA	YAQUI	TOLTEC	WAICURI
RAMA	ZOQUE	WOOLWA	ZACATEC
SERI			ZAPATEC
SUMO	AMUSGO	AMISHGO	
TECA	ARAWAK	BAKAIRI	
TECO	BORUCA	CARIBEE	CHANABAL
ULVA	BRIBRI	CHONTAL	CHAPANEC
VOTO	BRUNCA	CHUMULU	JACALTEC
WABI	CAHITA	COTONAM	MAZATECA
XOVA	CARIBI	GUALACA	MAZATECO
	CHOCHO	GUATUSO	MELCHORA
	DARIEN	HUASTEC	MOSQUITO
AZTEC	DIRIAN	HUATUSO	OROTINAN
CARIB	DORASK	JICAQUE	POKONCHI
CHUJE	EUDEVE	MAZAHUA	POPOLOCA
CUEVA	GUAYMI	MAZATEC	POPOLOCO
HUAVE	GUETAC	MIXTECA	TLASCALA
KICHE	KEKCHI	MIXTECO	TOTONACA
LENCA	LUCAYO	NAYARIT	TZUTUHIL
MOCOA	MANGUE	NICARAO	ZACATECO
			ZAPOTECA

SOUTH AMERICA

GES	INCA	ARARA	PASSE
ITE	INKA	ARAUA	PIOJE
ONA	ITEN	ARUAC	PIOXE
URO	IXIL	AUCAN	QUITU
URU	MAKU	BRAVO	SAMBO
YAO	MOJO	BUGRE	SENCI
	MOXO	CAITA	SIUSI
AGAZ	MURO	CAMPA	UAUPE
ANDE	MUSO	CHANE	VEJOZ
ANTA	MUZO	CHIMU	WAURA
ANTI	NUZO	CHOCO	YAGUA
AUCA	PEBA	CHOLO	YAMEO
BARE	PIRO	COLAN	YUNCA
BORO	PURU	CUNZA	
CAME	TAMA	GESAN	AMORUA
CANA	TAPA	GUANA	APALAI
CANE	TOBA	GUATO	APIACA
CARA	TRIO	HUARE	APIBON
CIXO	TUPI	INERI	ARAUNA
CORA	TUPY	MBAYA	ATORAI
DIAU	URAN	OYANA	AYMARA
DUIT	YNCA	PALTA	BANIVA
GHES		PAMPA	BETOYA

BORORO	OREJON	CASHIBO	TOTONAC
CANAPI	PIAROA	CHARRUA	UARAYCU
CANCHI	PURUHA	CHATINO	UGARONO
CANELO	QUICHE	CHIBCHA	WOYAWAY
CARAHO	SALIVA	CHIRINO	YUSTAGA
CARAJA	SAMUCU	CHOROTE	
CARIRI	SETIBO	CHOROTI	ALIKULUF
CAVINA	SHUARA	CHUNCHU	AMAHUACA
CAYAPA	SIPIBO	CHUROYA	APOLISTA
CAYAPO	TACANA	CIBONEY	ARAPAHOE
CHANCA	TAHAMI	FUEGIAN	BARBACOA
CHANGO	TAMOYO	GOAJIRO	BOTOCUDO
CHAYMA	TAPAJO	GUAHIBO	CADIUEIO
CHORTI	TAPUYA	GUARANI	CAINGANG
COCAMA	TARUMA	GUAYMIE	CANAMARY
COCOMA	TIMOTE	HUANUCO	CARICUNA
COFANE	TOTORO	HUANUCU	CHAMBIOA
COROPO	TUCANO	ITONAMA	CHAVANTE
COTOXO	TUNEBO	JAVAHAI	CHIQUITO
GALIBI	VILELA	LORENZO	CHIRIANA
GOYANA	WARRAU	MAIPURE	COCONUCO
HIBITO	WITOTO	MAPUCHE	CONCHULU
IXIANA	YAHGAN	MARIANA	CORABECA
JAPURA	YAHUNA	MIRANHA	COVARECA
JAVAHE	YARURO	MOLUCHE	GUARAUNO
JAVAHI	YURUNA	PAMPEAN	GUAYAQUI
JIVARO	ZAPARA	PATAGON	JAVITERO
JUCUNA	ZAPARO	PAUMARI	MAYORUNA
JUMANA		PAYAGUA	MOSETENA
KECHUA	ANDAQUI	PUELCHE	PICUNCHE
LAMANO	APALAII	PUINAVI	PURUPURU
MACUSI	ARAUCAN	QUECHUA	QUERENDI
MIRANA	ARECUNA	SARIGUE	TAMANACO
MUISCA	AREKUNA	SATIENO	TOROMONA
MUYACA	AYAHUCA	SINSIGA	TUMUPASA
MUYSCA	CABOCLO	TARIANA	YAMAMADI
NASCAN	CAINGUA	TEHUECO	YAUAPERY
NOCTEN	CAMACAN	TERRABA	YURUCARE
OMAGUA	CARANGA	TIMBIRA	YURUCARI

EUROPE

GEG	Alb.	GAEL	Celt.	REMI	Belg.
LAK	Russ.	GAUL	Fr.	RUSS	
LAZ	Russ.	GEAT	Swed.	SCOT	Celt.
VAN	Russ.	GHEG	Alb.	SERB	Slav.
VOD	Finn.	GOTH	Ger.	SLAV	
VOT	Finn.	IMER	Russ.	SORB	Slav.
		JUTE	Ger.	SVAN	Russ.
AVAR	Russ.	KAMI	Russ.	TOSK	Alb.
BALT	Lith.	KOMI	Russ.	UBII	Ger.
BOII	Celt.	KURI	Russ.	VEND	Slav.
CELT	Brit., Fr.	LAPP	Scan.	VEPS	Finn.
CHAM	Alb.	LAZE	Russ.	VOTE	Finn.
CHUD	Finn.	LAZI	Russ.	VOTH	Finn.
DANE		LETT	Lith.	WEND	Slav.
ESTH		MANX	Celt.	WOTE	Finn.
FINN		PICT	Brit.	ZIPS	Ger.
FLEM	Belg.	POLE			

AEQUI	It.	ABKHAS	Russ.	VOLSKI	It.
ALANI	Russ.	ADIGHE	Russ.	VOTYAK	Finn.
ALANS	Russ.	ALEMAN	Ger.	ZYRIAN	Russ.
ALMAN	Ger.	ALMAIN	Ger.		
ATTIC	Gr.	ANGLES	Ger.	AEOLIAN	Gr.
AVARS	Russ.	BASQUE	Sp., Fr.	AEQUIAN	It.
BESSI	Gr.	BATAVI	Ger.	BASHKIR	Russ.
BOIKO	Russ.	BOSHAS	Russ.	BELGIAN	
CAITI	Ger.	BRETON	Fr.	BOSNIAN	Slav.
CROAT	Slav.	BRITON		BRYTHON	Celt.
CYMRY	Celt.	BULGAR		BUKEYET	Russ.
CZECH	Slav.	CARIAN	Gr.	CANDIOT	Gr.
DARGO	Russ.	CHATTI	Ger.	CATALAN	Sp.
DIGOR	Russ.	DORIAN	Gr.	CHECHEN	Russ.
DUTCH		FRENCH		CHUVASH	Bulg.
ELYMI	It.	GASCON	Fr.	CYPRIOT	Gr.
ERSAR	Russ.	GEATAS	Swed.	DARDANI	Gr.
FRANK	Ger.	GERMAN		DARGHIN	Russ.
GALGA	Russ.	GOIDEL	Celt.	FALISCI	It.
GREEK		HANSAS	Ger.	FAROESE	Dan.
GUZUL	Russ.	HERULI	Ger.	FIRBOLG	Celt.
GYPSY		HRVATI	Slav.	FLEMING	Belg.
IBERI	Sp.	IBERES	Sp.	FRISIAN	Ger.
ICENI	Brit.	INGUSH	Russ.	GADITAN	Sp.
IJORE	Finn.	IONIAN	Gr.	GALLEGO	Sp.
IRISH	Celt.	KABARD	Russ.	GENOESE	It.
KAZAN	Russ.	KYURIN	Russ.	HELLENE	Gr.
KUMAN	Hung.	LADINO	Swiss	HESSIAN	Ger.
KUMYK	Turk.	LITVAK	Lith.	IBERIAN	Sp.
KYMRY	Celt.	MAGYAR	Hung.	ISTRIAN	It.
LADIN	Swiss	MORDVA	Russ.	ITALIAN	
MARSI	Ger., It.	MOSCHI	Russ.	KARTHLI	Russ.
MAZUR	Pol.	MOSCVA	Russ.	KARTVEL	Russ.
MORDV	Russ.	NEMEAN	Gr.	KASHUBE	Ger.
NOGAI	Russ.	NERVII	Celt.	LATVIAN	Lith.
NORSE	Scan.	NORMAN	Fr., Scan.	LEONESE	Sp.
OSCAN	It.	PADUAN	It.	LESBIAN	Gr.
OSSET	Russ.	PICARD	Fr.	LOMBARD	It.
PECHT	Celt.	POLACK	Pol.	MALTESE	
PISAN	It.	ROMANY	Gyp.	MANXMAN	Celt.
POLAB	Slav.	RUTULI	It.	MERCIAN	Eng.
POMAK	Bulg.	SABINE	It.	MORDVIN	Russ.
QUADI	Ger.	SAFINI	It.	OXONIAN	Eng.
ROMAN	It.	SALIAN	Dutch	PAPHIAN	Gr.
SAXON	Ger.	SAMIAN	Gr.	PARMESE	It.
SCIOT	Gr.	SATRAE	Gr.	PATARIN	It.
SICEL	It.	SICANI	It.	PELASGI	Gr.
SUEVI	Ger.	SICULI	It.	PERMIAK	Finn.
SVANE	Russ.	TAGAUR	Russ.	PERMIAN	Finn.
SWISS		TAVAST	Finn.	RAURACI	Fr.
TAULI	Russ.	TEUTON	Ger.	RAURICI	Fr.
USKOK	Slav.	THEBAN	Gr.	RHODIAN	Gr.
VANNI	Russ.	TUSCAN	It.	RUSSIAN	
VENED	Slav.	UGRJAN	Finn.	RUTHENE	Russ.
VEPSE	Finn.	VANDAL	Ger.	SABELLI	It.
VLACH	Rum.	VANNAI	Russ.	SAMNITE	It.
VOGUL	Finn.	VELIKA	Russ.	SENONES	Celt.
WELSH	Celt.	VENETI	It.	SEQUANI	Celt.
ZHMUD	Lith.	VOLCAE	Celt.	SERBIAN	Slav.

SIENESE	It.	CROATIAN	Slav.	PATAVIAN	It.
SILURES	Eng.	CYPRIOTE	Gr.	PELASGOI	Gr.
SLOVENE	Slav.	ETRUSCAN	It.	PHYRGIAN	Gr.
SPARTAN	Gr.	FRIULIAN	It.	POLABIAN	Slav.
SUEVIAN	Ger.	GALICLAN	Sp.	POLANDER	Pol.
SUIONES	Ger.	GALLEGAN	Sp.	PORTUGEE	
SULIOTE	Gr.	ILLYRIAN	Alb.	PRUSSIAN	Ger.
SWABIAN	Ger.	KARELIAN	Russ.	RHAETIAN	It.
TOLEDAN	Sp.	KASUBIAN	Ger.	RUMANIAN	
UMBRIAN	It.	KHALDIAN	Finn.	RUMELIAN	Bulg.
VAUDOIS	Swiss	KONARIOT	Turk.	RUSSNIAK	Russ.
VESTINI	It.	LEZGHIAN	Russ.	SALOPIAN	Eng.
WALLOON	Belg.	LIGURIAN	It.	SAVOYARD	Fr.
		LIVONIAN	Lith.	SEMNONES	Ger.
ALBANIAN		MAJORCAN	Sp.	SICAMBRI	Ger.
ANDORRAN	Sp.	MAZOVIAN	Ger.	SICILIAN	It.
ARMENIAN		MEGARIAN	Gr.	SILESIAN	Ger.
ASTURIAN	Sp.	MILANESE	It.	SPANIARD	Sp.
AUSTRIAN		MINORCAN	Sp.	THRACIAN	Gr.
BAVARIAN	Ger.	MORAVIAN	Slav.	TYROLESE	Aust.
BISCAYAN	Sp.	NORSEMAN	Scan.	ULTONIAN	Eng.
BOEOTIAN	Gr.	NORTHMAN	Scan.	USIPETES	Ger.
BOHEMIAN	Slav.	PANNONIC	Hung.	VENETIAN	It.
CHERUSCI	Ger.	PARISIAN	Fr.	VISIGOTH	Ger.
CORSICAN	Fr.	PARMESAN	It.	YUGOSLAV	Slav.
		PATARINE	It.		

AFRICA

GA	AFAR	FUNJ	RIFE
GI	AKAN	GALA	RORI
	AKIM	GOGO	SAAN
ABO	AKKA	GOLO	SAHO
ARO	AKRA	GOMA	SARA
EDO	ALUR	GUHA	SERE
EFE	ASHA	HABE	SHLU
EVE	BARI	HARB	SHOA
EWE	BAYA	HEHE	SOGA
FAN	BEJA	HIMA	SUKU
FON	BENI	HOVA	SUSU
FUL	BERI	HUMA	SUTO
FUR	BINI	IDJO	TEBJ
IBO	BOGO	IDYO	TEDA
IJO	BONI	IDZO	TIBU
JUR	BUBE	JAGA	TOMA
KRA	BUBI	KAFA	VILI
KRU	DAGO	KORA	VIRA
KUA	DAZA	KROO	VIRI
LUO	DOKO	LUBA	VITI
LVO	EBOE	LUOH	WAFD
LWO	EFIK	LURI	XOSA
RUA	EGBA	MABA	YAKA
SAN	EJAM	MADI	ZULU
SUK	EKOI	MARI	
VAI	FANG	NAMA	AFIFI
VEI	FIOT	NUBA	AMADI
YAO	FONG	NUPE	ATEBA
	FULA	QUNG	BALAO
ABSI	FUNG	RAVI	BANDA

BANTU	PYGMY	GABOON	ABABDEH
BASSA	RUNDI	GRIQUA	ACHANGO
BATWA	SAKAI	HAMITE	AKWAPIM
BENIN	SERER	HARARI	AMAKOSA
BONGO	SHLUH	HEIKUM	AMAZULU
BORAN	SHONA	HERERO	ANTAIVA
BRAVA	SONGO	IGBARA	ASHANTI
CHAGA	SOTHO	IGBIRA	BABONGO
CONGO	SOTIK	IKBERE	BACONGO
DADJO	SWAZI	KABYLE	BAGANDA
DINKA	TEMBU	KAFFIR	BAGARRA
DUALA	TEMNE	KANURI	BAGGARA
FANTI	TIBBU	KIKUYU	BAKALAI
FANWE	TINNI	KORANA	BAKALEI
FULAH	TONGA	KPUESI	BAKONGO
FULBE	VOLOF	LATUKA	BAKUNDA
FUNJE	WAASI	LIBYAN	BAKWIRI
FUNJI	WARRI	LOBALE	BALANTA
GABON	WARUA	LOTUKO	BALANTE
GALLA	WAYAO	MAKARI	BAMBARA
GANDA	WOLOF	MARAVI	BAMBUBA
GIBBI	YOLOF	MBONDO	BAMBUTE
GREBO	ZANDE	MBUNDA	BANGALA
HABAB		MPONDO	BANYORO
HABBE	ABABUA	MURREE	BARONGA
HAUSA	ABANTU	NUBIAN	BAROTSE
IDDIO	ABATOA	NYAMBE	BARUNDI
IGARA	ABATUA	NZAMBI	BASONGO
INKRA	ABATWA	OBONGA	BATEKES
JOLOF	ABONGO	OVAMPO	BATONGA
KAFFA	ACHIAS	PANGWE	BATUSSI
KAMBA	AMHARA	POKOMO	BEDOUIN
KHUAI	ANTEVA	SENUSI	BULANDA
KIOKO	AZANDE	SESUTO	BUNYORO
KONDE	BAFIOT	SHAGIA	BUSHMAN
KONGO	BAHIMA	SHILHA	CABINDA
KREPI	BAHUMA	SHURRI	CUSHITE
LANGO	BAHUTU	SOMALI	DADSCHO
LENDU	BAKELE	SONGOI	DAHOMAN
LUNDA	BAKUBA	SUKUMA	DANAGLA
LUREM	BAKUTU	SURHAI	DANAKIL
MAKUA	BALAWU	THONGA	DANKALI
MAKWA	BALOLO	TIMNEH	FALASHA
MANDE	BALUBA	TUAREG	FALLATA
MARRI	BANYAI	WABENA	GAETULI
MASAI	BASOGA	WABUMA	GETULAN
MAURI	BASUTO	WAGOGO	GUANCHE
MBUBA	BATOKA	WAGUHA	GUHAYNA
MENDE	BEDUIN	WAHABI	HARATIN
MENDI	BERBER	WAHEHE	IMOHAGH
MONGO	BERTAT	WASOGA	KABINDA
MOSGU	BORANA	WATUSI	KABONGA
MOSSI	BULLOM	WAVIRA	KIRUNDI
MUTER	CHAGGA	WOCHUA	KOLDAJI
NANDI	CHAWIA	YAKALA	KROOBOY
NEGRO	DAMARA	YORUBA	LOATUKO
NILOT	DOROBO	ZARAMO	LUGANDA
NYORO	FANTEE	ZEHUGA	MACHOGO
PONDO	FULANI	ZENAGA	MAIACCA

MAKONDE	SWAHILI	AUXUMITE	MOROCCAN
MAREHAN	TUKULER	BAGHIRMI	NEGRILLO
MASHONA	TURKANA	BAROLONG	NIAMNIAM
MOGRABI	UGANDAN	BATETELA	NIGERIAN
MPANGWE	WABUNGA	BECHUANA	NYAMWEZI
MUNANDI	WACHAGA	BISHARIN	RAHANVIN
NAMAQUA	WAGWENO	CANGUELA	SAKALAVA
NEGRITO	WAKAMBA	CONGOESE	SUDANESE
NEGROID	WAKWAFI	EGYPTIAN	TUNISIAN
NILOTIC	WAKWAVI	HADENDOA	WAMBUTTI
PAHOUIN	WAMBUBA	HARRATIN	WANGATTA
SANDAWE	WAMBUGA	IMOSHAGH	WAPOKOMO
SANDAWI	WANGONI	KABABISH	WASAGARA
SENOUSI	WANYASA	KARAMOJO	
SHAIGIA	WASANGO	KUKURUKU	DANAGALEH
SHAMMAR	WASEGUA	LIBERIAN	MANGBATTU
SHILLUH	WONGARA	MAGHRIBI	MATABELES
SHILLUK		MAKARAKA	MAUGRABIN
SHUKRIA	ALGERIAN	MALAGASY	OVAHERERO
SONGHAI	AMATEMBU	MANDINGO	WANDOROBO
SONGHAY	ANDOROBO	MATABELE	
SONGHOI	ANGOLESE	MOGREBEE	
SUKKIIM	ASHANTEE	MOMBOTTU	

ASIA, AUSTRONESIA
CHINA, MONGOLIA, SIBERIA

HEH	GOLDI	BALKAR	UIGHUR
HEI	HAKKA	BELTIR	YAOMIN
YAO	HOKLO	BURIAT	
	IGDYR	DUNGAN	ALTAIAN
CHUD	KALKA	DURBAN	AMOYESE
DAUR	KAZAK	GILIAK	BOUROUT
GOLD	LAMUT	HAINAN	BUKEYET
HAPU	MOGUL	KALMUK	CHUKCHI
LOLO	OLCHA	KALMYK	DZUNGAR
MANS	OLCHI	KASSAK	ITELMES
MIAO	SAGAI	KHALKA	KALMUCK
NOSU	SERES	KOIBAL	KALMYCK
SAKA	SOYOT	KORIAK	KAMASIN
SART	TATAR	MANCHU	KHALKHA
SHIK	TURKI	MANTZU	KIRGHIZ
TOBA	UIGUR	MONGOL	OROCHON
USUN	USSUN	OROKON	SAMOYED
UZUN	UZBEK	OSTYAK	TURKMAN
	YAKUT	SHARRA	YENISEI
BURUT	YURAK	TARTAR	YUKAGIR
CHUDE		TAVGHI	
DAURI	ALTAIC	TELEUT	TURKOMAN
ELEUT	AMOYAN	TUNGUS	YUKAGHIR

JAPAN, AUSTRALIA, PHILIPPINES

ATA	AINO	SULU	BICOL
ATI	AINU		BIKOL
GOA	FIJI	ARAWA	DIERI
	KOKO	BATAK	ILOCO
AETA	MORO	BATAN	ILOKO

KIWAI	IGOROT	DADAYAG	VISAYAN
LANAO	ITALON	GADDANG	
LUCHU	ITAVES	ILOCANO	AWABAKAL
MACRI	KANAKA	ILOKANO	BUKIDNON
NIUAN	KOIARI	ILONGOT	CHAMORRO
TAGAL	MANOBO	ILPIRRA	CHINHWAN
YAKAN	MONTES	JOLOANO	FORMOSAN
	PAPUAN	KALINGA	HAWAIIAN
	SAMBAL	KOITAPU	IGORROTE
APAYAO	SAMOAN	LUCHUAN	KANKANAI
ARUNTA	TAGALA	MANGYAN	MONTESCO
BALUGA	TONGAN	NABOLOT	PAMPANGA
BILAAN	VISAYA	NEGRITO	PAMPANGO
BISAYA	YAMATO	RINGATU	QUIANGAN
BONTOK	ZAMBAL	SANGGIL	TAHITIAN
GADDAN		SATSUMA	TINGGIAN
IBANAG	BISAYAN	SUBANUM	
IBILAO	BISHMAN	TAGALOG	
IFUGAO	CAGAYAN	TIRURAI	

INDIA, PAKISTAN, TIBET, NEPAL

AO	CHANG	AGHORI	RAJPUT
HO	COORG	ANGAMI	RAMUSI
	DAFLA	ARAINS	SANTAL
AKA	DARDI	ARLENG	SAVARA
GOR	DOGRA	ARORAS	SHERPA
JAT	DRUPA	BADAGA	SINDHI
KHA	GADDI	BALUCH	TANGUT
KOL	GUJAR	BEHARI	TELUGU
MEO	HINDI	BHOTIA	TIPURA
	HINDU	BHUMIJ	YERAVA
AHIR	JUANG	BHUTIA	YUECHI
AOUL	KANDE	BIHARI	
AWAN	KHASI	CHAMAR	
BHAR	KOERI	CHAMPA	BALUCHI
BHIL	KONDH	DROKPA	BANGASH
DARD	KORWA	DRUKPA	BAZIGAR
GARO	KOTAR	GURKHA	BENGALI
GOND	KUMNI	HINDOO	BHOTIYA
KOCH	KUNBI	HOLEYA	BHUTANI
KOLI	KURMI	JHURIA	DRAVIDA
KUKI	LIMBU	KALWAR	GUJRATI
MAGH	MIKIR	KANWAR	KACHARI
MAGI	MUNDA	KHARIA	KHARWAR
MARI	MUREE	KHASIA	KHASIYA
NAGA	NEWAR	KODAGU	KURUMBA
NAIR	NURMI	KOMATI	LAMBADI
RAIS	ORAON	KONYAK	MADRASI
REKI	ORIYA	KURUBA	MARATHA
TODA	SAORA	LEPCHA	MARWARI
TULU	SAURA	LOHANA	ORAKZAI
TURI	TAMIL	MADIGA	PUNJABI
	URIYA	MANGAR	SHERANI
ANGKA	VEDDA	MISHMI	TAGHLIK
BALTI	WAKHI	PAHARI	TIBETAN
		PANJAB	

MIDDLE EAST, AFGHANISTAN

AUS	MUKRI	GHEBER	DURZADA
LUR	NEJDI	GILAKI	GHILZAI
	OMANI	HAZARA	HADJEMI
ARAB	SHIAH	HEJAZI	IRANIAN
GHUZ	SUNNI	KAFFIR	ISRAELI
IBAD	TAJIK	MYSIAN	KHOKANI
KURD	TAULI	PAMIRI	OSMANLI
SAFI	TEKKE	PATHAN	OTTOMAN
SEID	YEZDI	SELJUK	PAKHTUN
SLEB	YURUK	SHIITE	PUKHTUN
TURK	ZIRAK	SULABA	PERSIAN
		SULAIB	SARACEN
FARSI	AFGHAN	SUNNEE	SOGDIAN
IHLAT	AFSHAR	SYRIAN	SUNNITE
IRAKI	AUSHAR	TUNGAN	VIDDHAL
IRAQI	BRAHUI	YEMINI	
KAFIR	DEHWAR	YEZIDI	
KAJAR	DUNGAN		ACHAZKAI
KHUZI	DURANI	BELUCHI	BACTRIAN
MAHRI	GALCHA	BELUCKI	LEBANESE

LAOS, CAMBODIA, VIETNAM, MYANMAR

WA	THO	KAREN	YAOYIN
		KHMER	
KAW	AHOM	MUONG	ANAMESE
KHA	AKIU		BURMESE
KUI	CHIN	BALAWA	LAOTIAN
LAI	KADU	BURMAN	MEITHEI
LAO	KUKI	KACHIN	PALAUNG
MEO	LOLO	KHAMTI	
MON	SHAM	LUSHAI	ANNAMESE
MRU	SHAN	PEGUAN	TONKINESE
TAI	TSIN		

INDONESIA, MALAYA

BUGI	KAYAN	REJANG	TORADJA
CHAM	MALAY	SAMSAN	
DYAK	MURUT	SASSAK	ACHINESE
IBAN	PUNAN	SELUNG	BALINESE
THAI	SAKAI	SEMANG	JAVANESE
	SAMAL	TORAJA	MACASSAR
BAJAU	SASAK		MADURESE
BATTA	TZAAM	BAKATAN	MAKASSAR
BUKAT		BORNEAN	SUDANESE
CHIAM	ALFURO	LAMPONG	SUMATRAN
DAYAK	BILAAN	MALAYAN	TAGBUANA
DUSUN	KALANG	NIASESE	TIMORESE
JAKUN	NESIOT	SIAMESE	

THE UNIVERSE
PLANETS AND SATELLITES

Planet	Satellite	Planet	Satellite	Planet	Satellite
Mars	DEIMOS		HYPERION		EUROPA
	PHOBOS		ENCELADUS		HESTIA
Earth	MOON	Uranus	ARIEL		DEMETER
Pluto			OBERON		ADRASTEA
Venus			MIRANDA		AMALTHEA
Saturn			TITANIA		CALLISTO
	RHEA		UMBRIEL		GANYMEDE
	DIONE		IO		POSEIDON
	MIMAS	Jupiter	PAN	Mercury	
	TITAN		HERA	Neptune	NEREID
	PHOEBE		HADES		TRITON
	TETHYS				
	IAPETUS				

STARS

SUN	ACRAB	NIHAL	GIENAH
YED	ACRUX	NUNKI	HYADES
	AGENA	PHACD	KOCHAB
ADIB	ALCOR	PHAET	LESATH
ALYA	ALGOL	RIGEL	MARFIK
ATIK	ALKES	SABIK	MARKAB
AZHA	ANCHA	SAIPH	MEGREZ
BEID	ARKAB	SPICA	MEISSA
CAPH	ARNEB	TANIA	MENKAR
DUHR	ATLAS	WEZEN	MENKIB
ENIF	BAHAM	ZOSMA	MERKEB
IZAR	BIHAM		MEROPE
JUGA	CHARA	ACAMAR	MIRACH
JUZA	CUJAM	ADHARA	MIRFAK
KAUS	CURSA	ALBALI	MURZIN
KEID	DABIH	ALGEDI	NEKKAR
KIDS	DELTA	ALHENA	PHECDA
MAIA	DENEB	ALIOTH	PLEIAD
MIRA	DIFDA	ALKAID	POLLUX
NAOS	DUBHE	ALMACH	PROPUS
NATH	ERRAI	ALNASI	SCHEAT
PHAD	FURUD	ALTAIR	SIRIUS
SADR	GEMMA	ALTAIS	SMYRNA
SALM	HAMAL	ALTARF	THUBAN
SKAT	HOMAN	ALUDRA	YILDUN
SOPT	KIFFA	ANCHAT	ZANIAH
UNUK	MATAR	ARIDED	ZAURAK
VEGA	MEDIA	BOTEIN	
WEGA	MERAK	CASTOR	DOGSTAR
WEZN	MIRAC	DHENEB	POLARIS
	MIRAK	ELNATH	
	MIZAR	ETAMIN	

ASTEROIDS

IDA	IRIS	FLORA	VESTA
EROS	JUNO	IRENE	EGERIA
HEBE	CERES	METIS	HYGEIA

ICARUS	THETIS	FORTUNA	STARFISH
PALLAS	ASTRAEA	LUTETIA	
PSYCHE	EUNOMIA	MASSALIA	

COMETS AND METEORS

ABE	IKEYA	HALLEY	HUMASON
	KIRCH	HOLMES	MECHAIN
FAYE	KOPFF	LAHIRE	PERRINE
GALE	MRKOS	LEXELL	STEARNS
SEIU	SWIFT	OLBERS	
TOBA	WELLS	OTERMA	BORRELLY
WILD		TEMPEL	GRISCHOW
WOLF	ALCOCK	TEWFIK	KOHOUTEK
	BROOKS	TUTTLE	WESTPHAL
AREND	COGGIA	ZIMMER	
BAADE	DANIEL		MOREHOUSE
BIELA	DONATI	BARNARD	
BRAHE	FINLAY	BRORSEN	
ENCKE	FORBES	DARREST	

CONSTELLATIONS

ARA	altar	AQUILA	eagle	SAGITTA	arrow
APUS	bird of paradise	AURIGA	wagoner	SERPENS	snake
ARGO	ship	BOOTES	herdsman	SEXTANS	sextant
CRUX	cross	CAELUM	tool	CIRCINUS	compasses
GRUS	crane	CARINA	keel	EQUULEUS	colt
LYNX	lynx	CORONA	crown	ERIDANUS	river
LYRA	lyre	CORVUS	crow	HERCULES	hero
PAVO	peacock	CRATER	cup	LEOMINOR	lesser lion
URSA	bear	CYGNUS	swan	SCULPTOR	
VELA	sails	DORADO	swordfish		sculptor's shop
CANIS	dog	FORNAX	furnace	ANDROMEDA	
CETUS	whale	HYDRUS	watersnake		chained lady
DRACO	dragon	OCTANS	octant	CENTAURUS	centaur
HYDRA	water monster	PICTOR	easel	DELPHINUS	dolphin
INDUS	Indian	PISCIS	fish	MONOCERUS	unicorn
LEPUS	hare	PUPPIS	stern	OPHIUCHUS	
LUPUS	wolf	SCUTUM	shield		serpent holder
MALUS	mast	TUCANA	toucan	RETICULUM	net
MENSA	table mountain	VOLANS	flying fish	VULPECULA	fox
MUSCA	fly	CEPHEUS	monarch	CASSIOPEIA	
NORMA	square	COLUMBA	dove		lady in the chair
ORION	hunter	LACERTA	lizard	CHAMAELEON	
PYXIS	compass	PEGASUS	flying horse		chameleon
ANTLIA	pump	PERSEUS	rescuer	HOROLOGIUM	clock
		PHOENIX	fabulous bird	TRIANGULUM	triangle

ZODIACAL CONSTELLATIONS

LEO	Lion	GEMINI	Twins	AQUARIUS	
ARIES	Ram	PISCES	Fishes		Water-Bearer
LIBRA	Scales	TAURUS	Bull	CAPRICORN	Ram
VIRGO	Virgin	SCORPIO	Scorpion	SAGITTARIUS	Archer
CANCER	Crab				

MAN'S PROBES INTO OUTER SPACE

*Indicates former USSR

ARTIFICIAL SATELLITES AND SPACESHIPS

OAO	INJUN	POLYOT*	TRANSIT
OGO	LOFTI	PROTON*	VOSKHOD*
OSO	LUNIK*	RANGER	
	MIDAS	SYNCOM	ALOUETTE
ECHO	RELAY	VOSTOK*	ELEKTRON*
ESSA	SAMOS	YANTAR*	EXPLORER
GREB	TIROS		INTELSAT
LUNA*	TOPSI	COURIER	LANIBIRD
MARS*	TRAAC	MARINER	SURVEYOR
SNAP		MERCURY	VANGUARD
VELA	APOLLO	MOLNIYA*	
ZOND*	COSMOS*	ORBITER	EARLYBIRD
	GEMINI	PIONEER	
ARIEL	NIMBUS	SPUTNIK*	DISCOVERER
IDCSP	PAGEOS	TELSTAR	FRIENDSHIP

ASTRONAUTS

APT	KIZIM*	LOVELL	SHEPARD
SEE	LAIKA*	NELSON	WILCUTT
	OCHOA	NEWMAN	YEGOROV*
CARR	SCOTT	SHIRRA	
JETT	SMITH	TANNER	BELYAYEV*
RIDE	TITOV*	TYURIN	BIKOVSKY*
ROSS	WEITZ		COCKRELL
VOSS	WHITE	BASSETT	KRIKALEV
WALZ	YOUNG	BLACKIE*	LINNEHAN
		BLUFORD	MCDIVITT
	ALORIN	BREEZIE*	POPOVICH*
ASHBY	ALTMAN	CLERVOY	ROMINGER
BAKER	BORMAN	COLLINS	SOLOVYOV*
BARRY	BURSCH	CRIPPEN	STAFFORD
BROWN	CABANA	GAGARIN*	
FOALE	CERNAN	GRISSOM	ARMSTRONG
FRICK	CONRAD	HALSELL	CARPENTER
GLENN	COOPER	KAVANDI	COSMONAUT
GORIE	CURRIE	KOMAROV*	NIKOLAYEV*
HELMS	GIBSON	LINDSEY	
IVINS	GODWIN	SCHIRRA	FEOKTISTOV*
JONES	GORDON		TERECHKOVA*
	LEONOV*		

MISSILES, ROCKETS
U.S.

ABLE	DELTA	POPEYE	LACROSS
AJAX	GENIE	REDEYE	PATRIOT
GAPA	HYDRA	SATURN	PENGUIN
HAWK	LANCE	SHRIKE	PHOENIX
NIKE	SCOUT		POLARIS
THOR	SNARK	BULLPUP	SIDEARM
ZUNI	TITAN	CENTAUR	SKIPPER
		HARPOON	SPARROW
AGENA	DRAGON	JAVELIN	SPARTAN
ATLAS	FALCON	JUPITER	STINGER

TERRIER	HOUNDDOG	SERGEANT	LITTLEJOHN
TRIDENT	LACROSSE	TOMAHAWK	SHILLELAGH
WALLEYE	MAVERICK		SIDEWINDER
	PERSHING	CHAPARRAL	PEACEKEEPER
CORPORAL	POSEIDON	MINUTEMAN	
HELLFIRE	REDSTONE	HONESTJOHN	

Russia and Former USSR

ASH	KERRY	KIPPER	SCUNNER
GOA	KOALA	MOSKIT	SHYSTER
	KOMET	SAGGER	SIBLING
AMOS	SABER	SALISH	SNAPPER
ANAB	SASIN	SAMLET	SPANKER
APEX	SATAN	SANDAL	SUNBURN
KELT	SCAMP	SAVAGE	SWATTER
KENT	SCARP	SAWFLY	
KYLE	SILEX	SCARAB	GAUNTLET
SARK	SIREN	SICKLE	KANGAROO
SCUD	SKEAN	SINNER	KICKBACK
SEGO	SKIFF	SPIDER	KINGBOLT
SERB	SNIPE	SPIGOT	KINGFISH
STYX		SPIRAL	SCRUBBER
	ALKALI		SONGSTER
ACRID	ARCHER	GAINFUL	SPANDREL
ADDER	GADFLY	GAZELLE	STALLION
ALAMO	GALOSH	GREMLIN	STARFISH
APHID	GAMMON	GRIZZLY	STILETTO
ATOLL	GASKIN	GRUMBLE	STINGRAY
GANEF	GIMLET	KITCHEN	STURGEON
GECKO	GOBLET	KRYPTON	
GIANT	GOPHER	SADDLER	SHIPWRECK
GOLEM	GORGON	SAMPSON	
GRAIL	GRISON	SANDBOX	SCALEBOARD
GUILD	GROUSE	SAPWOOD	STARBRIGHT
KAREN	KEGLER	SAXHORN	
KAZOO	KENNEL	SCALPEL	
KEDGE	KILTER	SCROOGE	

Other

COBRA	EXOCET	CROTALE	SKYFLASH
ENTAC	HARPON	JAVELIN	VIGILANT
IKARA	MARTEL	PENGUIN	BLUESTEEL
MAMBA	NODONG	SEADART	STARBURST
MARTE	OTOMAT	SEASKUA	SWINGFIRE
MILAN	PLUTON	SEAWOLF	BLOODHOUND
APACHE	RAPIER	BLOWPIPE	STARSTREAK
ASPIDE	ROLAND	KORMORAN	
ENZIAN	SEACAT	SEAEAGLE	

WEARING APPAREL

HISTORIC, ECCLESIASTIC

ALB	COPE	HUKE	COTTA
	COWL	PALL	EPHOD
ALBA	FANO		FANON
CEST	HOOD	AMICE	FANUM

FROCK	ALMUCE	BIRETTA	SOUTANE
MITER	CASULA	BUSKINS	SPENCER
MITRE	CESTUS	CALOTTE	SULTANE
ORALE	CHIMER	CAPUCHE	TUNICLE
PALLA	CHITON	CASSOCK	ZIMARRA
PHANO	CYCLAS	CHIMERE	
SCARF	FANNEL	CHLAMYS	BERRETTA
SIMAR	JESUIT	CHRISOM	CAPUCHIN
STOLA	LEVITE	CUCULLA	CHASUBLE
STOLE	MANTUA	MANIPLE	CINCTURE
SYRMA	ROCHET	MOZETTA	DALMATIC
TALMA	TABARD	ORARION	GAMBESON
TIARA	TIPPET	PAENULA	HIMATION
TUNIC	TUNICA	PALLIUM	MANTEVIL
VAGAS	VAKASS	PELLARD	MOZZETTA
		PIANETA	SCAPULAR
ABOLLA	ARISARD	PLANETA	SURPLICE

NATIVE, LOCAL

ABA	GREGO	CANDYS	TEMIAK
OBI	HAORI	CHAMMA	TOUSER
	JELAB	DIRNDL	
BAJU	JEMMY	DOLMAN	BURNOUS
HAIK	JIBBA	HUIPIL	CHUDDAH
IZAR	LUNGI	JELICK	CHUDDAR
KILT	PAGNE	JELLAB	CHUDDER
MALO	PAREU	JIBBAH	FILIBEG
MIND	PARKA	JIBBEH	GALABIA
SARI	SAGUM	JUBBAH	SARAFAN
SAYA	TOOSH	KAROSS	TABLIER
TOGA	TREWS	KIMONO	ZAMARRA
		LUNGEE	
BURKA	ANORAK	MOOCHA	BURNOOSE
CABAN	BARVEL	NETCHA	CHAQUETA
CHOGA	BIETLE	PONCHO	CHARSHAF
CHOLI	BYRRUS	RAILLY	JIRKINET
DHOTI	CABAAN	SARONG	

BODY

BRA	PALL	FICHU	SKIRT
HAP	ROBE	FROCK	SLOPS
TOP	SACK	GANSY	SMOCK
TUX	SARK	GILET	STAYS
	SASH	HABIT	STOLE
BELT	SLIP	JEANS	TALAR
BRAT	SUIT	JUMPS	TONGS
CAPA	TOBE	JUPON	TUNIC
CAPE	VEST	KHAKI	WAIST
COAT		MIDDY	WAMUS
DICK	APRON	MUFTI	
ETON	BENJY	PANTS	BANIAN
GOWN	BENNY	PATTE	BASQUE
JUMP	CAPOT	PLAID	BAVARY
JUPE	CLOAK	POLKA	BLAZER
MAXI	CYMAR	SHAWL	BLOUSE
MIDI	DICKY	SHIFT	BODICE
MINI	DRESS	SHIRT	BOLERO

BUSTLE	STEPIN	PYJAMAS	NEGLIGEE
CAFTAN	TIGHTS	RISTORI	OILSKINS
CAMAIL	TUXEDO	ROMPERS	OVERALLS
CAMISA	ULSTER	SHOOTER	OVERCOAT
CAMISE	UNDIES	SLICKER	PEIGNOIR
CAPOTE	VESTEE	SLIVERS	PELERINE
COATEE	VISITE	SPENCER	PINAFORE
CORSET	WAMMUS	STAMMEL	PULLOVER
DICKEY	WAMPUS	SURCOAT	TROUSERS
GANSEY		SURTOUT	VESTMENT
GIRDLE	BALDRIC	SWEATER	
HALTER	BANDEAU	TEAGOWN	BRASSIERE
JACKET	BEDGOWN	UNIFORM	BRUNSWICK
JERKIN	CAMISIA	WRAPPER	CRINOLINE
JOSEPH	CHEMISE		GABARDINE
KABAYA	CRISPIN	BENJAMIN	GABERDINE
KAFTAN	CUTAWAY	BLOOMERS	GARIBALDI
KIRTLE	DESSOUS	BREECHES	GREATCOAT
LINDER	DOUBLET	CAMISOLE	HOOPSKIRT
LIVERY	DRAWERS	CARDIGAN	INVERNESS
MANTLE	GSTRING	CARDINAL	LOINCLOTH
NAPRON	HAPPING	CEINTURE	NIGHTGOWN
PEPLUM	HARNESS	CLEADING	OVERSKIRT
PHAROS	NEGLIGE	CORSELET	PEAJACKET
RAGLAN	NORFOLK	JAQUETTE	PETTICOAT
SKILTS	PAJAMAS	KNICKERS	PLUSFOURS
SLACKS	PALETOT	LINGERIE	POMPADOUR
SLIPON	PALTOCK	MACKINAW	REDINGOTE
SONTAG	PELISSE	MANTILLA	UNIONSUIT

HEAD AND NECK

*Indicates Neckwear

BIB	MAUD*	JERRY	VITTA
BOA*	PARE	KULAH	VOLET
BOW	RUFF*	LAMBA*	
CAP	TECK	LUNGI*	AIGRET
DIP	TIAR	MILAN	ANALAV
FEZ	TILE	MITER	ANGORA*
HAT	TOPI	MITRE	ASMACK
HOW	VEIL	MUTCH	BARRAD
LID		NUBIA*	BARRET
TAJ	AMPYX	PATTU*	BEAVER
TAM	ASCOT*	RABAT*	BERTHA*
TIE*	BARBE*	RUCHE*	BIGGIN
	BENJY	SCARF*	BOATER
AGAL	BERET	SHAKO	BONNET
BAKU	BOINA	SNOOD	BOWLER
COIF	BOXER	SQUAM	BOWTIE*
COWL	BUSBY	STOCK*	BRUTUS
FELT	CADDY	STRAW	BURLET
FLAT	CROWN	TERAI	CADDIE
FLOP	DERBY	THROW	CALASH
HOOD	DICER	TIARA	CALPAC
HURA	FICHU*	TOPEE	CAMAIL
JOAN	GIBUS	TOQUE	CASTOR
KEPI	JABOT*	TOZIE	CHOKER*
MASK	JASEY	TUQUE	CLAQUE

CLOCHE	SARAPE*	FLANDAN	YASHMAK
COCKUP	SERAPE*	FORAGER	
CRAVAT*	SLOUCH	GALERUM	AIGRETTE
DIADEM	TAENIA	HOMBURG	BALMORAL
DOMINO	TAPALO*	LEGHORN	BEARSKIN
FAILLE	TIPPET*	MOLOKER	BIGGONET
FEDORA	TOPHAT	MONTERO	CAPELINE
FILLET	TRILBY	MORTIER	CAPUTIUM
GORGET*	TUCKER*	MUFFLER*	CARCANET
GUIMPE*	TURBAN	NECKTIE*	HAVELOCK
HENNIN	UPARNA	PAISLEY*	HEADGEAR
KULLAH		PETASOS	KERCHIEF
LUNGEE*	ANLIKAR*	PETASUS	MAHARMAH
MANDIL	BANDANA	PILLBOX	NIGHTCAP
MOBCAP	BANDEAU	RAMILIE	OPERAHAT
PANAMA	BANDORE	SALACOT	RAMILLIE
PEPLUM	BRIMMER	SOWBACK	REHOBOAM
PILEUS	CALOTTE	SUNDOWN	SKULLCAP
PINNER	CAUBEEN	TALLITH	STEPHANE
RABATO*	CEREVIS	THERESE	SOMBRERO
RABBAT*	CHAPEAU	TRESSON	TARBOOSH
RAFFIA	CHECHIA	TRICORN	YARMULKA
REBATO*	COMMODE	TUTULUS	
SAILOR	DOPATTA*	YASHMAC	STOVEPIPE

LEGS AND FEET

BAL	STOGA	PUTTEE	SHINNER
	STOGY	PUTTIE	SLIPPER
BOOT		RUBBER	SLOGGER
CACK	ANKLET	SANDAL	TOPBOOT
CLOG	ARCTIC	SECQUE	
GETA	BOOTEE	STOGIE	BABOUCHE
HOSE	BROGAN	SUEDES	BALMORAL
MULE	BROGUE		BOOTIKIN
PUMP	BUSKIN	BABOOSH	BOTTEKIN
SHOE	CALIGA	BLUCHER	COLONIAL
SOCK	CHOPIN	BOTTINE	FINNESKO
TABI	COBCAB	CHINELA	GAMASHES
	CRAKOW	CHOPINE	HALFBOOT
	CREOLE	COTHURN	HUARACHO
CAMIK	GAITER	CRUISER	LARRIGAN
CHAPS	GALOSH	GAMBADO	MOCCASIN
KAMIK	JULIET	GARTERS	NAPOLEON
MOYLE	KAMMIK	HESSIAN	OVERSHOE
PUTTY	MOGGAN	HOSIERY	POULAINE
ROMEO	MUKLUK	HUSHION	SABOTINE
SABOT	OXFORD	LEGGING	SNEAKERS
SHAPS	PATTEN	RULLION	STOCKING
SPATS	PEDULE		
	PINSON		

FURS

CAT	CALF	MINK	CIVET
DOG	FLIX	MOLE	FITCH
FOX	GOAT	PONY	GENET
KID	HARE	SEAL	KOALA
	LAMB	VAIR	LLAMA
BEAR	LYNX	WOLF	OTTER

PAHMI	MARMOT	CRIMMER	KANGAROO
PANDA	MARTEN	FITCHEW	KINKAJOU
SABLE	MONKEY	GUANACO	KOLINSKY
SHEEP	NUTRIA	HAMSTER	REINDEER
SKUNK	OCELOT	KARAKUL	SQUIRREL
	PELTRY	KRIMMER	VISCACHA
ALPACA	RABBIT	LEOPARD	
BADGER	SUSLIK	MINIVER	BASSARISK
BEAVER	VICUNA	MUSKRAT	WOLVERINE
DESMAN	WEASEL	OPOSSUM	WOODCHUCK
ERMINE	WOMBAT	RACCOON	
FISHER		WALLABY	CHINCHILLA
JACKAL	CARACAL		
JAGUAR	CHEETAH	ANTELOPE	

SECTION III
SOLVING "CRYPTIC" CROSSWORD PUZZLES

The hidden-clues puzzle originated in England in the early 1920s. The originator was Powys Mathers, whose pseudonym was Torquemada. The pseudonym became internationally famous; the name Mathers, because he so long concealed his connection with the puzzles, remained little known to crossword-puzzle solvers.

Torquemada's first puzzles had a considerable vogue and spread all over England where, in fact, the cryptic puzzle virtually replaced the conventional crossword puzzle as it is published in American newspapers, magazines, and books today. Unlike American-style crosswords, the English puzzles leave many of the letters unkeyed, and their definitions frequently content themselves with stating the clues, these having no connection with the defined term. Most American cryptic definitions contain both a clue and a straight definition, as described below.

Cryptic puzzles may appear under a variety of names, such as "Puns and Anagrams," "Doubletalk," or simply "cryptic." Any puzzles reprinted from English sources are likely to be cryptic, whether so titled or not. The essential difference between cryptic puzzles and conventional crossword puzzles is that the difficulty in solving lies in the definitions, which must be deciphered, rather than in the obscurity of the answer word. In cryptic puzzles the answers are almost always common words. Since the definition both defines and clues the answer word, the solver can always tell if the answer he has found is the right one.

We will describe here briefly the most frequently used methods of constructing cryptic definitions. Sometimes definitions provide only a clue as to the deciphering of the answer. More often in American and Canadian cryptic puzzles the definition, in addition to containing a clue to finding the answer word, also contains a straight definition of it. Often the definition is divided, one half (roughly) defining the answer, the other containing the answer disguised in some manner or telling how to obtain it. Punctuation and capitalization are designed to confuse and should be ignored (exception: See Puns, below).

1. ANAGRAM. This is the most common type of definition. The answer word is contained in the definition, but its letters are rearranged to form a new word or words. For example,

"A mixed diet is correct." Ans.: edit.
("Diet" is an anagram for "edit"; mixed tells us that the letters are rearranged. "Correct" is a definition of "edit.")
"Mad liar? Must be Yamamoto." Ans.: admiral.
("Mad liar" is an anagram for "admiral.")

Hint: Look for some word, or for some connected combination of words, that has the same number of letters as the word you need. Try rearranging the letters and see if suddenly the whole definition makes sense.

2. CHARADES. The syllables of a word are dealt with sequentially, as in charades. For example:

"It follows Ed is correct." Ans.: edit.
("It" follows "ed" = put "it" after "ed": ed-it.)
"Exclude Edward—he's been exposed." Ans.: bared.
("Exclude" = "bar", "Edward" = "Ed": bar-ed.)

3. SPLIT WORDS. Syllables are interlocked in a way described in the definition. For example:

"It's correct that ET embraced a princess." Ans.: edit.
(The letters "E" and "T" "embrace" princess "Di": "e-di-t.")
"A bloke in a bar." Ans.: beggar.
("Bloke" = "egg," placed in "bar": b-egg-ar.)

4. HIDDEN WORDS. The word is spelled out but is hidden among other words. Often this type of definition contains a hint that the word is hidden, through use of the word "hidden," "hiding," "concealed," etc. For example:

"To refine is within the grasp of all educat*ed Ital*ians." Ans.: edit.
("Within the grasp" suggests a hidden word clue.)
"The Nazis marched into Yugoslavi*a, then s*outhward through a city in Greece." Ans.: Athens.

5. BACKWARD SPELLINGS. The answer word is found in
the definition or in a word suggested by the definition but
reversed (backward or upside down). The definition always
tells the solver in some way that a reversal is involved.
For example:

> "It's correct that the tide has turned." Ans.: edit.
> ("Tide" "turned" around is "edit.")
> "Take your pay from the right drawer." Ans.: reward.
> ("Drawer" read from the right is "reward.")

6. PUNS. The sound of words is used, usually suggested
in the definition by a word such as "we hear," "orally,"
etc., or by the presence of an exclamation point (!) or a
question mark (?). For example:

> "I heard that the score was even! The reverse is cor-
> rect." Ans.: edit.
> ("score was even" = "tied"; sounds like "tide,"
> which reversed makes "edit.")
> "I take a whiskey but not straight!" Ans.: awry.
> ("A whisky" is "a rye"; sounds like "awry", a
> definition of which is "not straight.")

7. DOUBLE DEFINITIONS. The simplest kind of definition, in which the second clue is also a definition.
Example:

> "Amend copyreader's work." Ans.: edit.
> (Both "amend" and "copyreader's work" define
> "edit.")
> "Assist your subordinate." Ans.: second.
> (Both "assist" and "subordinate" define "second.")

8. PIECES OF WORDS. Clues may indicate part of a word:
"head" might indicate the first letter; "tail" the last;
"heart" the middle. Half of a word may be used, or part
of a word may be removed. There are in addition some
standard abbreviations: right = R; left = L; love = O; time,
temperature, etc. = T; loud = F; soft = P, thousand = G;
and Roman numerals are commonly used. Examples:

> "Revise edict by cutting the chapter head." Ans.:
> edit.

("Chapter head" = "c", which when cut from "edict" leaves "edit.")

"Redemption lost import here." Ans: Eden.
(Take the letters of "import" out of "redemption", what's left is "Eden.")

"Initially Em's daughter in Toledo was correct." Ans.: edit.
(First letters of "Em's daughter in Toledo": "edit.")

"Revise New York's summer time by one." Ans.: edit.
(One = I, added to EDT—Eastern Daylight Time, New York's summer time—makes "edit.")

"Is it correct that ET was around 501?" Ans.: edit.
(501 = "DI" in Roman numerals; surrounded by E and T: edit.)

THE NEW AMERICAN CROSSWORD
PUZZLE DICTIONARY AND CRYPTIC PUZZLES

While the deceptive nature of the cryptic clue makes use of a dictionary more difficult, the solver will find this book most helpful when the definition part of the clue has been determined. The dictionary can then be used to find possible answers, which can be checked by solving the cryptic part of the clue.

Philip D. Morehead is an editor, pianist, conductor and Head of Staff for the Lyric Opera of Chicago. Mr. Morehead, son of the late lexicographer and games expert Albert H. Morehead, is the author of *The New International Dictionary of Music* and the *Penguin Roget's College Thesaurus in Dictionary Form*. He has also edited several revisions of the *New American Handy College Dictionary*, the *New American Roget's College Thesaurus in Dictionary Form*, and the *New American Crossword Puzzle Dictionary*.